TWELVE CENTURIES

OF

ENGLISH POETRY AND PROSE

SELECTED AND EDITED

By

ALPHONSO GERALD NEWCOMER

PROFESSOR OF ENGLISH IN THE LELAND STANFORD JUNIOR UNIVERSITY

AND

ALICE E. ANDREWS

TEACHER OF ENGLISH IN THE CLEVELAND HIGH SCHOOL, ST. PAUL

SCOTT, FORESMAN AND COMPANY

CHICAGO   NEW YORK

820.8
N541

P. F. Pettibone & Co.
Printers and Binders
Chicago

INTRODUCTION

This book was undertaken in response to the desire, expressed in many quarters, for a large body of standard English literature in an accessible, compact form, to accompany and supplement the manuals of literary history in use. As the project gradually shaped itself in the editors' hands, it took on something like the following threefold purpose:

First, to include, as far as possible, those classics of our literature—the ballads, elegies, and odes, the *L'Allegros* and *Deserted Villages*—which afford the basis for an appreciation of the greatest English writers.

Second, to supplement these with a sufficient number of selections from every period of our literature to provide a perspective and make the volume fairly representative from a historical point of view.

Third, to go somewhat outside of the beaten track, though keeping still to standard literature, and make a liberal addition of selections, especially from the drama and prose, to enliven the collection and widen its human interest.

This comprehensive character is indicated by the title of the volume. A somewhat unusual feature is the inclusion of both poetry and prose. The two forms have not been indiscriminately mingled, but they have been deliberately set side by side in the belief that both will gain by their conjunction. It is scarcely to be denied that at the present time a volume made up wholly of verse gives the impression of a collection of enshrined "classics," meant either to be admired from a distance or studied with tedious minuteness. On the other hand, a miscellaneous collection of unrelieved prose lacks attractiveness by seeming to lack emotional appeal. Putting them together will not only afford the relief of variety, but should lead to a better understanding of both by showing that the difference between them is often more formal than real—that poetry, with all its concern for form, is primarily the medium of the simplest truth and feeling, and that prose, though by preference pedestrian, may at times both soar and sing.

In making the selections, it was considered best to exclude the modern novel, a form of literature that scarcely lends itself to selection at all. With this exception, pretty much the whole field has been covered, though it is not maintained that every important man or movement has been represented. The Restoration drama can, for obvious reasons, have no place in these pages; nor should the omissions be regarded with surprise if a volume of confessedly rather elementary purpose fails to include such men as Burton, Browne, Locke, and Newton, voyagers "on strange seas of thought, alone." The endeavor was simply to secure the widest representation consistent with the intended service of the book and compatible with a due regard for both amount and proportion. Inconclusive fragments have been studiously avoided. Here and there, where a specimen of form only was desired—of Surrey's blank verse, for example, or of Thomson's Spenserian manner—this principle has not been adhered to. But apart from such exceptional cases, even

iii

where wholes could not be given, enough has still been given, not only to set the reader going, but to take him somewhere.

The order is chronological, and the division into periods corresponds in general to the division adopted by the senior editor in his history of *English Literature*. The adherence to chronology, however, has not been rigid, either in the order of names or in the order of selections under the names. Prose has usually been separated from verse, and minor poems have often been placed together. In fact, wherever an unpleasant juxtaposition could be avoided, or a more effective grouping secured, there has been no hesitation to exercise some freedom. The dates of the various selections will in most instances be found in the table of contents.

Selections from Old English, from Latin, and from Middle English down to Chaucer, are given in translation. After Chaucer, the original text is followed, but spelling and punctuation are modernized—a course which is almost necessary if a writer like Mandeville is to be read with any ease, and which has every reason to support it in writers of a much later date. To this rule the customary exceptions in poetry are made: Chaucer, Langland, the Ballads, *Everyman,* and Spenser's artificially archaic *Faërie Queene,* are kept in the original form. Much care has been bestowed upon the text. It is really a matter of somewhat more than curiosity whether, in the poet's fancy, the lowing herd *wind* over the lea, or *winds* over the lea, and he ought by all means to be reported faithfully. At the same time it has seemed equally important in a few instances to correct a manifest and misleading error or to remove an extremely offensive epithet. The instances of such changes are perhaps not a dozen in all.

The notes have been placed at the bottom of the page, primarily for convenience, but also to insure brevity. It will be observed that they serve other purposes than those of a mere glossary. Every care has been taken to make them pertinent and really explanatory, and to avoid unduly distracting the reader's attention or affronting his intelligence. It seemed fair to assume, on the reader's part, the possession of a dictionary and a Bible, and some elementary knowledge of classical mythology. It is altogether too common an editorial mistake to regard every capital letter as a signal for a note. Allusions to matters of very slight relevancy are purposely left unexplained. For example, in such an isolated poem as *Deor's Lament,* it seemed more to the purpose, at least of the present volume, to give a bit of literary comment than to weight down the poem with notes on events in remote Germanic tradition. On the other hand, wherever a note, of whatever nature, seemed absolutely demanded, no pains have been spared to provide it. In the case of selections hitherto not specially edited, this frequently involved great labor, and the editors learned how much easier it is to make an anthology than to equip it for intelligent use.* Details of biography, as well as the larger matters of literary history and criticism, have necessarily been left to the manuals of literary history. For the convenience of those who use the *English Literature* referred to above, exact page references to that volume have sometimes been added. Finally, there are frequent cross-references within the present volume, and these may be

---

* For instance, one note is still fresh in mind—the next to the last in the book—which required the reading of nearly two volumes of Stevenson, to say nothing of the labor spent in searching on the wrong track. Even in such a classic as *Everyman,* there remained obscurities to be cleared up, and apparently no editor had yet hit upon the explanation of so simple a matter as to "take my tappe in my lappe" (page 93, line 801), the meaning of which the editors guessed and subsequently verified by Jamieson's *Scottish Dictionary.* The word "kenns," as used by Scott in *Old Mortality* (see page 504), is not recorded in any of the standard dictionaries, including Jamieson. These examples, which are typical of many others, will serve to show that the preparation of the notes, slight as they may seem, has been no perfunctory or uncritical task.

further extended by the use of the index to the notes. It is believed that this index will be found extremely useful.

Manifestly many advantages are to be derived from having so much material in a single volume. The book may even be used as a source-book for the study of English history, in a liberal interpretation of that subject. From the Anglo-Saxon period, for example, a sufficient diversity of literature is presented to give body and reality to that far-away time. In a later period, the constantly recurring terms and manners of feudalism and chivalry make that age also historically real, and the archaism of Spenser, as the age passes away, does not appear such a detached, unintelligible phenomenon. The concentric "spheres" of the old Ptolemaic astronomy may be seen revolving about this earth as a centre through all the poetry down to Milton, when science steps in with its inexorable logic and man is constrained to take a humbler view of his station in the universe. On the other hand, Utopia may change to Arcadia, and Arcadia to El Dorado, but the dream itself refuses to die. A juster conception of the writers themselves is likewise made possible. Shakespeare is removed from his position of lonely grandeur. Milton, so fallen on evil days, finds ample justification for his poetic complaint in the graphic prose descriptions of Pepys and Evelyn. Johnson is humanized by being presented as the friend of Boswell.

Again, in the detailed study of the literature there is the immense advantage of often having at hand, where each student can see it for himself, the source of an allusion, the echo of a sentiment, or the different play of diverse imaginations about the same theme. One passage of Milton can be set by the side of a similar passage in Caedmon, another can be paralleled in Marlowe, a third in Spenser. The story of the last fight of *The Revenge* can be read first in Raleigh's circumstantial narrative and then in Tennyson's martial ode. Malory's Arthur reappears in Tennyson, Scott's Bonny Dundee in Macaulay's account of the battle of Killiecrankie. If the line in Browning's *Saul* about the "locust-flesh steeped in the pitcher" reminds us of an incident in the life of John the Baptist, we turn with interest to Wyclif's curious version of that story. An unusual word, "brede," occurring in one of Keats's odes, is found to have been used in an ode by Collins, and its literary genealogy can scarcely be doubted. The paths of Addison and Carlyle lie far apart, and yet both appear to have been indebted, the one for a quaint fancy, the other for a striking figure, to the same record of a shipwreck on the frozen shores of Nova Zembla more than three centuries ago. By the discerning teacher these cross-references can be multiplied indefinitely, and for nearly every cross-reference there will be a decided gain in understanding and appreciation. The student will see what a network a national literature is, and get some conception of the ever increasing enjoyment that attends upon an increasing familiarity with it.

Indeed, it has been one of the chief pleasures in making this compilation to feel that along with the so-called English classics, of finished form and universal content, so much was being gathered which, though less familiar, is scarcely less worthy, and frequently of a more intimate human appeal. It may not be desirable to teach all this matter, nor would it be possible at any one time or place. The important thing is to have it in hand. The teacher is thus given a real freedom of choice and enabled to teach literature, as it should be taught, with the personal touch. For the student, too, there will always remain some tracts of *terra incognita*, with the delight of wandering, of his own free will, along unfrequented paths. To share, for example, in the early Northmen's vague terror of nickers and jotuns, to listen to the words of Alfred the Great, to observe the concern of the good bishop of Tarente for the spiritual welfare of the nuns under his charge, to stand by at the birth of the first printed English book and note the aged Caxton's enthusiasm in spite of worn fingers and weary eyes, to join with Jonson in mourning and praising the great fellow-craftsman whom he knew, to watch with Pepys the coronation of the king or hear him piously thank God for the money won at gaming—these are things, it should seem, to arouse the most torpid imagination. If, from excursions of this nature, the student learns that good literature and interesting reading matter meet, that the one is not confined to exalted odes nor the other to current magazine fiction, a very real service will have been done by widening the scope of this volume.

It is obvious that in pursuing the study of such diverse material, no single method will suffice. Sometimes, as has already been hinted, reading is all that is necessary. But when a writer like Bacon, let us say, or Pope, writes with the deliberate purpose of instruction, his work must be studied with close application and may be analyzed until it yields its last shade of meaning. On the other hand, when Keats sings pathetically of the enduring beauty of art and the transient life of man, or when Browning chants some message of faith and cheer, a minutely analytical or skeptical attitude would be not only futile but fatal. And when the various purposes of instruction, inspiration, and æsthetic delight are combined in one work, as in the supreme example of *Paradise Lost,* the student who hopes to attain to anything like full comprehension must return to it with various methods and in various moods. It is from considerations like these that the teacher must determine his course. One thing, however, cannot be too often repeated. The most successful teacher of literature is he who brings to it a lively sympathy springing from intimate knowledge, assured that method is of minor moment so long as there is the responsive spirit that evokes response.

For ourselves, we would say that while we have divided the labor of preparing both copy and notes, there has been close coöperation at every stage of the work. We owe thanks for suggestions and encouragement to more friends than we may undertake to name. To Dr. Frederick Klaeber, in particular, of the University of Minnesota, we are indebted for advice upon the rendering of certain passages in *Beowulf,* and to Professor Lindsay Todd Damon, of Brown University, for a critical vigilance that has worked to the improvement of almost every page. By courtesy of The Macmillan Company the translations which represent Cynewulf have been reprinted from Mr. Stopford A. Brooke's *History of Early English Literature;* and by a similar courtesy on the part of Messrs. Charles Scribner's Sons, who hold copyrights in the works of Stevenson, we have been able to include the selections which close the volume.

A. G. N.
A. E. A.

CONTENTS

INTRODUCTION iii

ANGLO-SAXON PERIOD

BEOWULF (c. 700)........................ 1
DEOR'S LAMENT 18
CAEDMON (fl. 670)
  Paraphrase of the Scriptures
    From Genesis: The Garden of Eden;
      The Fall of Satan................18, 19
    From Exodus: The Cloud by Day;
      The Drowning of Pharaoh..... 19
BEDE (673-735)
  From the Ecclesiastical History (finished
    731):
    The Britons Seek Succor from the
      Romans. The Roman Wall.... 20
    A Parable of Man's Life............ 21
    The Story of Cædmon............. 21
CYNEWULF (fl. 670)
  Riddles II, VI, XV................... 23
  From the Christ..................... 24
  From the Elene 24
ANGLO-SAXON CHRONICLE (begun about 850)
  Extracts 25
  The Battle of Brunanburh............ 26
ALFRED THE GREAT (849-901)
  Ohthere's Narrative.................. 27

ANGLO-NORMAN PERIOD

GEOFFREY OF MONMOUTH (c. 1100-1154)
  From the Historia Britonum Regum (c.
    1135):
    The Story of King Leir.......... 29
    Arthur Makes the Saxons His Tribu-
      taries 31
ANCREN RIWLE, From the (c. 1225)........ 32
PROVERBS OF KING ALFRED, From the... 35
CUCKOO SONG (c. 1250) 36

FOURTEENTH CENTURY—AGE OF CHAUCER

PEARL, From the (c. 1350)............... 37
WILLIAM LANGLAND (1332?-1400?)
  From The Vision of Piers the Plowman
    (1362 onward):
    The Prologue (B text, 1377)....... 39
    From Passus I.................... 40
THE WYCLIF BIBLE (c. 1380). THE KING
    JAMES BIBLE (1611) 41
GEOFFREY CHAUCER (1340?-1400)
  From The Canterbury Tales (c. 1386 on-
    ward):
    The Prologue 43
    The Nonne Preestes Tale.......... 53
  From the Legend of Good Women (c.
    1385): The Story of Thisbe of
    Babylon, Martyr.............. 60
  The Compleynt of Chaucer to His Purse
    (1399) 62
TRAVELS OF SIR JOHN MANDEVILLE, From the
    (written c. 1356; English trans-
    lation after 1400)............. 63

THE FIFTEENTH AND EARLY SIXTEENTH CENTURIES

BALLADS
  Robin Hood and the Monk (MS. c. 1450). 69
  The Hunting of the Cheviot............ 73
  Sir Patrick Spens..................... 77
  Johnie Cock........................... 77

Bonnie George Campbell............. 79
The Wife of Usher's Well............. 79
Katharine Jaffray. 79
The Nutbrown Mayde................. 80
EVERYMAN (before 1525)............... 84
WILLIAM CAXTON (1422?-1491)
  The Recuyell of the Histories of Troy (c.
    1474): Prologue, and Epilogue
    to Book III.................... 95
SIR THOMAS MALORY (died 1471)
  From Le Morte Darthur (finished 1470;
    printed 1485)................. 96
SIR THOMAS MORE (1478-1535)
  From Utopia (in Latin, 1516; English
    translation, 1551, 1556)....... 110
ROGER ASCHAM (1515-1568)
  Toxophilus (1545)
    From the Foreword............... 119
    The Ways of the Wind.......... 121
  The Schoolmaster (1570)
    From A Preface to the Reader...... 122
    A Gentle Teacher and Pupil...... 124

THE ELIZABETHAN AGE—POETRY

SIR THOMAS WYATT (1503-1542; poems pub-
    lished 1557)
  The Lover Having Dreamed, etc. (Son-
    net) 125
  Of His Love that Pricked Her Finger
    with a Needle................. 125
  The Lover Complaineth the Unkindness
    of His Love................... 125
HENRY HOWARD, EARL OF SURREY (1517?-
    1547; poems published 1557)
  Description of Spring, etc. (Sonnet).... 126
  A Praise of His Love, etc............. 126
  Departure of Æneas from Dido........ 126
EDMUND SPENSER (1552-1599)
  The Faerie Queene. Dedication, and
    parts of Book I (1590)........ 127
  Prothalamion (1596).................. 139
ELIZABETHAN SONNETS
  Edmund Spenser: Amoretti XV, XXXVII,
    LXI (1595) 142
  Sir Philip Sidney: Astrophel and Stella
    I, XXXI (1591)............. 142
  Samuel Daniel: To Delia LI (1592).... 142
  Michael Drayton: Idea LXI (1619)... 143
  William Shakespeare: Sonnets XXIX,
    XXX, LXIV, LXV, LXXIII,
    LXXIV (1609)............... 143
ELIZABETHAN LYRICS
  Sir Philip Sidney: Astrophel and Stella,
    First Song (1591).............. 144
  George Peele: Fair and Fair (c. 1581).. 144
  Thomas Lodge: Rosalind's Madrigal
    (1590) 145
  Robert Southwell: The Burning Babe
    (1595) 145
  Christopher Marlowe: The Passionate
    Shepherd to His Love (1590)... 146
  Sir Walter Raleigh (?): The Nymph's
    Reply to the Shepherd (1590).. 146
  Pilgrim to Pilgrim................... 146
  William Shakespeare: Under the Green-
    wood Tree (c. 1599)........... 147
  Blow, Blow, Thou Winter Wind (c.
    1599) 147
  Take, O, Take Those Lips Away
    (1604) 147
  Come Away, Come Away, Death (c.
    1600) 147

vii

CONTENTS

on beds in the bowers,[1] when it was shown
them, 140
truly declared by a manifest token,
the hall-thane's hate; held themselves after
farther and faster who the fiend escaped.

So Grendel ruled, and warred against right,
alone against all, until empty stood
that best of houses. Great was the while,
twelve winters' tide, the Scyldings' friend
endured his rage, every woe,
ample sorrow. Whence it became
openly known to the children of men, 150
sadly in songs, that Grendel warred
awhile against Hrothgar, enmity waged,
crime and feud for many years,
strife incessant; peace would not have
with any man of the Danish power,
nor remit for a fee the baleful levy;
nor any wight might hold a hope
for a glorious satisfaction at the murderer's
hands.
The fell wretch kept persecuting— 159
the dark death-shade—the noble and youthful,
oppressed and snared them. All the night
he roamed the mist-moors. Men know not
whither hell-sorcerers wander at times.

Thus many crimes the foe of mankind,
the fell lone-roamer, often accomplished,
cruel injuries. Heorot he held,
seat richly adorned, in the dark nights;
yet might not the gift-throne touch, that treasure,
because of the Lord, nor knew His design.
'Twas great distress to the Scyldings' friend,
grief of spirit; often the wise men 171
sat in assembly; counsel devised they
what for strong-souled men it were best
to do against the perilous horrors.
Sometimes they promised idolatrous honors
at the temples, prayed in words
that the spirit-slayer aid would afford
against their afflictions. Such was their custom,
the heathen's hope; hell they remembered,
but the Creator, the Judge of deeds, 180
they knew not—knew not the Lord God, knew
not
how to praise the heavens' Protector,
Glory's Ruler. Woe to him who
thro' cruel malice shall thrust his soul
in the fire's embrace; let him expect not
comfort to find. Well unto him who
after his death-day may seek the Lord,
and win to peace in his Father's bosom.

IV. BEOWULF'S RESOLVE

So Healfdene's son on sorrow brooded;
for all his wisdom the hero could not 190
avert the evil; that strife was too strong,
loathsome and tedious, that came on the people,
malice-brought misery, greatest of night-woes.
Then Hygelac's thane,* a Geatman good,
heard from his home of Grendel's deeds;
he of mankind was strongest in power
in that day of this life, noble and vigorous.
He bade for himself a good wave-rider
to be prepared; said he would go
over the swan-road to seek the war-king, 200
the prince renowned, since men he had need of.
Dear though he was, his prudent liegemen
little blamed him for that voyage,
whetted him rather, and noted the omen.

Then the good chief chose him champions
of the Geat-folk, whomso bravest
he could find, and, fourteen with him,
sought the vessel. Then the hero, 208
the sea-crafty man, led the way to the shore.
Time passed; the floater was on the waves,
the boat 'neath the hill; the ready warriors
stepped on the prow; the streams surged
the sea 'gainst the sand; the warriors bare
into the bark's bosom bright arms,
a rich war-array. The men shoved out
on the welcome voyage the wooden bark.

Most like to a bird the foamy-necked floater,
impelled by the wind, then flew o'er the waves
till about the same time on the second day
the twisted prow had sailed so far 220
that the voyagers land descried,
shining ocean-shores, mountains steep,
spacious sea-nesses. Then was the floater
at the end of its voyage. Up thence quickly
the Weders' people stept on the plain;
the sea-wood tied; their mail-shirts shook,
their martial weeds; thanked God that to them
the paths of the waves had been made easy.

When from the wall the Scyldings' warder,
who the sea-shores had to keep, 230
saw bright shields borne over the gunwale,
war-gear ready, wonder arose
within his mind what those men were.
Hrothgar's thane then went to the shore,
on his horse riding, stoutly shook
the stave in his hands, and formally asked
them:
"What are ye of arm-bearing men,
with byrnies protected, who thus come leading
a surgy keel over the water-street,
here o'er the seas? I for this, 240
placed at the land's end, have kept sea-ward,

---

[1] Apartments used mainly by the women.

* Beowulf. Hygelac was his uncle, and king of the
Geats, or Weder-Geats, who lived in Sweden.

that no enemies on the Danes' land
with a ship-force might do injury.
Never more openly hither to come
have shield-men attempted; nay, and ye knew not
surely the pass-word ready of warriors,
permission of kinsmen. Yet ne'er have I seen
earl upon earth more great than is one of you,
or warrior in arms: 'tis no mere retainer
honored in arms, unless his face belies him,
his aspect distinguished. Now your origin
must I know, ere ye farther,   252
as false spies, into the Danes' land
hence proceed. Now ye dwellers
afar, sea-farers, give ye heed to
my simple thought: best is it quickly
to make known whence your coming is.''

V. The Mission of the Geats

Him the chief of them answered then,
the band's war-leader his word-hoard unlocked:
"We are of race of the Geats' nation,   260
and hearth-enjoyers of Hygelac.
Well known to nations was my father,
a noble chieftain, Ecgtheow named;
abode many winters ere he departed
old from his courts; nigh every sage
thro' the wide earth remembers him well.
We in kindness of feeling have come
to seek thy lord, the son of Healfdene,
the folk-defender. Be a kind informant.
We have a great errand to the illustrious   270
lord of the Danes. Naught shall be secret
whereof my thought is. Thou knowest whether
it be in sooth as we have heard say,
that with the Scyldings I know not what wretch,
a secret ill-doer, in the dark nights
displays thro' terror unheard-of malice,
havoc and slaughter. For this may I teach,
thro' my large mind, counsel to Hrothgar,
how he, wise and good, shall o'ercome the foe,
if ever a change is to befal,   280
if relief from evil should ever come
and that care-welling calmer grow.
Else he ever after oppression will suffer,
a time of trouble, while standeth there
in its high place the noblest of houses.''
Then spake the warder, astride of his horse,
the officer fearless: "Between these two
should a sharp shield-warrior who thinketh well
the difference know—'tween words and works.
This band, I hear, is a friendly one   290
to the Scyldings' lord. Pass ye on
with weapons and weeds, I will direct you.
Likewise will I give to my fellow-
liegemen orders in honor to keep.

'gainst every foe, your new-tarred ship,
your bark on the sand, till back o'er the water
the vessel with twisted neck shall bear
to the Weder-march the man beloved.
To such a warrior shall it surely be given
the rush of war to escape from whole.   300
Then they set forth; the vessel still bode
firm in her berth, the wide-bosomed ship,
at anchor fast. A boar's likeness sheen
'bove their cheeks they bore, adorned with gold;
stained and fire-hardened, it held life in ward.*
In warlike mood the men hastened on,
descended together, until the well-timbered
hall they might see, adorned all with gold.
Unto earth's dwellers that was the grandest
of houses 'neath heav'n, where the ruler abode;   310
the light of it shone over many lands.
To them then the warrior pointed out clearly
the proud one's court, that they might thither
take their way; then did the warrior
turn his steed and speak these words:
" 'Tis time for me to go on my way.
May the all-ruling Father with honor hold you
safe in your fortunes. I will back to the sea,
ward to keep against hostile bands.''

VI. The Arrival at Heorot

The street was stone-paved, the path gav guidance   320
to the men in a body; the war-byrnie shone,
hard, hand-locked; the ringed iron bright
sang in their gear, as they to the hall
in their arms terrific came striding on.
Their ample shields, their flint-hard bucklers,
the sea-weary set 'gainst the mansion's wall,
then stooped to the benches; their byrnies rang,
the war-gear of men. In a sheaf together
the javelins stood, the seamen's arms,   329
ash-wood, grey-tipped. These ironclad men
were weaponed well.
    Then a proud chief asked
these sons of conflict concerning their lineage:
"Whence do ye bear your plated shields
and grey sarks hither, your visor-helms
and heap of war-shafts? I am Hrothgar's
servant and messenger. Never saw I
strangers so many and proud. I ween
that ye out of pride, of greatness of soul,
and not for exile, have sought Hrothgar.''
Him then answered the famed for valor;   340
the Weders' proud lord, bold 'neath his helmet,
spake words afterward: "We are Hygelac's
table-enjoyers—my name, Beowulf.
I my errand will relate

* Boar-images surmounted the helmets.

to the great lord, son of Healfdene,
to thy prince, if he will grant us
graciously to greet him here.''

Wulfgar spake (he was lord of the Wendels;
known to many was his spirit,   348
his valor and wisdom): ''I will therefore
ask the Danes' friend, lord of the Scyldings,
mighty prince and ring-distributor,
about thy voyage, as thou requestest,
and make quickly known the answer
that the prince thinks fit to give me.''

He then went quickly where Hrothgar sat,
old and gray, among his earls;
the brave chief stood before the shoulders
of the Danes' lord—he knew court-usage.
Wulfgar spake to his friendly lord: 360
''Hither are borne, come from afar
o'er ocean's course, people of the Geats.
Beowulf these sons of conflict
name their chief. They make petition
that they may hold with thee, my lord,
words of converse. Decree not, Hrothgar,
denial of the boon of answer.
Worthy seem they, in their war-gear,
of earls' esteem—at least the chieftain
who has led the warriors hither.''   370

VII. Hrothgar's Welcome

Hrothgar spake, the Scyldings' shield:
''Lo, I knew him when he was a boy.
His old father was named Ecgtheow,
to whom in his home gave Hrethel the Geat
his only daughter. Now his offspring
bold comes hither, has sought a kind friend.
For sea-farers—they who bore gift-treasures
unto the Geats gratuitously—
were wont to say of him, the war-famed,
that he the might of thirty men   380
has in his hand-grip. Holy God
hath in his mercies sent him to us,
to the West Danes, as I hope,
'gainst Grendel's horror. For his daring,
to the good chief gifts I'll offer.
Be thou speedy, bid these kinsmen,
assembled together, come in to see me.
Say moreover they are welcome
guests to the Danes. [Then to the hall-door
Wulfgar went.] He announced the words: 390
''My victor-lord, O prince of the East Danes,
bids me tell you he knows your nobleness;
that, boldly striving over the sea-billows,
ye come to him hither welcome guests.
Now ye may go in your war-accoutrements,
'neath martial helm, Hrothgar to see.
Let your battle-boards, spears, and shafts,
here await the council of words.''

Arose then the chief, his many men around
him,
a brave band of thanes. Some remained
there,   400
held the war-weeds, as the bold one bade them.
They hastened together where the warrior directed,
under Heorot's roof; the valiant one went,
bold 'neath his helmet, till he stood on the dais.
Beowulf spake; his byrnie shone on him,
his war-net sewed by the smith's devices:
''Hail to thee, Hrothgar; I am Hygelac's
kinsman and war-fellow; many great deeds
in my youth have I ventured. To me on my
native turf
Grendel's doings became clearly known.   410
Sea-farers say that this most excellent
house doth stand, for every warrior,
useless and void when the evening light
under heaven's serenity is concealed.
Then, prince Hrothgar, did my people,
the most excellent men, sagacious,
counsel me that I should seek thee,
because they knew the might of my craft.
Themselves beheld—when I came from their
snares,
blood-stained from the foes—where five I
bound,   420
the jotun-race ravaged, and slew on the billows
nickers by night; distress I suffered,
avenged the Weders (they had had misery),
crushed the fell foe. And now against Grendel,
that miserable being, will I hold council,
alone with the giant.

''Of thee now, therefore,
lord of the bright Danes, Scyldings' protector,
will I make this one petition:
now that I come so far, deny not,
O patron of warriors, friend of people,   430
that I alone with my band of earls,
with this bold company, may purge Heorot.
I have learned this, that the demon-like being
in his heedlessness recketh not of weapons.
I then will disdain (so may Hygelac,
my liege lord, be to me gracious of mood)
to bear a sword or round yellow shield
into the battle; but shall with the enemy
grip and grapple, and for life contend,
foe against foe. And he whom death taketh
there shall trust in the doom of the Lord.   441

''I ween that he, if he may prevail,
will fearlessly eat, in the martial hall,
the Geat's people, as oft he has done
the Hrethmen's[1] forces. Thou wilt not need
to shroud my head, for he will have me,
stained with gore, if death shall take me;

1 the Danes

will bear off my bloody corse to feast on it;
lonely, will eat it without compunction;
will mark out my moor-mound. Thou wilt not
need   450
care to take for my body's disposal.
If the conflict take me, send to Hygelac
this best of battle-coats shielding my breast,
of vests most excellent; 'tis Hrædla's legacy,
Weland's[2] work. Fate goes aye as it must.''

VIII. HROTHGAR'S LAMENT

Hrothgar spake, the Scyldings' shield:
''For battles thou, my friend Beowulf,
and for honor, us hast sought.
Thy father fought in the greatest feud:
he was of Heatholaf the slayer,   460
with the Wylfings, when the Weder-Geats
for fear of war-feud might not harbor him.
Thence he sought, o'er the rolling waves,
the South Danes' folk, the noble Scyldings,
when first I ruled the Danish people
and in my youth held spacious realms,
the hoard-burg of heroes. Dead was Heregar,
my elder brother, son of Healfdene,—
passed from the living; he was better than I.
Later, that quarrel I settled with money;   470
over the water's back old treasures
I sent to the Wylfings: he swore to me oaths.
''Sorry am I in my mind to say
to any man what Grendel has wrought me
in Heorot with his hostile designs,
what swift mischiefs done. My courtiers are
    minished,
my martial band; them fate has off-swept
to the horrors of Grendel. Yet God may easily
turn from his deeds the frenzied spoiler.
Oft have promised the sons of conflict,   480
with beer drunken, over the ale-cup,
that they in the beer-hall would await
with sharp sword-edges Grendel's warfare.
Then at morning, when the day dawned,
this princely mead-hall was stained with gore,
all the bench-floor with blood besteamed,
the hall with sword-blood: I owned the fewer
of dear, faithful nobles, whom death destroyed.
Sit now to the feast, and joyfully think
of victory for men, as thy mind may incite.'' 490
For the sons of the Geats then, all together,
in the beer-hall a bench was cleared.
There the strong-souled went to sit,
proudly rejoicing; a thane did duty,
who bare in his hand the ale-cup bedecked,
poured the bright liquor. Clear rose the glee-
    man's
song in Heorot. There was joy of warriors,
a noble band of Danes and Weders.

2 The divine smith, or Vulcan, of northern legend.

IX. HUNFERTH'S TAUNT. THE REPLY

Hunferth spake, the son of Ecglaf,   499
who sat at the feet of the Scyldings' lord,
unloosed his malice. To him was the voyage
of the bold sailor, Beowulf, a great displeasure,
because he grudged that another man
should ever 'neath heaven more glories hold
of this middle-earth, than he himself.
''Art thou the Beowulf who strove with
    Breca
on the wide sea, in a swimming-strife,
where ye from pride tempted the floods,
and, for foolish vaunt, in the deep water
ventured your lives? Nor might any man,
either friend or foe, restrain you from   511
the perilous voyage, when seaward ye swam
with arms outspread o'er the ocean-stream,
measured the sea-ways, smote with your hands,
o'er the main glided. With winter's fury
the ocean-waves boiled; for a sennight ye toiled
on the water's domain. He conquered thee
    swimming;
he had more strength. At morningtide then
the sea bore him up to the Heathoræmas,
whence he sought, beloved of his people,   520
his country dear, the Brondings' land,
his fair, peaceful burgh, where a people he
    owned,
a burgh and treasures. All his boast to thee
the son of Beanstan truly fulfilled.
Worse of thee, therefore, now I expect—
though everywhere thou hast excelled in grim
    war,
in martial exploits—if thou to Grendel
darest near abide for a night-long space.''
Beowulf spake, Ecgtheow's son:
''Well, my friend Hunferth, drunken with
    beer,   530
a deal hast thou spoken here about Breca,
about his adventure. The sooth I tell,
that I possessed greater endurance at sea,
strength on the waves, than any other.
We two agreed when we were striplings,
and made our boast (we were both as yet
in youthful life), that we on the ocean .
would venture our lives; and thus we did.
A naked sword we held in hand
when we swam on the deep, as we meant to
    defend us   540
against the whales. Far on the flood-waves
away from me he could not float,
in the sea more swiftly, and from him I would
    not.
Then we together were in the sea
a five night's space, till it drove us asunder.
Weltering waves, coldest of tempests,
cloudy night, and the fierce north wind

grimly assaulted us; rough were the billows.
The rage of the sea-fishes was aroused.
Then my body-sark, hard and hand-locked,
afforded me help against my foes;   551
my braided war-shirt lay on my breast,
with gold adorned. A speckled monster
drew me to bottom, a grim one held me
fast in his grasp. Yet was it granted
that with the point I reached the creature,
with my war-falchion. A deadly blow,
dealt by my hand, destroyed the sea-beast.

X. THE QUEEN'S GREETING. GLEE IN HEOROT

"Thus frequently me my hated foes
fiercely threatened; but I served them   560
with my dear sword as it was fitting.
Not of that gluttony had they joy,
foul destroyers, to sit round the feast
near the sea-bottom and eat my body;
but in the morning, with falchions wounded,
up they lay among the shore-drift,
put to sleep by the sword; so that ne'er after
stopt they the way for ocean-sailers
over the surge. Light came from the east,
God's bright beacon, the seas grew calm,   570
so that the sea-nesses I might see,
windy walls. Fate often saves
an undoomed man when his valor avails.

"Yes, 'twas my lot with sword to slay
nickers nine. I have heard of no harder
struggle by night 'neath heaven's vault,
nor of man more harried in ocean-streams.
Yet with life I escaped from the grasp of
      dangers,
aweary of toil. Then the sea bore me,
the flood with its current, the boiling fiords,
to the Finns' land.

            "Now never of *thee*   581
have I heard tell such feats of daring,
such falchion-terrors. Ne'er yet Breca
at game of war, nor either of you,
so valiantly performed a deed
with shining swords (thereof I boast not),
tho' thou of thy brothers wast murderer,
of thy chief kinsmen, wherefore in hell
shalt thou suffer damnation, keen tho' thy wit
      be.
In sooth I say to thee, son of Ecglaf,   590
that never had Grendel, the fiendish wretch,
such horrors committed against thy prince,
such harm in Heorot, were thy spirit,
thy mind, as war-fierce as thou supposest.
But he has found that he need not greatly
care for the hatred of your people,
the fell sword-strength of the victor-Scyldings.*

* The epithet appears to be ironical. It is noteworthy that Hrothgar takes it all in good
part.

He takes a forced pledge, has mercy on none
of the Danish people, but wars at pleasure,
slays and shends you, nor strife expects   60(
from the Spear-Danes. But now of the Geats
the strength and valor shall I unexpectedly
show him in battle. Thereafter may all go
elate to the mead, after the light
of the ether-robed sun on the second day
shines from the south o'er the children of
      men."†

Then was rejoiced the treasure-distributor;
hoary-locked, war-famed, the bright Danes' lord
trusted in succor; the people's shepherd
from Beowulf heard his steadfast resolve.   610
There was laughter of men, the din resounded
words were winsome. Wealhtheow came forth,
Hrothgar's queen; mindful of courtesy,
the gold-adorned greeted the men in the hall.
First then the woman, high-born, handed the
cup to the East-Danes' country's guardian,
bade him be blithe at the beer-drinking,
dear to his people. He gladly partook of
the feast, and the hall-cup, battle-famed king.
Round then went the dame of the Helm-
      ings[1]   620
on every side, among old and young,
costly cups proffered, till came occasion
that she, the high-minded, ring-adorned queen
the mead-cup bore unto Beowulf.
She greeted the lord of the Geats, thanked
      God,
sagacious in words, that her wish had befallen,
that she in any warrior might trust
for comfort 'gainst crimes. He took the cup,
the warrior fierce, from Wealhtheow's hand,
and then made speech, eager for battle,—
Beowulf spake, the son of Ecgtheow: 631
"I resolved, when I went on the main
with my warrior-band and sat in the seaboat,
that I would wholly accomplish the will
of your people in this, or bow in death,
fast in the foe's grasp. I shall perform
deeds of valor, or look to find
here in this mead-hall my last day."
The Geat's proud speech the woman liked
      well;
the high-born queen of the people went,   64(
adorned with gold, to sit by her lord.
Within the hall then again as before
were bold words spoken—the people's joy
the victor folk's clamor—up to the moment

[1] Name of the queen's family.
† "In this speech," says Dr. J. R. C. Hall, "in
less than fourscore passionate lines, we have
rude and outspoken repartee, proud and un-
blushing boast, a rapid narrative, Munchausen
episodes, flashes of nature, a pagan proverb,
a bitter taunt, a reckless insult to the Danish race, a picture of a peaceful time to
come."

when Healfdene's son was fain to go to
his evening rest. He knew that conflict
awaited the monster in the high hall
so soon as they might no longer see
the sun's light, and o'er all murk night,
the shadow-helm of men, came creeping,   650
dusk under heaven. The company rose.
Hrothgar then paid Beowulf reverence—
one hero the other—and bade him hail,
gave him command of the wine-hall and said:
"Never since hand and shield I could raise,
have I before entrusted to any
the hall of the Danes, save now to thee.
Have now and hold this best of houses;
be mindful of glory, show mighty valor,
keep watch for the foe. No wish shall be lacking   660
if thou from this venture escape with thy life."

XI. Beowulf's Vigil

Then Hrothgar departed, the Scyldings' protector,
out of the hall with his band of warriors;
the martial leader would seek his consort,
Wealhtheow the queen. The glory of kings
had set against Grendel, as men have heard tell,
a hall-ward; he held a special office
about the Dane-prince, kept guard 'gainst the
giant.
But the chief of the Geats well trusted in   669
his own proud might and the Creator's favor.
He doffed from him then his iron byrnie,
the helm from his head, and gave to a henchman
his sword enchased, choicest of irons,
bade him take charge of the gear of war.
Some words of pride then spake the good
chief,
Beowulf the Geat, ere he mounted his bed:
"I count me no feebler in martial vigor
of warlike works than Grendel himself.
Therefore I will not, tho' easy it were,   679
with sword destroy him or lull him to rest.
'Tis a warfare he knows not—to strike against
me
and hew my shield, renowned tho' he be
for hostile works; but we two to-night
shall do without sword, if he dare seek
war without weapon. And afterward God,
the wise, the holy, shall glory doom
to whichever hand it meet to him seemeth."
Then lay down the brave man,—the bolster
received
the warrior's cheek; and around him many
a seaman keen reclined on his hall-couch.   690
Not one of them thought that he should thence
seek ever again the home he loved,

the folk or free burg where he was nurtured:
since erst they had heard how far too many
folk of the Danes a bloody death
o'ertook in that wine-hall. But to them the
Lord
gave woven victory,* to the Weders' people
comfort and succor, so that they all
by the might of one, by his single powers,
their foe overcame. Shown is it truly   700
that mighty God ruleth the race of men.
Now in the murky night came stalking
the shadow-walker. All the warriors
who should defend that pinnacled mansion
slept, save one. To men it was known
that the sinful spoiler, when God willed not,
might not drag them beneath the shade.
Natheless, he, watching in hate for the foe,
in angry mood waited the battle-meeting.

XII. Grendel's Onslaught

Then came from the moor, under the mist-
hills,   710
Grendel stalking; he bare God's anger.
The wicked spoiler thought to ensnare
many a man in the lofty hall.
He strode 'neath the clouds until the wine-
house,
the gold-hall of men, he readily saw,
richly adorned. Nor was that time
the first that Hrothgar's home he had sought:
but ne'er in his life, before nor since,
found he a bolder man or hall-thanes.
So then to the mansion the man bereft   720
of joys came journeying; soon with his hands
undid the door, tho' with forged bands fast;
the baleful-minded, angry, burst open
the mansion's mouth. Soon thereafter
the fiend was treading the glittering floor,
paced wroth of mood; from his eyes started
a horrid light, most like to flame.
He in the mansion saw warriors many,
a kindred band, together sleeping,
fellow-warriors. His spirit exulted.   730
The fell wretch expected that ere day came
he would dissever the life from the body
of each, for in him the hope had risen
of a gluttonous feast. Yet 'twas not his fate
that he might more of the race of men
eat after that night. The mighty kinsman
of Hygelac watched how the wicked spoiler
would proceed with his sudden grasping.
Nor did the monster mean to delay;
for he at the first stroke quickly seized   740

* This is a characteristic Northern figure, as well
   as Greek; but it is not Christian. An interesting expansion of it may be found in
   Gray's poem of *The Fatal Sisters.*

a sleeping warrior, tore him unawares,
bit his bone-casings, drank his veins' blood,
in great morsels swallowed him. Soon had he
devoured all of the lifeless one,
feet and hands. He stepped up nearer,
took then with his hand the doughty-minded
warrior at rest; with his hand the foe
reached towards him. He instantly grappled
with the evil-minded, and on his arm rested.

Soon as the criminal realized   750
that in no other man of middle-earth,
of the world's regions, had he found
a stronger hand-grip, his mind grew fearful.
Yet not for that could he sooner escape.
He was bent on flight, would flee to his cavern,
the devil-pack seek; such case had never
in all his life-days befallen before.
Then Hygelac's good kinsman remembered
his evening speech; upright he stood,   759
and firmly grasped him; his fingers yielded.
The jotun was fleeing; the earl stept further.
The famed one considered whether he might
more widely wheel and thence away
flee to his fen-mound; he knew his fingers'
    power
in the fierce one's grasp. 'Twas a dire journey
the baleful spoiler made to Heorot.
The princely hall thundered; terror was
on all the Danes, the city-dwellers,
each valiant one, while both the fierce   769
strong warriors raged; the mansion resounded.

Then was it wonder great that the wine-hall
withstood the war-beasts, nor fell to the ground,
the fair earthly dwelling; yet was it too fast,
within and without, with iron bands,
cunningly forged, though where the fierce ones
fought, I have heard, many a mead-bench,
with gold adorned, from its sill started.
Before that, weened not the Scyldings' sages
that any man ever, in any wise,
in pieces could break it, goodly and bone-
    decked,   780
or craftily rive—only the flame's clutch
in smoke could devour it. Startling enough
the noise uprose. Over the North Danes
stood dire terror, on every one
of those who heard from the wall the whoop,
the dread lay sung by God's denier,
the triumphless song of the thrall of hell,
his pain bewailing. He held him fast,—
he who of men was strongest of might,
of them who in that day lived this life.   790

XIII. The Monster Repulsed

Not for aught would the refuge of earls
leave alive the deadly guest;
the days of his life he counted not useful

to any folk. There many a warrior
of Beowulf's drew his ancient sword;
they would defend the life of their lord,
of the great prince, if so they might.
They knew not, when they entered the strife,
the bold and eager sons of battle,
and thought to hew him on every side   800
his life to seek, that not the choicest
of irons on earth, no battle-falchion,
could ever touch the wicked scather,
since martial weapons he had forsworn,
every edge whatever. Yet on that day
of this life was his life-parting
wretched to be, and the alien spirit
to travel far into power of fiends.

Then he who before in mirth of mood
(he was God's foe) had perpetrated   810
many crimes 'gainst the race of men,
found that his body would not avail him,
for him the proud kinsman of Hygelac
had in hand; each was to the other
hateful alive. The fell wretch suffered
bodily pain; a deadly wound
appeared on his shoulder, his sinews started,
his bone-casings burst. To Beowulf was
the war-glory given; Grendel must thence,
death-sick, under his fen-shelters flee,   820
seek a joyless dwelling; well he knew
that the end of his life was come, his appointed
number of days. For all the Danes,
that fierce fight done, was their wish accom-
    plished.
So he then, the far-come, the wise and strong
of soul, had purified Hrothgar's hall,
saved it from malice; his night's work rejoiced
    him,
his valor-glories. The Geatish chieftain
had to the East-Danes his boast fulfilled,
had healed, to-wit, the preying sorrow   830
that they in that country before had suffered
and had to endure for hard necessity,
no small affliction. A manifest token
it was when the warrior laid down the hand—
arm and shoulder, Grendel's whole grappler
together there—'neath the vaulted roof.

XIV. Joy at Heorot

Then in the morning, as I have heard tell,
there was many a warrior around the gift hall:
folk-chiefs came, from far and near,
o'er distant ways, the wonder to see,   840
the tracks of the foe. His taking from life
seemed not grievous to any warrior
who the inglorious one's trail beheld,—
how, weary in spirit, o'ercome in the conflict,
death-doomed and fleeing, he bare death-traces
thence away to the nickers' mere.

There was the surge boiling with blood,
the dire swing of waves all commingled;
with clotted blood hot, with sword-gore it
     welled;
the death-doomed dyed it, when he joyless
laid down his life in his fen-asylum,   851
his heathen soul. There hell received him.

Thence again turned they, comrades old,
from the joyous journey, and many a younger,
proud from the mere, riding on horses,
warriors on steeds. Then was Beowulf's
glory celebrated. Many oft said
that south or north, between the seas
the wide world over, there was no other
'neath heaven's course who was a better   860
shield-bearer, or one more worthy of power.
Yet found they no fault with their lord beloved,
the joyful Hrothgar: he was their good king.

     .   .   .   .

           Then was morning light
sent forth and quickened. Many a retainer,
strong in spirit, to the high hall went,   919
to see the rare wonder. The king himself also
from his nuptial bower, guardian of ring-
     treasures,
with a large troop stept forth, rich in glory,
for virtues famed; and his queen with him
the meadow-path measured with train of
     maidens.

XV. HROTHGAR'S GRATITUDE

Hrothgar spake (he to the hall went,
stood near the threshold, saw the steep roof
shining with gold, and Grendel's hand):
"Now for this sight, to the Almighty thanks!
May it quickly be given! Much ill have I borne,
Grendel's snares; ever can God work   930
wonder on wonder, the King of Glory.
Not long was it since, that I little weened
for woes of mine through all my life,
reparation to know, when, stained with blood,
the best of houses all gory stood;
woe was wide-spread for each of my counsellors,
who did not ween that they evermore
from foes could defend the people's landwork,[1]
from devils and phantoms. Now this warrior,
through the might of the Lord, has done a deed
which we all together before could not   941
with cunning accomplish. Lo, this may say
whatever woman brought forth this son
among the nations, if yet she lives,
that the ancient Creator was gracious to her
at the birth of her son. Now will I, O Beowulf,
best of warriors, even as a son,
love thee in my heart. Keep henceforth well
our kinship new; no lack shalt thou have

[1] Heorot

of worldly desires, wherein I have power.
Full often for less have I dealt a reward,
an honor-gift, to a feebler warrior,   952
weaker in conflict. Thou for thyself
hast wrought so well, that thy glory shall live
through every age. May the All-wielder
with good reward thee, as now He has done."
Beowulf spake, Ecgtheow's son:
"We with great good will, that arduous work,
that fight, have achieved; we boldly ventured
in war with the monster. The more do I wish
that thou himself mightest have seen,   961
the foe in his trappings, full weary enough.
Him I quickly, with hard and fast fetters,
on his death-bed thought to have bound,
that through my hand-grips low he should lie,
struggling for life, but his body escaped.
I was not able, the Lord did not will it,
to keep him from going; I held him not firm
     enough,
the deadly foe: too strong on his feet
the enemy was. Yet his hand he left,   970
for his life's safety, to guard his track,
his arm and shoulder; yet not thereby
did the wretched creature comfort obtain;
nor will he, crime-doer, the longer live
with sins oppressed. For pain has him
in its grip compelling straitly clasped,
in its deadly bonds; there shall he await,
the crime-stained wretch, the Final Doom,
as the Lord of Splendor shall mete it to him."
Then less noisy was Ecglaf's son   980
in vaunting speech of words of war,
after the nobles, thro' might of the hero,
over the high roof had gazed on the hand,
the fingers of the foe, each for himself.*
Each finger-nail was firm as steel—
a heathen's hand-spurs and a warrior's,—
hideously monstrous. Every one said
that no excellent iron of the bold ones
would be able to touch the demon's hand,
would ever sever the bloody limb.   990

XVI. FEASTING AND SONG

Then quickly 'twas ordered, that Heorot
     within
by hand be adorned; many were they,
of men and women, who the wine-house,
the guest-hall, prepared; gold-shimmering shone
the webs on the walls, wondrous sights many
to each and all that gaze upon such.

* Beowulf, says Dr. Klaeber, "had placed Grendel's hand (on some projection perhaps)
above the door (outside) as high as he could
reach," where the nobles, looking from outside "in the direction of the high roof," behold it. Others think that it was hung up
within the hall.

That splendid dwelling much shattered was,
though bound within with bands of iron;
the hinges asunder were rent, the roof
alone was saved all sound, when the monster,
stained with foul deeds, turned him to flight,
hopeless of life. 1002

[The feast is held, gifts are bestowed on the hero, and Hrothgar's minstrel sings a song of a hundred lines about Finn, the king of the Frisians.]

XVIII. THE QUEEN'S SPEECH

. . . . The lay was sung, 1159
the gleeman's song. Pastime was resumed,
noise rose from the benches, the cup-boys served
     wine
from wondrous vessels. Then Wealhtheow came
     forth
'neath a gold diadem, to where the two good
cousins† sat; at peace were they still,
each true to the other; there Hunferth too sat
at the Scylding lord's feet,—all had faith in his
     spirit,
his courage, altho' to his kinsmen he had not
in sword-play been true.‡ Then the Scyldings'
     queen spake:
"Accept this beaker, my beloved lord,[1]
dispenser of treasure; may'st be joyful, 1170
gold-friend of men! And speak to the Geats
with gentle words! So man shall do.
Be kind toward the Geats, mindful of gifts;
near and far thou now hast safety.
Men have said that thou this warrior
wouldst have for a son. Heorot is purged,
the bright hall of rings: enjoy while thou may-
     est
the rewards of the many, and to thy sons leave
folk and realm, when thou shalt go forth
to see thy Creator. Well I know that 1180
my gracious Hrothulf will the youth
in honor maintain if thou sooner than he,
oh friend of the Scyldings, leavest the world.
I ween that he with good will repay
our offspring dear, if he remembers
all the favors that we for his pleasure
and honor performed when he was a child."
     Then she turned to the seat where were her
          sons,
Hrethric and Hrothmund, and the sons of the
     heroes, 1189
the youths all together; there sat the noble
Beowulf the Geat, beside the two brothers.

[1] Hrothgar
† Hrothgar, and his nephew, Hrothulf, who must
     have been older than the king's children (cp.
     lines 1180 ff), but who evidently did not re-
     main "true."
‡ He was said to have killed his brothers.

XIX. BEOWULF REWARDED. EVENTIDE

     The cup was brought him, and friendly greet-
          ing
in words was given and twisted gold
kindly proffered—bracelets two,
armor and rings, a collar the largest
of those that on earth I have heard tell of.
Never 'neath heaven have I heard of a better
treasure-hoard of men, since Hama bore off
to the glittering burg the Brosings' necklace,§
the jewel and casket (he fled the guileful 1200
hate of Eormenric, chose gain eternal[1]).
Hygelac the Geat wore this collar,
the grandson of Swerting, on his last raid,
when he 'neath his banner the treasure de-
     fended,
the slaughter-spoil guarded; fate took him off
when he out of pride sought his own woe,
war with the Frisians; he the jewels conveyed,
the precious stones, over the wave-bowl,
the powerful king; he fell 'neath his shield.
Then into the power of the Franks the king's
     life
went, and his breast-weeds, went too the collar;
warriors inferior plundered the fallen 1212
after the war-lot; the Geat-folk held
the abode of the slain.
                    The hall resounded.
Wealhtheow spake, before the warrior-band
     said:
"Use this collar, Beowulf dear,
oh youth, with joy, and use this mantle,
these lordly treasures, and thrive thou well;
prove thyself mighty, and be to these boys
gentle in counsels. I will reward thee. 1220
This hast thou achieved, that, far and near,
throughout all time, men will esteem thee,
even so widely as the sea encircles
the windy land-walls. Be while thou livest
a prosperous noble. I grant you well
precious treasures; be thou to my sons
gentle in deeds, thou who hast joy.
Here is each earl to the other true,
mild of mood, to his liege lord faithful;
the thanes are united, the people all ready. 1230
Warriors who have drunken, do as I bid."
     To her seat then she went. There was choic-
          est of feasts,
the warriors drank wine; Wyrd they knew not,
calamity grim, as it turned out
for many a man after evening had come
and Hrothgar had to his lodging departed,
the ruler to rest. There guarded the hall

[1] Perhaps entered a monastery (S. Bugge).
§ The famous necklace of Freyja, which Hama
     stole from Eormenric, the cruel king of the
     Goths.

countless warriors, as oft they had done.
They cleared the bench-floor; it soon was o'er-
    spread
with beds and bolsters. A certain beer-bearer,
ready and fated, bent to his rest.   1241
They set at their heads their disks of war,
their shield-wood bright; there on the bench,
over each noble, easy to see,
was his high martial helm, his ringed byrnie
and war-wood stout. It was their custom
that they were ever for war prepared,
at home, in the field, in both alike,
at whatever time to their liege lord
the need befel. 'Twas a ready people.   1250

XX. GRENDEL'S MOTHER

They sank then to sleep. One sorely paid
for his evening rest, as full oft had happened
since the gold-hall Grendel occupied,
unrighteousness did, until the end came,
death after sins. Then it was seen,
wide-known among men, that still an avenger
lived after the foe, for a long time
after the battle-care,—Grendel's mother.
The woman-demon remembered her misery,
she that the watery horrors, the cold streams,
had to inhabit, when Cain became   1261
slayer by sword of his only brother,
his father's son. Then he went forth blood-
    stained,
by murder marked, fleeing man's joy,
dwelt in the wilderness. Thence awoke many
fated demons; Grendel was one,
the hated fell wolf who at Heorot found
a watchful warrior awaiting the conflict;
and there the monster laid hold of him.
Yet was he mindful of his great strength, 1270
the generous gift that God had given him,
and trusted for help in him the All-wielder,
for comfort and aid; so slew he the fiend,
struck down the hell-spirit. Then humble he
    made off,
the foe of mankind, to seek his death-home,
of joy deprived. Natheless his mother,
greedy and gloomy, was bent on going
the sorrowful journey, her son's death to
    avenge.
    So came she to Heorot, to where the Ring-
        Danes   1279
throughout the hall slept. Forthwith there came
to the warriors a change, when in on them
    rushed
Grendel's mother; the terror was less
by just so much as the force of women is,
the war-dread from woman, than that from a
    man

when the hilt-bound sword, hammer-beaten,
stained with gore, and doughty of edges,
hews off the head of the boar on the helm.
    Then in the hall the hard edge was drawn,
the sword o'er the seats, many a broad shield
raised firm in hand; helms they forgot
and byrnies broad, when the terror seized them.
She was in haste,—would out from thence 1292
to save her life, since she was discovered.
One of the nobles she quickly had
with grip fast seized, as she went to fen;
he was to Hrothgar of heroes the dearest
in comradeship beside the two seas,
a mighty shield-warrior, whom she killed,
a hero renowned. (Beowulf was absent,
for another apartment had before been as-
    signed,   1300
after giving of treasures, to the great Geat.)
A cry was in Heorot. She took with its gore
the well known hand;[1] grief had become
renewed in the dwellings. 'Twas no good ex-
    change,
that those on both sides payment must make
with lives of their friends.
    Then was the old king,
the hoary war-hero, in stormy mood
when his highest thane, no longer living,
his dearest friend, he knew to be dead.
Quickly to his chamber was Beowulf summoned,
the victor-rich warrior. Together ere day 1311
he went with his earls, the noble champion
with his comrades went where the wise king
    awaited
whether for him the All-wielder would
after the woe-time a change bring about.
Then along the floor went the warlike man
with his body guard (the hall-wood resounded)
till he the wise prince greeted with words,
the lord of the Ingwins;[2] asked if he had had
according to his wish, an easy night.   1320

XXI. SORROW FOR ÆSCHERE. THE MONSTER'S MERE

Hrothgar spake, the Scyldings' protector:
"Ask not after happiness! Grief is renewed
to the folk of the Danes. Dead is Æschere,
of Yrmenlaf the elder brother,
my confidant and my counsellor,
my near attendant when we in war
defended our heads, when hosts contended,
and boar-crests crashed; such should an earl be,
preeminently good, as Æschere was.
He in Heorot has had for murderer   1330
a ghost-like death-spirit; I know not whether

[1] Grendel's (see l. 834)
[2] the Danes

the fell carrion-gloater her steps back has
    traced,
made known by her meal. She the feud has
    avenged,
that thou yester-night didst Grendel slay,
through thy fierce nature, with fetter-like
    grasps,
for that he too long my people diminished
and wrought destruction. He in battle suc-
    cumbed,
forfeiting life. And now comes another
mighty man-scather to avenge her son,—
has from afar warfare established,   1340
as it may seem to many a thane
who mourns in spirit his treasure-giver,
in hard heart-affliction. Now low lies the hand
which once availed you for every desire.

  "I have heard it said by the land-dwellers,
by my own subjects, my hall-counsellors,
that they have seen a pair of such
mighty march-stalkers holding the moors,
stranger-spirits, whereof the one,
so far as they could certainly know,   1350
was in form of a woman; the other, accurst,
trod an exile's steps in the figure of man
(save that he huger than other men was),
whom in days of yore the dwellers on earth
Grendel named. They know not a father.
whether any was afore-time born
of the dark ghosts. That secret land
they dwell in, wolf-dens, windy nesses,
the perilous fen-path, where the mountain
    stream
downward flows 'neath the mists of the nesses,
the flood under earth. 'Tis not far thence, 1361
a mile in measure, that the mere stands,
over which hang rustling groves;
a wood fast rooted the water o'ershadows.
  "There every night may be seen a dire won-
    der,
fire in the flood. None so wise lives
of the children of men, who knows the bottom.
Although the heath-stepper, wearied by hounds,
the stag strong of horns, seek that holtwood,
driven from far, he will give up his life,   1370
his breath, on the shore, ere he will venture
his head upon it. That is no pleasant place.
Thence surging of waters upwards ascends
wan to the welkin, when the wind stirs up
the hateful tempests, till air grows gloomy
and skies shed tears. Again now is counsel
in thee alone! The spot thou yet ken'st not,
the perilous place where thou may'st find
this sinful being. Seek if thou dare.
With riches will I for the strife reward thee,
with ancient treasures, as I before did,   1381
with twisted gold, if thou comest off safe.''

XXII. THE PURSUIT

  Beowulf spake, Ecgtheow's son:
''Sorrow not, sage man, 'tis better for each
to avenge his friend than greatly to mourn.
Each of us must an end await
of this world's life; let him work who can
high deeds ere death; that will be for the war-
    rior,
when he is lifeless, afterwards best.
Rise, lord of the realm, let us quickly go
to see the course of Grendel's parent.   1391
I promise thee, not to the sea shall she 'scape,
nor to earth's embrace, nor to mountain-wood,
nor to ocean's ground, go whither she will.
This day do thou endurance have
in every woe, as I expect of thee!''
  Up leapt the old man then, thanked God,
the mighty Lord, for what the man said.
For Hrothgar then a horse was bridled,
a steed with curled mane. The ruler wise
in state went forth; a troop strode on,   1401
bearing their shields. Tracks there were
along the forest paths widely seen,
her course o'er the ground; she had thither
    gone
o'er the murky moor. Of their fellow thanes
she bore the best one, soul-bereft,
of those that with Hrothgar defended their
    home.
  Then overpassed these sons of nobles
deep rocky gorges, a narrow road,
strait lonely paths, an unknown way,   1410
precipitous nesses, monster-dens many.
He went in advance, he and a few
of the wary men, to view the plain,
till suddenly he found mountain-trees
overhanging a hoary rock,
a joyless wood; there was water beneath,
gory and troubled. To all the Danes,
friends of the Scyldings, 'twas grievous in
    mind,
a source of sorrow to many a thane,
pain to each earl, when of Æschere,   1420
on the sea-shore, the head they found.
  The flood boiled with blood, the people looked
    on
at the hot glowing gore. The horn at times
    sang
a ready war-song. The band all sat.
They saw in the water a host of the worm-kind,
strange sea dragons sounding the deep;
in the headland-clefts also, nickers lying,
which in the morning oft-times keep
their sorrowful course upon the sail-road,
worms and wild beasts;—they sped away,
bitter and rage-swollen; they heard the sound,

the war-horn singing. The lord of the Geats
with a bolt from his bow took one from life,
from his wave-strife, and left in his vitals 1434
the hard war-shaft; he in the sea was
the slower in swimming, when death took him
    off.
Quickly on the waves, with hunting-spears
sharply hooked, he was strongly pressed,
felled by force, and drawn up on the headland,
the wonderful swimmer. The men there gazed
on the grisly guest.

    Beowulf girt himself   1441
in war-like weeds; for life he feared not;
his warrior-byrnie, woven by hands,
ample and inlaid, must tempt the deep;
it could well his body protect
that battle-grip might not scathe his breast,
the fierce one's wily grasp injure his life,
But the flashing helm guarded his head,
(which with the sea-bottom was to mingle, 1449
and seek the sea-surge) with jewels adorned,
encircled with chains, as in days of yore
the weapon-smith wrought it, wondrously
    framed,
set with swine-figures, so that thereafter
no brand nor war-sword ever could bite it.

    Nor then was that least of powerful aids
which Hrothgar's orator[1] lent him at need:
Hrunting was named the hafted falchion.
'Twas among the foremost of olden treasures;
its edge was iron, tainted with poison,   1459
harden'd with warrior-blood; ne'er in battle
had it failed any of those that brandished it,
who durst to travel the ways of terror,
the perilous trysts. 'Twas not the first time
that it a valorous deed should perform.

    Surely Ecglaf's son remembered not,
the mighty in power, what erst he had said,
drunken with wine, when the weapon he lent
to a better sword-warrior. He durst not himself
'mid the strife of the waves adventure his life,
a great deed perform; there lost he his credit
for valorous doing. Not so with the other 1471
when he had prepared himself for battle!

XXIII. The Fight Beneath the Waves

    Beowulf spake, Ecgtheow's son:
"Remember thou now, great son of Healfdene,
sagacious prince, now I am ready to go,
O gold-friend of men, the things we have
    spoken:
If I should lose my life for thy need,
that thou wouldst ever be to me,
when I am gone, in a father's stead.   1479
Be a guardian thou to my fellow thanes,

[1] Hunferth (cf. l. 499)

to my near comrades, if war take me off.
Also the treasures which thou hast given me,
beloved Hrothgar, to Hygelac send.
By that gold then may the lord of the Geats
    know,
may Hrethel's son see, when he looks on that
    treasure,
that I in man's virtue have found one pre-
    eminent,
a giver of rings, and rejoiced while I might.
And let Hunferth have the ancient relic,
the wondrous war-sword, let the far-famed man
the hard-of-edge have. I with Hrunting 1490
will work me renown, or death shall take me.'"

    After these words the Weder-Geats' lord
with ardor hastened, nor any answer
would he await. The sea-wave received
the warrior-hero. It was a day's space
ere he the bottom could perceive.
Forthwith she found—she who the flood's
    course
had blood-thirsty held a hundred years,
grim and greedy—that a man from above
was there exploring the realm of strange crea-
    tures.   1500
Then at him she grasped, the warrior seized
in her horrible claws. Nathless she crushed not
his unhurt body; the ring-mail guarded him,
so that she might not pierce that war-dress,
the lock-linked sark, with her hostile fingers.

    Then when the sea-wolf reached the bottom,
she bore to her dwelling the prince of rings
so that he might not, brave as he was,
his weapons wield; for many strange beings
in the deep oppressed him, many a sea-beast
with its battle tusks his war-sark broke; 1511
the wretches pursued him. Then the earl found
he was in he knew not what dread hall,
where him no water in aught could scathe,
nor because of the roof could the sudden grip
of the flood reach him; he saw a fire-light,
a brilliant beam brightly shining.
The hero perceived then the wolf of the deeps,
the mighty mere-wife; a powerful onslaught
he made with his falchion, the sword-blow with-
    held not,   1520
so on her head the ringed brand sang
a horrid war-song. The guest then discovered
how that the battle-beam would not bite,
would not scathe life, but that the edge failed
its lord at his need; erst had it endured
hand-conflicts many, slashed often the helm,
war-garb of the doomed; then was the first time
for the precious gift that its power failed.

    Still was he resolute, slacked not his ardor,
of great deeds mindful was Hygelac's kinsman.
Flung he the twisted brand, curiously bound,

the angry champion, that stiff and steel-edged
it lay on the earth; in his strength he trusted,
his powerful hand-grip. So shall man do, 1534
when he in battle thinks of gaining
lasting praise, nor cares for his life.
 By the shoulder then seized he (recked not of
  her malice),
the lord of the war-Geats, Grendel's mother;
the fierce fighter hurled, incensed as he was,
the mortal foe, that she fell to the ground.
She quickly repaid him again in full 1541
with her fierce grasps, and at him caught;
then stumbled he weary, of warriors the strongest,
the active champion, so that he fell.
She pressed down the hall-guest, and drew her
  dagger,
the broad gleaming blade,—would avenge her
  son,
her only child. On his shoulder lay
the braided breast-net which shielded his life
'gainst point, 'gainst edge, all entrance withstood.
 Then would have perished Ecgtheow's son
'neath the wide earth, champion of the Geats,
had not his war-byrnie help afforded, 1552
his battle-net hard, and holy God
awarded the victory. The wise Lord,
Ruler of Heaven, with justice decided it
easily, when he again stood up.

XXIV. Victory

 Then he saw 'mongst the arms a victorious
  falchion,
an old jotun-sword, of edges doughty,
the glory of warriors; of weapons 'twas choicest, 1559
save it was greater than any man else
to the game of war could carry forth,
good and gorgeous, the work of giants.
 The knotted hilt seized he, the Scyldings'
  warrior,—
fierce and deadly grim, the ringed sword swung;
despairing of life, he angrily struck,
that 'gainst her neck it griped her hard,
her bone-rings[1] brake. Thro' her fated carcass
the falchion passed; on the ground she sank.
The blade was gory, the man joy'd in his work.
 The sword-beam shone bright, light rayed
  within, 1570
even as from heaven serenely shines
the candle of the firmament. He looked down
  the chamber,
then turned by the wall; his weapon upraised
firm by the hilt Hygelac's thane,

angry and resolute. Nor was the edge
to the war-prince useless; for he would forthwith
Grendel requite for the many raids
that he had made upon the West Danes,
and not on one occasion only,
when he Hrothgar's hearth-companions 1580
slew in their rest, sleeping devoured
fifteen men of the folk of the Danes,
and as many others conveyed away,
hateful offerings. He had so repaid him
for that, the fierce champion, that at rest he
  saw,
weary of contest, Grendel lying   .
deprived of his life, as he had been scathed by
the conflict at Heorot; the corpse bounded far
when after death he suffered the stroke, 1589
the hard sword-blow, and his head it severed.
 Forthwith they saw, the sagacious men,
those who with Hrothgar kept watch on the
  water,
that the surge of the waves was all commingled,
the deep stained with blood. The grizzly-haired
old men together spake of the hero,
how they of the atheling hoped no more
that, victory-flush'd, he would come to seek
their famous king, since this seemed a sign
that him the sea-wolf had quite destroyed.
The noon-tide* came, they left the nesses,
the Scyldings bold; departed home thence
the gold-friend of men. The strangers sat,
sick of mood, and gazed on the mere, 1603
wished but weened not that they their dear lord
himself should see.
 Then that sword, the war-blade,
with its battle-gore like bloody icicles,
began to fade. A marvel it was,
how it all melted, most like to ice
when the Father relaxes the bands of the frost,
unwinds the flood-fetters, He who has power
over seasons and times; true Creator is that!
More treasures he took not, the Weder-Geats'
  lord, 1612
within those dwellings (though many he saw
  there)
except the head, and the hilt also,
with jewels shining;—the blade had all melted,
the drawn brand was burnt, so hot was the
  blood,
so venomous the demon, who down there had
  perished.
Afloat soon was he that at strife had awaited
the slaughter of foes; he swam up through the
  water.

---

[1] vertebrae

* An apparent admission of the exaggeration in
l. 1495, though noon meant formerly the
ninth hour of the day, which would bring it
near evening.

The ocean surges all were cleansed,   1620
the dwellings vast, when the stranger guest
her life-days left and this fleeting existence.
Then came to land the sailor's protector
stoutly swimming, rejoiced in his sea-spoil,
the mighty burden of what he brought with
    him.
Then toward him they went, with thanks to
    God,
the stout band of thanes, rejoiced in their lord,
because they beheld him safe and sound.
From the vigorous chief both helm and byrnie
were then soon loosed. The sea subsided—
the cloud-shadowed water with death-gore dap-
    pled.   1631
    Thence forth they went retracing their steps
happy at heart, the high-way measured,
the well-known road. The nobly bold men
up from the sea-shore bore the head,
not without labor for each of them,
the mightily daring. Four undertook
with toil to bear on the battle-spear,
up to the gold-hall, the head of Grendel;
until straightway to the hall they came,   1640
resolute, warlike, four and ten of them,
Geats all marching with their lord.
Proud amid the throng, he trod the meadows.
    Then entering came the prince of thanes,
the deed-strong man with glory honored,
the man bold in battle, Hrothgar's greet.
And into the hall, where men are drinking,
Grendel's head by the hair was borne,
a thing of terror to nobles and lady.
'Twas a wonderful sight men looked upon.

XXV. Hrothgar's Gratitude and Counsel

    Beowulf spake, Ecgtheow's son: 1651
"Lo, these sea-offerings, son of Healfdene,
lord of the Scyldings, we have joyfully brought,
in token of glory: thou seest them here.
Not easily did I escape with my life,
ventured with pain on the war under water.
Indeed the struggle would have been ended
outright, had not God me shielded.
Not able was I, in the conflict, with Hrunting
aught to accomplish, though that weapon was
    good;   1660
but the Ruler of men granted to me,
that I saw on the wall, all beautiful hanging,
an old heavy sword, (He has often directed
the friendless man,) and that weapon I drew.
Then I slew in that strife, as occasion afforded,
the wards of the house. That war-falchion then,
that drawn brand, was burnt, as the blood
    burst forth,
of strife-blood the hottest. Thence I the hilt
from the foes bore away, avenged the crimes,

the Danes' death-plague, as it was fitting. 1670
    "I promise thee now that thou in Heorot
mayest sleep secure with thy warrior-band,
and thy thanes, each one, thanes of thy people,
the tried and the youthful; that thou needest
    not,
oh prince of the Scyldings, fear from that side
life's bane to thy warriors as erst thou didst."
    Then the golden hilt, to the aged hero,
the hoar war-leader, in hand was given,
giant-work old; it passed to the keeping
(those devils once fallen) of the lord of the
    Danes,   1680
wonderful smith-work; when quitted this world
the fierce-hearted creature, God's adversary,
of murder guilty, and his mother also,
it passed to the keeping of the best
of the world-kings that by the two seas,
in Scania-land, treasures dealt.
Then Hrothgar spake; he gazed on the hilt,
old relic whereon was the origin written
of an ancient war, when the flood had slain—
the flowing ocean—the race of the giants;—
they had borne them boldly. That was a people
alien from God; them a final reward,   1692
through the rage of the water, the All-wielder
    gave.
On the mounting too, of shining gold,
in runic letters, was rightly marked,
was set and said, for whom first was wrought
that choicest of swords, with hilt bound round
and serpentine. Then spake the wise man,
the son of Healfdene, (all were silent):
    "Lo this may he say who practises truth
and right 'mong the people, far back all re-
    members,   1701
a land-warden old, that this earl was
nobly born. Thy fame is exalted,
through far and wide ways, Beowulf, my friend,
over every nation. Thou wearest with patience
thy might, and with prudence. I shall show
    thee my love,
e'en as we two have said: thou shalt be for a
    comfort
a very long time to thine own people,
a help unto warriors. Not so was Heremod[1]
to Ecgwela's children, the noble Scyldings;
he throve not for their weal, but for their
    slaughter,   1711
and for a death-plague to the folk of the Danes.
In angry mood slew he his table-sharers,
his nearest friends, till he lonely departed,
the very great prince, from the joys of men.
Though him Mighty God, with delights of
    power,
with strength had exalted, above all men

  1 A Danish King, banished for cruelty.

had advanced him, yet there grew in his heart
a bloodthirsty spirit; he gave no rings
to the Danes, as was custom; joyless continued
    he,   1720
so that of war he the misery suffered,
long bale to the people. Learn thou from him;
lay hold of man's virtue! For thee have I told
    this,
wise in winters. 'Tis wondrous to say,
how mighty God, to the race of men,
through his ample mind, dispenses wisdom,
lands and valor: He has power over all.
Sometimes He lets wander at their own will
the thoughts of a man of race renowned,
in his country gives him the joy of earth,   1730
a shelter-city of men to possess;
thus makes to him subject parts of the world,
ample kingdoms, that he himself may not,
because of his folly, think of his end.
He lives in plenty; no whit deters him
disease or old age, no uneasy care
darkens his soul, nor anywhere strife
breeds hostile hate; but for him the whole
    world
turns at his will; he the worse knows not,—

XXVI. HROTHGAR'S COUNSEL CONCLUDED

until within him a great deal of arrogance
grows and buds, when the guardian sleeps, 1741
the keeper of the soul. Too fast is the sleep,
bound down by cares; very near is the slayer,
who from his arrow-bow wickedly shoots.
Then he in the breast, 'neath the helm, will be
    stricken
with the bitter shaft; he cannot guard him
from strange evil orders of the Spirit accursed.
Too small seems to him what long he has held;
fierce minded he covets, gives not in his pride
many rich rings; and the future life   1750
he forgets and neglects, because God to him
    gave,
Ruler of glory, many great dignities.
In the final close at length it chances
that the body-home, inconstant, sinks,
fated falls. Another succeeds,
who without reluctance treasure dispenses,
old wealth of the warrior, terror heeds not.
   "From that evil keep thee, Beowulf dear,
best among warriors, and choose thee the better,
counsels eternal. Heed not arrogance,   1760
famous champion! Now is thy might
in flower for awhile; eftsoons will it be
that disease or the sword shall deprive thee of
    strength,
or the clutch of fire, or rage of flood,
or falchion's grip, or arrows' flight,
or cruel age; or brightness of eyes

shall fail and darken; sudden 'twill be,
that thee, noble warrior, death shall o'erpower.
   "Thus I the Ring-Danes half a hundred years
had ruled 'neath the welkin, and saved them in
    war   1776
from many tribes through this mid-earth,
with spears and swords, so that I counted
that under Heaven I had no foe.
Lo to me then came a reverse in my realm,
after merriment sadness, since Grendel became
my enemy old, and my assailant.
From that persecution have I constantly borne
great grief of mind. So thanks be to God
the Lord Eternal, that I have lived
till I on that head all clotted with gore,   1780
old conflict ended, might gaze with my eyes.
Go now to thy seat, the banquet enjoy,
O honored in battle; for us two shall be
many treasures in common, when morning shall
    come.''
   Glad was the Geat and straightway went
to take his seat, as the sage commanded.
   Then as before were the famed for valor,
the sitters at court right handsomely
set feasting afresh.   The night-helm grew
    murky,   1789
dark o'er the vassals; the courtiers all rose;
the grizzly-haired prince would go to his bed,
the aged Scylding; the Geat, exceedingly
famed shield-warrior, desired to rest.
Him, journey-weary, come from afar,
a hall-thane promptly guided forth
who in respect had all things provided
for a thane's need, such as in that day
farers over the sea should have.
   The great-hearted rested. High rose the hall
vaulted and gold-hued; therein slept the guest,
until the black raven, blithe-hearted, announced
the joy of heaven. Then came the bright sun
o'er the fields gliding.   1803
[Beowulf returns the sword Hrunting to
Hunferth, then goes to the king and announces
his intention of returning to his fatherland.
The king repeats his thanks and praises.]

XXVII. THE PARTING

   Then to him gave the warrior's protector,
the son of Healfdene, treasures twelve;
with those gifts bade him his own dear people
in safety to seek, and quickly return.   1869
The king, in birth noble, then kissed the prince,
the lord of the Scyldings the best of thanes;—
and round the neck clasped him; tears he shed,
the hoary headed; chances two
there were to the aged, the second stronger,
whether (or not) they should see each other
again in conference. So dear was the man

that his breast's heaving he could not restrain,
but in his bosom, in heart-bands fast,
for the man beloved his secret longing
burned in his blood. Beowulf thence,   1880
a gold-proud warrior, trod the greensward,
in treasure exulting. The sea-ganger awaited,
at anchor riding, its owner and lord.*

DEOR'S LAMENT†

Weland for a woman learned to know exile,
that haughty earl bowed unto hardship,
had for companions sorrow and longing,
the winter's cold sting, woe upon woe,
what time Nithhad laid sore need on him.
Withering sinew-wounds! Ill-starred man!   6
   That was o'erpassed; this may pass also.

On Beadohilde bore not so heavily
her brother's death as the dule in her own
   heart   9
when she perceived, past shadow of doubt,

her maidhood departed, and yet could nowise
clearly divine how it might be.   12
   That was o'erpassed; this may pass also.

Of Hild's fate we have heard from many.
Land-bereaved were the Geatish chieftains,
so that sorrow left them sleepless.
   That was o'erpassed; this may pass also.

Theodoric kept for thirty winters   18
in the burg of the Mærings; 'twas known of
   many.
   That was o'erpassed; this may pass also.

Heard have we likewise of Eormanric's mind,
wolfishly tempered; widely enthralled he
the folk of the Goth-realm; he was a grim king.
Many a warrior sat locked in his sorrow,   24
waiting on woe; wished, how earnestly!
the reign of that king might come to an end.
   That was o'erpassed; this may pass also.

. . Now of myself this will I say: 35
Erewhile I was Scôp of the Heodenings,
dear to my lord. Deor my name was.
A many winters I knew good service;
gracious was my lord. But now Heorrenda,
by craft of his singing, succeeds to the land-
   right
that Guardian of Men erst gave unto me.
   That was o'erpassed; this may pass also.

CAEDMON (fl. 670)

From the PARAPHRASE OF THE SCRIPTURES*

The Garden of Eden

Then beheld our Creator
the beauty of his works and the excellence of
   his productions,
of the new creatures. Paradise stood
good and spiritual, filled with gifts,
with forward benefits. Fair washed   216
the genial land the running water,
the well-brook: no clouds as yet
over the ample ground bore rains
lowering with wind; yet with fruits stood
earth adorn'd. Held their onward course
river-streams, four noble ones,
from the new Paradise.
These were parted, by the Lord's might,
all from one (when he this earth created)

---

* Is the poem of Beowulf in any sense mythological? Perhaps the latest and best opinion on the subject is that it is not.
"Undoubtedly one is here on the borderland of myth. But in the actual poem the border is not crossed. Whatever the remote connection of Beowulf the hero with Beowa the god, . . . to the poet of the epic its hero is a man, and the monsters are such as folk then believed to haunt sea and lake and moor."—Francis B. Gummere: *The Oldest English Epic.*
"The poem loses nothing of its picturesqueness in being denied its mythology. The firedrake and Grendel and the she-demon are more terrible when conceived as uncanny and abominable beings whose activities in the world can only be dimly imagined by men than they are when made mere personifications of the forces of nature. Beowulf is no less heroic as a mortal facing with undaunted courage these grisly phantoms of the moor and mere, than as a god subduing the sea or the darkness. And the proud words that he utters in his dying hour are more impressive from the lips of a man than from those of a being who still retains some of the glory of a god about him,—'In my home I awaited what time might bring me, held well my own, sought no treacherous feuds, swore no false oaths. In all this I can rejoice, though sick unto death with my wounds.' "—William W. Lawrence: *Pub. Mod. Lang. Association,* June, 1909.

Deor's Lament is one of the poems that may have been brought from the continent by the Angles in their early migrations. "Its form," says Stopford Brooke, "is remarkable. It has a refrain, and there is no other early English instance of this known to us. It is written in strophes, and one motive, constant throughout, is expressed in the refrain. This dominant cry of passion makes the poem a true lyric, . . . the Father of all English lyrics . . . Deor has been deprived of his rewards and lands, and has seen a rival set above his head. It is this whirling down of Fortune's wheel that he mourns in his song, and he compares his fate to that of others who have suffered, so that he may have some comfort. But the comfort is stern like that the Northmen take."

* These paraphrases of the Scriptures are commonly spoken of as Cædmon's, though ascribed to him on very uncertain grounds. Apart from their intrinsic worth they are interesting for their possible relation to *Paradise Lost.* See *Eng. Lit.,* p. 23. The translation is the literal one of Benjamin Thorpe.

water with beauty bright, and sent into the
world.   220

THE FALL OF SATAN

The All-powerful had angel tribes,
through might of hand, the holy Lord,
ten established, in whom he trusted well
that they his service would follow,
work his will; therefore gave he them wit,   250
and shaped them with his hands; the holy Lord.
He had placed them so happily, one he had
    made so powerful,
so mighty in his mind's thought, he let him
    sway over so much,
highest after himself in heaven's kingdom. He
    had made him so fair,
so beauteous was his form in heaven, that came
    to him from the Lord of hosts,
he was like to the light stars. It was his to
    work the praise of the Lord,
it was his to hold dear his joys in heaven, and
    to thank his Lord
for the reward that he had bestow'd on him in
    that light; then had he let him long pos-
    sess it;
but he turned it for himself to a worse thing,
    began to raise war upon him,
against the highest Ruler of heaven, who sitteth
    in the holy seat.   260

.   .   .   .   .   .

The fiend with all his comrades fell then from
    heaven above,
through as long as three nights and days,
the angels from heaven into hell, and them all
    the Lord
transformed to devils, because they his deed
    and word
would not revere; therefore them in a worse
    light,   310
under the earth beneath, Almighty God
had placed triumphless in the swart hell;
there they have at even, immeasurably long,
each of all the fiends, a renewal of fire;
then cometh ere dawn the eastern wind,
frost bitter-cold; ever fire or dart,
some hard torment they must have;
it was wrought for them in punishment.

.   .   .   .   .   .

Then spake the haughty king
who of angels erst was brightest,   338
fairest in heaven: . . .
"This narrow place is most unlike
that other that we ere knew,
high in heaven's kingdom, which my master
    bestow'd on me,
though we it, for the All-powerful, may not
    possess,
must cede our realm; yet hath he not done
    rightly   360
that he hath struck us down to the fiery abyss
of the hot hell, bereft us of heaven's kingdom,
hath it decreed with mankind
to people. That of sorrows is to me the
    greatest,
that Adam shall, who of earth was wrought,
my strong seat possess,
be to him in delight, and we endure this tor-
    ment,
misery in this hell. Oh had I power of my
    hands,
and might one season be without,
be one winter's space, then with this host I—370
But around me lie iron bonds,
presseth this cord of chain: I am powerless!
me have so hard the clasps of hell,
so firmly grasped! Here is a vast fire
above and underneath, never did I see
a loathlier landskip; the flame abateth not,
hot over hell. Me hath the clasping of these
    rings,
this hard-polish'd band, impeded in my course,
debarr'd me from my way; my feet are bound,
my hands manacled, of these hell-doors are   380
the ways obstructed, so that with aught I cannot
from these limb-bonds escape.''—From *Genesis*.

THE CLOUD BY DAY

Had the cloud, in its wide embrace,
the earth and firmament above alike divided:
it led the nation-host; quenched was the flame-
    fire,
with heat heaven-bright. The people were
    amazed,
of multitudes most joyous, their day-shield's
    shade
rolled over the clouds. The wise God had   80
the sun's course with a sail shrouded;
though the mast-ropes men knew not,
nor the sail-cross might they see,
the inhabitants of earth, all the enginery;
how was fastened that greatest of field-houses.

THE DROWNING OF PHARAOH AND HIS ARMY

The folk was affrighted, the flood-dread seized
    on
their sad souls; ocean wailed with death,
the mountain heights were with blood be-
    steamed,
the sea foamed gore, crying was in the waves,
the water full of weapons, a death-mist
    rose;   450
the Egyptians were turned back;
trembling they fled, they felt fear:
would that host gladly find their homes;

their vaunt grew sadder; against them as a
    cloud, rose
the fell rolling of the waves; there came not
    any
of that host to home, but from behind inclosed
    them
fate with the wave. Where ways ere lay,
sea raged. Their might was merged,
the streams stood, the storm rose
high to heaven; the loudest army-cry   460
the hostile uttered; the air above was thickened
with dying voices; blood pervaded the flood,
the shield-walls were riven, shook the firmament
that greatest of sea-deaths: the proud died,
kings in a body; the return prevailed
of the sea at length; their bucklers shone
high over the soldiers; the sea-wall rose,
the proud-ocean-stream, their might in death
    was
fastly fettered.—From *Exodus.*

BEDE (673-735)

From the ECCLESIASTICAL HISTORY.*

The Britons Seek Succor from the Romans The Roman Wall

From that time,[1] the south part of Britain, destitute of armed soldiers, of martial stores, and of all its active youth, which had been led away by the rashness of the tyrants, never to return, was wholly exposed to rapine, as being totally ignorant of the use of weapons. Whereupon they suffered many years under two very savage foreign nations, the Scots from the west, and the Picts from the north. We call these foreign nations, not on account of their being seated out of Britain, but because they were remote from that part of it which was possessed by the Britons; two inlets of the sea lying between them, one of which runs in far and broad into the land of Britain, from the Eastern Ocean, and the other from the Western, though they do not reach so as to touch one another. . .

On account of the irruption of these nations, the Britons sent messengers to Rome with letters in mournful manner, praying for succours, and promising perpetual subjection, provided that the impending enemy should be driven away. An armed legion was immediately sent them, which, arriving in the island, and engaging the enemy, slew a great multitude of them, drove the rest out of the territories of their allies, and having delivered them from their cruel oppressors, advised them to build a wall between the two seas across the island, that it might secure them, and keep off the enemy; and thus they returned home with great triumph. The islanders raising the wall, as they had been directed, not of stone, as having no artist capable of such a work, but of sods, made it of no use. However, they drew it for many miles between the two bays or inlets of the seas, which we have spoken of; to the end that where the defense of the water was wanting, they might use the rampart to defend their borders from the irruptions of the enemies. Of which work there erected, that is, of a rampart of extraordinary breadth and height, there are evident remains to be seen at this day. It begins at about two miles' distance from the monastery of Abercurnig,[2] and running westward, ends near the city Alcluith.[3]

But the former enemies, when they perceived that the Roman soldiers were gone, immediately coming by sea, broke into the borders, trampled and overran all places, and like men mowing ripe corn, bore down all before them. Hereupon messengers are again sent to Rome, imploring aid, lest their wretched country should be utterly extirpated, and the name of the Roman province, so long renowned among them, overthrown by the cruelties of barbarous foreigners, might become utterly contemptible. A legion is accordingly sent again, and, arriving unexpectedly in autumn, made great slaughter of the enemy, obliging all those that could escape, to flee beyond the sea; whereas before, they were wont yearly to carry off their booty without any opposition. Then the Romans declared to the Britons that they could not for the future undertake such troublesome expeditions for their sake, advising them rather to handle their weapons like men, and undertake themselves the charge of engaging their enemies, who would not prove too powerful for them, unless they were deterred by cowardice; and, thinking that it might be some help to the allies, whom they were forced to abandon, they built a strong stone wall from sea to sea, in a straight line between the towns that had been there built for fear of the enemy, and not far from the trench of Severus. This famous wall, which is still to be seen, was built at the public and private expense, the Britons also lending their assistance. It is eight feet in breadth, and twelve in height, in a straight line from

1 About 400 onward.
* See *Eng. Lit.*, p. 23.

2 Abercorn, a village on the south bank of the Firth of Forth.
3 Dumbarton.

east to west, as is still visible to beholders. This being finished, they gave that dispirited people good advice, with patterns to furnish them with arms. Besides, they built towers on the sea-coast to the southward, at proper distances, where their ships were, because there also the irruptions of the barbarians were apprehended, and so took leave of their friends, never to return again.—Book I, Chapter 12. (Translation from the Latin, edited by J. A. Giles.)

A Parable of Man's Life †

The king, hearing these words, answered, that he was both willing and bound to receive the faith which he taught; but that he would confer about it with his principal friends and counsellors, to the end that if they also were of his opinion, they might all together be cleansed in Christ the Fountain of life. Paulinus consenting, the king did as he said; for, holding a council with the wise men, he asked of everyone in particular what he thought of the new doctrine, and the new worship that was preached? To which the chief of his own priests, Coifi, immediately answered, "O king, consider what this is which is now preached to us; for I verily declare to you, that the religion which we have hitherto professed has, as far as I can learn, no virtue in it. For none of your people has applied himself more diligently to the worship of our gods than I; and yet there are many who receive greater favours from you, and are more preferred than I, and are more prosperous in all their undertakings. Now if the gods were good for anything, they would rather forward me, who have been more careful to serve them. It remains, therefore, that if upon examination you find those new doctrines, which are now preached to us, better and more efficacious, we immediately receive them without any delay."

Another of the king's chief men, approving of his words and exhortations, presently added: "The present life of man, O king, seems to me, in comparison of that time which is unknown to us, like to the swift flight of a sparrow through the room wherein you sit at supper in winter, with your commanders and ministers, and a good fire in the midst, whilst the storms of rain and snow prevail abroad; the sparrow I say, flying in at one door, and immediately out at another, whilst he is within, is safe from the wintry storm; but after a short space of fair weather, he immediately vanishes out of your sight, into the dark winter from which he had emerged. So this life of man appears for a short space, but of what went before, or what is to follow, we are utterly ignorant. If, therefore, this new doctrine contains something more certain, it seems justly to deserve to be followed." The other elders and king's counsellors by Divine inspiration, spoke to the same effect.—Book II, Chapter 13. (Translation from the Latin, edited by J. A. Giles.)

The Story of Cædmon ‡

In this Abbess's Minster was a certain brother extraordinarily magnified and honoured with a divine gift; for he was wont to make fitting songs which conduced to religion and piety; so that whatever he learned through clerks of the holy writings, that he, after a little space, would usually adorn with the greatest sweetness and feeling, and bring forth in the English tongue; and by his songs the minds of many men were often inflamed with contempt for the world, and with desire of heavenly life. And moreover, many others after him, in the English nation, sought to make pious songs; but yet none could do like him, for he had not been taught from men, nor through man, to learn the poetic art; but he was divinely aided, and through God's grace received the art of song. And he therefore never might make aught of leasing[4] or of idle poems, but just those only which conduced to religion, and which it became his pious tongue to sing. The man was placed in worldly life until the time that he was of mature age, and had never learned any poem; and he therefore often in convivial society, when, for the sake of mirth, it was resolved that they all in turn should sing to the harp, when he saw the harp approaching him, then for shame he would rise from the assembly and go home to his house.

When he so on a certain time did, that he left the house of the convivial meeting, and was gone out to the stall of the cattle, the care of which that night had been committed to him—when he there, at proper time, placed his limbs on the bed and slept, then stood some man by him, in a dream, and hailed and greeted him, and named him by his name, saying "Cædmon, sing me something." Then he an-

---

† This is an incident of the visit of Paulinus, who, in the year 625, during the reign of King Edwin (Eadwine) of Northumbria, came to England as a missionary from Pope Gregory.

4 lying
‡ See *Eng. Lit.*, p. 22. The "Minster" referred to was the monastery at Whitby, founded by the Abbess Hilda in 658.

swered and said, ''I cannot sing anything, and therefore I went out from this convivial meeting, and retired hither, because I could not.'' Again he who was speaking with him said, ''Yet thou must sing to me.'' Said he, ''What shall I sing?'' Said he, ''Sing me the origin of things.'' When he received this answer, then he began forthwith to sing, in praise of God the creator, the verses and the words which he had never heard, the order of which is this:

> ''Now must we praise
> the Guardian of heaven's kingdom,
> the Creator's might,
> and his mind's thought;
> glorious Father of men!
> as of every wonder he,
> Lord eternal,
> formed the beginning.
> He first framed
> for the children of earth
> the heaven as a roof;
> holy Creator!
> then mid-earth,
> the Guardian of mankind,
> the eternal Lord,
> afterwards produced;
> the earth for men,
> Lord Almighty!''

Then he arose from sleep, and had fast in mind all that he sleeping had sung, and to those words forthwith joined many words of song worthy of God in the same measure.

Then came he in the morning to the town-reeve, who was his superior, and said to him what gift he had received; and he forthwith led him to the abbess, and told, and made that known to her. Then she bade all the most learned men and the learners to assemble, and in their presence bade him tell the dream, and sing the poem; that, by the judgment of them all, it might be determined why or whence that was come. Then it seemed to them all, so as it was, that to him, from the Lord himself, a heavenly gift had been given. Then they expounded to him and said some holy history, and words of godly lore; then bade him, if he could, to sing some of them, and turn them into the melody of song. When he had undertaken the thing, then went he home to his house, and came again in the morning, and sang and gave to them, adorned with the best poetry, what had been entrusted to him.

Then began the abbess to make much of and love the grace of God in the man; and she then exhorted and instructed him to forsake worldly life and take to monkhood: and he that well approved. And she received him into the minster with his goods, and associated him with the congregation of those servants of God and caused him to be taught the series of the Holy History and Gospel; and he, all that he could learn by hearing, meditated with himself, and, as a clean[5] animal, ruminating, turned into the sweetest verse: and his song and his verse were so winsome to hear, that his teachers themselves wrote and learned from his mouth. He first sang of earth's creation, and of the origin of mankind, and all the history of Genesis, which is the first book of Moses, and then of the departure of the people of Israel from the Egyptians' land, and of the entrance of the land of promise, and of many other histories of the canonical books of Holy Writ; and of Christ's incarnation, and of his passion, and of his ascension into heaven; and of the coming of the Holy Ghost, and the doctrine of the Apostles. And also of the terror of the doom to come, and the fear of hell torment, and the sweetness of the heavenly kingdom, he made many poems; and, in like manner, many others of the divine benefits and judgments he made; in all which he earnestly took care to draw men from the love of sins and wicked deeds, and to excite to a love and desire of good deeds; for he was a very pious man, and to regular disciplines[6] humbly subjected; and against those who in otherwise would act, he was inflamed with the heat of great zeal. And he therefore with a fair end his life closed and ended.

For when the time approached of his decease and departure, then was he for fourteen days ere that oppressed and troubled with bodily infirmity; yet so moderately that, during all that time, he could both speak and walk. There was in the neighbourhood a house for infirm men, in which it was their custom to bring the infirm, and those who were on the point of departure, and there attend to them together. Then bade he his servant, on the eve of the night that he was going from the world, to prepare him a place in that house, that he might rest; whereupon the servant wondered why he this bade, for it seemed to him that his departure was not so near; yet he did as he said and commanded. And when he there went to bed, and in joyful mood was speaking some things, and joking together with those who were therein previously, then it was over midnight that he asked, whether they had the eucharist[7] within?

---

5 In the ceremonial sense (see *Leviticus*, xi).
6 penances   7 host, or consecrated bread

They answered, "What need is to thee of the eucharist? Thy departure is not so near, now thou thus cheerfully and thus gladly art speaking to us." Again he said, "Bring me nevertheless the eucharist."

When he had it in his hands, he asked, Whether they had all a placid mind and kind, and without any ill-will towards him? Then they all answered, and said, that they knew of no ill-will towards him, but they all were very kindly disposed and they besought him in turn that he would be kindly disposed to them all. Then he answered and said, "My beloved brethren, I am very kindly disposed to you and all God's men." And he thus was strengthening himself with the heavenly viaticum,[8] and preparing himself an entrance into another life. Again he asked, "How near it was to the hour that the brethren must rise and teach the people of God, and sing their nocturns?"[9] They answered, "It is not far to that." He said, "It is well, let us await the hour." And then he prayed, and signed himself with Christ's cross, and reclined his head on the bolster, and slept for a little space; and so with stillness ended his life. And thus it was, that as he with pure and calm mind and tranquil devotion had served God, that he, in like manner, left the world with as calm a death, and went to His presence; and the tongue that had composed so many holy words in the Creator's praise, he then in like manner its last words closed in His praise, crossing himself, and committing his soul into His hands. Thus it is seen that he was conscious of his own departure, from what we have now heard say.—Book IV., Chapter 24. (Translated from Latin into Anglo-Saxon by Alfred the Great. Modern English translation by Benjamin Thorpe.)

CYNEWULF (fl. 750)*

RIDDLE II.

Who so wary and so wise of the warriors lives,
That he dare declare who doth drive me on my way,
When I start up in my strength! Oft in stormy wrath,
Hugely then I thunder, tear along in gusts,

Fare above the floor of earth, burn the folk-halls down,   5
Ravage all the rooms! There the reek ariseth
Gray above the gables. Great on earth the din,
And the slaughter-qualm of men. Then I shake the woodland,
Forests rich in fruits; then I fell the trees;—
I with water over-vaulted—by the wondrous Powers   10
Sent upon my way, far and wide to drive along!
On my back I carry that which covered once
All the tribes of Earth's indwellers, spirits and all flesh,
In the sand together! Say who shuts me in,
Or what is my name—I who bear this burden!
           Answer: A Storm on Land.

RIDDLE VI.

I am all alone, with the iron wounded,
With the sword slashed into, sick of work of battle,
Of the edges weary. Oft I see the slaughter,
Oft the fiercest fighting. Of no comfort ween I,—
So that, in the battle-brattling,[1] help may bring itself to me;   5
Ere I, with the warriors, have been utterly fordone.
But the heritage of hammers[2] hews adown at me,
Stark of edges, sworded-sharp, of the smiths the handiwork,
On me biting in the burgs! Worse the battle is
I must bear for ever! Not one of the Leech-kin,[3]   10
In the fold-stead, could I find out,
Who, with herbs he has, then should heal me of my wound!
But the notching of my edges more and more becomes
Through the deadly strokes of swords, in the daylight, in the night.
           Of the Shield.

RIDDLE XV.

I a weaponed warrior was! Now in pride bedecks me
A young serving-man all with silver and fine gold,
With the work of waving gyres![4] Warriors sometimes kiss me;
Sometimes I to strife of battle summon with my calling
Willing war-companions! Whiles, the horse doth carry   5

---

8 provisions for a journey (in this case the eucharist)
9 service before daybreak
* These extracts from Cynewulf's writings are translations by Mr. Stopford Brooke, and have been taken from Mr. Brooke's *History of Early English Literature* by permission of the publishers, Messrs. Macmillan & Co.

1 battle uproar   3 physicians
2 swords   4 circles

Me the march-paths over, or the ocean-stallion
Fares the floods with me, flashing in my jew-
　　els—.
Often times a bower-maiden, all bedecked with
　　armlets,
Filleth up my bosom; whiles, bereft of covers,
I must, hard and heedless, (in the houses)
　　lie!　　　　　　　　　　　　　　　　10
Then, again, hang I, with adornments fretted,
Winsome on the wall where the warriors drink.
Sometimes the folk-fighters, as a fair thing on
　　warfaring,
On the back of horses bear me; then bedecked
　　with jewels
Shall I puff with wind from a warrior's
　　breast.　　　　　　　　　　　　　　15
Then, again, to glee-feasts I the guests invite
Haughty heroes to the wine—other whiles
　　shall I
With my shouting save from foes what is stolen
　　away,
Make the plundering scather flee. Ask what is
　　my name!

　　　　　　　　　　　　　Of the Horn.

From the CHRIST.†

Then the *Courage-hearted* quakes, when the
　　King he hears　　　　　　　　　　　797
Speak the words of wrath—Him the wielder of
　　the Heavens—

† The *Christ* is a poem dealing with the Nativity
and Ascension of Christ, and the Day of
Judgment. Our extracts are from the hymn-
like passage which presages the Judgment
and the poet's dread upon that day, and which
closes with a vision of the stormy voyage
of life ending in serenity. Cynewulf signed
some of his poems acrostically by inserting
runes which spelt his name. Runes were
characters which represented words as well
as letters, just as our letter "B" might stand
for the words *be* or *bee*. Those used in this
passage of which we give a portion are:

ᚳ　= C = cēne = keen, bold one

ᚣ　= Y = yfel = wretched

ᚾ　= N = nyd = need

ᛗ　= E = eh = horse

ᚹ　= W = wyn = joy

ᚢ　= U = ur = our

ᛚ　= L = lagu = water

ᚠ　= F = feoh = wealth

Speak to those who once on earth but obeyed
　　him weakly,
While as yet their *Yearning pain* and their
　　Need most easily
Comfort might discover. . . .
　　　　　　　　　　Gone is then the *Winsomeness*
Of the Earth's adornments! What to *Us* as
　　men belonged　　　　　　　　　　806
Of the joys of life was locked, long ago, in
　　Lake-Flood,[6]
All the *Fee*[7] on Earth. . . .

　　　　　　　　　　　　Mickle is our need
That in this unfruitful time, ere that fearful
　　Dread,
On our spirit's fairness we should studiously
　　bethink us!　　　　　　　　　　　850
Now most like it is as if we on lake of ocean,
O'er the water cold in our keels are sailing,
And through spacious sea, with our stallions
　　of the Sound,[8]
Forward drive the flood-wood. Fearful is the
　　stream
Of immeasurable surges that we sail on here,
Through this wavering world, through these
　　windy oceans,
O'er the path profound. Perilous our state of
　　life
E'er that we had sailed (our ship) to the shore
　　(at last),
O'er the rough sea-ridges. Then there reached
　　us help,
That to hithe[9] of Healing homeward led us
　　on—　　　　　　　　　　　　　860
He the Spirit-Son of God! And he dealt us
　　grace,
So that we should be aware, from the vessel's
　　deck,
Where our stallions of the sea we might stay
　　with ropes,
Fast a-riding by their anchors—ancient horses
　　of the waves!
Let us in that haven then all our hope estab-
　　lish,
Which the ruler of the Æther there has roomed
　　for us,
When He climbed to Heaven—Holy in the
　　Highest!

From the ELENE.‡

Forth then fared the folk-troop, and a fighting-
　　lay　　　　　　　　　　　　　　27

6 The Deluge　　7 property　　8 ships　　9 harbor
‡ The *Elene* is the story of St. Helena, the mother
of Constantine the Great, who made a pilgrimage to Jerusalem in search of the Holy
Cross. The lines quoted describe the battle in
which Constantine is victorious over the
Huns. See Brooke's *Early English Literature*,
pp. 405-406.

Sang the Wolf in woodland, wailed a slaughter-
rune!
Dewy-feathered, on the foes' track,
Raised the Earn[10] his song. . . .

Loud upsang the Raven
Swart, and slaughter-fell. Strode along the
war-host; 53
Blew on high the horn-bearers; heralds of the
battle shouted;
Stamped the earth the stallion; and the host
assembled
Quickly to the quarrel! . . .

Sang the trumpets
Loud before the war-hosts; loved the work the
raven: 110
Dewy-plumed, the earn looked upon the march;
. . . . Song the wolf uplifted,
Ranger of the holt![11] Rose the Terror of the
battle!
There was rush of shields together, crush of
men together,
Hard hand-swinging there, and of hosts down-
dinging,
After that they first encountered flying of the
arrows!
On that fated folk, full of hate the hosters[12]
grim
Sent the showers of arrows, spears above the
yellow shields;
Forth they shot then snakes of battle[13]
Through the surge of furious foes, by the
strength of fingers! 120
Strode the stark[14] in spirit, stroke on stroke
they pressed along;
Broke into the wall of boards[15], plunged the
bill[16] therein:
Thronged the bold in battle! There the banner
was uplifted;
(Shone) the ensign 'fore the host; victory's
song was sung.
Glittered there his javelins, and his golden
helm
On the field of fight! Till in death the heathen,
Joyless fell!

FROM THE ANGLO-SAXON CHRONICLE*

Anno 409. This year the Goths took the city
of Rome by storm, and after this the Romans
never ruled in Britain; and this was about
eleven hundred and ten years after it had been
built. Altogether they ruled in Britain four
hundred and seventy years since Caius Julius
first sought the land.

Anno 418. This year the Romans collected
all the treasures that were in Britain, and some
they hid in the earth, so that no one has since
been able to find them; and some they carried
with them into Gaul.

. . . .

Anno 443. This year the Britons sent over
sea to Rome, and begged for help against the
Picts; but they had none, because they were
themselves warring against Attila, king of the
Huns. And then they sent to the Angles, and
entreated the like of the athelings[1] of the
Angles.

. . . .

Anno 449. This year Martianus and Valen-
tinus succeeded to the empire, and reigned
seven years. And in their days Hengist and
Horsa, invited by Vortigern, king of the Britons, landed in Britain, on the shore which is
called Wippidsfleet; at first in aid of the Britons, but afterwards they fought against them.
King Vortigern gave them land in the south-
east of this country, on condition that they
should fight against the Picts. Then they fought
against the Picts, and had the victory wheresoever they came. They then sent to the Angles;
desired a larger force to be sent, and caused
them to be told the worthlessness of the Britons, and the excellencies of the land. Then
they soon sent thither a larger force in aid of
the others. At that time there came men from
three tribes in Germany; from the Old-Saxons,
from the Angles, from the Jutes. From the
Jutes came the Kentish-men and the Wight-
warians, that is, the tribe which now dwells in
Wight, and that race among the West-Saxons
which is still called the race of Jutes. From
the Old-Saxons came the men of Essex and
Sussex and Wessex. From Anglia, which has
ever since remained waste betwixt the Jutes
and Saxons, came the men of East Anglia, Middle Anglia, Mercia, and all North-humbria.
Their leaders were two brothers, Hengist and
Horsa: they were the sons of Wihtgils; Wihtgils son of Witta, Witta of Wecta, Wecta of
Woden: from this Woden sprang all our royal
families, and those of the South-humbrians
also.†

Anno 455. This year Hengist and Horsa
fought against King Vortigern at the place
which is called Ægels-threp[2] and his brother

10 eagle
11 wood
12 soldiers, host
13 darts

14 firm
15 shields
16 sword
* See *Eng. Lit.*, p. 28.

1 princes 2 Aylesford
† The language here appears to be that of a northern chronicler. The MS. of this portion has
been traced to Peterborough.

Horsa was there slain, and after that Hengist obtained the kingdom, and Æsc his son.

Anno 565. This year Ethelbert succeeded to the kingdom of the Kentish-men, and held it fifty-three years. In his days the holy pope Gregory sent us baptism, that was in the two and thirtieth year of his reign: and Columba, a mass-priest, came to the Picts, and converted them to the faith of Christ: they are dwellers by the northern mountains. And their king gave him the island which is called Ii[3]: therein are five hides‡ of land, as men say. There Columba built a monastery, and he was abbot there thirty-seven years, and there he died when he was seventy-two years old. His successors still have the place. The Southern Picts had been baptized long before: Bishop Ninia, who had been instructed at Rome, had preached baptism to them, whose church and his monastery is at Whitherne, consecrated in the name of St. Martin: there he resteth, with many holy men. Now in Ii there must ever be an abbot, and not a bishop; and all the Scottish bishops ought to be subject to him because Columba was an abbot and not a bishop.

Anno. 596. This year Pope Gregory sent Augustine to Britain, with a great many monks, who preached the word of God to the nation of the Angles.

Anno 871. . . . And about fourteen days after this, King Ethelred and Alfred his brother fought against the army[4] at Basing, and there the Danes obtained the victory. And about two months after this, King Ethelred and Alfred his brother fought against the army at Marden; and they[4] were in two bodies, and they[5] put both to flight, and during a great part of the day were victorious; and there was great slaughter on either hand; but the Danes had possession of the place of carnage: and there Bishop Heahmund was slain, and many good men: and after this battle there came a great army in the summer to Reading. And after this, over Easter, king Ethelred died; and he reigned five years and his body lies at Winburn-minster.

Then Alfred the son of Ethelwulf, his brother, succeeded to the kingdom of the West-Saxons. And about one month after this, king Alfred with a small band fought against the whole army at Wilton, and put them to flight for a good part of the day; but the Danes had

possession of the place of carnage. And this year nine general battles were fought against the army in the kingdom south of the Thames, besides which Alfred the king's brother, and single ealdormen,† and king's thanes, often times made incursions on them, which were not counted: and within the year nine earls and one king were slain. And that year the West Saxons made peace with the army.—(From the translation edited by J. A. Giles.)

THE BATTLE OF BRUNANBURH *

Anno 937. Here Athelstan the King, ruler of
    earls,
ring-giver to chieftains, and his brother eke,
Edmund Atheling,[1] lifelong honor
struck out with the edges of swords in battle
at Brunanburh: they cleft the shield-wall,[2]
hewed the war-lindens[3] with the leavings of
    hammers,[4]
these heirs of Edward; for fitting it was
to their noble descent that oft in the battle
'gainst foes one and all the land they should
    fend,
the hoards and the homes. The enemy fell,
Scot-folk and seamen,[5]   11
death-doomed they fell; slippery the field
with the blood of men, from sunrise
when at dawn the great star
stole o'er the earth, the bright candle of God
the Eternal Lord, till the noble creation
sank to its seat. There lay many a one
slain by a spear, many a Norseman
shot o'er his shield, many a Scotsman
weary and sated with strife. The men of
    Wessex   20
in troops the live-long day
followed on the footsteps of the hostile folk.
From the rear they fiercely struck the fleeing
with the sharp-ground swords. The Mercians
    did not stint
hard hand-play to any of the heroes
who with Anlaf o'er the wave-welter[6]
in the bosom of boats sought the land,
doomed to fall in the fight. On the field

† nobles
1 prince
2 The Germanic phalanx, in which the shields were
    overlapped.
3 shields made of linden wood
4 swords, hammered out
5 the Danes
6 ocean
* This poem is, says Professor Bright, "the most
    important of the poetic insertions in the Anglo-Saxon Chronicles." It records the victory
    of Athelstan, son of Edward, grandson of Alfred the Great and king of the West Saxons
    and the Mercians, over a combination including Danes from Northumbria and Ireland,
    Scots, and Welsh. The Danes were headed by
    Anlaf (or Olaf), the Scots by Constantine.

3 Iona   4 the Danes   5 Ethelred and Alfred
‡ Variously estimated at from 60 to 120 acres.

five young kings lay killed,

put to sleep by swords; and seven too   30

of the earls of Anlaf, and countless warriors

of the seamen and the Scotch: routed was

the Norsemen's king, forced by need

with a little band to the boat's bow.

The galley glided on the waves; the king fled forth

on the fallow flood; so he saved his life.

And so by flight to his northern kinsfolk

came that wise one, Constantine,

gray battle man; boast he durst not

of the strife of swords; shorn of kinsfolk was he,   40

fallen on the battle-field his friends,

slain were they in strife; and his son, young for war,

left he on the slaughter-spot sore wounded.

Gray-haired hero, hoary traitor,

boast he durst not of the brand-clash;[7]

nor could Anlaf with their armies shattered

laugh that they the better were in battle-work,

in the fight of banners on the battle-field,

in the meeting of the spears, in the mingling of the men,

in the strife of weapons on the slaughter-field 50

which they played with Edward's heirs.

Departed then the Northmen in the nailèd ships,

a dreary leaving of darts[8] on the dashing sea.

O'er the deep water Dublin they sought,

Ireland again, abashed.

So the brethren both together,

King and Atheling, sought their kinsfolk

and West-Saxon land, from war exultant;

left behind to share the slain

the dusky-coated, the dark raven   60

horny-beaked, and the eagle white behind,

gray-coated, the carrion to consume,

the greedy war-hawk, and that gray beast,

the wolf in the weald.[9]   Nor had greater slaughter

ever yet upon this island

e'er before a folk befallen

by sword-edges, say the books,

those old wise ones,[10] since from Eastward hither

Angles and Saxons on advanced,   69

o'er the waters wide sought the Britons,

warsmiths proud o'ercame the Welsh,

Earls honor-hungry got this homeland.[11]

---

[7] clashing of swords

[8] The few left alive.

[9] forest

[10] In apposition with "books."

[11] Referring to the Anglo-Saxon conquest of Britain in the fifth century.

ALFRED THE GREAT (849-901)

OHTHERE'S NARRATIVE.*

Ohthere told his lord King Alfred, that he dwelt northmost of all the Northmen. He said that he dwelt in the land to the northward, along the West-Sea; he said, however, that that land is very long north from thence, but it is all waste except in a few places where the Finns here and there dwell, for hunting in the winter, and in the summer for fishing in that sea. He said that he was desirous to try, once on a time, how far that country extended due north, or whether any one lived to the north of the waste. He then went due north along the country, leaving all the way the waste land on the right, and the wide sea on the left, for three days: he was as far north as the whale-hunters go at the farthest. Then he proceeded in his course due north as far as he could sail in another three days; then the land there inclined due east, or the sea into the land, he knew not which, but he knew that he there waited for a west wind, or a little north, and sailed thence eastward along that land as far as he could sail in four days; then he had to wait for a due north wind, because the land there inclined due south, or the sea in on that land, he knew not which; he then sailed along the coast due south, as far as he could sail in five days. There lay a great river[1] up in that land; they then turned up in that river, because they durst not sail on by that river, on account of hostility, because all that country was inhabited on the other side of that river; he had not before met with any land that was inhabited since he came from his own home; but all the way he had waste land on his right, except for fishermen, fowlers, and hunters, all of whom were Finns, and he had constantly a wide sea to the left. The Beormas[2] had well cultivated their country, but they did not dare to enter it; and the Terfinna land[3] was all waste, except where hunters, fishers, or fowlers had taken up their quarters.

The Beormas told him many particulars both of their own land, and of the other lands lying about them; but he knew not what was true, because he did not see it himself; it seemed

---

[1] The Dwina.

[2] A people east of the Dwina.

[3] The region between the Gulf of Bothnia and the North Cape.

* From the addition made by King Alfred to his translation of *Orosius' History of the World*; modern English translation by Benjamin Thorpe. Ohthere was a Norwegian sailor, who, straying to Alfred's court, was eagerly questioned. See *Eng. Lit.*, p. 26.

to him that the Finns and the Beormas spoke nearly one language. He went thither chiefly, in addition to seeing the country, on account of the walruses, because they have very noble bones in their teeth; some of those teeth they brought to the king; and their hides are good for ship-ropes. This whale is much less than other whales, it being not longer than seven ells; but in his own country is the best whale-hunting,—there they are eight and forty ells long, and the biggest of them fifty ells long; of these he said that he and five others had killed sixty in two days. He was a very wealthy man in those possessions in which their wealth consists, that is in wild deer. He had at the time he came to the king, six hundred unsold tame deer. These deer they call rein-deer, of which there were six decoy rein-deer, which are very valuable among the Finns, because they catch the wild rein-deer with them.

He was one of the foremost men in that country, yet he had not more than twenty horned cattle, and twenty sheep, and twenty swine, and the little that he ploughed he ploughed with horses.* But their wealth consists for the most part in the rent paid them by the Finns. That rent is in skins of animals, and birds' feathers, and whalebone, and in ship-ropes made of whales' hides, and of seals'. Everyone pays according to his birth; the best-born, it is said, pay the skins of fifteen martens, and five rein-deer's, and one bear's skin, ten ambers[4] of feathers, a bear's or otter's skin kirtle, and two ship-ropes, each sixty ells long, made either of whale-hide or of seal's.

He said that the Northmen's land was very long and narrow; all that his man could either pasture or plough lies by the sea, though that is in some parts very rocky; and to the east are wild mountains, parallel to the cultivated land. The Finns inhabit these mountains, and the cultivated land is broadest to the eastward, and continually narrower the more north. To the east it may be sixty miles broad, or a little broader, and towards the middle thirty, or broader; and northward, he said, where it is narrowest, that it might be three miles broad to the mountain, and the mountain then is in some parts so broad that a man may pass over in two weeks, and in some parts so broad that a man may pass over in six days. Then along this land southwards, on the other side of the mountain, is Sweden; to that land northwards, and along that land northwards, Cwenland.[5] The Cwenas sometimes make depredations on the Northmen over the mountain, and sometimes the Northmen on them; there are very large fresh meres amongst the mountains, and the Cwenas carry their ships over land into the meres, and thence make depredations on the Northmen; they have very little ships, and very light.

Ohthere said that the shire in which he dwelt is called Halgoland. He said that no one dwelt to the north of him; there is likewise a port to the south of that land, which is called Sciringes-heal;[6] thither, he said, no one could sail in a month, if he landed at night, and every day had a fair wind; and all the while he would sail along the land, and on the starboard will first be Iraland,[7] and then the islands which are between Iraland and this land.[8] Then it is this land until he come to Sciringes-heal, and all the way on the larboard, Norway. To the south of Sciringes-heal, a very great sea runs up into the land, which is broader than any one can see over; and Jutland is opposite on the other side, and then Zealand. This sea runs many miles up in that land. And from Sciringes-heal, he said that he sailed in five days to that port which is called Æt-Hæthum,[9] which is between the Wends, and Saxons, and Angles, and belongs to Denmark.

When he sailed thitherward from Sciringes-heal, Denmark was on his left, and on the right a wide sea for three days, and two days before he came to Hæthum he had on the right Jutland, Zealand, and many islands. In these lands the Angles dwelt before they came hither to this land. And then for two days he had on his left the islands which belong to Denmark.

5 Between the Gulf of Bothnia and the White Sea.
6 In the Gulf of Christiania.
7 Ireland (meaning Scotland; or possibly an error
    for Iceland).
8 England   9 Sleswig

4 forty bushels
* The Anglo-Saxons plowed with oxen.

ANGLO-NORMAN PERIOD

GEOFFREY OF MONMOUTH
(c. 1100-1154)

THE STORY OF KING LEIR.*

After this unhappy fate of Bladud, Leir, his son, was advanced to the throne, and nobly governed his country sixty years. He built upon the river Sore a city, called in the British tongue, Kaerleir, in the Saxon, Leircestre. He was without male issue, but had three daughters, whose names were Gonorilla, Regau, and Cordeilla, of whom he was dotingly fond, but especially of his youngest, Cordeilla. When he began to grow old, he had thoughts of dividing his kingdom among them, and of bestowing them on such husbands as were fit to be advanced to the government with them. But to make trial who was worthy to have the best part of his kingdom, he went to each of them to ask which of them loved him most. The question being proposed, Gonorilla, the eldest, made answer, "That she called heaven to witness, she loved him more than her own soul." The father replied, "Since you have preferred my declining age before your own life, I will marry you, my dearest daughter, to whomsoever you shall make choice of, and give with you the third part of my kingdom." Then Regau, the second daughter, willing, after the example of her sister, to prevail upon her father's good nature, answered with an oath, "That she could not otherwise express her thoughts, but that she loved him above all creatures." The credulous father upon this made her the same promise that he did to her eldest sister, that is, the choice of a husband, with the third part of his kingdom. But Cordeilla, the youngest, understanding how easily he was satisfied with the flattering expressions of her sisters, was desirous to make trial of his affection after a different manner. "My father," said she, "is there any daughter that can love her father more than duty requires?

* From the *Historia Britonum Regum*, Book II., Chapters XI.-XIV. Translation from the Latin edited by J. A. Giles. See *Eng. Lit.*, p. 37.

In my opinion, whoever pretends to it, must disguise her real sentiments under the veil of flattery. I have always loved you as a father, nor do I yet depart from my purposed duty; and if you insist to have something more extorted from me, hear now the greatness of my affection, which I always bear you, and take this for a short answer to all your questions; look how much you have, so much is your value, and so much do I love you." The father, supposing that she spoke this out of the abundance of her heart, was highly provoked, and immediately replied, "Since you have so far despised my old age as not to think me worthy the love that your sisters express for me, you shall have from me the like regard, and shall be excluded from any share with your sisters in my kingdom. Notwithstanding, I do not say but that since you are my daughter, I will marry you to some foreigner, if fortune offers you any such husband; but will never, I do assure you, make it my business to procure so honourable a match for you as for your sisters; because, though I have hitherto loved you more than them, you have in requital thought me less worthy of your affection than they." And, without further delay, after consultation with his nobility, he bestowed his two other daughters upon the dukes of Cornwall and Albania, with half the island at present, but after his death, the inheritance of the whole monarchy of Britain.

It happened after this, that Aganippus, king of the Franks, having heard of the fame of Cordeilla's beauty, forthwith sent his ambassadors to the king to demand her in marriage. The father, retaining yet his anger towards her, made answer, "That he was very willing to bestow his daughter, but without either money or territories; because he had already given away his kingdom with all his treasure to his eldest daughters, Gonorilla and Regau." When this was told Aganippus, he, being very much in love with the lady, sent again to king Leir, to tell him, "That he had money and territories enough, as he possessed the third part of Gaul, and desired no more than his daughter only, that he might have heirs by her." At last the match was concluded; Cordeilla was sent to Gaul, and married to Aganippus.

A long time after this, when Leir came to be infirm through old age, the two dukes, on whom he had bestowed Britain with his two daughters, fostered an insurrection against him, and deprived him of his kingdom, and of all regal authority, which he had hitherto exercised with great power and glory. At length, by mutual agreement, Maglaunus, duke of Albania, one of his sons-in-law, was to allow him a maintenance at his own house, together with sixty soldiers, who were to be kept for state. After two years' stay with his son-in-law, his daughter Gonorilla grudged the number of his men, who began to upbraid the ministers of the court with their scanty allowance; and, having spoken to her husband about it, she gave orders that the number of her father's followers should be reduced to thirty, and the rest discharged. The father, resenting this treatment, left Maglaunus, and went to Henuinus, duke of Cornwall, to whom he had married his daughter Regau. Here he met with an honourable reception, but before the year was at an end, a quarrel happened between the two families which raised Regau's indignation; so that she commanded her father to discharge all his attendants but five, and to be contented with their service. This second affliction was insupportable to him, and made him return again to his former daughter, with hopes that the misery of his condition might move in her some sentiments of filial piety, and that he, with his family, might find a subsistence with her. But she, not forgetting her resentment, swore by the gods he should not stay with her, unless he would dismiss his retinue, and be contented with the attendance of one man; and with bitter reproaches she told him how ill his desire of vainglorious pomp suited his age and poverty. When he found that she was by no means to be prevailed upon, he was at last forced to comply, and, dismissing the rest, to take up with one man only. But by this time he began to reflect more sensibly with himself upon the grandeur from which he had fallen, and the miserable state to which he was now reduced, and to enter upon thoughts of going beyond sea to his youngest daughter. Yet he doubted whether he should be able to move her commisseration, because (as was related above) he had treated her so unworthily. However, disdaining to bear any longer such base usage, he took ship for Gaul. In his passage he observed he had only the third place given him among the princes that were with him in the ship, at

which, with deep sighs and tears, he burst forth into the following complaint:—

"O irreversible decrees of the Fates, that never swerve from your stated course! why did you ever advance me to an unstable felicity, since the punishment of lost happiness is greater than the sense of present misery? The remembrance of the time when vast numbers of men obsequiously attended me in the taking the cities and wasting the enemy's countries, more deeply pierces my heart than the view of my present calamity, which has exposed me to the derision of those who were formerly prostrate at my feet. Oh! the enmity of fortune! Shall I ever again see the day when I may be able to reward those according to their deserts who have forsaken me in my distress? How true was thy answer, Cordeilla, when I asked thee concerning thy love to me, 'As much as you have, so much is your value, and so much do I love you.' While I had anything to give, they valued me, being friends, not to me, but to my gifts: they loved me then, but they loved my gifts much more: when my gifts ceased, my friends vanished. But with what face shall I presume to see you, my dearest daughter, since in my anger I married you upon worse terms than your sisters, who, after all the mighty favours they have received from me, suffer me to be in banishment and poverty?"

As he was lamenting his condition in these and the like expressions, he arrived at Karitia,[1] where his daughter was, and waited before the city while he sent a messenger to inform her of the misery he was fallen into, and to desire her relief for a father who suffered both hunger and nakedness. Cordeilla was startled at the news, and wept bitterly, and with tears asked how many men her father had with him. The messenger answered, he had none but one man, who had been his armour-bearer, and was staying with him without the town. Then she took what money she thought might be sufficient, and gave it to the messenger, with orders to carry her father to another city, and there give out that he was sick, and to provide for him bathing, clothes, and all other nourishment. She likewise gave orders that he should take into his service forty men, well clothed and accoutred, and that when all things were thus prepared he should notify his arrival to king Aganippus and his daughter. The messenger quickly returning, carried Leir to another city, and there kept him concealed, till he had done everything that Cordeilla had commanded.

1 Calais

As soon as he was provided with his royal apparel, ornaments, and retinue, he sent word to Aganippus and his daughter, that he was driven out of his kingdom of Britain by his sons-in-law, and was come to them to procure their assistance for recovering his dominions. Upon which they, attended with their chief ministers of state and the nobility of the kingdom, went out to meet him, and received him honourably, and gave into his management the whole power of Gaul, till such time as he should be restored to his former dignity.

In the meantime Aganippus sent officers over all Gaul to raise an army, to restore his father-in-law to his kingdom of Britain. Which done, Leir returned to Britain with his son and daughter and the forces which they had raised, where he fought with his sons-in-law and routed them. Having thus reduced the whole kingdom to his power, he died the third year after. Aganippus also died; and Cordeilla, obtaining the government of the kingdom, buried her father in a certain vault, which she ordered to be made for him under the river Sore, in Leicester, and which had been built originally under the ground to the honour of the god Janus.[2] And here all the workmen of the city, upon the anniversary solemnity of that festival, used to begin their yearly labours.

Arthur Makes the Saxons His Tributaries

After a few days they went to relieve the city Kaerliudcoit, that was besieged by the pagans; which being situated upon a mountain, between two rivers in the province of Lindisia, is called by another name Lindocolinum.[1] As soon as they arrived there with all their forces, they fought with the Saxons, and made a grievous slaughter of them, to the number of six thousand; part of whom were drowned in the rivers, part fell by the hands of the Britons. The rest in a great consternation quitted the siege and fled, but were closely pursued by Arthur, till they came to the wood of Celidon, where they endeavoured to form themselves into a body again, and make a stand. And here they again joined battle with the Britons, and made a brave defence, whilst the trees that were in the place secured them against the enemies' arrows. Arthur, seeing this, commanded the trees that were in that part of the wood to be cut down, and the trunks to be placed quite round them, so as to hinder their getting out; resolving to keep them pent up here till he could reduce them by famine. He then commanded his troops to besiege the wood, and continued three days in that place. The Saxons, having now no provisions to sustain them, and being just ready to starve with hunger, begged for leave to go out; in consideration whereof they offered to leave all their gold and silver behind them, and return back to Germany with nothing but their empty ships. They promised also that they would pay him tribute from Germany, and leave hostages with him. Arthur, after consultation about it, granted their petition; allowing them only leave to depart, and retaining all their treasures, as also hostages for payment of the tribute. But as they were under sail on their return home, they repented of their bargain, and tacked about again towards Britain, and went on shore at Totness. No sooner were they landed, than they made an utter devastation of the country as far as the Severn sea, and put all the peasants to the sword. From thence they pursued their furious march to the town of Bath, and laid siege to it. When the king had intelligence of it, he was beyond measure surprised at their proceedings, and immediately gave orders for the execution of the hostages. And desisting from an attempt which he had entered upon to reduce the Scots and Picts, he marched with the utmost expedition to raise the siege; but laboured under very great difficulties, because he had left his nephew Hoel sick at Alclud.[2] At length, having entered the province of Somerset, and beheld how the siege was carried on, he addressed himself to his followers in these words: "Since these impious and detestable Saxons have disdained to keep faith with me, I, to keep faith with God, will endeavour to revenge the blood of my countrymen this day upon them. To arms, soldiers, to arms, and courageously fall upon the perfidious wretches, over whom we shall, with Christ assisting us, undoubtedly obtain victory."

When he had done speaking, St. Dubricius, archbishop of Legions,[3] going to the top of a hill, cried out with a loud voice, "You that have the honour to profess the Christian faith, keep fixed in your minds the love which you owe to your country and fellow subjects, whose sufferings by the treachery of the pagans will be an everlasting reproach to you, if you do not courageously defend them. It is your country which you fight for, and for which you should, when required, voluntarily suffer death; for that itself is victory and the cure of the soul. For he that shall die for his brethren, offers himself a living sacrifice to God, and has Christ

2 During the Roman occupation.   1 Lincoln

2 Dumbarton
3 The City of Legions (now Newport) in South Wales, where the Roman legions wintered.

for his example, who condescended to lay down his life for his brethren. If therefore any of you shall be killed in this war, that death itself, which is suffered in so glorious a cause, shall be to him for penance and absolution of all his sins.'' At these words, all of them encouraged with the benediction of the holy prelate, instantly armed themselves, and prepared to obey his orders. Also Arthur himself, having put on a coat of mail suitable to the grandeur of so powerful a king, placed a golden helmet upon his head, on which was engraven the figure of a dragon; and on his shoulders his shield called Priwen; upon which the picture of the blessed Mary, mother of God, was painted, in order to put him frequently in mind of her. Then girding on his Caliburn,[4] which was an excellent sword made in the isle of Avallon, he graced his right hand with his lance, named Ron, which was hard, broad, and fit for slaughter. After this, having placed his men in order, he boldly attacked the Saxons, who were drawn out in the shape of a wedge, as their manner was. And they, notwithstanding that the Britons fought with great eagerness, made a noble defence all that day; but at length, towards sunsetting, climbed up the next mountain, which served them for a camp: for they desired no larger extent of ground, since they confided very much in their numbers. The next morning Arthur, with his army, went up the mountain, but lost many of his men in the ascent, by the advantage which the Saxons had in their station on the top, from whence they could pour down upon him with much greater speed than he was able to advance against them. Notwithstanding, after a very hard struggle, the Britons gained the summit of the hill and quickly came to a close engagement with the enemy, who again gave them a warm reception, and made a vigorous defence. In this manner was a great part of that day also spent; whereupon Arthur, provoked to see the little advantage he had yet gained and that victory still continued in suspense, drew out his Caliburn, and, calling upon the name of the blessed Virgin, rushed forward with great fury into the thickest of the enemy's ranks; of whom (such was the merit of his prayers) not one escaped alive that felt the fury of his sword; neither did he give over the fury of his assault until he had, with his Caliburn alone, killed four hundred and seventy men. The Britons, seeing this, followed their leader in great multitudes, and made slaughter on all sides; so that Colgrin, and Baldulph his

brother, and many thousands more fell before them. But Cheldric,[5] in this imminent danger of his men, betook himself to flight.—From the same; Book IX, Ch. III, IV.

FROM THE ANCREN RIWLE
(ANCHORESSES' RULE.)*

Do you now ask what rule you anchoresses should observe? Ye should by all means, with all your might and all your strength, keep well the inward rule, and for its sake the outward. The inward rule is always alike. The outward is various, because every one ought so to observe the outward rule as that the body may therewith best serve the inward. All may and ought to observe one rule concerning purity of heart, that is, a clean unstained conscience, without any reproach of sin that is not remedied by confession. This the body rule effects. This rule is framed not by man's contrivance, but by the command of God. Wherefore, it ever is and shall be the same, without mixture and without change; and all men ought ever invariably to observe it. But the external rule, which I called the handmaid, is of man's contrivance; nor is it instituted for any thing else but to serve the internal law. It ordains fasting, watching, enduring cold, wearing haircloth, and such other hardships as the flesh of many can bear and many cannot. Wherefore, this rule may be changed and varied according to every one's state and circumstances. For some are strong, some are weak, and may very well be excused, and please God with less; some are learned, and some are not, and must work the more, and say their prayers at the stated hours in a different manner; some are old and ill favoured, of whom there is less fear; some are young and lively, and have need to be more on their guard. Every anchoress must, therefore, observe the outward rule according to the advice of her confessor, and do obediently whatever he enjoins and commands her, who knows

* These "Rules and Duties of Monastic Life" were prepared (c. 1210) for the guidance of a little society of three nuns who dwelt at Tarente, in Dorsetshire—"gentlewomen, sisters, of one father and of one mother, who had in the bloom of their youth forsaken all the pleasures of the world and become anchoresses." The book consists of eight chapters, the first and last of which deal with the "outward rule," the others with the "inward rule." It is possibly the work of Richard Poor (d. 1237), Bishop of Salisbury, who was benefactor of the nunnery at Tarente. Very marked is the spirit of charity and tolerance in which it is written. Moreover, it is among the best examples of simple, eloquent prose in English antedating the English Bible. Our translation is that of James Morton.

[4] The famous Excalibur.
[5] Leader of the Saxons.

her state and strength. He may modify the outward rule, as prudence may direct, and as he sees that the inward rule may thus be best kept.

. . . .

When you first arise in the morning bless yourselves with the sign of the cross and say, "In the name of the Father, and of the Son, and of the Holy Ghost, Amen," and begin directly "Creator Spirit, Come," with your eyes and your hands raised up toward heaven, bending forward on your knees upon the bed, and thus say the whole hymn to the end, with the versicle, "Send forth Thy Holy Spirit," and the prayer, "God, who didst teach the hearts of thy faithful people," etc. After this, putting on your shoes and your clothes, say the Paternoster[1] and the Creed,[2] and then, "Jesus Christ, Son of the Living God, have mercy on us! Thou who didst condescend to be born of a virgin, have mercy on us!" Continue saying these words until you be quite dressed. Have these words much in use, and in your mouth as often as ye may, sitting and standing.

. . . .

True anchoresses are compared to birds; for they leave the earth; that is, the love of all earthly things; and through yearning of heart after heavenly things, fly upward toward heaven. And, although they fly high, with high and holy life, yet they hold the head low, through meek humility, as a bird flying boweth down its head, and accounteth all her good deeds and good works nothing worth, and saith, as our Lord taught all his followers, "*Cum omnia bene feceritis, dicite quod servi inutiles estis;*" "When ye have done all well," saith the Lord, "say that ye are unprofitable servants." Fly high, and yet hold the head always low.

The wings that bear them upward are, good principles, which they must move unto good works, as a bird, when it would fly, moveth its wings. Also the true anchoresses, whom we compare to birds,—yet not we, but God—spread their wings and make a cross of themselves, as a bird doth when it flieth; that is, in the thoughts of the heart, and the mortification of the flesh, they bear the Lord's cross. Those birds fly well that have little flesh, as the pelican hath, and many feathers. The ostrich, having much flesh, maketh a pretense to fly, and flaps his wings, but his feet always draw to the earth. In like manner, the carnal anchoress,

[1] The Lord's Prayer.
[2] The Confession of Faith, beginning, "Credo in unum Deum."

who loveth carnal pleasures, and seeketh her ease, the heaviness of her flesh and its desires deprive her of her power of flying; and though she makes a pretense and much noise with her wings; that is, makes it appear as if she flew, and were a holy anchoress, whoever looks at her narrowly, laughs her to scorn; for her feet, as doth the ostrich's, which are her lusts, draw her to the earth. Such are not like the meagre pelican, nor do they fly aloft, but are birds of the earth, and make their nests on the ground. But God called the good anchoresses birds of heaven, as I said before: "*Vulpes foveas habent et volucres cœli nidos.*" "Foxes have their holes, and birds of heaven their nests."

True anchoresses are indeed birds of heaven, that fly aloft, and sit on the green boughs singing merrily; that is, they meditate, enraptured, upon the blessedness of heaven that never fadeth, but is ever green; and sit on this green, singing right merrily; that is, in such meditation they rest in peace and have gladness of heart, as those who sing. A bird, however, sometimes alighteth down on the earth to seek his food for the need of the flesh; but while he sits on the ground he is never secure, and is often turning himself, and always looking cautiously around. Even so, the pious recluse, though she fly ever so high, must at times alight down to the earth in respect of her body—and eat, drink, sleep, work, speak, and hear, when it is necessary, of earthly things. But then, as the bird doth, she must look well to herself, and turn her eyes on every side, lest she be deceived, and be caught in some of the devil's snares, or hurt in any way, while she sits so low.

"The birds," saith our Lord, "have nests;" "*volucres cœli habent nidos.*" A nest is hard on the outside with pricking thorns, and is delicate and soft within; even so shall a recluse endure hard and pricking thorns in the flesh; yet so prudently shall she subdue the flesh by labour, that she may say with the Psalmist: "*Fortitudinem meam ad te custodiam;*" that is, "I will keep my strength, O Lord, to thy behoof;" and therefore the pains of the flesh are proportioned to every one's case. The nest shall be hard without and soft within; and the heart sweet. They who are of a bitter or hard heart, and indulgent towards their flesh, make their nest, on the contrary, soft without and thorny within. These are the discontented and fastidious anchoresses; bitter within, when they ought to be sweet; and delicate without, when they ought to be hard. These, in such a nest, may have hard rest, when they consider well. For, from such a nest, they will too late bring forth young birds, which are good works, that they may fly toward heaven. Job calleth a religious house a nest; and saith, as if he were a recluse: "*In nidulo meo moriar;*" that is, "I shall die in my nest, and be as dead therein;" for this relates to anchorites; and, to dwell therein until she die; that is, I will never cease, while my soul is in my body, to endure things hard outwardly, as the nest is, and to be soft within.

.   .   .   .

Hear now, as I promised, many kinds of comfort against all temptations, and, with God's grace, thereafter the remedies.

Whosoever leadeth a life of exemplary piety may be certain of being tempted. This is the first comfort. For the higher the tower is, it hath always the more wind. Ye yourselves are the towers, my dear sisters, but fear not while ye are so truly and firmly cemented all of you to one another with the lime of sisterly love. Ye need not fear any devil's blast, except the lime fail; that is to say, except your love for each other be impaired through the enemy. As soon as any of you undoeth her cement, she is soon swept forth; if the other do not hold her she is soon cast down, as a loose stone is from the coping of the tower, down into the deep pitch of some foul sin.

Here is another encouragement which ought greatly to comfort you when ye are tempted. The tower is not attacked, nor the castle, nor the city, after they are taken; even so the warrior of hell attacks, with temptation, none whom he hath in his hand; but he attacketh those whom he hath not. Wherefore, dear sisters, she who is not attacked may fear much lest she be already taken. . .

The sixth comfort is, that our Lord, when He suffereth us to be tempted, playeth with us, as the mother with her young darling: she flies from him, and hides herself, and lets him sit alone, and look anxiously around, and call Dame! dame! and weep a while, and then leapeth forth laughing, with outspread arms, and embraceth and kisseth him, and wipeth his eyes. In like manner, our Lord sometimes leaveth us alone, and withdraweth His grace, His comfort, and His support, so that we feel no delight in any good that we do, nor any satisfaction of heart; and yet, at that very time, our dear Father loveth us never the less, but does it for the great love that He hath to us.

.   .   .   .

Ye shall not possess any beast, my dear sisters, except only a cat. An anchoress that hath cattle appears as Martha was, a better housewife than anchoress; nor can she in any wise be Mary, with peacefulness of heart. For then she must think of the cow's fodder, and of the herdsman's hire, flatter the heyward,[1] defend herself when her cattle is shut up in the pinfold, and moreover pay the damage. Christ knoweth, it is an odious thing when people in the town complain of anchoresses' cattle. If, however, any one must needs have a cow, let her take care that she neither annoy nor harm any one, and that her own thoughts be not fixed thereon. An anchoress ought not to have any thing that draweth her heart outward. Carry ye on no traffic. An anchoress that is a buyer and seller selleth her soul to the chapman of hell. Do not take charge of other men's property in your house, nor of their cattle, nor their clothes, neither receive under your care the church vestments, nor the chalice, unless force compel you, or great fear, for oftentimes much harm has come from such care-taking.

Because no man seeth you, nor do ye see any man, ye may be well content with your clothes, be they white, be they black; only see that they be plain, and warm, and well made—skins well tawed;[2] and have as many as you need, for bed, and also for back. Next your flesh ye shall wear no flaxen cloth, except it be of hards[3] and of coarse canvass. Whoso will may have a stamin,[4] and whoso will may be without it. Ye shall sleep in a garment and girt. Wear no iron, nor haircloth, nor hedgehog-skins; and do not beat yourselves therewith, nor with a scourge of leather thongs, nor leaded; and do not with holly nor with briars cause yourselves to bleed without leave of your confessor; and do not, at one time, use too many flagellations. Let your shoes be thick and warm. In summer ye are at liberty to go and sit barefoot, and to wear hose without vamps,[5] and whoso liketh may lie in them. A woman may well enough wear an undersuit of haircloth very well tied with the strapples reaching down to her feet, laced tightly. If ye would dispense with wimples, have warm capes, and over them black veils. She who wishes to be seen, it is no great wonder though she adorn herself; but, in the eyes of God, she is more lovely who is unadorned outwardly for his sake. Have neither ring, nor broach, nor ornamented girdle, nor gloves, nor any such thing that is not proper for you to have.

.   .   .   .

1 A cattle-keeper on a common.
2 Prepared with oil, or without tan-liquor.
3 The coarser parts of flax or hemp.
4 A shirt of linsey-woolsey.
5 gaiters

In this book read every day, when ye are at leisure,—every day, less or more; for I hope that, if ye read it often, it will be very beneficial to you, through the grace of God, or else I shall have ill employed much of my time. God knows, it would be more agreeable to me to set out on a journey to Rome, than to begin to do it again. And, if ye find that ye do according to what ye read, thank God earnestly; and if ye do not, pray for the grace of God, and diligently endeavour that ye may keep it better, in every point, according to your ability. May the Father, and the Son, and the Holy Ghost, the one Almighty God, keep you under his protection! May he give you joy and comfort, my dear sisters, and for all that ye endure and suffer for him may he never give you a less reward than his entire self. May he be ever exalted from world to world, for ever and ever, Amen.

As often as ye read any thing in this book, greet the Lady with an Ave Mary for him that made this rule, and for him who wrote it, and took pains about it. Moderate enough I am, who ask so little.

PROVERBS OF KING ALFRED*

1

Many thanes sat at Seaford,
many bishops, book-learned men,
many proud earls, knights every one.
There was Earl Ælfric, wise in the law;
Alfred also, England's guardian,
England's darling, England's king.
He began, as ye may hear,
to teach them how to lead their lives.
He was king, and he was clerk;[1]
well he loved the Lord's work;   10
wise in word and cautious in deed,
he was the wisest man in England.

2

Thus quoth Alfred, England's comfort:
"Would ye, my people, give ear to your lord,
he would direct you wisely in all things,
how ye might win to worldly honour
and also unite your souls with Christ."

3

Wise were the words King Alfred spake.
"Humbly I rede[2] you, my dear friends,
poor and rich, all you my people,   20
that ye all fear Christ the Lord,

love him and please him, the Lord of Life.
He is alone good, above all goodness;
He is alone wise, above all wisdom;
He is alone blissful, above all bliss;
He is alone man's mildest Master;
He is alone our Father and Comfort." . .

4

Thus quoth Alfred:
"The earl and the lord
that heeds the king's word
shall rule o'er his land
with righteous hand;
and the clerk and the knight
shall give judgment aright,
to poor or to rich   80
it skilleth[3] not which.
For whatso men sow,
the same shall they mow,
and every man's doom
to his own door come." . .

12

Thus quoth Alfred:
"Small trust may be
in the flowing sea.
Though thou hast treasure
enough and to spare,
both gold and silver,   200
to nought it shall wear;
to dust it shall drive,
as God is alive.
Many a man for his gold
God's wrath shall behold,
and shall be for his silver
forgot and forlorn.
It were better for him
he had never been born." . .

14

Thus quoth Alfred:
"If thou hast sorrow,
tell it not to thy foe;
tell it to thy saddle-bow
and ride singing forth.   230
So will he think,
who knows not thy state,
that not unpleasing
to thee is thy fate.
If thou hast a sorrow
and he knoweth it,
before thee he'll pity,
behind thee will twit.
Thou mightest betray it
to such a one
as would without pity   240
thou madest more moan.
Hide it deep in thy heart

1 scholar   2 counsel
* The proverbs here translated from Middle English, some of them plainly Biblical, were popularly ascribed to King Alfred and were supposed to have been delivered by him to his Witenagemot at Seaford. See *Eng. Lit.*, p. 38.
3 matters

that it leave no smart;
nor let it be guessed
what is hid in thy breast.''   .   .

22

     Thus quoth Alfred: 410
''Boast shouldst thou not,
nor chide with a sot;
nor foolishly chatter
and idle tales scatter
at the freeman's board.
Be chary of word.
The wise man can store
few words with great lore.
Soon shot's the fool's bolt;
whence I count him a dolt   420
who saith all his will
when he should keep still.
For oft tongue breaketh bone,
though herself has none.''

CUCKOO SONG (c. 1250)*

Summer is y-comen in,
    Loudly sing Cuckoo!
Groweth seed and bloweth mead

And springeth wood anew.
    Sing Cuckoo!
Loweth after calf the cow,
    Bleateth after lamb the ewe,
Buck doth gambol, bullock amble,—
    Merry sing Cuckoo!
Cuckoo, Cuckoo! Well singest thou
Cuckoo! nor cease thou ever now.

(*Foot*)

Sing Cuckoo now, sing Cuckoo.
Sing Cuckoo, sing Cuckoo now.

* See *Eng. Lit.*, p. 42, for the Middle English, which is here somewhat modernized. The song was set to music, and the manuscript which contains the music adds the following directions, in Latin: "This part-song (*rota*) may be sung by four in company. It should not be sung by fewer than three, or at least two, in addition to those who sing the *Foot*. And it should be sung in this manner: One begins, accompanied by those who sing the *Foot*, the rest keeping silent. Then, when he has reached the first note after the cross [a mark on the musical score], another begins; and so on. The first line of the *Foot* one singer repeats as often as necessary, pausing at the end; the other line another man sings, pausing in the middle but not at the end, but immediately beginning again."

FOURTEENTH CENTURY—AGE OF CHAUCER

FROM THE PEARL (c. 1350)*

1

O pearl, for princes' pleasure wrought,
  In lucent gold deftly to set,
Never from orient realms was brought
  Its peer in price, I dare say, yet.
So beautiful, so fresh, so round,
  So smooth its sides, so slender shown,
Whatever gems to judge be found
  I needs must set it apart, alone.
But it is lost! I let it stray
  Down thro' the grass in an arbor-plot.
With love's pain now I pine away,
  Lorn of my pearl without a spot.   12

2

Since in that spot it slipt from my hand,
  Oft have I lingered there and yearned
For joy that once my sorrows banned
  And all my woes to rapture turned.
Truly my heart with grief is wrung,
  And in my breast there dwelleth dole;
Yet never song, methought, was sung
  So sweet as through that stillness stole.
O tide of fancies I could not stem!
  O fair hue fouled with stain and blot!
O mould, thou marrest a lovely gem,
  Mine own, own pearl without a spot. . .   24

> This anonymous poem is allegorical; possibly the
> "pearl" is the poet's daughter (*Eng. Lit.*, 44).
> The selection here given is translated, because
> the West Midland dialect of the original pre-
> sents more difficulties than the East Midland of
> Chaucer. The whole is a very interesting
> piece of construction, combining the Romance
> elements of meter and rhyme, as employed by
> Chaucer, with the old Saxon alliteration
> which the West Midland poets, like Langland,
> affected. Note also the refrain-like effects.
> In this translation, the exacting rhyme-
> scheme of the original, which permits but
> three rhyme sounds in a stanza, has been ad-
> hered to in the last three stanzas only. The
> first stanza of the original runs thus:
> Perle plesaunte to prynces paye,
>   To clanly clos in golde so clere,
> Out of oryent I hardyly saye,
>   Ne proved I never her precios pere,—
> So rounde, so reken in uche a raye,
>   So smal, so smothe her sydez were,—
> Queresoever I jugged gemmez gaye,
>   I sette hyr sengeley in synglere.
> Allas! I leste hyr in on erbere;
>   Thurgh gresse to grounde hit fro me yot;
> I dewyne for-dokked of luf-daungere,
>   Of that pryvy perle withouten spot.

4

Once to that spot I took my way
  And passed within the arbor green.
It was mid-August's festal day,
  When the corn is cut with sickles keen.
The mound that did my pearl embower
  With fair bright herbage was o'erhung,
Ginger and gromwell and gillyflower,
  And peonies sprinkled all among.
Yet if that sight was good to see,
  Goodlier the fragrance there begot
Where dwells that one so dear to me,
  My precious pearl without a spot.   48

5

Then on that spot my hands I wrung,
  For I felt the touch of a deadly chill,
And riotous grief in my bosom sprung,
  Tho' reason would have curbed my will.
I wailed for my pearl there hid away,
  While fiercely warred my doubts withal,
But tho' Christ showed where comfort lay,
  My will was still my sorrow's thrall.
I flung me down on that flowery mound,
  When so on my brain the fragrance wrought
I sank into a sleep profound,
  Above that pearl without a spot.   60

6

Then from that spot my spirit soared.
  My senses locked in slumber's spell,
My soul, by grace of God outpoured,
  Went questing where his marvels dwell.
I know not where that place may be,
  I know 'twas by high cliffs immured,
And that a forest fronted me
  Whose radiant slopes my steps allured.
Such splendor scarce might one believe—
  The goodly glory wherewith they shone;
No web that mortal hands may weave   71
  Has e'er such wondrous beauty known. . .

9

Yes, beautiful beyond compare,
  The vision of that forest-range
Wherein my fortune bade me fare—
  No tongue could say how fair, how strange.
I wandered on as one entranced,
  No bank so steep as to make me cower;
And the farther I went the brighter danced
  The light on grass and tree and flower.

Hedge-rows there were, and paths, and streams
 Whose banks were as fine threads of gold,
And I stood on the strand and watched the
     gleams
 Of one that downward in beauty rolled.   108

10

Dear Lord, the beauty of that fair burn!
 Its berylline banks were bright as day,
And singing sweetly at every turn
 The murmuring waters took their way.
On the bottom were stones a-shimmer with light
 As gleams through glass that waver and leap,
Or as twinkling stars on a winter night
 That watch in heaven while tired men sleep.
For every pebble there that laved
 Seemed like a rare and radiant gem;
Each pool was as with sapphires paved,   119
 So lustrous shone the beauty of them. . .

13

Then longing seized me to explore
 The farther margin of that stream,
For fair as was the hither shore
 Far fairer did the other seem.
About me earnestly I sought
 To find some way to win across,
But all my seeking availed me nought;
 There was no ford; I stood at loss.
Methought I must not daunted dwell
 In sight of such a blissful goal,
When lo, a strange thing there befell   155
 That still more deeply stirred my soul.

14

More wonder still my soul to daze!
 I saw beyond that lowly stream
A crystal cliff refulgent raise
 Its regal height, and, dazzling, gleam.
And at its foot there sat a child,
 A gracious maid, and debonair,
All in a white robe undefiled—
 Well had I known her otherwhere.
As glistening gold men use to spin,
 So shone that glory the cliff before.
Long did I drink her beauty in,   167
 And longed to call to her ever more. . .

16

But more than my longing was now my fright;
 I stood quite still; I durst not call;
With eyes wide open and lips shut tight,
 I stood as quiet as hawk in hall.
I weened it was some spectral shape,
 I dreaded to think what should ensue
If I should call her and she escape
 And leave me only my plight to rue.
When lo, that gracious, spotless may,[1]
 So delicate, so soft, so slight,

[1] maid

Uprose in all her queenly array,
 A priceless thing in pearls bedight.   192

17

Pearl-dight in royal wise, perdie,
 One might by grace have seen her there,
When all as fresh as a fleur-de-lys
 Adown the margent stepped that fair.
Her robe was white as gleaming snow,
 Unclasped at the sides and closely set
With the loveliest margarites, I trow,
 That ever my eyes looked on yet.
Her sleeves were broad and full, I ween,
 With double braid of pearls made bright.
Her kirtle shone with as goodly sheen,   203
 With precious pearls no less bedight. . .

20

Pearl-dight, that nature's masterpiece
 Came down the margent, stepping slow;
No gladder man from here to Greece
 When by the stream she stood, I trow.
More near of kin than aunt or niece,
 She made my gladness overflow;
She proffered me speech—Oh heart's release!—
 In womanly fashion bending low;
Caught off her crown of queenly show
 And welcomed me as a maiden might.
Ah well that I was born to know   239
 And greet that sweet one pearl-bedight!

21

"O pearl," quoth I, "all pearl-bedight,
 Art thou my Pearl, the Pearl I mourn
And long for through the lonely night?
 In weariness my days have worn
Since thou in the grass didst slip from sight.
 Pensive am I, heart-sick, forlorn,—
While thou hast won to pure delight
 In Paradise, of sorrow shorn.
What fate has hither my jewel borne
 And left me beggared to moan and cry?
For since we twain asunder were torn,
 A joyless jeweler am I."   252

22

That jewel then, with gems o'erspread,
 Upturned her face and her eyes gray,
Replaced the crown upon her head,
 And thus my longing did allay:
"Oh, sir, thou hast thy tale misread
 To say thy pearl is stolen away,
That is so safely casketed
 Here in this garden bright and gay,
Herein forever to dwell and play
 Where comes not sin nor sorrow's blight.
Such treasury [2] wouldst thou choose, parfay,
 Didst thou thy jewel love aright." *   264

[2] Compare *Matthew* vi. 21.
* A long religious dissertation follows and the
    dreamer awakes consoled.

WILLIAM LANGLAND ?
(1332?-1400)

THE VISION OF PIERS THE PLOWMAN.*

FROM THE PROLOGUE.

In a somer seson, whan soft was the sonne,
I shope[1] me in shroudes[2] as I a shepe[3] were,
In habite as an heremite unholy of workes,[4]
Went wyde[5] in this world wondres to here.
Ac[6] on a May mornynge, on Malverne hulles,[7]
Me byfel a ferly,[8] of fairy,[9] me thoughte;
I was wery forwandred[10] and went me to reste
Under a brode banke bi a bornes[11] side,   8
And as I lay and lened and loked in the wateres,
I slombred in a slepyng, it sweyved[12] so merye.
  Thanne gan I to meten[13] a merveilouse swevene,[14]
That I was in a wildernesse, wist I never where;
As I biheelde into the est an hiegh to[15] the sonne,
I seigh[16] a toure[17] on a toft[18] trielich[19] ymaked;
A depe dale binethe, a dongeon[20] there-inne,
With depe dyches and derke and dredful of sight.   16
A faire felde ful of folke[21] fonde I there bytwene,
Of alle maner of men, the mene and the riche,
Worchyng and wandryng as the worlde asketh.
Some putten hem[22] to the plow, pleyed ful selde,
In settyng[23] and in sowyng swonken[24] ful harde,
And wonnen that wastours with glotonye destruyeth.[25]   22

And some putten hem to pruyde, apparailed hem there-after,
In contenaunce of clothyng comen disgised.[26]
  In prayers and in penance putten hem manye,
Al for love of owre lorde lyveden ful streyte,[27]
In hope forto have hevenriche[28] blisse;
As ancres[29] and heremites that holden hem in here[33] selles,
And coveiten nought in contre to kairen[30] aboute,
For no likerous[31] liflode[32] her[33] lykam[34] to plese.   30
  And somme chosen chaffare;[35] they cheven[36] the bettere,
As it semeth to owre syght that suche men thryveth;
And somme murthes[37] to make as mynstralles conneth,[38]
And geten gold with here[33] glee, giltles, I leve.[39]
Ac iapers[40] and iangelers,[41] Iudas chylderen,
Feynen hem[42] fantasies and foles hem maketh,
And han here witte at wille to worche, yif thei sholde;
That Poule precheth of hem I nel nought preve it here;
Qui turpiloquium loquitur is luciferes hyne.[43]
  Bidders[44] and beggeres fast aboute yede,[45]
With her belies and her bagges of bred ful ycrammed;   41
Fayteden[46] for here fode, foughten atte ale;[47]
In glotonye, god it wote,[48] gon hij[49] to bedde,
And risen with ribaudye[50] tho roberdes knaves;[51]
Slepe and sori sleuthe[52] seweth[53] hem evre.[54]
Pilgrymes and palmers[55] plighted hem togidere
To seke seynt Iames[56] and seyntes in Rome.
Thei went forth in here wey with many wise tales,
And hadden leve to lye al here lyf after.
I seigh somme that seiden thei had ysought seyntes:

[1] arrayed
[2] rough garments
[5] shepherd
[4] not spiritual
[5] abroad
[6] but
[7] hills
[8] wonder
[9] enchantment
[10] weary from wandering
[11] brook's
[12] sounded
[13] to dream
[14] dream
[15] on high toward
[16] saw
[17] The tower of Truth, abode of God the Father.
[18] elevated place
[19] cunningly
[20] The "castel of care," abode of Falsehood (Lucifer).
[21] The world.
[22] them (selves)
[23] planting
[24] toiled
[25] and won that which wasteful men expend in gluttony.

[26] came strangely garbed
[27] strictly
[28] of the kingdom of heaven
[29] anchorites
[30] wander
[31] delicate
[32] livelihood, living
[33] their
[34] body
[35] trade
[36] succeed
[37] mirth
[38] know how
[39] believe
[40] jesters
[41] chatterers
[42] invent for themselves
[43] what Paul preaches about them I will

not show here, "for he who speaks slander is Lucifer's servant."
[44] beggars
[45] went
[46] cheated
[47] fought at the ale
[48] knows
[49] they
[50] ribaldry
[51] those robber villains
[52] sloth
[53] pursue
[54] ever
[55] Palmers made it their regular business to visit shrines.
[56] A shrine at Compostella in Galicia.

* In this long allegorical poem, the poet with the daring of a reformer attacks what he thinks to be the abuses in church, state, and society. The prologue, of which the first 82 lines are here given, sets the key-note of the poem by a description of the suffering, weakness, and crimes of the world as seen by the poet in a vision. Then in Passus (Chapter) I, of which a few lines are given, the poet begins his narrative interpretation of his vision. Our text is the B-text as printed by Dr. Skeat.

To eche a[57] tale that thei tolde here tonge was
    tempred to lye   51
More than to sey soth[58] it semed bi here speche.
    Heremites on[59] an heep, with hoked staves,
Wenten to Walsyngham,* and here wenches
    after[60];
Grete lobyes[61] and longe,[62] that loth were to
    swynke,[63]
Clotheden hem in copis[64] to ben knowen fram
    othere;
And shopen hem[65] heremites here ese to have.
    I fonde there Freris, alle the foure ordres,[66]
Preched the peple for profit of hem-selven,
Glosed[67] the gospel as hem good lyked,[68]   60
For coveitise[69] of copis construed it as thei
    wolde.
Many of this maistres Freris[70] mowe[71] clothen
    hem at lykyng,
For here money and marchandise marchen
    togideres.
For sith[72] charite hath be chapman[73] and chief
    to shryve lordes,†
Many ferlis[74] han fallen in a fewe yeris.[75]
But[76] holychirche and hij holde better togideres,
    The most myschief on molde[77] is mountyng wel
    faste.[78]
    There preched a Pardonere[79] as he a prest
      were,
Broughte forth a bulle[80] with bishopes seles,
And seide that hym-self myghte assoilen[81]
    hem alle
Of falshed of fastyng,[82] of vowes ybroken.   71
    Lewed[83] men leved[84] hym wel and lyked his
    wordes,
Comen up knelyng to kissen his bulles;
He bonched[85] hem with his brevet[86] and blered
    here eyes,

And raughte[87] with his ragman[88] rynges and
    broches;
Thus they geven here golde, glotones to
    kepe. . . .
Were the bischop yblissed[89] and worth bothe
    his eres,
His seel[90] shulde nought be sent to deceyve
    the peple.
Ac it is naught by[91] the bischop that the boy[92]
    precheth,   80
For the parisch prest and the pardonere
    parten[93] the silver,
That the poraille[94] of the parisch sholde have,
    yif thei nere.[95] . . .

From Passus I.

What this montaigne bymeneth,[1] and the merke
    dale,
And the felde ful of folke, I shal yow faire
    schewe.
A loveli ladi of lere,[2] in lynnen yclothed,
Come down fram a castel and called me faire,
And seide, 'Sone, slepestow,[3] sestow[4] this
    poeple,
How bisi thei ben abouten the mase[5]?
The moste partie of this poeple that passeth on
    this erthe,
Have thei worschip[6] in this worlde, thei wilne
    no better;
Of other hevene than here holde thei no tale[7].'
    I was aferd of her face theigh[8] she faire
    were,   10
And seide, 'Mercy, Madame, what is this to
    mene?'
'The toure up the toft,' quod she, 'Treuthe is
    there-inne,
And wolde that ye wroughte as his worde
    techeth;
For he is fader of feith, fourmed yow alle,
Bothe with fel[9] and with face, and yaf[10] yow
    fyve wittis
Forto worschip hym ther-with the while that ye
    ben here.

57 at every
58 truth
59 in
60 in their train
61 lubbers
62 tall
63 toil
64 friars' capes
65 arrayed themselves as
66 Dominicans, Franciscans, Carmelites, Augustines
67 interpreted
68 as it pleased them
69 covetousness
70 these master friars
71 may

72 since
73 pedlar
74 wonders
75 years
76 unless
77 earth
78 will increase rapidly
79 One commissioned to grant pardons
80 a Papal mandate
81 absolve
82 failure in fasting
83 ignorant
84 believed
85 struck
86 letter of indulgence

* The shrine of Our Lady of Walsingham (Norfolk) was almost more celebrated than that of Thomas à Becket.
† So worldly were the friars seeking money for hearing confessions and peddling their wares, that they often quarreled with the priests as to which should hear the confession.

87 got
88 bull with bishop's seals
89 righteous
90 seal
91 not against

92 i. e., the pardoner
93 divide
94 poor
95 if they (the pardoner and the priest) did not exist

1 means
2 face
3 sleepest thou
4 seest thou
5 confused throng

6 if they have honor
7 account
8 though
9 skin
10 gave

THE WYCLIF BIBLE (c. 1380)

ATTHEW III. THE COMING OF JOHN THE BAPTIST.

In tho daies Joon Baptist cam and prechid a the desert of Judee, and seide, Do ye penunce, for the kyngdom of hevenes schal nygh. 'or this is he of whom it is seid bi Isaie the rofete, seiynge, A vois of a crier in desert, Iake ye redi the weyes of the Lord, make ye ght the pathis of hym. And this Joon hadde othing of camels heris, and a girdil of skyn boute his leendis, and his mete was hony oukis[1] and hony of the wode. Thanne Jeru-alem wente out to hym, and al Judee, and al 1e countre aboute Jordan, and thei werun aischen of hym in Jordan, and knowlechiden er synnes.

But he sigh many of Farisies and of Saduces omynge to his baptem, and seide to hem, Gen-raciouns of eddris,[2] who schewid to you to e fro wrath that is to come? Therfor do ye vorthi fruytis of penaunce. And nyle ye seie[3] vith ynne you, We han Abraham to fadir: for seie to you that God is myghti to reise up of hes stones the sones of Abraham. And now he axe is putte to the root of the tre: therfor very tre that makith not good fruyt schal be utte doun, and schal be cast in to the fire.

I waisch you in watyr in to penaunce: but e that schal come aftir me is stronger than , whos schoon I am not worthi to bere: he chal baptise you in the Holi Goost, and fier. Vhos wenewynge[4] clooth is in his hond, and ie schal fulli clense his corn floor, and schal radere his whete in to his berne; but the chaf ie schal brenne with fier that mai not be quenchid.

Thanne Jhesus cam fro Galilee in to Jordan o Joon, to be baptisid of him. Jon forbede aym and seide, I owe to be baptisid of thee, and thou comest to me? But Jhesus answerid and seide to hym, Suffre now: for thus it fall-th to us to fulfille alle rightfulnesse. Then Joon suffrid hym. And whanne Jhesus was oaptisid, anon he wente up fro the watir: and o, hevenes weren opened to hym, and he say che spirit of God comynge doun as a dowve, and comynge on him. And lo, a vois fro hevenes, seiynge, This is my loved sone, in whiche I have plesid to me. *(Punctuation and capitalization modernized.)*

1 honey-suckles (Wyclif, translating from the Vulgate, evidently mistook the meaning of the Latin *locustæ*)
2 adders
3 will not ye to say
4 winnowing

THE KING JAMES BIBLE (1611)

MATTHEW III. THE COMING OF JOHN THE BAPTIST.

In those daies came John the Baptist, preach-ing in the wildernesse of Judea, and saying, Repent yee: for the kingdome of heaven is at hand. For this is he that was spoken of by the Prophet Esaias, saying, The voyce of one cry-ing in the wildernesse, Prepare ye the way of the Lord, make his paths straight. And the same John had his raiment of camels haire, and a leatherne girdle about his loynes, and his meate was locusts and wilde honie. Then went out to him Hierusalem, and all Judea, and all the region round about Jordane. And were baptized of him in Jordane, confessing their sinnes.

But when he saw many of the Pharisees and Sadducees come to his Baptisme, he said unto them, O generation of vipers, who hath warned you to flee from the wrath to come? Bring forth therefore fruits meete for repentance. And thinke not to say within your selves, Wee have Abraham to *our* father: For I say unto you, that God is able of these stones to raise up children unto Abraham. And now also the axe is layd unto the roote of the trees: There-fore every tree which bringeth not foorth good fruite, is hewen downe, and cast into the fire.

I indeed baptize you with water unto re-pentance: but he that commeth after mee, is mightier than I, whose shooes I am not worthy to beare, hee shall baptize you with the holy Ghost, and with fire. Whose fanne is in his hand, and he will throughly purge his floore, and gather his wheate into the garner: but wil burne up the chaffe with unquenchable fire. Then commeth Jesus from Galilee to Jordane, unto John, to be baptized of him: But John forbade him, saying, I have need to bee bap-tized of thee, and commest thou to me?

And Jesus answering, said unto him, Suffer it to be so now: for thus it becommeth us to fulfill all righteousnesse. Then he suffered him. And Jesus, when hee was baptized, went up straightway out of the water: and loe, the heavens were opened unto him, and he saw the Spirit of God descending like a dove, and light-ing upon him. And loe, a voice from heaven, saying, This is my beloved Soone, in whom I am well pleased. *(Verse numbering omitted.)*

CHAUCER'S PRONUNCIATION

a long = *ah* as in *father: bathed* [bahth-ed].

a short = *ah* without prolongation, as in *aha: at* [aht].

ai, ay = *ah'ee* (nearly equal to modern long *i*): *day* [dah'ee].

ɪu, aw = *ah'oo* (nearly equal to modern *ou* in *house:* straunge [strahwnjë].

e long = *ai* as in *pair: bere* [bearë].

e short = *e* as in *ten: hem* [hem].

e final = *ë* (pronounced as a very light separate syllable, like the final *e* in the German *eine.* So also is *es* of the plural.): *soote* [sohtë]. It is regularly elided before a following vowel, before *he, his, him, hire* (her), *here* (their), *hem* (them), and occasionally before other words beginning with *h;* also in *hire, here, oure,* etc.

ea, ee = our long *a; eek* [āke].

ei, ey = *ah' ee* (or our long *i*, aye): *wey* [wy].

eu, ew = French *u: hewe* [hü-e].

i long = *ee* (nearly): *shires* [sheer-es].

i short = *i* in *pin: with* [with].

o, oo long = *oa* in *oar: roote* [nearly rōtë].

o short = *o* in *not:* [not].

oi, oy = *oo' ee* (near equal to modern *oi*): *floytinge* [floiting].

ou, ow = our *oo* in *roōd* in words that in Mod. Eng. have taken the sound of *ou* in *loud: hous* [hoos].

ou, ow = *oh' oo* in words that now have the *ō* sound: *soule, knowe* [sōlë, knowë].

u long = French *u* (found only in French words): *vertu* [vehrtü].

u short = *u* in *pull: but* [bŏot].

c = *k* before *a, o, u* or any consonant.
  = *s* before *e, i, y.*

g = hard in words not of French origin.
  = *j* before *e, i* in words of French origin.

gh = *kh,* like the German *ch* in *nicht.*

h initial = omitted in unaccented *he, his, him, hire, hem.*

r = trilled.

s = often sharp when final.
  = never *sh* or *zh* (*vision* has therefore three syllables, *condicioun* four, etc.).

t = as at present; but final *-tion* = two syllables (si-oon).

th = *th* in *thin* or *th* in *this,* as in Mod. Eng.

w = sometimes *oo* as in *herberw.*

The following may serve to illustrate the approximate pronunciation of a few lines, without attempting Mr. Skeat's finer distinctions such as *vahyn* for *veyne,* etc. Note that *ë* is a separate syllable lightly pronounced, that *ʋ* equals *u* in *full,* and *ü* is French *u.*

Whan that Ahpreellë with 'is shoorës sohtë
The drookht of March hath persëd toh the rohtë,
And bahthëd evree vyne in swich lecoor
Of which vertü engendred is the floor;
Whan Zephirus aik with 'is swaitë braith
Inspeerëd hath in evry holt and haith
The tendre croopës, and the yungë sunnë
Hath in the Ram 'is halfë coors irunnë,
And smahlë foolës makhen melodeeë
That slaipen al the nikht with ohpen eeë,—
So priketh 'em nahtür in her corahgës,—
Than longen folk toh gohn on pilgrimahgës,
And palmerz for toh saiken strahwngë strondës,
Toh férnë halwës kooth in sondree londës;
And spesialee, from evree sheerës endë
Of Engëlond, toh Cahwnterberee thy wendë,
The hohlee blisful marteer for toh saikë,
That hem hath holpen whan that thy wair saikë.

CHAUCER'S METRE

A large part of Chaucer's work is written in heroic couplets: every two consecutive lines rhyming, and each line containing five iambic feet, that is, five groups of two syllables each, with the accent on the second syllable of each foot; e. g.

And bath'|ed eve'|ry veyn'|in swich'|li cour'|

An extra syllable is often added at the end of the line: e. g.

Whan that| Aprill|le with| his shou|res soo|te

Sometimes the first foot is shortened to one long syllable: e. g.

Twen|ty bo|kes clad| in blak| or reed|

THE TEXT

We have followed, with a few changes, the text of *The Canterbury Tales* printed by Dr. W. W. Skeat in the Clarendon Press Series, which is based on the Ellesmere MS.

GEOFFREY CHAUCER
(1340?-1400) *

From THE CANTERBURY TALES

The Prologue.

han that[1] Aprille with his shoures soote[2]
he droghte[3] of Marche hath perced to the
   roote,
nd bathed every veyne[4] in swich licour[5],
f which vertu[6] engendred is the flour[7];
Vhan Zephirus[8] eek[9] with his swete breeth
nspired hath in every holt[10] and heeth
he tendre croppes[11], and the yonge sonne
Iath in the Ram his halfe cours y-ronne[12],
nd smale fowles[13] maken melodye,
hat slepen al the night with open yë[14],   10
So priketh hem [15] nature in hir[16] corages[17]):
han[18] longen [19] folk to goon on pilgrimages,
And palmers for to seken[20] straunge strondes[21],
o ferne[22] halwes[23], couthe[24] in sondry londes;
And specially, from every shires ende
Of Engelond, to Caunterbury they wende,
The holy blisful martir[25] for to seke,
That hem hath holpen, whan that they were
   seke[26].
  Bifel that, in that sesoun on a day,
n Southwerk at the Tabard [27] as I lay   20
Redy to wenden on my pilgrimage
To Caunterbury with ful devout corage[28],
At night was come in-to that hostelrye
Wel[29] nyne and twenty in a compaignye,
Of sondry folk, by aventure[30] y-falle[31]

In felawshipe, and pilgrims were they alle,
That toward Caunterbury wolden ryde;
The chambres and the stables weren wyde,
And wel we weren esed[32] atte beste.
And shortly, whan the sonne was to[33] reste,   30
So hadde I spoken with hem everichon[34],
That I was of hir felawshipe anon,
And made forward[35] erly for to ryse,
To take our wey, ther as[36] I yow devyse[37].
  But natheles, whyl I have tyme and space,
Er that I ferther in this tale pace,
Me thinketh it acordaunt [38] to resoun,
To telle yow al the condicioun
Of ech of hem, so as it semed me,   39
And whiche they weren[39], and of what degree;
And eek in what array[40] that they were inne:
And at a knight than wol I first biginne.
  A Knight there was, and that a worthy man,
That fro the tyme that he first bigan
To ryden out, he loved chivalrye,
Trouthe and honour, fredom[41] and curteisye.
Ful worthy was he in his lordes werre[42],
And therto hadde he riden (no man ferre[43])
As wel in cristendom as hethenesse,
And evere honoured for his worthinesse.   50
At Alisaundre[44] he was, whan it was wonne;
Ful ofte tyme he hadde the bord bigonne[45]
Aboven alle naciouns in Pruce[46].
In Lettow[47] hadde he reysed[48] and in Ruce[49],
No cristen man so ofte of his degree[50].
In Gernade[51] at the sege eek hadde he be
Of Algezir[52], and riden in Belmarye[53].
At Lyeys[54] was he, and at Satalye[54]
Whan they were wonne; and in the Grete See[55]
At many a noble armee[56] hadde he be.   60
At mortal batailles hadde he been fiftene,
And foughten for our feith at Tramissene[57]
In listes[58] thryes, and ay slayn his foo. ·
This ilke[59] worthy knight hadde been also
Somtyme with the lord of Palatye[60],
Ageyn[61] another hethen in Turkye:
And everemore he hadde a sovereyn prys[62].
And though that he were worthy, he was wys,

1 when
2 sweet showers
3 drought
4 vein
5 such sap
6 power
7 flower
8 the west-wind
9 also
10 wood
11 shoots
12 when the spring sun
   has passed through
   the second, or
   April, half of his
   course in that con-
   stellation of the
   zodiac called the
   Ram, i. e., about
   April 11
13 birds

14 eyes
15 them
16 their
17 hearts
18 then
19 Indicative plural of
   the verb "long".
20 seek
21 shores
22 distant
23 shrines
24 known
25 Thomas à Becket
26 sick
27 An inn (a tabard was
   a short coat).
28 heart
29 full
30 chance
31 fallen

* "I take unceasing delight in Chaucer. How exquisitely tender he is, and yet how perfectly
free from the least touch of sickly melancholy
or morbid drooping! The sympathy of the
poet with the subjects of his poetry is particularly remarkable in Shakespeare and
Chaucer; but what the first effects by a strong
act of imagination and mental metamorphosis,
the last does without any effort, merely by
the inborn kindly joyousness of his nature.
How well we seem to know Chaucer! How
absolutely nothing do we know of Shakespeare!"—Coleridge. See also Dryden "On
Chaucer" in the present volume.

32 made easy: i. e., ac-
   commodated in the
   best manner
33 at
34 every one
35 agreement
36 where
37 tell
38 according
39 what sort of people
   they were
40 dress
41 liberality
42 war
43 further
44 Alexandria (1365)
45 sat at the head of the
   table
46 Prussia

47 Lithuania (a western
   province of Russia)
48 forayed
49 Russia
50 rank
51 Granada
52 Algeciras
53 A Moorish kingdom
   in Africa.
54 A town in Asia Minor.
55 Mediterranean
56 armed expedition
57 In Asia Minor.
58 tournaments
59 same
60 In Asia Minor.
61 against
62 high praise

And of his port[1] as meek as is a mayde.
He nevere yet no vileinye[2] ne sayde
In al his lyf, un-to no maner wight.   70
He was a verray parfit gentil knight.
But for to tellen yow of his array,
His hors[3] were goode, but he was nat gay[4].
Of fustian[5] he wered a gipoun[6]
Al bismotered[7] with his habergeoun[8].
For he was late y-come from his viage[9],
And wente for to doon his pilgrimage[10].
    With him ther was his sone, a yong Squyer,
A lovyer, and a lusty bacheler[11],   80
With lokkes crulle[12], as[13] they were leyd in
    presse.
Of twenty yeer of age he was, I gesse.
Of his stature he was of evene lengthe[14],
And wonderly delivere[15], and greet of
    strengthe.
And he hadde been somtyme in chivachye[16],
In Flaundres, in Artoys[17], and Picardye[17],
And born him wel, as of so litel space[18],
In hope to stonden in his lady[19] grace.
Embrouded[20] was he, as it were a mede[21]
Al ful of fresshe floures, whyte and rede.   90
Singinge he was, or floytinge[22], al the day;
He was as fresh as is the month of May.
Short was his goune, with sleves longe and
    wyde.
Wel coude he sitte on hors, and faire ryde.
He coude songes make and wel endyte[23],
Iuste[24] and eek daunce, and wel purtreye[25] and
    wryte.
So hote[26] he lovede, that by nightertale[27]
He sleep namore than doth a nightingale.
Curteys he was, lowly, and servisable,
And carf[28] biforn his fader at the table.   100
    A Yeman hadde he[29], and servaunts namo[30]
At that tyme, for him liste[31] ryde so;
And he was clad in cote and hood of grene;
A sheef of pecok arwes brighte and kene
Under his belt he bar ful thriftily,
(Wel coude he dresse his takel yemanly[33]:

His arwes drouped noght with fetheres lowe),
And in his hand he bar a mighty bowe.
A not-heed[34] hadde he, with a broun visage.
Of wode-craft[35] wel coude[36] he al the usage.   110
Upon his arm he bar a gay bracer[37],
And by his syde a swerd and a bokeler[38],
And on that other syde a gay daggere,
Harneised[39] wel, and sharp as point of spere;
A Cristofre[40] on his brest of silver shene[41].
An horn he bar, the bawdrik[42] was of grene;
A forster[43] was he, soothly[44], as I gesse.
    Ther was also a Nonne, a Prioresse,
That of hir smyling was ful simple and coy;
Hir gretteste ooth was but by sëynt Loy[45];   120
And she was cleped[46] madame Eglentyne.
Ful wel she song the service divyne,
Entuned in hir nose ful semely;
And Frensh she spak ful faire and fetisly[47],
After the scole of Stratford atte Bowe*,
For Frensh of Paris was to hir unknowe.
At mete wel y-taught was she with-alle;
She leet no morsel from hir lippes falle,
Ne wette hir fingres in hir sauce depe.
Wel coude she carie a morsel, and wel kepe,   130
That no drope ne fille[48] up-on hir brest.
In curteisye was set ful moche hir lest[49],
Hir over lippe wyped she so clene,
That in hir coppe[50] was no ferthing sene
Of grece, whan she dronken hadde hir draughte.
Ful semely after hir mete she raughte[51],
And sikerly[52] she was of greet disport[53],
And ful plesaunt, and amiable of port[54],
And peyned[55] hir to countrefete[56] chere[57]
Of court, and been estatlich[58] of manere,   140
And to ben holden digne[59] of reverence.
But, for to speken of hir conscience,
She was so charitable and so pitous[60],
She wolde wepe, if that she sawe a mous
Caught in a trappe, if it were deed or bledde.
Of smale houndes had she, that she fedde
With rosted flesh, or milk and wastel breed[61].
But sore weep she if oon of hem were deed,

1 bearing
2 unbecoming word
3 horses
4 gaily dressed
5 coarse cloth
6 a short tight-fitting
    coat
7 spotted
8 coat of mail
9 voyage
10 In order to give
    thanks for his safe
    return.
11 An aspirant for
    knighthood.
12 curly
13 as if
14 average height
15 nimble
16 military expeditions
17 An ancient province
    of France.

18 considering the
    shortness of the
    time
19 lady's
20 embroidered
21 meadow
22 playing the flute
23 compose
24 joust (engage in a
    tournament)
25 draw
26 hotly
27 night-time
28 carved
29 the knight
30 no more
31 it pleased him
32 arrows
33 order his tackle
    (equipment) in
    yeomanlike man-
    ner

34 nut-head, a closely
    cropped head
35 wood-craft
36 knew
37 guard for the arm
38 shield
39 equipped
40 image of St. Christo-
    pher
41 bright
42 girdle worn over the
    shoulder
43 forester
44 truly
45 St. Eloy or Loy or
    Eligius, patron
    saint of gold-
    smiths.

46 named
47 daintily, exactly
48 fell
49 pleasure
50 cup
51 reached
52 surely
53 good humor
54 bearing
55 took pains
56 imitate
57 behavior
58 to be dignified
59 worthy
60 compassionate
61 bread made of the
    best flour—cake-
    bread

* Stratford le Bow, where there was a Benedic-
    tine nunnery, and where Anglo-French would
    be spoken, rather than the Parisian kind.

if men smoot it with a yerde[1] smerte[2]:
d al was conscience and tendre herte.   150
l semely hir wimpel[3] pinched[4] was;
r nose tretys[5]; hir eyen greye as glas;
r mouth ful smal, and ther-to softe and reed;
t sikerly[6] she hadde a fair forheed.
was almost a spanne brood, I trowe;
r, hardily[7], she was nat undergrowe.
l fetis[8] was hir cloke, as I was war[9].
: smal coral aboute hir arm she bar
peire of bedes[10], gauded[11] al with grene;   159
d ther-on heng a broche of gold ful shene,
which ther was first write a crowned A,
d after, *Amor vincit omnia*[12].
Another Nonne with hir hadde she,
at was hir chapeleyne, and Preestes thre.
A Monk ther was, a fair for the maistrye[13],
n out-rydere, that lovede venerye[14],
manly man, to been an abbot able.
l many a deyntee[15] hors hadde he in stable:
d, whan he rood, men mighte his brydel here
nglen in a whistling wynd as clere,   170
d eek as loude as doth the chapel-belle.
ere-as[16] this lord was keper of the celle,
e reule of seint Maure or of seint Beneit[18],
y-cause that it was old and som-del streit[19],
is ilke monk leet olde thinges[20] pace[21],
d held after the newe world the space[22].
e yaf nat of that text a pulled[23] hen,
at seith, that hunters been nat holy men;
e that a monk, whan he is recchelees[24],
likned til a fish that is waterlees;   180
is is to seyn, a monk out of his cloistre.
t thilke text held he nat worth an oistre.
nd I seyde his opinioun was good.
hat[25] sholde he studie, and make him selven wood[26],
pon a book in cloistre alwey to poure,
swinken[27] with his handes, and laboure,
s Austin bit[28]? How shal the world be served?
t Austin have his swink[27] to him reserved.

Therfor he was a pricasour[29] aright;
Grehoundes he hadde, as swifte as fowel in flight;
Of priking and of hunting for the hare   191
Was al his lust[30], for no cost wolde he spare.
I seigh[31] his sleves purfiled[32] at the hond
With grys[33], and that the fyneste of a lond;
And, for to festne his hood under his chin,
He hadde of gold y-wroght a curious pin:
A love-knot in the gretter ende ther was.
His heed was balled[34], that shoon as any glas,
And eek his face, as he hadde been anoint.
He was a lord ful fat and in good point[35];   200
His eyen stepe[36], and rollinge in his heed,
That stemed as a forneys of a leed[37],
His botes souple, his hors in greet estat.
Now certeinly he was a fair prelat;
He was nat pale as a for-pyned goost[38].
A fat swan loved he best of any roost.
His palfrey was as broun as is a berye.
A Frere[39] ther was, a wantown[40] and a merye,
A limitour[41], a ful solempne[42] man.
In alle the ordres foure[43] is noon that can[44]
So moche of daliaunce and fair langage.   211
He hadde maad ful many a mariage
Of yonge wommen, at his owne cost.
Un-to his ordre he was a noble post.
Ful wel biloved and famulier was he
With frankeleyns[45] over-al in his contree,
And eek with worthy wommen of the toun:
For he had power of confessioun,
As seyde him-self, more than a curat,
For of his ordre he was licentiat[46].   220
Ful swetely herde he confessioun,
And plesaunt was his absolucioun;
He was an esy man to yeve[47] penaunce
Ther-as he wiste to han a good pitaunce[48];
For unto a povre ordre for to yive[49]
Is signe that a man is wel y-shrive.
For if he[50] yaf, he[51] dorste make avaunt[52],
He wiste that a man was repentaunt.
For many a man so hard is of his herte[53],   229
He may nat wepe al-thogh him sore smerte[54].
Therfore, in stede of weping and preyeres,

tick
harply
eck covering
laited
vell proportioned
urely
ertainly
vell made
ware
a set of beads, a rosary
having the gawdies or large beads green
"Love conquers all."
a very fine monk indeed
hunting
fine
where
A smaller religious

house dependent on a monastery.
18 The oldest forms of monastic discipline were based on the rules of St. Maur and of St. Benet or Benedict.
19 somewhat strict
20 (these rules)
21 pass
22 pace, way
23 plucked (he would not give a straw for that text that—)
24 wandering or vagrant
25 why
26 crazy
27 work
28 bids

29 hard rider
30 pleasure
31 saw
32 bordered
33 grey fur
34 bald
35 *en bon point,* fat
36 bright
37 glow like the fire under a cauldron
38 tormented ghost
39 friar
40 brisk
41 One licensed to beg within certain limits.
42 pompous
43 Dominicans (Black Friars); Francis-
cans (Grey Friars); Carmelites (White Friars); Augustin (or Austin) Friars.
44 knows
45 country gentlemen
46 One licensed to give absolution.
47 give, assign
48 where he knew he could get a good gift
49 give
50 the man
51 the friar
52 boast
53 heart
54 he suffer sorely

Men moot[1] yeve silver to the povre freres.
His tipet[2] was ay[3] farsed[4] ful of knyves
And pinnes, for to yeven faire wyves.
And certeinly he hadde a mery note;
Wel coude he singe and pleyen on a rote[5].
Of yeddinges[6] he bar utterly the prys[7].
His nekke whyt was as the flour-de-lys[8].
Ther-to he strong was as a champioun.
He knew the tavernes wel in every toun,   240
And everich hostiler[9] and tappestere[10]
Bet[11] than a lazar[12] or a beggestere[13];
For un-to swich a worthy man as he
Acorded nat, as by his facultee[14],
To have with seke[15] lazars aqueyntaunce.
It is nat honest[16], it may nat avaunce[17]
For to delen with no swich poraille[18],
But al with riche and sellers of vitaille.
And over-al[19], ther-as[20] profit sholde aryse,
Curteys he was, and lowly of servyse.   250
Ther nas no man nowher so vertuous[21].
He was the beste beggere in his hous;
For thogh a widwe hadde noght a sho[22],
So plesaunt was his *In principio*[23],
Yet wolde he have a ferthing[24], er he wente,
His purchas[25] was wel bettre than his rente[26].
And rage[27] he coude as it were right a
   whelpe[28].
In love-dayes[29] ther coude he mochel helpe.
For ther he was nat lyk a cloisterer
With a thredbare cope, as in a povre scoler,   260
But he was lyk a maister or a pope.
Of double worsted was his semi-cope[30],
That rounded as a belle out of the presse.
Somwhat he lipsed, for his wantownesse[31],
To make his English swete up-on his tonge;
And in his harping, whan that he had songe,
His eyen twinkled in his heed aright,
As doon the sterres in the frosty night.
This worthy limitour was cleped Huberd.

   A Marchant was ther with a forked berd, 270
In mottelee[32], and hye on horse he sat,

Up-on his heed a Flaundrish bever hat;
His botes clasped faire and fetisly.
His resons[33] he spak ful solempnely[34],
Sowninge[35] alway thencrees[36] of his winning.
He wolde the see were kept[37] for any thing[38]
Bitwixe Middelburgh and Orewelle[39].
Wel coude[40] he in eschaunge sheeldes[41] selle.
This worthy man ful wel his wit bisette[42];
Ther wiste no wight that he was in dette,   2
So estatly[43] was he of his governaunce[44],
With his bargaynes, and with his chevisaunce.
For sothe he was a worthy man with-alle,
But sooth to seyn, I noot[46] how men him cal[
   A Clerk[47] ther was of Oxenford also,
That un-to logik hadde longe y-go[48].
As lene was his hors as is a rake,
And he nas[49] nat right fat, I undertake[50];
But loked holwe[51], and ther-to soberly[52].
Ful thredbar was his overest[53] courtepy[54]   2
For he had geten him yet no benefice[55],
Ne was so worldly for to have office[56].
For him was levere[57] have at his beddes heed
Twenty bokes, clad in blak or reed
Of Aristotle and his philosophye,
Than robes riche, or fithele[58], or gay sautrye[5
But al be that he was a philosophre[60],
Yet hadde he but litel gold in cofre;
But al that he mighte of his frendes hente[61];
On bokes and on lerninge he it spente,   30
And bisily gan for the soules preye
Of hem that yaf him where-with to scoleye[62].
Of studie took he most cure[63] and most hede.
Noght o word spak he more than was nede,
And that was seyd in forme and reverence,
And short and quik, and ful of hy sentence[64]
Sowninge[65] in moral vertu was his speche,
And gladly wolde he lerne, and gladly teche.
   A Sergeant of the Lawe[66], war[67] and wys,
That often hadde been at the parvys[68],   31

1 ought to
2 hood, cowl
3 ever
4 stuffed
5 fiddle
6 songs
7 he took the prize
8 lily
9 innkeeper
10 bar maid
11 better
12 leper
13 female beggar
14 it was unsuitable, considering his ability
15 sick
16 creditable
17 profit
18 poor people
19 everywhere
20 where
21 energetic
22 shoe
23 *St. John I.* 1, "In the beginning," etc. (the opening of the friar's address)
24 half a cent
25 proceeds of his begging
26 regular income
27 play
28 just like a puppy
29 arbitration days (for settling differences without lawsuit)
30 short cape
31 lisped a little out of whimsical jolliness
32 dress of variegated color
33 opinions
34 pompously
35 proclaiming, sounding
36 the increase
37 guarded
38 at any cost, by all means
39 The first a port in the Netherlands, opposite Harwich in England; the second a town near the mouth of the river Orwell in England.
40 knew how to
41 French crowns (he was a money-changer)
42 employed
43 dignified
44 management
45 agreements
46 ne+wot (know not)
47 student, scholar
48 devoted himself
49 ne+was (was not)
50 affirm
51 hollow
52 solemn
53 outer
54 coat
55 ecclesiastical living
56 secular office
57 he had rather
58 fiddle
59 psaltery, harp
60 The word meant both philosopher and alchemist.
61 get
62 devote himself to study
63 care
64 meaning
65 tending to
66 king's lawyer
67 wary
68 portico (of St. Paul's, where lawyers met for consultation)

ᴉer was also, ful riche of excellence.
ᴉscreet he was, and of greet reverence[1]:
e semed swich, his wordes weren so wyse,
stice he was ful often in assyse[2],
y patente[3] and by pleyn[4] commissioun;
or his science, and for his heigh renoun
f fees and robes hadde he many oon.
, greet a purchasour[5] was nowher noon[6].
l was fee simple[7] to him in effect,
is purchasing mighte nat been infect[8].   320
owher so bisy a man as he ther nas,
nd yet he semed bisier than he was.
ᴉ termes hadde he caas and domes alle[9],
ᴉat from the tyme of king William were
    falle[10].
herto he coude endyte, and make a thing,
her coude no wight pinche[11] at his wryting;
nd every statut coude[12] he pleyn by rote.
e rood but hoomly in a medlee cote
irt with a ceint[13] of silk, with barres[14] smale;
f his array telle I no lenger tale.   330
  A Frankeleyn[15] was in his compaignye;
ᴊhyt was his berd[16], as is the dayesye[17].
f his complexioun[18] he was sangwyn[19].
ᴊel loved he by the morwe[20] a sop[21] in wyn.
o liven in delyt was evere his wone[22],
ᴉor he was Epicurus[23] owne sone,
ᴉat heeld opinioun that pleyn delyt
ᴊas verraily felicitee parfyt.
n housholdere, and that a greet, was he;
eynt Iulian[24] he was in his contree.   340
ᴉis breed, his ale, was alwey after oon[25];
 bettre envyned[26] man was nevere noon.
ᴊith-oute bake mete was nevere his hous,
ᴉf fish and flesh, and that so plentevous,
t snewed[27] in his hous of mete and drinke,
ᴉf alle deyntees that men coude thinke.
ᴉfter the sondry sesons of the yeer,
ᴊo chaunged he his mete and his soper.
ᴉul many a fat partrich hadde he in mewe[28],

And many a breem[29] and many a luce in
    stewe[30].   350
Wo[31] was his cook, but-if[32] his sauce were
Poynaunt and sharp, and redy al his gere[33].
His table dormant[34] in his halle alway
Stood redy covered al the longe day.
At sessiouns[35] ther was he lord and sire.
Ful ofte tyme he was knight of the shire[36].
An anlas[37] and a gipser[38] al of silk
Heng at his girdel, whyt as morne milk
A shirreve hadde he been, and a countour[39];
Was nowher such a worthy vavasour[40].   360
  An Haberdassher[41] and a Carpenter,
A Webbe,[42] a Dyere, and a Tapicer[43],
And they were clothed alle in o liveree,
Of a solempne and greet fraternitee.
Ful fresh and newe hir gere apyked[44] was;
Hir knyves were y-chaped[45] noght with bras,
But al with silver wroght ful clene and weel,
Hir girdles and hir pouches everydeel.
Wel semed ech of hem a fair burgeys[46],
To sitten in a yeldhalle[47] on a deys[48].   370
Everich[49], for the wisdom that he can[50],
Was shaply[51] for to been an alderman.
For catel[52] hadde they ynogh and rente[53],
And eek hir wyves wolde it wel assente[54];
And elles certein were they to blame.
It is ful fair to been y-clept *ma dame*,
And goon[55] to vigilyës[56] al bifore,
And have a mantel roialliche y-bore[57].
  A Cook they hadde with hem for the nones[58],
To boille chiknes[59] with the mary-bones,   380
And poudre-marchant[60] tart[61], and galingale[62].
Wel coude he knowe[63] a draughte of London
    ale.
He coude roste, and sethe[64], and broille, and
    frye,
Maken mortreux[65], and wel bake a pye.
But greet harm was it, as it thoughte me,
That on his shine[66] a mormal[67] hadde he;

For blankmanger[1], that made he with the beste.

A Shipman was ther, woning[2] fer by weste:
For aught I woot[3], he was of Dertemouthe.
He rood up-on a rouncy[4], as he couthe[5],   390
In a gowne of falding[6] to the knee.
A daggere hanging on a laas[7] hadde he
Aboute his nekke under his arm adoun.
The hote somer had maad his hewe al broun;
And, certeinly, he was a good felawe.
Ful many a draughte of wyn had he y-drawe
From Burdeux-ward, whyl that the chapman[8] sleep.
Of nyce[9] conscience took he no keep[10].
If that he faught, and hadde the hyer hond,
By water he sente hem hoom to every lond[11].
But of his craft[12] to rekene wel his tydes   401
His stremes and his daungers him bisydes,
His herberwe[13] and his mone[14], his lodemenage[15],
Ther nas noon swich from Hulle to Cartage.
Hardy he was, and wys to undertake;
With many a tempest hadde his berd been shake.
He knew wel alle the havenes, as they were,
From Gootlond[16] to the cape of Finistere[17],
And every cryke in Britayne and in Spayne;
His barge y-cleped was the Maudelayne.   410

With us ther was a Doctour of Phisyk[18],
In al this world ne was ther noon him lyk
To speke of phisik and of surgerye;
For he was grounded in astronomye[19].
He kepte his pacient a ful greet del
In houres[20], by his magik naturel.
Wel coude he fortunen[21] the ascendent
Of his images[22] for his pacient*.
He knew the cause of everich maladye,
Were it of hoot or cold, or moiste, or drye†,   420
And where engendred, and of what humour;
He was a verrey parfit practisour.
The cause y-knowe, and of his harm the rote[23],
Anon he yaf the seke man his bote[24].
Ful redy hadde he his apothecaries,

To sende him drogges, and his letuaries[25],
For ech of hem made other for to winne[26];
Hir frendschipe nas nat newe to biginne[27].
Wel knew he the olde Esculapius*,
And Deiscorides, and eek Rufus;   4
Old Ypocras, Haly, and Galien;
Serapion, Razis, and Avicen;
Averrois, Damascien, and Constantyn;
Bernard, and Gatesden, and Gilbertyn.
Of his diete mesurable[28] was he,
For it was of no superfluitee,
But of greet norissing and digestible.
His studie was but litel on the Bible.
In sangwin[29] and in pers[30] he clad was al,
Lyned with taffata[31] and with sendal[31]   4
And yet he was but esy of dispence[32];
He kepte that he wan in pestilence.
For gold in phisik is a cordial[33],
Therfor he lovede gold in special.

A Good Wyf was ther of bisyde Bathe,
But she was som-del deef, and that wa scathe[34].
Of cloth-making she hadde swiche an haunt[35],
She passed hem of Ypres[36] and of Gaunt[37].
In al the parisshe wyf ne was ther noon
That to the offring[38] bifore hir sholde goon;   45
And if ther dide, certeyn, so wrooth was she,
That she was out of alle charitee.
Hir coverchiefs[39] ful fyne were of ground[40];
I dorste swere they weyeden ten pound[41]
That on a Sonday were upon hir heed.
Hir hosen weren of fyn scarlet reed,
Ful streite y-teyd, and shoes ful moiste[42] an newe.
Bold was hir face, and fair, and reed of hewe
She was a worthy womman al hir lyve,   45
Housbondes at chirche-dore[43] she hadde fyve,
Withouten[44] other compaignye in youthe;
But thereof nedeth nat to speke as nouthe[45].
And thryes hadde she been at Ierusalem;
She hadde passed many a straunge streem;

1 minced capon, cream, sugar and flour
2 dwelling
3 know
4 common hackney
5 as well as he could
6 coarse cloth
7 cord
8 merchant
9 over scrupulous
10 heed
11 made them walk the plank
12 skill
13 harbor
14 moon
15 pilotage
16 Jutland, Denmark
17 On the coast of Spain.
18 medicine
19 astrology
20 he treated his patient at favorable astrological times
21 forecast
22 talismans
23 the root of the evil
24 remedy
25 medicines mixed with confections
26 the doctor and the druggist each made business for the other
27 of recent date
28 moderate
29 reddish
30 light blue
31 thin silk
32 moderate in spending
33 Gold in medicine was supposed to render it especially efficacious.
34 a pity
35 skill
36 In West Flanders
37 Ghent
38 The ceremony of offering gifts t relics on "Relic Sunday."
39 kerchiefs for th head
40 texture
41 Because ornamentee with gold and sil ver.
42 soft
43 People were marrie at the church porch.
44 without counting
45 at present

* Figures or talismans made when a favorable star was rising above the horizon, i. e., was in the ascendant, could, it was believed, cause good or evil to a patient.
† Diseases were thought to be caused by an excess of one or another of these humours.
* The god of medicine, son of Apollo. The others named in lines 430-43- are all famous physicians and scholars of antiquity and mediæva times. Gatisden of Oxford was almost a contemporary of Chaucer.

At Rome she hadde been, and at Boloigne[1],
In Galice at seint Iame[2], and at Coloigne[3].
She coude moche of wandring by the weye.
Gat-tothed[4] was she, soothly for to seye.
Up-on an amblere[5] esily she sat,
Y-wimpled wel, and on hir heed an hat   470
As brood as is a bokeler[6] or a targe;
A foot-mantel[7] aboute hir hipes large,
And on hir feet a paire of spores sharpe.
In felaweschip wel coude she laughe and carpe[8].
Of remedies of love[9] she knew per-chaunce,
For she coude of that art the olde daunce.

A good man was ther of religioun,
And was a povre Persoun[10] of a toun;
But riche he was of holy thoght and werk.
He was also a lerned man, a clerk,   480
That Cristes gospel trewely wolde preche;
His parisshens devoutly wolde he teche.
Benigne he was, and wonder diligent,
And in adversitee ful pacient;
And swich he was y-preved[11] ofte sythes[12].
Ful looth were him to cursen for his tythes[13],
But rather wolde he yeven, out of doute,
Un-to his povre parisshens aboute
Of his offring[14], and eek of his substaunce[15].
He coude in litel thing han suffisaunce.   490
Wyd was his parisshe, and houses fer a-sonder,
But he ne lafte nat[16], for reyn ne thonder,
In siknes nor in meschief[17] to visyte
The ferreste[18] in his parisshe, moche and lyte[19],
Up-on his feet, and in his hand a staf.
This noble ensample to his sheep he yaf,
That first he wroghte, and afterward he
       taughte;
Out of the gospel he tho[20] wordes caughte;
And this figure he added eek ther-to,
That if gold ruste, what shal yren[21] do?   500
For if a preest be foul, on whom we truste,
No wonder is a lewed[22] man to ruste;
And shame it is, if a preest take keep[23],
A [spotted] shepherde and a clene sheep.
Wel oghte a preest ensample for to yive,
By his clennesse, how that his sheep shold live.
He sette nat his benefice to hyre[24],
And leet his sheep encombred in the myre,

And ran to London, un-to sëynt Poules,
To seken him a chaunterie[25] for soules,
Or with a bretherhed to been withholde[26],   510
But dwelte at hoom, and kepte wel his folde,
So that the wolf ne made it nat miscarie;
He was a shepherde and no mercenarie[27].
And though he holy were, and vertuous,
He was to sinful man nat despitous[28],
Ne of his speche daungerous[29] ne digne[30],
But in his teching discreet and benigne.
To drawen folk to heven by fairnesse
By good ensample, this was his bisynesse: 520
But it were any persone obstinat,
What so he were, of heigh or lowe estat,
Him wolde he snibben[31] sharply for the nones[32].
A bettre preest, I trowe that nowher non is.
He wayted after no pompe and reverence,
Ne maked him a spyced[33] conscience,
But Cristes lore, and his apostles twelve,
He taughte, but first he folwed it him-selve.

With him ther was a Plowman, was his
       brother,   529
That hadde y-lad[34] of dong ful many a fother[35],
A trewe swinkere[36] and a good was he,
Livinge in pees and parfit charitee.
God loved he best with al his hole herte
At alle tymes, thogh him gamed or smerte[37],
And thanne his neighebour right as him-selve.
He wolde thresshe, and ther-to dyke[38] and
       delve,
For Cristes sake, for every povre wight,
Withouten hyre[39], if it lay in his might.
His tythes payed he ful faire and wel,
Bothe of his propre[40] swink and his catel[41].   540
In a tabard he rood upon a mere[42].

Ther was also a Reve[43] and a Millere,
A Somnour[44] and a Pardoner[45] also,
A Maunciple[46], and my-self; there were namo[47].
The Miller was a stout carl[48], for the
       nones[49],
Ful big he was of braun, and eek of bones;
That proved wel, for over-al ther[50] he cam,
At wrastling he wolde have alwey the ram[51].
He was short-sholdred, brood, a thikke knarre[52],

1 Where there was an image of the Virgin.
2 to the shrine of St. James in Galicia in Spain
3 Where according to legend the bones of the Three Wise Men of the East were kept.
4 gap-toothed: i. e., with teeth wide apart
5 nag
6 shield
7 riding skirt
8 chatter
9 love-charms
10 parson
11 proved
12 times
13 he was loath to ex-communicate those who would not pay their tithes
14 gifts made to him
15 property
16 ceased not
17 trouble
18 farthest
19 rich and poor
20 those
21 iron
22 ignorant
23 notice
24 he did not sub-let his parish
25 a position to sing mass
26 maintained
27 hireling
28 merciless
29 over-bearing
30 proud
31 reprove
32 on occasion
33 sophisticated
34 led
35 load
36 laborer
37 whether his luck were good or bad
38 dig ditches
39 pay
40 own
41 property
42 mare (then the humble man's steed)
43 bailiff
44 A summoner to ecclesiastical courts.
45 One commissioned to grant pardons.
46 A purchaser of food for lawyers at inns of court or for colleges.
47 no more
48 churl, fellow
49 for you
50 everywhere
51 The prize.
52 knotted, thick-set fellow

Ther nas no dore that he nolde heve of harre[1],
Or breke it, at a renning, with his heed.   551
His berd as any sowe or fox was reed,
And ther-to brood, as though it were a spade.
Up-on the cop[2] right of his nose he hade
A werte[3], and ther-on stood a tuft of heres,
Reed as the bristles of a sowes eres[4];
His nose-thirles[5] blake were and wyde.
A swerd and bokeler bar he by his syde;
His mouth as greet was as a greet forneys.
He was a Ianglere[6] and a goliardeys[7],   560
And that was most of sinne and harlotryes[8].
Wel coude he stelen corn, and tollen thryes[9];
And yet he hadde a thombe of gold[10], pardee.
A whyt cote and a blew hood wered he.
A baggepype wel coude he blowe and sowne[11],
And therwithal he broghte us out of towne.

    A gentil Maunciple was ther of a temple[12],
Of which achatours[13] mighte take exemple
For to be wyse in bying of vitaille.   569
For whether that he payde, or took by taille[14],
Algate he wayted[15] so in his achat[16],
That he was ay biforn and in good stat.
Now is nat that of God a ful fair grace,
That swich a lewed[17] mannes wit shal pace[18]
The wisdom of an heep of lerned men?
Of maistres hadde he mo[19] than thryes ten,
That were of lawe expert and curious;
Of which ther were a doseyn in that hous,
Worthy to been stiwardes of rente and lond
Of any lord that is in Engelond,   580
To make him live by his propre good,
In honour dettelees, but he were wood[20],
Or live as scarsly[21] as him list desire;
And able for to helpen al a shire
In any cas that mighte falle or happe;
And yit this maunciple sette hir aller cappe[22].

    The Reve was a sclendre colerik[23] man,
His berd was shave as ny as ever he can.
His heer was by his eres round y-shorn.
His top was dokked[24] lyk a preest biforn.   590
Ful longe were his legges, and ful lene,
Y-lyk a staf, ther was no calf y-sene.
Wel coude he kepe a gerner[25] and a binne;
Ther was noon auditour coude on him winne.
Wel wiste he, by the droghte, and by the reyn.
The yeldyng of his seed, and of his greyn.

His lordes sheep, his neet[26], his dayerye,
His swyn, his hors, his stoor[27], and his pultrye,
Was hoolly in this reves governing,
And by his covenaunt yaf the rekening[28]   600
Sin[29] that his lord was twenty yeer of age;
Ther coude no man bringe him in arrerage[30].
Ther nas baillif, ne herde[31], ne other hyne[32],
That he ne knew his sleighte and his covyne[33];
They were adrad of him, as of the deeth.
His woning[34] was ful fair up-on an heeth,
With grene treës shadwed was his place.
He coude bettre than his lord purchace.
Ful riche he was astored prively,
His lord wel coude he plesen subtilly,   610
To yeve and lene him of his owne good,
And have a thank, and yet a cote, and hood[35].
In youthe he lerned hadde a good mister[36];
He was a wel good wrighte, a carpenter.
This reve sat up-on a ful good stot[37],
That was al pomely[38] grey, and highte Scot.
A long surcote of pers[39] up-on he hade,
And by his syde he bar a rusty blade.
Of Northfolk was this reve, of which I telle,
Bisyde a toun men clepen Baldeswelle.   620
Tukkéd[40] he was, as is a frere, aboute,
And evere he rood the hindreste of our route.

    A Somnour was ther with us in that place,
That hadde a fyr-reed cherubinnes face,
For sauceflem[41] he was, with eyen narwe,
. . . .
With scalled[42] browes blake, and piled[43] berd;
Of his visage children were aferd.
Ther nas quik-silver, litarge[44], ne brimstoon,
Boras[45], ceruce[44], ne oille of tartre noon,   630
Ne oynement that wolde clense and byte,
That him mighte helpen of his whelkes[46] whyte,
Ne of the knobbes sitting on his chekes.
Wel loved he garleek, oynons, and eek lekes,
And for to drinken strong wyn, reed as blood.
Thanne wolde he speke, and crye as he were
    wood[47].
And whan that he wel dronken hadde the wyn,
Than wolde he speke no word but Latyn.
A fewe termes hadde he, two or thre,
That he had lerned out of som decree;   640
No wonder is, he herde it al the day;

---

1 could not heave off its hinges
2 tip
3 wart
4 ears
5 nostrils
6 bold talker
7 buffoon
8 ribaldries
9 take toll three times (instead of once)
10 worth gold (because with it he tested his flour)
11 play upon
12 lawyers' quarters
13 buyers
14 tally, i. e., on credit
15 always he was so careful
16 purchase
17 ignorant
18 surpass
19 more
20 crazy
21 economically
22 cheated them all
23 irascible
24 cut short
25 granary
26 cattle
27 stock
28 rendered account
29 since
30 find him in arrears
31 herder
32 servant
33 whose craft and deceit he did not know
34 dwelling
35 lend his lord's own property to him and receive gratitude and interest as well
36 trade
37 stallion
38 spotted, dappled
39 blue
40 his coat was tucked up by means of a girdle
41 pimpled
42 scurfy
43 plucked (thin)
44 white lead
45 borax
46 blotches
47 mad

And eek ye knowen wel, how that a Iay
Can clepen 'Watte,'[1] as well as can the pope.
But who-so coude in other thing him grope[2],
Thanne hadde he spent al his philosophye;
Ay '*Questio quid iuris*'[3] wolde he crye.
He was a gentil harlot[4] and a kynde;
A bettre felawe sholde men noght fynde.
He wolde suffre for[5] a quart of wyn
A good felawe to have his [wikked sin]   650
A twelf-month, and excuse him atte fulle:
And prively a finch eek coude he pulle[6].
And if he fond owher[7] a good felawe,
He wolde techen him to have non awe,
In swich cas, of the erchedeknes curs[8],
But-if[9] a mannes soule were in his purs[10];
For in his purs he sholde y-punisshed be.
'Purs is the erchedeknes helle,' seyde he.
But wel I woot he lyed right in dede;   659
Of cursing oghte ech gulty man him drede[11]—
For curs wol slee right as assoilling[12] saveth—
And also war him of a *significavit*[13].
In daunger[14] hadde he at his owne gyse[15]
The yonge girles[16] of the diocyse,
And knew hir counseil, and was al hir reed[17].
A gerland hadde he set up-on his heed,
As greet as it were for an ale-stake[18];
A bokeler hadde he maad him of a cake.
  With him ther rood a gentil Pardoner
Of Rouncivale[19], his frend and his compeer,   670
That streight was comen fro the court of Rome.
Ful loude he song, 'Com hider, love, to me.'
This somnour bar to him a stif burdoun[20],
Was nevere trompe[21] of half so greet a soun.
This pardoner hadde heer as yelow as wex,
But smothe it heng, as doth a strike of flex[22];
By ounces[23] henge his lokkes that he hadde[24],
And ther-with he his shuldres overspradde;
But thinne it lay, by colpons[25] oon and oon;
But hood, for Iolitee, ne wered he noon,   680
For it was trussed up in his walet.
Him thoughte[26], he rood al of the newe Iet[27];
Dischevele, save his cappe, he rood al bare.
Swiche glaringe eyen hadde he as an hare.

A vernicle[28] hadde he sowed on his cappe.
His walet lay biforn him in his lappe,
Bret-ful[29] of pardoun come from Rome al hoot.
A voys he hadde as smal as hath a goot.
No berd hadde he, ne nevere sholde have,
As smothe it was as it were late y-shave;   690

.   .   .   .

But of his craft, fro Berwik unto Ware[30],
Ne was ther swich another pardoner.
For in his male[31] he hadde a pilwe-beer[32],
Which that, he seyde, was our lady veyl[33]:
He seyde, he hadde a gobet[34] of the seyl[35]
That seynt Peter hadde, whan that he wente
Up-on the see, til Iesu Crist him hente[36].
He hadde a croys[37] of latoun[38], ful of stones,
And in a glas he hadde pigges bones.   700
But with thise relikes, whan that he fond
A povre person dwelling up-on lond[39],
Up-on a day he gat him more moneye
Than that the person gat in monthes tweye.
And thus with feyned flaterye and Iapes[40],
He made the person and the peple his apes.
But trewely to tellen, atte laste,
He was in chirche a noble ecclesiaste.
Wel coude he rede a lessoun or a storie,
But alderbest[41] he song an offertorie;   710
For wel he wiste, whan that song was songe,
He moste preche, and wel affyle[42] his tonge,
To winne silver, as he ful wel coude;
Therefore he song so meriely and loude.
  Now have I told you shortly, in a clause,
Thestat, tharray, the nombre, and eek the cause
Why that assembled was this compaignye
In Southwerk, at this gentil hostelrye,
That highte the Tabard, faste by the Belle.
But now is tyme to yow for to telle   720
How that we baren us that ilke night,.
Whan we were in that hostelrye alight.
And after wol I telle of our viage,
And al the remenaunt of our pilgrimage.
But first I pray yow of your curteisye,
That ye narette it nat my vileinye[43],
Thogh that I pleynly speke in this matere,
To telle yow hir wordes and hir chere[44];
Ne thogh I speke hir wordes proprely[45].
For this ye knowen al-so wel as I,   730
Who-so shal telle a tale after a man,

1 Walter (then a very
   common name in
   England)
2 test
3 "The question is,
   What is the law?"
4 good fellow
5 in return for
6 pluck a pigeon for
   himself
7 anywhere
8 excommunication
9 unless
10 purse
11 (reflexive) fear for
   himself
12 absolution
13 writ of excommuni-
   cation
14 in his jurisdiction

15 control
16 young people of
   either sex
17 the adviser of them
   all
18 sign-pole of an inn
   (often a bush hung
   up in front)
19 Possibly the Hospi-
   tal of Rouncyvalle
   in London.
20 accompaniment
21 trumpet
22 handful of flax
23 small portions
24 such as he had
25 shreds
26 it seemed to him
27 fashion

28 a St. Veronica (a
   cloth bearing a pic-
   ture of Christ)
29 brimful
30 from the north to
   the south of Eng-
   land
31 valise
32 pillow-case
33 the veil of the Vir-
   gin
34 piece
35 sail

36 caught, i. e., con-
   verted
37 cross
38 brass
39 in the country
40 tricks
41 best of all
42 file, polish
43 attribute it not to
   my ill-breeding
44 appearance
45 exactly

He moot reherce, as ny[1] as evere he can,
Everich a[2] word, if it be in his charge[3],
Al[4] speke he never so rudeliche and large[5];
Or elles he moot telle his tale untrewe,
Or feyne thing, or fynde wordes newe.
He may nat spare, al-thogh he were his brother;
He moot as wel seye o word as another.
Crist spak him-self ful brode in holy writ,
And wel ye woot, no vileinye is it.   740
Eek Plato seith, who-so that can him rede[6],
The wordes mote[7] be cosin to the dede.
Also I prey yow to foryeve it me,
Al[8] have I nat set folk in hir degree
Here in this tale, as that they sholde stonde;
My wit is short, ye may wel understonde.

    Greet chere[9] made our hoste us everichon[10],
And to the soper sette he us anon;
And served us with vitaille at the beste.
Strong was the wyn, and wel to drinke us leste[11].

A semely man our hoste was with-alle   751
For to han been a marshal in an halle;
A large man he was with eyen stepe[12],
A fairer burgeys[13] was ther noon in Chepe[14]:
Bold of his speche, and wys, and wel y-taught,
And of manhod him lakkede right naught.
Eek therto he was right a mery man,
And after soper pleyen[15] he bigan,
And spak of mirthe amonges othere thinges,
Whan that we hadde maad our rekeninges[16]; 760
And seyde thus: 'Now, lordinges, trewely
Ye ben to me right welcome hertely:
For by my trouthe, if that I shal nat lye,
I ne saugh[17] this yeer so mery a compaignye
At ones in this herberwe[18] as is now.
Fayn wolde I doon yow mirthe, wiste I how[19].
And of a mirthe I am right now bithoght,
To doon yow ese[20], and it shal coste noght.
Ye goon to Caunterbury; God yow spede, 769
The blisful martir[21] quyte[22] yow your mede[23].
And wel I woot, as ye goon by the weye,
Ye shapen[24] yow to talen[25] and to pleye;
For trewely, confort ne mirthe is noon
To ryde by the weye doumb as a stoon;
And therefor wol I maken yow disport,

As I seyde erst, and doon yow som confort.
And if yow lyketh alle, by oon assent,
Now for to stonden at[26] my Iugement,
And for to werken as I shal yow seye,
To-morwe, whan ye ryden by the weye,   780
Now, by my fader soule, that is deed,
But[27] ye be merye, I wol yeve yow myn heed.
Hold up your hond, withoute more speche.'
Our counseil was nat longe for to seche[28];
Us thoughte it was noght worth to make it wys[29],
And graunted him with-outen more avys[30],
And bad him seye his verdit, as him leste.
    'Lordinges,' quod he, 'now herkneth for the beste;
But tak it not, I prey yow, in desdeyn;
This is the poynt, to speken short and pleyn,
That ech of yow, to shorte with our weye[31],
In this viage, shal telle tales tweye,   792
To Caunterbury-ward, I mene it so,
And hom-ward he shal tellen othere two,
Of aventures that whylom han bifalle.
And which of yow that bereth him best of alle,
That is to seyn, that telleth in this cas
Tales of best sentence and most solas[32],
Shal han a soper at our aller cost
Here in this place, sitting by this post,   800
Whan that we come agayn fro Caunterbury.
And for to make yow the more mery,
I wol my-selven gladly with yow ryde,
Right at myn owne cost, and be your gyde.
And who-so wol my Iugement withseye[33]
Shal paye al that we spenden by the weye.
And if ye vouche-sauf that it be so,
Tel me anon, with-outen wordes mo,
And I wol erly shape[34] me therfore.'
    This thing was graunted, and our othes swore   810
With ful glad herte, and preyden him also
That he wold vouche-sauf for to do so,
And that he wolde been our governour,
And of our tales Iuge and reportour,
And sette a soper at a certeyn prys;
And we wold reuled been at his devys[35],
In heigh and lowe; and thus, by oon assent,
We been acorded to his Iugement.
And ther-up-on the wyn was fet[36] anoon;
We dronken, and to reste wente echoon,   820
With-outen any lenger taryinge.
A-morwe, whan that[37] day bigan to springe,
Up roos our host, and was our aller cok[33],

---

1 nearly
2 every
3 i. e., in the tale committed to him
4 although
5 freely
6 Chaucer could not read Greek
7 must
8 although
9 entertainment
10 every one
11 it pleased
12 bright
13 citizen
14 A market square in London (now a street, Cheapside).
15 to play, jest
16 paid our bills
17 saw not
18 inn
19 give you fun if I knew how
20 give you recreation
21 Thomas à Becket
22 requite (give)
23 reward
24 plan
25 to tell tales
26 by
27 unless
28 seek
29 a matter of deliberation
30 consideration
31 to shorten our way with
32 amusement
33 gainsay
34 prepare
35 decision
36 fetched
37 when
38 cock of us all (who woke them up)

And gadrede us togidre, alle in a flok,
And forth we riden, a litel more than pas[1],
Un-to the watering of seint Thomas[2].
And there our host bigan his hors areste,
And seyde; 'Lordinges, herkneth if yow leste.
Ye woot your forward[3], and I it yow recorde[4].
If even-song and morwe-song acorde,   830
Lat se now who shal telle the firste tale.
As evere mote I drinke wyn or ale,
Who-so be rebel to my Iugement
Shal paye for al that by the weye is spent.
Now draweth cut[5], er that we ferrer[6]
    twinne[7];
He which that hath the shortest shal biginne.'
'Sire knight,' quod he, 'my maister and my
    lord,
Now draweth cut, for that is myn acord[8].
Cometh neer[9],' quod he, 'my lady prioresse;
And ye, sir clerk, lat be your shamfast-
    nesse,   840
Ne studieth noght[10]; ley hond to, every man.'
    Anon to drawen every wight bigan,
And shortly for to tellen, as it was,
Were it by averture[11], or sort[12], or cas[13],
The sothe[14] is this, the cut fil to the knight,
Of which ful blythe and glad was every wight;
And telle he moste his tale, as was resoun,
By forward and by composicioun[15],
As ye han herd; what nedeth wordes mo?
And whan this goode man saugh it was so,
As he that wys was and obedient   851
To kepe his forward by his free assent,
He seyde: 'Sin[16] I shal beginne the game,
What, welcome be the cut, a[17] Goddes name!
Now lat us ryde, and herkneth what I seye.'
    And with that word we riden forth our weye;
And he bigan with right a mery chere[18]
His tale anon, and seyde in this manere.

THE NONNE PREESTES TALE*

*Here biginneth the Nonne Preestes Tale of the
Cok and Hen, Chauntecleer and
Pertelote.*

A povre widwe somdel stope[19] in age,
Was whylom[20] dwelling in a narwe[21] cotage,
Bisyde a grove, stondyng in a dale.
This widwe, of which I telle yow my tale,

Sin thilke[22] day that she was last a wyf,
In pacience ladde a ful simple lyf,
For litel was hir catel and hir rent[23];
By housbondrye, of such as God hir sente,
She fond[24] hir-self, and eek hir doghtren[25] two.
Three large sowes hadde she, and namo,   10
Three kyn, and eek a sheep that highte[26]
    Malle.
Ful sooty was hir bour, and eek hir halle[27],
In which she eet ful many a sclendre meel.
Of poynaunt sauce hir neded[28] never a deel.
No deyntee morsel passed thurgh hir throte;
Hir dyete was accordant to hir cote.
Repleccioun[29] ne made hir nevere syk;
Attempree dyete was al hir physyk,
And exercyse, and hertes suffisaunce.
The goute lette[30] hir no-thing for to daunce, 20
No poplexye shente[31] nat hir heed;
No wyn ne drank she, neither whyt ne reed;
Hir bord was served most with whyt and blak,
Milk and broun breed, in which she fond no
    lak,
Seynd[32] bacoun, and somtyme an ey[33] or
    tweye,
For she was as it were a maner deye[34].
    A yerd she hadde, enclosed al aboute
With stikkes, and a drye dich with-oute,
In which she hadde a cok, hight Chauntecleer,
In al the land of crowing nas[35] his peer.   30
His vois was merier than the merye orgon[36]
On messe-dayes[37] that in the chirche gon;
Wel sikerer[38] was his crowing in his logge[39],
Than is a clokke, or an abbey orlogge[40].
By nature knew he ech ascensioun[41]
Of equinoxial in thilke toun;
For whan degrees fiftene were ascended,
Thanne crew he, that it mighte nat ben
    amended[42].
His comb was redder than the fyn coral,
And batailed[43], as it were a castel-wal.   40
His bile[44] was blak, and as the Ieet[45] it shoon;
Lyk asur were his legges, and his toon[46];
His nayles whytter than the lilie flour,

1 faster than a walk
2 Two miles on the way
    to Canterbury.
3 agreement
4 remind you of it
5 lots
6 further
7 separate
8 decision
9 nearer
10 don't meditate
11 chance
12 fate
13 accident
14 truth
15 contract
16 since
17 in
18 expression
19 advanced
20 once upon a time
21 narrow
22 since that
23 her property (chat-
    tels) and her in-
    come
24 supported
25 daughters
26 was called
27 Bower and hall are
    terms applicable
    to a castle; used
    here humorously
    of the probably
    one-room cottage.
28 (reflexive) she need-
    ed
29 surfeit
30 hindered
31 hurt
32 singed (broiled)
33 egg
34 sort of dairy-woman
35 was not
36 organs
37 mass-days
38 surer
39 lodging
40 horologe
41 he knew the time
    every hour of the
    day (for 15° of
    the equinoctial are
    passed each hour
    of the twenty-four)
42 so that it couldn't
    be improved upon
43 embattled
44 bill
45 jet
46 toes

* In the Ellesmere MS. this is the twentieth tale.
Sir John, the "Nun's Priest," was an escort
of Madame Eglentyne: see *Prologue*, 164. His
tale is an old one, found in various languages.

And lyk the burned[1] gold was his colour.
This gentil cok hadde in his governaunce
Sevene hennes, for to doon all his plesaunce,
Whiche were his sustres and his paramours,
And wonder lyk to him, as of[2] colours.
Of whiche the faireste hewed on hir throte
Was cleped[3] faire damoysele Pertelote.   50
Curteys she was, discreet, and debonaire[4],
And compaignable, and bar hir-self so faire,
Sin thilke day that she was seven night old,
That trewely she hath the herte in hold
Of Chauntecleer loken in every lith[5],
He loved hir so, that wel him was therwith.
But such a Ioye was it to here hem singe,
Whan that the brighte sonne gan to springe,
In swete accord, 'my lief is faren in londe[6].'
For thilke[7] tyme, as I have understonde,   60
Bestes and briddes coude speke and singe.

    And so bifel, that in a dawenynge,
As Chauntecleer among his wyves alle
Sat on his perche, that was in the halle,
And next him sat this faire Pertelote,
This Chauntecleer gan gronen in his throte,
As man that in his dreem is drecched[8] sore.
And whan that Pertelote thus herde him rore,
She was agast, and seyde, 'o herte deere,
What eyleth yow, to grone in this manere? 70
Ye ben a verray sleper, fy for shame!'
And he answerde and seyde thus, 'madame,
I pray yow, that ye take it nat agrief[9]:
By God, me mette[10] I was in swich meschief
Right now, that yet myn herte is sore afright.
Now God,' quod he, 'my swevene[11] rede[12]
    aright,
And keep my body out of foul prisoun!
Me mette, how that I romed up and doun
Withinne our yerde, wher as I saugh a beste,
Was lyk an hound, and wolde han maad
    areste[13]   80
Upon my body, and wolde han had me deed.
His colour was bitwixe yelwe and reed;
And tipped was his tail, and bothe his eres
With blak, unlyk the remenant of his heres;
His snowte smal, with glowinge eyen tweye.
Yet of his look for fere almost I deye;
This caused me my groning, douteles.'

    'Avoy[14]!' quod she, 'fy on yow, herteles[15]!
Allas!' quod she, 'for, by that God above,
Now han ye lost myn herte and al my love;   90
I can nat love a coward, by my feith.
For certes, what so any womman seith,

We alle desyren, if it mighte be,
To han housbondes hardy, wyse, and free[16],
And secree[17], and no nigard, ne no fool,
Ne him that is agast of every tool[18],
Ne noon avauntour[19], by that God above!
How dorste ye sayn for shame unto youre love,
That any thing mighte make yow aferd?
Have ye no mannes herte, and han a berd?   100
Allas! and conne ye been agast of swevenis?
No-thing, God wot, but vanitee, in sweven is.
Swevenes engendren of replecciouns,
And ofte of fume, and of complecciouns[20],
Whan humours[21] been to[22] habundant in a
    wight.
Certes this dreem, which ye han met[23] to-night,
Cometh of the grete superfluitee
Of youre rede *colera*[24], pardee,
Which causeth folk to dremen in here[25] dremes
Of arwes[26], and of fyr with rede lemes[27],   110
Of grete bestes, that they wol hem byte,
Of contek[28], and of whelpes grete and lyte;
Right as the humour of malencolye[29]
Causeth ful many a man, in sleep, to crye,
For fere of blake beres, or boles[30] blake,
Or elles, blake develes wole him take.
Of othere humours coude I telle also,
That werken many a man in sleep ful wo;
But I wol passe as lightly as I can.   119

    Lo Catoun[31], which that was so wys a man,
Seyde he nat thus, ne do no fors[32] of dremes?
Now, sire,' quod she, 'whan we flee fro the
    bemes,
For Goddes love, as[33] tak som laxatyf;
Up peril of my soule, and of my lyf,
I counseille yow the beste, I wol nat lye,
That both of colere, and of malencolye[29]
Ye purge yow; and for ye shul nat tarie,
Though in this toun is noon apotecarie,
I shal my-self to herbes techen yow,   129
That shul ben for your hele, and for your
    prow[34];
And in our yerd tho herbes shal I fynde,
The whiche han of here propretee, by kynde[35],
To purgen yow binethe, and eek above.
Forget not this, for Goddes owene love!
Ye been ful colerik of compleccioun.
Ware[36] the sonne in his ascencioun
Ne fynde yow nat repleet of humours hote;

16 liberal
17 trusty
18 weapon
19 boaster
20 temperaments
21 The four causes and
    classes of disease
    (see *Prologue*,
    420).
22 too
23 dreamed
24 red cholera (caused
    by too much bile
    and blood)
25 their
26 arrows
27 gleams
28 contest
29 Due to excess of bile.
30 bulls
31 Dionysius Cato
32 take no notice
33 do now (pleonastic)
34 profit
35 nature
36 beware

1 burnished
2 in respect to
3 named
4 gracious
5 locked in every limb
6 my beloved is gone to
    the country, gone
    away
7 at that
8 troubled
9 amiss
10 I dreamed
11 dream
12 interpret
13 seizure
14 away
15 heartless one

And if it do, I dar wel leye a grote[1],
That ye shul have a fevere terciane[2],
Or an agu, that may be youre bane.　140
A day or two ye shul have digestyves
Of wormes, er ye take your laxatyves,
Of lauriol, centaure, and fumetere[3],
Or elles of ellebor[4], that groweth there,
Of catapuce[5], or of gaytres[6] beryis,
Of erbe yve, growing in our yerd, that mery is;
Pekke hem up right as they growe, and ete
　　hem in.
Be mery, housbond, for your fader kyn!
Dredeth no dreem; I can say yow namore.'
　'Madame,' quod he, '_graunt mercy_[7] of your
　　lore.
But natheles, as touching daun[8] Catoun,　151
That hath of wisdom such a gret renoun,
Though that he bad no dremes for to drede,
By God, men may in olde bokes rede
Of many a man, more of auctoritee
Than evere Catoun was, so moot I thee[9],
That al the revers[10] seyn of this sentence[11],
And han wel founden by experience,
That dremes ben significaciouns,
As wel of Ioye as tribulaciouns　160
That folk enduren in this lyf present.
Ther nedeth make of this noon argument;
The verray preve[12] sheweth it in dede.
Oon of the gretteste auctours that men rede[13]
Seith thus, that whylom two felawes wente
On pilgrimage, in a ful good entente;
And happed so, thay come into a toun,
Wher as ther was swich congregacioun
Of peple, and eek so streit[14] of herbergage[15],
That they ne founde as muche as o cotage,　170
In which they bothe mighte y-logged be.
Wherfor thay mosten, of necessitee,
As for that night, departen compaignye;
And ech of hem goth to his hostelrye,
And took his logging as it wolde falle.
That oon of hem was logged in a stalle,
Fer[16] in a yerd, with oxen of the plough;
That other man was logged wel y-nough,
As was his aventure[17], or his fortune,
That us governeth alle as in commune[18].　180
And so bifel, that, long er it were day,
This man mette in his bed, ther as he lay,
How that his felawe gan up-on him calle,
And seyde, 'allas! for in an oxes stalle

This night I shal be mordred ther[19] I lye.
Now help me, dere brother, or I dye;
In alle haste com to me,' he sayde.
This man out of his sleep for fere abrayde[20];
But whan that he was wakned of his sleep,
He turned him, and took of this no keep[21];　190
Him thoughte[22] his dreem nas but a vanitee.
Thus twyes in his sleping dremed he.
And atte thridde tyme yet his felawe
Com, as him thoughte, and seide, 'I am now
　　slawe[23];
Bihold my bloody woundes, depe and wyde!
Arys up erly in the morwe-tyde[24],
And at the west gate of the toun,' quod he,
'A carte ful of donge ther shaltow see,
In which my body is hid ful prively;
Do thilke carte arresten[25] boldely.　200
My gold caused my mordre, sooth to sayn;'
And tolde him every poynt how he was slayn,
With a ful pitous face, pale of hewe.
And truste wel, his dreem he fond ful trewe;
For on the morwe, as sone as it was day,
To his felawes in he took the way;
And whan that he cam to this oxes stalle,
After his felawe he bigan to calle.
The hostiler answerde him anon,
And seyde, 'sire, your felawe is agon,　210
As sone as day he wente out of the toun.'
This man gan fallen in suspecioun,
Remembring on his dremes that he mette,
And forth he goth, no lenger wolde he lette[26],
Unto the west gate of the toun, and fond
A dong-carte, as it were to donge lond,
That was arrayed in that same wyse
As ye han herd the dede man devyse[27];
And with an hardy herte he gan to crye
Vengeaunce and Iustice of this felonye:—　220
'My felawe mordred is this same night,
And in this carte he lyth gapinge upright.
I crye out on the ministres[28],' quod he,
'That sholden kepe and reulen this citee;
Harrow! allas! her lyth my felawe slayn!'
What sholde I more un-to this tale sayn?
The peple out-sterte, and caste the cart to
　　grounde,
And in the middel of the dong they founde
The dede man, that mordred was al newe.　229
'O blisful God, that art so Iust and trewe!
Lo, how that thou biwreyest[29] mordre alway!
Mordre wol out, that se we day by day.
Mordre is so wlatsom[30] and abhominable
To God, that is so Iust and resonable,

1 wager a groat (four
　　pence)
2 tertian (every third
　　day)
3 laurel, centaury, fumi-
　　tory
4 hellebore
5 spurge
6 dog-wood
7 great thanks
8 lord, master (Latin
　　dominus)

9 so may I thrive (a
　　strong affirmative;
　　cp. l. 246)
10 opposite
11 opinion
12 proof
13 Cicero
14 scant
15 lodging-places
16 afar
17 luck
18 in general

19 murdered where
20 started up
21 heed
22 it seemed to him
23 slain
24 morning-time

25 have..stopped
26 delay
27 relate
28 officers
29 makest known
30 hateful

That he ne wol nat suffre it heled[1] be;
Though it abyde a yeer, or two, or three,
Mordre wol out, this[2] my conclusioun.
And right anoon, ministres of that toun
Han hent the carter, and so sore him pyned[3],
And eek the hostiler so sore engyned[4],   240
That thay biknewe[5] hir wikkednesse anoon,
And were an-hanged by the nekke-boon.
  'Here may men seen that dremes been to
      drede.
And certes, in the same book I rede,
Right in the nexte chapitre after this,
(I gabbe[6] nat, so have I Ioye or blis,)
Two men that wolde han passed over see,
For certeyn cause, in-to a fer contree,
If that the wind ne hadde been contrarie,
That·made hem in a citee for to tarie,   250
That stood ful mery upon an haven-syde.
But on a day, agayn[7] the even-tyde,
The wind gan chaunge, and blew right as hem
      leste.
Iolif and glad they wente un-to hir reste,
And casten hem[8] ful erly for to saille;
But to that oo[9] man fel a greet mervaille[10].
That oon of hem, in sleping as he lay,
Him mette a wonder ·dreem, agayn[7] the day;
Him thoughte a man stood by his beddes syde,
And him comaunded, that he sholde abyde[11],
And seyde him thus, 'if thou to-morwe
      wende,   261
Thou shalt be dreynt[12]; my tale is at an ende.'
He wook, and tolde his felawe what he mette,
And preyde him his viage for to lette[13];
As[14] for that day, he preyde him to abyde.
His felawe, that lay by his beddes syde,
Gan for to laughe, and scorned him ful faste.
'No dreem,' quod he, 'may so myn herte
      agaste[15],
That I wol lette[13] for to do my thinges[16].
I sette not a straw by thy dreminges,   270
For swevenes been but vanitees and Iapes[17].
Men dreme al-day[18] of owles or of apes,
And eek of many a mase[19] therwithal;
Men dreme of thing that nevere was ne shal.
But sith[20] I see that thou wolt heer abyde,
And thus for-sleuthen[21] wilfully thy tyde,
God wot it reweth[22] me; and have good day.'
And thus he took his leve, and wente his way.
But er that he hadde halfe his cours y-seyled,

Noot[23] I nat why, ne what mischaunce it
      eyled[24],
But casuelly[25] the shippes botme rente,   281
And ship and man under the water wente
In sighte of othere shippes it byside,
That with hem seyled at the same tyde.
And therfor, faire Pertelote so dere,
By swiche ensamples olde maistow[26] lere[27],
That no man sholde been to recchelees[28]
Of dremes, for I sey thee, douteless,
That many a dreem ful sore is for to drede.
  'Lo, in the lyf of seint Kenelm, I rede,   290
That was Kenulphus sone, the noble king
Of Mercenrike[29], how Kenelm mette a thing;
A lyte[30] er he was mordred, on a day,
His mordre in his avisioun[31] he say[32].
His norice[33] him expouned every del
His swevene, and bad him for to kepe him wel
For[34] traisoun; but he nas but seven yeer
      old,
And therfore litel tale[35] hath he told[36]
Of any dreem, so holy was his herte.
By God, I hadde levere[37] than my sherte   300
That ye had rad[38] his legende, as have I.
Dame Pertelote, I sey yow trewely,
Macrobeus, that writ the avisioun[39]
In Affrike of the worthy Cipioun,
Affermeth dremes, and seith that they been
Warning of thinges that men after seen.
And forther-more, I pray yow loketh wel
In the olde testament, of Daniel,
If he held dremes any vanitee.
Reed eek of Ioseph, and ther shul ye see   310
Wher[40] dremes ben somtyme (I sey nat alle)
Warning of thinges that shul after falle.
Loke of Egipt the king, daun[41] Pharao,
His bakere and his boteler[42] also,
Wher[40] they ne felte noon effect in dremes.
Who so wol seken actes[43] of sondry remes[44]
May rede of dremes many a wonder thing.
  'Lo Cresus, which that was of Lyde[45] king,
Mette he nat that he sat upon a tree,
Which signified he sholde anhanged be?   320
Lo heer Andromacha, Ectores wyf,
That day that Ector sholde lese[46] his lyf,
She dremed on the same night biforn,
How that the lyf of Ector sholde be lorn[47],

1 hidden
2 this is
3 tormented
4 racked
5 confessed
6 lie
7 toward
8 planned
9 one
10 marvel
11 tarry
12 drowned
13 delay
14 at least
15 frighten
16 business matters
17 jests
18 all the time
19 wild fancy
20 since
21 lose through sloth
22 grieveth
23 know not
24 ailed it
25 accidentally
26 mayest thou
27 learn
28 careless
29 Mercia
30 little
31 vision
32 saw
33 nurse
34 for fear of
35 heed
36 taken
37 rather
38 read
39 Cicero's *Dream of Scipio*, annotated by the grammarian Macrobius.
40 whether
41 lord
42 butler
43 the history
44 realms
45 L y d i a (in A s i a Minor)
46 lose
47 lost

f thilke day he wente in-to bataille;
She warned him, but it mighte nat availle;
He wente for to fighte natheles,
But he was slayn anoon[1] of[2] Achilles.
But thilke tale is al to long to telle,
And eek it is ny[3] day, I may nat dwelle. 330
Shortly I seye, as for conclusioun,
That I shal han of this avisioun
Adversitee; and I seye forther-more,
That I ne telle of laxatyves no store[4],
For they ben venimous[5], I woot it wel;
I hem defye, I love hem nevere a del.
  'Now let us speke of mirthe, and stinte al
    this;
Madame Pertelote, so have I blis[6],
Of o thing God hath sent me large grace;
For whan I see the beautee of your face, 340
Ye ben so scarlet-reed about youre yën,
It maketh al my drede for to dyen;
For, also siker[7] as *In principio*,
Mulier est hominis confusio[8];
Madame, the sentence of this Latin is—
Womman is mannes Ioye and al his blis;
  .   .   .   .   .   .
I am so ful of Ioye and of solas   350
That I defye bothe sweven and dreem.'
And with that word he fley[9] doun fro the
    beem,
For it was day, and eek his hennes alle;
And with a chuk he gan hem for to calle,
For he had founde a corn, lay in the yerd.
Roial he was, he was namore aferd;
  .   .   .   .   .   .
He loketh as it were a grim leoun;
And on his toos he rometh up and doun, 360
Him deyned[10] not to sette his foot to grounde.
He chukketh, whan he hath a corn y-founde,
And to him rennen[11] thanne his wyves alle.
Thus roial, as a prince is in his halle,
Leve I this Chauntecleer in his pasture;
And after wol I telle his aventure.
  Whan that the month in which the world
    bigan,
That highte March, whan God first maked man,
Was complet, and y-passed were also,
Sin March bigan, thritty dayes and two, 370
Bifel that Chauntecleer, in al his pryde,
His seven wyves walking by his syde,
Caste up his eyen to the brighte sonne,
That in the signe of Taurus hadde y-ronne
Twenty degrees and oon, and somwhat more;
And knew by kynde, and by noon other lore,

That it was pryme[12], and crew with blisful
    stevene[13].
'The sonne,' he sayde, 'is clomben up on
    hevene
Fourty degrees and oon, and more, y-wis.
Madame Pertelote, my worldes blis,   380
Herkneth thise blisful briddes[14] how they singe,
And see the fresshe floures how they springe;
Ful is myn hert of revel and solas.'
But sodeinly him fil a sorweful cas[15];
For evere the latter ende of Ioye is wo.
God woot that worldly Ioye is sone ago[16];
And if a rethor[17] coude faire endyte[18],
He in a chronique saufly[19] mighte it write,
As for a sovereyn notabilitee[20].   389
Now every wys man, lat him herkne me;
This storie is al-so trewe, I undertake[21],
As is the book of Launcelot de Lake[22],
That wommen holde in ful gret reverence.
Now wol I torne agayn to my sentence.
  A col[23]-fox, ful of sly iniquitee,
That in the grove hadde woned yeres three,
By heigh imaginacioun forn-cast[24],
The same night thurgh-out the hegges[25] brast[26]
Into the yerd, ther Chauntecleer the faire
Was wont, and eek his wyves, to repaire; 400
And in a bed of wortes[27] stille he lay,
Til it was passed undern[28] of the day,
Wayting his tyme on Chauntecleer to falle
As gladly doon thise homicydes alle,
That in awayt liggen[29] to mordre men.
O false mordrer, lurking in thy den!
O newe Scariot[30], newe Genilon[31]!
False dissimilour[32], O Greek Sinon[33],
That broghtest Troye al-outrely[34] to sorwe!
O Chauntecleer, acursed be that morwe,   410
That thou into that yerd flough fro the bemes!
Thou were ful wel y-warned by thy dremes,
That thilke day was perilous to thee.
But what that God forwot[35] mot nedes be,
After the opinioun of certeyn clerkis.
Witnesse on[36] him, that any perfit clerk is,
That in scole is gret altercacioun
In this matere, and greet disputisoun,

quickly	7 sure
by	8 In the beginning wo-
nigh	man is man's de-
set no value upon	struction.
laxatives	9 flew
poisonous	10 he deigned
as I hope for bliss	11 run

12 nine o'clock	26 burst
13 voice	27 herbs
14 birds	28 about eleven a. m.
15 fate	29 lie
16 gone	30 Judas Iscariot
17 rhetorician	31 The traitor that
18 relate	caused the defeat
19 safely	of Charlemagne
20 a thing especially	and the death of
worthy to be	Roland.
known	32 deceiver
21 affirm	33 Designer of the
22 A romance of chiv-	wooden horse by
alry, obviously	which Troy was
false.	entered.
23 coal black	34 entirely
24 pre-ordained by the	35 foreknows
supreme conception	36 by
25 hedges	

And hath ben of an hundred thousand men.
But I ne can not bulte it to the bren[1],   420
As can the holy doctour Augustyn[2],
Or Boece[3], or the bishop Bradwardyn[4],
Whether that Goddes worthy forwiting
Streyneth[5] me nedely for to doon a thing,
(Nedely clepe I simple necessitee);
Or elles, if free choys be graunted me
To do that same thing, or do it noght,
Though God forwot it, er that it was wroght;
Or if his witing streyneth nevere a del
But by necessitee condicionel[6].   430
I wol not han to do of swich matere;
My tale is of a cok, as ye may here,
That took his counseil of his wyf, with sorwe,
To walken in the yerd upon that morwe
That he had met the dreem, that I of tolde.
Wommennes counseils been ful ofte colde[7];
Wommannes counseil broghte us first to wo,
And made Adam fro paradys to go,
Ther as he was ful mery, and wel at ese.
But for I noot[8], to whom it mighte displese,
If I counseil of wommen wolde blame,   441
Passe over, for I seyde it in my game[9].
Rede auctours, wher they trete of swich matere,
And what thay seyn of wommen ye may here.
Thise been the cokkes wordes, and nat myne;
I can noon harme of no womman divyne.

Faire in the sond, to bathe hire merily,
Lyth Pertelote, and alle hir sustres by,
Agayn[10] the sonne; and Chauntecleer so free
Song merier than the mermayde in the
      see;   450
For Phisiologus[11] seith sikerly,
How that they singen wel and merily.
And so bifel, that as he caste his yë[12],
Among the wortes, on a boterflye,
He was war[13] of this fox that lay ful lowe.
No-thing ne liste him thanne for to crowe,
But cryde anon, 'cok, cok,' and up he sterte,
As man that was affrayed in his herte.
For naturelly a beest desyreth flee
Fro his contrarie[14], if he may it see,   460
Though he never erst had seyn it with his yë.
This Chauntecleer, whan he gan him espye[15],

He wolde han fled, but that the fox anon
Seyde, 'Gentil sire, allas! wher wol ye gon?
Be ye affrayed of me that am your freend?
Now certes, I were worse than a feend,
If I to yow wolde harm or vileinye.
I am nat come your counseil for tespye;
But trewely, the cause of my cominge
Was only for to herkne how that ye singe.   47[0]
For trewely ye have as mery a stevene[16],
As eny aungel hath, that is in hevene;
Therwith ye han in musik more felinge
Than hadde Boece, or any that can singe.
My lord your fader (God his soule blesse!)
And eek your moder, of hir gentilesse,
Han in myn hous y-been, to my gret ese[17];
And certes, sire, ful fayn wolde I yow plese.
But for men speke of singing, I wol saye,
So mote I brouke[18] wel myn eyen tweye,   48[0]
Save yow, I herde nevere man so singe,
As dide your fader in the morweninge;
Certes, it was of herte[19], al that he song.
And for to make his voys the more strong,
He wolde so peyne him[20], that with both his
      yën
He moste winke[21], so loude he wolde cryen,
And stonden on his tiptoon therwithal,
And strecche forth his nekke long and smal.
And eek he was of swich discrecioun,
That ther nas no man in no regioun   490
That him in song or wisdom mighte passe.
I have weel rad in daun[22] Burnel the Asse,
Among his vers, how that ther was a cok,
For that a prestes sone yaf him a knok
Upon his leg, whyl he was yong and nyce[23],
He made him for to lese his benefyce[24].
But certeyn, ther nis no comparisoun
Bitwix the wisdom and discrecioun
Of your fader, and of his subtiltee.
Now singeth, sire, for seinte charitee,   500
Let se, conne ye your fader countrefete?'
This Chauntecleer his winges gan to bete,
As man that coude his tresoun nat espye,
So was he ravisshed with his flaterye.

Allas! ye lordes, many a fals flatour[25]
Is in your courtes, and many a losengeour[26],
That plesen yow wel more, by my feith,
Than he that soothfastnesse unto yow seith.
Redeth Ecclesiaste[27] of flaterye;
Beth war, ye lordes, of hir trecherye.   51[0]

1 boult it to the bran;
  i. e., thoroughly
  sift the question
2 St. Augustine
3 Boethius, a Roman
  statesman and
  philosopher of the
  fifth century A. D.
4 Chancellor at Oxford
  in the fourteenth
  century.
5 foreknowledge con-
  strains
6 except by conditional
  (as opposed to sim-
  ple or absolute)

necessity (The old
  question whether
  foreknowledge con-
  stitutes foreordina-
  tion.)
7 baneful
8 know not
9 jest
10 in
11 Theobaldus' *Physio-
  logus*, or "Natural
  History of Twelve
  Animals."
12 eyes
13 aware
14 opponent, foe
15 to espy

16 voice
17 to my great pleas-
  ure; i. e., the fox
  had eaten them
18 have the use of
19 from his heart
20 strain himself
21 he must shut both
  eyes

22 lord (This was an
  old story.)
23 foolish
24 i. e., by crowing so
  late that the youth
  did not awake in
  time
25 flatterer
26 deceiver
27 *Ecclesiasticus*, xii. 10.

This Chauntecleer stood hye up-on his toos,
Strecching his nekke, and held his eyen cloos,
And gan to crowe loude for the nones[1];
And daun Russel[2] the foxe sterte up at ones,
And by the gargat[3] hente Chauntecleer,
And on his bak toward the wode him beer[4],
For yet ne was ther no man that him sewed[5].
O destinee, that mayst nat ben eschewed!
Allas, that Chauntecleer fleigh fro the bemes!
Allas, his wyf ne roghte[6] nat of dremes!   520
And on a Friday fil al this meschaunce.
O Venus, that art goddesse of plesaunce,
Sin that thy servant was this Chauntecleer,

        .   .   .   .   .

Why woldestow suffre him on thy day to dye?
O Gaufred, dere mayster soverayn[7],
That, whan thy worthy king Richard was slayn
With shot, compleynedest his deth so sore,
Why ne hadde I now thy sentence[8] and thy
                lore,
The Friday for to chide, as diden ye?   531
(For on a Friday soothly slayn was he.)
Than wolde I shewe yow how that I coude
        pleyne[9]
For Chauntecleres drede, and for his peyne.
   Certes, swich cry ne lamentacioun
Was nevere of ladies maad, whan Ilioun
Was wonne, and Pirrus[10] with his streite[11]
        swerd,
Whan he hadde hent king Priam by the berd,
And slayn him (as saith us Eneydos)[12],
As maden alle the hennes in the clos[13],   540
Whan they had seyn of Chauntecleer the sighte.
But sovereynly[14] dame Pertelote shrighte[15],
Ful louder than dide Hasdrubales[16] wyf,
Whan that hir housbond hadde lost his lyf,
And that the Romayns hadde brend Cartage,
She was so ful of torment and of rage,
That wilfully into the fyr she sterte[17],
And brende[18] hir-selven with a stedfast herte.
O woful hennes, right so cryden ye,
As, whan that Nero brende the citee   550
Of Rome, cryden senatoures wyves,
For that hir housbondes losten alle hir lyves;
Withouten gilt[19] this Nero hath hem slayn.
Now wol I torne to my tale agayn:
This sely[20] widwe, and eek hir doghtres two,

Herden thise hennes crye and maken wo,
And out at dores sterten thay anoon,
And syen the fox toward the grove goon,
And bar upon his bak the cok away;
And cryden, 'Out! harrow! and weylaway!   560
Ha, ha, the fox!' and after him they ran,
And eek with staves many another man;
Ran Colle our dogge, and Talbot[21], and Ger-
        land[21],
And Malkin[22], with a distaf in hir hand;
Ran cow and calf, and eek the verray hogges
So were they fered for berking of the dogges
And shouting of the men and wimmen eke,
They ronne so, hem thoughte hir herte breke.
They yelleden as feendes doon in helle;
The dokes cryden as men wolde hem quelle[23];
The gees for fere flowen over the trees;   571
Out of the hyve cam the swarm of bees;
So hidous was the noyse, a! benedicite![24]
Certes, he Iakke Straw[25], and his meynee[26],
Ne maden nevere shoutes half so shrille,
Whan that they wolden any Fleming kille,
As thilke day was maad upon the fox.
Of bras thay broghten bemes[27] and of box[28],
Of horn, of boon, in whiche they blewe and
        pouped[29],
And therwithal thay shryked and they houped[30];
It semed as that hevene sholde falle.   581
Now, gode men, I pray yow herkneth alle!
   Lo, how fortune turneth sodeinly
The hope and pryde eek of his enemy!
This cok, that lay upon the foxes bak,
In al his drede, un-to the fox he spak,
And seyde, 'sire, if that I were as ye,
Yet sholde I seyn (as wis[31] God helpe me),
Turneth agayn, ye proude cherles alle!
A verray pestilence up-on yow falle!   590
Now am I come un-to this wodes syde,
Maugree[32] your heed, the cok shal heer abyde;
I wol him ete in feith, and that anon.'—
The fox answerde, 'In feith, it shal be don,'—
And as he spak that word, al sodeinly
This cok brak from his mouth deliverly[33],
And heighe up-on a tree he fleigh anon.
And whan the fox saugh that he was y-gon,
'Allas!' quod he, 'O Chauntecleer, allas!
I have to yow,' quod he, 'y-doon trespas,   600
In-as-muche as I maked yow aferd,
Whan I yow hente, and broghte out of the
        yerd;

occasion
As the ass was called
   Burnel because he
   is brown, so the
   fox was called Rus-
   sell because he is
   red.
throat
bore
followed
did not care for
Chaucer is making fun
   of an old writer,

Geoffrey de Vin-
   sauf.
8 power of expression
9 complain
10 Pyrrhus
11 drawn
12 The Aeneid.
13 enclosure
14 surpassingly
15 shrieked
16 A king of Carthage.
17 leaped
18 burned
19 guilt
20 pious

21 a dog (?)
22 a servant girl
23 kill
24 bless ye
25 Jack Straw, leader
   with Wat Tyler in
   the Peasants' Re-
   volt of 1381; said
   to have killed
   "many Flemings,"

competitors in
   trade.
26 followers
27 horns
28 wood
29 made a noise with a
   horn
30 whooped
31 certainly
32 in spite of
33 quickly

But, sire, I dide it in no wikke[1] entente;
Com doun, and I shal telle yow what I mente.
I shal seye sooth to yow, God help me so.'
'Nay than,' quod he, 'I shrewe[2] us bothe two,
And first I shrewe my-self, bothe blood and
    bones,
If thou bigyle me ofter than ones.
Thou shalt namore, thurgh thy flaterye
Do[3] me to singe and winke with myn yë.   610
For he that winketh, whan he sholde see,
Al wilfully, God lat him never thee[4]!
'Nay,' quod the fox, 'but God yive him
    meschaunce,
That is so undiscreet of governaunce,
That iangleth[5] whan he sholde holde his pees.'
    Lo, swich it is for to be recchelees,
And necligent, and truste on flaterye.
But ye that holden this tale a folye,
As of a fox, or of a cok and hen,
Taketh the moralitee therof, good men.   620
For seint Paul seith, that al that writen is,
To our doctryne[6] it is y-write, y-wis.
Taketh the fruyt, and lat the chaf be stille.
Now, gode God, if that it be thy wille,
As seith my lord, so make us alle good men;
And bringe us to his heighe blisse. Amen[7].

From THE LEGEND OF GOOD WOMEN.

The Story of Thisbe of Babylon, Martyr

Incipit Legende Tesba Babilon, Martiris

At Babiloyne whilom fil it[8] thus,—
The whiche toun the queene Semyramus[9]
Leet dichen al about, and walles make[10]
Ful hye, of harde tiles wel y-bake: 709
There were dwellynge in this noble toune
Two lordes, which that were of grete renoune,
And woneden[11] so neigh upon a grene,
That ther nas but a stoon wal hem betwene,
As ofte in grette tounes is the wone.
And sooth to seyn, that o man had a sone,
Of al that londe oon of the lustieste;
That other had a doghtre, the faireste
That esteward in the worlde was tho[12]
    dwellynge.   718
The name of everyche[13] gan to other sprynge[14],
By wommen that were neyghebores aboute;
For in that contre yit, withouten doute,

Máydens ben y-kept for jelousye
Ful streyte[15], leste they diden somme folye.
    This yonge man was cleped Piramus,
And Tesbe highte the maide,—Naso[16] seith
    thus.
And thus by reporte was hir name y-shove[17],
That as they wex in age, wex hir love.
And certeyn, as by reson of hir age,
Ther myghte have ben betwex hem marïage,
But that hir fadres nold[18] it not assente,   73
And both in love y-like soore they brente[19],
That noon of al hir frendes myghte it lette[20]
But prevely[21] somtyme yit they mette
By sleight, and spoken somme of hir desire,
As wre the glede[22] and hotter is the fire;
Forbeede a love, and it is ten so woode[23].
    This wal, which that bitwixe hem bothe
    stoode,
Was cloven a-two, right fro the toppe adoun,
Of olde tyme, of his foundacioun.   739
But yit this clyfte was so narwe and lite[24]
It was nat seene, deere ynogh a myte[25];
But what is that that love kannat espye?
Ye lovers two, if that I shal nat lye,
Ye founden first this litel narwe clifte,
And with a soune as softe as any shryfte[26],
They leete hir wordes thurgh the clifte pace,
And tolden, while they stoden in the place,
Al hire compleynt of love, and al hire wo,
At every tyme whan they dorste so.   749
Upon the o syde of the walle stood he,
And on that other syde stood Tesbe,
The swoote soun of other to receyve.
    And thus here[27] wardeyn wolde they disceyve,
And every day this walle they wolde threete[28],
And wisshe to God that it were doun y·bete.
Thus wolde they seyn: 'Allas, thou wikked
    walle!
Thurgh thyn envye thow us lettest[29] alle!
Why nyltow cleve[30], or fallen al a-two?
Or at the leeste, but thow wouldest so[31],
Yit woldestow but ones let us meete,   760
Or ones that we myghte kyssen sweete,
Than were we covered[32] of oure cares colde.
But natheles, yit be we to thee holde[33],
In as muche as thou suffrest for to goon
Our wordes thurgh thy lyme and eke thy stoon;

1 wicked
2 curse
3 cause
4 prosper
5 chatters
6 instruction
7 A sort of benediction; the "my lord" refers probably to the Archbishop of Canterbury.
8 it happened
9 Semiramis, wife of Ninus, the mythical king and founder of Nineveh.
10 caused to be surrounded by ditches and walls
11 dwelt (*wone* in 714 = custom)
12 then
13 each
14 came to the ears of the other
15 strictly
16 Ovid (Publius Ovidius Naso) in *Metamorphoses* iv 55, ff., whence this story is taken.
17 their names were brought forward (literally *pushed*)
18 would not
19 burned
20 prevent
21 secretly
22 cover the glowing coal
23 ten times as passionate
24 little
25 scarcely at all
26 confession
27 their
28 threaten
29 hinderest
30 wilt thou not cleave in two
31 if thou wouldest not do that
32 recovered
33 beholden

Yet oghte we with the ben wel apayede[1].'
And whan these idel wordes weren sayde,
The colde walle they wolden kysse of stoon,
And take hir leve, and forth they wolden goon.
And this was gladly in the evetyde,   770
Or wonder erly, lest men it espyede.
And longe tyme they wroght in this manere,
Til on a day, whan Phebus[2] gan to clere[3]—
Aurora with the stremes of hire hete[4]
Had dried uppe the dewe of herbes wete—
Unto this clyfte, as it was wont to be,
Come Piramus, and after come Tesbe.
And plighten trouthe[5] fully in here faye[6],
That ilke same nyght to steele awaye,
And to begile hire wardeyns everychone,   780
And forth out of the citee for to gone.
And, for the feeldes ben so broode and wide,
For to meete in o place at o tyde
They sette markes, hire metyng sholde bee
Ther[7] kyng Nynus was graven[8], under a tree,—
For olde payens[9], that ydoles heriede[10],
Useden tho in feeldes to ben beriede[11],—
And faste by his grave was a welle.
And, shortly of this tale for to telle,
This covenaunt was affermed wonder faste,   790
And longe hem thoghte that the sonne laste,
That it nere goon[12] under the see adoun.

This Tesbe hath so greete affeccioun,
And so grete lykynge Piramus to see,
That whan she seigh hire tyme myghte bee,
At nyght she stale[13] awey ful prevely,
With hire face y-wympled subtilly.
For al hire frendes, for to save hire trouthe,
She hath forsake; allas, and that is routhe[14],
That ever woman wolde be so trewe   800
To trusten man, but she the bet hym knewe[15]!
And to the tree she goth a ful goode paas[16],
For love made hir so hardy in this caas;
And by the welle adoun she gan hir dresse[17].
Allas! than comith a wilde leonesse
Out of the woode, withouten more arreste[18],
With blody mouth, of strangelynge of a beste,
To drynken of the welle ther as she sat.
And whan that Tesbe had espyed that,
She ryst[19] hir up, with a ful drery herte,   810
And in a cave with dredful foot she sterte,
For by the moone she saugh it wel withalle.
And as she ranne, hir wympel leet she falle,
And tooke noon hede, so sore she was awhaped[20],

And eke so glade that she was escaped;
And ther she sytte, and darketh[21] wonder stille.
Whan that this lyonesse hath dronke hire fille,
Aboute the welle gan she for to wynde[22],
And ryght anon the wympil gan she fynde,
And with hir blody mouth it al to-rente.   820
Whan this was don, no lenger she ne stente[23],
But to the woode hir wey than hath she nome[24].

And at the laste this Piramus is come,
But al to longe, allas, at home was hee!
The moone shone, men myghte wel y-see,
And in his wey, as that he come ful faste,
His eyen to the grounde adoun he caste;
And in the sonde as he behelde adoun[25],
He seigh the steppes broode of a lyoun;
And in his herte he sodeynly agroos[26],   830
And pale he wex, therwith his heer aroos,
And nere he come, and founde the wympel torne.
'Allas,' quod he, 'the day that I was borne!
This o nyght wol us lovers bothe slee!
How shulde I axen mercy of Tesbee,
Whan I am he that have yow slayne, allas?
My byddyng hath i-slayn yow in this caas!
Allas, to bidde a woman goon by nyghte
In place ther as[27] peril fallen myghte!
And I so slowe! allas, I ne hadde be[28]   840
Here in this place, a furlong wey or ye[29]!
Now what lyon that be in this foreste,
My body mote he renten[30], or what beste
That wilde is, gnawen mote he now my herte!'
And with that worde he to the wympel sterte,
And kiste it ofte, and wepte on it ful sore;
And seyde, 'Wympel, allas! ther nys no more[31],
But thou shalt feele as wel the blode of me,
As thou hast felt the bledynge of Tesbe.'
And with that worde he smot hym to the herte;   850
The blood out of the wounde as brode sterte
As water, whan the conduyte broken is.

Now Tesbe, which that wyste[32] nat of this,
But syttyng in hire drede, she thoghte thus:
'If it so falle that my Piramus
Be comen hider, and may me nat y-fynde,
He may me holden fals, and eke unkynde.'
And oute she comith, and after hym gan espien
Bothe with hire herte and with hire eyen;
And thoghte, 'I wol him tellen of my drede,
Bothe of the lyonesse and al my dede.'   861
And at the laste hire love than hath she founde,
Betynge with his helis[33] on the grounde,
Al blody; and therwithal abak she sterte,

---

pleased
Apollo, the sun-god
shine clearly
heat
troth
faith
where
buried
pagans
) worshipped

11 then used to be buried in fields
12 were not gone
13 stole
14 pity
15 unless she knew him better
16 quickly
17 took her station
18 delay
19 riseth

20 amazed
21 lies hid
22 roam
23 stopped
24 taken
25 looked down
26 shuddered
27 where

28 that I had not been
29 a short time before you
30 may he rend
31 nothing remains
32 who knew
33 i. e., still pulsating

And lyke the wawes[1] quappe[2] gan hir herte,
And pale as boxe[3] she wax, and in a throwe[4]
Avised hir[5], and gan him wel to knowe,
That it was Piramus, hire herte dere.
　Who koude write which a dedely chere
Hath Tesbe now? and how hire heere[6] she
　　rente?　　　　　　　　　　　　　　870
And how she gan hir-selve to turmente?
And how she lyth and swowneth on the
　　grounde?
And how she wepe of teres ful his wounde?
How medleth[7] she his blood with hir com-
　　pleynte?
How with his blood hir-selven gan she peynte?
How clippeth[8] she the dede corps? allas!
How doth this woful Tesbe in this cas?
How kysseth she his frosty mouthe so colde?
Who hath don this? and who hath ben so
　　bolde　　　　　　　　　　　　　879
To sleen my leefe? O speke, Piramus!
I am thy Tesbe, that thee calleth thus!'
And therwithal she lyfteth up his heed.
　This woful man, that was nat fully deed,
Whan that he herde the name of Tesbe crien[9],
On hire he caste his hevy dedely eyen,
And doun agayn, and yeldeth up the goste.
　Tesbe rist uppe, withouten noyse or boste[10],
And saugh hir wympel and his empty shethe,
And eke his swerde, that him hath don to
　　dethe.
Than spake she thus: 'Thy woful hande,' quod
　　she,　　　　　　　　　　　　　　890
'Is strong ynogh in swiche a werke to me;
For love shal me yive strengthe and hardy-
　　nesse,
To make my wounde large ynogh, I gesse.
I wole the[11] folowen ded, and I wol be
Felawe and cause eke of thy deeth,' quod she.
'And thogh that nothing save the deth only
Myghte the fro me departe[12] trewely,
Thou shal no more departe now fro me
Than fro the deth, for I wol go with the.
　'And now, ye wrecched jelouse fadres oure,
Wé, that weren whilome children youre,　901
We prayen yow, withouten more envye,
That in o grave i-fere[13], we moten lye,
Syn love hath broght us to this pitouse ende.
And ryghtwis God to every lover sende,
That loveth trewely, more prosperite
Than ever hadde Piramus and Tesbe.
And let no gentile woman hire assure,
To putten hire in swiche an áventure.
But God forbede but a woman kan　　　910
Ben also trewe and lovynge as a man,

And for my parte I shal anon it kythe[14]!'
And with that worde his swerde she took as
　　swithe[15],
That warme was of hire loves blood, and hote,
And to the herte she hire-selven smote.
　And thus are Tesbe and Piramus ago[16].
Of trewe men I fynde but fewe mo
In al my bookes, save this Piramus,
And therfore have I spoken of hym thus
For it is deyntee to us men to fynde　　920
A man that kan in love be trewe and kynde.
Here may ye seen, what lover so he be,
A woman dar and kan as wel as he.

THE COMPLEYNT OF CHAUCER TO HIS PURSE

To you, my purse, and to noon other wyght
　Compleyne I, for ye be my lady dere!
I am so sorry now that ye been light;
　For, certes, but ye make me hevy chere[17],
　Me were as leef be leyd upon my bere[18],
For whiche unto your mercy thus I crye,—
Beth[19] hevy ageyn, or elles mot[20] I dye!

Now voucheth sauf[21] this day or hit[22] be nyght
　That I of you the blisful soun[23] may here[24]
Or see your colour lyk the sonne bright,　1(
　That of yelownesse hadde never pere[25],
　Ye be my lyf! ye be myn hertes stere[26]!
Quene of comfort and of good companye!
Beth hevy ageyn, or elles mot I dye.

Now, purse, that be to me my lyves light
　And saveour, as doun[27] in this worlde here,
Out of this toun help me throgh your myght,
　Syn[28] that ye wole not been my tresorere[29],
　For I am shave as nye as is a frere[30].
But yet I pray unto your curtesye,
Beth hevy ageyn, or elles mot I dye!

L'Envoye De Chaucer

O conquerour of Brutes Albioun[31],
Which that by lyne and free eleccioun
　Ben verray kyng, this song to you I sende
　And ye that mowen[32] al myn harm amende
Have mynde upon my supplicacioun!

14 show	23 sound
15 quickly	24 hear
16 gone	25 peer
17 unless you put on for me a heavy look (with a play on the word *heavy*, which usually in this connection means *sad*)	26 helm, guide
	27 down
	28 since
	29 treasurer
	30 shaven as close as a friar (terribly hard pinched)
18 I would as soon be laid upon my bier	31 Henry IV. had just been made king Brutus was a legendary king of England (Albion)
19 be	
20 must	
21 vouchsafe, grant	
22 before it	32 can

1 waves		
2 flutter		
3 box-wood	6 hair	10 outcry
4 moment	7 mingleth	11 thee
5 considered	8 embraceth	12 separate
	9 spoken	13 together

FROM THE TRAVELS OF SIR JOHN MANDEVILLE *

PROLOGUE

Forasmuch as the land beyond the sea, that is to say the Holy Land, that men call the Land of Promission or of Behest[1], passing all other lands, is the most worthy land, most excellent, and lady and sovereign of all other lands, and is blessed and hallowed of the precious body and blood of our Lord Jesus Christ; in the which land it liked him to take flesh and blood of the Virgin Mary, to environ[2] that holy land with his blessed feet; . . . and forasmuch as it is long time passed that there was no general passage ne voyage over the sea; and many men desire for to hear speak of the Holy Land, and have thereof great solace and comfort;—I, John Mandeville, Knight, albeit I be not worthy, that was born in England, in the town of St. Albans, and passed the sea in the year of our Lord Jesu Christ, 1322, in the day of St. Michael; and hitherto have been long time over the sea, and have seen and gone through many diverse lands, and many provinces and kingdoms and isles; and have passed throughout Turkey, Armenia the little and the great; through Tartary, Persia, Syria, Arabia, Egypt the high and the low; through Libya, Chaldea, and a great part of Ethiopia; through Amazonia, Ind the less and the more†, a great part; and throughout many other isles that be about Ind, where dwell many diverse folks, and of diverse manners and laws, and of diverse shapes of men; . . . I shall tell the way that they shall hold thither. For I have oftentimes passed and ridden that way, with good company of many lords. God be thanked!

And ye shall understand that I have put this book out of Latin into French, and translated it again out of French into English, that every man of my nation may understand it. But lords and knights and other noble and worthy men that con[3] Latin but little, and have been beyond the sea, know and understand if I say truth or no, and if I err in devising[4], for forgetting or else, that they may redress it and amend it. For things passed out of long time from a man's mind or from his sight, turn soon into forgetting; because that[5] the mind of man ne may not be comprehended ne withholden, for the frailty of mankind.‡

OF THE CROSS OF OUR LORD JESU CHRIST

At Constantinople is the cross of our Lord Jesu Christ, and his coat without seams, that is clept *tunica inconsutilis*[6], and the sponge, and the reed, of the which the Jews gave our Lord eisel[7] and gall, in[8] the cross. And there is one of the nails that Christ was nailed with on the cross. And some men trow that half the cross, that Christ was done on, be in Cyprus, in an abbey of monks, that men call the Hill of the Holy Cross; but it is not so. For that cross, that is in Cyprus, is the cross in the which Dismas the good thief was hanged on. But all men know not that; and that is evil y-done[9]. For for profit of the offering they say that it is the cross of our Lord Jesu Christ.

And ye shall understand that the cross of our Lord was made of four manner of trees, as it is contained in this verse,—*In cruce fit palma, cedrus, cypressus, oliva.* For that piece that went upright from the earth to the head was of cypress; and the piece that went overthwart, to the which his hands were nailed, was of palm; and the stock, that stood within the earth, in the which was made the mortise, was of cedar; and the table above his head, that was a foot and an half long, on the which the title was written in Hebrew, Greek, and Latin, that was of olive. . . .

And the Christian men, that dwell beyond the sea, in Greece, say that the tree of the cross, that we call cypress, was of that tree that Adam ate the apple off; and that find they written. And they say also that their scripture saith that Adam was sick, and said to his son Seth, that he should go to the angel that kept Paradise, that he would send him oil of mercy, for to anoint with his members, that he might have health. And Seth went. But the angel would not let him come in; but said

---

Land of Promise   3 know
go about

This book, which was extremely popular in its day, was accepted then and long after in good faith. We now know it to be mainly a compilation from other books of travel, ingeniously passed off as a record of original experience. "Mandeville" is probably a fictitious name. The oldest MS. is in French, dated 1371. The English translation from which our selections are taken was made after 1400, and therefore represents the language of the generation succeeding Chaucer. The spelling is modernized. See *Eng. Lit.*, p. 44.
Mandeville here couples the fabulous land of the Amazons with the actual Lesser and Greater India.

4 relating
5 because
6 called "the tunic unsewn"
7 vinegar
8 on
9 Old past participle; y equals German ge.

‡ Possibly "Sir John" means to give the reader a sly hint here that it is also one of the frailties of mankind to tell big stories.

to him, that he might not have the oil of mercy. But he took him three grains of the same tree that his father ate the apple off; and bade him, as soon as his father was dead, that he should put these three grains under his tongue, and grave[1] him so: and so he did. And of these three grains sprang a tree, as the angel said that it should, and bare a fruit, through the which fruit Adam should be saved. And when Seth came again, he found his father near dead. And when he was dead, he did with the grains as the angel bade him; of the which sprung three trees, of the which the cross was made, that bare good fruit and blessed, our Lord Jesu Christ; through whom Adam and all that come of him should be saved and delivered from dread of death without end, but[2] it be their own default.

How Roses came first into the World

And a little from Hebron is the mount of Mamre, of the which the valley taketh his name. And there is a tree of oak, that the Saracens clepe[3] *Dirpe*, that is of Abraham's time: the which men clepe the Dry Tree. And they say that it hath been there since the beginning of the world, and was some-time green and bare leaves, unto the time that our Lord died on the cross, and then it dried: and so did all the trees that were then in the world. And some say, by their prophecies, that a lord, a prince of the west side of the world, shall win the Land of Promission, that is the Holy Land, with help of Christian men, and he shall do sing[4] a mass under that dry tree; and then the tree shall wax green and bear both fruit and leaves, and through that miracle many Jews and Saracens shall be turned to Christian faith: and therefore they do great worship thereto, and keep it full busily[5]. And, albeit so, that it be dry, natheless[6] yet he[7] beareth great virtue, for certainly he that hath a little thereof upon him, it healeth him of the falling evil, and his horse shall not be afoundered. And many other virtues it hath; wherefore men hold it full precious.

From Hebron men go to Bethlehem in half a day, for it is but five mile; and it is full fair way, by plains and woods full delectable. Bethlehem is a little city, long and narrow and well walled, and in each side enclosed with good ditches: and it was wont to be clept Ephrata, as holy writ saith, *Ecce, audivimus eum in Ephrata,* that is to say, 'Lo, we heard him in Ephrata.' And toward the east end of the city is a full fair church and a gracious and it hath many towers, pinnacles and corners, full strong and curiously made; and within that church be forty-four pillars of marble, great and fair.

And between the city and the church is the field *Floridus,* that is to say, the 'field flourished[8].' Forasmuch as a fair maiden was blamed with wrong, and slandered; for which cause she was demned to death, and to be burnt in that place, to the which she was led. And as the fire began to burn about her, she made her prayers to our Lord, that as wisely as she was not guilty of that sin, that he would help her and make it to be known to all men, of his merciful grace. And when she had thus said, she entered into the fire, and anon was the fire quenched and out; and the brands that were burning became red rose-trees, and the brands that were not kindled became white rose-trees, full of roses. And these were the first rose-trees and roses, both white and red, that ever any man saw; and thus was this maiden saved by the grace of God. And therefore is that field clept the field of God flourished, for it was full of roses.

How the Earth and Sea be of round Form and Shape, by proof of the Star that is clept Antarctic, that is fixed in the South*

In that land, ne in many other beyond that, no man may see the Star Transmontane, that is clept the Star of the Sea, that is unmovable and that is toward the north, that we clepe the Lode-star. But men see another star, the contrary to him, that is toward the south, that is clept Antarctic. And right as the ship-men take their advice here and govern them by the Lode-star, right so do the men beyond those parts by the star of the south, the which star appeareth not to us. And this star that is toward the north, that we clepe the Lode-star, ne appeareth not to them. For which cause men may well perceive that the land and the sea be of round shape and form; for the part of the firmament showeth in one country that showeth not in another country. And men may well prove by experience and subtle compassment of wit, that if a man found passages by ships that would go to search the world, men might go by ship all about the world and above and beneath.

[1] bury
[2] unless
[3] call
[4] cause to be sung
[5] very attentively
[6] nevertheless
[7] it
[8] in flower
[9] certainly
* An example of the speculations that were rife long before Columbus undertook his voyage.

The which thing I prove thus after that I have seen. For I have been toward the parts of Brabant[1], and beholden the Astrolabe that the star that is clept the Transmontane is fifty-three degrees high; and more further in Almayne[2] and Bohemia it hath fifty-eight degrees; and more further toward the parts septentrional[3] it is sixty-two degrees of height and certain minutes; for I myself have measured it by the Astrolabe. Now shall ye know, that against the Transmontane is the tother star that is clept Antartic, as I have said before. And those two stars ne move never, and by them turneth all the firmament right as doth a wheel that turneth by his axle-tree. So that those stars bear the firmament in two equal parts, so that it hath as much above as it hath beneath. After this I have gone toward the parts meridional, that is, toward the south, and I have found that in Libya men see first the star Antarctic. And so far I have gone more further in those countries, that I have found that star more high; so that toward the High Libya it is eighteen degrees of height and certain minutes (of the which sixty minutes make a degree). After going by sea and by land toward this country of that I have spoken, and to other isles and lands beyond that country, I have found the Star Antarctic of thirty-three degrees of height and more minutes. And if I had had company and shipping for to go more beyond, I trow well, in certain, that we should have seen all the roundness of the firmament all about. . . .

And wit well, that, after that[4] I may perceive and comprehend, the lands of Prester John,* Emperor of Ind, be under us. For in going from Scotland or from England toward Jerusalem men go upwards always. For our land is in the low part of the earth toward the west, and the land of Prester John is in the low part of the earth toward the east. And they have there the day when we have the night; and also, high to the contrary, they have the night when we have the day. For the earth and the sea be of round form and shape, as I have said before; and that that men go upward to one coast[5], men go downward to another coast.

Also ye have heard me say that Jerusalem is in the midst of the world. And that may men prove, and show there by a spear, that is pight[6] into the earth, upon the hour of midday, when it is equinox, that showeth no shadow on no side. And that it should be in the midst of the world, David witnesseth it in the Psalter, where he saith, *Deus operatus est salutem in medio terrae.*[7] Then, they that part from those parts of the west for to go toward Jerusalem, as many journeys[8] as they go upward for to go thither, in as many journeys may they go from Jerusalem unto other confines of the superficialty of the earth beyond. And when men go beyond those journeys toward Ind and to the foreign isles, all is environing[9] the roundness of the earth and of the sea under our countries on this half.

And therefore hath it befallen many times of one thing that I have heard counted[10] when I was young, how a worthy man departed sometime from our countries for to go search the world. And so he passed Ind and the isles beyond Ind, where be more than 5000 isles. And so long he went by sea and land, and so environed the world by many seasons, that he found an isle where he heard speak his own language, calling an oxen in the plough such words as men speak to beasts in his own country; whereof he had great marvel, for he knew not how it might be. But I say that he had gone so long by land and by sea, that he had environed all the earth; that he was come again environing, that is to say, going about, unto his own marches[11], and if he would have passed further, he would have found his country and his own knowledge. But he turned again from thence, from whence he was come from. And so he lost much painful labor, as himself said a great while after that he was come home. For it befell after, that he went into Norway. And there tempest of the sea took him, and he arrived in an isle. And when he was in that isle, he knew well that it was the isle where he had heard speak his own language before, and the calling of oxen at the plow; and that was possible thing.

But now it seemeth to simple men unlearned, that men ne may not go under the earth, and also that men should fall toward the heaven from under. But that may not be, upon less than[12] we may fall toward heaven from the earth where we be. For from what part of the earth that men dwell, either above or beneath, it seemeth always to them that dwell that they

---

1 Holland
2 Germany
3 north
4 And know well that, according to what
5 and that as men go upward to one region
* Prester is "presbyter," an elder or priest. This fabulous Christian monarch was supposed to have conquered the Saracens in the East.
6 set
7 The Lord wrought salvation in the midst of the earth. (See *Psalms,* 74 :12.)
8 days' travel
9 they are all the while encircling
10 recounted
11 borders
12 unless

go more right than any other folk. And right as it seemeth to us that they be under us, right so it seemeth to them that we be under them. For if a man might fall from the earth unto the firmament, by greater reason the earth and the sea that be so great and so heavy should fall to the firmament: but that may not be, and therefore saith our Lord God, *Non timeas me, qui suspendi terram ex nihilo!*[13]

And albeit that it be possible thing that men may so environ all the world, natheless, of a thousand persons, one ne might not happen to return into his country. For the greatness of the earth and of the sea, men may go by a thousand and a thousand other ways, that no man could ready him[14] perfectly toward the parts that he came from, but if it were by adventure and hap, or by the grace of God. For the earth is full large and full great, and holds in roundness and about environ[15], by above and by beneath, 20425 miles, after the opinion of old wise astronomers; and their sayings I reprove nought. But, after my little wit, it seemeth me, saving their reverence, that it is more.

And for to have better understanding I say thus. Be there imagined a figure that hath a great compass. And, about the point of the great compass that is clept the centre, be made another little compass. Then after, be the great compass devised by lines in many parts, and that all the lines meet at the centre. So, that in as many parts as the great compass shall be departed[16], in as many shall be departed the little, that is about the centre, albeit that the space be less. Now then, be the great compass represented for the firmament, and the little compass represented for the earth. Now then, the firmament is devised by astronomers in twelve signs, and every sign is devised in thirty degrees; that is, 360 degrees that the firmament hath above. Also, be the earth devised in as many parts as the firmament, and let every part answer to a degree of the firmament. And wit it well, that, after the authors of astronomy, 700 furlongs of earth answer to a degree of the firmament, and those be eighty-seven miles and four furlongs. Now be that here multiplied by 360 sithes[17], and then they be 31,500 miles every[18] of eight furlongs, after[19] miles of our country. So much hath the earth in roundness and of

height environ, after mine opinion and mine understanding.

Of the Trees that Bear Meal, Honey, Wine, and Venom; and of Other Marvels

After that isle, in going by sea, men find another isle, good and great, that men clepe Pathen[1], that is a great kingdom full of fair cities and full of towns. In that land grow trees that grow meal, whereof men make good bread and white and of good savor; and it seemeth as it were of wheat, but it is not allinges[2] of such savor. And there be other trees that bear honey good and sweet, and other trees that bear venom, against the which there is no medicine but one; and that is to take their proper[3] leaves and stamp them and temper them with water and then drink it, and else he shall die; for triacle[4] will not avail, ne none other medicine. Of this venom the Jews had let seek of[5] one of their friends for to empoison all Christianity, as I have heard them say in their confession before their dying: but thanked be Almighty God! they failed of their purpose; but always they[6] make great mortality of people. And other trees there be also that bear wine of noble sentiment[7]. And if you like to hear how the meal cometh out of the trees I shall say you. Men hew the trees with an hatchet, all about the foot of the tree, till that the bark be parted in many parts, and then cometh out thereof a thick liquor, the which they receive in vessels, and dry it at the heat of the sun; and then they have it to a mill to grind and it becometh fair meal and white[8]. And the honey and the wine and the venom be drawn out of other trees in the same manner, and put in vessels for to keep.

In that isle is a dead sea, that is a lake that hath no ground[9]: and if anything fall into that lake it shall never come up again. In that lake grow reeds, that be canes, that they clepe Thaby[10], that be thirty fathoms long; and of these canes men make fair houses. And there be other canes that be not so long, that grow near the land and have so long roots that endure well a four quarters[11] of a furlong or

---

1 Some region of the East Indies; the island described just before this is Java. But India and China are themselves spoken of as islands.
2 altogether
3 own
4 Or treacle; a compound in ancient medicine supposed to be a universal antidote.
5 had caused to be sought by
6 i.e., the venomous trees
7 taste
8 Tapioca is prepared thus from cassava roots.
9 bottom
10 bamboos
11 extend quite one-fourth (?)

13 Have no fear of me, who hanged the earth upon nothing. (See *Job*, 26:7.)
14 direct himself
15 approximately
16 divided
17 times
18 each
19 according to

more; and at the knots of those roots men find precious stones that have great virtues. And he that beareth any of them upon him, iron ne steel may not hurt him, ne draw no blood upon him; and therefore, they that have those stones upon them fight full hardily both upon sea and land, for men may not harm them on no part. And therefore, they that know the manner, and shall fight with them, they shoot to them arrows and quarrels without iron or steel, and so they hurt them and slay them. And also of those canes they make houses and ships and other things, as we have here, making houses and ships of oak or of any other trees. And deem no man that I say it but for a trifle, for I have seen of the canes with mine own eyes, full many times, lying upon the river of that lake, of the which twenty of our fellows ne might not lift up ne bear one to the earth.

OF THE PARADISE TERRESTRIAL

And beyond the land and the isles and the deserts of Prester John's lordship, in going straight toward the east, men find nothing but mountains and rocks, full great. And there is the dark region, where no man may see, neither by day ne by night, as they of the country say. And that desert and that place of darkness dure from this coast unto Paradise terrestrial, where that[1] Adam, our foremost[2] father, and Eve were put, that dwelled there but little while; and that is towards the east at the beginning of the earth. But that is not that east that we clepe our east on this half, where the sun riseth to us. For when the sun is east in those parts towards Paradise terrestrial, it is then midnight in our part on this half, for the roundness of the earth, of the which I have touched[3] to you of before. For our Lord God made the earth all round in the mid place of the firmament. And there as[1] mountains and hills be and valleys, that is not but only of[4] Noah's flood, that wasted the soft ground and the tender, and fell down into valleys, and the hard earth and the rocks abide[5] mountains, when the soft earth and tender waxed nesh[6] through the water, and fell and became valleys. Of Paradise ne can I not speak properly. For I was not there. It is far beyond. And that forthinketh me[7]. And also I was not worthy. But as I have heard say of[8] wise men beyond, I shall tell you with good will.

Paradise terrestrial, as wise men say, is the highest place of earth, that is in all the world. And it is so high that it toucheth nigh to the circle of the moon, there as the moon maketh her turn; for she is so high that the flood of Noah ne might not come to her, that would have covered all the earth of the world all about and above and beneath, save Paradise only alone. And this Paradise is enclosed all about with a wall, and men wit not whereof it is; for the walls be covered all over with moss, as it seemeth. And it seemeth not that the wall is stone of nature, ne of none other thing that the wall is. And that wall stretcheth from the south to the north, and it hath not but one entry that[9] is closed with fire, burning; so that no man that is mortal ne dare not enter.

And in the most high place of Paradise, even in the middle place, is a well that casteth out the four floods that run by divers lands. Of the which the first is clept Pison, or Ganges, that is all one; and it runneth throughout Ind or Emlak, in the which river be many precious stones, and much of lignum aloes[10] and much gravel of gold. And that other river is clept Nilus or Gison, that goeth by Ethiopia and after by Egypt. And that other is clept Tigris, that runneth by Assyria and by Armenia the great. And that other is clept Euphrates, that runneth also by Media and Armenia and by Persia. And men there beyond say, that all the sweet waters of the world, above and beneath, take their beginning of the well of Paradise, and out of that well all waters come and go.

The first river is clept Pison, that is to say in their language, Assembly; for many other rivers meet them there, and go into that river. And some men clepe it Ganges, for a king that was in Ind, that hight[11] Gangeres, and that it ran throughout his land. And that water is in some place clear, and in some place troubled, in some place hot, and in some place cold.

The second river is clept Nilus or Gison; for it is always trouble[12]; and Gison, in the language of Ethiopia, is to say, trouble, and in the language of Egypt also.

The third river, that is clept Tigris, is as much for to say as, fast-running; for he runneth more fast than any of the tother; and also there is a beast, that is clept Tigris, that is fast-running.

The fourth river is clept Euphrates, that is to say, well-bearing; for here grow many goods

1 where
2 first
3 related
4 from nothing else than
5 remained
6 soft
7 causes me regret
8 by
9 which
10 A fragrant oriental wood.
11 was called
12 troubled, murky

upon that river, as corn, fruits, and other goods enough plenty.

And ye shall understand that no man that is mortal ne may not approach to that Paradise. For by land no man may go for wild beasts that be in the desert, and for the high mountains and great huge rocks that no man may pass by, for the dark places that be there, and that many. And by the rivers may no man go. For the water runneth so rudely and so sharply, because that it cometh down so outrageously from the high places above, that it runneth in so great waves, that no ship may not row ne sail against it. And the water roareth so, and maketh so huge a noise and so great tempest, that no man may hear other in the ship, though he cried with all the craft that he could in the highest voice that he might. Many great lords have assayed with great will, many times, for to pass by those rivers towards Paradise, with full great companies. But they might not speed on their voyage. And many died for weariness of rowing against those strong waves. And many of them became blind, and many deaf, for the noise of the water. And some were perished and lost within the waves. So that no mortal man may approach to that place, without special grace of God, so that of that place I can say you no more; and therefore I shall hold me still, and return to that that I have seen.

CONCLUSION

And ye shall understand, if it like you, that at mine home-coming I came to Rome, and showed my life to our holy father the pope, and was assoiled[1] of all that lay in my conscience, of many a diverse grievous point; as men must needs that be in company, dwelling amongst so many a diverse folk of diverse sect and of belief, as I have been. And amongst all I showed him this treatise, that I had made after information of men that knew of things that I had not seen myself, and also of marvels and customs that I had seen myself, as far as God would give me grace; and besought his holy fatherhood that my book might be examined and proved by the advice of his said council. And our holy father, of his special grace, remitted my book to be examined and proved by the advice of his said counsel. By the which my book was proved for true, insomuch that they showed me a book, that my book was examined by, that comprehended full more, by an hundred part, by the which the *Mappa Mundi*[2] was made after. And so my book (albeit that many men ne list not to give credence to nothing but to that that they see with their eye, ne be the author ne the person never so true) is affirmed and proved by our holy father, in manner and form as I have said.

And I, John Mandeville, knight, abovesaid (although I be unworthy), that departed from our countries and passed the sea, the year of grace a thousand three hundred and twenty-two, that have passed many lands and many isles and countries, and searched many full strange places, and have been in many a full good honorable country, and at many a fair deed of arms (albeit that I did none myself, for mine unable insufficience), now I am come home, maugre myself, to rest, for gouts arthritic that me distrain[3] that define[4] the end of my labor; against my will (God knoweth).

And thus, taking solace in my wretched rest, recording the time past, I have fulfilled these things, and put them written in this book, as it would come into my mind, the year of grace a thousand three hundred and fifty-six, in the thirty-fourth year that I departed from our countries. Wherefore I pray to all the readers and hearers of this book, if it please them, that they would pray to God for me; and I shall pray for them.

---

1 absolved

2 Map of the World.   4 mark
3 afflict

THE FIFTEENTH AND EARLY SIXTEENTH CENTURIES

BALLADS

ROBIN HOOD AND THE MONK.*

1 In somer, when the shawes[1] be sheyne[2],
   And leves be large and long,
   Hit is full mery in feyre foreste
   To here the foulys[3] song:

2 To se the dere draw to the dale,
   And leve the hilles hee,
   And shadow hem in the levës grene,
   Under the grene-wode tre.

3 Hit befel on Whitsontide,
   Erly in a May mornyng,
   The son up feyre can[4] shyne,
   And the briddis mery can syng.

4 'This is a mery mornyng,' seid Litull John,
   'Be[5] hym that dyed on tre;
   A more mery man then[6] I am one
   Lyves not in Christiantë.

5 'Pluk up thi hert, my dere mayster,'
   Litull John can[4] sey,
   And thynk hit is a full fayre tyme
   In a mornyng of May.'

6 'Ye, on[7] thyng greves me,' seid Robyn,
   'And does my hert mych woo;
   That I may not no solem day
   To mas nor matyns goo.

7 'Hit is a fourtnet and more,' seid he,
   'Syn I my savyour see[8];
   Today wil I to Notyngham,
   With the myght of mylde Marye.'

8 Than spake Moche, the mylner sun[9],
   Ever more wel hym betyde!

'Take twelve of thi wyght yemen[10],
   Well weppynd, be thi side.
   Such on wolde thi selfe slon[11],
   That twelve dar not abyde[12].'

9 'Of all my mery men,' seid Robyn,
   'Be my feith I wil non have,
   But Litull John shall beyre my bow,
   Til that me list[13] to drawe.'

10 'Thou shall beyre thin own,' seid Litull Jon,
   'Maister, and I wyl beyre myne,
   And we well shete a peny[14],' seid Litull Jon,
   'Under the grene-wode lyne[15].'

11 'I wil not shete a peny,' seyd Robyn Hode,
   'In feith, Litull John, with the,
   But ever for on as[16] thou shetis,' seide Robyn,
   'In feith I holde[17] the thre.'

12 Thus shet thei forth, these yemen too[18],
   Bothe at buske[19] and brome[20],
   Til Litull John wan of his maister
   Five shillings to[21] hose and shone[22].

13 A ferly[23] strife fel them betwene,
   As they went bi the wey;
   Litull John seid he had won five shillings,
   And Robyn Hode seid schortly nay.

14 With that Robyn Hode lyed[24] Litul Jon,
   And smote hym with his hande;
   Litul Jon waxed wroth therwith,
   And pulled out his bright bronde.

15 'Were thou not my maister,' seid Litull John,

---

1 woods
2 beautiful
3 birds'
4 did
5 by
6 than
7 one
8 partook of the sacrament
9 miller's son
10 brave yeomen
11 slay
12 who would not dare withstand twelve
13 it pleases me
14 shoot for a penny
15 linden
16 unless for each one that
17 wager
18 two
19 bush
20 broom (heather)
21 for
22 shoes
23 strange
24 gave the lie to

* From a MS. of about 1450, though the ballad is probably much earlier. See *Eng. Lit.*, p. 63.

'Thou shuldis by[25] hit ful sore;
Get the a man wher thou wilt,
For thou getis me no more.'

16   Then Robyn goes to Notyngham,
     Hym selfe mornyng allone,
     And Litull John to mery Scherwode,
     The pathes he knew ilkone[26].

17   Whan Robyn came to Notyngham,
     Sertenly withouten layn[27],
     He prayed to God and myld Mary
     To bryng hym out save[28] agayn.

18   He gos in to Seynt Mary chirch,
     And kneled down before the rode[29];
     Alle that ever were the church within
     Beheld wel Robyn Hode.

19   Beside hym stod a gret-hedid munke,
     I pray to God woo[30] he be!
     Fful sone he knew gode Robyn,
     As sone as he hym se.

20   Out at the durre he ran,
     Fful sone and anon;
     Alle the gatis of Notyngham
     He made to be sparred[31] everychon.

21   'Rise up,' he seid, 'thou prowde schereff,
     Buske[32] the and make the bowne[33];
     I have spyed the kynggis felon,
     Ffor sothe he is in this town.

22   'I have spyed the false felon,
     As he stondis at his masse;
     Hit is long[34] of the,' seide the munke,
     'And[35] ever he fro us passe.

23   'This traytur name is Robyn Hode,
     Under the grene-wode lynde;
     He robbyt me onys[36] of a hundred pound,
     Hit shalle never out of my mynde.'

24   Up then rose this prowde shereff,
     And radly[37] made hym yare[33];
     Many was the moder son
     To the kyrk with hym can fare.

25   In at the durres thei throly[38] thrast,
     With staves ful gode wone[39];

'Alas, alas,' seid Robyn Hode,
'Now mysse I Litull John.'

26   But Robyn toke out a too-hond sworde,
     That hangit down be his kne;
     Ther as[1] the schereff and his men stode
         thyckust,
     Thedurwarde wolde he.

27   Thryes thorowout them he ran then
     For sothe as I yow sey,
     And woundyt mony a moder son,
     And twelve he slew that day.

28   His sworde upon the schireff hed
     Sertanly he brake in too;
     'The smyth that the made,' seid Robyn,
     'I pray God wyrke hym woo.

29   'Ffor now am I weppynlesse,' seid Robyn
     'Alasse! agayn my wylle;
     But if[2] I may fle these traytors fro,
     I wot thei wil me kyll.'

30   Robyn in to the churchë ran,
     Throout hem everilkon,*

.   .   .   .   .   .

31   Sum[3] fel in swonyng as thei were dede,
     And lay stil as any stone;
     Non of theym were in her mynde
     But only Litull Jon.

32   'Let be your rule[4],' seid Litull Jon,
     'Ffor his luf that dyed on tre,
     Ye that shulde be dughty men;
     Het is gret shame to se.

33   'Oure maister has bene hard bystode[5]
     And yet scapyd away;
     Pluk up your hertis, and leve this mone,
     And harkyn what I shal say.

34   'He has servyd Oure Lady many a day,
     And yet wil, securly[6];
     Therfor I trust in hir specialy
     No wyckud deth shal he dye.

35   'Therfor be glad,' seid Litul John,
     'And let this mournyng be;
     And I shal be the munkis gyde,
     With the myght of mylde Mary.

25 aby, atone for
26 each one
27 lying   33 ready
28 safe   34 because
29 rood, cross   35 if
30 unhappy   36 once
31 barred   37 quickly
32 prepare thee   38 stoutly
                            39 number

1 where   4 folly ? Some would
2 unless   read *dule = grief*)
3 Robin   Hood's men,   5 pressed
    who have heard of   6 surely
    the capture of Rob-
    in.
* A leaf is missing, some twelve stanzas. Similar
    gaps occur later.

       .   .   .   .   .

'We will go but we too;
And I mete hym,' seid Litul John,

       .   .   .   .   .

37 'Loke that ye kepe wel owre tristil-tre[7],
     Under the levys smale,
And spare non of this venyson,
     That gose in thys vale.'

38 Fforthe then went these yemen too,
     Litul John and Moche on fere[8],
And lokid on Moch emys hows[9],
     The hye way lay full nere.

39 Litul John stode at a wyndow in the
         mornyng,
     And lokid forth at a stage[10];
He was war wher the munke came ridyng,
     And with hym a litul page.

40 'Be my feith,' seid Litul John to Moch,
     'I can the tel tithyngus[11] gode;
I se wher the munke cumys rydyng,
     I know hym be his wyde hode.'

41 They went in to the way, these yemen
         bothe,
     As curtes men and hende[12];
Thei spyrred[13] tithyngus at [14] the munke,
     As they hade bene his frende[15].

42 'Ffro whens come ye?' seid Litull Jon,
     'Tel us tithyngus, I yow pray,
Off a false owtlay, callid Robyn Hode,
     Was takyn yisterday.

43 'He robbyt me and my felowes bothe
     Of twenti marke[16] in serten;
If that false owtlay be takyn,
     Ffor sothe we wolde be fayn[17].'

44 'So did he me,' seid the munke,
     Of a hundred pound and more;
I layde furst hande hym apon,
     Ye may thonke me therfore.'

45 'I pray God thanke you,' seid Litull John,
     'And we will when we may;
We will go with you, with your leve,
     And bryng yow on your way.

46 'Ffor Robyn Hode hase many a wilde
         felow,
     I tell you in certen;
If thei wist ye rode this way,
     In feith ye shulde be slayn.'

47 As thei went talking be the way,
     The munke and Litull John,
John toke the munkis horse be the hede,
     Fful sone and anon.

48 Johne toke the munkis horse be the hed,
     Ffor sothe as I yow say;
So did Much the litull page,
     Ffor he shulde not scape away.

49 Be the golett[18] of the hode
     John pulled the munke down;
John was nothyng of hym agast,
     He lete hym falle on his crown.

50 Litull John was sore agrevyd,
     And drew owt his swerde in hye;
This munke saw he shulde be ded,
     Lowd mercy can he crye.

51 'He was my maister,' seid Litull John,
     'That thou hase browght in bale[19];
Shalle thou never cum at our kyng,
     Ffor to telle hym tale.'

52 John smote of the munkis hed,
     No longer wolde he dwell;
So did Moch the litull page,
     Ffor ferd lest he wolde tell.

53 Ther thei beryed hem bothe,
     In nouther mosse nor lyng[20],
And Litull John and Much infere
     Bare the letturs to oure kyng.

       .   .   .   .   .

     He knelid down upon his kne:
'God yow save, my lege lorde,
     Jhesus yow save and se!

55 'God yow save, my lege kyng!'
     To speke John was full bolde;
He gaf hym the letturs in his hond,
     The kyng did hit unfold.

56 The kyng red the letturs anon,
     And seid, 'So mot I the[21],
Ther was never yoman in mery Inglond
     I longut so sore to se.

---

7 trysting-tree
8 in company
9 in on Much's uncle's house
10 from an (upper) story
11 tidings
12 civil
13 asked
14 of
15 friends
16 A mark was 13s. 4d
17 glad
18 throat-band
19 harm
20 neither moss nor heather
21 may I thrive

57 'Wher is the munke that these shuld have
          brought?'
      Oure kyng can say:
      'Be my trouth,' seid Litull John,
      'He dyed after[22] the way.'

58 The kyng gaf Moch and Litul Jon
      Twenti pound in sertan,
 And made theim yemen of the crown,
      And bade theim go agayn.

59 He gaf John the seel in hand,
      The sheref for to bere,
 To bryng Robyn hym to,
      And no man do hym dere[23].

60 John toke his leve at[24] oure kyng,
      The sothe as I yow say;
 The next way to Notyngham
      To take, he yede[25] the way.

61 Whan John came to Notyngham
      The gatis were sparred ychon;
 John callid up the porter,
      He answerid sone anon.

62 'What is the cause,' seid Litul Jon,
      'Thou sparris the gates so fast?'
 'Because of Robyn Hode,' seid the porter,
      'In depe prison is cast.

63 'John and Moch and Wyll Scathlok,
      Ffor sothe as I yow say,
 Thei slew oure men upon our wallis,
      And sawten[26] us every day.'

64 Litull John spyrred after the schereff,
      And sone he hym fonde;
 He oppyned the kyngus prive seell,
      And gaf hym in his honde.

65 Whan the sheref saw the kyngus seell,
      He did of[27] his hode anon:
 'Wher is the munke that bare the letturs?'
      He seid to Litull John.

66 'He[28] is so fayn of[29] hym,' seid Litul
        John,
      'Ffor sothe as I yow say,
 He has made hym abot of Westmynster,
      A lorde of that abbay.'

67 The scheref made John gode chere,
      And gaf hym wyne of the best;

      At nyght thei went to her bedde,
      And every man to his rest.

68 When the scheref was on slepe,
      Dronken of wyne and ale,
 Litul John and Moch for sothe
      Toke the way unto the jale.

69 Litul John callid up the jayler,
      And bade hym rise anon;
 He seyd Robyn Hode had brokyn prison,
      And out of hit was gon.

70 The porter rose anon sertan,
      As sone as he herd John calle;
 Litul John was redy with a swerd,
      And bare hym to the walle.

71 'Now wil I be porter,' seid Litul John,
      'And take the keyes in honde':
 He toke the way to Robyn Hode,
      And sone he hym unbonde.

72 He gaf hym a gode swerd in his hond,
      His hed therwith for to kepe[1],
 And ther as[2] the walle was lowyst
      Anon down can thei lepe.

73 Be that the cok began to crow,
      The day began to spryng;
 The scheref fond the jaylier ded,
      The comyn[3] bell made he ryng.

74 He made a crye thoroout al the town,
      Wheder he be yoman or knave,
 That cowthe bryng hym Robyn Hode,
      His warison[4] he shuld have.

75 'Ffor I dar never,' said the scheref,
      'Cum before oure kyng;
 Ffor if I do, I wot serten
      Ffor sothe he wil me heng.'

76 The scheref made to seke Notyngham,
      Bothe be strete and stye[5],
 And Robyn was in mery Scherwode,
      As light as lef on lynde[6].

77 Then bespake gode Litull John,
      To Robyn Hode can he say,
 'I have done the a gode turn for an evyll,
      Quyte[7] the whan thou may.

78 'I have done the a gode turne,' seid Litull
        John,

---

22 upon   26 assault
23 harm   27 put off
24 of   28 i. e., the king
25 went   29 pleased with

1 guard   5 alley
2 where   6 linden tree
3 public   7 quit (i. e., clear the
4 reward   debt)

'Ffor sothe as I yow say;
I have brought the under grene-wode lyne[6];
Ffare wel, and have gode day.'

79 'Nay, be my trouth,' seid Robyn Hode,
'So shall hit never be;
I make the maister,' seid Robyn Hode,
'Off alle my men and me.'

80 'Nay, be my trouth,' seid Litull John,
'So shalle hit never be;
But lat me be a felow,' seid Litull John,
'No noder kepe I be[8].'

81 Thus John gate Robyn Hod out of prison;
Sertan withoutyn layn[9],
Whan his men saw hym hol and sounde,
Ffor sothe they were full fayne.

82 They filled in wyne, and made hem glad,
Under the levys smale,
And gete[10] pastes of venyson,
That gode was with ale.

83 Than worde came to oure kyng
How Robyn Hode was gon,
And how the scheref of Notyngham
Durst never loke hym upon.

84 Then bespake oure cumly kyng,
In an angur hye:
'Litull John hase begyled the schereff,
In faith so hase he me.

85 'Litul John has begyled us bothe,
And that full wel I se;
Or ellis the schereff of Notyngham
Hye hongut[11] shulde he be.

86 'I made hem yemen of the crowne,
And gaf hem fee[12] with my hond;
I gaf hem grith[13],' seid oure kyng,
'Thorowout all mery Inglond.

87 'I gaf theym grith,' then seid oure kyng;
'I say, so mot I the,
Ffor sothe soch a yeman as he is on[14]
In all Inglond ar not thre.

88 'He is trew to his maister,' seid our kyng;
'I sey, be swete Seynt John,
He lovys better Robyn Hode
Then he dose us ychon.'

89 'Robyn Hode is ever bond to hym,
Bothe in strete and stalle[15];
Speke no more of this mater,' seid our
kyng,
'But John has begyled us alle.'

90 Thus endys the talkyng of the munke
And Robyn Hode i-wysse[16];
God, that is ever a crowned kyng,
Bryng us all to his blisse.'

THE HUNTING OF THE CHEVIOT*

1 The Persë[1] owt[2] off Northombarlonde,
and avowe to God mayd he
That he wold hunte in the mowntayns
off Chyviat within days thre,
In the magger of[3] doughtë Dogles,
and all that ever with him be.

2 The fattiste hartes in all Cheviat
he sayd he wold kyll, and cary them
away:
"Be my feth," sayd the dougheti Doglas
agayn,
"I wyll let[4] that hontyng yf that I
may."

3 Then the Persë owt off Banborowe cam,
with him a myghtee meany[5],
With fifteen hondrith archares bold off
blood and bone;
the[6] wear chosen owt of shyars[7] thre.

4 This begane on a Monday at morn,
in Cheviat the hillys so he;
The chylde may rue that ys unborn,
it wos the more pittë.

5 The dryvars[8] thorowe the woodës went,
for to reas the dear;
Bomen byckarte[9] uppone the bent[10]
with ther browd aros cleare[11].

6 Then the wyld[12] thorowe the woodës went,
on every sydë shear[13];
Greahondës thorowe the grevis[14] glent[15],
for to kyll thear dear.

15 i. e., abroad and at home
16 indeed

---

1 The family of Percy was an old one of northern
England.
2 came out
3 maugre, in spite of
4 prevent
5 band
6 they
7 shires
8 stalkers
9 skirmished
10 field
11 bright
12 game
13 several, separate
14 groves
15 darted

8 no other care I to be
9 lying (i. e., truly)
10 got
11 hanged
12 money
13 security
14 one

*Probably old in 1550. Sidney mentions "the olde
song of Percy and Duglas." There is a later
version which is commonly known as **Chevy
Chace.**

7 This begane in Chyviat the hyls abone[16],
    yerly[17] on a Monnyn-day;
Be that[18] it drewe to the oware off none,
    a hondrith fat hartës ded ther lay.

8 The blewe a mort[19] uppone the bent,
    the semblyde on sydis shear;
To the quyrry[20] then the Persë went,
    to se the bryttlynge[21] off the deare.

9 He sayd, "It was the Duglas promys,
    this day to met me hear;
But I wyste he wolde faylle, verament[22];"
    a great oth the Persë swear.

10 At the laste a squyar off Northomberlonde
    lokyde at his hand full ny;
He was war a the doughetie Doglas
    commynge,
    with him a myghttë meany.

11 Both with spear, bylle[23], and brande,
    yt was a myghtti sight to se;
Hardyar men, both off hart nor hande,
    wear not in Cristiantë.

12 The wear twenti hondrith spear-men good,
    withoute any feale[24],
The wear borne along be the watter a
    Twyde,
    yth[25] bowndës of Tividale.

13 "Leave of the brytlyng of the dear," he
    sayd,
    "and to your boys[26] lock ye tayk good
    hede;
For never sithe ye wear on your mothars
    borne
    had ye never[27] so mickle nede."

14 The dougheti Dogglas on a stede,
    he rode alle his men beforne;
His armor glytteryde as dyd a glede[28];
    a boldar barne[29] was never born.

15 "Tell me whos men ye ar," he says,
    "or whos men that ye be:
Who gave youe leave to hunte in this
    Chyviat chays,
    in the spyt of myn and of me."

16 The first mane[1] that ever him an answear
    mayd,
    yt was the good lord Persë:
"We wyll not tell the[2] whoys[3] men we ar,"
    he says,
    "nor whos men that we be;
But we wyll hounte hear in this chays,
    in the spyt of thyne and of the.

17 "The fattiste hartës in all Chyviat
    we have kyld, and cast[4] to carry them
    away.
"Be my troth," sayd the doughetë Dogglas
    agayn,
    "therfor the ton[5] of us shall de[6] this
    day."

18 Then sayd the doughtë Doglas
    unto the lord Persë:
"To kyll alle thes giltles men,
    alas, it wear great pittë!

19 "But, Persë, thowe art a lord of lande,
    I am a yerle callyd within my contrë;
Let all our men uppone a parti[7] stande,
    and do[8] the battell off the and of me."

20 "Nowe Cristes cors[9] on his crowne[10],"
    sayd the lord Persë,
"who-so-ever ther-to says nay;
Be[11] my troth, doughttë Doglas," he says,
    "thow shalt never se that day[12].

21 "Nethar in Ynglonde, Skottlonde, nar
    France,
    nor for no man of a woman born[13],
But, and[14] fortune be my chance,
    I dar met him, on[15] man for on[15]."

22 Then bespayke a squyar off Northombar-
    londe,
    Richard Wytharyngton was his nam:
"It shall never be told in Sothe-Ynglonde,"
    he says,
    "to Kyng Herry the Fourth for sham.

23 "I wat[16] youe byn[17] great lordës twaw,
    I am a poor squyar of lande:
I wylle never se my captayne fyght on a
    fylde,
    and stande my selffe and loocke on,
But whylle I may my weppone welde,
    I wylle not fayle both hart and hande."

16 above
17 early
18 by the time
19 death-note
20 slaughtered game
21 cutting up
22 truly
23 sword
24 fail
25 in the
26 bows
27 ever
28 glowing coal
29 man

1 man
2 thee
3 whose
4 intend
5 one
6 die
7 to one side
8 let us do
9 curse
10 head
11 by
12 sc., when I say nay
13 sc., will I shrink
14 if
15 one
16 know
17 be

24 That day, that day, that dredfull day!
    the first fit[18] here I fynde;
And[19] youe wyll here any mor a[20] the
      hountyng a the Chyviat,
    yet ys ther mor behynde.

25 The Yngglyshe men hade ther bowys
      yebent,
    ther hartes wer good yenoughe;
The first off arros that the[21] shote off,
    seven skore spear-men the sloughe.

26 Yet byddys[22] the yerle Doglas uppon the
      bent,
    a captayne good yenoughe,
And that was sene verament,
    for he wrought hom[23] both woo and
      wouche[24].

27 The Dogglas partyd his ost[25] in thre,
    lyk a cheffe cheften off pryde;
With suar spears off myghttë tre[26],
    the[21] cum in on every syde:

28 Thrughe our Yngglyshe archery[27]
    gave many a wounde fulle wyde;
Many a doughetë[28] the[21] garde[29] to dy,
    which ganyde them no pryde.

29 The Ynglyshe men let ther boys be,
    and pulde owt brandes that wer brighte;
It was a hevy syght to se
    bryght swordes on basnites[30] lyght.

30 Thorowe ryche male[31] and myneyeple[32],
    many sterne[33] the[21] strocke done[34]
      streght;
Many a freyke[35] that was fulle fre[36],
    ther undar foot dyd lyght.

31 At last the Duglas and the Persë met,
    lyk to captayns of myght and of mayne;
The[21] swapte[37] togethar tylle the both
      swat[38],
    with swordes that wear of fyn myllan[39].

32 Thes worthë freckys for to fyght,
    ther-to[40] the wear fulle fayne[41],

Tylle the bloode owte off thear basnetes
      sprente[42]
    as ever dyd heal[43] or rayn.

33 "Yelde the, Persë," sayde the Doglas,
    "and i feth[44] I shalle the brynge
Wher thowe shalte have a yerls wagis[45]
    of Jamy our Skottish kynge.

34 "Thou shalte have thy ransom fre,
    I hight[46] the hear[47] this thinge;
For the manfullyste man yet art thowe
    that ever I conqueryd in filde fight-
      tynge."

35 "Nay," sayd the lord Persë,
    "I tolde it the beforne,
That I wolde never yeldyde be
    to no man of a woman born."

36 With that ther cam an arrowe hastely,
    forthe off a myghttë wane[48];
Hit hathe strekene the yerle Duglas
    in at the brest-bane.

37 Thorowe lyvar and longës[1] bathe[2]
    the sharpe arrowe ys gane,
That never after in all his lyffe-days
    he spayke mo wordës but ane:
That was, "Fyghte ye, my myrry men,
      whyllys ye may,
    for my lyff-days ben gan."

38 The Persë leanyde on his brande,
    and sawe the Duglas de;
He tooke the dede mane by the hande,
    and sayd, "Wo ys me for the!

39 "To have savyde thy lyffe, I wolde have
      partyde with
    my landes for years thre,
For a better man, of hart nare of hande,
    was nat in all the north contrë."

40 Off all that se[3] a Skottishe knyght,
    was callyd Ser Hewe the Monggom-
      byrry[4];
He sawe the Duglas to the deth was
      dyght[5],
    he spendyd[6] a spear, a trusti tre.

41 He rod uppone a corsiare[7]
    throughe a hondrith archery:

18 division of the song	30 helmets		
19 if	31 armor		
20 of	32 gauntlet		
21 they	33 stubborn ones		
22 abides	34 down		
23 them	35 man		
24 harm	36 noble		
25 host	37 smote		
26 wood	38 sweat		
27 archers	39 Milan steel		
28 doughty man	40 i. e., to fight		
29 caused	41 glad		

42 sprang	1 lungs		
43 hail	2 both		
44 in faith	3 saw		
45 earl's wages	4 Montgomery		
46 promise	5 doomed		
47 here	6 spanned, seized		
48 multitude (? Skeat)	7 courser		

He never stynttyde[8], nar never blane[9],
 tylle he cam to the good lord Persë.

42 He set uppone the lorde Persë
 a dynte that was full soare;
 With a suar spear of a myghttë tre
 clean thorow the body he the Persë ber[10],

43 A[11] the tothar syde that a man myght se
 a large cloth-yard and mare:
 Towe bettar captayns wear nat in Cristiantë
 then that day slan wear ther.

44 An archar off Northomberlonde
 say[12] slean was the lord Persë;
 He bar a bende bowe in his hand,
 was made off trusti tre.

45 An arow, that a cloth-yarde was lang,
 to the harde stele halyde[13] he;
 A dynt that was both sad and soar
 he sat[14] on Ser Hewe the Monggombyrry.

46 The dynt yt was both sad and sar,
 that he of Monggomberry sete;
 The swane-fethars that his arrowe bar
 with his hart-blood the wear wete.

47 Ther was never a freake[15] wone foot wolde
 fle,
 but still in stour[16] dyd stand,
 Heawyng on yche othar, whylle the myghte
 dre[17],
 with many a balfull brande.

48 This battell begane in Chyviat
 an owar befor the none,
 And when even-songe bell was rang,
 the battell was nat half done.

49 The tocke[18] . . . on ethar hande
 be the lyght off the mone;
 Many hade no strenght for to stande,
 in Chyviat the hillys abon.

50 Of fifteen hondrith archars of Ynglonde
 went away but seventi and thre;
 Of twenti hondrith spear-men of Skotlonde,
 but even five and fifti.

51 But all wear slayne Cheviat within;
 the hade no strengthe to stand on hy;

The chylde may rue that ys unborne,
 it was the mor pittë.

52 Thear was slayne, withe the lord Persë,
 Sir Johan of Agerstone,
 Ser Rogar, the hinde[19] Hartly,
 Ser Wyllyam, the bolde Hearone.

53 Ser Jorg, the worthë Loumle,
 a knyghte of great renowen,
 Ser Raff[20], the ryche Rugbe,
 with dyntes wear beaten dowene.

54 For Wetharryngton my harte was wo,
 that ever he slayne shulde be;
 For when both his leggis wear hewyne in
 to,
 yet he knyled and fought on hys kny.

55 Ther was slayne, with the dougheti Duglas,
 Ser Hewe the Monggombyrry,
 Ser Davy Lwdale, that worthë was,
 his sistars son was he.

56 Ser Charls a Murrë[21] in that place,
 that never a foot wolde fle;
 Ser Hewe Maxwelle, a lorde he was,
 with the Doglas dyd he dey.

57 So on the morrowe the mayde them
 byears[22]
 off birch and hasell so gray;
 Many wedous, with wepyng tears,
 cam to fache ther makys[23] away.

58 Tivydale may carpe off[24] care,
 Northombarlond may mayk great mon,
 For towe such captayns as slayne wear
 thear,
 on the March-parti[25] shall never be non.

59 Word ys commen to Eddenburrowe,
 to Jamy the Skottische kynge,
 That dougheti Duglas, lyff-tenant of the
 Marches,
 he lay slean Chyviot within.

60 His handdës dyd he weal[26] and wryng,
 he sayd, "Alas, and woe ys me!
 Such an othar captayn Skotland within,"
 he sayd, "ye-feth shuld never be."*

---

8 stopped
9 ceased
10 pierced
11 on
12 saw that
13 drew
14 set
15 man
16 stress of battle
17 endure
18 they took (count?)
19 gentle
20 Ralph
21 Murray
22 biers
23 mates
24 sing of
25 border side
26 clench
* This lament, contrasted with King Harry's boast that follows, may be taken as an amusing indication of English authorship of the ballad.

61 Worde ys commyn to lovly Londone,
    till[27] the fourth Harry our kynge,
That lord Persë, leyff-tenante of the
    Marchis,
    he lay slayne Chyviat within.

62 "God have merci on his solle," sayde
    Kyng Harry,
    "good Lord, yf thy will it be!
I have a hondrith captayns in Ynglonde,"
    he sayd,
    "as good as ever was he:
But, Persë, and I brook[28] my lyffe,
    thy deth well quyte[29] shall be."

63 As our noble kynge mayd his avowe,
    lyke a noble prince of renowen,
For the deth of the lord Persë
    he dyde the battell of Hombyll-down;

64 Wher syx and thrittë Skottishe knyghtes
    on a day wear beaten down:
Glendale glytteryde on[30] ther armor bryght,
    over castille, towar, and town.

65 This was the hontynge off the Cheviat,
    that tear[31] begane this spurn[32],
Old men that knowen the grownde well
    yenoughe
    call it the battell of Otterburn.

66 At Otterburn begane this spurne
    uppone a Monnynday;
Ther was the doughtë Doglas slean,
    the Persë never went away.

67 Ther was never a tym on the Marche-
    partës
    sen[33] the Doglas and the Persë met,
But yt ys mervele and[34] the rede blude
    ronne not,
    as the reane doys[35] in the stret.

68 Jhesue Crist our balys[36] bete[37],
    and to the blys us brynge!
Thus was the hountynge of the Chivyat:
    God send us alle good endyng!

SIR PATRICK SPENS

1 The king sits in Dumferling toune[1],
    Drinking the blude-reid wine:
"O whar will I get guid sailor,
    To sail this schip of mine?"

2 Up and spak an eldern[2] knicht,
    Sat at the kings richt kne:
"Sir Patrick Spence is the best sailor,
    That sails upon the se."

3 The king has written a braid[3] letter,
    And signd it wi his hand,
And sent it to Sir Patrick Spence,
    Was walking on the sand.

4 The first line that Sir Patrick red,
    A loud lauch[4] lauched he;
The next line that Sir Patrick red,
    The teir blinded his ee.

5 "O wha is this has don this deid,
    This ill deid don to me,
To send me out this time o' the yeir,
    To sail upon the se!

6 "Mak hast, mak haste, my mirry men all,
    Our guid schip sails the morne:"
"O say na sae, my master deir,
    For I feir a deadlie storme.

7 "Late, late yestreen I saw the new moone,
    Wi the auld moone in hir arme,
And I feir, I feir, my deir master,
    That we will cum to harme."

8 O our Scots nobles wer richt laith
    To weet their cork-heild schoone;
Bot[5] lang owre[6] a' the play wer playd,
    Thair hats they swam aboone[7].

9 O lang, lang may their ladies sit,
    Wi thair fans into their hand,
Or eir they se Sir Patrick Spence
    Cum sailing to the land.

10 O lang, lang may the ladies stand,
    Wi thair gold kems[8] in their hair,
Waiting for thair ain deir lords,
    For they'll se thame na mair.

11 Haf owre, haf owre to Aberdour,
    It's fiftie fadom deip,
And thair lies guid Sir Patrick Spence,
    Wi the Scots lords at his feit.

JOHNIE COCK.*

1 Up Johnie raise in a May morning,
    Calld for water to wash his hands

27 to
28 if I enjoy
29 paid for
30 in, with (Humbleton is in Glendale district)
31 that ere, erewhile

32 trouble
33 since
34 if
35 rain does
36 evil
37 remedy, better

1 Dunfermline, northwest of Edinburgh, once a royal residence.

2 old
3 broad, open
4 laugh
5 but

6 before
7 swam in over their hats (so to speak)
8 combs

* Our text of this vigorous ballad follows the admirable combination made by Professor F. B. Gummere from various versions.

And he has calld for his gude gray hunds
That lay bund in iron bands, bands,
That lay bund in iron bands.

2 'Ye 'll busk[1], ye 'll busk my noble dogs,
Ye 'll busk and mak them boun[2],
For I 'm going to the Braidscaur hill
To ding[3] the dun[4] deer doun.'

3 Johnie 's mother has gotten word o that,
And care-bed she has taen[5]:
'O Johnie, for my benison[6],
I beg you 'l stay at hame;
For the wine so red, and the well-baken
bread,
My Johnie shall want nane.

4 'There are seven forsters at Pickeram
Side,
At Pickeram where they dwell,
And for a drop of thy heart 's bluid
They wad ride the fords of hell.'

5 But Johnie has cast off the black velvet,
And put on the Lincoln twine[7],
And he is on to gude greenwud
As fast as he could gang.

6 Johnie lookit east, and Johnie lookit west,
And he lookit aneath the sun,
And there he spied the dun deer sleeping
Aneath a buss o whuns[8].

7 Johnie shot, and the dun deer lap[9],
And she lap wondrous wide,
Until they came to the wan water,
And he stemd[10] her of her pride.

8 He 'as taen out the little pen-knife,
'Twas full three quarters[11] long,
And he has taen out of that dun deer
The liver bot[12] and the tongue.

9 They eat of the flesh, and they drank of
the blood,
And the blood it was so sweet,
Which caused Johnie and his bloody hounds
To fall in a deep sleep.

10 By then came an old palmer,
And an ill death may he die!
For he 's away to Pickram Side
As fast as he can drie[13].

11 'What news, what news?' says the Seven
Forsters,
'What news have ye brought to me?'
'I have noe news,' the palmer said,
'But what I saw with my eye.

12 'As I cam in by Braidisbanks,
And down among the whuns,
The bonniest youngster eer I saw
Lay sleepin amang his hunds.

13 'The shirt that was upon his back
Was o the holland[14] fine;
The doublet[15] which was over that
Was o the Lincoln twine.'

14 Up bespake the Seven Forsters,
Up bespake they ane and a':
'O that is Johnie o Cockleys Well,
And near him we will draw.'

15 O the first stroke that they gae him,
They struck him off by the knee;
Then up bespake his sister 's son:
'O the next 'll gar[16] him die!'

16 'O some they count ye well-wight[17] men,
But I do count ye nane;
For you might well ha wakend me,
And askd gin I wad be taen.

17 'The wildest wolf in aw this wood
Wad not ha done so by me;
She 'd ha wet her foot ith wan water,
And sprinkled it oer my brae[18],
And if that wad not ha wakend me,
She wad ha gone and let me be.

18 'O bows of yew, if ye be true,
In London, where ye were bought,
Fingers five, get up belive[19],
Manhuid shall fail me nought.'

19 He has killd the Seven Forsters,
He has killd them all but ane,
And that wan[20] scarce to Pickeram Side,
To carry the bode-words[21] hame.

20 'Is there never a [bird] in a' this wood
That will tell what I can say;
That will go to Cockleys Well,
Tell my mither to fetch me away?'

21 There was a [bird] into that wood,
That carried the tidings away,
And many ae[22] was the well-wight man
At the fetching o Johnie away.

1 make ready
2 ready
3 strike
4 dark brown
5 i. e., is sick with anxiety
6 blessing
7 cloth
8 bush of furze
9 leaped
10 stript
11 of a yard
12 as well as
13 hold out
14 linen
15 waistcoat
16 make
17 very brave
18 brow
19 quick
20 won, made his way
21 message
22 a one

BONNIE GEORGE CAMPBELL.

1 High upon Highlands,
    and low upon Tay,
Bonnie George Campbell
    rade out on a day.

2 Saddled and bridled
    and gallant rade he;
Hame cam his guid horse,
    but never cam he.

3 Out cam his auld mither
    greeting fu' sair[1],
And out cam his bonnie bride
    riving[2] her hair.

4 Saddled and bridled
    and booted rade he;
Toom[3] hame cam the saddle,
    but never cam he.

5 'My meadow lies green,
    and my corn is unshorn,
My barn is to build,
    and my babe is unborn.'

6 Saddled and bridled
    and booted rade he;
Toom hame cam the saddle,
    but never cam he.

THE WIFE OF USHER'S WELL.

1 There lived a wife at Usher's Well,
    And a wealthy wife was she;
She had three stout and stalwart sons,
    And sent them oer the sea.

2 They hadna been a week from her,
    A week but barely ane,
When word came to the carline[4] wife
    That her three sons were gane.

3 They hadna been a week from her,
    A week but barely three,
When word came to the carlin wife
    That her sons she'd never see.

4 'I wish the wind may never cease,
    Nor fashes[5] in the flood,
Till my three sons come hame to me,
    In earthly flesh and blood.'

5 It fell about the Martinmass[6],
    When nights are lang and mirk[7],

The carlin wife's three sons came hame,
    And their hats were o the birk[8].

6 It neither grew in syke[9] nor ditch,
    Nor yet in ony sheugh[10],
But at the gates o Paradise,
    That birk grew fair eneugh.

7 'Blow up the fire, my maidens!
    Bring water from the well!
For a' my house shall feast this night,
    Since my three sons are well.'

8 And she has made to them a bed,
    She's made it large and wide,
And she's ta'en her mantle her about,
    Sat down at the bed-side.

9 Up then crew the red, red cock,
    And up and crew the gray;
The eldest to the youngest said,
    ' 'Tis time we were away.'

10 The cock he hadna craw'd but once,
    And clappd his wings at a',
When the youngest to the eldest said,
    'Brother, we must awa.

11 'The cock doth craw, the day doth daw,
    The channerin[11] worm doth chide;
Gin[12] we be mist out o our place,
    A sair pain we maun bide.

12 'Fare ye weel, my mother dear!
    Fareweel to barn[13] and byre[14]!
And fare ye weel, the bonny lass
    That kindles my mother's fire!'*

KATHARINE JAFFRAY.†

1 There livd a lass in yonder dale,
    And doun in yonder glen, O,
And Kathrine Jaffray was her name,
    Well known by many men, O.

2 Out came the Laird of Lauderdale,
    Out frae the South Countrie,
All for to court this pretty maid,
    Her bridegroom for to be.

---

1 weeping full sore
2 tearing
3 empty
4 old

5 troubles (storms)
6 November 11
7 dark

8 birch
9 marsh
10 furrow
11 fretting

12 if
13 granary
14 stable

* "The beauty of reticence in this last farewell is
    as delicate as anything in literature."—F. B.
    Gummere.
† Scott's "Lochinvar" is based upon this ballad.

3   He has teld[1] her father and mither baith,
      And a' the rest o her kin,
    And has teld the lass hersell,
      And her consent has win.

4   Then came the Laird of Lochinton,
      Out frae the English border,
    All for to court this pretty maid,
      Well mounted in good order.

5   He's teld her father and mither baith,
      As I hear sindry say,
    But he has nae teld the lass her sell,
      Till on her wedding day.

6   When day was set, and friends were met,
      And married to be,
    Lord Lauderdale came to the place,
      The bridal for to see.

7   'O are you come for sport, young man?
      Or are you come for play?
    Or are you come for a sight o our bride,
      Just on her wedding day?'

8   'I'm nouther come for sport,' he says,
      'Nor am I come for play;
    But if I had one sight o your bride,
      I'll mount and ride away.'

9   There was a glass of the red wine
      Filld up them atween,
    And ay she drank to Lauderdale,
      Wha her true-love had been.

10 Then he took her by the milk-white hand,
      And by the grass-green sleeve,
    And he mounted her high behind him there,
      At the bridegroom he askt nae leive.

11 Then the blude run down by the Cowden
        Banks,
      And down by Cowden Braes,
    And ay she[2] gard[3] the trumpet sound,
      'O this is foul, foul play!'

12 Now a' ye that in England are,
      Or are in England born,
    Come nere to Scotland to court a lass,
      Or else ye'l get the scorn.

13 They haik ye up[4] and settle ye by[5],
      Till on your wedding day,
    And gie ye frogs instead o fish,*
      And play ye foul, foul play.

1 told   3 caused
2 Perhaps this should be 4 haul you up
  he, referring to the   5 set you aside (lead you
  Laird of Lochinton   on and deceive you)
* In the ballad of *Lord Randal*, the lord is poisoned with eels.

THE NUTBROWN MAYDE.*

Be it right or wronge, thes men amonge[1]
  On wymen do complayn,
Affermyng this, how that it is
  A laboure spent in vayn
To love them welle; for never a dele
  They love a man agayn.
For late a man do what he can
  Ther favoure to attayn,
Yet yf a newe do them pursue,
  Ther ferste trew lover than[2]   10
Laboureth for nought; for from her[3] thought
  He is a banysshed man.

I say not nay, but that alle day
  It is both wreten and said
That woman's feyth is, as who seyth,
  Alle utturly decayde;
But nevertheless right good witnes
  In this case myght be layde,
That they love trew, and contenewe,—
  Recorde the Nutbrown Mayde,   20
Which, whan her love cam her to prove,
  To her to make his mone,
Wolde not departe, for in her hart
  She loved but hym alone.

Than betwen us let us discusse
  What was alle the manere
Between them two: we wille also
  Telle alle the payn in fere[4]
That she was in. Now I begyn,
  So that ye me answere;   30
Wherfor alle ye that present be,
  I pray you, geve an ere.
I am the knyght; I com by nyght,
  As secrete as I can,
Saying, 'Alas! thus stondith the caas,
  I am a banysshed man.'

1 all the while   3 their
2 then   4 i-fere, together
* This poem is essentially a little drama, of which
  the first three stanzas constitute a kind of
  prologue and the last stanza an epilogue. In
  the first stanza one speaker propounds the
  general theme of the fickleness of womankind.
  In the second stanza, another speaker cites
  in refutation the story of the Nutbrown
  Mayde. Then the first speaker proposes that
  they two enact that story, and he begins by
  assuming the part of the man who pretended
  to be outlawed in order to "prove" the maid's
  love. The second speaker takes the part of
  the maid, and the dialogue continues regularly
  in alternate stanzas. It is readily seen that
  the poem, though for convenience grouped
  here with the ballads, is of a very different character from the folk-ballads proper, and a product of much more conscious art. Our text
  is that of the Balliol MS., with some very
  slight changes of spelling and the regular
  substitution of MAYDE for the more frequent
  marginal PUELLA of the manuscript.

MAYDE

And I your wille for to fulfille
  In this wille not refuse,
Trustyng to shew in wordis fewe
  That men have an ylle use[5]   40
(To ther own shame) wymen to blame,
  And causelesse them accuse.
Therfor to you I answere now,
  Alle wymen to excuse,—
Myn own hart dere, with you what chere?
  I pray you, telle me anon;
For in my mynd, of alle mankynd
  I love but you alon.

SQUYRE

It stondith so; a dede is doo
  Wherof gret harme shalle grow: 50
My destynye ys for to dye
  A shamfulle deth, I trow,
Or ellis to flee; the on[6] muste be;
  Non other way I know
But to withdraw as an outlawe,
  And take me to my bow.
Wherfor adewe, myn own hart trew!
  Non other rede I can[7],
For I muste to the grenwode go,
  Alon, a banysshed man.   60

MAYDE

O Lorde, what is this worldis blis
  That changith as the mone?
The[8] somers day in lusty may
  Is darke beffore the none.
I here you say, Farewelle. Nay, nay,
  We departe[9] not so sone.
Why say ye so? Whether[10] wille ye go?
  Alas, what have ye done?
Alle my welfare to sorrow and care
  Shuld chaunge yf ye were gon;   70
For in my mynde, of alle mankynd
  I love but you alon.

SQUYRE

I can beleve it shalle you greve,
  And sumwhat you dystreyne,
But afterward your paynes harde,
  Within a day or twayn,
Shalle sone aslake, and ye shalle take
  Conforte to you agayn.
Why should you ought for to take thought[11]?
  Your laboure were in vayn.   80
And thus I doo, and pray you to,
  As hartely as I can;
For I muste to the grenwode go,
  Alon, a banysshed man.

MAYDE

Now sith[12] that ye have shewed to me
  The secrete of your mynde,
I shalle be playn to you agayn[13],
  Lyke as ye shalle me fynde.
Sith it is so that ye wille go,
  I wille not bide behynde;   90
Shalle it never be said the Nut Brown Mayde
  Was to here love unkynde.
Make you redy, for so am I,
  Alle though it were anon[14];
For in my mynd, of alle mankynd
  I love but you alon.

SQUYRE

Yet I you rede to take good hede
  What men wille thynke and say:
Of[15] yong, of olde, hit shalle be told
  That ye be gon away,   100
Your wanten wille for to fulfille,
  In grenwode you to play,
And that ye myght for your delite
  Ne lengar make delay.
Rather than ye shuld thus for me
  Be called a mysse[16] woman,
Yet wold I to the grenwode go,
  Alon, a banysshed man.

MAYDE

Though it be songe of olde and yonge
  That I shuld be to blame,   110
Thers be the charge that speke so large
  In hurtyng of my name;
For I wille prove that feythfulle love
  Hit is devoyed of shame,
In your distresse and hevynesse,
  To parte[17] with you the same,—
To shewe all tho that do not so
  Trew lovers are they non;
For in my mynd, of alle mankynd
  I love but you alon.   120

SQUYRE

I counsaille you, remembre how
  Hit is no maydyns lawe
Nothyng to doute, but to renne out
  To wode with an outlawe.
For ye muste ther in your hond bere
  A bowe redy to drawe,
And, as a theff, thus must ye leve
  Ever in drede and awe.
Wherby to you gret harm myght grow;
  Yet hade I lever than   130
That I had to the grenwod go,
  Alon, a banysshed man.

---

5 evil custom
6 one
7 no   other   counsel   I
    know
8 Variant reading: my.
9 part
10 whither
11 at all take anxiety
12 since
13 in return
14 at once
15 by
16 Variant: ylle.
17 share

MAYDE

I say not nay, but as ye say,
    Yt is no maydyns lore;
But love may make me to forsake,
    As I have sayd beffore,
To cum on fote, to hunte and shote,
    To get us mete in store;
For so that I your company
    May have, I aske no more.   140
From which to parte it makyth my harte
    As colde as any ston;
For in my mynde, of alle mankynd
    I love but you alon.

SQUYRE

For an outlawe this is the lawe,
    That men hym take and bynde,
Without pité, hangid to be,
    And waver with the wynde.
Yf I had nede, (as God forbede!)
    What soccours could ye fynde?   150
Forsoth, I trow, ye and your bowe
    For fere wold draw behynde.
And no mervayle, for littille avayle
    Were in your counselle than;
Wherfor I wille to the grenwod go,
    Alon, a banysshed man.

MAYDE

Right welle know ye that wymen be
    But feeble for to fight;
No womanhede it is indede
    To be bolde as a knyght.   160
Yet in such fere yf that ye were,
    With ennemyes day or nyght,
I wold withstond, with bow in honde,
    To helpe you with my myght,
And you to save, as wymen have
    From deth many [an] one;
For in my mynd, of alle mankynd
    I love but you alon.

SQUYRE

Yet take good hede, for ever I drede
    That ye could not susteyn   170
The thorny wayes, the depe valeyes,
    The snowe, the froste, the rayn,
The colde, the hete; for drye and wete
    We muste logge on the playn,
And, us above, non other roffe
    But a brake, bushe, or twayn;
Which sone shuld greve you, I beleve,
    And ye wold gladly than
That I had to the grenwode goo,
    Alon, a banysshed man.   180

MAYDE

Sith I have here ben partynere
    With you [in] yoye and blisse,

I muste also parte of your woo
    Endure, as reason is.
Yet am I sure of on pleasure,
    And shortly it is this:
That wher ye be, me semeth, pardé,
    I could not fare amysse.
Without more speche I you beseche
    That we were shortly gon;   190
For in my mynd, of alle mankynd
    I love but you alon.

SQUYRE

Iff ye go thyder, ye must consider,
    Whan ye have luste to dyne,
Ther shalle no mete be for to gete,
    Nether bere, ale, ne wyne;
Ne shetes clen, to lay betwen,
    Made of threde and twyne;
Non other hous, but levis and boues,
    To cover your hede and myne.   200
Loo, myn hart swete, this ille dyett
    Shuld make you pale and wan;
Wherfor I wille to the grenwod go,
    Alon, a banysshed man.

MAYDE

Amonge the wilde dere, suche an archere
    As men say that ye be
May not faylle of good vytaylle,
    Wher is so gret plenté.
And water clere of the rivere
    Shalle be fulle swete to me,   210
With which in hele[18] I shalle right welle
    Endure, as ye shalle see.
And, or we go, a bedde or two
    I can provide anon;
For in my mynde, of alle mankynd
    I love but you alon.

SQUYRE

Loo! yet beffore, ye must do more,
    Yf ye wille goo with me:
As, cute your here up by your ere,
    Your kyrtyll by your knee,   220
With bow in honde, for to withstonde
    Your enymyes, yf nede be;
And this same nyght, beffore daylight,
    To wodewarde wille I flee.
Yff that ye wille alle this fulfille,
    Do it as shortly as ye can;
Els wille I to the grenwode go,
    Alon, a banysshed man.

MAYDE

I shalle as now[19] do more for you
    Than longith to womanhede,   230
To shorte myn here, a bowe to bere,
    To shote in tyme of nede.

18 health   19 now (redundant *as*)

O my swete moder, beffore alle oder
  For you I have moste drede;
But now, adewe! I must ensue
  Wher fortune doth me lede.
Alle this make ye; now lat us flee,
  The day commeth fast upon;
For in my mynd, of alle mankynd
  I love but you alon.

SQUYRE

Nay, nay, not so; ye shalle not go,
  And I shalle telle you whye:
Your appetite is to be light
  Of love, I welle espye;
For like as ye have said to me,
  In likewyse hardely20
Ye wolde answere, whosoever it were,
  In way of companye.
It is said of olde, Son whot, sone colde,   250
  And so is a woman;
For I muste to the grenwode goo,
  Alon, a banysshed man.

MAYDE

Yf ye take hede, it is no nede
  Such wordis to say to me,
For ofte ye prayd, and long assayed,
  Or I you loved, pardé.
And though that I of auncetrye
  A barons doughter be,
Yet have ye proved how I ye loved,
  A squyre of lowe degre,   260
And ever shalle, what so befalle,
  To dye therefor anon;
For in my mynd, of alle mankynd
  I love but you alon.

SQUYRE

A baron's child to be begiled,
  It were a cursèd dede.
To be felowe with an outlawe,
  Almyghty God forbede!
Yet better were, the pore squyer
  Alon to foreste yede21,   270
Than ye shuld say, another day,
  That by my cursèd rede
Ye were betrayde. Wherefor, good mayd,
  The best rede that I can,
Ys that I to the grenwod go,
  Alon, a banysshed man.

MAYDE

Whatever befalle, I never shalle
  Of this thyng you outbrayde;
But yf ye go and leve me so,
  Than have ye me betrayde.   280

Remembre you welle how that ye dele,
  For yf ye be as ye said,
Ye were unkynd to leve me behynd,
  Your love, the Nutbrown Mayde.
Truste [me] truly, that I shalle dye
  Sone after ye be gon;
For in my mynd, of all mankynd
  I love but you alon.

SQUYRE

If that you went, ye shuld repent,
  For in the foreste nowe   290
I have purveyde22 me of a mayde
  Whom I love more than you,—
Another more fayre than ever ye were,
  I dare it welle avowe;
And of you both, eche wille be wroth
  With other, as I trowe.
It were myn eas to leve23 in peas,
  So wille I, yf I can;
Wherefor I wille to the grenwod goo,
  Alon, a banysshed man.   300

MAYDE

Though in the wode I understode
  Ye had a paramoure,
Alle this may nought remeve my thought,
  But that I wille be your;
And she shalle fynd me softe and kynd,
  And curteys every oure,
Glad to fulfille alle that she wille
  Comaund me to my powere.
For had ye, loo! an hundredth mo,
  Yet wolde I be that on;   310
For in my mynd, of alle mankynd
  I love but you alon.

SQUYRE

Myn own der love, I se thee prove
  That ye be kynde and trewe;
Of mayde and wyf, in alle my lyff,
  The best that ever I knew.
Be mery and glade, be no more sade,
  The case is chaunged newe,
For it were rewth that for your trewth
  Ye shuld have cause to rewe.   320
Be not dysmayde, whatsoever I said
  To you whan I began;
I wille not to the grenwode go;
  I am no banysshed man.

MAYDE

Thes tydingis be more gladder to me
  Than to be made a quene,
Yf I were sure they shuld endure;
  But it is often seen,
When men wille24 breke promyse, they speke
  The wordis on the splene25.   330

Ye shape som wyle me to begile,
And stele from me, I wene;
Than were the caas wors than it was,
And I more woo-begon;
For in my mynd, of alle mankynd
I love but you alon.

SQUYRE

Ye shalle not nede further to drede;
I wille not disparage
You, God defende, sith ye descende
Of so gret a lynage.   340
Now understond; to Westmorelond,
Which is myn herytage,
I wille you bryng, and with a rynge
By way of maryage
I wille you take, and lady make,
As shortly as I can;
Than have ye wonne an erles sonne,
And not a banysshed man.

Here may ye see that women be,
In love, meke, kynd, and stable;   350
Latt never man repreve them than
Or calle them variable,
But rather pray God that we may
To them be confortable.
God sumtyme provith such as he lovith,
Yf they be charytable;
For sith men wold that women shuld
Be meke to them echone,
Moche more aught they to God obey,
And serve but hym alon.   360

EVERYMAN

*Here begynneth a treatyse how the hye Fader
of Heven sendeth Dethe to somon every
creature to come and gyve a counte of
theyr lyves in this worlde, and is
in maner of a moral playe.**

MESSENGER.

I pray you all gyve your audyence,
And here[1] this mater[2] with reverence,
By fygure[3] a morall[4] playe;
The somonynge of Everyman called it is,
That of our lyves and endynge shewes

[1] hear   [3] in form
[2] matter   [4] A Morality

* This play exists also in Dutch, entitled "Elcker-
lijk," printed about 1495, and attributed to
Petrus Dorlandus. The earliest known English editions date about 1525. From the dates
and the almost entire lack of humor in the
play, it is most probable that the English
form is a free translation from the Dutch.
We follow the text of the Skot copy in the
Britwell Library, as reprinted by W. W. Greg,
with capitals and punctuation added. On
Moralities and Miracle Plays, see *Eng. Lit.*,
64-67.

How transytory we be all daye[5].
This mater is wonders[6] precyous,
But the entent[7] of it is more gracyous,
And swete to bere awaye.   9
The story sayth:—Man, in the begynnynge
Loke well, and take good heed to the endynge,
Be you never so gay;
Ye thynke synne in the begynnynge full swete,
Whiche in the ende causeth the soule to wepe,
Whan the body lyeth in claye.
Here shall you se how Felawshyp and Jolyte,
Bothe Strengthe, Pleasure and Beaute,
Wyll fade from thes[8] as floure in Maye.   18
For ye shall here, how our heven kynge
Calleth Everyman to a generall rekenynge.
Gyve audyence, and here what he doth saye.

GOD *speketh.*

I perceyve here in my majeste
How that all creatures be to me unkynde,
Lyvynge without drede in worldely prosperyte;
Of ghostly[9] syght the people be so blynde,
Drowned in synne they know me not for theyr
    God;
In worldely ryches is all theyr mynde.
They fere not my ryghtwysnes, the sharpe
    rood;
My lawe that I shewed whan I for them dyed
They forgete clene, and shedynge of my blode
    rede;   30
I hanged bytwene two, it can not be denyed;
To gete them lyfe I suffred to be deed.
I heled theyr fete; with thornes hurt was my
    heed;
I coude do no more than I dyde truely.
And nowe I se the people do clene for sake me:
They use[10] the seven deedly synnes dampnable.
As pryde, coveytyse, wrathe and lechery,
Now in the worlde be made commendable,
And thus they leve of aungelles the hevenly
    company,   39
Every man lyveth so after his owne pleasure;
And yet of theyr lyfe they be nothinge sure.
I se, the more that I them forbere,
The worse they be fro yere to yere;
All that lyveth appayreth[11] faste.
Therefore I wyll in all the haste
Have a rekenynge of every mannes persone.
For, and[12] I leve the people thus alone
In theyr lyfe and wycked tempestes,
Veryly they wyll become moche worse than
    beestes:
For now one wolde by envy another up ete;
Charyte they do all clene forgete.   51

[5] always   [9] spiritual
[6] wondrously   [10] practise
[7] purpose   [11] degenerates
[8] thee   [12] if

I hoped well that every man
In my glory shulde make his mansyon,
And thereto I had them all electe;
But now I se, like traytours dejecte,
They thanke me not for the pleasure that I to
them ment,
Nor yet for theyr beynge that I them have lent.
I profered the people grete multytude of mercy,
And fewe there be that asketh it hertly[13];
They be so combred with worldly ryches   60
That nedes on them I must do justyce,
On every man lyvynge without fere.—
Where arte thou, Deth, thou myghty messen-
gere?
    DETHE. Almyghty God, I am here at your
wyll,
Your commaundement to fulfyll.
    GOD. Go thou to Everyman,
And shewe hym in my name
A pylgrymage he must on hym take,
Which he in no wyse may escape,   69
And that he brynge with hym a sure rekenynge,
Without delay or ony taryenge.
    DETHE. Lorde, I wyll in the worlde go
renne[14] over all,
And cruelly out serche bothe grete and small.
Every man wyll I beset that lyveth beestly
Out of Goddes lawes and dredeth not foly.
He that loveth rychesse I wyll stryke with my
darte,
His syght to blynde, and fro heven to departe[15],
Excepte that almes be his good frende,
In hell for to dwell, worlde without ende.
Loo, yonder I se Everyman walkynge,   80
Full lytell he thynketh on my comynge!
His mynde is on flesshely lustes, and his treas-
ure;
And grete payne it shall cause hym to endure
Before the Lorde, heven kynge.—

        [EVERYMAN enters.]

Everyman, stande styll. Whyder arte thou
goynge,
Thus gayly? hast thou thy Maker forgete?
    EVERYMAN. Why askest thou?
Woldest thou wete?[16]
    DETHE. Ye, syr, I wyll shewe you:
In grete hast I am sende to the   90
Fro God, out of his mageste.
    EVERYMAN. What, sente to me?
    DETHE. Ye, certaynly.
Thoughe thou have forgete hym here,
He thynketh on the in the hevenly spere,
As, or[17] we departe, thou shalte knowe.
    EVERYMAN. What desyreth God of me?

DETHE. That shall I shewe thee:
A rekenynge he wyll nedes have,
Without ony lenger respyte.
    EVERYMAN. To gyve a rekenynge longer lay-
ser[18] I crave;
This blynde mater troubleth my wytte.
    DETHE. On the thou must take a longe
journey,
Therfore thy boke of counte with the thou
brynge,
For turne agayne thou can not by no waye;
And loke thou be sure of thy rekenynge,
For before God thou shalte answere and shewe
Thy many badde dedes and good but a fewe,
How thou hast spente thy lyfe, and in what
wyse,
Before the chefe lorde of paradyse.   110
Have I do[19] we were in that waye,
For, wete thou well, thou shalte make none
attournay[20].
    EVERYMAN. Full unredy I am suche reken-
ynge to gyve.
I knowe the not. What messenger arte thou?
    DETHE. I am Dethe, that no man dredeth.
For every man I rest[21], and no man spareth,
For it is Goddes commaundement
That all to me sholde be obedyent.
    EVERYMAN. O Dethe, thou comest whan I
had thee leest in mynde!
In thy power it lyeth me to save;   120
Yet of my good wyl I gyve the, if thou wyl
be kynde,
Ye, a thousande pounde shalte thou have,
And dyfferre[22] this mater tyll an other daye.
    DETHE. Everyman, it may not be by no waye.
I set not by[23] golde, sylver, nor rychesse,
Ne by pope, emperour, kynge, duke ne prynces;
For, and I wolde receyve gyftes grete,
All the worlde I myght gete;
But my custome is clene contrary.   129
I gyve the no respyte, come hens and not tary.
    EVERYMAN. Alas! shall I have no lenger
respyte?
I may saye Deth geveth no warnynge!
To thynke on the it maketh my herte seke;
For all unredy is my boke of rekenynge.
But, xii yere and I myght have abydynge,
My countynge boke I wolde make so clere,
That my rekenynge I sholde not nede to fere.
Wherfore, Deth, I praye the, for Goddes mercy,
Spare me tyll I be provyded of remedy.
    DETHE. The avayleth not to crye, wepe and
praye.   140

13 heartily
14 run
15 separate
16 know
17 before
18 leisure
19 For "have ado": have
    done with, that we
    may be on our way
20 find no intercessor
21 arrest
22 defer
23 care not for

But hast[1] the lyghtly that thou were[2] gone that
    journaye.
And preve[3] thy frendes, yf thou can.
For, wete thou well, the tyde abydeth no man,
And in the worlde eche lyvynge creature
For Adams synne must dye of nature.
    EVERYMAN. Dethe, yf I sholde this pylgrym-
        age take,
And my rekenynge suerly make,
Shewe me, for saynt Charyte,
Sholde I not come agayne shortly?
    DETHE. No, Everyman, and thou be ones
        there,
Thou mayst never more come here,   151
Trust me veryly.
    EVERYMAN. O gracyous God, in the hye sete
        celestyall,
Have mercy on me in this moost nede.—
Shall I have no company fro this vale teres-
    tryall
Of myne acqueynce[4] that way me to lede?
    DETHE. Ye, yf ony be so hardy
That wolde go with the and bere the company.
Hye the, that thou were gone to Goddes mag-
    nyfycence,
Thy rekenynge to gyve before His presence. 160
What, wenest thou thy lyve is gyven the
And thy worldely gooddes also?
    EVERYMAN. I had wende so veryle.
    DETHE. Nay, nay, it was but lende the,
For as soone as thou arte go,
Another a whyle shall have it and than go ther
    fro,
Even as thou hast done.
Everyman, thou arte made[5]! Thou hast thy
    wyttes fyve,
And here on erthe wyll not amende thy lyve!
For sodeynly I do come.   170
    EVERYMAN. O wretched caytyfe[6], wheder
        shall I flee,
That I myght scape this endles sorowe?
Now, gentyll Deth, spare me tyll to morowe,
That I may amende me
With good advysement.
    DETHE. Naye, thereto I wyll not consent,
Nor no man wyll I respyte;
But to the herte sodeynly I shall smyte
Without ony advysement.
And now out of thy syght I wyll me hy.   180
Se thou make the redy shortely,
For thou mayst saye this is the daye
That no man lyvynge may scape awaye.
    EVERYMAN. Alas! I may well wepe with
        syghes depe;
Now have I no maner of company

To helpe me in my journey, and me to kepe;
And also my wrytynge[7] is full unredy.
How shall I do now for to excuse me?
I wolde to God I had never begete[8]!   189
To my soule a full grete profyte it had be,
For now I fere paynes huge and grete.
The tyme passeth, Lorde, helpe, that all
    wrought!
For though I mourne it avayleth nought.
The day passeth, and is almoost ago[9],
I wote not well what for to do.
To whome were I best my complaynt to make?
What and I to Felawshyp therof spake,
And shewed hym of this sodeyne chaunce?
For in hym is all myne affyaunce[10].   199
We have in the worlde so many a daye
Be good frendes in sporte and playe.
I se hym yonder certaynely;
I trust that he wyll bere me company,
Therfore to hym wyll I speke to ese my sorowe.
Well mette, good Felawshyp, and good morowe.
    FELAWSHYP *speketh:* Everyman, good morowe!
        By this day,
Syr, why lokest thou so pyteously?
If ony thynge be a mysse I praye the me saye,
That I may helpe to remedy.
    EVERYMAN. Ye, good Felawshyp, ye,   210
I am in greate jeoparde.
    FELAWSHYP. My true frende, shewe to me
        your mynde;
I wyll not forsake the to my lyves ende,
In the waye of good company.
    EVERYMAN. That was well spoken, and
        lovyngly.
    FELAWSHYP. Syr, I must nedes knowe your
        hevynesse,
I have pyte[11] to se you in ony dystresse.
If ony have you wronged ye shall revenged be,
Thoughe I on the grounde be slayne for the,
Though that I knowe before that I sholde
    dye.   220
    EVERYMAN. Veryly, Felawshyp, gramercy[12]
    FELAWSHYP. Tusshe! by thy thankes I set
        not a strawe.
Shewe me your grefe and saye no more.
    EVERYMAN. If I my herte sholde to you
        breke,
And than you to tourne your mynde fro me,
And wolde not me comforte whan ye here me
    speke,
Than sholde I ten tymes soryer be.
    FELAWSHYP. Syr, I saye as I wyll do in dede.
    EVERYMAN. Than be you a good frende at
    nede.
I have founde you true here before.   230

---

1 haste
2 may be
3 prove
4 acquaintance
5 mad
6 captive, **wretch**
7 (his account)
8 been born
9 gone
10 trust
11 pity
12 great **thanks**

FELAWSHYP. And so ye shall evermore,
For, in fayth, and thou go to hell
I wyll not forsake the by the waye.

    EVERYMAN. Ye speke lyke a good frende, I
      byleve you well,
I shall deserve it, and I may.

    FELAWSHYP. I speke of no deservynge, by
      this daye,
For he that wyll saye and nothynge do
Is not worthy with good company to go.
Therfore shewe me the grefe of your mynde
As to your frende mooste lovynge and
    kynde.   240

    EVERYMAN. I shall shewe you how it is:
Commaunded I am to go a journaye,
A long waye, harde and daungerous,
And gyve a strayte counte, without delaye,
Before the hye Juge Adonay[3].
Wherfore, I pray you, bere me company,
As ye have promysed, in this journaye.

    FELAWSHYP. That is mater in dede! Promyse
      is duty.
But and I sholde take suche a vyage on me,
I knowe it well, it shulde be to my payne; 250
Also it make me aferde, certayne.
But let us take counsell here as well as we can,
For your wordes wolde fere[4] a stronge man.

    EVERYMAN. Why, ye sayd, yf I had nede,
Ye wolde me never forsake, quycke[5] ne deed,
Thoughe it were to hell, truely.

    FELAWSHYP. So I sayd certaynely.
But such pleasures be[6] set a syde the sothe[7]
    to saye,
And also, yf we toke suche a journaye,
Whan sholde we come agayne?   260

    EVERYMAN. Naye, never agayne, tyll the
      daye of dome[8].

    FELAWSHYP. In fayth, than wyll not I come
there,
Who hath you these tydynges brought?

    EVERYMAN. In dede, Deth was with me here.

    FELAWSHYP. Now, by God that all hathe
      bought,
If Deth were the messenger,
For no man that is lyvynge to daye
I wyll not go that lothe[9] journaye,
Not for the fader that bygate me.   269

    EVERYMAN. Ye promysed other wyse, parde[10].

    FELAWSHYP. I wote well I say[11] so, truely,
And yet yf thou wylte ete, drynke and make
    good chere
Or haunt to women the lusty company,
I wolde not forsake you, whyle the daye is
    clere,

Truste me veryly.

    EVERYMAN. Ye, therto ye wolde be redy:
To go to myrthe, solas, and playe,
Your mynde wyll soner apply,
Than to bere me company in my longe jour-
    naye.

    FELAWSHYP. Now, in good fayth, I wyll not
      that waye;   280
But, and thou wyll murder, or ony man kyll,
In that I wyll helpe the with a good wyll.

    EVERYMAN. O that is a symple[12] advyse in
      dede!
Gentyll felawe, help me in my necessyte;
We have loved longe, and now I nede!
And now, gentyll Felawshyp, remember me.

    FELAWSHYP. Wheder ye have loved me or no,
By saynt John, I wyll not with the go.

    EVERYMAN. Yet I pray the, take the labour
      and do so moche for me,
To brynge me forwarde, for saynt Charyte, 290
And comforte me tyll I come without the
    towne.

    FELAWSHYP. Nay, and thou wolde gyve me
      a newe gowne,
I wyll not a fote with the go;
But and thou had taryed, I wolde not have
    lefte the so:
And as now, God spede the in thy journaye!
For from the I wyll departe as fast as I maye.

    EVERYMAN. Wheder a waye, Felawshyp?
      wyll thou forsake me?

    FELAWSHYP. Ye, by my faye[13]! To God I
      betake[14] the.

    EVERYMAN. Farewell, good Fellawshyp! For
      the my herte is sore!
A dewe for ever, I shall se the no more. 300

    FELAWSHYP. In fayth, Everyman, fare well
      now at the ende,
For you I wyll remember that partynge is
    mournynge.

    EVERYMAN. A lacke! shall we thus departe[15]
      in dede?
A! Lady, helpe! without ony more comforte,
Lo, Felawshyp forsaketh me in my moost nede.
For helpe in this worlde wheder shall I re-
    sorte?
Felawshyp here before with me wolde mery
    make,
And now lytell sorowe for me dooth he take.
It is sayd, in prosperyte men frendes may
    fynde
Whiche in adversyte be full unkynde.   310
Now wheder for socoure shall I flee,
Syth that Felawshyp hath forsaken me?
To my kynnesmen I wyll truely,
Prayenge them to helpe me in my necessyte.

---

3 God
4 frighten
5 alive
6 are (now)
7 truth
8 judgment
9 loathsome
10 One of the many forms
    of the oath *pardieu*
11 said
12 foolish
13 faith
14 commend
15 separate

I byleve that they wyll do so,
For kynde[2] wyll crepe where it may not go[3].
I wyll go saye; for yonder I se them go:—
Where be ye now, my frendes and kynnesmen?
   KYNREDE. Here be we now at your com-
    maundement.
Cosyn, I praye you, shewe us your entent   320
In ony wyse, and not spare.
   COSYN. Ye, Everyman, and to us declare
If ye be dysposed to go ony whyder;
For, wete you well, wyll lyve and dye to gyder.
   KYNREDE. In welth and wo we wyll with
    you holde;
For over his kynne a man may be bolde.
   EVERYMAN. Gramercy, my frendes and kynnes-
    men kynde!
Now shall I shewe you the grefe of my mynde.
I was commaunded by a messenger,
That is a hye kynges chefe offycer;   330
He bad me go a pylgrymage to my payne,
And, I knowe well, I shall never come agayne.
Also I must gyve a rekenynge strayte;
For I have a grete enemy that hath me in
    wayte[4],
Whiche entendeth me for to hynder.
   KYNREDE. What a counte is that whiche ye
    must render?
That wolde I knowe.
   EVERYMAN. Of all my workes I must shewe,
How I have lyved, and my dayes spent;
Also of yll dedes that I have used   340
In my tyme, syth lyfe was me lent,
And of all vertues that I have refused.
Therefore, I praye you, go thyder with me
To helpe to make myn accounte, for saynt
    Charyte.
   COSYN. What, to go thyder! Is that the
    mater?
Nay, Everyman, I had lever[5] fast[6] brede and
    water,
All this fyve yere and more.
   EVERYMAN. Alas, that ever I was bore[7],
For now shall I never be mery,
If that you forsake me.   350
   KYNREDE. A! syr, what, ye be a mery man!
Take good herte to you, and make no mone.
But one thynge I warne you, by saynt Anne,
As for me ye shall go alone.
   EVERYMAN. My Cosyn, wyll you not with
    me go?
   COSYN. No, by our Lady! I have the crampe
    in my to:
Trust not to me; for, so God me spede,

I wyll deceyve you in your moost nede.
   KYNREDE. It avayleth not us to tyse[8]:   359
Ye shall have my mayde, with all my herte;
She loveth to go to feestes there to be nyse[9],
And to daunce, and a brode to sterte[10],
I wyll gyve her leve to helpe you in that
    journey,
If that you and she may a gree.
   EVERYMAN. Now shewe me the very effecte
    of your mynde;
Wyll you go with me, or abyde be hynde?
   KYNREDE. Abyde behynde! ye[11], that wyll
    I and I maye;
Therfore farewell tyll another daye.
   EVERYMAN. Howe sholde I be mery or gladde?
For fayre promyses men to me make,   370
But, whan I have moost nede, they me for-
    sake;
I am deceyved, that maketh me sadde.
   COSYN. Cosyn Everyman, farewell now,
For, veryly, I wyll not go with you.
Also of myne owne an unredy rekenynge
I have to accounte, therfore I make taryenge;
Now God kepe the, for now I go.
   EVERYMAN. A! Jesus, is all come here to?
Lo, fayre wordes maketh fooles fayne;   379
They promyse, and nothynge wyll do certayne.
My kynnesmen promysed me faythfully
For to a byde with me stedfastly;
And now fast a waye do they flee;
Even so Felawshyp promysed me.
What frende were best me of to provyde?
I lose my tyme here longer to abyde;
Yet in my mynde a thynge there is,—
All my lyfe I have loved ryches;
Yf that my Good now helpe me myght,
He wolde make my herte full lyght;   390
I wyll speke to hym in this dystresse,—
Where arte thou, my Gooddes and Ryches?
   GOODES. Who calleth me? Everyman? What
    hast thou haste?
I lye here in corners, trussed and pyled so hye,
And in chestes I am locked so fast,
Also sacked in bagges, thou mayst se with thyn
    eye,
I can not styre; in packes lowe I lye.
What wolde ye have? Lyghtly me saye.
   EVERYMAN. Come hyder, Good, in al the hast
    thou may,
For of counseyll I must desyre the.   400
   GOODES. Syr, and ye in the worlde have
    sorowe or adversyte,
That can I helpe you to remedy shortly.
   EVERYMAN. It is another dysease that greveth
    me;

---

2 nature, kinship
3 walk (i. e., will do all
   in its power)
4 is lying in wait for me
5 rather
6 fast on
7 born
8 entice
9 wanton
10 abroad to run
11 yea

In this worlde it is not, I tell the so,
I am sent for an other way to go,
To gyve a strayte counte generall
Before the hyest Jupyter of all.
And all my lyfe I have had joye and pleasure
  in the,
Therfore I pray the go with me;
For, paraventure, thou mayst before God al-
  myghty   410
My rekenynge helpe to clene, and puryfye,
For it is sayd ever amonge[1]
That money maketh all ryght that is wronge.
  GOODES. Nay, Everyman, I synge an other
    songe;
I folowe no man in suche vyages,
For, and I wente with the,
Thou sholdes fare moche the worse for me:
For bycause on me thou dyd set thy mynde,
Thy rekenynge I have made blotted and blynde,
That thyne accounte thou can not make truly;
And that hast thou for the love of me.   421
  EVERYMAN. That wolde greve me full sore,
Whan I sholde come to that ferefull answere.
Up! let us go thyther to gyder.
  GOODES. Nay, not so: I am to brytell[2], I
    may not endure:
I wyll folowe [no] man one fote be ye sure.
  EVERYMAN. Alas, I have the loved, and had
    grete pleasure
All my lyfe dayes on good and treasure.
  GOODES. That is to thy dampnacyon without
    lesynge[3],   429
For my love is contrary to the love ever-
  lastynge;
But yf thou had me loved moderately durynge[4]
As to the poore gyve parte of me,
Than sholdest thou not in this dolour be,
Nor in this grete sorowe and care.
  EVERYMAN. Lo, now was I deceyved or I
    was ware,
And all I may wyte[5] my spendynge of tyme.
  GOODES. What, wenest thou that I am thyne?
  EVERYMAN. I had went[6] so.
  GOODES. Naye, Everyman, I saye no:
As for a whyle I was lente the;   440
A season thou hast had me in prosperyte;
My condycyon is mannes soule to kyll,
If I save one a thousande I do spyll[7].
Wenest thou that I wyll folowe the?
Nay, fro this worlde not veryle.
  EVERYMAN. I had wende otherwyse.
  GOODES. Therfore to thy soule Good is a
    thefe,
For whan thou arte deed, this is my gyse[8]:

Another to deceyve in this same wyse
As I have done the, and all to his soules
  reprefe[9].   450
  EVERYMAN. O false Good, cursed thou be,
Thou traytour to God, that hast deceyved me
And caught me in thy snare.
  GOODES. Mary[10], thou brought thy self in care,
Wherof I am gladde;
I must nedes laugh, I can not be sadde.
  EVERYMAN. A! Good, thou hast had longe
    my hertely love;
I gave the that whiche sholde be the Lordes
  above:
But wylte thou not go with me in dede?
I praye the trouth to saye.   460
  GOODES. No, so God me spede;
Therfore fare well, and have good daye.
  EVERYMAN. O to whome shall I make my
    mone
For to go with me in that hevy journaye?
Fyrst Felawshyp sayd he wolde with me gone;
His wordes were very pleasaunte and gaye,
But afterwarde he lefte me alone.
Than spake I to my kynnesmen all in despayre,
And also they gave me wordes fayre,—
They lacked no fayre spekynge;   470
But all forsake me in the endynge.
Than wente I to my Goodes, that I loved best,
In hope to have comforte, but there had I
  leest;
For my Goodes sharpely dyd me tell
That he bryngeth many in to hell.
Than of my selfe I was ashamed,
And so I am worthy to be blamed.
Thus may I well my selfe hate.
Of whome shall I now counseyll take?
I thynke that I shall never spede
Tyll that I go to my Good-dede.
But, alas, she is so weke
That she can nother go[11] nor speke.
Yet wyll I venter on her now.—
My Good-dedes, where be you?
  GOOD-DEDES. Here I lye, colde in the grounde;
Thy synnes hath me sore bounde
That I can not stere[12].
  EVERYMAN. O Good-dedes, I stande in fere;
I must you pray of counseyll,   490
For helpe now sholde come ryght well.
  GOOD-DEDES. Everyman, I have understandynge
That ye be somoned a counte to make
Before Myssyas[13] of Jherusalem kynge,
And you do by me[14] that journay with you wyll
  I take.

1 everywhere   4 the whyle
2 brittle   5 blame to
3 without lying, i, e., 6 thought
    truly   7 destroy

8 custom
9 reproof
10 An oath by the Virgin
    Mary.
11 neither walk
12 stir

13 Messiah
14 if you will act by my
    advice (Pollard. Or
    possibly by = buy,
    ransom: if you de-
    liver me.)

EVERYMAN. Therefore I come to you my
moone to make.
I pray you that ye wyll go with me.
GOOD-DEDES. I wolde full fayne, but I can
not stande veryly.
EVERYMAN. Why, is there ony thynge on
you fall?
GOOD-DEDES. Ye, syr, I may thanke you of
all.   500
If ye had parfytely chered[1] me,
Your boke of counte full redy had be.
Loke, the bokes of your workes and dedes eke
A! se how they lye under the fete,
To your soules hevynes.
EVERYMAN. Our Lord Jesus, helpe me,
For one letter here I can not se.
GOOD-DEDES. There is a blynde rekenynge in
tyme of dystress.
EVERYMAN. Good-dedes, I praye you helpe
me in this nede,
Or elles I am for ever dampned in dede;   510
Therfore helpe me to make rekenynge
Before the Redemer of all thynge,
That kynge is, and was, and ever shall.
GOOD-DEDES. Everyman, I am sory of your
fall,
And fayne wolde I helpe you, and I were
able.
EVERYMAN. Good-dedes, your counseyll I
pray you gyve me.
GOOD-DEDES. That shall I do veryly,
Thoughe that on my fete I may not go.
I have a syster that shall with you also,   519
Called Knowledge, whiche shall with you abyde,
To help you to make that dredefull rekenynge.
KNOWLEDGE. Everyman, I wyll go with the,
and be thy gyde,
In thy moost nede to go by thy syde.
EVERYMAN. In good condycyon I am now in
every thynge,
And am hole content with this good thynge,
Thanked by[2] God my creature[3].
GOOD-DEDES. And whan he hath brought you
there,
Where thou shalte hele the of thy smarte,
Than go you with your rekenynge and your
good dedes togyder,
For to make you joyfull at herte   530
Before the blessyd Trynyte.
EVERYMAN. My Good-dedes, gramercy;
I am well content certaynly
With your wordes swete.
KNOWLEDGE. Now go we togyder lovyngly
To Confessyon, that clensynge ryvere.
EVERYMAN. For joy I wepe: I wolde we
were there;

But, I pray you, gyve me cognycyon[4]
Where dwelleth that holy man Confessyon?
KNOWLEDGE. In the hous of salvacyon;   540
We shall fynde hym in that place,
That shall us comforte by Goddes grace.—
Lo, this is Confessyon; knele downe, & aske
mercy,
For he is in good conceyte[5] with God almyghty.
EVERYMAN. O gloryous fountayne that all
unclennes doth claryfy,
Wasshe fro me the spottes of vyce unclene,
That on me no synne may be sene;
I come with Knowlege for my redempcyon,
Redempte with herte and full contrycyon,   549
For I am commaunded a pylgrymage to take,
And grete accountes before God to make.
Now I praye you, Shryfte[6], moder of sal-
vacyon,
Helpe my good dedes for my pyteous ex-
clamacyon.
CONFESSYON. I knowe your sorowe well,
Everyman:
Bycause with Knowlege ye come to me,
I wyll you comforte as well as I can;
And a precyous jewell I wyll gyve the,
Called penaunce, [voyce] voyder[7] of adversyte;
Therwith shall your body chastysed be
With abstynence and perseveraunce in Goddes
servyce: 560
Here shall you receyve that scourge of me
Whiche is penaunce stronge that ye must en-
dure,
To remembre thy Savyour was scourged for the
With sharpe scourges, and suffred it pacyently;
So must thou, or thou scape that paynful
pylgrymage.—
Knowledge, kepe hym in this vyage,
And by that tyme Good-dedes wyll be with
the;
But in ony wyse be seker of mercy,
For your tyme draweth fast; and ye wyll saved
be,
Aske God mercy, and he wyll graunte truely:
Whan with the scourge of penaunce man doth
hym bynde,   571
The oyle of forgyvenes than shall he fynde.
EVERYMAN. Thanked be God for his gracyous
werke,
For now I wyll my penaunce begyn;
This hath rejoysed and lyghted my herte,
Though the knottes be paynfull and harde
within.
KNOWLEDGE. Everyman, loke your penaunce
that ye fulfyll,
What payne that ever it to you be;

1 entertained
2 be   3 creator

4 information
5 favor   7 expeller (voyce is prob-
6 absolution   ably an error)

And Knowledge shall gyve you counseyll at
    wyll,
How your accounte ye shall make clerely. 580
  EVERYMAN. O eternall God, O hevenly fygure,
O way of ryghtwysnes, O goodly vysyon,
Whiche descended downe in a vyrgyn pure
Because he wolde Everyman redeme,
Whiche Adam forfayted by his dysobedyence,
O blessyd Godheed, electe and hye devyne,
Forgyve my grevous offence;
Here I crye the mercy in this presence;
O ghostly treasure, O raunsomer and redemer!
Of all the worlde, hope and conduyter[1],   590
Myrrour of joye, foundatour[2] of mercy,
Whiche enlumyneth heven and erth therby,
Here my clamorous complaynt, though it late
  be!
Receyve my prayers; unworthy in this hevy
  lyfe
Though I be, a synner moost abhomynable,
Yet let my name be wryten in Moyses table.[3]
O Mary, praye to the maker of all thynge
Me for to helpe at my endynge,
And save me fro the power of my enemy;
For Deth assayleth me strongly: 600
And, Lady, that I may by meane of thy prayer
Of your sones glory to be partynere,
By the meanes of his passyon[4], I it crave;
I beseche you, helpe my soule to save!—
Knowledge, gyve me the scourge of penaunce,
My flesshe therwith shall gyve acqueyntaunce;
I wyll now begyn, yf God gyve me grace.
  KNOWLEDGE. Everyman, God gyve you tyme
    and space;
Thus I bequeth you in the handes of our
    Savyour;
Now may ye make your rekenynge sure. 610
  EVERYMAN. In the name of the holy Trynyte
My body sore punysshyd shall be,
Take this, body, for the synne of the flesshe;
Also thou delytest to go gay and fresshe;
And in the way of dampnacyon thou dyd me
  brynge;
Therfore suffre now strokes of punysshynge;
Now of penaunce I wyll wade the water clere,
To save me from purgatory, that sharpe fyre.
  GOOD-DEDES. I thanke God, now I can walke
    and go,   619
And am delyvered of my sykenesse and wo:
Therfore with Everyman I wyll go, and not
  spare.
His good workes I wyll helpe hym to declare.
  KNOWLEDGE. Now, Everyman, be mery and
    glad;

Your Good-dedes cometh now, ye may not be
  sad;
Now is your Good-dedes hole and sounde,
Goynge upryght upon the grounde.
  EVERYMAN. My herte is lyght, and shalbe
    evermore;
Now wyll I smyte faster than I dyde before.
  GOOD-DEDES. Everyman, pylgryme, my spe-
    cyall frende,
Blessyd be thou without ende;   630
For the is preparate the eternall glory.
Ye have me made hole and sounde,
Therfore I will byde by the in every stounde[5].
  EVERYMAN. Welcome, my Good-dedes! Now
    I here thy voyce
I wepe for very sweteness of love.
  KNOWLEDGE. Be no more sad, but ever rejoyce.
God seeth thy lyvynge in his trone above;
Put on this garment to thy behove[6],
Whiche is wette with your teres,
Or elles before God you may it mysse,   640
Whan ye to your journeys ende come shall.
  EVERYMAN. Gentyll Knowledge, what do ye
    it call?
  KNOWLEDGE. It is a garmente of sorowe,
Fro payne it wyll you borowe[7];
Contrycyon it is,
That getteth forgyvenes,
He pleasyth God passynge well.
  GOOD-DEDES. Everyman, wyll you were it for
    your hele[8]?
  EVERYMAN. Now blessyd be Jesu, Maryes
    sone,
For now have I on true contrycyon,   650
And lette us go now without taryenge.—
Good-dedes, have we clere our rekenynge?
  GOOD-DEDES. Ye, in dede, I have here.
  EVERYMAN. Than I trust we nede not fere.
Now, frendes, let us not parte in twayne.
  KYNREDE.[9] Nay, Everyman, that wyll we not
    certayne.
  GOOD-DEDES. Yet must thou led[10] with t
Thre persones of grete myght.
  EVERYMAN. Who sholde they be?
  GOOD-DEDES. Dyscrecyon and Strength they
    hyght[11],   660
And thy Beaute may not abyde behynde.
  KNOWLEDGE. Also ye must call to mynde
Your Fyve-wyttes[12], as for your counseylours.
  GOOD-DEDES. You must have them redy at
    all houres.
  EVERYMAN. Howe shall I gette them hyder?

---

1 leader
2 founder
3 Apparently meaning
  the Book of Life
4 death on the cross

5 hour
6 profit
7 redeem
8 wear it for your heal-
  ing
9 Probably error for
  KNOWLEDGE
10 lead
11 are called
12 The five senses

KYNREDE. You must call them all togyder,
And they wyll here you in contynent[1].

EVERYMAN. My frendes, come hyder, and be present,
Dyscrecyon, Strengthe, my Fyve-wyttes and Beaute.

BEAUTE. Here at your wyll we be all redy.
What wyll ye that we sholde do?   671

GOOD-DEDES. That ye wolde with Everyman go,
And helpe hym in his pylgrymage.
Advyse you, wyll ye with him or not in that vyage?

STRENGTHE. We wyll brynge hym all thyder
To his helpe and comforte, ye may beleve me.

DYSCRECYON. So wyll we go with hym all togyder.

EVERYMAN. Almyghty God, loved myght thou be;
I gyve the laude[2] that I have hyder brought
Strength, Dyscrecyon, Beaute, & Fyve-wyttes, lacke I nought: 680
And my Good-dedes, with Knowledge clere,
All be in my company at my wyll here;
I desyre no more to my besynes.

STRENGTHE. And I, Strength, wyll by you stande in dystres,
Though thou wolde in batayle fyght on the ground.

FYVE-WYTTES. And though it were thrugh the worlde rounde,
We wyll not departe for swete ne soure,

BEAUTE. No more wyll I unto dethes houre,
What so ever therof befall.

DYSCRECYON. Everyman, advyse you fyrst of all,   690
Go with a good advysement and delyberacyon.
We all gyve you vertuous monycyon[3]
That all shall be well.

EVERYMAN. My frendes, harken what I wyll tell;
I praye God rewarde you in his heven spere.
Now herken all that be here,
For I wyll make my testament
Here before you all present;
In almes, halfe my good I wyll gyve with my handes twayne
In the way of charyte with good entent,   700
And the other halfe styll shall remayne
In queth[4] to be retourned there[5] it ought to be.
This I do in despyte of the fende of hell,
To go quyte out of his perell[6]
Ever after and this daye.

KNOWLEDGE. Everyman, herken what I saye;
Go to presthode I you advyse,
And receyve of him in ony wyse
The holy sacrament and oyntement togyder,
Than shortly se ye tourne agayne hyder,   710
We wyll all abyde you here.

FYVE-WYTTES. Ye, Everyman, hye you that ye redy were[7].
There is no Emperour, King, Duke, ne Baron
That of God hath commycyon
As hath the leest preest in the worlde beynge[8];
For of the blessyd sacramentes pure and benynge
He bereth the keyes, and thereof hath the cure[9].
For mannes redempcyon it is ever sure
Whiche God for our soules medycyne   719
Gave us out of his herte with grete payne.
Here in this transytory lyfe, for the and me
The blessyd sacramentes vii. there be:
Baptym, confyrmacyon, with preesthode good,
And the sacrament of Goddes precyous flesshe and blod,
Maryage, the holy extreme unccyon[10] and penaunce:
These seven be good to have in remembraunce,
Gracyous sacramentes of hye devynyte.

EVERYMAN. Fayne wolde I receyve that holy body
And mekely to my ghostly fader I wyll go.

FYVE-WYTTES. Everyman, that is the best that ye can do;   730
God wyll you to salvacyon brynge,
For preesthode excedeth all other thyng
To us holy scrypture they do teche,
And converteth man fro synne, heven to reche;
God hath to them more power gyven
Than to ony aungell that is in heven.
With v. wordes he may consecrate
Goddes body in flesshe and blode to make,
And handeleth his Maker bytwene his handes.
The preest byndeth and unbyndeth all bandes
Both in erthe and in heven.   741
Thou mynystres[11] all the sacramentes seven.
Though we kysse thy fete thou were worthy.
Thou arte surgyon that cureth synne deedly.
No remedy we fynde under God
Bute all onely preesthode.
Every man, God gave preest that dygnyte
And setteth them in his stede amonge us to be.
Thus be they above aungelles in degree.

KNOWLEDGE. If preestes be good, it is so suerly,   750
But whan Jesu hanged on the crosse with grete smarte,
There he gave out of his blessyd herte
The same sacrament in grete tourment;

---

1 without delay
2 praise
3 admonition
4 under promise
5 where
6 out of his power
7 haste that ye may be ready
8 living
9 care
10 last anointing
11 administerest

He solde them not to us, that Lorde omnyp-
otent;
Therfore saynt Peter the apostell dothe saye
That Jesus curse hath all they
Whiche God theyr Savyour do by[1] or sell,
Or they for[2] ony money do take or tell[3].
Synfull preestes gyveth the synners example
bad; . . .
These be with synne made blynde.   763
   FYVE-WYTTES. I trust to God, no suche may
we fynde;
Therfore let us preesthode honour,
And folowe theyr doctryne for our soules
socoure.
We be theyr shepe, and they shepeherdes be,
By whome we all be kepte in suerte.—
Peas! for yonder I se Everyman come,
Which hath made true satysfaccyon.   770
   GOOD-DEDES. Me thynke, it is he in dede.
   EVERYMAN. Now Jesu be your alder spede[4]!
I have receyved the sacrament for my re-
dempcyon,
And than myne extreme unccyon.
Blessyd be all they that counseyled me to take
it!
And now frendes, let us go without longer
respyte.
I thanke God, that ye have taryed so longe.
Now set eche of you on this rodde[5] your
honde,
And shortely folowe me.
I go before there I wolde be. God be your
gyde.   780
   STRENGTH. Everyman, we wyll not fro you go
Tyll we have done this vyage longe.
   DYSCRECYON. I, Dyscrecyon, wyll byde by
you also.
   KNOWLEDGE. And though this pylgrymage be
never so stronge[6]
I wyll never parte you fro.
Everyman, I wyll be as sure by the
As ever I dyde by Judas Machabee[7].
   EVERYMAN. Alas! I am so faynt I may not
stande,
My lymmes under me doth folde.
Frendes, let us not tourne agayne to this lande,
Not for all the worldes golde,   791
For in to this cave must I crepe,
And tourne to erth and there to slepe.
   BEAUTE. What, in to this grave, alas!
   EVERYMAN. Ye, there shall ye consume, more
and lesse.[8]

   BEAUTE. And what, sholde I smoder here?
   EVERYMAN. Ye, by my fayth, and never more
appere!
In this worlde lyve no more we shall,
But in heven before the hyest Lorde of all.
   BEAUTE. I crosse out all this! adewe, by
saynt Johan!   800
I take my tappe[9] in my lappe, and am gone.
   EVERYMAN. What, Beaute, whyder wyll ye?
   BEAUTE. Peas! I am defe, I loke not be-
hynde me,
Not and thou woldest gyve me all the golde
in thy chest.
   EVERYMAN. Alas! whereto may I truste?
Beaute gothe fast awaye fro me.
She promysed with me to lyve and dye.
   STRENGTHE. Everyman, I wyll the also for-
sake and denye,
Thy game lyketh[10] me not at all.
   EVERYMAN. Why than ye wyll forsake me
all!   810
Swete Strength, tary a lytell space.
   STRENGTHE. Nay, syr, by the rode of grace,
I wyll hye me from the fast,
Though thou wepe to[11] thy herte to brast[12].
   EVERYMAN. Ye wolde ever byde by me, ye
sayd.
   STRENGTHE. Ye, I have you ferre[13] ynoughe
conveyde.
Ye be olde ynoughe, I understande,
Your pylgrymage to take on hande.
I repent me, that I hyder came.
   EVERYMAN. Strength, you to dysplease I am
to blame;   820
Wyll ye breke promyse that is dette[14]?
   STRENGTHE. In fayth, I care not!
Thou arte but a foole to complayne;
You spende your speche, and wast your brayne;
Go, thryst[15] the into the grounde!
   EVERYMAN. I had wende[16] surer I shulde
you have founde:
He that trusteth in his Strength,
She hym deceyveth at the length;
Bothe Strength and Beaute forsaketh me,
Yet they promysed me fayre and lovyngly. 830
   DYSCRECION. Everyman, I wyll after Strength
be gone;
As for me I wyll leve you alone.
   EVERYMAN. Why, Dyscrecyon, wyll ye for-
sake me?
   DYSCRECION. Ye, in fayth, I wyll go fro the;
For whan Strength goth before,
I folowe after ever more.

[1] buy
[2] Possibly *they for* should be *therfor*.
[3] count
[4] the help of you all
[5] rood, cross
[6] difficult
[7] Leader of the Jews against the Syrians in the recovery of Jerusalem, 164 B. C. See I. *Maccabees*, iii.
[8] high and low alike
[9] bunch of tow (for spinning: an old wives' saying)
[10] pleases
[11] until
[12] break to pieces
[13] far
[14] See l. 248.
[15] thrust
[16] weened, thought

EVERYMAN. Yet, I pray the, for the love of the Trynyte,

Loke in my grave ones pyteously.

DYSCRECION. Nay, so nye wyll I not come!

Fare well, everychone.[1] 840

EVERYMAN. O all thynge fayleth, save God alone,

Beaute, Strength, and Dyscrecyon;

For, whan Deth bloweth his blast,

They all renne fro me full fast.

FYVE-WYTTES. Everyman, my leve now of the I take;

I wyll folowe the other, for here I the forsake.

EVERYMAN. Alas, than may I wayle and wepe,

For I toke you for my best frende.

FYVE-WYTTES. I wyll no lenger the kepe; 850

Now farewell, and there an ende.

EVERYMAN. O Jesu, helpe! all hath forsaken me.

GOOD-DEDES. Nay, Everyman, I wyll byde with the,

I wyll not forsake the in dede;

Thou shalte fynde me a good frende at nede.

EVERYMAN. Gramercy, Good-dedes, now may I true frendes se;

They have forsaken me everychone,

I loved them better than my Good-dedes alone.

Knowlege, wyll ye forsake me also?

KNOWLEDGE. Ye, Everyman, whan ye to deth shall go;

But not yet for no maner of daunger. 860

EVERYMAN. Gramercy, Knowledge, with all my herte.

KNOWLEDGE. Nay, yet I wyll not from hens[2] departe,

Tyll I se where ye shall be come.

EVERYMAN. Me thynke, alas, that I must be gone

To make my rekenynge and my dettes paye;

For I se my tyme is nye spent awaye.—

Take example, all ye that this do here or se,

How they that I love best do forsake me,

Excepte my Good-dedes, that bydeth truely.

GOOD-DEDES. All erthly thynges is but vanyte, 870

Beaute, Strength, and Dyscrecyon, do man forsake,

Folysshe frendes, and kynnesmen that fayre spake,

All fleeth save Good-dedes and that am I.

EVERYMAN. Have mercy on me, God moost myghty,—

And stande by me, thou moder & mayde, holy Mary.

GOOD-DEDES. Fere not, I wyll speke for the.

EVERYMAN. Here I crye, God mercy.

GOOD-DEDES. Shorte[3] our ende and mynysshe[4] our payne;

Let us go and never come agayne.

EVERYMAN. Into thy handes, Lorde, my soule I commende, 880

Receyve it, Lorde, that it be not lost!

As thou me boughtest, so me defende,

And save me from the fendes boost[5],

That I may appere with that blessyd hoost

That shall be saved at the day of dome.

In manus tuas[6], of myghtes moost,

For ever commendo spiritum meum[7].

KNOWLEDGE. Now hath he suffred that[8] we all shall endure,

The Good-dedes shall make all sure.

Now hath he made endynge, 890

Me thynketh that I here aungelles synge,

And make grete joy and melody,

Where every mannes soule receyved shall be.

THE AUNGELL. Come excellente electe spouse to Jesu!

Here above thou shalt go,

Bycause of thy synguler vertue.

Now the soule is taken the body fro

Thy rekenynge is crystall clere;

Now shalte thou in to the hevenly spere,

Unto the whiche all ye shall come 900

That lyveth well before the daye of dome.

DOCTOUR.* This morall, men may have in mynde;

Ye herers, take it of worth, olde and yonge,

And forsake Pryde, for he deceyveth you in the ende,

And remembre Beaute, Fyve-wyttes, Strength, and Dyscrecyon,

They all at the last do Everyman forsake,

Save[9] his Good-dedes there doth he take.

But be ware, and[10] they be small,

Before God he hath no helpe at all.

None excuse may be there for Everyman! 910

Alas! how shall he do than?

For after dethe amendes may no man make,

For than mercy and pyte doth hym forsake.

If his rekenynge be not clere whan he doth come,

God wyll saye—Ite maledicti, in ignem aeternum[11].

And he that hath his accounte hole and sounde

Hye in heven he shall be crounde;

3 shorten   8 what
4 diminish   9 only
5 fiend's boast   10 for if
6 into Thy hands   11 go, ye accursed, into
7 I commend my spirit   everlasting fire
* To the Doctour (i. e., learned man, or teacher)
   is assigned the epilogue, which emphasizes the
   moral of the play.

Unto whiche place God brynge us all thyder,
That we may lyve body and soule togyder!
Therto helpe the Trynyte!   920
Amen, saye ye, for saynt Charyte!

FINIS

Thus endeth this morall playe of Everyman.

WILLIAM CAXTON (1422?-1491)

THE RECUYELL OF THE HISTORIES OF TROY.*

PROLOGUE

When I remember that every man is bounden by the commandment and counsel of the wise man to eschew sloth and idleness, which is mother and nourisher of vices, and ought to put myself unto virtuous occupation and business, then I, having no great change of occupation, following the said counsel took a French book, and read therein many strange and marvellous histories[1], wherein I had great pleasure and delight, as well for the novelty of the same, as for the fair language of the French, which was in prose so well and compendiously set and written, which methought I understood the sentence[2] and substance of every matter. And for so much of this book was new and late made and drawn into French, and never had seen it in our English tongue, I thought in myself it should be a good business to translate it into our English, to the end that it might be had as well in the royaume[3] of England as in other lands, and also for to pass therewith the time, and thus concluded in myself to begin this said work. And forthwith took pen and ink, and began boldly to run forth as blind Bayard† in this present work, which is named ''The Recuyell of the Trojan Histories.'' And afterward when I remembered myself of my simpleness and unperfectness that I had in both languages, that is to wit in French and in English, for in France was I never, and was born and learned my English in Kent, in the Weald, where I doubt not is spoken as broad and rude English as in any place of England; and have continued by the space of thirty years for the most part in the countries of Brabant, Flanders, Holland, and Zealand; and thus when all these things came before me, after that[4] I had made and written five or six quires, I fell in despair of this work, and purposed no more to have continued therein, and those laid apart, and in two years after labored no more in this work, and was fully in will to have left it, till on a time it fortuned that the right high, excellent, and right virtuous princess, my right redoubted Lady, my Lady Margaret, by the grace of God sister unto the King of England and of France, my sovereign lord, Duchess of Burgundy, of Lotryk, of Brabant, of Limburg, and of Luxembourg, Countess of Flanders, of Artois, and of Burgundy, Palatine of Hainault, of Holland, of Zealand, and of Namur, Marquesse of the Holy Empire, Lady of Frisia, of Salins, and of Mechlin, sent for me to speak with her good Grace of divers matters, among the which I let her Highness have knowledge of the foresaid beginning of this work, which[5] anon commanded me to show the said five or six quires to her said Grace; and when she had seen them, anon she found a default in my English, which she commanded me to amend, and moreover commanded me straitly[6] to continue and make an end of the residue then not translated; whose dreadful[7] commandment I durst in no wise disobey, because I am a servant unto her said Grace and receive of her yearly fee and other many good and great benefits, (and also hope many more to receive of her Highness), but forthwith went and labored in the said translation after my simple and poor cunning, also[8] nigh as I can follow my author, meekly beseeching the bounteous Highness of my said Lady that of her benevolence list[9] to accept and take in gree[10] this simple and rude work here following; and if there be anything written or said to her pleasure, I shall think my labor well employed, and whereas[11] there is default, that she arette[12] it to the simpleness of my cunning, which is full small in this behalf; and require and pray all them that shall read this said work to correct it, and to hold me excused of the rude and simple translation.

And thus I end my prologue.

EPILOGUE TO BOOK III.

Thus end I this book, which I have translated after mine Author as nigh as God hath

---

1 stories
2 sense   3 realm
* ''The collection of the stories of Troy.'' This book, printed at Bruges in Flanders about 1474, was the first book printed in English. See *Eng. Lit.*, p. 68. The spelling is here modernized.
† A legendary horse in the Charlemagne romances. ''As bold as blind Bayard'' was an old proverb for recklessness.

4 after
5 who
6 strictly
7 revered
8 just as
9 she please
10 graciously
11 where
12 may she attribute

given me cunning, to whom be given the laud and praising. And for as much as in the writing of the same my pen is worn, my hand weary and not steadfast, mine eyne dimmed with overmuch looking on the white paper, and my courage not so prone and ready to labor as it hath been, and that age creepeth on me daily and feebleth all the body, and also because I have promised to divers gentlemen and to my friends to address[13] to them as hastily as I might this said book, therefore I have practised and learned at my great charge and dispense to ordain[14] this said book in print, after the manner and form as ye may here see, and is not written with pen and ink as other books be; to the end that every man may have them at once. For all the books of this story, named "The Recule of the Histories of Troy" thus imprinted as ye here see, were begun in one day and also finished in one day, which book I have presented to my said redoubted Lady, as afore is said. And she hath well accepted it, and largely rewarded me, wherefore I beseech Almighty God to reward her said Grace with everlasting bliss after this life, praying her said Grace and all them that shall read this book not to disdain the simple and rude work, neither to reply against the saying of the matters touched in this book, though it accord not unto the translation of others which have written it. For divers men have made divers books which in all points accord not, as Dictes, Dares,[15] and Homer. For Dictes and Homer, as Greeks, say and write favorably for the Greeks, and give them more worship than to the Trojans; and Dares writeth otherwise than they do. And also as for the proper names, it is no wonder that they accord not, for some one name in these days have divers equivocations after the countries that they dwell in; but all accord in conclusion the general destruction of that noble city of Troy, and the death of so many noble princes, as kings, dukes, earls, barons, knights, and common people, and the ruin irreparable of that city that never since was re-edified; which may be example to all men during the world how dreadful and jeopardous it is to begin a war, and what harms, losses, and death followeth. Therefore the Apostle saith: "All that is written is written to our doctrine[16]," which doctrine for the common weal I beseech God may be taken in such place and time as shall be most needful in increasing of peace, love, and charity; which grant us He that suffered for the same to be crucified on the rood tree. And say we all Amen for charity!

SIR THOMAS MALORY (d. 1471)

FROM LE MORTE DARTHUR.*

HOW ARTHUR WAS CHOSEN KING. BOOK I, CHAPTERS IV-VII

And then King Uther fell passing[1] sore sick, so that three days and three nights he was speechless: wherefore all the barons made great sorrow, and asked Merlin what counsel were best. There is none other remedy, said Merlin, but God will have his will. But look ye all barons be before King Uther to-morn, and God and I shall make him to speak. So on the morn all the barons with Merlin came before the king; then Merlin said aloud unto King Uther, Sir, shall your son Arthur be king after your days, of this realm with all the appurtenance? Then Uther Pendragon turned him, and said in hearing of them all, I give him God's blessing and mine, and bid him pray for my soul, and righteously and worshipfully that he claim the crown, upon forfeiture of my blessing; and therewith he yielded up the ghost, and then was he interred as longed to a king. Wherefore the queen, fair Igraine, made great sorrow, and all the barons.

Then stood the realm in great jeopardy long while, for every lord that was mighty of men made him strong, and many weened to have been king. Then Merlin went to the Archbishop of Canterbury, and counselled him for to send for all the lords of the realm, and all the gentlemen of arms, that they should to London come by Christmas, upon pain of cursing; and for this cause, that Jesus, that was born on that night, that he would of his great mercy show some miracle, as he was come to be

---

13 send
14 prepare
15 Reputed authors of Trojan tales which are found only in late Latin, and
which, though popular in the Middle Ages, have sunk into obscurity
16 for our instruction

1 exceeding (surpassing)
2 A magician, Arthur's adviser.
* Of the hundred books printed by Caxton, this was in every way one of the most important —in size, in intrinsic literary value, and in the influence it was destined to have upon succeeding literature. Its author compiled it out of the enormous amount of material which had grown up in Western Europe about the legends of King Arthur and the Holy Grail, drawing mainly from French sources, but bringing to it original constructive and imaginative elements and in particular an admirable narrative style. See *Eng. Lit.*, p. 68. The spelling of our text, as in all the succeeding prose of this volume, is modernized.

king of mankind, for to show some miracle who should be rightwise king of this realm. So the Archbishop, by the advice of Merlin, sent for all the lords and gentlemen of arms that they should come by Christmas even unto London. And many of them made them clean of their life[3], that their prayer might be the more acceptable unto God.

So in the greatest church of London, whether it were Paul's* or not the French book maketh no mention, all the estates[4] were long or[5] day in the church for to pray. And when matins and the first mass was done, there was seen in the churchyard, against the high altar, a great stone four square, like unto a marble stone, and in midst thereof was like an[6] anvil of steel a foot on high, and therein stuck a fair sword, naked, by the point, and letters there were written in gold about the sword that said thus: —Whoso pulleth out this sword of this stone and anvil, is rightwise king born of all England. Then the people marvelled, and told it to the Archbishop. I command, said the Archbishop, that ye keep you within your church, and pray unto God still; that no man touch the sword till the high mass be all done. So when all masses were done all the lords went to behold the stone and the sword. And when they saw the scripture, some assayed[7]; such as would have been king. But none might stir the sword nor move it. He is not here, said the Archbishop, that shall achieve[8] the sword, but doubt not God will make him known. But this is my counsel, said the Archbishop, that we let purvey[9] ten knights, men of good fame, and they to keep this sword. So it was ordained, and then there was made a cry, that every man should assay that would, for to win the sword.

And upon New Year's Day the barons let make a jousts[10] and a tournament, that all knights that would joust or tourney there might play, and all this was ordained for to keep the lords together and the commons, for the Archbishop trusted that God would make him known that should win the sword. So upon New Year's Day, when the service was done, the barons rode unto the field, some to joust and some to tourney, and so it happened that Sir Ector, that had great livelihood about London, rode unto the jousts, and with him rode Sir Kay his son, and young Arthur that was his nourished[11] brother; and Sir Kay was[12] made knight at All Hallowmass afore.

So as they rode to the jousts-ward, Sir Kay lost his sword, for he had left it at his father's lodging, and so he prayed young Arthur for to ride for his sword. I will well, said Arthur, and rode fast after the sword, and when he came home, the lady and all were out to see the jousting. Then was Arthur wroth, and said to himself, I will ride to the churchyard, and take the sword with me that sticketh in the stone, for my brother Sir Kay shall not be without a sword this day. So when he came to the churchyard, Sir Arthur alit and tied his horse to the stile, and so he went to the tent, and found no knights there, for they were at the jousting; and so he handled the sword by the handles, and lightly and fiercely pulled it out of the stone, and took his horse and rode his way until he came to his brother Sir Kay, and delivered him the sword.

And as soon as Sir Kay saw the sword, he wist[13] well it was the sword of the stone, and so he rode to his father Sir Ector, and said: Sir, lo here is the sword of the stone, wherefore I must be king of this land. When Sir Ector beheld the sword, he returned again and came to the church, and there they alit all three, and went into the church. And anon he made Sir Kay to swear upon a book how he came to that sword. Sir, said Sir Kay, by my brother Arthur, for he brought it to me. How gat ye this sword? said Sir Ector to Arthur. Sir, I will tell you. When I came home for my brother's sword, I found nobody at home to deliver me his sword, and so I thought my brother Sir Kay should not be swordless, and so I came hither eagerly and pulled it out of the stone without any pain. Found ye any knights about this sword? said Sir Ector. Nay, said Arthur. Now, said Sir Ector to Arthur, I understand ye must be king of this land. Wherefore I, said Arthur, and for what cause? Sir, said Ector, for God will have it so, for there should[14] never man have drawn out this sword, but he that shall be rightwise king of this land. Now let me see whether ye can put the sword there as it was, and pull it out again.

3 were shriven of their sins
4 The three estates, clergy, lords, and commons.
5 before
6 a kind of
7 tried
8 attain
9 cause to be provided
10 tilting-match (usually single combat, as distinct from a tourney or tournament).

* The present site of St. Paul's has been occupied by various churches; there is even a tradition that before the introduction of Christianity a temple of Diana stood on the spot. King Ethelbert erected a cathedral there in 607 and dedicated it to St. Paul. It was burned in 1086. Then was built the old St. Paul's which Malory knew, and which lasted until the great fire of 1666, to be followed by the present structure designed by Sir Christopher Wren.

11 foster
12 had been
13 knew
14 could (was fated)

That is no mastery[15], said Arthur, and so he put it in the stone, wherewithal Sir Ector assayed to pull out the sword and failed. Now assay, said Sir Ector unto Sir Kay. And anon he pulled at the sword with all his might, but it would not be.

Now shall ye assay, said Sir Ector to Arthur. I will well, said Arthur, and pulled it out easily. And therewithal Sir Ector knelt down to the earth, and Sir Kay. Alas, said Arthur, my own dear father and brother, why kneel ye to me? Nay, nay, my lord Arthur, it is not so; I was never your father nor of your blood, but I wot well ye are of an higher blood than I weened ye were. And then Sir Ector told him all, how he was betaken[16] him for to nourish him, and by whose commandment, and by Merlin's deliverance. Then Arthur made great dole when he understood that Sir Ector was not his father. Sir, said Ector unto Arthur, will ye be my good and gracious lord when ye are king? Else were I to blame, said Arthur, for ye are the man in the world that I am most beholden to, and my good lady and mother your wife, that as well as her own hath fostered me and kept. And if ever it be God's will that I be king as ye say, ye shall desire of me what I may do, and I shall not fail you, God forbid I should fail you. Sir, said Sir Ector, I will ask no more of you, but that ye will make my son, your foster brother, Sir Kay, seneschal of all your lands. That shall be done, said Arthur, and more, by the faith of my body, that never man shall have that office but he, while he and I live.

Therewithal they went unto the Archbishop, and told him how the sword was achieved, and by whom; and on Twelfth-day[17] all the barons came thither, and to assay to take the sword, who that would assay. But there afore them all, there might none take it out but Arthur; wherefore there were many lords wroth, and said it was a great shame unto them all and the realm, to be overgoverned with a boy of no high blood born, and so they fell out[18] at that time that it was put off till Candlemas[19], and then all the barons should meet there again; but always the ten knights were ordained to watch the sword day and night, and so they set a pavilion over the stone and the sword, and five always watched.

So at Candlemas many more great lords came thither for to have won the sword, but there might none prevail. And right as Arthur did at Christmas, he did at Candlemas, and pulled out the sword easily, whereof the barons were sore aggrieved and put it off in delay till the high feast of Easter. And as Arthur sped[20] before, so did he at Easter, yet there were some of the great lords had indignation that Arthur should be king, and put it off in a delay till the feast of Pentecost. Then the Archbishop of Canterbury by Merlin's providence[21] let purvey then of the best knights that they might get, and such knights as Uther Pendragon loved best and most trusted in his days. And such knights were put about Arthur as Sir Baudwin of Britain, Sir Kay, Sir Ulfius, Sir Brastias. All these with many other were always about Arthur, day and night, till the feast of Pentecost.

And at the feast of Pentecost all manner of men assayed to pull at the sword that would assay, but none might prevail but Arthur, and pulled it out afore all the lords and commons that were there, wherefore all the commons cried at once, We will have Arthur unto our king, we will put him no more in delay, for we all see that it is God's will that he shall be our king, and who that[22] holdeth against it, we will slay him. And therewith all they kneeled at once, both rich and poor, and cried Arthur mercy because they had delayed him so long, and Arthur forgave them, and took the sword between both his hands, and offered it upon the altar, where the Archbishop was, and so was he made knight of[23] the best man that was there. And so anon was the coronation made. And there was he sworn unto his lords and the commons for to be a true king, to stand with true justice from thenceforth the days of this life.

How Arthur by the Mean of Merlin Gat Excalibur His Sword of the Lady of the Lake. Book I, Chapter XXV.

Right so the king and he departed, and went unto an hermit that was a good man and a great leech[24]. So the hermit searched all his wounds and gave him good salves; so the king was there three days, and there were his wounds well amended that he might ride and go[25], and so departed. And as they rode, Arthur said, I have no sword. No force[26], said Merlin, hereby is a sword that shall be yours, an I may[27]. So they rode till they came to a lake, the which was a fair water and broad,

15 feat
16 entrusted to
17 The festival of the Epiphany, twelfth
18 were so dissatisfied
19 Feb. 2.
day after Christmas.
20 succeeded
21 prudence
22 whoever
23 by (viz., the Archbishop)
24 physician
25 walk
26 no matter
27 if I have power

and in the midst of the lake Arthur was ware of an arm clothed in white samite[28], that held a fair sword in that hand. Lo! said Merlin, yonder is that sword that I spake of. With that they saw a damosel going[29] upon the lake. What damosel is that? said Arthur. That is the Lady of the Lake, said Merlin; and within that lake is a rock, and therein is as fair a place as any on earth, and richly beseen[30]; and this damosel will come to you anon, and then speak ye fair to her that she will give you that sword. Anon withal came the damosel unto Arthur, and saluted him, and he her again. Damosel, said Arthur, what sword is that, that yonder the arm holdeth above the water? I would it were mine, for I have no sword. Sir Arthur, king, said the damosel, that sword is mine, and if ye will give me a gift when I ask it you, ye shall have it. By my faith, said Arthur, I will give you what gift ye will ask. Well! said the damosel, go ye into yonder barge, and row yourself to the sword, and take it and the scabbard with you, and I will ask my gift when I see my time. So Sir Arthur and Merlin alit and tied their horses to two trees, and so they went into the ship, and when they came to the sword that the hand held, Sir Arthur took it up by the handles, and took it with him, and the arm and the hand went under the water.

And so they came unto the land and rode forth, and then Sir Arthur saw a rich pavilion. What signifieth yonder pavilion? It is the knight's pavilion, said Merlin, that ye fought with last, Sir Pellinore; but he is out, he is not there. He hath ado with a knight of yours that hight[31] Egglame, and they have foughten together, but at the last Egglame fled, and else he had been dead, and he hath chased him even to Carlion[32], and we shall meet with him anon in the highway. That is well said, said Arthur, now have I a sword, now will I wage battle with him, and be avenged on him. Sir, you shall not so, said Merlin, for the knight is weary of fighting and chasing, so that ye shall have no worship[33] to have ado with him; also he will not be lightly matched of one[34] knight living, and therefore it is my counsel, let him pass, for he shall do you good service in short time, and his sons after his days. Also ye shall see that day in short space, you shall be right glad to give him your sister to wed. When I see him, I will do as ye advise, said Arthur.

Then Sir Arthur looked on the sword, and liked it passing well. Whether liketh[35] you better, said Merlin, the sword or the scabbard? Me liketh better the sword, said Arthur. Ye are more unwise, said Merlin, for the scabbard is worth ten of the swords, for whiles ye have the scabbard upon you, ye shall never lose no blood be ye never so sore wounded, therefore keep well the scabbard always with you. So they rode unto Carlion, and by the way they met with Sir Pellinore; but Merlin had done such a craft[36], that Pellinore saw not Arthur, and he passed by without any words. I marvel, said Arthur, that the knight would not speak. Sir, said Merlin, he saw you not, for an[37] he had seen you, ye had not lightly departed. So they came unto Carlion, whereof his knights were passing glad. And when they heard of his adventures, they marvelled that he would jeopard his person so, alone. But all men of worship said it was merry to be under such a chieftain, that would put his person in adventure as other poor knights did.

How King Arthur Took a Wife, and Wedded Guenever, Daughter to Leodegrance, King of the Land of Cameliard, with Whom He Had the Round Table. Book III, Chapter I

In the beginning of Arthur, after he was chosen king by adventure and by grace, for the most part of the barons knew not that he was Uther Pendragon's son, but as Merlin made it openly known, but yet many kings and lords held great war against him for that cause. But well Arthur overcame them all, for[1] the most part the days of his life he was ruled much by the counsel of Merlin. So it fell on a time King Arthur said unto Merlin, My barons will let me have no rest, but needs I must take a wife, and I will none take but by thy counsel and by thine advice. It is well done, said Merlin, that ye take a wife, for a man of your bounty[2] and noblesse should not be without a wife. Now is there any that ye love more than another? Yea, said King Arthur, I love Guenever the king's daughter, Leodegrance of the land of Cameliard, the which holdeth in his house the Table Round that ye told he had of my father Uther. And this damosel is the most valiant and fairest lady that I know living, or yet that ever I could find. Sir, said Merlin, as of[3] her beauty and fairness she is one of the fairest on live[4], but, an ye loved her not so

---

28 A rich silk fabric.
29 walking
30 appointed
31 is called

32 Carleon-upon-Usk in Wales, one of Arthur's courts.
33 honor
34 by any

35 which pleaseth
36 worked such magic

37 if

1 because
2 prowess

3 as for
4 alive

well as ye do, I should find you a damosel of
beauty and of goodness that should like[5] you
and please you, an your heart were not set;
but there as a man's heart is set, he will be loth
to return. That is truth, said King Arthur.
But Merlin warned the king covertly that
Guenever was not wholesome for him to take
to wife, for he warned him that Launcelot
should love her, and she him again[6]; and so he
turned his tale to the adventures of the Sangreal.

Then Merlin desired of the king for to have
men with him that should enquire of Guenever,
and so the king granted him, and Merlin went
forth unto King Leodegrance of Cameliard,
and told him of the desire of the king that he
would have unto his wife Guenever his daughter. That is to me, said King Leodegrance, the
best tidings that ever I heard, that so worthy
a king of prowess and noblesse will wed my
daughter. And as for my lands, I will give
him, wist I it might please him, but he hath
lands enow, him needeth none, but I shall send
him a gift shall please him much more, for I
shall give him the Table Round, the which
Uther Pendragon gave me, and when it is full
complete, there is an hundred knights and fifty.
And as for an hundred good knights I have
myself, but I fawte[7] fifty, for so many have
been slain in my days. And so Leodegrance delivered his daughter Guenever unto Merlin, and
the Table Round with the hundred knights, and
so they rode freshly[8], with great royalty, what
by water and what by land, till that they came
nigh unto London.

When King Arthur heard of the coming of
Guenever and the hundred knights with the
Table Round, then King Arthur made great
joy for her coming, and that rich present, and
said openly, This fair lady is passing welcome
unto me, for I have loved her long, and therefore there is nothing so lief[9] to me. And these
knights with the Round Table please me more
than right great riches. And in all haste the
king let ordain[10] for the marriage and the
coronation in the most honourable wise that
could be devised.

How an Old Man Brought Galahad to the
Siege Perilous and Set Him Therein.
Book XIII, Chapters I-IV

At the vigil of Pentecost[1], when all the fellowship of the Round Table were come unto
Camelot[2] and there heard their service, and the
tables were set ready to[3] the meat, right so
entered into the hall a full fair gentlewoman
on horseback, that had ridden full fast, for
her horse was all besweated. Then she there
alit, and came before the king and saluted
him; and he said: Damosel, God thee bless.
Sir, said she, for God's sake say me where Sir
Launcelot is. Yonder ye may see him, said
the king. Then she went unto Launcelot and
said: Sir Launcelot, I salute you on King
Pelles' behalf, and I require you to come on
with me hereby into a forest. Then Sir
Launcelot asked her with whom she dwelled.
I dwell, said she, with King Pelles[4]. What will
ye with me? said Launcelot. Ye shall know,
said she, when ye come thither. Well, said he,
I will gladly go with you. So Sir Launcelot
bad his squire saddle his horse and bring his
arms; and in all haste he did his commandment. Then came the queen unto Launcelot,
and said: Will ye leave us at this high feast?
Madam, said the gentlewoman, wit[5] ye well he
shall be with you tomorn[6] by dinner time. If
I wist, said the queen, that he should not be
with us tomorn he should not go with you
by my good will.

Right so departed Sir Launcelot with the
gentlewoman, and rode until that he came into
a forest and into a great valley, where they
saw an abbey of nuns; and there was a squire
ready and opened the gates, and so they entered and descended off their horses; and there
came a fair fellowship about Sir Launcelot,
and welcomed him, and were passing glad of
his coming. And then they led him unto the
Abbess's chamber and unarmed him; and right
so he was ware upon a bed lying two of his
cousins, Sir Bors and Sir Lionel, and then he
waked them; and when they saw him they
made great joy. Sir, said Sir Bors unto Sir
Launcelot, what adventure hath brought you
hither, for we weened tomorn to have found
you at Camelot? As God me help, said Sir
Launcelot, a gentlewoman brought me hither,
but I know not the cause.

In the meanwhile that they thus stood talking together, therein came twelve nuns that
brought with them Galahad,[7] the which was
passing fair and well made, that unnethe[8] in
the world men might not find his match: and
all those ladies wept. Sir, said they all, we
bring you here this child the which we have

---

5 suit
6 in return
7 lack (fault)

8 gaily
9 dear
10 ordered preparation

1 Whitsunday (the seventh Sunday after Easter),
  commemorating the descent of the Holy Spirit
  upon the Apostles.

2 The legendary seat of   of Arimathæa."
    Arthur's court.   (Malory.)
3 for   5 know
4 "King of the foreign   6 to-morrow morning
    country and cousin   7 The son of Launcelot.
    nigh unto Joseph   8 scarcely

nourished, and we pray you to make him a knight, for of a more worthier man's hand may he not receive the order of knighthood. Sir Launcelot beheld the young squire and saw him seemly and demure as a dove, with all manner of good features, that he weened of his age never to have seen so fair a man of form. Then said Sir Launcelot: Cometh this desire of himself? He and all they said yea. Then shall he, said Sir Launcelot, receive the high order of knighthood as[11] tomorn at the reverence[9] of the high feast. That night Sir Launcelot had passing good cheer; and on the morn at the hour of prime,[10] at Galahad's desire, he made him knight and said: God make him a good man, for of beauty faileth you not as any that liveth.

Now fair sir, said Sir Launcelot, will ye come with me unto the court of King Arthur? Nay, said he, I will not go with you as[11] at this time. Then he departed from them and took his two cousins with him, and so they came unto Camelot by the hour of underne[12] on Whitsunday. By that time the king and the queen were gone to the minster to hear their service. Then the king and the queen were passing glad of Sir Bors and Sir Lionel, and so was all the fellowship.

So when the king and all the knights were come from service, the barons espied in the sieges[13] of the Round Table all about, written with golden letters: Here ought to sit he,[14] and he[14] ought to sit here. And thus they went so long till that they came to the Siege Perilous,[15] where they found letters newly written of gold which said: Four hundred winters and four and fifty accomplished after the passion[16] of our Lord Jesu Christ ought this siege to be fulfilled.[17] Then all they said: This is a marvellous thing and an adventurous. In the name of God, said Sir Launcelot; and then accounted the term of the writing[18] from the birth of our Lord unto that day. It seemeth me, said Sir Launcelot, this siege ought to be fulfilled this same day, for this is the feast of Pentecost after the four hundred and four and fifty year; and if it would please all parties, I would none of these letters were seen this day, till he be come that ought to achieve this adventure. Then made they to ordain a cloth of silk, for to cover these letters in the Siege Perilous.

Then the king bad haste unto dinner. Sir, said Sir Kay the Steward, if ye go now unto your meat ye shall break your old custom of your court, for ye have not used on this day to sit at your meat or that [19] ye have seen some adventure. Ye say sooth, said the king, but I had so great joy of Sir Launcelot and of his cousins, which be come to the court whole[20] and sound, so that I bethought me not of mine old custom. So, as they stood speaking, in came a squire and said unto the king: Sir, I bring unto you marvellous tidings. What be they? said the king. Sir, there is here beneath at the river a great stone which I saw fleet[21] above the water, and therein I saw sticking a sword. The king said: I will see that marvel.

So all the knights went with him, and when they came to the river they found there a stone fleeting, as it were of red marble, and therein stuck a fair rich sword, and in the pommel thereof were precious stones wrought with subtil[22] letters of gold. Then the barons read the letters which said in this wise: Never shall man take me hence, but only he by whose side I ought to hang, and he shall be the best knight of the world. When the king had seen the letters, he said unto Sir Launcelot: Fair sir, this sword ought to be yours, for I am sure ye be the best knight of the world. Then Sir Launcelot answered full soberly: Certes, sir, it is not my sword; also, Sir, wit ye well I have no hardiness to set my hand to it, for it longed[23] not to hang by my side. Also, who that assayeth to take the sword and faileth of it, he shall receive a wound by that sword that he shall not be whole[20] long after. And I will that ye wit that this same day shall the adventures of the Sangreal, that is called the Holy Vessel, begin.*

19 before   20 hale, well   21 float   22 cunning
23 Probably for *longeth*, belongs.
* "Though the earliest French accounts of the Holy Grail differ in many details, from them all we can make up a story somewhat as follows: Joseph of Arimathæa, after taking Christ's body from the cross, collected his blood in the Grail, a dish or cup which our Lord had used at the Last Supper. Then, because Joseph had buried Christ reverently, he was thrown into prison by the angry Jews, who tried to starve him; but Joseph was solaced and fed by the Grail, miraculously presented to him by Christ in person. Released after forty years, Joseph set out from Jerusalem with his wife and kindred, who, having accepted his faith, were ready to follow him and his sacred vessel to far-off lands. He went through various adventures, principally conversions of heathen, the most important being of the King of Sarras and his people." (Howard Maynadier: *The Arthur of the English Poets*.) After the disappearance of the holy relic (which was reported to be of emerald), the quest of it was a visionary search often undertaken, according to the legends, as a test of purity. It was a wave of fanaticism prompting this search that broke up Arthur's goodly fellowship of knights.

9 observance
10 at the first hour
11 The word is redundant.
12 late forenoon
13 seats
14 So-and-so
15 Seat of Peril
16 suffering, crucifixion
17 occupied
18 calculated the time set down in the writing

Now, fair nephew, said the king unto Sir Gawaine, assay ye, for my love. Sir, he said, save your good grace[24] I shall not do that. Sir, said the king, assay to take the sword and at my commandment. Sir, said Gawaine, your commandment I will obey. And therewith he took up the sword by the handles, but he might not stir it. I thank you, said the king to Sir Gawaine. My lord Sir Gawaine, said Sir Launcelot, now wit ye well this sword shall touch you so sore that ye shall will ye had never set your hand thereto for the best castle of this realm. Sir, he said, I might not with-say mine uncle's will and commandment. But when the king heard this he repented it much, and said unto Sir Percivale that he should as-say, for his love. And he said: Gladly, for to bear Sir Gawaine fellowship. And therewith he set his hand on the sword and drew it strongly, but he might not move it. Then were there [no[25]] more that durst be so hardy to set their hands thereto. Now may ye go to your dinner, said Sir Kay unto the king, for a marvellous adventure have ye seen.

So the king and all went unto the court, and every knight knew his own place, and set him therein, and young men that were knights served them. So when they were served, and all sieges fulfilled save only the Siege Perilous, anon there befell a marvellous adventure, that[26] all the doors and windows of the palace shut by themself. Not for then [27] the hall was not greatly darked; and therewith they [were all[25]] abashed both one and other. Then King Arthur spake first and said: By God, fair fellows and lords, we have seen this day marvels, but or[28] night I suppose we shall see greater marvels.

In the meanwhile came in a good old man, and an ancient, clothed all in white, and there was no knight knew from whence he came. And with him he brought a young knight, both on foot, in red arms, without sword or shield, save a scabbard hanging by his side. And these words he said: Peace be with you, fair lords. Then the old man said unto Arthur: Sir, I bring here a young knight, the which is of king's lineage, and of the kindred of Joseph of Aramathie, whereby the marvels of this court, and of strange realms, shall be fully accomplished. The king was right glad of his words, and said unto the good man: Sir, ye be right welcome, and the young knight with you.

Then the old man made the young man to unarm him, and he was in a coat of red sen-dal,[29] and bare a mantle upon his shoulder that was furred with ermine, and put that upon him. And the old knight said unto the young knight: Sir, follow me. And anon he led him unto the Siege Perilous, where beside sat Sir Launcelot; and the good man lift up the cloth, and found there letters that said thus: This is the siege of Galahad, the haut[30] prince. Sir, said the old knight, wit ye well that place is yours. And then he set him down surely in that siege. And then he said to the old man: Sir, ye may now go your way, for well have ye done that ye were commanded to do; and recommend me unto my grandsire, King Pelles, and unto my lord Petchere, and say them on my behalf, I shall come and see them as soon as ever I may. So the good man departed; and there met him twenty noble squires, and so took their horses and went their way. Then all the knights of the Table Round marvelled greatly of Sir Gala-had, that he durst sit there in that Siege Peril-ous, and was so tender of age; and wist not from whence he came but all only[31] by God; and said: This is he by whom the Sangreal shall be achieved, for there sat never none but he, but he were mischieved.[32]

Then Sir Launcelot beheld his son and had great joy of him. Then Bors told his fellows: Upon pain of my life this young knight shall come unto great worship.[33] This noise was great in all the court, so that it came to the queen. Then she had marvel what knight it might be that durst adventure him to sit in the Siege Perilous. Many said unto the queen he resembled much unto Sir Launcelot. I may well suppose, said the queen, that Sir Launce-lot, being won by enchantment, had him of King Pelles' daughter, and his name is Gala-had. I would fain see him, said the queen, for he must needs be a noble man, for so is his father, I report me unto[34] all the Table Round. So when the meat was done that the king and all were risen, the king yede[35] unto the Siege Perilous and lift up the cloth, and found there the name of Galahad; and then he shewed it unto Sir Gawaine, and said: Fair nephew, now have we among us Sir Galahad, the good knight that shall worship[33] us all; and upon pain of my life he shall achieve the Sangreal, right as Sir Launcelot had done[36] us to understand. Then came King Arthur unto Galahad and said: Sir, ye be welcome, for ye shall move

24 A deprecatory phrase.
25 Inserted in the second edition by Caxton's successor. Wynkyn de Worde.
26 in that
27 nevertheless
28 ere
29 thin silk
30 high
31 unless it were
32 harmed
33 honor
34 call to witness
35 went
36 caused

many good knights to the quest of the Sangreal, and ye shall achieve that never knights
might bring to an end. Then the king took
him by the hand, and went down from the
palace to shew Galahad the adventures of the
stone.

How Sir Launcelot Was Tofore the Door of the Chamber Wherein the Holy Sangreal Was. Book XVII. Chapters XIII-XV.

Now saith the history, that when Launcelot
was come to the water of Mortoise, as it is
rehearsed before, he was in great peril, and so
he laid him down and slept, and took the adventure that God would send him. So when he
was asleep there came a vision unto him and
said: Launcelot, arise up and take thine armour, and enter into the first ship that thou
shalt find. And when he heard these words he
start up and saw great clearness about him.
And then he lift up his hand and blessed him,[1]
and so took his arms and made him ready; and
so by adventure he came by a strand, and
found a ship the which was without sail or oar.
And as soon as he was within the ship there
he felt the most sweetness that ever he felt,
and he was fulfilled with all thing that he
thought on or desired. Then he said: Fair
sweet Father, Jesu Christ, I wot not in what
joy I am, for this joy passeth all earthly joys
that ever I was in. And so in this joy he laid
him down to the ship's board, and slept till
day.

And when he awoke he found there a fair
bed, and therein lying a gentlewoman dead,
the which was Sir Percivale's sister.* And as
Launcelot devised[2] her, he espied in her right
hand a writ, the which he read, the which told
him all the adventures that ye have heard tofore, and of what lineage she was come. So
with this gentlewoman Sir Launcelot was a
month and more. If ye would ask how he
lived, He that fed the people of Israel with
manna in the desert, so was he fed; for every
day when he had said his prayers he was sustained with the grace of the Holy Ghost.

So on a night he went to play him by the
water side, for he was somewhat weary of the

ship. And then he listened and heard an horse
come, and one riding upon him. And when he
came nigh he seemed a knight. And so he let
him pass, and went thereas[3] the ship was; and
there he alit, and took the saddle and the
bridle and put the horse from him, and went
into the ship. And then Launcelot dressed[4]
unto him, and said: Ye be welcome. And he
answered and saluted him again,[5] and asked
him: What is your name? for much my heart
giveth[6] unto you. Truly, said he, my name is
Launcelot du Lake. Sir, said he, then be ye
welcome, for ye were the beginner of me in
this world. Ah, said he, are ye Galahad? Yea,
forsooth, said he; and so he kneeled down and
asked him his blessing, and after took off his
helm and kissed him.

And there was great joy between them, for
there is no tongue can tell the joy that they
made either of other, and many a friendly
word spoken between, as kin would, the which
is no need here to be rehearsed. And there
every each[7] told other of their adventures and
marvels that were befallen to them in many
journeys sith[8] that they departed from the
court. Anon, as Galahad saw the gentlewoman
dead in the bed, he knew her well enough, and
told great worship of her, that she was the best
maid living, and it was great pity of her death.
But when Launcelot heard how the marvellous
sword was gotten, and who made it, and all the
marvels rehearsed afore, then he prayed Galahad, his son, that he would show him the
sword†, and so he did; and anon he kissed the
pommel, and the hilt, and the scabbard. Truly,
said Launcelot, never erst knew I of so high
adventures done, and so marvellous and
strange.

So dwelt Launcelot and Galahad within that
ship half a year, and served God daily and
nightly with all their power; and often they
arrived in isles far from folk, where there repaired none but wild beasts, and there they
found many strange adventures and perilous,
which they brought to an end; but for[9] those
adventures were with wild beasts, and not in
the quest of the Sangreal, therefore the tale
maketh here no mention thereof, for it would
be too long to tell of all those adventures that
befell them.

So after, on a Monday, it befell that they arrived in the edge of a forest tofore a cross;

1 crossed himself   3 where
2 gazed upon
* She had given her blood to heal a lady and had
made this dying request of her brother: "As
soon as I am dead, put me in a boat at the
next haven, and let me go as adventure will
lead me; and as soon as ye three come to
the city of Sarras, there to achieve the Holy
Grail, ye shall find me under a tower arrived,
and there bury me in the spiritual place."

4 addressed himself (or   7 each one
  simply "went")   8 since
5 in return   9 because
6 goeth out
† The sword of King David, which had been put
by Solomon into this miraculous ship, and
which maimed or slew all who attempted to
draw it, until Galahad came.

and then saw they a knight armed all in white, and was richly horsed, and led in his right hand a white horse; and so he came to the ship, and saluted the two knights on the High Lord's behalf, and said: Galahad, sir, ye have been long enough with your father, come out of the ship, and start upon this horse, and go where the adventures shall lead thee in the quest of the Sangreal. Then he went to his father and kissed him sweetly, and said: Fair sweet father, I wot not when I shall see you more till I see the body of Jesu Christ. I pray you, said Launcelot, pray ye to the High Father that He hold me in His service. And so he took his horse, and there they heard a voice that said: Think for to do well, for the one shall never see the other before the dreadful day of doom. Now, son Galahad, said Launcelot, syne[10] we shall depart, and never see other, I pray to the High Father to conserve me and you both. Sir, said Galahad, no prayer availeth so much as yours. And therewith Galahad entered into the forest.

And the wind arose, and drove Launcelot more than a month throughout the sea, where he slept but little, but prayed to God that he might see some tidings of the Sangreal. So it befell on a night, at midnight, he arrived afore a castle, on the back side, which was rich and fair, and there was a postern opened toward the sea, and was open without any keeping, save two lions kept the entry; and the moon shone clear. Anon Sir Launcelot heard a voice that said: Launcelot, go out of this ship and enter into the castle, where thou shalt see a great part of thy desire.

Then he ran to his arms, and so armed him, and so went to the gate and saw the lions. Then set he hand to his sword and drew it. Then there came a dwarf suddenly, and smote him on the arm so sore that the sword fell out of his hand. Then heard he a voice say: O man of evil faith and poor belief, wherefore trowest[11] thou more on thy harness than in thy Maker, for He might more avail thee than thine armour, in whose service that thou art set. Then said Launcelot: Fair Father Jesu Christ, I thank thee of Thy great mercy that Thou reprovest me of my misdeed; now see I well that ye hold me for your servant. Then took he again his sword and put it up in his sheath, and made a cross in his forehead, and came to the lions, and they made semblant[12] to do him harm. Notwithstanding he passed by them without hurt, and entered into the

castle to the chief fortress, and there were they all at rest.

Then Launcelot entered in so armed, for he found no gate nor door but it was open. And at the last he found a chamber whereof the door was shut, and he set his hand thereto to have opened it, but he might not. Then he enforced him mickle[13] to undo the door. Then he listened and heard a voice which sang so sweetly that it seemed none earthly thing; and him thought the voice said: Joy and honour be to the Father of Heaven. Then Launcelot kneeled down tofore the chamber, for well wist he that there was the Sangreal within that chamber. Then said he: Fair sweet Father, Jesu Christ, if ever I did thing that pleased Thee, Lord for Thy pity never have me not in despite for my sins done aforetime, and that thou show me something of that I seek. And with that he saw the chamber door open, and there came out a great clearness, that the house was as bright as[14] all the torches of the world had been there. So came he to the chamber door, and would have entered. And anon a voice said to him, Flee, Launcelot, and enter not, for thou oughtest not to do it; and if thou enter thou shalt forthink[15] it. Then he withdrew him aback right heavy.[16]

Then looked he up in the middes of the chamber, and saw a table of silver, and the holy vessel, covered with red samite, and many angels about it, whereof one held a candle of wax burning, and the other held a cross, and the ornaments of an altar. And before the holy vessel he saw a good man clothed as a priest. And it seemed that he was at the sacring of the mass.[17] And it seemed to Launcelot that above the priest's hands were three men, whereof the two put the youngest by likeness between the priest's hands; and so he lift it up right high, and it seemed to show so to the people. And then Launcelot marvelled not a little, for him thought the priest was so greatly charged of[18] the figure that him seemed that he should fall to the earth. And when he saw none about him that would help him, then came he to the door a great pace,[19] and said: Fair Father Jesu Christ, ne take it for no sin though I help the good man which hath great need of help. Right so entered he into the chamber, and came toward the table of silver; and when he came nigh he felt a breath, that him thought it was intermeddled[20]

---

10 since
11 trustest
12 semblance (made as if)
13 tried hard
14 as if
15 repent
16 sad
17 the communion service
18 burdened with
19 quickly
20 intermingled

with fire, which smote him so sore in the visage that him thought it brent[21] his visage; and therewith he fell to the earth, and had no power to arise, as he that was so araged,[22] that had lost the power of his body, and his hearing, and his seeing. Then felt he many hands about him, which took him up and bare him out of the chamber door, without any amending of his swoon, and left him there, seeming dead to all people.

So upon the morrow when it was fair day they within were arisen, and found Launcelot lying afore the chamber door. All they marvelled how that he came in, and so they looked upon him, and felt his pulse to wit whether there were any life in him; and so they found life in him, but he might not stand nor stir no member that he had. And so they took him by every part of the body, and bare him into a chamber, and laid him in a rich bed, far from all folk; and so he lay four days. Then the one said he was on live, and the other said, Nay. In the name of God, said an old man, for I do you verily to wit he is not dead, but he is so full of life as the mightiest of you all; and therefore I counsel you that he be well kept till God send him life again.

How Galahad and His Fellows Were Fed of the Holy Sangreal, and how Galahad Was Made King. Book XVII. Chapters XIX-XXII

So departed Galahad from thence, and rode five days till that he came to the maimed king.[23] And ever followed Percivale the five days, asking where he had been; and so one told him how the adventures of Logris were achieved. So on a day it befell that they came out of a great forest, and there they met at traverse[24] with Sir Bors, the which rode alone. It is none need to tell if they were glad; and them he saluted, and they yielded him honour and good adventure,[25] and every each told other. Then said Bors: It is more than a year and a half that I ne lay ten times where men dwelled, but in wild forests and in mountains, but God was ever my comfort. Then rode they a great while till that they came to the castle of Carbonek. And when they were entered within the castle King Pelles knew them; then there was great joy, for they wist well by their coming that they had fulfilled the quest of the Sangreal.

Then Eliazar, King Pelles' son, brought tofore them the broken sword wherewith Joseph was stricken through the thigh. Then Bors set his hand thereto, if that he might have soldered it again; but it would not be. Then he took it to Percivale, but he had no more power thereto than he. Now have ye it again, said Percivale to Galahad, for an it be ever achieved by any bodily man ye must do it. And then he took the pieces and set them together, and they seemed that they had never been broken, and as well as it had been first forged. And when they within espied that the adventure of the sword was achieved, then they gave the sword to Bors, for it might not be better set[26]; for he was a good knight and a worthy man.

And a little afore even, the sword arose great and marvellous, and was full of great heat that many men fell for dread. And anon alit a voice among them, and said: They that ought not to sit at the table of Jesu Christ arise, for now shall very[27] knights be fed. So they went thence, all save King Pelles and Eliazar, his son, the which were holy men, and a maid which was his niece; and so these three fellows and they three were there, no more.

Anon they saw knights all armed come in at the hall door, and did off their helms and their arms, and said unto Galahad: Sir, we have hied right much for to be with you at this table where the holy meat shall be departed.[28] Then said he: Ye be welcome, but of whence be ye? So three of them said they were of Gaul, and other three said they were of Ireland, and the other three said they were of Denmark. So as they sat thus there came out a bed of tree,[29] of[30] a chamber, the which four gentlewomen brought; and in the bed lay a good man sick, and a crown of gold upon his head; and there in the middes of the place they set him down, and went again their way. Then he lift up his head, and said: Galahad, Knight, ye be welcome, for much have I desired your coming, for in such pain and in such anguish I have been long. But now I trust to God the term is come that my pain shall be allayed, that I shall pass out of this world so as it was promised me long ago.

Therewith a voice said: There be two among you that be not in the quest of the Sangreal, and therefore depart ye. Then King Pelles and his son departed. And therewithal beseemed them that there came a man, and four angels from heaven, clothed in likeness of a bishop, and had a cross in his hand; and these four

21 burnt
22 like one so angry
23 Pelles, who had attempted to draw the miraculous sword.
24 crossed paths
25 A salutation, *buona ventura,* "good luck."
26 placed
27 true
28 divided, distributed
29 wood
30 from

angels bare him up in a chair, and set him down before the table of silver whereupon the Sangreal was; and it seemed that he had in middes of his forehead letters the which said: See ye here Joseph, the first bishop of Christendom, the same which Our Lord succoured in the city of Sarras in the spiritual place. Then the knights marvelled, for that bishop was dead more than three hundred year tofore. O knights, said he, marvel not, for I was sometime[31] an earthly man.

With that they heard the chamber door open, and there they saw angels; and two bare candles of wax, and the third a towel, and the fourth a spear which bled marvellously, and three drops fell within a box which he held with his other hand. And they set the candles upon the table, and the third the towel upon the vessel, and the fourth the holy spear even upright upon the vessel. And then the bishop made semblant as though he would have gone to the sacring of the mass. And then he took an ubbly[32] which was made in likeness of bread. And at the lifting up there came a figure in likeness of a child, and the visage was as red and as bright as any fire, and smote himself into the bread, so that they all saw it that the bread was formed of a fleshly man; and then he put it into the holy vessel again, and then he did that longed[33] to a priest to do to a mass. And then he went to Galahad and kissed him, and bad him go and kiss his fellows: and so he did anon. Now, said he, servants of Jesu Christ, ye shall be fed afore this table with sweetmeats that never knights tasted. And when he had said, he vanished away. And they set them at the table in great dread, and made their prayers.

Then looked they and saw a man come out of the holy vessel, that had all the signs of the passion[34] of Jesu Christ, bleeding all openly, and said: My knights, and my servants, and my true children, which be come out of deadly life into spiritual life, I will now no longer hide me from you, but ye shall see now a part of my secrets and of my hidden things: now hold and receive the high meat which ye have so much desired. Then took he himself the holy vessel and came to Galahad; and he kneeled down, and there he received his Saviour, and after him so received all his fellows; and they thought it so sweet that it was marvellous to tell.

Then said he to Galahad: Son, wotest thou what I hold betwixt my hands? Nay, said he,

but if[35] ye will tell me. This is, said he, the holy dish wherein I ate the lamb on Sher-Thursday[36]. And now hast thou seen that thou most desired to see, but yet hast thou not seen it so openly as thou shalt see it in the city of Sarras in the spiritual place. Therefore thou must go hence and bear with thee this holy vessel; for this night it shall depart from the realm of Logris, that it shall never be seen more here. And wotest thou wherefore? For he is not served nor worshipped to his right by them of this land, for they be turned to evil living; therefore I shall disherit them of the honour which I have done them. And therefore go ye three to-morrow unto the sea, where ye shall find your ship ready, and with you take the sword with the strange girdles, and no more with you but Sir Percivale and Sir Bors. Also I will that ye take with you of the blood of this spear for to anoint the maimed king, both his legs and all his body, and he shall have his health.

Sir, said Galahad, why shall not these other fellows go with us? For this cause: for right as I departed[37] my apostles one here and another there, so I will that ye depart; and two of you shall die in my service, but one of you shall come again and tell tidings. Then gave he them his blessing and vanished away. And Galahad went anon to the spear which lay upon the table, and touched the blood with his fingers, and came after to the maimed king and anointed his legs. And therewith he clothed him[38] anon, and start upon his feet out of his bed as an whole man, and thanked Our Lord that He had healed him. . . .

Right so departed Galahad, Percivale and Bors with him; and so they rode three days, and then they came to a rivage,[39] and found the ship whereof the tale speaketh of tofore. And when they came to the board[40] they found in the middes the table of silver which they had left with the maimed king, and the Sangreal which was covered with red samite. Then were they glad to have such things in their fellowship; and so they entered and made great reverence thereto; and Galahad fell in his prayer long time to Our Lord, that at what time he asked, that he should pass out of this world. So much he prayed till a voice said to him: Galahad, thou shalt have thy request; and when thou askest the death of thy body thou shalt have it, and then shalt thou find the life of the soul.

---

31 once
32 wafer
33 what belonged
34 crucifixion
35 unless
36 the day before Good Friday
37 parted
38 himself
39 shore
40 aboard

Percivale heard this, and prayed him, of[41] fellowship that was between them, to tell him wherefore he asked such things. That shall I tell you, said Galahad; the other day when we saw a part of the adventures of the Sangreal I was in such a joy of heart, that I trow never man was that was earthly. And therefore I wot well, when my body is dead my soul shall be in great joy to see the blessed Trinity every day, and the Majesty of Our Lord, Jesu Christ. So long were they in the ship that they said to Galahad: Sir, in this bed ought ye to lie, for so saith the scripture. And so he laid him down and slept a great while; and when he awaked he looked afore him and saw the city of Sarras.

And as they would have landed they saw the ship wherein Percivale had put his sister in. Truly, said Percivale, in the name of God, well hath my sister holden us covenant. Then took they out of the ship the table of silver, and he took it to Percivale and to Bors, to go tofore, and Galahad came behind. And right so they went to the city, and at the gate of the city they saw an old man crooked. Then Galahad called him and bad him help to bear this heavy thing. Truly, said the old man, it is ten year ago that I might not go but with crutches. Care thou not, said Galahad, and arise up and shew thy good will. And so he assayed, and found himself as whole as ever he was. Then ran he to the table, and took one part against[42] Galahad. And anon arose there great noise in the city, that a cripple was made whole by knights marvellous that entered into the city. Then anon after, the three knights went to the water, and brought up into the palace Percivale's sister, and buried her as richly as a king's daughter ought to be.

And when the king of the city, which was cleped[43] Estorause, saw the fellowship, he asked them of whence they were, and what thing it was that they had brought upon the table of silver. And they told him the truth of the Sangreal, and the power which that God had set there. Then the king was a tyrant, and was come of the line of paynims, and took them and put them in prison in a deep hole. But as soon as they were there Our Lord sent them the Sangreal, through whose grace they were alway fulfilled while that they were in prison.

So at the year's end it befel that this King Estorause lay sick, and felt that he should die. Then he sent for the three knights, and they came afore him; and he cried them mercy of

that he had done to them, and they forgave it him goodly; and he died anon. When the king was dead all the city was dismayed, and wist not who might be their king. Right so as they were in counsel there came a voice among them, and bad them choose the youngest knight of them three to be their king: For he shall well maintain you and all yours. So they made Galahad king by all the assent of the holy city, and else they would have slain him. And when he was come to behold the land, he let make above the table of silver a chest of gold and of precious stones, that hylled[44] the holy vessel. And every day early the three fellows would come afore it, and make their prayers. Now at the year's end, and the self day after Galahad had borne the crown of gold, he arose up early and his fellows, and came to the palace, and saw tofore them the holy vessel, and a man kneeling on his knees in likeness of a bishop, that had about him a great fellowship of angels as it had been Jesu Christ himself; and then he arose and began a mass of Our Lady. And when he came to the sacrament of the mass, and had done, anon he called Galahad, and said to him: Come forth, the servant of Jesu Christ, and thou shalt see that[45] thou hast much desired to see. And then he began to tremble right hard when the deadly[46] flesh began to behold the spiritual things. Then he held up his hands toward heaven and said: Lord, I thank thee, for now I see that that hath been my desire many a day. Now, blessed Lord, would I not longer live, if it might please thee, Lord.

And therewith the good man took Our Lord's body betwixt his hands, and proffered it to Galahad, and he received it right gladly and meekly. Now wotest thou what I am? said the good man. Nay, said Galahad. I am Joseph of Aramathie, the which Our Lord hath sent here to thee to bear thee fellowship; and wotest thou wherefore that he hath sent me more than any other? For thou hast resembled me in two things; in that thou hast seen the marvels of the Sangreal, and in that thou hast been a clean maiden,[47] as I have been and am. And when he had said these words Galahad went to Percivale and kissed him, and commended him to God; and so he went to Sir Bors and kissed him, and commended him to God, and said: Fair lord, salute me to my lord, Sir Launcelot, my father, and as soon as ye see him, bid him remember of this unstable world.[48] And therewith he kneeled down tofore the table and

41 by the
42 the part opposite
43 who was called
44 covered
45 that which
46 mortal
47 pure youth
48 remember the insta-
bility of life

made his prayers, and then suddenly his soul departed to Jesu Christ, and a great multitude of angels bare his soul up to heaven, that the two fellows might well behold it. Also the two fellows saw come from heaven an hand, but they saw not the body. And then it came right to the Vessel, and took it and the spear, and so bare it up to heaven. Sithen was there never man so hardy to say that he had seen the Sangreal.

How Mordred Was Slain and Arthur Hurt to the Death. Book XXI. Chapters IV-VII

Then were they condescended[1] that King Arthur and Sir Mordred* should meet betwixt both their hosts, and every each of them should bring fourteen persons; and they came with this word unto Arthur. Then said he: I am glad that this is done, and so he went into the field. And when Arthur should depart, he warned all his host that an they see any sword drawn: Look ye come on fiercely, and slay that traitor, Sir Mordred, for I in no wise trust him. In likewise Sir Mordred warned his host that: An ye see any sword drawn, look that ye come on fiercely, and so slay all that ever before you standeth; for in no wise I will not trust for this treaty, for I know well my father will be avenged on me. And so they met as their appointment was, and so they were agreed and accorded thoroughly; and wine was fetched, and they drank.

Right soon came an adder out of a little heath bush, and it stung a knight on the foot. And when the knight felt him stung, he looked down and saw the adder, and then he drew his sword to slay the adder, and thought of none other harm. And when the host on both parties saw that sword drawn, then they blew beamous,[2] trumpets, and horns, and shouted grimly. And so both hosts dressed them[3] together. And King Arthur took his horse, and said: Alas this unhappy day! and so rode to his party. And Sir Mordred in likewise.

And never was there seen a more dolefuller battle in no Christian land; for there was but rushing and riding, foining[4] and striking, and many a grim word was there spoken either to other, and many a deadly stroke. But ever

King Arthur rode throughout the battle[5] of Sir Mordred many times, and did full nobly as a noble king should, and at all times he fainted never; and Sir Mordred that day put him in devoir,[6] and in great peril. And thus they fought all the long day, and never stinted till the noble knights were laid to the cold earth; and ever they fought still till it was near night, and by that time was there an hundred thousand laid dead upon the down.[7]

Then was Arthur wood[8] wroth out of measure, when he saw his people so slain from him. Then the king looked about him, and then was he ware, of all his host and of all his good knights, were left no more on live but two knights; that one was Sir Lucan the Butler, and his brother Sir Bedivere, and they were full sore wounded. Jesu mercy, said the king, where are all my noble knights become? Alas that ever I should see this doleful day, for now, said Arthur, I am come to mine end. But would to God that I wist where were that traitor Sir Mordred, that hath caused all this mischief.

Then was King Arthur ware where Sir Mordred leaned upon his sword amongst a great heap of dead men. Now give me my spear, said Arthur unto Sir Lucan, for yonder I have espied the traitor that all this woe hath wrought. Sir, let him be, said Sir Lucan, for he is unhappy;[9] and if ye pass this unhappy day ye shall be right well revenged upon him. Good lord, remember ye of your night's dream, and what the spirit of Sir Gawaine told you this night, yet God of his great goodness hath preserved you hitherto. Therefore, for God's sake, my lord, leave off by this, for blessed be God ye have won the field, for here we be three on live, and with Sir Mordred is none on live; and if ye leave off now this wicked day of destiny is past. Tide[10] me death, betide me life, saith the king, now I see him yonder alone he shall never escape mine hands, for at a better avail shall I never have him. God speed you well, said Sir Bedivere.

Then the king gat his spear in both his hands, and ran toward Sir Mordred, crying: Traitor, now is thy death day come. And when Sir Mordred heard Sir Arthur, he ran until him with his sword drawn in his hand. And there King Arthur smote Sir Mordred under the shield, with a foin of his spear, throughout the body, more than a fathom. And when Sir Mordred felt that he had his death wound he

1 agreed
2 beaumes (a kind of trumpet)
3 rushed
4 thrusting
* During Arthur's absence his nephew Mordred (or son, as he is sometimes called) usurped his throne and gave battle to Arthur upon his return.
5 ranks
6 did his best (his utmost endeavor)
7 high plain
8 madly
9 of evil omen
10 befall

thrust himself with the might that he had up to the bur of King Arthur's spear. And right so he smote his father Arthur, with his sword holden in both his hands, on the side of the head, that the sword pierced the helmet and the brain pan, and therewithal Sir Mordred fell stark dead to the earth.

And the noble Arthur fell in a swoon to the earth, and there he swooned ofttimes. And Sir Lucan the Butler and Sir Bedivere ofttimes heaved him up. And so weakly they led him betwixt them both, to a little chapel not far from the seaside. And when the king was there he thought him well eased. Then heard they people cry in the field. Now go thou, Sir Lucan, said the king, and do me to wit[11] what betokens that noise in the field. So Sir Lucan departed, for he was grievously wounded in many places. And so as he yede,[12] he saw and hearkened by the moonlight, how that pillers[13] and robbers were come into the field, to pill and to rob many a full noble knight of brooches, and beads, of many a good ring, and of many a rich jewel; and who that were not dead all out,[14] there they slew them for their harness and their riches. When Sir Lucan understood this work, he came to the king as soon as he might, and told him all what he had heard and seen. Therefore by my rede,[15] said Sir Lucan, it is best that we bring you to some town. I would it were so, said the king, but I may not stand, mine head works so. Ah Sir Launcelot, said King Arthur, this day have I sore missed thee: alas, that ever I was against thee, for now have I my death, whereof Sir Gawaine me warned in my dream.

Then Sir Lucan took up the king the one part, and Sir Bedivere the other part, and in the lifting the king swooned; and Sir Lucan fell in a swoon with the lift, that the part of his bowels fell out of his body, and therewith the noble knight's heart brast.[16] And when the king awoke, he beheld Sir Lucan, how he lay foaming at the mouth, and part of his bowels lay at his feet. Alas, said the king, this is to me a full heavy sight, to see this noble duke so die for my sake, for he would have holpen me, that had more need of help than I. Alas, he would not complain him, his heart was so set to help me: now Jesu have mercy upon his soul!

Then Sir Bedivere wept for the death of his brother. Leave this mourning and weeping, said the king, for all this will not avail me, for wit thou well an I might live myself, the death

of Sir Lucan would grieve me evermore; but my time hieth fast, said the king. Therefore, said Arthur unto Sir Bedivere, take thou Excalibur, my good sword, and go with it to yonder water side, and when thou comest there I charge thee throw my sword in that water, and come again and tell me what thou there seest. My lord, said Bedivere, your commandment shall be done, and lightly bring you word again.

So Sir Bedivere departed, and by the way he beheld that noble sword, that the pommel and the haft was all of precious stones; and then he said to himself: If I throw this rich sword in the water, thereof shall never come good, but harm and loss. And then Sir Bedivere hid Excalibur under a tree. And so, as soon as he might, he came again unto the king, and said he had been at the water, and had thrown the sword in the water. What saw thou there? said the king. Sir, he said, I saw nothing but waves and winds. That is untruly said of thee, said the king, therefore go thou lightly again, and do my commandment; as thou art to me lief and dear, spare not, but throw it in.

Then Sir Bevidere returned again, and took the sword in his hand; and then him thought sin and shame to throw away that noble sword, and so eft[17] he hid the sword, and returned again, and told to the king that he had been at the water, and done his commandment. What saw thou there? said the king. Sir, he said, I saw nothing but the waters wappe and waves wanne.[18] Ah, traitor untrue, said King Arthur, now hast thou betrayed me twice. Who would have weened that, thou that hast been to me so lief and dear? and thou art named a noble knight, and would betray me for the richness of the sword. But now go again lightly, for thy long tarrying putteth me in great jeopardy of my life, for I have taken cold. And but if[19] thou do now as I bid thee, if ever I may see thee I shall slay thee with mine own hands; for thou wouldst for my rich sword see me dead.

Then Sir Bedivere departed, and went to the sword, and lightly took it up, and went to the water side; and there he bound the girdle about the hilts, and then he threw the sword as far into the water as he might; and there came an arm and an hand above the water and met it, and caught it, and so shook it thrice and brandished, and then vanished away the hand with the sword in the water. So Sir Bedivere came again to the king, and told him

11 let me know
12 went
13 pillagers
14 outright
15 advice
16 burst
17 again
18 lap and ebb (ebb and flow)
19 unless

what he saw. Alas, said the king, help me
hence, for I dread me I have tarried over long.

Then Sir Bedivere took the king upon his
back, and so went with him to that water side.
And when they were at the water side, even
fast by the bank hoved a little barge with
many fair ladies in it, and among them all was
a queen, and all they had black hoods, and all
they wept and shrieked when they saw King
Arthur. Now put me into the barge, said the
king. And so he did softly; and there received
him three queens with great mourning; and so
they set them down, and in one of their laps
King Arthur laid his head. And then that
queen said: Ah, dear brother, why have ye tarried so long from me? alas, this wound on
your head hath caught over-much cold. And
so then they rowed from the land, and Sir
Bedivere beheld all those ladies go from him.
Then Sir Bedivere cried: Ah my lord Arthur,
what shall become of me, now ye go from me
and leave me here alone among mine enemies?
Comfort thyself, said the king, and do as well
as thou mayest, for in me is no trust for to
trust in; for I will into the vale of Avilion[20] to
heal me of my grievous wound: and if thou
hear never more of me, pray for my soul. But
ever the queens and ladies wept and shrieked,
that it was pity to hear.

And as soon as Sir Bedivere had lost the
sight of the barge, he wept and wailed, and so
took the forest; and so he went all that night,
and in the morning he was ware, betwixt two
holts hoar,[21] of a chapel and an hermitage.
Then was Sir Bedivere glad, and thither he
went; and when he came into the chapel, he
saw where lay an hermit grovelling on all
four, there fast by a tomb was new graven.
When the hermit saw Sir Bedivere he knew
him well, for he was but little tofore Bishop of
Canterbury, that Sir Mordred flemed.[22] Sir,
said Bedivere, what man is there interred that
ye pray so fast for? Fair son, said the hermit,
I wot not verily, but by deeming.[23] But this
night, at midnight, here came a number of
ladies, and brought hither a dead corpse, and
prayed me to bury him; and here they offered
an hundred tapers, and there they gave me an hundred besants.[24] Alas, said Sir Bedivere, that
was my lord King Arthur, that here lieth buried in this chapel.

Then Sir Bedivere swooned; and when he
awoke he prayed the hermit he might abide
with him still there, to live with fasting and
prayers. For from hence will I never go, said
Sir Bedivere, by my will, but all the days of
my life here to pray for my lord Arthur. Ye
are welcome to me, said the hermit, for I know
you better than ye ween that I do. Ye are the
bold Bedivere, and the full noble duke, Sir
Lucan the Butler, was your brother. Then Sir
Bedivere told the hermit all as ye have heard
tofore. So there bode Sir Bedivere with the
hermit that was tofore Bishop of Canterbury,
and there Sir Bedivere put upon him poor
clothes, and served the hermit full lowly in
fasting and in prayers.

Yet some men say in many parts of England that King Arthur is not dead, but had[25]
by the will of our Lord Jesu into another place;
and men say that he shall come again, and he
shall win the holy cross. I will not say it shall
be so, but rather I will say, here in this world
he changed his life. But many men say that
there is written upon his tomb this verse: *Hic
jacet Arthurus, Rex quondam, Rexque futurus.*[26]
Thus leave I here Sir Bedivere with the hermit,
that dwelled that time in a chapel beside Glas-
tonbury, and there was his hermitage. And so
they lived in their prayers, and fastings, and
great abstinence.

SIR THOMAS MORE (1478-1535)

FROM UTOPIA.*

THE EPISTLE

Thomas More to Peter Giles,† sendeth greeting:
I am almost ashamed, right well-beloved
Peter Giles, to send unto you this book of the
Utopian commonwealth, well nigh after a
year's space, which I am sure you looked for
within a month and a half. And no marvel.
For you knew well enough that I was already
disburdened of all the labor and study belonging to the invention in this work, and that I
had no need at all to trouble my brains about
the disposition or conveyance of the mat-

20 Or Avalon, the Celtic Land of the Blessed, or
  Earthly Paradise.
21 two gray wooded hills
22 put to flight   24 a gold coin (named
23 I can only conjecture   from Byzantium)

25 taken
26 *Here lies Arthur, king that was and shall be.*
* This book was written and published in Latin
  in 1516. It was translated by Ralph Robinson in 1551. The extracts here given are
  from the second edition of Robinson's translation, 1556. "Utopia" is a word made from
  the Greek, meaning "nowhere." As the imaginary commonwealth is pictured in such attractive colors, it is easy to regard the first
  syllable of the name as representing the
  Greek *eu*, "well," instead of *ou*, "not," and
  "Utopian" has come to mean "perfect," as
  well as "visionary."
† A friend of More who lived at Antwerp.

ter, and therefore had herein nothing else to do but only to rehearse those things which you and I together heard master Raphael‡ tell and declare. Wherefore there was no cause why I should study to set forth the matter with eloquence: forasmuch as his talk could not be fine and eloquent, being first not studied for, but sudden and unpremeditate, and then, as you know, of a man better seen[1] in the Greek language than in the Latin tongue. And my writing, the nigher it should approach to his homely, plain, and simple§ speech, so much the nigher should it go to the truth, which is the only mark whereunto I do and ought to direct all my travail and study herein.

I grant and confess, friend Peter, myself discharged of so much labor, having all these things ready done to my hand, that almost there was nothing left for me to do. Else either the invention or the disposition of this matter might have required of a wit neither base, neither at all unlearned, both some time and leisure, and also some study. But if it were requisite and necessary that the matter should also have been written eloquently, and not alone truly, of a surety that thing could I have performed by no time nor study. But now seeing all these cares, stays, and lets[2] were taken away, wherein else so much labor and study should have been employed, and that there remained no other thing for me to do but only to write plainly the matter as I heard it spoken, that indeed was a thing light and easy to be done.

Howbeit, to the dispatching of this so little business my other cares and troubles did leave almost less than no leisure. Whiles I do daily bestow my time about law matters, some to plead, some to hear, some as an arbitrator with mine award to determine, some as an umpire or a judge, with my sentence finally to discuss; whiles I go one way to see and visit my friend, another way about mine own private affairs; whiles I spend almost all the day abroad amongst other, and the residue at home among mine own: I leave to myself, I mean to my book, no time. For when I am come home, I must commen[3] with my wife, chat with my children, and talk with my servants. All the which things I reckon and account among business, forasmuch as they must of necessity be done: and done must they needs be, unless a man will be a stranger in his own house. And in any wise a man must so fashion and order his conditions, and so appoint and dispose himself, that he be merry, jocund, and pleasant among them whom either nature hath provided, or chance hath made, or he himself hath chosen, to be the fellows and companions of his life, so that with too much gentle behavior and familiarity he do not mar them, and by too much sufferance of his servants make them his masters.

Among these things now rehearsed stealeth away the day, the month, the year. When do I write then? And all this while have I spoken no word of sleep, neither yet of meat, which among a great number doth waste no less time than doth sleep, wherein almost half the lifetime of man creepeth away. I therefore do win and get only that time which I steal from sleep and meat. Which time because it is very little, and yet somewhat it is, therefore have I once at the last, though it be long first, finished Utopia, and have sent it to you, friend Peter, to read and peruse, to the intent that if anything have escaped me, you might put me in remembrance of it. For though in this behalf I do not greatly mistrust myself (which would God I were somewhat in wit and learning as I am not all of the worst and dullest memory) yet have I not so great trust and confidence in it that I think nothing could fall out of my mind.

For John Clement, my boy,* who as you know was there present with us, whom I suffer to be away from no talk wherein may be any profit or goodness (for out of this young bladed and new shot up corn, which hath already begun to spring up both in Latin and Greek learning, I look for plentiful increase at length of goodly ripe grain),—he, I say, hath brought me into a great doubt. For whereas Hythloday (unless my memory fail me) said that the bridge of Amaurote, which goeth over the river of Anyder, is five hundred paces, that is to say, half a mile in length, my John sayeth that two hundred of those paces must be plucked away, for that the river containeth there not above three hundred paces in breadth. I pray you heartily, call the matter to your remembrance. For if you agree with him, I also will say as you say, and confess myself deceived. But if you cannot remember the thing,

---

1 versed
2 hindrances   3 commune
‡ Raphael Hythloday, the imaginary narrator, whom More professes to have met in Antwerp. His name means "teller of idle tales."
§ To use two or three words thus for the same idea was a common practice of writers of the time, and especially of translators, who often took this means of giving both the Latin derivative and its Saxon equivalent. More's Latin is much terser than his translator's English.

* He was a tutor in More's household.

then surely I will write as I have done and as mine own remembrance serveth me. For as I will take good heed that there be in my book nothing false, so if there be anything doubtful, I will rather tell a lie than make a lie; because I had rather be good, than wily.

Howbeit, this matter may easily be remedied if you will take the pains to ask the question of Raphael himself by word of mouth, if he be now with you, or else by your letters. Which you must needs do for another doubt also that hath chanced,—through whose fault I cannot tell, whether through mine, or yours, or Raphael's. For neither we remembered to inquire of him, nor he to tell us, in what part of the new world Utopia is situate. The which thing, I had rather have spent no small sum of money than that it should thus have escaped us: as well for that I am ashamed to be ignorant in what sea that island standeth, whereof I write so long a treatise, as also because there be with us certain men, and especially one virtuous and godly man, and a professor of divinity, who is exceeding desirous to go unto Utopia; not for a vain and curious desire to see news,[4] but to the intent he may further and increase our religion, which is there already luckily begun. And that he may the better accomplish and perform this his good intent, he is minded to procure that he may be sent thither by the high Bishop; yea, and that he himself may be made Bishop of Utopia: being nothing scrupulous herein, that he must obtain this Bishopric with suit.[5] For he counteth that a godly suit which proceedeth not of the desire of honor or lucre, but only of a godly zeal.

Wherefore I most earnestly desire you, friend Peter, to talk with Hythloday, if you can, face to face, or else to write your letters to him, and so to work in this matter that in this my book there may neither anything be found which is untrue, neither anything be lacking which is true.

And I think verily it shall be well done that you show unto him the book itself. For if I have missed or failed in any point, or if any fault have escaped me, no man can so well correct and amend it as he can: and yet that can he not do unless he peruse and read over my book written. Moreover, by this means shall you perceive whether he be well willing and content that I should undertake to put this work in writing. For if he be minded to publish and put forth his own labors and travails himself, perchance he would be loth, and so would

I also, that in publishing the Utopian weal public,[6] I should prevent[7] him, and take from him the flower and grace of the novelty of this his history.

Howbeit, to say the very truth, I am not yet fully determined with myself whether I will put forth my book or no. For the natures of men be so diverse, the fantasies of some so wayward, their minds so unkind, their judgments so corrupt, that they which lead a merry and a jocund life, following their own sensual pleasures and carnal lusts, may seem to be in a much better state or case than they that vex and unquiet themselves with cares and study for the putting forth and publishing of some thing that may be either profit or pleasure to others: which others nevertheless will disdainfully, scornfully, and unkindly accept the same. The most part of all be unlearned. And a great number hath learning in contempt. The rude and barbarous alloweth nothing but that which is very barbarous indeed. If it be one that hath a little smack of learning, he rejecteth as homely gear and common ware whatsoever is not stuffed full of old moth-eaten terms, and that be worn out of use. Some there be that have pleasure only in old rustic antiquities; and some only in their own doings. One is so sour, so crabbed, and so unpleasant, that he can away with[8] no mirth nor sport. Another is so narrow between the shoulders that he can bear no jests nor taunts. Some silly poor souls be so afeard that at every snappish word their nose shall be bitten off, that they stand in no less dread of every quick and sharp word than he that is bitten of a mad dog feareth water. Some be so mutable and wavering that every hour they be in a new mind, saying one thing sitting and another thing standing. Another sort sitteth upon their ale-benches, and there among their cups they give judgment of the wits of writers, and with great authority they condemn, even as pleaseth them, every writer according to his writing, in most spiteful manner mocking, louting, and flouting them; being themselves in the mean season safe, and, as sayeth the proverb, out of all danger of gun-shot. For why,[9] they be so smug and smooth that they have not so much as one hair of an honest man whereby one may take hold of them. There be, moreover, some so unkind and ungentle that though they take great pleasure and delectation in the work, yet, for all that, they cannot find in their hearts to love the author thereof, nor to afford him a

---

4 new things
5 not scrupling at all to ask for it
6 commonwealth
7 anticipate
8 endure
9 because

good word: being much like uncourteous, unthankful, and churlish guests, which, when they have with good and dainty meats well filled their bellies, depart home, giving no thanks to the feast-maker. Go your ways now, and make a costly feast at your own charges for guests so dainty-mouthed, so divers in taste, and besides that of so unkind and unthankful natures.

But nevertheless, friend Peter, do, I pray you, with Hythloday as I willed you before. And as for this matter, I shall be at my liberty afterwards to take new advisement. Howbeit, seeing I have taken great pains and labor in writing the matter, if it may stand with his mind and pleasure, I will, as touching the edition or publishing of the book, follow the counsel and advice of my friends, and specially yours. Thus fare you well, right heartily beloved friend Peter, with your gentle wife: and love me as you have ever done, for I love you better than ever I did.

OF THE CITIES, AND NAMELY OF AMAUROTE.[10]
BOOK II. CHAPTER II

As for their cities, whoso knoweth one of them, knoweth them all: they be all so like one to another, as farforth as the nature of the place permitteth. I will describe therefore to you one or other of them, for it skilleth[11] not greatly which; but which rather than Amaurote? Of them all this is the worthiest and of most dignity. For the residue 'knowledge it for the head city, because there is the Councilhouse. Nor to me any of them all is better beloved, as wherein I lived five whole years together.

The city of Amaurote standeth upon the side of a low hill, in fashion almost four square. For the breadth of it beginneth a little beneath the top of the hill, and still continueth by the space of two miles, until it come to the river of Anyder.[12] The length of it, which lieth by the river's side, is somewhat more.

The river of Anyder riseth four and twenty miles above Amaurote out of a little spring. But being increased by other small rivers and brooks that run into it, and, among other, two somewhat big ones, before the city it is half a mile broad, and farther, broader. And forty miles beyond the city it falleth into the ocean sea. By all that space that lieth between the sea and the city, and certain miles also above the city, the water ebbeth and floweth six hours together with a swift tide. When the sea floweth in, for the length of thirty miles it filleth all the Anyder with salt water, and driveth back the fresh water of the river. And somewhat further it changeth the sweetness of the fresh water with saltness. But a little beyond that the river waxeth sweet, and runneth forby[13] the city fresh and pleasant. And when the sea ebbeth and goeth back again, the fresh water followeth it almost even to the very fall into the sea. There goeth a bridge over the river made not of piles or of timber, but of stonework, with gorgeous and substantial arches at that part of the city that is farthest from the sea; to the intent that ships may pass along forby all the side of the city without let.

They have also another river, which indeed is not very great. But it runneth gently and pleasantly. For it riseth even out of the same hill that the city standeth upon, and runneth down a slope through the midst of the city into Anyder. And because it riseth a little without the city, the Amaurotians have enclosed the head spring of it with strong fences and bulwarks, and so have joined it to the city. This is done to the intent that the water should not be stopped, nor turned away, or poisoned, if their enemies should chance to come upon them. From thence the water is derived and conveyed down in canals of brick divers ways into the lower parts of the city. Where that cannot be done, by reason that the place will not suffer it, there they gather the rain-water in great cisterns, which doth them as good service.

The city is compassed about with a high and thick stone wall full of turrets and bulwarks. A dry ditch, but deep, and broad, and overgrown with bushes, briers, and thorns, goeth about three sides or quarters of the city. To the fourth side the river itself serveth for a ditch.

The streets be appointed[14] and set forth very commodious and handsome, both for carriage,[15] and also against the winds. The houses be of fair and gorgeous building, and on the street side they stand joined together in a long row through the whole street without any partition or separation. The streets be twenty foot broad.* On the back side of the houses, through the whole length of the street, lie large gardens, inclosed round about with the back part of the streets. Every house hath

---

10 The name means "dark, unknown."
11 matters   12 i. e., waterless

13 past (German *vorbei*)   15 transportation
14 arranged
* To More this width seemed generous. Some of the busiest streets of London were, until a recent date, scarcely wider.

two doors, one into the street, and a postern door on the back side into the garden. These doors be made with two leaves, never locked nor bolted, so easy to be opened that they will follow the least drawing of a finger, and shut again alone. Whoso will, may go in, for there is nothing within the houses that is private, or any man's own. And every tenth year they change their houses by lot.

They set great store by their gardens. In them they have vineyards, all manner of fruit, herbs, and flowers, so pleasant, so well furnished, and so finely kept, that I never saw thing more fruitful, nor better trimmed in any place. Their study and diligence herein cometh not only of pleasure, but also of a certain strife and contention that is between street and street, concerning the trimming, husbanding, and furnishing of their gardens—every man for his own part. And verily you shall not lightly find in all the city anything that is more commodious, either for the profit of the citizens, or for pleasure. And therefore it may seem that the first founder of the city minded nothing so much as these gardens.

For they say that king Utopus himself, even at the first beginning, appointed and drew forth the platform[16] of the city into this fashion and figure that it hath now, but the gallant garnishing, and the beautiful setting forth of it, whereunto he saw that one man's age would not suffice, that he left to his posterity. For their chronicles, which they keep written with all diligent circumspection, containing the history of one thousand seven hundred and sixty years, even from the first conquest of the island, record and witness that the houses in the beginning were very low, and, like homely cottages or poor shepherd houses, made at all adventures[17] of every rude piece of timber that came first to hand, with mud walls, and ridged roofs, thatched over with straw. But now the houses be curiously builded after a gorgeous and gallant sort, with three stories one over another. The outsides of the walls be made either of hard flint, or of plaster, or else of brick, and the inner sides be well strengthened with timber-work. The roofs be plain and flat, covered with a certain kind of plaster that is of no cost, and yet so tempered that no fire can hurt or perish it, and withstandeth the violence of the weather better than any lead. They keep the wind out of their windows with glass, for it is there much used, and somewhere also with fine linen cloth dipped in oil or amber, and that for two com-

modities. For by this means more light cometh in, and the wind is better kept out.†

OF SCIENCES, CRAFTS AND OCCUPATIONS. BOOK II. CHAPTER IV

Husbandry is a science common to them all in general, both men and women, wherein they be all expert and cunning. In this they be all instructed even from their youth, partly in their schools with traditions and precepts, and partly in the country nigh the city, brought up[18] as it were in playing, not only beholding the use of it, but, by occasion of exercising their bodies, practicing it also. Besides husbandry, which (as I said) is common to them all, every one of them learneth one or other several[19] and particular science as his own proper craft. That is most commonly either cloth-working in wool or flax, or masonry, or the smith's craft, or the carpenter's science. For there is none other occupation that any number to speak of doth use there.

For[20] their garments, which throughout all the island be of one fashion (saving that there is a difference between the man's garment and the woman's, between the married and the unmarried), and this one continueth for ever more unchanged, seemly and comely to the eye, no let to the moving and wielding of the body, also fit both for winter and summer,—as for these garments (I say), every family maketh their own. But of the other aforesaid crafts every man learneth one. And not only the men, but also the women. But the women, as the weaker sort, be put to the easier crafts, as to work wool and flax. The more laborsome sciences be committed to the men. For the most part every man is brought up in his father's craft. For most commonly they be naturally thereto bent and inclined. But if a man's mind stand to any other, he is by adoption put into a family of that occupation which he doth most fantasy. Whom not only his father, but also the magistrates do diligently look to, that he be put to a discreet and an honest householder. Yea, and if any person, when he hath learned one craft, be desirous to learn also another, he is likewise suffered and permitted. When he hath learned both, he occupieth whether he will,[21] unless the city have more need of the one than of the other.

---

[18] The Latin reads *educti* and should have been translated "led out."
[19] separate
[20] as for   [21] practises whichever he wishes
† Glass windows were introduced into the wealthier houses in England probably in More's time. Other houses continued to use slat and wicker lattices and panels of horn.

The chief and almost the only office of the Syphogrants‡ is to see and take heed that no man sit idle, but that every one apply his own craft with earnest diligence; and yet for all that, not to be wearied from early in the morning to late in the evening with continual work, like laboring and toiling beasts. For this is worse than the miserable and wretched condition of bondmen. Which nevertheless is almost everywhere the life of workmen and artificers, saving in Utopia. For they, dividing the day and the night into twenty-four just hours, appoint and assign only six of those hours to work, three before noon, upon the which they go straight to dinner; and after dinner, when they have rested two hours, then they work three hours, and upon that they go to supper.§ About eight of the clock in the evening (counting one of the clock at the first hour after noon), they go to bed: eight hours they give to sleep. All the void time that is between the hours of work, sleep, and meat, that they be suffered to bestow, every man as he liketh best himself. Not to th' intent that they should misspend this time in riot or slothfulness, but, being then licensed[22] from the labor of their own occupations, to bestow the time well and thriftily upon some other science, as shall please them. For it is a solemn custom there to have lectures daily early in the morning, where to be present they only be constrained that be namely chosen and appointed to learning. Howbeit, a great multitude of every sort of people, both men and women, go to hear lectures, some one, and some another, as every man's nature is inclined. Yet, this notwithstanding, if any man had rather bestow this time upon his own occupation (as it chanceth in many whose minds rise not in the contemplation of any science liberal), he is not letted nor prohibited, but is also[23] praised and commended, as profitable to the commonwealth.

After supper they bestow one hour in play, in summer in their gardens, in winter in their common halls, where they dine and sup. There they exercise themselves in music, or else in honest and wholesome communication. Diceplay, and such other foolish and pernicious games, they know not. But they use two games not much unlike the chess. The one is the Battle of Numbers, wherein one number

stealeth away another. The other is wherein Vices fight with Virtues, as it were in battle array, or a set field. In the which game is very properly showed, both the strife and discord that vices have among themselves, and again their unity and concord against virtues; and also what vices be repugnant to what virtues—with what power and strength they assail them openly, by what wiles and subtlety they assault them secretly; with what help and aid the virtues resist and overcome the puissance of the vices; by what craft they frustrate their purposes; and finally by what sleight or means the one getteth the victory.

But here, lest you be deceived, one thing you must look more narrowly[24] upon. For seeing they bestow but six hours in work, perchance you may think that the lack of some necessary things hereof may ensue. But this is nothing so. For that small time is not only enough, but also too much, for the store and abundance of all things that be requisite either for the necessity or commodity of life. The which thing you also shall perceive if you weigh and consider with yourselves how great a part of the people in other countries liveth idle. First, almost all women, which be the half of the whole number: or else if the women be somewhere occupied, there most commonly in their stead the men be idle. Besides this, how great and how idle a company is there of priests, and religious men[25], as they call them. Put thereto all rich men, specially all landed men, which commonly be called gentlemen and noblemen. Take into this number also their servants; I mean all that flock of stout, bragging rush-bucklers.[26] Join to them also sturdy and valiant beggars, cloaking their idle life under the color of some disease or sickness. And truly you shall find them[27] much fewer than you thought, by whose labor all these things are wrought that in men's affairs are now daily used and frequented.

Now consider with yourself, of these few that do work, how few be occupied in necessary works. For where money beareth all the swing, there many vain and superfluous occupations must needs be used to serve only for riotous superfluity and unhonest pleasure. For the same multitude that now is occupied in work, if they were divided into so few occupations as the necessary use of nature requireth, in so great plenty of things as then of necessity would ensue, doubtless the prices would be

22 freed   23 even
‡ Officers, two hundred in number, each elected by and ruling over thirty families. The word, like Tranibore and other supposed words of the old Utopian tongue, is meaningless.
§ In England, in More's time summer working hours were from 5 a. m. to 7 p. m.

24 closely   26 swashbucklers
25 men attached to some   27 those
   religious order;
   monks, etc.

too little for the artificers to maintain their livings. But if all these that be now busied about unprofitable occupations, with all the whole flock of them that live idly and slothfully, which consume and waste every one of them more of these things that come by other men's labor than two of the workmen themselves do; if all these (I say) were set to profitable occupations, you easily perceive how little time would be enough, yea and too much, to store us with all things that may be requisite either for necessity or for commodity, yea or for pleasure, so that the same pleasure be true and natural.

And this in Utopia the thing itself maketh manifest and plain. For there, in all the city, with the whole country or shire adjoining to it, scarcely five hundred persons of all the whole number of men and women, that be neither too old nor too weak to work, be licensed and discharged from labor. Among them be the Syphogrants, who, though they be by the laws exempt and privileged from labor, yet they exempt not themselves; to the intent that they may the rather by their example provoke others to work. The same vacation from labor do they[27] also enjoy to whom the people, persuaded by the commendation of the priests and secret election of the Syphogrants, have given a perpetual licence from labor to learning. But if any one of them prove not according to the expectation and hope of him conceived, he is forthwith plucked back to the company of artificers. And, contrariwise, often it chanceth that a handicraftsman doth so earnestly bestow his vacant and spare hours in learning, and through diligence so profiteth therein, that he is taken from his handy[28] occupation and promoted to the company of the learned. Out of this order of the learned be chosen ambassadors, priests, Tranibores,* and finally the prince himself, whom they in their old tongue call Barzanes, and by a newer name, Adamus.[29] The residue of the people being neither idle, nor yet occupied about unprofitable exercises, it may be easily judged in how few hours how much good work by them may be done and dispatched towards those things that I have spoken of.

This commodity they have also above others, that in the most part of necessary occupations they need not so much work as other nations do. For first of all the building or repairing of houses asketh everywhere so many men's continual labor, because that the unthrifty heir suffereth the houses that his father builded in continuance of time to fall in decay. So, that which he might have upholden with little cost, his successor is constrained to build it again anew, to his great charge. Yea, many times also the house that stood one man in[30] much money, another is of so nice and so delicate a mind that he setteth nothing by it. And it being neglected, and therefore shortly falling into ruin, he buildeth up another in another place with no less cost and charge. But among the Utopians, where all things be set in a good order, and the commonwealth in a good stay,[31] it very seldom chanceth that they choose a new plot to build an house upon. And they do not only find speedy and quick remedies for present faults, but also prevent them that be like to fall. And by this means their houses continue and last very long with little labor and small reparations, in so much that this kind of workmen sometimes have almost nothing to do, but that they be commanded to hew timber at home, and to square and trim up stones, to the intent that if any work chance, it may the speedlier rise.

Now, sir, in their apparel, mark (I pray you) how few workmen they need. First of all, whiles they be at work, they be covered homely with leather or skins that will last seven years. When they go forth abroad, they cast upon them a cloak, which hideth the other homely apparel. These cloaks throughout the whole island be all of one color, and that is the natural color of the wool. They therefore do not only spend much less woolen cloth than is spent in other countries, but also the same standeth them in much less cost. But linen cloth is made with less labor, and is therefore had more in use. But in linen cloth only whiteness, in woolen only cleanliness, is regarded. As for the smallness or fineness of the thread, that is nothing passed for.[32] And this is the cause wherefore in other places four or five cloth gowns of divers colors, and as many silk coats, be not enough for one man. Yea, and if he be of the delicate and nice sort, ten be too few; whereas there one garment will serve a man most commonly two years. For why should he desire more? Seeing if he had them, he should not be the better hapt[33] or covered from cold, neither in his apparel any whit the comelier.

Wherefore, seeing they be all exercised in profitable occupations, and that few artificers

---

28 manual   29 Or Ademus, "folkless"
* Magistrates, twenty in number, superior to the   30 cost   32 not at all heeded
    Syphogrants.   31 state   33 wrapt

n the same crafts be sufficient, this is the
ause that, plenty of all things being among
hem, they do sometimes bring forth an innu-
nerable company of people to amend the highways, if any be broken. Many times also,
vhen they have no such work to be occupied
bout, an open proclamation is made that they
hall bestow fewer hours in work. For the
nagistrates do not exercise their citizens
gainst their wills in unneedful labors. For
vhy, in the institution of that weal public this
nd is only and chiefly pretended[34] and minded,
hat what time may possibly be spared from
he necessary occupations and affairs of the
ommonwealth, all that the citizens should
vithdraw from the bodily service to the free
iberty of the mind and garnishing of the
ame. For herein they suppose the felicity of
nis life to consist.

F THEIR JOURNEYINGS OR TRAVELLING ABROAD,
WITH DIVERS OTHER MATTERS. BOOK II.
CHAPTER VI

But if any be desirous to visit either their
riends dwelling in another city, or to see the
lace itself, they easily obtain licence of their
yphograntes and Traniboures, unless there be
ome profitable let.[35] No man goeth out alone;
ut a company is sent forth together with their
rince's letters, which do testify that they have
cence to go that journey, and prescribeth also
ne day of their return. They have a wagon
iven them, with a common bondman,* which
riveth the oxen, and taketh charge of them.
ut unless they have women in their company,
ney send home the wagon again, as an im-
ediment and a let. And though they carry
othing forth with them, yet in all their jour-
ey they lack nothing. For wheresoever they
ome, they be at home. If they tarry in a
lace longer than one day, then there every one
f them falleth to his own occupation, and be
ery genteelly entertained of[36] the workmen
nd companies of the same crafts. If any man
f his own head and without leave walk out
f his precinct and bounds, taken without the
rince's letters, he is brought again for a
igitive or a runaway with great shame and
buke, and is sharply punished. If he be
ken in that fault again, he is punished with
ondage.
If any be desirous to walk abroad into the
elds, or into the country that belongeth to

the same city that he dwelleth in, obtaining the
good will of his father, and the consent of his
wife, he is not prohibited. But into what part
of the country soever he cometh he hath no
meat given him until he have wrought out his
forenoon's task, or dispatched so much work as
there is wont to be wrought before supper.
Observing this law and condition, he may go
whither he will within the bound of his own
city. For he shall be no less profitable to the
city than if he were within it.
Now you see how little liberty they have
to loiter; how they can have no cloak or pretence to idleness. There be neither wine-tav-
erns, nor ale-houses, nor stews,[37] nor any occasion of vice or wickedness, no lurking corners,
no places of wicked counsels or unlawful assemblies. But they be in the present sight and
under the eyes of every man. So that of necessity they must either apply[38] their accustomed
labors, or else recreate themselves with honest
and laudable pastimes. This fashion and trade
of life being used among the people, it cannot
be chosen but that they must of necessity have
store and plenty of all things. . .
They keep at home all the treasure which
they have, to be holpen and succored by it
either in extreme jeopardies, or in sudden dangers; but especially and chiefly to hire therewith, and that for unreasonable great wages,
strange soldiers. For they had rather put
strangers in jeopardy than their own countrymen; knowing that for money enough their
enemies themselves many times may be bought
or sold, or else through treason be set together
by the ears among themselves. For this cause
they keep an inestimable treasure; but yet not
as a treasure; but so they have it, and use it,
as in good faith I am ashamed to show, fearing that my words shall not be believed. And
this I have more cause to fear, for that I know
how difficultly and hardly I myself would have
believed another man telling the same if I had
not presently seen it with mine own eyes. For
it must needs be that how far a thing is dissonant and disagreeing from the guise and
trade[39] of the hearers, so far shall it be out
of their belief. Howbeit, a wise and indifferent esteemer[40] of things will not greatly marvel, perchance, seeing all their other laws and
customs do so much differ from ours, if the use
also of gold and silver among them be applied
rather to their own fashions than to ours. I
mean in that they occupy[41] not money them-

aimed at   36 by
business hindrance
Transgressors of the law in Utopia were made
   slaves and attached to the soil. Each farm
   had at least two bondmen.

37 low resorts   40 impartial judge
38 ply   41 use
39 manners and practice

selves, but keep it for that chance; which as it may happen, so it may be that it shall never come to pass.

In the meantime gold and silver, whereof money is made, they do so use, as none of them doth more esteem it than the very nature of the thing deserveth. And then who doth not plainly see how far it is under iron? as without the which men can no better live than without fire and water. Whereas to gold and silver nature hath given no use that we may not well lack if that[42] the folly of men had not set it in higher estimation for the rareness' sake. But of[43] the contrary part, nature, as a most tender and loving mother, hath placed the best and most necessary things open abroad: as the air, the water, and the earth itself; and hath removed and hid farthest from us vain and unprofitable things. Therefore if these metals among them should be fast locked up in some tower, it might be suspected that the prince and the Council (as the people is ever foolishly imagining) intended by some subtlety to deceive the commons, and to take some profit of it to themselves. Furthermore, if they should make thereof plate and such other finely and cunningly wrought stuff; if at any time they should have occasion to break it, and melt it again, therewith to pay their soldiers wages, they see and perceive very well that men would be loth to part from those things that they once began to have pleasure and delight in.

To remedy all this they have found out a means, which, as it is agreeable to all their other laws and customs, so it is from ours (where gold is so much set by, and so diligently kept) very far discrepant and repugnant; and therefore uncredible, but only to them that be wise. For wher as they eat and drink in earthen and glass vessels, which indeed be curiously and properly made, and yet be of very small value; of gold and silver they make commonly other vessels that serve for vile uses, not only in their common halls, but in every man's private house. Furthermore, of the same metals they make great chains, fetters, and gyves, wherein they tie their bondmen. Finally, whosoever for any offense be infamed,[44] by their ears hang rings of gold; upon their fingers they wear rings of gold, and about their necks chains of gold; and, in conclusion, their heads be tied about with gold. Thus by all means possible they procure to have gold and silver among them in reproach and infamy. And these metals which other

nations do so grievously and sorrowfully forego as in a manner their own lives, if they should altogether at once be taken from the Utopians, no man there would think that he had lost the worth of one farthing.

They gather also pearls by the seaside, and diamonds and carbuncles upon certain rocks, and yet they seek not for them; but by chance finding them, they cut and polish them. And therewith they deck their young infants. Which, like as in the first years of their childhood they make much and be fond and proud of such ornaments, so when they be a little more grown in years and discretion, perceiving that none but children do wear such toys and trifles, they lay them away even of their own shamefastness, without any bidding of their parents; even as our children, when they wax big, do cast away nuts, brooches, and puppets. Therefore these laws and customs, which be so far different from all other nations, how divers fantasies also and minds they do cause, did I never so plainly perceive, as in the ambassadors of the Anemolians.

These ambassadors came to Amaurote whilst I was there. And because they came to entreat of great and weighty matters, those three citizens apiece out of every city* were comen thither before them. But all the ambassadors of the next countries which had been there before and knew the fashions and manners of the Utopians, among whom they perceived no honor given to sumptuous apparel, silks to be contemned, gold also to be infamed and reproachful, were wont to come thither in very homely and simple array. But the Anemolians, because they dwell far thence and had very little acquaintance with them, hearing that they were all apparelled alike, and that very rudely and homely, thinking them not to have the things which they did not wear, being therefore more proud than wise, determined in the gorgeousness of their apparel to represent very gods, and with the bright shining and glistering of their gay clothing to dazzle the eyes of the silly[45] poor Utopians.

So there came in three ambassadors with one hundred servants all apparelled in changeable colors, the most of them in silks, the ambassadors themselves (for at home in their own country they were noblemen) in cloth of gold, with great chains of gold, with gold hanging at their ears, with gold rings upon their fingers, with brooches and aiglets of gold upon

---

42 it   44 disgraced
47 of

45 simple
* Utopian delegates mentioned in a previous chapter.

their caps, which glistered full of pearls and precious stones; to be short, trimmed and adorned with all those things which among the Utopians were either the punishment of bond-men, or the reproach of infamed persons, or else trifles for young children to play withal.[46] Therefore it would have done a man good at his heart to have seen how proudly they dis-played their peacocks' feathers, how much they made of their painted sheaths,[47] and how loft-ly they set forth and advanced themselves when they compared their gallant apparel with the poor raiment of the Utopians. For all the peo-ple were swarmed forth into the streets.

And on the other side it was no less pleasure to consider how much they were deceived, and how far they missed of their purpose, being contrariwise taken than they thought they should have been. For to the eyes of all the Utopians, except very few which had been in other countries for some reasonable cause, all that gorgeousness of apparel seemed shameful and reproachful. In so much that they most reverently saluted the vilest and most abject of them for lords; passing over the ambassadors themselves without any honor, judging them by their wearing of gold chains to be bondmen. Yea, you should have seen children also, that had cast away their pearls and precious stones, when they saw the like sticking on the ambassadors' caps, dig and push their mothers under the sides, saying thus to them: "Look, mother, how great a lubber doth yet wear pearls and precious stones, as though he were a little child still." But the mother, yea and that also in good earnest: "Peace, son," saith she, "I think he be some of the ambassadors' fools." Some found fault at their golden chains, as to no use nor purpose, being so small and weak that a bondman might easily break them, and again so wide and large that, when it pleased him, he might cast them off and run away at liberty whither he would.

But when the ambassadors had been there a day or two and saw so great abundance of gold so lightly esteemed, yea in no less re-proach than it was with them in honor; and besides that, more gold in the chains and gyves of one fugitive bondman than all the costly ornaments of them three was worth; they be-gan to abate their courage, and for very shame laid away all that gorgeous array whereof they were so proud; and specially when they had talked familiarly with the Utopians, and had learned all their fashions and opinions. For they marvel that any men be so foolish as to

have delight and pleasure in the doubtful glis-tering of a little trifling stone, which[48] may behold any of the stars, or else the sun itself; or that any man is so mad as to count him-self the nobler for the smaller or finer thread of wool, which self-same wool (be it now in never so fine a spun thread) a sheep did once wear; and yet was she all that time no other thing than a sheep. . . .

These and such like opinions have they con-ceived, partly by education, being brought up in that commonwealth whose laws and customs be far different from these kinds of folly, and partly by good literature and learning. For though there be not many in every city which be exempt and discharged from all other labors and appointed only to learning, that is to say, such in whom even from their very childhood they have perceived a singular towardness, a fine wit, and a mind apt to good learning; yet all in their childhood be instruct in learning. And the better part of the people, both men and women, throughout all their whole life do bestow in learning those spare hours which we said they have vacant from bodily labors.*

ROGER ASCHAM (1515-1568)

TOXOPHILUS†

FROM THE FOREWORD

To all Gentlemen and Yeomen of England:

Bias, the wise man, came to Croesus, the rich king, on a time when he was making new ships, purposing to have subdued by water the out isles lying betwixt Greece and Asia Minor. "What news now in Greece?" saith the king

[48] who

* It may be worth noting that our word "school" is derived from *schola*, "leisure."
† "Toxophilus" means "a lover of the bow," and the book is in the form of a dialogue between Toxophilus, an archer, and Philologus, a scholar. Two centuries before, at the battle of Crecy, the British yeomen had shown the superiority of the long bow in battle to the equipment of the armed knight, and archery had been assiduously cultivated, though when Ascham wrote this (1545) it was, for purposes of war, gradually giving way to fire-arms. If Ascham was conservative in clinging to this old-time weapon, in another respect he was courageously radical. That is in his employ-ment of the English vernacular for a learned prose treatise. That he was conscious of making a literary departure is manifest in this Preface, and also in the dedication to King Henry which preceded it, where he de-fended himself for having "written this Eng-lish matter in the English tongue for English men," although to have written it "either in Latin or Greek had been more easier." See *Eng. Lit.*, p. 81.

with

47 coverings

to Bias. "None other news but these," saith Bias, "that the isles of Greece have prepared a wonderful company of horsemen to overrun Lydia withal." "There is nothing under heaven," saith the king, "that I would so soon wish, as that they durst be so bold to[1] meet us on the land with horse." "And think you," saith Bias, "that there is anything which they would sooner wish than that you should be so fond[2] to meet them on the water with ships?" And so Croesus, hearing not the true news, but perceiving the wise man's mind and counsel, both gave then over making of his ships, and left also behind him a wonderful example for all commonwealths to follow: that is, evermore to regard and set most by that thing whereunto nature hath made them most apt and use hath made them most fit.

By this matter I mean the shooting in the long bow, for English men. Which thing with all my heart I do wish, and if I were of authority I would counsel, all the gentlemen and yeomen of England not to change it with any other thing, how good soever it seem to be, but that still, according to the old wont of England, youth should use it for the most honest pastime in peace, that men might handle it as a most sure weapon in war. Other strong weapons which both experience doth prove to be good, and the wisdom of the King's Majesty and his Council provides to be had, are not ordained to take away shooting; but that both, not compared together whether[3] should be better than the other, but so joined together that the one should be always an aid and help for the other, might so strengthen the realm on all sides that no kind of enemy, in any kind of weapon, might pass and go beyond us.

For this purpose, I, partly provoked by the counsel of some gentlemen, partly moved by the love which I have always borne toward shooting, have written this little treatise, wherein if I have not satisfied any man, I trust he will the rather be content with my doing, because I am, I suppose, the first which hath said anything in this matter; and few beginnings be perfect, saith wise men. And also because, if I have said amiss, I am content that any man amend it, or if I have said too little, any man that will to add what him pleaseth to it.

My mind is, in profiting and pleasing every man, to hurt or displease no man, intending none other purpose but that youth might be stirred to labor, honest pastime, and virtue, and, as much as lay in me, plucked from idleness, unthrifty games, and vice. Which thing I have labored only in this book, showing ho[w] fit shooting is for all kinds of men, how hon[est] a pastime for the mind, how wholesome a exercise for the body, not vile for great me[n] to use, not costly for poor men to sustain, n[o] lurking in holes and corners for ill men a[nd] their pleasure to misuse it, but abiding in th[e] open sight and face of the world for good me[n] if it fault, by their wisdom to correct it. An[d] here I would desire all gentlemen and yeome[n] to use this pastime in such a mean that th[e] outrageousness of gaming should not hurt th[e] honesty[4] of shooting, which of his own natu[re] is always joined with honesty, yet for men[s] faults oftentimes blamed unworthily, as a[ll] good things have been and evermore shall be.

If any man would blame me, either for ta[k]ing such a matter in hand, or else for writin[g] it in the English tongue, this answer I ma[y] make him, that what the best of the real[m] think it honest[5] for them to use, I, one of th[e] meanest[6] sort, ought not to suppose it vile fo[r] me to write. And though to have written in another tongue had been both more profi[t]able for my study and also more honest[5] fo[r] my name, yet I can think my labor well b[e]stowed if, with a little hindrance of my pro[fit] and name, may come any furtherance to th[e] pleasure or commodity of the gentlemen an[d] yeomen of England, for whose sake I took th[e] matter in hand. And as for the Latin or Gree[k] tongue, everything is so excellently done i[n] them that none can do better; in the Englis[h] tongue, contrary, everything in a manner [so] meanly, both for the matter and handling, tha[t] no man can do worse. For therein the lea[st] learned for the most part have been alway[s] most ready to write, and they which had lea[st] hope in Latin have been most bold in Englis[h] when surely every man that is most ready [to] talk is not most able to write. He that wi[ll] write well in any tongue must follow this cou[n]sel of Aristotle:—to speak as the common pe[o]ple do, to think as wise men do; and so shou[ld] every man understand him, and the judgme[nt] of wise men allow[7] him.

Many English writers have not done so, b[ut] using strange words, as Latin, French, a[nd] Italian, do make all things dark and har[d]. Once I communed with a man which reasone[d] the English tongue to be enriched and i[n]creased thereby, saying: Who will not prai[se] that feast where a man shall drink at a dinn[er] both wine, ale, and beer? Truly, quoth I, th[ey] be all good, every one taken by himself alo[ne] but if you put malmsey and sack, red wine a[nd] white, ale and beer, and all in one pot, you shall make a drink neither easy to be known nor yet wholesome for the body. Cicero, in following Isocrates, Plato, and Demosthenes, increased the Latin tongue after another sort. This way[8] because divers men that write do not know, they can neither follow it, because of their ignorancy, nor yet will praise it, for very arrogancy—two faults, seldom the one out of the other's company.

English writers, by diversity of time, have taken diverse matters in hand. In our fathers' time nothing was read but books of feigned chivalry, wherein a man by reading should be led to none other end but only to manslaughter and bawdry. If any man suppose they were good enough to pass the time withal, he is deceived. For surely vain words do work no small thing thereunto of their own nature. These books, as I have heard say, were made the most part in abbeys and monasteries, a very likely and fit fruit of such an idle and blind kind of living.*

In our time now, when every man is given to know much rather than to live well, very many do write, but after such a fashion as very many do shoot. Some shooters take in hand stronger bows than they be able to maintain. This thing maketh them sometime to outshoot the mark, sometime to shoot far wide, and perchance hurt some that look on. Other that never learned to shoot, nor yet knoweth good shaft nor bow, will be as busy as the best, but such one commonly plucketh down[9] a side, and crafty archers which be against him will be both glad of him, and also ever ready to lay[10] and bet with him; it were better for such one to sit down than shoot. Other there be which have very good bow and shafts and good knowledge in shooting, but they have been brought up in such evil-favored shooting that they can neither shoot fair nor yet near. If any man will apply these things together, he shall not see the one far differ from the other.

And I also, among all other, in writing this little treatise, have followed some young shooters, which both will begin to shoot for a little money, and also will use to shoot once or twice about the mark for nought afore they begin agood. And therefore did I take this little matter in hand to assay[11] myself, and hereafter, by the grace of God, if the judgment of wise men that look on think that I can do any

good, I may perhaps cast my shaft among other for better game.

THE WAYS OF THE WIND. FROM BOOK II

The wind is sometimes plain up and down, which is commonly most certain, and requireth least knowledge, wherein a mean shooter with mean gear,[1] if he can shoot home, may make best shift. A side wind tryeth an archer and good gear very much. Sometime it bloweth aloft, sometime hard by the ground; sometime it bloweth by blasts, and sometime it continueth all in one; sometime full side wind, sometime quarter with him and more, and likewise against him, as a man with casting up light grass, or else if he take good heed, shall sensibly learn by experience.

To see the wind with a man his[2] eyes, it is impossible, the nature of it is so fine and subtle; yet this experience of the wind had I once myself, and that was in the great snow that fell four years ago. I rode in the highway betwixt Topcliffe-upon-Swale and Boroughbridge, the way being somewhat trodden before by wayfaring men. The fields on both sides were plain and lay almost yard deep with snow; the night afore had been a little frost, so that the snow was hard and crusted above. That morning the sun shone bright and clear, the wind was whistling aloft, and sharp, according to the time of the year. The snow in the highway lay loose and trodden with horse' feet: so as the wind blew, it took the loose snow with it, and made it so slide upon the snow in the field, which was hard and crusted by reason of the frost over night, that thereby I might see very well the whole nature of the wind as it blew that day. And I had a great delight and pleasure to mark it, which maketh me now far better to remember it.

Sometime the wind would be not past two yards broad, and so it would carry the snow as far as I could see. Another time the snow would blow over half the field at once. Sometime the snow would tumble softly, by and by it would fly wonderful fast. And this I perceived also, that the wind goeth by streams and not whole together. For I should see one stream within a score[3] of me, then the space of two score no snow would stir, but after so much quantity of ground another stream of snow at the same very time should be carried likewise, but not equally; for the one would

---

8 Construe after "know." 10 wager
9 lowers the score of 11 try
* Ascham is manifestly condemning such romances as Malory's *Le Morte Darthur*. England was at this time Protestant, and the dissolution of the monasteries a recent event.

1 ordinary equipment
2 man's (a pedantic form, due to the erroneous idea that the possessive s was a contraction of *his*).
3 twenty yards

stand still when the other flew apace, and so continue, sometime swiftlier, sometime slowlier, sometime broader, sometime narrower, as far as I could see. Nor it flew not straight, but sometime it crooked this way, sometime that way, and sometime it ran round about in a compass. And some time the snow would be lifted clean from the ground up in the air; and by and by it would be all clapped to the ground as though there had been no wind at all; straightway it would rise and fly again.

And—that which was the most marvelous of all—at one time two drifts of snow flew, the one out of the west into the east, the other out of the north into the east. And I saw two winds by reason of the snow, the one cross over the other, as it had been two highways. And again I should hear the wind blow in the air when nothing was stirred at the ground. And when all was still where I rode, not very far from me the snow should be lifted wonderfully. This experience made me more marvel at the nature of the wind, than it made me cunning in the knowledge of the wind; but yet thereby I learned perfectly that it is no marvel at all, although men in a wind lease[4] their length[5] in shooting, seeing so many ways the wind is so variable in blowing.

THE SCHOOLMASTER*

FROM A PREFACE TO THE READER

When the great plague was at London, the year 1563, the Queen's Majesty, Queen Elizabeth, lay at her castle of Windsor; where, upon the tenth day of December, it fortuned that in Sir William Cecil's chamber (her Highness' Principal Secretary), there dined together these personages: Mr. Secretary himself, Sir William Peter, Sir J. Mason, D. Wotton, Sir Richard Sackville, Treasurer of the Exchequer, Sir Walter Mildmay, Chancellor of the Exchequer, Mr. Haddon, Master of Requests, Mr. John Astley, Master of the Jewel House, Mr. Bernard Hampton, Mr. Nicasius, and I. Of which number the most part were of her Majesty's most honorable Privy Council, and the rest serving her in very good place. I was

glad then, and do rejoice yet to remember, that my chance was so happy to be there that day in the company of so many wise and good men together as hardly then could have been picked out again out of all England beside.

Mr. Secretary hath this accustomed manner, though his head be never so full of most weighty affairs of the realm, yet at dinner time he doth seem to lay them always aside, and findeth ever fit occasion to talk pleasantly of other matters, but most gladly of some matter of learning; wherein he will courteously hear the mind of the meanest[1] at his table.

Not long after our sitting down, "I have strange news brought me," saith Mr. Secretary, "this morning, that divers scholars of Eton be run away from the school for fear of beating." Whereupon Mr. Secretary took occasion to wish that some more discretion were in many schoolmasters, in using correction than commonly there is; who many times punish rather the weakness of nature than the fault of the scholar; whereby many scholars that might else prove well, be driven to hate learning before they know what learning meaneth, and so are made willing to forsake their book and be glad to be put to any other kind of living.

Mr. Peter, as one somewhat severe of nature, said plainly that the rod only[2] was the sword that must keep the school in obedience and the scholar in good order. Mr. Wotton, a man mild of nature, with soft voice and few words inclined to Mr. Secretary's judgment, and said "In mine opinion, the schoolhouse should be indeed, as it is called by name,[3] the house of play and pleasure, and not of fear and bondage. And as I do remember, so saith Socrates in one place of Plato.[4] And therefore, if a rod carry the fear of a sword, it is no marvel if those that be fearful of nature choose rather to forsake the play, than to stand always within the fear of a sword in a fond[5] man's handling.

Mr. Mason, after his manner, was very merry with both parties, pleasantly playing both with the shrewd touches[6] of many curst[7] boys, and with the small discretion of many lewd[8] schoolmasters. Mr. Haddon was fully of Mr. Peter's opinion, and said that the best schoolmaster of our time was the greatest beater; and named the person. "Though," quoth I, "it was his good fortune to send from his school unto the university one of the best scholars indeed of all our time, yet wise men do think that that came

4 lose
5 distance between the archer and the target
* While Ascham belongs to the generation preceding the Elizabethans, this last work of his was written and published (posthumously, 1570) well within the Virgin Queen's reign, and the little glimpse behind the curtain which its preface affords may serve both to introduce and to exemplify what Tennyson has so happily called "the spacious times of great Elizabeth."

1 humblest
2 alone
3 See note on "school," page 119.
4 i. e., of Plato's works
5 foolish
6 mischievous traits
7 perverse
8 ignorant

to pass rather by the great towardness of the scholar than by the great beating of the master; and whether this be true or no, you yourself are best witness.'' I said somewhat further in the matter how and why young children were sooner allured by love, than driven by beating, to attain good learning; wherein I was the bolder to say my mind because Mr. Secretary courteously provoked me thereunto, or else in such a company, and namely in his presence, my wont is to be more willing to use mine ears than to occupy my tongue. Sir Walter Mildmay, Mr. Astley, and the rest, said very little; only Sir Richard Sackville said nothing at all.

After dinner I went up to read with the Queen's Majesty. We read then together in the Greek tongue, as I well remember, that noble oration of Demosthenes against Aeschines for his false dealing in his embassage to King Philip of Macedonia. Sir Richard Sackville came up soon after, and finding me in her Majesty's privy chamber, he took me by the hand, and carrying me to a window said: Mr. Ascham, I would not for a good deal of money have been this day absent from dinner, where though I said nothing, yet I gave as good ear, and do consider as well the talk that passed, as any one did there. Mr. Secretary said very wisely, and most truly, that many young wits be driven to hate learning before they know what learning is. I can be good witness to this myself. For a fond schoolmaster, before I was fully fourteen years old, drave me so, with fear of beating, from all love of learning, as⁹ now—when I know what difference it is to have learning, and to have little or none at all—I feel it my greatest grief, and find it my greatest hurt that ever came to me, that it was my so ill chance to light upon so lewd a schoolmaster. But seeing it is but in vain to lament things past, and also wisdom to look to things to come, surely, God willing, if God lend me life, I will make this my mishap some occasion of good hap to little Robert Sackville, my son's son. For whose bringing up I would gladly, if it so please you, use specially your good advice. I hear say you have a son much of his age. We will deal thus together. Point you out a schoolmaster who by your order shall teach my son and yours, and for all the rest I will provide; yea, though they three do cost me a couple of hundred pounds by year. And beside, you shall find me as fast a friend to you and yours as perchance any you have.'' Which promise the worthy

gentleman surely kept with me until his dying day.

We had then further talk together of bringing up of children; of the nature of quick and hard wits;[10] of the right choice of a good wit; of fear and love in teaching children. We passed from children and came to young men, namely Gentlemen. We talked of their too much liberty to live as they lust[11]; of their letting loose too soon to overmuch experience of ill, contrary to the good order of many good old commonwealths of the Persians and Greeks; of wit[12] gathered and good fortune gotten by some only by experience, without learning. And lastly, he required of me very earnestly to show what I thought of the common going of English men into Italy.

''But,'' saith he, ''because this place and this time will not suffer so long talk as these good matters require, therefore I pray you, at my request, and at your leisure, put in some order of writing the chief points of this our talk concerning the right order of teaching and honesty of living, for the good bringing up of children and young men. And surely, beside contenting me, you shall both please and profit very many others.'' I made some excuse by lack of ability and weakness of body. ''Well,'' saith he, ''I am not now to learn what you can do. Our dear friend, Mr. Goodrick, whose judgment I could well believe, did once for all satisfy me fully therein. Again, I heard you say not long ago that you may thank Sir John Cheke* for all the learning you have. And I know very well myself that you did teach the Queen. And therefore seeing God did so bless you, to make you the scholar of the best master, and also the schoolmaster of the best scholar, that ever were in our time, surely you should please God, benefit your country, and honest[13] your own name, if you would take the pains to impart to others what you learned of such a master, and how ye taught such a scholar. And in uttering the stuff ye received of the one, in declaring the order ye took with the other, ye shall never lack neither matter nor manner, what to write nor how to write, in this kind of argument.'' I, beginning some farther excuse, suddenly was called to come to the Queen.

The night following I slept little, my head was so full of this our former talk, and I so mindful somewhat to satisfy the honest request of so dear a friend. I thought to prepare some little treatise for a New Year's gift

10 intellects   12 knowledge
11 like   13 honor
* A famous teacher at St. John's, Cambridge, who gave a great impulse to classical learning.

that

that Christmas. But, as it chanceth to busy builders, so, in building this my poor school-house (the rather because the form of it is somewhat new, and differing from others), the work rose daily higher and wider than I thought it would in the beginning. And though it appear now, and be in very deed, but a small cottage, poor for the stuff and rude for the workmanship, yet in going forward I found the site so good as I was loth to give it over, but the making so costly, outreaching my ability, as many times I wished that some one of those three my dear friends with full purses, Sir Thomas Smith, Mr. Haddon, or Mr. Watson, had had the doing of it. Yet nevertheless I myself, spending gladly that little that I gat at home by good Sir John Cheke, and that that I borrowed abroad of my friend Sturmius, beside somewhat that was left me in reversion by my old masters Plato, Aristotle, and Cicero, I have at last patched it up as I could, and as you see.

A GENTLE TEACHER AND PUPIL. FROM BOOK I.

And one example whether love or fear doth work more in a child for virtue and learning, I will gladly report; which may be heard with some pleasure, and followed with more profit. Before I went into Germany I came to Broadgate in Leicestershire, to take my leave of that noble Lady Jane Grey, to whom I was exceeding much beholden. Her parents, the duke and duchess, with all the household, gentlemen and gentlewomen, were hunting in the park. I found her in her chamber reading "Phaedon Platonis"[1] in Greek, and that with as much delight as some gentlemen would read a merry tale in Bocase.[2] After salutation and duty done, with some other talk, I asked her why she would lose such pastime in the park? Smiling she answered me, "I wis,[3] all their

sport in the park is but a shadow to that pleasure that I find in Plato. Alas! good folk, they never felt what true pleasure meant." "And how came you, madam," quoth I, "to this deep knowledge of pleasure, and what did chiefly allure you unto it, seeing, not many women, but very few men, have attained thereunto?" "I will tell you," quoth she; "and tell you a truth which, perchance, ye will marvel at. One of the greatest benefits that ever God gave me is that he sent me so sharp and severe parents and so gentle a schoolmaster. For when I am in presence of either father or mother, whether I speak, keep silence, sit, stand, or go, eat, drink, be merry or sad, be sewing, playing, dancing, or doing anything else, I must do it, as it were, in such weight, measure, and number, even so perfectly as God made the world, or else I am so sharply taunted, so cruelly threatened, yea presently sometimes with pinches, nips, and bobs,[4] and other ways which I will not name for the honor I bear them, so without measure misordered,[5] that I think myself in hell till time come that I must go to Mr. Elmer, who teacheth me so gently, so pleasantly, with such fair allurements to learning, that I think all the time nothing whilst I am with him. And when I am called from him I fall on[6] weeping, because whatsoever I do else but learning, is full of grief, trouble, fear, and whole misliking unto me. And thus my book hath been so much my pleasure, and bringeth daily to me more pleasure and more, that in respect of it all other pleasures, in very deed, be but trifles and troubles unto me."

I remember this talk gladly, both because it is so worthy of memory, and because also it was the last talk that ever I had and the last time that ever I saw that noble and worthy lady.

---

1 Plato's *Phaedo,* on the Immortality of the Soul.
2 Boccaccio.　　　3 y-wis, certainly

4 raps
5 ill disciplined

6 to (a-weeping)

THE ELIZABETHAN AGE—POETRY

SIR THOMAS WYATT
(1503-1542)*

THE LOVER HAVING DREAMED OF ENJOYMENT
OF HIS LOVE, COMPLAINETH THAT THE DREAM
IS NOT EITHER LONGER OR TRUER

Unstable dream, according to the place,†
Be steadfast once, or else at least be true.
By tasted sweetness make me not to rue
The sudden loss of thy false feigned grace.
By good respect in such a dangerous case
Thou broughtst not her into these tossing seas,
But madest my spirit to live, my care t'en-
    crease,
My body in tempest her delight t'embrace.
The body dead, the spirit had his desire;
Painless was the one, the other in delight.
Why then, alas! did it not keep it right,
But thus return to leap into the fire,
And where it was at wish, could not remain?
Such mocks of dreams do turn to deadly pain.

OF HIS LOVE THAT PRICKED HER FINGER WITH
    A NEEDLE

She sat and sewed, that hath done me the
    wrong
Whereof I plain, and have done many a day;
And whilst she heard my plaint in piteous
    song,
She wished my heart the sampler[1], that[2] it
    lay.
The blind master whom I have served so long,
Grudging to hear that[3] he did hear her say,
Made her own weapon do[4] her finger bleed,
To feel if pricking were so good indeed!

1 needle-work pattern   3 that which
2 as   4 make

* Though Wyatt and Surrey were, in strictness,
pre-Elizabethans, their poems, first published
in 1557, were manifest harbingers of the
creative impulse we associate with Elizabeth's
reign. Thirty years later Sidney called these
poets "the two chief lanterns of light to all
others that have since employed their pens
upon English poesy." Wyatt introduced the
Petrarchian sonnet form into England; Surrey devised the variation used later by Shakespeare: and Surrey was the first to employ
heroic blank verse. See *Eng. Lit.*, p. 84.
† This phrase appears to have more rhyme than
reason. Possibly *place = text*, referring to
1 Cor., xv, 58.

THE LOVER COMPLAINETH THE UNKINDNESS OF
    HIS LOVE

My lute, awake, perform the last
Labour that thou and I shall waste,
And end that[1] I have now begun.
And when this song is sung and past,
My lute, be still, for I have done.

As to be heard where ear is none,
As lead to grave[2] in marble stone,
My song may pierce her heart as soon.
Should we then sigh or sing or moan?
No, no, my lute, for I have done.

The rocks do not so cruelly
Repulse the waves continually,
As she my suit and affection;
So that I am past remedy,
Whereby my lute and I have done.

Proud of the spoil that thou hast got
Of simple hearts through Lovës shot,
By whom unkind thou hast them won,
Think not he hath his bow forgot,
Although my lute and I have done.

Vengeance shall fall on thy disdain
That makest but game on earnest pain.
Think not alone under the sun
Unquit[3] to cause thy lovers plain[4],
Although my lute and I have done.

May chance thee lie withered and old
In winter nights that are so cold,
Plaining in vain unto the moon;
Thy wishes then dare not be told.
Care then who list, for I have done.

And then may chance thee to repent
The time that thou hast lost and spent
To cause thy lovers sigh and swoon;
Then shalt thou know beauty but lent,
And wish and want, as I have done.

Now cease, my lute, this is the last
Labour that thou and I shall waste,
And ended is that we begun.
Now is this song both sung and past,
My lute, be still, for I have done.

1 that which   3 unrepaid
2 cut, engrave   4 to complain

HENRY HOWARD, EARL OF SURREY (1517?-1547)*

DESCRIPTION OF SPRING, WHEREIN EACH THING RENEWS, SAVE ONLY THE LOVER

The soote[1] season that bud and bloom forth
    brings
With green hath clad the hill and eke the vale;
The nightingale with feathers new she sings;
The turtle to her make[2] hath told her tale:
Summer is come, for every spray now springs;
The hart hath hung his old head on the pale;
The buck in brake his winter cote he flings;
The fishes flete with new repaired scale;
The adder all her slough away she slings;
The swift swallow pursueth the flies smale;
The busy bee her honey now she mings[3].
Winter is worn, that was the flowers' bale:
And thus I see among these pleasant things
Each care decays, and yet my sorrow springs.

A PRAISE OF HIS LOVE, WHEREIN HE REPROVETH THEM THAT COMPARE THEIR LADIES WITH HIS

Give place, ye lovers, here before,
    That spent your boasts and brags in vain;
My Lady's beauty passeth more
    The best of yours, I dare well sayen,
Than doth the sun the candle light,
Or brightest day the darkest night.

And thereto hath a troth as just
    As had Penelope the fair;
For what she saith, ye may it trust
    As it by writing sealed were.
And virtues hath she many moe
Than I with pen have skill to show.

I could rehearse, if that I would,
    The whole effect[4] of Nature's plaint
When she had lost the perfect mold,
    The like to whom she could not paint.
With wringing hands how she did cry,
And what she said, I know it, I.

I know she swore with raging mind,
    Her kingdom only set apart,
There was no loss, by law of kind[5],
    That could have gone so near her heart.
And this was chiefly all her pain:
She could not make the like again.

Sith[6] nature thus gave her the praise
    To be the chiefest work she wrought,

In faith, methink, some better ways
    On your behalf might well be sought,
Than to compare, as ye have done,
To match the candle with the sun.

DEPARTURE OF AENEAS FROM DIDO

Such great complaints brake forth out o
    her breast;
Whiles Aeneas full minded to depart,
All things prepared, slept in the poop on high
To whom in sleep the wonted godhead's for
'Gan aye appear, returning in like shape[1]
As seemed him, and 'gan him thus advise,
Like unto Mercury in voice and hue,
With yellow bush[2], and comely limbs of youth
    "O goddess' son, in such case canst the
    sleep,
Ne yet, bestraught[3], the dangers dost foresee
That compass thee, nor hear'st the fair wind
    blow?
Dido in mind rolls vengeance and deceit;
Determ'd to die, swells with unstable ire.
Wilt thou not flee whiles thou hast time o
    flight?
Straight shalt thou see the seas covered wi
    sails,
The blazing brands the shore all spread wi
    flame,
And if[4] the morrow steal upon thee here.
Come off, have done, set all delay aside;
For full of change these women be alway."
This said, in the dark night he 'gan him hi
    Aeneas, of this sudden vision
Adread, starts up out of his sleep in haste,
Calls up his feres[5]: "Awake, get up, n
    men!
Aboard your ships, and hoise up sail wi
    speed.
A god me wills, sent from above again,
To haste my flight and wreathen cables cut.
O holy god, whatso thou art, we shall
Follow thee, and all blithe obey thy will.
Be at our hand and friendly us assist;
Address[6] the stars with prosperous influence
And with that word his glistering sword w
    sheaths,
With which drawn he the cables cut in twa
The like desire the rest embraced all.
All things in haste they cast, and forth th
    whirl;
The shores they leave; with ships the seas a
    spread:
Cutting the foam by the blue seas thay swe
    (From the *Translation of the Fou*
      Book of Virgil's Aeneid.)

---

1 sweet   4 tenor
2 turtle-dove to her mate   5 nature
3 mixes   6 since
* See note on preceding page.

1 (as before)   4 an if, if
2 locks   5 comrades
3 nor yet, distracted   6 endue

EDMUND SPENSER (1552-1599)*

THE FAERIE QUEENE

THE DEDICATION

TO THE MOST HIGH,

MIGHTIE, AND MAGNIFICENT EMPRESSE

RENOWMED FOR PIETIE, VERTUE,

AND ALL GRATIOUS GOVERNMENT

ELIZABETH

BY THE GRACE OF GOD

QUEENE OF ENGLAND, FRAUNCE, AND IRELAND,

AND OF VIRGINIA,

DEFENDOUR OF THE FAITH, &C.

HER MOST HUMBLE SERVAUNT

EDMUND SPENSER

DOTH IN ALL HUMILITIE

DEDICATE, PRESENT, AND CONSECRATE

THESE HIS LABOURS

TO LIVE WITH THE ETERNITIE

OF HER FAME.

1

Lo I the man, whose Muse whilome[1] did maske,
As time her taught, in lowly Shepheards
weeds[2],
Am now enforst a far unfitter taske,
For trumpets sterne to chaunge mine Oaten
reeds,
And sing of Knights and Ladies gentle[3] deeds;
Whose prayses having slept in silence long,
Me, all too meane, the sacred Muse areeds[4]
To blazon broad emongst her learned throng:
    Fierce warres and faithfull loves shall moral-
        ize my song.

2

Helpe then, O holy Virgin chiefe of nine[5],
Thy weaker Novice to performe thy will;
Lay forth out of thine everlasting scryne[6]
The antique rolles, which there lye hidden still,
Of Faerie knights and fairest Tanaquill[7],
Whom that most noble Briton Prince[8] so long
Sought through the world, and suffered so
        much ill,
That I must rue his undeserved wrong:
    O helpe thou my weake wit, and sharpen my
        dull tong.

3

And thou most dreaded impe[9] of highest Jove,
Faire Venus sonne, that with thy cruell dart
At that good knight so cunningly didst rove,
That glorious fire it kindled in his hart,
Lay now thy deadly Heben[10] bow apart,
And with thy mother milde come to mine ayde;
Come both, and with you bring triumphant
    Mart[11],
In loves and gentle jollities arrayd,
    After his murdrous spoiles and bloudy rage
        allayd.

4

And with them eke, O Goddesse heavenly
    bright,
Mirrour of grace and Majestie divine,
Great Lady of the greatest Isle, whose light
Like Phoebus lampe[12] throughout the world
    doth shine,
Shed thy faire beames into my feeble eyne,
And raise my thoughts, too humble and too
    vile,
To thinke of that true glorious type of thine,
The argument of mine afflicted stile[13]:
    The which to heare, vouchsafe, O dearest
        dred[14], a-while.

*Formerly
[1] referring to the *Shepheardes Calender,* a pastoral poem. See *Eng. Lit.,* 89-90.
The Faerie Queene is an allegory designed to set forth "a gentleman or noble person in virtuous and gentle discipline." The central characters are Gloriana, the queen of an imaginary ("faerie") court, who symbolizes Glory, and her suitor Prince Arthur, who stands for Magnificence (Munificence), "which virtue is the perfection of all the rest." Besides these, the twelve moral virtues were to have been separately represented by twelve knights, each performing deeds and overcoming temptations according to his character. But as the poet's design was never finished, only half these virtues get representation, and the central characters receive rather less prominence than the six several virtues which are set forth in the six completed books. Each of these books, consisting of twelve cantos, is practically a complete story in itself. The first deals with the Knight of the Red Cross, or Holiness, who, clad in the armor of the Christian faith, is sent forth by his Queen as the champion of Una (Truth) to deliver her parents, "who had been by an huge dragon many years shut up in a brasen castle." Beneath the moral allegory may be read also a political one, according to which Gloriana is Queen Elizabeth, Prince Arthur is Lord Leicester, Duessa is Mary Queen of Scots, etc. But after all, the poetry of the poem is worth far more than the elaborate allegory. The language and spelling are deliberately and sometimes falsely archaic. See *Eng. Lit.,* pp. 91-94.

[3] noble (as distinguished from rustic)
[4] urges
[5] Clio, Muse of History.
[6] shrine, chest
[7] The daughter of Oberon; here another name for Gloriana.

[8] Prince Arthur
[9] child
[10] ebony
[11] Mars
[12] the sun
[13] subject of my lowly pen
[14] object of reverence

The Knight of the Red Cross and his Fight
with the Monster Error. The Wiles
of Archimago. From Book I, Canto I.

1

A gentle Knight was pricking[1] on the plaine,
Ycladd in mightie armes and silver shielde,
Wherein old dints of deepe wounds did re-
maine,
The cruell markes of many a bloudy fielde;
Yet armes till that time did he never wield:
His angry steede did chide his foming bitt,
As much disdayning to the curbe to yield:
Full jolly[2] knight he seemd, and faire did sitt,
  As one for knightly giusts[3] and fierce en-
    counters fitt.

2

But on his brest a bloudie Crosse he bore,
The deare remembrance of his dying Lord,
For whose sweete sake that glorious badge he
wore,
And dead as living ever him ador'd:
Upon his shield the like was also scor'd,
For soveraine hope, which in his helpe he had:
Right faithfull true he was in deede and word,
But of his cheere[4] did seeme too solemne sad;
  Yet nothing did he dread, but ever was
    ydrad[5].

3

Upon a great adventure he was bond,
That greatest Gloriana to him gave,
That greatest Glorious Queene of Faerie lond,
To winne him worship[6], and her grace to have,
Which of all earthly things he most did crave;
And ever as he rode, his hart did earne[7]
To prove his puissance in battell brave
Upon his foe, and his new force to learne;
  Upon his foe, a Dragon horrible and stearne.

4

A lovely Ladie[8] rode him faire beside,
Upon a lowly Asse more white then snow,
Yet she much whiter, but the same did hide
Under a vele, that wimpled was full low,
And over all a blacke stole she did throw,
As one that inly mournd: so was she sad,
And heavie sat upon her palfrey slow;

Seemed in heart some hidden care she had,
  And by her in a line a milke white lambe
    she lad.*

5

So pure and innocent, as that same lambe,
She was in life and every vertuous lore,
And by descent from Royall lynage came
Of ancient Kings and Queenes, that had of
yore
Their scepters stretcht from East to Westerne
shore,
And all the world in their subjection held;
Till that infernall feend with foule uprore
Forwasted all their land, and them expeld:
  Whom to avenge, she had this Knight from
    far compeld[9].

6

Behind her farre away a Dwarfe did lag,
That lasie seemd in being ever last,
Or wearied[10] with bearing of her bag
Of needments at his backe. Thus as they past,
The day with cloudes was suddeine overcast,
And angry Jove an hideous storme of raine
Did poure into his Lemans[11] lap so fast,
That every wight[12] to shroud[13] it did constrain,
  And this faire couple eke to shroud them-
    selves were fain.

7

Enforst to seeke some covert nigh at hand,
A shadie grove not far away they spide,
That promist ayde the tempest to withstand:
Whose loftie trees yclad with sommers pride
Did spred so broad, that heavens light did
hide,
Not perceable with power of any starre:
And all within were pathes and alleies wide,
With footing worne, and leading inward farre:
  Faire harbour that them seemes; so in they
    entred arre.

8

And foorth they passe, with pleasure forward
led,
Joying to heare the birdes sweete harmony,
Which therein shrouded from the tempest dred,

1 riding, spurring
2 handsome
3 jousts
4 countenance
5 dreaded

6 honor
7 yearn
8 Una, personification of
  Truth.

9 summoned
10 Pronounce "wea-ri-ed."
11 beloved one (the
  earth).

12 person
13 shelter

* "That lamb we never see again! It was a
  thought that rose and passed away from the
  poet's soul; but the image had shown us the
  character of Una in her simplicity, as if it
  had been a dove that hung for a moment over
  her head, and while a voice spoke, disappeared—This is my beloved *daughter*, in
  whom I am well pleased."—Christopher
  North.

Seemd in their song to scorne the cruell sky.
Much can[14] they prayse the trees so straight
    and hy,
The sayling Pine[15], the Cedar proud and tall,
The vine-prop Elme, the Poplar never dry,
The builder Oake, sole king of forrests all,
  The Aspine good for staves, the Cypresse
    funerall.

9

The Laurell, meed of mightie Conquerours
And Poets sage, the firre that weepeth still,
The Willow worne of forlorne Paramours,
The Eugh[16] obedient to the benders will,
The Birch for shaftes, the Sallow for the mill,
The Mirrhe sweete bleeding in the bitter
    wound,
The warlike Beech, the Ash for nothing ill,
The fruitful Olive, and the Platane round,
  The carver Holme, the Maple seeldom inward
    sound.*

10

Led with delight, they thus beguile the way,
Untill the blustring storme is overblowne;
When weening to returne, whence they did
    stray,
They cannot finde that path, which first was
    showne,
But wander too and fro in wayes unknowne,
Furthest from end then, when they neerest
    weene,
That makes them doubt their wits be not their
    owne:
So many pathes, so many turnings seene,
  That which of them to take, in diverse doubt
    they been.

11

At last resolving forward still to fare,
Till that some end they finde or in or out,
That path they take, that beaten seemd most
    bare,
And like to lead the labyrinth about;
Which when by tract[17] they hunted had
    throughout,
At length it brought them to a hollow cave
Amid the thickest woods. The Champion stout
Eftsoones[18] dismounted from his courser brave,
  And to the Dwarfe awhile his needlesse spere
    he gave.

12

Be well aware, quoth then that Ladie milde,
Least suddaine mischiefe ye too rash provoke:
The danger hid, the place unknowne and wilde,

Breedes dreadfull doubts: Oft fire is without
    smoke,
And peril without show: therefore your stroke,
Sir Knight, with-hold, till further triall made.
Ah Ladie, (said he) shame were to revoke
The forward footing for an hidden shade:
  Vertue gives her selfe light, through darke-
    nesse for to wade[19].

13

Yea but (quoth she) the perill of this place
I better wot then you, though now too late
To wish you backe returne with foule disgrace,
Yet wisdome warnes, whilest foot is in the
    gate[20],
To stay the steppe, ere forced to retrate.
This is the wandring wood[21], this Errours den,
A monster vile, whom God and man does hate:
Therefore I read[22] beware. Fly, fly (quoth then
  The fearefull Dwarfe) this is no place for
    living men.

14

But full of fire and greedy hardiment,
The youthfull knight could not for ought be
    staide,
But forth unto the darksome hole he went,
And looked in: his glistring armor made
A litle glooming light, much like a shade,
By which he saw the ugly monster plaine,
Halfe like a serpent horribly displaide,
But th'other halfe did womans shape retaine,
  Most lothsom, filthie, foule, and full of vile
    disdaine[23].

15

And as she lay upon the durtie ground,
Her huge long taile her den all overspred,
Yet was in knots and many boughtes[24] up-
    wound,
Pointed with mortall sting. Of her there
    bred
A thousand yong ones[25], which she dayly fed,
Sucking upon her poisnous dugs, eachone
Of sundry shapes, yet all ill favored:
Soone as that uncouth light upon them shone,
  Into her mouth they crept, and suddain all
    were gone.

16

Their dam upstart, out of her den effraide,
And rushed forth, hurling her hideous taile
About her cursed head, whose folds displaid
Were stretcht now forth at length without
    entraile[24].

4 did
5 Cp. *Paradise Lost*, I. 292-294.   17 trace
6 yew   18 forthwith
* Perhaps such a diversity of trees may be allowed
    in the Wood of Error. Spenser is nothing if
    not imaginative.

19 Cp. *Comus*, 373.   23 disgusting vileness
20 way   24 coils
21 wood of wandering   25 Lies, the children of
22 counsel   Error.

She lookt about, and seeing one in mayle
Armed to point26, sought backe to turne
   againe;
For light she hated as the deadly bale,
Ay wont in desert darknesse to remaine,
   Where plain none might her see, nor she see
   any plaine.

17

Which when the valiant Elfe perceiv'd, he lept
As Lyon fierce upon the flying pray,
And with his trenchand blade her boldly kept
From turning backe, and forced her to stay:
Therewith enrag'd she loudly gan to bray,
And turning fierce, her speckled taile advaunst,
Threatning her angry sting, him to dismay:
Who nought aghast his mightie hand en-
   haunst27:
   The stroke down from her head unto her
   shoulder glaunst.

18

Much daunted with that dint28, her sence was
   dazd,
Yet kindling rage, her selfe she gathered round,
And all attonce her beastly body raizd
With doubled forces high above the ground:
Tho29 wrapping up her wrethed sterne arownd,
Lept fierce upon his shield, and her huge traine
All suddenly about his body wound,
That hand or foot to stirre he strove in vaine:
   God helpe the man so wrapt in Errours end-
   lesse traine.

19

His Lady sad to see his sore constraint,
Cride out, Now now Sir knight, shew what ye
   bee,
Add faith unto your force, and be not faint:
Strangle her, else she sure will strangle thee.
That when he heard, in great perplexitie,
His gall did grate for grief30 and high dis-
   daine,
And knitting all his force got one hand free,
Wherewith he grypt her gorge with so great
   paine51,
   That soone to loose her wicked bands did
   her constraine.*

. . . . . .

26 completely
27 raised
28 blow
29 then
30 his anger was stirred
   through pain
31 effort

* Stanzas 20-26 describe, in language made purposely coarse for the sake of the allegory, the
monster's foul tactics in self-defense, until
from her body the knight "raft her hatefull
heade without remorse," and the young ones
gorged themselves to death upon her blood.

27

His Ladie seeing all that chaunst, from farre
Approcht in hast to greet his victorie,
And said, Faire knight, borne under happy
   starre,
Who see your vanquisht foes before you lye:
Well worthie be you of that Armorie32,
Wherein ye have great glory wonne this day,
And proov'd your strength on a strong enimie:
Your first adventure: many such I pray,
   And henceforth ever wish that like succeed it
   may.

28

Then mounted he upon his Steede againe,
And with the Lady backward sought to wend;
That path he kept which beaten was most
   plaine,
Ne33 ever would to any by-way bend,
But still did follow one unto the end,
The which at last out of the wood them
   brought.
So forward on his way (with God to frend)
He passed forth, and new adventure sought;
   Long way he travelled, before he heard of
   ought.

29

At length they chaunst to meet upon the way
An aged Sire34, in long blacke weedes yclad,
His feete all bare, his beard all hoarie gray,
And by his belt his booke he hanging had;
Sober he seemde, and very sagely sad,
And to the ground his eyes were lowly bent,
Simple in shew, and voyde of malice bad,
And all the way he prayed, as he went,
   And often knockt his brest, as one that did
   repent.

30

He faire the knight saluted, louting35 low,
Who faire him quited36, as that courteous was:
And after asked him, if he did know
Of straunge adventures, which abroad did pas.
Ah my deare Sonne (quoth he) how should,
   alas,
Silly37 old man, that lives in hidden cell,
Bidding his beades38 all day for his trespas,
Tydings of warre and worldly trouble tell?
   With holy father sits39 not with such things
   to mell40.

31

But if of daunger which hereby doth dwell,
And homebred evil ye desire to heare,
Of a straunge man I can you tidings tell,

32 armor
33 nor
34 The enchanter Archi-
  mago, or Hypoc-
  risy, who stands
  for false religion.
35 bowing
36 requited
37 simple
38 praying his prayers
39 befits
40 meddle

That wasteth all this countrey farre and neare.
Of such (said he) I chiefly do inquere,
And shall you well reward to shew the place,
In which that wicked wight his dayes doth
  weare:
For to all knighthood it is foule disgrace,
  That such a cursed creature lives so long a
  space.

32

Far hence (quoth he) in wastfull wildernesse
His dwelling is, by which no living wight
May ever passe, but thorough[41] great distresse.
Now (sayd the Lady) draweth toward night,
And well I wote, that of your later fight
Ye all forwearied be: for what so strong,
But wanting rest will also want of might?
The Sunne that measures heaven all day long,
  At night doth baite[42] his steedes the Ocean
  waves emong.

33

Then with the Sunne take Sir, your timely
  rest,
And with new day new worke at once begin:
Untroubled night they say gives counsell best.
Right well Sir knight ye have advised bin,
(Quoth then that aged man;) the way to win
Is wisely to advise[43]: now day is spent;
Therefore with me ye may take up your In
For this same night. The knight was well con-
  tent:
  So with that godly father to his home they
  went.

34

A little lowly Hermitage it was,
Downe in a dale, hard by a forests side,
Far from resort of people, that did pas
In travell to and froe: a little wyde[44]
There was an holy Chappell edifyde[45],
Wherein the Hermite dewly wont to say
His holy things each morne and eventyde:
Thereby a Christall streame did gently play,
  Which from a sacred fountaine welled forth
  alway.

35

Arrived there, the little house they fill,
Ne looke for entertainment, where none was:
Rest is their feast, and all things at their will:
The noblest mind the best contentment has.
With faire discourse the evening so they pas:
For that old man of pleasing wordes had store,
And well could file his tongue as smooth as
  glas,
He told of Saintes and Popes, and evermore
He strowd an *Ave-Mary* after and before.

36

The drouping Night thus creepeth on them
  fast,
And the sad humour[46] loading their eye liddes,
As messenger of Morpheus on them cast
Sweet slombring deaw, the which to sleepe
  them biddes.
Unto their lodgings then his guestes he
  riddes[47]:
Where when all drownd in deadly sleepe he
  findes,
He to this study goes, and there amiddes
His Magick bookes and artes of sundry kindes,
  He seekes out mighty charmes, to trouble
  sleepy mindes.

37

Then choosing out few words most horrible,
(Let none them read) thereof did verses
  frame,
With which and other spelles like terrible,
He bad awake blacke Plutoes griesly Dame[48],
And cursed heaven and spake reprochfull shame
Of highest God, the Lord of life and light;
A bold bad man, that dar'd to call by name
Great Gorgon[49], Prince of darknesse and dead
  night,
  At which Cocytus quakes, and Styx is put to
  flight.

38

And forth he cald out of deepe darknesse dred
Legions of Sprights[50], the which like little
  flyes
Fluttring about his ever damned hed,
Awaite whereto their service he applyes,
To aide his friends, or fray[51] his enimies:
Of those he chose out two, the falsest twoo,
And fittest for to forge true-seeming lyes;
The one of them he gave a message too,
  The other by him selfe staide other worke to
  doo.

39

He making speedy way through spersed[52] ayre,
And through the world of waters wide and
  deepe,
To Morpheus house doth hastily repaire.
Amid the bowels of the earth full steepe,
And low, where dawning day doth never peepe,
His dwelling is; there Tethys[53] his wet bed
Doth ever wash, and Cynthia[54] still doth steepe
In silver deaw his ever-drouping hed,
  Whiles sad Night over him her mantle black
  doth spred.

41 except through   44 distant
42 feed   45 built
43 consider

46 dew of sleep   50 sprites, spirits
47 dismisses   51 affright
48 Proserpine, or Hecate. 52 widespread
49 Cp. *Paradise Lost*, 53 the ocean
    II, 965.   54 the moon

40

Whose double gates[55] he findeth locked fast,
The one faire fram'd of burnisht Yvory,
The other all with silver overcast;
And wakeful dogges before them farre do lye,
Watching to banish Care their enimy,
Who oft is wont to trouble gentle Sleepe.
By them the Sprite doth passe in quietly,
And unto Morpheus comes, whom drowned deepe
  In drowsie fit he findes: of nothing he takes keepe[56].

41

And more, to lulle him in his slumber soft,
A trickling streame from high rock tumbling downe,
And ever-drizzling raine upon the loft,
Mixt with a murmuring winde, much like the sowne
Of swarming Bees, did cast him in a swowne:
No other noyse, nor peoples troublous cryes,
As still are wont t'annoy the walled towne,
Might there be heard: but carelesse Quiet lyes,
  Wrapt in eternall silence farre from enemyes.*

42

The messenger approching to him spake,
But his wast wordes returnd to him in vaine:
So sound he slept, that nought mought him awake.
Then rudely he him thrust, and pusht with paine
Whereat he gan to stretch: but he againe
Shooke him so hard, that forced him to speake.
As one then in a dreame, whose dryer[57] braine
Is tost with troubled sights and fancies weake,
  He mumbled soft, but would not all his silence breake.

43

The Sprite then gan more boldly him to wake,
And threatned unto him the dreaded name
Of Hecate: whereat he gan to quake,
And lifting up his lumpish head, with blame
Halfe angry asked him, for what he came.
Hither (quoth he) me Archimago sent,
He that the stubborne Sprites can wisely tame,
He bids thee to him send for his intent
  A fit false dreame, that can delude the sleepers sent[58].

55 of false and true dreams   57 feverish
56 care   58 sense
* A stanza not easily matched in literature for
adaptation of sound to sense. It has been
much admired and imitated. See Thomson's
Castle of Indolence, I. 3-6; also Tennyson's
The Lotos-Eaters.

44

The God obayde, and, calling forth straight way
A diverse dreame out of his prison darke,
Delivered it to him, and downe did lay
His heavie head, devoide of carefull carke[59]
Whose sences all were straight benumbed and starke.
He backe returning by the Yvorie dore,
Remounted up as light as chearefull Larke,
And on his litle winges the dreame he bore
  In hast unto his Lord, where he him left afore.

45

Who all this while with charmes and hidden artes,
Had made a Lady of that other Spright,
And fram'd of liquid ayre her tender partes
So lively[60], and so like in all mens sight,
That weaker sence it could have ravisht quight:
The maker selfe, for all his wondrous witt,
Was nigh beguiled with so goodly sight:
Her all in white he clad, and over it
  Cast a black stole, most like to seeme for Una fit.

46

Now when that ydle dreame was to him brought,
Unto that Elfin knight he bad him fly,
Where he slept soundly void of evill thought,
And with false shewes abuse his fantasy,
In sort as he him schooled privily:
And that new creature, borne without her dew[61],
Full of the makers guile, with usage sly
He taught to imitate that Lady trew,
  Whose semblance she did carrie under feigned hew.

[The knight, deceived by the dream into thinking his lady Una false, flees with the Dwarf, until meeting on the way a Sarazin (Saracen, Pagan), named Sansfoy (Faithless), he slays him, and proceeds in the company of Sansfoy's lady, Duessa (Falsehood), who passes herself off as Fidessa (Faith).]

UNA AND THE LION. FROM BOOK I, CANTO III.

1

Nought is there under heav'ns wide hollownesse,
That moves more deare compassion of mind,
Then beautie brought t' unworthy wretchednesse

59 anxious care (with characteristic Spenserian tautology)
60 lifelike   61 unnaturally

Through envies snares, or fortunes freakes un-
    kind.
I, whether lately through her brightnesse blind,
Or through alleageance and fast fealtie,
Which I do owe unto all woman kind.
Feele my heart perst with so great agonie,
    When such I see, that all for pittie I could
    die.

2

And now it is empassioned so deepe,
For fairest Unaes sake, of whom I sing,
That my fraile eyes these lines with teares do
    steepe,
To thinke how she through guilefull handeling,
Though true as touch[1], though daughter of a
    king,
Though faire as ever living wight was faire,
Though nor in word nor deede ill meriting,
Is from her knight divorced in despaire,
    And her due loves deriv'd[2] to that vile
    witches share.

3

Yet she most faithfull Ladie all this while
Forsaken, wofull, solitarie mayd
Far from all peoples prease[3], as in exile,
In wildernesse and wastfull deserts strayd,
To seeke her knight; who subtilly betrayd
Through that late vision, which th' Enchaunter
    wrought,
Had her abandond. She of nought affrayd,
Through woods and wastnesse wide him daily
    sought;
    Yet wished tydings none of him unto her
    brought.

4

One day nigh wearie of the yrkesome way,
From her unhastie beast she did alight,
And on the grasse her daintie limbes did lay
In secret shadow, farre from all mens sight:
From her faire head her fillet she undight,
And laid her stole aside. Her angels face
As the great eye of heaven shyned bright,
And made a sunshine in the shadie place;
    Did never mortall eye behold such heavenly
    grace.

5

It fortuned out of the thickest wood
A ramping Lyon rushed suddainly,
Hunting full greedy after salvage blood;
Soone as the royall virgin he did spy,
With gaping mouth at her ran greedily,
To have attonce devourd her tender corse:
But to the pray when as he drew more ny,

His bloody rage asswaged with remorse,
    And with the sight amazd, forgat his furious
    forse.

6

In stead thereof he kist her wearie feet,
And lickt her lilly hands with fawning tong,
As he her wronged innocence did weet[4].
O how can beautie maister the most strong,
And simple truth subdue avenging wrong?
Whose yeelded pride and proud submission,
Still dreading death, when she had marked
    long,
Her hart gan melt in great compassion,
    And drizling teares did shed for pure affec-
    tion.

7

The Lyon Lord of every beast in field,
Quoth she, his princely puissance doth abate,
And mightie proud to humble weake does yield,
Forgetfull of the hungry rage, which late
Him prickt, in pittie of my sad estate:
But he my Lyon, and my noble Lord,
How does he find in cruell hart to hate,
Her that him lov'd, and ever most adord,
    As the God of my life? why hath he me
    abhord?

8

Redounding[5] teares did choke th' end of her
    plaint,
Which softly ecchoed from the neighbour wood;
And sad to see her sorrowfull constraint
The kingly beast upon her gazing stood;
With pittie calmd, downe fell his angry mood.
At last in close hart shutting up her paine,
Arose the virgin borne of heavenly brood,
And to her snowy Palfrey got againe,
    To seeke her strayed Champion, if she might
    attaine.

9

The Lyon would not leave her desolate,
But with her went along, as a strong gard
Of her chast person, and a faithfull mate
Of her sad troubles and misfortunes hard:
Still when she slept, he kept both watch and
    ward,
And when she wakt, he waited diligent,
With humble service to her will prepard:
From her faire eyes he tooke commaundement,
    And ever by her lookes conceived her in-
    tent.

[Una is overtaken by Archimago, disguised
as the Redcross Knight, and accompanies him
therefore trustingly. But they are met by
Sansloy (Lawless, a brother of Sansfoy), who
overcomes both Archimago and the Lion and
takes Una as his prey.]

---

1 as if tested by the touchstone
2 the love which is her due diverted
3 press, crowd

4 wit, know   5 overflowing

THE KNIGHT OF THE RED CROSS AT THE HOUSE
OF PRIDE. FROM BOOK I, CANTO IV

1

Young knight whatever that dost armes pro-
fesse,
And through long labours huntest after fame,
Beware of fraud, beware of ficklenesse,
In choice, and change of thy deare loved Dame,
Least thou of her beleeve too lightly blame,
And rash misweening doe thy hart remove:
For unto knight there is no greater shame,
Then lightnesse and inconstancie in love;
    That doth this Redcrosse knights ensample
    plainly prove.

2

Who after that he had faire Una lorne,
Through light misdeeming of her loialtie,
And false Duessa in her sted had borne,
Called Fidess', and so supposed to bee;
Long with her traveild, till at last they see
A goodly building, bravely garnished,
The house of mightie Prince it seemd to bee:
And towards it a broad high way that led,
    All bare through peoples feet, which thither
    traveiled.

3

Great troupes of people traveild thitherward
Both day and night, of each degree and place,
But few returned, having scaped hard,
With balefull beggerie, or foule disgrace;
Which ever after in most wretched case,
Like loathsome lazars,[1] by the hedges lay.
Thither Duessa bad him bend his pace.
For she is wearie of the toilesome way,
    And also nigh consumed is the lingring day.

4

A stately Pallace built of squared bricke,
Which cunningly was without morter laid,
Whose wals were high, but nothing strong, nor
    thick,
And golden foile all over them displaid,
That purest skye with brightnesse they dismaid:
High lifted up were many loftie towres,
And goodly galleries farre over laid,
Full of faire windowes and delightful bowres;
    And on the top a Diall told the timely
    howres.

5

It was a goodly heape for to behould,
And spake the praises of the workmans wit;
But full great pittie, that so faire a mould
Did on so weake foundation ever sit:
For on a sandie hill, that still did flit
And fall away, it mounted was full hie,

That every breath of heaven shaked it:
And all the hinder parts, that few could spie
    Were ruinous and old, but painted cunningly.

6

Arrived there, they passed in forth right;
For still to all the gates stood open wide:
Yet charge of them was to a Porter hight[1]
Cald Malvenù,* who entrance none denide:
Thence to the hall, which was on every side
With rich array and costly arras dight:
Infinite sorts[2] of people did abide
There waiting long, to win the wished sight
    Of her that was the Lady of that Pallace
    bright.

7

By them they passe, all gazing on them round,
And to the Presence mount; whose glorious
    vew[3]
Their frayle amazed senses did confound:
In living Princes court none ever knew
Such endlesse richesse, and so sumptuous shew;
Ne Persia selfe, the nourse of pompous pride
Like ever saw. And there a nobel crew
Of Lordes and Ladies stood on every side,
    Which with their presence faire the place
    much beautifide.

8

High above all a cloth of State was spred,
And a rich throne, as bright as sunny day,
On which there sate most brave embellished
With royall robes and gorgeous array,
A mayden Queene, that shone as Titans ray,
In glistring gold, and peerelesse pretious stone:
Yet her bright blazing beautie did assay
To dim the brightnesse of her glorious throne,
    As envying her selfe, that too exceeding
    shone.

9

Exceeding shone, like Phœbus fairest childe,[4]
That did presume his fathers firie wayne,
And flaming mouthes of steedes unwonted wilde
Through highest heaven with weaker hand to
    rayne;
Proud of such glory and advancement vaine,
While flashing beames do daze his feeble eyen,
He leaves the welkin way most beaten plaine,
And rapt with whirling wheeles, inflames the
    skyen,
    With fire not made to burne, but fairely for
    to shyne.

10

So proud she shyned in her Princely state,
Looking to heaven; for earth she did disdayne:

1 assigned   3 the vision of whose
2 throngs   glory
              4 Phaethon
* I. e., Ill-come, the opposite of Welcome.

1 lepers

nd sitting high; for lowly she did hate:
o underneath her scornefull feete was layne
A dreadfull Dragon with an hideous trayne,
nd in her hand she held a mirrhour bright,*
Vherein her face she often vewed fayne,
nd in her selfe-lov'd semblance tooke de-
    light;
  For she was wondrous faire, as any living
    wight.

11

)f griesly Pluto she the daughter was,
nd sad Proserpina the Queene of hell;
et did she thinke her pearlesse worth to pas
hat parentage, with pride so did she swell;
nd thundring Jove, that high in heaven doth
    dwell,
nd wield the world, she claymed for her syre,
)r if that any else did Jove excell:
  'or to the highest she did still aspyre,
  Or if ought higher were then that, did it
    desyre.

12

nd proud Lucifera men did her call,
hat made her selfe a Queene, and crowned to
    be,
et rightfull kingdome she had none at all,
Ne heritage of native soveraintie,
But did usurpe with wrong and tyrannie
Jpon the scepter, which she now did hold:
Ne ruld her Realmes with lawes, but pollicie,
nd strong advizement of six wizards old,†
  That with their counsels bad her kingdome
    did uphold.

13

Soone as the Elfin knight in presence came,
And false Duessa seeming Lady faire,
A gentle Husher, Vanitie by name
Made rowme, and passage for them did pre-
    paire:
o goodly brought them to the lowest staire
)f her high throne, where they on humble
    knee
Making obeyssance, did the cause declare,
Vhy they were come, her royall state to see,
  To prove the wide report of her great
    Majestee.

14

With loftie eyes, halfe loth to looke so low,
She thanked them in her disdainefull wise;
Ne other grace vouchsafed them to show
)f Princesse worthy, scarse them bad arise.
Her Lordes and Ladies all this while devise
Themselves to setten forth to straungers sight:

Some frounce their curled haire in courtly
    guise,
Some prancke their ruffes, and others trimly
    dight
  Their gay attire: each others greater pride
    does spight.

15

Goodly they all that knight do entertaine,
Right glad with him to have increast their
    crew:
But to Duess' each one himselfe did paine
All kindnesse and faire courtesie to shew;
For in that court whylome her well they knew:
Yet the stout Faerie mongst the middest crowd
Thought all her glorie vaine in knightly vew,
And that great Princesse too exceeding prowd,
  That to strange knight no better counte-
    nance allowd.

[Sansjoy (Joyless, third of the pagan brotherhood) appears, seeking vengeance for the
death of Sansfoy, and, secretly encouraged by
Duessa, challenges the Knight to combat.]

THE COMBAT BETWEEN THE KNIGHT OF THE RED CROSS AND SANSJOY. FROM BOOK I, CANTO V.

1

The noble hart, that harbours vertuous thought,
And is with child of glorious great intent,
Can never rest, untill it forth have brought
Th' eternall brood of glorie excellent.
Such restlesse passion did all night torment
The flaming corage[1] of that Faery knight,
Devizing, how that doughtie turnament
With greatest honour he atchieven might;
  Still did he wake, and still did watch for
    dawning light.

2

At last the golden Orientall gate,
Of greatest heaven gan to open faire,
And Phoebus fresh, as bridegrome to his mate,
Came dauncing forth, shaking his deawie haire:
And hurls his glistring beams through gloomy
    aire.
Which when the wakeful Elfe perceiv'd,
    streightway
He started up, and did him selfe prepaire,
In sunbright armes, and battailous array:
  For with that Pagan proud he combat will
    that day.

3

And forth he comes into the commune hall,
Where earely waite him many a gazing eye,
To weet what end to straunger knights may
    fall.
There many Minstrales maken melody,

Court ladies used to carry mirrors.
† Pride and her six counsellors, Idleness, Gluttony,
Lechery, Avarice, Envy, and Wrath, constitute
the "seven deadly sins."

1 heart

To drive away the dull melancholy,
And many Bardes, that to the trembling chord
Can tune their timely voyces cunningly,
And many Chroniclers that can record
 Old loves, and warres for Ladies doen by
  many a Lord.

4

Soon after comes the cruell Sarazin,
In woven maile all armed warily,
And sternly lookes at him, who not a pin
Does care for looke of living creatures eye.
They bring them wines of Greece and Araby,
And daintie spices fecht from furthest Ynd,
To kindle heat of corage privily:
And in the wine a solemne oth they bynd
 T' observe the sacred lawes of armes, that
  are assynd.

5

At last forth comes that far renowned Queene,
With royall pomp and Princely majestie;
She is ybrought unto a paled greene,[2]
And placed under stately canapee,
The warlike feates of both those knights to
 see.
On th' other side in all mens open vew
Duessa placed is, and on a tree
Sans-foy his[3] shield is hangd with bloody hew:
 Both those the lawrell girlonds[4] to the vic-
  tor dew.

6

A shrilling trompet sownded from on hye,
And unto battaill bad them selves addresse:
Their shining shieldes about their wrestes they
 tye,
And burning blades about their heads do
 blesse,[5]
The instruments of wrath and heavinesse:
With greedy force each other doth assayle,
And strike so fiercely, that they do impresse
Deepe dinted furrowes in the battred mayle;
 The yron walles to ward their blowes are
  weak and fraile.

7

The Sarazin was stout, and wondrous strong,
And heaped blowes like yron hammers great;
For after bloud and vengeance he did long.
The knight was fiers, and full of youthly heat,
And doubled strokes, like dreaded thunders
 threat:
For all for prayse and honour he did fight.
Both stricken strike, and beaten both do beat,
That from their shields forth flyeth firie light,
 And helmets hewen deepe show marks of
  eithers might.

8

So th' one for wrong, the other strives for
 right;
As when a Gryfon seized of[5] his pray,
A Dragon fiers encountreth in his flight,
Through widest ayre making his ydle way,
That would his rightfull ravine rend away;
With hideous horror both together smight,
And souce[6] so sore that they the heavens affray:
The wise Soothsayer seeing so sad sight,
 Th' amazed vulgar tels[7] of warres and mor-
  tall fight.

9

So th' one for wrong, the other strives for
 right,
And each to deadly shame would drive his foe,
The cruell steele so greedily doth bight
In tender flesh that streames of bloud down
 flow,
With which the armes, that earst so bright
 did show,
Into a pure vermillion now are dyde:
Great ruth in all the gazers harts did grow,
Seeing the gored woundes to gape so wyde,
 That victory they dare not wish to either
  side.

10

At last the Paynim chaunst to cast his eye,
His suddein eye, flaming with wrathful fyre,
Upon his brothers shield, which hong thereby:
Therewith redoubled was his raging yre,
And said, Ah wretched sonne[8] of wofull syre,
Doest thou sit wayling by blacke Stygian lake,
Whilest here thy shield is hangd for victors
 hyre,
And sluggish german[9] doest thy forces slake
 To after-send his foe, that him may over-
  take?

11

Goe captive Elfe, him quickly overtake,
And soone redeeme from his long wandring
 woe;
Goe guiltie ghost, to him my message make,
That I his shield have quit[10] from dying foe:
Therewith upon his crest he stroke him so,
That twise he reeled, readie twise to fall;
End of the doubtful battell deemed tho[11]
The lookers on, and lowd to him gan call
 The false Duessa, Thine the shield, and I,
  and all.

2 inclosed field
3 Sansfoy's
4 Both Duessa and the
5 brandish
shield are the
prizes of victory.

6 swoop (term from fal-
 conry)
7 prophesies to the
 amazed people.
8 Addressed to his
 brother.

9 Addressed to himself
 (german means
 brother)
10 redeemed
11 then

12

Soone as the Faerie heard his Ladie speake,
Out of his swowning dreame he gan awake,
And quickning faith, that earst was woxen
weake,
The creeping deadly cold away did shake:
Tho mov'd with wrath, and shame, and Ladies
sake,
Of all attonce he cast[10] avengd to bee,
And with so' exceeding furie at him strake,
That forced him to stoupe upon his knee;
  Had he not stouped so, he should have
    cloven bee.

13

And to him said, Goe now proud Miscreant,
Thy selfe thy message doe to german deare;
Alone he wandring thee too long doth want:
Goe say, his foe thy shield with his doth beare.
Therewith his heavie hand he high gan reare,
Him to have slaine; when loe a darkesome
clowd
Upon him fell: he no where doth appeare,
But vanisht is. The Elfe him calls alowd,
  But answer none receives: the darkness him
    does shrowd.

14

In haste Duessa from her place arose,
And to him running said, O prowest knight,
That ever Ladie to her love did chose,
Let now abate the terror of your might,
And quench the flame of furious despight,
And bloudie vengeance; lo th' infernall
powres,
Covering your foe with cloud of deadly night,
Have borne him hence to Plutoes balefull
bowres.
  The conquest yours, I yours, the shield, the
    glory yours.

15

Not all so satisfide, with greedie eye
He sought all round about, his thristie[11] blade
To bath in bloud of faithlesse enemy;
Who all that while lay hid in secret shade:
He standes amazed, how he thence should fade.
At last the trumpets Triumph sound on hie,
And running Heralds humble homage made,
Greeting him goodly with new victorie,
  And to him brought the shield, the cause of
    enmitie.

16

Wherewith he goeth to that soveraine Queene,
And falling her before on lowly knee,
To her makes present of his service seene:
Which she accepts, with thankes, and goodly
gree,[12]
Greatly advauncing[13] his gay chevalree.

So marcheth home, and by her takes the knight,
Whom all the people follow with great glee,
Shouting, and clapping all their hands on
hight,
  That all the aire it fils, and flyes to heaven
    bright.

17

Home is he brought, and laid in sumptuous
bed:
Where many skilfull leaches him abide,
To salve his hurts, that yet still freshly bled.
In wine and oyle they wash his woundes wide,
And softly can[14] embalme on every side.
And all the while, most heavenly melody
About the bed sweet musicke did divide,[15]
Him to beguile of griefe and agony:
  And all the while Duessa wept full bitterly.

[The Knight and the Dwarf escape from the
house of Pride, but the Knight is captured by
the giant Orgoglio (another impersonator of
Pride) and thrown into a dungeon. Meanwhile
Una, having escaped from Sansloy, meets the
Dwarf, who tells her what has befallen. Just
then appears Prince Arthur, seeking the court
of the Faerie Queene. He hears their story,
fights with Orgoglio, and frees his prisoner. Reunited, the Knight and Una proceed on their
way. After further trial in the Cave of Despair, and wholesome discipline at the House of
Holiness, they reach the goal of their journey—
the wasted kingdom, and the brazen tower where
Una's parents are imprisoned by the Dragon.
The Knight engages in a desperate conflict with
the Dragon, and only on the third day succeeds
in conquering him.]

THE DRAGON SLAIN. THE BETROTHAL OF UNA.
FROM BOOK I, CANTO XII.

1

Behold I see the haven nigh at hand,
To which I meane my wearie course to bend;
Vere the maine shete, and beare up with[1] the
land,
The which afore is fairely to be kend,
And seemeth safe from storms that may of-
fend;
There this faire virgin wearie of her way
Must landed be, now at her journeyes end:
There eke my feeble barke a while may stay
  Till merry wind and weather call her thence
    away.

10 resolved   12 good will
11 thirsty   13 lauding

14 did   1 make for
15 descant, perform in
   musical "divisions"

2

Scarsely had Phœbus in the glooming East
Yet harnessed his firie-footed teeme,
Ne reard above the earth his flaming creast;
When the last deadly smoke aloft did steeme
That signe of last outbreathed life did seeme
Unto the watchman on the castle wall,
Who thereby dead that balefull Beast did deeme,
And to his Lord and Ladie lowd gan call,
　To tell how he had seene the Dragons fatall fall.

3

Uprose with hastie joy, and feeble speed
That aged Sire, the Lord of all that land,
And looked forth, to weet if true indeede
Those tydings were, as he did understand,
Which whenas true by tryall he out found,
He bad to open wyde his brazen gate,
Which long time had been shut, and out of hond
Proclaymed joy and peace through all his state;
　For dead now was their foe which them forrayed late.

4

Then gan triumphant Trompets sound on hie,
That sent to heaven the ecchoed report
Of their new joy, and happie victorie
Gainst him, that had them long opprest with tort,[2]
And fast imprisoned in sieged fort.
Then all the people, as in solemne feast,
To him assembled with one full consort,
Rejoycing at the fall of that great beast,
　From whose eternall bondage now they were releast.

5

Forth came that auncient Lord and aged Queene,
Arayd in antique robes downe to the ground,
And sad habiliments right well beseene[3];
A noble crew about them waited round
Of sage and sober Peres[4], all gravely gownd;
Whom farre before did march a goodly band
Of tall young men, all hable armes to sownd[5],
But now they laurell braunches bore in hand;
　Glad signe of victorie and peace in all their land.

6

Unto that doughtie Conqueror they came,
And him before themselves prostrating low,
Their Lord and Patrone loud did him proclame,
And at his feet their laurell boughes did throw.
Soone after them all dauncing on a row
The comely virgins came, with girlands dight,
As fresh as flowres in medow greene do grow,
When morning deaw upon their leaves doth light:
　And in their hands sweet Timbrels all upheld on hight.

．　　．　　．　　．　　．　　．

17

Then sayd the royall Pere in sober wise;
Deare Sonne, great beene the evils which ye bore
From first to last in your late enterprise,
That I note[6] whether prayse, or pitty more:
For never living man, I weene, so sore
In sea of deadly daungers was distrest;
But since now safe ye seised have the shore,
And well arrived are, (high God be blest)
　Let us devize of ease and everlasting rest.

18

Ah, dearest Lord, said then that doughty knight,
Of ease or rest I may not yet devize,
For by the faith, which I to armes have plight,
I bounden am streight after this emprize,
As that your daughter can ye well advize,
Backe to returne to that great Faerie Queene,
And her to serve six yeares in warlike wize,
Gainst that proud Paynim king that workes her teene[7]:
　Therefore I ought crave pardon, till I there have beene.

19

Unhappie falles that hard necessitie,
(Quoth he) the troubler of my happie peace,
And vowed foe of my felicitie;
Ne I against the same can justly preace:[8]
But since that band ye cannot now release,
Nor doen undo;[9] (for vowes may not be vaine),
Soone as the terms of those six yeares shall cease,
Ye then shall hither backe returne againe,
　The marriage to accomplish vowd betwixt you twain.

20

Which for my part I covet to performe,
In sort as through the world I did proclame,
That whoso kild that monster most deforme,
And him in hardy battaile overcame,
Should have mine onely daughter to his Dame,
And of my kingdome heyre apparaunt bee:
Therefore since now to thee perteines the same,
By dew desert of noble chevalree,
　Both daughter and eke kingdome, lo, I yield to thee.

．　　．　　．　　．　　．　　．

---

2 wrong
3 arrayed
4 peers, princes
5 clash, wield
6 ne wot. know not
7 causes her grief
8 press
9 cause to be undone

[Archimago, in a last spiteful effort, comes
disguised as a messenger and attempts to prevent the betrothal by producing a letter from
Duessa in which she asserts that the Knight is
plighted to her. His ruse, however, is exposed.]

36

But they him layd full low in dungeon deepe,
And bound him hand and foote with yron
chaines
And with continual watch did warely keepe:
Who then would thinke, that by his subtile
trains
He could escape fowle death or deadly paines?
Thus when that princes wrath was pacifide,
He gan renew the late forbidden banes[10],
And to the knight his daughter dear he tyde,
    With sacred rites and vowes for ever to
    abyde.

37

His owne two hands the holy knots did knit,
That none but death for ever can devide;
His owne two hands, for such a turne most fit,
The housling[11] fire did kindle and provide,
And holy water thereon sprinckled wide;
At which the bushy Teade[12] a groome did light,
And sacred lamp in secret chamber hide,
Where it should not be quenched day nor night,
    For feare of evill fates, but burnen ever
    bright.

38

Then gan they sprinckle all the posts with
wine,
And made great feast to solemnize that day;
They all perfumde with frankencense divine,
And precious odours fetcht from far away,
That all the house did sweat with great aray:
And all the while sweete Musicke did apply
Her curious skill, the warbling notes to play,
To drive away the dull Melancholy;
    The whiles one sung a song of love and
    jollity.

39

During the which there was an heavenly noise
Heard sound through all the Pallace pleasantly,
Like as it had bene many an Angels voice
Singing before th' eternall Majesty,
In their trinall triplicities[13] on hye;
Yet wist no creature whence that heavenly
sweet
Proceeded, yet eachone felt secretly
Himselfe thereby reft of his sences meet,
    And ravished with rare impression in his
    sprite.

40

Great joy was made that day of young and
old,
And solemne feast proclaimd throughout the
land,
That their exceeding merth may not be told:
Suffice it heare by signes to understand
The usuall joyes at knitting of loves band.
Thrise happy man the knight himselfe did
hold,
Possessed of his Ladies hart and hand,
And ever, when his eye did her behold,
    His heart did seeme to melt in pleasures
    manifold.

41

Her joyous presence, and sweet company
In full content he there did long enjoy;
Ne wicked envie, ne vile gealosy,
His deare delights were able to annoy:
Yet swimming in that sea of blissfull joy,
He nought forgot how he whilome had sworne,
In case he could that monstrous beast destroy,
Unto his Faerie Queene backe to returne;
    The which he shortly did, and Una left to
    mourne.

42

Now strike your sailes ye jolly Mariners,
For we be come unto a quiet rode,
Where we must land some of our passengers,
And light this wearie vessell of her lode.
Here she a while may make her safe abode,
Till she repaired have her tackles spent,
And wants supplide. And then againe abroad
On the long voyage whereto she is bent:
    Well may she speede and fairely finish her
    intent.

PROTHALAMION*

Calm was the day, and through the trembling
air
Sweet-breathing Zephyrus did softly play—
A gentle spirit, that lightly did delay
Hot Titan's beams, which then did glister
fair;
When I, (whom sullen care,
Through discontent of my long fruitless stay
In princes' court, and expectation vain
Of idle hopes, which still do fly away
Like empty shadows, did afflict my brain)

* A "Spousall Verse" made in honor of the approaching double marriage of the Ladies
Elizabeth and Katherine Somerset in 1596,
and apparently celebrating some visit of
theirs to Essex House. F. T. Palgrave says
of this poem: "Nowhere has Spenser more
emphatically displayed himself as the very
poet of Beauty: The Renaissance impulse in
England is here seen at its highest and
purest."

10 banns   11 sacramental   12 torch
13 The thrice three orders of the celestial hier-
    archy: Seraphim, Cherubim, Thrones, Domin-
    ions, Virtues, Powers, Princedoms, Arch-
    angels, Angels.

Walk'd forth to ease my pain   10
Along the shore of silver-streaming Thames;
Whose rutty[1] bank, the which his river hems,
Was painted all with variable flowers,
And all the meads adorn'd with dainty gems
Fit to deck maidens' bowers,
And crown their paramours
Against the bridal day, which is not long:
   Sweet Thames! run softly, till I end my
    song.

There in a meadow by the river's side
A flock of nymphs I chancéd to espy,   20
All lovely daughters of the flood thereby,
With goodly greenish locks all loose untied
As each had been a bride;
And each one had a little wicker basket
Made of fine twigs, entailéd curiously.
In which they gather'd flowers to fill their
    flasket,
And with fine fingers cropt full feateously[2]
The tender stalks on high.
Of every sort which in that meadow grew
They gather'd some; the violet, pallid blue, 30
The little daisy that at evening closes,
The virgin lily and the primrose true,
With store of vermeil roses,
To deck their bridegrooms' posies
Against the bridal day, which was not long:
   Sweet Thames! run softly, till I end my
    song.

With that I saw two swans† of goodly hue
Come softly swimming down along the Lee[3];
Two fairer birds I yet did never see;
The snow which doth the top of Pindus strow
Did never whiter show,   41
Nor Jove himself, when he a swan would be
For love of Leda, whiter did appear;
Yet Leda was (they say) as white as he,
Yet not so white as these, nor nothing near;
So purely white they were
That even the gentle stream, the which them
    bare,
Seem'd foul to them, and bade his billows
    spare
To wet their silken feathers, lest they might
Soil their fair plumes with water not so fair. 50
And mar their beauties bright
That shone as Heaven's light

1 rooty
2 plucked very dexterously
3 stream
† "The critics blame him because in his *Prothalamion* the subjects of it enter on the Thames as swans and leave it at Temple Gardens as noble damsels; but to those who are grown familiar with his imaginary world such a transformation seems as natural as in the old legend of the Knight of the Swan."—Lowell.

Against their bridal day, which was not long:
   Sweet Thames! run softly, till I end my
    song.

Eftsoons the nymphs, which now had flowers
    their fill,
Ran all in haste to see that silver brood
As they came floating on the crystal flood;
Whom when they saw, they stood amazéd still
Their wondering eyes to fill;   59
Them seem'd they never saw a sight so fair
Of fowls, so lovely, that they sure did deem
Them heavenly born, or to be that same pair
Which through the sky draw Venus' silver
    team;
For sure they did not seem
To be begot of any earthly seed,
But rather Angels, or of Angels' breed;
Yet were they bred of summer's heat[4], they
    say,
In sweetest season, when each flower and weed
The earth did fresh array;
So fresh they seem'd as day,   70
Ev'n as their bridal day, which was not long:
   Sweet Thames! run softly, till I end my
    song.

Then forth they all out of their baskets drew
Great store of flowers, the honour of the field,
That to the sense did fragrant odours yield,
All which upon those goodly birds they threw
And all the waves did strew,
That like old Peneus' waters they did seem
When down along by pleasant Tempe's shore
Scatter'd with flowers, through Thessaly they
    stream,   80
That they appear, through lilies' plenteous
    store,
Like a bride's chamber-floor.
Two of those nymphs meanwhile two garlands
    bound
Of freshest flowers which in that mead they
    found,
The which presenting all in trim array,
Their snowy foreheads therewithal they
    crown'd;
Whilst one did sing this lay
Prepared against that day,
Against their bridal day, which was not long:
   Sweet Thames! run softly till I end my
    song.   90

'Ye gentle birds! the world's fair ornament,
And Heaven's glory, whom this happy hour
Doth lead unto your lovers' blissful bower,

4 Spenser spelled it Somer's heat (Somerset) and the pun was no doubt regarded as an ornament.

Joy may you have, and gentle hearts' content
Of your love's couplement;
And let fair Venus, that is queen of love,
With her heart-quelling son upon you smile,
Whose smile, they say, hath virtue to remove
All love's dislike, and friendship's faulty guile
For ever to assoil.   100
Let endless peace your steadfast hearts accord,
And blessèd plenty wait upon your board;
And let your bed with pleasures chaste abound,
That fruitful issue may to you afford
Which may your foes confound, .
And make your joys redound
Upon your bridal day, which is not long:
   Sweet Thames! run softly, till I end my
     song.'

So ended she; and all the rest around
To her redoubled that her undersong,   110
Which said their bridal day should not be long:
And gentle Echo from the neighbour ground
Their accents did resound.
So 'forth those joyous birds did pass along
Adown the Lee that to them murmur'd low,
As he would speak but that he lack'd a tongue;
Yet did by signs his glad affection show,
Making his stream run slow.
And all the fowl which in his flood did dwell
'Gan flock about these twain, that did excel
The rest, so far as Cynthia doth shend[5]   121
The lesser stars. So they, enrangèd well,
Did on those two attend,
And their best service lend
Against their wedding day, which was not long!
   Sweet Thames! run softly, till I end my song.

At length they all to merry London came,
To merry London, my most kindly nurse,
That to me gave this life's first native source,
Though from another place I take my name,   130
An house of ancient fame:
There when she came whereas[6] those bricky
   towers
The which on Thames' broad agèd back do
   ride,
Where now the studious lawyers have their
   bowers,
There whilome wont the Templar-knights to
   bide,
Till they decay'd through pride;
Next whereunto there stands a stately place,
Where oft I gainèd gifts and goodly grace
Of that great lord[7], which therein wont to
   dwell,

Whose want too well now feels my friendless
   case;
But ah! here fits not well   141
Old woes, but joys to tell
Against the bridal day, which is not long:
   Sweet Thames! run softly, till I end my song.

Yet therein now doth lodge a noble peer,[8]
Great England's glory and the world's wide
   wonder,
Whose dreadful name late through all Spain
   did thunder,
And Hercules' two pillars standing near
Did make to quake and fear:
Fair branch of honour, flower of chivalry! 150
That fillest England with thy triumphs' fame
Joy have thou of thy noble victory,[9]
And endless happiness of thine own name[10]
That promiseth the same;
That through thy prowess and victorious arms
Thy country may be freed from foreign harms,
And great Elisa's glorious name may ring
Through all the world, fill'd with thy wide
   alarms,
Which some brave Muse may sing
To ages following: 160
Upon the bridal day, which is not long:
   Sweet Thames! run softly, till I end my song!

From those high towers this noble lord issuing
Like Radiant Hesper, when his golden hair
In th' ocean billows he hath bathèd fair,
Descended to the river's open viewing
With a great train ensuing.
Above the rest were goodly to be seen
Two gentle knights of lovely face and feature,
Beseeming well the bower of any queen,   170
With gifts of wit and ornaments of nature,
Fit for so goodly stature,
That like the twins of Jove[11] they seem'd in
   sight
Which deck the baldric of the Heavens bright;
They two, forth pacing to the river's side,
Received those two fair brides, their love's
   delight;
Which, at th' appointed tide,
Each one did make his bride
Against their bridal day, which is not long:
   Sweet Thames! run softly, till I end my song.

5 the moon doth shame
6 where
7 Lord Leicester, Spenser's patron, whose death left him in "friendless case."
8 Robert Devereux, second Earl of Essex
9 At Cadiz, 1596.
10 Apparently an allusion to the fact that the words *ever* and *heureux* (Fr., "happy") can be seen in the name *Devereux*.
11 Castor and Pollux, who were placed among the stars as the constellation Gemini.

ELIZABETHAN SONNETS*

EDMUND SPENSER (1552-1599)

AMORETTI XV.

Ye tradeful merchants that with weary toil
Do seek most precious things to make your gain,
And both the Indias of their treasures spoil,
What needeth you to seek so far in vain?
For lo, my love doth in herself contain
All this world's riches that may far be found:
If sapphires, lo, her eyes be sapphires plain;
If rubies, lo, her lips be rubies sound;
If pearls, her teeth be pearls, both pure and
    round;
If ivory, her forehead ivory ween;
If gold, her locks are finest gold on ground;
If silver, her fair hands are silver sheen.
But that which fairest is, but few behold—
Her mind adorned with virtues manifold.

AMORETTI XXXVII.

What guile is this, that those her golden
    tresses
She doth attire under a net of gold,
And with sly skill so cunningly them dresses
That which is gold or hair may scarce be told?
Is it that men's frail eyes, which gaze too bold,
She may entangle in that golden snare,
And, being caught, may craftily enfold
Their weaker hearts, which are not well aware?
Take heed, therefore, mine eyes, how ye do stare
Henceforth too rashly on that guileful net,
In which if ever ye entrappéd are,
Out of her bands ye by no means shall get.
Fondness[1] it were for any, being free,
To covet fetters, though they golden be!

AMORETTI LXI.

The glorious image of the Maker's beauty,
My sovereign saint, the idol of my thought,
Dare not henceforth, above the bounds of duty,
T' accuse of pride, or rashly blame for ought.
For being, as she is, divinely wrought,
And of the brood of angels heavenly born,
And with the crew of blessed saints upbrought,
Each of which did her with their gifts adorn—
The bud of joy, the blossom of the morn,
The beam of light, whom mortal eyes admire;
What reason is it then but she should scorn

Base things that to her love too bold aspire!
Such heavenly forms ought rather worshipt be
Than dare be loved by men of mean degree.

SIR PHILIP SIDNEY (1554-1586)

ASTROPHEL AND STELLA I.†

Loving in truth, and fain in verse my love to
    show,
That she, dear she, might take some pleasure
    of my pain,—
Pleasure might cause her read, reading might
    make her know,
Knowledge might pity win, and pity grace
    obtain,—
I sought fit words to paint the blackest face
    of woe;
Studying inventions fine, her wits to entertain,
Oft turning others' leaves, to see if thence
    would flow
Some fresh and fruitful showers upon my sun-
    burn'd brain.
But words came halting forth, wanting Inven-
    tion's stay[2];
Invention, Nature's child, fled step-dame
    Study's blows;
And others' feet still seem'd but strangers in
    my way.
Thus, great with child to speak, and helpless
    in my throes,
Biting my truant pen, beating myself for spite;
Fool, said my Muse to me, look in thy heart
    and write.

ASTROPHEL AND STELLA XXXI.

With how sad steps, O Moon, thou climb'st the
    skies!
How silently, and with how wan a face!
What, may it be that e'en in heavenly place
That busy archer his sharp arrows tries!
Sure, if that long-with-love-acquainted eyes
Can judge of love, thou feel'st a lover's case,
I read it in thy looks; thy languish'd grace,
To me, that feel the like, thy state descries.
Then, e'en of fellowship, O Moon, tell me,
Is constant love deem'd there but want of wit?
Are beauties there as proud as here they be?
Do they above love to be loved, and yet
Those lovers scorn whom that love doth possess?
Do they call virtue, there, ungratefulness?

SAMUEL DANIEL (1562-1619)

TO DELIA LI.

Care-charmer Sleep, son of the sable Night,
Brother to Death, in silent darkness born,

---

1 folly
* Sonnet groups or sequences were a marked
  feature of Elizabethan verse. The *Amoretti*
  are a series of eighty-eight, recording Spenser's
  courtship of Elizabeth Boyle, his marriage to
  whom in 1594 was the occasion of his
  Epithalamion. The *Astrophel and Stella*
  series, of one hundred and ten, chronicles Sidney's love for Penelope Devereux. The in-
  spirers of most of the other series seem more
  or less imaginary. See *Eng. Lit.,* pp. 95, 107.

† See last note. "After Shakespeare's sonnets, Sidney's *Astrophel and Stella* offers the most intense and powerful picture of the passion of
  love in the whole range of our poetry."—F. T.
  Palgrave. 2 support

Relieve my languish, and restore the light;
With dark forgetting of my care return.
And let the day be time enough to mourn
The shipwreck of my ill-adventured youth:
Let waking eyes suffice to wail their scorn,
Without the torment of the night's untruth.
Cease, dreams, the images of day-desires,
To model forth the passions of the morrow;
Never let rising Sun approve you liars,
To add more grief to aggravate my sorrow:
Still let me sleep, embracing clouds in vain,
And never wake to feel the day's disdain.

MICHAEL DRAYTON (1563-1631)

IDEA LXI.

Since there's no help, come let us kiss and
part,—
Nay I have done, you get no more of me;
And I am glad, yea, glad with all my heart,
That thus so cleanly I myself can free;
Shake hands for ever, cancel all our vows,
And when we meet at any time again,
Be it not seen in either of our brows
That we one jot of former love retain.
Now at the last gasp of love's latest breath,
When his pulse failing, passion speechless lies,
When faith is kneeling by his bed of death,
And innocence is closing up his eyes,
—Now if thou would'st, when all have given
him over,
From death to life thou might'st him yet
recover!

WILLIAM SHAKESPEARE (1564-1616)

SONNET XXIX.

When in disgrace with fortune and men's eyes
I all alone beweep my outcast state,
And trouble deaf heaven with my bootless
cries,
And look upon myself, and curse my fate;
Wishing me like to one more rich in hope,
Featured like him, like him with friends possest,
Desiring this man's art, and that man's scope,
With what I most enjoy contented least;
Yet in these thoughts myself almost despising,
Haply I think on thee;—and then my state,
Like to the lark at break of day arising
From sullen earth, sings hymns at heaven's
gate;
For thy sweet love remember'd, such wealth
brings
That then I scorn to change my state with
kings.

SONNET XXX.

When to the sessions[3] of sweet silent thought
I summon up remembrance of things past,
I sigh the lack of many a thing I sought,
And with old woes new wail my dear time's
waste;
Then can I drown an eye, unused to flow,
For precious friends hid in death's dateless
night,
And weep afresh love's long-since-cancell'd woe,
And moan the expense[4] of many a vanished
sight.
Then can I grieve at grievances foregone,
And heavily from woe to woe tell o'er
The sad account of fore-bemoanéd moan,
Which I new pay as if not paid before:
—But if the while I think on thee, dear
Friend,
All losses are restored, and sorrows end.

SONNET LXIV.

When I have seen by Time's fell hand defaced
The rich proud cost of out-worn buried age;
When sometime lofty towers I see down-razed,
And brass eternal slave to mortal rage;
When I have seen the hungry ocean gain
Advantage on the kingdom of the shore,
And the firm soil win of the watery main,
Increasing store with loss, and loss with store;
When I have seen such interchange of state,
Or state itself confounded to decay,
Ruin hath taught me thus to ruminate—
That Time will come and take my Love away:
—This thought is as a death, which cannot
choose
But weep to have that which it fears to lose.

SONNET LXV.

Since brass, nor stone, nor earth, nor boundless
sea,
But sad mortality o'ersways their power,
How with this rage shall beauty hold a plea,
Whose action is no stronger than a flower?
O how shall summer's honey breath hold out
Against the wreckful siege of battering days,
When rocks impregnable are not so stout
Nor gates of steel so strong, but time decays?
O fearful meditation! where, alack!
Shall Time's best jewel[5] from Time's chest lie
hid?
Or what strong hand can hold his swift foot back,
Or who his spoil of beauty can forbid?
O! none, unless this miracle have might,
That in black ink my love may still shine
bright.

3 Legal phraseology   5 i. e., the poet's friend.
4 the cost (in grief)

SONNET LXXIII.

That time of year thou may'st in me behold
When yellow leaves, or none, or few, do hang
Upon those boughs which shake against the cold,
Bare ruin'd choirs, where late the sweet birds
    sang:
In me thou see'st the twilight of such day
As after sunset fadeth in the west,
Which by and by black night doth take away,
Death's second self, that seals up all in rest:
In me thou see'st the glowing of such fire,
That on the ashes of his youth doth lie
As the death-bed whereon it must expire,
Consumed with that which it was nourish'd by:
  —This thou perceiv'st, which makes thy love
    more strong,
  To love that well which thou must leave ere
    long.

SONNET LXXIV.

But be contented: when that fell arrest
Without all bail[6] shall carry me away,
My life hath in this line some interest,
Which for memorial still with thee shall stay.
When thou reviewest this, thou dost review
The very part was consecrate to thee:
The earth can have but earth, which is his due;
My spirit is thine, the better part of me:
So then thou hast but lost the dregs of life,
The prey of worms, my body being dead,
The coward conquest of a wretch's knife,
Too base of thee to be remembered.
  The worth of that is that which it contains,
  And that is this, and this with thee remains.

ELIZABETHAN LYRICS

SIR PHILIP SIDNEY (1554-1586)

ASTROPHEL AND STELLA, FIRST SONG

Doubt you to whom my Muse these notes
    intendeth,
Which now my breast surcharged to music
    lendeth?
  To you, to you, all song of praise is due,
Only in you my song begins and endeth.

Who hath the eyes which marry state with
    pleasure?
Who keeps the keys of Nature's chiefest
    treasure?
  To you, to you, all song of praise is due,
Only for you the heaven forgat all measure.[1] 8

Who hath the lips where wit in fairnes
    reigneth?
Who womankind at once both decks an
    staineth[2]?
  To you, to you, all song of praise is due,
Only by you Cupid his crown maintaineth.

Who hath the feet whose step all sweetnes
    planteth?
Who else, for whom Fame worthy trumpet
    wanteth?
  To you, to you, all song of praise is due,
Only to you her scepter Venus granteth.   1

Who hath the breast whose milk doth patienc
    nourish?
Whose grace is such that when it chides dot
    cherish?
  To you, to you, all song of praise is due,
Only through you the tree of life doth flourisl

Who hath the hand which without strok
    subdueth?
Who long-dead beauty with increase reneweth
  To you, to you, all song of praise is due,
Only at you all envy hopeless rueth.[3]   2

Who hath the hair which, loosest, fastest tieth
Who makes a man live then glad when h
    dieth?
  To you, to you, all song of praise is due,
Only of you the flatterer never lieth.

Who hath the voice which soul from sense
    sunders?
Whose force but yours the bolts of beaut
    thunders?
  To you, to you, all song of praise is due,
Only with you not miracles are wonders.[4] 3

Doubt you to whom my Muse these note
    intendeth?
Which now my breast o'ercharged to musi
    lendeth?
  To you, to you, all song of praise is due,
Only in you my song begins and endeth.

GEORGE PEELE (1558?-1597?)

FROM THE ARRAIGNMENT OF PARIS

Œnone

Fair and fair, and twice so fair,
  As fair as any may be,
The fairest shepherd on our green,
  A love for any lady.

---

6 refusing bail

1 was immeasurably lavish

2 i. e., by comparison 4 miracles are not wonder
3 sorrows

Paris

Fair and fair, and twice so fair,
  As fair as any may be;
Thy love is fair for thee alone,
  And for no other lady.

Œnone

My love is fair, my love is gay,
  And fresh as bin the flowers in May,
And of my love my roundelay,
  My merry, merry roundelay,
Concludes with Cupid's curse,—
  "They that do change old love for new,
Pray gods they change for worse!"

Ambo Simul[5]

They that do change old love for new,
  Pray gods they change for worse!

Œnone

Fair and fair, and twice so fair,
  As fair as any may be,
The fairest shepherd on our green,
  A love for any lady.

Paris

Fair and fair, and twice so fair,
  As fair as any may be;
Thy love is fair for thee alone,
  And for no other lady.

Œnone

My love can pipe, my love can sing,
My love can many a pretty thing,
And of his lovely praises ring
  My merry, merry roundelay.
  Amen to Cupid's curse,—
  "They that do change old love for new,
Pray gods they change for worse!"

Paris

They that do change old love for new,
  Pray gods they change for worse!

Ambo Simul

Fair and fair, and twice so fair,
  As fair as any may be;
Thy love is fair for thee alone,
  And for no other lady.

THOMAS LODGE (1558?-1625)

ROSALIND'S MADRIGAL

Love in my bosom, like a bee,
  Doth suck his sweet;
Now with his wings he plays with me,
  Now with his feet.

Within mine eyes he makes his nest,
His bed amidst my tender breast;
My kisses are his daily feast,
And yet he robs me of my rest:
    Ah! wanton, will ye?   9

And if I sleep, then percheth he
    With pretty flight,
And makes his pillow of my knee
    The livelong night.
  Strike I my lute, he tunes the string;
  He music plays if so I sing;
  He lends me every lovely thing,
  Yet cruel he my heart doth sting.
    Whist, wanton, still ye!   1:

Else I with roses every day
    Will whip you hence,
And bind you, when you long to play,
    For your offense;
  I'll shut my eyes to keep you in;
  I'll make you fast it for your sin;
  I'll count your power not worth a pin;
  —Alas! what hereby shall I win,
    If he gainsay me?   27

What if I beat the wanton boy
    With many a rod?
He will repay me with annoy,
    Because a god.
  Then sit thou safely on my knee,
  And let thy bower my bosom be;
  Lurk in mine eyes, I like of[6] thee;
  O Cupid, so thou pity me,
    Spare not, but play thee!   36

ROBERT SOUTHWELL (1561?-1595)

THE BURNING BABE

As I in hoary winter's night
  Stood shivering in the snow,
Surprised I was with sudden heat
  Which made my heart to glow;
And lifting up a fearful eye
  To view what fire was near,
A pretty Babe all burning bright
  Did in the air appear,
Who, scorched with excessive heat,
  Such floods of tears did shed,   10
As tho' His floods should quench His flames
  Which with His tears were fed.
"Alas!" quoth He, "but newly born
  In fiery heats I fry,
Yet none approach to warm their hearts
  Or feel my fire but I!
My faultless breast the furnace i.,
  The fuel, wounding thorns;

_____
5 Both together   6 am pleased with

Love is the fire and sighs the smoke,
   The ashes, shame and scorns;   20
The fuel Justice layeth on,
   And Mercy blows the coals;
The metal in this furnace wrought
   Are men's defiled souls;
For which, as now on fire I am
   To work them to their good,
So will I melt into a bath
   To wash them in my blood.''
With this He vanish'd out of sight,
   And swiftly shrunk away,   30
And straight I called unto mind
   That it was Christmas-day.

CHRISTOPHER MARLOWE (1564-1593)

THE PASSIONATE SHEPHERD TO HIS LOVE

Come live with me and be my love,
And we will all the pleasures prove
That valleys, groves, hills and fields,
Woods or steepy mountain yields.

And we will sit upon the rocks,
Seeing the shepherds feed their flocks,
By shallow rivers, to whose falls
Melodious birds sing madrigals.   8

And I will make thee beds of roses,
And a thousand fragrant posies,
A cap of flowers, and a kirtle
Embroider'd all with leaves of myrtle;

A gown made of the finest wool,
Which from our pretty lambs we pull;
Fair linéd slippers for the cold,
With buckles of the purest gold;   16

A belt of straw and ivy buds
With coral clasps and amber studs:
And if these pleasures may thee move,
Come live with me and be my love.

The shepherd swains shall dance and sing
For thy delight each May-morning:
If these delights thy mind may move,
Then live with me and be my love.   24

SIR WALTER RALEIGH (1552?-1618)*

THE NYMPH'S REPLY TO THE SHEPHERD

If all the world and love were young,
And truth in every shepherd's tongue,
These pretty pleasures might me move
To live with thee and be thy love.

* Neither of the two poems here given as Raleigh's can be ascribed to him with much confidence. The first appeared in *England's Helicon* over the name "Ignoto." The MS. of the second bears the initials "Sr. W. R."

Time drives the flocks from field to fold,
When rivers rage, and rocks grow cold;
And Philomel becometh dumb;
The rest complains of cares to come.

The flowers do fade, and wanton fields
To wayward Winter reckoning yields;
A honey tongue, a heart of gall,
Is fancy's spring, but sorrow's fall.

Thy gowns, thy shoes, thy beds of roses,
Thy cap, thy kirtle, and thy posies,
Soon break, soon wither, soon forgotten,
In folly ripe, in reason rotten.   1

Thy belt of straw and ivy buds,
Thy coral clasps and amber studs,
All these in me no means can move
To come to thee and be thy love.

But could youth last, and love still breed,
Had joys no date[7], nor age no need,
Then these delights my mind might move
To live with thee and be thy love.   2

PILGRIM TO PILGRIM

As you came from the holy land
   Of Walsinghame,†
Met you not with my true love
   By the way as you came?

How shall I know your true love,
   That have met many one,
As I went to the holy land,
   That have come, that have gone?   8

She is neither white nor brown,
   But as the heavens fair;
There is none hath a form so divine
   In the earth or the air.

Such a one did I meet, good sir,
   Such an angel-like face,
Who like a queen, like a nymph, did appear,
   By her gait, by her grace.   16

She hath left me here all alone,
   All alone, as unknown,
Who sometimes did me lead with herself,
   And me loved as her own.

7 end
† An ancient Priory in Norfolk, with a famous shrine of Our Lady, the object of many pilgrimages until its dissolution in 1538 (*Eng. Lit.*, p. 79). "A lover growing or grown old, it would seem, has been left in the lurch by the object of his affections. As all the world thronged to Walsingham the lover supposes that she too must have gone that way; and meeting a pilgrim returning from that English Holy Land, asks him if he has seen anything of her runaway ladyship."—J. W. Hales.

hat's the cause that she leaves you alone,
And a new way doth take,
ho loved you once as her own,
And her joy did you make? 24

have loved her all my youth,
But now old, as you see,
ove likes not the falling fruit
From the withered tree.

now that Love is a careless child,
And forgets promise past;
e is blind, he is deaf when he list,
And in faith never fast. 32

is desire is a dureless[1] content,
And a trustless joy;
e is won with a world of despair
And is lost with a toy.[2]

f womankind such indeed is the love,
Or the word love abusèd,
nder which many childish desires
And conceits are excusèd. 40

ut true love is a durable fire,
In the mind ever burning,
Never sick, never old, never dead,
From itself never turning.

WILLIAM SHAKESPEARE (1564-1616)

FROM AS YOU LIKE IT

Under the greenwood tree
Who loves to lie with me,
And turn[3] his merry note
Unto the sweet bird's throat—
Come hither, come hither, come hither!
Here shall he see
No enemy
But winter and rough weather.

Who doth ambition shun
And loves to live i' the sun,
Seeking the food he eats
And pleased with what he gets—
Come hither, come hither, come hither!
Here shall he see
No enemy
But winter and rough weather.

FROM AS YOU LIKE IT

Blow, blow, thou winter wind,
Thou art not so unkind
As man's ingratitude;
Thy tooth is not so keen
Because thou art not seen,
Although thy breath be rude.

Heigh ho! sing heigh ho! unto the green holly:
Most friendship is feigning, most loving mere
folly:
Then, heigh ho! the holly!
This life is most jolly.

Freeze, freeze, thou bitter sky,
Thou dost not bite so nigh
As benefits forgot:
Though thou the waters warp,
Thy sting is not so sharp
As friend remember'd not.

Heigh ho! sing heigh ho! unto the green holly:
Most friendship is feigning, most loving mere
folly:
Then, heigh ho! the holly!
This life is most jolly.

FROM MEASURE FOR MEASURE

Take, O, take those lips away,
That so sweetly were forsworn;
And those eyes, the break of day,
Lights that do mislead the morn:
But thy kisses bring again,
Bring again,
Seals of love, but sealed in vain,
Sealed in vain!

FROM TWELFTH NIGHT

Come away, come away, Death,
And in sad cypress let me be laid;
Fly away, fly away, breath;
I am slain by a fair cruel maid.
My shroud of white, stuck all with yew,
O prepare it!
My part of death, no one so true
Did share it.

Not a flower, not a flower sweet
On my black coffin let there be strown;
Not a friend, not a friend greet
My poor corpse, where my bones shall be
thrown:
A thousand thousand sighs to save,
Lay me, O where
Sad true lover never find my grave,
To weep there.

FROM HAMLET

How should I your true love know
From another one?
By his cockle hat and staff,
And his sandal shoon.[4]

[4] Pilgrims wore cockle shells in their hats in sign
of their having crossed the sea to the Holy
Land, and lovers not infrequently assumed
this disguise.

1 unenduring   2 trifle   3 modulate

He is dead and gone, lady,
    He is dead and gone;
At his head a grass-green turf,
    At his heels a stone.

White his shroud as the mountain snow,
    Larded[5] with sweet flowers,
Which bewept to the grave did go
    With true-love showers.

From Cymbeline

Hark, hark! the lark at heaven's gate sings,
    And Phoebus 'gins arise,
His steeds to water at those springs
    On chaliced flowers that lies;
And winking Mary-buds begin
    To ope their golden eyes:
With everything that pretty is,
        My lady sweet, arise!
        Arise, arise!

THOMAS DEKKER (1570?-1641?)

From Patient Grissell

Art thou poor, yet hast thou golden slumbers?
    O sweet content!
Art thou rich, yet is thy mind perplexed?
    O punishment!
Dost thou laugh to see how fools are vexed
To add to golden numbers golden numbers?
    O sweet content, O sweet, O sweet content!
    Work apace! apace! apace! apace!
    Honest labour bears a lovely face.
    Then hey noney, noney, hey noney, noney!

Canst drink the waters of the crispèd spring?
    O sweet content!
Swim'st thou in wealth, yet sink'st in thine
        own tears?
    O punishment!
Then he that patiently want's burden bears
No burden bears, but is a king, a king.
    O sweet content, O sweet, O sweet content!

    Work apace! apace! apace! apace!
    Honest labour bears a lovely face.
    Then hey noney, noney, hey noney, noney!

THOMAS CAMPION (d. 1619)

Cherry-Ripe

There is a garden in her face
    Where roses and white lilies grow;
A heavenly paradise is that place,
    Wherein all pleasant fruits do flow;

5 thickly strewn

There cherries grow that none may buy,
Till "Cherry-Ripe" themselves do cry.

Those cherries fairly do enclose
    Of orient pearl a double row,
Which when her lovely laughter shows,
    They look like rose-buds fill'd with snow:
Yet them no peer nor prince may buy,
Till "Cherry-Ripe" themselves do cry.

Her eyes like angels watch them still;
    Her brows like bended bows do stand,
Threat'ning with piercing frowns to kill
    All that attempt with eye or hand
Those sacred cherries to come nigh,
Till "Cherry-Ripe" themselves do cry!

MICHAEL DRAYTON (1563-1631)

Agincourt*

Fair stood the wind for France,
    When we our sails advance;
Nor now to prove our chance
        Longer will tarry;
But putting to the main,
At Caux, the mouth of Seine,
With all his martial train
        Landed King Harry.   8

And taking many a fort,
    Furnished in warlike sort,
Marcheth towards Agincourt
        In happy hour;
Skirmishing, day by day,
With those that stopped his way,
Where the French general lay
        With all his power..   16

Which[6], in his height of pride,
    King Henry to deride,
His ransom to provide
        To the King sending[7];
Which he neglects the while,
As from a nation vile,
Yet with an angry smile,
        Their fall portending.   24

6 who (the French general)
7 i. e., sending an order.
* In the course of the Hundred Years' War the English won three great victories over the French in the face of enormous odds—Crécy in 1346, Poitiers in 1356, and Agincourt in 1415. The last was won by Henry the Fifth, and so well was the glory of it remembered that after nearly two hundred years Drayton could celebrate it in this ballad, which bids fair to stand as the supreme national ballad of England. Breathless from the first word to the last, rude and rhythmic as the tread of an army, it arouses the martial spirit as few things but its imitators can.

And turning to his men,
Quoth our brave Henry then:
"Though they to one be ten
    Be not amazèd!
Yet have we well begun:
Battles so bravely won
Have ever to the sun
    By Fame been raisèd!   32

"And for myself," quoth he,
"This my full rest[8] shall be:
England ne'er mourn for me,
    Nor more esteem me!
Victor I will remain,
Or on this earth lie slain;
Never shall She sustain
    Loss to redeem me!   40

"Poitiers and Cressy tell,
When most their pride did swell,
Under our swords they fell.
    No less our skill is,
Than when our Grandsire great,
Claiming the regal seat,
By many a warlike feat
    Lopped the French lilies."   48

The Duke of York so dread
The eager vanward led;
With the main, Henry sped
    Amongst his henchmen:
Exeter had the rear,
A braver man not there!
O Lord, how hot they were
    On the false Frenchmen!   56

They now to fight are gone;
Armour on armour shone;
Drum now to drum did groan:
    To hear, was wonder;
That, with the cries they make,
The very earth did shake;
Trumpet to trumpet spake;
    Thunder to thunder.   64

Well it thine age became,
O noble Erpingham,
Which didst the signal aim
    To our hid forces!
When, from a meadow by,
Like a storm suddenly,
The English archery
    Stuck the French horses.   72

With Spanish yew so strong;
Arrows a cloth-yard long,

That like to serpents stung,
    Piercing the weather.
None from his fellow starts;
But, playing manly parts,
And like true English hearts,
    Stuck close together.   80

When down their bows they threw,
And forth their bilboes[9] drew,
And on the French they flew:
    Not one was tardy.
Arms were from shoulders sent,
Scalps to the teeth were rent,
Down the French peasants went:
    Our men were hardy.   88

This while our noble King,
His broad sword brandishing,
Down the French host did ding,
    As to o'erwhelm it;
And many a deep wound lent;
His arms with blood besprent,
And many a cruel dent
    Bruised his helmet.   96

Gloucester, that duke so good,
Next of the royal blood,
For famous England stood
    With his brave brother;
Clarence, in steel so bright,
Though but a maiden knight,
Yet in that furious fight
    Scarce such another!   104

Warwick in blood did wade,
Oxford, the foe invade,
And cruel slaughter made,
    Still as they ran up.
Suffolk his axe did ply;
Beaumont and Willoughby
Bare them right doughtily;
    Ferrers and Fanhope.   112

Upon Saint Crispin's Day
Fought was this noble Fray;
Which Fame did not delay
    To England to carry.
O when shall English men
With such acts fill a pen?
Or England breed again
    Such a King Harry?   120

BEN JONSON (1573?-1637)

To Celia

Drink to me only with thine eyes,
    And I will pledge with mine;
Or leave a kiss but in the cup
    And I'll not look for wine.

The thirst that from the soul doth rise
  Doth ask a drink divine;
But might I of Jove's nectar sup,
  I would not change for thine.

I sent thee late a rosy wreath,
  Not so much honouring thee
As giving it a hope that there
  It could not wither'd be;
But thou thereon didst only breathe
  And sent'st it back to me;
Since when it grows, and smells, I swear,
  Not of itself but thee!

THE TRIUMPH OF CHARIS

See the chariot at hand here of Love,
  Wherein my lady rideth!
Each that draws is a swan or a dove,
  And well the car Love guideth.
As she goes, all hearts do duty
    Unto her beauty;
And enamour'd, do wish, so they might
    But enjoy such a sight,
That they still were to run by her side,

Through swords, through seas, whither she
  would ride.   10

Do but look on her eyes, they do light
  All that Love's world compriseth!
Do but look on her hair, it is bright
  As Love's star when it riseth!
Do but mark, her forehead smoother
    Than words that soothe her;
And from her arched brows, such a grace
    Sheds itself through the face
As alone there triumphs to the life
All the gain, all the good, of the elements'
  strife.   20

Have you seen but a bright lily grow,
  Before rude hands have touched it?
Have you marked but the fall of the snow
  Before the soil hath smutched it?
Have you felt the wool of the beaver?
    Or swan's down ever?
Or have smelt o' the bud of the briar?
    Or the nard in the fire?
Or have tasted the bag of the bee?
Oh so white! Oh so soft! Oh so sweet is she!

THE ELIZABETHAN AGE—DRAMA

CHRISTOPHER MARLOWE
(1564-1593)

FROM
THE TRAGICAL HISTORY OF DOCTOR FAUSTUS.*

Enter Chorus.

CHORUS. Not marching in the fields of Thrasymene,[1]

Where Mars did mate[2] the warlike Carthagens;

Nor sporting in the dalliance of love,

In courts of kings where state[3] is overturn'd;

Nor in the pomp of proud audacious deeds,

Intends our Muse to vaunt her heavenly verse:

Only this, gentles,—we must now perform

The form of Faustus' fortunes, good or bad:

And now to patient judgments we appeal,

And speak for Faustus in his infancy.   10

Now is he born of parents base of stock,

In Germany, within a town call'd Rhodes:[4]

At riper years, to Wittenberg he went,

Whereas[5] his kinsmen chiefly brought him up.

So much he profits in divinity,

That shortly he was grac'd with doctor's name,

Excelling all, and sweetly can dispute

In th' heavenly matters of theology;

Till swoln with cunning,[6] of a self-conceit,

His waxen wings did mount above his reach,[7]   20

And, melting, heavens conspir'd his overthrow;

For, falling to a devilish exercise,

And glutted now with learning's golden gifts,

He surfeits upon cursèd necromancy;

Nothing so sweet as magic is to him,

Which he prefers before his chiefest bliss:

And this the man that in his study sits. [*Exit.*

[SCENE I.]

Faustus *discovered in his study.*

FAUSTUS. Settle[8] thy studies, Faustus, and begin

To sound the depth of that thou wilt profess:[9]

Having commenc'd,[10] be a divine in show,

Yet level at the end[11] of every art,

And live and die in Aristotle's works.

Sweet Analytics, 'tis thou hast ravish'd me!

Bene disserere est finis logices.[12]

Is, to dispute well, logic's chiefest end?

Affords this art no greater miracle?

Then read no more; thou hast attain'd that end: 16

A greater subject fitteth Faustus' wit:

Bid Economy farewell, and Galen[13] come:

Be a physician, Faustus; heap up gold,

And be eterniz'd for some wondrous cure:

Summum bonum medicinæ sanitas,

The end of physic is our body's health.

Why, Faustus, hast thou not attain'd that end?

Are not thy bills[14] hung up as monuments,

Whereby whole cities have escap'd the plague,

---

1 The scene of Hannibal's defeat of the Romans, 217 B. C. Marlowe means that his drama is not to deal, like others, with wars and intrigues.
2 cope with   4 Roda, near Weimar.
3 statehood, majesty   5 where
* The Faust legend, which embodies the old fancy of a compact with the Evil One, had its origin in the life of a certain German doctor, Johann Faustus, who, dying about 1538, was reputed to have been carried off by the devil. The tales that grew up about his memory were collected in "The History of Dr. Faustus, the Notorious Magician and Master of the Black Art," published at Frankfort-on-the-Main in 1587. A translation was printed in England and Marlowe immediately dramatized it (1588); since then the story has appeared in many forms. Marlowe's drama was probably not printed in his lifetime. The editions dated 1604 and 1616 differ in many particulars and certainly neither of them gives us the text as he left it. It is possible that none of the comic scenes, the mingling of which with tragedy came to be one of the characteristics of Elizabethan drama, were from his pen. The extracts given above present only the central tragic theme. The 1616 text is followed, with scene numbers inserted to correspond with A. W. Ward's divisions of the 1604 text.

6 knowledge
7 Alluding to the story of Icarus.
8 fix upon
9 choose for a profession
10 taken the doctor's degree
11 aim at the goal (viz., metaphysics)
12 "To dispute well is the end of logic."
13 A famous physician of the second century.
14 prescriptions

And thousand desperate maladies been
cur'd? 20
Yet art thou still but Faustus, and a man.
Couldst thou make men to live eternally,
Or, being dead, raise them to life again,
Then this profession were to be esteem'd.
Physic, farewell! Where is Justinian?[15]

[*Reads.*

*Si una eademque res legatur duobus, alter
rem, alter valorem rei, &c.*[16]
A petty case of paltry legacies! [*Reads.*
*Exhæreditare filium non potest pater, nisi,
&c.*[17]
Such is the subject of the institute,
And universal body of the law: 30
This study fits a mercenary drudge,
Who aims at nothing but external trash;
Too servile and illiberal for me.
When all is done, divinity is best:
Jerome's Bible,[18] Faustus; view it well.

[*Reads.*

Stipendium peccati mors est. Ha! *Stipen-
dium, &c.* The reward of sin is death; that's
hard. [*Reads.*
*Si peccasse negamus, fallimur, et nulla est
in nobis veritas;* If we say that we have
no sin, we deceive ourselves, and there is
no truth in us. Why, then, belike we must
sin, and so consequently die: 42
Ay, we must die an everlasting death.
What doctrine call you this, *Che sera, sera,*
What will be, shall be? Divinity, adieu![19]
These metaphysics of magicians,
And necromantic books are heavenly;
Lines, circles, scenes, letters, and characters;
Ay, these are those that Faustus most desires.
O, what a world of profit and delight, 50
Of power, of honour, and omnipotence,
Is promis'd to the studious artizan!
All things that move between the quiet poles
Shall be at my command: emperors and
kings
Are but obeyed in their several provinces;
But his dominion that exceeds in this,
Stretcheth as far as doth the mind of man;
A sound magician is a demigod:
Here tire, my brains, to gain a deity.

Enter Wagner.

Wagner, commend me to my dearest friends, 60
The German Valdes and Cornelius;
Request them earnestly to visit me.

WAG. I will, sir. [*Exit.*
FAUST. Their conference[10] will be a greater
help to me
Than all my labours, plod I ne'er so fast.
Enter Good Angel *and* Evil Angel.
G. ANG. O, Faustus, lay that damnèd book
aside,
And gaze not on it, lest it tempt thy soul,
And heap God's heavy wrath upon thy head!
Read, read the Scriptures:—that is blas-
phemy.
E. ANG. Go forward, Faustus, in that famous
art[21] 70
Wherein all Nature's treasure is contain'd:
Be thou on earth as Jove is in the sky,
Lord and commander of these elements.

[*Exeunt* Angels.

FAUST. How am I glutted with conceit of this!
Shall I make spirits fetch me what I please,
Resolve me of[22] all ambiguities,
Perform what desperate enterprise I will?
I'll have them fly to India for gold,
Ransack the ocean for orient pearl,
And search all corners of the new-found
world[23] 80
For pleasant fruits and princely delicates;[24]
I'll have them read me strange philosophy,
And tell the secrets of all foreign kings;
I'll have them wall all Germany with brass,
And make swift Rhine circle fair Witten-
berg;
I'll have them fill the public schools with silk,
Wherewith the students shall be bravely clad;
I'll levy soldiers with the coin they bring,
And chase the Prince of Parma* from our
land,
And reign sole king of all the provinces; 90
Yea, stranger engines for the brunt of war,
Than was the fiery keel at Antwerp-bridge,†
I'll make my servile spirits to invent.

Enter Valdes *and* Cornelius.

Come, German Valdes, and Cornelius,
And make me blest with your sage conference.
Valdes, sweet Valdes, and Cornelius,
Know that your words have won me at the
last
To practise magic and concealèd arts.
Philosophy is odious and obscure;
Both law and physic are for petty wits: 100
'Tis magic, magic that hath ravish'd me.

Then, gentle friends, aid me in this attempt;
And I, that have with subtle syllogisms
Gravell'd[25] the pastors of the German church,
And made the flowering pride of Wittenberg
Swarm to my problems, as th' infernal spirits
On sweet Musæus when he came to hell,[26]
Will be as cunning as Agrippa[27] was,
Whose shadow made all Europe honour him.

VALD. Faustus, these books, thy wit, and our
    experience,   110
Shall make all nations to canonize us.
As Indian Moors[28] obey their Spanish lcrds,
So shall the spirits of every element
Be always serviceable to us three;
Like lions shall they guard us when we
    please;
Like Almain rutters[29] with their horsemen's
    staves,
Or Lapland giants, trotting by our sides;
Sometimes like women, or unwedded maids,
Shadowing more beauty in[30] their airy brows
Than have the white breasts of the queen of
    love: 120
From Venice shall they drag huge argosies,
And from America the golden fleece
That yearly stuffs old Philip's treasury;
If learnèd Faustus will be resolute.

FAUST. Valdes, as resolute am I in this
As thou to live: therefore object it not.[1]

CORN. The miracles that magic will perform
Will make thee vow to study nothing else.
He that is grounded in astrology,
Enrich'd with tongues, well seen[2] in min-
    erals,   130
Hath all the principles magic doth require:
Then doubt not, Faustus, but to be renown'd,
And more frequented for this mystery
Than heretofore the Delphian oracle.
The spirits tell me they can dry the sea,
And fetch the treasure of all foreign wrecks,
Yea, all the wealth that our forefathers hid
Within the massy entrails of the earth;
Then tell me, Faustus, what shall we three
    want?

FAUST. Nothing, Cornelius. O, this cheers my
    soul!   140
Come, show me some demonstrations magical,
That I may conjure in some bushy grove,
And have these joys in full possession.

VALD. Then haste thee to some solitary grove,
And bear wise Bacon's and Albertus'[3] works,

The Hebrew Psalter, and New Testament;
And whatsoever else is requisite
We will inform thee ere our conference cease.

CORN. Valdes, first let him know the words of
    art;
And then, all other ceremonies learn'd,   150
Faustus may try his cunning by himself.

VALD. First I'll instruct thee in the rudiments,
And then wilt thou be perfecter than I.

FAUST. Then come and dine with me, and
    after meat,
We'll canvass every quiddity[4] thereof;
For, ere I sleep, I'll try what I can do;
This night I'll conjure, though I die there-
    fore.   *[Exeunt.*

[SCENE II.]

Enter two Scholars.

FIRST SCHOL. I wonder what's become of Faustus, that was wont to make our schools
ring with *sic probo.*[5]

SEC. SCHOL. That shall we presently know;
here comes his boy.

Enter Wagner.

FIRST SCHOL. How now, sirrah! where's thy
    master?

WAG. God in heaven knows.

SEC. SCHOL. Why, dost not thou know, then?

WAG. Yes, I know; but that follows not.

FIRST SCHOL. Go to, sirrah! leave your jesting,
    and tell us where he is. . . .   10

WAG. Truly, my dear brethren, my master is
within at dinner, with Valdes and Cornelius,
as this wine, if it could speak, would inform
your worships: and so, the Lord bless you,
preserve you, and keep you, my dear brethren!   *[Exit.*

FIRST SCHOL. O Faustus!   35
Then I fear that which I have long suspected,
That thou art fall'n into that damnèd art
For which they two are infamous through the
    world.

SEC. SCHOL. Were he a stranger, not allied
    to me,
The danger of his soul would make me
    mourn.
But, come, let us go and inform the Rector;
It may be his grave counsel may reclaim
    him.   40

FIRST SCHOL. I fear me nothing will reclaim
    him now.

SEC. SCHOL. Yet let us see what we can do.
    [Exeunt.

---

25 puzzled
26 See *Æneid* VI., 666.
27 A magician at the time of Johann Faustus.
28 American Indians
29 German horsemen
30 Perhaps *in = under*

---

1 make it no objection
2 skilled
3 Roger Bacon and Albertus Magnus, mediæval scholars popularly reputed to have practiced magic.
4 matter
5 "Thus I prove" (a formula in logical demonstration.

[SCENE III.]

Enter Faustus.

FAUST. Now that the gloomy shadow of the night,
Longing to view Orion's drizzling look,*
Leaps from th' antarctic world unto the sky,
And dims the welkin with her pitchy breath,
Faustus, begin thine incantations,
And try if devils will obey thy hest,
Seeing thou hast pray'd and sacrific'd to them.
Within this circle is Jehovah's name,
Forward and backward anagrammatiz'd,⁶
Th' abbreviated names of holy saints,   10
Figures of every adjunct to the heavens,
And characters of signs and erring⁷ stars,
By which the spirits are enforc'd to rise:
Then fear not, Faustus, to be resolute,
And try the utmost magic can perform.
                                    [*Thunder.*
*Sint mihi dii Acherontis propitii! Valeat
numen triplex Jehovæ! Ignei, äerii, aquatani
spiritus, salvete! Orientis princeps Belzebub,
inferni ardentis monarcha, et Demogorgon,
propitiamus vos, ut appareat et surgat Mephistophilis Dragon, quod tumeraris: per Je-
hovam, Gehennam, et consecratam aquam
quam nunc spargo, signumque crucis quod
nunc facio, et per vota nostra, ipse nunc surgat nobis dicatus Mephistophilis!†*   23

     Enter Mephistophilis.

I charge thee to return, and change thy shape;
Thou art too ugly to attend on me:
Go, and return an old Franciscan friar;
That holy shape becomes a devil best.⁸
          [*Exit* Mephistophilis.
I see there's virtue in my heavenly words.
Who would not be proficient in this art?
How pliant is this Mephistophilis,   30

6 written as an anagram
7 wandering (i. e., planets)
8 A Protestant fling at monasticism.
* The rising and setting of the constellation of
   Orion was said to be accompanied by rain.
† "May the gods of Acheron [river of pain, in
   Hades], be propitious to me! May the triple
   name of Jehovah avail! Hail, spirits of fire,
   air, and water! Beelzebub, prince of the east,
   monarch of burning hell, and Demogorgon,
   we propitiate you, that Mephistophilis the
   Dragon, *quod tumeraris* [text corrupt and un-
   translatable], may appear and arise: in the
   name of Jehovah, Gehenna and the holy water
   which I now sprinkle, and the sign of the
   cross which I now make and in the name of
   our vows, let Mephistophilis himself at our
   command, now arise." Beelzebub, etc., were
   members of the infernal hierarchy, of which
   Lucifer (Satan) was commonly regarded as
   chief. Marlowe makes Mephistophilis the
   servant of Lucifer, to whom he later gives
   the title of prince of the east, here given to
   Beelzebub.

Full of obedience and humility!
Such is the force of magic and my spells.

Re-enter Mephistophilis *like a Franciscan friar.*

MEPH. Now, Faustus, what wouldst thou have me do?
FAUST. I charge thee wait upon me whilst I live,
To do whatever Faustus shall command,
Be it to make the moon drop from her sphere,
Or the ocean to overwhelm the world.
MEPH. I am a servant to great Lucifer,
And may not follow thee without his leave:
No more than he commands must we per-
   form.   40
FAUST. Did not he charge thee to appear to me?
MEPH. No, I came hither of mine own accord.
FAUST. Did not my conjuring speeches raise thee? speak!
MEPH. That was the cause, but yet *per acci-
dens;*⁹
For, when we hear one rack¹⁰ the name of God,
Abjure the Scriptures and his Saviour Christ,
We fly, in hope to get his glorious soul;
Nor will we come, unless he use such means
Whereby he is in danger to be damn'd.
Therefore the shortest cut for conjuring   50
Is stoutly to abjure all godliness,
And pray devoutly to the prince of hell.
FAUST. So Faustus hath
Already done; and holds this principle,
There is no chief but only Belzebub;
To whom Faustus doth dedicate himself.
This word "damnation" terrifies not me,
For I confound hell in Elysium:¹¹
My ghost be with the old philosophers!   59
But, leaving these vain trifles of men's souls,
Tell me what is that Lucifer thy Lord?
MEPH. Arch-regent and commander of all spirits.
FAUST. Was not that Lucifer an angel once?
MEPH. Yes, Faustus, and most dearly lov'd of God.
FAUST. How comes it, then, that he is prince of devils?
MEPH. O, by aspiring pride and insolence;
For which God threw him from the face of heaven.
FAUST. And what are you that live with Luci-
fer?
MEPH. Unhappy spirits that fell with Lucifer,
Conspired against our God with Lucifer,   70
And are for ever damn'd with Lucifer.
FAUST. Where are you damn'd?

9 by accident   10 torture (in anagrams)
11 count hell and Elysium the same

MEPH. In hell.

FAUST. How comes it, then, that thou art out of hell?

MEPH. Why, this is hell, nor am I out of it:[12]
Think'st thou that I, that saw the face of God,
And tasted the eternal joys of heaven,
Am not tormented with ten thousand hells,
In being depriv'd of everlasting bliss?
O, Faustus, leave these frivolous demands, 80
Which strike a terror to my fainting soul!

FAUST. What, is great Mephistophilis so passionate
For being depriv**è**d of the joys of heaven?
Learn thou of Faustus manly fortitude,
And scorn those joys thou never shalt possess.
Go bear these tidings to great Lucifer:
Seeing Faustus hath incurr'd eternal death
By desperate thoughts against Jove's deity,
Say, he surrenders up to him his soul,
So he will spare him four and twenty years, 90
Letting him live in all voluptuousness;
Having thee ever to attend on me,
To give me whatsoever I shall ask,
To tell me whatsoever I demand,
To slay mine enemies, and to aid my friends,
And always be obedient to my will.
Go, and return to mighty Lucifer,
And meet me in my study at midnight,
And then resolve me of thy master's mind.

MEPH. I will, Faustus. [Exit. 100

FAUST. Had I as many souls as there be stars,
I'd give them all for Mephistophilis.
By him I'll be great emperor of the world,
And make a bridge thorough the moving air,
To pass the ocean with a band of men;
I'll join the hills that bind the Afric shore,
And make that country continent[13] to Spain,
And both contributary to my crown:
The Emperor shall not live but by my leave,
Nor any potentate of Germany. 110
Now that I have obtain'd what I desir'd,
I'll live in speculation of this art,
Till Mephistophilis return again. [Exit.

. . . .

[SCENE V.]

Faustus discovered in his study.

FAUST. Now, Faustus,
Must thou needs be damn'd, canst thou not be sav'd.
What boots it, then, to think on God or heaven?
Away with such vain fancies, and despair;
Despair in God, and trust in Belzebub:

Now, go not backward, Faustus, be resolute:
Why waver'st thou? O, something soundeth in mine ear,
"Abjure this magic, turn to God again!"
Why, he loves thee not;
The god thou serv'st is thine own appetite, 10
Wherein is fix'd the love of Belzebub:
To him I'll build an altar and a church,
And offer lukewarm blood of new-born babes.
Enter Good Angel and Evil Angel.

E. ANG. Go forward, Faustus, in that famous art.

G. ANG. Sweet Faustus, leave that execrable art.

FAUST. Contrition, prayer, repentance—what of these?

G. ANG. O, they are means to bring thee unto heaven.

E. ANG. Rather illusions, fruits of lunacy,
That make men foolish that do use them most.

G. ANG. Sweet Faustus, think of heaven and heavenly things. 20

E. ANG. No, Faustus; think of honour and of wealth. [Exeunt Angels.

FAUST. Wealth!
Why, the signiory[14] of Embden[15] shall be mine.
When Mephistophilis shall stand by me,
What power can hurt me? Faustus, thou art safe.
Cast no more doubts.—Mephistophilis, come,
And bring glad tidings from great Lucifer;—
Is't not midnight?—come Mephistophilis,
Veni,[16] veni, Mephistophile!

Enter Mephistophilis.

Now tell me what saith Lucifer, thy lord? 30

MEPH. That I shall wait on Faustus whilst he lives,
So he will buy my service with his soul.

FAUST. Already Faustus hath hazarded that for thee.

MEPH. But now thou must bequeath it solemnly,
And write a deed of gift with thine own blood;
For that security craves Lucifer.
If thou deny it, I must back to hell.

FAUST. Stay, Mephistophilis, and tell me, what good will my soul do thy lord?

MEPH. Enlarge his kingdom. 40

FAUST. Is that the reason why he tempts us thus?

12 Compare *Paradise Lost*, I. 254.
13 connected
14 dominion
15 A town of Hanover, Germany, formerly **very** prosperous.
16 come

MEPH. *Solamen miseris socios habuisse do-*
       loris.[17]

FAUST. Why, have you any pain that torture
        others?

MEPH. As great as have the human souls of
       men.
       But, tell me, Faustus, shall I have thy soul?
       And I will be thy slave, and wait on thee,
       And give thee more than thou hast wit to ask.

FAUST. Ay, Mephistophilis, I'll give it thee.

MEPH. Then, Faustus, stab thine arm cour-
       ageously,
       And bind thy soul, that at some certain day
       Great Lucifer may claim it as his own;   51
       And then be thou as great as Lucifer.

FAUST. [*Stabbing his arm*] Lo, Mephistophilis,
        for love of thee,
        Faustus hath cut his arm, and with his
        proper blood
        Assures his soul to be great Lucifer's,
        Chief lord and regent of perpetual night!
        View here this blood that trickles from mine
        arm,
        And let it be propitious for my wish.

MEPH. But, Faustus,
       Write it in manner of a deed of gift.   60

FAUST. [*Writing*] Ay, so I do. But, Mephis-
        tophilis,
        My blood congeals, and I can write no more.

MEPH. I'll fetch thee fire to dissolve it
       straight.   [*Exit.*

FAUST. What might the staying of my blood
        portend?
        Is it unwilling I should write this bill?
        Why streams it not, that I may write afresh?
        Faustus gives to thee his soul: O, there it
        stay'd!
        Why shouldst thou not? is not thy soul thine
        own?
        Then write again, *Faustus gives to thee his
        soul.*

Re-enter Mephistophilis *with the chafer*[18] *of fire.*

MEPH. See, Faustus, here is fire; set it on.   70

FAUST. So, now the blood begins to clear
        again;
        Now will I make an end immediately. [*Writes.*

MEPH. What will not I do to obtain his soul?
                                      [*Aside.*

FAUST. *Consummatum est;*[19] this bill is ended,
        And Faustus hath bequeath'd his soul to
        Lucifer.
        But what is this inscription on mine arm?
        Homo, fuge:[20] whither should I fly?

If unto God, he'll throw me down to hell.
My senses are deceiv'd; here's nothing
writ:—
O, yes, I see it plain; even here is writ,   80
Homo, fuge: yet shall not Faustus fly.

MEPH. I'll fetch him somewhat to delight his
       mind.   [*Aside, and then exit.*

Enter Devils, *giving crowns and rich apparel to
Faustus. They dance, and then depart.*

Re-enter Mephistophilis.

FAUST. What means this show? speak, Mephis-
        tophilis.

MEPH. Nothing, Faustus, but to delight thy
       mind,
       And let thee see what magic can perform.

FAUST. But may I raise such spirits when I
        please?

MEPH. Ay, Faustus, and do greater things
       than these.

FAUST. Then, Mephistophilis, receive this scroll,
        A deed of gift of body and of soul:
        But yet conditionally that thou perform   90
        All covenants and articles between us both!

MEPH. Faustus, I swear by hell and Lucifer
       To effect all promises between us both!

FAUST. Then hear me read it, Mephistophilis.
                                      [*Reads.*

*On these conditions following. First, that
Faustus may be a spirit in form and substance. Secondly, that Mephistophilis shall be
his servant, and be by him commanded.
Thirdly, that Mephistophilis shall do for him,
and bring him whatsoever he desires.
Fourthly, that he shall be in his chamber or
house invisible. Lastly, that he shall appear
to the said John Faustus, at all times, in
what shape and form soever he please. I,
John Faustus, of Wittenberg, Doctor, by
these presents, do give both body and soul to
Lucifer prince of the east, and his minister
Mephistophilis; and furthermore grant unto
them, that, four-and-twenty years being expired, and these articles above-written being
inviolate, full power to fetch or carry the
said John Faustus, body and soul, flesh and
blood, into their habitation wheresoever. By
me, John Faustus.*

MEPH. Speak, Faustus, do you deliver this as
       your deed?   110

FAUST. Ay, take it, and the devil give thee
        good of it!

MEPH. So, now, Faustus, ask me what thou
       wilt.

FAUST. First I will question with thee about
        hell.

---

[17] "It is a comfort to the miserable to have asso-
     ciates in their pain."
[18] vessel
[19] "It is done."   [20] "Man, flee!"

Tell me, where is the place that men call
    hell?

MEPH. Under the heavens.

FAUST. Ay, so are all things else; but where-
    abouts?

MEPH. Within the bowels of these elements,
Where we are tortur'd and remain for ever:
Hell hath no limits, nor is circumscrib'd
In one self-place; but where we are is hell,
And where hell is, there must we ever be: 121
And, to be short, when all the world dissolves,
And every creature shall be purified,
All places shall be hell that are not heaven.

FAUST. I think hell's a fable.

MEPH. Ay, think so still, till experience change
thy mind.

FAUST. Why, dost thou think that Faustus
    shall be damn'd?

MEPH. Ay, of necessity, for here's the scroll
In which thou hast given thy soul to Lucifer.

FAUST. Ay, and body too; and what of that?
Think'st thou that Faustus is so fond to
    imagine   131
That, after this life, there is any pain?
No, these are trifles and mere old wives'
    tales.

MEPH. But I am an instance to prove the contrary,
For I tell thee I am damn'd and now in hell.

   .   .   .   .   .   .

Here, take this book, peruse it well:
The iterating of these lines brings gold; 160
The framing of this circle on the ground
Brings thunder, whirlwinds, storm, and light-
    ning;
Pronounce this thrice devoutly to thyself,
And men in harness[21] shall appear to thee,
Ready to execute what thou command'st.

FAUST. Thanks, Mephistophilis, for this sweet
    book:
This will I keep as chary as my life. [Exeunt.

[SCENE VI.]

Enter Faustus, in his study, and Mephistophilis.

FAUST. When I behold the heavens, then I
    repent,
And curse thee, wicked Mephistophilis,
Because thou hast depriv'd me of those joys.

MEPH. 'Twas thine own seeking, Faustus;
thank thyself.
But think'st thou heaven is such a glorious
    thing?
I tell thee, Faustus, it is not half so fair
As thou, or any man that breathes on earth.

FAUST. How prov'st thou that?

MEPH. 'Twas made for man; then he's more
excellent.

FAUST. If heaven was made for man, 'twas
made for me: 10
I will renounce this magic and repent.

Enter Good Angel *and* Evil Angel.

G. ANG. Faustus, repent; yet God will pity
thee.

E. ANG. Thou art a spirit; God cannot pity
thee.

FAUST. Who buzzeth in mine ears I am a
spirit?
Be I a devil, yet God may pity me;
Yea, God will pity me, if I repent.

E. ANG. Ay, but Faustus never shall repent.
                    [Exeunt Angels.

FAUST. My heart is harden'd, I cannot repent;
Scarce can I name salvation, faith, or heaven:
Swords, poisons, halters, and envenom'd steel
Are laid before me to despatch myself;   21
And long ere this I should have done the
deed,
Had not sweet pleasure conquer'd deep
despair.
Have not I made blind Homer sing to me
Of Alexander's[22] love and Œnon's[23] death?
And hath not he, that built the walls of
Thebes[24]
With ravishing sound of his melodious harp,
Made music with my Mephistophilis?
Why should I die, then, or basely despair?
I am resolv'd; Faustus shall not repent.—
Come Mephistophilis, let us dispute again,
And reason of divine astrology.   32
Speak, are there many spheres above the
moon?
Are all celestial bodies but one globe,
As is the substance of this centric[25] earth?

MEPH. As are the elements, such are the heav-
ens,
Even from the moon unto th' empyreal orb,[26]
Mutually folded in each other's spheres,
And jointly move upon one axletree,
Whose termine[27] is term'd the world's wide
pole;   40
Nor are the names of Saturn, Mars, or
Jupiter
Feign'd, but are erring[28] stars.

FAUST. But have they all one motion, both
situ et tempore?[29]

MEPH. All move from east to west in four-
and-twenty hours upon the poles of the

---

21 armor | 22 Another name for Paris, whose love for Helen
                          caused the Trojan war.
                       23 Wife of Paris, who took her own life.
                       24 Amphion.   27 terminal
                       25 central   28 See note, p. 154
                       26 the sun   29 in place and time

world; but differ in their motions upon the poles of the zodiac.

FAUST. These slender questions Wagner can decide:
Hath Mephistophilis no greater skill?
Who knows not the double motion of the planets? 50
That the first is finish'd in a natural day;
The second thus: Saturn in thirty years;
Jupiter in twelve; Mars in four; the Sun,
Venus, and Mercury in a year; the Moon in twenty-eight days. These are freshmen's questions. But tell me, hath every sphere a dominion or *intelligentia?*[30]

MEPH. Ay.

FAUST. How many heavens or spheres are there?

MEPH. Nine; the seven planets, the firmament, and the empyreal heaven.* 60

FAUST. But is there not *cœlum igneum et crystallinum?*

MEPH. No, Faustus, they be but fables.

FAUST. Resolve[31] me, then, in this one question; why are not conjunctions, oppositions, aspects, eclipses, all at one time, but in some years we have more, in some less?

MEPH. *Per inæqualem motum respectu totius.*[32]

FAUST. Well, I am answered. Now tell me who made the world? 70

MEPH. I will not.

FAUST. Sweet Mephistophilis, tell me.

MEPH. Move me not, Faustus.

FAUST. Villain, have not I bound thee to tell me anything?

MEPH. Ay, that is not against our kingdom; this is.
Thou art damned; think thou of hell.

FAUST. Think, Faustus, upon God that made the world.

MEPH. Remember this. [*Exit.*

FAUST. Ay, go, accursèd spirit, to ugly hell! 80
'Tis thou hast damn'd distressèd Faustus' soul.
Is't not too late?

Re-enter Good Angel *and* Evil Angel.

E. ANG. Too late.

G. ANG. Never too late, if Faustus will repent.

E. ANG. If thou repent, devils will tear thee in pieces.

G. ANG. Repent, and they shall never raze thy skin. [*Exeunt* Angels.

30 sovereign authority and intellect
31 free me from doubt
32 "Because of their unequal motion with respect to the whole."
* According to the Ptolemaic system, these were nine concentric spheres, with the earth at the centre. A tenth sphere, the "fiery and crystalline heaven" mentioned in the next question, was sometimes added.

FAUST. O Christ, my Saviour, my Saviour,
Help to save distressèd Faustus' soul!

Enter Lucifer, Belzebub, *and* Mephistophilis.

LUC. Christ cannot save thy soul, for he is just:
There's none but I have interest in the same.

FAUST. O, what art thou that look'st so terribly? 91

LUC. I am Lucifer.
And this is my companion-prince in hell.

FAUST. O Faustus, they are come to fetch thy soul!

BELZ. We are come to tell thee thou dost injure us.

LUC. Thou call'st on Christ, contrary to thy promise.

BELZ. Thou shouldst not think on God.

LUC. Think on the devil.

BELZ. And his dam too.

FAUST. Nor will Faustus henceforth: pardon him for this, 100
And Faustus vows never to look to heaven.

LUC. So shalt thou show thyself an obedient servant,
And we will highly gratify thee for it.

BELZ. Faustus, we are come from hell in person to show thee some pastime: sit down, and thou shalt behold the Seven Deadly Sins appear to thee in their own proper shapes and likeness.

FAUST. That sight will be as pleasant unto me,
As Paradise was to Adam the first day 110
Of his creation.

LUC. Talk not of Paradise or creation; but mark the show.—
Go, Mephistophilis, and fetch them in.

Mephistophilis *brings in the* Seven Deadly Sins.

BELZ. Now, Faustus, question them of their names and dispositions.

FAUST. That shall I soon.—What art thou, the first? 117

PRIDE. I am Pride. I disdain to have any parents. . . . But, fie, what a smell is here! I'll not speak a word more for a king's ransom, unless the ground be perfumed, and covered with cloth of arras.

FAUST. Thou art a proud knave, indeed.—What art thou, the second? 129

COVET. I am Covetousness, begotten of an old churl, in a leather bag: and, might I now obtain my wish, this house, you, and all, should turn to gold, that I might lock you safe into my chest: O my sweet gold!

FAUST. And what art thou, the third? 135

ENVY. I am Envy, begotten of a chimney-sweeper and an oyster-wife. I cannot read, and therefore wish all books burned. I am lean with seeing others eat. O, that there would come a famine over all the world, that all might die, and I live alone! then thou shouldst see how fat I'd be. But must thou sit, and I stand? come down with a vengeance!

FAUST. Out, envious wretch!—But what art thou, the fourth? 145

WRATH. I am Wrath. I had neither father nor mother: I leapt out of a lion's mouth when I was scarce an hour old; and ever since have run up and down the world with this case of rapiers, wounding myself when I could get none to fight withal. I was born in hell; and look to it, for some of you shall be³³ my father.

FAUST. And what art thou, the fifth? 153

GLUT. I am Gluttony. My parents are all dead, and the devil a penny have they left me, but a small pension, and that buys me thirty meals a day and ten bevers,³⁴—a small trifle to suffice nature. I come of a royal pedigree: my father was a Gammon of Bacon, and my mother was a Hogshead of Claret-wine; my godfathers were these, Peter Pickled-herring and Martin Martlemas-beef;³⁵ and my godmother, O, she was an ancient gentlewoman; her name was Margery March-beer.³⁶ Now, Faustus, thou hast heard all my progeny; wilt thou bid me to supper? 165

FAUST. Not I.

GLUT. Then the devil choke thee!

FAUST. Choke thyself, glutton!—What art thou, the sixth?

SLOTH. Heigho! I am Sloth. I was begotten on a sunny bank. Heigho! I'll not speak a word more for a king's ransom. . . .

LUC. Away to hell, away! On, piper!

[Exeunt the Sins.

FAUST. O, how this sight doth delight my soul! 180

LUC. Tut, Faustus, in hell is all manner of delight.

FAUST. O, might I see hell, and return again safe,
How happy were I then!

LUC. Faustus, thou shalt; at midnight I will send for thee.
Meanwhile peruse this book and view it thoroughly,
And thou shalt turn thyself into what shape thou wilt.

FAUST. Thanks, mighty Lucifer!
This will I keep as chary³⁷ as my life.

LUC. Now Faustus, farewell.

FAUST. Farewell, great Lucifer.

[Exeunt Lucifer and Belzebub,
Come, Mephistophilis. [Exeunt.*

. . . .

[SCENE XIII.]

Thunder and lightning. Enter Devils with covered dishes; Mephistophilis leads them into Faustus' study, then enter Wagner.

WAG. I think my master means to die shortly; he has made his will, and given me his wealth, his house, his goods, and store of golden plate, besides two thousand ducats ready-coined. I wonder what he means: if death were nigh, he would not frolic thus. He's now at supper with the scholars, where there's such belly-cheer as Wagner in his life ne'er saw the like: and, see where they come! belike the feast is ended.† [Exit.

Enter FAUSTUS, Mephistophilis, and two or three Scholars.

FIRST SCHOL. Master Doctor Faustus, since our conference about fair ladies, which³⁸ was the beautifulest in all the world, we have determined with ourselves that Helen of Greece was the admirablest lady that ever lived: therefore, Master Doctor, if you will do us so much favour as to let us see that peerless dame of Greece, whom all the world admires for majesty, we should think ourselves much beholding unto you.

FAUST. Gentlemen,
For that³⁹ I know your friendship is unfeigh'd, 20
It is not Faustus' custom to deny
The just request of those that wish him well:
You shall behold that peerless dame of Greece,
No otherwise for pomp or majesty
Than when Sir Paris cross'd the seas with her,
And brought the spoils to rich Dardania.
Be silent, then, for danger is in words.

Music sounds. Mephistophilis brings in Helen; she passeth over the stage.

SEC. SCHOL. Was this fair Helen, whose admirèd worth

---

³⁸ as to which   ³⁹ because
* In the succeeding scenes are given, partly in relation by the Chorus, partly in action, Faustus' further adventures in the enjoyment of his new power, including a chariot-journey through the stellar heavens, and a ride on the back of a dragon to Rome, where, in disguise, or altogether invisible, he takes huge delight in playing pranks on the Pope and his Cardinals. But at length the twenty-four years of the compact draw to an end.
† This speech is almost regular blank verse and was probably written as such.

³³ must be   ³⁴ luncheons
³⁵ beef cured at Martlemas (Nov. 11)
³⁶ choice beer brewed in March
³⁷ carefully

Made Greece with ten years' war afflict poor
    Troy?
THIRD SCHOL. Too simple is my wit to tell
    her worth,   30
Whom all the world admires for majesty.
FIRST SCHOL. Now we have seen the pride of
    Nature's work,
We'll take our leaves: and, for this blessèd
    sight,
Happy and blest be Faustus evermore!
FAUST. Gentlemen, farewell: the same wish I
    to you.   [*Exeunt Scholars.*

Enter an Old Man.

OLD MAN. O gentle Faustus, leave this damnèd
    art,
This magic, that will charm thy soul to hell,
And quite bereave thee of salvation!
Though thou hast now offended like a man,
Do not persèver in it like a devil: 40
Yet, yet thou hast an amiable soul,
If sin by custom grow not into nature;
Then, Faustus, will repentance come too late;
Then thou art banish'd from the sight of
    heaven:
No mortal can express the pains of hell.
It may be, this my exhortation
Seems harsh and all unpleasant: let it not;
For, gentle son, I speak it not in wrath,
Or envy of thee, but in tender love,
And pity of thy future misery;   50
And so have hope that this my kind rebuke,
Checking thy body, may amend thy soul.
FAUST. Where art thou, Faustus? wretch, what
    hast thou done?
Hell claims his right, and with a roaring voice
Says, "Faustus, come; thine hour is almost
    come;"
And Faustus now will come to do thee right.
        [*Mephistophilis gives him a dagger.*
OLD MAN. O stay, good Faustus, stay thy des-
    perate steps!
I see an angel hover o'er thy head,
And, with a vial full of precious grace,
Offers to pour the same into thy soul: 60
Then call for mercy, and avoid despair.
FAUST. O friend, I feel
Thy words to comfort my distressèd soul!
Leave me a while to ponder on my sins.
OLD MAN. Faustus, I leave thee; but with
    grief of heart,
Fearing the enemy of thy hapless soul. [*Exit.*
FAUST. Accursèd Faustus, wretch, what hast
    thou done?
I do repent; and yet I do despair:
Hell strives with grace for conquest in my
    breast: c9
What shall I do to shun the snares of death?

MEPH. Thou traitor, Faustus, I arrest thy soul
For disobedience to my sovereign lord:
Revolt, or I'll in piece-meal tear thy flesh.
FAUST. I do repent I e'er offended him.
Sweet Mephistophilis, entreat thy lord
To pardon my unjust presumption,
And with my blood again I will confirm
The former vow I made to Lucifer.
MEPH. Do it, then, Faustus, with unfeignèd
    heart,
Lest greater dangers do attend thy drift.   80
FAUST. Torment, sweet friend, that base and
    aged man,
That durst dissuade me from thy Lucifer,
With greatest torments that our hell affords.
MEPH. His faith is great; I cannot touch his
    soul;
But what I may afflict his body with
I will attempt, which is but little worth.
FAUST. One thing, good servant, let me crave
    of thee,
To glut the longing of my heart's desire,—
That I may have unto my paramour
That heavenly Helen which I saw of late,   90
Whose sweet embraces may extinguish clean
Those thoughts that do dissuade me from my
    vow,
And keep my oath I made to Lucifer.
MEPH. This, or what else my Faustus shall
    desire,
Shall be perform'd in twinkling of an eye.

Re-enter Helen, *passing over the stage between
    two Cupids.*

FAUST. Was this the face that launch'd a
    thousand ships,
And burnt the topless towers of Ilium[1]?
Sweet Helen, make me immortal with a
    kiss.—   [*Kisses her.*
Her lips suck forth my soul: see, where it
    flies.
Come, Helen, come, give me my soul again. 100
Here will I dwell, for heaven is in these lips,
And all is dross that is not Helena.
I will be Paris, and for love of thee,
Instead of Troy, shall Wittenberg be sack'd;
And I will combat with weak Menelaus,
And wear thy colours on my plumèd crest;
Yea, I will wound Achilles in the heel,
And then return to Helen for a kiss.
O, thou art fairer than the evening air
Clad in the beauty of a thousand stars;   110
Brighter art thou than flaming Jupiter
When he appear'd to hapless Semele;
More lovely than the monarch of the sky
In wanton Arethusa's azur'd arms;

1 unsurpassable towers of Troy

And none but thou shalt be my paramour!

[*Exeunt.*

[SCENE XIV.]

Thunder. Enter Lucifer, Belzebub *and* Mephistophilis.

LUC. Thus from infernal Dis[2] do we ascend
To view the subjects of our monarchy,
Those souls which sin seals the black sons of hell;
'Mong which, as chief, Faustus, we come to thee,
Bringing with us lasting damnation
To wait upon thy soul: the time is come
Which makes it forfeit.

MEPH. And, this gloomy night,
Here, in this room, will wretched Faustus be.

BELZ. And here we'll stay, 10
To mark him how he doth demean himself.

MEPH. How should he but in desperate lunacy?
Fond worldling, now his heart-blood dries with grief;
His conscience kills it; and his labouring brain
Begets a world of idle fantasies
To over-reach the devil; but all in vain;
His store of pleasures must be sauc'd with pain.
He and his servant Wagner are at hand;
Both come from drawing Faustus' latest will.
See, where they come! 20

Enter Faustus *and* Wagner.

FAUST. Say, Wagner,—thou hast perus'd my will,
How dost thou like it?

WAG. Sir, so wondrous well,
As in all humble duty I do yield
My life and lasting service for your love.

FAUST. Gramercy,[3] Wagner.

Enter Scholars.
Welcome, gentlemen.

[*Exit* Wagner.

FIRST SCHOL. Now, worthy Faustus, methinks your looks are chang'd.

FAUST. O gentlemen!

SEC. SCHOL. What ails Faustus?

FAUST. Ah, my sweet chamber-fellow, had I lived with thee, then had I lived still! but now must die eternally. Look, sirs, comes he not? comes he not? 31

FIRST SCHOL. O my dear Faustus, what imports this fear?

SEC. SCHOL. Is all our pleasure turn'd to melancholy?

THIRD SCHOL. He is not well with being over-solitary.

SEC. SCHOL. If it be so, we'll have physicians, And Faustus shall be cur'd.

THIRD SCHOL. 'Tis but a surfeit, sir; fear nothing.

FAUST. A surfeit of deadly sin, that hath damned both body and soul.

SEC. SCHOL. Yet, Faustus, look up to heaven, and remember mercy is infinite. 41

FAUST. But Faustus' offense can ne'er be pardoned: the serpent that tempted Eve may be saved, but not Faustus. O gentlemen, hear me with patience, and tremble not at my speeches! Though my heart pant and quiver to remember that I have been a student here these thirty years, O, would I had never seen Wittenberg, never read book! and what wonders I have done, all Germany can witness, yea, all the world; for which Faustus hath lost both Germany and the world, yea, heaven itself, heaven, the seat of God, the throne of the blessed, the kingdom of joy; and must remain in hell for ever, hell, O hell, for ever! Sweet friends, what shall become of Faustus, being in hell for ever?

SEC. SCHOL. Yet, Faustus, call on God. 58

FAUST. On God, whom Faustus hath abjured! on God, whom Faustus hath blasphemed! O my God, I would weep! but the devil draws in my tears. Gush forth blood, instead of tears! yea, life and soul! O, he stays my tongue! I would lift up my hands; but see, they hold 'em, they hold 'em?

ALL. Who, Faustus?

FAUST. Why, Lucifer and Mephistophilis. O gentlemen, I gave them my soul for my cunning! 70

ALL. O, God forbid!

FAUST. God forbade it, indeed; but Faustus hath done it: for the vain pleasure of four-and-twenty years hath Faustus lost eternal joy and felicity. I writ them a bill[4] with mine own blood: the date is expired; this is the time, and he will fetch me.

FIRST SCHOL. Why did not Faustus tell us of this before, that divines might have prayed for thee? 81

FAUST. Oft have I thought to have done so; but the devil threatened to tear me in pieces, if I named God, to fetch me body and soul, if I once gave ear to divinity: and now 'tis too late. Gentlemen, away, lest you perish with me.

SEC. SCHOL. O, what may we do to save Faustus?

2 Another name for Pluto and his kingdom.
3 great thanks
4 bond

FAUST. Talk not of me, but save yourselves, and depart.   90

THIRD SCHOL. God will strengthen me; I will stay with Faustus.

FIRST SCHOL. Tempt not God, sweet friend; but let us into the next room, and pray for him.

FAUST. Ay, pray for me, pray for me; and what noise soever you hear, come not unto me, for nothing can rescue me.

SEC. SCHOL. Pray thou, and we will pray that God may have mercy upon thee.   100

FAUST. Gentlemen, farewell: if I live till morning, I'll visit you; if not, Faustus is gone to hell.

ALL. Faustus, farewell.   [*Exeunt* Scholars.

MEPH. Ay, Faustus, now thou hast no hope of heaven;
Therefore despair; think only upon hell,
For that must be thy mansion, there to dwell.

FAUST. Oh thou bewitching fiend, 'twas thy temptation
Hath robb'd me of eternal happiness!

MEPH. I do confess it, Faustus, and rejoice: 110
'Twas I that, when thou wert i' the way to heaven,
Damm'd up thy passage; when thou took'st the book
To view the Scriptures, then I turn'd the leaves,
And led thine eye.
What, weep'st thou? 'tis too late; despair! Farewell:
Fools that will laugh on earth must weep in hell.   [*Exit.*

Enter Good Angel *and* Evil Angel
at several doors.

G. ANG. O Faustus, if thou hadst given ear to me,
Innumerable joys had follow'd thee!
But thou didst love the world.

E. ANG. Gave ear to me,   119
And now must taste hell-pains perpetually.

G. ANG. O, what will all thy riches, pleasures, pomps,
Avail thee now?

E. ANG. Nothing, but vex thee more,
To want in hell, that had on earth such store.

G. ANG. O, thou hast lost celestial happiness,
Pleasures unspeakable, bliss without end.
Hadst thou affected[5] sweet divinity,
Hell or the devil had had no power on thee:
Hadst thou kept on that way, Faustus, behold,

         [*Music, while a throne descends.*

In what resplendent glory thou hadst sit
In yonder throne, like those bright-shining saints,   130
And triumph'd over hell! That hast thou lost;
And now, poor soul, must thy good angel leave thee:
The jaws of hell are open to receive thee.
         [*Exit. The throne ascends.*

E. ANG. Now, Faustus, let thine eyes with horror stare   [*Hell is discovered.*
Into that vast perpetual torture-house:
There are the Furies tossing damnèd souls
On burning forks; there bodies boil in lead;
There are live quarters broiling on the coals,
That ne'er can die; this ever-burning chair
Is for o'er-tortur'd souls to rest them in;   140
These that are fed with sops[6] of flaming fire,
Were gluttons, and lov'd only delicates,
And laugh'd to see the poor starve at their gates:
But yet all these are nothing; thou shalt see
Ten thousand tortures that more horrid be.

FAUST. O, I have seen enough to torture me!

E. ANG. Nay, thou must feel them, taste the smart of all:
He that loves pleasure must for pleasure fall:
And so I leave thee, Faustus, till anon;
Then wilt thou tumble in confusion.   150
         [*Exit. Hell disappears.—The clock strikes eleven.*

FAUST. O Faustus!
Now hast thou but one bare hour to live,
And then thou must be damn'd perpetually!
Stand still, you ever-moving spheres of heaven,
That time may cease, and midnight never come;
Fair Nature's eye, rise, rise again, and make Perpetual day; or let this hour be but
A year, a month, a week, a natural day,
That Faustus may repent and save his soul!
O lente, lente currite, noctis equi![7]   160
The stars move still, time runs, the clock will strike,
The devil will come, and Faustus must be damn'd.
O, I'll leap up to heaven!—Who pulls me down?—
See, where Christ's blood streams in the firmament!
One drop of blood will save me; O my Christ!—
Rend not my heart for naming of my Christ;
Yet will I call on him: O spare me, Lucifer!—

---

5 applied yourself to   7 "O slowly, slowly run,
6 morsels   ye steeds of night."

Where is it now? 'tis gone:
And see, a threatening arm, an angry brow!
Mountains and hills, come, come, and fall
    on me,   170
And hide me from the heavy wrath of heaven!
No!
Then will I headlong run into the earth:
Gape, earth! O, no, it will not harbour me!
You stars that reign'd at my nativity,
Whose influence hath allotted death and hell,
Now draw up Faustus, like a foggy mist,
Into the entrails of yon labouring cloud,
That, when you vomit forth into the air,
My limbs may issue from your smoky
    mouths;   180
But let my soul mount and ascend to heaven!
    [The clock strikes the half-hour.
O, half the hour is past! 'twill all be past
    anon.
O, if my soul must suffer for my sin,
Impose some end to my incessant pain;
Let Faustus live in hell a thousand years,
A hundred thousand, and at last be sav'd!
No end is limited to damnèd souls.
Why wert thou not a creature wanting soul?
Or why is this immortal that thou hast?
O, Pythagoras' metempsychosis,[8] were that
    true,   190
This soul should fly from me, and I be
    chang'd
Into some brutish beast! all beasts are happy,
For, when they diè,
Their souls are soon dissolv'd in elements;
But mine must live, still to be plagu'd in
    hell.
Curs'd be the parents that engender'd me!
No, Faustus, curse thyself, curse Lucifer
That hath depriv'd thee of the joys of
    heaven.
    [The clock strikes twelve.
It strikes, it strikes! Now, body, turn to air,
Or Lucifer will bear thee quick to hell! 200
O soul, be chang'd into small water-drops,
And fall into the ocean, ne'er be found!

    Thunder. Enter Devils.

O, mercy, heaven! look not so fierce on me!
Adders and serpents, let me breathe a while!
Ugly hell, gape not! come not, Lucifer!
I'll burn my books!—O Mephistophilis!
    [Exeunt Devils *with* Faustus.

[Scene XV.]

    Enter Scholars.

FIRST SCHOL. Come, gentlemen, let us go visit
    Faustus,
For such a dreadful night was never seen;
Since first the world's creation did begin,
Such fearful shrieks and cries were never
    heard:
Pray heaven the doctor have escap'd the
    danger.
SEC. SCHOL. O, help us, heaven! see, here are
    Faustus' limbs,
All torn asunder by the hand of death!
THIRD SCHOL. The devils whom Faustus serv'd
    have torn him thus;
For, twixt the hours of twelve and one, me-
    thought
I heard him shriek and call aloud for help;
At which self time the house seem'd all on
    fire   11
With dreadful horror of these damnèd fiends.
SEC. SCHOL. Well, gentlemen, though Faustus'
    end be such
As every Christian heart laments to think on,
Yet, for he was a scholar once admir'd
For wondrous knowledge in our German
    schools,
We'll give his mangled limbs due burial;
And all the students, cloth'd in mourning
    black,
Shall wait upon his heavy[9] funeral.
    [Exeunt.

    Enter Chorus.

CHOR. Cut is the branch that might have
    grown full straight,   20
And burnèd is Apollo's laurel-bough,[10]
That sometime grew within this learnèd man.
Faustus is gone: regard his hellish fall,
Whose fiendful fortune may exhort the wise
Only to wonder at unlawful things,
Whose deepness doth entice such forward
    wits
To practise more than heavenly power
    permits.   *[Exeunt.*
Terminat hora diem; terminat auctor opus.[11]

8 The theory held by Pythagoras, the Greek philosopher, that the soul, at death, passes into
  another body.

9 sad
10 The laurel was sacred to Apollo. Symbolic here
  for distinction in science or poetry.
11 "The hour ends the day, the author ends the
  work."

WILLIAM SHAKESPEARE
(1564-1616)

THE TEMPEST*

DRAMATIS PERSONÆ.

ALONSO, King of Naples.

SEBASTIAN, his brother.

PROSPERO, the right Duke of Milan.

ANTONIO, his brother, the usurping Duke of Milan.

FERDINAND, son to the King of Naples.

GONZALO, an honest old Counsellor.

ADRIAN, } Lords.
FRANCISCO,

CALIBAN, a savage and deformed Slave.

TRINCULO, a Jester.

STEPHANO, a drunken Butler.

Master of a Ship.   Boatswain.   Mariners.

MIRANDA, daughter to Prospero.

ARIEL, an airy Spirit.

IRIS,
CERES,
JUNO,   } presented by Spirits.
Nymphs,
Reapers,

Other Spirits attending on Prospero.

ACT I.
SCENE I.

On a ship at sea: a tempestuous noise of thunder and lightning heard.

Enter a SHIP-MASTER *and a* BOATSWAIN.

MAST. Boatswain!

BOATS. Here, master: what cheer?

MAST. Good,[1] speak to the mariners: fall to 't, yarely,[2] or we run ourselves aground: bestir, bestir.   [*Exit.*

Enter MARINERS.

BOATS. Heigh, my hearts! cheerly, cheerly, my hearts! yare, yare! Take in the topsail. Tend[3] to the master's whistle. Blow, till thou burst thy wind,[4] if room enough![5]

Enter ALONSO, SEBASTIAN, ANTONIO, FERDINAND, GONZALO, *and others.*

ALON. Good boatswain, have care. Where's the master? Play the men.   11

BOATS. I pray now, keep below.

ANT. Where is the master, boatswain?

BOATS. Do you not hear him? You mar our labour: keep your cabins: you do assist the storm.

GON. Nay, good, be patient.

BOATS. When the sea is. Hence! What cares† these roarers for the name of king? To cabin: silence! trouble us not.   19

GON. Good, yet remember whom thou hast aboard.

BOATS. None that I more love than myself. You are a counsellor; if you can command these elements to silence, and work the peace of the present,[6] we will not hand[7] a rope more; use your authority: if you cannot, give thanks you have lived so long, and make yourself ready in your cabin for the mischance of the

* *The Tempest* is one of Shakespeare's maturest productions, and is commonly assigned to the year 1610 or 1611. It may have had its origin in the spur given to the imagination by the widespread interest in the newly discovered Bermudas, where in the year 1609 the vessel of Sir George Somers was wrecked. A romantic play, with elements of both tragedy and comedy, and an included masque (if that be Shakespeare's); and with characters ranging from a brutish monster through the lowest and highest ranks of men to a creature of the spirit world, it contains perhaps in itself the best epitome of its creator's varied powers.

"The persons in this play," writes Edward Dowden, "while remaining real and living, are conceived in a more abstract way, more as types, than those in any other work of Shakespeare. Prospero is the highest wisdom and moral attainment; Gonzalo is humorous common-sense incarnated; all that is meanest and most despicable appears in the wretched conspirators; Miranda, whose name seems to suggest wonder, is almost an elemental being, framed in the purest and simplest type of womanhood, yet made substantial by contrast with Ariel, who is an unbodied joy, too much a creature of light and air to know human affection or human sorrow: Caliban (the name formed from cannibal) stands at the other extreme, with all the elements in him—appetites, intellect, even imagination—out of which man emerges into early civilization, but with a moral nature that is still gross and malignant. Over all presides Prospero like a providence. And the spirit of reconciliation, of forgiveness, harmonizing the contentions of men, appears in *The Tempest* in the same noble manner that it appears in *The Winter's Tale, Cymbeline,* and *Henry VIII.*"

"Nowhere," says Sidney Lee, "did Shakespeare give rein to his imagination with more imposing effect than in *The Tempest.* As in *A Midsummer Night's Dream,* magical or supernatural agencies are the mainsprings of the plot. But the tone is marked at all points by a solemnity and profundity of thought and sentiment which are lacking in the early comedy. . . . In Prospero, the guiding providence of the romance, who resigns his magic power in the closing scene, traces have been sought of the lineaments of the dramatist himself, who in this play probably bade farewell to the enchanted work of his life."

1 Good fellow
2 smartly
3 attend
4 Cp. *Lear,* III. ii. 1; *Pericles,* III. i. 44.
5 so long as we have sea-room
6 Supply "moment."
7 touch

† Such grammatical freedom is not unusual in Shakespeare and other writers of his time; compare the second line of Ariel's song, I. ii. 397, and the fourth line of "Hark, hark!" *Cymbeline,* II. iii. 24. The "roarers" here are of course the waves, but as the term was also applied to "bullies" we get a lively picture of their rudeness as well as their noise.

hour, if it so hap. Cheerly, good hearts! Out of our way, I say.   [*Exit.* 29

GON. I have great comfort from this fellow: methinks he hath no drowning mark upon him; his complexion is perfect gallows. Stand fast, good Fate, to his hanging: make the rope of his destiny our cable, for our own doth little advantage.[8] If he be not born to be hanged, our case is miserable.   [*Exeunt.*

Re-enter BOATSWAIN.

BOATS. Down with the topmast! yare! lower, lower! Bring her to try[9] with main-course.[10] [*A cry within.*] A plague upon this howling! they are louder than the weather or our office.   40

Re-enter SEBASTIAN, ANTONIO, *and* GONZALO.

Yet again! what do you here? Shall we give o'er, and drown? Have you a mind to sink?

SEB. A pox o' your throat, you bawling, blasphemous, incharitable dog!

BOATS. Work you, then.

ANT. Hang, cur! hang, you insolent noisemaker. We are less afraid to be drown'd than thou art.

GON. I'll warrant him for[11] drowning; though the ship were no stronger than a nutshell.   50

BOATS. Lay her a-hold,[9] a-hold! set her two courses off to sea again; lay her off.

Enter MARINERS, *wet.*

MARINERS. All lost! to prayers, to prayers! all lost!

BOATS. What, must our mouths be cold?

GON. The king and prince at prayers! let's assist them,
For our case is as theirs.

SEB.   I'm out of patience.

ANT. We are merely[12] cheated of our lives by drunkards:
This wide-chapped rascal,—would thou mightst lie drowning   60
The washing of ten tides!‡

GON.   He'll be hang'd yet,
Though every drop of water swear against it,
And gape at widest to glut him.

[*A confused noise within:* 'Mercy on us!'—
'We split, we split!'——'Farewell my wife and children!'——

'Farewell, brother!'——'We split, we split, we split!']

ANT. Let's all sink with the king.

SEB. Let's take leave of him.[13]

[*Exeunt* ANT. *and* SEB.

GON. Now would I give a thousand furlongs of sea for an acre of barren ground, long heath, brown furze, any thing. The wills above be done! but I would fain die a dry death.
                                        [*Exeunt.*

SCENE II.

The island. Before PROSPERO'S *cell.*

Enter PROSPERO *and* MIRANDA.

MIR. If by your art,[14] my dearest father, you have
Put the wild waters in this roar, allay them.
The sky, it seems, would pour down stinking pitch,
But that the sea, mounting to the welkin's cheek,
Dashes the fire out. O, I have suffer'd
With those that I saw suffer! a brave[15] vessel,
Who had, no doubt, some noble creature[16] in her,
Dash'd all to pieces. O, the cry did knock
Against my very heart! Poor souls, they perish'd!
Had I been any god of power, I would   10
Have sunk the sea within the earth, or ere[17]
It should the good ship so have swallowed and
The fraughting[18] souls within her.

PROS.   Be collected:
No more amazement: tell your piteous heart
There's no harm done.

MIR.   O, woe the day!

PROS.   No harm.
I have done nothing but in care of thee,
Of thee, my dear one, thee, my daughter, who
Art ignorant of what thou art, nought knowing
Of whence I am, nor that I am more better
Than Prospero, master of a full poor cell   20
And thy no greater father.

MIR.   More to know
Did never meddle[19] with my thoughts.

PROS.   'Tis time
I should inform thee farther. Lend thy hand,
And pluck my magic garment from me.—So:
                    [*Lays down his mantle.* *
Lie there, my art. Wipe thou thine eyes; have comfort.
The direful spectacle of the wreck, which touch'd
The very virtue of compassion in thee,
I have with such provision[20] in mine art .

---

8 help (verb)
9 close to the wind
10 main-sail
11 against
12 simply, absolutely
13 bid him farewell
‡ Pirates were hanged at low water mark and left during the washing of three tides.
14 magic (Note the respectful "you" in her address, the familiar "thou" in her father's.)
15 splendid
16 Collective for "creatures."
17 sooner than
18 freight-composing
19 mingle
20 foresight
* Prospero wears the mantle only in his capacity as magician.

So safely ordered, that there is no soul,
No, not so much perdition as an hair   30
Betid to any creature in the vessel
Which thou heard'st cry, which thou saw'st
  sink. Sit down;
For thou must now know farther.

MIR.   You have often
Begun to tell me what I am; but stopp'd,
And left me to a bootless inquisition,[21]
Concluding 'Stay: not yet.'

PROS.   The hour's now come;
The very minute bids thee ope thine ear;
Obey, and be attentive. Canst thou remember
A time before we came unto this cell?
I do not think thou canst, for then thou wast
  not   40
Out[22] three years old.

MIR.   Certainly, sir, I can.

PROS. By what? by any other house or
  person?
Of any thing the image tell me, that
Hath kept with thy remembrance.

MIR.   'Tis far off,
And rather like a dream than an assurance
That my remembrance warrants. Had I not
Four or five women once that tended me?

PROS. Thou hadst, and more, Miranda. But
  how is it
That this lives in thy mind? What seest thou
  else
In the dark backward and abysm of time?   50
If thou remember'st aught ere thou camest
  here,
How thou camest here thou mayst.

MIR.   But that I do not.

PROS. Twelve year since, Miranda, twelve
  year since,
Thy father was the Duke of Milan, and
A prince of power.

MIR.   Sir, are not you my father?

PROS. Thy mother was a piece of virtue, and
She said thou wast my daughter; and thy
  father
Was Duke of Milan; and his only heir
A princess, no worse issued.[23]

MIR.   O the heavens!
What foul play had we, that we came from
  thence?
Or blessed was't we did?

PROS.   Both, both, my girl: 61
By foul play, as thou say'st, were we heaved
  thence;
But blessedly holp thither.

MIR.   O, my heart bleeds
To think o' the teen[24] that I have turn'd you to,

Which is from[25] my remembrance! Please you
  farther.

PROS. My brother, and thy uncle, call'd
  Antonio,—
I pray thee, mark me,—that a brother should
Be so perfidious!—he whom, next thyself,
Of all the world I loved, and to him put
The manage of my state; as at that time   70
Through all the signories[26] it was the first,
And Prospero the prime duke, being so reputed
In dignity, and for the liberal arts
Without a parallel; those being all my study,
The government I cast upon my brother,
And to my state grew stranger, being trans-
  ported
And rapt in secret studies. Thy false uncle—
Dost thou attend me?

MIR.   Sir, most heedfully.

PROS. Being once perfected how to grant
  suits,
How to deny them, who to advance, and who 80
To trash[27] for over-topping,[28] new created
The creatures[29] that were mine, I say, or
  changed 'em,
Or else new form'd 'em; having both the key
Of officer and office, set all hearts i' the state
To what tune pleased his ear; that now he was
The ivy which had hid my princely trunk,
And suck'd my verdure out on't.[30] Thou
  attend'st not.

MIR. O, good sir, I do.

PROS.   I pray thee, mark me.
I, thus neglecting worldly ends, all dedicated
To closeness[31] and the bettering of my mind 90
With that which, but[32] my being so retired,
O'er-prized all popular rate,[33] in my false
  brother
Awaked an evil nature; and my trust,
Like a good parent, did beget of him
A falsehood in its contrary, as great
As my trust was; which had indeed no limit,
A confidence sans[34] bound. He being thus
  lorded,
Not only with what my revenue[35] yielded,
But what my power might else exact, like one
Who having into truth, by telling of it,   100
Made such a sinner of his memory,
To credit his own lie,[36] he did believe

21 vain inquiry
22 fully
23 descended
24 grief
25 out of
26 seignories, lordships
27 check (said of
  hounds; or it may
  be a figure from
  gardening — to
  "top," lop)
28 outrunning
29 followers, lords
30 out of it
31 seclusion
32 except
33 out-valued all popu-
  lar esteem (was
  better than any
  popularity, except
  that it enforced
  seclusion)
34 without
35 Pronounce *reven'ue.*
36 like one who has told an untruth until his false
  memory makes it seem truth (perhaps *into*
  should be *unto*.)

He was indeed the duke; out o' the[37] substitu-
tion,
And executing the outward face of royalty,
With all prerogative—hence his ambition
growing,—
Dost thou hear?

MIR.   Your tale, sir, would cure deafness.

PROS. To have no screen between this part
he play'd
And him he play'd it for, he needs will be
Absolute Milan.[38] Me, poor man, my library
Was dukedom large enough: of temporal
royalties
He thinks me now incapable; confederates,   111
So dry he was for sway, wi' the King of Naples
To give him annual tribute, do him homage,
Subject his coronet to his crown, and bend
The dukedom, yet unbow'd,—alas, poor Milan!—
To most ignoble stooping.

MIR.   O the heavens!

PROS. Mark his condition,[39] and the event;[40]
then tell me
If this might be a brother.

MIR.   I should sin
To think but[41] nobly of my grandmother:
Good wombs have borne bad sons.

PROS.   Now the condition.   120
This King of Naples, being an enemy
To me inveterate, hearkens my brother's suit;
Which was, that he, in lieu o' the premises[42]
Of homage and I know not how much tribute,
Should presently[43] extirpate me and mine
Out of the dukedom, and confer fair Milan,
With all the honours, on my brother: whereon,
A treacherous army levied, one midnight
Fated to the purpose, did Antonio open
The gates of Milan; and, i' the dead of
darkness,   130
The ministers for the purpose hurried thence
Me and thy crying self.

MIR.   Alack, for pity!
I, not remembering how I cried out then,
Will cry it o'er again: it is a hint
That wrings mine eyes to 't.

PROS.   Hear a little further,
And then I'll bring thee to the present business
Which now's upon's; without the which, this
story
Were most impertinent.[44]

MIR.   Wherefore did they not
That hour destroy us?

PROS.   Well demanded, wench:[45]

My tale provokes that question. Dear, they
durst not,
So dear the love my people bore me; nor set   141
A mark so bloody on the business; but
With colours fairer painted their foul ends.
In few,[46] they hurried us aboard a bark,
Bore us some leagues to sea; where they
prepared
A rotten carcass of a butt, not rigg'd,
Nor tackle, sail, nor mast; the very rats
Instinctively have quit it: there they hoist us,
To cry to the sea that roar'd to us; to sigh
To the winds, whose pity, sighing back again, 150
Did us but loving wrong.

MIR.   Alack, what trouble
Was I then to you!

PROS.   O, a cherubin
Thou wast that did preserve me. Thou didst
smile,
Infused with a fortitude from heaven,
When I have deck'd[47] the sea with drops full
salt,
Under my burthen groan'd; which raised in me
An undergoing stomach,[48] to bear up
Against what should ensue.

MIR.   How came we ashore?

PROS. By Providence divine.
Some food we had, and some fresh water, that
A noble Neapolitan, Gonzalo,   161
Out of his charity, who being then appointed
Master of this design, did give us, with
Rich garments, linens, stuffs and necessaries,
Which since have steaded much; so, of his
gentleness,
Knowing I loved my books, he furnish'd me
From mine own library with volumes that
I prize above my dukedom.

MIR.   Would I might
But ever see that man!

PROS.   Now I arise: [Resumes his mantle.
Sit still, and hear the last of our sea-sorrow.
Here in this island we arrived; and here   171
Have I, thy schoolmaster, made thee more profit
Than other princess'[49] can, that have more time
For vainer hours, and tutors not so careful.

MIR. Heavens thank you for 't! And now,
I pray you, sir,
For still 'tis beating in my mind, your reason
For raising this sea-storm?

PROS.   Know thus far forth.
By accident most strange, bountiful Fortune,
Now my dear lady, hath mine enemies
Brought to this shore; and by my prescience 180
I find my zenith doth depend upon
A most auspicious star, whose influence
If now I court not, but omit, my fortunes

---

37 in consequence of the
38 Duke of Milan. (So
  Cleopatra is called
  Egypt, etc.)
39 terms of confedera-
  tion
40 outcome
41 otherwise than
42 in return for the
  guarantees
43 at once
44 not pertinent
45 girl (with none of
  the modern con-
  temptuous sense)
46 in brief
47 covered
48 an enduring courage
49 princesses

168 THE ELIZABETHAN AGE

Will ever after droop. Here cease more questions:
Thou art inclined to sleep; 'tis a good dulness,
And give it way: I know thou canst not choose.
[MIRANDA *sleeps.*
Come away, servant, come. I am ready now.
Approach, my Ariel, come.

Enter ARIEL.

ARI. All hail, great master! grave sir, hail!
I come
To answer thy best pleasure; be 't to fly, 190
To swim, to dive into the fire, to ride
On the curl'd clouds, to thy strong bidding task
Ariel and all his quality.[50]

PROS. Hast thou, spirit,
Perform'd to point the tempest that I bade thee?

ARI. To every article.
I boarded the king's ship; now on the beak,
Now in the waist, the deck, in every cabin,
I flamed amazement: sometime I'ld divide,
And burn in many places; on the topmast,
The yards and bowsprit, would I flame distinctly,[51] 200
Then meet and join. Jove's lightnings, the precursors
O' the dreadful thunder-claps, more momentary
And sight-outrunning were not: the fire and cracks
Of sulphurous roaring the most mighty Neptune
Seem to besiege, and make his bold waves tremble,
Yea, his dread trident shake.

PROS. My brave spirit!
Who was so firm, so constant, that this coil[52]
Would not infect his reason?

ARI. Not a soul
But felt a fever of the mad, and play'd
Some tricks of desperation. All but mariners 210
Plunged in the foaming brine, and quit the vessel,
Then all afire with me: the king's son, Ferdinand,
With hair up-staring,—then like reeds, not hair,—
Was the first man that leap'd; cried, 'Hell is empty,
And all the devils are here.'

PROS. Why, that's my spirit!
But was not this nigh shore?

ARI. Close by, my master.

PROS. But are they, Ariel, safe?

ARI. Not a hair perish'd;
On their sustaining garments not a blemish,
But fresher than before: and, as thou badest me,

In troops I have dispersed them 'bout the isle
The king's son have I landed by himself; 22
Whom I left cooling of the air with sighs
In an odd angle of the isle, and sitting,
His arms in this sad knot.

PROS. Of the king's ship
The mariners, say how thou hast disposed,
And all the rest o' the fleet.

ARI. Safely in harbour
Is the king's ship; in the deep nook, where one
Thou call'dst me up at midnight to fetch dew
From the still-vex'd Bermoothes,[53] there she hid:
The mariners all under hatches stow'd; 23
Who, with a charm join'd to their suffer'd labour,
I have left asleep: and for the rest o' the fleet
Which I dispersed, they all have met again,
And are upon the Mediterranean flote,[54]
Bound sadly home for Naples;
Supposing that they saw the king's ship wreck'd,
And his great person perish.

PROS. Ariel, thy charge
Exactly is perform'd: but there's more work.
What is the time o' the day?

ARI. Past the mid season

PROS. At least two glasses. The time 'twixt six and now 24
Must by us both be spent most preciously.

ARI. Is there more toil? Since thou dost give me pains,
Let me remember thee what thou hast promised,
Which is not yet perform'd me.

PROS. How now? moody
What is 't thou canst demand?

ARI. My liberty.

PROS. Before the time be out? no more!

ARI. I prithee
Remember I have done thee worthy service;
Told thee no lies, made thee no mistakings, served
Without or grudge or grumblings: thou didst promise
To bate me a full year.

PROS. Dost thou forget 25
From what a torment I did free thee?

ARI. No.

PROS. Thou dost, and think'st it much to tread the ooze
Of the salt deep,
To run upon the sharp wind of the north,
To do me business in the veins o' the earth
When it is baked with frost.

ARI. I do not, sir.

[50] associates
[51] separately
[52] turmoil
[53] the ever tempestuous Bermudas (see introductory note)
[54] flood, sea

Pros. Thou liest, malignant thing! Hast
thou forgot
the foul witch Sycorax, who with age and envy
Was grown into a hoop? hast thou forgot her?
Ari. No, sir.
Pros.   Thou hast. Where was she born?
speak; tell me.   260
Ari. Sir, in Argier.⁵⁵
Pros.   O, was she so? I must
once in a month recount what thou hast been,
Which thou forget'st. This damn'd witch
Sycorax,
for mischiefs manifold, and sorceries terrible
To enter human hearing, from Argier,
thou know'st, was banish'd: for one thing she
did
they would not take her life. Is not this true?
Ari. Ay, sir.
Pros. This blue-eyed⁵⁶ hag was hither
brought with child,   269
and here was left by the sailors. Thou, my slave,
as thou report'st thyself, wast then her servant;
and, for⁵⁷ thou wast a spirit too delicate
To act her earthy and abhorr'd commands,
refusing her grand hests, she did confine thee,
By help of her more potent ministers,
and in her most unmitigable rage,
into a cloven pine; within which rift
imprison'd thou didst painfully remain
a dozen years; within which space she died, 279
and left thee there; where thou didst vent thy
groans
as fast as mill-wheels strike. Then was this
island—
save for the son that she did litter here,
a freckled whelp hag-born—not honour'd with
a human shape.
Ari.   Yes, Caliban, her son.
Pros. Dull thing, I say so; he, that Caliban,
Whom now I keep in service. Thou best
know'st
What torment I did find thee in; thy groans
Did make wolves howl, and penetrate the
breasts
Of ever-angry bears: it was a torment
To lay upon the damn'd, which Sycorax   290
Could not again undo: it was mine art,
When I arrived and heard thee, that made gape
The pine, and let thee out.
Ari.   I thank thee, master.
Pros. If thou more murmur'st, I will rend
an oak,
And peg thee in his knotty entrails, till
Thou hast howl'd away twelve winters.
Ari.   Pardon, master:
I will be correspondent to command,

And do my spiriting gently.
Pros.   Do so; and after two days
I will discharge thee.
Ari.   That's my noble master!
What shall I do? say what; what shall I do?
Pros. Go make thyself like a nymph o' the
sea: be subject   301
To no sight but thine and mine; invisible
To every eyeball else. Go take this shape,
And hither come in't: go hence with diligence!
[Exit Ariel.
Awake, dear heart, awake! thou hast slept well;
Awake!
Mir. The strangeness of your story put
Heaviness in me.
Pros.   Shake it off. Come on;
We'll visit Caliban my slave, who never
Yields us kind answer.
Mir.   'Tis a villain, sir,
I do not love to look on.
Pros.   But, as 'tis,   310
We cannot miss⁵⁸ him: he does make our fire,
Fetch in our wood, and serves in offices
That profit us. What, ho! slave! Caliban!
Thou earth, thou! speak.
Cal. [Within] There's wood enough within.
Pros. Come forth, I say! there's other
business for thee:
Come, thou tortoise! when?
Re-enter Ariel like a water-nymph.
Fine apparition! My quaint⁵⁹ Ariel,
Hark in thine ear.
Ari.   My lord, it shall be done. [Exit.
Pros. Thou poisonous slave, got by the devil
himself
Upon thy wicked dam, come forth!   320

Enter Caliban.

Cal. As wicked dew as e'er my mother
brush'd
With raven's feather from unwholesome fen
Drop on you both! a south-west blow on ye
And blister you all o'er!
Pros. For this, be sure, to-night thou shalt
have cramps,
Side-stitches that shall pen thy breath up;
urchins⁶⁰
Shall, for that vast of night that⁶¹ they may
work,
All exercise on thee; thou shalt be pinch'd
As thick as honeycomb, each pinch more
stinging
Than bees that made 'em.
Cal.   I must eat my dinner. 330
This island's mine, by Sycorax my mother,

55 Algiers   57 because
56 with blue-circled eyes

58 do without   61 that waste and void
59 dainty   of night wherein
60 goblins

Which thou takest from me. When thou camest
  first,
Thou strokedst me, and madest much of me;
  wouldst give me
Water with berries in 't;* and teach me how
To name the bigger light, and how the less,
That burn by day and night: and then I loved
  thee,
And show'd thee all the qualities o' th' isle,
The fresh springs, brine-pits, barren places and
  fertile:
Cursed be I that did so! All the charms
Of Sycorax, toads, beetles, bats, light on you!
For I am all the subjects that you have,   341
Which[62] first was mine own king: and here
  you sty me
In this hard rock, whiles you do keep from me
The rest o' th' island.
    PROS.   Thou most lying slave,
Whom stripes may move, not kindness! I have
  used thee,
Filth as thou art, with human care; and lodged
  thee
In mine own cell, till thou didst seek to violate
The honour of my child.
    CAL. O ho, O ho! would 't had been done!
Thou didst prevent me; I had peopled else   350
This isle with Calibans.
    PROS.   Abhorred slave,
Which any print of goodness wilt not take,
Being capable of all ill! I pitied thee,
Took pains to make thee speak, taught thee
  each hour
One thing or other: when thou didst not,
  savage,
Know thine own meaning, but wouldst gabble
  like
A thing most brutish, I endow'd thy purposes
With words that made them known. But thy
  vile race,[63]
Though thou didst learn, had that in 't which
  good natures
Could not abide to be with; therefore wast
  thou   360
Deservedly confined into this rock,
Who hadst deserved more than a prison.
    CAL. You taught me language; and my
  profit on 't
Is, I know how to curse. The red plague rid[64]
  you
For learning me your language!
    PROS.   Hag-seed, hence!

Fetch us in fuel; and be quick, thou'rt best,
To answer[65] other business. Shrug'st tho
  malice?
If thou neglect'st, or dost unwillingly
What I command, I'll rack thee with o
  cramps,
Fill all thy bones with aches,† make thee roa
That beasts shall tremble at thy din.   37
    CAL.   No, pray thee
[Aside] I must obey: his art is of such powe
It would control my dam's god, Setebos,[66]
And make a vassal of him.
    PROS.   So, slave, hence! [Exit CALIBAN

Re-enter ARIEL, invisible, playing and singing
  FERDINAND following.

ARIEL'S song.

  Come unto these yellow sands,
    And then take hands:
  Courtsied when you have and kiss'd
    The wild waves whist:[67]
  Foot it featly here and there;   38
  And, sweet sprites, the burthen bear.[68]
    Hark, hark!
    BURTHEN [dispersedly]. Bow-wow.
  ARI. The watch dogs bark:
    BURTHEN [dispersedly]. Bow-wow.
  ARI. Hark, hark! I hear
  The strain of strutting chanticleer
  Cry, Cock-a-diddle-dow.

  FER. Where should this music be? i' th' air
  or th' earth?
It sounds no more: and, sure, it waits upon
Some god o' th' island. Sitting on a bank,
Weeping again the king my father's wreck,   390
This music crept by me upon the waters,
Allaying both their fury and my passion[69]
With its sweet air: thence I have follow'd it,
Or it hath drawn me rather. But 'tis gone.
No, it begins again.
      ARIEL sings.
  Full fathom five thy father lies;
    Of his bones are coral[70] made;
  Those are pearls that were his eyes:
    Nothing of him that doth fade,
  But doth suffer a sea-change   400
  Into something rich and strange.
  Sea-nymphs hourly ring his knell:
    BURTHEN. Ding-dong.

---

62 who (antecedent I)   64 destroy
63 nature
*Coffee was at this time hardly known in Eng-
  land. In William Strachey's account of the
  shipwreck of Sir George Somers, the men are
  said to have made a pleasant drink of an infusion of berries of the cedar.

65 perform   69 suffering (from Latin
66 A Patagonian deity.   patior)
67 into silence   70 Perhaps used collec-
68 take up the refrain   tively (but see note
                 on I. i. 17).
† Pronounced aitches or atches. The ch was pronounced like k only in the verb; compare
  bake, batch, break, breach.

ARI. Hark! now I hear them,—Ding-dong, bell.

FER. The ditty does remember[71] my drown'd father.

This is no mortal business, nor no sound
That the earth owes:[72]—I hear it now above me.

PROS. The fringed curtains of thine eye advance,[73]
And say what thou seest yond.

MIR.   What is 't? a spirit?
Lord, how it looks about! Believe me, sir,   410
It carries a brave[74] form. But 'tis a spirit.

PROS. No, wench; it eats and sleeps and hath such senses
As we have, such. This gallant which thou seest
Was in the wreck; and, but he's something stain'd
With grief, that's beauty's canker, thou mightst call him
A goodly person: he hath lost his fellows,
And strays about to find 'em.

MIR.   I might call him
A thing divine; for nothing natural
I ever saw so noble.

PROS.   [Aside] It goes on, I see,   419
As my soul prompts it. Spirit, fine spirit! I'll free thee
Within two days for this.

FER.   Most sure the goddess
On whom these airs attend! Vouchsafe my prayer
May know if you remain upon this island;
And that you will some good instruction give
How I may bear me here; my prime request,
Which I do last pronounce, is, O you wonder!
If you be maid or no?

MIR.   No wonder, sir;
But certainly a maid.

FER.   My language! heavens!
I am the best of them that speak this speech,
Were I but where 'tis spoken.

PROS.   How? the best?   430
What wert thou, if the King of Naples heard thee?

FER. A single[75] thing, as I am now, that wonders
To hear thee speak of Naples.[76] He does hear me;
And that he does I weep: myself am Naples,
Who with mine eyes, never since at ebb, beheld
The king my father wreck'd.

MIR.   Alack, for mercy!

FER. Yes, faith, and all his lords; the Duke of Milan
And his brave son* being twain.

PROS.   [Aside] The Duke of Milan
And his more braver daughter could control[77] thee,
If now 'twere fit to do it. At the first sight   440
They have changed eyes. Delicate Ariel,
I'll set thee free for this. [To FER.] A word, good sir;
I fear you have done yourself some wrong:[78] a word.

MIR. Why speaks my father so ungently? This
Is the third man that e'er I saw; the first
That e'er I sigh'd for: pity move my father
To be inclined my way!

FER.   O, if a virgin,
And your affection not gone forth, I'll make you
The queen of Naples.

PROS.   Soft, sir! one word more.
[Aside] They are both in either's powers: but this swift business   450
I must uneasy[79] make, lest too light winning
Make the prize light. [To FER.] One word more; I charge thee
That thou attend me: thou dost here usurp
The name thou owest[80] not; and hast put thyself
Upon this island as a spy, to win it
From me, the lord on 't.

FER.   No, as I am a man.

MIR. There's nothing ill can dwell in such a temple:
If the ill spirit have so fair a house,
Good things will strive to dwell with 't.

PROS.   Follow me.
Speak not you for him; he's a traitor. Come;
I'll manacle thy neck and feet together: 461
Sea-water shalt thou drink; thy food shall be
The fresh-brook muscles, wither'd roots, and husks
Wherein the acorn cradled. Follow.

FER.   No;
I will resist such entertainment till
Mine enemy has more power.

        [Draws, and is charmed from moving.

MIR.   O dear father,
Make not too rash a trial of him, for
He's gentle, and not fearful.[81]

PROS.   What! I say,

---

71 commemorate
72 owns
73 raise
74 fine
75 solitary; also, miserable
76 See note 38.

77 confute
78 made a mistake
79 difficult
80 ownest
* Possibly an oversight, for no such character appears.
81 mild and harmless (or possibly, high-spirited and not afraid)

My foot my tutor? Put thy sword up, traitor;
Who makest a show, but darest not strike, thy
   conscience
Is so possess'd with guilt: come from thy
   ward;[82]   471
For I can here disarm thee with this stick
And make thy weapon drop.
   MIR.   Beseech you, father.
   PROS.   Hence! hang not on my garments.
   MIR.   Sir, have pity;
I'll be his surety.
   PROS.   Silence! one word more
Shall make me chide thee, if not hate thee.
   What!
An advocate for an impostor! hush!
Thou think'st there is no more such shapes
   as he,
Having seen but him and Caliban: foolish
   wench!
To[83] the most of men this is a Caliban,   480
And they to him are angels.
   MIR.   My affections
Are, then, most humble; I have no ambition
To see a goodlier man.
   PROS.   Come on; obey:
Thy nerves[84] are in their infancy again,
And have no vigour in them.
   FER.   So they are:
My spirits, as in a dream, are all bound up.
My father's loss, the weakness which I feel,
The wreck of all my friends, nor[85] this man's
   threats,
To whom I am subdued, are but light to me,
Might I but through my prison once a day   490
Behold this maid: all corners else o' th' earth
Let liberty make use of; space enough
Have I in such a prison.
   PROS.   [Aside] It works. [To FER.] Come
on.
Thou hast done well, fine Ariel! [To FER.]
   Follow me.
[To ARI.] Hark what thou else shalt do me.
   MIR.   Be of comfort;
My father's of a better nature, sir,
Than he appears by speech: this is unwonted
Which now came from him.
   PROS.   Thou shalt be as free
As mountain winds: but then exactly do
All points of my command.
   ARI.   To the syllable. 500
PROS. Come, follow. Speak not for him.
                      [Exeunt.

ACT II.

SCENE I.

Another part of the island.

Enter ALONSO, SEBASTIAN, ANTONIO, GONZALO
   ADRIAN, FRANCISCO, *and others.*

   GON. Beseech you, sir, be merry; you have
   cause,
So have we all, of joy; for our escape
Is much beyond our loss. Our hint[1] of woe
Is common; every day, some sailor's wife,
The masters of some merchant,[2] and the mer-
   chant,
Have just our theme of woe; but for the
   miracle,
I mean our preservation, few in millions
Can speak like us: then wisely, good sir, weigh
Our sorrow with our comfort.
   ALON.   Prithee, peace.
   SEB.* He receives comfort like cold porridge
   ANT. The visitor[3] will not give him o'er so
   SEB. Look, he's winding up the watch of his
wit; by and by it will strike.
   GON. Sir,—
   SEB. One: tell.[4]
   GON. When every grief is entertain'd that's
   offer'd,
Comes to the entertainer—
   SEB. A dollar.
   GON. Dolour comes to him, indeed: you have
spoken truer than you purposed.   20
   SEB. You have taken it wiselier than I meant
you should.
   GON. Therefore, my lord,—
   ANT. Fie, what a spendthrift is he of his
tongue!
   ALON. I prithee, spare.
   GON. Well, I have done: but yet,—
   SEB. He will be talking.
   ANT. Which, of he or Adrian, for a good
wager, first begins to crow?
   SEB. The old cock.   30
   ANT. The cockerel.
   SEB. Done. The wager?
   ANT. A laughter.
   SEB. A match!
   ADR. Though this island seem to be desert,—
   SEB. Ha, ha, ha!—So, you're paid.
   ADR. Uninhabitable, and almost inacces-
sible,—
   SEB. Yet,—
   ADR. Yet,—

1 occasion
2 vessel
3 comforter (Gonzalo: the word was used of parish
   visitors of the sick)
4 keep count
* The conversation of Sebastian and Antonio takes
   place aside.

82 posture of defence   85 Used, by confusion of
83 compared to   construction, for
84 sinews   "and."

ANT. He could not miss 't.5   40

ADR. It must needs be of subtle, tender and
[de]licate temperance.6

ANT. Temperance7 was a delicate wench.

SEB. Ay, and a subtle; as he most learnedly
[de]livered.

ADR. The air breathes upon us here most
[sw]eetly.

SEB. As if it had lungs, and rotten ones.

ANT. Or as 'twere perfumed by a fen.

GON. Here is everything advantageous to
[lif]e.

ANT. True; save means to live.   50

SEB. Of that there's none, or little.

GON. How lush and lusty the grass looks!
[ho]w green!

ANT. The ground, indeed, is tawny.

SEB. With an eye8 of green in 't.

ANT. He misses not much.

SEB. No; he doth but mistake the truth
[to]tally.

GON. But the rarity of it is,—which is in-
ed almost beyond credit,—

SEB. As many vouched rarities are.   60

GON. That our garments, being, as they
[we]re, drenched in the sea, hold, notwithstand-
[in]g, their freshness and glosses, being rather
[ne]w-dyed than stained with salt water.

ANT. If but one of his pockets could speak,
[wo]uld it not say he lies?

SEB. Ay, or very falsely pocket up his
[re]port.

GON. Methinks our garments are now as
[fr]esh as when we put them on first in Afric,
[at] the marriage of the king's fair daughter
[Cl]aribel to the King of Tunis.   71

SEB. 'Twas a sweet marriage, and we pros-
[pe]r well in our return.

ADR. Tunis was never graced before with
[su]ch a paragon to9 their queen.

GON. Not since widow Dido's time.

ANT. Widow! a pox o' that! How came
[th]at widow in? widow Dido!

SEB. What if he had said 'widower Æneas'
[t]o? Good Lord, how you take it!   80

ADR. 'Widow Dido' said you? you make me
[st]udy of that: she was of Carthage, not of
[Tu]nis.

GON. This Tunis, sir, was Carthage.

ADR. Carthage?

GON. I assure you, Carthage.

ANT. His word is more than the miraculous
[ha]rp.10

SEB. He hath raised the wall, and houses too.

ANT. What impossible matter will he make
easy next?   89

SEB. I think he will carry this island home
in his pocket, and give it his son for an apple.

ANT. And, sowing the kernels of it in the
sea, bring forth more islands.

GON. Ay.

ANT. Why, in good time.

GON. Sir, we were talking that our garments
seem now as fresh as when we were at Tunis
at the marriage of your daughter, who is now
queen.

ANT. And the rarest that e'er came there.

SEB. Bate,11 I beseech you, widow Dido.   100

ANT. O, widow Dido! ay, widow Dido.

GON. Is not, sir, my doublet as fresh as the
first day I wore it? I mean, in a sort.

ANT. That sort was well fished for.

GON. When I wore it at your daughter's
marriage?

ALON. You cram these words into mine ears
against
The stomach of my sense. Would I had never
Married my daughter there! for, coming thence,
My son is lost, and, in my rate,12 she too,
Who is so far from Italy removed   110
I ne'er again shall see her. O thou mine heir
Of Naples and of Milan, what strange fish
Hath made his meal on thee?

FRAN.   Sir, he may live:
I saw him beat the surges under him,
And ride upon their backs; he trod the water,
Whose enmity he flung aside, and breasted
The surge most swoln that met him; his bold
head
'Bove the contentious waves he kept, and oar'd
Himself with his good arms in lusty stroke
To the shore, that o'er his13 wave-worn basis
bow'd,   120
As stooping to relieve him: I not doubt
He came alive to land:

ALON.   No, no, he's gone.

SEB. Sir, you may thank yourself for this
great loss,
That would not bless our Europe with your
daughter,
But rather lose her to an African;
Where she, at least, is banish'd from your eye
Who14 hath cause to wet the grief on 't.15

ALON.   Prithee, peace.

SEB. You were kneel'd to, and importuned
otherwise,
By all of us; and the fair soul herself
Weigh'd 16 between loathness and obedience, at

.. e., could not fail to   8 tinge
   say just what you   9 for
   anticipated   10 Amphion's harp,
 temperature   which raised the
 A proper name among   walls of Thebes
   the Puritans

11 except   14 which
12 opinion   15 to weep over it
13 its   16 balanced

Which end o' the beam should[17] bow. We have
　　lost your son,　　　　　　　　　　　131
I fear, for ever: Milan and Naples have
Mo widows in them of this business' making
Than we bring men to comfort them:
The fault 's your own.

　　ALON.　　　　　So is the dear 'st[18] o' the loss.
　　GON. My lord Sebastian,
The truth you speak doth lack some gentleness,
And time[19] to speak it in: you rub the sore,
When you should bring the plaster.

　　SEB.　　　　　　　　　Very well.
　　ANT. And most chirurgeonly.[20]　　　140
　　GON. It is foul weather in us all, good sir,
When you are cloudy.

　　SEB.　　　　　　Foul weather?
　　ANT.　　　　　　　　　Very foul.
　　GON. Had I plantation[21] of this isle, my
　　lord,—
　　ANT. He 'ld sow 't with nettle-seed.
　　SEB.　　　　　　Or docks, or mallows.
　　GON. And were the king on 't, what would
　　I do?
　　SEB. 'Scape being drunk for want of wine.
　　GON. I' the commonwealth I would by con-
　　traries
Execute all things; for no kind of traffic
Would I admit; no name of magistrate;
Letters[22] should not be known; riches, poverty,
And use of service,[23] none; contract, suc-
　　cession,　　　　　　　　　　　　　151
Bourn, bound of land, tilth, vineyard, none;
No use of metal, corn, or wine, or oil;
No occupation; all men idle, all;
And women too, but innocent and pure;
No sovereignty;—

　　SEB.　　　　　Yet he would be king on 't.
　　ANT. The latter end of his commonwealth
forgets the beginning.
　　GON. All things in common nature should
　　produce　　　　　　　　　　　　　159
Without sweat or endeavour: treason, felony,
Sword, pike, knife, gun, or need of any en-
　　gine,[24]
Would I not have; but nature should bring
　　forth,
Of it own kind,[25] all foison,[26] all abundance,
To feed my innocent people.

　　　.　　.　　.　　.　　.　　.
I would with such perfection govern, sir,
To excel the golden age.
　　SEB.　　　　　　　'Save his majesty!
　　ANT. Long live Gonzalo!

　　GON.　　　　　And,—do you mark me, si
　　ALON. Prithee, no more: thou dost ta
nothing to me.　　　　　　　　　　　1
　　GON. I do well believe your highness; a
did it to minister occasion to these gentleme
who are of such sensible[27] and nimble lun
that they always use to laugh at nothing.
　　ANT. 'Twas you we laughed at.
　　GON. Who in this kind of merry fooling a
nothing to you: so you may continue, and lau
at nothing still.
　　ANT. What a blow was there given!　18
　　SEB. An[28] it had not fallen flat-long.[29]
　　GON. You are gentlemen of brave mettle
you would lift the moon out of her sphere,
she would continue in it five weeks witho
changing.

Enter ARIEL *(invisible), playing solemn musi*
　　SEB. We would so, and then go a bat-fow
ing.[30]
　　ANT. Nay, good my lord, be not angry.
　　GON. No, I warrant you; I will not adve
ture my discretion so weakly. Will you laug
me asleep, for I am very heavy?
　　ANT. Go sleep, and hear us.*　　　　19
　　　　[*All sleep except* ALON., SEB., *and* AN
　　ALON. What, all so soon asleep! I wis
　　mine eyes
Would, with themselves, shut up my thoughts
　　I find
They are inclined to do so.
　　SEB.　　　　　　　Please you, sir,
Do not omit[31] the heavy offer of it:
It seldom visits sorrow; when it doth,
It is a comforter.
　　ANT.　　　　We two, my lord,
Will guard your person while you take you
　　rest,
And watch your safety.
　　ALON.　　　　Thank you.—Wondrous heav
　　　　[ALONSO *sleeps. Exit* ARIE
　　SEB. What a strange drowsiness possesse
them!
　　ANT. It is the quality o' the climate.
　　SEB.　　　　　　　　　Why　20
Doth it not then our eyelids sink? I find n
Myself disposed to sleep.
　　ANT.　　　　Nor I; my spirits are nimbl
They fell together all, as by consent;
They dropp'd, as by a thunder-stroke. Wha
　　might,

---

17 Supply "she."
18 heaviest
19 Supply "proper."
20 surgeon-like
21 colonization
22 literature
23 practice of servitude
24 of war
25 spontaneously
26 plenty

27 sensitive
28 if
29 flatwise
30 catching birds a
　　night by beatin
　　the bushes
31 let pass
* This passage is obscure. Perhaps it is a collo
　quial inversion for "Hear us, and go t
　sleep."

orthy Sebastian?—O, what might?—No
  more:—
nd yet methinks I see it in thy face,
hat thou shouldst be: the occasion speaks32
  thee; and
y strong imagination sees a crown
ropping upon thy head.

SEB.   What, art thou waking?

ANT. Do you not hear me speak?

SEB.   I do; and surely 210
is a sleepy language, and thou speak'st
at of thy sleep. What is it thou didst say?
iis is a strange repose, to be asleep
ith eyes wide open; standing, speaking, moving,
nd yet so fast asleep.

ANT.   Noble Sebastian,
iou let'st thy fortune sleep—die, rather;
  wink'st
hiles thou art waking.

SEB.   Thou dost snore distinctly;33
iere's meaning in thy snores.

ANT. I am more serious than my custom:
  you
ust be so too, if heed me; which to do 220
rebles thee o'er.34

SEB.   Well, I am standing water.

ANT. I'll teach you how to flow.

SEB.   Do so: to ebb
ereditary sloth instructs me.

ANT.   O,
' you but knew how you the purpose cherish
'hiles thus you mock it! how, in stripping it,
ou more invest it!35 Ebbing men, indeed,
ost often do so near the bottom run
y their own fear or sloth.

SEB.   Prithee, say on:
he setting of thine eye and cheek proclaim
  matter from thee; and a birth, indeed, 230
'hich throes 36 thee much to yield.37

ANT.   Thus, sir:
lthough this lord of weak remembrance, this,
'ho shall be of as little memory
hen he is earth'd, hath here almost persuaded,—
or he's a spirit of persuasion, only
rofesses38 to persuade,—the king his son's
  alive,
'is as impossible that he's undrown'd
s he that sleeps here swims.

SEB.   I have no hope
iat he's undrown'd.

ANT.   O, out of that 'no hope'

What great hope have you! no hope that
  way is 240
Another way so high a hope that even
Ambition cannot pierce a wink beyond,
But doubt39 discovery there. Will you grant
  with me
That Ferdinand is drown'd?

SEB.   He's gone.

ANT.   Then, tell me,
Who's the next heir of Naples?

SEB.   Claribel.

ANT. She that is queen of Tunis; she that
  dwells
Ten leagues beyond man's life; she that from
  Naples
Can have no note, unless the sun were post,—
The man i' the moon's too slow,—till new-born
  chins 249
Be rough and razorable; she that from whom40
We all were sea-swallow'd, though some cast
  again,
And by that destiny, to perform an act
Whereof what's past is prologue; what to
  come,
In yours and my discharge.

SEB.   What stuff is this! how say you?
'Tis true, my brother's daughter's queen of
  Tunis;
So is she heir of Naples; 'twixt which regions
There is some space.

ANT.   A space whose every cubit
Seems to cry out, 'How shall that Claribel
Measure us41 back to Naples? Keep in Tunis,
And let Sebastian wake.' Say, this were
  death 260
That now hath seized them; why, they were no
  worse
Than now they are. There be that can rule
  Naples
As well as he that sleeps; lords that can prate
As amply and unnecessarily
As this Gonzalo; I myself could make
A chough of as deep chat.42 O, that you bore
The mind that I do! what a sleep were this
For your advancement! Do you understand me?

SEB. Methinks I do.

ANT.   And how does your content
Tender43 your own good fortune?

SEB.   I remember 270
You did supplant your brother Prospero.

ANT.   True:
And look how well my garments sit upon me;
Much feater than before: my brother's servants

Invites
significantly
will treble thy for-
tunes

35 more alluringly clothe
  it
36 pains
37 bring forth
38 his sole profession is

39 but must doubt (the
  possibility of)
40 Supply "coming."
41 traverse us (the cu-
  bits)

42 a jackdaw talk as
  deeply
43 regard

Were then my fellows: now they are my men.

SEB. But, for your conscience?

ANT. Ay, sir; where lies that? if 'twere a kibe,[44]
'Twould put me to my slipper: but I feel not
This deity in my bosom: twenty consciences,
That stand 'twixt me and Milan, candied be they,
And melt, ere they molest! Here lies your brother, 280
No better than the earth he lies upon,
If he were that which now he's like, that's dead;
Whom I, with this obedient steel, three inches of it,
Can lay to bed for ever; whiles you, doing thus,
To the perpetual wink for aye might put
This ancient morsel, this Sir Prudence, who
Should not upbraid our course. For all the rest,
They'll take suggestion as a cat laps milk;
They'll tell the clock[45] to any business that
We say befits the hour.

SEB. Thy case, dear friend, 290
Shall be my precedent; as thou got'st Milan,
I'll come by Naples. Draw thy sword: one stroke
Shall free thee from the tribute which thou payest;
And I the king shall love thee.

ANT. Draw together;
And when T rear my hand, do you the like,
To fall it on Gonzalo.

SEB. O, but one word.
[They talk apart.
Re-enter ARIEL *(invisible)*.

ARI. My master through his art foresees the danger
That you, his friend, are in; and sends me forth,—
For else his project dies,—to keep them living.
[*Sings in* GONZALO'S *ear.*
While you here do snoring lie,
Open-eyed conspiracy
His time doth take.
If of life you keep a care,
Shake off slumber, and beware:
Awake, awake!

ANT. Then let us both be sudden.

GON. Now, good angels
Preserve the king! [They awake.

ALON. Why, how now? ho, awake!—Why are you drawn?
Wherefore this ghastly looking?

GON. What's the matte

SEB. Whiles we stood here securing yo repose, 3
Even now, we heard a hollow burst of bellowi
Like bulls, or rather lions: did't not wake yo
It struck mine ear most terribly.

ALON. I heard nothir

ANT. O, 'twas a din to fright a monste ear,
To make an earthquake! sure, it was the ro
Of a whole herd of lions.

ALON. Heard you this, Gonzal

GON. Upon mine honour, sir, I heard a hu ming,
And that a strange one too, which did awa me:
I shaked you, sir, and cried: as mine ey open'd, 3
I saw their weapons drawn:—there was a noi
That's verily. 'Tis best we stand upon o guard,
Or that we quit this place: let's draw o weapons.

ALON. Lead off this ground; and let make further search
For my poor son.

GON. Heavens keep him from these beast
For he is, sure, i' th' island.

ALON. Lead away.

ARI. Prospero my lord shall know what have done:
So, king, go safely on to seek thy son. [*Exeu*

SCENE II.

Another part of the island.

Enter CALIBAN *with a burden of wood. A no of thunder heard.*

CAL. All the infections that the sun sucks
From bogs, fens, flats, on Prosper fall, a make him
By inch-meal[46] a disease! His spirits hear n
And yet I needs must curse. But they'll n pinch,
Fright me with urchin-shows, pitch me i' t mire,
Nor lead me, like a firebrand, in the dark
Out of my way, unless he bid 'em: but
For every trifle are they set upon me;
Sometime like apes, that mow and chatter me,
And after bite me; then like hedgehogs, whi
Lie tumbling in my barefoot way, and mount
Their pricks at my footfall; sometime am I
All wound with adders, who with cloven tongu
Do hiss me into madness.

44 heel-sore   45 count time (make the hour fit)   46 piece-meal

Enter TRINCULO.

Lo, now, lo!
[he]re comes a spirit of his, and to torment me
[fo]r bringing wood in slowly. I'll fall flat;
[pe]rchance he will not mind me. 17

TRIN. Here's neither bush nor shrub, to bear
[of] any weather at all, and another storm brew-
[in]g; I hear it sing i' the wind: yond same
[bl]ack cloud, yond huge one, looks like a foul
[bo]mbard[47] that would shed his liquor. If it
[sh]ould thunder as it did before, I know not
[wh]ere to hide my head: yond same cloud can-
[no]t choose but fall by pailfuls. What have we
[he]re? a man or a fish? dead or alive? A fish:
[he] smells like a fish; a very ancient and fish-
[li]ke smell; a kind of not of the newest Poor-
[Jo]hn.[48] A strange fish! Were I in England
[no]w, as once I was, and had but this fish
[pa]inted, not a holiday fool there but would give
[a] piece of silver: there would this monster
[m]ake[49] a man; any strange beast there makes
[a] man: when they will not give a doit[50] to re-
[li]eve a lame beggar, they will lay out ten to
[se]e a dead Indian. Legged like a man! and
[hi]s fins like arms! Warm o' my troth! I do
[no]w let loose my opinion; hold it no longer:
[th]is is no fish, but an islander, that hath lately
[su]ffered by a thunderbolt. [*Thunder.*] Alas,
[th]e storm is come again! my best way is to
[cr]eep under his gaberdine;[51] there is no other
[sh]elter hereabout: misery acquaints a man with
[st]range bed-fellows. I will here shroud till the
[dr]egs of the storm be past. 43

[E]nter STEPHANO, *singing: a bottle in his hand.*

STE. I shall no more to sea, to sea,
Here shall I die a-shore—
[T]his is a very scurvy tune to sing at a man's
[f]uneral: well, here's my comfort. [*Drinks.*

Sings.

[T]he master, the swabber, the boatswain and I,
The gunner, and his mate,
[L]oved Moll, Meg, and Marian, and Margery, 50
But none of us cared for Kate;
For she had a tongue with a tang,
Would cry to a sailor, Go hang!
[S]he loved not the savour of tar nor of pitch;—
Then, to sea, boys, and let her go hang!

[T]his is a scurvy tune too: but here's my com-
[f]ort. [*Drinks.*

CAL. Do not torment me:—O! 58

STE. What's the matter? Have we devils
[h]ere? Do you put tricks upon 's with salvages

and men of Ind, ha? I have not escaped drowning, to be afeard now of your four legs; for it
hath been said, As proper a man as ever went
on four legs cannot make him give ground;
and it shall be said so again, while Stephano
breathes at nostrils.

CAL. The spirit torments me:—O!

STE. This is some monster of the isle with
four legs, who hath got, as I take it, an ague.
Where the devil should he learn[52] our language?
I will give him some relief, if it be but for
that. If I can recover him, and keep him tame,
and get to Naples with him, he's a present for
any emperor that ever trod on neat's-leather.

CAL. Do not torment me, prithee; I'll bring
my wood home faster. 75

STE. He's in his fit now, and does not talk
after the wisest. He shall taste of my bottle:
if he have never drunk wine afore, it will go
near to remove his fit. If I can recover him,
and keep him tame, I will not take[53] too much
for him; he shall pay for him that hath him,
and that soundly.

CAL. Thou dost me yet but little hurt; thou
wilt anon, I know it by thy trembling: now
Prosper works upon thee. 84

STE. Come on your ways: open your mouth;
here is that which will give language to you,
cat:[54] open your mouth; this will shake your
shaking, I can tell you, and that soundly: you
cannot tell who's your friend: open your chaps
again.

TRIN. I should know that voice: it should
be—but he is drowned; and these are devils:—
O defend me! 92

STE. Four legs and two voices,—a most delicate monster! His forward voice, now, is to
speak well of his friend; his backward voice
is to utter foul speeches and to detract. If all
the wine in my bottle will recover him, I will
help his ague. Come:—Amen! I will pour
some in thy other mouth.

TRIN. Stephano! 100

STE. Doth thy other mouth call me? Mercy,
mercy! This is a devil, and no monster: I
will leave him; I have no long spoon.[55]

TRIN. Stephano! If thou beest Stephano,
touch me, and speak to me; for I am Trinculo,
—be not afeard,—thy good friend Trinculo.

STE. If thou beest Trinculo, come forth:
I'll pull thee by the lesser legs: if any be
Trinculo's legs, these are they. Thou art very
Trinculo indeed! How camest thou to be the

---

[47] large leathern liquor-vessel
[48] salted hake
[49] Used punningly, "to make the fortune of."
[50] A small Dutch coin.
[51] long cloak
[52] can he have learned
[53] cannot ask
[54] Proverb: "Good liquor will make a cat speak."
[55] Proverb: "He must have a long spoon that would eat with the devil."

siege of this moon-calf[56]? can he vent[57] Trinculos?   111

TRIN. I took him to be killed with a thunder-stroke. But art thou not drowned, Stephano? I hope, now, thou art not drowned. Is the storm overblown? I hid me under the dead moon-calf's gaberdine for fear of the storm. And art thou living, Stephano? O Stephano, two Neapolitans scaped!

STE. Prithee, do not turn me about; my stomach is not constant.

CAL. [*Aside*] These be fine things, an if they
        be not sprites.   ·   121
That's a brave god, and bears celestial liquor:
I will kneel to him.   .   ·

STE. How didst thou scape? How camest thou hither? swear, by this bottle, how thou camest hither. I escaped upon a butt of sack, which the sailors heaved o'erboard, by this bottle! which I made of the bark of a tree with mine own hands, since I was cast ashore.

CAL. I'll swear, upon that bottle, to be thy true subject; for the liquor is not earthly.   130

STE. Here; swear, then, how thou escapedst.

TRIN. Swum ashore, man, like a duck: I can swim like a duck, I'll be sworn.

STE. Here, kiss the book. Though thou canst swim like a duck, thou art made like a goose.

TRIN. O Stephano, hast any more of this?

STE. The whole butt, man: my cellar is in a rock by the sea-side, where my wine is hid. How now, moon-calf! how does thine ague?

CAL. Hast thou not dropp'd from heaven?

STE. Out o' the moon, I do assure thee: I was the man i' the moon when time was.   142

CAL. I have seen thee in her, and I do adore thee: my mistress show'd me thee, and thy dog, and thy bush.

STE. Come, swear to that; kiss the book: I will furnish it anon with new contents: swear.

TRIN. By this good light, this is a very shallow monster! I afeard of him! A very weak monster! The man i' the moon! A most poor credulous monster! Well drawn,[58] monster, in good sooth!   151

CAL. I will show thee every fertile inch o' th' island; and I will kiss thy foot: I prithee, be my god.

TRIN. By this light, a most perfidious and drunken monster! when's god's asleep, he'll rob his bottle.

CAL. I'll kiss thy foot; I'll swear myself thy subject.

STE. Come on, then; down, and swear.

TRIN. I shall laugh myself to death at this

puppy-headed monster. A most scurvy monste... I could find it in my heart to beat him,— 1...

STE. Come, kiss.

TRIN. But that the poor monster's in drin... An abominable monster!

CAL. I'll show thee the best springs; I'
  · pluck thee berries;
I'll fish for thee, and get thee wood enough.
A plague upon the tyrant that I serve!
I'll bear him no more sticks, but follow thee,
Thou wondrous man.

TRIN. A most ridiculous monster, to make wonder of a poor drunkard!   17

CAL. I prithee, let me bring thee whe...
        crabs[59] grow;
And I with my long nails will dig thee pi...
        nuts;[60]
Show thee a jay's nest, and instruct thee how
To snare the nimble marmoset; I'll bring the
To clustering filberts, and sometimes I'll g...
        thee
Young scamels[61] from the rock. Wilt thou g...
        with me?

STE. I prithee now, lead the way, witho... any more talking. Trinculo, the king and a... our company else being drowned, we will i... herit here: here; bear my bottle: fellow Tri... culo, we'll fill him by and by again.   18

CAL. [*sings drunkenly*]
    Farewell, master; farewell, farewell!

TRIN. A howling monster; a drunken mo... ster.

CAL. No more dams I'll make for fish;
          Nor fetch in firing
          At requiring;
      Nor scrape trencher, nor wash dish:
          'Ban, 'Ban, Cacaliban
      Has a new master:—get a new man.
Freedom, hey-day! hey-day, freedom! fre... dom, hey-day, freedom!   19

STE. O brave monster! Lead the way.
                                      [*Exeun...*

ACT III.

SCENE I.

Before Prospero's cell.

Enter FERDINAND, *bearing a log.*

FER. There be some sports are painful, an... their labour
Delight in them sets off:* some kinds of bas... ness[1]

59 crab apples   61 Meaning   unkn 9 w
60 edible roots   (possibly for se
                                   mell, sea-mew).

---

1 menial work
* This sentence yields various meanings, accordi... as "labour" is subject or object, and accor... ing as "sets off" means "heightens" or "o... sets."

---

56 the offscum of this   57 spawn
     monstrosity   58 well drunk, well
                                drained

re nobly undergone, and most poor matters
oint to rich ends. This my mean task
/ould be as heavy to me as odious, but
he mistress which I serve quickens what's
  dead,
nd makes my labours pleasures: O, she is
en times more gentle than her father's
  crabbed,
nd he's composed of harshness. I must remove
ome thousands of these logs, and pile them
  up,   10
'pon a sore injunction:[2] my sweet mistress
/eeps when she sees me work, and says, such
  baseness
[ad never like executor. I forget:
ut these sweet thoughts do even refresh my
  labours,
[ost busy lest,† when I do it.

nter MIRANDA; *and* PROSPERO, *at a distance,*
unseen.

MIR.   Alas, now, pray you,
/ork not so hard: I would the lightning had
urnt up those logs that you are enjoin'd to
  pile!
ray, set it down, and rest you: when this
  burns,
[will weep for having wearied you. My father
s hard at study; pray, now, rest yourself;   20
.e's safe for these three hours.

FER.   O most dear mistress,
he sun will set before I shall discharge
/hat I must strive to do.

MIR.   If you'll sit down,
'll bear your logs the while: pray, give me
  that;
'll carry it to the pile.

FER.   No, precious creature;
had rather crack my sinews, break my back,
han you should such dishonour undergo,
/hile I sit lazy by.

MIR.   It would become me
s well as it does you: and I should do it
/ith much more ease; for my good will is
  to it,   30
nd yours it is against.

PROS.   Poor worm, thou art infected!
his visitation[3] shows it.

MIR.   You look wearily.

FER. No, noble mistress; 'tis fresh morning with me
/hen you are by at night. I do beseech you,—
hiefly that I might set it in my prayers,—
/hat is your name?

MIR.   Miranda.—O my father,

I have broke your hest to say so!

FER.   Admired Miranda!
Indeed the top of admiration! worth
What's dearest to the world! Full many a lady
I have eyed with best regard, and many a
  time   40
The harmony of their tongues hath into bond-
  age
Brought my too diligent ear: for several vir-
  tues
Have I liked several women; never any
With so full soul, but some defect in her
Did quarrel with the noblest grace she owed,
And put it to the foil:[4] but you, O you,
So perfect and so peerless, are created
Of every ceature's best!

MIR.   I do not know
One of my sex; no woman's face remember,
Save, from my glass, mine own; nor have I
  seen   50
More that I may call men than you, good
  friend,
And my dear father: how features are abroad,
I am skilless[5] of; but, by my modesty,
The jewel in my dower, I would not wish
Any companion in the world but you;
Nor can imagination form a shape,
Besides yourself, to like of. But I prattle
Something too wildly, and my father's precepts
I therein do forget.

FER.   I am, in my condition,
A prince, Miranda; I do think, a king;   60
I would, not so!—and would no more endure
This wooden slavery than to suffer
The flesh-fly blow my mouth. Hear my soul
  speak:
The very instant that I saw you, did
My heart fly to your service; there resides,
To make me slave to it; and for your sake
Am I this patient log-man.

MIR.   Do you love me?

FER. O heaven, O earth, bear witness to this
  sound,
And crown what I profess with kind event,[6]
If I speak true! if hollowly, invert   70
What best is boded me to mischief! I,
Beyond all limit of what else i' the world
Do love, prize, honour you.

MIR.   I am a fool
To weep at what I am glad of.

PROS.   Fair encounter
Of two most rare affections! Heavens rain
  grace
On that which breeds between 'em!

FER.   Wherefore weep you?

behest   3 visit
Another very obscure passage. The later Folios
  read *least*, Theobald conjectures *busyless*, Holt
  busiest

4 disadvantage   6 outcome
5 ignorant

MIR. At mine unworthiness, that dare not
    offer
What I desire to give; and much less take
What I shall die to want.[7] But this is trifling;
And all the more it seeks to hide itself,   80
The bigger bulk it shows. Hence, bashful cun-
    ning!
And prompt me, plain and holy innocence!
I am your wife, if you will marry me;
If not, I 'll die your maid: to be your fellow
You may deny me; but I 'll be your servant,
Whether you will or no.
    FER.   My mistress, dearest;
And I thus humble ever.
    MIR.   My husband, then?
    FER. Ay, with a heart as willing
As bondage e'er of freedom: here 's my hand.
    MIR. And mine, with my heart in 't: and
    now farewell
Till half an hour hence.
    FER.   A thousand thousand! 91
           [*Exeunt* FER. *and* MIR. *severally.*
PROS. So glad of this as they I cannot be,
Who are surprised withal; but my rejoicing
At nothing can be more. I 'll to my book;
For yet, ere supper-time, must I perform
Much business appertaining.   [*Exit.*

SCENE II.

Another part of the Island.

Enter CALIBAN, STEPHANO, *and* TRINCULO.

STE. Tell not me;—when the butt is out, we
will drink water; not a drop before: therefore
bear up, and board 'em.[8] Servant-monster,
drink to me.

TRIN. Servant-monster! the folly of this
island! They say there 's but five upon this
isle: we are three of them; if th' other two
be brained like us, the state totters.

STE. Drink, servant-monster, when I bid
thee: thy eyes are almost set[9] in thy head. 10

TRIN. Where should they be set else? he
were a brave monster indeed, if they were set
in his tail.

STE. My man-monster hath drowned his
tongue in sack: for my part, the sea cannot
drown me; I swam, ere I could recover the
shore, five-and-thirty leagues off and on. By
this light, thou shalt be my lieutenant, monster,
or my standard.[10]

TRIN. Your lieutenant, if you list; he 's no
standard.   20

STE. We 'll not run, Monsieur Monster.

TRIN. Nor go neither; but you 'll lie, li
dogs, and yet say nothing neither.

STE. Moon-calf, speak once in thy life,
thou beest a good moon-calf.

CAL. How does thy honour? Let me lick th
shoe. I 'll not serve him, he is not valiant.

TRIN. Thou liest, most ignorant monster:
am in case to justle[11] a constable. Why, tho
deboshed[12] fish, thou, was there ever man
coward that hath drunk so much sack as
to-day? Wilt thou tell a monstrous lie, bei
but half a fish and half a monster?

CAL. Lo, how he mocks me! wilt thou l
him, my lord?

TRIN. 'Lord,' quoth he! That a monst
should be such a natural![13]

CAL. Lo, lo, again! bite him to death,
prithee.

STE. Trinculo, keep a good tongue in yo
head: if you prove a mutineer,—the next tre
The poor monster 's my subject, and he sha
not suffer indignity.   4

CAL. I thank my noble lord. Wilt thou b
pleased to hearken once again to the suit
made to thee?

STE. Marry, will I: kneel and repeat it;
will stand, and so shall Trinculo.

Enter ARIEL *(invisible)*

CAL. As I told thee before, I am subject t
a tyrant, a sorcerer, that by his cunning hat
cheated me of the island.

ARI. Thou liest.

CAL. Thou liest, thou jesting monkey, thou
I would my valiant master would destroy thee
I do not lie.

STE. Trinculo, if you trouble him any mor
in 's tale, by this hand, I will supplant some o
your teeth.

TRIN. Why, I said nothing.

STE. Mum, then, and no more. Proceed.

CAL. I say, by sorcery he got this isle; 6
From me he got it. If thy greatness will
Revenge it on him,—for I know thou darest,
But this thing dare not,—

STE. That 's most certain.

CAL. Thou shalt be lord of it, and I 'll serv
thee.

STE. How now shall this be compassed
Canst thou bring me to the party?

CAL. Yea, yea, my lord: I 'll yield him the
    asleep,
Where thou mayst knock a nail into his head.

ARI. Thou liest; thou canst not. 7

CAL. What a pied ninny 's[14] this! Tho
    scurvy patch![15]

---

7 lack
8 sail up and attack
    them (the cups)
9 fixed
10 standard-bearer
11 in trim to jostle
12 debauched
13 simpleton
14 motley-coated fool
15 fool

do beseech thy greatness, give him blows,
And take his bottle from him: when that's
  gone,
He shall drink nought but brine; for I'll not
  show him
Where the quick freshes are.

STE. Trinculo, run into no further danger:
interrupt the monster one word further, and,
by this hand, I'll turn my mercy out o' doors,
and make a stock-fish[16] of thee.

TRIN. Why, what did I? I did nothing. I'll
  go farther off. 81

STE. Didst thou not say he lied?

ARI. Thou liest.

STE. Do I so? take thou that. [Beats him.]
As you like this, give me the lie another time.

TRIN. I did not give the lie. Out o' your
wits, and hearing too? A pox o' your bottle!
this can sack and drinking do. A murrain on
your monster, and the devil take your fingers!

CAL. Ha, ha, ha! 90

STE. Now, forward with your tale.—Prithee,
stand farther off.

CAL. Beat him enough: after a little time,
I'll beat him too.

STE. Stand farther.—Come, proceed.

CAL. Why, as I told thee, 'tis a custom with
  him
' th' afternoon to sleep: there thou mayst
  brain him,
Having first seized his books; or with a log
Batter his skull, or paunch him with a stake,
Or cut his wezand[17] with thy knife. Remember
First to possess his books; for without them
He's but a sot, as I am, nor hath not 101
One spirit to command: they all do hate him
As rootedly as I. Burn but his books.
He has brave utensils,—for so he calls them,—
Which, when he has a house, he'll deck withal.
And that[18] most deeply to consider is
The beauty of his daughter; he himself
Calls her a nonpareil: I never saw a woman,
But only Sycorax my dam and she;
But she as far surpasseth Sycorax 110
As great'st does least.

STE.   Is it so brave a lass?

CAL. Ay, lord; she will become thy bed, I
  warrant,
And bring thee forth brave brood.

STE. Monster, I will kill this man: his
daughter and I will be king and queen,—save
our graces!—and Trinculo and thyself shall be
viceroys. Dost thou like the plot, Trinculo?

TRIN. Excellent.

STE. Give me thy hand: I am sorry I

beat thee; but, while thou livest, keep a good
tongue in thy head. 121

CAL. Within this half hour will he be
  asleep:
Wilt thou destroy him then?

STE.   Ay, on mine honour.

ARI. This will I tell my master.

CAL. Thou makest me merry; I am full of
  pleasure:
Let us be jocund; will you troll the catch[19]
You taught me but while-ere?

STE. At thy request, monster, I will do reason, any reason.—Come on, Trinculo, let us
sing. [Sings.
    Flout 'em and scout 'em, 130
      And scout 'em and flout 'em;
        Thought is free.

CAL. That's not the tune.
    [ARIEL plays the tune on a tabor and pipe.

STE. What is this same?

TRIN. This is the tune of our catch, played
by the picture of Nobody.[20]

STE. If thou beest a man, show thyself in
thy likeness: if thou beest a devil, take 't as
thou list.

TRIN. O, forgive me my sins!

STE. He that dies pays all debts: I defy
  thee. Mercy upon us! 141

CAL. Art thou afeard?

STE. No, monster, not I.

CAL. Be not afeard; the isle is full of
  noises,
Sounds and sweet airs, that give delight, and
  hurt not.
Sometimes a thousand twangling instruments
Will hum about mine ears; and sometime voices,
That, if I then had waked after long sleep,
Will make me sleep again: and then, in dream-
  ing,
The clouds methought would open, and show
  riches
Ready to drop upon me; that, when I waked,
I cried to dream again. 152

STE. This will prove a brave kingdom to
  me, where
I shall have my music for nothing.

CAL. When Prospero is destroyed.

STE. That shall be by and by: I remember
the story.

TRIN. The sound is going away; let's follow it, and after do our work.

STE. Lead, monster; we'll follow. I would
I could see this taborer; he lays it on. 160

TRIN. Wilt come? I'll follow, Stephano.
    [Exeunt.

---

16 dried cod (which is
    beaten before
    boiled)
17 wind-pipe
18 that which
19 part-song
20 Alluding to a print
    (of merely head,
    legs, and arms)
    prefixed to an old
    comedy.

SCENE III.

Another part of the island.

Enter ALONSO, SEBASTIAN, ANTONIO, GONZALO, ADRIAN, FRANCISCO, *and others.*

GON. By 'r lakin,[21] I can go no further, sir;
My old bones ache: here's a maze trod, indeed,
Through forth-rights and meanders! By your patience,
I needs must rest me.
ALON.   Old lord, I cannot blame thee,
Who am myself attach'd[22] with weariness,
To the dulling of my spirits: sit down, and rest.
Even here I will put off my hope, and keep it
No longer for[23] my flatterer: he is drown'd
Whom thus we stray to find; and the sea mocks   9
Our frustrate search on land. Well, let him go.
ANT. [*Aside to* SEB.] I am right glad that he's so out of hope.
Do not, for one repulse, forego the purpose
That you resolved to effect.
SEB. [*Aside to* ANT.] The next advantage
Will we take thoroughly.
ANT. [*Aside to* SEB.] Let it be to-night;
For, now they are oppress'd with travel, they
Will not, nor cannot, use such vigilance
As when they are fresh.
SEB. [*Aside to* ANT.] I say, to-night: no more.   [*Solemn and strange music.*
ALON. What harmony is this?—My good friends, hark!
GON. Marvellous sweet music!

Enter PROSPERO *above (invisible). Enter several strange* SHAPES, *bringing in a banquet: they dance about it with gentle actions of salutations; and, inviting the King, etc., to eat, they depart.*

ALON. Give us kind keepers, heavens!—What were these?
SEB. A living drollery.[24] Now I will believe   21
That there are unicorns; that in Arabia
There is one tree, the phœnix' throne; one phœnix
At this hour reigning there.
ANT.   I'll believe both;
And what does else want credit,[25] come to me,
And I'll be sworn 'tis true: travellers ne'er did lie,
Though fools at home condemn 'em.

GON.   If in Naple
I should report this now, would they believ me?
If I should say, I saw such islanders,—
For, certes, these are people of the island,— 3
Who, though they are of monstrous shape, yet note,
Their manners are more gentle-kind than of
Our human generation you shall find
Many, nay, almost any.
PROS.   [*Aside*] Honest lord,
Thou has said well; for some of you there present
Are worse than devils.
ALON.   I cannot too much muse[2]
Such shapes, such gesture, and such sound, ex pressing—
Although they want the use of tongue—a kind
Of excellent dumb discourse.
PROS.   [*Aside*.] Praise in departing.[27]
FRAN. They vanish'd strangely.
SEB.   No matter, since 4
They have left their viands behind; for we have stomachs.—
Will 't please you taste of what is here?
ALON.   Not I
GON. Faith, sir, you need not fear. Wher we were boys,
Who would believe that there were mountain eers
Dew-lapp'd like bulls, whose throats had hang ing at 'em
Wallets of flesh? or that there were such men
Whose heads stood in their breasts? which now we find
Each putter-out of five for one* will bring us
Good warrant of.
ALON.   I will stand to, and feed,
Although my last: no matter, since I feel   5(
The best is past. Brother, my lord the duke,
Stand to, and do as we.
Thunder and lightning. Enter ARIEL, *like a harpy; claps his wings upon the table, and, with a quaint device, the banquet van ishes.*

ARI. You are three men of sin, whom Des tiny,—
That hath to[28] instrument this lower world
And what is in 't,—the never-surfeited sea
Hath caused to belch up you; and on this island,
Where man doth not inhabit,—you 'mongst men
[26] wonder at
[27] Proverb: "Save your praises till you go."
[28] for

---

21 ladykin (little lady, the Virgin Mary)
22 attacked
23 as

24 puppet show
25 whatever else is in credible

* Referring to travellers going on a perilous jour ney, who sometimes made over their property on condition that if they returned safe it should be restored to them two, three, or even five fold.

eing most unfit to live. I have made you mad;
nd even with such-like valour men hang and
  drown
heir proper selves.

> [ALON., SEB., *etc., draw their swords.*
>   You fools! I and my fellows 60
re ministers of Fate: the elements,
f whom your swords are temper'd, may as
  well
Vound the loud winds, or with bemock'd-at
  stabs
Kill the still-closing waters, as diminish
ne dowle29 that's in my plume: my fellow-
  ministers
re like invulnerable. If you could hurt,
our swords are now too massy for your
  strengths,
nd will not be uplifted. But remember,—
'or that's my business to you,—that you three
rom Milan did supplant good Prospero;   70
xposed unto the sea, which hath requit it,
Iim and his innocent child: for which foul
  deed
he powers, delaying, not forgetting, have
ncensed the seas and shores, yea, all the creatures,
Against your peace. Thee of thy son, Alonso,
hey have bereft; and do pronounce by me:
Lingering perdition—worse than any death
Can be at once—shall step by step attend
You and your ways; whose wraths to guard
  you from,—
Vhich here, in this most desolate isle, else
  falls   80
Upon your heads,—is nothing but30 heart-sor-
  row
And a clear life ensuing.

*He vanishes in thunder; then, to soft music,
  enter the* SHAPES *again and dance, with
  mocks and mows, and carrying out the
  table.*

PROS. Bravely the figure of this harpy hast
  thou
Perform'd, my Ariel; a grace it had, devour-
  ing:
Of my instruction hast thou nothing bated
In what thou hadst to say: so, with good life
And observation strange,31 my meaner minis-
  ters
Their several kinds32 have done. My high
  charms work,
And these mine enemies are all knit up
In their distractions: they now are in my
  power;   90
And in these fits I leave them, while I visit

Young Ferdinand,—whom33 they suppose is
  drown'd,—
And his and mine loved darling. [*Exit above.*
GON. I' the name of something holy, sir,
  why stand you
In this strange stare?
ALON.   O, it is monstrous, monstrous!
Methought the billows spoke, and told me of it;
The winds did sing it to me; and the thunder,
That deep and dreadful organ-pipe, pronounced
The name of Prosper: it did bass my trespass.
Therefore my son i' th' ooze is bedded; and 100
I'll seek him deeper than e'er plummet sounded,
And with him there lie mudded.   [*Exit.*
SEB.   But one fiend at a time,
I'll fight their legions o'er.
ANT.   I'll be thy second.
              [*Exeunt* SEB. *and* ANT.
GON. All three of them are desperate: their
  great guilt,
Like poison given to work a great time after,
Now 'gins to bite the spirits. I do beseech you,
That are of suppler joints, follow them swiftly,
And hinder them from what this ecstasy34
May now provoke them to.
ADR.   Follow, I pray you. [*Exeunt.*

ACT IV.

SCENE I.

Before Prospero's cell.

Enter PROSPERO, FERDINAND *and* MIRANDA.

PROS. If I have too austerely punish'd you,
Your compensation makes amends; for I
Have given you here a third1 of mine own life,
Or that for which I live; who once again
I tender to thy hand: all thy vexations
Were but my trials of thy love, and thou
Hast strangely stood the test: here, afore
  Heaven,
I ratify this my rich gift. O Ferdinand,
Do not smile at me that I boast her off,
For thou shalt find she will outstrip all praise 10
And make it halt behind her.
FER.   I do believe it2
Against an oracle.
PROS. Then, as my gift, and thine own ac-
  quisition
Worthily purchased, take my daughter: but
If thou dost break her virgin-knot3 before

33 For "who."   34 madness

1 Commonly taken to mean that he himself and
   his dukedom (or his wife) are the two other
   thirds; but some editors read *thread.*
2 Supply "and should."   3 girdle worn as mark
                              of maidenhood

29 filament of down   31 rare observance
30 nothing will avail but   32 appropriate functions

All sanctimonious ceremonies may
With full and holy rite be minister'd,
No sweet aspersion³ shall the heavens let fall
To make this contract grow; but barren hate,
Sour-eyed disdain and discord shall bestrew 20
The union of your bed with weeds so loathly
That you shall hate it both: therefore take heed,
As Hymen's lamps shall light you.⁴
FER. As I hope
For quiet days, fair issue and long life,
With such love as 'tis now, the murkiest den,
The most opportune place, the strong'st suggestion
Our worser genius can, shall never melt
Mine honour into lust, to take away
The edge of that day's celebration
When I shall think, or⁵ Phœbus' steeds are founder'd,
Or Night kept chain'd below.
PROS. Fairly spoke. 31
Sit, then, and talk with her; she is thine own.
What, Ariel! my industrious servant, Ariel!
Enter ARIEL.
ARI. What would my potent master? here I am.
PROS. Thou and thy meaner fellows your last service
Did worthily perform; and I must use you
In such another trick. Go bring the rabble,
O'er whom I give thee power, here to this place:
Incite them to quick motion; for I must
Bestow upon the eyes of this young couple 40
Some vanity⁶ of mine art: it is my promise,
And they expect it from me.
ARI. Presently?⁷
PROS. Ay, with a twink.
ARI. Before you can say 'come,' and 'go,'
And breathe twice, and cry, 'so, so,'
Each one, tripping on his toe,
Will be here with mop⁸ and mow.
Do you love me, master? no?
PROS. Dearly, my delicate Ariel. Do not approach
Till thou dost hear me call.
ARI. Well, I conceive. [*Exit.* 50
PROS. Look thou be true; do not give dalliance
Too much the rein: the strongest oaths are straw
To the fire i' the blood: be more abstemious,
Or else, good night your vow!

FER. I warrant you, sir
The white cold virgin snow upon my heart
Abates the ardour of my liver.⁹
PROS. Well.
Now come, my Ariel! bring a corollary,¹⁰
Rather than want a spirit: appear, and pertly!¹¹
No tongue! all eyes! be silent. [*Soft music*
Enter IRIS.
IRIS. Ceres, most bounteous lady, thy ric˹
leas
Of wheat, rye, barley, vetches, oats, and pease
Thy turfy mountains, where live nibbling sheep
And flat meads thatch'd with stover,¹² them t
keep;
Thy banks with pioned and twilled¹³ brims,
Which spongy April at thy hest betrims,
To make cold nymphs chaste crowns; and th
broom-groves,
Whose shadow the dismissed bachelor loves,
Being lass-lorn; thy pole-clipt¹⁴ vineyard;
And thy sea-marge, sterile and rocky-hard,
Where thou thyself dost air;—the queen o
the sky,¹⁵
Whose watery arch and messenger am I, 7
Bids thee leave these; and with her sovereig
grace,
Here, on this grass-plot, in this very place,
To come and sport:—her peacocks fly amain
Approach, rich Ceres, her to entertain.
Enter CERES.
CER. Hail, many-colour'd messenger, tha
ne'er
Dost disobey the wife of Jupiter;
Who, with thy saffron wings, upon my flower
Diffusest honey-drops, refreshing showers; 7
And with each end of thy blue bow dost crow
My bosky¹⁶ acres and my unshrubb'd down,¹
Rich scarf to my proud earth;—why hath th
queen
Summon'd me hither, to this short-grass'
green?
IRIS. A contract of true love to celebrate;
And some donation freely to estate¹⁸
On the blest lovers.
CER. Tell me, heavenly bow,
If Venus or her son, as thou dost know,
Do now attend the queen? Since they did pio
The means that dusky Dis¹⁹ my daughter got,
Her and her blind boy's scandal'd company
I have forsworn.
IRIS. Of her society

---

3 sprinkling
4 as you hope to be blessed by the god of marriage
5 either
6 illusion
7 at once
8 grimace (about the same as "mow")
9 Then regarded as the seat of passion.
10 surplusage
11 nimbly
12 coarse hay
13 peonied and reedy (?)
14 pole-entwined
15 Juno
16 woody
17 cleared slopes
18 bestow
19 Pluto (who carrie˻ off Proserpina)

Be not afraid: I met her deity
Cutting the clouds towards Paphos, and her son
Dove-drawn with her. Here thought they to
    have done
Some wanton charm upon this man and maid,
Whose vows are, that no bed-right shall be paid
Till Hymen's torch be lighted: but in vain;
Mar's hot minion[20] is return'd again;
Her waspish-headed son has broke his arrows,   99
Swears he will shoot no more, but play with
    sparrows,
And be a boy right out.
    CER.   High'st queen of state,
Great Juno, comes; I know her by her gait.
            Enter JUNO.
    JUNO. How does my bounteous sister? Go
    with me
To bless this twain, that they may prosperous be,
And honour'd in their issue.   [*They sing:*
    JUNO. Honour, riches, marriage-blessing,
        Long continuance, and increasing,
        Hourly joys be still upon you!
        Juno sings her blessings on you.

    CER. Earth's increase, foison[21] plenty,   110
        Barns and garners never empty;
        Vines with clustering bunches growing;
        Plants with goodly burthen bowing;
        Spring come to you at the farthest
        In the very end of harvest!
        Scarcity and want shall shun you;
        Ceres' blessing so is on you.

    FER. This is a most majestic vision, and
Harmonious charmingly. May I be bold
To think these spirits?
    PROS.   Spirits, which by mine art   120
I have from their confines call'd to enact
My present fancies.
    FER.   Let me live here ever;
So rare a wonder'd father and a wise
Makes this place Paradise.
        [JUNO *and* CERES *whisper, and send*
                    IRIS *on employment.*
    PROS.   Sweet, now, silence!
Juno and Ceres whisper seriously;
There's something else to do: hush, and be
    mute,
Or else our spell is marr'd.
    IRIS. You nymphs, call'd Naiads, of the
    winding brooks,
With your sedged crowns and ever-harmless
    looks,
Leave your crisp[22] channels, and on this green
    land   130
Answer your summons; Juno does command:

Come, temperate nymphs, and help to celebrate
A contract of true love; be not too late.
            Enter certain NYMPHS.
You sunburn'd sicklemen, of August weary,
Come hither from the furrow, and be merry:
Make holiday; your rye-straw hats put on,
And these fresh nymphs encounter every one
In country footing.[23]

Enter certain REAPERS, *properly habited: they
    join with the* NYMPHS *in a graceful dance;
    towards the end whereof* PROSPERO *starts
    suddenly, and speaks; after which, to a
    strange, hollow, and confused noise, they
    heavily vanish.*

    PROS. [*Aside*] I had forgot that foul con-
        spiracy
Of the beast Caliban and his confederates   140
Against my life: the minute of their plot
Is almost come. [*To the* SPIRITS.] Well done!
    avoid;[24] no more!
    FER. This is strange: your father's in some
        passion
That works him strongly.
    MIR.   Never till this day
Saw I him touch'd with anger so distemper'd.
    PROS. You do look, my son, in a moved sort.
As if you were dismay'd: be cheerful, sir.
Our revels now are ended. These our actors,
As I foretold you, were all spirits, and
Are melted into air, into thin air: 150
And, like the baseless fabric of this vision,
The cloud-capp'd towers, the gorgeous palaces,
The solemn temples, the great globe itself,
Yea, all which it inherit, shall dissolve,
And, like this insubstantial pageant faded,
Leave not a rack[25] behind. We are such stuff
As dreams are made on;[26] and our little life
Is rounded with a sleep. Sir, I am vex'd;
Bear with my weakness; my old brain is
    troubled:
Be not disturbed with my infirmity: 160
If you be pleased, retire into my cell,
And there repose: a turn or two I'll walk,
To still my beating mind.
    FER. MIR.   We wish you peace. [*Exeunt.*
    PROS. Come with a thought.[27] I thank thee,
    Ariel: come.
            Enter ARIEL.
    ARI. Thy thoughts I cleave to. What's thy
        pleasure?
    PROS.   Spirit,
We must prepare to meet with[28] Caliban.
    ARI. Ay, my commander: when I presented
    Ceres,

---

20 darling (Venus)   22 waveleted
21 abundance

23 dancing   26 of
24 depart   27 quick as thought
25 shred of vapor   28 meet, frustrate

I thought to have told thee of it; but I fear'd
Lest I might anger thee.
    PROS. Say again, where didst thou leave
      these varlets?   170
    ARI. I told you, sir, they were red-hot with
      drinking;
So full of valour that they smote the air
For breathing in their faces; beat the ground
For kissing of their feet; yet always bending
Towards their project. Then I beat my tabor;
At which, like unback'd[29] colts, they prick'd
    their ears,
Advanced their eyelids, lifted up their noses
As they smelt music: so I charm'd their ears,
That, calf-like, they my lowing follow'd
    through
Tooth'd briers, sharp furzes, pricking goss,[30]
    and thorns,   180
Which enter'd their frail shins: at last I left
    them
I' the filthy-mantled pool beyond your cell,
There dancing up to the chins, that the foul lake
O'erstunk their feet.
    PROS.   This was well done, my bird.
Thy shape invisible retain thou still:
The trumpery in my house, go bring it hither,
For stale[31] to catch these thieves.
    ARI.   I go, I go. [*Exit.*
    PROS. A devil, a born devil, on whose nature
Nurture can never stick; on whom my pains,
Humanely taken, all, all lost, quite lost;   190
And as with age his body uglier grows,
So his mind cankers. I will plague them all,
Even to roaring.

    Re-enter ARIEL, *loaden with glistering
                apparel, etc.*

          Come, hang them on this line.[32]
    PROSPERO *and* ARIEL *remain, invisible.*

Enter CALIBAN, STEPHANO, *and* TRINCULO, *all
              wet.*
    CAL. Pray you, tread softly, that the blind
mole may not hear a foot fall: we now are near
his cell.
    STE. Monster, your fairy, which you say is a
harmless fairy, has done little better than
played the Jack with us.
    TRIN. Monster, my nose is in great indigna-
tion.   200
    STE. So is mine. Do you hear, monster? If
I should take a displeasure against you, look
you,—
    TRIN. Thou wert but a lost monster.
    CAL. Good my lord, give me thy favour still.
Be patient, for the prize I'll bring thee to

Shall hoodwink[33] ~~this~~ mischance: therefore
    speak softly.
All's hush'd as midnight yet.
    TRIN. Ay, but to lose our bottles in the
pool,—
    STE. There is not only disgrace and dis-
honour in that, monster, but an infinite loss. 210
    TRIN. That's more to me than my wetting:
yet this is your harmless fairy, monster.
    STE. I will fetch off my bottle, though I be
o'er ears for my labour.
    CAL. Prithee, my king, be quiet. See'st thou
here,
This is the mouth o' the cell: no noise, and
    enter.
Do that good mischief which may make this
    island
Thine own for ever, and I, thy Caliban,
For aye thy foot-licker.
    STE. Give me thy hand. I do begin to have
bloody thoughts.   220
    TRIN. O King Stephano! O peer! O worthy
Stephano! look what a wardrobe here is for
thee!
    CAL. Let it alone, thou fool; it is but trash.
    TRIN. O, ho, monster! we know what be-
longs to a frippery.[34] O King Stephano!
    STE. Put off that gown, Trinculo; by this
hand, I'll have that gown.
    TRIN. Thy grace shall have it.
    CAL. The dropsy drown this fool! what do
    you mean   230
To dote thus on such luggage? Let's alone,[35]
And do the murder first: if he awake,
From toe to crown he'll fill our skins with
    pinches,
Make us strange stuff.
    STE. Be you quiet, monster. Mistress line,
is not this my jerkin? Now is the jerkin
under the line: now, jerkin, you are like to
lose your hair, and prove a bald jerkin.*
    TRIN. Do, do: we steal by line and level,[36]
an 't like your grace.   240
    STE. I thank thee for that jest; here's a
garment for 't: wit shall not go unrewarded
while I am king of this country. 'Steal by
line and level' is an excellent pass of pate;[37]
there's another garment for 't.
    TRIN. Monster, come, put some lime[38] upon
your fingers, and away with the rest.

33 blind you to   editors,   "let's
34 old-clothes shop   alone.")
35 Supply "go;" (*alone*   36 by rule
    may be an error for   37 thrust of wit
    along; or read, with   38 bird-lime
    Rowe and other
* Perhaps alluding to the frequent loss of hair
    from fevers contracted in crossing the line,
    or equator.

29 unridden   31 decoy
30 gorse   32 lime-tree, linden

CAL. I will have none on 't: we shall lose
our time.
And all be turn'd to barnacles, or to apes
With foreheads villanous low.   250
STE. Monster, lay-to your fingers: help to
bear this away where my hogshead of wine is,
or I'll turn you out of my kingdom: go to,
carry this.
TRIN. And this.
STE. Ay, and this.
[nois. of hunters heard. Enter divers SPIRITS,
in shape of dogs and hounds, hunting them
about; PROSPERO and ARIEL setting them
on.
PROS. Hey, Mountain, hey!
AR. Silver! there it goes, Silver!
PROS. Fury, Fury! there, Tyrant, there!
hark, hark!
[CAL., STE., and TRIN. are driven out.
Go charge my goblins that they grind their
joints
With dry convulsions; shorten up their sinews
With aged cramps; and more pinch-spotted
make them   261
Than pard or cat o' mountain.
ARI.   Hark, they roar!
PROS. Let them be hunted soundly. At this
hour
Lie at my mercy all mine enemies:
Shortly shall all my labours end, and thou
Shalt have the air at freedom: for a little
Follow, and do me service.   [Exeunt.

ACT V.
SCENE I.
Before the cell of Prospero.

Enter PROSPERO in his magic robes, and ARIEL.

PROS. Now does my project gather to a head:
My charms crack[1] not; my spirits obey; and
time
Goes upright with his carriage.[2] How's the
day?
ARI. On the sixth hour; at which time, my
lord,
You said our work should cease.
PROS.   I did say so,
When first I raised the tempest. Say, my
spirit,
How fares the king and 's followers?
ARI.   Confined together
In the same fashion as you gave in charge,
Just as you left them; all prisoners, sir,
In the line-grove which weather-fends your cell;
They cannot budge till your release. The king, 11

His brother, and yours, abide all three dis-
tracted,
And the remainder mourning over them,
Brimful of sorrow and dismay; but chiefly
Him that you term'd, sir, 'The good old lord,
Gonzalo';
His tears run down his beard, like winter's
drops
From eaves of reeds. Your charm so strongly
works 'em,
That if you now beheld them, your affections
Would become tender.
PROS.   Dost thou think so, spirit?
ARI. Mine would, sir, were I human.
PROS.   And mine shall. 20
Hast thou, which art but air, a touch, a feeling
Of their afflictions, and shall not myself,
One of their kind, that relish all as sharply,[3]
Passion[4] as they, be kindlier moved than thou
art?
Though with their high wrongs[5] I am struck to
the quick,
Yet with my nobler reason 'gainst my fury
Do I take part: the rarer action is
In virtue than in vengeance: they being peni-
tent,
The sole drift of my purpose doth extend
Not a frown further. Go release them, Ariel: 30
My charms I'll break, their senses I'll restore,
And they shall be themselves.
ARI.   I'll fetch them, sir. [Exit.
PROS. Ye elves of hills, brooks, standing
lakes, and groves;
And ye that on the sands with printless foot
Do chase the ebbing Neptune, and do fly him
When he comes back; you demi-puppets that
By moonshine do the green sour ringlets[6] make,
Whereof the ewe not bites; and you whose
pastime
Is to make midnight mushrooms, that rejoice
To hear the solemn curfew; by whose aid—   40
Weak masters though ye be—I have bedimm'd
The noontide sun, call'd forth the mutinous
winds,
And 'twixt the green sea and the azured vault
Set roaring war: to the dread rattling thunder
Have I given fire, and rifted Jove's stout oak
With his own bolt; the strong-based promon-
tory
Have I made shake, and by the spurs pluck'd up
The pine and cedar: graves at my command
Have waked their sleepers, oped, and let 'em
forth
By my so potent art. But this rough magic 50
I here abjure; and, when I have required

---

1 break, fail   2 carries all through well
3 feel quite as keenly   6 of grass ("fairy rings")
4 have passions
5 crimes

Some heavenly music,—which even now I do,—
To work mine end upon their senses, that
This airy charm is for, I'll break my staff,
Bury it certain fathoms in the earth,
And deeper than did ever plummet sound
I'll drown my book.   [*Solemn music.*

Re-enter ARIEL *before: then* ALONSO, *with a frantic gesture, attended by* GONZALO; SEBASTIAN *and* ANTONIO *in like manner, attended by* ADRIAN *and* FRANCISCO: *they all enter the circle which* PROSPERO *had made, and there stand charmed; which* PROSPERO *observing, speaks:*

A solemn air, and the best comforter
To an unsettled fancy, cure thy brains,
Now useless, boil'd within thy skull! There stand,
For you are spell-stopp'd.   61
Holy Gonzalo, honourable man,
Mine eyes, even sociable to[7] the show of thine,
Fall fellowly drops. The charm dissolves apace;
And as the morning steals upon the night
Melting the darkness, so their rising senses
Begin to chase the ignorant fumes that mantle
Their clearer reason. O good Gonzalo,
My true preserver, and a loyal sir   69
To him thou follow'st! I will pay thy graces
Home[8] both in word and deed. Most cruelly
Didst thou, Alonso, use me and my daughter:
Thy brother was a furtherer in the act.
Thou art pinch'd for 't now, Sebastian. Flesh and blood,
You, brother mine, that entertain'd ambition,
Expell'd remorse and nature; who, with Sebastian,—
Whose inward pinches therefore are most strong,—
Would here have kill'd your king; I do forgive thee,
Unnatural though thou art. Their understanding
Begins to swell; and the approaching tide   80
Will shortly fill the reasonable shore,[9]
That now lies foul and muddy. Not one of them
That yet looks on me, or would know me:
Ariel,
Fetch me the hat and rapier in my cell:
I will discase me, and myself present
As I was sometime Milan: quickly, spirit;
Thou shalt ere long be free.

ARIEL *sings and helps to attire him.*

Where the bee sucks, there suck I:
In a cowslip's bell I lie;

There I couch when owls do cry.   90
On the bat's back I do fly
After summer merrily.
Merrily, merrily shall I live now
Under the blossom that hangs on the bough.

PROS. Why, that's my dainty Ariel! I shall miss thee;
But yet thou shalt have freedom: so, so, so.
To the king's ship, invisible as thou art:
There shalt thou find the mariners asleep
Under the hatches; the master and the boatswain
Being awake, enforce them to this place,   100
And presently, I prithee.
ARI. I drink the air before me, and return
Or ere your pulse twice beat.   [*Exit.*
GON. All torment, trouble, wonder and amazement
Inhabits here: some heavenly power guide us
Out of this fearful country!
PROS.   Behold, sir king,
The wronged Duke of Milan, Prospero:
For more assurance that a living prince
Does now speak to thee, I embrace thy body;
And to thee and thy company I bid   110
A hearty welcome.
ALON.   Whether thou be'st he or no,
Or some enchanted trifle to abuse[10] me,
As late I have been, I not know: thy pulse
Beats, as of flesh and blood; and, since I saw thee,
The affliction of my mind amends, with which,
I fear, a madness held me: this must crave—
An if this be at all—a most strange story.
Thy dukedom I resign, and do entreat
Thou pardon me my wrongs.—But how should Prospero
Be living and be here?
PROS.   First, noble friend,   120
Let me embrace thine age, whose honour cannot
Be measured or confined.
GON.   Whether this be
Or be not, I'll not swear.
PROS.   You do yet taste
Some subtilties[11] o' the isle, that will not let you
Believe things certain. Welcome, my friends all!
[*Aside to* SEB. *and* ANT.] But you, my brace of lords, were I so minded,
I here could pluck his highness' frown upon you,
And justify[12] you traitors: at this time
I will tell no tales.
SEB.   [*Aside*] The devil speaks in him.
PROS.   No.

For you, most wicked sir, whom to call brother
Would even infect my mouth, I do forgive 131
Thy rankest fault,—all of them; and require
My dukedom of thee, which perforce, I know,
Thou must restore.

ALON.   If thou be'st Prospero,
Give us particulars of thy preservation;
How thou hast met us here, who three hours
    since
Were wreck'd upon this shore; where I have
    lost—
How sharp the point of this remembrance is!—
My dear son Ferdinand.

PROS.   I am woe for 't, sir.

ALON. Irreparable is the loss; and patience
Says it is past her cure.

PROS.   I rather think 141
You have not sought her help, of whose soft
    grace
For the like loss I have her sovereign aid,
And rest myself content.

ALON.   You the like loss!

PROS. As great to me as late; and, sup-
    portable
To make the dear loss, have I means much
    weaker
Than you may call to comfort you, for I
Have lost my daughter.

ALON.   A daughter?
O heavens, that they were living both in Naples,
The king and queen there! that they were, I
    wish
Myself were mudded in that oozy bed 151
Where my son lies. When did you lose your
    daughter?

PROS. In this last tempest. I perceive, these
    lords
At this encounter do so much admire,[13]
That they devour their reason, and scarce think
Their eyes do offices of truth, their words
Are natural breath: but, howsoe'er you have
Been justled from your senses, know for certain
That I am Prospero, and that very duke
Which was thrust forth of Milan; who most
    strangely 160
Upon this shore, where you were wreck'd, was
    landed.
To be the lord on 't. No more yet of this;
For 'tis a chronicle of day by day,
Not a relation for a breakfast, nor
Befitting this first meeting. Welcome, sir;
This cell's my court: here have I few
    attendants,
And subjects none abroad: pray you, look in.
My dukedom since you have given me again,
I will requite you with as good a thing;

At least bring forth a wonder, to content ye 170
As much as me my dukedom.

Here PROSPERO *discovers* FERDINAND *and*
    MIRANDA *playing at chess.*

MIR. Sweet lord, you play me false.

FER.   No, my dear'st love,
I would not for the world.

MIR. Yes,[14] for a score of kingdoms you
    should[15] wrangle,
And I would call it fair play.

ALON.   If this prove
A vision of the island, one dear son
Shall I twice lose.

SEB.   A most high miracle!

FER. Though the seas threaten, they are
    merciful;
I have cursed them without cause.   [*Kneels.*

ALON.   Now all the blessings
Of a glad father compass thee about! 180
Arise, and say how thou camest here.

MIR.   O, wonder!
How many goodly creatures are there here!
How beauteous mankind is! O brave new
    world,
That has such people in 't!

PROS.   'Tis new to thee.

ALON. What is this maid with whom thou
    wast at play?
Your eld'st acquaintance cannot be three hours:
Is she the goddess that hath sever'd us,
And brought us thus together?

FER.   Sir, she is mortal;
But by immortal Providence she's mine:
I chose her when I could not ask my father 190
For his advice, nor thought I had one. She
Is daughter to this famous Duke of Milan,
Of whom so often I have heard renown,
But never saw before; of whom I have
Received a second life; and second father
This lady makes him to me.

ALON.   I am hers:
But, O, how oddly will it sound that I
Must ask my child forgiveness!

PROS.   There, sir, stop:
Let us not burthen our remembrances with
A heaviness that's gone.

GON.   I have inly wept, 200
Or should have spoke ere this. Look down,
    you gods,
And on this couple drop a blessed crown!
For it is you that have chalk'd forth the way
Which brought us hither.

ALON.   I say, Amen, Gonzalo!

GON. Was Milan thrust from Milan, that his
    issue

---

14 Supply   "but   what   15 might
             then?"

Should become kings of Naples? O, rejoice
Beyond a common joy! and set it down
With gold on lasting pillars: In one voyage
Did Claribel her husband find at Tunis,
And Ferdinand, her brother, found a wife   210
Where he himself was lost, Prospero his duke-
dom
In a poor isle, and all of us ourselves
When no man was his own.

    ALON.   [*To* FER. *and* MIR.] Give me your
hands:
Let grief and sorrow still embrace his heart
That doth not wish you joy!

    GON.   Be it so! Amen!
Re-enter ARIEL *with the* MASTER *and*
    BOATSWAIN *amazedly following.*

O, look, sir, look, sir! here is more of us:
I prophesied, if a gallows were on land,
This fellow could not drown. Now, blasphemy,
That swear'st grace o'erboard, not an oath on
    shore?
Hast thou no mouth by land? What is the
    news?

    BOATS.   The best news is, that we have
safely found   221
Our king and company; the next, our ship—
Which, but three glasses since, we gave out
    split—16
Is tight and yare and bravely rigged, as when
We first put out to sea.

    ARI.   [*Aside to* PROS.] Sir, all this service
Have I done since I went.

    PROS.   [*Aside to* ARI.] My tricksy spirit!

    ALON.   These are not natural events; they
strengthen
From strange to stranger. Say, how came you
    hither?

    BOATS.   If I did think, sir, I were well
awake,
I 'ld strive to tell you. We were dead of sleep,
And—how we know not—all clapp'd under
    hatches;   231
Where, but even now, with strange and several
    noises
Of roaring, shrieking, howling, jingling chains,
And mo diversity of sounds, all horrible,
We were awaked; straightway, at liberty;
Where we, in all her trim, freshly beheld
Our royal, good, and gallant ship; our master
Capering to eye her:—on a trice, so please you,
Even in a dream, were we divided from them,
And were brought moping hither.   239

    ARI.   [*Aside to* PROS.] Was 't well done?

    PROS.   [*Aside to* ARI.] Bravely, my diligence.
Thou shalt be free.

    ALON.   This is as strange a maze as e'er
men trod;
And there is in this business more than nature
Was ever conduct[17] of: some oracle
Must rectify our knowledge.

    PROS.   Sir, my liege,
Do not infest[18] your mind with beating on
The strangeness of this business; at pick'd
    leisure
Which shall be shortly, single I 'll resolve you,[19]
Which to you shall seem probable, of every
These happen'd accidents; till when, be
    cheerful,
And think of each thing well. [*Aside to* ARI.]
    Come hither, spirit: 251
Set Caliban and his companions free;
Untie the spell. [*Exit* ARIEL.] How fares my
    gracious sir?
There are yet missing of your company
Some few odd lads that you remember not.
Re-enter ARIEL, *driving in* CALIBAN, STEPHANO,
    and TRINCULO, *in their stolen apparel.*

    STE.   Every man shift for all the rest, and
let no man take care for himself;[20] for all is but
fortune.—Coragio, bully-monster, coragio!

    TRIN.   If these be true spies which I wear in
my head, here's a goodly sight.   266

    CAL.   O Setebos, these be brave spirits
indeed!
How fine my master is! · I am afraid
He will chastise me.

    SEB.   Ha, ha!
What things are these, my lord Antonio?
Will money buy 'em?

    ANT.   Very like; one of them
Is a plain fish, and, no doubt, marketable.

    PROS.   Mark but the badges[21] of these men,
my lords,
Then say if they be true. This mis-shapen
    knave,
His mother was a witch; and one so strong
That could control the moon, make flows and
    ebbs,   270
And deal in her command, without[22] her power.
These three have robb'd me; and this demi-
    devil—
For he's a bastard one—had plotted with them
To take my life. Two of these fellows you
Must know and own; this thing of darkness I
Acknowledge mine.

    CAL.   I shall be pinch'd to death.

    ALON.   Is not this Stephano, my drunken
butler?

---

16 declared wrecked

17 conductor
18 trouble
19 give you explanation
20 A drunkenly dis-
   torted speech.

21 i. e., the stolen ap-
   parel
22 act in her place, be-
   yond

SEB. He is drunk now: where had he wine?

ALON. And Trinculo is reeling ripe: where should they

Find this grand liquor that hath gilded 'em?—
How camest thou in this pickle?   281

TRIN. I have been in such a pickle since I saw you last, that, I fear me, will never out of my bones: I shall not fear fly-blowing.

SEB. Why, how now, Stephano!

STE. O, touch me not;—I am not Stephano, but a cramp.

PROS. You 'ld be king o' the isle, sirrah?

STE. I should have been a sore one, then.

ALON. This is a strange thing as e'er I look'd on.   [Pointing to CALIBAN.

PROS. He is as disproportion'd in his manners.   290

As in his shape. Go, sirrah, to my cell;
Take with you your companions; as you look
To have my pardon, trim it handsomely.

CAL. Ay, that I will; and I'll be wise hereafter,

And seek for grace. What a thrice-double ass
Was I, to take this drunkard for a god,
And worship this dull fool!

PROS.   Go to; away!

ALON. Hence, and bestow your luggage where you found it.

SEB. Or stole it, rather.

          [Exeunt CAL., STE., and TRIN.

PROS. Sir, I invite your Highness and your train   300

To my poor cell, where you shall take your rest
For this one night; which, part of it, I'll waste
With such discourse as, I not doubt, shall make it
Go quick away: the story of my life,
And the particular accidents gone by
Since I came to this isle: and in the morn
I'll bring you to your ship, and so to Naples,
Where I have hope to see the nuptial
Of these our dear-beloved solemnized;
And thence retire me to my Milan, where   310
Every third thought shall be my grave.

ALON.   I long

To hear the story of your life, which must
Take23 the ear strangely.

PROS.   I'll deliver all;

And promise you calm seas, auspicious gales,
And sail so expeditious, that shall catch
Your royal fleet far off. [Aside to ARI.] My Ariel, chick,
That is thy charge: then to the elements
Be free, and fare thou well! Please you, draw near.   [Exeunt.

23 captivate

Spoken by PROSPERO.

Now my charms are all o'erthrown,
And what strength I have's mine own,
Which is most faint: now, 'tis true,
I must be here confined by you,
Or sent to Naples. Let me not,
Since I have my dukedom got,
And pardon'd the deceiver, dwell
In this bare island by your spell;
But release me from my bands
With the help of your good hands: 10
Gentle breath of yours my sails
Must fill, or else my project fails,
Which was to please. Now I want24
Spirits to enforce, art to enchant;
And my ending is despair,
Unless I be relieved by prayer,
Which pierces so, that it assaults
Mercy itself, and frees all faults.
As you from crimes would pardon'd be,
Let your indulgence set me free.   20

BEN JONSON (1573?-1637)

TO THE MEMORY OF MY BELOVED MASTER WILLIAM SHAKESPEARE AND WHAT HE HATH LEFT US.†

To draw no envy, Shakespeare, on thy name,
Am I thus ample1 to thy book and fame;

24 lack
* Probably not written by Shakespeare.

1 liberal
† Written after Shakespeare's death, which took place in April, 1616. Beaumont died in March and was buried in Westminster Abbey by the side of Chaucer and Spenser, where twenty-one years later Jonson himself was to lie. Shakespeare, however, was buried at Stratford. (*Eng. Lit.*, p. 411.) Lines 19-21 refer to the following "Epitaph on Shakespeare" which was written by William Basse:
"Renowned Spenser, lie a thought more nigh
To learned Chaucer; and, rare Beaumont, lie
A little nearer Spenser, to make room
For Shakespeare in your threefold, fourfold tomb.
To lodge all four in·one bed make a shift,
For until doomsday hardly will a fifth,
Betwixt this day and that, by fates be slain,
For whom your curtains need be drawn again.
But if precedency in death doth bar
A fourth place in your sacred sepulchre,
Under this sable marble of thine own,
Sleep, rare tragedian, Shakespeare, sleep alone:
Thy unmolested peace, in an unshared cave,
Possess as lord, not tenant, of thy grave:
That unto us, and others, it may be
Honour hereafter to be laid by thee."
The tenor of Jonson's praise appears to be that other English poets, though great, are "disproportioned," that is, inferior to Shakespeare: his peers are to be found only among the ancients, though he himself knew little about them.

While I confess thy writings to be such,
As neither man, nor Muse, can praise too much.
'Tis true, and all men's suffrage.[2] But these ways
Were not the paths I meant unto thy praise;
For silliest ignorance on these may light,
Which, when it sounds at best, but echoes right;
Or blind affection, which doth ne'er advance
The truth, but gropes, and urgeth all by chance; 10
Or crafty malice might pretend this praise,
And think to ruin, where it seem'd to raise.

. . . . . .

But thou art proof against them, and, indeed,
Above the ill fortune of them, or the need.
 I therefore will begin: Soul of the age!
The applause! delight! the wonder of our stage!
My Shakespeare rise! I will not lodge thee by
Chaucer, or Spenser, or bid Beaumont lie 20
A little further off, to make thee room:
Thou art a monument without a tomb,
And art alive still, while thy book doth live,
And we have wits to read, and praise to give.
That I not mix thee so, my brain excuses,
I mean with great, but disproportion'd Muses:
For if I thought my judgment were of years,[3]
I should commit thee surely with thy peers,
And tell how far thou didst our Lyly outshine,
Or sporting Kyd, or Marlowe's mighty line. 30
And though thou hadst small Latin and less Greek,
From thence to honour thee, I will not seek[4]
For names: but call forth thund'ring Æschylus,
Euripides, and Sophocles to us,
Pacuvius, Accius, him of Cordova dead,[5]
To live again, to hear thy buskin[6] tread,
And shake a stage: or when thy socks[7] were on,
Leave thee alone for the comparison
Of all, that insolent Greece, or haughty Rome
Sent forth, or since did from their ashes come.
Triumph, my Britain, thou hast one to show, 41
To whom all scenes of Europe homage owe.
He was not of an age, but for all time!
And all the Muses still were in their prime,
When, like Apollo, he came forth to warm
Our ears, or like a Mercury to charm!
Nature herself was proud of his designs,
And joyed to wear the dressing of his lines!
Which were so richly spun, and woven so fit,
As, since, she will vouchsafe no other wit. 50

The merry Greek, tart Aristophanes,
Neat Terence, witty Plautus, now not please;
But antiquated and deserted lie,
As they were not of nature's family.
 Yet must I not give nature all; thy art,
My gentle Shakespeare, must enjoy a part.
For though the poet's matter nature be,
His art doth give the fashion: and, that he
Who casts to write a living line, must sweat,
(Such as thine are) and strike the second heat
Upon the Muses' anvil; turn the same, 61
And himself with it, that he thinks to frame;
Or for the laurel, he may gain a scorn;
For a good poet's made as well as born.
And such wert thou! Look how the father's face
Lives in his issue, even so the race
Of Shakespeare's mind and manners brightly shines
In his well turnèd, and true filèd lines;
In each of which he seems to shake a lance,
As brandish'd at the eyes of ignorance. 70
 Sweet Swan of Avon! what a sight it were
To see thee in our water yet appear,
And make those flights upon the banks of Thames,
That so did take Eliza,[8] and our James!
But stay, I see thee in the hemisphere
Advanced, and made a constellation there!
Shine forth, thou Star of poets, and with rage,
Or influence, chide, or cheer the drooping stage,
Which, since thy flight from hence, hath mourn'd like night, 79
And despairs day, but for thy volume's light.

FROM VOLPONE; OR, THE FOX
THE ARGUMENT*

Volpone, childless, rich, feigns sick, despairs,
Offers his state to hopes of several heirs,
Lies languishing: his parasite receives
Presents of all, assures, deludes; then weaves
Other cross plots, which ope themselves, are told.
New tricks for safety are sought; they thrive: when bold,
Each tempts the other again, and all are sold.

8 captivate Queen Elizabeth
* This Argument—which is in the form of an acrostic, the initial letters of the seven lines spelling the title—gives in condensed form the plot of the play. The purpose is to present instructively some of the worst passions of men, especially avarice. Volpo'ne, the rich, hypocritical old "fox," assisted by his paras'te, Mosca ("fly"), amuses himself with deluding those who hope to become his heirs, namely, the advocate Voltore ("vulture"), Corbaccio ("old raven"), etc.; but all come to grief in the end. The selection here printed constitutes the major portion of Act I. On Jonson's use of "humours," see *Eng. Lit.*, p. 122.

2 verdict
3 mature
4 will not be at a loss
5 Three Roman tragic poets (the Cordovan is Seneca)
6 A high boot worn by ancient tragic actors; figurative for "tragedy."
7 A low shoe worn by ancient comedians; hence "comedy."

ACT I.

Scene I.—*A Room in* Volpone's *House.*
Enter Volpone *and* Mosca.

Volpone. Good morning to the day; and
    next, my gold!
Open the shrine, that I may see my saint.
    [Mosca *withdraws the curtain, and*
        discovers piles of gold, plate,
        jewels, etc.
Hail the world's soul, and mine! more glad   10
    than is
The teeming earth to see the longed-for sun
Peep through the horns of the celestial Ram[1]
Am I, to view thy splendour darkening his;
That lying here, amongst my other hoards,
Show'st like a flame by night, or like the day
Struck out of chaos, when all darkness fled
Unto the centre. O thou son of Sol,
But brighter than thy father, let me kiss,
With adoration, thee, and every relic
Of sacred treasure in this blessed room.   20
Well did wise poets, by thy glorious name,
Title that age which they would have the best;
Thou being the best of things; and far tran-
    scending
All style of joy, in children, parents, friends,
Or any other waking dream on earth:
Thy looks when they to Venus did ascribe,
They should have given her twenty thousand
    Cupids;
Such are thy beauties and our loves! Dear saint,
Riches, the dumb god, that giv'st all men
    tongues,
That canst do nought, and yet mak'st men do
    all things;   30
The price of souls; even hell, with thee to boot,
Is made worth heaven. Thou art virtue, fame,
Honour, and all things else. Who can get thee,
He shall be noble, valiant, honest, wise——
  Mos. And what he will, sir. Riches are in
    fortune
A greater good than wisdom is in nature.
  Volp. True, my beloved Mosca. Yet I glory
More in the cunning purchase of my wealth,
Than in the glad possession, since I gain
No common way; I use no trade, no venture;   40
I wound no earth with ploughshares, fat no
    beasts
To feed the shambles; have no mills for iron,
Oil, corn, or men, to grind them into powder:
I blow no subtle glass, expose no ships
To threat'nings of the furrow-faced sea;
I turn no monies in the public bank,
Nor usure private.[2] . . . .

. . . . . What should I do,
But cocker up[3] my genius, and live free
To all delights my fortune calls me to?   50
I have no wife, no parent, child, ally,
To give my substance to; but whom I make
Must be my heir; and this makes men observe
    me:
This draws new clients daily to my house,
Women and men of every sex and age,
That bring me presents, send me plate, coin,
    jewels,
With hope that when I die (which they expect
Each greedy minute) it shall then return
Tenfold upon them; whilst some, covetous
Above the rest, seek to engross me whole,   60
And counter-work the one unto the other,
Contend in gifts, as they would seem in love:
All which I suffer, playing with their hopes,
And am content to coin them into profit,
And look upon their kindness, and take more,
And look on that; still bearing them in hand,[4]
Letting the cherry knock against their lips,
And draw it by their mouths, and back again.—
How now! . . . .
               [*Knocking without.*
Who's that? . . Look, Mosca. . .   70
  Mos. 'Tis Signior Voltore, the advocate;
    I know him by his knock.
  Volp. Fetch me my gown,
My furs, and night-caps; say my couch is
    changing,
And let him entertain himself awhile
Without i' the gallery. [*Exit* Mosca.] Now,
    now my clients
Begin their visitation! Vulture, kite,
Raven, and gorcrow, all my birds of prey,
That think me turning carcase, now they come:
I am not for them yet.
    Re-enter Mosca, *with the gown, etc.*
How now! the news?   80
  Mos. A piece of plate, sir.
  Volp. Of what bigness?
  Mos. Huge,
Massy, and antique, with your name inscribed,
And arms engraven.
  Volp. Good! and not a fox
Stretched on the earth, with fine delusive
    sleights,
Mocking a gaping crow? ha, Mosca!
  Mos. Sharp, sir.
  Volp. Give me my furs.   90
             [*Puts on his sick dress.*
Why dost thou laugh so, man?
  Mos. I cannot choose, sir, when I apprehend
What thoughts he has without now, as he walks:

---

1 The first sign of the   2 practice   no private
  zodiac, ascendant at   usury
  the vernal equinox.

3 pamper   4 leading them on

That this might be the last gift he should give;
That this would fetch you; if you died to-day,
And gave him all, what he should be to-morrow;
What large return would come of all his
    ventures;
How he should worshipped be, and reverenced;
Ride with his furs, and foot-cloths; waited on
By herds of fools and clients; have clear way   100
Made for his mule, as lettered as himself;
Be called the great and learned advocate:
And then concludes, there's nought impossible.
    Volp. Yes, to be learned, Mosca.
    Mos. O, no: rich
Implies it. Hood an ass with reverend purple,
So you can hide his two ambitious ears,
And he shall pass for a cathedral doctor.5
    Volp. My caps, my caps, good Mosca. Fetch
    him in.
    Mos. Stay, sir; your ointment for your
    eyes.   110
    Volp. That's true;
Dispatch, dispatch: I long to have possession
Of my new present.
    Mos. That, and thousands more,
I hope to see you lord of.
    Volp. Thanks, kind Mosca.
    Mos. And that, when I am lost in blended
    dust,
And hundreds such as I am, in succession—
    Volp. Nay, that were too much, Mosca.
    Mos. You shall live   120
Still to delude these harpies.
    Volp. Loving Mosca!
'Tis well; my pillow now, and let him enter.
                           [*Exit* Mosca.
Now, my feigned cough, my phthisic, and my
    gout,
My apoplexy, palsy, and catarrhs,
Help, with your forced functions, this my pos-
    ture,
Wherein, this three year, I have milked their
    hopes.
He comes; I hear him—Uh! [*coughing.*] uh!
    uh! uh! O——
Re-enter Mosca, *introducing* Voltore *with a*
    piece of Plate.
    Mos. You still are what you were, sir. Only
    you,
Of all the rest, are he6 commands his love,   130
And you do wisely to preserve it thus,
With early visitation, and kind notes7
Of your good meaning to him, which, I know,
Cannot but come most grateful. Patron! sir!
Here's Signior Voltore is come——

5 learned man worthy   6 he that
   to occupy the seat   7 tokens
   (*cathedra*) of au-
   thority

    Volp. [*faintly*] What say you?
    Mos. Sir, Signior Voltore is come th...
    morning
To visit you.
    Volp. I thank him.
    Mos. And hath brought   14...
A piece of antique plate, bought of St. Mark...
With which he here presents you.
    Volp. He is welcome.
Pray him to come more often.
    Mos. Yes.
    Volt. What says he?
    Mos. He thanks you, and desires you to se...
    him often.
    Volp. Mosca.
    Mos. My patron!
    Volp. Bring him near, where is he?   15...
I long to feel his hand.
    Mos. The plate is here, sir.
    Volt. How fare you, sir?
    Volp. I thank you, Signior Voltore.
Where is the plate? mine eyes are bad.
    Volt. [*putting it into his hands.*] I'm sorr...
To see you still thus weak.
    Mos. That he's not weaker.   [*Asid...*
    Volp. You are too munificent.
    Volt. No, sir; would to heaven,   16...
I could as well give health to you, as tha...
    plate!
    Volp. You give, sir, what you can; I than...
    you. Your love
Hath taste in this, and shall not be una...
    swered:
I pray you see me often.
    Volt. Yes, I shall, sir.
    Volp. Be not far from me.
    Mos. Do you observe that, sir?
    Volp. Hearken unto me still; it will co...
    cern you.
    Mos. You are a happy man, sir; know yo...
    good.   17...
    Volp. I cannot now last long——
    Mos. You are his heir, sir.
    Volt. Am I?
    Volp. I feel me going: Uh! uh! uh! uh!
I'm sailing to my port, Uh! uh! uh! uh!
And I am glad I am so near my haven.
    Mos. Alas, kind gentleman! Well, we mu...
    all go—
    Volt. But, Mosca——
    Mos. Age will conquer.
    Volt. Pray thee, hear me;   18...
Am I inscribed his heir for certain?
    Mos. Are you!
I do beseech you, sir, you will vouchsafe

8 The great square and mart of Venice.

To write me in your family.⁹ All my hopes
Depend upon your worship: I am lost
Except the rising sun do shine on me.
  Volt. It shall both shine, and warm thee,
        Mosca.
  Mos. Sir,
I am a man that hath not done your love
All the worst offices: here I wear your keys, 190
See all your coffers and your caskets locked,
Keep the poor inventory of your jewels,
Your plate, and monies; am your steward, sir,
Husband your goods here.
  Volt. But am I sole heir?
  Mos. Without a partner, sir: confirmed this
        morning:
The wax is warm yet, and the ink scarce dry
Upon the parchment.
  Volt. Happy, happy me!
By what good chance, sweet Mosca?   200
  Mos. Your desert, sir;
I know no second cause.
  Volt. Thy modesty
Is not to know it¹⁰; well, we shall requite it.
  Mos. He ever liked your course, sir; that
        first took him.
I oft have heard him say how he admired
Men of your large profession, that could speak
To every cause, and things mere contraries,
Till they were hoarse again, yet all be law;
That, with most quick agility, could turn, 210
And return; make knots, and undo them;
Give forked counsel; take provoking¹¹ gold
On either hand, and put it up¹²; these men,
He knew, would thrive with their humility.
And, for his part, he thought he should be blest
To have his heir of such a suffering spirit,
So wise, so grave, of so perplexed a tongue,
And loud withal, that would **not** wag, nor
        scarce
Lie still, without a fee; when every word
Your worship but lets fall, is a chequin¹³! 220
        [*Knocking without.*
Who's that? one knocks; I would not have you
        seen, sir.
And yet—pretend you came, and went in haste;
I'll fashion an excuse—and, gentle sir,
When you do come to swim in golden lard,
Up to the arms in honey, that your chin
Is borne up stiff with fatness of the flood,
Think on your vassal; but remember me:
I have not been your worst of clients.
  Volt. Mosca!—
  Mos. When will you have your inventory
        brought, sir?   230

Or see a copy of the Will?—Anon¹⁴!—
I'll bring them to you, sir. Away, begone,
Put business in your face.   [*Exit* Voltore.
  Volp.[*springing up.*] Excellent Mosca!
Come hither, let me kiss thee.
  Mos. Keep you still, sir.
Here is Corbaccio.
  Volp. Set the plate away:
The vulture's gone, and the old raven's come.
  Mos. Betake you to your silence, and your
        sleep.   240
Stand there and multiply. [*Putting the plate
        to the rest.*] Now we shall see
A wretch who is indeed more impotent
Than this can feign to be; yet hopes to hop
Over his grave.
        Enter Corbaccio.
        Signior Corbaccio!
You're very welcome, sir.
  Corb. How does your patron?
  Mos. Troth, as he did, sir, no amends.
  Corb. What! mends he?
  Mos. No, sir: he's rather worse.
  Corb. That's well. Where is he?   250
  Mos. Upon his couch, sir, newly fall'n
        asleep.
  Corb. Does he sleep well?
  Mos. No wink, sir, all this night,
Nor yesterday; but slumbers.
  Corb. Good! he should take
Some counsel of physicians: I have brought
        him
An opiate here, from mine own doctor.
  Mos. He will not hear of drugs.
  Corb. Why? I myself
Stood by while it was made, saw all the in-
        gredients;   260
And know it cannot but most gently work:
My life for his, 'tis but to make him sleep.
  Volp. Ay, his last sleep, if he would take it.
        [*Aside.*
  Mos. Sir,
He has no faith in physic.
  Corb. Say you, say you?
  Mos. He has no faith in physic: he does
        think
Most of your doctors are the greater danger,
And worse disease, to escape. I often have
Heard him protest that your¹⁵ physician 270
Should never be his heir.
  Corb. Not I his heir?
  Mos. Not your physician, sir.
  Corb. O, no, no, no.
I do not mean it.
  Mos. No, sir, nor their fees
He cannot brook: he says they flay a man

⁹ engage me as your servant ¹¹ alluring ¹² pouch it ¹⁰ it is your modesty that speaks thus ¹³ sequin; an Italian coin worth about 9s ¹⁴ at once (addressed to the one knocking) ¹⁵ a

Before they kill him.
  Corb. Right, I do conceive you.
  Mos. And then they do it by experiment; 280
For which the law not only doth absolve them,
But gives them great reward: and he is loth
To hire his death so.
  Corb. It is true, they kill
With as much licence as a judge.
  Mos. Nay, more;
For he but kills, sir, where the law condemns,
And these can kill him too.
  Corb. Ay, or me;
Or any man. How does his apoplex? 290
Is that strong on him still?
  Mos. Most violent.
His speech is broken, and his eyes are set,
His face drawn longer than 'twas wont——
  Corb. How! how!
Stronger than he was wont?
  Mos. No, sir; his face
Drawn longer than 'twas wont.
  Corb. O, good!
  Mos. His mouth 300
Is ever gaping, and his eyelids hang.
  Corb. Good.
  Mos. A freezing numbness stiffens all his joints,
And makes the colour of his flesh like lead.
  Corb. 'Tis good.
  Mos. His pulse beats slow, and dull.
  Corb. Good symptoms still.
  Mos. And from his brain——
  Corb. I conceive you; good.
  Mos. Flows a cold sweat, with a continual rheum, 310
Forth the resolved[16] corners of his eyes.
  Corb. Is't possible? Yet I am better, ha!
How does he with the swimming of his head?
  Mos. O, sir, 'tis past the scotomy;[17] he now
Hath lost his feeling, and hath left[18] to snort:
You hardly can perceive him, that he breathes.
  Corb. Excellent, excellent! sure I shall out-last him:
This makes me young again, a score of years.
  Mos. I was a-coming for you, sir.
  Corb. Has he made his Will? 320
What has he given me?
  Mos. No, sir.
  Corb. Nothing! ha?
  Mos. He has not made his Will, sir.
  Corb. Oh, oh, oh!
What then did Voltore, the lawyer, here?
  Mos. He smelt a carcase, sir, when he but heard
My master was about his testament;

As I did urge him to it for your good——
  Corb. He came unto him, did he? I thought so. 33●
  Mos. Yes, and presented him this piece o plate.
  Corb. To be his heir?
  Mos. I do not know, sir.
  Corb. True:
I know it too.
  Mos. By your own scale,[19] sir. [*Aside*
  Corb. Well,
I shall prevent him yet. See, Mosca, look,
Here I have brought a bag of bright chequines
Will quite weigh down his plate. 34●
  Mos. [*taking the bag.*] Yea, marry, sir.
This is true physic, this your sacred medicine
No talk of opiates to[20] this great elixir!
  Corb. 'Tis aurum palpabile, if not pot abile.[21]
  Mos. It shall be ministered to him in his bowl.
  Corb. Ay, do, do, do.
  Mos. Most blessed cordial!
This will recover him.
  Corb. Yes, do, do, do.
  Mos. I think it were not best, sir. 35●
  Corb. What?
  Mos. To recover him.
  Corb. O, no, no, no; by no means.
  Mos. Why, sir, this
Will work some strange effect, if he but feel it.
  Corb. 'Tis true, therefore forbear; I'll take my venture:
Give me it again.
  Mos. At no hand:[22] pardon me:
You shall not do yourself that wrong, sir. I
Will so advise you, you shall have it all. 36●
  Corb. How?
  Mos. All, sir; 'tis your right, your own; no man
Can claim a part: 'tis yours without a rival,
Decreed by destiny.
  Corb. How, how, good Mosca?
  Mos. I'll tell you, sir. This fit he shall recover.
  Corb. I do conceive you.
  Mos. And on first advantage
Of his gained sense, will I re-importune him
Unto the making of his testament: 37●
And show him this. [*Pointing to the money.*
  Corb. Good, good.
  Mos. 'Tis better yet,
If you will hear, sir.

16 relaxed
17 dizziness
18 ceased
19 judging him by yourself
20 compared to
21 Gold that can be felt, though not drunk (potable gold was believed to have medicinal value).
22 by no means

Corb. Yes, with all my heart.

Mos. Now would I counsel you, make home
    with speed;

There, frame a Will; whereto you shall inscribe

My master your sole heir.

Corb. And disinherit

My son!   380

Mos. O, sir, the better: for that colour[23]

Shall make it much more taking.

Corb. O, but colour?

Mos. This Will, sir, you shall send it unto
    me.

Now, when I come to inforce, as I will do,

Your cares, your watchings, and your many
    prayers,

Your more than many gifts, your this day's
    present,

And last, produce your Will; where, without
    thought,

Or least regard, unto your proper issue,

A son so brave, and highly meriting,   390

The stream of your diverted love hath thrown
    you

Upon my master, and made him your heir:

He cannot be so stupid, or stone-dead,

But out of conscience and mere gratitude——

Corb. He must pronounce me his?

Mos. 'Tis true.

Corb. This plot

Did I think on before.

Mos. I do believe it.

Corb. Do you not believe it?   400

Mos. Yes, sir.

Corb. Mine own project.

Mos. Which, when he hath done, sir——

Corb. Published me his heir?

Mos. And you so certain to survive him——

Corb. Ay.

Mos. Being so lusty a man——

Corb. 'Tis true.

Mos. Yes, sir——

Corb. I thought on that too. See, how he
    should be   410

The very organ to express my thoughts!

Mos. You have not only done yourself a
    good——

Corb. But multiplied it on my son.

Mos. 'Tis right, sir.

Corb. Still, my invention.

Mos. 'Las, sir! heaven knows,

It hath been all my study, all my care,

(I e'en grow gray withal,) how to work
    things——

Corb. I do conceive, sweet Mosca.

Mos. You are he   420

For whom I labour here.

Corb. Ay, do, do, do:

I'll straight about it.   [*Going.*

Mos. Rook go with you, raven![24]   [*Aside.*

Corb. I know thee honest.

Mos. You do lie, sir!

Corb. And——

Mos. Your knowledge is no better than your
    ears, sir.

Corb. I do not doubt to be a father to thee.

Mos. Nor I to gull my brother of his bless-
    ing.   430

Corb. I may have my youth restored to me,
    why not?

Mos. Your worship is a precious ass!

Corb. What sayest thou?

Mos. I do desire your worship to make haste,
    sir.

Corb. 'Tis done, 'tis done; I go.   [*Exit.*

Volp. [*leaping from his couch.*] O, I shall
    burst!

Let out my sides, let out my sides——

Mos. Contain

Your flux[25] of laughter, sir: you know this
    hope

Is such a bait, it covers any hook.   440

Volp. O, but thy working, and thy placing it!

I cannot hold; good rascal, let me kiss thee:

I never knew thee in so rare a humour.

Mos. Alas, sir, I but do as I am taught;

Follow your grave instructions; give them
    words;

Pour oil into their ears, and send them hence.

Volp. 'Tis true, 'tis true. What a rare
    punishment

Is avarice to itself!

BEAUMONT AND FLETCHER
(1584-1616) (1579-1625)

FROM THE KNIGHT OF THE BURNING
PESTLE.*

INDUCTION.

*Several Gentlemen sitting on Stools upon the
    Stage. The Citizen, his Wife, and Ralph
    sitting below among the audience.*

Enter Speaker of the Prologue.

S. of Prol. "From all that's near the court,
    from all that's great,

24 may cheat pursue you,   25 flow
    cheat!

* This play was written and acted about 1611.
Like Shakespeare's *A Midsummer Night's
Dream*, it is made up of diverse elements—a
romantic comedy and a burlesque. Herein are
given a few scenes of the latter, which can
easily be detached from the main plot. It

Within the compass of the city-walls,
We now have brought our scene——''
    Citizen leaps on the Stage.
    Cit. Hold your peace, goodman boy!
    S. of Prol. What do you mean, sir?
    Cit. That you have no good meaning: this
seven years[1] there hath been plays at this
house, I have observed it, you have still[2] girds
at citizens; and now you call your play ''The
London Merchant.'' Down with your title,
boy! down with your title!
    S. of Prol. Are you a member of the noble
city?
    Cit. I am.
    S. of Prol. And a freeman?[3]
    Cit. Yea, and a grocer.
    S. of Prol. So, grocer, then, by your sweet
favour, we intend no abuse to the city.
    Cit. No, sir! yes, sir: if you were not re-
solved to play the Jacks,[4] what need you study
for new subjects, purposely to abuse your betters? why could not you be contented, as well
as others, with ''The Legend of Whittington,''
or ''The Life and Death of Sir Thomas Gres-
ham, with the building of the Royal Exchange,'' or ''The story of Queen Eleanor,
with the rearing of London Bridge upon wool-
sacks?''†
    S. of Prol. You seem to be an understand-
ing man: what would you have us do, sir?
    Cit. Why, present something notably in
honour of the commons[5] of the city.
    S. of Prol. Why, what do you say to ''The
Life and Death of fat Drake, or the Repairing
of Fleet Sewers?''
    Cit. I do not like that; but I will have a
citizen, and he shall be of my own trade.
    S. of Prol. Oh, you should have told us
your mind a month since; our play is ready
to begin now.
    Cit. 'Tis all one for that; I will have a

grocer, and he shall do admirable things.
    S. of Prol. What will you have him do?
    Cit. Marry, I will have him——
    Wife. [below.] Husband, husband!
    Ralph. [below.] Peace, mistress.
    Wife. [below.] Hold thy peace, Ralph; I
know what I do, I warrant ye.—Husband, husband!
    Cit. What sayest thou, cony?[6]
    Wife [below.] Let him kill a lion with a
pestle, husband! let him kill a lion with a
pestle!
    Cit. So he shall.—I'll have him kill a lion
with a pestle.
    Wife. [below.] Husband! shall I come up,
husband?
    Cit. Ay, cony.—Ralph, help your mistress
this way.—Pray, gentlemen, make her a little
room.—I pray you, sir, lend me your hand to
help up my wife: I thank you, sir.—So.
        [*Wife comes on the Stage.*
    Wife. By your leave, gentlemen all; I'm
something troublesome: I'm a stranger here;
I was ne'er at one of these plays, as they say,
before; but I should have seen ''Jane Shore''
once; and my husband hath promised me, any
time this twelvemonth, to carry me to ''The
Bold Beauchamps,'' but in truth he did not.
I pray you, bear with me.
    Cit. Boy, let my wife and I have a couple of
stools, and then begin; and let the grocer do
rare things.   [*Stools are brought.*
    S. of Prol. But, sir, we have never a boy
to play him: every one hath a part already.
    Wife. Husband, husband, for God's sake, let
Ralph play him! beshrew me, if I do not think
he will go beyond them all.
    Cit. Well remembered, wife.—Come up,
Ralph.—I'll tell you, gentlemen; let them but
lend him a suit of reparel and necessaries,[7] and,
by gad, if any of them all put him to shame,
I'll be hanged.
        [*Ralph comes on the Stage.*
    Wife. I pray you, youth, let him have a
suit of reparel!—I'll be sworn, gentlemen, my
husband tells you true: he will act you sometimes at our house, that all the neighbours cry
out on him; he will fetch you up a couraging[6]
part so in the garret, that we are all as feared,
I warrant you, that we quake again: we'll fear[9]
our children with him; if they be never so
unruly, do but cry, ''Ralph comes, Ralph
comes!'' to them, and they'll be as quiet as
lambs.—Hold up thy head, Ralph; show the

must be understood that it was the custom
at theaters to admit gallants and others who
liked to be conspicuous, and who were willing
to pay an extra sixpence, to seats on the
stage, where they often abused their privilege
by indulging in audible criticism of the play
and players. The authors of the present drama
ingeniously staged that custom as a part of
their own play and took the opportunity to
satirize both the taste and understanding of
their dunce-critics. Furthermore, they wove
in a burlesque upon the romantic extravagance of knight-errantry, presenting in Ralph,
the grocer's apprentice, another Don Quixote,
like him whose immortal deeds had been given
to the world's laughter but a few years before.

1 Supply ''that.''
2 always
3 one invested with full
    citizen's rights
† These are titles of old plays, more or less distorted; the reference to London Bridge is a
jesting addition. The title proposed five lines
farther down is of course a jest.

4 play the knave (cp.
    The Tempest, IV.,
    i., 918)
5 ordinary citizens

6 rabbit (a term of en-
    dearment)
7 The grocer means to

    say ''apparel and
    accessories.''
8 valiant
9 scare

gentlemen what thou canst do; speak a huffing[10] part; I warrant you, the gentlemen will accept of it.

Cit. Do, Ralph, do.

Ralph. "By Heaven, methinks, it were an easy leap
To pluck bright honour from the pale-faced moon;
Or dive into the bottom of the sea,
Where never fathom-line touched any ground,
And pluck up drowned honour from the lake of hell.'"[11]

Cit. How say you, gentlemen, is it not as I told you?

Wife. Nay, gentlemen, he hath played before, my husband says, Mucedorus,[12] before the wardens of our company.

Cit. Ay, and he should have played Jeronimo[12] with a shoemaker for a wager.

S. of Prol. He shall have a suit of apparel, if he will go in.

Cit. In, Ralph, in Ralph; and set out the grocery in their kind,[13] if thou lovest me.
[*Exit Ralph.*

Wife. I warrant, our Ralph will look finely when he's dressed.

S. of Prol. But what will you have it called?

Cit. "The Grocer's Honour."

S. of Prol. Methinks "The Knight of the Burning Pestle" were better.

Wife. I'll be sworn, husband, that's as good a name as can be.

Cit. Let it be so.—Begin, begin; my wife and I will sit down.

S. of Prol. I pray you, do.

Cit. What stately music have you? you have shawms?

S. of Prol. Shawms! no.

Cit. No! I'm a thief, if my mind did not give[14] me so. Ralph plays a stately part, and he must needs have shawms: I'll be at the charge of them myself, rather than we'll go without them.

S. of Prol. So you are like to be.

Cit. Why, and so I will be: there's two shillings;—[*Gives money.*]—let's have the waits[15] of Southwark; they are as rare fellows as any are in England; and that will fetch them all o'er the water[16] with a vengeance, as if they were mad.

S. of Prol. You shall have them. Will you sit down, then?

Cit. Ay.—Come, wife.

Wife. Sit you merry all, gentlemen; I'm bold to sit amongst you for my ease.
[*Citizen and wife sit down.*

S. of Prol. "From all that's near the court, from all that's great,
Within the compass of the city-walls,
We now have brought our scene. Fly far from hence
All private taxes,[17] immodest phrases,
Whatever may but show like vicious!
For wicked mirth never true pleasure brings,
But honest minds are pleased with honest things."—

Thus much for that we do; but for Ralph's part you must answer for yourself.

Cit. Take you no care for Ralph; he'll discharge himself, I warrant you.
[*Exit Speaker of Prologue.*

Wife. I'faith, gentlemen, I'll give my word for Ralph.

ACT I, SCENE III.

A Grocer's Shop.

Enter Ralph, as a Grocer, reading Palmerin of England,[18] with Tim and George.

[*Wife.* Oh, husband, husband, now, now! there's Ralph, there's Ralph.

Cit. Peace, fool! let Ralph alone.—Hark you, Ralph; do not strain yourself too much at the first.—Peace!—Begin, Ralph.]

Ralph. [*Reads.*] Then Palmerin and Trineus, snatching their lances from their dwarfs, and clasping their helmets, galloped amain after the giant; and Palmerin, having gotten a sight of him, came posting amain, saying, "Stay, traitorous thief! for thou mayst not so carry away her, that is worth the greatest lord in the world;" and, with these words, gave him a blow on the shoulder, that he struck him besides[19] his elephant. And Trineus, coming to the knight that had Agricola behind him, set him soon besides his horse, with his neck broken in the fall; so that the princess, getting out of the throng, between joy and grief, said, "All happy knight, the mirror of all such as follow arms, now may I be well assured of the love thou bearest me."—I wonder why the kings do not raise an army of fourteen or fifteen hundred thousand men, as big as the army that the Prince of Portigo brought against Rosicleer,[20] and destroy these giants; they do much

---

10 swaggering
11 Hotspur's speech in 1 *Henry IV.*, I, iii., somewhat distorted.
12 A character in an

Elizabethan comedy.
13 proper garb
14 tell
15 professional carolers
16 The Thames.

17 personal hits
18 A Spanish romance, then lately translated.

19 by the side of
20 A character in another Spanish romance.

hurt to wandering damsels, that go in quest of their knights.

[*Wife.* Faith, husband, and Ralph says true; for they say the King of Portugal cannot sit at his meat, but the giants and the ettins[21] will come and snatch it from him.

Cit. Hold thy tongue.—On, Ralph!]

Ralph. And certainly those knights are much to be commended, who, neglecting their possessions, wander with a squire and a dwarf through the deserts to relieve poor ladies.

[*Wife.* Ay, by my faith, are they, Ralph; let 'em say what they will, they are indeed. Our knights neglect their possessions well enough, but they do not the rest.] . . .

Ralph. But what brave spirit could be content to sit in his shop, with a flappet[22] of wood, and a blue apron before him, selling mithridatum and dragon's-water[23] to visited[24] houses, that might pursue feats of arms, and, through his noble achievements, procure such a famous history to be written of his heroic prowess?

[*Cit.* Well said, Ralph; some more of those words, Ralph.

Wife. They go finely, by my troth.]

Ralph. Why should not I, then, pursue this course, both for the credit of myself and our company? for amongst all the worthy books of achievements, I do not call to mind that I yet read of a grocer-errant: I will be the said knight.—Have you heard of any that hath wandered unfurnished of his squire and dwarf? My elder prentice Tim shall be my trusty squire, and little George my dwarf. Hence, my blue apron! Yet, in remembrance of my former trade, upon my shield shall be portrayed a Burning Pestle, and I will be called the Knight of the Burning Pestle.

[*Wife.* Nay, I dare swear thou wilt not forget thy old trade; thou wert ever meek.]

Ralph. Tim!

Tim. Anon.

Ralph. My beloved squire, and George my dwarf, I charge you that from henceforth you never call me by any other name but "the right courteous and valiant Knight of the Burning Pestle;" and that you never call any female by the name of a woman or wench, but "fair lady," if she have her desires, if not, "distressed damsel;" that you call all forests and heaths "deserts," and all horses "palfreys."

[*Wife.* This is very fine, faith.—Do the gentlemen like Ralph, think you, husband?

Cit. Ay, I warrant thee; the players would

give all the shoes in their shop for him.]

Ralph. My beloved squire Tim, stand out. Admit this were a desert, and over it a knight-errant pricking,[25] and I should bid you inquire of his intents, what would you say?

Tim. Sir, my master sent me to know whither you are riding?

Ralph. No, thus: "Fair sir, the right courteous and valiant Knight of the Burning Pestle commanded me to inquire upon what adventure you are bound, whether to relieve some distressed damsel, or otherwise."

[*Cit.* Scurvy blockhead, cannot remember!

Wife. I'faith, and Ralph told him on't before: all the gentlemen heard him.—Did he not, gentlemen? did not Ralph tell him on't?]

George. Right courteous and valiant Knight of the Burning Pestle, here is a distressed damsel to have a halfpenny-worth of pepper.

[*Wife.* That's a good boy! see, the little boy can hit it; by my troth, it's a fine child.]

Ralph. Relieve her, with all courteous language. Now shut up shop; no more my prentices, but my trusty squire and dwarf. I must bespeak[26] my shield and arming pestle.

[*Exeunt Tim and George.*

[*Cit.* Go thy ways, Ralph! As I'm a true man, thou art the best on 'em all.

Wife. Ralph, Ralph!

Ralph. What say you, mistress?

Wife. I prithee, come again quickly, sweet Ralph.

Ralph. By and by.] [*Exit.*

* * * * * *

[In the main plot, Jasper Merrythought has been dismissed by his employer for falling in love with his employer's daughter. His father takes his part, but his mother is incensed, and taking her younger son, Michael, and her money and jewels, she leaves her home, and the two are wandering in Waltham Forest, when Ralph comes on the scene.]

ACT II, SCENE II.

Waltham Forest.

Enter Mistress Merrythought and Michael.

Mist. Mer. Come, Michael; art thou not weary, boy?

Mich. No, forsooth, mother, not I.

Mist. Mer. Where be we now, child?

Mich. Indeed, forsooth, mother, I cannot tell, unless we be at Mile-End: Is not all the world Mile-End, mother?

Mist. Mer. No, Michael, not all the world, boy; but I can assure thee, Michael, Mile-End

---

21 giants
22 small p i e c e (here pestle)
23 popular medicines of the time
24 plague-stricken
25 riding
26 order

a goodly matter: there has been a pitch-
ld,27 my child, between the naughty Spaniels
d the Englishmen; and the Spaniels ran
ay, Michael, and the Englishmen followed:
y neighbour Coxstone was there, boy, and
lled them all with a birding-piece.

Mich. Mother, forsooth—

Mist. Mer. What says my white boy28?

Mich. Shall not my father go with us too?

Mist. Mer. No, Michael, let thy father go
ick-up;29 . . let him stay at home, and
ng for his supper, boy. Come, child, sit down,
d I'll show my boy fine knacks, indeed.
They sit down: and she takes out a casket.]
ook here, Michael; here's a ring, and here's
brooch, and here's a bracelet, and here's two
ags more, and here's money and gold by th'
e,30 my boy.

Mich. Shall I have all this, mother?

Mist. Mer. Ay, Michael, thou shalt have all,
ichael.

[*Cit.* How likest thou this, wench?

Wife. I cannot tell; I would have Ralph,
eorge; I'll see no more else, indeed, la; and
pray you, let the youths understand so much
word of mouth; for, I tell you truly, I'm
raid o' my boy. Come, come, George, let's
merry and wise: the child's a fatherless
ild; and say they should put him into a
rait pair of gaskins,31 'twere worse than knot-
ass;32 he would never grow after it.]

Enter Ralph, Tim, and George.

[*Cit.* Here's Ralph, here's Ralph!

Wife. How do you do, Ralph? you are wel-
me, Ralph, as I may say; it's a good boy,
ld up thy head, and be not afraid; we are
y friends, Ralph; the gentlemen will praise
ee, Ralph, if thou playest thy part with
dacity. Begin, Ralph, a' God's name!]

Ralph. My trusty squire, unlace my helm;
ve me my hat. Where are we, or what desert
ay this be?

George. Mirror of knighthood, this is, as I
ke it, the perilous Waltham-down; in whose
ttom stands the enchanted valley.

Mist. Mer. Oh, Michael, we are betrayed,
e are betrayed! here be giants! Fly, boy!
r, boy, fly!

[*Exit with Michael, leaving the casket.*

Ralph. Lace on my helm again. What noise
is this?
gentle lady, flying the embrace
f some uncourteous knight! I will relieve her.

Go, squire, and say, the Knight, that wears
this Pestle
In honour of all ladies, swears revenge
Upon that recreant coward that pursues her;
Go, comfort her, and that same gentle squire
That bears her company.

Tim. I go, brave knight. [*Exit.*

Ralph. My trusty dwarf and friend, reach
me my shield;
And hold it while I swear. First, by my
knighthood;
Then by the soul of Amadis de Gaul,33
My famous ancestor; then by my sword
The beauteous Brionella girt about me;
By this bright burning Pestle, of mine honour
The living trophy; and by all respect
Due to distressèd damsels; here I vow
Never to end the quest of this fair lady
And that forsaken squire till by my valour
I gain their liberty!

George. Heaven bless the knight
That thus relieves poor errant gentlewomen!

[*Exeunt.*

[*Wife.* Ay, marry, Ralph, this has some
savour in 't; I would see the proudest of them
all offer to carry his books after him. But,
George, I will not have him go away so soon;
I shall be sick if he go away, that I shall: call
Ralph again, George, call Ralph again; I
prithee, sweetheart, let him come fight before
me, and let's ha' some drums and some trumpets, and let him kill all that comes near him,
an34 thou lov'st me, George!

Cit. Peace a little, bird: he shall kill them
all, an they were twenty more on 'em than there
are.]

. . . . . .

[Jasper enters and, finding the casket, carries
it off.]

ACT II, SCENE III.

Another part of the Forest.

Enter Ralph and George.

[*Wife.* But here comes Ralph, George; thou
shalt hear him speak as he were an emperal.]

Ralph. Comes not sir squire again?

George. Right courteous knight,
Your squire doth come, and with him comes the
lady,
And the Squire of Damsels, as I take it.

*Enter Tim, Mistress Merrythought, and
Michael.*

Ralph. Madam, if any service or devoir35
Of a poor errant knight may right your wrongs,

---

pitched battle (probably only a mock battle,
for the Spanish never fought the English
there)
dear boy
go hang
galore
breeches

32 Supposed, when tak-
en as an infusion,
to retard growth.

33 A hero of medieval
romance, "Knight
of the Burning
Sword."

34 if
35 duty

Command it; I am prest[36] to give you succour;
For to that holy end I bear my armour.

Mist. Mer. Alas, sir, I am a poor gentle-woman, and I have lost my money in this forest.

Ralph. Desert, you would say, lady; and not lost
Whilst I have sword and lance. Dry up your tears,
Which ill befit the beauty of that face,
And tell the story, if I may request it,
Of your disastrous fortune.

Mist. Mer. Out, alas! I left a thousand pound, a thousand pound, e'en all the money I had laid up for this youth, upon the sight of your mastership, you looked so grim, and, as I may say it, saving your presence, more like a giant than a mortal man.

Ralph. I am as you are, lady; so are they;
All mortal. But why weeps this gentle squire?

Mist. Mer. Has he not cause to weep, do you think, when he hath lost his inheritance?

Ralph. Young hope of valour, weep not; I am here
That will confound thy foe, and pay it dear
Upon his coward head, that dares deny
Distressèd squires and ladies equity.
I have but one horse, on which shall ride
The fair lady behind me, and before
This courteous squire: fortune will give us more
Upon our next adventure. Fairly speed
Beside us, squire and dwarf, to do us need!
[*Exeunt.*

[*Cit.* Did not I tell you, Nell, what your man would do? by the faith of my body, wench, for clean action and good delivery, they may all cast their caps at him.

Wife. And so they may, i' faith; for I dare speak it boldly, the twelve companies[37] of London cannot match him, timber for timber. Well, George, an he be not inveigled by some of these paltry players, I ha' much marvel: but, George, we ha' done our parts, if the boy have any grace to be thankful.

Cit. Yes, I warrant thee, duckling.]

. . . .

[Ralph encounters Jasper, who knocks him down with his own pestle, whereupon Ralph and his party seek shelter at the Bell Inn.]

ACT II, SCENE VI.

Before the Bell-Inn, Waltham.

Enter Ralph, Mistress Merrythought, Michael, Tim and George.

[*Wife.* Oh, husband, here's Ralph again!—

Stay, Ralph, let me speak with thee. H[ow] dost thou, Ralph? art thou not shrewdly hur[t] the foul great lungies¹ laid unmercifully [on] thee: there's some sugar-candy for thee. Pr[o]ceed; thou shalt have another bout with him.

Cit. If Ralph had him at the fencing-scho[ol,] if he did not make a puppy of him, and dri[ve] him up and down the school, he should ne'[er] come in my shop more.]

Mist. Mer. Truly, Master Knight of t[he] Burning Pestle, I am weary.

Mich. Indeed, la, mother, and I am ve[ry] hungry.

Ralph. Take comfort, gentle dame, and yo[u] fair squire;
For in this desert there must needs be plac[ed]
Many strong castles held by courteous knight[s]
And till I bring you safe to one of those,
I swear by this my order ne'er to leave you. .

George. I would we had a mess of potta[ge,]
and a pot of drink, squire, and were going [to] bed!

Tim. Why, we are at Waltham-town's en[d,]
and that's the Bell-Inn.

George. Take courage, valiant knight, da[m]sel, and squire!
I have discovered, not a stone's cast off,
An ancient castle, held by the old knight
Of the most holy order of the Bell,
Who gives to all knights-errant entertain:
There plenty is of food, and all prepared
By the white hands of his own lady dear.
He hath three squires that welcome all h[is] guests;
The first, hight² Chamberlino, who will see
Our beds prepared, and bring us snowy shee[ts,]
Where never footman stretched his butter[ed] hams;³
The second, hight Tapstero, who will see
Our pots full fillèd, and no froth therein;
The third, a gentle squire, Ostlero hight,
Who will our palfreys slick with wisps [of] straw,
And in the manger put them oats enough,
And never grease their teeth with cand[le] snuff.⁴

[*Wife.* That same dwarf's a pretty boy, b[ut] the squire's a groutnol.⁵]

Ralph. Knock at the gates, my squire, wi[th] stately lance.
[*Tim knocks at the do[or.]
Enter Tapster.*

Tap. Who's there?—You're welcome, ge[n]tlemen: will you see a room?

---

36 ready
37 licensed companies of players
1 lubber
2 called
3 Footmen anointed their calves with grease.
4 A trick to prevent horses from eating
5 blockhead

George. Right courteous and valiant Knight
f the Burning Pestle, this is the Squire Tap-
tero.

Ralph. Fair Squire Tapstero, I a wandering
knight,
light of the Burning Pestle, in the quest
Of this fair lady's casket and wrought purse,
Losing myself in this vast wilderness,
Am to this castle well by fortune brought;
Where, hearing of the goodly entertain
Your knight of holy order of the Bell
Gives to all damsels and all errant knights,
thought to knock, and now am bold to enter.

Tap. An't please you see a chamber, you
re very welcome.   [*Exeunt.*

[*Wife.* George, I would have something
lone, and I cannot tell what it is.

Cit. What is it, Nell?

Wife. Why, George, shall Ralph beat no-
ody again? prithee, sweetheart, let him.

Cit. So he shall, Nell; and if I join with
im, we'll knock them all.]

ACT III, SCENE II.

A Room in the Bell-Inn, Waltham.

Enter Mistress Merrythought, Ralph, Michael, Tim, George, Host and Tapster.

[*Wife.* Oh, Ralph! how dost thou, Ralph?
How hast thou slept to-night? has the knight
used thee well?

Cit. Peace, Nell; let Ralph alone.]

Tap. Master, the reckoning is not paid.

Ralph. Right courteous knight, who, for the
order's sake
Which thou hast ta'en, hang'st out the holy
Bell,
As I this flaming Pestle bear about,
We render thanks to your puissant self,
Your beauteous lady, and your gentle squires,
For thus refreshing of our wearied limbs,
Stiffened with hard achievements in wild de-
sert.

Tap. Sir, there is twelve shillings to pay.

Ralph. Thou merry Squire Tapstero, thanks
to thee
For comforting our souls with double jug:
And, if adventurous fortune prick thee forth,
Thou jovial squire, to follow feats of arms,
Take heed thou tender⁶ every lady's cause,
Every true knight, and every damsel fair;
But spill the blood of treacherous Saracens,
And false enchanters that with magic spells
Have done to death full many a noble knight.

Host. Thou valiant Knight of the Burning

Pestle, give ear to me; there is twelve shillings
to pay, and, as I am a true knight, I will not
bate a penny.

[*Wife.* George, I prithee, tell me, must
Ralph pay twelve shillings now?

Cit. No, Nell, no; nothing but the old
knight is merry with Ralph.

Wife. Oh, is't nothing else? Ralph will be
as merry as he.]

Ralph. Sir Knight, this mirth of yours be-
comes you well;
But, to requite this liberal courtesy,
If any of your squires will follow arms,
He shall receive from my heroic hand
A knighthood, by the virtue of this Pestle.

Host. Fair knight, I thank you for your
noble offer:
Therefore, gentle knight,
Twelve shillings you must pay, or I must cap⁷
you.

[*Wife.* Look, George! did not I tell thee as
much? the knight of the Bell is in earnest.
Ralph shall not be beholding to him: give him
his money, George, and let him go snick up.⁸

Cit. Cap Ralph! no.—Hold your hand, Sir
Knight of the Bell; there's your money [*gives
money*]: have you any thing to say to Ralph
now? Cap Ralph!

Wife. I would you should know it, Ralph
has friends that will not suffer him to be capt
for ten times so much, and ten times to the
end of that.—Now take thy course, Ralph.]

Mist. Mer. Come, Michael; thou and I will
go home to thy father; he hath enough left to
keep us a day or two, and we'll set our fellows
abroad to cry our purse and our casket: shall
we, Michael?

Mich. Ay, I pray, mother; in truth my feet
are full of chilblains with travelling.

[*Wife.* Faith, and those chilblains are a
foul trouble. Mistress Merrythought, when
your youth comes home, let him rub all the
soles of his feet, and his heels, and his ankles,
with a mouse-skin; or, if none of your people
can catch a mouse, when he goes to bed let him
roll his feet in the warm embers, and, I warrant you, he shall be well. . .]

Mist. Mer. Master Knight of the Burning
Pestle, my son Michael and I bid you farewell:
I thank your worship heartily for your kindness.

Ralph. Farewell, fair lady, and your tender
squire.
If pricking through these deserts I do hear
Of any traitorous knight, who through his guile
Hath light upon your casket and your purse,
I will despoil him of them, and restore them.

Mist. Me. I thank your worship.

[*Exit with Michael.*

Ralph. Dwarf, bear my shield; squire, elevate my lance:—

And now farewell, you Knight of holy Bell.

[*Cit.* Ay, ay, Ralph, all is paid.]

Ralph. But yet, before I go, speak, worthy knight,

If aught you do of sad adventures know,

Where errant knight may through his prowess win

Eternal fame, and free some gentle souls

From endless bonds of steel and lingering pain.

Host. Sirrah, go to Nick the barber, and bid him prepare himself, as I told you before, quickly.

Tap. I am gone, sir.   [*Exit.*

Host. Sir Knight, this wilderness affordeth none

But the great venture, where full many a knight

Hath tried his prowess, and come off with shame;

And where I would not have you lose your life

Against no man, but furious fiend of hell.

Ralph. Speak on, Sir Knight; tell what he is and where:

For here I vow, upon my blazing badge,

Never to blaze[9] a day in quietness,

But bread and water will I only eat,

And the green herb and rock shall be my couch,

Till I have quelled that man, or beast, or fiend,

That works such damage to all errant knights.

Host. Not far from hence, near to a craggy cliff,

At the north end of this distressèd town,

There doth stand a lowly house,

Ruggedly builded, and in it a cave

In which an ugly giant now doth won,[10]

Ycleped[11] Barbarossa: in his hand

He shakes a naked lance of purest steel,

With sleeves turned up; and him before he wears

A motley garment, to preserve his clothes

From blood of those knights which he massacres

And ladies gent:[12] without his door doth hang

A copper basin on a prickant[13] spear;

At which no sooner gentle knights can knock,

But the shrill sound fierce Barbarossa hears,

And rushing forth, brings in the errant knight,

And sets him down in an enchanted chair;

Then with an engine[14], which he hath prepared,

With forty teeth, he claws his courtly crown;

Next makes him wink, and underneath his chin

He plants a brazen piece of mighty bord[15],

And knocks his bullets[16] round about his cheeks

Whilst with his fingers, and an instrument

With which he snaps his hair off, he doth fill

The wretch's ears with a most hideous noise:

Thus every knight-adventurer he doth trim,

And now no creature dares encounter him.

Ralph. In God's name, I will fight with him Kind sir,

Go but before me to this dismal cave,

Where this huge giant Barbarossa dwells,

And, by that virtue that brave Rosicleer

That damnéd brood of ugly giants slew,

And Palmerin Frannarco overthrew,

I doubt not but to curb this traitor foul,

And to the devil send his guilty soul.

Host. Brave-sprighted knight, thus far I will perform

This your request; I'll bring you within sight

Of this most loathsome place, inhabited

By a more loathsome man; but dare not stay

For his main force swoops all he sees away.

Ralph. Saint George, set on before! march squire and page.   [*Exeunt*

[*Wife.* George, dost think Ralph will confound the giant?

Cit. I hold my cap to a farthing he does: why, Nell, I saw him wrestle with the great Dutchman, and hurl him.

Wife. Faith, and that Dutchman was a goodly man, if all things were answerable[17] to his bigness. And yet they say there was a Scotchman higher than he, and that they two and a knight met, and saw one another for nothing. . . .]

ACT III, SCENE IV.

Before a Barber's Shop, Waltham.

Enter Ralph, Host, Tim, and George.

[*Wife.* Oh, Ralph's here, George!—God send thee good luck, Ralph!]

Host. Puissant knight, yonder his mansion is.

Lo, where the spear and copper basin are!

Behold that string, on which hangs many a tooth,

Drawn from the gentle jaw of wandering knights![18]

I dare not stay to sound; he will appear. [*Exit.*

Ralph. Oh, faint not, heart! Susan, my lady dear,

The cobbler's maid in Milk-street, for whose sake

9 shine
10 dwell
11 called

12 gentle, courteous
13 pointing upward
14 instrument

15 broad rim (i. e., a barber's basin)
16 soap-balls
17 in proportion

18 Barbers were also surgeons and dentists.

take these arms, oh, let the thought of thee
Carry thy knight through all adventurous
    deeds;
And, in the honour of thy beauteous self,
May I destroy this monster Barbarossa!—
Knock, squire, upon the basin, till it break
With the shrill strokes, or till the giant speak.

[*Tim knocks upon the basin.*

Enter Barber.

[*Wife.* Oh, George, the giant, the giant!—
Now, Ralph, for thy life!]

Bar. What fond[19] unknowing wight is this,
    that dares
To rudely knock at Barbarossa's cell,
Where no man comes but leaves his fleece be-
    hind?

Ralph. I, traitorous caitiff, who am sent by
    fate
To punish all the sad enormities
Thou hast committed against ladies gent
And errant knights. Traitor to God and men,
Prepare thyself; this is the dismal hour
Appointed for thee to give strict account
Of all thy beastly treacherous villanies.

Bar. Fool-hardy knight, full soon thou shalt
    aby[20]
This fond reproach: thy body will I bang;
                [*Takes down his pole.*
And lo, upon that string thy teeth shall hang!
Prepare thyself, for dead soon shalt thou be.

Ralph. Saint George for me!   [*They fight.*
Bar. Gargantua[21] for me!

[*Wife.* To him, Ralph, to him! hold up the
giant; set out thy leg before, Ralph!

Cit. Falsify a blow, Ralph, falsify a blow!
The giant lies open on the left side.

Wife. Bear't off, bear't off still! there,
boy!—Oh, Ralph's almost down, Ralph's almost
down!]

Ralph. Susan, inspire me! now have up again.

Wife. Up, up, up, up, up! so, Ralph! down
with him, down with him, Ralph!

Cit. Fetch him o'er the hip, boy!

[*Ralph knocks down the Barber.*

Wife. There, boy! kill, kill, kill, kill, kill,
Ralph!

19 foolish
20 pay for

21 A giant in Rabelais'
    satire.

Cit. No, Ralph; get all out of him first.]

Ralph. Presumptuous man, see to what des-
    perate end
Thy treachery hath brought thee! The just
    gods,
Who never prosper those that do despise them,
For all the villanies which thou hast done
To knights and ladies, now have paid thee
    home
By my stiff arm, a knight adventurous.
But say, vile wretch, before I send thy soul
To sad Avernus, (whither it must go)
What captives holdst thou in thy sable cave?

Bar. Go in, and free them all; thou hast the
day.

Ralph. Go, squire and dwarf, search in this
    dreadful cave,
And free the wretched prisoners from their
    bonds.

.   .   .   .   .   .

[*Exeunt Tim and George, who presently
    re-enter.*

[*Cit.* Cony, I can tell thee, the gentlemen
like Ralph.

Wife. Ay, George, I see it well enough.—
Gentlemen, I thank you all heartily for gracing
my man Ralph; and I promise you, you shall
see him oftener.]

Bar. Mercy, great knight! I do recant my
    ill,
And henceforth never gentle blood will spill.

Ralph. I give thee mercy; but yet shalt
    thou swear
Upon my Burning Pestle, to perform
Thy promise utterèd.

Bar. I swear and kiss.   [*Kisses the Pestle.*
Ralph. Depart, then, and amend.——
                          [*Exit Barber.*
Come, squire and dwarf; the sun grows toward
    his set,
And we have many more adventures yet.
                                [*Exeunt.*

[*Cit.* Now Ralph is in this humour, I know
he would ha' beaten all the boys in the house,
if they had been set on him.

Wife. Ay, George, but it is well as it is: I
warrant you, the gentlemen do consider what
it is to overthrow a giant.]

THE ELIZABETHAN AGE—PROSE

SIR PHILIP SIDNEY (1554-1586)

FROM THE COUNTESS OF PEMBROKE'S ARCADIA*

To My Dear Lady and Sister, the Countess of Pembroke:

Here now have you, most dear, and most worthy to be most dear, Lady, this idle work of mine, which, I fear, like the spider's web, will be thought fitter to be swept away than worn to any other purpose. For my part, in very truth, as the cruel fathers among the Greeks were wont to do to the babes they would not foster, I could well find in my heart to cast out in some desert of forgetfulness this child, which I am loath to father. But you desired me to do it; and your desire, to my heart, is an absolute commandment. Now it is done only for you, only to you. If you keep it to yourself, or to such friends as will weigh errors in the balance of goodwill, I hope, for the father's sake, it will be pardoned, perchance made much of, though in itself it have deformities; for, indeed, for severer eyes it is not, being but a trifle, and that triflingly handled. Your dear self can best witness the manner, being done in loose sheets of paper, most of it in your presence, the rest by sheets sent unto you as fast as they were done. In sum, a young head, not so well stayed[1] as I would it were, and shall be when God will, having many, many fancies begotten in it, if it had not been in some way delivered, would have

---

[1] steadied

* Sidney did not mean to "walk abroad" into print with his book. This will partly explain the loose style in which it is written. But Elizabethan prose in general was much inferior to Elizabethan poetry. Scholars—the writer class—still clung to Latin, and even Bacon's vigorous English is marred by Latinisms; men of action, like Raleigh, wrote in English, but naturally were little concerned for style; while the work of conscious stylists, like Lyly and Sidney, suffered from "Euphuism," that fashion of affectation and conceits that so weakened the prose of the age. (*Eng. Lit.*, p. 128.) The brief selection given here lacks narrative interest, but will exemplify this curious style and also give a glimpse of that Arcadia which has been idealized in poetry and romance into an imaginary paradise of the simple, natural life.

grown a monster, and more sorry I might be that they came in than that they gat out. But his chief safety shall be the not walking abroad, and his chief protection the bearing the livery of your name, which, if my goodwill do not deceive me, is worthy to be a sanctuary for a greater offender. This say I because I know thy virtue so; and this say I because I know it may be ever so, or, to say better, because it will be ever so. Read it then, at your idle times, and the follies your good judgment will find in it blame not, but laugh at; and so looking for no better stuff than, as in a haberdasher's shop, glasses or feathers, you will continue to love the writer, who doth exceedingly love you, and most, most heartily prays you may long live to be a principal ornament to the family of the Sidneys.

Your loving Brother,
PHILIP SIDNEY.

FROM BOOK I

It was in the time that the earth begins to put on her new apparel against the approach of her lover, and that the sun running a most even course becomes an indifferent arbiter between the night and the day, when the hopeless shepherd Strephon was come to the sands which lie against the island of Cithera,[†] where viewing the place with a heavy kind of delight, and sometimes casting his eyes to the isleward, he called his friendly rival the pastor[2] Claius unto him; and, setting first down in his darkened countenance a doleful copy of what he would speak,[‡]

"O my Claius," said he, "hither we are now come to pay the rent for which we are so called unto by overbusy remembrance; remembrance, restless remembrance, which claims not only this duty of us, but for it will have us

---

[2] shepherd

† As the native isle of Aphrodite, this is a fitting place for Urania, the "heavenly," to be referred to. It lies south of Greece, and Arcadia is a country of Greece; but in Arcadian romances geography matters little.

‡ A good example of the "conceits" which marked the prose and often the poetry of this period. See *Eng. Lit.*, p. 129.

rget ourselves. I pray you, when we were
aid our flock, and that,[3] of other shepherds,
me were running after their sheep, strayed
eyond their bounds, some delighting their
res with seeing them nibble upon the short
ad sweet grass, some medicining their sick
ves, some setting a bell for an ensign of a
.eepish squadron, some with more leisure in-
enting new games for exercising their bodies,
ad sporting their wits,—did remembrance
rant us an holiday, either for pastime or de-
otion, nay, either for necessary food or
atural rest, but that still it forced our
aoughts to work upon this place, where we
.st—alas, that the word 'last' should so long
.st—did grace our eyes upon her ever-flour-
 shing beauty; did it not still cry within us:
Ah, you base-minded wretches! are your
aoughts so deeply bemired in the trade of
rdinary worldlings, as, for respect of gain
ome paltry wool may yield you, to let so much
ime pass without knowing perfectly her es-
ate, especially in so troublesome a season; to
eave that shore unsaluted from whence you
aay see to the island where she dwelleth; to
eave those steps unkissed wherein Urania
rinted the farewell of all beauty?'

"Well, then, remembrance commanded, we
beyed, and here we find that as our remem-
rance came ever clothed unto us in the form
f this place, so this place gives new heat to
he fever of our languishing remembrance.
Yonder, my Claius, Urania alighted; the very
orse methought bewailed to be so disbur-
lened; and as for thee, poor Claius, when thou
ventest to help her down, I saw reverence and
lesire so divide thee that thou didst at one
nstant both blush and quake, and instead of
pearing her wert ready to fall down thyself.
There she sate, vouchsafing[4] my cloak (then
most gorgeous) under her; at yonder rising of
he ground she turned herself, looking back
toward her wonted abode, and because of her
parting, bearing much sorrow in her eyes, the
lightsomeness whereof had yet so natural a
cheerfulness as it made even sorrow seem to
smile; at the turning she spake to us all, open-
ng the cherry of her lips, and, Lord! how
greedily mine ears did feed upon the sweet
words she uttered! And here she laid her
hand over those eyes, when she saw the tears
springing in them, as if she would conceal them
from other[5] and yet herself feel some of thy
sorrow. But woe is me! yonder, yonder did
she put her foot into the boat, at that instant,
as it were, dividing her heavenly beauty between the earth and the sea. But when she
was embarked did you not mark how the winds
whistled, and the seas danced for joy, how the
sails did swell with pride, and all because they
had Urania? O Urania, blessed be thou,
Urania, the sweetest fairness and fairest
sweetness!''

With that word his voice brake so with sobbing that he could say no farther; and Claius
thus answered, ''Alas, my Strephon,'' said he,
''what needs this score to reckon up only our
losses? What doubt is there but that the
sight of this place doth call our thoughts to
appear at the court of affection, held by that
racking steward Remembrance? As well may
sheep forget to fear when they spy wolves, as
we can miss such fancies, when we see any
place made happy by her treading. Who can
choose that saw her but think where she stayed,
where she walked, where she turned, where she
spoke? But what is all this? Truly no more
but, as this place served us to think of those
things, so those things serve as places to call
to memory more excellent matters. No, no,
let us think with consideration, and consider
with acknowledging, and acknowledge with
admiration, and admire with love, and love
with joy in the midst of all woes; let us in
such sort think, I say, that our poor eyes were
so enriched as to behold, and our low hearts so
exalted as to love, a maid who is such, that as
the greatest thing the world can show is her
beauty, so the least thing that may be praised
in her is her beauty. Certainly, as her eyelids are more pleasant to behold than two
white kids climbing up a fair tree, and browsing
on his tenderest branches, and yet are nothing
compared to the day-shining stars contained in
them; and as her breath is more sweet than a
gentle southwest wind, which comes creeping
over flowery fields and shadowed waters in the
extreme heat of summer, and yet is nothing
compared to the honey-flowing speech that
breath doth carry,—no more all that our eyes
can see of her—though when they have seen
her, what else they shall ever see is but dry
stubble after clover-grass—is to be matched
with the flock of unspeakable virtues laid up
delightfully in that best builded fold.

''But, indeed, as we can better consider the
sun's beauty by marking how he gilds these
waters and mountains than by looking upon
his own face, too glorious for our weak eyes;
so it may be our conceits—not able to bear her
sun-staining excellency—will better weigh it
by her works upon some meaner subject employed. And, alas, who can better witness

3 when   5 others
4 allowing

that than we, whose experience is grounded upon feeling? Hath not the only[6] love of her made us, being silly ignorant shepherds, raise up our thoughts above the ordinary level of the world, so as great clerks[7] do not disdain our conference?[8] Hath not the desire to seem worthy in her eyes made us, when others were sleeping, to sit viewing the course of the heavens; when others were running at base,[9] to run over learned writings; when others mark their sheep, we to mark our selves? Hath not she thrown reason upon our desires, and, as it were, given eyes unto Cupid? Hath in any, but in her, love-fellowship maintained friendship betwee rivals, and beauty taught the beholders chastity?'' . . .

[The shepherds rescue the shipwrecked Musidorus and undertake to lead him to the home of a hospitable man in their native country of Arcadia.]

So that the third day after, in the time that the morning did strow roses and violets in the heavenly floor against the coming of the sun, the nightingales, striving one with the other which could in most dainty variety recount their wrong-caused sorrow, made them put off their sleep; and, rising from under a tree, which that night had been their pavilion, they went on their journey, which by-and-by welcomed Musidorus' eyes with delightful prospects. There were hills which garnished their proud heights with stately trees; humble valleys whose base estate seemed comforted with the refreshing of silver rivers; meadows enamelled with all sorts of eye-pleasing flowers; thickets which, being lined with most pleasant shade, were witnessed so to, by the cheerful disposition of many well-tuned birds; each pasture stored with sheep, feeding with sober security, while the pretty lambs, with bleating oratory, craved the dam's comfort; here a shepherd's boy piping, as though he should never be old; there a young shepherdess knitting, and withal singing: and it seemed that her voice comforted her hands to work, and her hands kept time to her voice-music.

As for the houses of the country—for many houses came under their eye—they were all scattered, no two being one by the other, and yet not so far off as that it barred mutual succor; a show, as it were, of an accompanable[10] solitariness, and of a civil wildness.

''I pray you,'' said Musidorus, then first unsealing his long-silent lips, ''what countries be these we pass through, which are so diverse show, the one wanting no store, the other ha ing no store but of want?''

''The country,'' answered Claius, ''whe you were cast ashore, and now are passe through, is Laconia, not so poor by the ba renness of the soil—though in itself not pa ing fertile—as by a civil war, which bei these two years within the bowels of that e tate, between the gentlemen and the peasants— by them named Helots—hath in this sort, as were, disfigured the face of nature and mad it so unhospitable as now you have found i the towns neither of the one side nor the oth willingly opening their gates to strangers, n strangers willingly entering, for fear of bei mistaken. But this country where now you s your foot, is Arcadia; and even hard by the house of Kalander, whither we lead yo This country being thus decked with peace, an the child of peace, good husbandry, the houses you see so scattered are of men, as w two are, that live upon the commodity of thei sheep, and therefore, in the division of the A cadian estate, are termed shepherds—a happ people, wanting little because they desire n much.''

SIR WALTER RALEIGH
(1552?-1618)

THE LAST FIGHT OF THE REVENGE.[*]

The Lord Thomas Howard, with six of he Majesty's ships, six victuallers of London, th bark *Raleigh,* and two or three pinnaces, rid ing at anchor near unto Flores, one of th westerly islands of the Azores, the last o August in the afternoon, had intelligence b one Captain Middleton, of the approach of th Spanish Armada.[1] Which Middleton, being i a very good sailer, had kept them compan three days before, of good purpose both to dis

[1] Armada=fleet; armado=single warship.
[*] In the fall of 1591 a small fleet of English ves sels lay at the Azores to intercept the Spanis treasure-ships from the Indies. On the ap pearance of the Spanish war-vessels the English vessel took to flight, with the exception of th *Revenge,* the Vice Admiral of the fleet, com manded by Sir Richard Grenville. The stor of the fight of the *Revenge* was written b Raleigh, a cousin of Grenville's, and pub lished anonymously in 1591; it was include eight years later, in Hakluyt's *Voyages.* Ba con also celebrated the fight as ''a defea exceeding a victory,'' ''memorable even be yond credit and to the hight of some heroica fable,'' in which ''the ship for the span o fifteen hours sat like a stag amongst hound at the bay, and was sieged and fought with i turn by fifteen great ships of Spain.'' Se also Froude's essay on *England's Forgotte Worthies,* and Tennyson's ballad, *The Revenge*

6 mere
7 scholars
8 conversation
9 prisoner's base
10 companionable

cover their forces the more, as also to give advice to my Lord Thomas of their approach.

He had no sooner delivered the news but the fleet was in sight. Many of our ships' companies were on shore in the island, some providing ballast for their ships, others filling of water and refreshing themselves from the land with such things as they could either for money or by force recover.[2] By reason whereof our ships being all pestered, and rummaging every thing out of order,[†] very light for want of ballast, and that which was most to our disadvantage, the one half of the men of every ship sick and utterly unserviceable. For in the *Revenge* there were ninety diseased; in the *Bonaventure*, not so many in health as could handle her mainsail—for had not twenty men been taken out of a bark of Sir George Cary's, his being commanded to be sunk, and those appointed to her, she had hardly ever recovered[3] England. The rest, for the most part, were in little better state.

The names of her Majesty's ships were these, as followeth: the *Defiance*, which was Admiral, the *Revenge*, Vice Admiral, the *Bonaventure*, commanded by Captain Crosse, the *Lion*, by George Fenner, the *Foresight*, by Thomas Vavisour, and the *Crane*, by Duffield; the *Foresight* and the *Crane* being but small ships only—the other were of middle size. The rest, besides the bark *Raleigh*, commanded by Captain Thin, were victuallers, and of small force or none.

The Spanish fleet, having shrouded their approach by reason of the island, were now so soon at hand as[4] our ships had scarce time to weigh their anchors, but some of them were driven to let slip their cables and set sail. Sir Richard Grenville was the last weighed, to recover the men that were upon the island, which otherwise had been lost. The Lord Thomas with the rest very hardly recovered the wind, which Sir Richard Grenville not being able to do, was persuaded[5] by the master and others to cut[6] his mainsail and cast[7] about, and to trust to the sailing of his ship: for the squadron of Seville were on his weather bow. But Sir Richard utterly refused to turn from the enemy, alleging that he would rather choose to die, than to dishonor himself, his country, and her Majesty's ship, persuading his company that he would pass through the two

squadrons in despite of them, and enforce those of Seville to give him way. Which he performed upon divers of the foremost, who, as the mariners term it, sprang their luff,[8] and fell under the lee of the *Revenge*. But the other course had been the better, and might right well have been answered in so great an impossibility of prevailing. Notwithstanding out of the greatness of his mind he could not be persuaded.[‡]

In the meanwhile, as he attended those which were nearest him, the great *San Philip*, being in the wind of him, and coming towards him, becalmed his sails in such sort as the ship could neither weigh nor feel the helm: so huge and high carged[9] was the Spanish ship, being of a thousand and five hundred tons; who afterlaid the *Revenge* aboard.[10] When he was thus bereft of his sails, the ships that were under his lee, luffing up, also laid him aboard; of which the next was the admiral of the Biscayans, a very mighty and puissant ship commanded by Brittan Dona. The said *Philip* carried three tier of ordinance on a side, and eleven pieces in every tier. She shot[11] eight forthright out of her chase,[12] besides those of her stern ports.

After the *Revenge* was entangled with this *Philip*, four other boarded her, two on her larboard, and two on her starboard. The fight thus beginning at three of the clock in the afternoon continued very terrible all that evening. But the great *San Philip*, having received the lower tier of the *Revenge*, discharged with crossbarshot, shifted herself with all diligence from her sides, utterly misliking her first entertainment. Some say that the ship foundered, but we cannot report it for truth, unless we were assured.

The Spanish ships were filled with companies of soldiers, in some two hundred besides the mariners, in some five, in others eight hundred. In ours there were none at all besides the mariners, but the servants of the commanders and some few voluntary gentlemen only.

After many interchanged volleys of great ordinance and small shot, the Spaniards deliberated to enter the *Revenge*, and made divers attempts, hoping to force her by the multitudes of their armed soldiers and musketeers, but were still repulsed again and again, and at all

---

2 obtain
3 regained
4 that
5 advised
6 spread
7 turn
† I. e., were all cumbered, and badly stowed. The syntax of this sentence, as of others that follow, is very faulty. Cp. note on the style of the preceding selection.

8 kept close to the wind by means of the helm
9 Or *carqued* (a nautical term of uncertain meaning, possibly high-carved or built)
10 came alongside of (from behind)
11 could shoot
12 a joint in the stern
‡ He was a fierce man, "of nature very severe," who in his day had the reputation of eating the wine-glasses after he drank the wine.

times beaten back into their own ships or into the seas. In the beginning of the fight, the *George Noble* of London, having received some shot through her by the armados, fell under the lee of the Revenge, and asked Sir Richard what he would command him, being but one of the victuallers and of small force. Sir Richard bade him save himself, and leave him to his fortune.

After the fight had thus without intermission continued while the day lasted and some hours of the night, many of our men were slain and hurt, and one of the great galleons of the Armada and the admiral of the Hulks[13] both sunk, and in many other of the Spanish ships great slaughter was made. Some write that Sir Richard was very dangerously hurt almost in the beginning of the fight, and lay speechless for a time ere he recovered. But two of the *Revenge's* own company brought home in a ship of lime from the islands, examined by some of the Lords and others, affirmed that he was never so wounded as that he forsook the upper deck, till an hour before midnight; and then being shot into the body with a musket, as he was a-dressing[14] was again shot into the head, and withal his chirurgeon[15] wounded to death. This agreeth also with an examination, taken by Sir Francis Godolphin, of four other mariners of the same ship being returned, which examination the said Sir Francis sent unto master William Killigrew, of her Majesty's Privy Chamber.

But to return to the fight, the Spanish ships which attempted to board the *Revenge*, as they were wounded and beaten off, so always others came in their places, she having never less than two mighty galleons by her sides and aboard her. So that ere the morning from three of the clock the day before, there had fifteen several armados assailed her; and all so ill approved their entertainment, as they were by the break of day far more willing to hearken to a composition[16] than hastily to make any more assaults or entries. But as the day increased, so our men decreased; and as the light grew more and more, by so much more grew our discomforts. For none appeared in sight but enemies, saving one small ship called the *Pilgrim*, commanded by Jacob Whiddon, who hovered all night to see the success;[17] but in the morning, bearing with the *Revenge*, was hunted like a hare among many ravenous hounds, but escaped.

All the powder of the *Revenge* to the last barrel was now spent, all her pikes broken, forty of her best men slain, and the most part of the rest hurt.. In the beginning of the fight she had but one hundred free from sickness, and fourscore and ten sick, laid in hold upon the ballast. A small troop to man such a ship, and a weak garrison to resist so mighty an army! By those hundred all was sustained, the volleys, boardings, and enterings of fifteen ships of war, besides those which beat her at large. On the contrary the Spanish were always supplied with soldiers brought from every squadron, all manner of arms and powder at will. Unto ours there remained no comfort at all, no hope, no supply either of ships, men, or weapons; the masts all beaten overboard, all her tackle cut asunder, her upper work altogether razed; and, in effect, evened she was with the water, but[18] the very foundation or bottom of a ship, nothing being left overhead either for flight or defence.

Sir Richard finding himself in this distress, and unable any longer to make resistance, having endured in this fifteen hours' fight the assault of fifteen several armados, all by turns aboard him, and by estimation eight hundred shot of great artillery, besides many assaults and entries, and that himself and the ship must needs be possessed by the enemy, who were now cast in a ring round about him, the *Revenge* not able to move one way or other but as she was moved by the waves and billows of the sea,—commanded the master gunner, whom he knew to be a most resolute man, to split and sink the ship, that thereby nothing might remain of glory or victory to the Spaniards, seeing in so many hours' fight, and with so great a navy, they were not able to take her, having had fifteen hours' time, fifteen thousand men, and fifty and three sail of men-of-war to perform it withal; and persuaded the company, or as many as he could induce, to yield themselves unto God, and to the mercy of none else, but, as they had, like valiant resolute men, repulsed so many enemies, they should not now shorten the honor of their nation by prolonging their own lives for a few hours or a few days.

The master gunner readily condescended,[19] and divers others. But the Captain and the Master were of another opinion and besought Sir Richard to have care of them, alleging that the Spaniard would be as ready to entertain a composition as they were willing to offer the same, and that there being divers sufficient and valiant men yet living, and whose wounds were not mortal, they might do their country and prince acceptable service hereafter. And (that

13 heavy ships   15 also his surgeon
14 having the wound   16 agreement, terms
   dressed   17 outcome

18 nothing but   19 agreed

where Sir Richard had alleged that the Spaniards should never glory to have taken one ship of her Majesty's, seeing that they had so long and so notably defended themselves) they answered that the ship had six foot of water in hold, three shot under water which were so weakly stopped as, with the first working of the sea, she must needs sink, and was besides so crushed and bruised as she could never be removed out of the place.

And as the matter was thus in dispute, and Sir Richard refusing to hearken to any of those reasons, the Master of the *Revenge* (while the Captain won unto him the greater party) was convoyed aboard the *General Don Alfonso Bassan*. Who finding none over hasty to enter the *Revenge* again, doubting lest Sir Richard would have blown them up and himself, and perceiving by the report of the Master of the *Revenge* his dangerous disposition, yielded that all their lives should be saved, the company sent for England, and the better sort to pay such reasonable ransom as their estate would bear, and in the mean season to be free from galley or imprisonment. To this he so much the rather condescended, as well, as I have said, for fear of further loss and mischief to themselves, as also for the desire he had to recover Sir Richard Grenville; whom for his notable valor he seemed greatly to honor and admire.

When this answer was returned, and that safety of life was promised, the common sort being now at the end of their peril, the most drew back from Sir Richard and the gunner, being no hard matter to dissuade men from death to life. The master gunner finding himself and Sir Richard thus prevented and mastered by the greater number, would have slain himself with a sword had he not been by force withheld and locked into his cabin. Then the *General* sent many boats aboard the *Revenge*, and divers of our men, fearing Sir Richard's disposition, stole away aboard the *General* and other ships. Sir Richard, thus overmatched, was sent unto by Alfonso Bassan to remove out of the *Revenge*, the ship being marvellous unsavory, filled with blood and bodies of dead and wounded men like a slaughter-house. Sir Richard answered that he might do with his body what he list,[20] for he esteemed it not; and as he was carried out of the ship he swoonded,[21] and reviving again desired the company to pray for him. The General used Sir Richard with all humanity, and left nothing unattempted that tended to his recovery, highly commending his valor and worthiness,

and greatly bewailed the danger wherein he was, being unto them a rare spectacle, and a resolution seldom approved,[22] to see one ship turn toward so many enemies, to endure the charge and boarding of so many huge armados, and to resist and repel the assaults and entries of so many soldiers. All which, and more, is confirmed by a Spanish captain of the same Armada, and a present actor in the fight, who, being severed from the rest in a storm, was by the *Lion of London*, a small ship, taken, and is now prisoner in London.

The General Commander of the Armada was Don Alfonso Bassan, brother to the Marquis of Santa Cruce. The Admiral of the Biscayan squadron was Britan Dona; of the squadron of Seville, Marquis of Arumburch. The Hulks and Fly-boats[23] were commanded by Luis Cutino. There were slain and drowned in this fight well near two thousand of the enemies, and two especial Commanders, Don Luis de Sant John, and Don George de Prunaria de Malaga, as the Spanish Captain confesseth, besides divers others of special account, whereof as yet report is not made.

The admiral of the Hulks and the *Ascension* of Seville were both sunk by the side of the *Revenge;* one other recovered the road of Saint Michaels, and sunk also there; a fourth ran herself with the shore to save her men. Sir Richard died, as it is said, the second or third day aboard the *General*, and was by them greatly bewailed. What became of his body, whether it was buried in the sea or on the land we know not: the comfort that remaineth to his friends is, that he hath ended his life honorably in respect of the reputation won to his nation and country, and of the same to his posterity, and that, being dead, he hath not outlived his own honor.§

22 experienced
23 Dutch boats that had   been impressed into the Spanish service.

§ The account of his death by another contemporary, Jan Huyghen van Linschoten, runs thus: "He was borne into the ship called the Saint Paul, wherein was the Admiral of the Fleet, Don Alonso de Barsan. There his wounds were dressed by the Spanish surgeons, but Don Alonso himself would neither see him nor speak with him. All the rest of the captains and gentlemen went to visit him and to comfort him in his hard fortune, wondering at his courage and stout heart, for that he shewed not any sign of faintness nor changing of color. But feeling the hour of death to approach, he spake these words in Spanish, and said: 'Here die I, Richard Grenville, with a joyful and quiet mind, for that I have ended my life as a true soldier ought to do that hath fought for his country, queen, religion, and honor, whereby my soul most joyful departeth out of this body, and shall always leave behind it an everlasting fame of a valiant and true soldier that hath done his duty as he was bound to do.'"

FRANCIS BACON (1561-1626)

ESSAYS*

OF STUDIES

Studies serve for delight, for ornament, and for ability. Their chief use for delight is in privateness and retiring; for ornament, is in discourse; and for ability, is in the judgment and disposition of business. For expert men can execute, and perhaps judge of particulars, one by one; but the general counsels, and the plots and marshalling of affairs, come best from those that are learned. To spend too much time in studies is sloth; to use them too much for ornament, is affectation; to make judgment wholly by their rules, is the humour of a scholar. They perfect nature, and are perfected by experience: for natural abilities are like natural plants, that need pruning by study; and studies themselves do give forth directions too much at large, except they be bounded in[1] by experience. Crafty men[2] contemn studies, simple men admire[3] them, and wise men use them; for they teach not their own use; but that is a wisdom without[4] them, and above them, won by observation. Read not to contradict and confute; nor to believe and take for granted; nor to find talk and discourse; but to weigh and consider. Some books are to be tasted,† others to be swallowed, and some few to be chewed and digested; that is, some books are to be read only in parts; others to be read, but not curiously; and some few to be read wholly, and with diligence and attention. Some books also may be read by deputy, and extracts made of them by others; but that would be only in the less important arguments, and the meaner sort of books; else distilled books are like common distilled waters, flashy[5] things. Reading maketh a full man; conference[6] a ready man; and writing an exact man. And therefore, if a man write little, he had need have a great memory; if he

confer little, he had need have a present wit; and if he read little, he had need have much cunning, to seem to know that[7] he doth not. Histories make men wise; poets witty;[8] the mathematics subtile; natural philosophy deep; moral grave; logic and rhetoric able to contend. *Abeunt studia in mores.*[9] Nay, there is no stond[10] or impediment in the wit but may be wrought out[11] by fit studies; like as diseases of the body may have appropriate exercises. Bowling is good for the stone[12] and reins; shooting[13] for the lungs and breast; gentle walking for the stomach; riding for the head; and the like. So if a man's wit be wandering, let him study the mathematics; for in demonstrations, if his wit be called away never so little, he must begin again. If his wit be not apt to distinguish or find differences, let him study the Schoolmen;[14] for they are *cymini sectores.* If he be not apt to beat over matters, and to call up one thing to prove and illustrate another, let him study the lawyers' cases. So every defect of the mind may have a special receipt.

OF DISCOURSE

Some in their discourse[1] desire rather commendation of wit, in being able to hold all arguments, than of judgment, in discerning what is true; as if it were a praise to know what might be said, and not what should be thought. Some have certain common places and themes wherein they are good, and want variety; which kind of poverty is for the most part tedious, and when it is once perceived ridiculous. The honorablest part of talk is to give the occasion; and again to moderate and pass to somewhat else; for then a man leads the dance. It is good, in discourse and speech of conversation, to vary and intermingle speech of the present occasion with arguments, tales with reasons, asking of questions with telling of opinions, and jest with earnest: for it is a dull thing to tire, and, as we say now, to jade any thing too far. As for jest, there be certain things which ought to be privileged from it; namely, religion, matters of state, great persons, any man's present business of importance, and any case that deserveth pity. Yet there be some that think their wits have been asleep

---

1 checked
2 craftsmen, men of practical skill (much like "expert men" above)
3 wonder at
4 outside of
5 insipid
6 conversation

* The first edition of Bacon's *Essays* (ten in number) was printed in 1597; revised and enlarged editions appeared in 1612 and 1625. The first two essays given here were in the first edition, the next two in the second, the last two in the third; but all follow the text of the third. The spelling is modernized, the paragraphing not; as the essays consist often of detached thoughts, a change of thought may be expected at any point.

† Of the six sentences beginning here Macaulay said: "We do not believe Thucydides himself has anywhere compressed so much thought in so small a space."

7 that which
8 imaginative
9 "Studies are transmuted into character."
10 stand, obstacle
11 removed
12 gravel (a disease of

the kidneys, or reins)
13 archery
14 medieval theologians who were "splitters of cumin-seeds," hair-splitters

---

1 conversation

xcept they dart out somewhat that is piquant, nd to the quick. That is a vein which would[2] e bridled;

Parce, puer, stimulis, et fortius utere loris.[3]

And generally, men ought to find the differ- nce between saltness and bitterness. Cer- ainly, he that hath a satirical vein, as he mak- th others afraid of his wit, so he had need be fraid of others' memory. He that question- th much shall learn much, and content much; ut especially if he apply[4] his questions to the kill of the persons whom he asketh; for he hall give them occasion to please themselves n speaking, and himself shall continually ather knowledge. But let his questions not be roublesome; for that is fit for a poser.[5] And et him be sure to leave other men their turns o speak. Nay, if there be any that would eign and take up all the time, let him find 1eans to take them off, and to bring others on; s musicians use to do with those that dance oo long galliards.[6] If you dissemble some- imes your knowledge of that you are thought o know, you shall be thought another time to now that you know not. Speech of a man's elf ought to be seldom, and well chosen. I new one was wont to say in scorn, *He must eeds be a wise man, he speaks so much of him- elf:* and there is but one case wherein a man 1ay commend himself with good grace; and hat is in commending virtue in another; espe- ially if it be such a virtue whereunto himself retendeth. Speech of touch towards others hould be sparingly used; for discourse ought o be as a field, without coming home to any 1an. I knew two noblemen, of the west part f England, whereof the one was given to coff, but kept ever royal cheer in his house; he other would ask of those that had been at he other's table, *Tell truly, was there never a 'out or dry[7] blow given?* To which the guest vould answer, *Such and such a thing passed.* 'he lord would say, *I thought he would mar a 'ood dinner.* Discretion of speech is more than loquence; and to speak agreeably to him with vhom we deal, is more than to speak in good vords or in good order. A good continued peech, without a good speech of interlocution, hows slowness: and a good reply or second peech, without a good settled speech, showeth hallowness and weakness. As we see in beasts, hat those that are weakest in the course are yet nimblest in the turn; as it is betwixt the greyhound and the hare. To use too many cir- cumstances ere one come to the matter, is wearisome; to use none at all, is blunt.

Of Friendship

It had been hard for him[1] that spake it to have put more truth and untruth together in few words, than in that speech, *Whosoever is delighted in solitude is either a wild beast or a god.* For it is most true that a natural and secret hatred and aversation towards[2] society in any man, hath somewhat of the savage beast; but it is most untrue that it should have any character at all of the divine nature; ex- cept it proceed, not out of a pleasure in soli- tude, but out of a love and desire to sequester a man's self for higher conversation: such as is found to have been falsely and feignedly in some of the heathen; as Epimenides the Can- dian, Numa the Roman, Empedocles the Sicil- ian, and Apollonius of Tyana;* and truly and really in divers of the ancient hermits and holy fathers of the church. But little do men per- ceive what solitude is, and how far it extend- eth. For a crowd is not company; and faces are but a gallery of pictures; and talk but a tinkling cymbal, where there is no love. The Latin adage meeteth[3] with it a little: *Magna civitas, magna solitudo;*[4] because in a great town friends are scattered; so that there is not that fellowship, for the most part, which is in less neighborhoods. But we may go further, and affirm most truly that it is a mere[5] and miserable solitude to want true friends; with- out which the world is but a wilderness; and even in this sense also of solitude, whosoever in the frame of his nature and affections is unfit for friendship, he taketh it of the beast, and not from humanity.

A principal fruit of friendship is the ease and discharge of the fulness and swellings of the heart, which passions of all kinds do cause and induce. We know diseases of stoppings and suffocations are the most dangerous in the body; and it is not much otherwise in the mind; you may take sarza[6] to open the liver, steel to open the spleen, flowers[7] of sulphur for the lungs, castoreum for the brain; but no re- ceipt openeth the heart, but a true friend; to

should
"Spare the whip, boy, and hold more firm- ly the reins." Ovid, *Met.* ii. 127.

4 adapt
5 examiner
6 A lively French dance for two.
7 hard

1 Aristotle, *Politics,* i. 2.
2 aversion for
3 agrees
4 "A great town is a great solitude."

5 pure, complete
6 sarsaparilla
7 flower (i. e., flour, ed. 1639)

* Epimenides, the Cretan poet, was said to have slept in a cave for fifty-seven years; Numa was instructed by the Muse Egeria in a sacred grove; Empedocles surrounded himself with mystery; Apollonius was an ascetic.

whom you may impart griefs, joys, fears, hopes, suspicions, counsels, and whatsoever lieth upon the heart to oppress it, in a kind of civil shrift or confession.

It is a strange thing to observe how high a rate great kings and monarchs do set upon this fruit of friendship whereof we speak: so great, as[8] they purchase it many times at the hazard of their own safety and greatness. For princes, in regard of the distance of their fortune from that of their subjects and servants, cannot gather this fruit, except (to make themselves capable thereof) they raise some persons to be as it were companions and almost equals to themselves, which many times sorteth to[9] inconvenience. The modern languages give unto such persons the name of favorites, or privadoes; as if it were matter of grace, or conversation. But the Roman name attaineth the true use and cause thereof, naming them *participes curarum;*[10] for it is that which tieth the knot. And we see plainly that this hath been done, not by weak and passionate princes only, but by the wisest and most politic that ever reigned; who have oftentimes joined to themselves some of their servants; whom both themselves have called friends, and allowed others likewise to call them in the same manner; using the word which is received between private men.

L. Sylla, when he commanded Rome, raised Pompey (after surnamed the Great) to that height, that Pompey vaunted himself for Sylla's over-match. For when he had carried the consulship for a friend of his,[11] against the pursuit of Sylla, and that Sylla did a little resent thereat, and began to speak great, Pompey turned upon him again, and in effect bade him be quiet; *for that more men adored the sun rising than the sun setting.* With Julius Cæsar, Decimus Brutus had obtained that interest, as[12] he set him down in his testament for heir in remainder after his nephew. And this was the man that had power with him to draw him forth to his death. For when Cæsar would have discharged the senate, in regard of some ill presages, and specially a dream of Calpurnia; this man lifted him gently by the arm out of his chair, telling him he hoped he would not dismiss the senate till his wife had dreamt a better dream. And it seemeth his favor was so great, as Antonius, in a letter which is recited *verbatim* in one of Cicero's Philippics, calleth him *venefica, witch;* as if he

had enchanted Cæsar. Augustus raised Agripp (though of mean birth) to that height, as whe he consulted with Mæcenas about the mar riage of his daughter Julia, Mæcenas took th liberty to tell him, *that he must either marr his daughter to Agrippa, or take away his life there was no third way, he had made him s great.* With Tiberius Cæsar, Sejanus had as cended to that height, as they two were terme and reckoned as a pair of friends. Tiberiu in a letter to him saith, *Hæc pro amiciti nostrâ non occultavi;*[13] and the whole senat dedicated an altar to Friendship, as to a god dess, in respect of the great dearness of friend ship between them two. The like or more wa between Septimius Severus and Plautianus For he forced his eldest son to marry th daughter of Plautianus; and would often main tain Plautianus in doing affronts to his son and did write also in a letter to the senate, b these words: *I love the man so well, as I wis he may over-live me.* Now if these princes ha been as a Trajan or a Marcus Aurelius, a ma might have thought that this had proceeded o an abundant goodness of nature; but bein men so wise, of such strength and severity o mind, and so extreme lovers of themselves, a all these were, it proveth most plainly tha they found their own felicity (though as grea as ever happened to mortal men) but as a half piece,[14] except they mought have a frien to make it entire; and yet, which is more, the were princes that had wives, sons, nephews and yet all these could not supply the comfor of friendship.

It is not to be forgotten what Comineus ob serveth of his first master, Duke Charles th Hardy; namely, that he would communicate hi secrets with none; and least of all, those secret which troubled him most. Whereupon he goet on and saith that towards his latter time tha *closeness did impair and a little perish his un derstanding.* Surely Comineus mought hav made the same judgment also, if it had please him, of his second master, Louis the Eleventh whose closeness was indeed his tormentor. Th parable of Pythagoras is dark, but true; *Co ne edito: Eat not the heart.* Certainly, if man would give it a hard phrase, those tha want friends to open themselves unto are can nibals of their own hearts. But one thing i most admirable[15] (wherewith I will conclud this first fruit of friendship), which is, tha this communicating of a man's self to hi

---

8 that
9 results in
10 "partners of cares"

11 Lepidus
12 such interest that

13 "Because of our friendship I have not concealed this."

14 a half-coin (which sometimes circulated)
15 wonderful

friend works two contrary effects; for it re-
doubleth joys, and cutteth griefs in halves.
For there is no man that imparteth his joys
to his friend, but he joyeth the more; and
no man that imparteth his griefs to his friend,
but he grieveth the less. So that it is, in truth,
of[16] operation upon a man's mind, of like
virtue as the alchemists use[17] to attribute to
their stone[18] for man's body; that it worketh
all[19] contrary effects, but still to the good and
benefit of nature. But yet without praying in
aid of[20] alchemists, there is a manifest image
of this in the ordinary course of nature. For
in bodies, union strengtheneth and cherisheth
any natural action; and on the other side
weakeneth and dulleth any violent impression:
and even so is it of minds.

The second fruit of friendship is healthful
and sovereign for the understanding, as the first
is for the affections.[21] For friendship maketh
indeed a fair day in the affections, from storm
and tempests; but it maketh daylight in the
understanding, out of darkness and confusion
of thoughts. Neither is this to be understood
only of faithful counsel, which a man receiveth
from his friend; but before you come to that,
certain it is that whosoever hath his mind
fraught with many thoughts, his wits and understanding do clarify and break up, in the
communicating and discoursing with another;
he tosseth his thoughts more easily; he mar-
shalleth them more orderly; he seeth how they
look when they are turned into words: finally,
he waxeth wiser than himself; and that more
by an hour's discourse than by a day's meditation. It was well said of Themistocles to
the king of Persia, *That speech was like cloth
of Arras opened and put abroad, whereby
the imagery doth appear in figure; whereas in
thoughts they lie but as in packs.* Neither is
this second fruit of friendship, in opening the
understanding, restrained only to such friends
as are able to give a man counsel; (they indeed are best;) but even without that, a man
learneth of himself, and bringeth his own
thoughts to light, and whetteth his wits as
against a stone, which itself cuts not. In a
word, a man were better relate[22] himself to a
statue or picture, than to suffer his thoughts
to pass in smother.

Add now, to make this second fruit of friendship complete, that other point which lieth more
open and falleth within vulgar[23] observation;

which is faithful counsel from a friend. Her-
aclitus saith well in one of his enigmas, *Dry
light is ever the best.* And certain it is, that
the light that a man receiveth by counsel from
another is drier and purer than that which
cometh from his own understanding and judgment; which is ever infused and drenched in
his affections and customs. So as[24] there is as
much difference between the counsel that a
friend giveth, and that a man giveth himself,
as there is between the counsel of a friend
and of a flatterer. For there is no such flatterer as is a man's self; and there is no such
remedy against flattery of a man's self as the
liberty of a friend. Counsel is of two sorts:
the one concerning manners, the other concerning business. For the first, the best preservative to keep the mind in health is the faithful
admonition of a friend. The calling of a
man's self to a strict account is a medicine,
sometime too piercing and corrosive. Reading
good books of morality is a little flat and dead.
Observing our faults in others is sometimes
improper for our case. But the best recipe
(best, I say, to work, and best to take) is the
admonition of a friend. It is a strange thing
to behold what gross errors and extreme absurdities many (especially of the greater sort)
do commit, for want of a friend to tell them
of them; to the great damage both of their
fame and fortune: for, as St. James saith,[25]
they are as men *that look sometimes into a
glass, and presently forget their own shape
and favor.*[26] As for business, a man may
think, if he will, that two eyes see no more
than one; or that a gamester seeth always
more than a looker-on; or that a man in anger
is as wise as he that hath said over the four
and twenty letters;* or that a musket may
be shot off as well upon the arm as upon a
rest; and such other fond and high imaginations, to think himself all in all. But when all
is done, the help of good counsel is that which
setteth business straight. And if any man
think that he will take counsel, but it shall be
by pieces; asking counsel in one business of
one man, and in another business of another
man; it is well (that is to say, better perhaps
than if he asked none at all); but he runneth
two dangers: one, that he shall not be faithfully counselled; for it is a rare thing, except
it be from a perfect and entire friend, to have
counsel given, but such as shall be bowed and

6 in its
7 are wont
8 T h e   "philosopher's
     stone."
9 wholly

20 calling upon (a legal
     term)
21 feelings
22 unbosom
23 common

24 so that   26 features
25 *Epistle* I, 23
* The number in the Greek alphabet, as also in
   the English when J and U were not differen-
   tiated from I and V.

crooked to some ends which he hath that giveth it. The other, that he shall have counsel given, hurtful and unsafe (though with good meaning), and mixed partly of mischief and partly of remedy; even as if you would call a physician that is thought good for the cure of the disease you complain of, but is unacquainted with your body; and therefore may put you in way for a present cure, but overthroweth your health in some other kind; and so cure the disease and kill the patient. But a friend that is wholly acquainted with a man's estate will beware, by furthering any present business, how he dasheth upon other inconvenience. And therefore rest not upon scattered counsels; they will rather distract and mislead, than settle and direct.

After these two noble fruits of friendship (peace in the affections, and support of the judgment), followeth the last fruit; which is like the pomegranate, full of many kernels; I mean aid and bearing a part in all actions and occasions. Here the best way to represent to life the manifold use of friendship is to cast[27] and see how many things there are which a man cannot do himself; and then it will appear that it was a sparing speech of the ancients, to say, *that a friend is another himself;* for that a friend is far more than himself. Men have their time,[28] and die many times in desire of[29] some things which they principally take to heart; the bestowing of a child,[30] the finishing of a work, or the like. If a man have a true friend, he may rest almost secure that the care of those things will continue after him. So that a man hath, as it were, two lives in his desires. A man hath a body, and that body is confined to a place; but where friendship is, all offices of life are as it were granted to him and his deputy. For he may exercise them by his friend. How many things are there which a man cannot, with any face or comeliness, say or do himself? A man can scarce allege his own merits with modesty, much less extol them; a man cannot sometimes brook to supplicate or beg; and a number of the like. But all these things are graceful in a friend's mouth, which are blushing in a man's own. So again, a man's person hath many proper relations which he cannot put off. A man cannot speak to his son but as a father; to his wife but as a husband; to his enemy but upon terms: whereas a friend may speak as the case requires, and not as it sorteth with the person. But to enumerate these things were

endless; I have given the rule, where a man cannot fitly play his own part; if he have not a friend, he may quit the stage.

OF RICHES

I cannot call riches better than the baggage of virtue. The Roman word is better, *impedimenta.* For as the baggage is to an army, so is riches to virtue. It cannot be spared nor left behind, but it hindereth the march; yea, and the care of it sometimes loseth or disturbeth the victory. Of great riches there is no real use, except it be in the distribution; the rest is but conceit.[1] So saith Solomon, *Where much is, there are many to consume it; and what hath the owner but the sight of it with his eyes?* The personal fruition[2] in any man cannot reach to feel great riches: there is a custody of them; or a power of dole and donative[3] of them; or a fame of them; but no solid use to the owner. Do you not see what feigned prices are set upon little stones[4] and rarities? and what works of ostentation are undertaken, because there might seem to be some use of great riches? But then you will say, they may be of use to buy men out of dangers or troubles. As Solomon saith, *Riches are as a strong hold, in the imagination of the rich man.* But this is excellently expressed that it is in imagination, and not always in fact. For certainly great riches have sold more men than they have bought out. Seek not proud riches, but such as thou mayest get justly, use soberly, distribute cheerfully, and leave contentedly. Yet have no abstract nor friarly contempt of them. But distinguish, as Cicero saith well of Rabirius Posthumus, *In studio rei amplificandæ apparebat, non avaritiæ prædam, sed instrumentum bonitati quæri.*[5] Harken also to Solomon, and beware of hasty gathering of riches: *Qui festinat ad divitias non erit insons.*[6] The poets feign that when Plutus (which is Riches) is sent from Jupiter he limps and goes slowly; but when he is sent from Pluto, he runs and is swift of foot. Meaning that riches gotten by good means and just labor pace slowly; but when they come by the death of others (as by the course of inheritance, testaments, and the like), they come tumbling upon a man. But it mought

27 consider
28 appointed time
29 often die while still desiring
30 in marriage

1 fancy
2 enjoyment
3 distribution and gift
4 Cp. *Utopia*, p. 118.
5 "In his endeavor to increase his wealth, it was evident that he sought not what should be a mere prey for avarice, but an instrument of good."
6 "Who hastens to become rich shall not be innocent."

applied likewise to Pluto, taking him for
 devil. For when riches come from the
vil (as by fraud and oppression and unjust
 ans), they come upon[7] speed. The ways
 enrich are many, and most of them foul.
rsimony is one of the best, and yet is not
 1ocent; for it withholdeth men from works
 liberality and charity. The improvement of
 ground is the most natural obtaining of
hes; for it is our great mother's blessing,
 earth's; but it is slow. And yet where
 n of great wealth do stoop to husbandry, it
 ltiplieth riches exceedingly. I knew a no-
 man in England, that had the greatest audits
 any man in my time; a great grazier, a
 eat sheepmaster, a great timber man, a great
 lier, a great corn-master, a great lead-man,
 d so of iron, and a number of the like points
 husbandry. So as[8] the earth seemed a sea
 him, in respect of the perpetual importation.
 was truly observed by one, that himself came
 ry hardly to a little riches, and very easily
 great riches. For when a man's stock is
 ne to that, that he can expect[9] the prime
 markets, and overcome[10] those bargains
 ich for their greatness are few men's money,
 d be partner in the industries of younger
 n, he cannot but increase mainly.[11] The
 ins of ordinary trades and vocations
  honest; and furthered by two things
 iefly: by diligence, and by a good name for
 od and fair dealing. But the gains of bar-
 ins are of a more doubtful nature, when men
 all wait upon[12] others' necessity, broke[13] by
 vants and instruments to draw them on, put
 others cunningly that would be better chap-
 n,[14] and the like practices, which are crafty
 d naught.[15] As for the chopping[16] of bar-
 ins, when a man buys not to hold but to sell
 er again, that commonly grindeth double,
 th upon the seller and upon the buyer. Shar-
 gs do greatly enrich, if the hands be well
 osen that are trusted. Usury is the certain-
  means of gain, though one of the worst:
 that whereby a man doth eat his bread in
 lore vultus alieni;[17] and besides, doth plough
 on Sundays. But yet certain though it be,
 hath flaws; for that[18] the scriveners and
 okers do value[19] unsound men to serve their
 n turn. The fortune in being the first in an
 vention or in a privilege doth cause some-

times a wonderful overgrowth in riches; as it
was with the first sugar man in the Canaries.
Therefore if a man can play the true logician,
to have as well judgment as invention, he may
do great matters; especially if the times be fit.
He that resteth upon gains certain shall
hardly[20] grow to great riches; and he that
puts all upon adventures doth oftentimes break
and come to poverty: it is good therefore to
guard adventures with certainties, that may
uphold losses. Monopolies, and coemption[21] of
wares for re-sale, where they are not restrained,[22] are great means to enrich; especially if the party have intelligence what
things are like to come into request, and so
store himself beforehand. Riches gotten by
service, though it be of the best rise,[23] yet
when they are gotten by flattery, feeding
humours,[24] and other servile conditions, they
may be placed amongst the worst. As for fishing for testaments and executorships (as Tacitus saith of Seneca, *testamenta et orbos tam-
quam indagine capi*[25]), it is yet worse, by how
much men submit themselves to meaner persons than in service. Believe not much them
that seem to despise riches; for they despise
them that[26] despair of them; and none worse
when they come to them. Be not penny-wise;
riches have wings, and sometimes they fly away
of themselves, sometimes they must be set flying to bring in more. Men leave their riches
either to their kindred, or to the public; and
moderate portions prosper best in both. A
great state left to an heir, is as a lure to all
the birds of prey round about to seize on him,
if he be not the better stablished in years and
judgment. Likewise glorious[27] gifts and foundations are like *sacrifices without salt;* and but
the painted sepulchres of alms, which soon will
putrefy and corrupt inwardly.[28] Therefore
measure not thine advancements by quantity,
but frame them by measure: and defer not
charities till death; for, certainly, if a man
weigh it rightly, he that doth so is rather liberal of another man's than of his own.

Of Revenge

Revenge is a kind of wild justice; which the
more man's nature runs to, the more ought law
to weed it out. For as for the first wrong, it
doth but offend the law; but the revenge of
that wrong putteth the law out of office.[29] Cer-

---

ith
o that
ait for
command
greatly
must watch for
negotiate
buyers
bad

16 bartering, dealing in
17 "in the sweat of an-
    other man's face"
18 because
19 represent them to be
    financially s o u n d
    (for the sake of
    getting a commis-
    sion on the loan)

20 with difficulty
21 cornering
22 i. e., by law
23 source
24 catering to whims
25 "He took wills and
    wardships as with a
    net."

26 who (antecedent is
    they)
27 vain-glorious
28 See *Mark* ix. 49;
    Matthew xxiii. 27.
29 i. e., by assuming its
    function

tainly, in taking revenge, a man is but even with his enemy; but in passing it over, he is superior; for it is a prince's part to pardon. And Solomon, I am sure, saith, *It is the glory of a man to pass by an offense.* That which is past is gone, and irrevocable; and wise men have enough to do with things present and to come; therefore they do but trifle with themselves, that labor in past matters. There is no man doth a wrong for the wrong's sake; but thereby to purchase himself profit, or pleasure, or honor, or the like. Therefore why should I be angry with a man for loving himself better than me? And if any man should do wrong merely out of ill-nature, why, yet it is but like the thorn or briar, which prick and scratch, because they can do no other. The most tolerable sort of revenge is for those wrongs which there is no law to remedy; but then let a man take heed the revenge be such as there is no law to punish; else a man's enemy is still before hand, and it is two for one. Some, when they take revenge, are desirous the party should know whence it cometh. This is the more generous. For the delight seemeth to be not so much in doing the hurt as in making the party repent. But base and crafty cowards are like the arrow that flieth in the dark. Cosmus, duke of Florence, had a desperate saying against perfidious or neglecting friends, as if those wrongs were unpardonable; *You shall read* (saith he) *that we are commanded to forgive our enemies; but you never read that we are commanded to forgive our friends.* But yet the spirit of Job was in a better tune: *Shall we* (saith he) *take good at God's hands, and not be content to take evil also?* And so of friends in a proportion. This is certain, that a man that studieth revenge, keeps his own wounds green, which otherwise would heal and do well. Public revenges are for the most part fortunate;[30] as that for the death of Cæsar; for the death of Pertinax; for the death of Henry the Third of France; and many more. But in private revenges it is not so. Nay rather, vindictive persons live the life of witches; who, as they are michievous, so end they infortunate.

OF GARDENS

God Almighty first planted a garden. And indeed it is the purest of human pleasures. It is the greatest refreshment to the spirits of man; without which buildings and palaces are but gross handiworks: and a man shall ever see that when ages grow to civility and elegancy,

men come to build stately sooner than to garden finely; as if gardening were the greater perfection. I do hold it,[1] in the royal ordering of gardens, there ought to be gardens for all the months in the year; in which several things of beauty may be then in season.[2] For December, and January, and the latter part of November, you must take such things as are green all winter: holly; ivy; bays; juniper; cypress-trees; yew; pine-apple-trees;[3] fir-trees; rosemary; lavender; periwinkle, the white, the purple, and the blue; germander; flags; orange-trees; lemon-trees; and myrtles, if they be stoved;[4] and sweet marjoram, warm set. There followeth, for the latter part of January and February, the mezereon-tree,[6] which then blossoms; crocus vernus,[7] both the yellow and the grey; primroses; anemones; the early tulippa; hyacinthus orientalis; chamaïris;[8] fritellaria. For March, there come violets, specially the single blue, which are the earliest; the yellow daffodil; the daisy; the almond-tree in blossom; the peach-tree in blossom; the cornelian-tree in blossom; sweet-briar. In April follow the double white violet; the wall-flower; the stock-gilliflower; the cowslip; flower-delices,[9] and lilies of all natures; rosemary-flowers; the tulippa; the double peony; the pale daffodil; the French honeysuckle; the cherry-tree in blossom; the damson and plum-trees in blossom; the white thorn in leaf; the lilac-tree. In May and June come pinks of all sorts, specially the blush-pink; roses of all kinds, except the musk, which comes later; honeysuckles; strawberries; bugloss; columbine; the French marigold; flos Africanus;[10] cherry-tree in fruit; ribes;[11] figs in fruit; rasps;[12] vine-flowers; lavender in flowers; the sweet satyrian, with the white flower; herba muscaria;[14] lilium convallium; the apple-tree in blossom. In June come gilliflowers of all varieties; musk-roses; the lime-tree in blossom; early pears and plums in fruit; jennetings;[15] codlins. In August come plums of all sorts in fruit; pears; apricocks; berberries; filberds; musk-melons; monks-hoods of all colors. In September come grapes; apples; poppies of all colors; peaches; melocotones;[16] nectarines; cornelians; wardens; quinces. In October and the beginning of N

---

30 of good result

1 maintain
2 Cp. *Winter's Tale*, iv. 4, 72 ff.
3 pines (cones being called pine-apples)
4 kept in a hot-house
5 warmly placed
6 a shrub-laurel
7 spring crocus
8 dwarf iris
9 fleur-de-lis
10 African marigold
11 currants
12 raspberries
13 orchis
14 grape hyacinth
15 early apples
16 a variety of peach
17 late pears

mber come services;[18] medlars; bullaces;[19]
ses cut or removed to come late; holly-hocks;
d such like. These particulars are for the
mate of London; but my meaning is per-
ived, that you may have *ver perpetuum*,[20] as
e place affords.

And because the breath of flowers is far
reeter in the air (where it comes and goes
ke the warbling of music) than in the hand,
erefore nothing is more fit for that delight,
an to know what be the flowers and plants
at do best perfume the air. Roses, damask
d red, are fast[21] flowers of their smells; so
at you may walk by a whole row of them,
d find nothing of their sweetness; yea though
be in a morning's dew. Bays likewise yield
smell as they grow. Rosemary little; nor
eet marjoram. That which above all others
elds the sweetest smell in the air is the violet,
ecially the white double violet, which comes

twice a year; about the middle of April, and
about Bartholomew-tide.[22] Next to that is the
muskrose. Then the strawberry-leaves dying,
which [yield] a most excellent cordial smell.
Then the flower of the vines; it is a little dust,
like the dust of a bent,[23] which grows upon
the cluster in the first coming forth. Then
sweet-briar. Then wall-flowers, which are very
delightful to be set under a parlor or lower
chamber window. Then pinks and gilliflowers,
specially the matted pink and clove gilliflower.
Then the flowers of the lime-tree. Then the
honeysuckles, so they be somewhat afar off.
Of bean-flowers I speak not, because they are
field flowers. But those which perfume the air
most delightfully, not passed by as the rest,
but being trodden upon and crushed, are three;
that is, burnet, wild-thyme, and watermints.
Therefore you are to set whole alleys[24] of them,
to have the pleasure when you walk or tread.

s o r b, mountain-ash,   20 "perpetual spring"
   rowan   21 frugal
a plum

22 August   24 paths
23 grass-stalk or rush

THE SEVENTEENTH CENTURY

CAROLINE LYRICS

GEORGE HERBERT (1593-1633)

VIRTUE

1

Sweet day, so cool, so calm, so bright,
    The bridal of the earth and sky!
The dew shall weep thy fall to-night;
    For thou must die.

2

Sweet rose, whose hue, angry and brave, .
    Bids the rash gazer wipe his eye,
Thy root is ever in its grave,
    And thou must die.

3

Sweet spring, full of sweet days and roses,
    A box where sweets compacted lie,
My music shows ye have your closes,
    And all must die.

4

Only a sweet and virtuous soul,
    Like seasoned timber, never gives;
But though the whole world turn to coal,
    Then chiefly lives.

THOMAS CAREW (1598?-1639?)

SONG*

1

Ask me no more where Jove bestows,
When June is past, the fading rose,
For in your beauty's orient deep
These flowers, as in their causes, sleep.

2

Ask me no more whither do stray
The golden atoms of the day,
For, in pure love, heaven did prepare
Those powders to enrich your hair.

* In stanza 3, "dividing" means running musical
   divisions; for "sphere," st. 4, see note on *Par.
   Lost,* II, 1030.

3

Ask we no more whither doth haste
The nightingale when May is past,
For in your sweet dividing throat
She winters and keeps warm her note.

4

Ask me no more where those stars light
That downwards fall in dead of night,
For in your eyes they sit, and there
Fixèd become as in their sphere.

5

Ask me no more if east or west
The phoenix builds her spicy nest,
For unto you at last she flies,
And in your fragrant bosom dies.

SIR JOHN SUCKLING (1609-1642)

SONG FROM AGLAURA

1

Why so pale and wan, fond lover?
    Prithee, why so pale?
Will, when looking well can't move her,
    Looking ill prevail?
    Prithee, why so pale?

2

Why so dull and mute, young sinner?
    Prithee, why so mute?
Will, when speaking well can't win her,
    Saying nothing do't?
    Prithee, why so mute?

3

Quit, quit for shame! This will not move
    This cannot take her.
If of herself she will not love,
    Nothing can make her:
    The devil take her!

RICHARD LOVELACE (1618-1658)

TO LUCASTA. GOING TO THE WARS

1

Tell me not, sweet, I am unkind,
    That from the nunnery
Of thy chaste breast and quiet mind
    To war and arms I fly.

2

True, a new mistress now I chase,
    The first foe in the field;
And with a stronger faith embrace
    A sword, a horse, a shield.

3

Yet this inconstancy is such
    As you, too, shall adore;
I could not love thee, dear, so much,
    Loved I not honour more.

TO ALTHEA, FROM PRISON*

1

When Love with unconfinèd wings
    Hovers within my gates,
And my divine Althea brings
    To whisper at the grates;
When I lie tangled in her hair
    And fettered to her eye,
The birds that wanton in the air
    Know no such liberty.

2

When flowing cups run swiftly round
    With no allaying Thames,
Our careless heads with roses bound,
    Our hearts with loyal flames;
When thirsty grief in wine we steep,
    When healths and draughts go free—
Fishes that tipple in the deep
    Know no such liberty.

3

When, like committed linnets, I
    With shriller throat shall sing
The sweetness, mercy, majesty,
    And glories of my King;
When I shall voice aloud how good
    He is, how great should be,
Enlargèd winds, that curl the flood,
    Know no such liberty.

4

Stone walls do not a prison make,
    Nor iron bars a cage;
Minds innocent and quiet take
    That for an hermitage;
If I have freedom in my love
    And in my soul am free,

Lovelace, the gallant cavalier and poet, was, for
his devotion to King Charles, twice behind
bars—a "committed" song-bird. In line 7, the
original reading is "gods," but the emenda-
tion "birds" is too plausible to be dismissed,
especially in view of the sequence—birds,
fishes, winds, angels. In stanza 2, "allaying"
means diluting.

Angels alone, that soar above,
    Enjoy such liberty.

ROBERT HERRICK (1591-1674)

CORINNA'S GOING A-MAYING†

Get up, get up for shame, the blooming morn
Upon her wings presents the god unshorn.
    See how Aurora throws her fair
    Fresh-quilted colours through the air;
    Get up, sweet slug-a-bed, and see
    The dew bespangling herb and tree.
Each flower has wept and bowed toward the
        east
Above an hour since: yet you not dress'd;
    Nay! not so much as out of bed?
    When all the birds have matins said   10
    And sung their thankful hymns, 'tis sin,
    Nay, profanation, to keep in,
Whenas a thousand virgins on this day
Spring, sooner than the lark, to fetch in May.

Rise and put on your foliage, and be seen
To come forth, like the spring-time, fresh and
        green,
    And sweet as Flora. Take no care
    For jewels for your gown or hair:
    Fear not; the leaves will strew
    Gems in abundance upon you: 20
Besides, the childhood of the day has kept,
Against you come, some orient pearls unwept;
    Come and receive them while the light
    Hangs on the dew-locks of the night:
    And Titan on the eastern hill
    Retires himself, or else stands still
Till you come forth. Wash, dress, be brief in
        praying:
Few beads are best when once we go a-Maying.

Come, my Corinna, come; and, coming, mark
How each field turns a street, each street a
        park   30
    Made green and trimmed with trees; see how
    Devotion gives each house a bough
    Or branch: each porch, each door ere this
    An ark, a tabernacle is,
Made up of white-thorn, neatly interwove;
As if here were those cooler shades of love.
    Can such delights be in the street
    And open fields and we not see't?
    Come, we'll abroad; and let's obey
The proclamation made for May: 40

† The "god unshorn" of line 2 is Titan with all
his beams; "May" (14) is hawthorne and
other May blossoms; "beads" (28) are prayers;
"green-gown" (51) is a tumble on the
grass.

And sin no more, as we have done, by staying;
But, my Corinna, come, let's go a-Maying.

There's not a budding boy or girl this day
But is got up, and gone to bring in May.
    A deal of youth, ere this, is come
    Back, and with white-thorn laden home.
    Some have despatched their cakes and cream
    Before that we have left to dream:
And some have wept, and woo'd, and plighted
    troth,
And chose their priest, ere we can cast off
    sloth: 50
    Many a green-gown has been given;
    Many a kiss, both odd and even:
    Many a glance, too, has been sent
    From out the eye, love's firmament;
Many a jest told of the keys betraying
This night, and locks picked, yet we're not
    a-Maying.

Come, let us go while we are in our prime;
And take the harmless folly of the time.
    We shall grow old apace, and die
    Before we know our liberty.   60
    Our life is short, and our days run
    As fast away as does the sun;
And, as a vapour or a drop of rain,
Once lost, can ne'er be found again,
    So when or you or I are made
    A fable, song, or fleeting shade,
    All love, all liking, all delight
    Lies drowned with us in endless night.
Then while time serves, and we are but de-
    caying,
Come, my Corinna, come, let's go a-Maying.   70

TO THE VIRGINS, TO MAKE MUCH OF TIME

1

Gather ye rosebuds while ye may,
    Old time is still a-flying;
And this same flower that smiles to-day,
    To-morrow will be dying.

2

The glorious lamp of heaven, the sun,
    The higher he's a-getting,
The sooner will his race be run,
    And nearer he's to setting.

3

That age is best which is the first,
    When youth and blood are warmer;
But being spent, the worse and worst
    Times still succeed the former.

4

Then be not coy, but use your time,
    And while ye may, go marry;
For, having lost but once your prime,
    You may forever tarry.

TO ELECTRA

1

I dare not ask a kiss,
    I dare not beg a smile,
Lest having that or this,
    I might grow proud the while.

2

No, no, the utmost share
    Of my desire shall be
Only to kiss that air
    That lately kissèd thee.

HOW ROSES CAME RED

1

Roses at first were white,
    Till they could not agree,
Whether my Sapho's breast
    Or they more white should be.

2

But being vanquished quite,
    A blush their cheeks bespread;
Since which, believe the rest,
    The roses first came red.

EDMUND WALLER (1606-1687)

Go, Lovely Rose

1

Go, lovely Rose!
Tell her that wastes her time and me,
    That now she knows,
When I resemble her to thee,
How sweet and fair she seems to be.

2

Tell her that's young,
And shuns to have her graces spied,
    That hadst thou sprung
In deserts, where no men abide,
Thou must have uncommended died.

3

Small is the worth
Of beauty from the light retired;
    Bid her come forth,
Suffer herself to be desired,
And not blush so to be admired.

4

Then die! that she
The common fate of all things rare
  May read in thee;
How small a part of time they share
That are so wondrous sweet and fair.

ON A GIRDLE

1

That which her slender waist confined,
[A]ll now my joyful temples bind;
[N]o monarch but would give his crown,
[H]is arms might do what this has done.

2

It was my heaven's extremest sphere,
[Th]e pale which held that lovely deer.
[M]y joy, my grief, my hope, my love,
[Di]d all within this circle move.

3

A narrow compass! and yet there
[D]welt all that's good, and all that's fair;
[Gi]ve me but what this ribband bound,
[Ta]ke all the rest the sun goes round.

HENRY VAUGHAN (1622-1695)

THE RETREAT

[H]appy those early days, when I
[Sh]ined in my angel infancy!
[B]efore I understood this place
[A]ppointed for my second race,
[O]r taught my soul to fancy ought
[B]ut a white, celestial thought;
[W]hen yet I had not walked above
[A] mile or two from my first love,
[A]nd looking back—at that short space—
[C]ould see a glimpse of His bright face;
[W]hen on some gilded cloud or flower   11
[M]y gazing soul would dwell an hour,
[A]nd in those weaker glories spy
[So]me shadows of eternity;
[B]efore I taught my tongue to wound
[M]y conscience with a sinful sound,
[O]r had the black art to dispense,
[A] several sin to every sense,
[Bu]t felt through all this fleshly dress
[B]right shoots of everlastingness.   20
[O] how I long to travel back,
[A]nd tread again that ancient track!
[Th]at I might once more reach that plain,
[W]here first I left my glorious train;
[Fr]om whence the enlightened spirit sees

That shady city of palm trees.
But ah! my soul with too much stay
Is drunk, and staggers in the way!
Some men a forward motion love,
But I by backward steps would move;   30
And when this dust falls to the urn,
In that state I came, return.

JOHN MILTON (1608-1674)

ON THE MORNING OF CHRIST'S NATIVITY

Composed 1629.

This is the month, and this the happy morn,
Wherein the Son of Heaven's eternal King,
Of wedded maid and virgin mother born,
Our great redemption from above did bring;
  For so the holy sages[1] once did sing,
    That he our deadly forfeit[2] should release,
    And with his Father work us a perpetual peace.

That glorious form, that light unsufferable,
And that far-beaming blaze of majesty,
Wherewith he wont[3] at Heaven's high council-
    table
To sit the midst of Trinal Unity,   11
He laid aside; and here with us to be,
    Forsook the courts of everlasting day,
    And chose with us a darksome house of mortal
        clay.

Say, Heavenly Muse, shall not thy sacred vein
Afford a present to the Infant God?
Hast thou no verse, no hymn, or solemn strain,
To welcome him to this his new abode,
Now while the heaven, by the sun's team un-
    trod,
    Hath took no print of the approaching
        light,   20
And all the spangled host keep watch in
        squadrons bright?

See how from far upon the eastern road
The star-led wizards[4] haste with odours sweet!
O run, prevent[5] them with thy humble ode,
And lay it lowly at his blessed feet;
Have thou the honour first thy Lord to greet,
    And join thy voice unto the angel quire,
    From out his secret altar touched with hal-
        lowed fire.

1 The Old Testament   4 Wise Men from the
  prophets.   East.
2 penalty for sin   5 anticipate
3 was wont

THE HYMN

It was the winter wild,
While the heaven-born child 30
 All meanly wrapt in the rude manger lies;
Nature, in awe to him,
Had doffed her gaudy trim,
 With her great Master so to sympathize:
It was no season then for her
 To wanton with the sun, her lusty paramour.

Only with speeches fair
She woos the gentle air
 To hide her guilty front with innocent snow,
And on her naked shame, 40
Pollute with sinful blame,
 The saintly veil of maiden white to throw;
Confounded, that her Maker's eyes
Should look so near upon her foul deformities.

But he, her fears to cease,
Sent down the meek-eyed Peace:
 She, crowned with olive green, came softly
  sliding
Down through the turning sphere,[6]
His ready harbinger[7]
 With turtle[8] wing the amorous clouds divid-
  ing;
And waving wide her myrtle wand, 51
She strikes a universal peace through sea and
  land.

No war, or battle's sound,
Was heard the world around;
 The idle spear and shield were high uphung;
The hookèd[9] chariot stood
Unstained with hostile blood;
 The trumpet spake not to the armèd throng;
And kings sat still with awful[10] eye,
As if they surely knew their sovran Lord was
  by. 60

But peaceful was the night
Wherein the Prince of Light
 His reign of peace upon the earth began:
The winds, with wonder whist,[11]
Smoothly the waters kissed,
 Whispering new joys to the mild ocean,
Who now hath quite forgot to rave,
While birds of calm sit brooding on the
  charmèd wave.

The stars, with deep amaze,
Stand fixed in steadfast gaze, 70
 Bending one way their precious influence,

And will not take their flight,
For all the morning light,
 Or Lucifer[12] that often warned them thenc[e]
But in their glimmering orbs did glow,
Until their Lord himself bespake and bid th[em]
  go.

And though the shady gloom
Had given day her room,
 The sun himself withheld his wonted spe[ed],
And hid his head for shame,
As[13] his inferior flame
 The new-enlightened world no more sho[uld]
  need:
He saw a greater Sun appear
Than his bright throne or burning axlet[ree]
  could bear.

The shepherds on the lawn,[14]
Or ere the point of dawn,
 Sat simply chatting in a rustic row;
Full little thought they than[15]
That the mighty Pan[16]
 Was kindly come to live with them below:
Perhaps their loves, or else their sheep,
Was all that did their silly[17] thoughts so bu[sy]
  keep.

When such music sweet
Their hearts and ears did greet
 As never was by mortal finger strook,[18]
Divinely-warbled voice
Answering the stringèd noise,
 As all their souls in blissful rapture took:
The air, such pleasure loath to lose,
With thousand echoes still prolongs each hea[v]-
  enly close.

Nature, that heard such sound
Beneath the hollow round
 Of Cynthia's seat[19] the airy region thrilli[ng],
Now was almost won
To think her part was done,
 And that her reign had here its l[ast]
  fulfilling:
She knew such harmony alone
Could hold all heaven and earth in happ[ier]
  union.

At last surrounds their sight
A globe of circular light,
 That with long beams the shamefaced nig[ht]
  arrayed;

---

6 See note to *Par. Lost*,
 II, 1030, p. 255.
7 forerunner
8 turtle-dove

9 The axles of ancient
  war-chariots were
  armed with scythes.
10 full of awe
11 stilled

12 The morning star.
13 as if
14 untilled ground
15 then
16 The god of shepherds;
 here Christ, as the
 Good Shepherd.

17 From the same r[oot]
  as the German *se[lig]*
  holy; here, in[no]-
  cent.
18 struck
19 The moon's sphere.

The helmèd cherubim
And sworded seraphim
  Are seen in glittering ranks with wings displayed,
Harping in loud and solemn quire,
With unexpressive[20] notes, to Heaven's newborn heir.

Such music (as 'tis said)
Before was never made,
  But when of old the sons of morning sung,[21]
While the Creator great   120
His constellations set,
  And the well-balanced world on hinges hung,
And cast the dark foundations deep,
And bid the weltering waves their oozy channel keep.

Ring out, ye crystal spheres!
Once bless our human ears
  (If ye have power to touch our senses so),
And let your silver chime
Move in melodious time;
  And let the bass of heaven's deep organ blow;
And with your ninefold[22] harmony   131
Make up full consort to the angelic symphony.

For if such holy song
Enwrap our fancy long,
  Time will run back and fetch the age of gold;
And speckled Vanity
Will sicken soon and die,
  And leprous Sin will melt from earthly mould;
And Hell itself will pass away,
And leave her dolorous mansions to the peering day.   140

Yea, Truth and Justice then
Will down return to men,
  Orbed in a rainbow; and, like glories wearing,
Mercy will sit between,
Throned in celestial sheen,
  With radiant feet the tissued clouds down steering;
And heaven, as at some festival,
Will open wide the gates of her high palace-hall.

But wisest Fate says no,
This must not yet be so;   150

The Babe yet lies in smiling infancy
That on the bitter cross
Must redeem our loss,
  So both himself and us to glorify:
Yet first, to those ychained in sleep,
The wakeful trump of doom must thunder through the deep,[23]

With such a horrid clang
As on Mount Sinai rang,[24]
  While the red fire and smouldering clouds outbrake:
The aged earth, aghast   160
With terror of that blast,[25]
  Shall from the surface to the centre shake,
When, at the world's last session,
The dreadful Judge in middle air shall spread his throne.

And then at last our bliss
Full and perfect is,[26]
  But now begins; for from this happy day
The old Dragon under ground,
In straiter limits bound,
  Not half so far casts his usurpèd sway; 170
And wroth to see his kingdom fail,
Swinges[27] the scaly horror of his folded tail.

The oracles are dumb;[28]
No voice or hideous hum
  Runs through the archèd roof in words deceiving.
Apollo from his shrine
Can no more divine,
  With hollow shriek the steep of Delphos leaving.
No nightly trance, or breathèd spell,
Inspires the pale-eyed priest from the prophetic cell.   180

The lonely mountains o'er,
And the resounding shore,
  A voice of weeping heard and loud lament;
From haunted spring, and dale
Edged with poplar pale,
  The parting Genius[29] is with sighing sent;
With flower-inwoven tresses torn,
The Nymphs in twilight shade of tangled thickets mourn.

In consecrated earth,
And on the holy hearth,   190

---

20 inexpressible
21 "When the morning stars sang together." *Job*, xxxviii, 7.
22 See note on p. 255. The spheres were sometimes held to be only nine in number.
23 ? the air
24 When God gave Moses the ten commandments.
25 Cp. l. 156.
26 will be
27 lashes
28 Christ's coming is conceived as putting to naught the heathen divinities.
29 singular of *genii*—spirits

The Lars and Lemures[30] moan with midnight
        plaint;
In urns and altars round,
A drear and dying sound
    Affrights the flamens[31] at their service
        quaint;
And the chill marble seems to sweat,
While each peculiar power forgoes his wonted
        seat.

Peor[32] and Baälim[32]
Forsake their temples dim,
    With that twice-battered god of Palestine;[33]
And mooned Ashtaroth,[34]   200
Heaven's queen and mother both,
    Now sits not girt with tapers' holy shine;
The Libyc Hammon[35] shrinks his horn;
In vain the Tyrian maids their wounded Tham-
        muz[36] mourn.

And sullen Moloch,[37] fled,
Hath left in shadows dread
    His burning idol all of blackest hue;
In vain with cymbals' ring
They call the grisly king,
    In dismal dance about the furnace blue;   210
The brutish gods of Nile as fast,
Isis[38] and Orus[39] and the dog Anubis,[40] haste.

Nor is Osiris seen
In Memphian grove or green,
    Trampling the unshowered grass with low-
        ings loud;
Nor can he be at rest
Within his sacred chest;[41]
    Naught but profoundest Hell can be his
        shroud;
In vain, with timbreled anthems dark,
The sable-stoled sorcerers bear his worshiped
        ark.

He feels from Juda's land   221
The dreaded Infant's hand;

The rays of Bethlehem blind his dusky eyn;
Nor all the gods beside
Longer dare abide,
    Not Typhon[42] huge ending in snaky twine:
Our Babe, to show his Godhead true,
Can in his swaddling bands control the damned
    crew.

So when the sun in bed,
Curtained with cloudy red,   230
    Pillows his chin upon an orient wave,
The flocking shadows pale
Troop to the infernal jail,
    Each fettered ghost slips to his several grave,
And the yellow-skirted fays
Fly after the night-steeds, leaving their moon-
        loved maze.

But see! the Virgin blest
Hath laid her Babe to rest.
    Time is our tedious song should here have
        ending:
Heaven's youngest-teemed[43] star   240
Hath fixed her polished car,
    Her sleeping Lord with handmaid lamp at-
        tending;
And all about the courtly stable
Bright-harnessed angels sit in order serviceable.

ON SHAKESPEARE. 1630

WHAT needs my Shakespeare for his honoured
        bones
The labour of an age in piled stones?
Or that his hallowed reliques should be hid
Under a star-ypointing[44] pyramid?
Dear son of memory, great heir of fame,
What need'st thou such weak witness of thy
        name?
Thou in our wonder and astonishment
Hast built thyself a livelong monument.
For whilst to the shame of slow-endeavouring
        art,
Thy easy numbers flow, and that each heart   10
Hath from the leaves of thy unvalued[45] book
Those Delphic[46] lines with deep impression took;
Then thou, our fancy of itself bereaving,
Dost make us marble with too much conceiv-
        ing;[47]
And so sepulchred in such pomp dost lie,
That kings for such a tomb would wish to die.

---

30 spirits of the depart-
    ed (to whom sacri-
    fices would no
    longer be made).
31 Roman priests
32 Phœnician divinities.
33 Dagon (I Samuel, v,
    1-4.)
34 Phœnician goddess of
    the moon.
35 The Egyptian horned
    god Ammon.
36 Adonis, a god of the Syrians, who having been
    slain by a wild boar, was said to die every
    year and revive again.
37 Chief god of the Phœnicians; his image was of
    brass and filled with fire and into his arms
    children were thrown to be sacrificed.

38 Wife of Osiris, the
    god of the Nile,
    who is below con-
    fused with the bull-
    god Apis.
39 Their son.
40 An Egyptian divin-
    ity in the form of
    a dog.
41 He was captured by
    being lured to en-
    ter a chest.

42 A mythological snake-
    like monster.
43 born (the Star of
    Bethlehem)
44 The form has no war-
    rant, but the mean-
    ing is clear.

45 invaluable
46 oracular, wise
47 The thought is not
    very clear, but cp.
    lines 7, 8, and Il
    Penseroso, 42.

L'ALLEGRO[1]

HENCE, loathèd Melancholy,
  Of Cerberus[2] and blackest Midnight born
In Stygian cave forlorn,
  'Mongst horrid shapes and shrieks and sights
    unholy!
Find out some uncouth[3] cell,
  Where brooding darkness spreads his jealous
    wings,
And the night-raven sings;
  There under ebon shades and low-browed
    rocks,
As ragged as thy locks,
  In dark Cimmerian[4] desert ever dwell.   10
But come, thou Goddess fair and free,
  In heaven yclept Euphrosyne,
And by men heart-easing Mirth;
  Whom lovely Venus, at a birth,
With two sister Graces[5] more,
  To ivy-crownèd Bacchus bore;
Or whether (as some sager[6] sing)
  The frolic wind that breathes the spring,
Zephyr, with Aurora playing,
  As he met her once a-Maying,   20
There on beds of violets blue
  And fresh-blown roses washed in dew,
Filled her with thee, a daughter fair,
  So buxom,[7] blithe, and debonair.
Haste thee, nymph, and bring with thee
  Jest, and youthful Jollity,
Quips, and cranks[8] and wanton wiles,
  Nods and becks[9] and wreathèd smiles,
Such as hang on Hebe's[10] cheek,
  And love to live in dimple sleek;   30
Sport that wrinkled Care derides,
  And Laughter holding both his sides.
Come, and trip it as you go,
  On the light fantastic toe;
And in thy right hand lead with thee
  The mountain-nymph, sweet Liberty;
And if I give thee honour due,
  Mirth, admit me of thy crew,
To live with her, and live with thee,
  In unreprovèd pleasures free: 40
To hear the lark begin his flight,
  And singing, startle the dull night,
From his watch-tower in the skies,
  Till the dappled dawn doth rise;

Then to come[11] in spite of sorrow,
  And at my window bid good-morrow,
Through the sweet-briar or the vine,
  Or the twisted eglantine;[12]
While the cock, with lively din,
  Scatters the rear of darkness thin;   50
And to the stack, or the barn-door,
  Stoutly struts his dames before:
Oft listening how the hounds and horn
  Cheerly rouse the slumbering morn,
From the side of some hoar hill,
  Through the high wood echoing shrill:
Sometime walking, not unseen,
  By hedge-row elms, on hillocks green,
Right against the eastern gate
  Where the great sun begins his state,   60
Robed in flames and amber light,
  The clouds in thousand liveries dight;[13]
While the ploughman, near at hand,
  Whistles o'er the furrowed land,
And the milkmaid singeth blithe,
  And the mower whets his scythe,
And every shepherd tells his tale[14]
  Under the hawthorn in the dale.
Straight mine eye hath caught new pleas-
    ures,
  Whilst the landskip round it measures: 70
Russet lawns and fallows[15] grey,
  Where the nibbling flocks do stray;
Mountains on whose barren breast
  The labouring clouds do often rest;
Meadows trim, with daisies pied,
  Shallow brooks and rivers wide;
Towers and battlements it sees
  Bosomed high in tufted trees,
Where perhaps some beauty lies,
  The cynosure[16] of neighbouring eyes.   80
Hard by, a cottage chimney smokes
  From betwixt two aged oaks,
Where Corydon and Thyrsis[17] met
  Are at their savoury dinner set
Of herbs and other country messes,
  Which the neat-handed Phillis[17] dresses;
And then in haste her bower she leaves,
  With Thestylis[17] to bind the sheaves;
Or, if the earlier season lead,
  To the tanned haycock in the mead.   90
Sometimes, with secure delight,
  The upland hamlets will invite,
When the merry bells ring round,
  And the jocund rebecks[18] sound
To many a youth and many a maid

1 The Cheerful Man.
2 The three-headed dog
    that guarded the
    entrance to Hades.
3 unknown
4 The Cimmerians of fa-
    ble lived beyond the
    ocean streams, out
    of reach of the
    sun.
5 Aglaia and Thalia,

goddesses of festive
  joy.
6 more sagely (The
    mythology that fol-
    lows is Milton's
    own invention).
7 lithe, lively
8 odd turns of speech
9 beckonings
10 Daughter of Jupiter
    and Juno; goddess
    of youth.

11 i. e., arise and go (to
    the window)
12 honeysuckle
13 decked
14 counts his sheep
15 untilled land

16 center of observation
17 Common names of
    rustics in pastoral
    poetry.
18 Instruments like vio-
    lins.

Dancing in the chequered shade;
And young and old come forth to play
On a sunshine holiday,
Till the livelong daylight fail:
Then to the spicy nut-brown ale,   100
With stories told of many a feat,
How Faery Mab the junkets eat
She[19] was pinched and pulled, she said;
And he, by Friar's[20] lantern led,
Tells how the drudging goblin[21] sweat
To earn his cream-bowl duly set,
When in one night, ere glimpse of morn,
His shadowy flail hath threshed the corn
That ten day-labourers could not end;
Then lies him down, the lubber fiend,   110
And, stretched out all the chimney's
        length,
Basks at the fire his hairy strength,
And crop-full out of doors he flings,
Ere the first cock his matin rings.
Thus done the tales, to bed they creep,
By whispering winds soon lulled asleep.
Towered cities please us then,
And the busy hum of men,
Where throngs of knights and barons bold,
In weeds[22] of peace high triumphs[23] hold,
With store of ladies, whose bright eyes   121
Rain influence, and judge the prize
Of wit or arms, while both contend
To win her grace whom all commend.
There let Hymen[24] oft appear
In saffron robe, with taper clear,
And pomp and feast and revelry,
With mask[25] and antique pageantry;
Such sights as youthful poets dream
On summer eves by haunted stream.   130
Then to the well-trod stage anon,
If Jonson's learnèd sock[26] be on,
Or sweetest Shakespeare, Fancy's child,
Warble his native wood-notes wild.
And ever, against eating cares,
Lap me in soft Lydian[27] airs,
Married to immortal verse,
Such as the meeting soul may pierce,
In notes with many a winding bout[28]
Of linkèd sweetness long drawn out,   140
With wanton heed[29] and giddy cunning,

The melting voice through mazes running,
Untwisting all the chains that tie
The hidden soul of harmony;
That Orpheus' self[30] may heave his head
From golden slumber on a bed
Of heaped Elysian flowers, and hear
Such strains as would have won the ear
Of Pluto to have quite set free
His half-regainèd Eurydice.   150
These delights if thou canst give,
Mirth, with thee I mean to live.

IL PENSEROSO.[1]

HENCE, vain deluding Joys,
    The brood of Folly without father bred!
How little you bested,[2]
    Or fill the fixèd mind with all your toys!
Dwell in some idle brain,
    And fancies fond[3] with gaudy shapes pos-
        sess,[4]
As thick and numberless
    As the gay motes that people the sun-beams,
Or likest hovering dreams,
    The fickle pensioners of Morpheus' train.[5]   10
But hail, thou Goddess sage and holy,
Hail, divinest Melancholy!
Whose saintly visage is too bright
To hit the sense of human sight,
And therefore to our weaker view
O'erlaid with black, staid Wisdom's hue;
Black, but such as in esteem
Prince Memnon's sister[6] might beseem,
Or that starred Ethiop queen[7] that strove
To set her beauty's praise above   20
The sea nymphs, and their powers offended.
Yet thou art higher far descended:
Thee bright-haired Vesta[8] long of yore
To solitary Saturn bore;
His daughter she (in Saturn's reign
Such mixture was not held a stain).
Oft in glimmering bowers and glades
He met her, and in secret shades
Of woody Ida's[9] inmost grove,

[30] Stones and trees and beasts followed his music
and by it he even drew his wife Eurydice
forth from Hades, but lost her because he
looked back to see whether she were coming.

19 One of the story-tel-
    lers. For the pranks
    of Faery Mab, see
    Romeo and Juliet,
    I, iv, 53, ff.
20 ? Will o' the wisp.
21 R o b i n Goodfellow,
    t h e mischievous
    fairy. People placed
    a bowl of cream at
    the door to insure
    his help, and to
    prevent his mis-
    chief.

22 dress
23 processions, s h o w s,
    revels
24 The god of marriage.
25 A form of entertain-
    ment.
26 low-heeled shoe, sym-
    bol of comedy
27 One of the three
    moods of Grecian
    music.
28 turn
29 freedom and c a r e
    combined

1 The Thoughtful Man.
2 bestead (profit)
3 foolish
4 captivate
5 followers of the god
    of dreams
6 Memnon was king of
    the Ethiopians at
    the time of the Tro-
    jan wars.
7 Cassiopea was carried
    by Perseus to heav-
    en, where she be-

came a constella-
    tion.
8 Goddess of the hearth
    or of fire, possibly
    signifying genius.
    The genealogy is
    Milton's invention.
9 Mt. Ida in Crete, the
    ancient kingdom of
    Saturn, from which
    he was driven by
    his son Jupiter.

Whilst yet there was no fear of Jove. 30
Come, pensive Nun, devout and pure,
Sober, steadfast, and demure,
All in a robe of darkest grain,
Flowing with majestic train,
And sable stole10 of cypress lawn11
Over thy decent12 shoulders drawn.
Come, but keep thy wonted state,
With even step, and musing gait,
And looks commercing with the skies,
Thy rapt soul sitting in thine eyes: 40
There, held in holy passion still,
Forget thyself to marble, till
With a sad leaden downward cast
Thou fix them on the earth as fast.
And join with thee calm Peace, and Quiet,
Spare Fast, that oft with gods doth diet,
And hears the Muses in a ring
Aye round about Jove's altar sing;
And add to these retired Leisure,
That in trim gardens takes his pleasure; 50
But first, and chiefest, with thee bring
Him that yon soars on golden wing,
Guiding the fiery-wheeled throne,
The cherub Contemplation;13
And the mute Silence hist14 along,
Less Philomel will deign a song,
In her sweetest, saddest plight,
Smoothing the rugged brow of Night,
While Cynthia checks her dragon yoke15
Gently o'er the accustomed16 oak: 60
Sweet bird, that shunn'st the noise of folly,
Most musical, most melancholy!
Thee, chauntress, oft the woods among,
I woo to hear thy even-song;
And missing thee, I walk unseen
On the dry smooth-shaven green,
To behold the wandering moon,
Riding near her highest noon,
Like one that had been led astray
Through the heaven's wide pathless way, 70
And oft, as if her head she bowed,
Stooping through a fleecy cloud.
Oft on a plat of rising ground,
I hear the far-off curfew17 sound,
Over some wide-watered shore,
Swinging slow with sullen roar;
Or if the air will not permit,
Some still removed place will fit,

Where glowing embers through the room
Teach light to counterfeit a gloom, 80
Far from all resort of mirth,
Save the cricket on the hearth,
Or the bellman's drowsy charm18
To bless the doors from nightly harm.
Or let my lamp at midnight hour
Be seen in some high lonely tower,
Where I may oft out-watch the Bear,19
With thrice-great Hermes;20 or unsphere
The spirit of Plato, to unfold
What worlds or what vast regions hold 90
The immortal mind that hath forsook
Her mansion in this fleshy nook;
And21 of those demons that are found
In fire, air, flood, or underground,
Whose power hath a true consent22
With planet or with element.
Sometime let gorgeous Tragedy
In sceptred pall23 come sweeping by,
Presenting Thebes,24 or Pelops'25 line,
Or the tale of Troy divine,26 100
Or what (though rare) of later age
Ennobled hath the buskined stage.27
But, O sad Virgin! that thy power
Might raise Musæus28 from his bower;
Or bid the soul of Orpheus29 sing
Such notes as, warbled to the string,
Drew iron tears down Pluto's cheek,
And made Hell grant what love did seek;
Or call up him that left half-told
The story of Cambuscan bold,30 110
Of Camball, and of Algarsife,
And who had Canace to wife,
That owned the virtuous31 ring and glass,
And of the wondrous horse of brass
On which the Tartar king did ride!
And if aught else great bards beside
In sage and solemn tunes have sung,
Of turneys, and of trophies hung,
Of forests, and enchantments drear,
Where more is meant than meets the ear.32 120
Thus, Night, oft see me in thy pale career,
Till civil-suited Morn appear,

10 robe
11 A thin texture.
12 seemly, modest
13 The name is Milton's, but cp. Ezekiel x.
14 lead hushed
15 Cynthia (Diana, goddess of the moon) was not drawn by dragons; Ceres, goddess of harvests, was.
16 frequented (by Philomel, the nightingale)
17 A bell rung in olden times at eight o'clock as a signal that fires were to be covered and lights put out.

18 The night watchman's hourly cry often ended with a benediction.
19 The constellation of the Great Dipper which remains in the heavens all night.
20 I. e., read the works of Hermes Trismegistus (thrice great), a mythical learned king of Egypt.
21 Supply "to tell" in the same construction with "to unfold."
22 con-sentio, agreement
23 mantle of state
24 Aeschylus's "Seven Against Thebes."
25 Sophocles' "Electra."
26 Homer's "Iliad."
27 Shakespeare? The buskin was the high-heeled shoe symbolical of tragedy.
28 son of Orpheus
29 See note 30, p. 228.
30 References in ll. 110-115 are all to Chaucer's "Squiere's Tale."
31 powerful
32 Spenser?

Not tricked and frounced[33] as she was wont
With the Attic boy[34] to hunt,
But kerchieft in a comely cloud,
While rocking winds are piping loud,
Or ushered with a shower still,
When the gust hath blown his fill,
Ending on the rustling leaves,
With minute-drops from off the eaves.   130
And when the sun begins to fling
His flaring beams, me, Goddess, bring
To archèd walks of twilight groves,
And shadows brown, that Sylvan[35] loves,
Of pine, or monumental oak,
Where the rude axe with heavèd stroke
Was never heard the nymphs to daunt,
Or fright them from their hallowed haunt.
There in close covert by some brook,
Where no profaner eye may look,   140
Hide me from day's garish eye,
While the bee with honeyed thigh,
That at her flowery work doth sing,
And the waters murmuring,
With such consort as they keep,
Entice the dewy-feathered Sleep;
And let some strange mysterious dream
Wave at his[36] wings in airy stream
Of lively portraiture displayed,
Softly on my eyelids laid[37];   150
And as I wake,[38] sweet music breathe
Above, about, or underneath,
Sent by some spirit to mortals good,
Or the unseen Genius of the wood.
But let my due feet never fail
To walk the studious cloister's pale,[39]
And love the high embowèd[40] roof,
With antique pillars massy proof,[41]
And storied[42] windows richly dight,
Casting a dim religious light.   160
There let the pealing organ blow,
To the full-voiced quire below,
In service high and anthems clear,
As may with sweetness, through mine ear,
Dissolve me into ecstasies,
And bring all Heaven before mine eyes.
And may at last my weary age
Find out the peaceful hermitage,
The hairy gown, and mossy cell,
Where I may sit and rightly spell[43]   170
Of every star that heaven doth shew,
And every herb that sips the dew,
Till old experience do attain
To something like prophetic strain.

33 curled
34 Cephalus, beloved by Aurora.
35 Sylvanus, a forest god.
36 Sleep's.
37 Modifies "dream.
38 Supply "let."
39 limits
40 vaulted
41 ? massively proof
42 painted to represent stories
43 strue, study

These pleasures, Melancholy, give,
And I with thee will choose to live.

LYCIDAS.*

YET once more,[1] O ye laurels,[2] and once more
Ye myrtles[2] brown, with ivy[2] never sere,
I come to pluck your berries harsh and crude
And with forced fingers rude
Shatter your leaves before the mellowing year
Bitter constraint and sad occasion dear
Compels me to disturb your season due;
For Lycidas is dead, dead ere his prime,
Young Lycidas, and hath not left his peer.
Who would not sing for Lycidas? he knew   10
Himself to sing, and build the lofty rhyme.
He must not float upon his watery bier
Unwept, and welter[3] to the parching wind,
Without the meed of some melodious tear.
  Begin then, Sisters of the sacred well[4]
That from beneath the seat of Jove doth
          spring;
Begin, and somewhat loudly sweep the string.
Hence with denial vain and coy excuse:
So may some gentle Muse
With lucky words favour my destined urn,   20
And as he passes turn,
And bid fair peace be to my sable shroud.
  For we were nursed upon the self-same hill,
Fed the same flock, by fountain, shade, and
          rill;
Together both, ere the high lawns[6] appeared
Under the opening eyelids of the morn,
We drove a-field, and both together heard
What time the gray-fly[7] winds her sultry horn
Battening[8] our flocks with the fresh dews of
          night,
Oft till the star that rose at evening, bright, 30
Toward heaven's descent had sloped his wes-
          tering wheel.
Meanwhile the rural ditties were not mute,
Tempered to the oaten flute;

1 Milton apparently had written nothing for three years.
2 Symbols of the poet's rewards.
3 toss, roll
4 The Pierian spring at the foot of Mt. Olympus, Jove's
seat; the birthplace of the nine muses
5 i. e., at the same college
6 pastures
7 The trumpet fly that makes a sharp hissing sound at noon
8 fattening
* This elegy was written in memory of Edward King, a fellow student of Milton's at Cambridge, who was drowned off the Welsh coast August, 1637. The sad event and the poet's sorrow are poetically set forth in the pastoral guise of one shepherd mourning for another. The fact, moreover, that King was destined for the Church enabled Milton to introduce St. Peter and voice, through him, a Puritan denunciation of the corruption among the clergy. See Eng. Lit., p. 149.

ough Satyrs danced, and Fauns with cloven
  heel
rom the glad sound would not be absent long;
nd old Damœtas[9] loved to hear our song.
  But O the heavy change, now thou art gone,
ow thou art gone, and never must return!
hee, Shepherd, thee the woods and desert
  caves,
/ith wild thyme and the gadding vine
  o'ergrown,
nd all their echoes, mourn.   41
he willows and the hazel copses green
hall now no more be seen,
anning their joyous leaves to thy soft lays.
s killing as the canker to the rose,
r taint-worm to the weanling[10] herds that
  graze,
r frost to flowers, that their gay wardrobe
  wear,
/hen first the white-thorn blows;
uch, Lycidas, thy loss to shepherd's ear.
  Where were ye, Nymphs, when the remorseless deep   50
losed o'er the head of your loved Lycidas?
or neither were ye playing on the steep
/here your old bards, the famous Druids, lie,
or on the shaggy top of Mona[11] high,
or yet where Deva[12] spreads her wizard
  stream.
y me, I fondly dream!
Iad ye been there—for what could that have
  done?
/hat could the Muse[13] herself that Orpheus
  bore,
he Muse herself, for her enchanting son,
/hom universal nature did lament,   60
/hen by the rout that made the hideous roar,
Iis gory visage down the stream was sent,
own the swift Hebrus to the Lesbian shore?[14]
  Alas! what boots it with uncessant care
o tend the homely, slighted, shepherd's
  trade,[15]
nd strictly meditate the thankless Muse?
/ere it not better done, as others use,
o sport with Amaryllis in the shade,
r with the tangles of Neæra's hair?[16]
ame is the spur that the clear spirit doth
  raise   70

(That last infirmity of noble mind)
To scorn delights and live laborious days;
But the fair guerdon[17] when we hope to find,
And think to burst out into sudden blaze,
Comes the blind Fury[18] with the abhorrèd
  shears,
And slits the thin-spun life. 'But not the
  praise,'
Phœbus[19] replied, and touched my trembling
  ears:
'Fame is no plant that grows on mortal soil,
Nor in the glistering foil   79
Set off to the world, nor in broad rumour lies;
But lives and spreads aloft by those pure eyes
And perfect witness of all-judging Jove;
As he pronounces lastly on each deed,
Of so much fame in heaven expect thy meed.'
  O fountain Arethuse,[20] and thou honoured
  flood,
Smooth-sliding Mincius,[21] crowned with vocal
  reeds,
That strain I heard was of a higher mood:
But now my oat proceeds,
And listens to the herald[22] of the sea,
That came in Neptune's plea.[23]   90
He asked the waves, and asked the felon winds,
What hard mishap hath doomed this gentle
  swain?
And questioned every gust of rugged wings
That blows from off each beakèd promontory:
They knew not of his story;
And sage Hippotades[24] their answer brings,
That not a blast was from his dungeon
  strayed;
The air was calm, and on the level brine
Sleek Panope[25] with all her sisters played.
It was that fatal and perfidious bark,   100
Built in the eclipse,* and rigged with curses
  dark,
That sunk so low that sacred head of thine.
  Next Camus,[26] reverend sire, went footing
  slow,
His mantle hairy, and his bonnet sedge,[27]

17 reward
18 Atropos, the third Fate, cuts the thread of life but (line 76) cannot cut off the praise.
19 Apollo, god of wisdom, music, and poetry.
20 Sung of by Theocritus, a pastoral poet of Sicily; invoked here because of this association.
21 A river near Mantua, the home of Virgil, and of which he sang.
22 Triton, son of Neptune.
23 To inquire in the name of Neptune, god of ocean.
24 Æolus, god of the winds, son of Hippotas.
25 One of the Nereids, or sea-nymphs.
26 The river Cam, that flows past Cambridge.
27 A rush-like reed which has on the edges of its leaf peculiar letter-like characters.

A pastoral disguise, doubtless, for some friend or tutor.
 young
1 Anglesey, an island county of N. Wales, which was also a seat of the Druids.
2 The River Dee, of legendary associations.
13 Calliope.
14 Orpheus having angered the Thracian Bacchantes, was torn into pieces by them.
15 poetry
16 i. e., live for pleasure (the names are imaginary)

* For this superstition, Cp. *Macbeth*, IV, I, 28.

Inwrought with figures dim, and on the edge
Like to that sanguine flower[28] inscribed with
     woe.
'Ah! who hath reft,' quoth he, 'my dearest
     pledge?'[29]
Last came, and last did go,
The pilot[30] of the Galilean lake;
Two massy keys he bore of metals twain   110
(The golden opes, the iron shuts amain).
He shook his mitred[31] locks, and stern
     bespake:[32]
'How well could I have spared for thee, young
     swain,
Enow of such as for their bellies' sake,
Creep and intrude and climb into the fold!
Of other care they little reckoning make
Than how to scramble at the shearers' feast,
And shove away the worthy bidden guest.
Blind mouths! † that scarce themselves know
     how to hold
A sheep-hook, or have learnt aught else the
     least   120
That to the faithful herdman's art belongs!
What recks[33] it them? What need they? They
     are sped;[34]
And when they list, their lean and flashy songs
Grate on their scrannel[35] pipes of wretched
     straw;
The hungry sheep look up, and are not fed,
But swoln with wind and the rank mist[36] they
     draw,
Rot inwardly, and foul contagion spread;
Besides what the grim wolf[37] with privy paw
Daily devours apace, and nothing said.
But that two-handed engine[38] at the door   130
Stands ready to smite once, and smite no more.'
   Return, Alpheus;[39] the dread voice is past
That shrunk thy streams; return, Sicilian
     Muse,[40]
And call the vales, and bid them hither cast
Their bells and flowrets of a thousand hues.
Ye valleys low, where the mild whispers use[41]
Of shades and wanton winds and gushing
     brooks,

On whose fresh lap the swart star[42] sparely
     looks,
Throw hither all your quaint enamelled eyes,
That on the green turf suck the honeyed show-
     ers,   140
And purple all the ground with vernal flowers
Bring the rathe[44] primrose that forsaken dies
The tufted crow-toe,[45] and pale jessamine,
The white pink, and the pansy freaked with
     jet,
The glowing violet,
The musk-rose, and the well-attired woodbine
With cowslips wan that hang the pensive head,
And every flower that sad embroidery wears;
Bid amaranthus[46] all his beauty shed,
And daffodillies fill their cups with tears,   150
To strew the laureate hearse[47] where Lycid lies
For so to interpose a little ease,
Let our frail thoughts dally with false surmise
Ay me! whilst thee the shores and sounding
     seas
Wash far away, where'er thy bones are hurled
Whether beyond the stormy Hebrides,[48]
Where thou perhaps under the whelming tide
Visit'st the bottom of the monstrous world;
Or whether thou, to our moist vows denied,
Sleep'st by the fable of Bellerus old,   160
Where the great vision of the guarded mount
Looks toward Namancos[51] and Bayona's[52] hold
Look homeward, Angel, now, and melt with
     ruth;
And O ye dolphins,[53] waft the hapless youth.
   Weep no more, woeful shepherds, weep no
     more,
For Lycidas, your sorrow, is not dead,
Sunk though he be beneath the watery floor;
So sinks the day-star in the ocean bed,
And yet anon repairs his drooping head,
And tricks[54] his beams, and with new-spangled
     ore   170
Flames in the forehead of the morning sky:
So Lycidas sunk low, but mounted high,
Through the dear might of him that walked the
     waves,

28 The hyacinth which was said to have the Greek words *ai ai* (alas) on its petals.
29 offspring
30 Peter.
31 Wearing the bishop's head-dress.
32 spoke out
33 concerns
34 cared for
35 lean, thin, therefore harsh (flashy means tasteless, worthless)
† See Ruskin's comment on this passage in his *Sesame and Lilies.*

36 false teachings
37 Milton's hostile characterization of the Church of Rome.
38 Perhaps the two Houses of Parliament.
39 The river god who pursued Arethusa and was made one with her in the fountain of Arethusa. Cp. l. 85.
40 The muse of pastoral poetry.
41 dwell

42 dog-star
43 sparingly
44 early
45 purple hyacinth
46 An imaginary flower that never fades.
47 garlanded bier
48 Islands north of Scotland.
49 world of monsters (the sea)
50 fable of Bellerus = fabled Bellerus. He is sometimes said to have been a Cornish giant. the western end of Cornwall is a rock called the Giant's Chair; and near Land's End a rock called St. Michael's Mount, said to guarded by the archangel himself.

51 In Spain.
52 Near Namancos; both found on ancient maps.
53 Dolphins rescued Arion the Greek poet when jealous sailors, coveting his treasure threw him overboard.
54 arranges

Where, other groves and other streams along,
With nectar pure his oozy locks he laves,
And hears the unexpressive[55] nuptial song,
In the blest kingdoms meek of joy and love.
There entertain him all the saints above,
In solemn troops and sweet societies,
That sing, and singing in their glory move, 180
And wipe the tears for ever from his eyes.
Now, Lycidas, the shepherds weep no more;
Henceforth thou art the Genius of the shore,
In thy large recompense,[56] and shalt be good
To all that wander in that perilous flood.

   Thus sang the uncouth[57] swain to the oaks
     and rills,
While the still morn went out with sandals
   gray;
He touched the tender stops of various quills,
With eager thought warbling his Doric[58] lay:
And now the sun had stretched out all the
   hills, 190
And now was dropt into the western bay.
At last he rose, and twitched his mantle blue:
To-morrow to fresh woods and pastures new.

SONNETS

WHEN THE ASSAULT WAS INTENDED TO THE CITY*

CAPTAIN, or Colonel, or Knight in arms,
  Whose chance on these defenceless doors[1] may
   seize,
   If ever deed of honour did thee please,
  Guard them, and him within protect from
   harms.
He can requite thee; for he knows the charms
  That call[2] fame on such gentle acts as these,
  And he can spread thy name o'er lands and
   seas,
  Whatever clime the sun's bright circle
   warms.
Lift not thy spear against the Muses' bower:
  The great Emathian conqueror[3] bid spare 10
  The house of Pindarus,[4] when temple and
   tower
Went to the ground; and the repeated air[5]
  Of sad Electra's poet had the power
  To save the Athenian walls from ruin bare.

55 inexpressible   57 unknown
56 as thy great reward   58 pastoral

1 of Milton's home   2 call forth
3 Alexander the Great; Emathia was a part of
   Macedonia.
4 The home of Pindar, the great Grecian lyric
   poet, was ordered saved when Thebes was destroyed, B. C. 333.
5 After the taking of Athens by the Lacedemo-
   nians in B. C. 404, the singing of part of
   Euripides' drama *Electra* so influenced the
   conquerors that the city was saved.
* When Charles I advanced upon London, which
   was largely Puritan.

TO THE LORD GENERAL CROMWELL, MAY, 1652

CROMWELL, our chief of men, who through a
  cloud
  Not of war only, but detractions[6] rude,
  Guided by faith and matchless fortitude,
  To peace and truth thy glorious way hast
   ploughed,
And on the neck of crownèd Fortune proud
  Hast reared God's trophies, and his work
   pursued,
While Darwen stream,[7] with blood of Scots
  imbrued,
  And Dunbar field, resounds thy praises loud,
And Worcester's laureate wreath: yet much
  remains
  To conquer still; peace hath her victories 10
  No less renowned than war: new foes arise,
Threatening to bind our souls with secular
  chains.[8]
  Help us to save free conscience from the paw
  Of hireling wolves, whose gospel is their
  maw.

ON THE LATE MASSACRE IN PIEDMONT*

AVENGE, O Lord, thy slaughtered saints, whose
  bones
  Lie scattered on the Alpine mountains cold;
  Even them who kept thy truth so pure of
   old,
  When all our fathers worshiped stocks and
   stones,
Forget not: in thy book record their groans
  Who were thy sheep, and in their ancient
   fold
  Slain by the bloody Piedmontese, that rolled
Mother with infant down the rocks. Their
  moans
The vales redoubled to the hills, and they
  To heaven. Their martyred blood and ashes
   sow 10
  O'er all the Italian fields, where still doth
  sway
The triple tyrant; that from these may grow
  A hundredfold, who, having learnt thy way,
  Early may fly the Babylonian woe.

6 Proceeding from Presbyterian opponents.
7 At the Darwen Cromwell defeated the Scotch in
  1648, at Dunbar in 1650; at Worcester he
  defeated Charles I. in 1651.
8 i. e. state control of religion
* The Protestant Vaudois or Waldenses in southern France were practically crushed out in
  1655 because of their refusal to accept the
  state religion. They were an ancient sect,
  originating in 1170; see line 3. In line 12,
  there is an allusion to the triple tiara of the
  Pope; in line 14, to the doom of the mystical
  Babylon of *Revelation* xvii and xviii.

ON HIS BLINDNESS

WHEN I consider how my light is spent
　Ere half my days, in this dark world and
　　wide,
　And that one talent which is death to hide
　Lodged with me useless, though my soul
　　more bent
To serve therewith my Maker, and present
　My true account, lest he returning chide;
　'Doth God exact day-labour, light denied?'
I fondly[9] ask. But Patience, to prevent
That murmur, soon replies, 'God doth not need
　Either man's work or his own gifts. Who
　　best　　　　　　　　　　　　　　10
　Bear his mild yoke, they serve him best. His
　　state
Is kingly: thousands at his bidding speed,
　And post o'er land and ocean without rest;
　They also serve who only stand and wait.'

TO CYRIACK SKINNER

CYRIACK, this three years' day these eyes,
　　though clear
　To outward view, of blemish or of spot,
　Bereft of light, their seeing have forgot;
　Nor to their idle orbs doth sight appear
Of sun or moon or star throughout the year,
　Or man or woman. Yet I argue not
　Against Heaven's hand or will, nor bate a jot
Of heart or hope, but still bear up and steer
Right onward. What supports me, dost thou
　ask?
　The conscience,[10] friend, to have lost them
　　overplied　　　　　　　　　　　10
　In liberty's defence,† my noble task,
Of which all Europe talks from side to side.
　This thought might lead me through the
　　world's vain mask
　Content, though blind, had I no better guide.

FROM PARADISE LOST

BOOK I

THE ARGUMENT

This First Book proposes, first in brief, the
whole subject: Man's disobedience, and the
loss thereupon of Paradise, wherein he was
placed: then touches the prime cause of his fall
—the Serpent, or rather Satan in the Serpent;
who, revolting from God, and drawing to his
side many legions of Angels, was by the command of God driven out of Heaven with all his
crew into the great Deep. Which action passed
over, the Poem hastens into the midst of
things; presenting Satan with his Angels now
fallen into Hell—described here, not in the
Centre[1] (for heaven and earth may be supposed
as yet not made, certainly not yet accursed),
but in a place of utter darkness, fitliest called
Chaos. Here Satan with his Angels lying on
the burning lake, thunderstruck and astonished,
after a certain space recovers, as from confusion; calls up him who, next in order and
dignity, lay by him: they confer of their miserable fall. Satan awakens all his legions, who
lay till then in the same manner confounded.
They rise: their numbers; array of battle;
their chief leaders named, according to the
idols known afterwards in Canaan and the
countries adjoining. To these Satan directs
his speech; comforts them with hope yet of
regaining Heaven; but tells them lastly of a
new world and new kind of creature to be
created, according to an ancient prophecy or
report in Heaven; for that Angels were long
before this visible creation was the opinion of
many ancient Fathers. To find out the truth
of this prophecy, and what to determine thereon, he refers to a full council. What his associates thence attempt. Pandemonium, the
palace of Satan, rises, suddenly built out of
the Deep: the infernal Peers there sit in
council.

OF Man's first disobedience, and the fruit
Of that forbidden tree, whose mortal taste
Brought death into the world, and all our woe,
With loss of Eden,* till one greater Man
Restore us, and regain the blissful seat,
Sing, Heavenly Muse,[2] that on the secret[3] top
Of Oreb,[4] or of Sinai, didst inspire
That shepherd who first taught the chosen seed[5]
In the beginning[6] how the Heavens and Earth
Rose out of Chaos: or, if Sion[7] hill　　　　10
Delight thee more, and Siloa's brook that
　flowed
Fast[8] by the oracle of God, I thence
Invoke thy aid to my adventurous song,
That with no middle flight intends to soar
Above the Aonian mount,[9] while it pursues
Things unattempted yet in prose or rhyme.

[1] Earth; see note on
　l. 74.
[2] See VII, 1-12, p. 258.
[3] hidden (Cowper), re-
　tired (Landor)
[4] Horeb, or Sinai,
　whereon God spoke
　　to Moses from the
　　burning bush.
[5] Deut. x, 15.
[6] Modifies "rose."
[7] Zion, in Jerusalem.
[8] close (by the Temple)
[9] Helicon (fig. for Gre-
　cian poetry).
* "And the Lord God planted a garden eastward
　in Eden."—Gen. ii, 8. Strictly, therefore,
　Eden is the region, Paradise the garden.

9 foolishly　　　　　　10 consciousness
† He wrote the answer to Salmasius (the Defensio
pro Populo Anglicano) in the face of warning
from physicians that he would become blind
unless he gave up work.

And chiefly Thou, O Spirit, that dost prefer
Before all temples the upright heart and pure,
Instruct me, for Thou know'st; Thou from the first
Wast present, and, with mighty wings out-
spread,   20
Dove-like sat'st brooding on the vast Abyss,
And mad'st it pregnant: what in me is dark
Illumine, what is low raise and support;
That to the highth of this great argument[10]
I may assert Eternal Providence,
And justify the ways of God to men.
  Say first—for Heaven hides nothing from
Thy view,
Nor the deep tract of Hell—say first what cause
Moved our grand parents, in that happy state,
Favored of Heaven so highly, to fall off   30
From their Creator, and transgress his will
For one restraint, lords of the world besides.
Who first seduced them to that foul revolt?
  The infernal Serpent; he it was, whose guile,
Stirred up with envy and revenge, deceived
The mother of mankind, what time his pride
Had cast him out from Heaven,[11] with all his host
Of rebel Angels, by whose aid, aspiring
To set himself in glory above his peers,
He trusted to have equalled the Most High,   40
If he opposed; and with ambitious aim
Against the throne and monarchy[12] of God
Raised impious war in Heaven, and battle proud,
With vain attempt. Him the Almighty Power
Hurled headlong flaming from the ethereal sky,
With hideous ruin and combustion, down
To bottomless perdition; there to dwell
In adamantine chains and penal fire,
Who durst defy the Omnipotent to arms.
  Nine times the space that measures day and night   50
To mortal men, he with his horrid crew
Lay vanquished, rolling in the fiery gulf,
Confounded, though immortal. But his doom
Reserved him to more wrath; for now the thought
Both of lost happiness and lasting pain
Torments him; round he throws his baleful eyes,
That witnessed[13] huge affliction and dismay,
Mixed with obdurate pride and steadfast hate.
At once, as far as Angels ken, he views
The dismal situation waste and wild: 60
A dungeon horrible on all sides round

As one great furnace flamed; yet from those flames
No light; but rather darkness visible
Served only to discover[14] sights of woe,
Regions of sorrow, doleful shades, where peace
And rest can never dwell, hope never comes
That comes to all; but torture without end
Still urges,[15] and a fiery deluge, fed
With ever-burning sulphur unconsumed.
Such place Eternal Justice had prepared   70
For those rebellious; here their prison ordained
In utter[16] darkness, and their portion set,
As far removed from God and light of Heaven
As from the centre thrice to the utmost pole.*
Oh how unlike the place from whence they fell!
There the companions of his fall, o'erwhelmed
With floods and whirlwinds of tempestuous fire,
He soon discerns; and, weltering by his side,
One next himself in power, and next in crime,
Long after known in Palestine, and named   80
Beëlzebub. To whom the Arch-Enemy,
And thence in Heaven called Satan,[17] with bold words
Breaking the horrid silence, thus began:—
  'If thou beest he—but Oh how fallen! how changed
From him, who in the happy realms of light,
Clothed with transcendent brightness, didst out-
shine
Myriads, though bright!—if he whom mutual league,
United thoughts and counsels, equal hope
And hazard in the glorious enterprise,
Joined with me once, now misery hath joined
In equal ruin—into what pit thou seest   91
From what highth fallen:[18] so much the stronger proved
He with his thunder: and till then who knew
The force of those dire arms? Yet not for those,
Nor what the potent Victor in his rage
Can else inflict, do I repent, or change,
Though changed in outward lustre, that fixed mind,
And high disdain from sense of injured merit,
That with the Mightiest raised me to contend,
And to the fierce contention brought along   100
Innumerable force of Spirits armed,
That durst dislike his reign, and, me pre-
ferring,

14 reveal
15 presses (a Latinism)
16 outer
17 i. e., Adversary
18 An exclamatory sentence without regular construction.
* According to the Ptolemaic system, the earth is the center of the physical universe. The utmost or outmost pole would be the outer boundary, the firmament. Milton, while disposed to accept the new Copernican theory, clung to the old system for poetic purposes.

10 theme
11 Cp. Caedmon's account, p. 19.
12 single rule
13 bore witness to (within himself)

His utmost power with adverse power opposed
In dubious battle on the plains of Heaven,
And shook his throne. What though the field
    be lost?
All is not lost: the unconquerable will,
And study of revenge, immortal hate,
And courage never to submit or yield,
And what is else not to be overcome;
That glory never shall his wrath or might 110
Extort from me. To bow and sue for grace
With suppliant knee, and deify his power
Who, from the terror of this arm, so late
Doubted his empire[19]—that were low indeed;
That were an ignominy and shame beneath
This downfall; since by fate the strength of
    gods
And this empyreal substance cannot fail;
Since, through experience of this great event,
In arms not worse, in foresight much advanced,
We may with more successful hope resolve 120
To wage by force or guile eternal war,
Irreconcilable to our grand Foe,
Who now triumphs, and in the excess of joy
Sole reigning holds the tyranny of Heaven.'
  So spake the apostate Angel, though in pain,
Vaunting aloud, but racked with deep despair;
And him thus answered soon his bold com-
    peer:—
  'O Prince! O Chief of many thronèd powers
That led the embattled Seraphim[20] to war
Under thy conduct, and, in dreadful deeds 130
Fearless, endangered Heaven's perpetual King,
And put to proof his high supremacy,
Whether upheld by strength, or chance, or
    fate!
Too well I see and rue the dire event
That with sad overthrow and foul defeat
Hath lost us Heaven, and all this mighty host
In horrible destruction laid thus low,
As far as gods and heavenly essences
Can perish: for the mind and spirit remains
Invincible, and vigor soon returns, 140
Though all our glory extinct, and happy state
Here swallowed up in endless misery.
But what if he our Conqueror (whom I now
Of force[21] believe almighty, since no less
Than such could have o'erpowered such force
    as ours)
Have left us this our spirit and strength entire,
Strongly to suffer and support our pains,
That we may so suffice his vengeful ire,
Or do him mightier service as his thralls
By right of war, whate'er his business be, 150
Here in the heart of Hell to work in fire,
Or do his errands in the gloomy Deep?

What can it then avail, though yet we feel
Strength undiminished, or eternal being
To undergo eternal punishment?'
    Whereto with speedy words the Arch-Fiend
    replied:—
'Fallen Cherub, to be weak is miserable,
Doing or suffering: but of this be sure—
To do aught good never will be our task,
But ever to do ill our sole delight, 160
As being the contrary to his high will
Whom we resist. If then his providence
Out of our evil seek to bring forth good,
Our labor must be to pervert that end,
And out of good still to find means of evil;
Which ofttimes may succeed so as perhaps
Shall grieve him, if I fail not, and disturb
His inmost counsels from their destined aim.
But see! the angry Victor hath recalled
His ministers of vengeance and pursuit 170
Back to the gates of Heaven; the sulphurous
    hail,
Shot after us in storm, o'erblown hath laid
The fiery surge that from the precipice
Of Heaven received us falling; and the
    thunder,
Winged with red lightning and impetuous rage,
Perhaps hath spent his shafts, and ceases now
To bellow through the vast and boundless
    Deep.*
Let us not slip the occasion, whether scorn
Or satiate fury yield it from our Foe.
Seest thou yon dreary plain, forlorn and wild,
The seat of desolation, void of light, 181
Save what the glimmering of these livid flames
Casts pale and dreadful? Thither let us tend[22]
From off the tossing of these fiery waves;
There rest, if any rest can harbor there;
And, reassembling our afflicted[23] powers,
Consult how we may henceforth most offend
Our Enemy, our own loss how repair,
How overcome this dire calamity,
What reinforcement we may gain from hope,
If not what resolution from despair.' 191
    Thus Satan, talking to his nearest mate,
With head uplift above the wave, and eyes
That sparkling blazed; his other parts besides,
Prone on the flood, extended long and large,
Lay floating many a rood, in bulk as huge
As whom the fables name of monstrous size,†

---

[22] make our way (a [23] beaten down (a
    Latinism)   Latinism)
* Even above the resonance to be felt everywhere
  through Milton's verse this line rises with a
  resonance of its own.
† The Titans were the children of Uranus and
  Gaea (Heaven and Earth). Briareos and Typhon were Gigantes, sometimes said to have
  been imprisoned beneath mountains, thus representing the forces of earthquake and volcano.

[19] sovereignty   [21] perforce
[20] See p. 139, note 13.

Titanian, or Earth-born, that warred on Jove,
Briareos or Typhon, whom the den
By ancient Tarsus held, or that sea-beast   200
Leviathan,[24] which God of all his works
Created hugest that swim the ocean-stream.
Him, haply slumbering on the Norway foam,
The pilot of some small night-foundered skiff
Deeming some island, oft, as seamen tell,
With fixed anchor in his scaly rind,
Moors by his side under the lee, while night
Invests the sea, and wished morn delays.
So stretched out huge in length the Arch-Fiend
      lay,   209
Chained[25] on the burning lake; nor ever thence
Had[26] risen or heaved his head, but that the will
And high permission of all-ruling Heaven
Left him at large to his own dark designs,
That with reiterated crimes he might
Heap on himself damnation, while he sought
Evil to others, and enraged might see
How all his malice served but to bring forth
Infinite goodness, grace, and mercy, shewn
On Man by him seduced; but on himself   219
Treble confusion, wrath, and vengeance poured.
  Forthwith upright he rears from off the pool
His mighty stature; on each hand the flames
Driven backward slope their pointing spires,
      and, rolled
In billows, leave i' the midst a horrid vale.
Then with expanded wings he steers his flight
Aloft, incumbent on the dusky air,
That felt unusual weight; till on dry land
He lights—if it were land that ever burned
With solid, as the lake with liquid fire,
And such appeared in hue, as when the force
Of subterranean wind transports a hill   231
Torn from Pelorus,[27] or the shattered side
Of thundering Ætna, whose combustible
And fuelled entrails thence conceiving fire,
Sublimed[28] with mineral fury, aid the winds,
And leave a singed bottom all involved
With stench and smoke: such resting found the sole
Of unblest feet. Him followed his next mate,
Both glorying to have scaped the Stygian flood
As gods, and by their own recovered strength,
Not by the sufferance of supernal power.   241
  'Is this the region, this the soil, the clime,'
Said then the lost Archangel, 'this the seat
That we must change for Heaven? this mournful gloom
For that celestial light? Be it so, since he
Who now is sovran can dispose and bid

What shall be right: farthest from him is best,
Whom reason hath equalled, force hath made
      supreme
Above his equals. Farewell, happy fields,
Where joy forever dwells! Hail, horrors! hail,
Infernal world! and thou, profoundest Hell, 251
Receive thy new possessor, one who brings
A mind not to be changed by place or time.
The mind is its own place, and in itself
Can make a Heaven of Hell, a Hell of Heaven.[28]
What matter where, if I be still the same,
And what I should be, all but[29] less than he
Whom thunder hath made greater? Here at least
We shall be free; the Almighty hath not built
Here for his envy, will not drive us hence: 260
Here we may reign secure, and in my choice
To reign is worth ambition, though in Hell:
Better to reign in Hell, than serve in Heaven.
But wherefore let we then our faithful friends,
The associates and co-partners of our loss,
Lie thus astonished on the oblivious pool,
And call them not to share with us their part
In this unhappy mansion, or once more
With rallied arms to try what may be yet
Regained in Heaven, or what more lost in
      Hell?'   270
  So Satan spake; and him Beëlzebub
Thus answered:—'Leader of those armies
      bright
Which but the Omnipotent none could have
      foiled,
If once they hear that voice, their liveliest
      pledge
Of hope in fears and dangers—heard so oft
In worst extremes, and on the perilous edge
Of battle when it raged, in all assaults
Their surest signal—they will soon resume
New courage and revive, though now they lie
Grovelling and prostrate on yon lake of fire, 280
As we erewhile, astounded and amazed:
No wonder, fallen such a pernicious highth!'
  He scarce had ceased when the superior Fiend
Was moving toward the shore; his ponderous
      shield,
Ethereal temper,[30] massy, large, and round,
Behind him cast. The broad circumference
Hung on his shoulders like the moon, whose orb
Through optic glass the Tuscan artist[31] views
At evening from the top of Fesole,[32]
Or in Valdarno,[33] to descry new lands,   290
Rivers, or mountains, in her spotty globe.

28 Cp. p. 155, l. 75.
29 only
30 of ethereal temper
31 scientist (though possibly referring to
Galileo as a *maker* of telescopes)
32 Fiesole, a hill above Florence.
33 Valley of the Arno.

24 *Psalms* civ. 26.
25 2 *Peter* ii, 4.
26 would have
27 A Sicilian cape, now Faro.
28 sublimated

His spear—to equal which the tallest pine
Hewn on Norwegian hills, to be the mast
Of some great ammiral,[34] were but a wand—
He walked with, to support uneasy steps
Over the burning marle, not like those steps
On Heaven's azure; and the torrid clime
Smote on him sore besides, vaulted with fire.
Nathless he so endured, till on the beach
Of that inflamed sea he stood, and called   300
His legions, Angel forms, who lay entranced,
Thick as autumnal leaves that strow the brooks
In Vallombrosa,[35] where the Etrurian shades
High over-arched embower; or scattered sedge
Afloat, when with fierce winds Orion[36] armed
Hath vexed the Red-Sea coast, whose waves
            o'erthrew
Busiris[37] and his Memphian chivalry,
While with perfidious hatred they pursued
The sojourners of Goshen,[38] who beheld
From the safe shore their floating carcases 310
And broken chariot-wheels: so thick bestrown,
Abject and lost, lay these, covering the flood,
Under amazement of their hideous change.
He called so loud that all the hollow deep
Of Hell resounded:—'Princes, Potentates,
Warriors, the Flower of Heaven—once yours,
            now lost,
If such astonishment as this can seize
Eternal Spirits! Or have ye chosen this place
After the toil of battle to repose
Your wearied virtue, for the ease you find 320
To slumber here, as in the vales of Heaven?
Or in this abject posture have ye sworn
To adore the Conqueror, who now beholds
Cherub and Seraph rolling in the flood
With scattered arms and ensigns, till anon
His swift pursuers from Heaven-gates discern
The advantage, and descending tread us down
Thus drooping, or with linked thunderbolts
Transfix us to the bottom of this gulf?
Awake, arise, or be forever fallen!'   330
    They heard, and were abashed, and up they
            sprung
Upon the wing, as when men wont to watch,
On duty sleeping found by whom they dread,
Rouse and bestir themselves ere well awake.
Nor did they not perceive the evil plight
In which they were, or the fierce pains not feel;
Yet to their General's voice they soon obeyed
Innumerable. As when the potent rod
Of Amram's son,[39] in Egypt's evil day,

Waved round the coast, up called a pitchy
            cloud   340
Of locusts, warping on the eastern wind,
That o'er the realm of impious Pharaoh hung
Like night, and darkened all the land of Nile:
So numberless were those bad Angels seen
Hovering on wing under the cope of Hell,
'Twixt upper, nether, and surrounding fires;
Till, as a signal given, the uplifted spear
Of their great Sultan waving to direct
Their course, in even balance down they light
On the firm brimstone, and fill all the plain: 350
A multitude like which the populous North
Poured never from her frozen loins, to pass
Rhene or the Danaw, when her barbarous sons[40]
Came like a deluge on the South, and spread
Beneath Gibraltar to the Libyan sands.
Forthwith, from every squadron and each band,
The heads and leaders thither haste where stood
Their great Commander; godlike shapes, and
            forms
Excelling human, princely Dignities,
And Powers that erst in Heaven sat on
            thrones;   360
Though of their names in Heavenly records
            now
Be no memorial, blotted out and rased
By their rebellion from the Books of Life.*
Nor had they yet among the sons of Eve
Got them new names, till, wandering o'er the
            Earth,
Through God's high sufferance for the trial of
            man,
By falsities and lies the greatest part
Of mankind they corrupted to forsake
God their Creator, and the invisible
Glory of him that made them, to transform 370
Oft to the image of a brute, adorned
With gay religions[41] full of pomp and gold,
And devils to adore for deities:
Then were they known to men by various names,
And various idols through the heathen world.
    Say, Muse, their names then known, who
            first, who last,
Roused from the slumber on that fiery couch,
At their great Emperor's call, as next in worth
Came singly where he stood on the bare strand,
While the promiscuous crowd stood yet
            aloof.   380
    The chief were those who, from the pit of
            Hell
Roaming to seek their prey on Earth, durst fix

34 admiral's flag-ship
35 N e a r Florence, i n
    Tuscany (Etruria).
36 A   Greek   hunter;
    then a constellation
    supposed to bring
    tempests.

37 One of the Pharaohs;
    used here for the
    Pharaoh of the
    time of the Exodus.
38 *Exod.* xii, 26, xiv,
    22-28.
39 Moses

40 Vandals from the Rhine and Danube, 429 A. D.
41 rites
* Three lines of infinite sadness. Conversely,
    Dante does not allow the name of Christ to be
    spoken in his Inferno.

Their seats, long after, next the seat of God,
Their altars by his altar, gods adored
Among the nations round, and durst abide
Jehovah thundering out of Sion, throned
Between the Cherubim; yea, often placed
Within his sanctuary itself their shrines,
Abominations; and with cursed things
His holy rites and solemn feasts profaned, 390
And with their darkness durst affront[42] his
    light.
First Moloch, horrid king, besmeared with
    blood
Of human sacrifice, and parents' tears,
Though, for the noise of drums and timbrels
    loud,
Their children's cries unheard that passed
    through fire[43]
To his grim idol. Him the Ammonite
Worshiped in Rabba and her watery plain,
In Argob and in Basan, to the stream
Of utmost Arnon. Nor content with such
Audacious neighborhood, the wisest[44] heart 400
Of Solomon he led by fraud to build
His temple right against the temple of God
On that opprobrious hill,[45] and made his grove
The pleasant valley of Hinnom,[46] Tophet thence
And black Gehenna called, the type of Hell.
Next Chemos, the obscene dread of Moab's
    sons,
From Aroar to Nebo and the wild
Of southmost Abarim; in Hesebon
And Horonaim, Seon's realm, beyond
The flowery dale of Sibma clad with vines, 410
And Elealè to the Asphaltic pool.[47]
Peor his other name, when he enticed
Israel in Sittim, on their march from Nile,
To do him wanton rites, which cost them woe.[48]
Yet thence his lustful orgies he enlarged
Even to that hill of scandal, by the grove
Of Moloch homicide, lust hard by hate,
Till good Josiah drove them thence to Hell.[49]
With these came they who, from the bordering
    flood
Of old Euphrates to the brook that parts 420
Egypt from Syrian ground, had general names
Of Baalim and Ashtaroth[50]—those male,
These feminine. For Spirits, when they please,
Can either sex assume, or both; so soft
And uncompounded is their essence pure,
Not tied or manacled with joint or limb,
Nor founded on the brittle strength of bones,
Like cumbrous flesh; but, in what shape they
    choose,
Dilated or condensed, bright or obscure,
Can execute their aery purposes,   430
And works of love or enmity fulfil.
For those the race of Israel oft forsook
Their living Strength, and unfrequented left
His righteous altar, bowing lowly down
To bestial gods; for which their heads as low
Bowed down in battle, sunk before the spear
Of despicable foes. With these in troop
Came Astoreth, whom the Phœnicians called
Astarte, Queen of Heaven, with crescent horns;
To whose bright image nightly by the moon 440
Sidonian virgins paid their vows and songs;
In Sion also not unsung, where stood
Her temple on the offensive mountain, built
By that uxorious king whose heart, though
    large,
Beguiled by fair idolatresses, fell[51]
To idols foul. Thammuz[52] came next behind,
Whose annual wound in Lebanon allured
The Syrian damsels to lament his fate
In amorous ditties all a summer's day,
While smooth Adonis[53] from his native rock 450
Ran purple to the sea, supposed with blood
Of Thammuz yearly wounded: the love-tale
Infected Sion's daughters with like heat,
Whose wanton passions in the sacred porch
Ezekiel saw, when, by the vision led,
His eye surveyed the dark idolatries
Of alienated Judah. Next came one
Who mourned in earnest, when the captive ark
Maimed his brute image, head and hands lopt
    off
In his own temple, on the grunsel-edge,[54]   460
Where he fell flat, and shamed his worshipers:
Dagon[55] his name, sea-monster, upward man
And downward fish; yet had his temple high
Reared in Azotus, dreaded through the coast
Of Palestine, in Gath and Ascalon,
And Accaron and Gaza's frontier bounds.
Him followed Rimmon, whose delightful seat
Was fair Damascus, on the fertile banks
Of Abbana and Pharphar, lucid streams.
He also against the house of God was bold: 470
A leper once he lost, and gained a king,[56]
Ahaz, his sottish conqueror, whom he drew
God's altar to disparage and displace
For one of Syrian mode, whereon to burn
His odious offerings, and adore the gods
Whom he had vanquished. After these ap-
    peared
A crew who, under names of old renown,

---

42 confront
43 Jer. xxxii, 35.
44 most wise
45 2 Kings xxiii, 13.
46 Jer. vii, 31.
47 Dead Sea.
48 Numb. xxv, 9.
49 2 Kings xxiii.
50 Singular: Baal, As-
    toreth, Phoenician
    deities.
51 1 Kings xi, 4.
52 Identified with the
    Greek Adonis.
53 A Phoenician stream,
    tinged red by soil
from the Libanus
    mountains.
54 ground-sill
55 God of the Philis-
    tines. 1 Sam. v, 4.
56 2 Kings v.

Osiris, Isis, Orus, and their train,
With monstrous shapes and sorceries abused
Fanatic Egypt and her priests, to seek   480
Their wandering gods disguised in brutish
    forms
Rather than human. Nor did Israel scape
The infection, when their borrowed gold com-
    posed
The calf in Oreb,[57] and the robel king[58]
Doubled that sin in Bethel and in Dan,
Likening his Maker to the grazed ox—
Jehovah, who, in one night, when he passed
From Egypt marching, equalled with one stroke
Both her first-born and all her bleating gods.[59]
Belial[60] came last, than whom a Spirit more
    lewd   490
Fell not from Heaven, or more gross to love
Vice for itself. To him no temple stood
Or altar smoked; yet who more oft than he
In temples and at altars, when the priest
Turns atheist, as did Eli's sons,[61] who filled
With lust and violence the house of God?
In courts and palaces he also reigns,*
And in luxurious cities, where the noise
Of riot ascends above their loftiest towers,
And injury and outrage; and when night   500
Darkens the streets, then wander forth the sons
Of Belial, flown with insolence and wine.
Witness the streets of Sodom, and that night
In Gibeah, when the hospitable door
Exposed a matron, to avoid worse rape.
    These were the prime in order and in might;
The rest were long to tell, though far renowned
The Ionian[62] gods—of[63] Javan's issue held
Gods, yet confessed later[64] than Heaven and
    Earth,
Their boasted parents;—Titan, Heaven's first-
    born,   510
With his enormous brood, and birthright seized
By younger Saturn; he from mightier Jove,
His own and Rhea's son, like measure found;
So Jove usurping reigned. These, first in Crete
And Ida known, thence on the snowy top
Of cold Olympus ruled the middle air,
Their highest Heaven; or on the Delphian cliff,
Or in Dodona, and through all the bounds
Of Doric land; or who with Saturn old
Fled over Adria to the Hesperian[65] fields,   520
And o'er the Celtic roamed the utmost isles.
    All these and more came flocking; but with
    looks

Downcast and damp, yet such wherein appeared
Obscure some glimpse of joy, to have found
    their Chief
Not in despair, to have found themselves not
    lost
In loss itself; which on his countenance cast
Like doubtful hue. But he, his wonted pride
Soon recollecting, with high words that bore
Semblance of worth, not substance, gently
    raised
Their fainting courage, and dispelled their
    fears: 530
Then straight commands that at the warlike
    sound
Of trumpets loud and clarions, be upreared
His mighty standard. That proud honor
    claimed
Azazel as his right, a Cherub tall:
Who forthwith from the glittering staff un-
    furled
The imperial ensign, which, full high advanced,
Shone like a meteor streaming to the wind,
With gems and golden lustre rich emblazed,
Seraphic arms and trophies; all the while
Sonorous metal blowing martial sounds: 540
At which the universal host up-sent
A shout that tore Hell's concave, and beyond
Frighted the reign of Chaos and old Night.
All in a moment through the gloom were seen
Ten thousand banners rise into the air,
With orient colors waving; with them rose
A forest huge of spears; and thronging helms
Appeared, and serried shields in thick array
Of depth immeasurable. Anon they move
In perfect phalanx to the Dorian mood[66]   550
Of flutes and soft recorders[67]—such as raised
To highth of noblest temper heroes old
Arming to battle, and instead of rage
Deliberate valor breathed, firm and unmoved
With dread of death to flight or foul retreat;
Nor wanting power to mitigate and swage,[68]
With solemn touches, troubled thoughts, and
    chase
Anguish and doubt and fear and sorrow and
    pain
From mortal or immortal minds. Thus they,
Breathing united force with fixed thought,   560
Moved on in silence to soft pipes that charmed
Their painful steps o'er the burnt soil; and
    now
Advanced in view they stand, a horrid front
Of dreadful length and dazzling arms, in guise
Of warriors old, with ordered spear and shield,
Awaiting what command their mighty Chief

57 *Exod.* xii, 35, xxxii, 4.
58 *1 Kings* xii. 28.
59 *Exod.* xii, 29.
60 "wickedness" (2 *Cor.* vi, 15; personified by Milton)
61 *1. Sam.* ii, 12.
* Perhaps alluding to conditions in England under Charles II. Cp. VII, 32, p. 258.

62 Grecian (a name traceable to Javan, Noah's grandson).
63 by
64 Referring to the successive dynasties.
65 western. Italian

66 A grave harmony, employed by the Spartans.
67 flageolets
68 assuage

ad to impose. He through the armed files
arts his experienced eye, and soon traverse
he whole battalion views—their order due,
heir visages and stature as of gods; 570
heir number last he sums. And now his heart
istends with pride, and hardening in his
    strength
lories; for never, since created man,69
et such embodied force as, named with these,
uld merit more than that small infantry70
arred on by cranes: though all the giant
    brood
f Phlegra71 with the heroic race were joined
hat fought at Thebes and Ilium, on each side
ixed with auxiliar gods; and what resounds
a fable or romance of Uther's son,72 580
egirt with British and Armoric knights;
nd all who since,73 baptized or infidel,
ousted in Aspramont, or Montalban,
amasco, or Marocco, or Trebisond;
r whom Biserta sent from Afric shore
hen Charlemain with all his peerage fell
y Fontarabbia.74 Thus far these beyond
ompare of mortal prowess, yet observed75
heir dread commander. He, above the rest
a shape and gesture proudly eminent, 590
tood like a tower; his form had yet not lost
ll her original brightness, nor appeared
ess than Archangel ruined, and the excess
f glory obscured: as when the sun new-risen
ooks through the horizontal misty air
horn of his beams, or from behind the moon,
a dim eclipse, disastrous twilight sheds
n half the nations, and with fear of change
erplexes monarchs. Darkened so, yet shone
bove them all the Archangel; but his face 600
eep scars of thunder had intrenched, and care
at on his faded cheek, but under brows
f dauntless courage, and considerate pride
aiting revenge. Cruel his eye, but cast
igns of remorse and passion, to behold
he fellows of his crime, the followers rather
Far other once beheld in bliss), condemned
orever now to have their lot in pain;
illions of Spirits for his fault amerced76
f Heaven, and from eternal splendors flung 610
or his revolt; yet faithful how77 they stood,

Their glory withered: as, when Heaven's fire
Hath scathed the forest oaks or mountain pines,
With singed top their stately growth, though
    bare,
Stands on the blasted heath. He now prepared
To speak; whereat their doubled ranks they
    bend
From wing to wing, and half enclose him round
With all his peers: attention held them mute.
Thrice he assayed, and thrice, in spite of scorn,
Tears, such as Angels weep, burst forth: at
    last 620
Words interwove with sighs found out their
    way:—
'O myriads of immortal Spirits! O Powers
Matchless, but with the Almighty!—and that
    strife
Was not inglorious, though the event78 was
    dire,
As this place testifies, and this dire change,
Hateful to utter. But what power of mind,
Foreseeing or presaging, from the depth
Of knowledge past or present, could have
    feared
How such united force of gods, how such
As stood like these, could ever know repulse?
For who can yet believe, though after loss, 631
That all these puissant legions, whose exile
Hath emptied Heaven, shall fail to reascend,
Self-raised, and repossess their native seat?
For me, be witness all the host of Heaven,
If counsels different, or danger shunned
By me, have lost our hopes. But he who reigns
Monarch in Heaven, till then as one secure
Sat on his throne, upheld by old repute,
Consent or custom, and his regal state 640
Put forth at full, but still his strength con-
    cealed;
Which tempted our attempt,* and wrought our
    fall.
Henceforth his might we know, and know our
    own
So as not either to provoke, or dread
New war provoked. Our better part remains
To work in close design, by fraud or guile,
What force effected not; that he no less
At length from us may find, who overcomes
By force hath overcome but half his foe.
Space may produce new worlds; whereof so
    rife 650
There went a fame in Heaven that he ere long
Intended to create, and therein plant
A generation whom his choice regard
Should favor equal to the Sons of Heaven.

---

69 since the creation of
    man (a Latinism)
70 The pigmies. Iliad
    III. 6.
71 In Thrace.
72 King Arthur.
73 As described in
    French and Italian
    mediaeval
    romances.

75 These (though) thus
    far beyond compare
    of mortal prowess,
    yet observed (rev-
    erenced).
76 deprived
77 Follows "behold," l.
    605.

74 Fontarabbia, in northern Spain (perhaps pur-
    posely substituted for the pass of Roncesvalles,
    where, according to tradition, Charlemagne's
    rear guard was cut to pieces, though Charle-
    magne did not fall).

78 issue
* This word-play was severely condemned by Lan-
    dor. Compare ll. 606, 666-667.

Thither, if but to pry, shall be perhaps
Our first eruption: thither or elsewhere;
For this infernal pit shall never hold
Celestial Spirits in bondage, nor the Abyss
Long under darkness cover. But these thoughts,
Full counsel must mature. Peace is despaired, 660
For who can think submission? War, then, war
Open or understood, must be resolved.'
  He spake; and, to confirm his words, out-flew
Millions of flaming swords, drawn from the thighs
Of mighty Cherubim; the sudden blaze
Far round illumined Hell. Highly they raged
Against the Highest, and fierce with grasped arms
Clashed on their sounding shields the din of war,
Hurling defiance toward the vault of Heaven.
  There stood a hill not far, whose grisly[79] top 670
Belched fire and rolling smoke; the rest entire
Shone with a glossy scurf, undoubted sign
That in his womb was hid metallic ore,
The work of sulphur.[80] Thither, winged with speed,
A numerous brigad hastened: as when bands
Of pioneers, with spade and pickaxe armed,
Forerun the royal camp, to trench a field,
Or cast a rampart. Mammon led them on,
Mammon, the least erected Spirit that fell
From Heaven, for even in Heaven his looks and thoughts 680
Were always downward bent, admiring more
The riches of Heaven's pavement, trodden gold,
Than aught divine or holy else enjoyed
In vision beatific. By him first
Men also, and by his suggestion taught,
Ransacked the Centre,[81] and with impious hands
Rifled the bowels of their mother Earth
For treasures better hid. Soon had his crew
Opened into the hill a spacious wound,
And digged out ribs of gold. Let none admire[82] 690
That riches grow in Hell; that soil may best
Deserve the precious bane. And here let those
Who boast in mortal things, and wondering tell
Of Babel, and the works of Memphian kings,
Learn how their greatest monuments of fame,
And strength, and art, are easily outdone
By Spirits reprobate, and in an hour

What in an age they, with incessant toil
And hands innumerable, scarce perform.
Nigh on the plain, in many cells prepared, 70
That underneath had veins of liquid fire
Sluiced from the lake, a second multitude
With wondrous art founded[83] the massy ore,
Severing each kind, and scummed the bullion dross.
A third as soon had formed within the ground
A various mould, and from the boiling cells
By strange conveyance filled each hollow nook
As in an organ, from one blast of wind,
To many a row of pipes the sound-board breathes.
Anon out of the earth a fabric huge 7
Rose like an exhalation, with the sound
Of dulcet symphonies and voices sweet—
Built like a temple, where pilasters round
Were set, and Doric pillars overlaid
With golden architrave; nor did there want
Cornice or frieze, with bossy[85] sculpture graven:
The roof was fretted gold. Not Babylon,
Nor great Alcairo,[86] such magnificence
Equalled in all their glories, to enshrine
Belus or Serapis their gods, or seat 7
Their kings, when Egypt with Assyria strove
In wealth and luxury. The ascending pile
Stood fixed her stately highth, and straight the doors,
Opening their brazen folds, discover, wide
Within, her ample spaces o'er the smooth
And level pavement: from the arched roof,
Pendent by subtle magic, many a row
Of starry lamps and blazing cressets, fed
With naphtha and asphaltus, yielded light
As from a sky. The hasty multitude 7
Admiring entered, and the work some praise,
And some the architect. His hand was known
In Heaven by many a towered structure high
Where sceptred Angels held their residence,
And sat as Princes, whom the supreme King
Exalted to such power, and gave to rule,
Each in his hierarchy, the Orders bright.
Nor was his name unheard or unadored
In ancient Greece; and in Ausonian[87] land
Men called him Mulciber;[88] and how he fell 7
From Heaven they fabled, thrown by angry Jove
Sheer o'er the crystal battlements: from morn
To noon he fell, from noon to dewy eve,
A summer's day; and with the setting sun
Dropt from the zenith, like a falling star,
On Lemnos, the Ægæan isle. Thus they relate

---

[79] griesly, terrifying
[80] An early chemical theory.
[81] Cf. l. 74.
[82] wonder
[83] melted
[84] base ore (used adjectively)
[85] in high relief
[86] Cairo.
[87] Italian.
[88] Vulcan.

ring; for he with this rebellious rout
ell long before; nor aught availed him now
o have built in Heaven high towers; nor did
   he scape
y all his engines,[89] but was headlong sent 750
Vith his industrious crew to build in Hell.
  Meanwhile the winged heralds, by command
f sovran power, with awful ceremony
nd trumpet's sound, throughout the host proclaim
solemn council forthwith to be held
t Pandemonium,[90] the high capital
f Satan and his peers. Their summons called
rom every band and squared regiment
y place or choice the worthiest; they anon
Vith hundreds and with thousands trooping
   came   760
ttended. All access was thronged; the gates
nd porches wide, but chief the spacious hall
Though like a covered field, where champions
   bold
Vont[91] ride in armed, and at the Soldan's[92]
   chair
efied the best of Panim chivalry
o mortal combat, or career with lance)
hick swarmed, both on the ground and in the
   air,
rushed with the hiss of rustling wings. As
   bees
n spring-time, when the Sun with Taurus rides,
our forth their populous youth about the
   hive   770
n clusters; they among fresh dews and flowers
ly to and fro, or on the smoothed plank,
he suburb of their straw-built citadel,
ew rubbed with balm, expatiate and confer[93]
heir state-affairs. So thick the aery crowd
warmed and were straitened;[94] till, the signal
   given,
ehold a wonder; they but now who seemed
n bigness to surpass Earth's giant sons,
Now less than smallest dwarfs, in narrow room
hrong numberless, like that pygmean race[95]
eyond the Indian mount; or faery elves, 781
Vhose midnight revels, by a forest-side
r fountain, some belated peasant sees,
r dreams he sees, while overhead the Moon
its arbitress, and nearer to the Earth
Vheels her pale course; they, on their mirth
   and dance
ntent, with jocund music charm his ear;
t once with joy and fear his heart rebounds.
hus incorporeal Spirits to smallest forms

Reduced their shapes immense, and were at
   large,   790
Though without number still, amidst the hall
Of that infernal court. But far within,
And in their own dimensions like themselves,
The great Seraphic Lords and Cherubim
In close recess and secret conclave sat,
A thousand demi-gods on golden seats,
Frequent and full.[96] After short silence then,
And summons read, the great consult[97] began.

BOOK II

THE ARGUMENT

THE consultation begun, Satan debates
whether another battle is to be hazarded for
the recovery of Heaven: some advise it, others
dissuade. A third proposal is preferred, mentioned before by Satan, to search the truth of
that prophecy or tradition in Heaven concerning another world, and another kind of
creature, equal, or not much inferior, to themselves, about this time to be created. Their
doubt who shall be sent on this difficult search:
Satan, their chief, undertakes alone the voyage;
is honored and applauded. The council thus
ended, the rest betake them several ways and
to several employments, as their inclinations
lead them, to entertain the time till Satan
return. He passes on his journey to Hell-
gates, finds them shut, and who sat there to
guard them; by whom at length they are
opened, and discover to him the great gulf between Hell and Heaven; with what difficulty
he passes through, directed by Chaos, the
Power of that place, to the sight of this new
World which he sought.

HIGH on a throne of royal state, which far
Outshone the wealth of Ormus[1] and of Ind,
Or where the gorgeous East with richest hand
Showers on her kings barbaric pearl and gold,
Satan exalted sat,* by merit raised
To that bad eminence; and, from despair
Thus high uplifted beyond hope, aspires
Beyond thus high, insatiate to pursue
Vain war with Heaven; and, by success[2] un-
   taught,
His proud imaginations thus displayed:— 10
'Powers and Dominions, Deities of Heaven!

---

96 close and all occupied   97 A noun, like "com-
                                  pare," l. 588.

---

1 An eastern island,   2 result
   once a diamond
   mart.
* The imagery and language of this famous periodic opening evidently owes something to *The
   Faerie Queene*, I. iv. st. 8. The "barbaric
   gold" is from *Æneid* II. 504.

---

contrivances   92 Sultan's.
"Hall of all Demons"   93 walk about and dis-
   (word coined by   cuss
   Milton after model   94 contracted
   of *Pantheon*).   95 Cf. l. 575.
used to

For since no deep within her gulf can hold
Immortal vigor, though oppressed and fallen,
I give not Heaven for lost: from this descent
Celestial Virtues rising will appear
More glorious and more dread than from no
    fall,
And trust themselves to fear no second fate.
Me though just right, and the fixed laws of
    Heaven,
Did first create your leader, next, free choice,
With what besides, in council or in fight,   20
Hath been achieved of merit, yet this loss,
Thus far at least recovered, hath much more
Established in a safe, unenvied throne,
Yielded with full consent. The happier state
In Heaven, which follows dignity, might draw
Envy from each inferior; but who here
Will envy whom the highest place exposes
Foremost to stand against the Thunderer's aim
Your bulwark, and condemns to greatest share
Of endless pain? Where there is then no good 30
For which to strive, no strife can grow up
    there
From faction; for none sure will claim in Hell
Precedence, none whose portion is so small
Of present pain that with ambitious mind
Will covet more. With this advantage then
To union, and firm faith, and firm accord,
More than can be in Heaven, we now return
To claim our just inheritance of old,
Surer to prosper than prosperity
Could have assured us; and by what best
    way,   40
Whether of open war or covert guile,
We now debate; who can advise may speak.'
    He ceased; and next him Moloch, sceptred
    king,
Stood up, the strongest and the fiercest Spirit
That fought in Heaven, now fiercer by despair.
His trust was with the Eternal to be deemed
Equal in strength, and rather than be less
Cared not to be at all; with that care lost
Went all his fear: of God, or Hell, or worse,
He recked not, and these words thereafter
    spake:—   50
'My sentence[3] is for open war. Of wiles,
More unexpert, I boast not: them let those
Contrive who need, or when they need; not now.
For while they sit contriving, shall the rest—
Millions that stand in arms, and longing wait
The signal to ascend—sit lingering here,
Heaven's fugitives, and for their dwelling-
    place
Accept this dark opprobrious den of shame,
The prison of his tyranny who reigns
By our delay? No! let us rather choose,   60

Armed with Hell-flames and fury, all at once
O'er Heaven's high towers to force resistless
    way,
Turning our tortures into horrid arms
Against the Torturer; when to meet the noise
Of his almighty engine he shall hear
Infernal thunder, and for lightning see
Black fire and horror shot with equal rage
Among his Angels, and his throne itself
Mixed with Tartarean sulphur and strange fire,
His own invented torments. But perhaps   70
The way seems difficult and steep to scale
With upright wing against a higher foe.
Let such bethink them, if the sleepy drench
Of that forgetful lake benumb not still,
That in our proper motion[4] we ascend
Up to our native seat; descent and fall
To us is adverse. Who but felt of late,
When the fierce foe hung on our broken rear
Insulting, and pursued us through the deep,
With what compulsion and laborious flight   80
We sunk thus low? The ascent is easy then;
The event is feared! Should we again provoke
Our stronger,[5] some worse way his wrath may
    find
To our destruction—if there be in Hell
Fear to be worse destroyed! What can be
    worse
Than to dwell here, driven out from bliss, con-
    demned
In this abhorred deep to utter woe;
Where pain of unextinguishable fire
Must exercise us, without hope of end.
The vassals of his anger, when the scourge   90
Inexorably, and the torturing hour,
Calls us to penance? More destroyed than
    thus,
We should be quite abolished, and expire.
What fear we then? what doubt we to incense
His utmost ire? which, to the highth enraged,
Will either quite consume us, and reduce
To nothing this essential[6]—happier far
Than miserable to have eternal being!—
Or if our substance be indeed divine,
And cannot cease to be, we are at worst   100
On this side nothing; and by proof we feel
Our power sufficient to disturb his Heaven,
And with perpetual inroads to alarm,
Though inaccessible, his fatal throne:
Which, if not victory, is yet revenge.'
    He ended frowning, and his look denounced
Desperate revenge, and battle dangerous
To less than gods. On the other side up rose
Belial, in act more graceful and humane;

---

[3] judgment

[4] Being of ethereal na-
   ture they would
   naturally rise.

[5] superior (put as an
   imaginary argu-
   ment)
[6] essence

A fairer person lost not Heaven; he seemed 110
'or dignity composed, and high exploit.
But all was false and hollow; though his tongue
Dropt manna,[7] and could make the worse appear
The better reason, to perplex and dash
Maturest counsels: for his thoughts were low;
To vice industrious, but to nobler deeds
Timorous and slothful; yet he pleased the ear:
And with persuasive accent thus began:—
'I should be much for open war, O Peers, 120
As not behind in hate, if what was urged
Main reason to persuade immediate war
Did not dissuade me most, and seem to cast
Ominous conjecture on the whole success;
When he who most excels in facts[8] of arms,
In what he counsels and in what excels
Mistrustful, grounds his courage on despair
And utter dissolution, as the scope
Of all his aim, after some dire revenge.
First, what revenge? The towers of Heaven are filled
With armed watch, that render all access 130
Impregnable: oft on the bordering deep
Encamp their legions, or with obscure wing
Scout far and wide into the realm of Night,
Scorning surprise. Or could we break our way
By force, and at our heels all Hell should rise
With blackest insurrection, to confound
Heaven's purest light, yet our great Enemy,
All incorruptible, would on his throne
Sit unpolluted, and the ethereal mould,
Incapable of stain, would soon expel 140
Her mischief, and purge off the baser fire,
Victorious. Thus repulsed, our final hope
Is flat despair: we must exasperate
The Almighty Victor to spend all his rage;
And that must end us, that must be our cure—
To be no more. Sad cure! for who would lose,
Though full of pain, this intellectual being,
Those thoughts that wander through eternity,
To perish rather, swallowed up and lost
In the wide womb of uncreated Night, 150
Devoid of sense and motion? And who knows,
Let this be good,[9] whether our angry foe
Can give it, or will ever? How he can
Is doubtful; that he never will is sure.
Will he, so wise, let loose at once his ire,
Belike through impotence, or unaware,
To give his enemies their wish, and end
Them in his anger, whom his anger saves
To punish endless? "Wherefore cease we then?"

Say they who counsel war; "we are decreed,
Reserved, and destined to eternal woe: 161
Whatever doing, what can we suffer more,
What can we suffer worse?" Is this then worst,
Thus sitting, thus consulting, thus in arms?
What when we fled amain, pursued and struck
With Heaven's afflicting thunder, and besought
The Deep to shelter us? this Hell then seemed
A refuge from those wounds. Or when we lay
Chained on the burning lake? That sure was worse.
What if the breath that kindled those grim fires, 170
Awaked, should blow them into sevenfold rage,
And plunge us in the flames; or from above
Should intermitted vengeance arm again
His red right hand to plague us? What if all
Her stores were opened, and this firmament
Of Hell should spout her cataracts of fire,
Impendent horrors, threatening hideous fall
One day upon our heads; while we perhaps
Designing or exhorting glorious war,
Caught in a fiery tempest, shall be hurled, 180
Each on his rock transfixed, the sport and prey
Of racking whirlwinds, or forever sunk
Under yon boiling ocean, wrapt in chains;
There to converse with everlasting groans,
Unrespited, unpitied, unreprieved,
Ages of hopeless end! This would be worse.
War therefore, open or concealed, alike
My voice dissuades: for what can[10] force or guile
With him, or who deceive his mind, whose eye
Views all things at one view? He from Heaven's highth 190
All these our motions vain sees and derides;
Not more almighty to resist our might
Than wise to frustrate all our plots and wiles.
Shall we then live thus vile, the race of Heaven
Thus trampled, thus expelled to suffer here
Chains and these torments? Better these than worse,
By my advice; since fate inevitable
Subdues us, and omnipotent decree,
The Victor's will. To suffer, as to do,
Our strength is equal, nor the law unjust 200
That so ordains: this[11] was at first resolved,
If we were wise, against so great a foe
Contending, and so doubtful what might fall.
I laugh, when those who at the spear are bold
And venturous, if that fail them, shrink, and fear
What yet they know must follow—to endure
Exile, or ignominy, or bonds, or pain,

7 A sweet gum, exuding from shrubs (not the Biblical manna).
8 feat
9 supposing annihilation good
10 avails
11 viz., to abide the issue

The sentence of their conqueror. This is now
Our doom; which if we can sustain and bear,
Our Supreme Foe in time may much remit   210
His anger, and perhaps, thus far removed,
Not mind us not offending, satisfied
With what is punished; whence these raging
    fires
Will slacken, if his breath stir not their flames.
Our purer essence then will overcome
Their noxious vapor, or, inured, not feel;
Or, changed at length, and to the place con-
    formed
In temper and in nature, will receive
Familiar the fierce heat; and, void of pain,
This horror will grow mild, this darkness
    light;   220
Besides what hope the never-ending flight
Of future days may bring, what chance, what
    change
Worth waiting,—since our present lot appears
For happy[12] though but ill, for ill not worst,
If we procure not to ourselves more woe.'
    Thus Belial, with words clothed in reason's
    garb,
Counselled ignoble ease, and peaceful sloth,
Not peace; and after him thus Mammon
    spake:—
'Either to disenthrone the King of Heaven
We war, if war be best, or to regain   230
Our own right lost. Him to unthrone we then
May hope, when everlasting Fate shall yield
To fickle Chance, and Chaos judge the strife.
The former, vain to hope, argues as vain
The latter; for what place can be for us
Within Heaven's bound, unless Heaven's Lord
    Supreme
We overpower? Suppose he should relent,
And publish grace to all, on promise made
Of new subjection; with what eyes could we
Stand in his presence, humble, and receive   240
Strict laws imposed, to celebrate his throne
With warbled hymns, and to his Godhead sing
Forced Halleluiahs; while he lordly sits
Our envied sovran, and his altar breathes
Ambrosial odors and ambrosial flowers,
Our servile offerings? This must be our task
In Heaven, this our delight. How wearisome
Eternity so spent in worship paid
To whom we hate! Let us not then pursue—
By force impossible, by leave obtained   250
Unacceptable[13]—though in Heaven, our state
Of splendid vassalage; but rather seek
Our own good from ourselves, and from our
    own[14]
Live to ourselves, though in this vast recess,

Free, and to none accountable, preferring
Hard liberty before the easy yoke
Of servile pomp. Our greatness will appe
Then most conspicuous, when great things (
    small,
Useful of hurtful, prosperous of adverse,
We can create, and in what place soe'er   2
Thrive under evil, and work ease out of pain
Through labor and endurance. This dee
    world
Of darkness do we dread? How oft amidst
Thick clouds and dark doth Heaven's a
    ruling Sire
Choose to reside, his glory unobscured,
And with the majesty of darkness round
Covers his throne, from whence deep thunde
    roar,
Mustering their rage, and Heaven resemble
    Hell!
As he our darkness, cannot we his light
Imitate when we please? This desert soil   27
Wants not her hidden lustre, gems and gold
Nor want we skill or art, from whence to rai
Magnificence; and what can Heaven sho
    more?
Our torments also may in length of time
Become our elements, these piercing fires
As soft as now severe, our temper changed
Into their temper; which must needs remove
The sensible[15] of pain. All things invite
To peaceful counsels, and the settled state
Of order, how in safety best we may   28
Compose our present evils, with regard
Of what we are and where, dismissing quite
All thoughts of war. Ye have what I advise
    He scarce had finished, when such murmu
    filled
The assembly, as when hollow rocks retain
The sound of blustering winds, which all nigl
    long
Had roused the sea, now with hoarse cadenc
    lull
Seafaring men o'erwatched, whose bark b
    chance,
Or pinnace, anchors in a craggy bay
After the tempest: such applause was heard 29
As Mammon ended, and his sentence please
Advising peace; for such another field
They dreaded worse than Hell; so much th
    fear
Of thunder and the sword of Michaël
Wrought still within them; and no less desir
To found this nether empire, which might ris
By policy, and long process[16] of time,
In emulation opposite to Heaven.
Which when Beëlzebub perceived, than whom

atan except, none higher sat, with grave 300
spect he rose, and in his rising seemed
 pillar of state; deep on his front engraven
eliberation sat and public care;
nd princely counsel in his face yet shone,
ajestic, though in ruin. Sage he stood,
ith Atlantean[17] shoulders fit to bear
he weight of mightiest monarchies; his look
rew audience and attention still as night
r summer's noontide air, while thus he
   spake:—
'Thrones and Imperial Powers, Offspring of
   Heaven, 310
thereal Virtues! or these titles now
ust we renounce, and, changing style,[18] be
   called
rinces of Hell? for so the popular vote
nclines—here to continue, and build up here
 growing empire; doubtless! while we dream,
nd know not that the King of Heaven hath
   doomed
his place our dungeon—not our safe retreat
eyond his potent arm, to live exempt
rom Heaven's high jurisdiction, in new league
anded against his throne, but to remain 320
strictest bondage, though thus far removed,
nder the inevitable curb, reserved[19]
is captive multitude. For he, be sure,
 highth or depth, still first and last will
   reign
le king, and of his kingdom lose no part
y our revolt, but over Hell extend
is empire, and with iron sceptre rule
s here, as with his golden those in Heaven.
hat[20] sit we then projecting peace and war?
ar hath determined us, and foiled with loss
reparable; terms of peace yet none 331
ouchsafed or sought; for what peace will be
   given
o us enslaved, but custody severe,
nd stripes, and arbitrary punishment
flicted? And what peace can we return,
ut, to[21] our power, hostility and hate,
ntamed reluctance, and revenge, though slow,
et ever plotting how the Conqueror least
ay reap his conquest, and may least rejoice 340
 doing what we most in suffering feel?
or will occasion want, nor shall we need
ith dangerous expedition to invade
eaven, whose high walls fear no assault or
   siege,
r ambush from the Deep. What if we find
ome easier enterprise? There is a place
f ancient and prophetic fame in Heaven

Err not), another World, the happy seat
Of some new race called Man, about this time
To be created like to us, though less
In power and excellence, but favored more 350
Of him who rules above; so was his will
Pronounced among the gods, and by an oath
That shook Heaven's whole circumference,
   confirmed.
Thither let us bend all our thoughts, to learn
What creatures there inhabit, of what mould
Or substance, how endued, and what their
   power,
And where their weakness: how attempted[22]
   best,
By force or subtlety. Though Heaven be shut,
And Heaven's high Arbitrator sit secure
In his own strength, this place may lie ex-
   posed, 360
The utmost border of his kingdom, left
To their defence who hold it; here, perhaps,
Some advantageous act may be achieved
By sudden onset: either with Hell-fire
To waste his whole creation, or possess
All as our own, and drive, as we were driven,
The puny[23] habitants; or if not drive,
Seduce them to our party,[24] that their God
May prove their foe, and with repenting hand
Abolish his own works. This would surpass 370
Common revenge, and interrupt his joy
In our confusion, and our joy upraise
In his disturbance; when his darling sons,
Hurled headlong to partake with us, shall curse
Their frail original, and faded bliss—
Faded so soon! Advise if this be worth
Attempting, or to sit in darkness here
Hatching vain empires.' Thus Beëlzebub
Pleaded his devilish counsel, first devised
By Satan, and in part proposed; for whence,
But from the author of all ill, could spring 381
So deep a malice, to confound the race
Of Mankind in one root, and Earth with Hell
To mingle and involve, done all to spite
The great Creator? But their spite still serves
His glory to augment. The bold design
Pleased highly those Infernal States,[25] and joy
Sparkled in all their eyes; with full assent
They vote: whereat his speech he thus re-
   news:—
'Well have ye judged, well ended long de-
   bate, 390
Synod of gods! and, like to what ye are,
Great things resolved; which from the lowest
   deep
Will once more lift us up, in spite of fate,

Atlas-like appellation reserved for (a Lat-inism; cf. *arrive*, 409)

20 why
21 to the extent of
22 assailed
23 From French *puis né*, later born.
24 side
25 lords

Nearer our ancient seat—perhaps in view
Of those bright confines, whence, with neigh-
    boring arms
And opportune excursion, we may chance
Re-enter Heaven; or else in some mild zone
Dwell not unvisited of Heaven's fair light,
Secure, and at the brightening orient beam
Purge off this gloom; the soft delicious air, 400
To heal the scar of these corrosive fires,
Shall breathe her balm. But first, whom shall
    we send
In search of this new world? whom shall we
    find
Sufficient? who shall tempt with wandering
    feet
The dark, unbottomed, infinite Abyss,
And through the palpable obscure[26] find out
His uncouth way, or spread his aery flight,
Upborne with indefatigable wings
Over the vast abrupt,[26] ere he arrive[27]
The happy isle? What strength, what art,
    can then   410
Suffice, or what evasion bear him safe
Through the strict senteries and stations thick
Of Angels watching round? Here he had
    need[28]
All circumspection, and we now no less[29]
Choice in our suffrage; for on whom we send,
The weight of all, and our last hope, relies.'
    This said, he sat; and expectation held
His look suspense, awaiting who appeared
To second, or oppose, or undertake
The perilous attempt; but all sat mute,   420
Pondering the danger with deep thoughts; and
    each
In other's countenance read his own dismay,
Astonished. None among the choice and prime
Of those Heaven-warring champions could be
    found
So hardy as to proffer or accept,
Alone, the dreadful voyage; till at last
Satan, whom now transcendent glory raised
Above his fellows, with monarchal pride
Conscious of highest worth, unmoved thus
    spake:—
'O Progeny of Heaven! Empyreal Thrones!
With reason hath deep silence and demur   431
Seized us, though undismayed. Long is the
    way
And hard, that out of Hell leads up to Light;
Our prison strong, this huge convex of fire,
Outrageous to devour, immures us round
Ninefold; and gates of burning adamant,

Barred over us, prohibit all egress.
These passed, if any pass, the void profound
Of unessential[30] Night receives him next,
Wide-gaping, and with utter loss of being   4
Threatens him, plunged in that abortive[31] gul
If thence he scape into whatever world,
Or unknown region, what remains him less
Than unknown dangers and as hard escape?
But I should ill become this throne, O Peer
And this imperial sovranty, adorned
With splendor, armed with power, if aug!
    proposed
And judged of public moment, in the shape
Of difficulty or danger, could deter
Me from attempting. Wherefore do I assum
These royalties, and not refuse to reign,   4!
Refusing[32] to accept as great a share
Of hazard as of honor, due alike
To him who reigns, and so much to him due
Of hazard more, as he above the rest
High honored sits? Go therefore, might
    Powers,
Terror of Heaven, though fallen; intend[33] a
    home,
While here shall be our home, what best ma
    ease
The present misery, and render Hell
More tolerable; if there be cure or charm   4(
To respite, or deceive, or slack the pain
Of this ill mansion; intermit no watch
Against a wakeful foe, while I abroad
Through all the coasts of dark destruction see
Deliverance for us all: this enterprise
None shall partake with me.' Thus saying
    rose
The Monarch, and prevented all reply;
Prudent, lest, from his resolution raised,[34]
Others among the chief might offer now
(Certain to be refused) what erst they feared
And, so refused, might in opinion stand   47
His rivals, winning cheap the high repute
Which he through hazard huge must earn. Bu
    they
Dreaded not more the adventure than his voic
Forbidding; and at once with him they rose.
Their rising all at once was as the sound
Of thunder heard remote. Towards him the
    bend
With awful reverence prone; and as a god
Extol him equal to the Highest in Heaven.
Nor failed they to express how much the;
    praised   48
That for the general safety he despised
His own; for neither do the Spirits damned

---

ose all their virtue,—lest bad men should35 boast
Their specious deeds on Earth, which glory excites,
Or close ambition varnished o'er with zeal.
  Thus they their doubtful consultations dark
Ended, rejoicing in their matchless Chief;
As when from mountain-tops the dusky clouds
Ascending, while the North-wind sleeps, o'er-spread
Heaven's cheerful face, the louring element 490
Scowls o'er the darkened landskip snow or shower;
If chance the radiant sun with farewell sweet
Extend his evening beam, the fields revive,
The birds their notes renew, and bleating herds
Attest their joy, that hill and valley rings.
O shame to men! Devil with devil damned
Firm concord holds; men only disagree
Of creatures rational, though under hope
Of heavenly grace; and, God proclaiming peace,
Yet live in hatred, enmity, and strife 500
Among themselves, and levy cruel wars,
Wasting the Earth, each other to destroy:
As if (which might induce us to accord)
Man had not hellish foes enow besides,
That day and night for his destruction wait!
  The Stygian council thus dissolved; and forth
In order came the grand Infernal Peers;
Midst came their mighty Paramount, and seemed
Alone36 the antagonist of Heaven, nor less
Than Hell's dread Emperor, with pomp supreme, 510
And god-like imitated state; him round
A globe of fiery Seraphim enclosed
With bright emblazonry, and horrent37 arms,
Then of their session ended they bid cry
With trumpet's regal sound the great result:
Toward the four winds four speedy Cherubim
Put to their mouths the sounding alchymy,38
By herald's voice explained; the hollow Abyss
Heard far and wide, and all the host of Hell
With deafening shout returned them loud acclaim. 520
  Thence more at ease their minds, and somewhat raised
By false presumptuous hope, the ranged powers
Disband; and, wandering, each his several way
Pursues, as inclination or sad choice
Leads him perplexed, where he may likeliest find
Truce to his restless thoughts, and entertain

The irksome hours, till his great Chief return.
Part on the plain, or in the air sublime,39
Upon the wing or in swift race contend, 529
As at the Olympian games or Pythian fields;
Part curb their fiery steeds, or shun the goal40
With rapid wheels, or fronted41 brigads form:
As when, to warn proud cities, war appears
Waged in the troubled sky, and armies rush
To battle in the clouds; before each van
Prick forth the aery knights, and couch their spears,
Till thickest legions close; with feats of arms
From either end of Heaven the welkin burns.
Others, with vast Typhœan42 rage more fell, 539
Rend up both rocks and hills, and ride the air
In whirlwind; Hell scarce holds the wild uproar:
As when Alcides,43 from Œchalia crowned
With conquest, felt the envenomed robe, and tore
Through pain up by the roots Thessalian pines,
And Lichas from the top of Œta threw
Into the Euboic sea. Others, more mild,
Retreated in a silent valley, sing
With notes angelical to many a harp
Their own heroic deeds and hapless fall
By doom of battle; and complain that Fate 556
Free Virtue should enthrall to Force or Chance.
Their song was partial, but the harmony
(What could it less when Spirits immortal sing?)
Suspended Hell, and took with ravishment
The thronging audience. In discourse more sweet
(For eloquence the soul, song charms the sense)
Others apart sat on a hill retired,
In thoughts more elevate, and reasoned high
Of providence, foreknowledge, will, and fate,
Fixed fate, free will, foreknowledge absolute;
And found no end, in wandering mazes lost. 561
Of good and evil much they argued then,
Of happiness and final misery,
Passion and apathy, and glory and shame,
Vain wisdom all, and false philosophy!—
Yet with a pleasing sorcery could charm
Pain for a while or anguish, and excite
Fallacious hope, or arm the obdured breast
With stubborn patience as with triple steel.
Another part, in squadrons and gross bands,
On bold adventure to discover wide 571

39 uplifted
40 avoid striking the column that marks the turning point (Description taken from the ancient Grecian national games, the Olympian, Pythian, etc.)
41 confronting
42 See Book I. 199.
43 Hercules (referring to the story of the revenge of Nessus)

35 as a warning lest bad men should (They are in the same class!)
36 in himself
37 bristling
38 metallic compound

That dismal world, if any clime perhaps
Might yield them easier habitation, bend
Four ways their flying march, along the banks
Of four infernal rivers that disgorge
Into the burning lake their baleful streams:
Abhorred Styx, the flood of deadly hate;
Sad Acheron of sorrow, black and deep;
Cocytus, named of lamentation loud   579
Heard on the rueful stream; fierce Phlegethon,
Whose waves of torrent fire inflame with rage.
Far off from these a slow and silent stream,
Lethe, the river of oblivion, rolls
Her watery labyrinth, whereof who drinks
Forthwith his former state and being forgets,
Forgets both joy and grief, pleasure and pain.
Beyond this flood a frozen continent
Lies dark and wild, beat with perpetual storms
Of whirlwind and dire hail, which on firm land
Thaws not, but gathers heap, and ruin seems
Of ancient pile;[44] all else deep snow and ice, 591
A gulf profound as that Serbonian bog[45]
Betwixt Damiata and Mount Casius old,
Where armies whole have sunk: the parching
    air
Burns frore,[46] and cold performs the effect of
    fire.
Thither, by harpy-footed Furies haled,
At certain revolutions all the damned
Are brought; and feel by turns the bitter
    change
Of fierce extremes, extremes by change more
    fierce,
From beds of raging fire to starve[47] in ice 600
Their soft ethereal warmth, and there to pine
Immovable, infixed, and frozen round
Periods of time; thence hurried back to fire.
They ferry over this Lethean sound
Both to and fro, their sorrow to augment,
And wish and struggle, as they pass to reach
The tempting stream, with one small drop to
    lose
In sweet forgetfulness all pain and woe,
All in one moment, and so near the brink;
But Fate withstands, and, to oppose the at-
    tempt   610
Medusa with Gorgonian terror guards
The ford, and of itself the water flies
All taste of living wight, as once it fled
The lip of Tantalus. Thus roving on
In confused march forlorn, the adventurous
    bands,
With shuddering horror pale, and eyes aghast,
Viewed first their lamentable lot, and found
No rest. Through many a dark and dreary vale

They passed, and many a region dolorous,
O'er many a frozen, many a fiery Alp,[48] 620
Rocks, caves, lakes, fens, bogs, dens, and
    shades of death—
A universe of death, which God by curse
Created evil, for evil only good;
Where all life dies, death lives, and Nature
    breeds,
Perverse, all monstrous, all prodigious things,
Abominable, inutterable, and worse
Than fables yet have feigned, or fear con-
    ceived,
Gorgons, and Hydras, and Chimæras dire.
  Meanwhile the Adversary of God and Man,
Satan, with thoughts inflamed of highest de-
    sign,   630
Puts on swift wings, and toward the gates of
    Hell
Explores his solitary flight; sometimes
He scours the right hand coast, sometimes the
    left;
Now shaves with level wing the deep, then soars
Up to the fiery concave towering high.
As when far off at sea a fleet descried
Hangs in the clouds, by equinoctial winds
Close sailing from Bengala, or the isles
Of Ternate and Tidore,[49] whence merchants
    bring
Their spicy drugs; they on the trading flood
Through the wide Ethiopian[50] to the Cape, 641
Ply stemming nightly toward the pole: so
    seemed
Far off the flying Fiend. At last appear
Hell-bounds, high reaching to the horrid roof,
And thrice threefold the gates; three folds
    were brass,
Three iron, three of adamantine rock
Impenetrable, impaled with circling fire,
Yet unconsumed. Before the gates there sat
On either side a formidable Shape.
The one seemed woman to the waist, and fair, 65[0]
But ended foul in many a scaly fold
Voluminous and vast, a serpent armed
With mortal sting. About her middle round
A cry of Hell-hounds never-ceasing barked
With wide Cerberean[51] mouths full loud, and
    rung
A hideous peal; yet, when they list, would
    creep
If aught disturbed their noise, into her womb,
And kennel there, yet there still barked and
    howled
Within unseen. Far less abhorred than these

44 masonry   46 frosty
45 Herodotus II. 6, III.   47 freeze
  5.

48 mount
49 Two of the Molucca
    islands.
50 Indian Ocean.

51 Like those of Cer-
    berus, the three
    headed monster
    that guarded
    Hades.

exed Scylla, bathing in the sea that parts 660
alabria from the hoarse Trinacrian shore;*
for uglier follow tne night hag, when, called
n secret, riding through the air she comes,
ured with the smell of infant blood, to dance
With Lapland witches, while the laboring moon
clipses at their charms. The other Shape—
f shape it might be called that shape had none
istinguishable in member, joint, or limb,
r substance might be called that shadow
    seemed,
or each seemed either—black it stood as
    Night, 670
ierce as ten Furies, terrible as Hell,
nd shook a dreadful dart; what seemed his
    head
he likeness of a kingly crown had on.
atan was now at hand, and from his seat
he monster moving onward came as fast,
With horrid strides; Hell trembled as he strode.
he undaunted Fiend what this might be
    admired—52
dmired, not feared—God and his Son except,
reated thing naught valued he nor shunned—
nd with disdainful look thus first began:— 680
'Whence and what art thou, execrable Shape,
hat dar'st, though grim and terrible, advance
hy miscreated front athwart my way
o yonder gates? Through them I mean to
    pass,
hat be assured, without leave asked of thee.
etire; or taste thy folly, and learn by proof,
ell-born, not to contend with Spirits of
    Heaven.'
o whom the Goblin, full of wrath, replied:—
Art thou that Traitor-Angel, art thou he
Vho first broke peace in Heaven and faith, till
    then 690
nbroken, and in proud rebellious arms
rew after him the third part of Heaven's
    sons,
onjured against the Highest, for which both
    thou
nd they, outcast from God, are here condemned
o waste eternal days in woe and pain?
nd reckon'st thou thyself with Spirits of
    Heaven,
Iell-doomed, and breath'st defiance here and
    scorn,
Vhere I reign king, and, to enrage thee more,
hy king and lord? Back to thy punishment,

False fugitive, and to thy speed add wings, 700
Lest with a whip of scorpions I pursue
Thy lingering, or with one stroke of this dart
Strange horror seize thee, and pangs unfelt
    before.'
So spake the grisly Terror, and in shape,
So speaking and so threatening, grew tenfold
More dreadful and deform. On the other side,
Incensed with indignation, Satan stood
Unterrified, and like a comet burned,
That fires the length of Ophiuchus huge53
In the arctic sky, and from his horrid hair 710
Shakes pestilence and war. Each at the head
Levelled his deadly aim; their fatal hands
No second stroke intend; and such a frown
Each cast at the other, as when two black
    clouds,
With Heaven's artillery fraught, come rat-
    tling on
Over the Caspian, then stand front to front
Hovering a space, till winds the signal blow
To join their dark encounter in mid-air:—
So frowned the mighty combatants, that Hell
Grew darker at their frown; so matched they
    stood; 720
For never but once more was either like
To meet so great a foe. And now great deeds
Had been achieved, whereof all Hell had rung,
Had not the snaky Sorceress that sat
Fast by Hell-gate and kept the fatal key,
Risen, and with hideous outcry rushed between.
'O father, what intends thy hand,' she cried,
'Against thy only son? What fury, O son,
Possesses thee to bend that mortal dart
Against thy father's head? and know'st for
    whom? 730
For him who sits above, and laughs the while
At thee ordained his drudge, to execute
Whate'er his wrath, which he calls justice,
    bids—
His wrath, which one day will destroy ye both!'
She spake, and at her words the hellish Pest
Forbore: then these to her Satan returned:—
'So strange thy outcry, and thy words so
    strange
Thou interposest, that my sudden hand,
Prevented, spares to tell thee yet by deeds
What it intends, till first I know of thee 740
What thing thou art, thus double-formed, and
    why,
In this infernal vale first met, thou call'st
Me father, and that phantasm call'st my son.
I know thee not, nor ever saw till now
Sight more detestable than him and thee.'
    To whom thus the Portress of Hell-gate
    replied:—

52 wondered
Through Circe's jealousy, says Ovid. the lower
part of Scylla's body was transformed into
barking dogs; whereupon, throwing herself
into the sea, she was changed into a rock.
The next simile is drawn from Scandinavian
superstition.

53 A northern constellation.

'Hast thou forgot me then, and do I seem
Now in thine eye so foul? once deemed so fair
In Heaven, when at the assembly, and in sight
Of all the Seraphim with thee combined   750
In bold conspiracy against Heaven's King,
All on a sudden miserable pain
Surprised thee; dim thine eyes, and dizzy swum
In darkness, while thy head flames thick and
    fast
Threw forth, till on the left side opening wide,
Likest to thee in shape and countenance bright,
Then shining heavenly fair, a goddess armed,
Out of thy head I sprung.* Amazement seized
All the host of Heaven: back they recoiled
    afraid
At first, and called me *Sin*, and for a sign   760
Portentous held me; but, familiar grown,
I pleased, and with attractive graces won
The most averse; thee chiefly, who full oft
Thyself in me thy perfect image viewing
Became'st enamoured; and such joy thou took'st
With me in secret, that my womb conceived
A growing burden. Meanwhile war arose,
And fields were fought in Heaven; wherein
    remained
(For what could else?) to our Almighty Foe
Clear victory, to our part loss and rout   770
Through all the Empyrean. Down they fell,
Driven headlong from the pitch of Heaven,
    down
Into this deep; and in the general fall
I also: at which time this powerful key
Into my hands was given, with charge to keep
These gates forever shut, which none can pass
Without my opening. Pensive here I sat
Alone; but long I sat not, till my womb,
Pregnant by thee, and now excessive grown,
Prodigious motion felt and rueful throes.   780
At last this odious offspring whom thou seest,
Thine own begotten, breaking violent way,
Tore through my entrails, that, with fear and
    pain
Distorted, all my nether shape thus grew
Transformed; but he, my inbred enemy,
Forth issued, brandishing his fatal dart,
Made to destroy. I fled, and cried out *Death!*
Hell trembled at the hideous name, and sighed
From all her caves, and back resounded *Death!*
I fled; but he pursued (though more, it
    seems,   790
Inflamed with lust than rage) and, swifter far,
Me overtook, his mother, all dismayed,
And, in embraces forcible and foul
Engendering with me, of that rape begot

* Milton draws from pagan myths with especial
    freedom in describing his evil characters and
    scenes.

These yelling monsters, that with ceaseless cr[y]
Surround me, as thou saw'st, hourly conceive[d]
And hourly born, with sorrow infinite
To me; for, when they list, into the womb
That bred them they return, and howl, an[d]
    gnaw
My bowels, their repast; then, burstin[g]
    forth   8[00]
Afresh, with conscious terrors vex me roun[d]
That rest or intermission none I find.
Before mine eyes in opposition sits
Grim Death, my son and foe, who sets them o[n]
And me, his parent, would full soon devour
For want of other prey, but that he knows
His end with mine involved, and knows that
Should prove a bitter morsel, and his bane,
Whenever that shall be: so Fate pronounced.
But thou, O father, I forewarn thee, shun   81[0]
His deadly arrow; neither vainly hope
To be invulnerable in those bright arms,
Though tempered heavenly; for that morta[l]
    dint,
Save he who reigns above, none can resist.'
  She finished; and the subtle Fiend his lore
Soon learned, now milder, and thus answere[d]
    smooth:—
  'Dear daughter—since thou claim'st me fo[r]
    thy sire,
And my fair son here show'st me, the dea[r]
    pledge
Of dalliance had with thee in Heaven, and joy[s]
Then sweet, now sad to mention, through di[re]
    change   82[0]
Befallen us unforeseen, unthought of—know,
I come no enemy, but to set free
From out this dark and dismal house of pain
Both him and thee, and all the Heavenly hos[t]
Of Spirits that, in our just pretences54 arme[d]
Fell with us from on high. From them I go
This uncouth errand sole, and one for all
Myself expose, with lonely steps to tread
The unfounded Deep, and through the voi[d]
    immense
To search with wandering quest a place fore
    told   83[0]
Should be—and by concurring signs, ere no[w]
Created vast and round—a place of bliss
In the purlieus of Heaven; and therein place
A race of upstart creatures, to supply
Perhaps our vacant room, though mor[e]
    removed,
Lest Heaven, surcharged with potent multitude[s]
Might hap to move new broils. Be this, o[r]
    aught
Than this more secret, now designed, I haste

54 claims

'o know; and, this once known, shall soon
    return,
nd bring ye to the place where thou and
    Death   840
hall dwell at ease, and up and down unseen
Ving silently the buxom⁵⁵ air, embalmed
Vith odors: there ye shall be fed and filled
nmeasurably; all things shall be your prey.'
  He ceased; for both seemed highly pleased,
    and Death
rinned horrible a ghastly smile, to hear
is famine should be filled, and blessed his
    maw
estined to that good hour. No less rejoiced
is mother bad, and thus bespake her sire:—
  'The key of this infernal pit, by due   850
nd by command of Heaven's all-powerful
    King,
keep, by him forbidden to unlock
hese adamantine gates; against all force
eath ready stands to interpose his dart,
earless to be o'ermatched by living might.
ut what owe I to his commands above,
Vho hates me, and hath hither thrust me down
ito this gloom of Tartarus profound,
o sit in hateful office here confined,
nhabitant of Heaven and Heavenly-born,   860
ere in perpetual agony and pain,
Vith terrors and with clamors compassed round
f mine own brood, that on my bowels feed?
hou art my father, thou my author, thou
y being gav'st me; whom should I obey
ut thee? whom follow? Thou wilt bring me
    soon
o that new world of light and bliss, among
he gods who live at ease, where I shall reign
t thy right hand voluptuous, as beseems
hy daughter and thy darling, without end.' 870
  Thus saying, from her side the fatal key,
ad instrument of all our woe, she took;
nd, towards the gate rolling her bestial train,
orthwith the huge portcullis high up-drew,
Vhich but herself not all the Stygian Powers
ould once have moved; then in the key-hole
    turns
he intricate wards, and every bolt and bar
f massy iron or solid rock with ease
nfastens. On a sudden open fly,
Vith impetuous recoil and jarring sound,   880
he infernal doors, and on their hinges grate
arsh thunder, that the lowest bottom shook
f Erebus.⁵⁶ She opened; but to shut
xcelled her power: the gates wide open stood,
hat with extended wings a bannered host,

Under spread ensigns marching, might pass
    through
With horse and chariots ranked in loose array;
So wide they stood, and like a furnace-mouth
Cast forth redounding smoke and ruddy flame.
Before their eyes in sudden view appear   890
The secrets of the hoary Deep, a dark
Illimitable ocean, without bound,
Without dimension; where length, breadth, and
    highth,
And time, and place, are lost; where eldest
    Night
And Chaos, ancestors of Nature, hold
Eternal anarchy, amidst the noise
Of endless wars, and by confusion stand.
For Hot, Cold, Moist, and Dry, four champions
    fierce,
Strive here for mastery, and to battle bring
Their embryon⁵⁷ atoms; they around the flag
Of each his faction, in their several clans,   901
Light-armed or heavy, sharp, smooth, swift,
    or slow,
Swarm populous, unnumbered as the sands
Of Barca or Cyrene's torrid soil,
Levied to side with warring winds, and poise
Their lighter wings. To whom these most
    adhere,
He rules a moment; Chaos umpire sits,
And by decision more embroils the fray
By which he reigns; next him, high arbiter,
Chance governs all. Into this wild Abyss,   910
The womb of Nature, and perhaps her grave,
Of neither sea, nor shore, nor air, nor fire,
But all these in their pregnant causes mixed
Confusedly, and which thus must ever fight,
Unless the Almighty Maker them ordain
His dark materials to create more worlds—
Into this wild Abyss the wary Fiend
Stood on the brink of Hell and looked awhile,
Pondering his voyage; for no narrow frith
He had to cross. Nor was his ear less pealed 920
With noises loud and ruinous (to compare
Great things with small) than when Bellona⁵⁸
    storms
With all her battering engines, bent to rase
Some capital city; or less than if this frame
Of Heaven were falling, and these elements
In mutiny had from her axle torn
The steadfast Earth. At last his sail-broad
    vans
He spreads for flight, and in the surging smoke
Uplifted spurns the ground; thence many a
    league,
As in a cloudy chair, ascending rides   930
Audacious; but, that seat soon failing, meets

---

5 yielding
6 "Darkness," the Virgilian name for hell.

57 rudimentary
58 Roman goddess of war.

A vast vacuity; all unawares,
Fluttering his pennons vain, plumb-down he
    drops
Ten thousand fathom deep, and to this hour
Down had been falling, had not by ill chance
The strong rebuff of some tumultuous cloud,
Instinct with fire and nitre, hurried him
As many miles aloft. That fury stayed—
Quenched in a boggy Syrtis,[59] neither sea,
Nor good dry land—nigh foundered, on he
    fares,   940
Treading the crude consistence, half on foot,
Half flying; behoves him[60] now both oar and
    sail.
As when a gryphon through the wilderness
With winged course, o'er hill or moory dale,
Pursues the Arimaspian,[61] who by stealth
Had from his wakeful custody purloined
The guarded gold: so eagerly the Fiend
O'er bog or steep, through strait, rough, dense,
    or rare,
With head, hands, wings, or feet, pursues his
    way,
And swims, or sinks, or wades, or creeps, or
    flies.   950
At length a universal hubbub wild
Of stunning sounds and voices all confused,
Borne through the hollow dark, assaults his
    ear
With loudest vehemence. Thither he plies
Undaunted, to meet there whatever Power
Or Spirit of the nethermost Abyss
Might in that noise reside, of whom to ask
Which way the nearest coast of darkness lies
Bordering on light; when straight behold the
    throne
Of Chaos, and his dark pavilion spread   960
Wide on the wasteful Deep! With him
    enthroned
Sat sable-vested Night, eldest of things,
The consort of his reign; and by them stood
Orcus and Ades, and the dreaded name
Of Demogorgon;[62] Rumor next, and Chance,
And Tumult, and Confusion, all embroiled,
And Discord with a thousand various mouths.
    To whom Satan, turning boldly, thus:—'Ye
        Powers
And Spirits of this nethermost Abyss,
Chaos and ancient Night, I come no spy,   970
With purpose to explore or to disturb

The secrets of your realm; but, by constrai
Wandering this darksome desert, as my way
Lies through your spacious empire up to ligh
Alone and without guide, half lost, I seek
What readiest path leads where your gloom
    bounds
Confine with[63] Heaven; or if some other plac
From your dominion won, the Ethereal King
Possesses lately, thither to arrive
I travel this profound. Direct my course: 98
Directed, no mean recompense it brings
To your behoof, if I that region lost,
All usurpation thence expelled, reduce
To her original darkness and your sway
(Which is my present journey), and once mo
Erect the standard there of ancient Night.
Yours be the advantage all, mine the revenge
    Thus Satan; and him thus the Anarch[64] ol
With faltering speech and visage incompose
Answered:—'I know thee, stranger, who tho
    art: 99
That mighty leading Angel, who of late
Made head against Heaven's King, thoug
    overthrown.
I saw and heard; for such a numerous host
Fled not in silence through the frighted dee
With ruin upon ruin, rout on rout,
Confusion worse confounded; and Heaven-gat
Poured out by millions her victorious bands,
Pursuing. I upon my frontiers here
Keep residence; if all I can will serve
That little which is left so to defend,   100
Encroached on still through our intestine bro
Weakening the sceptre of old Night: first Hel
Your dungeon, stretching far and wid
    beneath;
Now lately Heaven and Earth, another world
Hung o'er my realm, linked in a golden cha
To that side Heaven from whence your legio
    fell.
If that way be your walk, you have not far;
So much the nearer danger. Go, and speed!
Havoc, and spoil, and ruin, are my gain.'
    He ceased; and Satan stayed not
        reply,   10
But, glad that now his sea should find a shor
With fresh alacrity and force renewed
Springs upward, like a pyramid of fire,
Into the wild expanse, and through the shock
Of fighting elements, on all sides round
Environed, wins his way; harder beset
And more endangered, than when Argo pass
Through Bosporus betwixt the justling rocks;
Or when Ulysses on the larboard shunned

---

59 quicksand   60 needs he
61 "It is said the Arimaspians, a one-eyed people,
    steal gold from the griffins."—Herodotus III.
    116.
62 Names of rather vague significance, sufficiently
    defined in 969. It is said that the name of
    Demogorgon was never uttered until a Chris-
    tian writer of the fourth century broke the
    spell.

63 border on
64 Word first used by Milton.

Charybdis, and by the other whirlpool steered:
So he with difficulty and labor hard   1021
Moved on: with difficulty and labor he;
But, he once passed, soon after, when Man fell,
Strange alteration! Sin and Death amain,
Following his track (such was the will of
    Heaven)
Paved after him a broad and beaten way
Over the dark Abyss, whose boiling gulf
Tamely endured a bridge of wondrous length,
From Hell continued, reaching the utmost orb
Of this frail World;* by which the Spirits
    perverse   1030
With easy intercourse pass to and fro
To tempt or punish mortals, except whom
God and good Angels guard by special grace.
  But now at last the sacred influence[65]
Of light appears, and from the walls of Heaven
Shoots far into the bosom of dim Night
A glimmering dawn. Here Nature first begins
Her farthest verge, and Chaos to retire,
As from her outmost works, a broken foe,
With tumult less and with less hostile din; 1040
That[66] Satan with less toil, and now with ease,
Wafts on the calmer wave by dubious light,
And, like a weather-beaten vessel, holds
Gladly the port, though shrouds and tackle
    torn;
Or in the emptier waste, resembling air,
Weighs his spread wings, at leisure to behold
Far off the empyreal Heaven, extended wide
In circuit, undetermined square or round,
With opal towers, and battlements adorned
Of living sapphire, once his native seat; 1050
And, fast by, hanging in a golden chain,
This pendent World, in bigness as a star
Of smallest magnitude close by the moon.
Thither, full fraught with mischievous revenge,
Accurst, and in a cursed hour, he hies.

FROM BOOK III. INVOCATION TO LIGHT†

HAIL, holy Light, offspring of Heaven first-
    born!
Or of the Eternal coeternal beam
May I express thee unblamed? since God is
    light,

And never but in unapproached light
Dwelt from eternity—dwelt then in thee,
Bright effluence of bright essence increate![1]
Or hear'st thou rather[2] pure Ethereal stream,
Whose fountain who shall tell? Before the
    Sun,
Before the Heavens, thou wert, and at the voice
Of God, as with a mantle, didst invest   10
The rising World of waters dark and deep,
Won from the void and formless Infinite!
Thee I revisit now with bolder wing,
Escaped the Stygian Pool, though long detained
In that obscure sojourn, while in my flight,
Through utter and through middle Darkness
    borne,
With other notes than to the Orphean lyre
I sung of Chaos and eternal Night,
Taught by the Heavenly Muse to venture down
The dark descent, and up to re-ascend,   20
Though hard and rare. Thee I revisit safe,
And feel thy sovran vital lamp; but thou
Revisit'st not these eyes, that roll in vain
To find thy piercing ray, and find no dawn;
So thick a drop serene[3] hath quenched their
    orbs,
Or dim suffusion veiled. Yet not the more
Cease I to wander where the Muses haunt
Clear spring, or shady grove, or sunny hill,
Smit with the love of sacred song; but chief
Thee, Sion, and the flowery brooks beneath, 30
That wash thy hallowed feet, and warbling
    flow,
Nightly I visit: nor sometimes forget
Those other two equalled with me in fate,
So were I[4] equalled with them in renown,
Blind Thamyris and blind Mæonides,[5]
And Tiresias and Phineus, prophets old:
Then feed on thoughts that voluntary move
Harmonious numbers; as the wakeful bird
Sings darkling, and, in shadiest covert hid,
Tunes her nocturnal note. Thus with the
    year   40
Seasons return; but not to me returns
Day, or the sweet approach of even or morn
Or sight of vernal bloom, or summer's rose,
Or flocks, or herds, or human face divine;
But cloud instead and ever-during dark
Surrounds me, from the cheerful ways of men
Cut off, and, for the book of knowledge fair,
Presented with a universal blank
Of Nature's works, to me expunged and rased,
And wisdom at one entrance quite shut out. 50

5 Perhaps literally "in-   66 so that
  flow."
  By world is meant the starry universe with the
  earth at the center. The Ptolemaic theory
  held the universe to consist of ten concentric,
  transparent, revolving spheres, each carrying
  with it its own body—Moon, Mercury, Venus,
  Sun, Mars, Jupiter, Saturn, Fixed Stars, with
  finally the Crystalline Sphere, and the Primum
  Mobile ("first movable," primary source of
  motion). From their revolutions came, according to Pythagoras, the "music of the spheres."
† Milton speaks here in his own person; it is to be
  remembered that he was blind (Cf. line 23).

1 uncreated   4 would I were so
2 wouldst r a t h e r b e 5 Homer, who mentions
  called   Thamyris as an-
3 The *gutta serena*,   other blind bard.
  supposed cause of
  blindness.

So much the rather thou, Celestial Light,
Shine inward, and the mind through all her
    powers
Irradiate; there plant eyes; all mist from
    thence
Purge and disperse, that I may see and tell
Of things invisible to mortal sight.

FROM BOOK IV. SATAN IN SIGHT OF EDEN

SOMETIMES towards Eden, which now in his
    view
Lay pleasant, his grieved look he fixes sad;
Sometimes towards Heaven and the full-blazing
    Sun,
Which now sat high in his meridian tower: 30
Then, much revolving, thus in sighs began:—
"O thou that, with surpassing glory crowned,
Look'st from thy sole dominion like the god
Of this new World—at whose sight all the stars
Hide their diminished heads—to thee I call,
But with no friendly voice, and add thy name,
O Sun, to tell thee how I hate thy beams,
That bring to my remembrance from what
    state
I fell, how glorious once above thy sphere,
Till pride and worse ambition threw me
    down,   40
Warring in Heaven against Heaven's matchless
    King!
Ah, wherefore? He deserved no such return
From me, whom he created what I was
In that bright eminence, and with his good
Upbraided none; nor was his service hard.
What could be less than to afford him praise,
The easiest recompense, and pay him thanks,
How due? Yet all his good proved ill in me,
And wrought but malice. Lifted up so high,
I sdained[6] subjection, and thought one step
    higher   50
Would set me highest, and in a moment quit
The debt immense of endless gratitude,
So burdensome, still paying, still to owe;
Forgetful what from him I still received;
And understood not that a grateful mind
By owing owes not, but still pays, at once
Indebted and discharged—what burden then?
Oh, had his powerful destiny ordained
Me some inferior Angel, I had stood
Then happy; no unbounded hope had raised 60
Ambition. Yet why not? Some other Power
As great might have aspired, and me, though
    mean,
Drawn to his part. But other Powers as great
Fell not, but stand unshaken, from within

Or from without to all temptations armed!
Hadst thou the same free will and power t
    stand?
Thou hadst. Whom hast thou then, or what
    to accuse,
But Heaven's free love dealt equally to all?
Be then his love accursed, since, love or hate,
To me alike it deals eternal woe.   7
Nay, cursed be thou; since against his thy wil
Chose freely what it now so justly rues.
Me miserable! which way shall I fly
Infinite wrath and infinite despair?
Which way I fly is Hell; myself am Hell;
And, in the lowest deep, a lower deep
Still threatening to devour me opens wide,
To which the Hell I suffer seems a Heaven.
O, then, at last relent! Is there no place
Left for repentance, none for pardon left?   8
None left but by submission; and that word
Disdain forbids me, and my dread of shame
Among the Spirits beneath, whom I seduced
With other promises and other vaunts
Than to submit, boasting I could subdue
The Omnipotent. Ay me! they little know
How dearly I abide that boast so vain,
Under what torments inwardly I groan.
While they adore me on the throne of Hell,
With diadem and sceptre high advanced,   9
The lower still I fall, only supreme
In misery: such joy ambition finds!
But say I could repent, and could obtain,
By act of grace, my former state; how soon
Would highth recall high thoughts, how soo
    unsay
What feigned submission swore! Ease woul
    recant
Vows made in pain, as violent and void
(For never can true reconcilement grow
Where wounds of deadly hate have pierced s
    deep);
Which would but lead me to a worse relapse 10
And heavier fall: so should I purchase dear
Short intermission, bought with double smart.
This knows my Punisher; therefore as far
From granting he, as I from begging, peace.
All hope excluded thus, behold, instead
Of us, outcast, exiled, his new delight,
Mankind, created, and for him this World!
So farewell hope, and, with hope, farewell fea
Farewell remorse! All good to me is lost;
Evil, be thou my Good: by thee at least · 11
Divided empire with Heaven's King I hold,
By thee, and more than half perhaps wi
    reign;
As Man ere long, and this new World, sha
    know."

6 disdained

From Book IV. Evening in Paradise

Now came still Evening on, and Twilight
    gray
Had in her sober livery all things clad;
Silence accompanied; for beast and bird,   600
They to their grassy couch, these to their nests
Were slunk, all but the wakeful nightingale.
She all night long her amorous descant sung:
Silence was pleased.   Now glowed the firma-
    ment
With living sapphires; Hesperus, that led
The starry host, rode brightest, till the Moon,
Rising in clouded majesty, at length
Apparent queen, unveiled her peerless light,
And o'er the dark her silver mantle threw;
When Adam thus to Eve:—"Fair consort, the
    hour   610
Of night, and all things now retired to rest,
Mind us of like repose; since God hath set
Labor and rest, as day and night, to men
Successive, and the timely dew of sleep,
Now falling with soft slumberous weight,
    inclines
Our eye-lids.   Other creatures all day long
Rove idle, unemployed, and less need rest;
Man hath his daily work of body or mind
Appointed, which declares his dignity,
And the regard of Heaven on all his ways;   620
While other animals unactive range,
And of their doings God takes no account.
To-morrow, ere fresh morning streak the east
With first approach of light, we must be risen,
And at our pleasant labor, to reform
Yon flowery arbors, yonder alleys green,
Our walk at noon, with branches overgrown,
That mock our scant manuring, and require
More hands than ours to lop their wanton
    growth.
Those blossoms also, and those dropping gums,
That lie bestrewn, unsightly and unsmooth, 631
Ask riddance, if we mean to tread with ease.
Meanwhile, as Nature wills, Night bids us
    rest.''

From Book V. The Morning Hymn of Adam and Eve

''These are thy glorious works, Parent of
    good,
Almighty! thine this universal frame,
Thus wondrous fair: thyself how wondrous
    then!
Unspeakable! who sitt'st above these heavens
To us invisible, or dimly seen
In these thy lowest works; yet these declare
Thy goodness beyond thought, and power
    divine.

Speak, ye who best can tell, ye Sons of Light,
Angels—for ye behold him, and with songs
And choral symphonies, day without night,
Circle his throne rejoicing—ye in Heaven;
On Earth join, all ye creatures, to extol
Him first, him last, him midst, and without end.
Fairest of Stars, last in the train of Night,
If better thou belong not to the Dawn,
Sure pledge of day, that crown'st the smiling
    morn
With thy bright circlet, praise him in thy sphere
While day arises, that sweet hour of prime. 170
Thou Sun, of this great World both eye and
    soul,
Acknowledge him thy greater; sound his praise
In thy eternal course, both when thou climb'st,
And when high noon hast gained, and when
    thou fall'st.
Moon, that now meet'st the orient Sun, now
    fliest,
With the fixed Stars, fixed in their orb that
    flies;[1]
And ye five other wandering Fires, that move
In mystic dance, not without song, resound
His praise who out of Darkness called up
    Light.
Air, and ye Elements, the eldest birth   180
Of Nature's womb, that in quaternion[2] run
Perpetual circle, multiform, and mix
And nourish all things, let your ceaseless
    change
Vary to our great Maker still new praise.
Ye Mists and Exhalations, that now rise
From hill or steaming lake, dusky or gray,
Till the sun paint your fleecy skirts with gold,
In honor to the World's great Author rise;
Whether to deck with clouds the uncolored sky,
Or wet the thirsty earth with falling showers,
Rising or falling, still advance his praise.   191
His praise, ye Winds, that from ·four quarters
    blow,
Breathe soft or loud; and wave your tops, ye
    Pines,
With every Plant, in sign of worship wave.
Fountains, and ye, that warble, as ye flow,
Melodious murmurs, warbling tune his praise.
Join voices, all ye living Souls.   Ye Birds,
That, singing, up to Heaven-gate ascend,
Bear on your wings and in your notes his
    praise.
Ye that in waters glide, and ye that walk   200
The earth, and stately tread, or lowly creep,
Witness if I be silent, morn or even,
To hill or valley, fountain, or fresh shade,

1 See note on II. 1030.
2 In their fourfold character of Earth, Water, **Air**,
    and Fire.   See II. 898.

Made vocal by my song, and taught his praise.
Hail, universal Lord! Be bounteous still
To give us only good; and, if the night
Have gathered aught of evil, or concealed,
Disperse it, as now light dispels the dark.''

FROM BOOK VII. INVOCATION TO URANIA

DESCEND from Heaven, Urania, by that name
If rightly thou art called,* whose voice divine
Following, above the Olympian hill I soar,
Above the flight of Pegasean wing!
The meaning, not the name, I call; for thou
Nor of the Muses nine, nor on the top
Of old Olympus dwell'st; but, heavenly-born,
Before the hills appeared or fountain flowed,
Thou with Eternal Wisdom didst converse,
Wisdom thy sister, and with her didst play   10
In presence of the Almighty Father, pleased
With thy celestial song. Up led by thee,
Into the Heaven of Heavens I have presumed,
An earthly guest, and drawn empyreal air,
Thy tempering. With like safety guided down,
Return me to my native element;
Lest, from this flying steed unreined (as once
Bellerophon,† though from a lower clime)
Dismounted, on the Aleian field I fall,
Erroneous there to wander and forlorn.   20
Half yet remains unsung, but narrower bound
Within the visible Diurnal Sphere.
Standing on Earth, not rapt above the pole,
More safe I sing with mortal voice, unchanged
To hoarse or mute, though fallen on evil days,
On evil days though fallen, and evil tongues,
In darkness, and with dangers compassed
    round,
And solitude; yet not alone, while thou
Visit'st my slumbers nightly, or when Morn
Purples the East. Still govern thou my song, 30
Urania, and fit audience find, though few.
But drive far off the barbarous dissonance
Of Bacchus and his revellers, the race
Of that wild route that tore the Thracian bard‡
In Rhodope, where woods and rocks had ears
To rapture, till the savage clamor drowned
Both harp and voice; nor could the Muse defend
Her son. So fail not thou who thee implores;
For thou art heavenly, she an empty dream.

* Milton declares that the Urania whom he invokes is not the pagan Muse of that name,
but a loftier Christian Muse, the "heavenly
one."
† Bellerophon, the fabled rider of Pegasus, tried
to mount to heaven upon him, but was thrown
for his presumption and doomed to wander
in the Aleian ("wandering") field.
‡ Orpheus offended the Thracian Bacchantes and
was torn to pieces by them. Milton, blind,
and, since the Restoration, reviled as a Puritan, had "fallen on evil days" and might even
fear from the dissolute courtiers of Charles
a fate not unlike that of Orpheus.

FROM BOOK XII. THE EXPULSION FROM PARADISE

HE[1] ended, and they both descend the hill.
Descended, Adam to the bower where Eve
Lay sleeping ran before, but found her waked
And thus with words not sad she him
    received:—
''Whence thou return'st and whither went'
    I know;   6
For God is also in sleep, and dreams advise,
Which he hath sent propitious, some great good
Presaging, since, with sorrow and heart
    distress
Wearied, I fell asleep. But now lead on;
In me is no delay; with thee to go
Is to stay here; without thee here to stay
Is to go hence unwilling; thou to me
Art all things under Heaven, all places thou,
Who for my wilful crime art banished hence
This further consolation yet secure   6
I carry hence: though all by me is lost,
Such favor I unworthy am vouchsafed,
By me the Promised Seed shall all restore.''
    So spake our mother Eve; and Adam hear
Well pleased, but answered not; for now to
    nigh
The Archangel stood, and from the other hi
To their fixed station, all in bright array,
The Cherubim descended, on the ground
Gliding, meteorous, as evening mist
Risen from a river o'er the marish glides,   6
And gathers ground fast at the laborer's he
Homeward returning. High in front advance
The brandished sword of God before the
    blazed,
Fierce as a comet; which with torrid heat,
And vapor as the Libyan air adust,[2]
Began to parch that temperate clime; where
In either hand the hastening Angel caught
Our lingering parents, and to the eastern ga
Led them direct, and down the cliff as fast
To the subjected[3] plain—then disappeared.   6
They, looking back, all the eastern side behel
Of Paradise, so late their happy seat,
Waved over by that flaming brand; the gate
With dreadful faces thronged and fiery arm
Some natural tears they dropped, but wipe
    them soon;
The world was all before them, where to choo
Their place of rest, and Providence their guid
They, hand in hand, with wandering steps an
    slow,
Through Eden[4] took their solitary way.

1 Michael, the angel   2 scorched
    delegated to lead   3 underlying
    them forth.   4 See note on I, 4.

ON EDUCATION

O MASTER SAMUEL HARTLIB:*

I AM long since persuaded, Master Hartlib, [th]at to say or do aught worth memory and imita[ti]on, no purpose or respect should sooner move us [th]an simply the love of God and of mankind. . . . [I] will not resist, therefore, whatever it is either [o]f divine or human obligement that you lay [u]pon me; but will forthwith set down in writ[in]g, as you request me, that voluntary idea, [wh]ich hath long in silence presented itself to [m]e, of a better education, in extent and com[p]rehension far more large, and yet of time far [sh]orter and of attainment far more certain, [th]an hath been yet in practice. Brief I shall [en]deavour to be; for that which I have to say [as]suredly this nation hath extreme need should [b]e done sooner than spoken. . . .

The end, then, of learning is, to repair the [ru]ins of our first parents by regaining to know [G]od aright, and out of that knowledge to love [h]im, to imitate him, to be like him, as we may [th]e nearest by possessing our souls of true [vi]rtue,1 which, being united to the heavenly [g]race of faith, makes up the highest perfection. [B]ut because our understanding cannot in this [b]ody found itself but on sensible things,2 nor [ar]rive so clearly to the knowledge of God and [th]ings invisible as by orderly conning over the [v]isible and inferior creature, the same method [is] necessarily to be followed in all discreet [te]aching. And seeing every nation affords not [ex]perience and tradition enough for all kinds [o]f learning, therefore we are chiefly taught the [la]nguages of those people who have at any [ti]me been most industrious after wisdom; so [th]at language is but the instrument conveying [t]o us things useful to be known. And though [a] linguist should pride himself to have all the [to]ngues that Babel cleft the world into, yet if [h]e have not studied the solid things in them as [w]ell as the words and lexicons, he were nothing [s]o much to be esteemed a learned man as any [y]eoman or tradesman competently wise in his [m]other-dialect only. Hence appear the many [m]istakes which have made learning generally [s]o unpleasing and so unsuccessful. First, we [d]o amiss to spend seven or eight years merely [i]n scraping together so much miserable Latin

and Greek as might be learned otherwise easily and delightfully in one year. And that which casts our proficiency therein so much behind is our time lost partly in too oft idle vacancies given both to schools and universities; partly in a preposterous exaction, forcing the empty wits of children to compose themes, verses, and orations, which are the acts of ripest judgment, and the final work of a head filled by long reading and observing with elegant maxims and copious invention. These are not matters to be wrung from poor striplings, like blood out of the nose, or the plucking of untimely fruit; besides the ill habit which they get of wretched barbarising against the Latin and Greek idiom with their untutored Anglicisms, odious to be read, yet not to be avoided without a well-continued and judicious conversing among pure authors, digested, which they scarce taste. Whereas, if after some preparatory grounds of speech by their certain forms got into memory they were led to the praxis3 thereof in some chosen short book lessoned thoroughly to them, they might then forthwith proceed to learn the substance of good things and arts in due order, which would bring the whole language quickly into their power. . . .

I shall detain you now no longer in the demonstration of what we should not do, but straight conduct you to a hillside, where I will point you out the right path of a virtuous and noble education; laborious indeed at the first ascent, but else so smooth, so green, so full of goodly prospect and melodious sounds on every side, that the harp of Orpheus was not more charming. I doubt not but ye shall have more ado to drive our dullest and laziest youth, our stocks and stubs, from the infinite desire of such a happy nurture, than we have now to hale and drag our choicest and hopefullest wits to that asinine feast of sow-thistles and brambles which is commonly set before them as all the food and entertainment of their tenderest and most docile age. I call, therefore, a complete and generous education, that which fits a man to perform justly, skilfully, and magnanimously all the offices, both private and public, of peace and war. And how all this may be done between twelve and one-and-twenty, less time than is now bestowed in pure trifling at grammar and sophistry, is to be thus ordered:—

First, to find out a spacious house and ground about it fit for an academy, and big enough to lodge a hundred and fifty persons, whereof twenty or thereabout may be attend-

---

Which we may most readily do by putting our souls in possession of true virtue.
Things perceived by the senses.
Hartlib was a Pole, settled in England, who had had some discussions with Milton on the subject of education. The slight omissions made here from the beginning of the tractate are made with the purpose of enabling the reader to get more rapidly into the subject.

3 practical exercises

ants, all under the government of one who shall be thought of desert sufficient, and ability either to do all, or wisely to direct and oversee it done. This place should be at once both school and university, not needing a remove to any other house of scholarship, except it be some peculiar college of law or physic where[4] they mean to be practitioners; but as for those general studies which take up all our time from Lilly* to the commencing, as they term it, master of art, it should be absolute.[5] After this pattern as many edifices may be converted to this use as shall be needful in every city throughout this land, which would tend much to the increase of learning and civility[6] everywhere. This number, less or more, thus collected, to the convenience[7] of a foot-company or interchangeably two troops of cavalry, should divide their day's work into three parts as it lies orderly—their studies, their exercise, and their diet.

For their studies: first, they should begin with the chief and necessary rules of some good grammar, either that now used, or any better; and while this is doing, their speech is to be fashioned to a distinct and clear pronunciation, as near as may be to the Italian, especially in the vowels. For we Englishmen, being far northerly, do not open our mouths in the cold air wide enough to grace a southern tongue, but are observed by all other nations to speak exceeding close and inward; so that to smatter Latin with an English mouth is as ill a hearing as law French. Next, to make them expert in the usefullest points of grammar, and withal to season them and win them early to the love of virtue & true labour, ere any flattering seducement or vain principle seize them wandering, some easy and delightful book of education should be read to them, whereof the Greeks have store, as Cebes, Plutarch, and other Socratic discourses; but in Latin we have none of classic authority extant, except the two or three first books of Quintilian and some select pieces elsewhere. But here the main skill and groundwork will be to temper[8] them such lectures and explanations upon every opportunity as may lead and draw them in willing obedience, inflamed with the study of learning and the admiration of virtue, stirred up with high hopes of living to be brave men and worthy patriots, dear to God and famous to all ages: that they may despise and

scorn all their childish and ill-taught qualities to delight in manly and liberal exercises; which he who hath the art and proper eloquence to catch them with, what with mild and effectual persuasions, and what with the intimation of some fear, if need be,* but chiefly by his own example, might in a short space gain them to an incredible diligence and courage, infusing into their young breasts such an ingenuous and noble ardour as would not fail to make many of them renowned and matchless men. At the same time, some other hour of the day might be taught them the rules of arithmetic, and soon after, the elements of geometry, even playing, as the old manner was. After evening repast till bed-time their thoughts would be best taken up in the easy grounds of religion and the story of Scripture. The next step would be to the authors of agriculture, Cato, Varro, and Columella, for the matter is most easy; and if the language is difficult, so much the better; it is not a difficulty above their years. And here will be an occasion of inciting and enabling them hereafter to improve the tillage of their country, to recover the bad soil, and to remedy the waste that is made of good; for this was one of Hercules' praises. Ere half these authors be read (which will soon be with plying hard and daily) they cannot choose but be masters of any ordinary prose so that it will be then seasonable for them to learn in any modern author the use of the globes and all the maps, first with the old names and then with the new; or they might be then capable to read any compendious method of natural philosophy; and, at the same time, might be entering into the Greek tongue after the same manner as was before prescribed in the Latin; whereby the difficulties of grammar being soon overcome, all the historical physiology of Aristotle and Theophrastus are open before them, and, as I may say, under contribution. The like access will be to Vitruvius, to Seneca's "Natural Questions," to Mela, Celsus, Pliny, or Solinus. And having thus passed the principles of arithmetic, geometry, astronomy, and geography, with a general compact of physics, they may descend in mathematics to the instrumental science of trigonometry, and from thence to fortification, architecture, enginery, or navigation. And in natural philosophy they may proceed leisurely from the history of meteors, minerals, plants, and living creatures, as far as anatomy. Then also in course might be read to them out of some not

4 some special college . . . in case that
5 complete in itself
6 civilization
7 collective number
8 intermingle
* The author of a Latin grammar which was once a standard text-book.

* Compare this with Ascham's *Schoolmaster*, p. 122.

JOHN MILTON

261

edious writer the institution of physic;[9] that they may know the tempers, the humours, the seasons, and how to manage a crudity,[10] which he who can wisely and timely do is not only a great physician to himself and to his friends, but also may at some time or other save an army by this frugal and expenseless means only, and not let the healthy and stout bodies of young men rot away under him for want of this discipline, which is a great pity, and no less a shame to the commander. To set forward all these proceedings in nature and mathematics, what hinders but that they may procure, as oft as shall be needful, the helpful experiences of hunters, fowlers, fishermen, shepherds, gardeners, apothecaries; and in the other sciences, architects, engineers, mariners, anatomists, who, doubtless, would be ready, some for reward and some to favour such a hopeful seminary. And this will give them such a real tincture of natural knowledge as they shall never forget, but daily augment with delight.*

. . . .

These are the studies wherein our noble and our gentle youth ought to bestow their time in a disciplinary way from twelve to one-and-twenty, unless they rely more upon their ancestors dead than upon themselves living. In which methodical course it is so supposed they must proceed by the steady pace of learning onward, as at convenient times for memory's sake to retire back into the middle-ward, and sometimes into the rear of what they have been taught, until they have confirmed and solidly united the whole body of their perfected knowledge, like the last embattling of a Roman legion. Now will be worth the seeing what exercises and recreations may best agree and become these studies.

The course of study hitherto briefly described is, what[11] I can guess by reading, likest to those ancient and famous schools of Pythagoras, Plato, Isocrates, Aristotle, and such others, out of which were bred such a number of renowned philosophers, orators, historians, poets, and princes all over Greece, Italy, and Asia, besides the flourishing studies of Cyrene and Alexandria. But herein it shall exceed them, and supply a defect as great as that which Plato noted in the commonwealth of Sparta. Whereas that city trained up their youth most for war, and these in their acade-

mies and Lycæum[12] all for the gown,[13] this institution of breeding which I here delineate shall be equally good both for peace and war. Therefore, about an hour and a half ere they eat at noon should be allowed them for exercise, and due rest afterwards; but the time for this may be enlarged at pleasure, according as their rising in the morning shall be early.

The exercise which I commend first is the exact use of their weapon, to guard, and to strike safely with edge or point; this will keep them healthy, nimble, strong, and well in breath; is also the likeliest means to make them grow large and tall, and to inspire them with a gallant and fearless courage, which being tempered with seasonable lectures and precepts to make them of true fortitude and patience, will turn into a native and heroic valour, and make them hate the cowardice of doing wrong. They must be also practised in all the locks and gripes of wrestling, wherein Englishmen were wont to excel, as need may often be in fight to tug, to grapple, and to close. And this, perhaps, will be enough wherein to prove and heat their single strength. The interim of unsweating themselves regularly, and convenient rest before meat, may both with profit and delight be taken up in recreating and composing their travailed spirits with the solemn and divine harmonies of music heard or learned, either whilst the skilful organist plies his grave and fancied descant in lofty fugues, or the whole symphony with artful and unimaginable touches adorn and grace the well-studied chords of some choice composer; sometimes the lute or soft organ-stop, waiting on[14] elegant voices either to religious, martial, or civil ditties, which, if wise men and prophets be not extremely out,[15] have a great power over dispositions and manners to smooth and make them gentle from rustic harshness and distempered passions. The like also would not be unexpedient after meat, to assist and cherish nature in her first concoction,[16] and send their minds back to study in good tune and satisfaction. Where having followed it close under vigilant eyes till about two hours before supper, they are, by a sudden alarum or watchword, to be called out to their military motions, under sky or covert, according to the season, as was the Roman wont; first on foot, then, as their age permits, on horseback to all the art of cavalry; that having in sport, but with much

---

9 the elements of physiology and medicine
10 indigestion
11 so far as
* At this point Milton takes up, in rapid succession, ethics, politics, theology, history, logic, and poetry.

12 The exercise ground and grove of Athens, where Aristotle taught.
13 philosophy
14 accompanying
15 mistaken
16 digestion

exactness and daily muster, served out the rudiments of their soldiership in all the skill of embattling, marching, encamping, fortifying, besieging, and battering, with all the helps of ancient and modern stratagems, tactics, and warlike maxims, they may, as it were out of a long war, come forth renowned and perfect commanders in the service of their country. They would not then, if they were trusted with fair and hopeful armies, suffer them for want of just and wise discipline to shed away from about them like sick feathers, though they be never so oft supplied; they would not suffer their empty and unrecruitable[17] colonels of twenty men in a company to quaff out or convey into secret hoards the wages of a delusive list[18] and miserable remnant; yet in the meanwhile to be overmastered with a score or two of drunkards, the only soldiery left about them, or else to comply with all rapines and violences. No, certainly, if they knew aught of that knowledge that belongs to good men or good governors they would not suffer these things.

But to return to our own institute: besides these constant exercises at home, there is another opportunity of gaining experience to be won from pleasure itself abroad: in those vernal seasons of the year, when the air is calm and pleasant, it were an injury and sullenness against nature not to go out and see her riches and partake in her rejoicing with heaven and earth. I should not, therefore, be a persuader to them of studying much then, after two or three years that they have well laid their grounds, but to ride out in companies with prudent and staid guides to all the quarters of the land, learning and observing all places of strength, all commodities of building and of soil for towns and tillage, harbours, and ports for trade; sometimes taking sea as far as to our navy, to learn there also what they can in the practical knowledge of sailing and of sea-fight. These ways would try all their peculiar gifts of nature, and if there were any secret excellence among them, would fetch it out and give it fair opportunities to advance itself by, which could not but mightily redound to the good of this nation, and bring into fashion again those old admired virtues and excellencies, with far more advantage now in this purity of Christian knowledge. Nor shall we then need the monsieurs of Paris to take our hopeful youth into their slight and prodigal custodies, and send them over back again trans-

formed into mimics, apes, and kickshaws.[19] But if they desire to see other countries at three or four and twenty years of age, not to learn principles, but to enlarge experience and make wise observation, they will by that time be such as shall deserve the regard and honour of all men where they pass, and the society and friendship of those in all places who are best and most eminent. And perhaps then other nations will be glad to visit us for their breeding, or else to imitate us in their own country.

Now, lastly, for their diet there cannot be much to say, save only that it would be best in the same house; for much time else would be lost abroad, and many ill habits got; and that it should be plain, healthful, and moderate I suppose is out of controversy.

Thus, Mr. Hartlib, you have a general view in writing, as your desire was, of that which at several times I had discoursed with you concerning the best and noblest way of education not beginning, as some have done, from the cradle, which yet might be worth many considerations, if brevity had not been my scope. Many other circumstances also I could have mentioned, but this, to such as have the worth in them to make trial, for light and direction may be enough. Only I believe that this is not a bow for every man to shoot in that count himself a teacher, but will require sinews almost equal to those which Homer gave Ulysses;[*] yet I am withal persuaded that it may prove much more easy in the assay[20] than it now seems at distance, and much more illustrious howbeit not more difficult than I imagine, and that imagination presents me with nothing but very happy and very possible according to best wishes, if God have so decreed, and this age have spirit and capacity enough to apprehend.

From AREOPAGITICA.[‡]

A SPEECH FOR THE LIBERTY OF UNLICENSED PRINTING, TO THE PARLIAMENT OF ENGLAND.

If ye be thus resolved, as it were injury to think ye were not, I know not what should

---

[17] incapable of recruiting their forces ("quaff out" in the next line appears to mean "spend for drink")
[18] "stuffed pay-roll"

[19] triflers   [20] trial
[*] Referring to the bow which none of the suitors could draw, but which Ulysses slew them with on his return.
[†] This sentence is a good example of Milton's awkwardness in prose, in which he said he had but the use of his "left hand." See Eng. Lit., p. 147.

[‡] The title is taken from that of a speech by the Greek orator, Isocrates, addressed to the Great Council of Athens, which was called the

withhold me from presenting ye with a fit instance wherein to show both that love of truth which ye eminently profess, and that uprightness of your judgment which is not wont to be partial to yourselves; by judging over again that Order which ye have ordained *to regulate Printing: That no book, pamphlet, or paper shall be henceforth printed, unless the same be first approved and licensed by such,* or at least one of such as shall be thereto appointed. For that part which preserves justly every man's copy[1] to himself, or provides for the poor, I touch not, only wish they be not made pretences to abuse and persecute honest and painful[2] men, who offend not in either of these particulars. But that other clause of Licensing Books, which we thought had died with his brother quadragesimal and matrimonial[3] when the prelates expired, I shall now attend with such a homily, as shall lay before ye, first the inventors of it to be those whom ye will be loth to own; next what is to be thought in general of reading, whatever sort the books be; and that this Order avails nothing to the suppressing of scandalous, seditious, and libellous books, which were mainly intended to be suppressed. Last, that it will be primely to the discouragement of all learning, and the stop of Truth, not only by disexercising and blunting our abilities in what we know already, but by hindering and cropping the discovery that might be yet further made both in religious and civil Wisdom.

I deny not, but that it is of greatest concernment in the Church and Commonwealth, to have a vigilant eye how books demean themselves as well as men; and thereafter to confine, imprison, and do sharpest justice on them as malefactors: For books are not absolutely dead things, but do contain a potency of life in them to be as active as that soul was whose progeny they are; nay, they do preserve as in a vial the purest efficacy and extraction of that living intellect that bred them. I know they are as lively, and as vigorously productive, as

those fabulous dragon's teeth;[4] and being sown up and down, may chance to spring up armed men. And yet, on the other hand, unless wariness be used, as good almost kill a man as kill a good book: who kills a man kills a reasonable creature, God's image; but he who destroys a good book, kills reason itself, kills the image of God, as it were in the eye.* Many a man lives a burden to the earth; but a good book is the precious life-blood of a master spirit, embalmed and treasured up on purpose to a life beyond life. 'Tis true, no age can restore a life, whereof perhaps there is no great loss; and revolutions of ages do not oft recover the loss of a rejected truth, for the want of which whole nations fare the worse. We should be wary therefore what persecution we raise against the living labours of public men, how we spill that seasoned life of man, preserved and stored up in books; since we see a kind of homicide may be thus committed, sometimes a martyrdom, and if it extend to the whole impression,[5] a kind of massacre, whereof the execution ends not in the slaying of an elemental life, but strikes at that ethereal and fifth essence,† the breath of reason itself, slays an immortality rather than a life. But lest I should be condemned of introducing license, while I oppose licensing, I refuse not the pains to be so much historical, as will serve to show what hath been done by ancient and famous commonwealths against this disorder, till the very time that this project of licensing crept out of the inquisition, was catched up by our prelates, and hath caught some of our presbyters.

.   .   .   .   .   .

I conceive, therefore, that when God did enlarge the universal diet of man's body, saving ever the rules of temperance, He then also, as before, left arbitrary the dieting and repasting of our minds; as wherein every mature man might have to exercise his own leading capacity. How great a virtue is temperance, how much of moment through the whole life of man! Yet God commits the managing so great a trust, without particular law or prescription, wholly to the demeanour of every grown man. And therefore when He Himself tabled[6] the Jews from heaven, that omer, which was every man's daily portion of manna, is computed to have been more than might have well sufficed the

---

Areopagus because it held its meetings on the Areopagus, or "Hill of Ares" ("Mars' Hill," where Paul preached: *Acts* xvii. 22). The tract was written late in 1644. Parliament, in its long struggle with Charles, had brought about many changes, the Westminster Assembly even going so far as practically to abolish prelacy, or episcopacy, and establish Presbyterianism. But an ordinance had been enacted in 1643 re-establishing the censorship of the press. Milton pleads to have this revoked; and his opening words (here omitted) praise Parliament for its professed willingness to "obey the voice of reason."

[1] copyright
[2] painstaking
[3] Orders concerning the keeping of Lent and marriage.

[4] Sown by Cadmus of Thebes.
[5] edition
[6] fed (*Exodus* xvi. 16)
* The reason of man is, as it were, the eye of his divine nature.
† Aristotle's fifth element; "quintessence," ether, or spirit.

heartiest feeder thrice as many meals. For those actions which enter into a man, rather than issue out of him, and therefore defile not, God uses not to captivate under a perpetual childhood of prescription, but trusts him with the gift of reason to be his own chooser; there were but little work left for preaching, if law and compulsion should grow so fast upon those things which heretofore were governed only by exhortation. Solomon informs us, that much reading is a weariness to the flesh; but neither he nor other inspired author tells us that such, or such, reading is unlawful: yet certainly, had God thought good to limit us herein, it had been much more expedient to have told us what was unlawful, than what was wearisome. As for the burning of those Ephesian books[7] by St. Paul's converts; 'tis replied the books were magic, the Syriac so renders them. It was a private act, a voluntary act, and leaves us to a voluntary imitation: the men in remorse burnt those books which were their own; the magistrate by this example is not appointed: these men practised the books, another might perhaps have read them in some sort usefully. Good and evil we know in the field of this world grow up together almost inseparably; and the knowledge of good is so involved and interwoven with the knowledge of evil, and in so many cunning resemblances hardly to be discerned, that those confused seeds which were imposed upon Psyche as an incessant labour to cull out, and sort asunder, were not more intermixed. It was from out the rind of one apple tasted, that the knowledge of good and evil, as two twins cleaving together, leaped forth into the world. And perhaps this is that doom which Adam fell into of knowing good and evil, that is to say of knowing good by evil. As therefore the state of man now is, what wisdom can there be to choose, what continence to forbear without the knowledge of evil? He that can apprehend and consider vice with all her baits and seeming pleasures, and yet abstain, and yet distinguish, and yet prefer that which is truly better, he is the true warfaring Christian. I cannot praise a fugitive and cloistered virtue, unexercised and unbreathed, that never sallies out and sees her adversary, but slinks out of the race, where that immortal garland is to be run for, not without dust and heat.‡ Assuredly we bring not innocence into the world, we bring impurity much rather; that which purifies us is trial, and trial

is by what is contrary. That virtue therefor which is but a youngling in the contemplatio of evil, and knows not the utmost that vic promises to her followers, and rejects it, is bu a blank virtue, not a pure; her whiteness is bu an excremental[8] whiteness; which was th reason why our sage and serious poet Spenser whom I dare be known to think a better teache than Scotus or Aquinas,[9] describing true tem perance under the person of Guion,[10] bring him in with his palmer through the cave o Mammon, and the bower of earthly bliss, tha he might see and know, and yet abstain. Sinc therefore the knowledge and survey of vice i in this world so necessary to the constitutin of human virtue, and the scanning of error t the confirmation of truth, how can we mor safely, and with less danger scout into th regions of sin and falsity than by reading al manner of tractates and hearing all manner o reason? And this is the benefit which may b had of books promiscuously read.

IZAAK WALTON (1593-1683)

THE COMPLETE ANGLER

FROM CHAPTER IV. OF THE TROUT, AND HOW TO FISH FOR HIM. AND OF THE MILKMAID'S SONG

Venator.* Trust me, master, I see now it is a harder matter to catch a trout than a chub; for I have put on patience, and followed you these two hours, and not seen a fish stir, neither at your minnow nor your worm.

Piscator. Well, scholar, you must endure worse luck some time, or you will never make a good angler. But what say you now? There is a trout now, and a good one too, if I can but hold him, and two or three turns more will tire him. Now you see he lies still, and the sleight is to land him. Reach me that landing-net; so, Sir, now he is mine own. What say you now? is not this worth all my labour and your patience?

Ven. On my word, master, this is a gallant trout: what shall we do with him?

Pisc. Marry, e'en eat him to supper: we'll go to my hostess, from whence we came; she told me, as I was going out of door, that my

---

7 *Acts* xix. 19.

‡ This is one—but only one—of the noble sentiments so nobly expressed, which make the *Areopagitica* one of the most prized documents in our literature.

8 surface

9 Scholastic **philoso**- phers.

10 *Faerie Queene*, Bk. II.

* *The Complete Angler* is in the form of a dialogue, chiefly between a fisherman, *Piscator*, and a scholar-hunter, *Venator*.

rother Peter, a good angler and a cheerful
ompanion, had sent word that he would lodge
here to-night, and bring a friend with him.
My hostess has two beds, and I know you and
I may have the best: we'll rejoice with my
brother Peter and his friend, tell tales, or sing
ballads, or make a catch,[1] or find some harmless
sport to content us and pass away a little time,
without offence to God or man.

Ven. A match,[2] good master, let's go to
that house; for the linen looks white and smells
of lavender, and I long to lie in a pair of sheets
that smell so. Let's be going, good master,
or I am hungry again with fishing.

Pisc. Nay, stay a little, good scholar. I
caught my last trout with a worm; now I will
put on a minnow, and try a quarter of an hour
about yonder trees for another; and so walk
towards our lodging. Look you, scholar, thereabout we shall have a bite presently or not at
all. Have with you, Sir! o' my word I have
hold of him. Oh! it is a great logger-headed
chub; come hang him upon that willow twig,
and let's be going. But turn out of the way
a little, good scholar, towards yonder high
honeysuckle hedge; there we'll sit and sing,
whilst this shower falls so gently upon the
teeming earth, and gives yet a sweeter smell to
the lovely flowers that adorn these verdant
meadows.

Look! under that broad beech-tree I sat
down, when I was last this way a-fishing. And
the birds in the adjoining grove seemed to have
a friendly contention with an echo, whose dead
voice seemed to live in a hollow tree, near to
the brow of that primrose hill. There I sat
viewing the silver streams glide silently towards
their centre, the tempestuous sea; yet sometimes opposed by rugged roots and pebble-
stones, which broke their waves, and turned
them into foam. And sometimes I beguiled
time by viewing the harmless lambs; some leaping securely in the cool shade, whilst others
sported themselves in the cheerful sun; and
saw others craving comfort from the swollen
udders of their bleating dams. As I thus sat,
these and other sights had so fully possessed
my soul with content, that I thought, as the
poet hath happily expressed it,

"I was for that time lifted above earth,
And possess'd joys not promised in my birth,"

As I left this place, and entered into the
next field, a second pleasure entertained me;
'twas a handsome milkmaid, that had not yet
attained so much age and wisdom as to load

her mind with any fears of many things that
will never be, as too many men too often do;
but she cast away all care, and sang like a
nightingale: her voice was good, and the ditty
fitted for it: it was that smooth song which
was made by Kit Marlow, now at least fifty
years ago; and the milkmaid's mother sang
an answer to it, which was made by Sir Walter
Raleigh in his younger days.

They were old-fashioned poetry, but choicely
good, I think much better than the strong lines
that are now in fashion in this critical age.
Look yonder! on my word, yonder they both be
a-milking again. I will give her the chub, and
persuade them to sing those two songs to us.

God speed you, good woman! I have been
a-fishing, and am going to Bleak Hall to my
bed, and having caught more fish than will sup
myself and my friend, I will bestow this upon
you and your daughter, for I use to sell none.

Milk-W. Marry, God require you, Sir, and
we'll eat it cheerfully; and if you come this
way a-fishing two months hence, a[2] grace of
God, I'll give you a syllabub of new ver-
juice,[3] in a new-made hay-cock, for it, and my
Maudlin shall sing you one of her best ballads;
for she and I both love all anglers, they be
such honest, civil, quiet men: in the meantime
will you drink a draught of red cow's milk?
you shall have it freely.

Pisc. No, I thank you; but, I pray, do us
a courtesy that shall stand[4] you and your
daughter in nothing, and yet we will think
ourselves still something in your debt; it is
but to sing us a song that was sung by your
daughter when I last passed over this meadow,
about eight or nine days since.

Milk-W. What song was it, I pray? Was
it "Come, Shepherds, deck your heads"? or,
"As at noon Dulcina rested"? or, "Phillida
flouts me"? or "Chevy Chace"? or, "Johnny
Armstrong"? or, "Troy Town"?

Pisc. No, it is none of those; it is a song
that your daughter sang the first part, and
you sang the answer to it.

Milk-W. Oh, I know it now. I learned the
first part in my golden age, when I was about
the age of my poor daughter; and the latter
part, which indeed fits me best now, but two
or three years ago, when the cares of the world
began to take hold of me: but you shall, God
willing, hear them both, and sung as well as
we can, for we both love anglers. Come,
Maudlin, sing the first part to the gentlemen

1 a singing "round"   2 a bargain
2 by the
3 whipped cream and grape-juice
4 cost

with a merry heart, and I'll sing the second, when you have done.

THE MILKMAID'S SONG

Come, live with me, and be my love, etc.†

Ven. Trust me, master, it is a choice song, and sweetly sung by honest Maudlin. I now see it was not without cause that our good Queen Elizabeth did so often wish herself a milkmaid all the month of May, because they are not troubled with fears and cares, but sing sweetly all the day, and sleep securely all the night; and without doubt, honest, innocent, pretty Maudlin does so. I'll bestow Sir Thomas Overbury's milkmaid's wish upon her, "That she may die in the spring, and being dead, may have good store of flowers stuck round about her winding-sheet."‡

FROM CHAPTER XXI. A SERMON ON CONTENT

Piscator. Let me tell you, scholar, that Diogenes walked on a day, with his friend, to see a country fair; where he saw ribbons and looking-glasses, and nut-crackers, and fiddles, and hobby-horses, and many other gimcracks; and, having observed them, and all the other finnimbruns§ that make a complete country fair, he said to his friend, "Lord, how many things are there in this world of which Diogenes hath no need!" And truly it is so, or might be so, with very many who vex and toil themselves to get what they have no need of. Can any man charge God that He hath not given him enough to make his life happy? No, doubtless; for nature is content with a little. And yet you shall hardly meet with a man that complains not of some want; though he, indeed, wants nothing but his will; it may be, nothing but his will of his poor neighbour, for not worshipping or not flattering him: and thus, when we might be happy and quiet, we create trouble to ourselves. I have heard of a man that was angry with himself because he was no taller; and of a woman that broke her looking-glass because it would not show her face to be as young and handsome as her next neighbour's was. And I knew another to whom God had given health and plenty, but a wife that nature had made peevish, and her husband's riches had made purse-proud; and, must,

because she was rich, and for no other virtu sit in the highest pew in the church; whi being denied her, she engaged her husband in a contention for it, and at last into a la suit with a dogged neighbour who was as ri as he, and had a wife as peevish and purse proud as the other; and this law-suit beg higher oppositions, and actionable¹ words, a more vexations and law-suits; for you mu remember that both were rich, and must ther fore have their wills. Well, this wilful, purs proud law-suit lasted during the life of th first husband; after which his wife vext a chid, and chid and vext till she also chid a vext herself into her grave; and so the weal of these poor rich people was curst into punishment, because they wanted meek a thankful hearts; for those only can make happy. I knew a man that had health a riches, and several houses, all beautiful, ar ready furnished, and would often trouble hir self and family to be removing from one hou to another; and being asked by a friend wh he removed so often from one house to a other, replied, "It was to find content in son one of them." But his friend, knowing h temper, told him, if he would find content any of his houses, he must leave himself b hind him; for content will never dwell b in a meek and quiet soul. And this may a pear, if we read and consider what our Savio says in St. Matthew's Gospel; for He the says: "Blessed be the merciful, for they sha obtain mercy.—Blessed be the pure in hear for they shall see God.—Blessed be the po in spirit, for theirs is the kingdom of heaven. And, "Blessed be the meek, for they sha possess the earth." Not that the meek sha not also obtain mercy, and see God, and l comforted, and at last come to the kingdo of heaven; but in the meantime he, and l only, possesses the earth as he goes toward that kingdom of heaven, by being humble an cheerful, and content with what his good Go has allotted him. He has no turbulent, repi ing, vexatious thoughts that he deserves better nor is vext when he sees others possest of mo honour or more riches than his wise God ha allotted for his share; but he possesses wha he has with a meek and contented quietnes such a quietness as makes his very dream pleasing, both to God and himself.

My honest scholar, all this is told to inclin you to thankfulness; and to incline you th more, let me tell you, that though the prophe

---

† For this song, see p. 146.
‡ The mother then sings the answer, which may be found on p. 146. Overbury's milk-maid is one of the most famous of his "Characters;" see *Eng. Lit.*, p. 193, note.
§ Walton appears to have coined this word. It is found only here.

¹ affording cause for legal action

David was guilty of murder and, indeed, of many other of the most deadly sins, yet he was said to be a man after God's own heart, because he abounded more with thankfulness than any other that is mentioned in holy Scripture, as may appear in his book of Psalms; where there is such a commixture of his confessing of his sins and unworthiness, and such thankfulness for God's pardon and mercies, as did make him to be accounted, even by God Himself, to be a man after His own heart. And let us, in that, labour to be as like him as we can; let not the blessings we receive daily from God make us not to value or not praise Him because they be common; let us not forget to praise Him for the innocent mirth and pleasure we have met with since we met together. What would a blind man give to see the pleasant rivers, and meadows, and flowers, and fountains, that we have met with since we met together? I have been told, that if a man that was born blind could obtain to have his sight for but only one hour during his whole life, and should, at the first opening of his eyes, fix his sight upon the sun when it was in its full glory, either at the rising or setting of it, he would be so transported and amazed, and so admire the glory of it, that he would not willingly turn his eyes from that first ravishing object, to behold all the other various beauties this world could present to him. And this, and many other like blessings, we enjoy daily. And for most of them, because they be so common, most men forget to pay their praises; but let not us, because it is a sacrifice so pleasing to Him that made that sun and us, and still protects us, and gives us flowers and showers, and stomachs and meat, and content and leisure to go a-fishing.

JOHN BUNYAN (1628-1688)

FROM THE PILGRIM'S PROGRESS*

CHRISTIAN FLEES FROM THE CITY OF DESTRUCTION

As I walked through the wilderness of this world, I lighted on a certain place where was a den,[1] and I laid me down in that place to sleep; and as I slept I dreamed a dream. I dreamed, and behold, I saw a man clothed with rags standing in a certain place, with his face from his own house, a book in his hand, and a great burden upon his back. I looked and saw him open the book, and read therein; and as he read, he wept and trembled; and not being able longer to contain, he brake out with a lamentable cry, saying, "What shall I do?"

I saw also that he looked this way, and that way, as if he would run; yet he stood still, because, as I perceived, he could not tell which way to go. I looked then, and saw a man named Evangelist coming to him, and [he] asked, "Wherefore dost thou cry?"

He answered, "Sir, I perceive, by the book in my hand, that I am condemned to die, and after that to come to judgment; and I find that I am not willing to do the first, nor able to do the second."

Then said Evangelist, "Why not willing to die, since this life is attended with so many evils?" The man answered, "Because I fear that this burden that is upon my back will sink me lower than the grave, and I shall fall into Tophet.[2] And Sir, if I be not fit to go to prison, I am not fit (I am sure) to go to judgment, and from thence to execution; and the thoughts of these things make me cry."

Then said Evangelist, "If this be thy condition, why standest thou still?" He answered, "Because I know not whither to go." Then he gave him a parchment roll, and there was written within, "Fly from the wrath to come."

The man therefore read it, and, looking upon Evangelist very carefully, said, "Whither must I fly?" Then said Evangelist, pointing with his finger over a very wide field, "Do you see yonder wicket gate?" The man said, "No." Then said the other, "Do you see yonder shining light?" He said, "I think I do." Then said Evangelist, "Keep that light in your eye, and go up directly thereto, so shalt thou see the gate; at which when thou knockest, it shall be told thee what thou shalt do."

So I saw in my dream that the man began to run. Now he had not run far from his own door, but his wife and children, perceiving it, began to cry after him to return; but the man

[1] Bedford Jail (See *Eng. Lit.*, p. 159).
* "The Pilgrim's Progress from This World to That which is to come: Delivered under the Similitude of a Dream, wherein is Discovered the manner of his setting out, his Dangerous Journey, and safe Arrival at the Desired Country." Title of the first edition, 1678, whence our text is taken.

[2] hell
"The Pilgrim's Progress is composed in the lowest style of English without slang or false grammar. If you were to polish it, you would at once destroy the reality of the vision. For works of imagination should be written in very plain language; the more purely imaginative they are the more necessary it is to be plain." —Coleridge.

put his fingers in his ears and ran on, crying, "Life! life! eternal life!" So he looked not behind him, but fled towards the middle of the plain.

The neighbors also came out to see him run; and as he ran, some mocked, others threatened, and some cried after him to return. Now among those that did so, there were two that were resolved to fetch him back by force. The name of the one was Obstinate, and the name of the other Pliable. Now by this time the man was got a good distance from them; but, however, they were resolved to pursue him, which they did, and in a little time overtook him. Then said the man, "Neighbors, wherefore are you come?" They said, "To persuade you to go back with us." But he said, "That can by no means be. You dwell," said he, "in the City of Destruction (the place also where I was born): I see it to be so; and dying there, sooner or later, you will sink lower than the grave, into a place that burns with fire and brimstone: be content, good neighbors, and go along with me."

What, said Obstinate, and leave our friends and our comforts behind us!

Yes, said Christian (for that was his name), because that all is not worthy to be compared with a little of that that I am seeking to enjoy; and if you will go along with me, you shall fare as I myself; for there, where I go, is enough and to spare. Come away, and prove my words.

Obst. What are the things you seek, since you leave all the world to find them?

Chr. I seek an inheritance, incorruptible, undefiled, and that fadeth not away; and it is laid up in heaven, and fast there, to be bestowed, at the time appointed, on them that diligently seek it. Read it so, if you will, in my book.

Obst. Tush, said Obstinate, away with your book: will you go back with us or no?

Chr. No, not I, said the other, because I have laid my hand to the plough.

Obst. Come then, neighbor Pliable, let us turn again, and go home without him: there is a company of these craz'd-headed coxcombs, that when they take a fancy by the end, are wiser in their own eyes than seven men that can render a reason.

Then said Pliable, Don't revile; if what the good Christian says is true, the things he looks after are better than ours: my heart inclines to go with my neighbor.

Obst. What, more fools still! Be ruled by me, and go back; who knows whither such a brain-sick fellow will lead you? Go back, g[o] back, and be wise.

Chr. Come with me, neighbor Pliable, there are such things to be had which I spok[e] of, and many more glories besides. If yo[u] believe not me, read here in this book; an[d] for the truth of what is expressed therein, be[-] hold, all is confirmed by the blood of Hi[m] that made it.

Pli. Well, neighbor Obstinate, said Pliable I begin to come to a point; I intend to g[o] along with this good man, and to cast in m[y] lot with him; but, my good companion, do yo[u] know the way to this desired place?

Chr. I am directed by a man, whose name is Evangelist, to speed me to a little gate that is before us, where we shall receive in[-] struction about the way.

Pli. Come then, good neighbor, let us be going. Then they went both together.

Obst. And I will go back to my place, said Obstinate: I will be no companion of such misled, fantastical fellows.

Now I saw in my dream, that when Obstinate was gone back, Christian and Pliable went talking over the plain; and thus they began their discourse.

Chr. Come, neighbor Pliable, how do you do? I am glad you are persuaded to go along with me; and had even Obstinate himself but felt what I have felt of the powers and terrors of what is yet unseen, he would not thus lightly have given us the back.

Pli. Come, neighbor Christian, since there is none but us two here, tell me now further, what the things are, and how to be enjoyed, whither we are going.

Chr. I can better conceive of them with my mind, than speak of them with my tongue: but yet, since you are desirous to know, I will read of them in my book.

Pli. And do you think that the words of your book are certainly true?

Chr. Yes, verily; for it was made by him that cannot lie.

Pli. Well said; what things are they?

Chr. There is an endless kingdom to be inhabited, and everlasting life to be given us, that we may inhabit that kingdom forever.

Pli. Well said; and what else?

Chr. There are crowns of glory to be given us; and garments that will make us shine like the sun in the firmament of heaven.

Pli. This is excellent; and what else?

Chr. There shall be no more crying, nor sorrow; for he that is owner of the place will wipe all tears from our eyes.

Pli. And what company shall we have there?

Chr. There we shall be with seraphims and cherubims: creatures that will dazzle your eyes to look on them. There also you shall meet with thousands and ten thousands that have gone before us to that place; none of them are hurtful, but loving and holy; every one walking in the sight of God, and standing in his presence with acceptance forever. In a word, there we shall see the elders with their golden crowns; there we shall see the holy virgins with their golden harps; there we shall see men, that by the world were cut in pieces, burned in flames, eaten of beasts, drowned in the seas, for the love that they bare to the Lord of the place; all well, and clothed with immortality as with a garment.

Pli. The hearing of this is enough to ravish one's heart. But are these things to be enjoyed? How shall we get to be sharers hereof?

Chr. The Lord, the governor of that country, hath recorded that in this book; the substance of which is, If we be truly willing to have it, he will bestow it upon us freely.

Pli. Well, my good companion, glad am I to hear of these things: come on, let us mend our pace.

Chr. I cannot go so fast as I would, by reason of this burden that is upon my back.

Now I saw in my dream, that just as they had ended this talk, they drew near to a very miry slough that was in the midst of the plain: and they being heedless, did both fall suddenly into the bog. The name of the slough was Despond. Here, therefore, they wallowed for time, being grievously bedaubed with the dirt; and Christian, because of the burden that was on his back, began to sink in the mire.

Pli. Then said Pliable, Ah, neighbor Christian, where are you now?

Chr. Truly, said Christian, I do not know.

Pli. At that Pliable began to be offended, and angrily said to his fellow, Is this the happiness you have told me all this while of? If we have such ill speed at our first setting out, what may we expect 'twixt this and our journey's end? May I get out again with my life, you shall possess the brave country alone for me. And with that he gave a desperate struggle or two, and got out of the mire on that side of the slough which was next to his own house: so away he went, and Christian saw him no more.

Wherefore Christian was left to tumble in the Slough of Despond alone; but still he endeavored to struggle to that side of the slough that was still further from his own house, and next to the wicket gate; the which he did, but could not get out because of the burden that was upon his back: but I beheld in my dream, that a man came to him, whose name was Help, and asked him what he did there.

Chr. Sir, said Christian, I was directed this way by a man called Evangelist, who directed me also to yonder gate, that I might escape the wrath to come. And as I was going thither, I fell in here.

Help. But why did you not look for the steps?

Chr. Fear followed me so hard that I fled the next[3] way, and fell in.

Help. Give me thy hand.

So he gave him his hand, and he drew him out, and set him upon sound ground, and bid him go on his way.*

. . . .

THE HILL OF DIFFICULTY AND THE SINFUL SLEEP

I beheld then, that they all went on till they came to the foot of an hill, at the bottom of which was a spring. There was also in the same place two other ways besides that which came straight from the gate: one turned to the left hand, and the other to the right, at the bottom of the hill; but the narrow way lay right up the hill, and the name of the going up the side of the hill is called Difficulty. Christian now went to the spring and drank thereof to refresh himself, and then began to go up the hill, saying,

This hill, though high, I covet to ascend;
The difficulty will not me offend;
For I perceive the way to life lies here:
Come, pluck up, Heart, let's neither faint nor fear;
Better, though difficult, the right way to go,
Than wrong, though easy, where the end is wo.

The other two also came to the foot of the hill. But when they saw that the hill was steep and high, and that there was two other ways to go; and supposing also that these two ways might meet again with that up which Christian went, on the other side of the hill; therefore they were resolved to go in those ways. Now the name of one of those ways was Danger, and the name of the other Destruction. So the one took the way which is called Danger, which led him into a great

3 nearest
* Christian passes through the gate, where he gets instructions for his journey; visits the House of the Interpreter; loses his burden at the foot of the Cross; receives a Roll from three Shining Ones; and after falling in with Formalist and Hypocrisy, comes to the Hill of Difficulty.

wood; and the other took directly up the way to Destruction, which led him into a wide field, full of dark mountains, where he stumbled and fell, and rose no more.

I looked then after Christian, to see him go up the hill, where I perceived he fell from running to going,[1] and from going to clambering upon his hands and his knees, because of the steepness of the place. Now about the midway to the top of the hill was a pleasant arbor, made by the Lord of the hill for the refreshment of weary travellers. Thither, therefore, Christian got, where also he sat down to rest him. Then he pulled his Roll out of his bosom, and read therein to his comfort; he also now began afresh to take a review of the coat or garment that was given him as he stood by the cross. Thus pleasing himself awhile, he at last fell into a slumber, and thence into a fast sleep, which detained him in that place until it was almost night; and in his sleep his Roll fell out of his hand. Now, as he was sleeping, there came one to him, and awaked him, saying, "Go to the ant, thou sluggard; consider her ways, and be wise." And with that, Christian suddenly started up, and sped him on his way, and went apace till he came to the top of the hill.

Now when he was got up to the top of the hill, there came two men running against him amain; the name of the one was Timorous, and the name of the other Mistrust: to whom Christian said, Sirs, what's the matter? you run the wrong way. Timorous answered, that they were going to the City of Zion, and had got up that difficult place: but, said he, the further we go, the more danger we meet with; wherefore we turned, and are going back again.

Yes, said Mistrust, for just before us lie a couple of lions in the way, whether sleeping or waking we know not; and we could not think, if we came within reach, but they would presently pull us in pieces.

Chr. Then said Christian, You make me afraid; but whither shall I fly to be safe? If I go back to mine own country, that is prepared for fire and brimstone; and I shall certainly perish there. If I can get to the Celestial City, I am sure to be in safety there. I must venture. To go back is nothing but death: to go forward is fear of death, and life everlasting beyond it: I will yet go forward. So Mistrust and Timorous ran down the hill, and Christian went on his way. But thinking again of what he had heard from the men, he felt in his bosom for his Roll, that he

might read therein and be comforted; but he felt, and found it not.

Then was Christian in great distress, and knew not what to do; for he wanted that which used to relieve him, and that which should have been his pass into the Celestial City. Here, therefore, he began to be much perplexed, and knew not what to do. At last he bethought himself that he had slept in the arbor that is on the side of the hill; and falling down upon his knees, he asked God forgiveness for that his foolish fact,[2] and then went back to look for his roll. But all the way he went back, who can sufficiently set forth the sorrow of Christian's heart? Sometimes he sighed, sometimes he wept, and oftentimes he chid himself for being so foolish to fall asleep in that place, which was erected only for a little refreshment from his weariness. Thus therefore, he went back, carefully looking on this side and on that, all the way as he went, if happily he might find his Roll, that had been his comfort so many times in his journey. He went thus till he came again within sight of the arbor where he sat and slept; but that sight renewed his sorrow the more, by bringing again, even afresh, his evil of sleeping into his mind. Thus, therefore, he now went on bewailing his sinful sleep, saying, Oh, wretched man that I am, that I should sleep in the daytime! that I should sleep in the midst of difficulty! that I should so indulge the flesh as to use that rest for ease to my flesh which the Lord of the hill hath erected only for the relief of the spirits of pilgrims! How many steps have I taken in vain! Thus it happened to Israel; for their sin they were sent back again by the way of the Red Sea; and I am made to tread those steps with sorrow, which I might have trod with delight, had it not been for this sinful sleep. How far might I have been on my way by this time! I am made to tread those steps thrice over, which I needed not to have trod but once: yea, now also I am like to be benighted, for the day is almost spent. Oh, that I had not slept!

Now by this time he was come to the arbor again, where for a while he sat down and wept; but at last (as Providence would have it), looking sorrowfully down under the settle, there he espied his Roll, the which he with trembling and haste catched up, and put it into his bosom. But who can tell how joyful this man was when he had gotten his Roll again? For this Roll was the assurance of his life, and acceptance at the desired haven. Therefore he laid

[1] walking

[2] deed

up in his bosom, gave thanks to God for
recting his eye to the place where it lay,
d with joy and tears betook himself again
his journey. But oh, how nimbly now did
go up the rest of the hill! Yet before he
t up, the sun went down upon Christian;
d this made him again recall the vanity of
s sleeping to his remembrance; and thus he
ain began to condole with himself: Ah,
ou sinful sleep! how for thy sake am I like
be benighted in my journey! I must walk
thout the sun, darkness must cover the path
my feet, and I must hear the noise of dole-
l creatures, because of my sinful sleep!
ow also he remembered the story that Mis-
ust and Timorous told him of, how they were
ighted with the sight of the lions. Then
id Christian to himself again, These beasts
nge in the night for their prey; and if they
ould meet with me in the dark, how should
shift them? how should I escape being by
em torn in pieces? Thus he went on his
ay. But while he was thus bewailing his
nhappy miscarriage, he lift up his eyes, and
ehold, there was a very stately Palace before
im, the name whereof was Beautiful, and it
ood just by the highway-side.

SAMUEL PEPYS (1633-1703)

FROM HIS DIARY*

EPYS APPOINTED SECRETARY TO THE GENERALS
OF THE FLEET. THE RETURN OF
KING CHARLES

Jan. 1, 1660 (Lord's day). This morning
we living lately in the garret) I rose, put on
ly suit with great skirts, having not lately
orn any other clothes but them. Went to
Ir. Gunning's chapel at Exeter House, where
e made a very good sermon. Dined at home
n the garret, where my wife dressed the re-
nains of a turkey, and in the doing of it she
urned her hand. I stayed at home all the
fternoon, looking over my accounts; then went
vith my wife to my father's and in going
bserved the great posts which the City have
et up at the Conduit in Fleet Street.
Mar. 5th. To Westminster by water, only
eeing Mr. Pinkney at his own house, where he

showed me how he had always kept the lion
and unicorn, in the back of his chimney,
bright, in expectation of the King's coming
again. At home I found Mr. Hunt, who told me
how the Parliament had voted that the Covenant†
be printed and hung in churches again. Great
hopes of the King's coming again.

6th. Everybody now drinks the King's health
without any fear, whereas before it was very
private that a man dare do it.

22nd. To Westminster, and received my warrant of Mr. Blackburne to be secretary to the
two Generals of the Fleet.

23rd. My Lord,‡ Captain Isham, Mr. Thomas,
John Crewe, W. Howe, and I to the Tower, where
the barges stayed for us; my Lord and the Captain in one, and W. Howe and I, &c., in the other,
to the Long Reach, where the *Swiftsure* lay at
anchor; (in our way we saw the great breach
which the late high water had made, to the loss of
many £1,000 to the people about Limehouse).
Soon as my Lord on board, the guns went off
bravely from the ships. And a little while after
comes the Vice-Admiral Lawson, and seemed
very respectful to my Lord, and so did the
rest of the commanders of the frigates that
were thereabouts. I to the cabin allotted for
me, which was the best that any had that belonged to my Lord. We were late writing of
orders, for the getting of ships ready, &c.

May 1. To-day I hear they were very merry
at Deal,[1] setting up the King's flag upon one
of their maypoles, and drinking his health upon
their knees in the streets, and firing the guns,
which the soldiers of the castle threatened, but
durst not oppose.

2nd. In the morning at a breakfast of
radishes in the Purser's cabin. After that,
to writing till dinner. At which time comes
Dunne from London, with letters that tell us
the welcome news of the Parliament's votes
yesterday, which will be remembered for the
happiest May-day that hath been many a year
to England. The King's letter was read in
the House, wherein he submits himself and all
things to them, as to an Act of Oblivion to
all, unless they shall please to except any.

May 29th. Abroad to shore with my Lord
(which he offered me of himself, saying that
I had a great deal of work to do this month,
which was very true). On shore we took horses,

---

* Pepys's Diary belongs to what may be called
  unconscious literature. It was not intended
  for publication, is reckless in grammar, un-
  concerned for style, ignorant of any sort of
  propriety, yet famous for its portrayal of
  an interesting man in an interesting period.
  See *Eng. Lit.*, p. 156.

1 A port near Dover.
† The Scottish "Covenant with God," a declaration
  of resistance to the Roman Church. The next
  year it was ordered to be publicly burnt.
‡ Sir Edward Montagu, whose service Pepys had
  entered, and who, as admiral and general,
  was appointed to convey Charles II. from
  Holland to England.

my Lord and Mr. Edward, Mr. Hetly and I, and three or four servants, and had a great deal of pleasure in riding. . . At last we came upon a very high cliff by the sea-side, and rode under it, we having laid great wagers, I and Dr. Mathews, that it was not so high as Paul's,[2] my Lord and Mr. Hetly, that it was. But we riding under it, my Lord made a pretty good measure of it with two sticks, and found it to be not above thirty-five yards high, and Paul's is reckoned to be about ninety. From thence toward the barge again, and in our way found the people of Deal going to make a bonfire for joy of the day, it being the King's birthday, and had some guns which they did fire at my Lord's coming by. For which I did give twenty shillings among them to drink. While we were on the top of the cliff, we saw and heard our guns in the fleet go off for the same joy. And it being a pretty fair day, we could see above twenty miles into France. Being returned on board, my Lord called for Mr. Sheply's book of Paul's, by which we were confirmed in our wager. . . . This day, it is thought, the King do enter the City of London.

30th. All this morning making up my accounts, in which I counted that I had made myself now worth about £80, at which my heart was glad, and blessed God.

MATTERS PERSONAL AND DOMESTIC

Oct. 13th. I went out to Charing Cross, to see Major-General Harrison* hanged, drawn, and quartered; which was done there, he looking as cheerful as any man could do in that condition. He was presently cut down, and his head and heart shown to the people, at which there was great shouts of joy. It is said that he said that he was sure to come shortly at the right hand of Christ to judge them that now had judged him; and that his wife do expect his coming again. Thus it was my chance to see the King beheaded at Whitehall, and to see the first blood shed in revenge for the blood of the King at Charing Cross. From thence to my Lord's, and took Captain Cuttance and Mr. Sheply to the Sun Tavern, and did give them some oysters. After that I went by water home, where I was angry with my wife for her things lying about, and in my passion kicked the little fine basket, which I bought her in Holland, and broke it, which troubled me after I had done it. With-

in all the afternoon setting up shelves in my study. At night to bed.

Nov. 22nd. This morning come the carpenters to make me a door at the other side of my house, going into the entry, which I was much pleased with. At noon, my wife and I walked to the Old Exchange, and there she bought her a white whisk[1] and put it on, and I a pair of gloves, and so we took coach for Whitehall to Mr. Fox's, where we found Mrs. Fox within, and an alderman of London paying £1,000 or £1,400 in gold upon the table for the King, which was the most gold that ever I saw together in my life. Mr. Fox come presently and did receive us with a great deal of respect; and then did take my wife and I to the Queen's presence-chamber, where he got my wife placed behind the Queen's chair, and I got into the crowd, and by and by the Queen and the two Princesses come to dinner. The Queen a very little plain old woman,* and nothing more in her presence in any respect nor garb than any ordinary woman. The Princess of Orange I had often seen before. The Princess Henrietta is very pretty, but much below my expectation: and her dressing of herself with her hair frizzed short up to her ears, did make her seem so much the less to me. But my wife standing near her with two or three black patches on, and well dressed, did seem to me much handsomer than she.

Feb. 27th, 1661. I called for a dish of fish which we had for dinner, this being the first day of Lent; and I do intend to try whether I can keep it or no.

28th. I took boat at Whitehall for Redriffe but in my way overtook Captain Cuttance and Tiddiman in a boat and so ashore with them at Queenhithe, and so to a tavern with them to a barrel of oysters, and so away. Captain Cuttance and I walked from Redriffe to Deptford, and there we dined, and notwithstanding my resolution, yet for want of other victuals, I did eat flesh this Lent, but am resolved to eat as little as I can.

THE CORONATION OF CHARLES II

Apr. 23rd. Coronation Day. About four rose and got to the Abbey, where I followed Sir J. Denham, the Surveyor, with some company that he was leading in. And with much ado, by the favour of Mr. Cooper, his man, did get up into a great scaffold across the north end of the Abbey, where with a great deal of patience I sat from past four till

---

2 St. Paul's Cathedral, London.
* He had served under Cromwell, and had signed the warrant for the execution of Charles I.

1 neckerchief
* Henrietta Maria, mother of Charles. The princesses mentioned were two of her daughters.

ven before the King come in. And a great easure it was to see the Abbey raised in the ddle, all covered with red, and a throne hat is a chair) and foot-stool on the top of ; and all the officers of all kinds, so much the very fiddlers, in red vests.

At last comes in the Dean and Prebends of estminster, with the Bishops (many of them cloth-of-gold copes), and after them the obility, all in their Parliament robes, which is a most magnificent sight. Then the Duke d the King with a sceptre (carried by my ord Sandwich) and sword and wand before m, and the crown too. The King in his bes, bare-headed, which was very fine. And ter all had placed themselves, there was a rmon and the service; and then in the Choir the high altar, the King passed through the ceremonies of the Coronation, which my great grief I and most in the Abbey uld not see. The crown being put upon his ad, a great shout began, and he come forth the throne, and there passed more ceremo- es: as taking the oath, and having things ad to him by the Bishop; and his Lords who put on their caps as soon as the King it on his crown) and bishops come, and eeled before him. And three times the King Arms² went to the three open places on the affold, and proclaimed, that if any one could ow any reason why Charles Stewart should ot be King of England, that now he should me and speak. And a General Pardon also as read by the Lord Chancellor, and medals ung up and down by my Lord Cornwallis, of lver, but I could not come by any. But so reat a noise that I could make but little of e music; and indeed, it was lost to every- ody.

I went out a little while before the King ad done all his ceremonies, and went round e Abbey to Westminster Hall, all the way ithin rails, and 10,000 people, with the ground overed with blue cloth; and scaffolds all the ay. Into the Hall I got, where it was very ne with hangings and scaffolds one upon an- ther full of brave ladies; and my wife in one ttle one, on the right hand. Here I stayed alking up and down, and at last, upon one f the side stalls I stood and saw the King come n with all the persons (but the soldiers) that ere yesterday in the cavalcade; and a most leasant sight it was to see them in their sev- ral robes. And the King come in with his rown on, and his sceptre in his hand, under a canopy borne up by six silver staves, carried by Barons of the Cinque Ports,³ and little bells at every end.

And after a long time, he got up to the farther end, and all set themselves down at their several tables; and that was also a brave sight: and the King's first course carried up by the Knights of the Bath. And many fine ceremonies there was of the herald's leading up people before him, and bowing; and my Lord of Albemarle's going to the kitchen and eat a bit of the first dish that was to go to the King's table. But, above all, was these three Lords, Northumberland, and Suffolk, and the Duke of Ormond, coming before the courses on horseback, and staying so all dinner-time, and at last to bring up⁴ [Dymock] the King's champion, all in armour on horseback, with his spear and target carried before him. And a herald proclaims, ''That if any dare deny Charles Stewart to be lawful King of England, here was a champion that would fight with him;'' and with these words, the champion flings down his gauntlet, and all this he do three times in his going up towards the King's table. At last when he is come, the King drinks to him, and then sends him the cup, which is of gold, and he drinks it off, and then rides back again with the cup in his hand. I went from table to table to see the bishops and all others at their dinner, and was infinitely pleased with it. And at the Lord's table, I met with William Howe, and he spoke to my Lord for me, and he did give me four rabbits and a pullet, and so I got it and Mr. Creed and I got Mr. Minshell to give us some bread, and so we at a stall eat it, as everybody else did what they could get. I took a great deal of pleasure to go up and down, and look upon the ladies, and to hear the music of all sorts, but above all, the twenty-four violins.

About six at night they had dined, and I went up to my wife. And strange it is to think, that these two days have held up fair till now that all is done, and the King gone out of the Hall; and then it fell a-raining and thundering and lightening as I have not seen it do for some years; which people did take great notice of; God's blessing of the work of these two days, which is a foolery to take too much notice of such things. I ob- served little disorder in all this, only the King's footmen had got hold of the canopy, and would keep it from the Barons of the Cinque

---

The Garter King-at-Arms, head of the heralds.

³ The five English Channel ports, Hastings, Sand-wich, Dover, Romney, Hythe.
⁴ This ceremony is no longer observed.

Ports, which they endeavoured to force from them again, but could not do it till my Lord Duke of Albemarle caused it to be put into Sir R. Pye's hand till to-morrow to be decided.

At Mr. Bowyer's; a great deal of company, some I knew, other I did not. Here we stayed upon the leads[5] and below till it was late, expecting to see the fireworks, but they were not performed to-night: only the City had a light like a glory round about it with bonfires. At last I went to King Street, and there sent Crockford to my father's and my house, to tell them I could not come home to-night, because of the dirt, and a coach could not be had. And so I took my wife and Mrs. Frankleyn (who I proffered the civility of lying with my wife at Mrs. Hunt's to-night) to Axe Yard, in which at the farther end there were three great bonfires, and a great many great gallants, men and women; and they laid hold of us, and would have us drink the King's health upon our knees, kneeling upon a faggot, which we all did, they drinking to us one after another: which we thought a strange frolic; but these gallants continued thus a great while, and I wondered to see how the ladies did tipple. At last I sent my wife and her bedfellow to bed, and Mr. Hunt and I went in with Mr. Thornbury (who did give the company all their wine, he being yeoman of the winecellar to the King) to his home; and there, with his wife and two of his sisters, and some gallant sparks that were there, we drank the King's health, and nothing else, till one of the gentlemen fell down stark drunk, and there lay; and I went to my Lord's pretty well.

Thus did the day end with joy everywhere; and blessed be God, I have not heard of any mischance to anybody through it all, but only to Serjt. Glynne, whose horse fell upon him yesterday, and is like to kill him, which people do please themselves to see how just God is to punish the rogue at such a time as this: he being now one of the King's Serjeants, and rode in the cavalcade with Maynard, to whom people wish the same fortune.§ There was also this night in King Street, a woman had her eye put out by a boy's flinging a firebrand into the coach. Now, after all this, I can say that, besides the pleasure of the sight of these glorious things, I may now shut my eyes against any other objects, nor for the future trouble myself to see things of state and show

as being sure never to see the like again in this world.

24th. At night, set myself to write dow[n] these three days' diary, and while I am abou[t] it, I hear the noise of the chambers, and othe[r] things of the fireworks, which are now playin[g] upon the Thames before the King; and I wis[h] myself with them, being sorry not to see them

JOHN EVELYN (1620-1706)

From His Diary*

The Restoration of Charles II

May 29, 1660. This day his Majesty Charles I[I] came to London after a sad and long exil[e] and calamitous suffering both of the King an[d] Church, being 17 years. This was also h[is] birth-day, and with a triumph of above 20,00[0] horse and foot, brandishing their swords an[d] shouting with inexpressible joy; the way[s] strewed with flowers, the bells ringing, th[e] streets hung with tapestry, fountains runnin[g] with wine; the Mayor, Aldermen, and all th[e] Companies† in their liveries, chains of gol[d] and banners; Lords and Nobles clad in clot[h] of silver, gold, and velvet; the windows an[d] balconies all set with ladies; trumpets, musi[c] and myriads of people flocking, even so far a[s] from Rochester, so as they were seven hou[rs] in passing the City, even from 2 in the afte[r]noon till 9 at night.

I stood in the Strand and beheld it, an[d] blessed God. And all this was done withou[t] one drop of blood shed, and by that very arm[y] which rebelled against him; but it was th[e] Lord's doing, for such a Restoration was neve[r] mentioned in any history, ancient or moder[n] since the return of the Jews from the Babylon[n]ish captivity; nor so joyful a day and so brigh[t] ever seen in this nation, this happening whe[n] to expect or effect it was past all human policy[.]

July 6. His Majesty began first to *touch fo[r] the evil,‡* according to custom, thus: his Majest[y]

* John Evelyn, "a good man in difficult times," a favorite of Charles II., traveler, and member of the Royal Society of London, was [a] man of real culture and wide intellectual interests. His *Diary* extends from 1640 to 170[6] covering a much longer period than that o[f] Pepys. Austin Dobson says of it: "If it doe[s] not, like the Diary of Pepys, disclose th[e] inner character of the writer, it neverthele[ss] possesses a distinctive interest. Its entrie[s] have the precise value of veracious statements it is a magazine—a mine, Scott called it[—] of contemporary memories of a definite kind.
† The Livery Companies, or Guilds, established a[s] a part of the city government to protect th[e] members of the various crafts.
‡ The scrofula was familiarly known as "the king['s] evil," from the superstition that it could b[e] healed by the royal touch.

5 roof (of sheets of lead)
§ Both these men had served Cromwell during the Protectorate, but unscrupulously transferred their allegiance to Charles at the time of the Restoration.

tting under his State[1] in the Banqueting-
ouse, the chirurgeons cause the sick to be
rought or led to the throne, where they kneel-
g, the King strokes their faces or cheeks with
oth his hands at once, at which instant a chap-
in in his formalities says, 'He put his hands
oon them and he healed them.' This is said
o every one in particular. When they have
en all touched they come up again in the
me order, and the other chaplain kneeling,
ad having angel gold[2] strung on white ribbon
a his arm, delivers them one by one to his
ajesty, who puts them about the necks of the
uched as they pass, whilst the first chaplain
peats, 'That is the true light who came into
e world.' Then follows an epistle (as at first
gospel) with the liturgy, prayers for the sick,
ith some alteration, lastly the blessing; and
en the Lord Chamberlain and Comptroller of
e Household bring a basin, ewer, and towel,
r his Majesty to wash.

Jan. 30, 1661. Was the first solemn fast and
ay of humiliation to deplore the sins which so
ng had provoked God against this afflicted
urch and people, ordered by Parliament to be
nually celebrated to expiate the guilt of the
ecrable murder of the late King.
This day (O the stupendous and inscrutable
dgments of God!) were the carcasses of those
ch rebels, Cromwell, Bradshaw, the Judge
ho condemned his Majesty, and Ireton, son-in-
w to the Usurper, dragged out of their superb
mbs in Westminster among the Kings, to
yburn, and hanged on the gallows there from
in the morning till 6 at night, and then buried
der that fatal and ignominious monument in
deep pit; thousands of people who had seen
em in all their pride being spectators. Look
ck at October 22, 1658, [Oliver's funeral,]
d be astonished! and fear God and honour
e King; but meddle not with them who are
ven to change!
Nov. 11. I was so idle as to go see a play
lled *Love and Honour.*—Dined at Arundel
ouse; and that evening discoursed with his
ajesty about shipping, in which he was ex-
eding skilful.
26. I saw *Hamlet, Prince of Denmark*, played,
t now the old plays began to disgust this
fined age, since his Majesty's being so long
road.
Dec. 14. I saw otter hunting with the King,
d killed one.
23. I heard an Italian play and sing to the
itar with extraordinary skill before the Duke.
Jan. 6, 1662. This evening, according to
canopy of state
standard, or "guinea" gold (bearing the figure of
an angel)

custom, his Majesty opened the revels of that
night by throwing the dice himself in the privy
chamber, where was a table set on purpose, and
lost his £100. (The year before he won £1,500.)
The ladies also played very deep. I came away
when the Duke of Ormond had won about £1,000,
and left them still at *passage*,[3] *cards*, etc. At
other tables, both there and at the Groom-
porter's,[4] observing the wicked folly and monstrous excess of passion amongst some losers;
sorry I am that such a wretched custom as play
to that excess should be countenanced in a Court
which ought to be an example of virtue to the
rest of the kingdom.

THE GREAT PLAGUE

Aug. 2, 1665. A solemn fast thro' England
to deprecate God's displeasure against the land
by pestilence and war; our Doctor preaching
on 26 Levit. 41, 42, that the means to obtain
remission of punishment was not to repine at it,
but humbly submit to it.
28. The contagion still increasing and growing now all about us, I sent my wife and whole
family (two or three necessary servants ex-
cepted) to my brother's at Wotton, being resolved to stay at my house myself and to look
after my charge, trusting in the providence and
goodness of God.
Sept. 7. Came home, there perishing near
10,000 poor creatures weekly; however, I went
all along the City and suburbs from Kent Street
to St. James's, a dismal passage, and dangerous
to see so many coffins exposed in the streets,
now thin of people; the shops shut up, and all
in mournful silence, as not knowing whose turn
might be next. I went to the Duke of Albemarle for a pest-ship, to wait on our infected
men, who were not a few.
Dec. 31. Now blessed be God for his extraordinary mercies and preservation of me this year,
when thousands and ten thousands perished and
were swept away on each side of me, there dying
in our parish this year 406 of the pestilence!

THE GREAT FIRE

Sept. 2, 1666. This fatal night about ten,
began that deplorable fire near Fish Street in
London.
3. I had public prayers at home. The fire
continuing, after dinner I took coach with my
wife and son, and went to the Bankside in
Southwark, where we beheld the dismal spectacle, the whole City in dreadful flames near
the water side; all the houses from the Bridge,
all Thames Street, and upwards towards Cheapside, down to the Three Cranes, were now con-
3 A game of dice.
4 The royal director of games.

sumed: and so returned exceeding astonished what would become of the rest.

The fire having continued all this night (if I may call that night which was light as day for ten miles round about, after a dreadful manner) when conspiring with a fierce Eastern wind in a very dry season; I went on foot to the same place, and saw the whole South part of the City burning from Cheapside to the Thames, and all along Cornhill (for it likewise kindled back against the wind as well as forward), Tower Street, Fenchurch Street, Gracious Street, and so along to Baynard's Castle, and was now taking hold of St. Paul's Church, to which the scaffolds contributed exceedingly. The conflagration was so universal, and the people so astonished, that from the beginning, I know not by what despondency or fate, they hardly stirred to quench it, so that there was nothing heard or seen but crying out and lamentation, running about like distracted creatures, without at all attempting to save even their goods; such a strange consternation there was upon them, so as it burned both in breadth and length, the Churches, Public Halls, Exchange, Hospitals, Monuments, and ornaments, leaping after a prodigious manner from house to house and street to street, at great distances one from the other; for the heat with a long set of fair and warm weather had even ignited the air and prepared the materials to conceive the fire, which devoured after an incredible manner houses, furniture, and everything. Here we saw the Thames covered with goods floating, all the barges and boats laden with what some had time and courage to save, as, on the other side, the carts, etc., carrying out to the fields, which for many miles were strewed with movables of all sorts, and tents erecting to shelter both people and what goods they could get away. Oh, the miserable and calamitous spectacle! such as haply the world had not seen the like since the foundation of it, nor be outdone, till the universal conflagration of it. All the sky was of a fiery aspect, like the top of a burning oven, and the light seen above 40 miles round about for many nights. God grant mine eyes may never behold the like, who now saw above 10,000 houses all in one flame; the noise and cracking and thunder of the impetuous flames, and shrieking of women and children, the hurry of people, the fall of towers, houses and churches, was like an hideous storm, and the air all about so hot and inflamed that at the last one was not able to approach it, so that they were forced to stand still and let the flames burn on, which they did for near two miles in length and one in breadth. The clouds, also, of smoke were dismal, and reached, upon computation, near 50 miles in length. Thus left it this afternoon burning, a resemblance Sodom, or the last day. It forcibly called to mind that passage—*non enim hic habemus stabilem civitatem:*[1] the ruins resembling the picture of Troy. London was, but is no more. Thus I returned home.

THE DEATH OF COWLEY

Aug. 1, 1667. I received the sad news Abraham Cowley's death, that incomparable poet and virtuous man, my very dear friend and was greatly deplored.

3. Went to Mr. Cowley's funeral, whose corpse lay at Wallingford House, and was thence conveyed to Westminster Abbey in a hearse with six horses and all funeral decency, near an hundred coaches of noblemen and persons of quality following; among these all the wits[2] of the town, divers bishops and clergymen. He was interred next Geoffrey Chaucer and near Spenser. A goodly monument has been since erected to his memory.

POPULAR PASTIMES

June 16, 1670. I went with some friends the Bear Garden, where was cock-fighting, do fighting, bear and bull baiting, it being a famous day for all these butcherly sports, or rather barous cruelties. The bulls did exceeding well but the Irish wolf-dog exceeded, which was tall greyhound, a stately creature indeed, w beat a cruel mastiff. One of the bulls tossed dog full into a *lady's lap*, as she sate in one the boxes at a considerable height from t arena. Two poor dogs were killed, and so ended with the ape on horseback, and I mo heartily weary of the rude and dirty pastime which I had not seen, I think, in twenty yea before.

THE DEATH OF CHARLES II

Feb. 4, 1685. I went to London, hearing Majesty had been the Monday before (2 Feb surprised in his bed-chamber with an apoplectic fit. On Thursday hopes of recovery were signified in the public Gazette, but that day, about noon, the physicians thought him feverish. I passed Thursday night with great difficult when complaining of a pain in his side, he drew two ounces more of blood from him; th was by 6 in the morning on Friday, and it ga him relief, but it did not continue, for bein now in much pain, and struggling for breath, lay dozing, and after some conflicts, the phys cians despairing of him, he gave up the gho at half an hour after eleven in the mornin

1 "For we have no abiding city."
2 men of culture

being 6 Feb. 1685, in the 36th year of his reign, and 54th of his age.

Thus died King Charles II, of a vigorous and robust constitution, and in all appearance promising a long life. He was a Prince of many virtues, and many great imperfections; debonair, easy of access, not bloody nor cruel; his countenance fierce, his voice great, proper of person, every motion became him; a lover of the sea, and skilful in shipping; not affecting other studies, yet he had a laboratory and knew of many empirical[3] medicines, and the easier mechanical mathematics; he loved planting and building, and brought in a politer way of living, which passed to luxury and intolerable expense. He had a particular talent in telling a story, and facetious passages, of which he had innumerable; this made some buffoons and vicious wretches too presumptuous and familiar, not worthy the favour they abused. He took delight in having a number of little spaniels follow him and lie in his bed-chamber. . . .

Certainly never had King more glorious opportunities to have made himself, his people, and all Europe happy, and prevented innumerable mischiefs, had not his too easy nature resigned him to be managed by crafty men, and some abandoned and profane wretches who corrupted his otherwise sufficient parts, disciplined as he had been by many afflictions during his banishment, which gave him much experience and knowledge of men and things; but those wicked creatures took him off from all application becoming so great a King. The history of his reign will certainly be the most wonderful for the variety of matter and accidents, above any extant in former ages: the sad tragical death of his father, his banishment and hardships, his miraculous restoration, conspiracies against him, parliaments, wars, plagues, fires, comets, revolutions abroad happening in his time, with a thousand other particulars. He was ever kind to me, and very gracious upon all occasions, and therefore I cannot, without ingratitude, but deplore his loss, which for many respects, as well as duty, I do with all my soul. . . .

I can never forget the inexpressible luxury and profaneness, gaming and all dissoluteness, and as it were total forgetfulness of God (it being Sunday evening) which this day se'nnight I was witness of, the King sitting and toying with his concubines, Portsmouth, Cleaveland, and Mazarine, etc., a French boy singing love songs, in that glorious gallery, whilst about twenty of the great courtiers and other dissolute persons were at Basset[4] round a large table, a bank of

at least 2,000 in gold before them; upon which two gentlemen who were with me made reflections with astonishment. Six days after was all in the dust!

JOHN DRYDEN (1631-1700)

From ABSALOM AND ACHITOPHEL[*]

The inhabitants of old Jerusalem[1]
Were Jebusites;[2] the town so called from them,
And theirs the native right.
But when the chosen people[3] grew more strong,
The rightful cause at length became the wrong;
And every loss the men of Jebus bore,   90
They still were thought God's enemies the more.

Thus worn and weakened, well or ill content,
Submit they must to David's[4] government:
Impoverished and deprived of all command,
Their taxes doubled as they lost their land;
And, what was harder yet to flesh and blood,
Their gods disgraced, and burnt like common wood.
This set the heathen priesthood in a flame,
For priests of all religions are the same.
Of whatso'er descent their godhead be,   100
Stock, stone, or other homely pedigree,
In his defence his servants are as bold,
As if he had been born of beaten gold.
The Jewish Rabbins,[5] though their enemies,
In this conclude them honest men and wise:
For 'twas their duty, all the learned think,
To espouse his cause by whom they eat and drink.
From hence began that Plot,[6] the nation's curse,
Bad in itself, but represented worse,   109
Raised in extremes, and in extremes decried,
With oaths affirmed, with dying vows denied,

1 London.
2 Roman Catholics.
3 Used ironically of the Puritans.
4 Charles II.
5 Dignitaries of the Church of England.
6 The Popish Plot.

* This, the first of Dryden's satires, was directed against the Earl of Shaftesbury (Achitophel) and the opponents of the court. The strong excitement aroused by the "Popish Plot," an alleged attempt to strengthen Roman Catholic power in England by the murder of Charles II., had impelled Shaftesbury, a Whig, to endeavor to secure the succession to the Protestant Duke of Monmouth (Absalom), thus preventing the Catholic Duke of York from ascending the throne. Charles II., who was secretly a Catholic, and was receiving aid from France, waited a favorable moment: then, aided by the Tories, he recalled his brother, the Duke of York, and threw Shaftesbury into prison on the charge of high treason. The poem appeared November 17, 1681. Shaftesbury's case was to come up November 24.

3 Approved by unscientific observation.
4 A game at cards.

Not weighed or winnowed by the multitude,
But swallowed in the mass, unchewed and
    crude.
Some truth there was, but dashed and brewed
    with lies
To please the fools and puzzle all the wise:
Succeeding times did equal folly call
Believing nothing or believing all.
The Egyptian[7] rites the Jebusites embraced,
Where gods were recommended by their taste;
Such savoury deities must needs be good   120
As served at once for worship and for food.[8]
By force they could not introduce these gods,
For ten to one in former days was odds:
So fraud was used, the sacrificer's trade;
Fools are more hard to conquer than persuade.
Their busy teachers mingled with the Jews
And raked for converts even the court and
    stews:
Which Hebrew priests the more unkindly took,
Because the fleece accompanies the flock.
Some thought they God's anointed meant to
    slay   130
By guns, invented since full many a day:
Our author swears it not; but who can know
How far the Devil and Jebusites may go?
This plot, which failed for want of common
    sense,
Had yet a deep and dangerous consequence;
For as, when raging fevers boil the blood,
The standing lake soon floats into a flood,
And every hostile humour which before
Slept quiet in its channels bubbles o'er;
So several factions from this first ferment 140
Work up to foam and threat the government.
Some by their friends, more by themselves
    thought wise,
Opposed the power to which they could not rise.
Some had in courts been great and, thrown
    from thence,
Like fiends were hardened in impenitence.
Some by their Monarch's fatal mercy grown
From pardoned rebels kinsmen to the throne
Were raised in power and public office high;
Strong bands, if bands ungrateful men could
    tie.
Of these the false Achitophel was first,   150
A name to all succeeding ages curst:
For close designs and crooked counsels fit,
Sagacious, bold, and turbulent of wit,
Restless, unfixed in principles and place,
In power unpleased, impatient of disgrace;
A fiery soul, which working out its way,
Fretted the pigmy body to decay

And o'er-informed[9] the tenement of clay.
A daring pilot in extremity,
Pleased with the danger, when the waves went
    high,   160
He sought the storms; but, for a calm unfit,
Would steer too nigh the sands to boast his wit.
Great wits are sure to madness near allied
And thin partitions do their bounds divide;
Else, why should he, with wealth and honour
    blest,
Refuse his age the needful hours of rest?
Punish a body which he could not please,
Bankrupt of life, yet prodigal of ease?
And all to leave what with his toil he won
To that unfeathered two-legged thing, a son,
Got while his soul did huddled notions try,   171
And born a shapeless lump, like anarchy.[10]
In friendship false, implacable in hate,
Resolved to ruin or to rule the state;
To compass this the triple bond[11] he broke,
The pillars of the public safety shook,
And fitted Israel[12] for a foreign yoke;[13]
Then, seized with fear, yet still affecting fame,
Usurped a patriot's all-atoning name.
So easy still it proves in factious times   180
With public zeal to cancel private crimes.
How safe is treason and how sacred ill,
Where none can sin against the people's will,
Where crowds can wink and no offence be
    known,
Since in another's guilt they find their own!
Yet fame deserved no enemy can grudge;
The statesman we abhor, but praise the judge.
In Israel's court ne'er sat an Abbethdin[14]
With more discerning eyes or hands more clean,
Unbribed, unsought, the wretched to redress,
Swift of despatch and easy of access.   191
Oh! had he been content to serve the crown
With virtues only proper to the gown,
Or had the rankness of the soil been freed
From cockle that oppressed the noble seed,
David for him his tuneful harp had strung
And Heaven had wanted[15] one immortal song.
But wild ambition loves to slide, not stand,
And Fortune's ice prefers to Virtue's land.
Achitophel, grown weary to possess   200
A lawful fame and lazy happiness,
Disdained the golden fruit to gather free
And lent the crowd his arm to shake the tree.

---

7 French.
8 A reference to the doctrine of transubstantiation.
9 filled to excess
10 Shaftesbury's son was a weakling.
11 The alliance of England, Holland, and Sweden,
    broken by the alliance in 1670 of England and
    France against Holland.
12 England.
13 That of France.
14 Chief judge of the Jewish court (Shaftesbury
    had been Lord Chancellor in 1672-3).
15 lacked (Dryden is referring to his own poem)

Now, manifest of crimes contrived long since,
He stood at bold defiance with his Prince,
Held up the buckler of the people's cause
Against the crown, and skulked behind the laws.
The wished occasion of the Plot he takes;
Some circumstances finds, but more he makes;
By buzzing emissaries fills the ears   210
Of listening crowds with jealousies and fears
Of arbitrary counsels brought to light,
And proves the King himself a Jebusite.
Weak arguments! which yet he knew full well
Were strong with people easy to rebel.
For governed by the moon, the giddy Jews
Tread the same track when she the prime renews:
And once in twenty years, their scribes record,
By natural instinct they change their lord.
Achitophel still wants a chief, and none   220
Was found so fit as warlike Absalon.
Not that he wished his greatness to create,
For politicians neither love nor hate:
But, for he knew his title not allowed
Would keep him still depending on the crowd,
That kingly power, thus ebbing out, might be
Drawn to the dregs of a democracy.
Him he attempts with studied arts to please
And sheds his venom in such words as these:

.   .   .   .

He said, and this advice[16] above the rest
With Absalom's mild nature suited best;
Unblamed of life (ambition set aside),
Not stained with cruelty nor puffed with
          pride,   480
How happy had he been, if Destiny
Had higher placed his birth or not so high!
His kingly virtues might have claimed a throne
And blessed all other countries but his own;
But charming greatness since so few refuse,
'Tis juster to lament him than accuse.
Strong were his hopes a rival to remove,
With blandishments to gain the public love,
To head the faction while their zeal was hot,
And popularly prosecute the plot.   490
To further this, Achitophel unites
The malcontents of all the Israelites,
Whose differing parties he could wisely join
For several ends to serve the same design;
The best, (and of the princes some were such,)
Who thought the power of monarchy too much;
Mistaken men and patriots in their hearts,
Not wicked, but seduced by impious arts;
By these the springs of property were bent
And wound so high they cracked the government.   500

The next for interest sought to embroil the
          state
To sell their duty at a dearer rate,
And make their Jewish markets of the throne;
Pretending public good to serve their own.
Others thought kings an useless heavy load,
Who cost too much and did too little good.
These were for laying honest David by
On principles of pure good husbandry.
With them joined all the haranguers of the
          throng
That thought to get preferment by the tongue.
Who follow next a double danger bring,   511
Not only hating David, but the King;
The Solymæan rout,[17] well versed of old
In godly faction and in treason bold,
Cowering and quaking at a conqueror's sword,
But lofty to a lawful prince restored,
Saw with disdain an Ethnic[18] plot begun
And scorned by Jebusites to be outdone.
Hot Levites[19] headed these; who pulled before
From the ark, which in the Judges' days[20]
          they bore,   520
Resumed their cant, and with a zealous cry
Pursued their old beloved theocracy,
Where Sanhedrin and priest enslaved the
          nation
And justified their spoils by inspiration;
For who so fit for reign as Aaron's race,
If once dominion they could found in grace?
These led the pack; though not of surest scent,
Yet deepest mouthed against the government.
A numerous host of dreaming saints succeed
Of the true old enthusiastic breed: 530
'Gainst form and order they their power employ,
Nothing to build and all things to destroy.
But far more numerous was the herd of such
Who think too little and who talk too much.
These out of mere instinct, they knew not why,
Adored their fathers' God and property,
And by the same blind benefit of Fate
The Devil and the Jebusite did hate:
Born to be saved even in their own despite,
Because they could not help believing right.   540
Such were the tools; but a whole Hydra more
Remains of sprouting heads too long to score.
Some of their chiefs were princes of the land;
In the first rank of these did Zimri[21] stand,

[16] Achitophel has been urging Absalom to advance his cause by securing possession of the person of the king.
[17] The London populace (Jerusalem = Hierosolyma).
[18] Gentile (i. e., the Popish Plot).
[19] Presbyterian ministers deprived of their office by the act of Uniformity.
[20] The days of the Commonwealth, when (l. 523) the clergy were unusually prominent in affairs of state.
[21] The Duke of Buckingham, favorite, and former minister, of Charles II. He had ridiculed Dryden.

A man so various that he seemed to be
Not one, but all mankind's epitome:
Stiff in opinions, always in the wrong,
Was everything by starts and nothing long;
But in the course of one revolving moon
Was chemist, fiddler, statesman, and buffoon;
Then all for women, painting, rhyming, drink-
    ing,   551
Besides ten thousand freaks that died in think-
    ing.
Blest madman, who could every hour employ
With something new to wish or to enjoy!
Railing and praising were his usual themes,
And both, to show his judgment, in extremes:
So over violent or over civil
That every man with him was God or Devil.
In squandering wealth was his peculiar art;
Nothing went unrewarded but desert.   560
Beggared by fools whom still he found too
    late,
He had his jest, and they had his estate.
He laughed himself from Court; then sought
    relief
By forming parties, but could ne'er be chief:
For spite of him, the weight of business fell
On Absalom and wise Achitophel;
Thus wicked but in will, of means bereft,
He left not faction, but of that was left.

MAC FLECKNOE.*

All human things are subject to decay
And, when Fate summons, monarchs must obey.
This Flecknoe found, who, like Augustus,[1]
    young
Was called to empire and had governed long,
In prose and verse was owned without dispute
Through all the realms of Nonsense absolute.
This aged prince, now flourishing in peace
And blest with issue of a large increase,
Worn out with business, did at length debate
To settle the succession of the state;   10
And pondering which of all his sons was fit
To reign and wage immortal war with wit,
Cried, " 'Tis resolved, for Nature pleads that
    he
Should only rule who most resembles me.
Shadwell alone my perfect image bears,
Mature in dulness from his tender years;
Shadwell alone of all my sons is he
Who stands confirmed in full stupidity.

The rest to some faint meaning make pretence
But Shadwell never deviates into sense.   2
Some beams of wit on other souls may fall,
Strike through and make a lucid interval;
But Shadwell's genuine night admits no ray
His rising fogs prevail upon the day.
Besides, his goodly fabric[2] fills the eye
And seems designed for thoughtless majesty,
Thoughtless as monarch oaks that shade the
    plain
And, spread in solemn state, supinely reign.
Heywood and Shirley[3] were but types of thee
Thou last great prophet of tautology.   3
Even I, a dunce of more renown than they,
Was sent before but to prepare thy way,
And coarsely clad in Norwich drugget[4] came
To teach the nations in thy greater name.
My warbling lute, the lute I whilom strung,
When to King John of Portugal[5] I sung,
Was but the prelude to that glorious day,
When thou on silver Thames didst cut thy way
With well-timed oars before the royal barge,
Swelled with the pride of thy celestial charge,
And, big with hymn, commander of an host;   4
The like was ne'er in Epsom blankets tost.[7]
Methinks I see the new Arion[8] sail,
The lute still trembling underneath thy nail.
At thy well-sharpened thumb from shore to
    shore
The treble squeaks for fear, the basses roar
Echoes from Private-alley Shadwell call,
And Shadwell they resound from Aston-hall.
About thy boat the little fishes throng,
As at the morning toast that floats along.   5
Sometimes, as prince of thy harmonious band
Thou wieldst thy papers in thy threshing hand
St. André's[9] feet ne'er kept more equal time
Not even the feet of thy own "Psyche's"[10]
    rhyme:
Though they in number as in sense excel,
So just, so like tautology, they fell,
That, pale with envy, Singleton[11] forswore
The lute and sword which he in triumph bore
And vowed he ne'er would act Villerius[12]
    more.   5

---

[1] Successor of Caesar at the age of eighteen, and virtual emperor at thirty-two.

* "Son of Flecknoe." Dryden is satirizing Thomas Shadwell, a rival dramatist and personal enemy, by making him the son of a very dull poet, Flecknoe, who had died several years before the date of this poem (1682) at an advanced age.

[2] Shadwell was a corpulent man.
[3] Two 17th century dramatists.
[4] rough woollen cloth
[5] Flecknoe had visited the court of Lisbon.
[6] The precise occasion of this has not been traced, but Shadwell is known to have been proficient in music.
[7] A familiar form of punishment, with an allusion to the title of Shadwell's play *Epsom Wells*
[8] A Grecian musician who, when thrown into the sea, was saved by the dolphins.
[9] A French dancing master.
[10] An opera by Shadwell.
[11] A singer.
[12] The principal character in one of Davenant's plays.

Here stopped the good old sire and wept for joy,
In silent raptures of the hopeful boy.
All arguments, but most his plays, persuade
That for anointed dulness he was made.

Close to the walls which fair Augusta[13] bind,
(The fair Augusta much to fears[14] inclined,)
An ancient fabric raised to inform the sight
There stood of yore, and Barbican it hight;
A watch-tower once, but now, so fate ordains,
Of all the pile an empty name remains;

. . . .

Near these a Nursery[15] erects its head   74
Where queens are formed and future heroes bred,
Where unfledged actors learn to laugh and cry,
Where infant trulls their tender voices try,
And little Maximins[16] the gods defy.
Great Fletcher[17] never treads in buskins[18] here,
Nor greater Jonson dares in socks[19] appear; 80
But gentle Simkin just reception finds
Amidst this monument of vanished minds;
Pure clinches[20] the suburbian muse affords
And Panton waging harmless war with words.
Here Flecknoe, as a place to fame well known,
Ambitiously designed his Shadwell's throne.
For ancient Dekker prophesied long since
That in this pile should reign a mighty prince,
Born for a scourge of wit and flail of sense,
To whom true dulness should some "Psyches"[10] owe,   90
But worlds of "Misers"[21] from his pen should flow;
"Humorists"[21] and Hypocrites it should produce,
Whole Raymond families and tribes of Bruce.[22]
Now empress Fame had published the renown
Of Shadwell's coronation through the town.
Roused by report of fame, the nations meet
From near Bunhill and distant Watling-street.
No Persian carpets spread the imperial way,
But scattered limbs of mangled poets lay;
From dusty shops neglected authors come, 100
. . . .

Much Heywood, Shirley,[23] Ogleby[24] there lay.
But loads of Shadwell almost choked the way.
Bilked stationers for yeomen[25] stood prepared
And Herringman[26] was captain of the guard.
The hoary prince[27] in majesty appeared,
High on a throne of his own labours reared.
At his right hand our young Ascanius[28] sate,
Rome's other hope and pillar of the state. 109
His brows thick fogs instead of glories grace,
And lambent dulness played around his face.
As Hannibal did to the altars come,
Sworn by his sire a mortal foe to Rome;[29]
So Shadwell swore, nor should his vow be vain,
That he till death true dulness would maintain;
And, in his father's right and realm's defence,
Ne'er to have peace with wit nor truce with sense.
The king himself the sacred unction made,
As king by office and as priest by trade.
In his sinister[30] hand, instead of ball,   120
He placed a mighty mug of potent ale;
"Love's Kingdom"[31] to his right he did convey,
At once his sceptre and his rule of sway;
Whose righteous lore the prince had practised young
And from whose loins recorded "Psyche" sprung.
His temples, last, with poppies[32] were o'erspread,
That nodding seemed to consecrate his head.
Just at that point of time, if fame not lie,
On his left hand twelve reverend owls did fly.
So Romulus, 'tis sung, by Tiber's brook, 130
Presage of sway from twice six vultures took.
The admiring throng loud acclamations make
And omens of his future empire take.
The sire then shook the honours of his head,
And from his brows damps of oblivion shed
Full on the filial dulness: long he stood,
Repelling from his breast the raging god;
At length burst out in this prophetic mood:
"Heavens bless my son! from Ireland let him reign
To far Barbadoes on the western main; 140
Of his dominion may no end be known
And greater than his father's be his throne;
Beyond 'Love's Kingdom' let him stretch his pen!"

---

3 London.
4 Of Popish and other plots.
5 A school for training boys and girls to the stage.
6 A character, in one of Dryden's own early plays, who defies the gods.
7 Fletcher, Jonson, and Dekker were prominent dramatists contemporary with and later than Shakespeare. Simkin was "a stupid clown" in a farce (see Cambridge *Dryden*) and Panton a punster.
18 High-heeled shoes worn by tragic actors, hence "tragedy."
19 Low shoes worn by comic actors, hence "comedy"
20 puns
21 A play by Shadwell.
22 Characters in his plays.
23 Seventeenth century dramatists.
24 An inferior poet.
25 defrauded booksellers as guardsmen
26 Shadwell's publisher.
27 Flecknoe.
28 Shadwell (Ascanius was the son of Aeneas, the mythical founder of Rome).
29 Livy, Book xxi.
30 left
31 A play by Flecknoe.
32 "Perhaps in allusion to Shadwell's frequent use of opium, as well as to his dulness." (Scott). Poppies are symbolic of sleep.

He paused, and all the people cried "Amen."
Then thus continued he: "My son, advance
Still in new impudence, new ignorance.
Success let others teach, learn thou from me
Pangs without birth and fruitless industry.
Let 'Virtuosos'³³ in five years be writ,
Yet not one thought accuse thy toil of wit.   150
Let gentle George³⁴ in triumph tread the stage,
Make Dorimant betray, and Loveit rage;
Let Cully, Cockwood, Fopling, charm the pit,
And in their folly show the writer's wit.
Yet still thy fools shall stand in thy defence
And justify their author's want of sense.
Let them be all by thy own model made
Of dulness and desire no foreign aid,
That they to future ages may be known,
Not copies drawn, but issue of thy own.   160
Nay, let thy men of wit too be the same,
All full of thee and differing but in name.
But let no alien Sedley³⁵ interpose
To lard with wit thy hungry Epsom prose.
And when false flowers of rhetoric thou
      wouldst cull,
Trust nature, do not labour to be dull;
But write thy best and top,³⁶ and in each line
Sir Formal's³⁷ oratory will be thine.
Sir Formal, though unsought, attends thy quill
And does thy northern dedications fill.³⁸   170
Nor let false friends seduce thy mind to fame
By arrogating Jonson's hostile name;³⁹
Let father Flecknoe fire thy mind with praise
And uncle Ogleby²⁴ thy envy raise.
Thou art my blood, where Jonson has no part:
What share have we in nature or in art?
Where did his wit on learning fix a brand
And rail at arts he did not understand?
Where made he love in Prince Nicander's¹⁰
      vein
Or swept the dust in Psyche's humble
      strain?   180
. . . .
Promised a play and dwindled to a farce?
When did his Muse from Fletcher¹⁷ scenes
      purloin,
As thou whole Etherege³⁴ dost transfuse to
      thine?
But so transfused as oil on waters flow,
His always floats above, thine sinks below.

This is thy province, this thy wondrous way,
New humours to invent for each new play:
This is that boasted bias of thy mind,
By which one way to dulness 'tis inclined,
Which makes thy writings lean on one
      still,
And, in all changes, that way bends thy will,
Nor let thy mountain belly make pretence
Of likeness; thine's a tympany⁴¹ of sense.
A tun of man⁴² in thy large bulk is writ,
But sure thou'rt but a kilderkin⁴³ of wit.
Like mine, thy gentle numbers feebly creep;
Thy tragic Muse gives smiles, thy comic sl
With whate'er gall thou setst thyself to wr
Thy inoffensive satires never bite;
In thy felonious heart though venom lies,
It does but touch thy Irish⁴⁴ pen, and die
Thy genius calls thee not to purchase fame
In keen Iambics,⁴⁵ but mild Anagram.
Leave writing plays, and choose for thy c
      mand
Some peaceful province in Acrostic land.
There thou mayest wings display and al
      raise,
And torture one poor word ten thousand wa
Or, if thou wouldst thy different talents sui
Set thy own songs, and sing them to
      lute."
He said, but his last words were scarcely hea
For Bruce and Longville²² had a trap
      pared,
And down they sent the yet declaiming ba
Sinking he left his drugget robe behind,
Borne upwards by a subterranean wind.
The mantle fell to the young prophet's par
With double portion of his father's art.

A SONG FOR ST. CECILIA'S DAY.*

November 22, 1687.

1

From harmony, from heavenly harmony
      This universal frame began;
   When Nature underneath a heap
      Of jarring atoms lay,
   And could not heave her head,

33 A play by Shadwell.
34 Etherege, a comic dramatist; Dori-mant, etc., are characters in his plays.
35 Writer of the pro-logue to Shadwell's *Epsom Wells*.
36 excel
37 A character in Shad-well's *Virtuoso*.
38 Shadwell dedicated much of his work to the Duke of Newcastle.
39 i. e., by comparing him with Jonson, who was quite his contrary (see also l. 193)
40 A character in Shad-well's *Psyche*.
41 dropsy
42 Cp. *I Henry IV.*, II. iv. 493.
43 small barrel
44 Shadwell was not Irish and insisted that had never been in Ireland more than a hours.
45 Iambics were the standard verse-form of sa in classical poetry.

* St. Cecilia, as patroness of music, is commo represented in paintings with a harp organ, and Dryden makes her the inventor the latter. Public festivals in her honor w held annually at London at this period. C pare the following Ode, and also Pope's, 305.

tuneful voice was heard from high,
Arise, ye more than dead.

a cold and hot and moist and dry
a order to their stations leap,
And Music's power obey.   10
n harmony, from heavenly harmony
This universal frame began:
From harmony to harmony
ugh all the compass of the notes it ran,
diapason[1] closing full in Man.

2

at passion cannot Music raise and quell?
hen Jubal[2] struck the chorded shell,
is listening brethren stood around,
And, wondering, on their faces fell
o worship that celestial sound: 20
than a god they thought there could not
            dwell
ithin the hollow of that shell,
hat spoke so sweetly, and so well.
at passion cannot Music raise and quell?

3

he trumpet's loud clangor
    Excites us to arms
ith shrill notes of anger
    And mortal alarms.
he double, double, double beat
    Of the thundering drum   30
Cries, hark! the foes come;
harge, charge, 'tis too late to retreat.

4

soft complaining flute
a dying notes discovers
he woes of hopeless lovers,
se dirge is whispered by the warbling lute.

5

harp violins proclaim
ir jealous pangs and desperation,
y, frantic indignation,
th of pains and height of passion,   40
or the fair, disdainful dame.

6

But oh! what art can teach,
What human voice can reach
    The sacred organ's praise?
Notes inspiring holy love,
es that wing their heavenly ways
o mend the choirs above.

chord including all tones.
The father of all such as handle the harp or
    organ." *Gen.* 4:21.

7

Orpheus could lead the savage race,
And trees unrooted left their place,
    Sequacious of[3] the lyre;
But bright Cecilia raised the wonder higher:
When to her organ vocal breath was given,
An angel heard, and straight appeared
    Mistaking earth for heaven.

GRAND CHORUS.

As from the power of sacred lays
    The spheres began to move,
And sung the great Creator's praise
    To all the blessed above;
So when the last and dreadful hour
This crumbling pageant shall devour,   60
The trumpet shall be heard on high,
The dead shall live, the living die,
And Music shall untune the sky.

ALEXANDER'S FEAST; OR, THE POWER OF MUSIC.

A SONG IN HONOUR OF ST. CECILIA'S DAY: 1697.

1

Twas at the royal feast for Persia won
    By Philip's warlike son:[1]
    Aloft in awful state
    The godlike hero sate
    On his imperial throne.
His valiant peers were placed around;
Their brows with roses and with myrtles bound:
    (So should desert in arms be crowned.)
The lovely Thais, by his side,
Sate like a blooming Eastern bride,   10
In flower of youth and beauty's pride.
    Happy, happy, happy pair!
        None but the brave,
        None but the brave,
    None but the brave deserves the fair.

CHORUS.

Happy, happy, happy pair!
    None but the brave,
    None but the brave,
    None but the brave deserves the fair.

2

Timotheus[2] placed on high   20
    Amid the tuneful quire,
With flying fingers touched the lyre:
    The trembling notes ascend the sky,

3 following

---

1 Alexander the Great conquered Persia in 331
        B. C.
2 Musician to Alexander.

And heavenly joys inspire.
The song began from[3] Jove,
Who left his blissful seats above,
(Such is the power of mighty love.)
A dragon's fiery form belied the god:
Sublime on radiant spires he rode,
When he to fair Olympia[4] pressed: 30
And while he sought her snowy breast,
Then round her slender waist he curled,
And stamped an image of himself, a sovereign
          of the world.
The listening crowd admire the lofty sound,
A present deity, they shout around;
A present deity, the vaulted roofs rebound:
     With ravished ears
     The monarch hears,
     Assumes the god,
     Affects to nod,   40
And seems to shake the spheres.

CHORUS.

With ravished ears
The monarch hears,
Assumes the god,
Affects to nod,
And seems to shake the spheres.

3

The praise of Bacchus then the sweet musician
          sung,
Of Bacchus ever fair, and ever young.
     The jolly god in triumph comes;
     Sound the trumpets, beat the drums;   50
          Flushed with a purple grace
          He shows his honest face:
Now give the hautboys[5] breath; he comes, he
          comes.
Bacchus ever fair and young,
     Drinking joys did first ordain;
Bacchus' blessings are a treasure,
Drinking is the soldier's pleasure;
          Rich the treasure,
          Sweet the pleasure,
     Sweet is pleasure after pain.   60

CHORUS.

Bacchus' blessings are a treasure,
Drinking is the soldier's pleasure;
     Rich the treasure,
     Sweet the pleasure,
Sweet is pleasure after pain.

4

Soothed with the sound the king grew vain;
Fought all his battles o'er again;

And thrice he routed all his foes, and thrice
          he slew the slain.
     The master saw the madness rise,
     His glowing cheeks, his ardent eyes;
And while he heaven and earth defied,
Changed his hand, and checked his pride.
     He chose a mournful Muse,
          Soft pity to infuse;
     He sung Darius[6] great and good,
          By too severe a fate,
     Fallen, fallen, fallen, fallen,
          Fallen from his high estate,
     And weltering in his blood;
     Deserted at his utmost need
     By those his former bounty fed;
     On the bare earth exposed he lies,
     With not a friend to close his eyes.

With downcast looks the joyless victor sate,
     Revolving in his altered soul
          The various turns of chance below;
     And, now and then, a sigh he stole,
          And tears began to flow.

CHORUS.

Revolving in his altered soul
     The various turns of chance below;
And, now and then, a sigh he stole,
     And tears began to flow.

5

The mighty master smiled to see
That love was in the next degree;
'Twas but a kindred-sound to move,
For pity melts the mind to love.
     Softly sweet, in Lydian[7] measures,
     Soon he soothed his soul to pleasures,
War, he sung, is toil and trouble;
Honour but an empty bubble;   100
     Never ending, still beginning,
Fighting still, and still destroying:
     If the world be worth thy winning,
Think, O think it worth enjoying:
     Lovely Thais sits beside thee,
     Take the good the gods provide thee.

The many rend the skies with loud applause;
So Love was crowned, but Music won the cause.
     The prince, unable to conceal his pain,
          Gazed on the fair   110
          Who caused his care,
     And sighed and looked, sighed and looked,
     Sighed and looked, and sighed again;

---

3 sang first of   5 oboes
4 Alexander's mother.

6 King of the Persians.
7 A soft, pathetic mode of Grecian music.

t length, with love and wine at once op-
      pressed,
he vanquished victor sunk upon her breast.
CHORUS.
The prince, unable to conceal his pain,
  Gazed on the fair
  Who caused his care,
And sighed and looked, sighed and looked,
Sighed and looked, and sighed again;   120
t length, with love and wine at once op-
      pressed,
he vanquished victor sunk upon her breast.

6
Now strike the golden lyre again;
A louder yet, and yet a louder strain.
Break his bands of sleep asunder,
And rouse him, like a rattling peal of
      thunder.
  Hark, hark, the horrid sound
    Has raised up his head;
    As awaked from the dead,
  And amazed, he stares around.   130
Revenge, revenge, Timotheus cries,
  See the Furies[8] arise;
  See the snakes that they rear,
  How they hiss in their hair,
And the sparkles that flash from their eyes!
  Behold a ghastly band,
  Each a torch in his hand!
hose are Grecian ghosts, that in battle were
      slain,
    And unburied remain
    Inglorious on the plain: 140
    Give the vengeance due
    To the valiant crew.
Behold how they toss their torches on high,
How they point to the Persian abodes,
nd glittering temples of their hostile gods.
he princes applaud with a furious joy;
nd the king seized a flambeau with zeal to
      destroy;
    Thais led the way,
    To light him to his prey,   149
nd, like another Helen, fired another Troy.

CHORUS.
nd the king seized a flambeau with zeal to
    destroy;
    Thais led the way,
    To light him to his prey,
nd, like another Helen, fired another Troy.

7
    Thus long ago,
  Ere heaving bellows learned to blow,

The Eumenides, avenging spirits.

While organs yet were mute,
  Timotheus, to his breathing flute
    And sounding lyre,
Could swell the soul to rage, or kindle soft
  desire.   160
  At last divine Cecilia came,
  Inventress of the vocal frame;
The sweet enthusiast, from her sacred store,
  Enlarged the former narrow bounds,
  And added length to solemn sounds,
With Nature's mother-wit, and arts unknown
      before.
  Let old Timotheus yield the prize,
    Or both divide the crown:
  He raised a mortal to the skies;
    She drew an angel down.

GRAND CHORUS.
At last divine Cecilia came,   170
Inventress of the vocal frame;
The sweet enthusiast, from her sacred store,
  Enlarged the former narrow bounds,
  And added length to solemn sounds,
With Nature's mother-wit, and arts unknown
      before.
  Let old Timotheus yield the prize,
    Or both divide the crown:
  He raised a mortal to the skies;
    She drew an angel down.

LINES PRINTED UNDER THE ENGRAVED PORTRAIT OF MILTON.

Three poets,[9] in three distant ages born,
Greece, Italy, and England did adorn.
The first in loftiness of thought surpassed,
The next in majesty, in both the last;
The force of nature could no farther go;
To make a third she joined the former two.

SONG FROM THE INDIAN EMPEROR.

Ah fading joy! how quickly art thou past!
    Yet we thy ruin haste.
As if the cares of human life were few,
    We seek out new:
And follow fate, that does too fast pursue.

See, how on every bough the birds express,
  In their sweet notes, their happiness.
    They all enjoy, and nothing spare;   8
But on their mother nature lay their care:
Why then should man, the lord of all below,
    Such troubles choose to know,
As none of all his subjects undergo?

9 Homer, Virgil, Milton.

Hark, hark, the waters—fall, fall, fall,
And with a murmuring sound
  Dash, dash, upon the ground,
    To gentle slumbers call.   16

SONG OF THAMESIS.*

Old father Ocean calls my tide;
Come away, come away;
The barks upon the billows ride,
The master will not stay;
The merry boatswain from his side
His whistle takes, to check and chide
The lingering lads' delay,
And all the crew aloud has cried,   8
Come away, come away.

See, the god of seas attends thee,
Nymphs divine, a beauteous train;
All the calmer gales befriend thee,
In thy passage o'er the main;
Every maid her locks is binding,
Every Triton's horn is winding;
Welcome to the wat'ry plain!   16

SONG FROM CLEOMENES.

No, no, poor suff'ring heart, no change endeavour;
Choose to sustain the smart, rather than leave her:
My ravished eyes behold such charms about her,
I can die with her, but not live without her;
One tender sigh of hers to see me languish,
Will more than pay the price of my past anguish.
Beware, O cruel fair, how you smile on me;
'Twas a kind look of yours that has undone me.   8

Love has in store for me one happy minute,
And she will end my pain who did begin it:
Then, no day void of bliss or pleasure leaving,
Ages shall slide away without perceiving;
Cupid shall guard the door, the more to please us,

And keep out Time and Death, when would seize us;
Time and Death shall depart, and say in fly
Love has found out a way to live by dying.

THE SECULAR MASQUE.

Enter JANUS.[1]

JANUS.

Chronos, Chronos,[2] mend thy pace:
An hundred times the rolling sun
Around the radiant belt has run
  In his revolving race.
Behold, behold, the goal in sight;
Spread thy fans, and wing thy flight.

*Enter CHRONOS, with a scythe in his h
and a globe on his back, which he sets
down at his entrance.*

CHRONOS.

Weary, weary of my weight,
Let me, let me drop my freight,
  And leave the world behind.
    I could not bear,
    Another year,
  The load of humankind.

Enter MOMUS,[3] *laughing.*

MOMUS.

Ha! ha! ha! ha! ha! ha! well hast thou
  To lay down thy pack,
  And lighten thy back.
The world was a fool, e'er since it begun;
And since neither Janus, nor Chronos, nor
  Can hinder the crimes
  Or mend the bad times,
'Tis better to laugh than to cry.

Chorus of all three.

'Tis better to laugh than to cry.

JANUS.

Since Momus comes to laugh below,
  Old Time, begin the show,
That he may see, in every scene,
What changes in this age have been.

CHRONOS.

Then, goddess of the silver bow, begin.
  (*Horns, or hunting music wit*

* From the opera *Albion and Albanius*, 1685. Thamesis is the River God Thames, addressing Albanius, who represents the Duke of York (afterward James II.) The latter, in 1679, had been compelled to retire to Brussels, in temporary exile, until the excitement against the Roman Catholics, created by the "Popish plot," should die away. The flattery of James is evident; but the song has a haunting beauty which sets it apart from mere eulogy.

1 Anciently the highest divinity, who presided the beginnings of things.
2 The god of time; ruler of the world before
3 The personification of mockery.

Enter DIANA.

DIANA.

th horns and with hounds I waken the day,
d hie to my woodland-walks away;
ack up my robe, and am buskined⁴ soon,
d tie to my forehead a wexing moon.   30
ourse the fleet stag, unkennel the fox,
d chase the wild goats o'er summits of
     rocks,
th shouting and hooting we pierce through
     the sky,
d Echo turns hunter, and doubles the cry.

Chorus of all.

th shouting and hooting we pierce through
     the sky,
d Echo turns hunter, and doubles the cry.

JANUS.

en our age was in its prime:

CHRONOS.

ee from rage:

DIANA.

And free from crime.

MOMUS.

very merry, dancing, drinking,
ughing, quaffing, and unthinking time.   40

Chorus of all.

en our age was in its prime,
ee from rage, and free from crime,
very merry, dancing, drinking,
ughing, quaffing, and unthinking time.

Dance of DIANA's *attendants.*
Enter MARS.

MARS.

spire⁵ the vocal brass, inspire;
e world is past its infant age:
     Arms and honour,
     Arms and honour,
t the martial mind on fire,
And kindle manly rage.   50
     Mars has looked the sky to red;
And Peace, the lazy good, is fled.
Plenty, peace, and pleasure fly;
     The sprightly green
In woodland-walks no more is seen;
e sprightly green has drunk the Tyrian⁶ dye.

ooted
reathe into, blow   6 purple

Chorus of all.

Plenty, peace, and pleasure fly;
     The sprightly green
In woodland-walks no more is seen;
The sprightly green has drunk the Tyrian
     dye.   60

MARS.

Sound the trumpet, beat the drum;
     Through all the world around,
     Sound a reveille,⁷ sound, sound,
The warrior god is come.

Chorus of all.

Sound the trumpet, beat the drum;
     Through all the world around,
     Sound a reveille, sound, sound,
The warrior god is come.

MOMUS.

Thy sword within the scabbard keep,
     And let mankind agree;   70
Better the world were fast asleep,
     Than kept awake by thee.
The fools are only thinner,
     With all our cost and care;
But neither side a winner,
     For things are as they were.

Chorus of all.

The fools are only thinner,
     With all our cost and care;

But neither side a winner,
     For things are as they were.   80

Enter VENUS.

Calms appear when storms are past;
Love will have his hour at last;
Nature is my kindly care;
Mars destroys, and I repair;
Take me, take me, while you may,
Venus comes not every day.

Chorus of all.

Take her, take her, while you may,
Venus comes not every day.

CHRONOS.

The world was then so light,
     I scarcely felt the weight;   90
Joy ruled the day, and Love the night.
But, since the Queen of Pleasure left the
     ground,
     I faint, I lag,
     And feebly drag
The ponderous orb around.

7 morning call

MOMUS.

All, all, of a piece throughout:

(*Pointing to Diana.*

Thy chase had a beast in view;

(*To Mars.*

Thy wars brought nothing about;

(*To Venus.*

Thy lovers were all untrue.

JANUS.

'Tis well an old age is out.   100

CHRONOS.

And time to begin a new.

Chorus of all.

All, all, of a piece throughout:
Thy chase had a beast in view;
Thy wars brought nothing about;
Thy lovers were all untrue.
'Tis well an old age is out,
And time to begin a new.

(*Dance of huntsmen, nymphs, warriors, and lovers.*)

ON CHAUCER.

FROM THE PREFACE TO THE FABLES.*

It remains that I say somewhat of Chaucer in particular.

In the first place, as he is the father of English poetry, so I hold him in the same degree of veneration as the Grecians held Homer, or the Romans Virgil. He is a perpetual fountain of good sense, learned in all sciences, and therefore speaks properly on all subjects. As he knew what to say, so he knows also when to leave off; a continence which is practised by few writers, and scarcely by any of the ancients, excepting Virgil and Horace. One of our late great poets[1] is sunk in his reputation because he could never forgive any conceit which came in his way, but swept, like a drag-net, great and small. There was plenty enough, but the dishes were ill sorted; whole pyramids of sweetmeats for boys and women, but little of solid meat for men. All this proceeded, not from any want of knowledge, but of judgment. Neither did he want that in discerning the beauties and faults of other poets, but only indulged himself in the luxury of writing; and perhaps knew it was a fault but hoped the reader would not find it. For this reason, though he must always be thought a great poet, he is no longer esteemed a good writer; and for ten impressions,[2] which his works have had in so many successive years, yet at present a hundred books are scarcely purchased once a twelvemonth; for, as my last Lord Rochester said, though somewhat profanely, "Not being of God, he could not stand."

Chaucer followed nature everywhere, but was never so bold to go beyond her, and there is a great difference of being *poeta* and *nimis poeta*,[3] if we believe Catullus, as much as betwixt a modest behaviour and affectation. The verse of Chaucer, I confess, is not harmonious to us; but 't is like the eloquence of one whom Tacitus commends, it was *auribus istius temporis accommodata:*[4] they who lived with him and some time after him, thought it musical; and it continues so even in our judgment, if compared with the numbers of Lydgate and Gower, his contemporaries; there is the rude sweetness of a Scotch tune in it, which is natural and pleasing though not perfect. 'Tis true I cannot go so far as he who published the last edition of him,[5] for he would make us believe the fault is in our ears, and that there were really ten syllables in a verse where we find but nine; but this opinion is not worth confuting; 't is so gross and obvious an error that common sense (which is a rule in everything but matters of faith and revelation) must convince the reader that equality of numbers[6] in every verse which we call heroic was either not known or not always practised in Chaucer's age. It were an easy matter to produce some thousands of his verses which are lame for want of half a foot and sometimes a whole one, and which no pronunciation can make otherwise.† We can only say that he lived in the infancy of our poetry, and that nothing is brought to perfection at the first. We must be children before we grow men. There was an Ennius, and in process of time

---

* The *Fables*, published in 1700, the last year of Dryden's life, were metrical translations, or rather paraphrases, of stories from Homer, Ovid, Boccaccio, and Chaucer. The Preface, in addition to being excellent criticism, is a good example of Dryden's style in prose—the modern English prose which he did so much toward regulating (*Eng. Lit.*, 166-167). This particular example is characterized by Mr. George Saintsbury as "forcible without the slightest effort, eloquent without declamation, graceful yet thoroughly manly."

1 Abraham Cowley, who could not "forgive" (i. e. give up, forego) strained fancies and distorted forms of expression.
2 New printings.
3 "Overmuch a poet" (said by Martial, not Catullus).
4 "Suited to the ears of that time."
5 That of Thomas Speght, 1597-1602.
6 Measures.
7 The iambic pentameter couplet (see *Eng. Lit.* 58, 165, 187).
† Dryden did not understand Chaucer's pronunciation nor sufficiently allow for imperfections in the manuscripts.

a Lucilius and a Lucretius, before Virgil and Horace; even after Chaucer there was a Spenser, a Harrington, a Fairfax, before Waller and Denham were in being, and our numbers were in their nonage till these last appeared.‡

.   .   .   .   .

He must have been a man of a most wonderful comprehensive nature, because, as it has been truly observed of him, he has taken into the compass of his *Canterbury Tales* the various manners and humours (as we now call them) of the whole English nation in his age. Not a single character has escaped him. All his pilgrims are severally distinguished from each other, and not only in their inclinations but in their very physiognomies and persons. Baptista Porta° could not have described their natures better than by the marks which the poet gives them.

The matter and manner of their tales and of their telling are so suited to their different educations, humours, and callings that each of them would be improper in any other mouth.

° A Neapolitan physiognomist.
‡ Posterity has not sustained this verdict. But see *Eng. Lit.*, pp. 141, 165.

Even the grave and serious characters are distinguished by their several sorts of gravity; their discourses are such as belong to their age, their calling, and their breeding, such as are becoming of them and of them only. Some of his persons are vicious and some virtuous; some are unlearned, or (as Chaucer calls them) lewd, and some are learned. Even the ribaldry of the low characters is different: the Reeve, the Miller, and the Cook are several men, and distinguished from each other as much as the mincing Lady Prioress and the broad-speaking, gap-toothed Wife of Bath. But enough of this: there is such a variety of game springing up before me that I am distracted in my choice and know not which to follow. It is sufficient to say, according to the proverb, that here is God's plenty. We have our forefathers and great-grand-dames all before us as they were in Chaucer's days: their general characters are still remaining in mankind, and even in England, though they are called by other names than those of monks and friars and canons and lady abbesses and nuns; for mankind is ever the same, and nothing lost out of nature though everything is altered.

SIR RICHARD STEELE
(1672-1729)

PROSPECTUS.

The Tatler, No. 1.   Tuesday, April 12, 1709.

Quicquid agunt homines——
nostri est farrago libelli.
Juv. Sat. i. 85, 86.
Whate'er men do, or say, or think, or dream,
Our motley Paper seizes for its theme.

Though the other papers, which are published for the use of the good people of England,* have certainly very wholesome effects, and are laudable in their particular kinds, they do not seem to come up to the main design of such narrations, which, I humbly presume, should be principally intended for the use of politic persons, who are so public-spirited as to neglect their own affairs to look into transactions of state. Now these gentlemen, for the most part, being persons of strong zeal, and weak intellects, it is both a charitable and necessary work to offer something, whereby such worthy and well-affected members of the commonwealth may be instructed, after their reading, what to think; which shall be the end and purpose of this my paper, wherein I shall, from time to time, report and consider all matters of what kind soever that shall occur to me, and publish such my advices and reflections every Tuesday, Thursday, and Saturday in the week, for the convenience of the post. I resolve to have something which may be of entertainment to the fair sex, in honour of whom I have invented the title of this paper. I therefore earnestly desire all persons, without distinction, to take it in for the present *gratis,* and hereafter at the price of one penny, forbidding all hawkers to take more for it at their peril. And I desire all persons to consider, that I am at a very great charge for proper materials for this work, as well as that, before I resolved upon it, I had settled a correspondence in all parts of the known and knowing world. And forasmuch as this globe is not trodden upon by mere drudges of business only, but that men of spirit and genius are justly to be esteemed as considerable agents in it, we shall not, upon a dearth of news, present you with musty foreign edicts, and dull proclamations, but shall divide our relation of the passages which occur in action or discourse throughout this town, as well as elsewhere, under such dates of places as may prepare you for the matter you are to expect in the following manner.

All accounts of gallantry, pleasure, and entertainment, shall be under the article of White's Chocolate-house;† poetry under that of Will's Coffee-house; Learning, under the title of Grecian; foreign and domestic news, you will have from St. James's Coffee-house; and what else I have to offer on any other subject shall be dated from my own Apartment.

I once more desire my reader to consider, that as I cannot keep an ingenious man to go daily to Will's under two-pence each day, merely for his charges; to White's under six-pence; nor to the Grecian, without allowing him some plain Spanish,[1] to be as able as others at the learned table; and that a good observer cannot speak with even Kidney[2] at St. James's without clean linen; I say, these considerations will, I hope, make all persons willing to comply with my humble request (when my *gratis* stock is exhausted) of a penny apiece; especially since they are sure of some proper amusement, and that it is impossible for me to want means to entertain them, having, besides the force of my own parts, the

---

* Newspapers had been published for nearly a century. Steele proposed in *The Tatler* to publish periodical essays, stories, etc., which should serve something more than a merely practical purpose. See *Eng. Lit.,* p. 176.

1 Probably wine (which according to *The Tatler,* No. 252, "heightens conversation").
2 A waiter.
† The public coffee and chocolate houses of London were used as headquarters for the meetings of clubs. White's and St. James's were frequented by statesmen and men of fashion; Will's was a rendezvous for men of letters, and The Grecian for lawyers and scholars.

power of divination, and that I can, by casting a figure,[3] tell you all that will happen before it comes to pass.

But this last faculty I shall use very sparingly, and speak but of few things until they are passed, for fear of divulging matters which may offend our superiors.

MEMORIES

The Tatler, No. 181. Tuesday, June 6, 1710.

—— Dies, ni fallor, adest, quem semper acerbum,
Semper honoratum, sic dii voluistis habebo.
Virg. Æn. v. 49.

And now the rising day renews the year,
A day for ever sad, for ever dear.

There are those among mankind, who can enjoy no relish of their being, except the world is made acquainted with all that relates to them, and think every thing lost that passes unobserved; but others find a solid delight in stealing by the crowd, and modelling their life after such a manner, as is as much above the approbation as the practice of the vulgar. Life being too short to give instances great enough of true friendship or good will, some sages have thought it pious to preserve a certain reverence for the *Manes*[4] of their deceased friends; and have withdrawn themselves from the rest of the world at certain seasons, to commemorate in their own thoughts such of their acquaintance who have gone before them out of this life. And indeed, when we are advanced in years, there is not a more pleasing entertainment, than to recollect in a gloomy moment the many we have parted with, that have been dear and agreeable to us, and to cast a melancholy thought or two after those, with whom, perhaps, we have indulged ourselves in whole nights of mirth and jollity. With such inclinations in my heart I went to my closet[5] yesterday in the evening, and resolved to be sorrowful; upon which occasion I could not but look with disdain upon myself, that though all the reasons which I had to lament the loss of many of my friends are now as forcible as at the moment of their departure, yet did not my heart swell with the same sorrow which I felt at that time; but I could, without tears, reflect upon many pleasing adventures I have had with some, who have long been blended with common earth.

Though it is by the benefit of nature, that length of time thus blots out the violence of afflictions; yet with tempers too much given to pleasure, it is almost necessary to revive the old places of grief in our memory; and ponder step by step on past life, to lead the mind into that sobriety of thought which poises the heart, and makes it beat with due time, without being quickened with desire, or retarded with despair, from its proper and equal motion. When we wind up a clock that is out of order, to make it go well for the future, we do not immediately set the hand to the present instant, but we make it strike the round of all its hours, before it can recover the regularity of its time. Such, thought I, shall be my method this evening; and since it is that day of the year which I dedicate to the memory of such in another life as I much delighted in when living, an hour or two shall be sacred to sorrow and their memory, while I run over all the melancholy circumstances of this kind which have occurred to me in my whole life. The first sense of sorrow I ever knew was upon the death of my father, at which time I was not quite five years of age; but was rather amazed at what all the house meant, than possessed with a real understanding why nobody was willing to play with me. I remember I went into the room where his body lay, and my mother sat weeping alone by it. I had my battledore in my hand, and fell a-beating the coffin, and calling papa; for, I know not how, I had some slight idea that he was locked up there. My mother catched me in her arms, and, transported beyond all patience[6] of the silent grief she was before in, she almost smothered me in her embraces; and told me, in a flood of tears, "Papa could not hear me, and would play with me no more, for they were going to put him under ground, whence he could never come to us again." She was a very beautiful woman, of a noble spirit, and there was a dignity in her grief amidst all the wildness of her transport, which, methought, struck me with an instinct of sorrow, that, before I was sensible of what it was to grieve, seized my very soul, and has made pity the weakness of my heart ever since. The mind in infancy is, methinks, like the body in embryo, and receives impressions so forcible, that they are as hard to be removed by reason, as any mark, with which a child is born, is to be taken away by any future application. Hence it is, that good-nature in me is no merit; but having been so frequently overwhelmed with her tears before I knew the cause of any affliction, or could draw defences from my own judgment, I imbibed commiseration, remorse, and an unmanly gentleness of mind, which has since insnared me into ten thousand calamities; from whence I can reap no advantage, except it be, that, in such a humour as I am now in, I can the better indulge myself in the softnesses of humanity, and enjoy that sweet anxiety which arises from the memory of past afflictions.

We, that are very old, are better able to remember things which befel us in our distant youth, than the passages of later days. For this reason it is, that the companions of my strong and vigorous years present themselves more immediately to me in this office of sorrow. Untimely and unhappy deaths are what we are most apt to lament; so little are we able to make it indifferent when a thing happens, though we know it must happen. Thus we groan under life, and bewail those who are relieved from it. Every object that returns to our imagination raises different passions, according to the circumstances of their departure. Who can have lived in an army, and in a serious hour reflect upon the many gay and agreeable men that might long have flourished in the arts of peace, and not join with the imprecations of the fatherless and widow on the tyrant to whose ambition they fell sacrifices? But gallant men, who are cut off by the sword, move rather our veneration than our pity; and we gather relief enough from their own contempt of death, to make that no evil, which was approached with so much cheerfulness, and attended with so much honour. But when we turn our thoughts from the great parts of life on such occasions, and instead of lamenting those who stood ready to give death to those from whom they had the fortune to receive it; I say, when we let our thoughts wander from such noble objects, and consider the havoc which is made among the tender and the innocent, pity enters with an unmixed softness, and possesses all our souls at once.

Here (were there words to express such sentiments with proper tenderness) I should record the beauty, innocence and untimely death, of the first object my eyes ever beheld with love. The beauteous virgin! how ignorantly did she charm, how carelessly excel! Oh, Death! thou hast right to the bold, to the ambitious, to the high, and to the haughty;

but why this cruelty to the humble, to the meek, to the undiscerning, to the thoughtless? Nor age, nor business, nor distress, can erase the dear image from my imagination. In the same week, I saw her dressed for a ball, and in a shroud. How ill did the habit of death become the pretty trifler? I still behold the smiling earth——A large train of disasters were coming on to my memory, when my servant knocked at my closet-door, and interrupted me with a letter, attended with a hamper of wine, of the same sort with that which is to be put to sale, on Thursday next, at Garraway's coffee-house.* Upon the receipt of it, I sent for three of my friends. We are so intimate, that we can be company in whatever state of mind we meet, and can entertain each other without expecting always to rejoice. The wine we found to be generous and warming, but with such an heat as moved us rather to be cheerful than frolicsome. It revived the spirits, without firing the blood. We commended it until two of the clock this morning; and having to-day met a little before dinner,† we found, that though we drank two bottles a man, we had much more reason to recollect than forget what had passed the night before.

THE CLUB.

The Spectator, No. 2, Friday, March 2, 1711.

——Ast alii sex
Et plures uno conclamant ore——
Juv. Sat. vii. 167.
Six more at least join their consenting voice.

The first of our society is a gentleman of Worcestershire, of ancient descent, a baronet, his name Sir Roger de Coverley. His great grandfather was inventor of that famous country-dance which is called after him. All who know that shire are very well acquainted with the parts and merits of Sir Roger. He is a gentleman that is very singular in his behaviour, but his singularities proceed from his good sense, and are contradictions to the manners of the world, only as he thinks the world is in the wrong. However, this humour creates him no enemies, for he does nothing with sourness or obstinacy; and his being unconfined to modes and forms, makes him but the readier and more capable to please and oblige all who know him. When he is in town, he lives in

* This was a place where periodical auctions were held, and lotteries conducted.
† The fashionable dinner hour was four o'clock.

oho Square.[7] It is said, he keeps himself a achelor by reason he was crossed in love by a erverse beautiful widow of the next county o him. Before this disappointment, Sir Roger as what you call a fine gentleman, had often upped with my Lord Rochester[8] and Sir leorge Etherege,[9] fought a duel upon his first oming to town, and kicked bully Dawson[10] in public coffee-house for calling him youngster. ut being ill-used by the above-mentioned idow, he was very serious for a year and a alf; and though, his temper being naturally ovial, he at last got over it, he grew careless f himself, and never dressed afterwards. He ontinues to wear a coat and doublet of the ame cut that were in fashion at the time of is repulse, which, in his merry humours, he ells us, has been in and out twelve times since e first wore it. . . . He is now in his fifty-ixth year, cheerful, gay, and hearty; keeps a ood house both in town and country; a great ver of mankind; but there is such a mirthful ast in his behaviour, that he is rather beloved han esteemed.

His tenants grow rich, his servants look satis-ed, all the young women profess love to him, nd the young men are glad of his company. Vhen he comes into a house, he calls the ser-ants by their names, and talks all the way pstairs to a visit. I must not omit, that Sir Roger is a justice of the quorum;* that he fills he chair at a quarter-session with great abili-ies, and, three months ago, gained universal pplause by explaining a passage in the game ct.

The gentleman next in esteem and authority mong us is another bachelor, who is a member f the Inner Temple;[11] a man of great probity, vit, and understanding; but he has chosen his lace of residence rather to obey the direction f an old humoursome father, than in pursuit f his own inclinations. He was placed there o study the laws of the land, and is the most earned of any of the house in those of the tage. Aristotle and Longinus[12] are much bet-er understood by him than Littleton or Coke.[13] The father sends up every post questions relat-ng to marriage-articles, leases, and tenures, in

the neighborhood; all which questions he agrees with[14] an attorney to answer and take care of in the lump. He is studying the passions themselves, when he should be inquiring into the debates among men which arise from them. He knows the argument of each of the orations of Demosthenes and Tully,[15] but not one case in the reports of our own courts. No one ever took him for a fool; but none, except his in-timate friends, know he has a great deal of wit. This turn makes him at once both disin-terested and agreeable. As few of his thoughts are drawn from business, they are most of them fit for conversation. His taste of books is a little too just for the age he lives in; he has read all, but approves of very few. His familiarity with the customs, manners, actions, and writings of the ancients, makes him a very delicate observer of what occurs to him in the present world. He is an excellent critic, and the time of the play is his hour of business: exactly at five he passes through New-Inn,[16] crosses through Russel-court, and takes a turn at Will's till the play begins; he has his shoes rubbed and his periwig powdered at the bar-ber's as you go into the Rose.[17] It is for the good of the audience when he is at the play, for the actors have an ambition to please him.

The person of next consideration is Sir Andrew Freeport, a merchant of great eminence in the city of London: a person of indefatiga-ble industry, strong reason, and great ex-perience. His notions of trade are noble and generous, and (as every rich man has usually some sly way of jesting, which would make no great figure were he not a rich man) he calls the sea the British Common. He is acquainted with commerce in all its parts; and will tell you that it is a stupid and barbarous way to extend dominion by arms; for true power is to be got by arts and industry. He will often argue that, if this part of our trade were well cultivated, we should gain from one nation; and if another, from another. I have heard him prove, that diligence makes more lasting acquisitions than valour, and that sloth has ruined more nations than the sword. He abounds in several frugal maxims, among which the greatest favourite is, "A penny saved is a penny got." A general trader of good sense is pleasanter company than a general scholar; and Sir Andrew having a natural unaffected eloquence, the perspicuity of his discourse gives

---

Then a fashionable part of London.
A favorite of Charles II.
A Restoration dramatist.
0 A notorious character of the time.
1 One of the four great colleges of law in London.
2 Ancient Greek philosophers and critics.
3 Great English lawyers of the 15th and 16th centuries respectively.
Justices of the peace presided over the criminal
courts or quarter sessions. Those chosen to
sit with the higher court which met twice a
year were called "justices of the quorum."

14 engages
15 Cicero.
16 Part of one of the law colleges.
17 A dissolute tavern-resort.

the same pleasure that wit would in another man. He has made his fortune himself; and says, that England may be richer than other kingdoms, by as plain methods as he himself is richer than other men; though at the same time I can say this of him, that there is not a point in the compass but blows home a ship in which he is an owner.

Next to Sir Andrew in the club-room sits Captain Sentry, a gentleman of great courage, good understanding, but invincible modesty. He is one of those that deserve very well, but are very awkward at putting their talents within the observation of such as should take notice of them. He was some years a captain, and behaved himself with great gallantry in several engagements and at several sieges; but having a small estate of his own, and being next heir to Sir Roger, he has quitted a way of life in which no man can rise suitably to his merit who is not something of a courtier as well as a soldier. I have heard him often lament, that in a profession, where merit is placed in so conspicuous a view, impudence should get the better of modesty. When he has talked to this purpose, I never heard him make a sour expression, but frankly confess that he left the world because he was not fit for it. A strict honesty and an even regular behaviour are in themselves obstacles to him that must press through crowds, who endeavour at the same end with himself, the favour of a commander. He will, however, in his way of talk, excuse generals for not disposing according to men's desert, or inquiring into it; for, says he, that great man who has a mind to help me has as many to break through to come at me, as I have to come at him: therefore, he will conclude, that a man who would make a figure, especially in a military way, must get over all false modesty, and assist his patron against the importunity of other pretenders, by a proper assurance in his own vindication. He says it is a civil cowardice to be backward in asserting what you ought to expect, as it is a military fear to be slow in attacking when it is your duty. With this candour does the gentleman speak of himself and others. The same frankness runs through all his conversation. The military part of his life has furnished him with many adventures, in the relation of which he is very agreeable to the company; for he is never overbearing, though accustomed to command men in the utmost degree below him; nor ever too obsequious, from an habit of obeying men highly above him.

But that our society may not appear a of humourists,[18] unacquainted with the lantries and pleasures of the age, we among us the gallant Will Honeycomb, a tleman, who, according to his years, shoul in the decline of his life; but having ever very careful of his person, and always a very easy fortune, time has made but little impression, either by wrinkles on forehead, or traces in his brain. His pe is well turned, and of a good height. H very ready at that sort of discourse with w men usually entertain women. He has all life dressed very well; and remembers habi as others do men. He can smile when speaks to him, and laughs easily. He kr the history of every mode, and can inform from which of the French king's wenches wives and daughters had this manner of cur their hair, that way of placing their ho whose frailty was covered by such a sor petticoat; and whose vanity to show her made that part of the dress so short in a year. In a word, all his conversation knowledge has been in the female world. other men of his age will take notice to what such a minister said upon such and an occasion, he will tell you, when the D of Monmouth danced at court, such a wo was then smitten, another was taken with at the head of his troop in the park. In these important relations, he has ever al the same time received a kind glance, o blow of a fan, from some celebrated bea mother of the present Lord Such-a-one. If speak of a young commoner that said a li thing in the house, he starts up, "He has g blood in his veins; Tom Mirabel begot h the rogue cheated me in that affair: that yo fellow's mother used me more like a dog t any woman I ever made advances to." T way of talking of his very much enlivens conversation among us of a more sedate tu and I find there is not one of the compa but myself, who rarely speak at all, but spe of him as of that sort of man who is usu called a well-bred fine gentleman. To concl his character, where women are not concern he is an honest worthy man.

I cannot tell whether I am to account f whom I am next to speak of as one of company, for he visits us but seldom; when he does, it adds to every man else a n enjoyment of himself. He is a clergyman very philosophic man, of general learni

18 queer fellows   19 costumes

t sanctity of life, and the most exact good
ling. He has had the misfortune to be of
ry weak constitution, and, consequently,
ot accept of such cares and business as
erments in his function would oblige him
he is therefore among divines, what a
ber-counsellor is among lawyers. The
ity of his mind and the integrity of his
create him followers, as being eloquent or
advances others. He seldom introduces
subject he speaks upon; but we are so far
 in years, that he observes, when he is
ng us, an earnestness to have him fall on
 divine topic, which he always treats with
a authority, as one who has no interest in
world, as one who is hastening to the
ct of all his wishes, and conceives hope
 his decays and infirmities. These are my
nary companions.

OSEPH ADDISON (1672-1719)

SIR ROGER AT CHURCH.

Spectator, No. 112. Monday, July 9, 1711.

νάτους μὲν πρῶτα θεούς, νόμῳ ὡς διάκειται,
.   Pythag.

First, in obedience to thy country's rites,
Worship th' immortal gods.

am always very well pleased with a country
day, and think, if keeping holy the sev-
 day were only a human institution, it
ld be the best method that could have been
ght of for the polishing and civilizing of
kind. It is certain the country people
ld soon degenerate into a kind of savages
 barbarians, were there not such frequent
rns of a stated time, in which the whole
ge meet together with their best faces, and
heir cleanliest habits, to converse with one
ther upon indifferent subjects, hear their
es explained to them, and join together in
ration of the Supreme Being. Sunday clears
y the rust of the whole week, not only as it
eshes in their minds the notions of religion,
 as it puts both the sexes upon appearing
heir most agreeable forms, and exerting all
 qualities as are apt to give them a figure
the eye of the village. A country fellow
inguishes himself as much in the church-
d, as a citizen does upon the 'Change, the
le parish-politics being generally discussed
hat place either after sermon or before the
 rings.

My friend Sir Roger, being a good church-
man, has beautified the inside of his church
with several texts of his own choosing. He has
likewise given a handsome pulpit-cloth, and
railed in the communion-table at his own expense. He has often told me, that at his coming to his estate he found his parishioners very
irregular; and that in order to make them
kneel and join in the responses, he gave every
one of them a hassock and a common prayer-
book; and at the same time employed an itinerant singing-master, who goes about the country for that purpose, to instruct them rightly
in the tunes of the psalms: upon which they
now very much value themselves, and indeed
outdo most of the country churches that I have
ever heard.

As Sir Roger is landlord to the whole congregation, he keeps them in very good order,
and will suffer nobody to sleep in it besides
himself; for if by chance he has been surprised
into a short nap at sermon, upon recovering out
of it he stands up and looks about him, and if
he sees anybody else nodding, either wakes
them himself, or sends his servant to them.
Several other of the old knight's peculiarities
break out upon these occasions. Sometimes he
will be lengthening out a verse in the singing
psalms, half a minute after the rest of the congregation have done with it; sometimes when
he is pleased with the matter of his devotion,
he pronounces Amen three or four times to the
same prayer: and sometimes stands up when
everybody else is upon their knees, to count
the congregation, or see if any of his tenants
are missing.

I was yesterday very much surprised to hear
my old friend in the midst of the service calling out to one John Matthews to mind what he
was about, and not disturb the congregation.
This John Matthews it seems is remarkable for
being an idle fellow, and at that time was kick-
ing his heels for his diversion. This authority
of the knight, though exerted in that odd manner which accompanies him in all circumstances
of life, has a very good effect upon the parish,
who are not polite[1] enough to see anything
ridiculous in his behaviour; besides that the
general good sense and worthiness of his character make his friends observe these little
singularities as foils that rather set off than
blemish his good qualities.

As soon as the sermon is finished, nobody
presumes to stir till Sir Roger is gone out of
the church. The knight walks down from his

1 polished

seat in the chancel between a double row of his tenants, that stand bowing to him on each side: and every now and then inquires how such an one's wife, or mother, or son, or father do, whom he does not see at church; which is understood as a secret reprimand to the person that is absent.

The chaplain has often told me, that upon a catechising day, when Sir Roger has been pleased with a boy that answers well, he has ordered a Bible to be given him next day for his encouragement; and sometimes accompanies it with a flitch of bacon to his mother. Sir Roger has likewise added five pounds a-year to the clerk's place; and, that he may encourage the young fellows to make themselves perfect in the church service, has promised upon the death of the present incumbent, who is very old, to bestow it according to merit.

The fair understanding between Sir Roger and his chaplain, and their mutual concurrence in doing good, is the more remarkable, because the very next village is famous for the differences and contentions that rise between the parson and the squire, who live in a perpetual state of war. The parson is always preaching at the squire; and the squire, to be revenged on the parson, never comes to church. The squire has made all his tenants atheists and tithe-stealers;[2] while the parson instructs them every Sunday in the dignity of his order, and insinuates to them almost in every sermon that he is a better man than his patron. In short, matters are come to such an extremity, that the squire has not said his prayers either in public or private this half year; and that the parson threatens him, if he does not mend his manners, to pray for him in the face of the whole congregation.

Feuds of this nature, though too frequent in the country, are very fatal to the ordinary people; who are so used to be dazzled with riches, that they pay as much deference to the understanding of a man of an estate, as of a man of learning; and are very hardly brought to regard any truth, how important soever it may be, that is preached to them, when they know there are several men of five hundred a-year who do not believe it.

NED SOFTLY.

The Tatler, No. 163. Tuesday, April 25, 1710.

Idem inficeto est inficetior rure,
Simul poemata attigit; neque idem unquam

Æquè est beatus, ac poema cum scribit:
Tam gaudet in se, tamque se ipse miratur.
Nimirum idem omnes fallimur; neque est q
    quam
Quem non in aliquâ re videre Suffenum
Possis ——

                                   Catul. de Suffeno, xx. 14

Suffenus has no more wit than a mere clo when he attempts to write verses, and yet he never happier than when he is scribbling; much does he admire himself and his compo tions. And, indeed, this is the foible of eve one of us, for there is no man living who not a Suffenus in one thing or other.

I yesterday came hither[3] about two ho before the company generally make their a pearance, with a design to read over all newspapers; but, upon my sitting down, I w accosted by Ned Softly, who saw me from corner in the other end of the room, where found he had been writing something. "M Bickerstaff,"[4] says he, "I observe by a la Paper of yours, that you and I are just of humour; for you must know, of all i pertinences, there is nothing which I so mu hate as news. I never read a Gazette[5] in i life; and never trouble my head about o armies, whether they win or lose, or in wh part of the world they lie encamped." Wit out giving me time to reply, he drew a pap of verses out of his pocket, telling me, "th he had something which would entertain more agreeably; and that he would desire judgment upon every line, for that we h time enough before us until the compa came in."

Ned Softly is a very pretty poet, and a gre admirer of easy lines. Waller[6] is his favourit and as that admirable writer has the best a worst verses of any among our great Engli poets, Ned Softly, has got all the bad on without book; which he repeats upon occasio to show his reading, and garnish his convers tion. Ned is indeed a true English reader, i capable of relishing the great and master strokes of this art; but wonderfully please with the little Gothic[7] ornaments of epigra matical conceits, turns, points, and quibble which are so frequent in the most admired

2 Those who do not pay their church tax.

3 Will's Coffee House.
4 The assumed name of the editor of *The Tatler.* Steele had chosen it. See *Eng. Lit.,* p. 177.
5 The official court newspaper.
6 A very popular po of the 17th ce tury.
7 Used contemptuous as equivalent quaint or in ba taste.

ur English poets, and practised by those who want genius and strength to represent, after the manner of the ancients, simplicity in its natural beauty and perfection.

Finding myself unavoidably engaged in such a conversation, I was resolved to turn my pain into a pleasure, and to divert myself as well as I could with so very odd a fellow. "You must understand," says Ned, "that the sonnet I am going to read to you was written upon a lady, who showed me some verses of her own making, and is, perhaps, the best poet of our age. But you shall hear it."

Upon which he began to read as follows:

To Mira on Her Incomparable Poems.

When dress'd in laurel wreaths you shine,
    And tune your soft melodious notes,
You seem a sister of the Nine,
    Or Phœbus' self in petticoats.

I fancy, when your song you sing,
    (Your song you sing with so much art)
Your pen was plucked from Cupid's wing;
    For, ah! it wounds me like his dart.

"Why," says I, "this is a little nosegay of conceits, a very lump of salt: every verse has something in it that piques; and then the *dart* in the last line is certainly as pretty a sting in the tail of an epigram, for so I think you critics call it, as ever entered into the thought of a poet." "Dear Mr. Bickerstaff," says he, shaking me by the hand, "everybody knows you to be a judge of these things; and to tell you truly, I read over Roscommon's translation of 'Horace's Art of Poetry' three several times, before I sat down to write the sonnet which I have shown you. But you shall hear it again, and pray observe every line of it; for not one of them shall pass without your approbation.

When dress'd in laurel wreaths you shine,

"That is," says he, "when you have your garland on; when you are writing verses." To which I replied, "I know your meaning: a metaphor!" "The same," said he, and went on.

And tune your soft melodious notes.

Pray observe the gliding of that verse; there is scarce a consonant in it: I took care to make it run upon liquids. Give me your opinion of it." "Truly," said I, "I think it as good as the former." "I am very glad to hear you say so," says he; "but mind the next.

You seem a sister of the Nine.

"That is," says he, "you seem a sister of the Muses; for, if you look into ancient authors, you will find it was their opinion that there were nine of them." "I remember it very well," said I; "but pray proceed."

"Or Phœbus' self in petticoats."

"Phœbus," says he, "was the god of poetry. These little instances, Mr. Bickerstaff, show a gentleman's reading. Then, to take off from the air of learning, which Phœbus and the Muses had given to this first stanza, you may observe, how it falls all of a sudden into the familiar; 'in Petticoats'!

Or Phœbus' self in petticoats."

"Let us now," says I, "enter upon the second stanza; I find the first line is still a continuation of the metaphor,

I fancy, when your song you sing."

"It is very right," says he, "but pray observe the turn of words in those two lines. I was a whole hour in adjusting of them, and have still a doubt upon me, whether in the second line it should be 'Your song you sing;' or, 'You sing your song.' You shall hear them both:

I fancy, when your song you sing,
    (Your song you sing with so much art)
            or
I fancy, when your song you sing,
    (You sing your song with so much art.)"

"Truly," said I, "the turn is so natural either way, that you have made me almost giddy with it." "Dear sir," said he, grasping me by the hand, "you have a great deal of patience; but pray what do you think of the next verse?

Your pen was pluck'd from Cupid's wing."

"Think!" says I; "I think you have made Cupid look like a little goose." "That was my meaning," says he: "I think the ridicule is well enough hit off. But we come now to the last, which sums up the whole matter.

For, ah! it wounds me like his dart.

"Pray how do you like that *Ah!* doth it not make a pretty figure in that place? *Ah!*——it looks as if I felt the dart, and cried out as being pricked with it.

> For, ah! it wounds me like his dart.

"My friend Dick Easy," continued he, "assured me, he would rather have written that *Ah!* than to have been the author of the Æneid. He indeed objected, that I made Mira's pen like a quill in one of the lines, and like a dart in the other. But as to that——" "Oh! as to that," says I, "it is but supposing Cupid to be like a porcupine, and his quills and darts will be the same thing." He was going to embrace me for the hint; but half a dozen critics coming into the room, whose faces he did not like, he conveyed the sonnet into his pocket, and whispered me in the ear, "he would show it me again as soon as his man had written it over fair."

FROZEN WORDS.

The Tatler, No. 254   Thursday, November 23, 1710.

> Splendidè mendax——.
>   Hor. 2 Od. iii. 35.
> Gloriously false——.

There are no books which I more delight in than in travels, especially those that describe remote countries, and give the writer an opportunity of showing his parts without incurring any danger of being examined or contradicted. Among all the authors of this kind, our renowned countryman, Sir John Mandeville[1] has distinguished himself, by the copiousness of his invention, and the greatness of his genius. The second to Sir John I take to have been, Ferdinand Mendez Pinto,[2] a person of infinite adventure, and unbounded imagination. One reads the voyages of these two great wits, with as much astonishment as the travels of Ulysses in Homer, or of the Red-Cross Knight in Spenser. All is enchanted ground, and fairyland.

I have got into my hands, by great chance, several manuscripts of these two eminent authors, which are filled with greater wonders than any of those they have communicated to the public; and indeed, were they not so well attested, they would appear altogether improbable. I am apt to think the ingenious authors did not publish them with the rest of their works, lest they should pass for fictions and fables: a caution not unnecessary, when the reputation of their veracity was not yet established in the world. But as this reason has now no farther weight, I shall make the public a present of these curious pieces, at such times as I shall find myself unprovided with other subjects.

The present paper I intend to fill with an extract from Sir John's Journal, in which that learned and worthy knight gives an account of the freezing and thawing of several short speeches, which he made in the territories of Nova Zembla.[3] I need not inform my reader, that the author of "Hudibras"[4] alludes to this strange quality in that cold climate, when, speaking of abstracted notions clothed in a visible shape, he adds that apt simile,

> "Like words congeal'd in northern air."

Not to keep my reader any longer in suspense, the relation put into modern language, is as follows:

"We were separated by a storm in the latitude of seventy-three, insomuch, that only the ship which I was in, with a Dutch and French vessel, got safe into a creek of Nova Zembla. We landed, in order to refit our vessels, and store ourselves with provisions. The crew of each vessel made themselves a cabin of turf and wood, at some distance from each other, to fence themselves against the inclemencies of the weather, which was severe beyond imagination. We soon observed, that in talking to one another we lost several of our words, and could not hear one another at above two yards distance, and that too when we sat very near the fire. After much perplexity, I found that our words froze in the air, before they could reach the ears of the persons to whom they were spoken. I was soon confirmed in this conjecture, when, upon the increase of the cold, the whole company grew dumb, or rather deaf; for every man was sensible, as we afterwards found, that he spoke as well as ever; but the sounds no sooner took air than they were condensed and lost. It was now a miserable spectacle to see us nodding and gaping at one another, every man talking, and no man heard. One might observe a seaman that could hail

[1] See p. 63.
[2] A Portuguese adventurer and writer of the sixteenth century, now generally believed to have been veracious.

[3] An island in the Arctic ocean. The journal of William Barentz, a Dutch navigator who was shipwrecked there in 1596, may have afforded Addison a hint for this fancy.
[4] A poem satirizing the Puritans, by Samuel Butler.

a ship at a league's distance, beckoning with his hand, straining his lungs, and tearing his throat; but all in vain:

"—— Nec vox nec verba sequuntur.

"Nor voice, nor words ensued.

"We continued here three weeks in this dismal plight. At length, upon a turn of wind, the air about us began to thaw. Our cabin was immediately filled with a dry clattering sound, which I afterwards found to be the crackling of consonants that broke above our heads, and were often mixed with a gentle hissing, which I imputed to the letter *s*, that occurs so frequently in the English tongue. I soon after felt a breeze of whispers rushing by my ear; for those, being of a soft and gentle substance, immediately liquefied in the warm wind that blew across our cabin. These were soon followed by syllables and short words, and at length by entire sentences, that melted sooner or later, as they were more or less congealed; so that we now heard every thing that had been *spoken* during the whole three weeks that we had been *silent*, if I may use that expression. It was now very early in the morning, and yet, to my surprise, I heard somebody say, 'Sir John, it is midnight, and time for the ship's crew to go to-bed.' This I knew to be the pilot's voice; and, upon recollecting myself, I concluded that he had spoken these words to me some days before, though I could not hear them until the present thaw. My reader will easily imagine how the whole crew was amazed to hear every man talking, and see no man opening his mouth. In the midst of this great surprise we were all in, we heard a volley of oaths and curses, lasting for a long while, and uttered in a very hoarse voice, which I knew belonged to the boatswain, who was a very choleric fellow, and had taken his opportunity of cursing and swearing at me, when he thought I could not hear him; for I had several times given him the strappado[5] on that account, as I did not fail to repeat it for these his pious soliloquies, when I got him on shipboard.

"I must not omit the names of several beauties in Wapping,[6] which were heard every now and then, in the midst of a long sigh that accompanied them; as, 'Dear Kate!' 'Pretty Mrs. Peggy!' 'When shall I see my Sue again!' This betrayed several amours which had been concealed until that time, and furnished us with a great deal of mirth in our return to England.

"When this confusion of voices was pretty well over, though I was afraid to offer at speaking, as fearing I should not be heard, I proposed a visit to the Dutch cabin, which lay about a mile farther up in the country. My crew were extremely rejoiced to find they had again recovered their hearing; though every man uttered his voice with the same apprehensions that I had done,

"—— Et timidè verba intermissa retentat.

"And try'd his tongue, his silence softly broke.

"At about half-a-mile's distance from our cabin we heard the groanings of a bear, which at first startled us; but, upon enquiry, we were informed by some of our company, that he was dead, and now lay in salt, having been killed upon that very spot about a fortnight before, in the time of the frost. Not far from the same place, we were likewise entertained with some posthumous snarls, and barkings of a fox.

"We at length arrived at the little Dutch settlement; and, upon entering the room, found it filled with sighs that smelt of brandy, and several other unsavoury sounds, that were altogether inarticulate. My valet, who was an Irishman, fell into so great a rage at what he heard, that he drew his sword; but not knowing where to lay the blame, he put it up again. We were stunned with these confused noises, but did not hear a single word until about half-an-hour after; which I ascribed to the harsh and obdurate sounds of that language, which wanted more time than ours to melt, and become audible.

"After having here met with a very hearty welcome, we went to the cabin of the French, who, to make amends for their three weeks' silence, were talking and disputing with greater rapidity and confusion than I ever heard in an assembly, even of that nation. Their language, as I found, upon the first giving of the weather, fell asunder and dissolved. I was here convinced of an error, into which I had before fallen; for I fancied, that for the freezing of the sound, it was necessary for it to be wrapped up, and, as it were, preserved in breath: but I found my mistake when I heard the sound of a kit[7] playing a minuet over our heads. I

---

5 A severe form of military punishment which usually dislocated the arms.

6 A quarter of London along the Thames frequented by seamen.

7 A small fiddle.

asked the occasion of it; upon which one of the company told me that it would play there above a week longer; 'for,' says he, 'finding ourselves bereft of speech, we prevailed upon one of the company, who had his musical instrument about him, to play to us from morning to night; all which time was employed in dancing in order to dissipate our chagrin, and *tuer le temps.*"[8]

Here Sir John gives very good philosophical reason, why the kit could not be heard during the frost; but, as they are something prolix, I pass them over in silence, and shall only observe, that the honourable author seems, by his quotations, to have been well versed in the ancient poets, which perhaps raised his fancy above the ordinary pitch of historians, and very much contributed to the embellishment of his writings.

A COQUETTE'S HEART.

The Spectator, No. 281. Tuesday, January 22, 1712.

Pectoribus inhians spirantia consulit exta.
　　　　　　　　　　　Virg. Æn. iv. 64.
Anxious the reeking entrails he consults.

Having already given an account of the dissection of a beau's head, with the several discoveries made on that occasion; I shall here, according to my promise, enter upon the dissection of a coquette's heart, and communicate to the public such particularities as we observed in that curious piece of anatomy.

I should perhaps have waived this undertaking, had not I been put in mind of my promise by several of my unknown correspondents, who are very importunate with me to make an example of the coquette, as I have already done of the beau. It is therefore, in compliance with the request of friends, that I have looked over the minutes of my former dream, in order to give the public an exact relation of it, which I shall enter upon without farther preface.

Our operator, before he engaged in this visionary dissection, told us that there was nothing in his art more difficult than to lay open the heart of a coquette, by reason of the many labyrinths and recesses which are to be found in it, and which do not appear in the heart of any other animal.

He desired us first of all to observe the pericardium, or outward case of the heart,

which we did very attentively; and by the help of our glasses discerned in it millions of little scars, which seemed to have been occasioned by the points of innumerable darts and arrows that from time to time had glanced upon the outward coat; though we could not discover the smallest orifice by which any of them had entered and pierced the inward substance.

Every smatterer in anatomy knows that this pericardium, or case of the heart, contains in it a thin reddish liquor, supposed to be bred from the vapours which exhale out of the heart, and being stopped here, are condensed into this watery substance. Upon examining this liquor, we found that it had in it all the qualities of that spirit which is made use of in the thermometer to show the change of weather.

Nor must I here omit an experiment one of the company assured us he himself had made with this liquor, which he found in great quantity about the heart of a coquette whom he had formerly dissected. He affirmed to us that he had actually inclosed it in a small tube made after the manner of a weather-glass; but that, instead of acquainting him with the variations of the atmosphere, it showed him the qualities of those persons who entered the room where it stood. He affirmed also, that it rose at the approach of a plume of feathers, an embroidered coat, or a pair of fringed gloves; and that it fell as soon as an ill-shaped periwig, a clumsy pair of shoes, or an unfashionable coat came into his house. Nay, he proceeded so far as to assure us, that upon his laughing aloud when he stood by it, the liquor mounted very sensibly, and immediately sunk again upon his looking serious. In short, he told us that he knew very well by this invention, whenever he had a man of sense or a coxcomb in his room.

Having cleared away the pericardium, or the case, and liquor above-mentioned, we came to the heart itself. The outward surface of it was extremely slippery, and the mucro, or point, so very cold withal, that upon endeavouring to take hold of it, it glided through the fingers like a smooth piece of ice.

The fibres were turned and twisted in a more intricate and perplexed manner than they are usually found in other hearts; insomuch that the whole heart was wound up together like a Gordian knot, and must have had very irregular and unequal motions, while it was employed in its vital function.

One thing we thought very observable, namely, that upon examining all the vessels which ame into it, or issued out of it, we could not discover any communication that it had with the tongue.

We could not but take notice likewise that several of those little nerves in the heart which are affected by the sentiments of love, hatred, and other passions, did not descend to this before us from the brain, but from the muscles which lie about the eye.

Upon weighing the heart in my hand, I found it to be extremely light, and consequently very hollow, which I did not wonder at, when, upon looking into the inside of it, I saw multitudes of cells and cavities running one within another, as our historians describe the apartments of Rosamond's bower.* Several of these little hollows were stuffed with innumerable sorts of trifles, which I shall forbear giving any particular account of, and shall, therefore, only take notice of what lay first and uppermost, which, upon our unfolding it, and applying our microscopes to it, appeared to be a flame-coloured hood.

We are informed that the lady of this heart, when living, received the addresses of several who made love to her, and did not only give each of them encouragement, but made everyone she conversed with believe that she regarded him with an eye of kindness; for which reason we expected to have seen the impression of multitudes of faces among the several plaits and foldings of the heart; but to our great surprise not a single print of this nature discovered itself till we came into the very core and centre of it. We there observed a little figure, which, upon applying our glasses to it, appeared dressed in a very fantastic manner. The more I looked upon it, the more I thought I had seen the face before, but could not possibly recollect either the place or time; when at length one of the company, who had examined this figure more nicely than the rest, showed us plainly by the make of its face, and the several turns of its features, that the little idol which was thus lodged in the very middle of the heart was the deceased beau, whose head gave some account of in my last Tuesday's paper.

As soon as we had finished our dissection, we resolved to make an experiment of the heart, not being able to determine among ourselves the nature of its substance, which differed in so many particulars from that in the heart of other females. Accordingly, we laid it into a pan of burning coals, when we observed in it a certain salamandrine quality, that made it capable of living in the midst of fire and flame, without being consumed or so much as singed.

As we were admiring this strange phenomenon, and standing round the heart in a circle, it gave a most prodigious sigh, or rather crack, and dispersed all at once in smoke and vapour. This imaginary noise, which methought was louder than the burst of a cannon, produced such a violent shake in my brain, that it dissipated the fumes of sleep, and left me in an instant broad awake.

THE VISION OF MIRZA.

The Spectator, No. 159.   Saturday, September 1, 1711.

—Omnem, quæ nunc obducta tuenti
Mortales hebetat visus tibi, et humida circum
Caligat, nubem eripiam—

$$\text{Virg. Æn. ii. 604.}$$

The cloud, which, intercepting the clear light,
Hangs o'er thy eyes, and blunts thy mortal
    sight,
I will remove—

When I was at Grand Cairo, I picked up several Oriental manuscripts, which I have still by me. Among others I met with one entitled The Visions of Mirza, which I have read over with great pleasure. I intend to give it to the public when I have no other entertainment for them; and shall begin with the first vision, which I have translated word for word as follows:—

"On the fifth day of the moon, which according to the custom of my forefathers I always keep holy, after having washed myself, and offered up my morning devotions, I ascended the high hills of Bagdad, in order to pass the rest of the day in meditation and prayer. As I was here airing myself on the tops of the mountains, I fell into a profound contemplation on the vanity of human life; and passing from one thought to another, 'Surely,' said I, 'man is but a shadow, and life a dream.' Whilst I was thus musing, I cast my eyes towards the summit of a rock that was not far from me, where I discovered one in the habit of a shepherd, with a musical instrument in his hand. As I looked upon him he applied it to his lips, and began to play upon it. The sound of it was exceedingly sweet, and wrought into a variety of tunes that

Henry II., it was said, built a labyrinth to conceal the abode of "Fair Rosamond."

were inexpressibly melodious, and altogether different from anything I had ever heard. They put me in mind of those heavenly airs that are played to the departed souls of good men upon their first arrival in Paradise, to wear out the impressions of their last agonies, and qualify them for the pleasures of that happy place. My heart melted away in secret raptures.

"I had been often told that the rock before me was the haunt of a Genius;[1] and that several had been entertained with music who had passed by it, but never heard that the musician had before made himself visible. When he had raised my thoughts by those transporting airs which he played to taste the pleasures of his conversation, as I looked upon him like one astonished, he beckoned to me, and by the waving of his hand directed me to approach the place where he sat. I drew near with that reverence which is due to a superior nature; and as my heart was entirely subdued by the captivating strains I had heard, I fell down at his feet and wept. The Genius smiled upon me with a look of compassion and affability that familiarized him to my imagination, and at once dispelled all the fears and apprehensions with which I approached him. He lifted me from the ground, and taking me by the hand, 'Mirza,' said he, 'I have heard thee in thy soliloquies; follow me.'

"He then led me to the highest pinnacle of the rock, and placing me on the top of it, 'Cast thy eyes eastward,' said he, 'and tell me what thou seest.' 'I see,' said I, 'a huge valley, and a prodigious tide of water rolling through it.' 'The valley that thou seest,' said he, 'is the Vale of Misery, and the tide of water that thou seest is part of the great Tide of Eternity.' 'What is the reason,' said I, 'that the tide I see rises out of a thick mist at one end, and again loses itself in a thick mist at the other?' 'What thou seest,' said he, 'is that portion of eternity which is called time, measured out by the sun, and reaching from the beginning of the world to its consummation. Examine now,' said he, 'this sea that is bounded with darkness at both ends, and tell me what thou discoverest in it.' 'I see a bridge,' said I, 'standing in the midst of the tide.' 'The bridge thou seest,' said he, 'is Human Life: consider it attentively.' Upon a more leisurely survey of it, I found that it consisted of three-score and ten entire arches, with several broken arches, which added to those that were entire,

made up the number about a hundred. As I was counting the arches, the Genius told me that this bridge consisted at first of a thousand arches; but that a great flood swept away the rest, and left the bridge in the ruinous condition I now beheld it. 'But tell me farther,' said he, 'what thou discoverest on it.' 'I see multitudes of people passing over it,' said I, 'and a black cloud hanging on each end of it.' As I looked more attentively, I saw several of the passengers dropping through the bridge into the great tide that flowed underneath it; and upon farther examination, perceived there were innumerable trap-doors that lay concealed in the bridge, which the passengers no sooner trod upon, but they fell through them into the tide, and immediately disappeared. These hidden pit-falls were set very thick at the entrance of the bridge, so that throngs of people no sooner broke through the cloud, but many of them fell into them. They grew thinner towards the middle, but multiplied and lay closer together towards the end of the arches that were entire.

"There were indeed some persons, but their number was very small, that continued a kind of hobbling march on the broken arches, but fell through one after another, being quite tired and spent with so long a walk.

"I passed some time in the contemplation of this wonderful structure, and the great variety of objects which it presented. My heart was filled with a deep melancholy to see several dropping unexpectedly in the midst of mirth and jollity, and catching at everything that stood by them to save themselves. Some were looking up towards the heavens in a thoughtful posture, and in the midst of a speculation stumbled and fell out of sight. Multitudes were very busy in the pursuit of bubbles that glittered in their eyes and danced before them; but often when they thought themselves within the reach of them, their footing failed and down they sunk. In this confusion of objects, I observed some who ran to and fro upon the bridge, thrusting several persons on trap-doors which did not seem to lie in their way, and which they might have escaped had they not been thus forced upon them.

"The Genius seeing me indulge myself on this melancholy prospect, told me I had dwelt long enough upon it. 'Take thine eyes off the bridge,' said he, 'and tell me if thou yet seest anything thou dost not comprehend.' Upon looking up, 'What mean,' said I, 'those great flights of birds that are perpetually hovering

1 spirit

about the bridge, and settling upon it from time to time? I see vultures, harpies, ravens, cormorants, and among many other feathered creatures several little winged boys, that perch in great numbers upon the middle arches. 'These,' said the Genius, 'are Envy, Avarice, Superstition, Despair, Love, with the like cares and passions that infest human life.'

"I here fetched a deep sigh. 'Alas,' said I, 'Man was made in vain! how is he given away to misery and mortality! tortured in life, and swallowed up in death!' The Genius being moved with compassion towards me, bid me quit so uncomfortable a prospect. 'Look no more,' said he, 'on man in the first stage of his existence, in his setting out for eternity; but cast thine eye on that thick mist into which the tide bears the several generations of mortals that fall into it. I directed my sight as I was ordered, and (whether or no the good Genius strengthened it with any supernatural force, or dissipated part of the mist that was before too thick for the eye to penetrate) I saw the valley opening at the farther end, and spreading forth into an immense ocean, that had a huge rock of adamant running through the midst of it, and dividing it into two equal parts. The clouds still rested on one half of it, insomuch that I could discover nothing in it; but the other appeared to me a vast ocean planted with innumerable islands, that were covered with fruits and flowers, and interwoven with a thousand little shining seas that ran among them. I could see persons dressed in glorious habits with garlands upon their heads, passing among the trees, lying down by the sides of fountains, or resting on beds of flowers; and could hear a confused harmony of singing birds, falling waters, human voices, and musical instruments. Gladness grew in me upon the discovery of so delightful a scene. I wished for the wings of an eagle, that I might fly away to those happy seats; but the Genius told me there was no passage to them, except through the gates of death that I saw opening every moment upon the bridge. 'The islands,' said he, 'that lie so fresh and green before thee, and with which the whole face of the ocean appears spotted as far as thou canst see, are more in number than the sands on the sea-shore: there are myriads of islands behind those which thou here discoverest, reaching farther than thine eye, or even thine imagination can extend itself. These are the mansions of good men after death, who, according to the degree and kinds of virtue in which they

excelled, are distributed among these several islands, which abound with pleasures of different kinds and degrees, suitable to the relishes and perfections of those who are settled in them: every island is a paradise accommodated to its respective inhabitants. Are not these, O Mirza, habitations worth contending for? Does life appear miserable that gives thee opportunities of earning such a reward? Is death to be feared that will convey thee to so happy an existence? Think not man was made in vain, who has such an eternity reserved for him.' I gazed with inexpressible pleasure on these happy islands. At length, said I, 'Show me now, I beseech thee, the secrets that lie hid under those dark clouds which cover the ocean on the other side of the rock of adamant.' The Genius making me no answer, I turned me about to address myself to him a second time, but I found that he had left me; I then turned again to the vision which I had been so long contemplating; but instead of the rolling tide, the arched bridge, and the happy islands, I saw nothing but the long hollow valley of Bagdad, with oxen, sheep, and camels grazing upon the sides of it.''

MATTHEW PRIOR (1664-1721)

TO A CHILD OF QUALITY FIVE YEARS OLD

Lords, knights, and 'squires, the numerous band,
    That wear the fair Miss Mary's fetters,
Were summoned by her high command,
    To show their passions by their letters.

My pen among the rest I took,
    Lest those bright eyes that cannot read
Should dart their kindling fires, and look
    The power they have to be obeyed.   8

Nor quality, nor reputation,
    Forbid me yet my flame to tell,
Dear Five-years-old befriends my passion,
    And I may write till she can spell.

For, while she makes her silk-worms beds
    With all the tender things I swear;
Whilst all the house my passion reads
    In papers round her baby's hair;   16

She may receive and own my flame,
    For, though the strictest prudes should know it,
She'll pass for a most virtuous dame
    And I for an unhappy poet.

Then too, alas! when she shall tear
　The lines some younger rival sends,
She 'll give me leave to write, I fear,
　And we shall still continue friends.　24

For, as our different ages move,
　'Tis so ordained, (would Fate but mend it!)
That I shall be past making love,
　When she begins to comprehend it.

A SIMILE

Dear Thomas, didst thou never pop
Thy head into a tinman's shop?
There, Thomas, didst thou never see
('Tis but by way of simile)
A squirrel spend his little rage
In jumping round a rolling cage?
The cage, as either side turned up,
Striking a ring of bells a-top?

Moved in the orb, pleased with the chimes
The foolish creature thinks he climbs:　10
But here or there, turn wood or wire,
He never gets two inches higher.

So fares it with those merry blades,
That frisk it under Pindus'[1] shades.
In noble songs, and lofty odes,
They tread on stars, and talk with gods;
Still dancing in an airy round,
Still pleased with their own verses' sound;
Brought back, how fast soe'er they go
Always aspiring, always low.

AN ODE

The merchant, to secure his treasure,
　Conveys it in a borrowed name:
Euphelia serves to grace my measure;
　But Cloe is my real flame.

My softest verse, my darling lyre,
　Upon Euphelia's toilet lay;
When Cloe noted[2] her desire
　That I should sing, that I should play.　8

My lyre I tune, my voice I raise;
　But with my numbers[3] mix my sighs:
And whilst I sing Euphelia's praise,
　I fix my soul on Cloe's eyes.

Fair Cloe blushed: Euphelia frowned:
　I sung and gazed: I played and trembled:
And Venus to the Loves around
　Remarked, how ill we all dissembled.　16

[1] A mountain in Greece　[2] denoted, expressed
　sacred to the Muses.　[3] verses

A BETTER ANSWER*

Dear Cloe, how blubbered is that pretty fac[e]
　Thy cheek all on fire, and thy hair all u[n]
　curled:
Prythee quit this caprice; and (as old Falsta[ff]
　says[4])
　Let us e'en talk a little like folks of th[e]
　world.

How canst thou presume thou hast leave [to]
　destroy
　The beauties which Venus but lent to th[y]
　keeping?
Those looks were designed to inspire love an[d]
　joy:
　More ord'nary eyes may serve people f[or]
　weeping.

To be vext at a trifle or two that I writ,
　Your judgment at once and my passion yo[u]
　wrong:
You take that for fact which will scarce b[e]
　found wit:
　Odds life! must one swear to the truth of [a]
　song?

What I speak, my fair Cloe, and what I writ[e]
　shows
　The difference there is betwixt Nature an[d]
　Art:
I court others in verse; but I love thee i[n]
　prose:
　And they have my whimsies; but thou ha[st]
　my heart.

The god of us verse-men (you know, Chiid[,])
　the sun,
　How after his journeys he sets up his rest[:]
If at morning o'er earth 'tis his fancy to ru[n]
　At night he declines on his Thetis's breas[t.]

So when I am wearied with wandering all day[,]
　To thee, my delight, in the evening I come[:]
No matter what beauties I saw in my way;
　They were but my visits, but thou art m[y]
　home.

Then finish, dear Cloe, this pastoral war;
　And let us, like Horace and Lydia,[5] agree[:]
For thou art a girl so much brighter than he[r,]
　As he was a poet sublimer than me.

[4] See 2 *Henry IV.*, V,　[5] Horace addressed man[y]
　iii, 101.　　　　　　　of his odes t[o]
　　　　　　　　　　　　　"Lydia."
* This poem was preceded by one called *An Answe[r]
　to Cloe Jealous.* (Prior's "Cloe," perhaps fo[r]
　distinction, has no *h* in her name.)

JOHN GAY (1685-1732)

FROM FABLES

XLIV. THE HOUND AND THE HUNTSMAN

Impertinence at first is borne
With heedless slight, or smiles of scorn;
Teased into wrath, what patience bears
The noisy fool who perseveres?

The morning wakes, the Huntsman sounds,
At once rush forth the joyful hounds.
They seek the wood with eager pace,
Through bush, through brier, explore the chase.
Now scattered wide, they try the plain,
And snuff the dewy turf in vain.   10
What care, what industry, what pains!
What universal silence reigns!
Ringwood, a Dog of little fame,
Young, pert, and ignorant of game,
At once displays his babbling throat;
The pack, regardless of the note,
Pursue the scent; with louder strain
Still persists to vex the train.
The Huntsman to the clamour flies;
The smacking lash he smartly plies.   20
His ribs all welked,[6] with howling tone
The puppy thus expressed his moan:
"I know the music of my tongue
Long since the pack with envy stung.
What will not spite?[7] These bitter smarts
I owe to my superior parts."
"When puppies prate," the Huntsman cried,
"They show both ignorance and pride:
Fools may our scorn, not envy, raise,
For envy is a kind of praise.   30
Had not thy forward noisy tongue
Proclaimed thee always in the wrong,
Thou might'st have mingled with the rest,
And ne'er thy foolish nose confest.
But fools, to talking ever prone,
Are sure to make their follies known."

XLV. THE POET AND THE ROSE

I hate the man who builds his name
On ruins of another's fame.
Thus prudes, by characters o'erthrown,
Imagine that they raise their own.
Thus scribblers, covetous of praise,
Think slander can transplant the bays.
Beauties and bards have equal pride,
With both all rivals are decried.
Who praises Lesbia's eyes and feature,
Must call her sister awkward creature;   10
For the kind flattery's sure to charm,
When we some other nymph disarm.

6 Covered with ridges
7 Understand "do."

As in the cool of early day
A Poet sought the sweets of May,
The garden's fragrant breath ascends,
And every stalk with odour bends.
A rose he plucked, he gazed, admired,
Thus singing as the Muse inspired:

"Go Rose, my Chloe's bosom grace;
    How happy should I prove,   20
Might I supply that envied place
    With never-fading love!
There, Phœnix-like, beneath her eye,
Involved in fragrance, burn and die!

"Know, hapless flower, that thou shalt find
    More fragrant roses there;
I see thy withering head reclined
    With envy and despair!
One common fate we both must prove;
You die with envy, I with love."   30

"Spare your comparisons," replied
An angry Rose who grew beside.
"Of all mankind you should not flout us;
What can a Poet do without us?
In every love-song roses bloom;
We lend you colour and perfume.
Does it to Chloe's charms conduce,
To found her praise on our abuse?
Must we, to flatter her, be made
To wither, envy, pine, and fade?"   40

ALEXANDER POPE (1688-1744)

ODE ON ST. CECILIA'S DAY.*

1

Descend, ye Nine! descend and sing:
The breathing instruments inspire;
Wake into voice each silent string,
    And sweep the sounding lyre!
In a sadly-pleasing strain
Let the warbling lute complain:
    Let the loud trumpet sound,

* This ode, composed in 1708, when Pope was but twenty years of age, is interesting chiefly for comparison with the odes written by Dryden for similar occasions. Pope has drawn freely upon classical mythology—the nine Muses, Morpheus, god of dreams, the voyage of the Argonauts with Orpheus drawing the trees of Mt. Pelion down to the sea by the sweetness of his strain, and especially the sad story of Orpheus' descent into Hades to win back his lost Eurydice only to lose her again and wander forlorn until the jealous and enraged Bacchantes stoned him to death and threw his limbs into the Hebrus. It is pointed out by Mr. W. J. Courthope that Dryden, by weaving in history instead of legend, secured greater human interest.

Till the roofs all around
The shrill echoes rebound:
While in more lengthened notes and slow,   10
The deep, majestic, solemn organs blow.
Hark! the numbers soft and clear,
Gently steal upon the ear;
Now louder, and yet louder rise
And fill with spreading sounds the skies;
Exulting in triumph now swell the bold notes,
In broken air, trembling, the wild music floats;
Till, by degrees, remote and small,
The strains decay,
And melt away,   20
In a dying, dying fall.

2

By music, minds an equal temper know,
Nor swell too high, nor sink too low.
If in the breast tumultuous joys arise,
Music her soft, assuasive voice applies;
Or, when the soul is pressed with cares,
Exalts her in enlivening airs.
Warriors she fires with animated sounds;
Pours balm into the bleeding lover's wounds;
Melancholy lifts her head,   30
Morpheus rouses from his bed,
Sloth unfolds her arms and wakes,
Listening Envy drops her snakes;
Intestine war no more our passions wage,
And giddy factions hear away their rage.

3

But when our country's cause provokes to arms,
How martial music every bosom warms!
So when the first bold vessel dared the seas,
High on the stern the Thracian raised his
strain,
While Argo saw her kindred trees   40
Descend from Pelion to the main.
Transported demi-gods stood round,
And men grew heroes at the sound,
Inflamed with glory's charms:
Each chief his sevenfold shield displayed,
And half unsheathed the shining blade
And seas, and rocks, and skies rebound,
To arms, to arms, to arms!

4

But when through all th' infernal bounds,
Which flaming Phlegethon surrounds,   50
Love, strong as Death, the poet led
To the pale nations of the dead,
What sounds were heard,
What scenes appeared,
O'er all the dreary coasts!

Dreadful gleams
Dismal screams,
Fires that glow,
Shrieks of woe,
Sullen moans,
Hollow groans,
And cries of tortured ghosts!
But hark! he strikes the golden lyre;
And see! the tortured ghosts respire,
See, shady forms advance!
Thy stone, O Sisyphus, stands still,
Ixion rests upon his wheel,
And the pale spectres dance!
The Furies sink upon their iron beds,
And snakes uncurled hang listening round
heads.

5

By the streams that ever flow,
By the fragrant winds that blow
O'er th' Elysian flowers;
By those happy souls who dwell
In yellow meads of asphodel,
Or amaranthine bowers;
By the hero's armed shades,
Glittering through the gloomy glades,
By the youths that died for love,
Wandering in the myrtle grove,
Restore, restore Eurydice to life:
Oh take the husband, or return the wife!

He sung, and hell consented
To hear the poet's prayer:
Stern Proserpine relented,
And gave him back the fair.
Thus song could prevail
O'er death, and o'er hell,
A conquest how hard and how glorious!
Though fate had fast bound her
With Styx nine times round her,
Yet music and love were victorious.

6

But soon, too soon, the lover turns his eyes
Again she falls, again she dies, she dies!
How wilt thou now the fatal sisters[1] move
No crime was thine, if 'tis no crime to love
Now under hanging mountains,
Beside the fall of fountains,
Or where Hebrus wanders,
Rolling in meanders,
All alone,
Unheard, unknown,
He makes his moan;

1 The three fates.

And calls her ghost.
r ever, ever, ever lost!
w with Furies surrounded,
spairing, confounded,
 trembles, he glows,
iidst Rhodope's² snows;
wild as the winds, o'er the desert he flies;
! Hæmus² resounds with the Bacchanals'
    cries—
            Ah see, he dies!   112
 even in death Eurydice he sung,
dice still trembled on his tongue,
Eurydice the woods,
Eurydice the floods,
dice the rocks, and hollow mountains rung.

7

sic the fiercest grief can charm,
d fate's severest rage disarm:
sic can soften pain to ease,   120
d make despair and madness please:
Our joys below it can improve,
And antedate the bliss above.
 the divine Cecilia found,
to her Maker's praise confined the sound.
 the full organ joins the tuneful choir,
' immortal powers incline their ear,
 on the swelling notes our souls aspire,
 solemn airs improve the sacred fire;
d angels lean from heaven to hear.   130
rpheus now no more let poets tell,
right Cecilia greater power is given;
 numbers raised a shade from hell,
Iers lift the soul to heaven.

FROM AN ESSAY ON CRITICISM.

hard to say, if greater want of skill
r in writing or in judging ill;
of the two, less dangerous is th' offence
 e our patience, than mislead our sense.
 few in that, but numbers err in this,
 ensure wrong for one who writes amiss;
 l might once himself alone expose,
 one in verse makes many more in prose.
with our judgments as our watches, none
 st alike, yet each believes his own.   10
ets as true genius is but rare,
 taste as seldom is the critic's share;
 must alike from Heaven derive their light,
 born to judge, as well as those to write.
 uch teach others, who themselves excel.
 ensure freely who have written well.
 rs are partial to their wit, 'tis true,
 re not critics to their judgment too?
 untain of Thrace.

Yet if we look more closely we shall find
Most have the seeds of judgment in their
    mind: 20
Nature affords at least a glimmering light;
The lines, though touched but faintly, are
    drawn right.
But as the slightest sketch, if justly traced,
Is by ill-colouring but the more disgraced,
So by false learning is good sense defaced.
.   .   .   .
First follow Nature and your judgment
    frame
By her just standard, which is still the same:
Unerring Nature, still divinely bright,   70
One clear, unchanged, and universal light,
Life, force, and beauty, must to all impart,
At once the source, and end, and test of Art.
Art from that fund each just supply provides,
Works without show, and without pomp pre-
    sides;
In some fair body thus th' informing[1] soul
With spirits feeds, with vigour fills the whole,
Each motion guides, and every nerve sustains;
Itself unseen, but in th' effects, remains.
Some, to whom Heaven in wit* has been pro-
    fuse,
Want as much more to turn it to its use;   81
For wit and judgment often are at strife;
Though meant each other's aid, like man and
    wife.
'Tis more to guide, than spur the Muse's
    steed;
Restrain his fury, than provoke his speed;
The wingèd courser, like a generous horse,
Shows most true mettle when you check his
    course.
Those rules of old discovered, not devised,
Are nature still, but nature methodized;
Nature, like liberty, is but restrained   90
By the same laws which first herself ordained.
Hear how learn'd Greece her useful rules
    indites,
When to repress and when indulge our flights;
High on Parnassus' top² her sons she showed,
And pointed out those arduous paths they
    trod;
Held from afar, aloft, th' immortal prize,
And urged the rest by equal steps to rise.
Just precepts thus from great examples given,
She drew from them what they derived from
    Heaven.
The generous critic fanned the poet's fire,   100

1 animating
2 The abode of Apollo and the Muses; figurative
    for the heights of poetic fame.
* This word has here the rather special 18th cen-
    tury meaning of brilliancy of intellect. talent

And taught the world with reason to admire.
Then Criticism the Muse's handmaid proved,
To dress her charms and make her more be-
    loved:
But following wits from that intention strayed,
Who could not win the mistress, wooed the
    maid;
Against the poets their own arms they turned,
Sure to hate most the men from whom they
    learned.
So modern 'pothecaries, taught the art
By doctor's bills[3] to play the doctor's part,
Bold in the practice of mistaken rules,   110
Prescribe, apply, and call their masters fools.
Some on the leaves of ancient authors prey,
Nor time nor moths e'er spoiled so much as
    they.
Some drily plain without invention's aid,
Write dull receipts how poems may be made;
These leave the sense, their learning to display,
And those explain the meaning quite away.
  You then whose judgment the right course
    would steer,
Know well each ancient's proper character;
His fable,[4] subject, scope in every page;   120
Religion, country, genius of his age;
Without all these at once before your eyes,
Cavil you may, but never criticise.
Be Homer's works your study and delight,
Read them by day, and meditate by night;
Thence form your judgment, thence your max-
    ims bring,
And trace the Muses upward to their spring.
Still with itself compared, his text peruse;
And let your comment be the Mantuan Muse.[5]
  When first young Maro[5] in his boundless
    mind
A work t' outlast immortal Rome designed, 131
Perhaps he seemed above the critic's law,
And but from nature's fountains scorned to
    draw;
But when t' examine every part he came,
Nature and Homer were, he found, the same.
Convinced, amazed, he checks the bold design;
And rules as strict his laboured work confine,
As if the Stagirite[6] o'erlooked each line.
Learn hence for ancient rules a just esteem;
To copy nature is to copy them.   140
  Some beauties yet no precepts can declare,
For there's a happiness as well as care.
Music resembles poetry, in each
Are nameless graces which no methods teach,
And which a master-hand alone can reach.
If, where the rules not far enough extend,

(Since rules were made but to promote the
    end)
Some lucky licence answer to the full
Th' intent proposed, that licence is a rule.
Thus Pegasus,[7] a nearer way to take,
May boldly deviate from the common track.
Great wits sometimes may gloriously offend,
And rise to faults true critics dare not men[d]
From vulgar bounds with brave disorder pa[rt]
And snatch a grace beyond the reach of art,
Which, without passing through the judgme[nt]
    gains
The heart, and all its end at once attains.
In prospects thus, some objects please our ey[es]
Which out of nature's common order rise,
The shapeless rock, or hanging precipice.
But though the ancients thus their rules inva[de]
(As kings dispense with laws themselves ha[ve]
    made)
Moderns beware! or if you must offend
Against the precept, ne'er transgress its en[d]
Let it be seldom, and compelled by need;
And have, at least, their precedent to plead.
The critic else proceeds without remorse,
Seizes your fame and puts his laws in force.
  I know there are to whose presumptuo[us]
    thoughts
Those freer beauties, even in them, se[em]
    faults.
Some figures monstrous and mis-shaped appe[ar]
Considered singly, or beheld too near,
Which, but proportioned to their light or pla[ce]
Due distance reconciles to form and grace.
A prudent chief not always must display
His powers in equal ranks, and fair array,
But with th' occasion and the place comply,
Conceal his force, nay, seem sometimes to f[ly]
Those oft are stratagems which errors seem,
Nor is it Homer nods, but we that dream.

  .   .   .   .

  Of all the causes which conspire to blind
Man's erring judgment, and misguide the mi[nd]
What the weak head with strongest bias ru[les]
Is pride, the never-failing vice of fools.
Whatever nature has in worth denied,
She gives in large recruits of needful pride;
For as in bodies, thus in souls, we find
What wants in blood and spirits, swelled [with]
    wind:
Pride, where wit fails, steps in to our defen[ce]
And fills up all the mighty void of sense.
If once right reason drives that cloud away,
Truth breaks upon us with resistless day.
Trust not yourself; but your defects to kno[w]
Make use of every friend—and every foe.

3 prescriptions
4 story, plot
5 Virgil.
6 Aristotle, the foremost critic of ancient times.
7 The winged horse of the Muses.

A little learning is a dangerous thing;
Drink deep, or taste not the Pierian spring:[8]
There shallow draughts intoxicate the brain,
And drinking largely sobers us again.
Fired at first sight with what the Muse imparts,
In fearless youth we tempt[9] the heights of arts, 220
While from the bounded level of our mind
Short views we take, nor see the lengths behind;
But more advanced, behold with strange surprise
New distant scenes of endless science rise!
So pleased at first the towering Alps we try
Mount o'er the vales, and seem to tread the sky,
Th' eternal snows appear already past,
And the first clouds and mountains seem the last;
But, those attained, we tremble to survey
The growing labours of the lengthened way, 230
Th' increasing prospect tires our wandering eyes,
Hills peep o'er hills, and Alps on Alps arise!
A perfect judge will read each work of wit
With the same spirit that its author writ:
Survey the whole, nor seek slight faults to find
Where nature moves, and rapture warms the mind;
Nor lose, for that malignant dull delight,
The generous pleasure to be charmed with wit.
But in such lays as neither ebb nor flow,
Correctly cold, and regularly low, 240
That shunning faults, one quiet tenor keep,
We cannot blame indeed—but we may sleep.
In wit, as nature, what affects our hearts
Is not th' exactness of peculiar parts;
'Tis not a lip, or eye, we beauty call,
But the joint force and full result of all.
Thus when we view some well-proportioned dome,
(The world's just wonder, and even thine, O Rome!)
No single parts unequally surprise,
All comes united to th' admiring eyes; 250
No monstrous height, or breadth, or length appear;
The whole at once is bold, and regular.
Whoever thinks a faultless piece to see,
Thinks what ne'er was, nor is, nor e'er shall be.
In every work regard the writer's end,
Since none can compass more than they intend;
And if the means be just, the conduct true,

Applause, in spite of trivial faults, is due.
As men of breeding, sometimes men of wit,
T' avoid great errors, must the less commit:
Neglect the rules each verbal critic lays, 261
For not to know some trifles, is a praise.
Most critics, fond of some subservient art,
Still make the whole depend upon a part:
They talk of principles, but notions prize,
And all to one loved folly sacrifice.
Once on a time, La Mancha's knight,[10] they say,
A certain bard encountering on the way,
Discoursed in terms as just, with looks as sage,
As e'er could Dennis,[11] of the Grecian stage; 271
Concluding all were desperate sots and fools,
Who durst depart from Aristotle's rules.
Our author, happy in a judge so nice,
Produced his play, and begged the knight's advice;
Made him observe the subject, and the plot,
The manners, passions, unities;[12] what not?
All which, exact to rule, were brought about,
Were but a combat in the lists left out.
"What! leave the combat out?" exclaims the knight;
Yes, or we must renounce the Stagirite.[6] 280
"Not so, by Heaven" (he answers in a rage),
"Knights, squires, and steeds, must enter on the stage."
So vast a throng the stage can ne'er contain.
"Then build a new, or act it in a plain."
Thus critics, of less judgment than caprice,
Curious not knowing, not exact but nice,
Form short ideas; and offend in arts,
(As most in manners) by a love to parts.
Some to conceit[13] alone their taste confine,
And glittering thoughts struck out at every line; 290
Pleased with a work where nothing's just or fit;
One glaring chaos and wild heap of wit.
Poets like painters, thus unskilled to trace
The naked nature and the living grace,
With gold and jewels cover every part,
And hide with ornaments their want of art.
True wit is nature to advantage dressed,
What oft was thought, but ne'er so well expressed;
Something, whose truth convinced at sight we find,

8 At the foot of Mt. Olympus, reputed birthplace of the Muses.
9 attempt

10 Don Quixote (in a spurious addition to Cervantes' work).
11 John Dennis, a critic of the time, the author of unsuccessful tragedies.
12 Aristotle's three "unities" of time, place, and action. (See Eng. Lit., p. 99.)
13 extravagant fancy

That gives us back the image of our mind. 300
As shades more sweetly recommend the light,
So modest plainness sets off sprightly wit.
For works may have more wit than does them good,
As bodies perish through excess of blood.
 Others for language all their care express,
And value books, as women men, for dress:
Their praise is still,—the style is excellent:
The sense they humbly take upon content.14
Words are like leaves; and where they most abound,
Much fruit of sense beneath is rarely found:
False eloquence, like the prismatic glass, 311
Its gaudy colours spreads on every place;
The face of nature we no more survey,
All glares alike, without distinction gay:
But true expression, like th' unchanging sun,
Clears and improves whate'er it shines upon,
It gilds all objects, but it alters none.
Expression is the dress of thought, and still
Appears more decent, as more suitable;
A vile conceit in pompous words expressed, 320
Is like a clown in regal purple dressed:
For different styles with different subjects sort,
As several garbs with country, town, and court.
Some by old words to fame have made pretence,
Ancients in phrase, mere moderns in their sense;
Such laboured nothings, in so strange a style,
Amaze th' unlearn'd, and make the learnèd smile.
Unlucky, as Fungoso15 in the play,
These sparks with awkward vanity display
What the fine gentleman wore yesterday; 330
And but so mimic ancient wits at best,
As apes our grandsires in their doublets drest.
In words, as fashions, the same rule will hold;
Alike fantastic, if too new, or old:
Be not the first by whom the new are tried,
Nor yet the last to lay the old aside.

THE RAPE OF THE LOCK.*

CANTO I

What dire offence from amorous causes springs,
What mighty contests rise from trivial things,
I sing.—This verse to Caryll, Muse! is due;

14 on trust
15 A character in Jonson's *Every Man Out of His Humour* who vainly tries to keep up with court fashions.
* This mock-heroic, or, as Pope styled it, "heroi-comical poem," was published first in 1712

This, e'en Belinda may vouchsafe to view.
Slight is the subject, but not so the praise,
If she inspire, and he approve my lays.
 Say what strange motive, Goddess! coul[d] compel
A well-bred lord t' assault a gentle belle?
Oh, say what stranger cause, yet unexplored,
Could make a gentle belle reject a lord? 1[0]
In tasks so bold, can little men engage,
And in soft bosoms dwells such mighty rage?
 Sol through white curtains shot a timorou[s] ray,
And oped those eyes that must eclipse the day
Now lap-dogs give themselves the rousin[g] shake,
And sleepless lovers, just at twelve, awake.
Thrice rung the bell, the slipper knocked th[e] ground,1
And the pressed watch2 returned a silver soun[d]
Belinda still her downy pillow pressed,
Her guardian sylph prolonged the balmy rest
'Twas he had summoned to her silent bed 2[0]
The morning dream that hovered o'er her head
A youth more glittering than a birth-nigh[t] beau,3
(That e'en in slumber caused her cheek t[o] glow)
Seemed to her ear his winning lips to lay,
And thus in whispers said, or seemed to say:
 "Fairest of mortals, thou distinguished car[e]
Of thousand bright inhabitants of air!
If e'er one vision touched thy infant though[t]
Of all the nurse and all the priest have taugh[t]
Of airy elves by moonlight shadows seen, 3[0]
The silver token,4 and the circled green,
Or virgins visited by angel powers,
With golden crowns and wreaths of heavenl[y] flowers;
Hear and believe! thy own importance know,
Nor bound thy narrow views to things below.

and in the present enlarged form in 1714. Th[e] subject, proposed to Pope by one Mr. Caryl[l] was suggested by a trifling feud that ha[d] arisen between two families because Lor[d] Petre, a dapper little baron, had cut a loc[k] from the head of Miss Arabella Fermo[r] ("Belinda"). The opening is in imitation o[f] classic epics, more especially of Virgil's *Æneid*. The chief addition in the later form is th[e] machinery of sylphs, gnomes, nymphs, an[d] salamanders, spirits inhabiting air, earth, water, and fire, respectively. Dr. Johnson pr[o]nounced the poem "the most airy, the mos[t] ingenious, and the most delightful" of all th[e] author's compositions, and De Quincey went s[o] far as to declare it "the most exquisite monu[ment of playful fancy that universal literatur[e] offers."

1 Summoning the lady's-maid.
2 A striking-watch.
3 One befitting the royal birthday ball.
4 Silver pieces droppe[d] by fairies into the shoes of tidy maid[s]

Some secret truths, from learnèd pride con-
    cealed,
To maids alone and children are revealed
What though no credit doubting wits may give?
The fair and innocent shall still believe.   40
Know, then, unnumbered spirits round thee fly,
The light militia of the lower sky.
These, though unseen, are ever on the wing,
Hang o'er the box,5 and hover round the Ring.6
Think what an equipage thou hast in air,
And view with scorn two pages and a chair.7
As now your own, our beings were of old,
And once enclosed in woman's beauteous
    mould;
Thence, by a soft transition, we repair
From earthly vehicles to these of air.   50
Think not, when woman's transient breath is
    fled,
That all her vanities at once are dead;
Succeeding vanities she still regards,
And though she plays no more, o'erlooks the
    cards.
Her joy in gilded chariots, when alive,
And love of ombre,8 after death survive.
For when the fair in all their pride expire,
To their first elements their souls retire:
The sprites of fiery termagants in flame
Mount up, and take a salamander's name.   60
Soft yielding minds to water glide away,
And sip, with nymphs, their elemental tea.
The graver prude sinks downward to a gnome,
In search of mischief still on earth to roam.
The light coquettes in sylphs aloft repair,
And sport and flutter in the fields of air.
    "Know further yet: whoever fair and
        chaste
Rejects mankind, is by some sylph embraced;
For spirits, freed from mortal laws, with ease
Assume what sexes and what shapes they
    please.
What guards the purity of melting maids,   71
In courtly balls, and midnight masquerades,
Safe from the treacherous friend, the daring
    spark,9
The glance by day, the whisper in the dark,
When kind occasion prompts their warm de-
    sires,
When music softens, and when dancing fires?
'Tis but their sylph, the wise celestials know,
Though honour is the word with men below.
Some nymphs there are, too conscious of their
    face,
For life predestined to the gnomes' embrace. 80

These swell their prospects and exalt their
    pride,
When offers are disdained, and love denied:
Then gay ideas crowd the vacant brain,
While peers, and dukes, and all their sweeping
    train,
And garters, stars, and coronets appear,
And in soft sounds 'Your Grace' salutes their
    ear.
'Tis these that early taint the female soul,
Instruct the eyes of young coquettes to roll,
Teach infant cheeks a bidden blush to know,
And little hearts to flutter at a beau.   90
    "Oft when the world imagine women stray,
The sylphs through mystic mazes guide their
    way,
Through all the giddy circle they pursue,
And old impertinence expel by new.
What tender maid but must a victim fall
To one man's treat, but for another's ball?
When Florio speaks, what virgin could with-
    stand,
If gentle Damon did not squeeze her hand?
With varying vanities, from every part,
They shift the moving toyshop of their heart;
Where wigs with wigs, with sword-knots sword-
    knots strive,   101
Beaux banish beaux, and coaches coaches drive.
This erring mortals levity may call;
Oh, blind to truth! the sylphs contrive it all.
    "Of these am I, who thy protection claim,
A watchful sprite, and Ariel is my name.
Late, as I ranged the crystal wilds of air,
In the clear mirror of thy ruling star
I saw, alas! some dread event impend,
Ere to the main10 this morning sun descend, 110
But Heaven reveals not what, or how, or where.
Warned by the sylph, O pious maid, beware!
This to disclose is all thy guardian can:
Beware of all, but most beware of man!"
    He said; when Shock, who thought she slept
        too long,
Leaped up, and waked his mistress with his
    tongue.
'Twas then, Belinda, if report say true,
Thy eyes first opened on a billet-doux;
Wounds, charms, and ardours were no sooner
    read,
But all the vision vanished from thy head. 120
    And now, unveiled, the toilet stands dis-
        played,
Each silver vase in mystic order laid.
First, robed in white, the nymph intent adores,
With head uncovered, the cosmetic powers.
A heavenly image in the glass appears,

5 At the theater.   7 sedan-chair
6 A fashionable prome-   8 A game at cards.
    nade in Hyde Park.   9 gallant

10 sea

To that she bends, to that her eyes she rears;
Th' inferior priestess, at her altar's side,
Trembling begins the sacred rites of pride.
Unnumbered treasures ope at once, and here
The various offerings of the world appear; 130
From each she nicely culls with curious toil,
And decks the goddess with the glittering
    spoil.
This casket India's glowing gems unlocks,
And all Arabia breathes from yonder box.
The tortoise here and elephant unite,
Transformed to combs, the speckled, and the
    white.
Here files of pins extend their shining rows,
Puffs, powders, patches, bibles, billets-doux.
Now awful beauty puts on all its arms;   139
The fair each moment rises in her charms,
Repairs her smiles, awakens every grace,
And calls forth all the wonders of her face;
Sees by degrees a purer blush arise,
And keener lightnings quicken in her eyes.
The busy sylphs surround their darling care,
These set the head,11 and those divide the hair,
Some fold the sleeve, whilst others plait the
    gown;
And Betty's praised for labours not her own.

CANTO II

Not with more glories, in th' ethereal plain,
The sun first rises o'er the purpled main,
Than, issuing forth, the rival of his beams
Launched on the bosom of the silver Thames.
Fair nymphs, and well-dressed youths around
    her shone,
But every eye was fixed on her alone.
On her white breast a sparkling cross she wore,
Which Jews might kiss, and infidels adore.
Her lively looks a sprightly mind disclose,
Quick as her eyes, and as unfixed as those;   10
Favours to none, to all she smiles extends;
Oft she rejects, but never once offends.
Bright as the sun, her eyes the gazers strike,
And, like the sun, they shine on all alike.
Yet graceful ease, and sweetness void of pride,
Might hide her faults, if belles had faults to
    hide;
If to her share some female errors fall,
Look on her face, and you'll forget 'em all.
    This nymph, to the destruction of mankind,
Nourished two locks, which graceful hung be-
    hind
In equal curls, and well conspired to deck   21
With shining ringlets the smooth ivory neck.
Love in these labyrinths his slaves detains,

And mighty hearts are held in slender chains.
With hairy springes, we the birds betray,
Slight lines of hair surprise the finny prey,
Fair tresses man's imperial race ensnare,
And beauty draws us with a single hair.
    Th' adventurous baron the bright locks ad-
    mired;
He saw, he wished, and to the prize aspired. 30
Resolved to win, he meditates the way,
By force to ravish, or by fraud betray;
For when success a lover's toil attends,
Few ask, if fraud or force attained his ends.
    For this, ere Phœbus rose, he had implored
Propitious Heaven, and every power adored,
But chiefly Love; to Love an altar built,
Of twelve vast French romances,1 neatly gilt.
There lay three garters, half a pair of gloves,
And all the trophies of his former loves;   40
With tender billets-doux he lights the pyre,
And breathes three amorous sighs to raise the
    fire.
Then prostrate falls, and begs with ardent eyes
Soon to obtain, and long possess the prize.
The powers gave ear, and granted half his
    prayer;
The rest the winds dispersed in empty air.
    But now secure the painted vessel glides,
The sunbeams trembling on the floating tides;
While melting music steals upon the sky,
And softened sounds along the waters die;   50
Smooth flow the waves, the zephyrs gently play,
Belinda smiled, and all the world was gay.
All but the sylph—with careful thoughts op-
    pressed,
Th' impending woe sat heavy on his breast.
He summons straight his denizens of air;
The lucid squadrons round the sails repair;
Soft o'er the shrouds aërial whispers breathe,
That seemed but zephyrs to the train beneath.
Some to the sun their insect wings unfold,
Waft on the breeze, or sink in clouds of gold;
Transparent forms, too fine for mortal sight, 61
Their fluid bodies half dissolved in light.
Loose to the wind their airy garments flew,
Thin glittering textures of the filmy dew,2
Dipt in the richest tincture of the skies,
Where light disports in ever-mingling dyes,
While every beam new transient colours flings,
Colours that change whene'er they wave their
    wings.
Amid the circle, on the gilded mast
Superior by the head, was Ariel placed;   70

11 head-dress

1 Ponderous romances,
    like Mlle. de Scu-
    déry's Le Grand
    Cyrus and Clélie,
    then in vogue.

2 gossamer (once sup-
    posed to be a prod-
    uct of dew)

is purple pinions opening to the sun,
e raised his azure wand, and thus begun:
"Ye sylphs and sylphids, to your chief give
    ear!
ys, fairies, genii, elves, and demons, hear!
e know the spheres, and various tasks as-
    signed
y laws eternal to th' aërial kind.
me in the fields of purest æther play,
nd bask and whiten in the blaze of day.
me guide the course of wandering orbs on
    high,
r roll the planets through the boundless sky.
me less refined, beneath the moon's pale
    light   81
irsue the stars that shoot athwart the night,
r suck the mists in grosser air below,
r dip their pinions in the painted bow,
r brew fierce tempests on the wintry main,
r o'er the glebe distil the kindly rain;
hers on earth o'er human race preside,
atch all their ways, and all their actions
    guide:
f these the chief the care of nations own,
nd guard with arms divine the British throne.
"Our humbler province is to tend the fair, 91
ot a less pleasing, though less glorious care;
save the powder from too rude a gale,
or let th' imprisoned essences exhale;
draw fresh colours from the vernal flowers;
steal from rainbows, ere they drop in
    showers,
brighter wash; to curl their waving hairs,
ssist their blushes, and inspire their airs;
ay, oft in dreams, invention we bestow,
change a flounce, or add a furbelow.   100
"This day, black omens threat the brightest
    fair
hat e'er deserved a watchful spirit's care;
me dire disaster, or by force, or sleight;
ut what, or where, the fates have wrapped in
    night.
hether the nymph shall break Diana's law,
r some frail china jar receive a flaw;
r stain her honour, or her new brocade;
orget her prayers, or miss a masquerade;
r lose her heart, or necklace, at a ball;
r whether Heaven has doomed that Shock
    must fall.   110
aste, then, ye spirits! to your charge repair;
he fluttering fan be Zephyretta's care;
he drops³ to thee, Brillante, we consign;
nd, Momentilla, let the watch be thine;
o thou, Crispissa, tend her favourite lock;
riel himself shall be the guard of Shock.
ar-rings

. . . .
"Whatever spirit, careless of his charge,
His post neglects, or leaves the fair at large,
Shall feel sharp vengeance soon o'ertake his
    sins,
Be stopped in vials, or transfixed with pins;
Or plunged in lakes of bitter washes lie,
Or wedged whole ages in a bodkin's eye;
Gums and pomatums shall his flight restrain,
While clogged he beats his silken wings in
    vain;
Or alum styptics with contracting power   131
Shrink his thin essence like a rivelled⁴ flower;
Or, as Ixion fixed, the wretch shall feel
The giddy motion of the whirling mill,⁵
In fumes of burning chocolate shall glow,
And tremble at the sea that froths below!"
He spoke; the spirits from the sails descend;
Some, orb in orb, around the nymph extend;
Some thrid the mazy ringlets of her hair;
Some hang upon the pendants of her ear;   140
With beating hearts the dire event they wait,
Anxiou and trembling for the birth of fate.

CANTO III

Close by those meads, forever crowned with
    flowers,
Where Thames with pride surveys his rising
    towers,
There stands a structure of majestic frame,¹
Which from the neighbouring Hampton takes
    its name.
Here Britain's statesmen oft the fall foredoom
Of foreign tyrants and of nymphs at home;
Here thou, great Anna! whom three realms
    obey,
Dost sometimes counsel take—and sometimes
    tea.
Hither the heroes and the nymphs resort,
To taste awhile the pleasures of a court;   10
In various talk th' instructive hours they
    passed,
Who gave the ball, or paid the visit last;
One speaks the glory of the British Queen,
And one describes a charming Indian screen;
A third interprets motions, looks, and eyes;
At every word a reputation dies.
Snuff, or the fan, supply each pause of chat,
With singing, laughing, ogling, and all that.
Meanwhile, declining from the noon of day,
The sun obliquely shoots his burning ray;   20
The hungry judges soon the sentence sign,

⁴ shriveled   ⁵ chocolate-mill
¹ Hampton Court, at times a royal residence.

And wretches hang that jurymen may dine;
The merchant from th' Exchange returns in
    peace,
And the long labours of the toilet cease.
Belinda now, whom thirst of fame invites,
Burns to encounter two adventurous knights,
At ombre singly to decide their doom;
And swells her breast with conquests yet to
    come.
Straight the three bands prepare in arms to
    join,
Each band the number of the sacred nine.[2]   30
Soon as she spreads her hand, th' aërial guard
Descend, and sit on each important card:
First, Ariel perched upon a Matadore,[3]
Then each, according to the rank they bore;
For sylphs, yet mindful of their ancient race,
Are, as when women, wondrous fond of place.
  Behold, four kings in majesty revered,
With hoary whiskers and a forky beard;
And four fair queens whose hands sustain a
    flower,
The expressive emblem of their softer power;
Four knaves in garbs succinct, a trusty band,   41
Caps on their heads, and halberts in their hand;
And parti-coloured troops, a shining train,
Draw forth to combat on the velvet plain.
  The skilful nymph reviews her force with
    care:
Let spades be trumps! she said, and trumps
    they were.
  Now move to war her sable Matadores,
In show like leaders of the swarthy Moors.
Spadillio first, unconquerable lord!
Led off two captive trumps and swept the
    board.   50
As many more Manillio forced to yield
And marched a victor from the verdant field.
Him Basto followed, but his fate more hard
Gained but one trump and one plebeian card.
With his broad sabre next, a chief in years,
The hoary majesty of spades appears,
Puts forth one manly leg, to sight revealed,
The rest his many-coloured robe concealed.
The rebel knave, who dares his prince engage,
Proves the just victim of his royal rage.
E'en mighty Pam,[4] that kings and queens o'er-
    threw,
And mowed down armies in the fights of Loo,
Sad chance of war! now destitute of aid,

Falls undistinguished by the victor spade!
  Thus far both armies to Belinda yield;
Now to the baron fate inclines the field.
His warlike Amazon her host invades,
The imperial consort of the crown of spade
The club's black tyrant first her victim died,
Spite of his haughty mien, and barbarous pri
What boots the regal circle on his head,
His giant limbs, in state unwieldy spread;
That long behind he trails his pompous robe,
And, of all monarchs, only grasps the globe?
  The baron now his diamonds pours apace;
Th' embroidered king who shows but half
    face,
And his refulgent queen, with powers combine
Of broken troops an easy conquest find.
Clubs, diamonds, hearts, in wild disorder see
With throngs promiscuous strew the lev
    green.
Thus when dispersed a routed army runs,
Of Asia's troops, and Afric's sable sons,
With like confusion different nations fly,
Of various habit, and of various dye,
The pierced battalions disunited fall,
In heaps on heaps; one fate o'erwhelms the
    all.
  The knave of diamonds tries his wily arts,
And wins (oh shameful chance!) the queen
    hearts.
At this the blood the virgin's cheek forsook,
A livid paleness spreads o'er all her look;
She sees, and trembles at th' approaching
Just in the jaws of ruin, and codille.[5]
And now (as oft in some distempered state)
On one nice trick depends the general fate.
An ace of hearts steps forth; the king unse
Lurked in her hand, and mourned his capti
    queen:
He springs to vengeance with an eager pace,
And falls like thunder on the prostrate ace.
The nymph exulting fills with shouts the sk
The walls, the woods, and long canals reply.
  Oh thoughtless mortals! ever blind to fate
Too soon dejected, and too soon elate.
Sudden, these honours shall be snatched aw
And cursed forever this victorious day.
  For lo! the board with cups and spoons
    crowned,
The berries[6] crackle, and the mill turns roun
On shining altars of Japan[7] they raise
The silver lamp; the fiery spirits blaze;
From silver spouts the grateful liquors glide,
While China's earth receives the smoking tid

---

[2] Each player holds nine cards.
[3] The three best cards—Spadillio, ace of spades;
    Manillio, a trump; and Basto, ace of clubs—
    were each called a Matadore (Spanish for the
    slayer in a bull-fight).
[4] Knave of clubs, the highest card in the game of
    Loo.

[5] A term signifying de- [6] coffee berries
    feat of the lone   [7] japanned tables
    hand, who loses the
    pool.

t once they gratify their scent and taste,   111
nd frequent cups prolong the rich repast.
traight hover round the fair her airy band;
me, as she sipped, the fuming liquor fanned,
me o'er her lap their careful plumes dis-
    played,
rembling, and conscious of the rich brocade.
offee (which makes the politician wise,
nd see through all things with his half-shut
    eyes)
ent up in vapours to the baron's brain
ew stratagems the radiant lock to gain.   120
, cease, rash youth! desist ere 'tis too late,
ear the just gods, and think of Scylla's[8] fate!
anged to a bird, and sent to flit in air,
e dearly pays for Nisus' injured hair!
But when to mischief mortals bend their will,
w soon they find fit instruments of ill!
st then Clarissa drew with tempting grace
two-edged weapon from her shining case:
ladies in romance assist their knight,   129
esent the spear, and arm him for the fight.
e takes the gift with reverence, and extends
e little engine on his fingers' ends;
is just behind Belinda's neck he spread,
 o'er the fragrant steams she bends her
    head.
ift to the lock a thousand sprites repair,
thousand wings, by turns, blow back the
    hair;
d thrice they twitched the diamond in her
    ear;
rice she looked back, and thrice the foe di ..
    near.
st in that instant, anxious Ariel sought
e close recesses of the virgin's thought;   140
on the nosegay in her breast reclined,
 watched th' ideas rising in her mind,
dden he viewed, in spite of all her art,
 earthly lover lurking at her heart.
azed, confused, he found his power expired,
signed to fate, and with a sigh retired.
The peer now spreads the glittering forfex[9]
    wide,
inclose the lock; now joins it, to divide.
en then, before the fatal engine closed,
wretched sylph too fondly interposed;   150
te urged the shears, and cut the sylph in
    twain,
ut airy substance soon unites again).[10]
e meeting points the sacred hair dissever
om the fair head, forever, and forever!

Then flashed the living lightning from her
    eyes,
And screams of horror rend th' affrighted
    skies.
Not louder shrieks to pitying Heaven are cast,
When husbands, or when lap-dogs breathe their
    last;
Or when rich China vessels, fallen from high,
In glittering dust and painted fragments lie!
"Let wreaths of triumph now my temples
    twine,"
The victor cried; "the glorious prize is mine!
While fish in streams, or birds delight in air,
Or in a coach and six the British fair,
As long as Atalantis[11] shall be read,
Or the small pillow grace a lady's bed,
While visits shall be paid on solemn days,
When numerous wax-lights in bright order
    blaze,
While nymphs take treats, or assignations give,
So long my honour, name, and praise shall live!
What Time would spare, from steel receives its
    date,[12]   171
And monuments, like men, submit to fate!
Steel could the labour of the gods destroy,
And strike to dust th' imperial towers of
    Troy;
Steel could the works of mortal pride confound,
And hew triumphal arches to the ground.
What wonder then, fair nymph! thy hairs
    should feel,
The conquering force of unresisted steel?"

CANTO IV

But anxious cares the pensive nymph oppressed,
And secret passions laboured in her breast.
Not youthful kings in battle seized alive,
Not scornful virgins who their charms survive,
Not ardent lovers robbed of all their bliss,
Not ancient ladies when refused a kiss,
Not tyrants fierce that unrepenting die,
Not Cynthia[1] when her manteau's pinned awry,
E'er felt such rage, resentment, and despair,
As thou, sad virgin, for thy ravished hair.   10
For, that sad moment, when the sylphs with-
    drew
And Ariel weeping from Belinda flew,
Umbriel, a dusky, melancholy sprite,
As ever sullied the fair face of light,
Down to the central earth, his proper scene,

---

ing Nisus' daughter,   9 shears (Latin)
   who betrayed her   10 A parody of *Paradise
   father by sending   Lost*, vi., 330.
   the enemy one of
   his hairs.

11 A scandalous novel of the time by Mrs. Manley.
12 fatal day

---

1 Any frivolous society woman.

Repaired to search the gloomy cave of Spleen.[2]
Swift on his sooty pinions flits the gnome,
And in a vapour reached the dismal dome.
No cheerful breeze this sullen region knows,
The dreaded east is all the wind that blows. 20
Here in a grotto, sheltered close from air,
And screened in shades from day's detested glare,
She sighs forever on her pensive bed,
Pain at her side, and Megrim[3] at her head.
Two handmaids wait[4] the throne, alike in place,
But differing far in figure and in face.
Here stood Ill-nature like an ancient maid,
Her wrinkled form in black and white arrayed;
With store of prayers, for mornings, nights, and noons
Her hand is filled; her bosom with lampoons. 30
There Affectation, with a sickly mien,
Shows in her cheek the roses of eighteen,
Practised to lisp, and hang the head aside,
Faints into airs, and languishes with pride,
On the rich quilt sinks with becoming woe,
Wrapped in a gown, for sickness, and for show.
The fair ones feel such maladies as these,
When each new night-dress gives a new disease.

A constant vapour o'er the palace flies;
Strange phantoms rising as the mists arise; 40
Dreadful, as hermit's dreams in haunted shades,
Or bright, as visions of expiring maids.
Now glaring fiends, and snakes on rolling spires,
Pale spectres, gaping tombs, and purple fires;
Now lakes of liquid gold, Elysian scenes,
And crystal domes, and angels in machines.[5]
Unnumbered throngs on every side are seen,
Of bodies changed to various forms by Spleen.
Here living tea-pots stand, one arm held out,
One bent; the handle this, and that the spout.
A pipkin there, like Homer's tripod, walks;[6] 51
Here sighs a jar, and there a goose-pie talks.

Safe past the gnome through this fantastic band,
A branch of healing spleenwort in his hand.
Then thus addressed the power: "Hail, wayward queen!
Who rule the sex, to fifty from fifteen:
Parent of vapours and of female wit;
Who give th' hysteric, or poetic fit; 60
On various tempers act by various ways,
Make some take physic, others scribble plays;
Who cause the proud their visits to delay,

And send the godly in a pet to pray.
A nymph there is, that all thy power disdains
And thousands more in equal mirth maintains
But oh! if e'er thy gnome could spoil a grace
Or raise a pimple on a beauteous face,
Like citron-waters matrons' cheeks inflame,
Or change complexions at a losing game. 7.

. . . .

Hear, me, and touch Belinda with chagrin,
That single act gives half the world the spleen.''
The goddess with a discontented air 7.
Seems to reject him, though she grants his prayer.
A wondrous bag with both her hands she binds,
Like that where once Ulysses held the winds;
There she collects the force of female lungs,
Sighs, sobs, and passions, and the war of tongues.
A vial next she fills with fainting fears,
Soft sorrows, melting griefs, and flowing tears
The gnome rejoicing bears her gifts away,
Spreads his black wings, and slowly mounts to day.
Sunk in Thalestris's[8] arms the nymph he found,
Her eyes dejected and her hair unbound.
Full o'er their heads the swelling bag he rent,
And all the furies issued at the vent.
Belinda burns with more than mortal ire,
And fierce Thalestris fans the rising fire.
"O wretched maid!" she spread her hands and cried,
(While Hampton's echoes, "Wretched maid!" replied)
"Was it for this you took such constant care
The bodkin, comb, and essence to prepare?
For this your locks in paper durance bound,
For this with torturing irons wreathed around
For this with fillets strained your tender head
And bravely bore the double loads of lead?[9]
Gods! shall the ravisher display your hair,
While the fops envy, and the ladies stare!
Honour forbid! at whose unrivalled shrine
Ease, pleasure, virtue, all our sex resign.
Methinks already I your tears survey,
Already hear the horrid things they say,
Already see you a degraded toast,
And all your honour in a whisper lost! 1.
How shall I, then, your helpless fame defend?
'Twill then be infamy to seem your friend!
And shall this prize, th' inestimable prize,
Exposed through crystal to the gazing eyes,

---

2 ill humor
3 low spirits
4 Supply "at."
5 stage devices
6 Iliad, xviii., 373.
7 Odyssey x., 20.
8 For Mrs. Morley, a sister of Sir George Brown, the "Sir Plume" of line 121.
9 leaded curl-papers

And heightened by the diamond's circling rays,
On that rapacious hand forever blaze?
Sooner shall grass in Hyde Park Circus[10] grow,
And wits take lodgings in the sound of Bow;[11]
Sooner let earth, air, sea, to chaos fall,   119
Men, monkeys, lap-dogs, parrots, perish all!''
    She said; then raging to Sir Plume repairs,
And bids her beau demand the precious hairs
(Sir Plume, of amber snuff-box justly vain,
And the nice conduct of a clouded[12] cane).
With earnest eyes, and round unthinking face,
He first the snuff-box opened, then the case,
And thus broke out—''My lord, why, what the
        devil?
Zounds! damn the lock! 'fore Gad, you must
        be civil!
Plague on't! 'tis past a jest—nay prithee, pox!
Give her the hair,'' he spoke, and rapped his
        box.   130
''It grieves me much,'' replied the peer again,
''Who speaks so well should ever speak in vain.
But by this lock, this sacred lock, I swear,
(Which never more shall join its parted hair;
Which never more its honours shall renew,
Clipped from the lovely head where late it
        grew)
That while my nostrils draw the vital air,
This hand, which won it, shall forever wear.''
He spoke, and speaking, in proud triumph
        spread
The long-contended honours of her head.   140
    But Umbriel, hateful gnome! forbears not
        so;
He breaks the vial whence the sorrows flow.
Then see! the nymph in beauteous grief ap-
        pears,
Her eyes half languishing, half drowned in
        tears;
On her heaved bosom hung her drooping head,
Which, with a sigh, she raised; and thus she
        said:
    ''Forever curs'd be this detested day,
Which snatched my best, my favourite curl
        away!
Happy! ah, ten times happy had I been,
If Hampton Court these eyes had never seen!
Yet am not I the first mistaken maid,   151
By love of courts to numerous ills betrayed.
Oh, had I rather unadmired remained
In some lone isle or distant northern land;
Where the gilt chariot never marks the way,
Where none learn ombre, none e'er taste
        bohea![13]

There kept my charms concealed from mortal
        eye,
Like roses, that in deserts bloom and die.
What moved my mind with youthful lords to
        roam?   159
Oh, had I stayed, and said my prayers at home!
'Twas this, the morning omens seemed to tell:
Thrice from my trembling hand the patch-
        box[14] fell;
The tottering china shook without a wind;
Nay, Poll sat mute, and Shock was most un-
        kind!
A sylph, too, warned me of the threats of fate,
In mystic visions, now believed too late!
See the poor remnants of these slighted hairs!
My hands shall rend what e'en thy rapine
        spares;
These in two sable ringlets taught to break,
Once gave new beauties to the snowy neck;   170
The sister lock now sits uncouth, alone,
And in its fellow's fate foresees its own;
Uncurled it hangs, the fatal shears demands,
And tempts once more, thy sacrilegious hands.
Oh, hadst thou, cruel! been content to seize
Hairs less in sight, or any hairs but these!''

CANTO V

She said: the pitying audience melt in tears.
But Fate and Jove had stopped the baron's
        ears.
In vain Thalestris with reproach assails,
For who can move when fair Belinda fails?
Not half so fixed the Trojan[1] could remain,
While Anna begged and Dido raged in vain.
Then grave Clarissa graceful waved her fan;
Silence ensued, and thus the nymph began:
    ''Say, why are beauties praised and honoured
        most,
The wise man's passion, and the vain man's
        toast?   10
Why decked with all that land and sea afford,
Why angels called, and angel-like adored?
Why round our coaches crowd the white-gloved
        beaux,
Why bows the side-box from its inmost rows?
How vain are all these glories, all our pains,
Unless good sense preserve what beauty gains;
That men may say, when we the front-box
        grace,
'Behold the first in virtue as in face!'
Oh! if to dance all night, and dress all day,
Charmed the small-pox, or chased old age away,

10 The ''Ring'' mentioned in I., 44.
11 Bow bells, the bells of St. Mary-le-bow in the
    cockney center of London.
12 mottled
13 A kind of black tea.

14 For face-patches.
_____
1 Æneas when repelling Dido's love and the en-
    treaties of her sister Anna. (Æneid iv., 440.)

Who would not scorn what housewife's cares
    produce, 21
Or who would learn one earthly thing of use?
To patch, nay ogle, might become a saint,
Nor could it sure be such a sin to paint.
But since, alas! frail beauty must decay;
Curled or uncurled, since locks will turn to
    grey;
Since painted, or not painted, all shall fade,
And she who scorns a man must die a maid;
What then remains but well our power to use,
And keep good humour still whate'er we
    lose? 30
And trust me, dear! good humour can prevail,
When airs, and flights, and screams, and scold-
    ing fail.
Beauties in vain their pretty eyes may roll;
Charms strike the sight, but merit wins the
    soul.''
    So spoke the dame, but no applause ensued;
Belinda frowned, Thalestris called her prude.
''To arms, to arms!'' the fierce virago cries,
And swift as lightning to the combat flies.
All side in parties, and begin th' attack;
Fans clap, silks rustle, and tough whalebones
    crack; 40
Heroes' and heroines' shouts confus'dly rise,
And bass and treble voices strike the skies.
No common weapons in their hands are found,
Like gods they fight, nor dread a mortal wound.
    So when bold Homer makes the gods engage,
And heavenly breasts with human passions
    rage;
'Gainst Pallas,[2] Mars,[3] Latona,[3] Hermes—Mars;
And all Olympus rings with loud alarms:
Jove's thunder roars, Heaven trembles all
    around,
Blue Neptune storms, the bellowing deeps re-
    sound: 50
Earth shakes her nodding towers, the ground
    gives way,
And the pale ghosts start at the flash of day!
    Triumphant Umbriel on a sconce's[4] height
Clapped his glad wings, and sat to view the
    fight;
Propped on their bodkin spears, the sprites
    survey
The growing combat, or assist the fray.
    While through the press enraged Thalestris
    flies,
And scatters death around from both her eyes,
A beau and witling perished in the throng,
One died in metaphor, and one in song. 60
''O cruel nymph! a living death I bear,''

Cried Dapperwit, and sunk beside his chair.
A mournful glance Sir Fopling upwards cas
''Those eyes are made so killing''—was h
    last.
Thus on Mæander's flowery margin lies
Th' expiring swan, and as he sings he dies.[5]
    When bold Sir Plume had drawn Clariss
    down,
Chloe stepped in and killed him with a frown
She smiled to see the doughty hero slain,
But, at her smile, the beau revived again.
    Now Jove suspends his golden scales in ai
Weighs the men's wits against the lady's hai
The doubtful beam long nods from side t
    side;
At length the wits mount up, the hairs subsid
    See, fierce Belinda on the Baron flies,
With more than usual lightning in her eyes;
Nor feared the chief th' unequal fight to try,
Who sought no more than on his foe to die.
But this bold lord with manly strength endue
She with one finger and a thumb subdued: 8
Just where the breath of life his nostrils drev
A charge of snuff the wily virgin threw;
The gnomes direct, to every atom just,
The pungent grains of titillating dust.
Sudden, with starting tears each eye o'erflow
And the high dome re-echoes to his nose.
    ''Now meet thy fate,'' incensed Belind
    cried,
And drew a deadly bodkin from her side.
(The same, his ancient personage to deck,
Her great great grandsire wore about his nec
In three seal-rings; which after, melte
    down, 9
Formed a vast buckle for his widow's gown;
Her infant grandame's whistle next it grew,
The bells she jingled, and the whistle blew;
Then in a bodkin graced her mother's hairs,
Which long she wore, and now Belinda wears.
    ''Boast not my fall,'' he cried, ''insultin
    foe!
Thou by some other shalt be laid as low;
Nor think to die dejects my lofty mind:
All that I dread is leaving you behind! 10
Rather than so, ah, let me still survive,
And burn in Cupid's flames—but burn alive.'
    ''Restore the lock!'' she cries; and a
    around
''Restore the lock!'' the vaulted roofs reboun
Not fierce Othello in so loud a strain
Roared for the handkerchief that caused hi
    pain.
But see how oft ambitious aims are crossed,
And chiefs contend till all the prize is lost!

2 Aider of the Greeks.   4 chandelier's
3 Aider of the Trojans.

5 Ovid's *Epistles*. vii., 1, 2.

e lock, obtained with guilt, and kept with
   pain, 109
every place is sought, but sought in vain:
ith such a prize no mortal must be blessed,
Heaven decrees! with Heaven who can contest?
Some thought it mounted to the lunar sphere,
nce all things lost on earth are treasured
   there.
ere heroes' wits are kept in ponderous vases,
nd beaux' in snuff-boxes and tweezer cases;
ere broken vows and death-bed alms are
   found,
nd lovers' hearts with ends of riband bound,
he courtier's promises, and sick man's prayers, 119
he smiles of harlots, and the tears of heirs,
ges for gnats, and chains to yoke a flea,
ried butterflies, and tomes of casuistry.
But trust the Muse—she saw it upward rise,
hough marked by none but quick, poetic eyes:
So Rome's great founder[6] to the heavens
   withdrew,
Proculus alone confessed in view)
sudden star, it shot through liquid air,
nd drew behind a radiant trail of hair.
ot Berenice's locks[7] first rose so bright,
he heavens bespangling with dishevelled light.
he sylphs behold it kindling as it flies, 131
nd pleased pursue its progress through the
   skies
This the beau monde shall from the Mall[8]
   survey,
nd hail with music its propitious ray.
his the blest lover shall for Venus take,
nd send up vows from Rosamonda's lake.[9]
his Partridge[10] soon shall view in cloudless
   skies,
hen next he looks through Galileo's eyes;
nd hence th' egregious wizard shall foredoom
he fate of Louis and the fall of Rome. 140
Then cease, bright nymph! to mourn thy
   ravished hair,
hich adds new glory to the shining sphere!
ot all the tresses that fair head can boast,
all draw such envy as the lock you lost.
or, after all the murders of your eye,
hen, after millions slain, yourself shall die;
hen those fair suns shall set, as set they
   must,

Romulus, carried to heaven by Mars, afterwards
   appeared to Proculus in great glory.
'Berenice's Hair," a group of seven stars in the
   constellation Leo.
A fashionable walk in St. James' Park.
n St. James' Park.
An almanac-maker of the time who yearly
   prophesied disaster.

And all those tresses shall be laid in dust:
This lock, the Muse shall consecrate to fame,
And 'midst the stars inscribe Belinda's
   name. 150

FROM AN ESSAY ON MAN.

EPISTLE I

Awake, my St. John![1] leave all meaner things
To low ambition, and the pride of kings.
Let us, since life can little more supply
Than just to look about us and to die,
Expatiate free o'er all this scene of man;
A mighty maze! but not without a plan;
A wild, where weeds and flowers promiscuous
   shoot;
Or garden, tempting with forbidden fruit.
Together let us beat this ample field,
Try what the open, what the covert yield; 10
The latent tracts, the giddy heights, explore
Of all who blindly creep, or sightless soar;
Eye nature's walks, shoot folly as it flies,
And catch the manners living as they rise;
Laugh where we must, be candid where we can;
But vindicate the ways of God to man.
  I. Say first, of God above, or man below,
What can we reason, but from what we know?
Of man, what see we but his station here
From which to reason or to which refer? 20
Through worlds unnumbered though the God
   be known,
'Tis ours to trace him only in our own.
He, who through vast immensity can pierce,
See worlds on worlds compose one universe,
Observe how system into system runs,
What other planets circle other suns,
What varied being peoples every star,
May tell why Heaven has made us as we are.
But of this frame the bearings, and the ties,
The strong connections, nice dependencies, 30
Gradations just, has thy pervading soul
Looked through? or can a part contain the
   whole?
  Is the great chain, that draws all to agree,
And drawn supports, upheld by God, or thee?
  II. Presumptuous man! the reason wouldst
   thou find,
Why formed so weak, so little, and so blind?
First, if thou canst, the harder reason guess,
Why formed no weaker, blinder, and no less?
Ask of thy mother earth, why oaks are made
Taller or stronger than the weeds they shade?

1 Henry St. John, Lord Bolingbroke, a politician
   and philosopher to whom Pope was indebted
   for the substance of this poem. The name is
   usually pronounced *Sin jun.*

Or ask of yonder argent fields above,   41
Why Jove's satellites are less than Jove.
  Of systems possible, if 'tis confessed
That wisdom infinite must form the best,
Where all must full or not coherent be,
And all that rises, rise in due degree;
Then, in the scale of reasoning life, 'tis plain,
There must be, somewhere, such a rank as
    man:
And all the question (wrangle e'er so long)
Is only this, if God has placed him wrong?   50
  Respecting man, whatever wrong we call,
May, must be right, as relative to all.
In human works, though laboured on with pain,
A thousand movements scarce one purpose
    gain;
In God's, one single can its end produce;
Yet serves to second too some other use.
So man, who here seems principal alone,
Perhaps acts second to some sphere unknown,
Touches some wheel, or verges to some goal;
'Tis but a part we see, and not a whole.   60
When the proud steed shall know why man
    restrains
His fiery course, or drives him o'er the plains;
When the dull ox, why now he breaks the clod,
Is now a victim, and now Egypt's god:[2]
Then shall man's pride and dullness compre-
    hend
His actions', passions', being's, use and end;
Why doing, suffering, checked, impelled; and
    why
This hour a slave, the next a deity.
  Then say not man's imperfect, Heaven in
    fault;
Say rather, man's as perfect as he ought: 70
His knowledge measured to his state and place,
His time a moment, and a point his space.
If to be perfect in a certain sphere,
What matter, soon or late, or here or there?
The blest to-day is as completely so,
As who began a thousand years ago.
  III. Heaven from all creatures hides the
    book of fate,
All but the page prescribed, their present state:
From brutes[3] what men, from men what
    spirits know:
Or who could suffer being here below?   80
The lamb thy riot dooms to bleed to-day,
Had he thy reason, would he skip and play?
Pleased to the last, he crops the flowery food,
And licks the hand just raised to shed his
    blood.
Oh, blindness to the future! kindly given,

That each may fill the circle marked b[y]
    Heaven:
Who sees with equal eye, as God of all,
A hero perish, or a sparrow fall,
Atoms or systems into ruin hurled,
And now a bubble burst, and now a world.
  Hope humbly then; with trembling pinio[ns]
    soar;
Wait the great teacher Death; and God ado[re]
What future bliss, he gives not thee to know,
But gives that hope to be thy blessing now.
Hope springs eternal in the human breast:
Man never is, but always to be blest.
The soul, uneasy and confined from home,
Rests and expatiates in a life to come.
  Lo, the poor Indian! whose untutored min[d]
Sees God in clouds, or hears him in the win[d];
His soul, proud science never taught [to]
    stray   1[00]
Far as the solar walk, or milky way;
Yet simple nature to his hope has given,
Behind the cloud-topped hill, an humbl[er]
    Heaven;
Some safer world in depths of woods embrace[d],
Some happier island in the watery waste,
Where slaves once more their native land b[e]-
    hold,
No fiends torment, no Christians thirst f[or]
    gold.
To be, contents his natural desire,
He asks no angel's wing, no seraph's fire;   1[10]
But thinks, admitted to that equal sky,
His faithful dog shall bear him company.
  IV. Go, wiser thou! and, in thy scale [of]
    sense
Weigh thy opinion against Providence;
Call imperfection what thou fanciest such,
Say, "Here he gives too little, there to[o]
    much;"
Destroy all creatures for thy sport or gust,[4]
Yet cry, "If man's unhappy, God's unjust;["]
If man alone engross not Heaven's high ca[re],
Alone made perfect here, immortal there, 1[20]
Snatch from his hand the balance and the ro[d],
Re-judge his justice, be the god of God.
In pride, in reasoning pride, our error lies;
All quit their sphere, and rush into the ski[es,]
Pride still is aiming at the blest abodes,
Men would be angels, angels would be gods.
Aspiring to be gods, if angels fell,
Aspiring to be angels, men rebel:
And who but wishes to invert the laws
Of order, sins against the Eternal Cause. 1[30]
  V. Ask for what end the heavenly bodi[es]
    shine,

2 Apis, the sacred bull   3 Supply "heaven hides."
    of Egypt.   Pope's verse is full
                                 of such ellipses.

4 delight

Earth for whose use? Pride answers, " 'Tis
    for mine:
For me kind nature wakes her genial power,
Suckles each herb, and spreads out every
    flower;
Annual for me, the grape, the rose renew
The juice nectareous, and the balmy dew;
For me, the mine a thousand treasures brings;
For me, health gushes from a thousand springs;
Seas roll to waft me, suns to light me rise;
My footstool earth, my canopy the skies."   140
    But errs not Nature from this gracious end,
From burning suns when livid deaths descend,
When earthquakes swallow, or when tempests
    sweep
Towns to one grave, whole nations to the deep?
No ('tis replied), the first Almighty Cause
Acts not by partial, but by general laws;
Th' exceptions few; some change, since all
    began:
And what created perfect?—Why then man?
If the great end be human happiness,   149
Then nature deviates; and can man do less?
As much that end a constant course requires
Of showers and sunshine, as of man's desires;
As much eternal springs and cloudless skies,
As men forever temperate, calm, and wise.
If plagues or earthquakes break not Heaven's
    design,
Why then a Borgia,5 or a Catiline?6
Who knows but He, whose hand the lightning
    forms,
Who heaves old ocean, and who wings the
    storms;
Pours fierce ambition in a Cæsar's mind,
Or turns young Ammon7 loose to scourge man-
    kind?   160
From pride, from pride, our very reasoning
    springs.
Account for moral, as for natural things:
Why charge we Heaven in those, in these
    acquit?
In both, to reason right is to submit,
    Better for us, perhaps, it might appear,
Were there all harmony, all virtue here;
That never air or ocean felt the wind,
That never passion discomposed the mind.
But all subsists by elemental strife;
And passions are the elements of life.   170
The general order, since the whole began,
Is kept in nature, and is kept in man.
    VI. What would this man? Now upward
        will he soar,

And little less than angel, would be more;
Now looking downwards, just as grieved ap-
    pears
To want the strength of bulls, the fur of bears.
Made for his use all creatures if he call,
Say what their use, had he the powers of all?
Nature to these, without profusion, kind,
The proper organs, proper powers assigned; 180
Each seeming want compensated of course,
Here with degrees of swiftness, there of force;
All in exact proportion to the state;
Nothing to add, and nothing to abate.
Each beast, each insect, happy in its own:
Is Heaven unkind to man, and man alone?
Shall he alone, whom rational we call,
Be pleased with nothing, if not blessed with
    all?
    The bliss of man (could pride that blessing
        find)
Is not to act or think beyond mankind;   190
No powers of body or of soul to share,
But what his nature and his state can bear.
Why has not man a microscopic eye?
For this plain reason, man is not a fly.
Say what the use, were finer optics given,
T' inspect a mite, not comprehend the heaven?
Or touch, if tremblingly alive all o'er,
To smart and agonize at every pore?
Or, quick effluvia darting through the brain,
Die of a rose in aromatic pain?   200
If nature thundered in his opening ears,
And stunned him with the music of the
    spheres,8
How would he wish that Heaven had left him
    still
The whispering zephyr and the purling rill!
Who finds not Providence all good and wise,
Alike in what it gives, and what denies?
    VII. Far as creation's ample range extends,
The scale of sensual, mental powers ascends.
Mark how it mounts, to man's imperial race,
From the green myriads in the peopled grass:
What modes of sight betwixt each wide ex-
    treme,   210
The mole's dim curtain, and the lynx's beam:
Of smell, the headlong lioness between
And hound sagacious on the tainted green:
Of hearing, from the life that fills the flood,
To that which warbles through the vernal
    wood:
The spider's touch, how exquisitely fine!
Feels at each thread, and lives along the line:
In the nice bee, what sense so subtly true

---

5 Gesare Borgia, son of
    Pope Alexander VI.,
    a notorious criminal
    and tyrant.

6 Roman conspirator.
7 Alexander the Great,
    who was flattering-
    ly styled the son of
    Jupiter Ammon.

8 Music, too fine or too mighty for mortal ears,
    supposed to be made by the revolution of the
    concentric spheres which, according to the old
    Ptolemaic system, composed the universe. (See
    note on *Doctor Faustus*, p. 158.)

From poisonous herbs extracts the healing dew?
How instinct varies in the groveling swine, 221
Compared, half-reasoning elephant, with thine!
'Twixt that and reason, what a nice barrier,
Forever separate, yet forever near!
Remembrance and reflection how allied;
What thin partitions sense from thought di-
  vide:
And middle natures, how they long to join,
Yet never pass th' insuperable line!
Without this just gradation, could they be
Subjected, these to those, or all to thee?   230
The powers of all subdued by thee alone,
Is not thy reason all these powers in one?

  VIII. See, through this air, this ocean, and
    this earth
All matter quick,[9] and bursting into birth.
Above, how high, progressive life may go!
Around, how wide! how deep extend below!
Vast chain of being! which from God began,
Natures ethereal, human, angel, man,
Beast, bird, fish, insect, what no eye can see,
No glass can reach; from infinite to thee, 240
From thee to nothing.—On superior powers
Were we to press, inferior might[10] on ours;
Or in the full creation leave a void,
Where, one step broken, the great scale's de-
  stroyed:
From nature's chain whatever link you strike,
Tenth, or ten thousandth, breaks the chain
  alike.

  And if each system in gradation roll
Alike essential to th' amazing whole,
The least confusion but in one, not all
That system only but the whole must fall.   250
Let earth unbalanced from her orbit fly,
Planets and suns run lawless through the sky;
Let ruling angels from their spheres be hurled,
Being on being wrecked, and world on world;
Heaven's whole foundations to their centre
  nod,
And nature tremble to the throne of God.
All this dread order break—for whom? for
  thee?
Vile worm!—Oh, madness! pride! impiety!

  IX. What if the foot, ordained the dust
    to tread,
Or hand, to toil, aspired to be the head? 260
What if the head, the eye, or ear repined
To serve mere engines to the ruling mind?
Just as absurd for any part to claim
To be another, in this general frame;[11]
Just as absurd, to mourn the tasks or pains,
The great directing Mind of all ordains.

All are but parts of one stupendous whole,
Whose body nature is, and God the soul;
That, changed through all, and yet in all the
  same;
Great in the earth, as in th' ethereal frame; 270
Warms in the sun, refreshes in the breeze,
Glows in the stars, and blossoms in the trees,
Lives through all life, extends through all ex-
  tent,
Spreads undivided, operates unspent;
Breathes in our soul, informs our mortal part,
As full, as perfect, in a hair as heart;
As full, as perfect, in vile man that mourns,
As the rapt seraph that adores and burns:
To him no high, no low, no great, no small;
He fills, he bounds, connects, and equals
  all.   280

  X. Cease then, nor order imperfection name:
Our proper bliss depends on what we blame.
Know thy own point: this kind, this due degree
Of blindness, weakness, Heaven bestows on
  thee.
Submit.—In this, or any other sphere,
Secure to be as blest as thou canst bear:
Safe in the hand of one disposing Power,
Or in the natal, or the mortal hour.
All nature is but art, unknown to thee;
All chance, direction, which thou canst not see;
All discord, harmony not understood;   291
All partial evil, universal good:
And, spite of pride, in erring reason's spite,
One truth is clear, whatever is, is right.

EPISTLE II

  I. Know then thyself, presume not God to
    scan:
The proper study of mankind is man.
Placed on this isthmus of a middle state,
A being darkly wise and rudely great:
With too much knowledge for the sceptic side,
With too much weakness for the stoic's pride,
He hangs between; in doubt to act, or rest;
In doubt to deem himself a god or beast;
In doubt his mind or body to prefer;
Born but to die, and reasoning but to err; 10
Alike in ignorance, his reason such,
Whether he thinks too little or too much:
Chaos of thought and passion, all confus'd;
Still by himself abused, or disabused;
Created half to rise, and half to fall;
Great lord of all things, yet a prey to all;
Sole judge of truth, in endless error hurled;
The glory, jest, and riddle of the world!
  Go, wondrous creature; mount where science
    guides,

---

9 alive   11 universe
10 Supply "press."

Λo, measure earth, weigh air, and state the
    tides;   20
Instruct the planets in what orbs to run,
Correct old Time, and regulate the sun;[1]
Go, soar with Plato to th' empyreal sphere,[2]
To the first good, first perfect, and first fair;
Or tread the mazy round his followers trod,
And quitting sense call imitating God;
As eastern priests in giddy circles run,[3]
And turn their heads to imitate the sun.
Go, teach Eternal Wisdom how to rule—
Then drop into thyself, and be a fool! 30
  Superior beings, when of late they saw
A mortal man unfold all nature's law,
Admired such wisdom in an earthly shape,
And showed a Newton, as we show an ape.
  Could he, whose rules the rapid comet bind,
Describe or fix one movement of his mind?
Who saw its fires here rise, and there descend,
Explain his own beginning or his end?
Alas! what wonder! Man's superior part
Unchecked may rise, and climb from art to
    art;
But when his own great work is but begun, 41
What reason weaves, by passion is undone.
  Trace science, then, with modesty thy guide;
First strip off all her equipage of pride;
Deduct what is but vanity or dress,
Or learning's luxury, or idleness,
Or tricks to show the stretch of human brain,
Mere curious pleasure, or ingenious pain;
Expunge the whole, or lop th' excrescent parts
Of all our vices have created arts;   50
Then see how little the remaining sum,
Which served the past, and must the times to
    come!

  II. Two principles in human nature reign;
Self-love to urge, and reason to restrain;
Nor this a good, nor that a bad we call,
Each works its end to move or govern all:
And to their proper operation still
Ascribe all good; to their improper, ill.
  Self-love, the spring of motion, acts[4] the
    soul;
Reason's comparing balance rules the whole. 60
Man, but for that, no action could attend,
And, but for this, were active to no end:
Fixed like a plant on his peculiar spot,
To draw nutrition, propagate, and rot;
Or, meteor-like, flame lawless thro' the void,

Destroying others, by himself destroyed.
  Most strength the moving principle requires;
Active its task, it prompts, impels, inspires:
Sedate and quiet, the comparing[5] lies,
Formed but to check, deliberate, and advise. 70
Self-love still stronger, as its objects nigh;
Reason's at distance and in prospect lie:
That sees immediate good by present sense;
Reason, the future and the consequence.
Thicker than arguments, temptations throng,
At best more watchful this, but that more
    strong.
The action of the stronger to suspend,
Reason still use, to reason still attend.
Attention, habit and experience gains; 79
Each strengthens reason, and self-love restrains.
  Let subtle schoolmen teach these friends to
    fight,
More studious to divide than to unite;
And grace and virtue, sense and reason split,
With all the rash dexterity of wit.
Wits, just like fools, at war about a name,
Have full as oft no meaning, or the same.
Self-love and reason to one end aspire,
Pain their aversion, pleasure their desire;
But greedy that, its object would devour,
This taste the honey, and not wound the
    flower: 90
Pleasure, or wrong or rightly understood,
Our greatest evil, or our greatest good.
  III. Modes of self-love the passions we
    may call;
'T is real good, or seeming, moves them all:
But since not every good we can divide,
And reason bids us for our own provide,
Passions, though selfish, if their means be fair,
List under reason, and deserve her care;
Those that imparted, court a nobler aim,
Exalt their kind, and take some virtue's name.
  In lazy apathy let stoics boast   101
Their virtue fixed; 't is fixed as in a frost;
Contracted all, retiring to the breast;
But strength of mind is exercise, not rest:
The rising tempest puts in act the soul,
Parts it may ravage, but preserves the whole.
On life's vast ocean diversely we sail,
Reason the card,[6] but passion is the gale;
Nor God alone in the still calm we find, 109
He mounts the storm, and walks upon the
    wind.
  Passions, like elements, though born to fight,
Yet, mixed and softened, in his work unite:
These 'tis enough to temper and employ;
But what composes man, can man destroy?
Suffice that reason keep to nature's road,

---

1 Alluding to the reformation of the calendar, which had fallen some twelve days behind the sun—a reformation then already generally adopted in Europe, though not in England till 1751.

2 Compare note on I. 202. (Bolingbroke held Plato in contempt.)

3 The dancing dervishes.

4 actuates, moves

5 Supply "principle."   6 compass

Subject, compound them, follow her and God.
Love, hope, and joy, fair pleasure's smiling
    train,
Hate, fear, and grief, the family of pain,
These, mixed with art, and to due bounds con-
    fined,   119
Make and maintain the balance of the mind:
The lights and shades, whose well-accorded
    strife
Gives all the strength and colour of our life.
  Pleasures are ever in our hands or eyes;
And when in act they cease, in prospect rise:
Present to grasp, and future still to find,
The whole employ of body and of mind.
All spread their charms, but charm not all
    alike;
On different senses different objects strike;
Hence different passions more or less inflame,
As strong or weak the organs of the frame; 130
And hence one master-passion in the breast,
Like Aaron's serpent, swallows up the rest.
  As man, perhaps, the moment of his breath,
Receives the lurking principle of death;
The young disease, that must subdue at length,
Grows with his growth, and strengthens with
    his strength:
So, cast and mingled with his very frame,
The mind's disease, its ruling passion, came;
Each vital humour which should feed the
    whole,
Soon flows to this, in body and in soul: 140
Whatever warms the heart, or fills the head,
As the mind opens, and its functions spread,
Imagination plies her dangerous art,
And pours it all upon the peccant part.
Nature its mother, habit is its nurse;
Wit, spirit, faculties, but make it worse;
Reason itself but gives it edge and pow'r;
As Heaven's blest beam turns vinegar more
    sour.
  We, wretched subjects, though to lawful
    sway,
In this weak queen some favorite still obey;
Ah! if she lend not arms as well as rules, 151
What can she more than tell us we are fools?
Teach us to mourn our nature, not to mend;
A sharp accuser, but a helpless friend!
Or from a judge turn pleader, to persuade
The choice we make, or justify it made;
Proud of an easy conquest all along,
She but removes weak passions for the strong.
So, when small humours gather to a gout,
The doctor fancies he has driven them out. 160
  Yes, nature's road must ever be preferred;
Reason is here no guide, but still a guard;
'T is hers to rectify, not overthrow,

And treat this passion more as friend than foe
A mightier power the strong direction sends,
And several men impels to several ends:
Like varying winds by other passions tossed,
This drives them constant to a certain coast.
Let power or knowledge, gold or glory, please
Or (oft more strong than all) the love
    ease;   17
Through life 't is followed, even at life's ex
    pense;
The merchant's toil, the sage's indolence,
The monk's humility, the hero's pride,
All, all alike find reason on their side.
  Th' Eternal Art, educing good from ill,
Grafts on this passion our best principle:
'T is thus the mercury of man is fixed,
Strong grows the virtue with his nature mixed
The dross cements what else were too refined
And in one interest body acts with mind.   18
  As fruits, ungrateful to the planter's care,
On savage stocks inserted, learn to bear,
The surest virtues thus from passions shoot,
Wild nature's vigour working at the root.
What crops of wit and honesty appear
From spleen, from obstinacy, hate, or fear!
See anger, zeal and fortitude supply;
Even avarice, prudence; sloth, philosophy;
Lust, through some certain strainers well re
    fined,
Is gentle love, and charms all womankind; 19
Envy, to which th' ignoble mind's a slave,
Is emulation in the learned or brave;
Nor virtue, male or female, can we name,
But what will grow on pride, or grow on shame
  Thus nature gives us (let it check our pride
The virtue nearest to our vice allied;
Reason the bias turns to good from ill,
And Nero reigns a Titus, if he will.[7]
The fiery soul abhorred in Catiline,
In Decius charms, in Curtius is divine:* 20
The same ambition can destroy or save,
And makes a patriot as it makes a knave.
  IV. This light and darkness in our chao
    joined,
What shall divide? The God within the mind
  Extremes in nature equal ends produce,
In man they join to some mysterious use;
Though each by turns the other's bound in
    vade,
As, in some well-wrought picture, light an
    shade,

[7] i. e., the tyrant turns benefactor.
* Decius voluntarily rushed into death because o
  a vision assuring victory to the side whos
  general should fall. Curtius is alleged to hav
  made a similar self-sacrifice, leaping into a
  chasm in the Roman forum.

And oft so mix, the difference is too nice
Where ends the virtue, or begins the vice.   210
  Fools! who from hence into the notion fall,
That vice or virtue there is none at all.
If white and black blend, soften, and unite
A thousand ways, is there no black or white?
Ask your own heart, and nothing is so plain;
'T is to mistake them costs the time and
    pain.
  V. Vice is a monster of so frightful mien,
As to be hated needs but to be seen;
Yet seen too oft, familiar with her face,
We first endure, then pity, then embrace.   220
But where th' extreme of vice, was ne'er
    agreed:
Ask where 's the north? at York, 't is on the
    Tweed;
In Scotland, at the Orcades; and there,
At Greenland, Zembla, or the Lord knows
    where.
No creature owns it in the first degree,
But thinks his neighbour further gone than he;
Even those who dwell beneath its very zone,
Or never feel the rage, or never own;
What happier natures shrink at with affright
The hard inhabitant contends is right.   230
  VI. Virtuous and vicious every man must
    be;
Few in th' extreme, but all in the degree:
The rogue and fool by fits is fair and wise;
And even the best, by fits, what they despise.
'T is but by parts we follow good or ill;
For, vice or virtue, self directs it still;
Each individual seeks a several goal;
But Heaven's great view is one, and that the
    whole.
That counterworks each folly and caprice;
That disappoints th' effect of every vice;   240
That, happy frailties to all ranks applied,
Shame to the virgin, to the matron pride,
Fear to the statesman, rashness to the chief,
To kings presumption, and to crowds belief:
That, virtue's ends from vanity can raise,
Which seeks no interest, no reward but praise;
And build on wants, and on defects of mind,
The joy, the peace, the glory of mankind.
  Heaven, forming each on other to depend,
A master, or a servant, or a friend,   250
Bids each on other for assistance call,
Till one man's weakness grows the strength of
    all.
Wants, frailties, passions, closer still ally
The common interest, or endear the tie.
To these we owe true friendship, love sincere,
Each home-felt joy that life inherits here;
Yet from the same we learn, in its decline,

Those joys, those loves, those interests to re-
    sign:
Taught half by reason, half by mere decay,
To welcome death, and calmly pass away.   260
  Whate'er the passion, — knowledge, fame, or
    pelf, —
Not one will change his neighbour with himself.
The learned is happy nature to explore,
The fool is happy that he knows no more;
The rich is happy in the plenty given,
The poor contents him with the care of Heaven.
See the blind beggar dance, the cripple sing,
The sot a hero, lunatic a king;
The starving chemist[8] in his golden views
Supremely blest, the poet in his Muse.   270
  See some strange comfort every state attend,
And pride bestowed on all, a common friend:
See some fit passion every age supply,
Hope travels through, nor quits us when we die.
  Behold the child, by Nature's kindly law,
Pleased with a rattle, tickled with a straw;
Some livelier plaything gives his youth delight,
A little louder, but as empty quite:
Scarfs, garters,[9] gold, amuse his riper stage, 279
And beads and prayer-books are the toys of
    age:
Pleased with this bauble still, as that before;
Till tired he sleeps, and life's poor play is
    o'er.
  Meanwhile Opinion gilds, with varying rays,
Those painted clouds that beautify our days;
Each want of happiness by hope supplied,
And each vacuity of sense by pride:
These build as fast as knowledge can destroy;
In Folly's cup still laughs the bubble joy;
One prospect lost, another still we gain;
And not a vanity is given in vain;   290
Even mean self-love becomes, by force divine,
The scale to measure others' wants by thine.
See, and confess, one comfort still must rise;
'T is this, Though man's a fool, yet God is
    wise!

THE UNIVERSAL PRAYER.

Father of all! in every age,
    In every clime adored,
By saint, by savage, and by sage,
    Jehovah, Jove, or Lord!

Thou Great First Cause, least understood:
    Who all my sense confined
To know but this, that Thou art good,
    And that myself am blind;   8

8 alchemist
9 The badge of the highest order of English knight-
    hood.

Yet gave me, in this dark estate,
  To see the good from ill;
And binding nature fast in fate,
  Left free the human will.

What conscience dictates to be done,
  Or warns me not to do,
This, teach me more than hell to shun,
  That, more than heaven pursue.   16

What blessings Thy free bounty gives,
  Let me not cast away;
For God is paid when man receives:
  T' enjoy is to obey.

Yet not to earth's contracted span
  Thy goodness let me bound,
Or think Thee Lord alone of man,
  When thousand worlds are round.   24

Let not this weak, unknowing hand
  Presume Thy bolts to throw,
And deal damnation round the land,
  On each I judge Thy foe.

If I am right, Thy grace impart,
  Still in the right to stay;
If I am wrong, oh! teach my heart
  To find that better way.   32

Save me alike from foolish pride,
  Or impious discontent,
At aught Thy wisdom has denied,
  Or aught Thy goodness lent.

Teach me to feel another's woe,
  To hide the fault I see;
That mercy I to others show,
  That mercy show to me.   40

Mean though I am, not wholly so,
  Since quickened by Thy breath;
Oh, lead me wheresoe'er I go,
  Through this day's life or death.

This day, be bread and peace my lot:
  All else beneath the sun,
Thou know'st if best bestowed or not,
  And let Thy will be done.   48

To Thee, whose temple is all space,
  Whose altar earth, sea, skies,
One chorus let all being raise,
  All nature's incense rise!

DANIEL DEFOE (1659-1731)

FROM ROBINSON CRUSOE

THE CASTAWAY[*]

Had I continued in the station I was now in, I had room for all the happy things to have yet befallen me for which my father so earnestly recommended a quiet, retired life, and of which he had so sensibly described the middle station of life to be full. But other things attended[1] me, and I was still to be the wilful agent of all my own miseries, and particularly to increase my fault and double the reflections upon myself, which in my future sorrows I should have leisure to make. All these miscarriages were procured by my apparent obstinate adherence to my foolish inclinations of wandering abroad, and pursuing that inclination in contradiction to the clearest views of doing myself good in a fair and plain pursuit of those prospects and those measures of life which Nature and Providence concurred to present me with and to make my duty.

As I had once done thus in my breaking away from my parents, so I could not be content now, but I must go and leave the happy view[2] I had of being a rich and thriving man in my new plantation, only to pursue a rash and immoderate desire of rising faster than the nature of the thing admitted; and thus I cast myself down again into the deepest gulf of human misery that ever man fell into, or perhaps could be consistent with life and a state of health in the world.

To come, then, by the just degrees to the particulars of this part of my story. You may suppose that having now lived almost four years in the Brazils, and beginning to thrive and prosper very well upon my plantation, I had not only learned the language, but had contracted acquaintance and friendship among my fellow-planters, as well as among the merchants at St. Salvador, which was our port, and that in my discourses among them I had frequently given them an account of my two voyages to the coast of Guinea, the manner of

---

1 awaited   2 prospect
* Crusoe, having run away to sea at the age of nineteen and been wrecked on the English coast, had next embarked on a trading vessel to the coast of Guinea. Upon a second voyage he was captured by the Moors. Escaping after two years of slavery, he was picked up by a Portuguese vessel and taken to the Brazils. There he set up as a planter and sent back to England for half of the two hundred pounds he had saved from his first venture.

ading with the negroes there, and how easy
was to purchase upon the coast for trifles—
ch as beads, toys, knives, scissors, hatchets,
ts of glass, and the like—not only gold-dust,
uinea grains,[3] elephants' teeth, etc., but
groes, for the service of the Brazils, in great
mbers.

They listened always very attentively to my
scourses on these heads, but especially to that
rt which related to the buying negroes;
ich was a trade, at that time, not only not
r entered into, but, as far as it was, had been
rried on by the *assiento*, or permission, of the
ngs of Spain and Portugal, and engrossed in
e public,[4] so that few negroes were brought,
d those excessive dear.

It happened, being in company with some
erchants and planters of my acquaintance,
d talking of those things very earnestly,
ree of them came to me the next morning,
d told me they had been musing very much
on what I had discoursed with them of, the
st night, and they came to make a secret pro-
sal to me. And after enjoining me secrecy,
ey told me that they had a mind to fit out a
ip to go to Guinea; that they had all planta-
ons as well as I, and were straitened for noth-
g so much as servants; that as it was a trade
at could not be carried on because they could
t publicly sell the negroes when they came
me, so they desired to make but one voyage,
bring the negroes on shore privately, and
vide them among their own plantations; and,
a word, the question was, whether I would
their supercargo in the ship, to manage the
ading part upon the coast of Guinea. And
ey offered me that I should have my equal
are of the negroes without providing any
rt of the stock.

This was a fair proposal, it must be con-
ssed, had it been made to any one that had
t had a settlement and plantation of his own
look after, which was in a fair way of com-
g to be very considerable, and with a good
ock upon it. But for me, that was thus en-
red and established, and had nothing to do
it go on as I had begun, for three or four
ears more, and to have sent for the other
undred pounds from England; and who, in
at time, and with that little addition, could
arce have failed of being worth three or
ur thousand pounds sterling, and that in-
easing too—for me to think of such a voyage,

was the most preposterous thing that ever man,
in such circumstances, could be guilty of.

But I, that was born to be my own destroyer,
could no more resist the offer than I could restrain my first rambling designs, when my
father's good counsel was lost upon me. In a
word, I told them I would go with all my
heart, if they would undertake to look after
my plantation in my absence, and would dispose of it to such as I should direct if I mis-
carried. This they all engaged to do, and entered into writings or covenants to do so; and
I made a formal will, disposing of my plantation and effects, in case of my death; making
the captain of the ship that had saved my
life, as before, my universal heir, but obliging
him to dispose of my effects as I had directed
in my will, one half of the produce being to
himself, and the other to be shipped to England.

In short, I took all possible caution to preserve my effects, and keep up my plantation.
Had I used half as much prudence to have
looked into my own interest, and have made a
judgment of what I ought to have done and
not to have done, I had certainly never gone
away from so prosperous an undertaking, leaving all the probable views of a thriving circumstance, and gone upon a voyage to sea, attended
with all its common hazards, to say nothing
of the reasons I had to expect particular misfortune to myself.

But I was hurried on, and obeyed blindly the
dictates of my fancy rather than my reason.
And accordingly, the ship being fitted out, and
the cargo furnished, and all things done as by
agreement by my partners in the voyage, I
went on board in an evil hour, the [first] of
[September 1659], being the same day eight
year that I went from my father and mother at
Hull, in order to act the rebel to their authority, and the fool to my own interest.

Our ship was about 120 tons burthen; carried six guns and fourteen men, besides the
master, his boy, and myself. We had on board
no large cargo of goods, except of such toys as
were fit for our trade with the negroes—such
as beads, bits of glass, shells, and odd trifles,
especially little looking-glasses, knives, scissors,
hatchets, and the like.

The same day I went on board we set sail,
standing away to the northward upon our own
coast, with design to stretch over for the
African coast, when they* came about ten or

---

aromatic seeds (used for spicing liquor)
held as a state monopoly (Possibly some word
like "stock" has been omitted.)

* This change of subject need not surprise. De-
foe's syntax is often very loose.

twelve degrees of northern latitude; which, it
seems, was the manner of their course in those
days. We had very good weather, only excessive hot, all the way upon our own coast,
till we came the height of[5] Cape St. Augustino;[6] from whence, keeping farther off at sea,
we lost sight of land, and steered as if we were
bound for the isle Fernando de Noronha, holding our course N.E. by N., and leaving those
isles on the east. In this course we passed the
line in about twelve days' time, and were, by
our last observation, in 7° 22′ northern latitude, when a violent tornado, or hurricane, took
us quite out of our knowledge. It began from
the south-east, came about to the north-west,
and then settled into the north-east, from
whence it blew in such a terrible manner, that
for twelve days together we could do nothing
but drive, and, scudding away before it, let
it carry us wherever fate and the fury of the
winds directed; and during these twelve days,
I need not say that I expected every day to be
swallowed up; nor, indeed, did any in the ship
expect to save their lives.

In this distress we had, besides the terror of
the storm, one of our men died of the calen-
ture,[7] and one man and the boy washed overboard. About the twelfth day, the weather
abating a little, the master made an observation as well as he could, and found that he
was in about 11 degrees north latitude, but that
he was 22 degrees of longitude difference west
from Cape St. Augustino; so that he found
he was gotten upon the coast of Guiana, or the
north part of Brazil, beyond the river Amazon,
toward that of the river Orinoco, commonly
called the Great River, and began to consult
with me what course he should take, for the
ship was leaky and very much disabled, and he
was going directly back to the coast of Brazil.

I was positively against that; and looking
over the charts of the sea-coast of America with
him, we concluded there was no inhabited country for us to have recourse to till we came
within the circle of the Caribbee Islands, and
therefore resolved to stand away for Barbadoes; which by keeping off at sea, to avoid
the indraft of the Bay or Gulf of Mexico, we
might easily perform, as we hoped, in about
fifteen days' sail; whereas we could not possibly make our voyage to the coast of Africa
without some assistance, both to our ship and
to ourselves.

With this design we changed our course, a[nd]
steered away N.W. by W. in order to rea[ch]
some of our English islands, where I hoped f[or]
relief; but our voyage was otherwise d[e-]
termined; for being in the latitude of 12 d[e-]
grees 18 minutes a second storm came upon [us]
which carried us away with the same im-
petuosity westward, and drove us so out of t[he]
very way of all human commerce, that had a[ll]
our lives been saved, as to the sea, we we[re]
rather in danger of being devoured by savag[es]
than ever returning to our own country.

In this distress, the wind still blowing ve[ry]
hard, one of our men early in the mornin[g]
cried out, "Land!" and we had no sooner r[un]
out of the cabin to look out, in hopes of se[e-]
ing whereabouts in the world we were, but t[he]
ship struck upon a sand, and in a moment, h[er]
motion being so stopped, the sea broke over h[er]
in such a manner, that we expected we shou[ld]
all have perished immediately; and we we[re]
immediately driven into our close quarters, [to]
shelter us from the very foam and spray of t[he]
sea.

It is not easy for any one, who has not be[en]
in the like condition, to describe or concei[ve]
the consternation of men in such circumstance[s.]
We knew nothing where we were, or upon wh[at]
land it was we were driven, whether an islan[d]
or the main, whether inhabited or not i[n-]
habited; and as the rage of the wind was sti[ll]
great, though rather less than at first, we coul[d]
not so much as hope to have the ship hold man[y]
minutes without breaking in pieces, unless t[he]
winds, by a kind of miracle, should turn immediately about. In a word, we sat lookin[g]
one upon another, and expecting death ever[y]
moment, and every man acting accordingly, a[nd]
preparing for another world; for there wa[s]
little or nothing more for us to do in this. Th[at]
which was our present comfort, and all th[e]
comfort we had, was that, contrary to our expectation, the ship did not break yet, and tha[t]
the master said the wind began to abate.

Now, though we thought that the wind did [a]
little abate, yet the ship having thus struc[k]
upon the sand, and sticking too fast for us t[o]
expect her getting off, we were in a dreadf[ul]
condition indeed, and had nothing to do b[ut]
to think of saving our lives as well as we coul[d.]
We had a boat at our stern just before th[e]
storm, but she was first staved by dashin[g]
against the ship's rudder, and in the nex[t]
place, she broke away, and either sunk, or wa[s]
driven off to sea, so there was no hope fro[m]
her. We had another boat on board, but ho[w]

5 reached the latitude of
6 Cape Sao Agostinhos, about four degrees north
  of Sao Salvador (Bahia).
7 A delirious fever.

o get off into the sea was a doubtful thing. However, there was no room to debate, for we fancied the ship would break in pieces every minute, and some told us she was actually broken already.

In this distress, the mate of our vessel lays hold of the boat, and with the help of the rest of the men they got her slung over the ship's side; and getting all into her, let go, and committed ourselves, being eleven in number, to God's mercy, and the wild sea; for though the storm was abated considerably, yet the sea went dreadful high upon the shore, and might well be called *den wild zee*, as the Dutch call the sea in a storm.

And now our case was very dismal indeed, for we all saw plainly that the sea went so high, that the boat could not live, and that we should be inevitably drowned. As to making sail, we had none; nor, if we had, could we have done anything with it: so we worked at the oar towards the land, though with heavy hearts, like men going to execution; for we all knew that when the boat came nearer the shore she would be dashed in a thousand pieces by the breach of the sea. However, we committed our souls to God in the most earnest manner; and the wind driving us towards the shore, we hastened our destruction with our own hands, pulling as well as we could towards land.

What the shore was, whether rock or sand, whether steep or shoal, we knew not; the only hope that could rationally give us the least shadow of expectation was, if we might happen into some bay or gulf, or the mouth of some river, where by great chance we might have run our boat in, or got under the lee of the land, and perhaps made smooth water. But there was nothing of this appeared; but as we made nearer and nearer the shore, the land looked more frightful than the sea.

After we had rowed, or rather driven, about a league and a half, as we reckoned it, a raging wave, mountain-like, came rolling astern of us, and plainly bade us expect the *coup de grâce*.[8] In a word, it took us with such a fury, that it overset the boat at once; and separating us, as well from the boat as from one another, gave us not time hardly to say, "O God!" for we were all swallowed up in a moment.

Nothing can describe the confusion of thought which I felt when I sunk into the water; for though I swam very well, yet I could not deliver myself from the waves so as to draw breath, till that wave having driven

me, or rather carried me, a vast way on towards the shore, and having spent itself, went back, and left me upon the land almost dry, but half dead with the water I took in. I had so much presence of mind, as well as breath left, that seeing myself nearer the mainland than I expected, I got upon my feet, and endeavoured to make on towards the land as fast as I could, before another wave should return and take me up again. But I soon found it was impossible to avoid it; for I saw the sea come after me as high as a great hill, and as furious as an enemy, which I had no means or strength to contend with. My business was to hold my breath, and raise myself upon the water, if I could; and so by swimming, to preserve my breathing, and pilot myself towards the shore, if possible; my greatest concern now being, that the sea, as it would carry me a great way towards the shore when it came on, might not carry me back again with it when it gave back towards the sea.

The wave that came upon me again, buried me at once 20 or 30 feet deep in its own body, and I could feel myself carried with a mighty force and swiftness towards the shore a very great way; but I held my breath, and assisted myself to swim still forward with all my might. I was ready to burst with holding my breath, when, as I felt myself rising up, so, to my immediate relief, I found my head and hands shoot out above the surface of the water; and though it was not two seconds of time that I could keep myself so, yet it relieved me greatly, gave me breath and new courage. I was covered again with water a good while, but not so long but I held it out; and finding the water had spent itself, and began to return, I struck forward against the return of the waves, and felt ground again with my feet. I stood still a few moments to recover breath, and till the water went from me, and then took to my heels and ran with what strength I had farther towards the shore. But neither would this deliver me from the fury of the sea, which came pouring in after me again, and twice more I was lifted up by the waves and carried forwards as before, the shore being very flat.

The last time of these two had well near been fatal to me; for the sea, having hurried me along as before, landed me, or rather dashed me, against a piece of a rock, and that with such force, as it left me senseless, and indeed helpless, as to my own deliverance; for the blow taking my side and breast, beat the breath as it were quite out of my body; and

8 finishing stroke

had it returned again immediately, I must have been strangled in the water. But I recovered a little before the return of the waves, and seeing I should be covered again with the water, I resolved to hold fast by a piece of the rock, and so to hold my breath, if possible, till the wave went back. Now as the waves were not so high as at first, being near land, I held my hold till the wave abated, and then fetched another run, which brought me so near the shore, that the next wave, though it went over me, yet did not so swallow me up as to carry me away, and the next run I took I got to the mainland, where, to my great comfort, I clambered up the cliffs of the shore, and sat me down upon the grass, free from danger, and quite out of the reach of the water.

I was now landed, and safe on shore, and began to look up and thank God that my life was saved in a case wherein there was some minutes before scarce any room to hope. I believe it is impossible to express to the life what the ecstasies and transports of the soul are when it is so saved, as I may say, out of the very grave; and I do not wonder now at that custom, namely, that when a malefactor, who has the halter about his neck, is tied up, and just going to be turned off, and has a reprieve brought to him,—I say, I do not wonder that they bring a surgeon with it, to let him blood[9] that very moment they tell him of it, that the surprise may not drive the animal spirits from the heart and overwhelm him:

"For sudden joys, like griefs, confound at
    first."

I walked about on the shore, lifting up my hands, and my whole being, as I may say, wrapt up in the contemplation of my deliverance, making a thousand gestures and motions which I cannot describe, reflecting upon all my comrades that were drowned, and that there should not be one soul saved but myself; for, as for them, I never saw them afterwards, or any sign of them, except three of their hats, one cap, and two shoes that were not fellows.

I cast my eyes to the stranded vessel, when the breach and froth of the sea being so big, I could hardly see it, it lay so far off, and considered, Lord! how was it possible I could get on shore?

After I had solaced my mind with the comfortable part of my condition, I began to look round me to see what kind of place I was in, and what was next to be done, and I soon

found my comforts abate, and that, in a word, I had a dreadful deliverance; for I was wet, had no clothes to shift me, nor anything either to eat or drink to comfort me, neither did I see any prospect before me but that of perishing with hunger, or being devoured by wild beasts; and that which was particularly afflicting to me was, that I had no weapon either to hunt and kill any creature for my sustenance, or to defend myself against any other creature that might desire to kill me for theirs. In a word, I had nothing about me but a knife, a tobacco-pipe, and a little tobacco in a box. This was all my provision; and this threw me into terrible agonies of mind, that for a while I ran about like a madman. Night coming upon me, I began, with a heavy heart, to consider what would be my lot if there were any ravenous beasts in that country, seeing at night they always come abroad for their prey.

All the remedy that offered to my thoughts at that time was, to get up into a thick bushy tree like a fir, but thorny, which grew near me, and where I resolved to sit all night, and consider the next day what death I should die, for as yet I saw no prospect of life. I walked about a furlong from the shore, to see if I could find any fresh water to drink, which I did, to my great joy; and having drank, and put a little tobacco in my mouth to prevent hunger, I went to the tree, and getting up into it, endeavoured to place myself so, as that if I should sleep I might not fall; and having cut me a short stick, like a truncheon, for my defence, I took up my lodging, and having been excessively fatigued, I fell fast asleep, and slept as comfortably as, I believe, few could have done in my condition, and found myself the most refreshed with it that I think I ever was on such an occasion.

JONATHAN SWIFT (1667-1745)

GULLIVER'S TRAVELS.*

FROM PART I. A VOYAGE TO LILLIPUT.

CHAPTER I.

My father had a small estate in Nottinghamshire; I was the third of five sons. He sent me to Emmanuel College in Cambridge at fourteen years old, where I resided three years, and

9 i. e., bleed him

*This apparently simple tale is in reality a continuous and sweeping satire. Says Sir Walter Scott: "No word drops from Gulliver's pen

applied myself close to my studies; but the charge of maintaining me, although I had a very scanty allowance, being too great for a narrow fortune, I was bound apprentice to Mr. James Bates, an eminent surgeon in London, with whom I continued four years; and my father now and then sending me small sums of money, I laid them out in learning navigation, and other parts of the mathematics useful to those who intend to travel, as I always believed it would be, some time or other, my fortune to do. When I left Mr. Bates, I went down to my father; where, by the assistance of him, and my uncle John and some other relations, I got forty pounds, and a promise of thirty pounds a year, to maintain me at Leyden. There I studied physic two years and seven months, knowing it would be useful in long voyages.

Soon after my return from Leyden, I was recommended by my good master, Mr. Bates, to be surgeon to *The Swallow*, Captain Abraham Pannell, commander; with whom I continued three years and a half, making a voyage or two into the Levant,[1] and some other parts. When I came back I resolved to settle in London; to which Mr. Bates, my master, encouraged me, and by him I was recommended to several patients. I took part of a small house in the Old Jewry;[2] and being advised to alter my condition, I married Mrs.[3] Mary Burton, second daughter to Mr. Edmund Burton, hosier in Newgate Street, with whom I received four hundred pounds for a portion.

But my good master, Bates, dying in two years after, and I having few friends, my business began to fail; for my conscience would not suffer me to imitate the bad practice of too many among my brethren. Having, there-

1 The Orient, especially the east coast of the Mediterranean.
2 A street in the heart of London.
3 Mistress, a title then given to both married and unmarried women.

in vain. Where his work ceases for a moment to satirize the vices of mankind in general, it becomes a stricture upon the parties, politics, and court of Britain; where it abandons that subject of censure, it presents a lively picture of the vices and follies of the fashionable world, or of the vain pursuits of philosophy, while the parts of the narrative which refer to the traveller's own adventures form a humorous and striking parody of the manner of old voyagers." Of Part I., the Voyage to Lilliput, the same writer says: "The satire is here levelled against the court and ministry of George I. In some points the parallel is very closely drawn, as where the parties in the church and state are described, and the mode in which offices and marks of distinction are conferred in the Lilliputian court." See also *Eng. Lit.*, pp. 174-175.

fore, consulted with my wife, and some of my acquaintance, I determined to go again to sea. I was surgeon successively in two ships, and made several voyages, for six years, to the East and West Indies, by which I got some addition to my fortune. My hours of leisure I spent in reading the best authors, ancient and modern, being always provided with a good number of books; and, when I was ashore, in observing the manners and dispositions of the people, as well as learning their language, wherein I had a great facility, by the strength of my memory.

The last of these voyages not proving very fortunate, I grew weary of the sea, and intended to stay at home with my wife and family. I removed from the Old Jewry to Fetter Lane, and from thence to Wapping, hoping to get business among the sailors; but it would not turn to account. After three years' expectation that things would mend, I accepted an advantageous offer from Captain William Prichard, master of *The Antelope*, who was making a voyage to the South Sea. We set sail from Bristol, May 4, 1699; and our voyage at first was very prosperous.

It would not be proper, for some reasons, to trouble the reader with the particulars of our adventures in those seas. Let it suffice to inform him, that, in our passage from thence to the East Indies, we were driven by a violent storm to the northwest of Van Diemen's Land. By an observation, we found ourselves in the latitude of 30 degrees 2 minutes south. Twelve of our crew were dead by immoderate labour and ill food; the rest were in a very weak condition.

On the fifth of November, which was the beginning of summer in those parts, the weather being very hazy, the seamen spied a rock within half a cable's length of the ship; but the wind was so strong, that we were driven directly upon it, and immediately split. Six of the crew, of whom I was one, having let down the boat into the sea, made a shift to get clear of the ship and the rock. We rowed, by my computation, about three leagues, till we were able to work no longer, being already spent with labour, while we were in the ship. We, therefore, trusted ourselves to the mercy of the waves; and, in about half an hour, the boat was overset by a sudden flurry from the north. What became of my companions in the boat, as well as of those who escaped on the rock, or were left in the vessel, I cannot tell, but conclude they were all lost.

For my own part, I swam as fortune directed me, and was pushed forward by wind and tide. I often let my legs drop, and could feel no bottom; but, when I was almost gone, and able to struggle no longer, I found myself within my depth; and, by this time, the storm was much abated.

The declivity was so small that I walked near a mile before I got to the shore, which I conjectured was about eight o'clock in the evening. I then advanced forward near half a mile, but could not discover any sign of houses or inhabitants; at least, I was in so weak a condition, that I did not observe them. I was extremely tired, and with that, and the heat of the weather, and about half a pint of brandy that I drank as I left the ship, I found myself much inclined to sleep. I lay down on the grass, which was very short and soft, where I slept sounder than ever I remembered to have done in my life, and, as I reckoned, above nine hours; for, when I awaked, it was just daylight. I attempted to rise, but was not able to stir: for as I happened to lie on my back, I found my arms and legs were strongly fastened on each side to the ground; and my hair, which was long and thick, tied down in the same manner. I likewise felt several slender ligatures across my body, from my armpits to my thighs. I could only look upwards; the sun began to grow hot, and the light offended my eyes.

I heard a confused noise about me; but, in the posture I lay, could see nothing except the sky. In a little time I felt something alive on my left leg, which, advancing gently forward over my breast, came almost up to my chin; when, bending my eyes downward as much as I could, I perceived it to be a human creature, not six inches high, with a bow and arrow in his hands, and a quiver at his back. In the meantime I felt at least forty more of the same kind (as I conjectured) following the first. I was in the utmost astonishment, and roared so loud that they all ran back in a fright; and some of them, as I was afterwards told, were hurt with the falls they got by leaping from my sides upon the ground. However, they soon returned, and one of them, who ventured so far as to get a full sight of my face, lifting up his hands and eyes by way of admiration, cried out in a shrill but distinct voice—*Hekinah degul!* The others repeated the same words several times, but I then knew not what they meant.

I lay all this while, as the reader may believe, in great uneasiness. At length, struggling to get loose, I had the fortune to break the strings, and wrench out the pegs, that fastened my left arm to the ground; for by lifting it up to my face, I discovered the methods they had taken to bind me, and, at the same time with a violent pull, which gave me excessive pain, I a little loosened the strings that tied down my hair on the left side, so that I was just able to turn my head about two inches.

But the creatures ran off a second time, before I could seize them; whereupon there was a great shout in a very shrill accent, and after it ceased, I heard one of them cry aloud, *Tolgo phonac;* when, in an instant, I felt above a hundred arrows discharged on my left hand which pricked me like so many needles; and besides, they shot another flight into the air as we do bombs in Europe, whereof many, I suppose, fell on my body (though I felt them not), and some on my face, which I immediately covered with my left hand.

When this shower of arrows was over, I fell a-groaning with grief and pain, and then striving again to get loose, they discharged another volley larger than the first, and some of them attempted with spears to stick me in the sides but by good luck I had on me a buff jerkin,[4] which they could not pierce. I thought it the most prudent method to lie still, and my design was to continue so till night, when, my left hand being already loose, I could easily free myself; and as for the inhabitants, I had reason to believe I might be a match for the greatest armies they could bring against me, if they were all of the same size with him that I saw.

But fortune disposed otherwise of me. When the people observed I was quiet, they discharged no more arrows: but, by the noise I heard, I knew their numbers increased; and about four yards from me, over against my right ear, I heard a knocking for above an hour, like that of people at work; when, turning my head that way, as well as the pegs and strings would permit me, I saw a stage erected about a foot and a half from the ground, capable of holding four of the inhabitants, with two or three ladders to mount it; from whence one of them, who seemed to be a person of quality, made me a long speech, whereof I understood not one syllable.

But I should have mentioned, that before the principal person began his oration, he cried

4 leather waistcoat

ut three times, *Langro dehul san* (these words, and the former, were afterwards repeated, and explained to me). Whereupon immediately about fifty of the inhabitants came and cut the strings that fastened the left side of my head, which gave me the liberty of turning it to the right, and of observing the person and gesture of him that was to speak. He appeared to be of a middle age, and taller than any of the other three who attended him, whereof one was a page that held up his train, and seemed to be somewhat longer than my middle finger; the other two stood one on each side, to support him. He acted every part of an orator, and I could observe many periods[5] of threatenings, and others of promises, pity, and kindness.

I answered in a few words, but in the most submissive manner, lifting up my left hand and both my eyes to the sun, as calling him for a witness: and, being almost famished with hunger, having not eaten a morsel for some hours before I left the ship, I found the demands of nature so strong upon me, that I could not forbear showing my impatience (perhaps against the strict rules of decency) by putting my finger frequently to my mouth, to signify that I wanted food. The *hurgo* (for so they call a great lord, as I afterwards learned) understood me very well. He descended from the stage, and commanded that several ladders should be applied to my sides; on which above an hundred of the inhabitants mounted, and walked towards my mouth, laden with baskets full of meat, which had been provided and sent thither by the king's orders, upon the first intelligence he received of me.

I observed there was the flesh of several animals, but could not distinguish them by the taste. There were shoulders, legs, and loins, shaped like those of mutton, and very well dressed, but smaller than the wings of a lark. I ate them by two or three at a mouthful, and took three loaves at a time, about the bigness of musket bullets. They supplied me as they could, showing a thousand marks of wonder and astonishment at my bulk and appetite. I then made another sign that I wanted drink.

They found by my eating that a small quantity would not suffice me; and being a most ingenious people, they slung up, with great dexterity, one of their largest hogsheads, then rolled it towards my hand, and beat out the top: I drank it off at a draught; which I might well do, for it did not hold half a pint, and tasted like a small[6] wine of Burgundy, but

much more delicious. They brought me a second hogshead, which I drank in the same manner, and made signs for more; but they had none to give me.

When I had performed these wonders, they shouted for joy, and danced upon my breast, repeating, several times, as they did at first, *Hekinah degul*. They made me a sign that I should throw down the two hogsheads, but first warning the people below to stand out of the way, crying aloud, *Borach mivola;* and, when they saw the vessels in the air, there was an universal shout of *Hekinah degul*.

I confess, I was often tempted, while they were passing backwards and forwards on my body, to seize forty or fifty of the first that came in my reach, and dash them against the ground. But the remembrance of what I had felt, which probably might not be the worst they could do, and the promise of honour I made them—for so I interpreted my submissive behaviour—soon drove out these imaginations. Besides, I now considered myself as bound, by the laws of hospitality, to a people who had treated me with so much expense and magnificence. However, in my thoughts I could not sufficiently wonder at the intrepidity of these diminutive mortals, who durst venture to mount and walk upon my body, while one of my hands was at liberty, without trembling at the very sight of so prodigious a creature as I must appear to them.

After some time, when they observed that I made no more demands for meat, there appeared before me a person of high rank from his imperial majesty. His excellency, having mounted on the small of my right leg, advanced forwards up to my face, with about a dozen of his retinue: and, producing his credentials under the signet-royal, which he applied close to my eyes, spoke about ten minutes, without any signs of anger, but with a kind of determinate resolution, often pointing forwards, which, as I afterwards found, was towards the capital city, about half a mile distant, whither it was agreed by his majesty in council that I must be conveyed. I answered in a few words, but to no purpose, and made a sign with my hand that was loose, putting it to the other (but over his excellency's head, for fear of hurting him or his train) and then to my own head and body, to signify that I desired my liberty.

It appeared that he understood me well enough, for he shook his head by way of disapprobation, and held his hands in a posture to show that I must be carried as a prisoner. However, he made other signs, to let me understand that I should have meat and drink enough, and very good treatment. Whereupon I once more thought of attempting to break my bonds; but again, when I felt the smart of their arrows upon my face and hands, which were all in blisters, and many of the darts still sticking in them, and observing, likewise, that the number of my enemies increased, I gave tokens to let them know that they might do with me what they pleased. Upon this the *hurgo* and his train withdrew, with much civility, and cheerful countenances.

Soon after, I heard a general shout, with frequent repetitions of the words, *Peplom selan*, and I felt great numbers of people on my left side, relaxing the cords to such a degree, that I was able to turn upon my right, and so get a little ease. But, before this, they had daubed my face and both my hands with a sort of ointment very pleasant to the smell, which, in a few minutes, removed all the smart of their arrows. These circumstances, added to the refreshment I had received by their victuals and drink, which were very nourishing, disposed me to sleep. I slept about eight hours, as I was afterwards assured; and it was no wonder, for the physicians, by the emperor's order, had mingled a sleepy potion in the hogsheads of wine.

It seems that, upon the first moment I was discovered sleeping on the ground, after my landing, the emperor had early notice of it by an express; and determined in council, that I should be tied in the manner I have related (which was done in the night, while I slept), that plenty of meat and drink should be sent to me, and a machine prepared to carry me to the capital city.

This resolution, perhaps, may appear very bold and dangerous, and I am confident would not be imitated by any prince in Europe on the like occasion. However, in my opinion, it was extremely prudent, as well as generous; for, supposing these people had endeavoured to kill me with their spears and arrows, while I was asleep, I should certainly have awaked with the first sense of smart, which might so far have roused my rage and strength, as to have enabled me to break the strings wherewith I was tied; after which, as they were not able to make resistance, so they could expect no mercy.

These people are most excellent mathematicians, and arrived to a great perfection in mechanics, by the countenance and encouragement of the emperor, who is a renowned patron of learning. This prince hath several machines fixed on wheels for the carriage of trees and other great weights. He often builds his largest men-of-war, whereof some are nine foot long, in the woods where the timber grows, and has them carried on these engines three or four hundred yards to the sea.* Five hundred carpenters and engineers were immediately set at work to prepare the greatest engine they had. It was a frame of wood, raised three inches from the ground, about seven feet long and four wide, moving upon twenty-two wheels. The shout I heard was upon the arrival of this engine, which, it seems, set out in four hours after my landing. It was brought parallel to me as I lay. But the principal difficulty was to raise and place me in this vehicle.

Eighty poles, each of one foot high, were erected for this purpose, and very strong cords, of the bigness of packthread, were fastened by hooks to many bandages, which the workmen had girt round my neck, my hands, my body, and my legs. Nine hundred of the strongest men were employed to draw up these cords by many pulleys fastened on the poles; and thus in less than three hours I was raised and slung into the engine, and there tied fast.

All this I was told; for, while the whole operation was performing, I lay in a profound sleep, by the force of that soporiferous medicine infused into my liquor. Fifteen hundred of the emperor's largest horses, each about four inches and a half high, were employed to draw me towards the metropolis, which, as I said, was half a mile distant.

About four hours after we began our journey, I awaked, by a very ridiculous accident; for the carriage being stopped a while, to adjust something that was out of order, two or three of the young natives had the curiosity to see how I looked, when I was asleep. They climbed up into the engine, and advancing very softly to my face, one of them, an officer in the guards, put the sharp end of his half-pike a good way up into my left nostril, which tickled my nose like a straw, and made me sneeze violently; whereupon they stole off, unperceived, and it was three weeks before I knew the cause of my awaking so suddenly.

We made a long march the remaining part

---

* Swift has been admired for the correctness of his figures. Compare the length of these men-of-war with the height of the Lilliputians.

of that day, and rested at night with five hundred guards on each side of me, half with torches, and half with bows and arrows, ready to shoot me, if I should offer to stir. The next morning, at sunrise, we continued our march, and arrived within two hundred yards of the city gates about noon. The emperor, and all his court, came out to meet us; but his great officers would by no means suffer his majesty to endanger his person by mounting on my body.

At the place where the carriage stopped there stood an ancient temple, esteemed to be the largest in the whole kingdom; which, having been polluted some years before by an unnatural murder, was, according to the zeal of those people, looked upon as profane, and therefore had been applied to common use, and all the ornaments and furniture carried away. In this edifice it was determined I should lodge. The great gate, fronting to the north, was about four feet high, and almost two feet wide, through which I could easily creep. On each side of the gate was a small window, not above six inches from the ground; into that on the left side the king's smith conveyed four score and eleven chains, like those that hang to a lady's watch in Europe, and almost as large, which were locked to my left leg with six-and-thirty padlocks.

Over against this temple, on the other side of the great highway, at twenty feet distance, there was a turret at least five feet high. Here the emperor ascended, with many principal lords of his court, to have an opportunity of viewing me, as I was told, for I could not see them. It was reckoned that above an hundred thousand inhabitants came out of the town upon the same errand; and, in spite of my guards, I believe there could not be fewer than ten thousand, at several times, who mounted my body, by the help of ladders. But a proclamation was soon issued, to forbid it, upon pain of death.

When the workmen found it was impossible for me to break loose, they cut all the strings that bound me; whereupon I rose up, with as melancholy a disposition as ever I had in my life. But the noise and astonishment of the people, at seeing me rise and walk, are not to be expressed. The chains that held my left leg were about two yards long, and gave me not only the liberty of walking backwards and forwards in a semicircle, but, being fixed within four inches of the gate, allowed me to creep in, and lie at my full length in the temple.

CHAPTER II.

When I found myself on my feet I looked about me, and must confess I never beheld a more entertaining prospect. The country around appeared like a continued garden, and the enclosed fields, which were generally forty foot square, resembled so many beds of flowers. These fields were intermingled with woods of half a stang,[1] and the tallest trees, as I could judge, appeared to be seven foot high. I viewed the town on my left hand, which looked like the painted scene of a city in a theatre. . . .

The emperor was already descended from the tower, and advancing on horseback towards me, which had like to have cost him dear; for the beast, though very well trained, yet wholly unused to such a sight, which appeared as if a mountain moved before him, reared up on his hinder feet. But that prince, who is an excellent horseman, kept his seat, till his attendants ran in and held the bridle, while his majesty had time to dismount.

When he alighted, he surveyed me round with great admiration, but kept without the length of my chain. He ordered his cooks and butlers, who were already prepared, to give me victuals and drink, which they pushed forward in a sort of vehicles upon wheels, till I could reach them. I took these vehicles, and soon emptied them all; twenty of them were filled with meat, and ten with liquor; each of the former afforded me two or three good mouthfuls; and I emptied the liquor of ten vessels, which was contained in earthen vials, into one vehicle, drinking it off at a draught; and so I did with the rest. The empress and young princes of the blood of both sexes, attended by many ladies, sat at some distance in their chairs;[2] but upon the accident that happened to the emperor's horse, they alighted, and came near his person, which I am now going to describe. He is taller, by almost the breadth of my nail, than any of his court, which alone is enough to strike an awe into the beholders. His features are strong and masculine, with an Austrian lip and arched nose, his complexion olive, his countenance erect, his body and limbs well proportioned, all his motions graceful, and his deportment majestic. He was then past his prime, being twenty-eight years and three-quarters old, of which he had reigned about seven in great felicity, and generally victorious.

1 half a rood (one-eighth of an acre)
2 sedan-chairs

For the better convenience of beholding him, I lay on my side, so that my face was parallel to his, and he stood but three yards off. However, I have had him since many times in my hand, and therefore cannot be deceived in the description.

His dress was very plain and simple, and the fashion of it between the Asiatic and the European; but he had on his head a light helmet of gold, adorned with jewels, and a plume on the crest. He held his sword drawn in his hand, to defend himself, if I should happen to break loose; it was almost three inches long; the hilt and scabbard were gold, enriched with diamonds. His voice was shrill, but very clear and articulate, and I could distinctly hear it, when I stood up.

The ladies and courtiers were all most magnificently clad; so that the spot they stood upon seemed to resemble a petticoat spread on the ground, embroidered with figures of gold and silver. His imperial majesty spoke often to me, and I returned answers, but neither of us could understand a syllable. There were several of his priests and lawyers present (as I conjectured by their habits[3]), who were commanded to address themselves to me; and I spoke to them in as many languages as I had the least smattering of, which were, High and Low Dutch, Latin, French, Spanish, Italian, and Lingua Franca;[4] but all to no purpose.

After about two hours the court retired, and J. was left with a strong guard, to prevent the impertinence, and probably the malice of the rabble, who were very impatient to crowd about me as near as they durst; and some of them had the impudence to shoot their arrows at me, as I sat on the ground by the door of my house, whereof one very narrowly missed my left eye. But the colonel ordered six of the ring-leaders to be seized, and thought no punishment so proper as to deliver them bound into my hands; which some of his soldiers accordingly did, pushing them forwards with the butt-ends of their pikes into my reach. I took them all in my right hand, put five of them into my coat-pocket; and as to the sixth, I made a countenance as if I would eat him alive. The poor man squalled terribly, and the colonel and his officers were in much pain, especially when they saw me take out my penknife; but I soon put them out of fear, for, looking mildly, and immediately cutting the strings he was bound with, I set him gently on the

ground, and away he ran. I treated the rest in the same manner, taking them one by one out of my pocket; and I observed both the soldiers and people were highly obliged at this mark of my clemency, which was represented very much to my advantage at court.

Towards night, I got with some difficulty into my house, where I lay on the ground, and continued to do so about a fortnight, during which time the emperor gave orders to have a bed prepared for me. Six hundred beds, of the common measure, were brought in carriages and worked up in my house; an hundred and fifty of their beds, sewn together, made up the breadth and length; and these were four double, which, however, kept me but very indifferently from the hardness of the floor, that was of smooth stone. By the same computation, they provided me with sheets, blankets, and coverlets, tolerable enough for one who had been so long inured to hardships as I.

As the news of my arrival spread through the kingdom, it brought prodigious numbers of rich, idle, and curious people to see me; so that the villages were almost emptied; and great neglect of tillage and household affairs must have ensued, if his imperial majesty had not provided, by several proclamations and orders of state, against this inconveniency. He directed that those who had already beheld me should return home, and not presume to come within fifty yards of my house without license from court; whereby the secretaries of state got considerable fees.

In the meantime, the emperor held frequent councils, to debate what course should be taken with me; and I was afterwards assured by a particular friend, a person of great quality, who was looked upon to be as much in the secret as any, that the court was under many difficulties concerning me. They apprehended my breaking loose; that my diet would be very expensive, and might cause a famine. Sometimes they determined to starve me, or at least to shoot me in the face and hands with poisoned arrows, which would soon dispatch me: but again they considered that the stench of so large a carcase might produce a plague in the metropolis, and probably spread through the whole kingdom.

In the midst of these consultations, several officers of the army went to the door of the great council-chamber, and two of them being admitted, gave an account of my behaviour to the six criminals above-mentioned, which made so favourable an impression in the breast of

---

[3] costumes
[4] A commercial jargon compounded then chiefly of Italian and Oriental languages.

majesty and the whole board in my behalf,
t an imperial commission was issued out,
iging all the villages nine hundred yards
nd the city to deliver in, every morning, six
ves, forty sheep, and other victuals, for my
tenance; together with a proportionable
antity of bread and wine, and other liquors;
the due payment of which his majesty gave
ignments upon his treasury. For this prince
es chiefly upon his own demesnes, seldom,
ept upon great occasions, raising any sub-
ies upon his subjects, who are bound to at-
d him in his wars at their own expense. An
ablishment was also made of six hundred
sons, to be my domestics, who had board-
ges allowed for their maintenance, and tents
lt for them very conveniently on each side
my door.

t was likewise ordered that three hundred
lors should make me a suit of clothes, after
fashion of the country; that six of his
jesty's greatest scholars should be employed
instruct me in their language; and lastly,
t the emperor's horses, and those of the
bility and troops of guards, should be fre-
ently exercised in my sight, to accustom
mselves to me.

All these orders were duly put in execution,
d in about three weeks I made a great
gress in learning their language; during
ich time the emperor frequently honoured
with his visits, and was pleased to assist
masters in teaching me. We began already
converse together in some sort; and the
st words I learnt were to express my desire
at he would please to give me liberty, which
every day repeated on my knees. His answer,
I could apprehend it, was, that this must
a work of time, not to be thought on with-
t the advice of his council, and that first I
st *lumos kelmin pesso desmar lon emposo;*
at is, swear a peace with him and his king-
m; however, that I should be used with all
ndness; and he advised me to acquire, by my
tience and discreet behaviour, the good
inion of himself and his subjects.

He desired I would not take it ill if he gave
ders to certain proper officers to search me;
r probably I might carry about me several
apons which must needs be dangerous things,
they answered the bulk of so prodigious a
rson. I said his majesty should be satisfied,
r I was ready to strip myself and turn up my
ckets before him. This I delivered, part in
ords, and part in signs.

He replied, that by the laws of the kingdom

I must be searched by two of his officers; that
he knew this could not be done without my
consent and assistance; that he had so good an
opinion of my generosity and justice, as to
trust their persons in my hands; that whatever they took from me should be returned
when I left the country, or paid for at the rate
which I should set upon them. I took up the
two officers in my hands, put them first into
my coat-pockets, and then into every other
pocket about me, except my two fobs and
another secret pocket I had no mind should be
searched, wherein I had some little necessaries
that were of no consequence to any but myself.
In one of my fobs there was a silver watch,
and in the other a small quantity of gold in
a purse.

These gentlemen having pen, ink, and paper
about them, made an exact inventory of everything they saw; and, when they had done, desired I would set them down, that they might
deliver it to the emperor. This inventory I
afterwards translated into English, and is
word for word as follows: *

Imprimis,[5] In the right coat-pocket of the
great man-mountain (for so I interpret the
words *quinbus flestrin*), after the strictest
search, we found only one great piece of
coarse cloth, large enough to be a foot-cloth
for your majesty's chief room of state. In the
left pocket we saw a huge silver chest, with a
cover of the same metal, which we the search-
ers were not able to lift. We desired it should
be opened, and one of us stepping into it,
found himself up to the mid-leg in a sort of
dust, some part whereof flying up to our faces,
set us both a sneezing for several times together. In his right waistcoat pocket we found
a prodigious bundle of white thin substances
folded one over another, about the bigness of
three men, tied with a strong cable, and marked
with black figures; which we humbly conceive
to be writings, every letter almost half as large
as the palm of our hands. In the left, there
was a sort of engine, from the back of which
were extended twenty long poles, resembling
the palisadoes before your majesty's court;
wherewith we conjecture the man-mountain
combs his head, for we did not always trouble
him with questions, because we found it a great
difficulty to make him understand us. In the

5 first
* This report may possibly satirize the reports of
the committees of secrecy on the Jacobite
plots.

large pocket on the right side of his middle cover (so I translate the word *ranfu-lo*, by which they meant my breeches), we saw a hollow pillar of iron, about the length of a man, fastened to a strong piece of timber, larger than the pillar; and upon one side of the pillar were huge pieces of iron sticking out, cut into strange figures, which we know not what to make of. In the left pocket, another engine of the same kind. In the smaller pocket on the right side were several round flat pieces of white and red metal, of different bulk; some of the white, which seemed to be silver, were so large and heavy that my comrade and I could hardly lift them. In the left pocket were two black pillars irregularly shaped; we could not without difficulty reach the top of them, as we stood at the bottom of his pocket. One of them was covered, and seemed all of a piece; but at the upper end of the other there appeared a white round substance, about twice the bigness of our heads. Within each of these was enclosed a prodigious plate of steel, which, by our orders, we obliged him to show us, because we apprehended they might be dangerous engines. He took them out of their cases, and told us that in his own country his practice was to shave his beard with one of these, and to cut his meat with the other. There were two pockets which we could not enter: these he called his fobs. Out of the right fob hung a great silver chain, with a wonderful kind of engine at the bottom. We directed him to draw out whatever was fastened to that chain, which appeared to be a globe, half silver, and half of some transparent metal; for on the transparent side we saw certain strange figures, circularly drawn, and thought we could touch them till we found our fingers stopped by that lucid substance. He put this engine to our ears, which made an incessant noise, like that of a water-mill; and we conjecture it is either some unknown animal, or the god that he worships; but we are more inclined to the latter opinion, because he assured us (if we understood him right, for he expressed himself very imperfectly), that he seldom did anything without consulting it. He called it his oracle, and said it pointed out the time for every action of his life. From the left fob he took out a net almost large enough for a fisherman, but contrived to open and shut like a purse, and served him for the same use; we found therein several massy pieces of yellow metal, which, if they be real gold, must be of immense value.

Having thus, in obedience to your majesty's

commands, diligently searched all his pocke[ts] we observed a girdle about his waist, made [of] the hide of some prodigious animal, fr[om] which, on the left side, hung a sword of t[he] length of five men; and on the right, a b[ag] or pouch, divided into two cells, each cell cap[a-] ble of holding three of your majesty's su[b-] jects. In one of these cells were several glob[es] or balls, of a most ponderous metal, about t[he] bigness of our heads, and required a stro[ng] hand to lift them; the other cell contained [a] heap of certain black grains, but of no gre[at] bulk or weight, for we could hold about fif[ty] of them in the palms of our hands.

This is an exact inventory of what we fou[nd] about the body of the man-mountain, who us[ed] us with great civility and due respect to yo[ur] majesty's commission. Signed and sealed, [on] the fourth day of the eighty-ninth moon of yo[ur] majesty's auspicious reign.

CLEFREN FRELOC,
MARSI FRELOC.

When this inventory was read over to t[he] emperor, he directed me, although in very ge[n-] tle terms, to deliver up the several particula[rs.]

He first called for my scimitar, which I to[ok] out, scabbard and all. In the meantime, [he] ordered three thousand of his choicest troo[ps] (who then attended him) to surround me at [a] distance, with their bows and arrows ju[st] ready to discharge; but I did not observe [it,] for mine eyes were wholly fixed upon h[is] majesty. He then desired me to draw m[y] scimitar, which, although it had got some ru[st] by the sea-water, was in most parts exceedi[ng] bright. I did so, and immediately all the troo[ps] gave a shout between terror and surprise; f[or] the sun shone clear, and the reflection dazzl[ed] their eyes, as I waved the scimitar to and f[ro] in my hand. His majesty, who is a most ma[g-] nanimous prince, was less daunted than I cou[ld] expect; he ordered me to return it into t[he] scabbard and cast it on the ground as gent[ly] as I could, about six foot from the end [of] my chain.

The next thing he demanded was one of t[he] hollow iron pillars, by which he meant m[y] pocket-pistols. I drew it out, and at his d[e-] sire, as well as I could, expressed to him t[he] use of it; and charging it only with powd[er,] which, by the closeness of my pouch, happen[ed] to escape wetting in the sea (an inconvenien[ce] against which all prudent mariners take speci[al] care to provide), I first cautioned the e[m-]

ror not to be afraid, and then I let it off in
e air.

The astonishment here was much greater
an at the sight of my scimitar. Hundreds
ll down as if they had been struck dead; and
en the emperor, although he stood his
ound, could not recover himself in some
me.

I delivered up both my pistols, in the same
anner as I had done my scimitar, and then my
uch of powder and bullets, begging him that
e former might be kept from the fire, for it
ould kindle with the smallest spark, and blow
his imperial palace into the air.

I likewise delivered up my watch, which the
mperor was very curious to see, and com-
anded two of his tallest yeomen of the guards
bear it on a pole upon their shoulders, as
aymen in England do a barrel of ale. He
as amazed at the continual noise it made and
e motion of the minute-hand, which he could
sily discern (for their sight is much more
ute than ours), and asked the opinions of his
arned men about it, which were various and
mote, as the reader may well imagine without
y repeating; although, indeed, I could not
ry perfectly understand them.

I then gave up my silver and copper money,
y purse, with nine large pieces of gold, and
me smaller ones; my knife and razor, my
mb and silver snuff-box, my handkerchief
d journal-book. My scimitar, pistols, and
uch were conveyed in carriages to his
ajesty's stores; but the rest of my goods
ere returned to me.

I had, as I before observed, one private
cket, which escaped their search, wherein
ere was a pair of spectacles (which I some-
mes use for the weakness of mine eyes), a
cket perspective,⁶ and several other little con-
eniences; which, being of no consequence to
e emperor, I did not think myself bound in
onour to discover; and I apprehended they
ight be lost or spoiled if I ventured them out
f my possession.

CHAPTER III

My gentleness and good behaviour had gained
far on the emperor and his court, and indeed
pon the army and people in general, that I
egan to conceive hopes of getting my liberty
a short time. I took all possible methods
cultivate this favourable disposition. The
atives came by degrees to be less apprehensive

telescope

of any danger from me. I would sometimes lie
down, and let five or six of them dance on my
hand; and at last the boys and girls would
venture to come and play at hide-and-seek in
my hair. I had now made a good progress in
understanding and speaking their language.

The emperor had a mind, one day, to entertain me with several of the country shows,
wherein they exceed all nations I have known,
both for dexterity and magnificence. I was
diverted with none so much as that of the rope-
dancers, performed upon a slender white
thread, extended about two feet, and twelve
inches from the ground. Upon which I shall
desire liberty, with the reader's patience, to
enlarge a little.

This diversion is only practised by those persons who are candidates for great employments
and high favour at court. They are trained in
this art from their youth, and are not always of
noble birth or liberal education. When a great
office is vacant, either by death or disgrace
(which often happens), five or six of those
candidates petition the emperor to entertain his
majesty and the court with a dance on the
rope; and whoever jumps the highest, without
falling, succeeds in the office. Very often the
chief ministers themselves are commanded to
show their skill, and to convince the emperor
that they have not lost their faculty. Flimnap,* the treasurer, is allowed to cut a caper
on the strait rope, at least an inch higher than
any other lord in the whole empire. I have
seen him do the summerset several times together upon a trencher, fixed on a rope, which
is no thicker than a common packthread in
England. My friend Reldresal, principal secretary for private affairs, is, in my opinion, if
I am not partial, the second after the treasurer; the rest of the great officers are much
upon a par.

These diversions are often attended with
fatal accidents, whereof great numbers are on
record. I myself have seen two or three candidates break a limb. But the danger is much
greater when the ministers themselves are commanded to show their dexterity! for, by contending to excel themselves and their fellows,
they strain so far that there is hardly one of
them who hath not received a fall, and some of
them two or three. I was assured that a year
or two before my arrival, Flimnap would have

* Flimnap stands for Sir Robert Walpole, at that
time Lord of the Treasury, who, when Swift
was a Whig—before 1710—had failed to aid
Swift to gain promotion.

infallibly broke† his neck if one of the king's cushions, that accidentally lay on the ground, had not weakened the force of his fall.‡

There is likewise another diversion, which is only shown before the emperor and empress and first minister, upon particular occasions. The emperor lays on the table three fine silken threads, of six inches long; one is purple, the other yellow, and the third white.§ These threads are proposed as prizes for those persons whom the emperor hath a mind to distinguish by a peculiar mark of his favour. The ceremony is performed in his majesty's great chamber of state, where the candidates are to undergo a trial of dexterity very different from the former, and such as I have not observed the least resemblance of in any other country of the old or the new world.

The emperor holds a stick in his hands, both ends parallel to the horizon, while the candidates, advancing one by one, sometimes leap over the stick, sometimes creep under it backwards and forwards several times, according as the stick is advanced or depressed. Sometimes the emperor holds one end of the stick, and his first minister the other; sometimes the minister has it entirely to himself. Whoever performs his part with most agility, and holds out the longest in leaping and creeping, is rewarded with the purple coloured silk; the yellow is given to the next, and the white to the third, which they all wear girt twice round about the middle; and you see few great persons about this court who are not adorned with one of these girdles.

The horses of the army, and those of the royal stables, having been daily led before me, were no longer shy, but would come up to my very feet without starting. The riders would leap them over my hand as I held it on the ground; and one of the emperor's huntsmen, upon a large courser, took my foot, shoe and all, which was indeed a prodigious leap.

I had the good fortune to divert the emperor one day after a very extraordinary manner. I desired he would order several sticks of

two feet high, and the thickness of an ordina[ry] cane, to be brought me; whereupon his majes[ty] commanded the master of his woods to gi[ve] directions accordingly; and the next morni[ng] six woodmen arrived with as many carriag[es] drawn by eight horses to each.

I took nine of these sticks, and fixing the[m] firmly in the ground in a quadrangular figu[re] two foot and a half square, I took four oth[er] sticks and tied them parallel at each corn[er] about two foot from the ground; then [I] fastened my handkerchief to the nine stic[ks] that stood erect, and extended it on all sid[es] till it was as tight as the top of a drum; a[nd] the four parallel sticks, rising about five inch[es] higher than the handkerchief, served as ledg[es] on each side.

When I had finished my work, I desired t[he] emperor to let a troop of his best hor[se,] twenty-four in number, come and exercise up[on] this plain. His majesty approved of the pr[o]posal, and I took them up one by one in m[y] hands, ready mounted and armed, with t[he] proper officers to exercise them. As soon [as] they got into order, they divided into two pa[r]ties, performed mock skirmishes, discharg[ed] blunt arrows, drew their swords, fled and pu[r]sued, attacked and retired, and, in short, d[is]covered the best military discipline I ever [be]held. The parallel sticks secured them a[nd] their horses from falling over the stage: a[nd] the emperor was so much delighted that [he] ordered this entertainment to be repeated se[v]eral days, and once was pleased to be lifted [up] and give the word of command; and, wi[th] great difficulty, persuaded even the empress he[r]self to let me hold her in her close chair with[in] two yards of the stage, from whence she w[as] able to take a full view of the whole perform[m]ance.

It was my good fortune that no ill accide[nt] happened in these entertainments; only on[ce] a fiery horse, that belonged to one of the ca[p]tains, pawing with his hoof, struck a hole [in] my handkerchief, and his foot slipping, [he] overthrew his rider and himself; but I i[m]mediately relieved them both, and covering t[he] hole with one hand, I set down the troop wi[th] the other, in the same manner as I took the[m] up. The horse that fell was strained in h[is] left shoulder, but the rider got no hurt, a[nd] I repaired my handkerchief as well as I coul[d;] however, I would not trust to the strength [of] it any more in such dangerous enterprises.

About two or three days before I was set [at] liberty, as I was entertaining the court wi[th]

---

† The preterit form for the participle was freely used in the eighteenth century. Note also below "these kind of feats."

‡ In 1717 Walpole was dismissed from office, but was probably saved from disastrous consequences through the influence of the Duchess of Kendal, favorite of George I.

§ In some editions these colors are given as blue, red, and green, the colors of the badges of the Orders of the Garter, Bath, and Thistle. The second named order, says Walpole's biographer, William Coxe, was revived by Walpole as "a cheap means of gratifying his political adherents."

these kind of feats, there arrived an express to inform his majesty that some of his subjects riding near the place where I was first taken up, had seen a great black substance lying on the ground, very oddly shaped, extending its edges round as wide as his majesty's bedchamber, and rising up in the middle as high as a man; that it was no living creature, as they at first apprehended, for it lay on the grass without motion; and some of them had walked round it several times; that, by mounting upon each other's shoulders, they had got to the top, which was flat and even, and, stamping upon it, they found it was hollow within; that they humbly conceived it might be something belonging to the man-mountain; and if his majesty pleased, they would undertake to bring it with only five horses.

I presently knew what they meant, and was glad at heart to receive this intelligence. It seems, upon my first reaching the shore after our shipwreck, I was in such confusion that, before I came to the place where I went to sleep, my hat, which I had fastened with a string to my head while I was rowing, and had stuck on all the time I was swimming, fell off after I came to land; the string, as I conjecture, breaking by some accident which I never observed, but thought my hat had been lost at sea. I entreated his imperial majesty to give orders it might be brought to me as soon as possible, describing to him the use and nature of it; and the next day the wagoners arrived with it, but not in a very good condition; they had bored two holes in the brim, within an inch and a half of the edge, and fastened two hooks in the holes; these hooks were tied by a long cord to the harness, and thus my hat was dragged along for above half an English mile; but the ground in that country being extremely smooth and level, it received less damage than I expected.

Two days after this adventure, the emperor, having ordered that part of the army which quarters in and about his metropolis to be in readiness, took a fancy of diverting himself in a very singular manner.* He desired I would stand like a colossus, with my legs as far asunder as I conveniently could. He then commanded his general (who was an old, experienced leader and a great patron of mine) to draw up the troops in close order and march them under me; the foot by twenty-four in a breast and the horse by sixteen, with drums beating, colours flying, and pikes advanced.

* George I. was especially fond of reviews.

This body consisted of three thousand foot and a thousand horse. . . . .

I had sent so many memorials and petitions for my liberty, that his majesty at length mentioned the matter, first in the cabinet, and then in a full council; where it was opposed by none, except Skyresh Bolgolam who was pleased, without any provocation, to be my mortal enemy. But it was carried against him by the whole board, and confirmed by the emperor. That minister was *galbet*, or admiral of the realm, very much in his master's confidence, and a person well versed in affairs, but of a morose and sour complexion. However, he was at length persuaded to comply; but prevailed that the articles and conditions upon which I should be set free, and to which I must swear, should be drawn up by himself.

These articles were brought to me by Skyresh Bolgolam in person, attended by two under-secretaries, and several persons of distinction. After they were read, I was demanded to swear to the performance of them, first in the manner of my own country, and afterwards in the method prescribed by their laws; which was, to hold my right foot in my left hand, and to place the middle finger of my right hand on the crown of my head, and my thumb on the tip of my right ear.

But because the reader may be curious to have some idea of the style and manner of expression peculiar to that people, as well as to know the articles upon which I recovered my liberty, I have made a translation of the whole instrument, word for word, as near as I was able, which I here offer to the public.

Golbasto Momaren Evlame Gurdilo Shefin Mully Ully Gue, most mighty Emperor of Lilliput, delight and terror of the universe, whose dominions extend five thousand *blustrugs* (about twelve miles in circumference) to the extremities of the globe; monarch of all monarchs, taller than the sons of men; whose feet press down to the center, and whose head strikes against the sun; at whose nod the princes of the earth shake their knees; pleasant as the spring, comfortable as the summer, fruitful as autumn, dreadful as winter. His most sublime Majesty proposeth to the Man-mountain, lately arrived to our celestial dominions, the following articles, which by a solemn oath he shall be obliged to perform.

First. The Man-mountain shall not depart from our dominions without our license under our great seal.

2d. He shall not presume to come into our

metropolis without our express order; at which time the inhabitants shall have two hours' warning to keep within their doors.

3d. The said Man-mountain shall confine his walks to our principal high roads, and not offer to walk or lie down in a meadow or field of corn.

4th. As he walks the said roads, he shall take the utmost care not to trample upon the bodies of any of our loving subjects, their horses or carriages, nor take any of our said subjects into his hands without their own consent.

5th. If an express requires extraordinary dispatch, the Man-mountain shall be obliged to carry in his pocket the messenger and horse a six-days' journey once in every moon, and return the said messenger back (if so required) safe to our imperial presence.

6th. He shall be our ally against our enemies in the island of Blefuscu, and do his utmost to destroy their fleet, which is now preparing to invade us.

7th. That the said Man-mountain shall at his times of leisure be aiding and assisting to our workmen, in helping to raise certain great stones towards covering the wall of the principal park, and other our royal buildings.

8th. That the said Man-mountain shall, in two moons' time, deliver in an exact survey of the circumference of our dominions, by a computation of his own paces round the coast.

Lastly. That upon his solemn oath to observe all the above articles, the said Man-mountain shall have a daily allowance of meat and drink sufficient for the support of 1724 of our subjects, with free access to our royal person, and other marks of our favour. Given at our palace at Belfaborac the twelfth day of the ninety-first moon of our reign.

I swore and subscribed to these articles with great cheerfulness and content, although some of them were not as honourable as I could have wished; which proceeded wholly from the malice of Skyresh Bolgolam the high admiral: whereupon my chains were immediately unlocked, and I was at full liberty; the Emperor himself in person did me the honour to be by at the whole ceremony. I made my acknowledgements by prostrating myself at his majesty's feet: but he commanded me to rise; and after many gracious expressions, which to avoid the censure of vanity, I shall not repeat, he added, that he hoped I should prove a useful servant, and well deserve all the favours he had already conferred upon me, or might do for the future.

The reader may please to observe, that in the last article for the recovery of my liberty the emperor stipulates to allow me a quantity of meat and drink sufficient for the support of 1724 Lilliputians. Some time after, asking a friend at court how they came to fix on that determined number, he told me that his majesty's mathematicians having taken the height of my body by the help of a quadrant, and finding it to exceed theirs in the proportion of twelve to one, they concluded, from the similarity of their bodies, that mine must contain at least 1724 of theirs, and consequently would require as much food as was necessary to support that number of Lilliputians. By which the reader may conceive an idea of the ingenuity of that people, as well as the prudent and exact economy of so great a prince.

JAMES THOMSON (1700-1748)

From THE SEASONS

SPRING

Come, gentle Spring, ethereal mildness, come;
And from the bosom of yon dropping cloud,
While music wakes around, veiled in a shower
Of shadowing roses, on our plains descend.

O Hertford, fitted or to shine in courts 5
With unaffected grace, or walk the plain
With innocence and meditation joined
In soft assemblage, listen to my song,
Which thy own season paints; when nature all
Is blooming, and benevolent, like thee. 10

And see where surly Winter passes off,
Far to the north, and calls his ruffian blasts:
His blasts obey, and quit the howling hill,
The shattered forest, and the ravaged vale;
While softer gales succeed, at whose kind touch, 15
Dissolving snows in livid torrents lost,
The mountains lift their green heads to the sky.

As yet the trembling year is unconfirmed,
And winter oft at eve resumes the breeze,

* The freshness of Thomson's poetry, derived from direct contact with nature, was recognized as early as 1756 by Joseph Warton, who wrote: "His descriptions have a distinctness and truth which are utterly wanting to those of poets who have only copied from each other and have never looked abroad on the objects themselves." Of the four sections of this poem, *Spring* was published last, in 1728; the Countess of Hertford, to whom it is dedicated, was a patroness of poetry whose interest in the author had been aroused by the publication of the preceding parts.

Chills the pale morn, and bids his driving
    sleets   20
Deform the day delightless: so that scarce
The bittern knows his time, with bill ingulfed,
To shake the sounding marsh; or from the
    shore
The plovers when to scatter o'er the heath,
And sing their wild notes to the listening
    waste.   25
    At last from Aries rolls the bounteous sun,[1]
And the bright Bull receives him. Then no
    more
The expansive atmosphere is cramped with
    cold;
But, full of life and vivifying soul,
Lifts the light clouds sublime, and spreads
    them thin,   30
Fleecy, and white, o'er all-surrounding Heaven.
Forth fly the tepid airs: and unconfined,
Unbinding earth, the moving softness strays,
Joyous the impatient husbandman perceives
Relenting Nature, and his lusty steers   35
Drives from their stalls, to where the well used
    plough
Lies in the furrow, loosened from the frost,
There, unrefusing, to the harnessed yoke
They lend their shoulder, and begin their toil,
Cheered by the simple song and soaring lark. 40
Meanwhile incumbent o'er the shining share[2]
The Master leans, removes the obstructing clay,
Winds[3] the whole work, and sidelong lays the
    glebe.
    White, through the neighbouring fields the
    sower stalks,
With measured step; and, liberal, throws the
    grain   45
Into the faithful bosom of the ground;
The harrow follows harsh, and shuts the scene.
    Be gracious, Heaven! for now laborious man
Has done his part. Ye fostering breezes, blow!
Ye softening dews, ye tender showers, de-
    scend!   50
And temper all, thou world-reviving sun,
Into the perfect year! Nor ye who live
In luxury and ease, in pomp and pride,
Think these last themes unworthy of your ear:
Such themes as these the rural Maro[4] sung   55
To wide-imperial Rome, in the full height
Of elegance and taste, by Greece refined.
In ancient times the sacred plough employed
The kings and awful fathers of mankind:
And some,[5] with whom compared your insect
    tribes   60

Are but the beings of a summer's day,
Have held the scale of empire, ruled the storm
Of mighty war; then, with victorious hand,
Disdaining little delicacies, seized
The plough, and, greatly independent, scorned
All the vile stores corruption can bestow.   66

    As rising from the vegetable world   570
My theme ascends, with equal wing ascend,
My panting Muse; and hark, how loud the
    woods
Invite you forth in all your gayest trim.
Lend me your song, ye nightingales! oh pour
The mazy-running soul of melody   575
Into my varied verse! while I deduce,
From the first note the hollow cuckoo sings,
The symphony of spring, and touch a theme
Unknown to fame—the passion of the groves.
    When first the soul of Love is sent abroad, 580
Warm through the vital air, and on the heart
Harmonious seizes, the gay troops begin,
In gallant thought, to plume the painted wing;
And try again the long-forgotten strain,
At first faint-warbled. But so sooner grows 585
The soft infusion prevalent and wide,
Than, all alive, at once their joy o'erflows
In music unconfined. Up-springs the lark,
Shrill-voiced and loud, the messenger of morn:
Ere yet the shadows fly, he mounted sings 590
Amid the dawning clouds, and from their
    haunts
Calls up the tuneful nations. Every copse
Deep-tangled, tree irregular, and bush
Bending with dewy moisture, o'er the heads
Of the coy quiristers[6] that lodge within,   595
Are prodigal of harmony. The thrush
And wood-lark, o'er the kind-contending throng
Superior heard, run through the sweetest
    length
Of notes; when listening Philomela[7] deigns
To let them joy, and purposes, in thought   600
Elate, to make her night excel their day.
The black-bird whistles from the thorny brake;
The mellow bull-finch answers from the grove:
Nor are the linnets, o'er the flowering furze 604
Poured out[8] profusely, silent. Joined to these,
Innumerous[9] songsters, in the freshening shade
Of new-sprung leaves, their modulations mix
Mellifluous. The jay, the rook, the daw,
And each harsh pipe, discordant heard alone,
Aid the full concert: while the stock-dove
    breathes   610
A melancholy murmur through the whole.
    'Tis Love creates their melody, and all
This waste of music 's the voice of Love.

[1] Passing from Aries, the first sign of the zodiac, to Taurus, the second (April 20).
[2] plowshare
[3] directs
[4] Virgil, in his *Georgics*.
[5] e. g., Cincinnatus.
[6] choristers
[7] the nightingale
[8] spread about
[9] innumerable

From THE CASTLE OF INDOLENCE*

1

O mortal man, who livest here by toil,
Do not complain of this thy hard estate;
That like an emmet thou must ever moil[1]
Is a sad sentence of an ancient date;[2]
And, certes, there is for it reason great;
For, though sometimes it makes thee weep
    and wail,
And curse thy star, and early drudge and late;
Withouten that would come a heavier bale,
    Loose life, unruly passions, and diseases pale.

2

In lowly dale, fast by a river's side
With woody hill o'er hill encompassed round,
A most enchanting wizard did abide,
Than whom a fiend more fell is nowhere found.
It was, I ween, a lovely spot of ground;
And there a season atween June and May,
Half prankt[3] with spring, with summer half
    imbrowned,
A listless climate made, where, sooth to say,
    No living wight could work, ne carèd even for
    play.

3

Was nought around but images of rest:
Sleep-soothing groves, and quiet lawns be-
    tween;
And flowery beds, that slumbrous influence
    kest,[4]
From poppies breathed; and beds of pleasant
    green,
Where never yet was creeping creature seen.
Meantime unnumbered glittering streamlets
    played,
And hurlèd everywhere their waters sheen;
That, as they bickered through the sunny glade,
    Though restless still themselves, a lulling
    murmur made.

4

Joined to the prattle of the purling rills,
Were heard the lowing herds along the vale,
And flocks loud-bleating from the distant hills,
And vacant[5] shepherds piping in the dale:
And now and then sweet Philomel would wail,
Or stock-doves plain[6] amid the forest deep,
That drowsy rustled to the sighing gale;

And still a coil[7] the grasshopper did keep:
    Yet all the sounds yblent[8] inclinèd all to
    sleep.

5

Full in the passage of the vale, above,
A sable, silent, solemn forest stood;
Where nought but shadowy forms was seen to
    move,
As Idless[9] fancied in her dreaming mood:
And up the hills, on either side, a wood
Of blackening pines, aye waving to and fro,
Sent forth a sleepy horror through the blood;
And where this valley winded out below,
    The murmuring main was heard, and scarcely
    heard, to flow.

6

A pleasing land of drowsy-hed[10] it was:
Of dreams that wave before the half-shut eye;
And of gay castles in the clouds that pass,
Forever flushing round a summer-sky.
There eke the soft delights, that witchingly
Instil a wanton sweetness through the breast,
And the calm pleasures, always hovered nigh;
But whate'er smackt of noyance, or unrest,
    Was far, far off expelled from this delicious
    nest.

7

The landskip such, inspiring perfect ease,
Where INDOLENCE (for so the wizard hight[11])
Close-hid his castle mid embowering trees,
That half shut out the beams of Phœbus bright,
And made a kind of checkered day and night.
Meanwhile, unceasing at the massy gate,
Beneath a spacious palm, the wicked wight
Was placed; and to his lute, of cruel fate
    And labour harsh, complained, lamenting
    man's estate.

8

Thither continual pilgrims crowded still,
From all the roads of earth that pass there by:
For, as they chanced to breathe on neighbour-
    ing hill,
The freshness of this valley smote their eye,
And drew them ever and anon more nigh;
Till clustering round the enchanter false they
    hung,
Ymolten[12] with his syren melody;
While o'er the enfeebling lute his hand he
    flung,
    And to the trembling chords these tempting
    verses sung:

---

1 labor   4 cast
2 *Genesis* iii., 19.   5 care-free
3 adorned   6 mourn
* "This poem being writ in the manner of Spenser,
the obsolete words, and the simplicity of diction in some of the lines, which borders on
the ludicrous, were necessary to make the imitation more perfect." (Thomson's note.) The
influence of the poem in turn upon Tennyson's
The Lotos-Eaters is also to be observed.

7 a noise, a stir   10 drowsiness
8 blended   11 was named
9 idleness   12 melted

9

'Behold! ye pilgrims of this earth, behold!
See all but man with unearned pleasure gay:
See her bright robes the butterfly unfold,
Broke from her wintry tomb in prime of May!
What youthful bride can equal her array?
Who can with her for easy pleasure vie?
From mead to mead with gentle wing to stray,
From flower to flower on balmy gales to fly,
    Is all she has to do beneath the radiant sky.

10

'Behold the merry minstrels of the morn,
The swarming songsters of the careless grove;
Ten thousand throats that, from the flowering
        thorn,
Hymn their good God, and carol sweet of love,
Such grateful kindly raptures them emove!
They neither plough, nor sow; ne, fit for flail,
E'er to the barn the nodding sheaves they
        drove;
Yet theirs each harvest dancing in the gale,
    Whatever crowns the hill, or smiles along the
        vale.

11

'Outcast of Nature, man! the wretched thrall
Of bitter-dropping sweat, of sweltry[13] pain,
Of cares that eat away thy heart with gall,
And of the vices, an inhuman train,
That all proceed from savage thirst of gain:
For when hard-hearted Interest first began
To poison earth, Astræa[14] left the plain;
Guile, Violence, and Murder, seized on man,
    And, for soft milky streams, with blood the
        rivers ran.

12

"Come, ye who still the cumbrous load of life
Push hard up-hill; but as the farthest steep
You trust to gain, and put an end to strife,
Down thunders back the stone with mighty
        sweep,
And hurls your labours to the valley deep,
Forever vain: come, and, withouten fee,
I in oblivion will your sorrows steep,
Your cares, your toils; will steep you in a sea
    Of full delight: O come, ye weary wights,
        to me!"

13 sultry
14 The goddess of justice, who in the golden age
    lived among men.

RULE, BRITANNIA

FROM THE MASQUE OF "ALFRED."

1

When Britain first, at Heaven's command,
    Arose from out the azure main,
This was the charter of the land,
    And guardian angels sang this strain:
        Rule, Britannia, rule the waves,
        Britons never will be slaves.

2

The nations not so blest as thee,
    Must in their turns to tyrants fall,
Whilst thou shalt flourish great and free,
    The dread and envy of them all.
        Rule, Britannia, rule the waves,
        Britons never will be slaves.

3

Still more majestic shalt thou rise,
    More dreadful from each foreign stroke;
As the loud blast that tears the skies
    Serves but to root thy native oak.
        Rule, Britannia, rule the waves,
        Britons never will be slaves.

4

Thee haughty tyrants ne'er shall tame;
    All their attempts to bend thee down
Will but arouse thy generous flame,
    But work their woe and thy renown.
        Rule, Britannia, rule the waves,
        Britons never will be slaves.

5

To thee belongs the rural reign;
    Thy cities shall with commerce shine;
All thine shall be the subject main,
    And every shore it circles thine.
        Rule, Britannia, rule the waves,
        Britons never will be slaves.

6

The Muses, still with freedom found,
    Shall to thy happy coast repair;
Blest isle, with matchless beauty crowned,
    And manly hearts to guard the fair!
        Rule, Britannia, rule the waves,
        Britons never will be slaves.

LATER EIGHTEENTH CENTURY

WILLIAM COLLINS (1721-1759)

A SONG FROM SHAKESPEARE'S CYMBELINE*

1

To fair Fidele's grassy tomb
    Soft maids and village hinds¹ shall bring
Each opening sweet, of earliest bloom,
    And rifle all the breathing spring.

2

No wailing ghost shall dare appear,
    To vex with shrieks this quiet grove;
But shepherd lads assemble here,
    And melting virgins own their love.

3

No withered witch shall here be seen,
    No goblins lead their nightly crew;
The female fays shall haunt the green,
    And dress thy grave with pearly dew.

4

The redbreast oft at evening hours
    Shall kindly lend his little aid,
With hoary moss, and gathered flowers,
    To deck the ground where thou art laid.

5

When howling winds, and beating rain,
    In tempests shake the sylvan cell,

¹ rustics, peasants
* This song, which flows almost like an improvisation, Collins constructed from the scene in *Cymbeline* IV. ii, 215-229, in which Guiderius and Arviragus speak over the body of their sister Imogen, who is disguised as Fidele and whom they suppose to be dead:

    Gui.   Why, he but sleeps:
If he be gone, he'll make his grave a bed;
With female fairies will his tomb be haunted,
And worms will not come to thee.
    Arv.   With fairest flowers
Whilst summer lasts and I live here, Fidele,
I'll sweeten thy sad grave: thou shalt not lack
The flower that's like thy face, pale primrose, nor
The azured harebell, like thy veins, no, nor
The leaf of eglantine, whom not to slander,
Out-sweetened not thy breath: the ruddock would,
With charitable bill, . . . bring thee all this;
Yea, and furr'd moss besides, when flowers are none,
To winter-ground thy corse,

Or midst the chase on every plain,
    The tender thought on thee shall dwell.

6

Each lonely scene shall thee restore,
    For thee the tear be duly shed:
Beloved, till life could charm no more;
    And mourned, till Pity's self be dead.

ODE †

1

How sleep the brave who sink to rest
By all their country's wishes blest!
When Spring, with dewy fingers cold,
Returns to deck their hallowed mold,
She there shall dress a sweeter sod
Than Fancy's feet have ever trod.

2

By fairy hands their knell is rung,
By forms unseen their dirge is sung;
There Honour comes, a pilgrim grey,
To bless the turf that wraps their clay;
And Freedom shall awhile repair,
To dwell a weeping hermit there!

ODE TO EVENING ‡

1

If ought of oaten stop,² or pastoral song,
May hope, chaste Eve, to soothe thy modest ear
    Like thy own solemn springs,
    Thy springs and dying gales,

2

O nymph reserved, while now the bright-haired sun
Sits in yon western tent, whose cloudy skirts,
    With brede³ ethereal wove,
    O'erhang his wavy bed:

² musical pipe   ³ embroidery
† "Written," says Collins, "in the beginning of the year 1746." The British troops had lately suffered losses in the War of the Austrian Succession, e. g., at Fontenoy in 1745, and Falkirk, January, 1746.
‡ "Although less popular than *The Deserted Village* and Gray's *Elegy*, the *Ode to Evening* is yet like them in embodying in exquisite form sights, sounds, and feelings of such permanent beauty that age cannot wither them nor custom stale."—W. C. Bronson. See also *Eng. Lit.*, 219-220.

3

Now air is hushed, save where the weak-eyed
    bat,
With short shrill shriek, flits by on leathern
    wing,
  Or where the beetle winds
  His small but sullen horn,

4

As oft he rises 'midst the twilight path,
Against the pilgrim borne in heedless hum:
  Now teach me, maid composed,
  To breathe some softened strain,

5

Whose numbers, stealing thro' thy darkening
    vale
May not unseemly with its stillness suit,
  As, musing slow, I hail
  Thy genial loved return!

6

For when thy folding-star4 arising shows
His paly circlet, at his warning lamp
  The fragrant Hours, and elves
  Who slept in flowers the day,

7

And many a nymph who wreathes her brows
    with sedge,
And sheds the freshening dew, and, lovelier
    still,
  The pensive Pleasures sweet,
  Prepare thy shadowy car.

8

Then lead, calm votaress, where some sheety
    lake
Cheers the lone heath, or some time-hallowed
    pile
  Or upland fallows grey
  Reflect its last cool gleam.

9

But when chill blustering winds, or driving
    rain,
Forbid my willing feet, be mine the hut
  That from the mountain's side
  Views wilds, and swelling floods,

10

And hamlets brown, and dim-discovered spires,
And hears their simple bell, and marks o'er all
  Thy dewy fingers draw
  The gradual dusky veil.

11

While Spring shall pour his showers, as oft he
    wont,
  Marking the time for folding the flocks.

And bathe thy breathing tresses, meekest Eve;
  While Summer loves to sport
  Beneath thy lingering light;

12

While sallow Autumn fills thy lap with leaves;
Or Winter, yelling thro' the troublous air,
  Affrights thy shrinking train,
  And rudely rends thy robes;

13

So long, sure-found beneath the sylvan shed,
Shall Fancy, Friendship, Science, rose-lipped
    Health,
  Thy gentlest influence own,
  And hymn thy favourite name!

THOMAS GRAY (1716-1771)

ELEGY WRITTEN IN A COUNTRY CHURCHYARD

1

The curfew tolls the knell of parting day,
  The lowing herd wind slowly o'er the lea,
The plowman homeward plods his weary way,
  And leaves the world to darkness and to me.

2

Now fades the glimmering landscape on the
    sight,
  And all the air a solemn stillness holds,
Save where the beetle wheels his droning flight,
  And drowsy tinklings lull the distant folds;

3

Save that from yonder ivy-mantled tower
  The moping owl does to the moon complain
Of such, as wandering near her secret bower,
  Molest her ancient solitary reign.

4

Beneath those rugged elms, that yew-tree's
    shade,
  Where heaves the turf in many a mouldering
    heap,
Each in his narrow cell for ever laid,
  The rude forefathers of the hamlet sleep.

5

The breezy call of incense-breathing morn,
  The swallow twittering from the straw-built
    shed,
The cock's shrill clarion, or the echoing horn,
  No more shall rouse them from their lowly
    bed.

6

For them no more the blazing hearth shall burn,
  Or busy housewife ply her evening care:

No children run to lisp their sire's return,
  Or climb his knees the envied kiss to share.

7

Oft did the harvest to their sickle yield,
  Their furrow oft the stubborn glebe has
    broke;
How jocund did they drive their team afield!
  How bowed the woods beneath their sturdy
    stroke!

8

Let not ambition mock their useful toil,
  Their homely joys, and destiny obscure;
Nor grandeur hear with a disdainful smile,
  The short and simple annals of the poor.

9

The boast of heraldry, the pomp of power,
  And all that beauty, all that wealth e'er gave,
Awaits alike th' inevitable hour.[1]
  The paths of glory lead but to the grave.

10

Nor you, ye proud, impute to these the fault,
  If memory o'er their tomb no trophies raise,
Where thro' the long-drawn aisle and fretted
    vault
  The pealing anthem swells the note of praise.

11

Can storied urn[2] or animated bust
  Back to its mansion call the fleeting breath?
Can honour's voice provoke[3] the silent dust,
  Or flattery soothe the dull cold ear of death?

12

Perhaps in this neglected spot is laid
  Some heart once pregnant with celestial fire;
Hands, that the rod of empire might have
    swayed,
  Or waked to ecstasy the living lyre.

13

But knowledge to their eyes her ample page
  Rich with the spoils of time did ne'er unroll;
Chill penury repressed their noble rage,
  And froze the genial[4] current of the soul.

14

Full many a gem of purest ray serene
  The dark unfathomed caves of ocean bear:
Full many a flower is born to blush unseen,
  And waste its sweetness on the desert air.

15

Some village Hampden,[5] that with dauntless
    breast

The little tyrant of his fields withstood;
  Some mute inglorious Milton here may rest,
    Some Cromwell guiltless of his country's
      blood.*

16

Th' applause of listening senates to command
  The threats of pain and ruin to despise,
To scatter plenty o'er a smiling land,
  And read their history in a nation's eyes.

17

Their lot forbade: nor circumscribed alone
  Their growing virtues, but their crimes con
    fined;
Forbade to wade through slaughter to a throne
  And shut the gates of mercy on mankind,

18

The struggling pangs of conscious truth to hide
  To quench the blushes of ingenuous shame,
Or heap the shrine of luxury and pride
  With incense kindled at the Muse's flame.

19

Far[7] from the madding crowd's ignoble strife
  Their sober wishes never learned to stray;
Along the cool sequestered vale of life
  They kept the noiseless tenor of their way.

20

Yet even these bones from insult to protect,
  Some frail memorial still erected nigh,
With uncouth rhymes and shapeless sculptur
    decked,
  Implores the passing tribute of a sigh.

21

Their name, their years, spelt by th' unlettere
    Muse,[8]
  The place of fame and elegy supply:
And many a holy text around she strews,
  That teach the rustic moralist to die.

22

For who to dumb forgetfulness a prey,
  This pleasing anxious being e'er resigned,
Left the warm precincts of the cheerful day,
  Nor cast one longing lingering look behind

23

On some fond breast the parting soul relies,
  Some pious drops the closing eye requires;
Even from the tomb the voice of nature crie
  Even in our ashes live their wonted fires.

1 Subject of "awaits."   4 natural
2 A burial urn, pictori-   5 A Puritan leader who
ally decorated.   resisted Charles I.
3 call forth

6 i. e., write flattering   7 i.e., being far
  verses to win favor   8 untaught poet
* Until a comparatively recent time Cromwell wa
  very generally regarded as a man who sacr
  ficed everything to his own inordinate amb
  tion. In the first draft of this stanza, Gr
  had written the names of Romans—Cat
  Tully (Cicero), and Caesar

24

'or thee, who mindful of th' unhonoured dead
  Dost in these lines their artless tale relate;
f chance,[9] by lonely contemplation led,
  Some kindred spirit shall inquire thy fate,

25

Iaply some hoary-headed swain may say,
  "Oft have we seen him at the peep of dawn
3rushing with hasty steps the dews away
  To meet the sun upon the upland lawn.

26

" There at the foot of yonder nodding beech
  That wreathes its old fantastic roots so high,
Iis listless length at noontide would he stretch,
  And pore upon the brook that babbles by.

27

" Hard by yon wood, now smiling as in scorn,
  Muttering his wayward fancies he would rove,
Vow drooping, woeful wan, like one forlorn,
  Or crazed with care, or crossed in hopeless
      love.

28

" One morn I missed him on the customed hill,
  Along the heath and near his favourite tree;
another came; nor yet beside the rill,
  Nor up the lawn, nor at the wood was he;

29

" The next with dirges due in sad array
  Slow thro' the church-way path we saw him
      borne.
approach and read (for thou canst read) the
      lay,
  Graved on the stone beneath yon aged thorn.' '

THE EPITAPH

30

Iere rests his head upon the lap of earth
  A youth to fortune and to fame unknown.
'air science frowned not on his humble birth,
  And melancholy marked him for her own.

31

,arge was his bounty, and his soul sincere,
  Heaven did a recompense as largely send:
Ie gave to misery all he had, a tear,
  He gained from Heaven ('twas all he wished)
      a friend.

32

'o farther seek his merits to disclose,
  Or draw his frailties from their dread abode,
There they alike in trembling hope repose)
  The bosom of his Father and his God.

perchance

THE PROGRESS OF POESY

A PINDARIC ODE*

I. 1

Awake, Æolian lyre, awake,
And give to rapture all thy trembling strings.
From Helicon's harmonious springs
A thousand rills their mazy progress take:
The laughing flowers, that round them blow,
Drink life and fragrance as they flow.
Now the rich stream of music winds along
Deep, majestic, smooth, and strong,
Thro' verdant vales, and Ceres' golden reign:
Now rolling down the steep amain,
Headlong, impetuous, see it pour:
The rocks, and nodding groves rebellow to the
    roar.

I. 2

Oh! sovereign of the willing soul,
Parent of sweet and solemn-breathing airs,
Enchanting shell![1] the sullen cares,
And frantic passions hear thy soft control.
On Thracia's hills the Lord of War[2]
Has curbed the fury of his car,
And dropped his thirsty lance at thy command.
Perching on the sceptred hand
Of Jove, thy magic lulls the feathered king[3]
With ruffled plumes, and flagging wing:
Quenched in dark clouds of slumber lie
The terror of his beak, and lightnings of his
    eye.

I. 3

Thee the voice, the dance, obey,
Tempered to thy warbled lay.
O'er Idalia's velvet-green[4]

---

[1] The lyre, said to have been made by Hermes from a tortoise shell.
[2] Mars
[3] Jove's eagle
[4] In Cyprus, sacred to Venus (Cytherea).
* The odes of Pindar, the most renowned lyric poet of ancient Greece, were mostly constructed in symmetrical triads, each triad containing a strophe, antistrophe, and epode, or turn, counter-turn, and after-song. Metrically the strophes and antistrophes all corresponded exactly throughout, and likewise the epodes. The livelier odes were written in what was known as the Æolian mood, in contrast to the graver Dorian mood and the more tender Lydian measures. Gray has borrowed freely from Pindar, even translating a portion of the first Pythian Ode. The following is a condensation of Gray's notes to his own poem: I. 1. The various sources of poetry, which gives life and lustre to all it touches.—I. 2. Power of harmony to calm the turbulent sallies of the soul.—I. 3. Power of harmony to produce all the graces of motion in the body. II. 1. Poetry given to mankind to compensate the real and imaginary ills of life.—II. 2. Extensive influence of poetic genius over the remotest and most uncivilized nations.—II. 3. Progress of Poetry from Greece to Italy, and from Italy to England.—III. 1. 2. 3. Shakespeare. Milton, Dryden.

The rosy-crownèd Loves are seen
On Cytherea's day
With antic Sports, and blue-eyed Pleasures,
Frisking light in frolic measures;
Now pursuing, now retreating,
Now in circling troops they meet:
To brisk notes in cadence beating
Glance their many-twinkling feet.
Slow-melting strains their queen's approach
    declare:
Where'er she turns the Graces homage pay.
With arms sublime,5 that float upon the air,
In gliding state she wins her easy way:
O'er her warm cheek, and rising bosom, move
The bloom of young desire, and purple light of
    love.

II. 1.

Man's feeble race what ills await,
Labour, and penury, the racks of pain,
Disease, and sorrow's weeping train,
And death, sad refuge from the storms of fate!
The fond6 complaint, my song, disprove,
And justify the laws of Jove.
Say, has he given in vain the heavenly Muse?
Night, and all her sickly dews,
Her spectres wan, and birds of boding cry,
He gives to range the dreary sky:
Till down the eastern cliffs afar
Hyperion's march they spy, and glittering
    shafts of war.

II. 2

In climes beyond the solar road,
Where shaggy forms o'er ice-built mountains
    roam,
The Muse has broke the twilight-gloom
To cheer the shivering native's dull abode.
And oft, beneath the odorous shade
Of Chili's boundless forests laid,
She deigns to hear the savage youth repeat
In loose numbers wildly sweet
Their feather-cinctured chiefs, and dusky loves.
Her track, where'er the goddess roves,
Glory pursue, and generous shame,
Th' unconquerable mind, and freedom's holy
    flame.

II. 3.

Woods, that wave o'er Delphi's steep,
Isles, that crown th' Ægean deep,
Fields, that cool Ilissus laves,
Or where Mæander's amber waves
In lingering labyrinths creep,
How do your tuneful echoes languish,
Mute, but to the voice of anguish?
Where each old poetic mountain
Inspiration breathed around:

Every shade and hallowed fountain
Murmured deep a solemn sound:
Till the sad Nine in Greece's evil hour
Left their Parnassus for the Latian plains.
Alike they scorn the pomp of tyrant-power,
And coward vice, that revels in her chains.
When Latium had her lofty spirit lost,
They sought, O Albion! next thy sea-encircle
    coast.

III. 1

Far from the sun and summer-gale,
In thy green lap was nature's darling laid,
What time, where lucid Avon strayed,
To him the mighty mother did unveil
Her awful face: the dauntless child
Stretched forth his little arms, and smiled.
This pencil take (she said) whose colours clea
Richly paint the vernal year:
Thine too these golden keys, immortal boy!
This can unlock the gates of joy;
Of horror that, and thrilling fears,
Or ope the sacred source of sympathetic tear

III. 2.

Nor second he, that rode sublime
Upon the seraph-wings of ecstacy,
The secrets of th' abyss to spy.
He passed the flaming bounds of place an
    time:
The living throne, the sapphire-blaze,7
Where angels tremble, while they gaze,
He saw; but blasted with excess of light,
Closed his eyes in endless night.
Behold, where Dryden's less presumptuous ca
Wide o'er the fields of glory bear
Two coursers of ethereal race,8
With necks in thunder clothed,9 and lon
    resounding pace.

III. 3

Hark, his hands the lyre explore!
Bright-eyed Fancy hovering o'er
Scatters from her pictured urn
Thoughts that breathe, and words that bur
But ah! 'tis heard no more ————
O lyre divine, what daring spirit
Wakes thee now? tho' he inherit
Nor the pride, nor ample pinion,
That the Theban Eagle10 bear
Sailing with supreme dominion
Thro' the azure deep of air:
Yet oft before his infant eyes would run
Such forms, as glitter in the Muse's ray
With orient hues, unborrowed of the sun:

7 *Ezekiel* i. 26
8 "Meant to express the stately march and soun
    ing energy of Dryden's rhymes." (Gray).
9 *Job* xxxix. 19
10 Pindar

5 uplifted   6 foolish

Yet shall he mount, and keep his distant way
Beyond the limits of a vulgar fate,
Beneath the good how far—but far above the
    great.

"OSSIAN"

JAMES MACPHERSON
(1736-1796)

OINA-MORUL.*

As flies the inconstant sun, over Larmon's
grassy hill, so pass the tales of old, along my
soul by night! When bards are removed to
their place: when harps are hung in Selma's
hall;[1] then comes a voice to Ossian, and
awakes his soul! It is the voice of years that
are gone! they roll before me, with all their
deeds! I seize the tales as they pass, and pour
them forth in song. Nor a troubled stream is
the song of the king, it is like the rising of
music from Lutha of the strings. Lutha of
many strings, not silent are thy streamy rocks,
when the white hands of Malvina move upon
the harp! Light of the shadowy thoughts, that
fly across my soul, daughter of Toscar of helmets, wilt thou not hear the song? We call
back, maid of Lutha, the years that have rolled
away!

It was in the days of the king, while yet
my locks were young, that I marked Con-
cathlin,[2] on high, from ocean's nightly wave.
My course was towards the isle of Fuarfed,
woody dweller of seas! Fingal had sent me to
the aid of Mal-orchol, king of Fuarfed wild:
for war was around him, and our fathers had
met at the feast.

In Col-coiled, I bound my sails; I sent my
sword to Mal-orchol of shells.[3] He knew the
signal of Albion, and his joy arose. He came
from his own high hall, and seized my hand

1 The royal residence of Fingal.
2 A star, perhaps the pole-star.
3 See note 1 to Gray's ode just preceding.
* The rhythmical prose pieces published by James
Macpherson in 1760-1763 as translations from
the ancient Gaelic bard Ossian (Oisin), son
of Fingal (Finn), were apparently based upon
genuine Gaelic, though probably not Ossianic,
remains, with liberal additions by Macpherson
himself. See *Eng. Lit.* 223. In the poem here
given, Ossian, addressing his daughter-in-law
Malvina, "maid of Lutha," relates a generous
deed of his youthful days. Sent by his father
to the assistance of the king of Fuarfed, he
defeated the foe, Ton-thormod, and was promised the king's daughter, Oina-morul. But dis-
covering that she loved Ton-thormod, he
yielded his claim and brought about a reconciliation of the foes. The rather excessive
punctuation of the piece is meant to empha-
size its rhythmical character.

in grief. "Why comes the race of heroes to a
falling king? Ton-thormod of many spears is
the chief of wavy Sar-dronlo. He saw and
loved my daughter, white-bosomed Oina-morul.
He sought; I denied the maid! for our fathers
had been foes. He came, with battle, to Fuarfed; my people are rolled away. Why comes
the race of heroes to a falling king?"

"I come not," I said, "to look, like a boy,
on the strife. Fingal remembers Mal-orchol,
and his hall for strangers. From his waves,
the warrior descended on thy woody isle. Thou
wert no cloud before him. Thy feast was
spread with songs. For this my sword shall
rise; and thy foes perhaps may fail. Our
friends are not forgot in their danger, though
distant is our land."

"Descendant of the daring Trenmor, thy
words are like the voice of Cruth-loda,[4] when
he speaks, from his parting cloud, strong
dweller of the sky! Many have rejoiced at my
feast; but they all have forgot Mal-orchol. I
have looked towards all the winds; but no
white sails were seen. But steel resounds in
my hall; and not the joyful shells. Come to
my dwelling, race of heroes! dark-skirted night
is near. Hear the voice of songs, from the
maid of Fuarfed wild."

We went. On the harp arose the white hands
of Oina-morul. She waked her own sad tale,
from every trembling string. I stood in
silence; for bright in her locks was the daughter of many isles! Her eyes were two stars,
looking forward through a rushing shower. The
mariner marks them on high, and blesses the
lovely beams. With morning we rushed to
battle, to Tormul's resounding stream: the foe
moved to the sound of Ton-thormod's bossy
shield. From wing to wing the strife was
mixed. I met Ton-thormod in flight. Wide
flew his broken steel. I seized the king in war.
I gave his hand, bound fast with thongs, to
Mal-orchol, the giver of shells. Joy rose at
the feast of Fuarfed, for the foe had failed.
Ton-thormod turned his face away, from Oina-
morul of isles!

"Son of Fingal," began Mal-orchol, "not
forgot shalt thou pass from me. A light shall
dwell in thy ship, Oina-morul of slow-rolling
eyes. She shall kindle gladness, along thy
mighty soul. Nor unheeded shall the maid
move in Selma, through the dwelling of
kings!"

In the hall I lay in night. Mine eyes were
half-closed in sleep. Soft music came to mine
ear: it was like the rising breeze, that whirls,

4 Odin.

at first, the thistle's beard; then flies, dark
shadowy, over the grass. It was the maid of
Fuarfed wild! she raised the nightly song; she
knew that my soul was a stream, that flowed
at pleasant sounds. "Who looks," she said,
"from his rock on ocean's closing mist? His
long locks, like the raven's wing, are wandering on the blast. Stately are his steps in grief!
The tears are in his eyes! His manly breast is
heaving over his bursting soul! Retire, I am
distant far; a wanderer in lands unknown.
Though the race of kings are around me, yet
my soul is dark. Why have our fathers been
foes, Ton-thormod, love of maids?"

"Soft voice of the streamy isle," I said,
"why dost thou mourn by night? The race
of daring Trenmor are not the dark in soul.
Thou shalt not wander, by streams unknown,
blue-eyed Oina-morul! Within this bosom is a
voice; it comes not to other ears: it bids Ossian
hear the hapless, in their hour of woe. Retire,
soft singer by night! Ton-thormod shall not
mourn on his rock!"

With morning I loosed the king. I gave the
long-haired maid. Mal-orchol heard my words,
in the midst of his echoing halls. "King of
Fuarfed wild, why should Ton-thormod mourn?
He is of the race of heroes, and a flame in war.
Your fathers have been foes, but now their
dim ghosts rejoice in death. They stretch
their hands of mist to the same shell in Loda.[5]
Forget their rage, ye warriors! it was the cloud
of other years."

Such were the deeds of Ossian, while yet his
locks were young: though loveliness, with a
robe of beams, clothed the daughter of many
isles. We call back, maid of Lutha, the years
that have rolled away!

From CARTHON

OSSIAN'S ADDRESS TO THE SUN

O thou that rollest above, round as the shield
of my fathers! Whence are thy beams, O sun!
thy everlasting light? Thou comest forth, in
thy awful beauty; the stars hide themselves in
the sky; the moon, cold and pale, sinks in the
western wave. But thou thyself movest alone:
who can be a companion of thy course? The
oaks of the mountains fall: the mountains
themselves decay with years; the ocean shrinks
and grows again: the moon herself is lost in
heaven; but thou art for ever the same; rejoicing in the brightness of thy course. When
the world is dark with tempests; when thunder
rolls, and lightning flies; thou lookest in thy

[5] The Hall of Odin.

beauty from the clouds, and laughest at the
storm. But to Ossian, thou lookest in vain;
for he beholds thy beams no more; whether
thy yellow hair flows on the eastern clouds, or
thou tremblest at the gates of the west. But
thou art, perhaps, like me, for a season; thy
years will have an end. Thou shalt sleep in
thy clouds, careless of the voice of the morning.
Exult then, O sun! in the strength of thy
youth: Age is dark and unlovely; it is like the
glimmering light of the moon, when it shines
through broken clouds, and the mist is on the
hills; the blast of the north is on the plain, the
traveler shrinks in the midst of his journey.

THOMAS CHATTERTON*
(1752-1770)

EPITAPH ON ROBERT CANYNGE

Thys Morneynge Starre of Radcleves rysynge
    Raie,
A True Man, Good of Mynde, and Canynge
    hyghte,[1]
Benethe thys Stone lies moltrynge ynto Claie
Untylle the darke Tombe sheene an aeterne
    Lyghte,
Thyrde from hys Loyns the present Canynge
    came;†
Houton[2] are wordes for to telle his doe;[3]
For aie shall lyve hys Heaven-recorded Name,
Ne shalle ytte die whanne Tyme shall be ne
    moe;[4]
Whan Mychael's Trompe shall sounde to rize
    the Soulle,

1 named   3 deeds
2 hollow   4 no more
* The "Rowley poems" of Chatterton, ascribed to
  him to a fictitious priest called Rowley, of the
  fifteenth century, are written in a spurious
  archaic dialect, not a few of the forms being
  pure inventions, sometimes merely for convenience of rhyme. In the selections here
  given (except the *Epitaph*, which is left unaltered) the spelling and some words are modernized, in accordance with Professor Skeat's
  edition, the better to show what genuine
  powers the youthful poet possessed. Chatterton wrote after this fashion:

  "In Virgyne the sweltrie sun gan sheene,
    And hotte upon the mees did caste his raie
    The apple rodded from its palie greene," etc.

This Spenserian manner, as in the poetry of
  Thomson a generation earlier, is in marked
  contrast to the prevailing classicism of the
  age. See *Eng. Lit.*, p. 223.
† William Canning, an actual mayor of Bristol in
  the time of Edward IV., who with his grand-
  father rebuilt the beautiful church of St
  Mary Redcliffe ("Radcleves rysynge Raie")
  It does not appear that the great-grandfather
  Robert, had any share in it. William Can-
  ning was asserted by Chatterton to have been
  Rowley's patron.

He'lle wynge toe heaven with kynne, and
   happie be ther dolle.[5]

AN EXCELENTE BALADE OF CHARITIE

As Written by the Good Priest Thomas
Rowley, 1464)

1

n Virgo now the sultry sun did sheene,
And hot upon the meads did cast his ray;
The apple reddened from its paly green,
And the soft pear did bend the leafy spray;
The pied chelandry[6] sang the livelong day;
Twas now the pride, the manhood of the year,
   And eke the ground was decked in its most
      deft aumere.[7]

2

The sun was gleaming in the midst of day,
Dead-still the air, and eke the welkin blue,
When from the sea arose in drear array
A heap of clouds of sable sullen hue,
The which full fast unto the woodland drew,
Hiding at once the sunnès festive face,
   And the black tempest swelled, and gathered
      up apace.

3

Beneath a holm,[8] fast by a pathway-side,
Which did unto Saint Godwin's convent lead,
A hapless pilgrim moaning did abide,
Poor in his view, ungentle in his weed,[9]
Long brimful of the miseries of need.
Where from the hailstorm could the beggar fly?
   He had no houses there, nor any convent
      nigh.

4

Look in his gloomèd face, his sprite there scan;
How woe-begone, how withered, dwindled, dead!
Haste to thy church-glebe-house, accursèd man!
Haste to thy shroud, thy only sleeping bed.
Cold as the clay which will grow on thy head
Are Charity and Love among high elves;
   For knights and barons live for pleasure and
      themselves.

5

The gathered storm is ripe; the big drops fall,
The sun-burnt meadows smoke, and drink the
   rain;
The coming ghastness[10] doth the cattle 'pall,[11]
And the full flocks are driving o'er the plain;
Dashed from the clouds, the waters fly again;
The welkin opes; the yellow lightning flies,
   And the hot fiery steam in the wide flashings
      dies.

6

List! now the thunder's rattling noisy sound
Moves slowly on, and then full-swollen clangs,
Shakes the high spire, and lost, expended,
   drowned,
Still on the frighted ear of terror hangs;
The winds are up; the lofty elm tree swangs;
Again the lightning, and the thunder pours,
   And the full clouds are burst at once in
      stony showers.

7

Spurring his palfrey o'er the watery plain,
The Abbot of Saint Godwin's convent came;
His chapournette[12] was drenchèd with the rain,
His painted girdle met with mickle shame;
He aynewarde told his bederoll[13] at the same;
The storm increases, and he drew aside,
   With the poor alms-craver near to the holm
      to bide.

8

His cope was all of Lincoln cloth so fine,
With a gold button fastened near his chin,
His autremete[14] was edged with golden twine,
And his shoe's peak a noble's might have been;
Full well it shewèd he thought cost no sin.
The trammels of his palfrey pleased his sight,
   For the horse-milliner his head with roses
      dight.[15]

9

"An alms, sir priest!" the drooping pilgrim
   said,
"Oh! let me wait within your convent-door,
Till the sun shineth high above our head,
And the loud tempest of the air is o'er.
Helpless and old am I, alas! and poor.
No house, no friend, nor money in my pouch,
   All that I call my own is this my silver
      crouche."[16]

10

"Varlet!" replied the Abbot, "cease your
   din;
This is no season alms and prayers to give,
My porter never lets a beggar in;
None touch my ring who not in honour live."
And now the sun with the black clouds did
   strive,
And shot upon the ground his glaring ray;
   The Abbot spurred his steed, and eftsoons
      rode away.

11

Once more the sky was black, the thunder
   rolled,
Fast running o'er the plain a priest was seen;

---

5 their dole (lot)
6 goldfinch
Misused for "apparel";
   properly "a purse."

8 holm oak
9 rustic in his dress
10 For "ghastliness."
11 appal

12 small round hat
13 backward told his
   beads, i. e., cursed
   (Chatterton)

14 loose white robe
15 arrayed
16 cross

Not dight full proud, nor buttoned up in gold,
His cope and jape[17] were grey, and eke were
    clean;
A Limitor[18] he was of order seen;
And from the pathway-side then turnèd he,
    Where the poor beggar lay beneath the hol-
    man tree.

12

"An alms, sir priest!" the drooping pilgrim
    said,
"For sweet Saint Mary and your order's
    sake."
The Limitor then loosened his pouch-thread,
And did thereout a groat of silver take;
The needy pilgrim did for gladness shake,
"Here, take this silver, it may ease thy care,
    We are God's stewards all, naught of our
    own we bear.

13

"But ah! unhappy pilgrim, learn of me.
Scarce any give a rentroll to their lord;
Here, take my semicope,[19] thou'rt bare, I see,
'Tis thine; the saints will give me my reward."
He left the pilgrim, and his way aborde.[20]
Virgin and holy Saints, who sit in gloure,[21]
    Or give the mighty will, or give the good man
    power!

From THE BATTLE OF HASTINGS*

17

And now Duke William marèshall'd his band,
And stretched his army out, a goodly row.
First did a rank of arcublastries[1] stand,
Next those on horseback drew th' ascending
    flo;[2]
Brave champions, each well learnèd in the bow,
Their asenglave[3] across their horses tied;
Or[4] with the loverds[5] squires behind did go,
Or waited, squire-like, at the horse's side.
When thus Duke William to a monk did say,
    "Prepare thyself with speed, to Harold
    haste away.

18

"Tell him from me one of these three to take:
That he to me do homage for this land,
Or me his heir, when he deceaseth, make,
Or to the judgment of Christ's vicar[6] stand."

He said; the monk departed out of hand,
And to King Harold did this message bear,
Who said, "Tell thou the duke, at his likand,[ ]
If he can get the crown, he may it wear."
He said, and drove the monk out of his sight
    And with his brothers roused each man to
    bloody fight.

19

A standard made of silk and jewels rare,
Wherein all colours, wrought about in bighes,[ ]
An armèd knight was seen death-doing there,
Under this motto—"He conquers or he dies."[ ]
This standard rich, endazzling mortal eyes,
Was borne near Harold at the Kenters' head
Who charged his brothers for the great em
    prise,
That straight the hest[10] for battle should be
    spread.
To every earl and knight the word is given,
    And cries "a guerre!"[11] and slogans shake
    the vaulted heaven.

20

As when the earth,[12] torn by convulsions dire
In realms of darkness hid from human sight
The warring force of water, air and fire,
Bursts from the regions of eternal night,
Through the dark caverns seeks the realms of
    light;
Some lofty mountain, by its fury torn,
Dreadfully moves, and causes great affright;
Now here, now there, majestic nods the
    bourne,[13]
And awful shakes, moved by th' almighty
    force;
    Whole woods and forests nod, and rivers
    change their course.

21

So did the men of war at once advance,
Linked man to man, appeared one body light
Above, a wood, y-formed of bill and lance,
That nodded in the air, most strange to sight
Hard as the iron were the men of might,
No need of slogans to enrouse their mind;
Each shooting spear made ready for the fight
More fierce than falling rocks, more swift than
    wind;
With solemn step, by echo made more dire,
    One single body all, they marched, their eyes
    on fire.

22

And now the grey-eyed morn with violets drest
Shaking the dewdrops on the flowery meads,

---

17 A short surplice (?).   20 For "pursued."
18 licensed begging friar   21 For "glory."
19 short cape

---

1 cross-bowmen   4 either
2 arrow   5 lords
3 lance? (Skeat)   6 the Pope
* There are two versions of this poem, one of
  which Chatterton admitted to be his own.
  The other, from which the stanzas above are
  taken, he declared to be Rowley's. There are
  seventy-two stanzas in all, but the battle is
  not brought to an end.

7 pleasure   11 "To battle!"
8 jewels   12 Sentence grammatic
9 See *Eng. Lit.*, p. 35.   ally defective
10 command   13 For "cliff."

Fled with her rosy radiance to the west.
Forth from the eastern gate the fiery steeds
Of the bright sun awaiting spirits leads.[12]
The sun, in fiery pomp enthroned on high,
Swifter than thought along his journey
    gledes,[14]
And scatters night's remains from out the sky.
He saw the armies make for bloody fray,
    And stopped his driving steeds, and hid his
      lightsome ray.

23

King Harold high in air majestic raised
His mighty arm, decked with a manchyn[15]
    rare;
With even hand a mighty javelin peised,[16]
Then furious sent it whistling through the air.
It struck the helmet of the Sieur de Beer.
In vain did brass or iron stop its way;
Above his eyes it came, the bones did tear,
Piercing quite through, before it did allay.[17]
He tumbled, screeching with his horrid pain,
    His hollow cuishes[18] rang upon the bloody
      plain.

24

This William saw, and, sounding Roland's song,
He bent his iron interwoven bow,
Making both ends to meet with might full
    strong;
From out of mortal's sight shot up the flo.
Then swift as falling stars to earth below,
It slanted down on Alfwold's painted shield,
Quite through the silver-bordured cross did go,
Nor lost its force, but stuck into the field;
The Normans, like their sovereign, did prepare,
    And shot ten thousand floes uprising in the
      air.

25

As when a flight of cranes that take their way
In household armies through the archèd sky,
Alike[19] the cause, or company or prey,
If that perchance some boggy fen is nigh,
Soon as the muddy nation[20] they espy,
In one black cloud they to the earth descend;
Fierce as the falling thunderbolt they fly,
In vain do reeds the speckled folk defend;
So prone to heavy blow the arrows fell,
    And pierced through brass, and sent many
      to heaven or hell.

26

Ælan Adelfred, of the stow[21] of Leigh,
Felt a dire arrow burning in his breast;
Before he died, he sent his spear away,

Then sank to glory and eternal rest.
Neville, a Norman of all Normans best,
Through the joint cuishè did the javelin feel,
As he on horseback for the fight addressed,
And saw his blood come smoking o'er the steel;
He sent the avenging flo into the air,
    And turned his horse's head, and did to leech
      repair.

27

And now the javelins, barbed with deathès
    wings,
Hurled from the English hands by force
    aderne,[22]
Whizz drear along, and songs of terror sings,
Such songs as always closed in life eterne.
Hurled by such strength along the air they
    burn,
Not to be quenchèd but in Normans' blood.
Where'er they came, they were of life forlorn,
And always followed by a purple flood.
Like clouds the Norman arrows did descend,
    Like clouds of carnage full, in purple drops
      did end.

SAMUEL JOHNSON (1709-1784)

From the PLAN OF AN ENGLISH DICTIONARY*

*To the Right Honourable Philip Dormer, Earl
of Chesterfield, One of His Majesty's
Principal Secretaries of State.*

My Lord,

    When first I undertook to write an English
Dictionary, I had no expectation of any higher
patronage than that of the proprietors of the
copy, nor prospect of any other advantage than
the price of my labour. I knew that the work
in which I engaged is generally considered as
drudgery for the blind, as the proper toil of
artless industry; a task that requires neither
the light of learning, nor the activity of genius,
but may be successfully performed without any
higher quality than that of bearing burthens
with dull patience, and beating the track of the
alphabet with sluggish resolution.

    Whether this opinion, so long transmitted,

---

22 cruel

---

* Johnson's ponderous diction may have been in
some measure due to his labors in the field
of lexicography, though doubtless much more
to his habit of thinking in general and abstract terms. It was jestingly said in his
time that he used hard words in the *Rambler*
papers on purpose to make his forthcoming
Dictionary indispensable. Yet the diction
confers a not unpleasing dignity upon the
wisdom it clothes; and it grew more chast-
ened with time, as is shown by the admirable
style of his *Lives of the Poets.* See *Eng. Lit.,*
208-209.

---

14 For "glides."
15 sleeve
16 poised
17 For "stop."
18 armour for the thighs
19 whatever
20 frogs (a manifest 18th century para-phrase)
21 place

and so widely propagated, had its beginning from truth and nature, or from accident and prejudice; whether it be decreed by the authority of reason, or the tyranny of ignorance, that of all the candidates for literary praise, the unhappy lexicographer holds the lowest place, neither vanity nor interest incited me to enquire. It appeared that the province allotted me was, of all the regions of learning, generally confessed to be the least delightful, that it was believed to produce neither fruit nor flowers; and that, after a long and laborious cultivation, not even the barren laurel† had been found upon it.

Yet on this province, my Lord, I entered, with the pleasing hope that, as it was low, it likewise would be safe. I was drawn forward with the prospect of employment, which, though not splendid, would be useful; and which, though it could not make my life envied, would keep it innocent; which would awaken no passion, engage me in no contention, nor throw in my way any temptation to disturb the quiet of others by censure, or my own by flattery.

I had read indeed of times in which princes and statesmen thought it part of their honour to promote the improvement of their native tongues; and in which dictionaries were written under the protection of greatness. To the patrons of such undertakings I willingly paid the homage of believing that they, who were thus solicitous for the perpetuity of their language, had reason to expect that their actions would be celebrated by posterity, and that the eloquence which they promoted would be employed in their praise. But I consider such acts of beneficence as prodigies, recorded rather to raise wonder than expectation; and content with the terms that I had stipulated, had not suffered my imagination to flatter me with any other encouragement, when I found that my design had been thought by your Lordship of importance sufficient to attract your favour.

How far this unexpected distinction can be rated among the happy incidents of life, I am not yet able to determine. Its first effect has been to make me anxious lest it should fix the attention of the public too much upon me, and, as it once happened to an epic poet of France,‡ by raising the reputation of the attempt, obstruct the reception of the work. I imagine what the world will expect from a scheme

prosecuted under your Lordship's influence and I know that expectation, when her wing are once expanded, easily reaches heights which performance never will attain; and when she has mounted the summit of perfection, derides her follower, who dies in the pursuit.

Not therefore to raise expectation, but to repress it, I here lay before your Lordship the Plan of my undertaking, that more may not be demanded than I intend; and that, before it is too far advanced to be thrown into a new method, I may be advertised of its defects or superfluities. Such informations I may justly hope, from the emulation with which those, who desire the praise of elegance or discernment, must contend in the promotion of a design that you, my Lord, have not thought unworthy to share your attention with treaties and with wars. . .

[Then follows the plan, with many details of vocabulary, orthography, pronunciation, etc.]

When I survey the Plan which I have laid before you, I cannot, my Lord, but confess that I am frighted at its extent, and, like the soldiers of Cæsar, look on Britain as a new world which it is almost madness to invade. But I hope that though I should not complete the conquest, I shall at least discover the coast, civilize part of the inhabitants, and make it easy for some other adventurer to proceed farther, to reduce them wholly to subjection and settle them under laws.

We are taught by the great Roman orator that every man should propose to himself the highest degree of excellence, but that he may stop with honour at the second or third: though therefore my performance should fall below the excellence of other dictionaries, I may obtain at least, the praise of having endeavoured well nor shall I think it any reproach to my diligence that I have retired, without a triumph from a contest with united academies and long successions of learned compilers. I cannot hope, in the warmest moments, to preserve so much caution through so long a work, as not often to sink into negligence, or to obtain so much knowledge of all its parts as not frequently to fail by ignorance. I expect that sometimes the desire of accuracy will urge me to superfluities, and sometimes the fear of prolixity betray me to omissions: that in the extent of such variety, I shall be often bewildered; and in the mazes of such intricacy, be frequently entangled: that in one part refinement will be subtilized beyond exactness, and evidence dilated in another beyond perspicuity Yet I do not despair of approbation from those

---

† The actual laurel is not barren, whatever be thought of the triumphs it symbolizes.
‡ Chapelain's *La Pucelle*, heralded for many years, was coldly received after publication.

who, knowing the uncertainty of conjecture, the scantiness of knowledge, the fallibility of memory, and the unsteadiness of 'attention, can compare the causes of error with the means of avoiding it, and the extent of art with the capacity of man; and whatever be the event of my endeavours, I shall not easily regret an attempt which has procured me the honour of appearing thus publicly,

My Lord,
Your Lordship's most obedient,
and most humble servant,
SAM. JOHNSON.

LETTER TO LORD CHESTERFIELD*

(Feb. 7, 1755)

To the Right Honourable the Earl of Chesterfield.

MY LORD:

I have been lately informed by the proprietor of the *World*, that two papers, in which my Dictionary is recommended to the public, were written by your Lordship. To be so distinguished is an honour which, being very little accustomed to favours from the great, I know not well how to receive, or in what terms to acknowledge.

When, upon some slight encouragement, I first visited your Lordship, I was overpowered, like the rest of mankind, by the enchantment of your address, and could not forbear to wish that I might boast myself *Le vainqueur du vainqueur de la terre;*[1]—that I might obtain that regard for which I saw the world contending; but I found my attendance so little encouraged that neither pride nor modesty would suffer me to continue it. When I had once addressed your Lordship in public, I had ex-

[1] "The conqueror of the conqueror of the world" (Boileau).

* "Johnson told me," says Boswell, "that there never was any particular incident which produced a quarrel between Lord Chesterfield and him; but that his Lordship's continued neglect was the reason why he resolved to have no connection with him. When the Dictionary was upon the eve of publication, Lord Chesterfield, who, it is said, had flattered himself with expectations that Johnson would dedicate the work to him, attempted . . . to conciliate him, by writing two papers in 'The World,' in recommendation of the work." "Upon which," commented Johnson, "I wrote him a letter expressed in civil terms, but such as might show him that I did not mind what he said or wrote, and that I had done with him." Boswell later obtained a copy of 'this celebrated letter, and gave it to the world. Carlyle, in his essay on *Boswell's Life of Johnson,* speaks of it as "that far-famed Blast of Doom, proclaiming into the ear of Lord Chesterfield, and, through him, of the listening world, that patronage should be no more." See *Eng. Lit.,* p. 208.

hausted all the art of pleasing which a retired and uncourtly scholar can possess. I had done all that I could; and no man is well pleased to have his all neglected, be it ever so little.

Seven years, my Lord, have now passed since I waited in your outward rooms, or was repulsed from your door; during which time I have been pushing on my work through difficulties, of which it is useless to complain, and have brought it, at last, to the verge of publication without one act of assistance, one word of encouragement, or one smile of favour. Such treatment I did not expect, for I never had a Patron before.

The shepherd in Virgil grew at last acquainted with Love, and found him a native of the rocks.[2]

Is not a Patron, my Lord, one who looks with unconcern on a man struggling for life in the water, and when he has reached ground, encumbers him with help? The notice which you have been pleased to take of my labours, had it been early, had been kind; but it has been delayed till I am indifferent, and cannot enjoy it; till I am solitary, and cannot impart it; till I am known, and do not want it. I hope it is no very cynical asperity not to confess obligations where no benefit has been received, or to be unwilling that the Public should consider me as owing that to a Patron, which Providence has enabled me to do for myself.

Having carried on my work thus far with so little obligation to any favourer of learning, I shall not be disappointed though I should conclude it, if less be possible, with less; for I have been long wakened from that dream of hope, in which I once boasted myself with so much exultation,

My Lord,
Your Lordship's most humble,
Most obedient servant,
SAM. JOHNSON.

FROM THE PREFACE TO THE ENGLISH DICTIONARY, 1755

In hope of giving longevity to that which its own nature forbids to be immortal, I have devoted this book, the labour of years, to the honour of my country, that we may no longer yield the palm of philology, without a contest, to the nations of the continent. The chief glory of every people arises from its authors: whether I shall add anything by my own writings to the reputation of English literature, must be left to time: much of my life has

[2] *Eclogue* VIII, 43.

been lost under the pressure of disease; much has been trifled away;* and much has always been spent in provision for the day that was passing over me; but I shall not think my employment useless or ignoble, if by my assistance foreign nations and distant ages gain access to the propagators of knowledge, and understand the teachers of truth; if my labours afford light to the repositories of science, and add celebrity to Bacon, to Hooker, to Milton, and to Boyle.[3]

When I am animated by this wish, I look with pleasure on my book, however defective, and deliver it to the world with the spirit of a man that has endeavoured well. That it will immediately become popular I have not promised to myself: a few wild blunders and risible absurdities, from which no work of such multiplicity was ever free, may for a time furnish folly with laughter and harden ignorance into contempt;† but useful diligence will at last prevail, and there never can be wanting some who distinguish desert; who will consider that no dictionary of a living tongue ever can be perfect, since, while it is hastening to publication, some words are budding, and some falling away; that a whole life cannot be spent upon syntax and etymology, and that even a whole life would not be sufficient; that he, whose design includes whatever language can express, must often speak of what he does not understand; that a writer will sometimes be hurried by eagerness to the end, and sometimes faint with weariness under a task which Scaliger[4] compares to the labours of the anvil and the mine; that what is obvious is not always known, and what is known is not always present; that sudden fits of inadvertency will surprise vigilance, slight avocations will seduce attention, and casual eclipses of the mind will darken learning; and that the writer shall often in vain trace his memory, at the moment of need, for that which yesterday he knew with intuitive readiness, and which will come uncalled into his thoughts to-morrow.

In this work, when it shall be found that much is omitted, let it not be forgotten that much likewise is performed; and though no book was ever spared out of tenderness to the author, and the world is little solicitous to know whence proceed the faults of that which it condemns, yet it may gratify curiosity to inform it that the "English Dictionary" was written with little assistance of the learned and without any patronage of the great; not in the soft obscurities of retirement, or under the shelter of academic bowers, but amidst inconvenience and distraction, in sickness and in sorrow.‡ It may repress the triumph of malignant criticism to observe, that if our language is not here fully displayed, I have only failed in an attempt which no human powers have hitherto completed. If the lexicons of ancient tongues, now immutably fixed, and comprised in a few volumes, be yet, after the toil of successive ages, inadequate and delusive; if the aggregated knowledge and co-operating diligence of the Italian academicians did not secure them from the censure of Beni;§ if the embodied critics of France, when fifty years had been spent upon their work, were obliged to change its economy,[5] and give their second edition another form, I may surely be contented without the praise of perfection, which, if I could obtain, in this gloom of solitude, what would it avail me? I have protracted my work till most of those whom I wished to please have sunk into the grave, and success and miscarriage are empty sounds: I therefore dismiss it with frigid tranquillity, having little to fear or hope from censure or from praise.

FROM THE PREFACE TO AN EDITION OF SHAKESPEARE'S PLAYS, 1765-1768

The poet, of whose works I have undertaken the revision, may now begin to assume the dignity of an ancient, and claim the privilege of established fame and prescriptive veneration. He has long outlived his century, the term commonly fixed as the test of literary merit. Whatever advantages he might once derive from personal allusions, local customs, or temporary opinions, have for many years been lost; and every topic of merriment, or motive of sorrow, which the modes of artificial life

[3] Robert Boyle, the natural philosopher, 1627-1691.
[4] A European scholar of the 16th century.
* Boswell reports Johnson as saying: "I have been trying to cure my laziness all my life, and could not do it."
† Johnson spoke prophetically. Among amusing entries, some of course intentional, Boswell has noted the following:
  Lexicographer. A writer of dictionaries, a harmless drudge.
  Pension. An allowance made to any one without an equivalent. In England it is generally understood to mean pay given to a state hireling for treason to his country.
  Oats. A grain which in England is generally given to horses, but in Scotland supports the people.
  Network. Anything reticulated or decussated at equal distances, with interstices between the intersections.
[5] system
‡ Johnson's wife died March 17, 1752, and the anniversary of her death he spent "in prayer and self-examination."
§ He objected to their basing their lexicon on Tuscan usage.

fforded him, now only obscure the scenes which they once illuminated. The effects of favour and competition are at an end; the tradition of his friendships and his enmities has perished; his works support no opinion with arguments, nor supply any faction with invectives; they can neither indulge vanity, nor gratify malignity; but are read without any other reason than the desire of pleasure, and are therefore praised only as pleasure is obtained; yet, thus unassisted by interest or passion, they have passed through variations of taste and changes of manners, and, as they devolved from one generation to another, have received new honours at every transmission.

But because human judgment, though it be gradually gaining upon certainty, never becomes infallible, and approbation, though long continued, may yet be only the approbation of prejudice or fashion, it is proper to inquire by what peculiarities of excellence Shakespeare has gained and kept the favour of his countrymen.

Nothing can please many, and please long, but just representations of general nature. Particular manners can be known to few, and therefore few only can judge how nearly they are copied. The irregular combinations of fanciful invention may delight awhile, by that novelty of which the common satiety of life sends us all in quest; but the pleasures of sudden wonder are soon exhausted, and the mind can only repose on the stability of truth.

Shakespeare is, above all writers, at least above all modern writers, the poet of nature; the poet that holds up to his readers a faithful mirror of manners and of life. His characters are not modified by the customs of particular places, unpractised by the rest of the world; by the peculiarities of studies or professions which can operate but upon small numbers; or by the accidents of transient fashions or temporary opinions: they are the genuine progeny of common humanity, such as the world will always supply and observation will always find. His persons act and speak by the influence of those general passions and principles by which all minds are agitated, and the whole system of life is continued in motion. In the writings of other poets a character is too often an individual: in those of Shakespeare it is commonly a species.

It is from this wide extension of design that so much instruction is derived. It is this which fills the plays of Shakespeare with practical axioms and domestic wisdom. It was said of Euripides that every verse was a precept; and it may be said of Shakespeare, that from

his works may be collected a system of civil and economical prudence. Yet his real power is not shown in the splendour of particular passages, but by the progress of his fable,[6] and the tenor of his dialogue: and he that tries to recommend him by select quotations, will succeed like the pedant in Hierocles,[7] who, when he offered his house to sale, carried a brick in his pocket as a specimen.

It will not easily be imagined how much Shakespeare excels in accommodating his sentiments to real life, but by comparing him with other authors. It was observed of the ancient schools of declamation, that the more diligently they were frequented, the more was the student disqualified for the world, because he found nothing there which he should ever meet in any other place. The same remark may be applied to every stage but that of Shakespeare. The theatre, when it is under any other direction, is peopled by such characters as were never seen, conversing in a language which was never heard, upon topics which will never arise in the commerce of mankind. But the dialogue of this author is often so evidently determined by the incident which produces it, and is pursued with so much ease and simplicity, that it seems scarcely to claim the merit of fiction, but to have been gleaned by diligent selection out of common conversation and common occurrences.

Upon every other stage the universal agent is love, by whose power all good and evil is distributed, and every action quickened or retarded. To bring a lover, a lady, and a rival into a fable; to entangle them in contradictory obligations, perplex them with oppositions of interest, and harass them with violence of desires inconsistent with each other; to make them meet in rapture, and part in agony; to fill their mouths with hyperbolical joy and outrageous sorrow; to distress them as nothing human ever was distressed; to deliver them as nothing human ever was delivered,—is the business of a modern dramatist. For this, probability is violated, life is misrepresented, and language is depraved. But love is only one of many passions; and as it has no great influence upon the sum of life, it has little operation in the dramas of a poet who caught his ideas from the living world and exhibited only what he saw before him. He knew that any other passion, as it was regular or exorbitant, was a cause of happiness or calamity.

6 story, plot
7 An Alexandrian philosopher to whom were attributed certain jests which Johnson once translated.

Characters thus ample and general were not easily discriminated and preserved, yet perhaps no poet ever kept his personages more distinct from each other. I will not say with Pope that every speech may be assigned to the proper speaker, because many speeches there are which have nothing characteristical; but, perhaps, though some may be equally adapted to every person, it will be difficult to find that any can be properly transferred from the present possessor to any other claimant. The choice is right, when there is reason for choice.

Other dramatists can only gain attention by hyperbolical or aggravated characters, by fabulous and unexampled excellence or depravity, as the writers of barbarous romances invigorated the reader by a giant and a dwarf; and he that should form his expectations of human affairs from the play, or from the tale, would be equally deceived. Shakespeare has no heroes; his scenes are occupied only by men, who act and speak as the reader thinks that he should himself have spoken or acted on the same occasion: even where the agency is supernatural, the dialogue is level with life. Other writers disguise the most natural passions and most frequent incidents; so that he who contemplates them in the book will not know them in the world: Shakespeare approximates the remote, and familiarizes the wonderful; the event which he represents will not happen, but, if it were possible, its effects would probably be such as he has assigned; and it may be said that he has not only shown human nature as it acts in real exigencies, but as it would be found in trials to which it cannot be exposed.

This therefore is the praise of Shakespeare, that his drama is the mirror of life; that he who has mazed his imagination in following the phantoms which other writers raise up before him, may here be cured of his delirious ecstacies by reading human sentiments in human language, by scenes from which a hermit may estimate the transactions of the world, and a confessor predict the progress of the passions.

FROM THE LIVES OF THE ENGLISH POETS

THE CHARACTER OF ADDISON

The end of this useful life was now approaching. Addison had for some time been oppressed by shortness of breath, which was now aggravated by a dropsy; and, finding his danger pressing, he prepared to die conformably to his own precepts and professions.

During this lingering decay. he sent, as Pope relates, a message by the Earl of Warwick[8] to Mr. Gay,[9] desiring to see him. Gay, who had not visited him for some time before, obeyed the summons, and found himself received with great kindness. The purpose for which the interview had been solicited was then discovered: Addison told him that he had injured him; but that, if he recovered, he would recompense him. What the injury was he did not explain, nor did Gay ever know; but supposed that some preferment designed for him, had, by Addison's intervention, been withheld.

Lord Warwick was a young man of very irregular life, and perhaps of loose opinions, Addison, for whom he did not want respect, had very diligently endeavoured to reclaim him; but his arguments and expostulations had no effect. One experiment, however, remained to be tried: when he found his life near its end he directed the young lord to be called; and when he desired, with great tenderness, to hear his last injunctions, told him, ''I have sent for you that you may see how a Christian can die.'' What effect this awful scene had on the ear I know not; he likewise died himself in a short time.

In Tickell's[10] excellent elegy on his friend are these lines:

He taught us how to live; and, oh! too high
The price of knowledge, taught us how to die.

In which he alludes, as he told Dr. Young,[11] to this moving interview.

Having given directions to Mr. Tickell for the publication of his works, and dedicated them on his death-bed to his friend Mr. Craggs, he died June 17, 1719, at Holland House, leaving no child but a daughter.

Of his virtue it is a sufficient testimony that the resentment of party has transmitted no charge of any crime. He was not one of those who are praised only after death; for his merit was so generally acknowledged, that Swift, having observed that his election passed without a contest, adds, that if he had proposed himself for king, he would hardly have been refused.[12]

His zeal for his party did not extinguish his kindness for the merit of his opponents: when he was Secretary in Ireland he refused to intermit his acquaintance with Swift.*

[8] Addison's step-son.
[9] John Gay, the poet (*Eng. Lit.*, 182).
[10] Thomas Tickell, a contributor to the *Spectator*.
[11] Edward Young, the poet (*Eng. Lit.*, 182).
[12] Addison was elected to Parliament in 1708.
* Addison, a Whig, and Swift, a Tory, took opposite sides in political controversy.

Of his habits, or external manners, nothing is so often mentioned as that timorous or sullen taciturnity, which his friends called modesty by too mild a name. Steele mentions with great tenderness "that remarkable bashfulness, which is a cloak that hides and muffles merit;" and tells us, that "his abilities were covered only by modesty, which doubles the beauties which are seen, and gives credit and esteem to all that are concealed." Chesterfield affirms, that "Addison was the most timorous and awkward man that he ever saw." And Addison, speaking of his own deficiency in conversation, used to say of himself, that, with respect to intellectual wealth, "he could draw bills for a thousand pounds, though he had not a guinea in his pocket."

That he wanted current coin for ready payment, and by that want was often obstructed and distressed; that he was oppressed by an improper and ungraceful timidity, every testimony concurs to prove; but Chesterfield's representation is doubtless hyperbolical. That man cannot be supposed very unexpert in the arts of conversation and practice of life, who, without fortune or alliance, by his usefulness and dexterity, became Secretary of State; and who died at forty-seven, after having not only stood long in the highest rank of wit and literature, but filled one of the most important offices of State.

The time in which he lived had reason to lament his obstinacy of silence; for "he was," says Steele, "above all men in that talent called humour, and enjoyed it in such perfection, that I have often reflected, after a night spent with him apart from all the world, that I had had the pleasure of conversing with an intimate acquaintance of Terence and Catullus, who had all their wit and nature, heightened with humour more exquisite and delightful than any other man ever possessed." This is the fondness of a friend; let us hear what is told us by a rival. "Addison's conversation," says Pope, "had something in it more charming than I have found in any other man. But this was only when familiar: before strangers, or perhaps a single stranger, he preserved his dignity by a stiff silence."

This modesty was by no means inconsistent with a very high opinion of his own merit. He demanded to be the first name in modern wit;[13] and, with Steele to echo him, used to depreciate Dryden, whom Pope and Congreve defended against them. There is no reason to doubt that he suffered too much pain from the

[13] Used in the 18th century sense of "polite learning."

prevalence of Pope's poetical reputation; nor is it without strong reason suspected, that by some disingenuous acts he endeavoured to obstruct it; Pope was not the only man whom he insidiously injured, though the only man of whom he could be afraid.

His own powers were such as might have satisfied him with conscious excellence. Of very extensive learning he has indeed given no proofs. He seems to have had small acquaintance with the sciences, and to have read little except Latin and French; but of the Latin poets his *Dialogue on Medals* show that he had perused the works with great diligence and skill. The abundance of his own mind left him little need of adventitious sentiments; his wit always could suggest what the occasion demanded. He had read with critical eyes the important volume of human life, and knew the heart of man from the depths of stratagem to the surface of affectation.

What he knew he could easily communicate. "This," says Steele, "was particular in this writer, that, when he had taken his resolution, or made his plan for what he designed to write, he would walk about a room, and dictate it into language with as much freedom and ease as any one could write it down, and attend to the coherence and grammar of what he dictated."

Pope, who can be less suspected of favouring his memory, declares that he wrote very fluently, but was slow and scrupulous in correcting; that many of his *Spectators* were written very fast, and sent immediately to the press; and that it seemed to be for his advantage not to have time for much revisal.

"He would alter," says Pope, "anything to please his friends, before publication; but would not retouch his pieces afterwards: and I believe not one word in *Cato*, to which I made an objection, was suffered to stand."

The last line of *Cato* is Pope's, having been originally written

And, oh! 'twas this that ended Cato's life.

Pope might have made more objections to the six concluding lines.[†] In the first couplet the words *from hence* are improper; and the second line is taken from Dryden's Virgil. Of the next couplet, the first verse being included in the second, is therefore useless; and in the third *Discord* is made to produce *Strife*.

[†] "From hence let fierce contending nations know
What dire effects from civil discord flow.
'Tis this that shakes our country with alarms,
And gives up Rome a prey to Roman arms,
Produces fraud, and cruelty, and strife,
And robs the guilty world of Cato's life."
The rather trivial verbal criticism is characteristic of the time.

Of the course of Addison's familiar day, before his marriage, Pope has given a detail. He had in the house with him Budgell, and perhaps Philips. His chief companions were Steele, Budgell, Philips, Carey, Davenant, and Colonel Brett. With one or other of these he always breakfasted. He studied all morning; then dined at a tavern, and went afterwards to Button's.

Button had been a servant in the Countess of Warwick's family, who, under the patronage of Addison, kept a coffee-house on the south side of Russell Street, about two doors from Covent Garden. Here it was that the wits of that time used to assemble. It is said that when Addison suffered any vexation from the countess, he withdrew the company from Button's house.‡

From the coffee-house he went again to a tavern, where he often sat late, and drank too much wine. In the bottle, discontent seeks for comfort, cowardice for courage, and bashfulness for confidence. It is not unlikely that Addison was first seduced to excess by the manumission which he obtained from the servile timidity of his sober hours. He that feels oppression from the presence of those to whom he knows himself superior, will desire to set loose his powers of conversation; and who, that ever asked succour from Bacchus, was able to preserve himself from being enslaved by his auxiliary?

Among those friends it was that Addison displayed the elegance of his colloquial accomplishments, which may easily be supposed such as Pope represents them. The remark of Mandeville,[14] who, when he had passed an evening in his company, declared that he was a parson in a tie-wig,[15] can detract little from his character; he was always reserved to strangers, and was not incited to uncommon freedom by a character like that of Mandeville.

From any minute knowledge of his familiar manners, the intervention of sixty years has now debarred us. Steele once promised Congreve and the public a complete description of his character; but the promises of authors are like the vows of lovers. Steele thought no more on his design, or thought on it with anxiety that at last disgusted him, and left his friend in the hands of Tickell.

One slight lineament of his character Swift has preserved. It was his practice, when he

found any man invincibly wrong, to flatter h opinions by acquiescence, and sink him y deeper in absurdity. This artifice of mischie was admired by Stella;[16] and Swift seems t approve her admiration.

His works will supply some information. appears from his various pictures of the worl that, with all his bashfulness, he had converse with many distinct classes of men, had surveye their ways with very diligent observation, an marked with great acuteness the effects o different modes of life. He was a man in whos presence nothing reprehensible was out of dan ger; quick in discerning whatever was wron, or ridiculous, and not unwilling to expose i There are, says Steele, in his writings man oblique strokes upon some of the wittiest me of the age. His delight was more to excit merriment than detestation, and he detects fol lies rather than crimes.

If any judgment be made, from his books, o his moral character, nothing will be found bu purity and excellence. Knowledge of mankind indeed, less extensive than that of Addison will show that to write, and to live, are ver different. Many who praise virtue, do no mor than praise it. Yet it is reasonable to believ that Addison's professions and practice were a no great variance, since, amidst that storm o faction in which most of his life was passed though his station made him conspicuous, an his activity made him formidable, the characte given him by his friends was never contradicte by his enemies: of those with whom interes or opinion united him, he had not only th esteem, but the kindness; and of others, whom the violence of opposition drove against him, though he might lose the love, he retained th reverence.

It is justly observed by Tickell that he employed wit on the side of virtue and religion. He not only made the proper use of wit himself, but taught it to others; and from his time it has been generally subservient to the cause of reason and of truth. He has dissipated the prejudice that had long connected gaiety with vice, and easiness of manners with laxity of principles. He has restored virtue to its dignity, and taught innocence not to be ashamed. This is an elevation of literary character, *above all Greek, above all Roman fame.*[17] No greater felicity can genius attain than that of having purified intellectual pleasure, separated mirth from indecency, and wit from licentiousness; of having taught a succession of writers

---

[14] Bernard Mandeville, a poet and somewhat of a cynic.
[15] i. e., in the latest court-fashion (tie-wigs having just come in; moreover, the learned professions affected the loose, flowing wigs)
‡ Addison married the countess in 1716.

[16] Swift's inamorata.
[17] Quoted from Pope, *To Augustus.*

o bring elegance and gaiety to the aid of goodness; and, if I may use expressions yet more awful, of having *turned many to right-eousness.*[18]

JAMES BOSWELL (1740-1795)

FROM THE LIFE OF SAMUEL JOHNSON, LL.D.

JOHNSON AT SCHOOL

He was first taught to read English by Dame Oliver, a widow, who kept a school for young children in Lichfield. He told me she could read the black letter, and asked him to borrow for her, from his father, a Bible in that character. When he was going to Oxford, she came to take leave of him, brought him, in the simplicity of her kindness, a present of gingerbread, and said he was the best scholar she ever had. He delighted in mentioning this early compliment: adding, with a smile, that "this was as high a proof of his merit as he could conceive." His next instructor in English was a master whom, when he spoke of him to me, he familiarly called Tom Brown, who, said he, "published a spelling-book, and dedicated it to the Universe; but I fear no copy of it can now be had."

He began to learn Latin with Mr. Hawkins, usher, or undermaster, of Lichfield school—"a man" (said he) "very skilful in his little way." With him he continued two years, and then rose to be under the care of Mr. Hunter, the head master, who, according to his account, "was very severe and wrongheadedly severe. He used" (said he) "to beat us unmercifully; and he did not distinguish between ignorance and negligence; for he would beat a boy equally for not knowing a thing, as for neglecting to know it. He would ask a boy a question, and if he did not answer it, he would beat him, without considering whether he had an opportunity of knowing how to answer it. For instance, he would call up a boy and ask him Latin for a candlestick, which the boy could not expect to be asked. Now, Sir, if a boy could answer every question, there would be no need of a master to teach him."

However, . . . Johnson was very sensible how much he owed to Mr. Hunter. Mr. Langton one day asked him how he had acquired so accurate a knowledge of Latin, in which I believe he was exceeded by no man of his time; he said, "My master whipt me very well. Without that, sir, I should have done nothing." He

told Mr. Langton that while Hunter was flogging his boys unmercifully, he used to say, "And this I do to save you from the gallows." Johnson, upon all occasions, expressed his approbation of enforcing instruction by means of the rod. "I would rather" (said he) "have the rod to be the general terror to all, to make them learn, than tell a child, if you do thus, or thus, you will be more esteemed than your brothers or sisters. The rod produces an effect which terminates in itself. A child is afraid of being whipped, and gets his task, and there's an end on't: whereas, by exciting emulation and comparisons of superiority, you lay the foundation of lasting mischief; you make brothers and sisters hate each other." . . .

That superiority over his fellows, which he maintained with so much dignity in his march through life, was not assumed from vanity and ostentation, but was the natural and constant effect of those extraordinary powers of mind, of which he could not but be conscious by comparison; the intellectual difference, which in other cases of comparison of characters, is often a matter of undecided contest, being as clear in his case as the superiority of stature in some men above others. Johnson did not strut or stand on tiptoe; he only did not stoop. From his earliest years, his superiority was perceived and acknowledged. He was from the beginning *anax andrōn*, a king of men. His schoolfellow, Mr. Hector, has obligingly furnished me with many particulars of his boyish days; and assured me that he never knew him corrected at school but for talking and diverting other boys from their business. He seemed to learn by intuition; for though indolence and procrastination were inherent in his constitution, whenever he made an exertion he did more than any one else. In short, he is a memorable instance of what has been often observed, that the boy is the man in miniature; and that the distinguishing characteristics of each individual are the same through the whole course of life. His favourites used to receive very liberal assistance from him; and such was the submission and deference with which he was treated, such the desire to obtain his regard, that three of the boys, of whom Mr. Hector was sometimes one, used to come in the morning as his humble attendants, and carry him to school. One in the middle stooped while he sat upon his back, and one on each side supported him, and thus he was borne triumphant. Such a proof of the early predominance of intellectual vigour is very remarkable, and does honour to human nature.

---

[18] *Daniel,* xii, 3.

JOHNSON'S FRIENDS, 1752-53*

His acquaintance with Bennet Langton, Esq., of Langton, in Lincolnshire, another much valued friend, commenced soon after the conclusion of his *Rambler;* which that gentleman, then a youth, had read with so much admiration, that he came to London chiefly with the view of endeavouring to be introduced to its author. By a fortunate chance he happened to take lodgings in a house where Mr. Levet[1] frequently visited; and having mentioned his wish to his landlady, she introduced him to Mr. Levet, who readily obtained Johnson's permission to bring Mr. Langton to him; as, indeed, Johnson, during the whole course of his life, had no shyness, real or affected, but was easy of access to all who were properly recommended, and even wished to see numbers at his *levee,* as his morning circle of company might, with strict propriety, be called. Mr. Langton was exceedingly surprised when the sage first appeared. He had not received the smallest intimation of his figure, dress, or manner. From perusing his writings, he fancied he should see a decent, well-drest, in short, a remarkably decorous philosopher. Instead of which, down from his bed-chamber, about noon, came, as newly risen, a huge uncouth figure, with a little dark wig which scarcely covered his head, and his clothes hanging loose about him. But his conversation was so rich, so animated, and so forcible, and his religious and political notions so congenial with those in which Langton had been educated, that he conceived for him that veneration and attachment which he ever preserved. . . .

One night when Beauclerk[2] and Langton had supped at a tavern in London, and sat till about three in the morning, it came into their heads to go and knock up Johnson, and see if they could prevail on him to join them in a ramble. They rapped violently at the door of his chambers in the Temple, till at last he appeared in his shirt, with his little black wig on the top of his head, instead of a nightcap, and a poker in his hand, imagining, probably, that some ruffians were coming to attack him. When he discovered who they were, and was told their errand, he smiled, and with great good humour agreed to their proposal: "What, is it you, you dogs! I'll have a frisk with you." He was soon dressed, and they sallied forth together into Covent-Garden, where the greengrocers and fruiterers were beginning to arrange their hampers, just come in from the country. Johnson made some attempts to help them; but the honest gardeners stared so at his figure and manner, and odd interference, that he soon saw his services were not relished. They then repaired to one of the neighbouring taverns, and made a bowl of that liquor called *Bishop,*[3] which Johnson had always liked; while, in joyous contempt of sleep, from which he had been roused, he repeated the festive lines,

"Short, O short, then be thy reign,
And give us to the world again!"

They did not stay long, but walked down to the Thames, took a boat, and rowed to Billingsgate. Beauclerk and Johnson were so well pleased with their amusement that they resolved to persevere in dissipation for the rest of the day: but Langton deserted them, being engaged to breakfast with some young ladies. Johnson scolded him for "leaving his social friends, to go and sit with a set of wretched *un-idea'd* girls." Garrick being told of this ramble, said to him smartly, "I heard of your frolic t'other night. You'll be in the *Chronicle.*" Upon which Johnson afterwards observed, "*He* durst not do such a thing. His *wife* would not let him!"

He entered upon this year, 1753, with his usual piety, as appears from the following prayer, which I transcribed from that part of his diary which he burned a few days before his death:

"Jan. 1, 1753, N. S.,* which I shall use for the future.

"Almighty GOD, who hast continued my life to this day, grant that, by the assistance of thy Holy Spirit, I may improve the time which thou shalt grant me, to my eternal salvation. Make me to remember, to thy glory, thy judgments and thy mercies. Make me so to consider the loss of my wife, whom thou hast taken from me, that it may dispose me by thy grace, to lead the residue of my life in thy fear. Grant this, O LORD, for JESUS CHRIST'S sake. Amen."

JOHNSON AND GOLDSMITH, 1773

He and Mr. Langton and I went together to THE CLUB,[4] where we found Mr. Burke, Mr.

---

[1] A surgeon, and odd character, inmate of Dr. Johnson's house.

[2] A gentleman of elegant tastes but rather free manners and opinions.

* These dates indicate the period of Johnson's life under which the particular records are made. See any edition of Boswell's *Johnson.*

[3] Mulled wine, oranges and sugar

[4] The Literary Club. See *Eng. Lit.*, p. 207

* New style: referring to the change to the Gregorian calendar, which was adopted in England in 1752, when the dates between September 2nd and 14th were omitted.

arrick, and some other members, and amongst
hem our friend Goldsmith, who sat silently
rooding over Johnson's reprimand to him
fter dinner.† Johnson perceived this, and said
side to some of us, "I'll make Goldsmith
orgive me;" and then called to him in a loud
oice, "Dr. Goldsmith—something passed to-
ay where you and I dined: I ask your
ardon." Goldsmith answered placidly, "It
ust be much from you, Sir, that I take ill."
nd so at once the difference was over, and
hey were on as easy terms as ever, and Gold-
mith rattled away as usual.

In our way to the club to-night, when I
egretted that Goldsmith would, upon every
ccasion, endeavour to shine, by which he often
xposed himself, Mr. Langton observed that he
vas not like Addison, who was content with the
ame of his writings, and did not aim also at
xcellency in conversation, for which he found
imself unfit: and that he said to a lady who
omplained of his having talked little in com-
any, "Madam, I have but nine-pence in ready
noney, but I can draw for a thousand pounds."
observed that Goldsmith had a great deal of
old in his cabinet, but not content with that,
vas always taking out his purse. JOHNSON.
'Yes, Sir, and that so often an empty purse!"

Goldsmith's incessant desire of being con-
picuous in company was the occasion of his
ometimes appearing to such disadvantage as
ne should hardly have supposed possible in a
nan of his genius. When his literary reputa-
ion had risen deservedly high, and his society
vas much courted, he became very jealous of
he extraordinary attention which was every-
vhere paid to Johnson. One evening, in a
ircle of wits, he found fault with me for
alking of Johnson as entitled to the honour
f unquestionable superiority. "Sir, (said he,)
ou are for making a monarchy of what should
oe a republic."

He was still more mortified, when talking in
a company with fluent vivacity, and, as he
lattered himself, to the admiration of all who
vere present; a German who sat next him,
nd perceived Johnson rolling himself as if
bout to speak, suddenly stopped him, saying,
'Stay, stay—Toctor Shonson is going to say
something." This was, no doubt, very pro-
voking, especially to one so irritable as Goldsmith, who frequently mentioned it with strong
xpressions of indignation.

It may also be observed that Goldsmith was

sometimes content to be treated with an easy
familiarity, but upon occasions would be con-
sequential and important. An instance of this
occurred in a small particular. Johnson had a
way of contracting the names of his friends:
as Beauclerk, Beau; Boswell, Bozzy; Langton,
Lanky; Murphy, Mur; Sheridan,[5] Sherry. I
remember one day, when Tom Davies[6] was
telling that Dr. Johnson said, "We are all in
labour for a name to *Goldy's* play," Goldsmith
seemed displeased that such a liberty should
be taken with his name, and said, "I have
often desired him not to call me *Goldy*." Tom
was remarkably attentive to the most minute
circumstance about Johnson. I recollect his
telling me once, on my arrival in London, "Sir,
our great friend has made an improvement on
his appellation of old Mr. Sheridan. He calls
him now *Sherry derry*."

CRITICAL OPINIONS

1775. Johnson was in high spirits this
evening at the club, and talked with great
animation and success. He attacked Swift, as
he used to do upon all occasions. "The 'Tale
of a Tub' is so much superior to his other
writings, that one can hardly believe he was
the author of it: there is in it such a vigour
of mind, such a swarm of thoughts, so much of
nature, and art, and life." I wondered to
hear him say of "Gulliver's Travels," "When
once you have thought of big men and little
men, it is very easy to do all the rest." I
endeavoured to make a stand for Swift, and
tried to rouse those who were much more able
to defend him; but in vain. Johnson at last,
of his own accord, allowed very great merit to
the inventory of articles found in the pocket of
"the Man Mountain," particularly the description of his watch, which it was conjectured was
his GOD, as he consulted it upon all occasions.
He observed, that "Swift put his name to but
two things (after he had a name to put), 'The
Plan for the Improvement of the English Language,' and the last 'Drapier's Letter.'"

1775. Next day I dined with Johnson at
Mr. Thrale's. He attacked Gray, calling him
"a dull fellow." BOSWELL. "I understand
he was reserved, and might appear dull in company; but surely he was not dull in poetry."
JOHNSON. "Sir, he was dull in company, dull
in his closet, dull everywhere. He was dull in a
new way, and that made many people think him
GREAT. He was a mechanical poet." He then

---

† After one of Johnson's long discourses, Goldsmith had begged that somebody else might
be heard; whereupon Johnson called him impertinent.

5 Thomas Sheridan, father of the dramatist.
6 A bookseller and publisher who published a pir-
ated edition of Johnson's writings but was
forgiven by him.

repeated some ludicrous lines, which have escaped my memory, and said, "Is not that GREAT, like his Odes?" Mrs. Thrale maintained that his Odes were melodious; upon which he exclaimed,

    " 'Weave the warp, and weave the woof;' "

I added, in a solemn tone,

    " 'The winding-sheet of Edward's race.'

There is a good line."—"Ay, (said he,) and the next line is a good one (pronouncing it contemptuously),

    " 'Give ample verge and room enough.'

No, Sir, there are but two good stanzas in Gray's poetry, which are in his 'Elegy in a Country Churchyard.' " He then repeated the stanza,

"For who to dumb forgetfulness a prey," &c.,

mistaking one word; for instead of *precincts* he said *confines.* He added, "The other stanza I forget."

    1776. Talking of *The Spectator,* he said, "It is wonderful that there is such a proportion of bad papers in the half of the work which was not written by Addison; for there was all the world to write that half, yet not a half of that half is good."

TALK AT THE CLUB, 1778

On Friday, April 3, I dined with him in London, in a company where were present several eminent men, whom I shall not name, but distinguish their parts in the conversation by different letters.[*]

F. "I have been looking at this famous antique marble dog of Mr. Jennings,[†] valued at a thousand guineas, said to be Alcibiades's dog." JOHNSON. "His tail then must be docked. That was the mark of Alcibiades' dog." E. "A thousand guineas! The representation of no animal whatever is worth so much. At this rate a dead dog would indeed be better than a living lion." JOHNSON. "Sir, it is not the worth of the thing, but of the skill in forming it, which is so highly estimated. Everything that enlarges the sphere of human powers, that shows man he can do what he thought he could not do, is valuable. The first man who balanced a straw upon his nose Johnson who rode upon three horses at a time; in short, all such men deserved the applause of mankind, not on account of the use of what they did, but of the dexterity which they exhibited." BOSWELL. "Yet a misapplication of time and assiduity is not to be encouraged. Addison, in one of his *Spectators,* commends the judgment of a King, who as a suitable reward to a man that by long perseverance had attained to the art of throwing a barley-corn through the eye of a needle, gave him a bushel of barley." JOHNSON. "He must have been a King of Scotland, where barley is scarce." F. "One of the most remarkable antique figures of an animal is the boar at Florence." JOHNSON. "The first boar that is well made in marble, should be preserved as a wonder. When men arrive at a facility of making boars well, then the workmanship is not of such value, but they should however be preserved as examples, and as a greater security for the restoration of the art, should it be lost." .

E. "From the experience which I have had —and I have had a great deal—I have learnt to think *better* of mankind." JOHNSON. "From my experience I have found them worse in commercial dealings, more disposed to cheat than I had any notion of; but more disposed to do one another good than I had conceived." J. "Less just and more beneficent." JOHNSON. "And really it is wonderful, considering how much attention is necessary for men to take care of themselves, and ward off immediate evils which press upon them, it is wonderful how much they do for others. As it is said of the greatest liar, that he tells more truth than falsehood; so it may be said of the worst man, that he does more good than evil." BOSWELL. "Perhaps from experience men may be found *happier* than we suppose." JOHNSON. "No, Sir; the more we enquire we shall find men the less happy." P. "As to thinking better or worse of mankind from experience, some cunning people will not be satisfied unless they have put men to the test, as they think. There is a very good story told of Sir Godfrey

---

[*] "It appears, by the books of the Club, that the company on that evening consisted of Dr. Johnson, president, Mr. Burke, Mr. Boswell, Dr. George Fordyce, Mr. Gibbon, Sir Joshua Reynolds, Lord Upper Ossory, and Mr. R. B. Sheridan. In Mr. Boswell's account the letter E. no doubt stands for Edmund Burke; F., in allusion to his family name of Fitzpatrick, probably means Lord Upper Ossory; but the appropriation of the other letters is very difficult."—Croker.

[†] Henry C. Jennings, a collector of antiques. The marble dog was at this date an object of great curiosity in London. Johnson had in mind the story in Plutarch's *Lives:* "Alcibiades had a dog of uncommon size and beauty, which cost him seventy minae, and yet his tail, which was his principal ornament, he caused to be cut off."

neller,[7] in his character of a justice of the peace. A gentleman brought his servant before him, upon an accusation of having stolen some money from him; but it having come out that he had laid it purposely in the servant's way in order to try his honesty, Sir Godfrey sent the master to prison." JOHNSON. "To resist temptation once is not a sufficient proof of honesty. If a servant, indeed, were to resist the continued temptation of silver lying in a window, as some people let it lie, when he is sure his master does not know how much there is of it, he would give a strong proof of honesty. But this is a proof to which you have no right to put a man. You know, humanly speaking, there is a certain degree of temptation which will overcome any virtue. Now, in so far as you approach temptation to a man, you do him an injury; and, if he is overcome, you share his guilt."

JOHNSON'S CHARACTER

The character of SAMUEL JOHNSON has, I trust, been so developed in the course of this work, that they who have honoured it with a perusal may be considered as well acquainted with him. As, however, it may be expected that I should collect into one view the capital and distinguishing features of this extraordinary man, I shall endeavour to acquit myself of that part of my biographical undertaking, however difficult it may be to do that which many of my readers will do better for themselves.

His figure was large and well formed, and his countenance of the cast of an ancient statue; yet his appearance was rendered strange and somewhat uncouth, by convulsive cramps, by the scars of that distemper[8] which it was once imagined the royal touch could cure, and by a slovenly mode of dress. He had the use only of one eye; yet so much does mind govern, and even supply the deficiency of organs, that his visual perceptions, as far as they extended, were uncommonly quick and accurate. So morbid was his temperament,[9] that he never knew the natural joy of a free and vigorous use of his limbs: when he walked, it was like the struggling gait of one in fetters; when he rode, he had no command or direction of his horse, but was carried as if in a balloon. That with his constitution and habits of life he should have lived seventy-five years, is a proof

that an inherent *vivida vis*[10] is a powerful preservative of the human frame.

Man is, in general, made up of contradictory qualities; and these will ever show themselves in strange succession where a consistency, in appearance at least, if not in reality, has not been attained by long habits of philosophical discipline. In proportion to the native vigour of the mind, the contradictory qualities will be the more prominent, and more difficult to be adjusted; and, therefore, we are not to wonder that Johnson exhibited an eminent example of this remark which I have made upon human nature. At different times he seemed a different man, in some respects; not, however, in any great or essential article upon which he had fully employed his mind and settled certain principles of duty, but only in his manners, and in the display of argument and fancy in his talk. He was prone to superstition, but not to credulity. Though his imagination might incline him to a belief of the marvellous and the mysterious, his vigorous reason examined the evidence with jealousy. He was a sincere and zealous Christian, of high Church-of-England and monarchical principles, which he would not tamely suffer to be questioned; and had, perhaps, at an early period, narrowed his mind somewhat too much, both as to religion and politics. His being impressed with the danger of extreme latitude in either, though he was of a very independent spirit, occasioned his appearing somewhat unfavourable to the prevalence of that noble freedom of sentiment which is the best possession of man. Nor can it be denied that he had many prejudices; which, however, frequently suggested many of his pointed sayings, that rather show a playfulness of fancy than any settled malignity. He was steady and inflexible in maintaining the obligations of religion and morality; both from a regard for the order of society, and from a veneration for the GREAT SOURCE of all order; correct, nay, stern in his taste; hard to please and easily offended; impetuous and irritable in his temper, but of a most humane and benevolent heart, which showed itself not only in a most liberal charity, as far as his circumstances would allow, but in a thousand instances of active benevolence. He was afflicted with a bodily disease, which made him often restless and fretful; and with a constitutional melancholy, the clouds of which darkened the brightness of his fancy, and gave a gloomy cast to his whole course of thinking: we, therefore, ought not to wonder at his sallies of impatience

---

7 Portrait painter to Charles II. and William III.
8 Scrofula, or King's Evil. On the "royal touch,"
   see Evelyn's *Diary*, July 6, 1660 (p. 274).
9 so sickly was his constitution

10 living force, spiritual energy

and passion at any time; especially when provoked by obtrusive ignorance, or presuming petulance; and allowance must be made for his uttering hasty and satirical sallies even against his best friends. And, surely, when it is considered that "amidst sickness and sorrow" he exerted his faculties in so many works for the benefit of mankind, and particularly that he achieved the great and admirable DICTIONARY of our language, we must be astonished at his resolution. The solemn text, "Of him to whom much is given much will be required," seems to have been ever present to his mind, in a rigorous sense, and to have made him dissatisfied with his labours and acts of goodness, however comparatively great; so that the unavoidable consciousness of his superiority was, in that respect, a cause of disquiet. He suffered so much from this, and from the gloom which perpetually haunted him and made solitude frightful, that it may be said of him, "If in this life only he had hope, he was of all men most miserable."

He loved praise, when it was brought to him; but was too proud to seek for it. He was somewhat susceptible of flattery. As he was general and unconfined in his studies, he cannot be considered as master of any one particular science; but he had accumulated a vast and various collection of learning and knowledge, which was so arranged in his mind as to be ever in readiness to be brought forth. But his superiority over other learned men consisted chiefly in what may be called the art of thinking, the art of using his mind; a certain continual power of seizing the useful substance of all that he knew, and exhibiting it in a clear and forcible manner; so that knowledge, which we often see to be no better than lumber in men of dull understanding, was, in him, true, evident, and actual wisdom. His moral precepts are practical; for they are drawn from an intimate acquaintance with human nature. His maxims carry conviction: for they are founded on the basis of common sense and a very attentive and minute survey of real life. His mind was so full of imagery, that he might have been perpetually a poet; yet it is remarkable that however rich his prose is in this respect, his poetical pieces, in general, have not much of that splendour, but are rather distinguished by strong sentiment, and acute observation, conveyed in harmonious and energetic verse, particularly in heroic couplets.

Though usually grave, and even awful in his deportment, he possessed uncommon and peculiar powers of wit and humour; he frequently indulged himself in colloquial pleasantry; and the heartiest merriment was often enjoyed i his company; with this great advantage, that as it was entirely free from any poisonous tinc ture of vice or impiety, it was salutary to thos who shared in it. He had accustomed himsel to such accuracy in his common conversatior that he at all times expressed his thoughts wit great force and an elegant choice of language the effect of which was aided by his having loud voice, and a slow, deliberate utterance In him were united a most logical head with most fertile imagination, which gave him a extraordinary advantage in arguing: for h could reason close or wide, as he saw best fo the moment. Exulting in his intellectua strength and dexterity, he could, when h pleased, be the greatest sophist that ever con tended in the lists of declamation; and, from spirit of contradiction, and a delight in show ing his powers, he would often maintain the wrong side with equal warmth and ingenuity so that, when there was an audience, his rea opinions could seldom be gathered from hi talk; though when he was in company with single friend, he would discuss a subject witl genuine fairness; but he was too conscientiou to make error permanent and pernicious by deliberately writing it; and, in all his numerou works, he earnestly inculcated what appeared to him to be the truth; his piety being constant and the ruling principle of all his conduct.

Such was SAMUEL JOHNSON, a man whose talents, acquirements, and virtues were so extraordinary, that the more his character is considered, the more he will be regarded by the present age, and by posterity, with admiration and reverence.

OLIVER GOLDSMITH (1728-1774)

FROM THE CITIZEN OF THE WORLD*

LETTER I

To Mr. ——, Merchant in London.
Amsterdam.

SIR,—Yours of the 13th instant, covering two bills, one on Messrs. R. and D., value £478 10s. and the other on Mr. ——, value £285, duly came to hand, the former of which met with honour but the other has been trifled with, and I am afraid will be returned protested.

* These "Chinese Letters," as they were commonly called, 123 in number, were written for *The Public Ledger* in 1760 and 1761. The source of their popularity lay in the amusing social satire obtained by viewing the customs of one country through the eyes of a citizen of another. Lien Chi Altangi is of course fictitious, as are the other Chinese characters mentioned.

The bearer of this is my friend, therefore let m be yours. He is a native of Honan in hina, and one who did me signal services, hen he was a mandarin, and I a factor, at anton. By frequently conversing with the nglish there, he has learned the language, ough entirely a stranger to their manners and stoms. I am told he is a philosopher; I am re he is an honest man: that to you will be s best recommendation, next to the considera-on of his being the friend of, Sir,

Yours, etc.

LETTER II

rom Lien Chi Altangi to ——, Merchant in Amsterdam.

London.

FRIEND OF MY HEART,—May the wings of eace rest upon thy dwelling, and the shield of nscience preserve thee from vice and misery! or all thy favours accept my gratitude and teem, the only tributes a poor philosophic anderer can return. Sure, fortune is resolved make me unhappy, when she gives others a wer of testifying their friendship by actions, d leaves me only words to express the sin-rity of mine.

I am perfectly sensible of the delicacy with hich you endeavour to lessen your own merit d my obligations. By calling your late in-ances of friendship only a return for former vours, you would induce me to impute to your stice what I owe to your generosity.

The services I did you at Canton, justice, manity, and my office bade me perform; ose you have done me since my arrival at msterdam, no laws obliged you to, no justice quired. Even half your favours would have een greater than my most sanguine expecta-ons.

The sum of money, therefore, which you pri-ately conveyed into my baggage when I was aving Holland, and which I was ignorant of ll my arrival in London, I must beg leave to turn. You have been bred a merchant, and a scholar; you consequently love money better an I. You can find pleasure in superfluity; am perfectly content with what is sufficient: ake therefore what is yours: it may give you me pleasure, even though you have no occa-ion to use it; my happiness it cannot improve, or I have already all that I want.

My passage by sea from Rotterdam to Eng-and was more painful to me than all the ourneys I ever made on land. I have traversed he immeasurable wilds of Mogul Tartary; felt ll the rigours of Siberian skies: I have had my repose a hundred times disturbed by invad-ing savages, and have seen, without shrinking, the desert sands rise like a troubled ocean all around me. Against these calamities I was armed with resolution; but in my passage to England, though nothing occurred that gave the mariners any uneasiness, to one who was never at sea before all was a subject of aston-ishment and terror. To find the land disappear —to see our ship mount the waves, swift as an arrow from the Tartar bow—to hear the wind howling through the cordage—to feel a sickness which depresses even the spirits of the brave,— these were unexpected distresses, and conse-quently assaulted me, unprepared to receive them.

You men of Europe think nothing of a voy-age by sea. With us of China a man who has been from sight of land is regarded upon his return with admiration. I have known some provinces where there is not even a name for the ocean. What a strange people, therefore, am I got amongst, who have founded an empire on this unstable element, who build cities upon billows that rise higher than the mountains of Tipartala,[1] and make the deep more formidable than the wildest tempest!

Such accounts as these, I must confess, were my first motives for seeing England. These induced me to undertake a journey of seven hundred painful days, in order to examine its opulence, buildings, sciences, arts, and manu-factures, on the spot. Judge, then, my disap-pointment on entering London, to see no signs of that opulence so much talked of abroad: wherever I turn I am presented with a gloomy solemnity in the houses, the streets, and the inhabitants; none of that beautiful gilding which makes a principal ornament in Chinese architecture. The streets of Nankin are some-times strewed with gold leaf; very different are those of London: in the midst of their pave-ment a great lazy puddle moves muddily along; heavy-laden machines, with wheels of unwieldy thickness, crowd up every passage: so that a stranger, instead of finding time for observa-tion, is often happy if he has time to escape from being crushed to pieces.

The houses borrow very few ornaments from architecture; their chief decoration seems to be a paltry piece of painting hung out at their doors or windows,[2] at once a proof of their indigence and vanity: their vanity, in each having one of those pictures exposed to public view; and their indigence, in being unable to

1 Unidentified.
2 House or door signs were formerly extensively used in London in place of numbers.

get them better painted. In this respect the fancy of their painters is also deplorable. Could you believe it? I have seen five black lions and three blue boars in less than the circuit of half a mile; and yet you know that animals of these colours are nowhere to be found, except in the wild imaginations of Europe.

From these circumstances in their buildings, and from the dismal looks of the inhabitants, I am induced to conclude that the nation is actually poor; and that, like the Persians, they make a splendid figure everywhere but at home. The proverb of Xixofou is, that a man's riches may be seen in his eyes: if we judge of the English by this rule, there is not a poorer nation under the sun.

I have been here but two days, so will not be hasty in my decisions. Such letters as I shall write to Fipsihi in Moscow I beg you will endeavor to forward with all diligence; I shall send them open, in order that you may take copies or translations, as you are equally versed in the Dutch and Chinese languages. Dear friend, think of my absence with regret, as I sincerely regret yours; even while I write, I lament our separation. Farewell.

Letter III

From Lien Chi Altangi to the care of Fipsihi, resident in Moscow; to be forwarded by the Russian caravan to Fum Hoam, First President of the Ceremonial Academy at Pekin, in China.

Think not, O thou guide of my youth, that absence can impair my respect, or interposing trackless deserts blot your reverend figure from my memory. The farther I travel I feel the pain of separation with stronger force; those ties that bind me to my native country and you are still unbroken. By every remove I only drag a greater length of chain.

Could I find aught worth transmitting from so remote a region as this to which I have wandered, I should gladly send it; but, instead of this, you must be contented with a renewal of my former professions, and an imperfect account of a people with whom I am as yet but superficially acquainted. The remarks of a man who has been but three days in the country can only be those obvious circumstances which force themselves upon the imagination. I consider myself here as a newly created being introduced into a new world. Every object strikes with wonder and surprise. The imagination, still unsated, seems the only active principle of the mind. The most trifling occurrences give

pleasure till the gloss of novelty is worn awa When I have ceased to wonder, I may possibl grow wise; I may then call the reasonin principle to my aid, and compare those objec with each other, which were before examine without reflection.

Behold me, then, in London, gazing at th strangers, and they at me. It seems they fir somewhat absurd in my figure; and had I nev been from home, it is possible I might find a infinite fund of ridicule in theirs: but by lor travelling I am taught to laugh at folly alon and to find nothing truly ridiculous but villair and vice.

When I had just quitted my native countr and crossed the Chinese wall, I fancied ever deviation from the customs and manners China was a departing from nature. I smile at the blue lips and red foreheads of th Tonguese;[3] and could hardly contain when saw the Daures[4] dress their heads with horn The Ostiacs[5] powdered with red earth, and th Calmuck[6] beauties, tricked out in all the fine of sheepskin, appeared highly ridiculous. B I soon perceived that the ridicule lay not them but in me; that I falsely condemne others for absurdity, because they happened differ from a standard originally founded prejudice or partiality.

I find no pleasure, therefore, in taxing th English with departing from nature in the external appearance, which is all I yet know their character: it is possible they only e deavour to improve her simple plan, since eve extravagance in dress proceeds from a desire becoming more beautiful than nature made u and this is so harmless a vanity, that I not on pardon, but approve it. A desire to be mo excellent than others is what actually makes so; and as thousands find a livelihood in socie by such appetites, none but the ignorant invei against them.

You are not insensible, most reverend Fu Hoam, what numberless trades, even among th Chinese, subsist by the harmless pride of ea other. Your nose-borers, feet-swathers, teet stainers, eyebrow-pluckers, would all wa bread, should their neighbours want vanit These vanities, however, employ much few hands in China than in England; and a fi gentleman or a fine lady here, dressed up to th fashion, seems scarcely to have a single lim that does not suffer some distortions from an

To make a fine gentleman several trades a

[3] The Tunguses, Mongolians of eastern Siberia.
[4] The Daurians, in Manchuria.
[5] A tribe of western Siberia.
[6] Western Mongols.

quired, but chiefly a barber. You have un-
ubtedly heard of the Jewish champion[7] whose
rength lay in his hair. One would think that
e English were for placing all wisdom there.
> appear wise, nothing more is requisite here
an for a man to borrow hair from the heads
all his neighbours, and clap it like a bush on
s own. The distributors of law and physic
ick on such quantities, that it is almost impos-
>le, even in idea, to distinguish between the
ad and the hair.

Those whom I have now been describing
fect the gravity of the lion; those I am going
describe more resemble the pert vivacity of
aller animals. The barber, who is still mas-
r of the ceremonies, cuts their hair close to
e crown; and then, with a composition of
eal and hog's-lard, plasters the whole in such
manner as to make it impossible to distin-
ish whether the patient wears a cap or a
aster; but, to make the picture more perfectly
riking, conceive the tail of some beast, a
eyhound's tail, or a pig's tail, for instance,
pended to the back of the head, and reaching
wn to the place where tails in other animals
e generally seen to begin; thus betailed and
powdered, the man of taste fancies he im-
oves in beauty, dresses up his hard-featured
ce in smiles, and attempts to look hideously
nder. Thus equipped, he is qualified to make
ve, and hopes for success more from the
wder on the outside of his head than the
ntiments within.

Yet when I consider what sort of a creature
e fine lady is to whom he is supposed to pay
s addresses, it is not strange to find him thus
uipped in order to please. She is herself
ery whit as fond of powder, and tails, and
g's lard, as he. To speak my secret senti-
ents, most reverend Fum, the ladies here are
orridly ugly; I can hardly endure the sight of
em; they no way resemble the beauties of
hina: the Europeans have a quite different
ea of beauty from us. When I reflect on the
mall-footed perfections of an Eastern beauty,
ow is it possible I should have eyes for a
oman whose feet are ten inches long? I shall
ever forget the beauties of my native city of
angfew. How very broad their faces! how
ry short their noses! how very little their
es! how very thin their lips! how very black
eir teeth! the snow on the tops of Bao[s] is
ot fairer than their cheeks; and their eyebrows
re small as the line by the pencil of Quamsi.
ere a lady with such perfections would be
ightful. Dutch and Chinese beauties, indeed,

have some resemblance, but English women are
entirely different; red cheeks, big eyes, and
teeth of a most odious whiteness, are not only
seen here, but wished for; and then they have
such masculine feet, as actually serve *some* for
walking!

Yet, uncivil as nature has been, they seem
resolved to outdo her in unkindness: they use
white powder, blue powder, and black powder
for their hair, and a red powder for the face
on some particular occasions.

They like to have the face of various colours,
as among the Tartars of Koreki,[8] frequently
sticking on, with spittle, little black patches on
every part of it, except on the tip of the nose,
which I have never seen with a patch. You'll
have a better idea of their manner of placing
these spots when I have finished a map of an
English face patched up to the fashion, which
shall shortly be sent to increase your curious
collection of paintings, medals, and monsters.

But what surprises more than all the rest is
what I have just now been credibly informed
of by one of this country. "Most ladies here,"
says he, "have two faces; one face to sleep in,
and another to show in company. The first is
generally reserved for the husband and family
at home; the other put on to please strangers
abroad. The family face is often indifferent
enough, but the out-door one looks something
better; this is always made at the toilet, where
the looking-glass and toad-eater[9] sit in council,
and settle the complexion of the day."

I cannot ascertain the truth of this remark:
however, it is actually certain that they wear
more clothes within doors than without; and I
have seen a lady, who seemed to shudder at a
breeze in her own apartment, appear half naked
in the streets. Farewell.

LETTER IV
To the Same

THE English seem as silent as the Japanese,
yet vainer than the inhabitants of Siam. Upon
my arrival I attributed that reserve to modesty,
which, I now find, has its origin in pride. Condescend to address them first, and you are sure
of their acquaintance; stoop to flattery, and
you conciliate their friendship and esteem.
They bear hunger, cold, fatigue, and all the
miseries of life, without shrinking; danger only
calls forth their fortitude; they even exult in
calamity: but contempt is what they cannot
bear. An Englishman fears contempt more

Samson (*Judges* xvi, 17)

8 Unidentified; possibly invented.
9 flattering attendant

than death; he often flies to death as a refuge from its pressure, and dies when he fancies the world has ceased to esteem him.

Pride seems the source not only of their national vices, but of their national virtues also. An Englishman is taught to love his king as his friend, but to acknowledge no other master than the laws which himself has contributed to enact. He despises those nations who, that one may be free, are all content to be slaves; who first lift a tyrant into terror, and then shrink under his power as if delegated from Heaven. Liberty is echoed in all their assemblies: and thousands might be found ready to offer up their lives for the sound, though perhaps not one of all the number understands its meaning. The lowest mechanic, however, looks upon it as his duty to be a watchful guardian of his country's freedom, and often uses a language that might seem haughty even in the mouth of the great emperor who traces his ancestry to the Moon.

A few days ago, passing by one of their prisons, I could not avoid stopping, in order to listen to a dialogue which I thought might afford me some entertainment. The conversation was carried on between a debtor through the grate of his prison, a porter who had stopped to rest his burden, and a soldier at the window. The subject was upon a threatened invasion from France, and each seemed extremely anxious to rescue his country from the impending danger. "For my part," cries the prisoner, "the greatest of my apprehensions is for our freedom; if the French should conquer, what would become of English liberty? My dear friends, liberty is the Englishman's prerogative; we must preserve that at the expense of our lives; of that the French shall never deprive us. It is not to be expected that men who are slaves themselves would preserve our freedom should they happen to conquer." "Ay, slaves," cries the porter, "they are all slaves, fit only to carry burdens, every one of them. Before I would stoop to slavery may this be my poison (and he held the goblet in his hand), may this be my poison—but I would sooner list for a soldier."

The soldier, taking the goblet from his friend, with much awe fervently cried out, "It is not so much our liberties, as our religion, that would suffer by such a change: ay, our religion, my lads. May the devil sink me into flames (such was the solemnity of his adjuration), if the French should come over, but our religion would be utterly undone!" So saying, instead of a libation, he applied the goblet to

his lips, and confirmed his sentiments with ceremony of the most persevering devotion.

In short, every man here pretends to be politician; even the fair sex are sometime found to mix the severity of national alterca tion with the blandishments of love, and ofte become conquerors by more weapons of destru tion than their eyes.

This universal passion for politics is gratifie by daily gazettes, as with us in China. But a in ours the emperor endeavours to instruct h people, in theirs the people endeavour to i struct the administration. You must not, ho ever, imagine that they who compile the papers have any actual knowledge of the pol tics or the government of a state; they on collect their materials from the oracle of so coffee-house, which oracle has himself gather them the night before from a beau at a ga ing-table, who has pillaged his knowledge fro a great man's porter, who has had his inform tion from the great man's gentleman,[10] who h invented the whole story for his own amuseme the night preceding.

The English, in general, seem fonder gaining the esteem than the love of those th converse with. This gives a formality to the amusements: their gayest conversations ha something too wise for innocent relaxatio though in company you are seldom disguste with the absurdity of a fool, you are seldo lifted into rapture by those strokes of vivaci which give instant though not permane pleasure.

What they want, however, in gaiety, th make up in politeness. You smile at hearin me praise the English for their politeness; y who have heard very different accounts fro the missionaries at Pekin, who have seen su a different behaviour in their merchants a seamen at home. But I must still repeat it, t English seem more polite than any of the neighbours; their great art in this respect li in endeavouring, while they oblige, to lessen t force of the favour. Other countries are fo of obliging a stranger; but seem desirous th he should be sensible of the obligation. T English confer their kindness with an appea ance of indifference, and give away benefi with an air as if they despised them.

Walking, a few days ago, between an Engli and a French man, into the suburbs of the cit we were overtaken by a heavy shower of rai I was unprepared; but they had each larg coats, which defended them from what seeme

10 valet

o me a perfect inundation. The Englishman,
seeing me shrink from the weather, accosted me
thus: "Pshaw, man, what dost shrink at?
Here, take this coat; I don't want it; I find it
no way useful to me; I had as lief be without
t." The Frenchman began to show his politeness in turn. "My dear friend," cries he,
'why won't you oblige me by making use of
my coat? You see how well it defends me from
he rain; I should not choose to part with it to
thers, but to such a friend as you I could even
art with my skin to do him service."

From such minute instances as these, most
reverend Fum Hoam, I am sensible your sagaci-
ty will collect instruction. The volume of
nature is the book of knowledge; and he becomes most wise who makes the most judicious
election. Farewell.

THE DESERTED VILLAGE *

SWEET AUBURN![1] loveliest village of the
   plain,
Where health and plenty cheered the labouring
   swain,
Where smiling spring its earliest visit paid,
And parting summer's lingering blooms de-
   layed:
Dear lovely bowers of innocence and ease,
Seats of my youth, when every sport could
   please,
How often have I loitered o'er thy green,
Where humble happiness endeared each scene!
How often have I paused on every charm,
The sheltered cot, the cultivated farm,   10
The never-failing brook, the busy mill,
The decent church that topt the neighbouring
   hill,
The hawthorn bush, with seats beneath the
   shade,
For talking age and whispering lovers made!
How often have I blest the coming day,
When toil remitting lent its turn to play,
And all the village train, from labour free,
Led up their sports beneath the spreading tree,
While many a pastime circled in the shade,

The young contending as the old surveyed;   20
And many a gambol frolicked o'er the ground,
And sleights of art and feats of strength went
   round!
And still, as each repeated pleasure tired,
Succeeding sports the mirthful band inspired;
The dancing pair that simply sought renown
By holding out to tire each other down;
The swain mistrustless of his smutted face,
While secret laughter tittered round the place;
The bashful virgin's sidelong looks of love,
The matron's glance that would those looks
   reprove.   30
These were thy charms, sweet village! sports
   like these,
With sweet succession, taught even toil to
   please;
These round thy bowers their cheerful influence
   shed;
These were thy charms—but all these charms
   are fled.
  Sweet smiling village, loveliest of the lawn,
Thy sports are fled, and all thy charms with-
   drawn;
Amidst thy bowers the tyrant's[2] hand is seen,
And desolation saddens all thy green:
One only master grasps the whole domain,
And half a tillage stints thy smiling plain. 40
No more thy glassy brook reflects the day,
But choked with sedges, works its weedy way;
Along thy glades, a solitary guest,
The hollow-sounding bittern guards its nest;
Amidst thy desert walks the lapwing flies,
And tires their echoes with unvaried cries.
Sunk are thy bowers in shapeless ruin all,
And the long grass o'ertops the mouldering
   wall;
And, trembling, shrinking from the spoiler's
   hand,
Far, far away, thy children leave the land. 50
  Ill fares the land, to hastening ills a prey,
Where wealth accumulates, and men decay:
Princes and lords may flourish, or may fade—
A breath can make them, as a breath has made:
But a bold peasantry, their country's pride,
When once destroyed, can never be supplied.
  A time there was, ere England's griefs
   began,
When every rood of ground maintained its
   man;
For him light labour spread her wholesome
   store,
Just gave what life required, but gave no more:
His best companions, innocence and health,   61
And his best riches ignorance of wealth.

Probably Lissoy, where Goldsmith spent his
childhood.
This poem was inspired by Goldsmith's conviction of the steady depopulation of Ireland.
In the letter in which he inscribed the poem
to Sir Joshua Reynolds, he wrote: "In
regretting the depopulation of the country,
I inveigh against the increase of our luxuries:
and here also I expect a shout of modern
politicians against me. For twenty or thirty
years past, it has been the fashion to consider
luxury as one of the greatest national advantages. Still, I must continue to think those
luxuries prejudicial to states by which so
many vices are introduced, and so many
kingdoms have been undone."

[2] A certain English landlord who evicted many
tenants.

But times are altered; trade's unfeeling train
Usurp the land, and dispossess the swain:
Along the lawn, where scattered hamlets rose,
Unwieldy wealth and cumbrous pomp repose;
And every want to luxury allied,
And every pang that folly pays to pride.
Those gentle hours that plenty bade to bloom,
Those calm desires that asked but little room,
Those healthful sports that graced the peaceful
    scene,   71
Lived in each look, and brightened all the green
These, far departing, seek a kinder shore,
And rural mirth and manners are no more.
Sweet Auburn! parent of the blissful hour,
Thy glades forlorn confess the tyrant's power.
Here, as I take my solitary rounds,
Amidst thy tangling walks and ruined grounds,
And, many a year elapsed, return to view
Where once the cottage stood, the hawthorn
    grew,   80
Remembrance wakes with all her busy train,
Swells at my breast, and turns the past to pain.
  In all my wand'rings round this world of
    care,
In all my griefs—and God has given my
    share—
I still had hopes, my latest hours to crown,
Amidst these humble bowers to lay me down;
To husband out life's taper at the close,
And keep the flame from wasting by repose.
I still had hopes, for pride attends us still,
Amidst the swains to show my book-learned
    skill,   90
Around my fire an evening group to draw,
And tell of all I felt, and all I saw;
And, as a hare, whom hounds and horns pursue,
Pants to the place from whence at first he flew,
I still had hopes, my long vexations past,
Here to return—and die at home at last.
  O blest retirement, friend to life's decline,
Retreats from care, that never must be mine,
How blest is he who crowns, in shades like
    these,
A youth of labour with an age of ease;   100
Who quits a world where strong temptations
    try,
And, since 'tis hard to combat, learns to fly!
For him no wretches, born to work and weep,
Explore the mine, or tempt the dangerous deep;
Nor surly porter stands, in guilty state,
To spurn imploring famine from the gate;
But on he moves to meet his latter end,
Angels around befriending virtue's friend;
Sinks to the grave with unperceived decay,
While resignation gently slopes the way;   110
And, all his prospects brightening to the last,
His heaven commences, ere the world be past!

Sweet was the sound, when oft at evening's
    close
Up yonder hill the village murmur rose;
There, as I passed with careless steps and slow
The mingling notes came softened from below
The swain responsive as the milk-maid sung,
The sober herd that lowed to meet their young
The noisy geese that gabbled o'er the pool,
The playful children just let loose from school
The watch-dog's voice that bayed the whisper-
    ing wind,   12
And the loud laugh that spoke the vacant mind
These all in sweet confusion sought the shade
And filled each pause the nightingale had
    made;
But now the sounds of population fail,
No cheerful murmurs fluctuate in the gale,
No busy steps the grass-grown footway tread
For all the bloomy flush of life is fled.
All but yon widowed, solitary thing,
That feebly bends beside the plashy spring; 13
She, wretched matron—forced in age, for bread
To strip the brook with mantling cresses spread
To pick her wintry faggot from the thorn,
To seek her nightly shed, and weep till morn—
She only left of all the harmless train,
The sad historian of the pensive plain!
  Near yonder copse, where once the garden
    smiled,
And still where many a garden flower grows
    wild;
There, where a few torn shrubs the place dis-
    close,
The village preacher's modest mansion rose. 14
A man he was to all the country dear,[3]
And passing[4] rich with forty pounds a year;
Remote from towns he ran his godly race,
Nor e'er had changed, nor wished to change his
    place;
Unpractised he to fawn, or seek for power,
By doctrines fashioned to the varying hour;
Far other aims his heart had learned to prize
More skilled to raise the wretched than to rise
His house was known to all the vagrant train,
He chid their wanderings, but relieved their
    pain;   15
The long-remembered beggar was his guest,
Whose beard descending swept his aged breast
The ruined spendthrift, now no longer proud,
Claimed kindred there, and had his claim
    allowed;
The broken soldier, kindly bade to stay,
Sat by his fire, and talked the night away,
Wept o'er his wounds, or, tales of sorrow done

[3] A description drawn from the poet's father or
    brother.
[4] surpassingly

Shouldered his crutch and showed how fields
    were won.
Pleased with his guests, the good man learned
    to glow,
And quite forgot their vices in their woe; 160
Careless their merits or their faults to scan,
His pity gave ere charity began.
    Thus to relieve the wretched was his pride,
And e'en his failings leaned to virtue's side;
But in his duty, prompt at every call,
He watched and wept, he prayed and felt for
    all;
And, as a bird each fond endearment tries
To tempt its new-fledged offspring to the skies,
He tried each art, reproved each dull delay,
Allured to brighter worlds, and led the way. 170
    Beside the bed where parting life was laid,
And sorrow, guilt, and pain, by turns dismayed,
The reverend champion stood.5 At his control
Despair and anguish fled the struggling soul;
Comfort came down the trembling wretch to
    raise,
And his last faltering accents whispered praise.
    At church, with meek and unaffected grace,
His looks adorned the venerable place;
Truth from his lips prevailed with double sway,
And fools, who came to scoff, remained to pray.
The service past, around the pious man, 181
With steady zeal, each honest rustic ran;
E'en children followed, with endearing wile,
And plucked his gown, to share the good man's
    smile:
His ready smile a parent's warmth expressed,
Their welfare pleased him, and their cares
    distressed;
To them his heart, his love, his griefs were
    given,
But all his serious thoughts had rest in heaven.
As some tall cliff that lifts its awful form,
Swells from the vale, and midway leaves the
    storm, 190
Though round its breast the rolling clouds are
    spread,
Eternal sunshine settles on its head.
    Beside yon straggling fence that skirts the
    way
With blossomed furze unprofitably gay—
There, in his noisy mansion, skilled to rule,
The village master6 taught his little school;
A man severe he was, and stern to view,
I knew him well, and every truant knew;
Well had the boding tremblers learned to trace
The day's disasters in his morning face; 200
Full well they laughed with counterfeited glee
At all his jokes, for many a joke had he;

Full well the busy whisper, circling round,
Conveyed the dismal tidings when he frowned;
Yet he was kind, or if severe in aught,
The love he bore to learning was in fault.
The village all declared how much he knew;
'Twas certain he could write, and cipher too:
Lands he could measure, terms and tides pre-
    sage, 209
And even the story ran that he could gauge.7
In arguing, too, the parson owned his skill,
For e'en though vanquished, he could argue
    still;
While words of learnèd length and thund'ring
    sound
Amazed the gazing rustics ranged around,
And still they gazed, and still the wonder grew
That one small head could carry all he knew.
But past is all his fame. The very spot,
Where many a time he triumphed, is forgot.
    Near yonder thorn that lifts its head on high,
Where once the sign-post caught the passing
    eye, 220
Low lies that house where nut-brown draughts
    inspired,
Where gray-beard mirth and smiling toil re-
    tired,
Where village statesmen talked with looks pro-
    found,
And news much older than their ale went round.
Imagination fondly stoops to trace
The parlour splendours of that festive place;
The white-washed wall, the nicely sanded floor,
The varnished clock that clicked behind the
    door;
The chest contrived a double debt to pay,
A bed by night, a chest of drawers by day; 230
The pictures placed for ornament and use,
The twelve good rules,8 the royal game of
    goose;
The hearth, except when winter chilled the day,
With aspen boughs, and flowers and fennel
    gay;
While broken tea-cups, wisely kept for show,
Ranged o'er the chimney, glistened in a row.
    Vain transitory splendours! could not all
Reprieve the tottering mansion from its fall?
Obscure it sinks, nor shall it more impart
An hour's importance to the poor man's heart;
Thither no more the peasant shall repair 241
To sweet oblivion of his daily care;
No more the farmer's news, the barber's tale,
No more the woodman's ballad shall prevail;
No more the smith his dusky brow shall clear,

---

5 A striking metaphor, taken from the tourney.
6 Probably Thomas Byrne, Goldsmith's teacher,
    was the model for this portrait.
7 estimate the capacity of casks
8 "Urge no healths," "Pick no quarrels," etc.
    Commonly hung in public houses, and attrib-
    uted to Charles I. The game mentioned in this
    line was played with counters and dice.

Relax his ponderous strength and lean to hear;
The host himself no longer shall be found
Careful to see the mantling bliss go round;
Nor the coy maid, half-willing to be pressed,
Shall kiss the cup to pass it to the rest.   250

Yes! let the rich deride, the proud disdain,
These simple blessings of the lowly train,
To me more dear, congenial to my heart,
One native charm, than all the gloss of art;
Spontaneous joys, where nature has its play,
The soul adopts, and owns their first-born
    sway:
Lightly they frolic o'er the vacant mind,
Unenvied, unmolested, unconfined.
But the long pomp, the midnight masquerade,
With all the freaks of wanton wealth arrayed,
In these, ere triflers half their wish obtain, 261
The toiling pleasure sickens into pain;
And, even while fashion's brightest arts decoy,
The heart distrusting asks, if this be joy?

Ye friends to truth, ye statesmen who survey
The rich man's joys increase, the poor's decay,
'Tis yours to judge how wide the limits stand
Between a splendid and a happy land.
Proud swells the tide with loads of freighted
    ore,   269
And shouting Folly hails them from her shore;
Hoards even beyond the miser's wish abound,
And rich men flock from all the world around.
Yet count our gains. This wealth is but a name
That leaves our useful products still the same.
Not so the loss. The man of wealth and pride
Takes up a place that many poor supplied;
Space for his lake, his park's extended bounds,
Space for his horses, equipage, and hounds;
The robe that wraps his limbs in silken sloth
Has robbed the neighbouring fields of half their
    growth;   280
His seat, where solitary sports are seen,
Indignant spurns the cottage from the green;
Around the world each needful product flies,
For all the luxuries the world supplies:
While thus the land, adorned for pleasure, all
In barren splendour feebly waits the fall.

As some fair female, unadorned and plain,
Secure to please while youth confirms her reign,
Slights every borrowed charm that dress sup-
    plies,
Nor shares with art the triumph of her eyes;
But when those charms are past, for charms are
    frail,   291
When time advances, and when lovers fail,   .
She then shines forth, solicitous to bless,
In all the glaring impotence of dress;
Thus fares the land, by luxury betrayed:
In nature's simplest charms at first arrayed,
But verging to decline, its splendours rise,

Its vistas strike, its palaces surprise;
While, scourged by famine, from the smiling
    land   299
The mournful peasant leads his humble band;
And while he sinks, without one arm to save,
The country blooms—a garden and a grave.

Where then, ah! where shall poverty reside,
To 'scape the pressure of contiguous pride?
If to some common's fenceless limits strayed
He drives his flock to pick the scanty blade,
Those fenceless fields the sons of wealth divide,
And e'en the bare-worn common is denied.

If to the city sped—what waits him there?
To see profusion that he must not share;   310
To see ten thousand baneful arts combined
To pamper luxury and thin mankind;
To see each joy the sons of pleasure know,
Extorted from his fellow-creature's woe;
Here, while the courtier glitters in brocade,
There, the pale artist[9] plies the sickly trade;
Here, while the proud their long-drawn pomps
    display,
There, the black gibbet glooms beside the way.
The dome where pleasure holds her midnight
    reign,   319
Here, richly decked, admits the gorgeous train;
Tumultuous grandeur crowds the blazing square;
The rattling chariots clash, the torches glare.
Sure scenes like these no troubles e'er annoy;
Sure these denote one universal joy!
Are these thy serious thoughts?—Ah! turn thine
    eyes
Where the poor houseless shivering female lies.
She once, perhaps, in village plenty blessed,
Has wept at tales of innocence distressed;
Her modest looks the cottage might adorn,   329
Sweet as the primrose peeps beneath the thorn;
Now lost to all; her friends, her virtue fled,
Near her betrayer's door she lays her head—
And, pinched with cold, and shrinking from the
    shower,
With heavy heart deplores that luckless hour,
When idly first, ambitious of the town,
She left her wheel and robes of country brown.
    Do thine, sweet Auburn! thine the lovelier
    train,
Do thy fair tribes participate her pain?
E'en now, perhaps, by cold and hunger led,   339
At proud men's doors they ask a little bread.
    Ah, no! To distant climes, a dreary scene,
Where half the convex world intrudes between,
Through torrid tracts with fainting steps they
    go,
Where wild Altama[10] murmurs to their woe.

9 artisan
10 The Altamaha, a river of Georgia.

Far different there from all that charmed be-
    fore,
The various terrors of that horrid shore;
Those blazing suns that dart a downward ray,
And fiercely shed intolerable day;
Those matted woods where birds forget to sing;
But silent bats in drowsy clusters cling;   350
Those poisonous fields with rank luxuriance
    crowned,
Where the dark scorpion gathers death around;
Where at each step the stranger fears to wake
The rattling terrors of the vengeful snake;
Where crouching tigers[11] wait their hapless
    prey,
And savage men more murderous still than
    they;
While oft in whirls the mad tornado flies,
Mingling the ravaged landscape with the skies.
Far different these from every former scene,
The cooling brook, the grassy-vested green,   360
The breezy covert of the warbling grove,
That only sheltered thefts of harmless love.
    Good Heaven! what sorrows gloomed that
    parting day,
That called them from their native walks away;
When the poor exiles, every pleasure past,
Hung round the bowers, and fondly looked their
    last—
And took a long farewell, and wished in vain
For seats like these beyond the western main—
And, shuddering still to face the distant deep,
Returned and wept, and still returned to weep.
The good old sire the first prepared to go   371
To new-found worlds, and wept for others'
    woe;
But for himself, in conscious virtue brave,
He only wished for worlds beyond the grave.
His lovely daughter, lovelier in her tears,
The fond companion of his helpless years,
Silent went next, neglectful of her charms,
And left a lover's for a father's arms.
With louder plaints the mother spoke her woes,
And blessed the cot where every pleasure rose,
And kissed her thoughtless babes with many a
    tear,   381
And clasped them close, in sorrow doubly dear;
Whilst her fond husband strove to lend relief
In all the silent manliness of grief.
    O luxury! thou curst by Heaven's decree,
How ill exchanged are things like these for
    thee!
How do thy potions, with insidious joy,
Diffuse their pleasures only to destroy!
Kingdoms, by thee to sickly greatness grown,
Boast of a florid vigour not their own: 390

At every draught more large and large they
    grow,
A bloated mass of rank unwieldy woe;
Till, sapped their strength, and every part un-
    sound,
Down, down they sink, and spread a ruin round.
    Even now the devastation is begun
And half the business of destruction done;
Even now, methinks, as pondering here I stand,
I see the rural virtues leave the land.
Down where yon anchoring vessel spreads the
    sail
That idly waiting flaps with every gale,   400
Downward they move, a melancholy band,
Pass from the shore, and darken all the strand.
Contented toil, and hospitable care,
And kind connubial tenderness are there,
And piety with wishes placed above,
And steady loyalty, and faithful love.
And thou, sweet Poetry, thou loveliest maid,
Still first to fly where sensual joys invade;
Unfit, in these degenerate times of shame,   409
To catch the heart, or strike for honest fame:
Dear charming nymph, neglected and decried,
My shame in crowds, my solitary pride;
Thou source of all my bliss and all my woe,
Thou found'st me poor at first, and keep'st me
    so;
Thou guide, by which the nobler arts excel,
Thou nurse of every virtue, fare thee well!
Farewell; and oh! where'er thy voice be tried,
On Torno's[12] cliffs, or Pambamarca's[13] side,
Whether where equinoctial fervours glow,
Or winter wraps the polar world in snow,   420
Still let thy voice, prevailing over time,
Redress the rigours of the inclement clime;
Aid slighted truth with thy persuasive strain;
Teach erring man to spurn the rage of gain;
Teach him, that states of native strength pos-
    sessed,
Though very poor, may still be very blest;
That trade's proud empire hastes to swift
    decay,
As ocean sweeps the laboured mole away;
While self-dependent power can time defy,
As rocks resist the billows and the sky.   430

THE HAUNCH OF VENISON

A POETICAL EPISTLE TO LORD CLARE

Thanks, my Lord, for your venison, for finer
    or fatter
Never ranged in a forest, or smoked in a
    platter;

---

11 Here Goldsmith's imagination played him false,
    unless tigers may stand for panthers.

12 The Tornea, a river   13 A mountain peak in
    in Sweden.   Ecuador.

The haunch was a picture for painters to
     study,—
The fat was so white, and the lean was so
     ruddy;
Though my stomach was sharp, I could scarce
     help regretting
To spoil such a delicate picture by eating;
I had thoughts in my chambers to place it in
     view,
To be shown to my friends as a piece of virtù;
As in some Irish houses, where things are so-so,
One gammon of bacon hangs up for a show;—
But, for eating a rasher of what they take
     pride in,   11
They'd as soon think of eating the pan it is
     fried in.
But hold—let me pause—don't I hear you pro-
     nounce
This tale of the bacon a damnable bounce?[1]
Well, suppose it a bounce; sure a poet may try,
By a bounce now and then, to get courage to
     fly.
But, my Lord, it's no bounce: I protest in my
     turn
It's a truth—and your Lordship may ask Mr.
     Byrne.[2]
    To go on with my tale: as I gazed on the
     haunch,
I thought of a friend that was trusty and
     staunch;   21
So I cut it, and sent it to Reynolds[3] undrest,
To paint it or eat it, just as he liked best.
Of the neck and the breast I had next to dis-
     pose;
'Twas a neck and a breast that might rival
     Monroe's:[4]
But in parting with these I was puzzled again,
With the how, and the who, and the where, and
     the when.
There's Howard, and Coley, and H—rth, and
     Hiff,
I think they love venison,—I know they love
     beef.
There's my countryman Higgins—oh! let him
     alone,
For making a blunder, or picking a bone.   30
But hang it!—to poets who seldom can eat,
Your very good mutton's a very good treat;
Such dainties to them, their health it might
     hurt;
It's like sending them ruffles when wanting a
     shirt.
While thus I debated, in reverie centered,
An acquaintance, a friend as he called him-
     self, entered;

An under-bred, fine-spoken fellow was he,
And he smiled as he looked at the venison and
     me.
   "What have we got here?—Why this is
     good eating!
Your own, I suppose—or is it in waiting?"   40
"Why, whose should it be?" cried I with a
     flounce;
"I get these things often"—but that was a
     bounce:
"Some lords, my acquaintance, that settle the
     nation,
Are pleased to be kind—but I hate ostenta-
     tion."
   "If that be the case, then," cried he, very
     gay,
"I'm glad I have taken this house in my way.
To-morrow you take a poor dinner with me;
No words—I insist on't—precisely at three;
We'll have Johnson, and Burke; all the wits
     will be there;
My acquaintance is slight, or I'd ask my Lord
     Clare.   51
And now that I think on't, as I am a sinner!
We wanted this venison to make out the dinner.
What say you—a pasty? It shall, and it must,
And my wife, little Kitty, is famous for crust.
Here, porter! this venison with me to Mile-
     end;[5]
No stirring—I beg—my dear friend—my dear
     friend!"
Thus, snatching his hat, he brushed off like
     the wind,
And the porter and eatables followed behind.
   Left alone to reflect, having emptied my
     shelf,
And "nobody with me at sea but myself,"   60
Though I could not help thinking my gentle-
     man hasty,
Yet Johnson, and Burke, and a good venison
     pasty,
Were things that I never disliked in my life,
Though clogged with a coxcomb, and Kitty
     his wife.
So next day, in due splendour to make my ap-
     proach,
I drove to his door in my own hackney-coach.
   When come to the place where we all were
     to dine
(A chair-lumbered closet, just twelve feet by
     nine),
My friend bade me welcome, but struck me
     quite dumb
With tidings that Johnson and Burke would
     not come: 71

---

1 impudent falsehood
2 Lord Clare's nephew.
3 Sir Joshua Reynolds.
4 Dorothy Monroe, a celebrated beauty.
5 In East London, where the poorer classes lived.

"For I knew it," he cried: "both eternally fail,

The one with his speeches, and t'other with Thrale.[6]

But no matter, I'll warrant we'll make up the party

With two full as clever and ten times as hearty.

The one is a Scotchman, the other a Jew;

They're both of them merry, and authors like you;

The one writes the 'Snarler,' the other the 'Scourge;'

Some think he writes 'Cinna'—he owns to 'Panurge.' "[*]

While thus he described them by trade and by name,

They entered, and dinner was served as they came.   80

  At the top a fried liver and bacon were seen;

At the bottom was tripe, in a swingeing[7] tureen;

At the sides there was spinach and pudding made hot;

In the middle a place where the pasty—was not.

Now my lord, as for tripe, it's my utter aversion,

And your bacon I hate like a Turk or a Persian;

So there I sat stuck, like a horse in a pound,

While the bacon and liver went merrily round:

But what vexed me most was that d—d Scottish rogue,

With his long-winded speeches, his smiles, and his brogue,   90

And, "Madam," quoth he, "may this bit be my poison,

A prettier dinner I never set eyes on;

Pray a slice of your liver, though may I be curst,

But I've eat of your tripe till I'm ready to burst."

"The tripe!" quoth the Jew, with his chocolate cheek;

"I could dine on this tripe seven days in a week:

I like these here dinners so pretty and small;

But your friend there, the doctor, eats nothing at all."

"Oho!" quoth my friend, "he'll come on in a trice;

He's keeping a corner for something that's nice: 100

There's a pasty."—"A pasty!" repeated the Jew;

"I don't care if I keep a corner for't too."

"What the de'il, mon, a pasty!" re-echoed the Scot;

"Though splitting, I'll still keep a corner for that."

"We'll all keep a corner," the lady cried out;

"We'll all keep a corner," was echoed about.

While thus we resolved, and the pasty delayed,

With looks that quite petrified, entered the maid:

A visage so sad, and so pale with affright,

Waked Priam in drawing his curtains by night.[8]   110

But we quickly found out—for who could mistake her?—

That she came with some terrible news from the baker:

And so it fell out, for that negligent sloven

Had shut out the pasty on shutting his oven.

Sad Philomel thus—but let similes drop;

And now that I think on't, the story may stop.

To be plain, my good Lord, it's but labour misplaced

To send such good verses to one of your taste;

You've got an odd something—a kind of discerning,

A relish, a taste—sickened over by learning;[9]

At least, it's your temper, as very well known,

That you think very slightly of all that's your own.   122

So, perhaps, in your habits of thinking amiss,

You may make a mistake, and think slightly of this.

From RETALIATION[*]

Of old, when Scarron[1] his companions invited,

Each guest brought his dish, and the feast was united;

[8] See *2 Henry IV.*, I,   [9] See *Hamlet*, III., i. i. 72.   85.

[1] A French burlesque poet.
[*] Goldsmith, because of his vanity and frequently empty talk, was the occasion of much diversion among his friends, and sometimes a butt of ridicule. At a gathering at St. James's coffee-house, he desired to try with David Garrick, the actor, his skill at epigram, and each was to write the other's epitaph. Garrick immediately composed the well-known couplet:

"Here lies Nolly Goldsmith, for shortness called Noll,
Who wrote like an angel, but talked like poor Poll."

Goldsmith took his time to reply, and the

[6] Mrs. Thrale, Dr. Johnson's friend.
[7] immense
[*] These were signatures to contemporary letters addressed to the *Public Advertiser* in support of the government.

If our landlord supplies us with beef and with
   fish,
Let each guest bring himself—and he brings
   the best dish.
Our Dean shall be venison, just fresh from
   the plains;
Our Burke shall be tongue, with the garnish of
   brains;
Our Will shall be wild-fowl of excellent flavour,
And Dick with his pepper shall heighten the
   savour;
Our Cumberland's sweet-bread its place shall
   obtain,
And Douglas is pudding, substantial and plain;
Our Garrick's a salad; for in him we see   11
Oil, vinegar, sugar, and saltness agree:
To make out the dinner, full certain I am
That Ridge is anchovy, and Reynolds is lamb;
That Hickey's a capon, and, by the same rule,
Magnanimous Goldsmith a gooseberry fool.[2]
At a dinner so various, at such a repast,
Who'd not be a glutton, and stick to the last?
Here, waiter, more wine! let me sit while I'm
   able,
Till all my companions sink under the table; 20
Then, with chaos and blunders encircling my
   head,
Let me ponder, and tell what I think of the
   dead.

   Here lies the good Dean, reunited to earth,
Who mixed reason with pleasure, and wisdom
   with mirth:
If he had any faults, he has left us in doubt—
At least, in six weeks I could not find 'em out;
Yet some have declared, and it can't be denied
   'em,
That sly-boots was cursedly cunning to hide
   'em.

   Here lies our good Edmund, whose genius
   was such,
We scarcely can praise it, or blame it too
   much;   30
Who, born for the universe, narrowed his mind,
And to party gave up what was meant for
   mankind.
Though fraught with all learning, yet straining his throat

To persuade Tommy Townshend[3] to lend him
   a vote;
Who, too deep for his hearers, still went on
   refining,
And thought of convincing while they thought
   of dining:
Though equal to all things, for all things unfit,
Too nice for a statesman, too proud for a wit;
For a patriot too cool; for a drudge, disobe-
   dient,
And too fond of the right to pursue the expe-
   dient.   40
In short, 'twas his fate, unemployed or in
   place, sir,
To eat mutton cold, and cut blocks with a
   razor.

.   .   .   .

   Here Cumberland lies, having acted his parts,
The Terence[4] of England, the mender of
   hearts;
A flattering painter, who made it his care
To draw men as they ought to be, not as they
   are.
His gallants are all faultless, his women divine,
And comedy wonders at being so fine;
Like a tragedy queen he has dizened her out,
Or rather like tragedy giving a rout.[5]
His fools have their follies so lost in a crowd
Of virtues and feelings that folly grows proud;
And coxcombs, alike in their failings alone, 71
Adopting his portraits, are pleased with their
   own.
Say, where has our poet this malady caught,
Or wherefore his characters thus without fault?
Say, was it that, vainly directing his view
To find out men's virtues, and finding them
   few,
Quite sick of pursuing each troublesome elf,
He grew lazy at last, and drew from himself.

.   .   .   .   .   .

   Here lies David Garrick, describe me who
   can
An abridgment of all that was pleasant in
   man;
As an actor, confessed without rival to shine;
As a wit, if not first, in the very first line:
Yet, with talents like these, and an excellent
   heart,
The man had his failings, a dupe to his art.
Like an ill-judging beauty, his colours he
   spread,
And beplastered with rouge his own natural
   red.   100
On the stage he was natural, simple, affecting;

result was *Retaliation*, a poem which he left
unfinished, and which was published after his
death. The characters whom he imagines
gathered about the table are Thomas Barnard,
Dean of Derry; Edmund Burke, with William
Burke, a kinsman, and Richard, a younger
brother; Richard Cumberland, the dramatist;
John Douglas, a Scotch canon; David Garrick; John Ridge and Tom Hickey, two Irish
lawyers; Sir Joshua Reynolds, the painter;
and himself. A kindlier satire—if satire it
may be called—has scarcely been written.
2 A dish of crushed gooseberries.

3 An M. P., afterwards   **4** A Roman comic writer.
   Lord Sydney.   **5** gay party

'Twas only that when he was off he was acting.
With no reason on earth to go out of his way,
He turned and he varied full ten times a day:
Though secure of our hearts, yet confoundedly
   sick,
If they were not his own by finessing and
   trick:
He cast off his friends, as a huntsman his pack,
For he knew when he pleased he could whistle
   them back.
Of praise a mere glutton, he swallowed what
   came,
And the puff of a dunce, he mistook it for
   fame;   110
 'Till his relish grown callous, almost to dis-
   ease,
Who peppered the highest was surest to please.
But let us be candid, and speak out our mind:
If dunces applauded, he paid them in kind.
Ye Kenricks, ye Kellys, and Woodfalls so
   grave,6
What a commerce was yours, while you got and
   you gave!
How did Grub Street7 re-echo the shouts that
   you raised,
While he was be-Rosciused8 and you were be-
   praised!
But peace to his spirit, wherever it flies,
To act as an angel and mix with the skies: 120
Those poets who owe their best fame to his
   skill
Shall still be his flatterers, go where he will,
Old Shakespeare receive him with praise and
   with love,
And Beaumonts and Bens9 be his Kellys above.

  · · · · · ·

 Here Reynolds is laid, and, to tell you my
   mind,
He has not left a wiser or better behind;
His pencil was striking, resistless, and grand;
His manners were gentle, complying, and
   bland;   140
Still born to improve us in every part,
His pencil our faces, his manners our heart:
To coxcombs averse, yet most civilly steering;
When they judged without skill, he was still
   hard of hearing;
When they talked of their Raphaels, Correg-
   gios, and stuff,
He shifted his trumpet, and only took snuff.
By flattery unspoiled—*

---

6 Dramatists and critics
  of the time.
Hackwriterdom.
  8 Roscius was the great-
    est Roman comic
    actor.
  9 "Rare Ben" Jonson.
* Here Death took the pen from the poet's hand
 before he could write his own epitaph.

EDWARD GIBBON (1737-1794)

THE FALL OF CONSTANTINOPLE†

After a siege of forty days, the fate of Constantinople could no longer be averted. The diminutive garrison was exhausted by a double attack; the fortifications, which had stood for ages against hostile violence, were dismantled on all sides by the Ottoman cannon; many breaches were opened; and near the gate of St. Romanus four towers had been leveled with the ground. For the payment of his feeble and mutinous troops, Constantine was compelled to despoil the churches, with the promise of a fourfold restitution; and his sacrilege offered a new reproach to the enemies of the union. A spirit of discord impaired the remnant of the Christian strength; the Genoese and Venetian auxiliaries asserted the preeminence of their respective service; and Justiniani and the great Duke, whose ambition was not extinguished by the common danger, accused each other of treachery and cowardice.

During the siege of Constantinople, the words of peace and capitulation had been sometimes pronounced; and several embassies had passed between the camp and the city. The Greek emperor was humbled by adversity, and would have yielded to any terms compatible with religion and royalty. The Turkish sultan was desirous of sparing the blood of his soldiers; still more desirous of securing for his own use the Byzantine treasures; and he accomplished a sacred duty in presenting to the *Gabours*1 the choice of circumcision, of tribute, or of death. The avarice of Mahomet might have been satisfied with an annual sum of one hundred thousand ducats; but his ambition grasped the capital of the East; to the prince he offered a rich equivalent, to the people a free toleration or a safe departure; but, after some fruitless treaty, he declared his resolu-

1 Giaours, "infidels"
† From *The Decline and Fall of the Roman Empire*, chapter LXVIII. Long after Rome had fallen before the incursions of the barbarians, Constantinople, the capital of the Eastern Empire, "the decrepit daughter of ancient Rome, alone remained standing, and for ten centuries, like a rocky island, defied the fury of the waves." (Victor Duruy.) The last Christian emperor was a Greek, Constantine Palæol'ogus; and when the city was finally besieged, in 1453, by the Ottoman Turks under Mahomet II., the defence was conducted by an alliance of Greeks, Venetians, and Genoese, sadly divided by their own religious differences. Their foremost general was Justiniani, a Genoese nobleman. On the significance of this event to western literature, see *Eng. Lit.*, p. 77, and on Gibbon, see the same, p. 213.

tion of finding either a throne or a grave under the walls of Constantinople. A sense of
honour and the fear of universal reproach
forbade Palæologus to resign the city into the
hands of the Ottomans; and he determined to
abide the last extremities of war. Several
days were employed by the sultan in the
preparations of the assault; and a respite was
granted by his favourite science of astrology,
which had fixed on the twenty-ninth of May
as the fortunate and fatal hour. On the evening of the twenty-seventh, he issued his final
orders; assembled in his presence the military
chiefs; and dispersed his heralds through the
camp to proclaim the duty and the motives of
the perilous enterprise. Fear is the first principle of a despotic government; and his
menaces were expressed in the Oriental style,
that the fugitives and deserters, had they the
wings of a bird, should not escape from his
inexorable justice. The greatest part of his
bashaws[2] and Janizaries[3] were the offspring of
Christian parents; but the glories of the Turkish name were perpetuated by successive adoption; and, in the gradual change of individuals, the spirit of a legion, a regiment, or an
oda[4] is kept alive by imitation and discipline.
In this holy warfare, the Moslems were exhorted to purify their minds with prayer, their
bodies with seven ablutions; and to abstain
from food till the close of the ensuing day. A
crowd of dervishes visited the tents, to instil
the desire of martyrdom, and the assurance
of spending an immortal youth amidst the
rivers and gardens of paradise and in the
embraces of the black-eyed virgins.[5] Yet Mahomet principally trusted to the efficacy of
temporal and visible rewards. A double pay
was promised to the victorious troops: "The
city and the buildings," said Mahomet, "are
mine; but I resign to your valour the captives
and the spoil, the treasures of gold and
beauty; be rich and be happy. Many are the
provinces of my empire: the intrepid soldier
who first ascends the walls of Constantinople
shall be rewarded with the government of the
fairest and most wealthy; and my gratitude shall accumulate his honours and fortunes
above the measure of his own hopes." Such
various and potent motives diffused among the
Turks a general ardour, regardless of life and
impatient for action; the camp re-echoed with
the Moslem shouts of "God is God, there is
but one God, and Mahomet is the apostle of

God;" and the sea and land, from Galata[6] to
the seven towers,[7] were illuminated by the
blaze of their nocturnal fires.

Far different was the state of the Christians; who, with loud and impotent complaints,
deplored the guilt, or the punishment, of their
sins. The celestial image of the Virgin had
been exposed in solemn procession; but their
divine patroness was deaf to their entreaties;
they accused the obstinacy of the emperor for
refusing a timely surrender; anticipated the
horrors of their fate; and sighed for the repose and security of Turkish servitude. The
noblest of the Greeks, and the bravest of the
allies, were summoned to the palace, to prepare them, on the evening of the twenty-eighth,
for the duties and dangers of the general assault. The last speech of Palæologus was the
funeral oration of the Roman Empire: he
promised, he conjured, and he vainly attempted
to infuse the hope which was extinguished in
his own mind. In this world all was comfortless and gloomy; and neither the gospel
nor the church have proposed any conspicuous
recompense to the heroes who fall in the service of their country. But the example of their
prince and the confinement of a siege had
armed these warriors with the courage of despair; and the pathetic scene is described by
the feelings of the historian Phranza,[8] who was
himself present at this mournful assembly.
They wept, they embraced; regardless of their
families and fortunes, they devoted their lives
and each commander, departing to his station, maintained all night a vigilant and
anxious watch on the rampart. The emperor
and some faithful companions, entered the
dome of St. Sophia, which in a few hours was
to be converted into a mosque; and devoutly
received, with tears and prayers, the sacrament of the holy communion. He reposed
some moments in the palace, which resounded
with cries and lamentations; solicited the par
don of all whom he might have injured; and
mounted on horseback to visit the guards and
explore the motions of the enemy. The dis
tress and fall of the last Constantine are more
glorious than the long prosperity of the By
zantine Cæsars.[9]

In the confusion of darkness an assailant
may sometimes succeed; but in this great and
general attack, the military judgment and
astrological knowledge of Mahomet advised

2 ministers and generals
3 Ottoman infantry, especially the Sultan's body-
    guard.
4 company   5 houris

6 A northern suburb of   8 Chamberlain of Palæ-
    Constantinople.   ologus.
7 The southern gate.   9 i. e., the Emperors of
                               the East.

him to expect the morning, the memorable twenty-ninth of May, in the fourteen hundred and fifty-third year of the Christian era. The preceding night had been strenuously employed: the troops, the cannon, and the fascines[10] were advanced to the edge of the ditch, which, in many parts, presented a smooth and level passage to the breach; and his fourscore galleys almost touched, with the prows and their scaling-ladders, the less defensible walls of the harbour. Under pain of death, silence was enjoined; but the physical laws of motion and sound are not obedient to discipline or fear; each individual might suppress his voice and measure his footsteps; but the march and labour of thousands must inevitably produce a strange confusion of dissonant clamours, which reached the ears of the watchmen of the towers. At daybreak, without the customary signal of the morning gun, the Turks assaulted the city by sea and land; and the similitude of a twined or twisted thread has been applied to the closeness and continuity of their line of attack. The foremost ranks consisted of the refuse of the host, a voluntary crowd, who fought without order or command; of the feebleness of age or childhood, of peasants and vagrants, and of all who had joined the camp in the blind hope of plunder and martyrdom. The common impulse drove them onward to the wall; the most audacious to climb were instantly precipitated; and not a dart, not a bullet, of the Christians was idly wasted on the accumulated throng. But their strength and ammunition were exhausted in this laborious defense; the ditch was filled with the bodies of the slain; they supported the footsteps of their companions; and of this devoted vanguard the death was more serviceable than the life. Under their respective pashaws and sanjaks,[11] the troops of Anatolia and Romania were successively led to the charge; but, after a conflict of two hours, the Greeks still maintained and improved their advantage; and the voice of the emperor was heard, encouraging his soldiers to achieve, by a last effort, the deliverance of their country. In th t fatal moment the Janizaries arose, fresh, vigorous, and invincible. The sultan himself on horseback, with an iron mace in his hand, was the spectator and judge of their valour; he was surrounded by ten thousand of his domestic troops, whom he reserved for the decisive occasion; and the tide of battle was directed and impelled by his voice and eye. His numerous ministers of justice were posted behind the line, to urge, to restrain, and to punish; and, if danger was in the front, shame and inevitable death were in the rear of the fugitives. The cries of fear and of pain were drowned in the martial music of drums, trumpets, and attaballs;[12] and experience has proved that the mechanical operation of sounds, by quickening the circulation of the blood and spirits, will act on the human machine more forcibly than the eloquence of reason and honour. From the lines, the galleys, and the bridge, the Ottoman artillery thundered on all sides; and the camp and city, the Greeks and the Turks, were involved in a cloud of smoke, which could only be dispelled by the final deliverance or destruction of the Roman empire. The single combats of the heroes of history or fable amuse our fancy and engage our affections; the skillful evolutions of war may inform the mind, and improve a necessary though pernicious science. But, in the uniform and odious pictures of a general assault, all is blood, and horror, and confusion; nor shall I strive, at the distance of three centuries and a thousand miles, to delineate a scene of which there could be no spectators, and of which the actors themselves were incapable of forming any just or adequate idea.

The immediate loss of Constantinople may be ascribed to the bullet, or arrow, which pierced the gauntlet of John Justiniani. The sight of his blood, and the exquisite pain, appalled the courage of the chief, whose arms and counsels were the firmest rampart of the city. As he withdrew from his station in quest of a surgeon, his flight was perceived and stopped by the indefatigable emperor. "Your wound," exclaimed Palæologus, "is slight; the danger is pressing; your presence is necessary; and whither will you retire?" "I will retire," said the trembling Genoese, "by the same road which God has opened to the Turks;" and at these words he hastily passed through one of the breaches of the inner wall. By this pusillanimous act he stained the honours of a military life; and the few days which he survived in Galata, or the isle of Chios, were embittered by his own and the public reproach. His example was imitated by the greatest part of the Latin auxiliaries, and the defence began to slacken when the attack was pressed with redoubled vigour. The number of the Ottomans was fifty, perhaps a hundred, times superior to

---

0 bundles of sticks for filling ditches
1 provincial governors

12 kettle-drums

that of the Christians; the double walls were reduced by the cannon to a heap of ruins; in a circuit of several miles, some places must be found more easy of access or more feebly guarded; and, if the besiegers could penetrate in a single point, the whole city was irrecoverably lost. The first who deserved the sultan's reward was Hassan, the Janizary, of gigantic stature and strength. With his scimetar in one hand and his buckler in the other, he ascended the outward fortification; of the thirty Janizaries, who were emulous of his valour, eighteen perished in the bold adventure. Hassan and his twelve companions had reached the summit: the giant was precipitated from the rampart; he rose on one knee, and was again oppressed by a shower of darts and stones. But his success had proved that the achievement was possible: the walls and towers were instantly covered with a swarm of Turks; and the Greeks, now driven from the vantage ground, were overwhelmed by increasing multitudes. Amidst these multitudes, the emperor, who accomplished all the duties of a general and a soldier, was long seen, and finally lost. The nobles who fought round his person sustained, till their last breath, the honourable names of Palæologus and Cantacuzene:[13] his mournful exclamation was heard, "Cannot there be found a Christian to cut off my head?" and his last fear was that of falling alive into the hands of the infidels. The prudent despair of Constantine cast away the purple; amidst the tumult, he fell by an unknown hand, and his body was buried under a mountain of the slain. After his death, resistance and order were no more; the Greeks fled towards the city; and many were pressed and stifled in the narrow pass of the gate of St. Romanus. The victorious Turks rushed through the breaches of the inner wall; and, as they advanced into the streets, they were soon joined by their brethren, who had forced the gate Phenar on the side of the harbour. In the first heat of the pursuit, about two thousand Christians were put to the sword; but avarice soon prevailed over cruelty; and the victors acknowledged that they should immediately have given quarter, if the valour of the emperor and his chosen bands had not prepared them for a similar opposition in every part of the capital. In was thus, after a siege of fifty-three days, that Constantinople, which had defied the power of Chosroes,[14] the Cha-

gan,[15] and the caliphs,[16] was irretrievably subdued by the arms of Mahomet the Second. Her empire only had been subverted by the Latins; her religion was trampled in the dust by the Moslem conquerors.

GILBERT WHITE (1720-1793)

From THE NATURAL HISTORY OF SELBORNE

Selborne,* Nov. 23, 1773.

To the Honourable Daines Barrington.

DEAR SIR,

In obedience to your injunctions I sit down to give you some account of the house martin or martlet; and, if my monography of this little domestic and familiar bird should happen to meet with your approbation, I may probably soon extend my inquiries to the rest of the British *Hirundines*—the swallow, the swift, and the bank martin.

A few house martins begin to appear about the 16th of April; usually some few days later than the swallow. For some time after they appear, the *Hirundines* in general pay no attention to the business of nidification, but play and sport about either to recruit from the fatigue of their journey, if they do migrate at all, or else that their blood may recover its true tone and texture after it has been so long benumbed by the severities of winter. About the middle of May, if the weather be fine, the martin begins to think in earnest of providing a mansion for its family. The crust or shell of this nest seems to be formed of such dirt or loam as comes most readily to hand, and is tempered and wrought together with little bits of broken straws to render it tough and tenacious. As this bird often builds against a perpendicular wall without any projecting ledge under, it requires its utmost efforts to get the first foundation firmly fixed, so that it may safely carry the superstructure. On this occasion the bird not only clings with its claws but partly supports itself by strongly inclining its tail against the wall, making that a fulcrum; and thus steadied, it works and plasters the materials into the face of the brick or stone. But then, that this work may not, while it is soft and green, pull itself down by its own

15 Title of the king of the Avars, ally of Chosroes
16 Ottoman sovereigns.

* A parish in Hampshire, England, where Whit[e] lived and made the observations in natural history which were communicated to hi[s] friends, Thomas Pennant and Daines Bar[r]ington.

13 The names of several Byzantine emperors.
14 A Persian king, who in the seventh century besieged Constantinople for ten years.

weight, the provident architect has prudence and forbearance enough not to advance her work too fast; but by building only in the morning, and by dedicating the rest of the day to food and amusement, gives it sufficient time to dry and harden. About half an inch seems to be a sufficient layer for a day. Thus careful workmen when they build mud walls (informed at first perhaps by this little bird) raise but a moderate layer at a time, and then desist; lest the work should become top-heavy, and so be ruined by its own weight. By this method in about ten or twelve days is formed an hemispheric nest with a small aperture towards the top, strong, compact, and warm; and perfectly fitted for all the purposes for which it was intended. But then nothing is more common than for the house sparrow, as soon as the shell is finished, to seize on it as its own, to eject the owner, and to line it after its own manner.

After so much labour is bestowed in erecting a mansion, as Nature seldom works in vain, martins will breed on for several years together in the same nest, where it happens to be well sheltered and secure from the injuries of weather. The shell or crust of the nest is a sort of rustic-work full of knobs and protuberances on the outside: nor is the inside of those that I have examined smoothed with any exactness at all; but is rendered soft and warm, and fit for incubation, by a lining of small straws, grasses, and feathers; and sometimes by a bed of moss interwoven with wool. In this nest the hen lays from three to five white eggs. . .

As the young of small birds presently arrive at their *helikia*, or full growth, they soon become impatient of confinement, and sit all day with their heads out at the orifice, where the dams, by clinging to the nest, supply them with food from morning to night. For a time the young are fed on the wing by their parents; but the feat is done by so quick and almost imperceptible a sleight, that a person must have attended very exactly to their motions before he would be able to perceive it.

As soon as the young are able to shift for themselves, the dams immediately turn their thoughts to the business of a second brood: while the first flight, shaken off and rejected by their nurses, congregate in great flocks, and are the birds that are seen clustering and hovering on sunny mornings and evenings round towers and steeples, and on the roofs of churches and houses. These congregatings usually begin to take place about the first week in August; and therefore we may conclude that by that time the first flight is pretty well over. The young of this species do not quit their abodes all together, but the more forward birds get abroad some days before the rest. These, approaching the eaves of buildings, and playing about before them, make people think that several old ones attend one nest. They are often capricious in fixing on a nesting-place, beginning many edifices, and leaving them unfinished; but when once a nest is completed in a sheltered place, it serves for several seasons. Those which breed in a ready-finished house get the start, in hatching, of those that build new, by ten days or a fortnight. These industrious artificers are at their labours in the long days before four in the morning: when they fix their materials, they plaster them on with their chins, moving their heads with a quick vibratory motion. They dip and wash as they fly sometimes in very hot weather, but not so frequently as swallows. It has been observed that martins usually build to a north-east or north-west aspect, that the heat of the sun may not crack and destroy their nests: but instances are also remembered where they bred for many years in vast abundance in a hot stifled inn-yard, against a wall facing to the south.

Birds in general are wise in their choice of situation: but in this neighbourhood, every summer, is seen a strong proof to the contrary at a house without eaves in an exposed district where some martins build year by year in the corners of the windows. But, as the corners of these windows (which face to the south-east and south-west) are too shallow, the nests are washed down every hard rain; and yet these birds drudge on to no purpose from summer to summer, without changing their aspect or house. It is a piteous sight to see them labouring when half their nest is washed away, and bringing dirt—"*generis lapsi sarcire ruinas.*"[1] Thus is instinct a most wonderful unequal faculty, in some instances so much above reason, in other respects so far below it! Martins love to frequent towns, especially if there are great lakes and rivers at hand; nay, they even affect the close air of London. And I have not only seen them nesting in the Borough,[2] but even in the Strand and Fleet Street; but then it was obvious from the dinginess of their aspect that their feathers partook of the filth of that sooty atmosphere. Martins are by far the least agile of the four species; their wings and tails are short, and

[1] "To repair the wreck of the fallen house." Virgil: *Georgia*, iv. 249.

[2] A street extending north from London Bridge.

therefore they are not capable of such surprising turns and quick and glancing evolutions as the swallow. Accordingly they make use of a placid easy motion in a middle region of the air, seldom mounting to any great height, and never sweeping long together over the surface of the ground or water. They do not wander far for food, but affect sheltered districts, over some lake, or under some hanging wood, or in some hollow vale, especially in windy weather. They breed the latest of all the swallow kind; in 1772 they had nestlings on to October the 21st, and are never without unfledged young as late as Michaelmas.[3]

As the summer declines, the congregating flocks increase in numbers daily, by the constant accession of the second broods; till at last they swarm in myriads upon myriads round the villages on the Thames, darkening the face of the sky as they frequent the aits[4] of that river where they roost. They retire (the bulk of them, I mean) in vast flocks together, about the beginning of October: but have appeared of late years in a considerable flight in this neighbourhood, for one day or two, as late as November the 3rd and 6th after they were supposed to have been gone for more than a fortnight. They therefore withdraw with us the latest of any species. Unless these birds are very short-lived indeed, or unless they do not return to the district where they are bred, they must undergo vast devastations somehow, and somewhere; for the birds that return yearly bear no manner of proportion to the birds that retire.

House martins are distinguished from their congeners by having their legs covered with soft downy feathers down to their toes. They are no songsters; but twitter in a pretty inward soft manner in their nests. During the time of breeding, they are often greatly molested with fleas.—*Letter XVI* (or *LV*).

Selborne, April 21, 1780.
DEAR SIR,
The old Sussex tortoise, that I have mentioned to you so often, is become my property. I dug it out of its winter dormitory in March last, when it was enough awakened to express its resentment by hissing; and, packing it in a box with earth, carried it eighty miles in post chaises. The rattle and hurry of the journey so perfectly roused it, that, when I turned it out on a border, it walked twice down to the bottom of my garden: however, in the evening, the weather being cold, it buried itself in the loose mould, and continues still concealed.

As it will be under my eye, I shall now have an opportunity of enlarging my observations on its mode of life and propensities; and perceive already that, towards the time of coming forth, it opens a breathing place in the ground near its head, requiring, I conclude, a freer respiration as it becomes more alive. This creature not only goes under the earth from the middle of November to the middle of April, but sleeps great part of the summer; for it goes to bed in the longest days at four in the afternoon, and often does not stir in the morning till late. Besides, it retires to rest for every shower; and does not move at all in wet days.

When one reflects on the state of this strange being, it is a matter of wonder to find that Providence should bestow such a profusion of days, such a seeming waste of longevity, on a reptile that appears to relish it so little as to squander more than two-thirds of its existence in a joyless stupor, and be lost to all sensation for months together in the profoundest of slumbers.

While I was writing this letter, a moist and warm afternoon, with the thermometer at 50, brought forth troops of shell-snails; and, at the same juncture, the tortoise heaved up the mould and put out its head; and the next morning came forth, as it were raised from the dead; and walked about till four in the afternoon. This was a curious coincidence! a very amusing occurrence! to see such a similarity of feelings between the two *phereoikoi*! for so the Greeks call both the shell-snail and the tortoise.—*Letter L* (or *XCII*).

More Particulars Respecting the Old Family Tortoise.

Because we call this creature an abject reptile, we are too apt to undervalue his abilities, and depreciate his powers of instinct. Yet he is, as Mr. Pope says of his lord,*

　'Much too wise to walk into a well:'

and has so much discernment as not to fall down a haha;[5] but to stop and withdraw from the brink with the readiest precaution.

Though he loves warm weather, he avoids the hot sun; because his thick shell, when once heated, would, as the poet says of solid armour, 'scald with safety.' He therefore spends the more sultry hours under the umbrella of a

---

[3] Sept. 29.　　　　[4] Islets

[5] A hedge in a ditch.
* *Imitations of Horace*, II, ii, 191.

large cabbage leaf, or amidst the waving forests of an asparagus bed.

But as he avoids heat in the summer, so, in the decline of the year, he improves the faint autumnal beams, by getting within the reflection of a fruit-wall: and, though he never has read that planes inclining to the horizon receive a greater share of warmth, he inclines his shell by tilting it against the wall, to collect and admit every feeble ray.

Pitiable seems the condition of this poor embarrassed reptile; to be cased in a suit of ponderous armour, which he cannot lay aside; to be imprisoned, as it were, within his own shell,- must preclude, we should suppose, all activity and disposition for enterprise. Yet there is a season of the year (usually the beginning of June) when his exertions are remarkable. He then walks on tiptoe, and is stirring by five in the morning; and, traversing the garden, examines every wicket and interstice in the fences, through which he will escape if possible; and often has eluded the care of the gardener, and wandered to some distant field.—*The Antiquities of Selborne.*

EDMUND BURKE (1729-1797)

FROM THE SPEECH AT BRISTOL, 1780*

Since you have suffered me to trouble you so much on this subject, permit me, gentlemen, to detain you a little longer. I am indeed most solicitous to give you perfect satisfaction. I find there are some of a better and softer nature than the persons with whom I have supposed myself in debate, who neither think ill of the Act of Relief, nor by any means desire the repeal; yet who, not accusing but lamenting what was done, on account of the consequences, have frequently expressed their wish that the late Act had never been made. Some of this description, and persons of worth, I have met with in this city. They conceive that the prejudices, whatever they might be, of a large part of the people ought not to have been shocked; that their opinions ought to have been previously taken, and much attended to; and that thereby the late horrid scenes might have been prevented.

* In 1699 a most tyrannical law against Roman Catholics had been passed. The abolition of this law in 1778, by the Act of Relief, aroused some fanatical opposition expressed in cries of "No Popery", and in the Lord George Gordon riots. Burke is defending before his constituents his support of the repeal. Sir Samuel Romilly called the entire speech "perhaps the first piece of oratory in our language."

I confess my notions are widely different, and I never was less sorry for any action of my life. I like the bill the better on account of the events of all kinds that followed it. It relieved the real sufferers; it strengthened the state; and, by the disorders that ensued, we had clear evidence that there lurked a temper somewhere which ought not to be fostered by the laws. No ill consequences whatever could be attributed to the Act itself. We knew beforehand, or we were poorly instructed, that toleration is odious to the intolerant; freedom to oppressors; property to robbers; and all kinds and degrees of prosperity to the envious. We knew that all these kinds of men would gladly gratify their evil dispositions under the sanction of law and religion if they could; if they could not, yet, to make way to their objects, they would do their utmost to subvert all religion and all law. This we certainly knew; but, knowing this, is there any reason, because thieves break in and steal, and thus bring detriment to you, and draw ruin on themselves, that I am to be sorry that you are in the possession of shops, and of warehouses, and of wholesome laws to protect them? Are you to build no houses because desperate men may pull them down upon their own heads? Or, if a malignant wretch will cut his own throat because he sees you give alms to the necessitous and deserving, shall his destruction be attributed to your charity, and not to his own deplorable madness? If we repent of our good actions, what, I pray you, is left for our faults and follies? It is not the beneficence of the laws, it is the unnatural temper, which beneficence can fret and sour, that is to be lamented. It is this temper which, by all rational means, ought to be sweetened and corrected. If froward men should refuse this cure, can they vitiate anything but themselves? Does evil so react upon good as not only to retard its motion, but to change its nature? If it can so operate, then good men will always be in the power of the bad; and virtue, by a dreadful reverse of order, must lie under perpetual subjection and bondage to vice.

As to the opinion of the people, which some think, in such cases, is to be implicitly obeyed. —Nearly two years' tranquillity which followed the Act, and its instant imitation in Ireland, proved abundantly that the late horrible spirit was, in a great measure, the effect of insidious art, and perverse industry, and gross misrepresentation. But suppose that the dislike had been much more deliberate and much more general than I am persuaded it was,

When we know that the opinions of even the greatest multitudes are the standard of rectitude, I shall think myself obliged to make those opinions the masters of my conscience; but if it may be doubted whether Omnipotence itself is competent to alter the essential constitution of right and wrong, sure I am that such *things* as they and I are possessed of no such power. No man carries further than I do the policy of making government pleasing to the people; but the widest range of this politic complaisance is confined within the limits of justice. I would not only consult the interest of the people, but I would cheerfully gratify their humours. We are all a sort of children that must be soothed and managed. I think I am not austere or formal in my nature. I would bear, I would even myself play my part in, any innocent buffooneries to divert them; but I never will act the tyrant for their amusement. If they will mix malice in their sports, I shall never consent to throw them any living sentient creature whatsoever, no, not so much as a kitling, to torment.

''But, if I profess all this impolitic stubbornness, I may chance never to be elected into Parliament.'' It is certainly not pleasing to be put out of the public service; but I wish to be a member of Parliament to have my share of doing good and resisting evil. It would therefore be absurd to renounce my objects in order to obtain my seat. I deceive myself indeed most grossly if I had not much rather pass the remainder of my life hidden in the recesses of the deepest obscurity, feeding my mind even with the visions and imaginations of such things, than to be placed on the most splendid throne of the universe, tantalized with a denial of the practice of all which can make the greatest situation any other than the greatest curse. Gentlemen, I have had my day. I can never sufficiently express my gratitude to you for having set me in a place wherein I could lend the slightest help to great and laudable designs. If I have had my share in any measure giving quiet to private property and private conscience; if by my vote I have aided in securing to families the best possession, peace; if I have joined in reconciling kings to their subjects, and subjects to their prince; if I have assisted to loosen the foreign holdings of the citizen, and taught him to look for his protection to the laws of his country, and for his comfort to the good-will of his countrymen; if I have thus taken my part with the best of men in the best of their actions, I can shut the book—I might wish to read a page or two more, but this is enough for my measure—I have not lived in vain.

And now, gentlemen, on this serious day, when I come, as it were, to make up my account with you, let me take to myself some degree of honest pride on the nature of the charges that are against me. I do not here stand before you accused of venality, or of neglect of duty. It is not said that, in the long period of my service, I have in a single instance sacrificed the slightest of your interests to my ambition, or to my fortune. It is not alleged that, to gratify any anger or revenge of my own or of my party, I have had a share in wronging or oppressing any description of men, or any one man in any description. No! the charges against me are all of one kind: that I have pushed the principles of general justice and benevolence too far, further than a cautious policy would warrant, and further than the opinions of many would go along with me. In every accident which may happen through life—in pain, in sorrow, in depression and distress—I will call to mind this accusation, and be comforted.

From REFLECTIONS ON THE REVOLUTION IN FRANCE*

Yielding to reasons, at least as forcible as those which were so delicately urged in the compliment on the new year,† the king of France will probably endeavour to forget these events and that compliment. But history, who keeps a durable record of all our acts, and exercises her awful censure over the proceedings of all sorts of sovereigns, will not forget either those events, or the era of this liberal refinement[1] in the intercourse of mankind. History will record, that on the morning of the 6th of October, 1789, the king and queen of France, after a day of confusion, alarm, dismay, and slaughter, lay down, under the pledged security of public faith, to indulge nature in a few hours of respite, and troubled, melancholy repose. From this sleep the queen was first startled by the voice of the sentinel at her door, who cried out to her to save herself by flight—that this was the last proof of

[1] Spoken sarcastically; see beginning of third paragraph.
* These reflections grew out of a correspondence which Burke had with "a very young gentleman of Paris," and they retain the tone of a personal letter. They were published in 1790.
† An address from the Assembly had been presented to the King and Queen Jan. 3, 1790, felicitating them upon the new year and begging them to forget the past in view of the good they might do in the future.

idelity he could give—that they were upon him, and he was dead. Instantly he was cut down. A band of cruel ruffians and assassins, reeking with his blood, rushed into the chamber of the queen, and pierced with a hundred strokes of bayonets and poniards the bed, from whence this persecuted woman had but just time to fly almost naked, and, through ways unknown to the murderers, had escaped to seek refuge at the feet of a king and husband, not secure of his own life for a moment.

This king, to say no more of him, and this queen, and their infant children, (who once would have been the pride and hope of a great and generous people,) were then forced to abandon the sanctuary of the most splendid palace in the world, which they left swimming in blood, polluted by massacre, and strewed with scattered limbs and mutilated carcases. Thence they were conducted into the capital of their kingdom. Two had been selected from the unprovoked, unresisted, promiscuous slaughter, which was made of the gentlemen of birth and family who composed the king's body guard. These two gentlemen, with all the parade of an execution of justice, were cruelly and publicly dragged to the block, and beheaded in the great court of the palace. Their heads were stuck upon spears, and led the procession; whilst the royal captives who followed in the train were slowly moved along, amidst the horrid yells, and shrilling screams, and frantic dances, and infamous contumelies, and all the unutterable abominations of the furies of hell, in the abused shape of the vilest of women. After they had been made to taste, drop by drop, more than the bitterness of death, in the slow torture of a journey of twelve miles, protracted to six hours, they, were, under a guard, composed of those very soldiers who had thus conducted them through this famous triumph, lodged in one of the old palaces of Paris now converted into a bastile for kings.

Is this a triumph to be consecrated at altars? to be commemorated with grateful thanksgiving? to be offered to the divine humanity with fervent prayer and enthusiastic ejaculation?— These Theban and Thracian orgies,[2] acted in France, and applauded only in the Old Jewry,[3] I assure you, kindle prophetic enthusiasm in the minds but of very few people in this kingdom: although a saint and apostle, who may have revelations of his own, and who has so

completely vanquished all the mean superstitions of the heart, may incline to think it pious and decorous to compare it with the entrance into the world of the Prince of Peace, proclaimed in a holy temple by a venerable sage, and not long before not worse announced by the voice of angels to the quiet innocence of shepherds.

At first I was at a loss to account for this fit of unguarded transport. I knew, indeed, that the sufferings of monarchs make a delicious repast to some sort of palates. There were reflections which might serve to keep this appetite within some bounds of temperance. But when I took one circumstance into my consideration, I was obliged to confess, that much allowance ought to be made for the society, and that the temptation was too strong for common discretion; I mean, the circumstance of the Io Pæan[4] of the triumph, the animating cry which called "for all the BISHOPS to be hanged on the lamp-posts," might well have brought forth a burst of enthusiasm on the foreseen consequences of this happy day. I allow to so much enthusiasm some little deviation from prudence. I allow this prophet to break forth into hymns of joy and thanksgiving on an event which appears like the precursor of the Millennium, and the projected fifth monarchy,[5] in the destruction of all church establishments. There was, however, (as in all human affairs there is,) in the midst of this joy, something to exercise the patience of these worthy gentlemen, and to try the long-suffering of their faith. The actual murder of the king and queen, and their child, was wanting to the other auspicious circumstances of this "beautiful day." The actual murder of the bishops, though called for by so many holy ejaculations, was also wanting. A group of regicide and sacrilegious slaughter, was indeed boldly sketched, but it was only sketched. It unhappily was left unfinished, in this great history-piece of the massacre of innocents. What hardy pencil of a great master, from the school of the rights of men,* will finish it, is to be seen hereafter. The age has not yet the complete benefit of that diffusion of knowledge that has undermined superstition and error; and the king of France wants another object or two to consign to oblivion, in consideration of all the good which is to

2 Bacchanalian orgies of ancient Greece.
3 A London street, where Dr. Richard Price, of the Revolution Society, had preached a sermon in approbation of the Revolution in France.

4 Ancient shout of victory.
5 The dream of a Puritan sect of Cromwell's time, to establish a monarchy rivaling ancient Assyria, Persia, Macedonia and Rome.
* Ironically alluding to the philosophers who upheld revolutionary doctrines in the name of humanity. Burke's extreme conservatism on this subject must not be forgotten.

arise from his own sufferings, and the patriotic crimes of an enlightened age.

Although this work of our new light and knowledge did not go to the length that in all probability it was intended it should be carried, yet I must think that such treatment of any human creatures must be shocking to any but those who are made for accomplishing revolutions. But I cannot stop here. Influenced by the inborn feelings of my nature, and not being illuminated by a single ray of this new sprung modern light, I confess to you, Sir, that the exalted rank of the persons suffering, and particularly the sex, the beauty, and the amiable qualities of the descendant of so many kings and emperors, with the tender age of royal infants, insensible only through infancy and innocence of the cruel outrages to which their parents were exposed, instead of being a subject of exultation, adds not a little to my sensibility on that most melancholy occasion.

I hear that the august person, who was the principal object of our preacher's triumph, though he supported himself, felt much on that shameful occasion. As a man, it became him to feel for his wife and his children, and the faithful guards of his person, that were massacred in cold blood about him; as a prince, it became him to feel for the strange and frightful transformation of his civilized subjects, and to be more grieved for them than solicitous for himself. It derogates little from his fortitude, while it adds infinitely to the honour of his humanity. I am very sorry to say it, very sorry indeed, that such personages are in a situation in which it is not becoming in us to praise the virtues of the great.

I hear, and I rejoice to hear, that the great lady, the other object of the triumph, has borne that day, (one is interested that beings made for suffering should suffer well,) and that she bears all the succeeding days, that she bears the imprisonment of her husband, and her captivity, and the exile of her friends, and the insulting adulation of addresses, and the whole weight of her accumulated wrongs, with a serene patience, in a manner suited to her rank and race, and becoming the offspring of a sovereign[6] distinguished for her piety and her courage; that, like her, she has lofty sentiments; that she feels with the dignity of a Roman matron; that in the last extremity she will save herself from the last disgrace;[7] and that, if she must fall, she will fall by no ignoble hand.

It is now sixteen or seventeen years since I saw the queen of France, then the dauphiness at Versailles; and surely never lighted on this orb, which she hardly seemed to touch, a more delightful vision. I saw her just above the horizon, decorating and cheering the elevated sphere she just began to move in,—glittering like the morning-star, full of life, and splendour, and joy. Oh! what a revolution! and what a heart must I have to contemplate without emotion that elevation and that fall! Little did I dream when she added titles of veneration to those of enthusiastic, distant, respectful love, that she should ever be obliged to carry the sharp antidote against disgrace concealed in that bosom; little did I dream that I should have lived to see such disasters fallen upon her in a nation of gallant men, in a nation of men of honour, and of cavaliers. I thought ten thousand swords must have leaped from their scabbards to avenge even a look that threatened her with insult. But the age of chivalry is gone. That of sophisters, economists, and calculators, has succeeded; and the glory of Europe is extinguished for ever. Never, never more shall we behold that generous loyalty to rank and sex, that proud submission, that dignified obedience, that subordination of the heart, which kept alive, even in servitude itself the spirit of an exalted freedom. The unbought grace of life, the cheap defence of nations, the nurse of manly sentiment and heroic enterprise is gone! It is gone, that sensibility of principle, that chastity of honour, which felt a stain like a wound, which inspired courage whilst it mitigated ferocity, which ennobled whatever it touched, and under which vice itself lost half its evil, by losing all its grossness.

This mixed system of opinion and sentiment had its origin in the ancient chivalry; and the principle, though varied in its appearance by the varying state of human affairs, subsisted and influenced through a long succession of generations, even to the time we live in. If it should ever be totally extinguished, the loss I fear will be great. It is this which has given its character to modern Europe. It is this which has distinguished it under all its forms of government, and distinguished it to its advantage, from the states of Asia, and possibly from those states which flourished in the most brilliant periods of the antique world. It was this, which, without confounding ranks, had produced a noble equality, and handed it down through all the gradations of social life. It was this opinion which mitigated kings into

6 Maria Theresa

7 By poison, self-administered.

ompanions, and raised private men to be fel-
ows with kings. Without force or opposition,
subdued the fierceness of pride and power;
obliged sovereigns to submit to the soft
llar of social esteem, compelled stern authority
 submit to elegance, and gave a dominating
anquisher of laws to be subdued by manners.
But now all is to be changed. All the pleas-
g illusions, which made power gentle and
bedience liberal, which harmonized the difrent shades of life and which, by a bland
ssimilation, incorporated into politics the sen-
ments which beautify and soften private
ciety, are to be dissolved by this new con-
ering empire of light and reason. All the
ecent drapery of life is to be rudely torn off.
ll the superadded ideas, furnished from the
ardrobe of a moral imagination, which the
eart owns, and the understanding ratifies, as
ecessary to cover the defects of our naked,
ivering nature, and to raise it to dignity in
ir own estimation, are to be exploded as a
diculous, absurd, and antiquated fashion.

On this scheme of things, a king is but a
an, a queen is but a woman; a woman is but
a animal, and an animal not of the highest
der. All homage paid to the sex in general
s such, and without distinct views, is to be
garded as romance and folly. Regicide, and
arricide, and sacrilege, are but fictions of
perstition, corrupting jurisprudence by de-
roying its simplicity. The murder of a king,
 a queen, or a bishop, or a father, are only
mmon homicide; and if the people are by
y chance, or in any way, gainers by it, a
rt of homicide much the most pardonable, and
to which we ought not to make too severe a
rutiny.

On the scheme of this barbarous philosophy,
hich is the offspring of cold hearts and muddy
nderstandings, and which is as void of solid
isdom as it is destitute of all taste and ele-
ance, laws are to be supported only by their
vn terrors, and by the concern which each
dividual may find in them from his own pri-
te speculations, or can spare to them from
s own private interests. In the groves of
eir academy,* at the end of every vista, you
e nothing but the gallows. Nothing is left
hich engages the affections on the part of the
mmonwealth. On the principles of this me-
anic philosophy, our institutions can never be
nbodied, if I may use the expression, in per-
ns; so as to create in us love, veneration,

—————
The Athenian philosophers conducted their instruction walking in the groves of the
Academe. See Newman, *Site of a University*,
in the present volume.

admiration, or attachment. But that sort of
reason which banishes the affections is incapable of filling their place. These public affections, combined with manners, are required
sometimes as supplements, sometimes as cor-
rectives, always as aids to law. The precept
given by a wise man, as well as a great critic,
for the construction of poems, is equally true
as to states:—*Non satis est pulchra esse
poemata, dulcia sunto.*[8] There ought to be a
system of manners in every nation, which a
well-formed mind would be disposed to relish.
To make us love our country, our country ought
to be lovely.

WILLIAM COWPER (1731-1800)

From OLNEY HYMNS
XXXV. LIGHT SHINING OUT OF DARKNESS

1

GOD moves in a mysterious way
  His wonders to perform;
He plants his footsteps in the sea,
  And rides upon the storm.

2

Deep in unfathomable mines
  Of never-failing skill
He treasures up his bright designs,
  And works his sovereign will.

3

Ye fearful saints, fresh courage take,
  The clouds ye so much dread
Are big with mercy, and shall break
  In blessings on your head.

4

Judge not the Lord by feeble sense,
  But trust him for his grace:
Behind a frowning providence
  He hides a smiling face.

5

His purposes will ripen fast,
  Unfolding every hour;
The bud may have a bitter taste,
  But sweet will be the flower.

6

Blind unbelief is sure to err,
  And scan his work in vain:
God is his own interpreter,
  And he will make it plain.

—————
8 "It is not enough that poems be beautiful, they
must have sweetness." Horace: *Ars Poetica*,
99.

ON THE LOSS OF THE ROYAL GEORGE *

1

Toll for the brave!
  The brave that are no more!
All sunk beneath the wave,
  Fast by their native shore!

2

Eight hundred of the brave,
  Whose courage well was tried,
Had made the vessel heel,
  And laid her on her side.

3

A land-breeze shook the shrouds,
  And she was overset:
Down went the Royal George,
  With all her crew complete.

4

Toll for the brave!
  Brave Kempenfelt is gone;
His last sea-fight is fought;
  His work of glory done.

5

It was not in the battle;
  No tempest gave the shock;
She sprang no fatal leak;
  She ran upon no rock.

6

His sword was in its sheath;
  His fingers held the pen
When Kempenfelt went down
  With twice four hundred men.

7

Weigh the vessel up,
  Once dreaded by our foes!
And mingle with our cup
  The tear that England owes:

8

Her timbers yet are sound,
  And she may float again,
Full charged with England's thunder,
  And plough the distant main.

9

But Kempenfelt is gone,
  His victories are o'er;
And he and his eight hundred
  Shall plough the wave no more.

* A man-of-war which, in 1782, while undergoing repairs, turned over, filled, and sank, with Admiral Kempenfelt and over eight hundred men on board. This poem takes a place among the great poems written about the British navy, like Campbell's *Ye Mariners of England* and Tennyson's *The Revenge*.

THE JACKDAW †

1

There is a bird, who, by his coat,
And by the hoarseness of his note,
  Might be supposed a crow;
A great frequenter of the church,
Where bishop-like he finds a perch,
  And dormitory too.

2

Above the steeple shines a plate,
That turns and turns to indicate
  From what point blows the weather;
Look up—your brains begin to swim,
'Tis in the clouds—that pleases him;
  He chooses it the rather.

3

Fond of the speculative height,
Thither he wings his airy flight,
  And thence securely sees
The bustle and the raree-show[1]
That occupy mankind below,
  Secure and at his ease.

4

You think, no doubt, he sits and muses
On future broken bones and bruises,
  If he should chance to fall.
No; not a single thought like that
Employs his philosophic pate,
  Or troubles it at all.

5

He sees that this great roundabout,
The world, with all its motley rout,
  Church, army, physic, law,
Its customs, and its businesses,
Is no concern at all of his,
  And says—what says he?—"Caw.'

6

Thrice happy bird! I too have seen
Much of the vanities of men;
  And, sick of having seen 'em,
Would cheerfully these limbs resign
For such a pair of wings as thine,
  And such a head between 'em.

ON THE RECEIPT OF MY MOTHER'S PICTURE, OUT OF NORFOLK; THE GIFT OF MY COUSIN, ANN BODHAM

O that those lips had language! Life has
  passed
With me but roughly since I heard thee last.
Those lips are thine—thy own sweet smile I see,

1 A show that can be carried about in a box.
† Translated from the Latin of Cowper's teacher, Vincent Bourne.

The same that oft in childhood solaced me;
Voice only fails, else how distinct they say,
'Grieve not, my child, chase all thy fears
    away!''
The meek intelligence of those dear eyes
 Blest be the art that can immortalize,
The art that baffles Time's tyrannic claim
To quench it) here shines on me still the same.
    Faithful remembrancer of one so dear,   11
O welcome guest, though unexpected here!
Who bidst me honour with an artless song,
Affectionate, a mother lost so long,
I will obey, not willingly alone,
But gladly, as the precept were her own:
And, while that face renews my filial grief,
Fancy shall weave a charm for my relief,
Shall steep me in Elysian reverie,
A momentary dream that thou art she.   20
    My mother! when I learned that thou wast
        dead,
Say, wast thou conscious of the tears I shed?
Hovered thy spirit o'er thy sorrowing son,
Wretch even then, life's journey just begun?
Perhaps thou gavest me, though unfelt, a kiss:
Perhaps a tear, if souls can weep in bliss—
Ah, that maternal smile! It answers—Yes.
I heard the bell tolled on thy burial day,
I saw the hearse that bore thee slow away,
And, turning from my nursery window, drew 30
A long, long sigh, and wept a last adieu!
But was it such?—It was.—Where thou art
    gone,
Adieus and farewells are a sound unknown.
May I but meet thee on that peaceful shore,
The parting word shall pass my lips no more!
Thy maidens, grieved themselves at my concern,
Oft gave me promise of thy quick return.
What ardently I wished I long believed,
And, disappointed still, was still deceived.
By expectation every day beguiled,   40
Dupe of *to-morrow* even from a child.
Thus many a sad to-morrow came and went,
Till, all my stock of infant sorrow spent,
I learned at last submission to my lot;
But, though I less deplored thee, ne'er forgot.
    Where once we dwelt our name is heard no
        more,
Children not thine have trod my nursery floor;
And where the gardener Robin, day by day,
Drew me to school along the public way,   50
Delighted with my bauble coach, and wrapped
In scarlet mantle warm, and velvet capped,
'Tis now become a history little known
That once we called the pastoral house our own.
Short-lived possession! but the record fair
That memory keeps, of all thy kindness there,
Still outlives many a storm, that has effaced
A thousand other themes less deeply traced.

Thy nightly visits to my chamber made,
That thou might'st know me safe and warmly
    laid;
Thy morning bounties ere I left my home,   60
The biscuit, or confectionery plum;
The fragrant waters on my cheeks bestowed
By thy own hand, till fresh they shone and
    glowed;
All this, and more endearing still than all,
Thy constant flow of love, that knew no fall,
Ne'er roughened by those cataracts and brakes,
That humour interposed too often makes;
All this still legible in memory's page,
And still to be so to my latest age,
Adds joy to duty, makes me glad to pay   70
Such honours to thee as my numbers may;
Perhaps a frail memorial, but sincere,
Not scorned in heaven, though little noticed
    here.
    Could Time, his flight reversed, restore the
        hours
When, playing with thy vesture's tissued
    flowers,
The violet, the pink, and jessamine,
I pricked them into paper with a pin
(And thou wast happier than myself the while,
Wouldst softly speak, and stroke my head and
    smile),
Could those few pleasant days again appear, . 80
Might one wish bring them, would I wish them
    here?
I would not trust my heart—the dear delight
Seems so to be desired, perhaps I might—
But no—what here we call our life is such
So little to be loved, and thou so much,
That I should ill requite thee to constrain
Thy unbound spirit into bonds again.
    Thou, as a gallant bark from Albion's coast
(The storms all weathered and the ocean
    crossed)
Shoots into port at some well-havened isle,   90
Where spices breathe, and brighter seasons
    smile,
There sits quiescent on the floods that show
Her beauteous form reflected clear below,
While airs impregnated with incense play
Around her, fanning light her streamers gay;
So thou, with sails how swift! hast reached the
    shore,
"Where tempests never beat nor billows roar,"
And thy loved consort on the dangerous tide
Of life long since has anchored by thy side.
But me, scarce hoping to attain that rest,   100
Always from port withheld, always distressed—
Me howling blasts drive devious, tempest tost,
Sails ripped, seams opening wide, and compass
    lost,
And day by day some current's thwarting force

Sets me more distant from a prosperous course.
Yet oh the thought that thou art safe, and he!
That thought is joy, arrive what may to me.
My boast is not, that I deduce my birth
From loins enthroned, and rulers of the earth;
But higher far my proud pretensions rise—— 110
The son of parents passed into the skies!
And now, farewell. Time unrevoked has run
His wonted course, yet what I wished is done.
By contemplation's help, not sought in vain,
I seem to have lived my childhood o'er again;
To have renewed the joys that once were mine,
Without the sin of violating thine:
And, while the wings of Fancy still are free
And I can view this mimic show of thee,
Time has but half succeeded in his theft—— 120
Thyself removed, thy power to soothe me left.

TO MRS. UNWIN *

MARY! I want a lyre with other strings,
Such aid from heaven as some have feigned
　　they drew,
An eloquence scarce given to mortals, new
And undebased by praise of meaner things,
That, ere through age or woe I shed my wings,
I may record thy worth with honour due,
In verse as musical as thou art true,
And that immortalizes whom it sings.
But thou hast little need. There is a book
By seraphs writ with beams of heavenly light,
On which the eyes of God not rarely look,
A chronicle of actions just and bright;
There all thy deeds, my faithful Mary, shine,
And, since thou own'st that praise, I spare thee
　　mine.

THE CASTAWAY †

1

Obscurest night involved the sky,
　　The Atlantic billows roared,
When such a destined wretch as I,
　　Washed headlong from on board,
Of friends, of hope, of all bereft,
His floating home forever left.

2

No braver chief could Albion boast
　　Than he with whom he went,
Nor ever ship left Albion's coast
　　With warmer wishes sent.
He loved them both, but both in vain,
Nor him beheld, nor her again.

* The friend and constant companion of Cowper
　for thirty-four years.
† The last poem that Cowper wrote; founded on
　an incident in Admiral Anson's *Voyages*. It
　portrays imaginatively his own melancholy
　condition.

3

Not long beneath the whelming brine,
　　Expert to swim, he lay;
Nor soon he felt his strength decline,
　　Or courage die away;
But waged with death a lasting strife,
Supported by despair of life.

4

He shouted; nor his friends had failed
　　To check the vessel's course,
But so the furious blast prevailed
　　That, pitiless perforce,
They left their outcast mate behind,
And scudded still before the wind.

5

Some succour yet they could afford;
　　And such as storms allow,
The cask, the coop, the floated cord,
　　Delayed not to bestow;
But he, they knew, nor ship nor shore,
Whate'er they gave, should visit more.

6

Nor, cruel as it seemed, could he
　　Their haste himself condemn,
Aware that flight, in such a sea,
　　Alone could rescue them;
Yet bitter felt it still to die
Deserted, and his friends so nigh.

7

He long survives, who lives an hour
　　In ocean, self-upheld:
And so long he, with unspent power,
　　His destiny repelled;
And ever, as the minutes flew,
Entreated help, or cried "Adieu!"

8

At length, his transient respite past,
　　His comrades, who before
Had heard his voice in every blast,
　　Could catch the sound no more;
For then, by toil subdued, he drank
The stifling wave, and then he sank.

9

No poet wept him; but the page
　　Of narrative sincere,
That tells his name, his worth, his age
　　Is wet with Anson's tear:
And tears by bards or heroes shed
Alike immortalise the dead.

10

I therefore purpose not, or dream,
　　Descanting on his fate,
To give the melancholy theme

A more enduring date:
But misery still delights to trace
Its semblance in another's case.

11

No voice divine the storm allayed,
    No light propitious shone,
When, snatched from all effectual aid,
    We perished, each alone;
But I beneath a rougher sea,
And whelmed in deeper gulfs than he.

GEORGE CRABBE (1754-1832)

From THE BOROUGH*

Letter I

"Describe the Borough."—Though our idle tribe
May love description, can we so describe,
That you shall fairly streets and buildings trace,
And all that gives distinction to a place?
This cannot be; yet, moved by your request,
A part I paint—let fancy form the rest.
    Cities and towns, the various haunts of men,
Require the pencil; they defy the pen.
Could he, who sang so well the Grecian fleet,[1]
So well have sung of alley, lane, or street?   10
Can measured lines these various buildings show,
The Town-Hall Turning, or the Prospect Row?
Can I the seats of wealth and want explore,
And lengthen out my lays from door to door?
    Then, let thy fancy aid me.—I repair
From this tall mansion of our last-year's mayor,
Till we the outskirts of the Borough reach,
And these half-buried buildings next the beach;
Where hang at open doors the net and cork,
While squalid sea-dames mend the meshy work;
Till comes the hour, when, fishing through the tide,   21
The weary husband throws his freight aside—
A living mass, which now demands the wife,
The alternate labours of their humble life.

1 Homer, *Iliad* II.
* This poem was inscribed to the Duke of Rutland, to whom Crabbe had been chaplain, and takes the form of Letters from a resident of a sea-port (Crabbe was a native of Aldeburgh, Suffolk) to the owner of an inland country-seat. The date of the poem is 1810. Crabbe's reputation, however, was established by *The Village* in 1783, and his place is with those later 18th century poets who clung to the 18th century forms, though reacting against the artificiality and frigid conventionalism that had so long reigned. In homeliness of themes and naked realism of treatment, the poet of *The Village* and *The Borough* stands quite alone. See *Eng. Lit.* p. 226.

Can scenes like these withdraw thee from thy wood,
Thy upland forest or thy valley's flood?
Seek, then, thy garden's shrubby bound, and look,
As it steals by, upon the bordering brook:
That winding streamlet, limpid, lingering, slow,
Where the reeds whisper when the zephyrs blow;   30
Where in the midst, upon her throne of green,
Sits the large lily as the water's queen;
And makes the current, forced awhile to stay,
Murmur and bubble as it shoots away;
Draw then the strongest contrast to that stream,
And our broad river will before thee seem.
    With ceaseless motion comes and goes the tide;
Flowing, it fills the channel vast and wide;
Then back to sea, with strong majestic sweep
It rolls, in ebb yet terrible and deep;   40
Here sampire-banks and salt-wort bound the flood;
There stakes and sea-weeds, withering on the mud;
And, higher up, a ridge of all things base,
Which some strong tide has rolled upon the place.
    Thy gentle river boasts its pigmy boat,
Urged on by pains, half grounded, half afloat;
While at her stern an angler takes his stand,
And marks the fish he purposes to land,
From that clear space, where, in the cheerful ray
Of the warm sun, the scaly people play.   50
    Far other craft our prouder river shows,
Hoys, pinks and sloops; brigs, brigantines and snows:
Nor angler we on our wide stream descry,
But one poor dredger where his oysters lie:
He, cold and wet, and driving with the tide,
Beats his weak arms against his tarry side,
Then drains the remnant of diluted gin,
To aid the warmth that languishes within;
Renewing oft his poor attempts to beat
His tingling fingers into gathering heat.   60
    He shall again be seen when evening comes,
And social parties crowd their favourite rooms,
Where on the table pipes and papers lie,
The steaming bowl or foaming tankard by.
'Tis then, with all these comforts spread around,
They hear the painful dredger's welcome sound;
And few themselves the savoury boon deny,
The food that feeds, the living luxury.
    Yon is our quay! those smaller hoys from town,   69
Its various wares, for country-use, bring down;

Those laden waggons, in return, impart
The country-produce to the city mart;
Hark to the clamour in that miry road,
Bounded and narrowed by yon vessel's load;
The lumbering wealth she empties round the
　　place,
Package, and parcel, hogshead, chest, and case;
While the loud seaman and the angry hind,
Mingling in business, bellow to the wind.
　　Near these a crew amphibious, in the docks,
Rear, for the sea, those castles on the stocks:
See the long keel, which soon the waves must
　　hide;　　　　　　　　　　　　　　　　81
See the strong ribs which form the roomy side;
Bolts yielding slowly to the sturdiest stroke,
And planks which curve and crackle in the
　　smoke.
Around the whole rise cloudy wreaths, and far
Bear the warm pungence of o'er-boiling tar.
　　Dabbling on shore half-naked sea-boys crowd,
Swim round a ship, or swing upon the shroud;
Or, in a boat purloined, with paddles play,
And grow familiar with the watery way.　　90
Young though they be, they feel whose sons
　　they are;
They know what British seamen do and dare;
Proud of that fame, they raise and they enjoy
The rustic wonder of the village boy.

　　·　·　·　·　·　·　·　·

　　Turn to the watery world!—but who to thee
(A wonder yet unviewed) shall paint—the sea?
Various and vast, sublime in all its forms,
When lulled by zephyrs, or when roused by
　　storms;
Its colours changing, when from clouds and sun
Shades after shades upon the surface run;
Embrowned and horrid[2] now, and now serene,
In limpid blue, and evanescent green;　　170
And oft the foggy banks on ocean lie,
Lift the fair sail, and cheat the experienced
　　eye.
　　Be it the summer-noon: a sandy space
The ebbing tide has left upon its place;
Then just the hot and stony beach above,
Light twinkling streams in bright confusion
　　move
(For heated thus, the warmer air ascends,
And with the cooler in its fall contends);
Then the broad bosom of the ocean keeps
An equal motion, swelling as it sleeps,　　180
Then slowly sinking; curling to the strand,
Faint, lazy waves o'ercreep the ridgy sand,
Or tap the tarry boat with gentle blow,
And back return in silence, smooth and slow.
Ships in the calm seem anchored; for they glide
On the still sea, urged solely by the tide;
Art thou not present, this calm scene before,
2 rough

Where all beside is pebbly length of shore,
And far as eye can reach, it can discern n
　　more?
　　Yet sometimes comes a ruffling cloud, t
　　make　　　　　　　　　　　　　　　　19
The quiet surface of the ocean shake;
As an awakened giant with a frown
Might show his wrath, and then to sleep sin
　　down.
View now the winter-storm, above, one cloud
Black and unbroken, all the skies o'ershroud
The unwieldy porpoise through the day befor
Had rolled in view of boding men on shore;
And sometimes hid, and sometimes showed, hi
　　form,
Dark as the cloud, and furious as the storm.
　　All where the eye delights, yet dreads, t
　　roam,　　　　　　　　　　　　　　　　20
The breaking billows cast the flying foam
Upon the billows rising—all the deep
Is restless change; the waves so swelled an
　　steep,
Breaking and sinking, and the sunken swells
Nor one, one moment, in its station dwells.
But, nearer land, you may the billows trace,
As if contending in their watery chase;
May watch the mightiest till the shoal they
　　reach,
Then break and hurry to their utmost stretch;
Curled as they come, they strike with furious
　　force,　　　　　　　　　　　　　　　　21
And then, re-flowing, take their grating course
Raking the rounded flints, which ages past
Rolled by their rage, and shall to ages last.
　　Far off, the petrel in the troubled way
Swims with her brood, or flutters in the spray;
She rises often, often drops again,
And sports at ease on the tempestuous main.
　　High o'er the restless deep, above the reach
Of gunner's hope, vast flights of wild-ducks
　　stretch;
Far as the eye can glance on either side,　220
In a broad space and level line they glide;
All in their wedge-like figures from the north,
Day after day, flight after flight, go forth.
　　In-shore their passage tribes of sea-gulls
　　urge,
And drop for prey within the sweeping surge;
Oft in the rough opposing blast they fly
Far back, then turn, and all their force apply,
While to the storm they give their weak com-
　　plaining cry;
Or clap the sleek white pinion to the breast,
And in the restless ocean dip for rest.　　230
　　Darkness begins to reign; the louder wind
Appals the weak and awes the firmer mind;
But frights not him, whom evening and the
　　spray

part conceal—yon prowler on his way.
o! he has something seen; he runs apace,
s if he feared companion in the chase;
e sees his prize, and now he turns again,
owly and sorrowing—"Was your search in
   vain?"
ruffly he answers, " 'Tis a sorry sight!
  seaman's body; there'll be more to-night!"
 Hark to those sounds! they're from distress
   at sea;   241
ow quick they come! What terrors may there
  be!
es, 'tis a driven vessel: I discern
ights, signs of terror, gleaming from the
   stern;
thers behold them too, and from the town
 various parties seamen hurry down;
heir wives pursue, and damsels urged by
   dread,
est men so dear be into danger led;
heir head the gown has hooded, and their call
 this sad night is piercing like the squall;
hey feel their kinds of power, and when they
   meet,   251
hide, fondle, weep, dare, threaten, or entreat.
 See one poor girl, all terror and alarm,
as fondly seized upon her lover's arm;
Thou shalt not venture;" and he answers,
  "No!
will not"—still she cries, "Thou shalt not
  go."
No need of this; not here the stoutest boat
an through such breakers, o'er such billows
   float;
et may they view these lights upon the beach,
'hich yield them hope, whom help can never
   reach,   260
From parted clouds the moon her radiance
   throws
n the wild waves, and all the danger shows;
ut shows them beaming in her shining vest,
errific splendour! gloom in glory dressed!
his for a moment, and then clouds again
ide every beam, and fear and darkness reign.
 But hear we now those sounds? Do lights
  appear?
see them not! the storm alone I hear:
nd lo! the sailors homeward take their way;
an must endure—let us submit and pray. 270
 Such are our winter-views; but night comes
  on—
ow business sleeps, and daily cares are gone;
ow parties form, and some their friends assist
o waste the idle hours at sober whist;
he tavern's pleasure or the concert's charm
nnumbered moments of their sting disarm;
lay-bills and open doors a crowd invite,

To pass off one dread portion of the night;
And show and song and luxury combined
Lift off from man this burthen of mankind. 280
 Others adventurous walk abroad and meet
Returning parties pacing through the street;
When various voices, in the dying day,
Hum in our walks, and greet us in our way;
When tavern-lights flit on from room to room,
And guide the tippling sailor, staggering home:
There as we pass, the jingling bells betray
How business rises with the closing day:
Now walking silent, by the river's side,
The ear perceives the rippling of the tide; 290
Or measured cadence of the lads who tow
Some entered hoy, to fix her in her row;
Or hollow sound, which from the parish-bell
To some departed spirit bids farewell!
 Thus shall you something of our BOROUGH
  know.
Far as a verse, with Fancy's aid, can show;
Of sea or river, of a quay or street,
The best description must be incomplete;
But when a happier theme succeeds, and when
Men are our subjects and the deeds of men; 300
Then may we find the Muse in happier style,
And we may sometimes sigh and sometimes
  smile.

WILLIAM BLAKE (1757-1827)

SONG

1

How sweet I roamed from field to field,
  And tasted all the summer's pride,
Till I the Prince of Love beheld,
  Who in the sunny beams did glide.

2

He showed me lilies for my hair,
  And blushing roses for my brow;
And led me through his gardens fair
  Where all his golden pleasures grow.

3

With sweet May-dews my wings were wet,
  And Phoebus fired my vocal rage;
He caught me in his silken net,
  And shut me in his golden cage.

4

He loves to sit and hear me sing,
  Then, laughing, sports and plays with me;
Then stretches out my golden wing,
  And mocks my loss of liberty.

TO THE MUSES

1

Whether on Ida's[1] shady brow,
Or in the chambers of the East,
The chambers of the sun, that now
From ancient melody have ceased;

2

Whether in Heaven ye wander fair,
Or the green corners of the earth,
Or the blue regions of the air
Where the melodious winds have birth;

3

Whether on crystal rocks ye rove,
Beneath the bosom of the sea
Wandering in many a coral grove,
Fair Nine, forsaking Poetry!

4

How have you left the ancient love
That bards of old enjoyed in you!
The languid strings do scarcely move,
The sound is forced, the notes are few.

INTRODUCTION TO SONGS OF INNOCENCE

1

Piping down the valleys wild,
Piping songs of pleasant glee,
On a cloud I saw a child,
And he, laughing, said to me:

2

"Pipe a song about a Lamb!"
So I piped with merry cheer.
"Piper, pipe that song again:"
So I piped: he wept to hear.

3

"Drop thy pipe, thy happy pipe;
Sing thy songs of happy cheer:"
So I sang the same again,
While he wept with joy to hear.

4

"Piper, sit thee down and write
In a book, that all may read."
So he vanished from my sight;
And I plucked a hollow reed,

5

And I made a rural pen,
And I stained the water clear,
And I wrote my happy songs
Every child may joy to hear.

THE TIGER *

1

Tiger, Tiger, burning bright
In the forest of the night,
What immortal hand or eye
Could frame thy fearful symmetry?

2

In what distant deeps or skies
Burnt the fire of thine eyes?
On what wings dare he aspire?
What the hand dare seize the fire?

3

And what shoulder, and what art,
Could twist the sinews of thy heart?
When thy heart began to beat,
What dread hand forged thy dread feet?

4

What the hammer? What the chain?
In what furnace was thy brain?
What the anvil? What dread grasp
Dared its deadly terrors clasp?

5

When the stars threw down their spears,
And watered heaven with their tears,
Did he smile his work to see?
Did he who made the Lamb make thee?

6

Tiger, Tiger, burning bright
In the forest of the night,
What immortal hand or eye
Dare frame thy fearful symmetry?

AH, SUNFLOWER

1

Ah, Sunflower! weary of time,
Who countest the steps of the Sun;
Seeking after that sweet golden clime
Where the traveller's journey is done;

2

Where the Youth, pined away with desire,
And the pale Virgin, shrouded in snow,
Arise from their graves, and aspire
Where my Sunflower wishes to go!

---

[1] A mountain of the Troad; also one in Crete. Helicon, in Bœotia, is more properly the mountain of the Muses.

* The Text is that of Malkin, 1806.

SCOTTISH LYRICS

ROBERT FERGUSSON (1750-1774)

Elegy on the Death of Scots Music*

1

n Scotia's plains, in days of yore,
When lads and lasses tartan wore,
aft music rang on ilka[1] shore,
    In hamely weid;[2]
ut harmony is now no more,
    And music dead.

2

ound her the feathered choir would wing,
ae bonnily she wont to sing,
nd sleely[3] wake the sleeping string,
    Their sang to lead,
weet as the zephyrs o' the spring;
    But now she's dead.

3

Mourn, ilka nymph and ilka swain,
k sunny hill and dowie[4] glen;
et weeping streams and Naiads drain
    Their fountain head;
et Echo swell the dolefu' strain,
    Sin' music's dead.

4

Whan the saft vernal breezes ca'
he grey-haired winter's fogs awa',
aebody than is heard to blaw,
    Near hill or mead,
n chaunter[5] or on aiten straw,[6]
    Sin' music's dead.

5

ae lasses now, on simmer days,
Will lilt[7] at bleaching o' their claes;
ae herds[8] on Yarrow's bonny braes,[9]
    Or banks o' Tweed,
elight to chaunt their hameil[10] lays,
    Sin' music's dead.

6

t glomin now the bagpipe's dumb,
Whan weary owsen[11] hameward come;

Sae sweetly as it wont to bum,[12]
    And pibrochs[13] skreed;[14]
We never hear its weirlike[15] hum,
    For music's dead.

7

Macgibbon's[16] gane: Ah! wae's my heart!
The man in music maist expert,
Wha cou'd sweet melody impart,
    And tune the reed,
Wi' sic a slee and pawky[17] art;
    But now he's dead.

8

Ilk carline[18] now may grunt and grane,
Ilk bonny lassie make great mane;
Sin' he's awa, I trow there's nane
    Can fill his stead;
The blythest sangster on the plain,
    Alack, is dead!

9

Now foreign sonnets bear the gree,[19]
And crabbit[20] queer variety
O' sounds fresh sprung frae Italy,
    A bastard breed!
Unlike that saft-tongued melody
    Whilk[21] now lies dead.

10

Cou'd lav'rocks[22] at the dawning day,
Cou'd linties chirming[23] frae the spray,
Or todling burns[24] that smoothly play
    O'er gowden[25] bed,
Compare wi' *Birks of Invermay?*[26]
    But now they're dead.

11

O Scotland! that cou'd yence[27] afford
To bang the pith[28] o' Roman sword,
Winna your sons, wi' joint accord,
    To battle speed,
And fight till Music be restor'd,
    Whilk now lies dead!

LADY ANNE LINDSAY (1750-1825)

Auld Robin Gray

1

When the sheep are in the fauld, and the kye
    at hame,
And a' the warld to rest are gane,

---

[1] every	[6] oaten reed
[2] homely garb	[7] sing cheerily
[3] skillfully	[8] shepherds
[4] gloomy	[9] slopes
[5] finger-pipe (of a bag-pipe)	[10] homely
	[11] oxen

Native Scottish music and poetry were for a long time eclipsed by the popularity of English and foreign modes. But they never died out completely; and at the very time when Fergusson wrote his lament (about 1773) they were experiencing a revival which reached its culmination some fifteen years later in the poems and songs of Burns.

[12] drone	[20] crabbed
[13] martial tunes	[21] which
[14] quaver forth	[22] sky-larks
[15] warlike	[23] linnets chirping
[16] Wm. Macgibbon, a musician of Edinburgh.	[24] loitering brooks
	[25] golden
[17] cunning	[26] A popular song.
[18] old woman	[27] once
[19] victory	[28] surpass the might

The waes o' my heart fa' in showers frae my
   e'e,
While my gudeman lies sound by me.

2

Young Jamie lo'ed me weel, and sought me for
   his bride;
But saving a croun he had naething else beside;
To make the croun a pund, young Jamie gaed
   to sea;
And the croun and the pund were baith for me.

3

He hadna been awa' a week but only twa,
When my father brak his arm, and the cow was
   stown[29] awa';
My mother she fell sick,—and my Jamie at the
   sea—
And auld Robin Gray came a-courtin' me.

4

My father couldna work, and my mother
   couldna spin;
I toiled day and night, but their bread 1
   couldna win;
Auld Rob maintained them baith, and wi'
   tears in his e'e
Said, "Jennie, for their sakes, O, marry me!"

5

My heart it said nay; I looked for Jamie back;
But the wind it blew high, and the ship it was
   a wrack;
His ship it was a wrack—why didna Jamie dee?
Or why do I live to cry, Wae's me!

6

My father urged me sair: my mother didna
   speak;
But she looked in my face till my heart was
   like to break:
They gi'ed him my hand, tho' my heart was in
   the sea;
Sae auld Robin Gray he was gudeman to me.

7

I hadna been a wife a week but only four,
When mournfu' as I sat on the stane at the
   door,
I saw my Jamie's wraith,—for I couldna think
   it he,
Till he said, "I'm come hame to marry thee."

8

O sair, sair did we greet,[30] and mickle[31] say
   of a';
We took but ae kiss, and I bade him gang
   awa';

I wish that I were dead, but I'm no like t
   dee;
And why was I born to say, Wae's me!

9

I gang like a ghaist, and I carena to spin;
I daurna think on Jamie, for that wad be a sin
But I'll do my best a gude wife aye to be,
For auld Robin Gray he is kind unto me.

ISOBEL PAGAN (d. 1821)

CA' THE YOWES

1

As I gaed down the water side,
There I met my shepherd lad,
He rowed[1] me sweetly in his plaid,
   And he ca'd me his dearie.

Ca' the yowes[2] to the knowes,[3]
Ca' them where the heather grows,
Ca' them where the burnie rows,[4]
   My bonnie dearie.

2

"Will ye gang down the water side,
And see the waves sae sweetly glide
Beneath the hazels spreading wide?
   The moon it shines fu' clearly."

   Ca' the yowes, etc.

3

"I was bred up at nae sic school,
My shepherd lad, to play the fool;
And a' the day to sit in dool,[5]
   And naebody to see me."

4

"Ye shall get gowns and ribbons meet,
Cauf-leather shoon upon your feet,
And in my arms ye'se[6] lie and sleep,
   And ye shall be my dearie."

5

"If ye'll but stand to what ye've said,
I'se gang wi' you, my shepherd lad,
And ye may row me in your plaid,
   And I shall be your dearie."

6

"While waters wimple to the sea,
While day blinks in the lift[7] sae hie,
Till clay-cauld death shall blin' my e'e,
   Ye aye shall be my dearie."

29 stolen
30 cry
31 much (or possibly "little")

1 rolled
2 ewes
3 knolls
4 brook flows
5 sorrow
6 ye shall
7 sky

LADY NAIRNE (1766—1845)

THE LAND O' THE LEAL

1

I'm wearin' awa', John,
Like snaw-wreaths in thaw, John,
I'm wearin' awa'
   To the land o' the leal.[8]
There's nae sorrow there, John,
There's neither cauld nor care, John,
The day is aye fair
   In the land o' the leal.

2

Our bonnie bairn's there, John,
She was baith gude and fair, John;
And oh! we grudged her sair
   To the land o' the leal.
But sorrow's sel' wears past, John,
And joy's a-coming fast, John,
The joy that's aye to last
   In the land o' the leal.

3

Sae dear that joy was bought, John,
Sae free the battle fought, John,
That sinfu' man e'er brought
   To the land o' the leal.
Oh, dry your glistening e'e, John!
My saul langs to be free, John,
And angels beckon me
   To the land o' the leal.

4

Oh, haud[9] ye leal and true, John!
Your day it's wearin' through, John,
And I'll welcome you
   To the land o' the leal.
Now fare-ye-weel, my ain John,
This warld's cares are vain, John,
We'll meet, and we'll be fain,[10]
   In the land o' the leal.

ROBERT BURNS (1759-1796)

THE COTTER'S SATURDAY NIGHT *

INSCRIBED TO ROBERT AIKEN, ESQ.

Let not Ambition mock their useful toil,
  Their homely joys, and destiny obscure;
Nor Grandeur hear, with a disdainful smile,
  The short and simple annals of the poor.
                GRAY.

1

My lov'd, my honour'd, much respected friend!
No mercenary bard his homage pays;
With honest pride, I scorn each selfish end,
My dearest meed, a friend's esteem and praise;[†]
To you I sing, in simple Scottish lays,
The lowly train in life's sequester'd scene,
The native feelings strong, the guileless ways,
What Aiken in a cottage would have been;
  Ah! tho' his worth unknown, far happier
     there, I ween!

2

November chill blaws loud wi' angry sugh;[1]
The short'ning winter day is near a close;
The miry beasts retreating frae the pleugh;
The black'ning trains o' craws to their repose:
The toil-worn Cotter[2] frae his labour goes,—
This night his weekly moil[3] is at an end,—
Collects his spades, his mattocks, and his hoes,
Hoping the morn in ease and rest to spend,
  And weary, o'er the moor, his course does
     hameward bend.

3

At length his lonely cot appears in view,
Beneath the shelter of an aged tree;
Th' expectant wee-things, toddlin, stacher[4]
   through
To meet their dad, wi' flichterin[5] noise an'
   glee.
His wee bit ingle,[6] blinkin bonilie,
His clean hearth-stane, his thrifty wifie's smile,
The lisping infant prattling on his knee,
Does a' his weary kiaugh[7] and care beguile,
  An' makes him quite forget his labour an'
     his toil.

4

Belyve,[8] the elder bairns come drappin in,
At service out, amang the farmers roun';
Some ca'[9] the pleugh, some herd, some tentie[10]
   rin

---

8 loyal, faithful   10 happy
  hold

1 sough   6 fire-place or fire
2 cottager   7 anxiety
3 labor   8 by and by
4 stagger   9 drive
5 fluttering   10 heedful

---

* Of this poem, Gilbert Burns, Robert's brother, writes: "Robert had frequently remarked to me that he thought there was something peculiarly venerable in the phrase, 'Let us worship God,' used by a decent, sober head of a family, introducing family worship. To this sentiment of the author, the world is indebted for *The Cotter's Saturday Night*. The cotter is an exact copy of my father, in his manners, his family devotion, and exhortations; yet the other parts of the description do not apply to our family. None of us were 'at service out among the farmers roun'. Instead of our depositing our 'sair-won penny-fee' with our parents, my father laboured hard, and lived with the most rigid economy, that he might be able to keep his children at home." Mr. J. L. Robertson, commenting on the fact that less than half the poem is in English, says: "An unusually elevated or serious train of thought in the mind of a Scottish peasant seems to demand for its expression the use of a speech which one may describe as Sabbath Scotch."

† Aiken was not only a patron, but a genuine friend, of Burns.

A cannie[11] errand to a neibor town:
Their eldest hope, their Jenny, woman-grown,
In youthfu' bloom, love sparkling in her e'e,
Comes hame, perhaps to shew a braw[12] new
    gown,
Or deposite her sair-won penny-fee,
    To help her parents dear, if they in hard-
        ship be.

5

With joy unfeign'd, brothers and sisters meet,
And each for other's weelfare kindly spiers:[13]
The social hours, swift-wing'd, unnotic'd fleet;
Each tells the uncos[14] that he sees or hears.
The parents, partial, eye their hopeful years;
Anticipation forward points the view;
The mother, wi' her needle an' her sheers,
Gars[15] auld claes look amaist as weel's the
    new;
    The father mixes a' wi' admonition due.

6

Their master's an' their mistress's command
The younkers a' are warnèd to obey;
An' mind their labours wi' an eydent[16] hand,
An' ne'er, tho' out o' sight, to jauk or play;
"An' O! be sure to fear the Lord alway,
An' mind your duty, duly, morn an' night;
Lest in temptation's path ye gang astray,
Implore His counsel and assisting might:
    They never sought in vain that sought the
        Lord aright!"

7

But hark! a rap comes gently to the door;
Jenny, wha kens the meaning o' the same,
Tells how a neibor lad cam o'er the moor,
To do some errands, and convoy her hame.
The wily mother sees the conscious flame
Sparkle in Jenny's e'e, and flush her cheek;
Wi' heart-struck, anxious care, inquires his
    name,
While Jenny hafflins[17] is afraid to speak;
    Weel pleas'd the mother hears it's nae wild
        worthless rake.

Wi' kindly welcome Jenny brings him ben,[18]
A strappin youth; he takes the mother's eye;
Blythe Jenny sees the visit's no ill taen;
The father cracks[19] of horses, pleughs, and kye.
The youngster's artless heart o'erflows wi' joy,
But blate[20] and laithfu',[21] scarce can weel
    behave;
The mother, wi' a woman's wiles, can spy

What makes the youth sae bashfu' and sa
    grave,
    Weel-pleas'd to think her bairn's respecte
        like the lave.[22]

9

O happy love! where love like this is found!
O heart-felt raptures! bliss beyond compare!
I've pacèd much this weary, mortal round,
And sage experience bids me this declare,—
"If Heaven a draught of heavenly pleasur
    spare,
One cordial in this melancholy vale,
'Tis when a youthful, loving, modest pair
In other's arms breathe out the tender tale,
    Beneath the milk-white thorn that scents th
        ev'ning gale.''

10

Is there, in human form, that bears a heart,
A wretch! a villain! lost to love and truth!
That can, with studied, sly, ensnaring art,
Betray sweet Jenny's unsuspecting youth?
Curse on his perjur'd arts! dissembling smooth
Are honour, virtue, conscience, all exil'd?
Is there no pity, no relenting ruth,
Points to the parents fondling o'er their child
    Then paints the ruin'd maid, and their di
        traction wild?

11

But now the supper crowns their simple boar
The halesome parritch, chief of Scotia's foo
The sowpe[1] their only hawkie[2] does afford,
That yont[3] the hallan[4] snugly chows her coo
The dame brings forth, in complimental moo
To grace the lad, her weel-hain'd kebbuck
    fell;[6]
An' aft he's prest, an' aft he ca's it guid:
The frugal wifie, garrulous, will tell
    How 'twas a towmond auld, sin' lint was
        the bell.[7]

12

The cheerfu' supper done, wi' serious face,
They round the ingle form a circle wide;
The sire turns o'er, with patriarchal grace
The big ha's[8] Bible, ance his father's pride:
His bonnet rev'rently is laid aside,
His lyart haffets[9] wearing thin and bare;
Those strains that once did sweet in Zion glid
He wales[10] a portion with judicious care;

22 rest

---

11 careful
12 handsome
13 asks
14 strange things
15 makes
16 diligent

17 partly
18 into the parlor
19 talks
20 shamefaced
21 bashful

1 sup. portion (of milk)
2 cow
3 beyond
4 partition
5 well saved cheese
6 biting
7 a twelve-month old, since flax was in flower

8 hall (In ancier
    usage, the "hal
    was the general a
    sembly room of t
    house, as oppos
    to the privat
    "bowers.")
9 grey temples
10 chooses

And ''Let us worship God!'' he says with
  solemn air.

13

They chant their artless notes in simple guise,
They tune their hearts, by far the noblest aim;
Perhaps 'Dundee's' wild-warbling measures
  rise,
Or plaintive 'Martyrs,' worthy of the name;
Or noble 'Elgin' beets[11] the heaven-ward flame,
The sweetest far of Scotia's holy lays:
Compar'd with these, Italian trills are tame:
The tickl'd ears no heart-felt raptures raise;
  Nae unison hae they with our Creator's
  praise.

14

The priest-like father reads the sacred page,
How Abram was the friend of God on high;
Or Moses bade eternal warfare wage
With Amalek's ungracious progeny;
Or how the royal bard[12] did groaning lie
Beneath the stroke of Heaven's avenging ire;
Or Job's pathetic plaint, and wailing cry;
Or rapt Isaiah's wild, seraphic fire;
  Or other holy seers that tune the sacred lyre.

15

Perhaps the Christian volume is the theme,
How guiltless blood for guilty man was shed;
How He, who bore in Heav'n the second name,
Had not on earth whereon to lay His head:
How His first followers and servants sped;
The precepts sage they wrote to many a land:
How he,[13] who lone in Patmos banishèd,
Saw in the sun a mighty angel stand,
  And heard great Bab'lon's doom pronounc'd
  by Heav'n's command.

16

Then kneeling down to Heaven's Eternal King,
The saint, the father, and the husband prays:
Hope ''springs exulting on triumphant wing,''[14]
That thus they all shall meet in future days,
There ever bask in uncreated rays,
No more to sigh, or shed the bitter tear,
Together hymning their Creator's praise,
In such society, yet still more dear,
  While circling Time moves round in an eter-
  nal sphere.

17

Compar'd with this, how poor Religion's pride
In all the pomp of method and of art,
When men display to congregations wide
Devotion's ev'ry grace, except the heart!

The Pow'r, incens'd, the pageant will desert,
The pompous strain, the sacerdotal stole;
But haply, in some cottage far apart,
May hear, well-pleas'd, the language of the
  soul;
  And in His Book of Life the inmates poor
  enrol.

18

Then homeward all take off their sev'ral way;
The youngling cottagers retire to rest;
The parent-pair their secret homage pay,
And proffer up to Heav'n the warm request,
That He who stills the raven's clam'rous nest,
And decks the lily fair in flow'ry pride,
Would, in the way His wisdom sees the best,
For them and for their little ones provide;
  But chiefly, in their hearts with grace divine
  preside.

19

From scenes like these old Scotia's grandeur
  springs,
That makes her lov'd at home, rever'd abroad:
Princes and lords are but the breath of kings,
''An honest man's the noblest work of
  God;''[15]
And certes, in fair Virtue's heavenly road,
The cottage leaves the palace far behind;
What is a lordling's pomp? a cumbrous load,
Disguising oft the wretch of human kind,
  Studied in arts of hell, in wickedness refin'd!

20

O Scotia! my dear, my native soil!
For whom my warmest wish to Heaven is sent,
Long may thy hardy sons of rustic toil
Be blest with health, and peace, and sweet con-
  tent!
And oh! may Heaven their simple lives prevent
From luxury's contagion, weak and vile!
Then, howe'er crowns and coronets be rent,
A virtuous populace may rise the while,
  And stand a wall of fire around their much-
  lov'd isle.

21

O Thou! who pour'd the patriotic tide
That stream'd thro' Wallace's undaunted heart,
Who dar'd to nobly stem tyrannic pride,
Or nobly die, the second glorious part,—
(The patriot's God peculiarly thou art,
His friend, inspirer, guardian, and reward!)
O never, never Scotia's realm desert,
But still the patriot, and the patriot-bard,
  In bright succession raise, her ornament and
  guard!

---

11 adds fuel to, fans   14 Pope, *Windsor For-*
12 David   *est*, 112.
13 John

15 Pope, *Essay on Man*, iv. 248.

ADDRESS TO THE DEIL *

"O Prince! O chief of many thronéd pow'rs
That led th' embattled seraphim to war."
MILTON.

1

O THOU! whatever title suit thee—
Auld Hornie, Satan, Nick, or Clootie[1]—
Wha in yon cavern grim an' sootie,
    Clos'd under hatches,
Spairges† about the brunstane[2] cootie,
    To scaud[3] poor wretches!

2

Hear me, auld Hangie,[4] for a wee,
An' let poor damnèd bodies be;
I'm sure sma' pleasure it can gie,
    E'en to a deil,
To skelp[5] an' scaud poor dogs like me,
    An' hear us squeel!

3

Great is thy pow'r an' great thy fame;
Far kenn'd an' noted is thy name;
An' tho' yon lowin[6] heugh's[7] thy hame,
    Thou travels far;
An' faith! thou's neither lag[8] nor lame,
    Nor blate[9] nor scaur.[10]

4

Whyles,[11] rangin like a roarin lion,
For prey a' holes and corners tryin;
Whyles, on the strong-wing'd tempest flyin,
    Tirlin[12] the kirks;
Whyles, in the human bosom pryin,
    Unseen thou lurks.

5

I've heard my rev'rend graunie say,
In lanely[13] glens ye like to stray;

1 From *cloot*, one of the
    divisions of a clo-
    ven hoof.
2 brimstone
3 scald
4 hangman
5 slap
6 blazing

7 pit
8 slow
9 bashful
10 timid
11 sometimes
12 unroofing
13 lonely

* "The humorous satire of the piece is at the expense of popular Scottish Calvinism."—J L. Robertson.
† "*Spairges* is the best Scots word in its place I ever met with. The deil is not standing flinging the liquid brimstone on his friends with a ladle, but we see him standing at a large boiling vat, with something like a golf-bat, striking the liquid this way and that way aslant, with all his might, making it fly through the whole apartment, while the inmates are winking and holding up their arms to defend their faces." (James Hogg.) This interpretation admirably fits the word *spairges* (Latin, *spargere*, to sprinkle; English, *asperge, asperse*); if it is correct, the word *cootie*, which properly means a wooden kitchen dish of any size from a ladle to a small tub, is used rather boldly for the contents of the cootie.

Or where auld ruin'd castles gray
    Nod to the moon,
Ye fright the nightly wand'rer's way
    Wi' eldritch[14] croon.[15]

6

When twilight did my graunie summon
To say her pray'rs, douce[16] honest woman!
Aft yont[17] the dyke she's heard you bummin,[1]
    Wi' eerie[14] drone;
Or, rustlin, thro' the boortrees[19] comin,
    Wi' heavy groan.

7

Ae dreary, windy, winter night,
The stars shot down wi' sklentin[20] light,
Wi' you mysel I gat a fright
    Ayont[17] the lough;[21]
Ye like a rash-buss[22] stood in sight,
    Wi' waving sough.

8

The cudgel in my nieve[23] did shake,
Each bristl'd hair stood like a stake,
When wi' an eldritch, stoor[24] "Quaick, quaick,"
    Amang the springs,
Awa ye squatter'd[25] like a drake,
    On whistlin wings.

9

Let warlocks[26] grim, an' wither'd hags,
Tell how wi' you, on ragweed nags,
They skim the muirs[27] an' dizzy crags,
    Wi' wicked speed;
And in kirk-yards renew their leagues,
    Owre howket[28] dead.

10

Thence, countra wives wi' toil and pain
May plunge an' plunge the kirn[29] in vain;
For oh! the yellow treasure's ta'en
    By witchin skill;
An' dawtet,[30] twal[31]-pint hawkie's[32] gaen
    As yell's[33] the bill.[34]

11

Thence, mystic knots mak great abuse
On young guidmen, fond, keen, an' crouse;[35]

14 ghostly
15 moan
16 grave
17 beyond
18 buzzing
19 elders
20 slanting
21 lake
22 bush of rushes
23 fist
24 harsh

25 fluttered
26 wizards
27 moors
28 dug up
29 churn
30 doted on, dear
31 twelve
32 cow
33 dry as
34 bull
35 spirited

When the best wark-lume i' the house,
    By cantrip[1] wit,
Is instant made no worth a louse,
    Just at the bit.[2]

12

When thowes dissolve the snawy hoord,
An' float the jinglin icy boord,
Then water-kelpies[3] haunt the foord,
    By your direction,
An' 'nighted trav'lers are allur'd
    To their destruction.

13

And aft your moss-traversing spunkies[4]
Decoy the wight that late an' drunk is:
The bleezin,[5] curst, mischievous monkies
    Delude his eyes,
Till in some miry slough he sunk is,
    Ne'er mair to rise.

14

When masons' mystic word an' grip
In storms an' tempests raise you up,
Some cock or cat your rage maun stop,
    Or, strange to tell!
The youngest brither ye wad whip
    Aff straught to hell.

15

Lang syne,[6] in Eden's bonie* yard,
When youthfu' lovers first were pair'd,
An' all the soul of love they shar'd,
    The raptur'd hour,
Sweet on the fragrant flow'ry swaird,
    In shady bow'r;

16

Then you, ye auld snick[7]-drawing dog!
Ye cam to Paradise incog,
An' play'd on man a cursèd brogue,[8]
    (Black be your fa'![9])
An' gied the infant warld a shog,[10]
    'Maist ruin'd a'.

17

D'ye mind that day when, in a bizz,[11]
Wi' reeket duds, an' reestet gizz,[12]
Ye did present your smoutie phiz
    'Mang better folk,

An' sklented on the man of Uz[1]
    Your spitefu' joke?

18

An' how ye gat him i' your thrall,
An' brak him out o' house an hal',
While scabs and blotches did him gall,
    Wi' bitter claw;
An' lows'd[2] his ill-tongu'd wicked scaul',[3]
    Was warst ava?

19

But a' your doings to rehearse,
Your wily snares an' fechtin[4] fierce,
Sin' that day Michael did you pierce,[5]
    Down to this time,
Wad ding a Lallan[6] tongue, or Erse,[7]
    In prose or rhyme.

20

An' now, auld Cloots,[8] I ken ye're thinkin,
A certain bardie's rantin, drinkin,
Some luckless hour will send him linkin[9]
    To your black pit;
But faith! he'll turn a corner jinkin,[10]
    An' cheat you yet.

21

But fare you weel, auld Nickie-ben!
O wad ye tak a thought an' men'!
Ye aiblins[11] might—I dinna ken—
    Still hae a stake:
I'm wae[12] to think upo' yon den,
    Ev'n for your sake!

ADDRESS TO THE UNCO GUID†
OR THE RIGIDLY RIGHTEOUS

My Son, these maxims make a rule,
    An' lump them aye thegither;
The *Rigid Righteous* is a fool,
    The *Rigid Wise* anither:
The cleanest corn that e'er was dight[13]
    May hae some pyles o' caff[14] in;
So ne'er a fellow-creature slight
    For random fits o' daffin.[15]
       SOLOMON.—Eccles. vii, 16.

1

O ye wha are sae guid yoursel',
    Sae pious and sae holy,

1 magic	8 trick
2 nick of time	9 lot
3 spirits	10 shock
4 will-o'-the-wisps	11 bustle
5 blazing	12 smoked garments and
6 since	singed face
7 latch	

1 Job	9 tripping
2 loosed	10 dodging
3 scold	11 perhaps
4 fighting	12 sad
5 *Par. Lost* vi, 325	13 dressed, winnowed
6 baffle a lowland	14 grains of chaff
7 Gaelic	15 merriment
8 hoofs (Satan)	

* This spelling represents the broad Scotch pronunciation rather better than the spelling *bonny*.

† The word *unco* (for *uncouth*, "unknown") is used both as an adjective, meaning "unusual, strange," and as an adverb, meaning "extremely, wonderfully."

Ye've nought to do but mark and tell
    Your neibours' fauts and folly!
Whase life is like a weel-gaun[1] mill,
    Supplied wi' store o' water;
The heapet happer's ebbing still,
    An' still the clap[2] plays clatter,—

2

Hear me, ye venerable core,[3]
    As counsel for poor mortals
That frequent pass douce[4] Wisdom's door
    For glaiket[5] Folly's portals:
I, for their thoughtless, careless sakes,
    Would here propone[6] defences—
Their donsie[7] tricks, their black mistakes,
    Their failings and mischances.

3

Ye see your state wi' theirs compar'd,
    And shudder at the niffer;[8]
But cast a moment's fair regard,
    What makes the mighty differ?[9]
Discount what scant occasion gave,
    That purity ye pride in;
And (what's aft mair than a' the lave)
    Your better art o' hidin.

4

Think, when your castigated pulse
    Gies now and then a wallop,
What ragings must his veins convulse
    That still eternal gallop!
Wi' wind and tide, fair i' your tail,
    Right on ye scud your sea-way;
But in the teeth o' baith to sail,
    It makes an unco lee-way.

5

See Social Life and Glee sit down,
    All joyous and unthinking,
Till, quite transmugrified,[10] they're grown
    Debauchery and Drinking:
O would they stay to calculate
    Th' eternal consequences;
Or—your more dreaded hell to state—
    Damnation of expenses! . . . .

7

Then gently scan your brother man,
    Still gentler sister woman;
Tho' they may gang a kennin[11] wrang,
    To step aside is human;
One point must still be greatly dark,—
    The moving *Why* they do it;
And just as lamely can ye mark,
    How far perhaps they rue it.

8

Who made the heart, 'tis He alone
    Decidedly can try us;
He knows each chord, its various tone,
    Each spring, its various bias:
Then at the balance let's be mute,
    We never can adjust it;
What's *done* we partly may compute,
    But know not what's *resisted*.

TO A MOUSE

ON TURNING HER UP IN HER NEST WITH THE
PLOUGH, NOVEMBER, 1785

1

Wee, sleekit,[1] cowrin, tim'rous beastie,
O, what a panic's in thy breastie!
Thou need na start awa sae hasty
        Wi' bickering[2] brattle![3]
I wad be laith to rin an' chase thee
        Wi' murd'rin pattle![4]

2

I'm truly sorry man's dominion
Has broken nature's social union,
An' justifies that ill opinion
        Which makes thee startle
At me, thy poor, earth-born companion,
        An' fellow-mortal!

3

I doubt na, whyles,[5] but thou may thieve;
What then? poor beastie, thou maun live!
A daimen[6] icker[7] in a thrave[8]
        'S a sma' request;
I'll get a blessin wi' the lave,[9]
        An' never miss't!

4

Thy wee bit housie, too, in ruin!
It's silly wa's the win's are strewin!
An' naething, now, to big[10] a new ane,
        O' foggage[11] green!
An' bleak December's winds ensuin,
        Baith snell[12] an' keen!

5

Thou saw the fields laid bare and waste,
An' weary winter comin fast,
An' cozie here, beneath the blast,
        Thou thought to dwell,
Till crash! the cruel coulter[13] past
        Out thro' thy cell.

1 well-going   7 mischievous
2 clapper   8 exchange
3 corps, company   9 difference
4 grave   10 transformed
5 giddy   11 a little
6 propose

1 sleek   8 twenty-four sheaves
2 hastening   9 rest
3 scamper   10 build
4 plough-staff, or scraper 11 herbage
5 sometimes   12 sharp
6 occasional   13 plough
7 ear of corn

6

That wee bit heap o' leaves an' stibble
Has cost thee mony a weary nibble!
Now thou's turn'd out, for a' thy trouble,
        But[1] house or hald,[2]
To thole[3] the winter's sleety dribble
        An' cranreuch[4] cauld!

7

But, Mousie, thou art no thy lane[5]
In proving foresight may be vain;
The best laid schemes o' mice an' men
        Gang aft a-gley,[6]
An' lea'e us nought but grief an' pain,
        For promis'd joy.

8

Still thou art blest, compar'd wi' me;
The present only toucheth thee:
But och! I backward cast my e'e
        On prospects drear!
An' forward, tho' I canna see,
        I guess an' fear!

TO A LOUSE

ON SEEING ONE ON A LADY'S BONNET AT CHURCH

1

Ha! whaur ye gaun, ye crowlin[7] ferlie?[8]
Your impudence protects you sairly;[9]
I canna say but ye strunt[10] rarely,
        Owre gauze and lace;
Tho', faith! I fear ye dine but sparely
        On sic a place.

2

Ye ugly, creepin, blastit[11] wonner,[12]
Detested, shunn'd by saunt an' sinner,
How daur ye set your fit[13] upon her—
        Sae fine a lady?
Gae somewhere else and seek your dinner
        On some poor body.

3

Swith![14] in some beggar's haffet[15] squattle;[16]
There ye may creep, and sprawl, and sprattle.[17]
Wi' ither kindred, jumping cattle,
        In shoals and nations;
Whaur horn[18] nor bane[19] ne'er daur unsettle
        Your thick plantations.

4

Now haud[20] you there, ye're out o' sight,
Below the fatt'rels,[21] snug and tight;
Na, faith ye yet! ye'll no be right
        Till ye've got on it—
The vera tapmost, tow'rin height
        O' Miss's bonnet.

5

My sooth![22] right bauld ye set your nose out,
As plump an' grey as ony grozet[23]
O for some rank, mercurial rozet,[24]
        Or fell, red smeddum,[25]
I'd gie you sic a hearty dose o't,
        Wad dress your droddum.[26]

6

I wad na been surpris'd to spy
You on an auld wife's flainen toy;[27]
Or aiblins some bit duddie[28] boy,
        On's wyliecoat;[29]
But Miss's fine Lunardi![30] fye!
        How daur ye do't?

7

O Jenny, dinna toss your head,
An' set your beauties a' abread!
Ye little ken what cursed speed
        The blastie's makin!
Thae winks an' finger-ends, I dread,
        Are notice takin!

8

O wad some Power the giftie gie us
To see oursels as ithers see us!
It wad frae mony a blunder free us,
        An' foolish notion:
What airs in dress an' gait wad lea'e us,
        An' ev'n devotion!

TO A MOUNTAIN DAISY

ON TURNING ONE DOWN WITH THE PLOUGH, IN APRIL, 1786

Wee, modest, crimson-tippèd flow'r,
Thou's met me in an evil hour;
For I maun[31] crush amang the stoure[32]
        Thy slender stem:
To spare thee now is past my pow'r,
        Thou bonie gem.

1 without	11 blasted, "confounded"
2 abode	12 marvel
3 endure	13 foot
4 hoar-frost	14 quick
5 alone	15 temple
6 awry	16 sprawl
7 crawling	17 struggle
8 wonder	18 horn-comb
9 greatly	19 poison
10 strut	
20 hold	27 flannel cap
21 ribbon-ends	28 ragged
22 truth	29 flannel vest
23 gooseberry	30 A bonnet named for
24 rosin	an aeronaut.
25 powder	31 must
26 back	32 flying dust

2

Alas! it's no thy neibor sweet,
The bonie lark, companion meet,
Bending thee 'mang the dewy weet
    Wi' spreckl'd breast,
When upward-springing, blythe, to greet
    The purpling east.

3

Cauld blew the bitter-biting north
Upon thy early, humble birth;
Yet cheerfully thou glinted forth
    Amid the storm,
Scarce rear'd above the parent-earth
    Thy tender form.

4

The flaunting flow'rs our gardens yield,
High shelt'ring woods an' wa's[1] maun shield;
But thou, beneath the random bield[2]
    O' clod or stane,
Adorns the histie[3] stibble field
    Unseen, alane.

5

There, in thy scanty mantle clad,
Thy snawie bosom sun-ward spread,
Thou lifts thy unassuming head
    In humble guise;
But now the share uptears thy bed,
    And low thou lies!

6

Such is the fate of artless maid,
Sweet flow'ret of the rural shade!
By love's simplicity betray'd,
    And guileless trust;
Till she, like thee, all soil'd, is laid
    Low i' the dust.

7

Such is the fate of simple bard,
On life's rough ocean luckless starr'd!
Unskilful he to note the card[4]
    Of prudent lore,
Till billows rage, and gales blow hard,
    And whelm him o'er!

8

Such fate to suffering Worth is giv'n,
Who long with wants and woes has striv'n,
By human pride or cunning driv'n
    To mis'ry's brink;
Till wrench'd of ev'ry stay but Heav'n,
    He ruin'd sink!

1 walls
2 shelter
3 barren
4 compass-card

9

Ev'n thou who mourn'st the Daisy's fate,
That fate is thine—no distant date;
Stern Ruin's plough-share drives elate,
    Full on thy bloom,
Till crush'd beneath the furrow's weight
    Shall be thy doom!

TAM O' SHANTER

A TALE

"Of Brownyis and of Bogillis full is this Buke."
         —GAWIN DOUGLAS.

When chapman[1] billies[2] leave the street,
And drouthy[3] neibors neibors meet,
As market-days are wearing late,
And folk begin to tak the gate;
While we sit bousin[4] at the nappy,[5]   5
An' getting fou[6] and unco[7] happy,
We think na on the lang Scots miles,
The mosses, waters, slaps,[8] and stiles,
That lie between us and our hame,
Whare sits our sulky, sullen dame,   10
Gathering her brows like gathering storm,
Nursing her wrath to keep it warm.

    This truth fand[9] honest Tam o' Shanter,
As he frae Ayr ae night did canter:
(Auld Ayr, wham ne'er a town surpasses,   15
For honest men and bonie lasses).

    O Tam! had'st thou but been sae wise,
As taen thy ain wife Kate's advice!
She tauld thee weel thou was a skellum,[10]
A bletherin,[11] blusterin, drunken blellum;[12]   20
That frae November till October,
Ae market-day thou was na sober;
That ilka melder[13] wi' the miller,
Thou sat as lang as thou had siller;
That ev'ry naig was ca'd[14] a shoe on,   25
The smith and thee gat roarin fou on;
That at the Lord's house, ev'n on Sunday,
Thou drank wi' Kirkton Jean till Monday.
She prophesied that, late or soon,
Thou would be found, deep drown'd in Doon,   30
Or catch'd wi' warlocks[15] in the mirk,[16]
By Alloway's auld, haunted kirk.

    Ah, gentle dames! it gars me greet,[17]
To think how mony counsels sweet,

1 pedlar
2 fellows
3 thirsty
4 drinking
5 ale
6 full
7 very
8 gates
9 found
10 rascal
11 idly-talking
12 babbler
13 every grinding of corn
14 driven
15 wizards
16 dark
17 make me weep

How mony lengthen'd', sage advices,   35
The husband frae the wife despises!

But to our tale:—Ae market night,
Tam had got planted unco right,
Fast by an ingle, bleezin finely,
Wi' reamin swats[1] that drank divinely;   40
And at his elbow, Souter[2] Johnie,
His ancient, trusty, drouthy crony:
Tam lo'ed him like a vera brither.
They had been fou for weeks thegither.
The night drave on wi' sangs and clatter;   45
And ay the ale was growing better:
The landlady and Tam grew gracious,
Wi' secret favours, sweet and precious:
The souter tauld his queerest stories;
The landlord's laugh was ready chorus;   50
The storm without might rair and rustle,
Tam did na mind the storm a whistle.

Care, mad to see a man sae happy,
E'en drown'd himsel amang the nappy:
As bees flee hame wi' lades o' treasure,   55
The minutes wing'd their way wi' pleasure;
Kings may be blest, but Tam was glorious,
O'er a' the ills o' life victorious!

But pleasures are like poppies spread,
You seize the flow'r, its bloom is shed;   60
Or like the snow falls[3] in the river,
A moment white—then melts for ever;
Or like the borealis race,
That flit ere you can point their place;
Or like the rainbow's lovely form   65
Evanishing amid the storm.—
Nae man can tether time or tide:
The hour approaches Tam maun ride;
That hour, o' night's black arch the key-stane,
That dreary hour he mounts his beast in;   70
And sic a night he taks the road in,
As ne'er poor sinner was abroad in.

The wind blew as 'twad blawn its last;
The rattling show'rs rose on the blast;
The speedy gleams the darkness swallow'd;   75
Loud, deep, and lang the thunder bellow'd:
That night, a child might understand,
The Deil had business on his hand.

Weel-mounted on his grey mare, Meg,
A better never lifted leg,   80
Tam skelpit[4] on thro' dub[5] and mire,
Despising wind, and rain, and fire;
Whiles holding fast his gude blue bonnet,
Whiles crooning o'er some auld Scots sonnet,
Whiles glow'rin round wi' prudent cares,   85

Lest bogles catch him unawares.
Kirk-Alloway was drawing nigh,
Where ghaists and houlets[1] nightly cry.

By this time he was cross the ford,
Whare in the snaw the chapman smoor'd;[2]   90
And past the birks[3] and meikle[4] stane,
Whare drucken Charlie brak's neck-bane;
And thro' the whins,[5] and by the cairn,[6]
Whare hunters fand the murder'd bairn;
And near the thorn, aboon the well,   95
Whare Mungo's mither hang'd hersel.
Before him Doon pours all his floods;
The doubling storm roars thro' the woods,
The lightnings flash from pole to pole,
Near and more near the thunders roll;   100
When, glimmering thro' the groaning trees,
Kirk-Alloway seem'd in a bleeze,[7]
Thro' ilka bore[8] the beams were glancing,
And loud resounded mirth and dancing.

Inspiring bold John Barleycorn!   105
What dangers thou canst make us scorn!
Wi' tippenny,[9] we fear nae evil;
Wi' usquabae,[10] we'll face the devil!
The swats sae ream'd in Tammie's noddle,
Fair play, he car'd na deils a boddle,[11]   110
But Maggie stood, right sair astonish'd,
Till, by the heel and hand admonish'd,
She ventur'd forward on the light;
And, wow! Tam saw an unco[12] sight!

Warlocks and witches in a dance;   115
Nae cotillon brent[13] new frae France,
But hornpipes, jigs, strathspeys, and reels[14]
Put life and mettle in their heels.
A winnock-bunker[15] in the east,
There sat Auld Nick, in shape o' beast;   120
A towzie tyke,[16] black, grim, and large,
To gie them music was his charge;
He screw'd the pipes and gart them skirl,[17]
Till roof and rafters a' did dirl.[18]
Coffins stood round, like open presses,   125
That shaw'd the dead in their last dresses;
And by some devilish cantraip[19] sleight
Each in its cauld hand held a light,
By which heroic Tam was able
To note upon the haly table   130
A murderer's banes in gibbet-airns;
Twa span-lang, wee, unchristened bairns;
A thief, new-cutted frae the rape,[20]

Wi' his last gasp his gab[1] did gape;
Five tomahawks, wi' blude red-rusted: 135
Five scymitars, wi' murder crusted;
A garter, which a babe had strangled:
A knife, a father's throat had mangled,
Whom his ain son o' life bereft,
The grey hairs yet stack to the heft;   140
Wi' mair o' horrible and awfu',
Which ev'n to name wad be unlawfu'.

As Tammie glowr'd,[2] amaz'd, and curious,
The mirth and fun grew fast and furious;
The piper loud and louder blew,   145
The dancers quick and quicker flew;
They reel'd, they set, they cross'd, they cleekit,[3]
Till ilka carlin[4] swat[5] and reekit,[6]
And coost[7] her duddies[8] to the wark,[9]
And linket[10] at it in her sark![11]   150

Now, Tam, O Tam; had thae been queans,[12]
A' plump and strapping in their teens!
Their sarks, instead o' creeshie[13] flannen,
Been snaw-white seventeen hunder linen!*
Thir[14] breeks o' mine, my only pair,   155
That ance were plush, o' gude blue hair,
I wad hae gien them aff my hurdies,[15]
For ae blink o' the bonie burdies![16]
But wither'd beldams, auld and droll,
Rigwoodie[17] hags wad spean[18] a foal,   160
Lowping[19] an' flinging on a crummock,[20]
I wonder didna turn thy stomach.

But Tam ken'd what was what fu' brawlie:[21]
There was ae winsome wench and walie[22]
That night enlisted in the core[23]   165
(Lang after ken'd on Carrick shore:
For mony a beast to dead she shot,
And perish'd mony a bonie boat,
And shook baith meikle corn and bear,[24]
And kept the country-side in fear);   170
Her cutty sark, o' Paisley harn,[25]
That while a lassie she had worn,
In longitude tho' sorely scanty,
It was her best, and she was vauntie.[26]

Ah! little ken'd thy reverend grannie,   175
That sark she coft[1] for her wee Nannie,
Wi' twa pund Scots† ('twas a' her riches),
Wad ever grac'd a dance of witches!

But here my Muse her wing maun cow'r,
Sic flights are far beyond her pow'r;   180
To sing how Nannie lap and flang
(A souple jade she was and strang),
And how Tam stood, like one bewitch'd,
And thought his very een[2] enrich'd:
Even Satan glowr'd, and fidg'd[3] fu' fain,   185
And hotch'd[4] and blew wi' might and main:
Till first ae caper, syne[5] anither,
Tam tint[6] his reason a' thegither,
And roars out, "Weel done, Cutty-sark!"
And in an instant all was dark: 190
And scarcely had he Maggie rallied,
When out the hellish legion sallied.

As bees bizz out wi' angry fyke,[7]
When plundering herds assail their byke;[8]
As open pussie's[9] mortal foes,   195
When, pop! she starts before their nose;
As eager runs the market-crowd,
When "Catch the thief!" resounds aloud;
So Maggie runs, the witches follow,
Wi' mony an eldritch[10] skriech and hollo.   200

Ah, Tam! Ah, Tam! thou'll get thy fairin![11]
In hell they'll roast thee like a herrin!
In vain thy Kate awaits thy comin!
Kate soon will be a woefu' woman!
Now, do thy speedy utmost, Meg,   205
And win the key-stane of the brig;[12]
There, at them thou thy tail may toss,
A running stream they dare na cross.
But ere the key-stane she could make,
The fient[13] a tail she had to shake!   210
For Nannie, far before the rest,
Hard upon noble Maggie prest,
And flew at Tam wi' furious ettle;[14]
But little wist she Maggie's mettle—
Ae spring brought aff her master hale,   215
But left behind her ain grey tail:
The carlin claught her by the rump,
And left poor Maggie scarce a stump.

Now, wha this tale o' truth shall read,
Ilk man, and mother's son, take heed: 220
Whene'er to drink you are inclin'd,
Or cutty-sarks run in your mind,

1 mouth	15 hips
2 stared	16 lasses
3 joined hands	17 bony
4 old woman	18 that would wean (by disgust)
5 sweated	
6 steamed	19 leaping
7 cast off	20 staff
8 clothes	21 well
9 work	22 goodly
10 tripped	23 company
11 smock	24 barley
12 girls	25 short shirt, of Paisley yarn
13 greasy	
14 these	26 proud

* Very fine linen, woven in a reed of 1700 divisions, or 46 to the inch.

1 bought	8 hive
2 eyes	9 the hare's
3 fidgeted	10 ghostly
4 squirmed	11 reward
5 then	12 bridge
6 lost	13 devil
7 fuss	14 intent

† A pound Scots is one shilling, eight pence—about forty cents.

Think, ye may buy the joys owre dear;
Remember Tam o' Shanter's mare.

GREEN GROW THE RASHES

There's nought but care on ev'ry han',
   In ev'ry hour that passes, O:
What signifies the life o' man,
   An 'twere na for the lasses, O.

Chor.—Green grow the rashes,[1] O;
     Green grow the rashes, O;
     The sweetest hours that e'er I spend
     Are spent among the lasses, O.

The war'ly[2] race may riches chase,
   An' riches still may fly them, O;
An' tho' at last they catch them fast,
   Their hearts can ne'er enjoy them, O.
                Green grow, &c.

But gie me a cannie[3] hour at e'en,
   My arms about my dearie, O;
An' war'ly cares, an' war'ly men,
   May a' gae tapsalteerie,[4] O!
                Green grow, &c.

For you sae douce,[5] ye sneer at this;
   Ye're nought but senseless asses, O:
The wisest man the warl' e'er saw,
   He dearly lov'd the lasses, O.
                Green grow, &c.

Auld Nature swears, the lovely dears
   Her noblest work she classes, O:
Her prentice han' she try'd on man,
   An' then she made the lasses, O.
                Green grow, &c.

AULD LANG SYNE

Should auld acquaintance be forgot,
   And never brought to min'?
Should auld acquaintance be forgot
   And auld lang syne![6]

Chorus—For auld lang syne, my dear,
     For auld lang syne,
     We'll tak a cup o' kindness yet
     For auld lang syne.

And surely ye'll be your pint-stowp![7]
   And surely I'll be mine!
And we'll tak a cup o' kindness yet,
   For auld lang syne.
                For auld, &c.

We twa hae run about the braes,[1]
   And pu'd the gowans[2] fine;
But we've wander'd mony a weary fit,[3]
   Sin' auld lang syne.
                For auld, &c.

We twa hae paidl'd i' the burn,[4]
   From mornin' sun till dine;[5]
But seas between us braid[6] hae roar'd
   Sin' auld lang syne.
                For auld, &c.

And there's a hand, my trusty fier![7]
   And gie's a hand o' thine!
And we'll tak a right guid-willie waught,[8]
   For auld lang syne.
                For auld, &c.

JOHN ANDERSON MY JO

John Anderson my jo,[9] John,
   When we were first acquent,
Your locks were like the raven,
   Your bonie brow was brent;[10]
But now your brow is beld,[11] John,
   Your locks are like the snaw;
But blessings on your frosty pow,[12]
   John Anderson my jo.

John Anderson my jo, John,
   We clamb the hill thegither;
And mony a canty[13] day, John
   We've had wi' ane anither::
Now we maun totter down, John,
   And hand in hand we'll go,
And sleep thegither at the foot,
   John Anderson my jo.

WHISTLE O'ER THE LAVE O'T

First when Maggie was my care,
Heav'n, I thought, was in her air,
Now we're married—speir[14] nae mair,
   But whistle o'er the lave[15] o't!
Meg was meek, and Meg was mild,
Sweet and harmless as a child—
Wiser men than me's beguil'd;
   Whistle o'er the lave o't!

How we live, my Meg and me,
How we love, and how we gree,

1 rushes		9 sweetheart (joy)
2 worldly		10 smooth
3 quiet	6 old long since (old	11 bald
4 topsy-turvy	times)	12 head
5 grave	7 be good for (stand for)	13 merry
	your three-pint	14 ask
	measure	15 rest
	8 hearty draught	

I care na by how few may see—
　Whistle o'er the lave o't!
Wha I wish were maggot's meat,
Dish'd up in her winding-sheet,
I could write—but Meg maun see't—
　Whistle o'er the lave o't!

TO MARY IN HEAVEN*

Thou ling'ring star, with less'ning ray,
　That lov'st to greet the early morn,
Again thou usher'st in the day
　My Mary from my soul was torn.
O Mary! dear departed shade!
　Where is thy place of blissful rest?
See'st thou thy lover lowly laid?
　Hear'st thou the groans that rend his
　　breast?　　　　　　　　　　　　8

That sacred hour can I forget,
　Can I forget the hallowed grove,
Where by the winding Ayr we met
　To live one day of parting love?
Eternity will not efface
　Those records dear of transports past,
Thy image at our last embrace—
　Ah! little thought we 'twas our last!　16

Ayr, gurgling, kiss'd his pebbled shore,
　O'erhung with wild woods, thick'ning green;
The fragrant birch and hawthorn hoar
　'Twin'd amorous round the raptur'd scene:
The flow'rs sprang wanton to be prest,
　The birds sang love on every spray,
Till too, too soon the glowing west
　Proclaim'd the speed of wingèd day.　24

Still o'er these scenes my mem'ry wakes,
　And fondly broods with miser care!
Time but th' impression stronger makes,
　As streams their channels deeper wear.
My Mary, dear departed shade!
　Where is thy place of blissful rest?
See'st thou thy lover lowly laid?
　Hear'st thou the groans that rend his
　　breast?　　　　　　　　　　　　32

MY HEART'S IN THE HIGHLANDS

Farewell to the Highlands, farewell to the
　North,
The birth-place of valour, the country of
　worth;
Wherever I wander, wherever I rove,
The hills of the Highlands for ever I love.

* Mary Campbell, who died in 1786; Burns's
"Highland Mary."

My heart's in the Highlands, my heart is
　not here;
My heart's in the Highlands, a-chasing the
　deer;
A-chasing the wild deer, and following the
　roe,
My heart's in the Highlands wherever I go.

Farewell to the mountains, high-cover'd with
　snow;
Farewell to the straths[1] and green valleys be-
　low;
Farewell to the forests and wild-hanging woods,
Farewell to the torrents and loud-pouring
　floods.

My heart's in the Highlands, my heart is
　not here;
My heart's in the Highlands, a-chasing the
　deer;
A-chasing the wild deer, and following the
　roe,
My heart's in the Highlands wherever I go.

THE BANKS O' DOON

Ye flowery banks o' bonie Doon,
　How can ye blume sae fair?
How can ye chant, ye little birds,
　And I sae fu' o' care?

Thou'll break my heart, thou bonie bird,
　That sings upon the bough;
Thou minds me o' the happy days,
　When my fause luve was true.　　　8

Thou'll break my heart, thou bonie bird,
　That sings beside thy mate;
For sae I sat, and sae I sang,
　And wist na o' my fate.

Aft hae I rov'd by bonie Doon
　To see the woodbine twine,
And ilka bird sang o' its luve,
　And sae did I o' mine.　　　　　16

Wi' lightsome heart I pu'd a rose,
　Frae aff its thorny tree,
And my fause luver staw[2] my rose
　But left the thorn wi' me.

AFTON WATER

Flow gently, sweet Afton, among thy green
　braes,[3]
Flow gently, I'll sing thee a song in thy
　praise;

1 broad vales　　　　　　3 hills, slopes
2 stole

My Mary's asleep by thy murmuring stream,
Flow gently, sweet Afton, disturb not her
dream.

Thou stock-dove whose echo resounds thro' the
glen,
Ye wild whistling blackbirds in yon thorny den,
Thou green-crested lapwing, thy screaming
forbear,
I charge you, disturb not my slumbering
fair.   8

How lofty, sweet Afton, thy neighbouring hills,
Far mark'd with the courses of clear, winding
rills;
There daily I wander as noon rises high,
My flocks and my Mary's sweet cot in my eye.

How pleasant thy banks and green valleys
below,
Where wild in the woodlands the primroses
blow;
There oft, as mild Evening weeps over the lea,
The sweet-scented birk[1] shades my Mary and
me.   16

Thy crystal stream, Afton, how lovely it glides,
And winds by the cot where my Mary resides;
How wanton thy waters her snowy feet lave,
As gathering sweet flow'rets she stems thy
clear wave.

Flow gently, sweet Afton, among thy green
braes,
Flow gently, sweet river, the theme of my lays;
My Mary's asleep by thy murmuring stream,
Flow gently, sweet Afton, disturb not her
dream.   24

HIGHLAND MARY

Ye banks, and braes, and streams around
    The castle o' Montgomery,
Green be your woods, and fair your flowers,
    Your waters never drumlie![2]
There simmer first unfald[3] her robes,
    And there the langest tarry;
For there I took the last fareweel
    O' my sweet Highland Mary.   8

How sweetly bloom'd the gay green birk,
    How rich the hawthorn's blossom,
As underneath their fragrant shade
    I clasp'd her to my bosom!
The golden hours on angel wings,
    Flew o'er me and my dearie;
For dear to me, as light and life,
    Was my sweet Highland Mary.   16

Wi' monie a vow, and lock'd embrace,
    Our parting was fu' tender;
And, pledging aft to meet again,
    We tore oursels asunder;
But O, fell death's untimely frost,
    That nipt my flower sae early!
Now green's the sod, and cauld's the clay,
    That wraps my Highland Mary!   24

O pale, pale now, those rosy lips,
    I aft hae kiss'd sae fondly!
And closed for aye the sparkling glance
    That dwelt on me sae kindly!
And mould'ring now in silent dust,
    That heart that lo'ed me dearly!
But still within my bosom's core
    Shall live my Highland Mary.   32

BANNOCKBURN

ROBERT BRUCE'S ADDRESS TO HIS ARMY

Scots, wha hae wi' Wallace bled,
Scots, wham Bruce has aften led;
Welcome to your gory bed,
    Or to victory!

Now's the day, and now's the hour;
See the front o' battle lour;
See approach proud Edward's' power—
    Chains and slavery!   8

Wha will be a traitor knave?
Wha can fill a coward's' grave?
Wha sae base as be a slave?
    Let him turn and flee!

Wha for Scotland's king and law
Freedom's sword will strongly draw,
Freeman stand, or Freeman fa',
    Let him follow me!   16

By oppression's woes and pains!
By your sons in servile chains!
We will drain our dearest veins,
    But they shall be free!

Lay the proud usurpers low!
Tyrants fall in every foe!
Liberty's in every blow!—
    Let us do or die!   24

CONTENTED WI' LITTLE AND CANTIE WI' MAIR

Contented wi' little, and cantie[1] wi' mair,
Whene'er I forgather[2] wi' Sorrow and Care,
I gie them a skelp[3] as they're creeping alang,

1 birch   3 i. e., may summer un-
2 muddy   fold

1 merry   3 slap
2 meet

Wi' a cog[1] o' gude swats[2] and an auld Scottish sang.

I whiles claw[3] the elbow o' troublesome
    Thought;
But man is a soger, and life is a faught;
My mirth and gude humour are coin in my
    pouch,
And my freedom's my lairdship nae monarch
    dare touch.   8

A towmond[4] o' trouble, should that be my fa'[5]
A night o' gude fellowship sowthers[6] it a';
When at the blythe end of our journey at last,
Wha the deil ever thinks o' the road he has
    past?

Blind Chance, let her snapper and stoyte[7] on
    her way;
Be 't to me, be 't frae me, e'en let the jade
    gae:
Come ease or come travail, come pleasure or
    pain,
My warst word is ''Welcome, and welcome
    again!''   16

A MAN'S A MAN FOR A' THAT

Is there,[8] for honest poverty,
    That hings his head, an' a' that?
The coward slave, we pass him by,
    We dare be poor for a' that!
For a' that, an' a' that,
    Our toils obscure, an' a' that;
The rank is but the guinea's stamp;
    The man's the gowd[9] for a' that.   8

What though on hamely fare we dine,
    Wear hodden-grey,[10] an' a' that;
Gie fools their silks, and knaves their wine,
    A man's a man for a' that.
For a' that, an' a' that,
    Their tinsel show, an' a' that;
The honest man, tho' e'er sae poor,
    Is king o' men for a' that.   16

1 cup
2 ale
3 scratch
4 twelve month
5 lot
6 solders, mends
7 stumble and stagger
8 Supply ''a man.''
9 gold
10 coarse cloth

Ye see yon birkie,[1] ca'd a lord,
    Wha struts, an' stares, an' a' that;
Tho' hundreds worship at his word,
    He's but a coof[2] for a' that.
For a' that, an'. a' that,
    His riband, star, an' a' that,
The man o' independent mind,
    He looks and laughs at a' that.   24

A prince can mak a belted knight,
    A marquis, duke, an' a' that;
But an honest man's aboon his might,
    Guid faith, he mauna fa'[3] that!
For a' that, an' a' that,
    Their dignities, an' a' that,
The pith o' sense, an' pride o' worth,
    Are higher rank than a' that.   32

Then let us pray that come it may,
    As come it will for a' that,
That sense and worth, o'er a' the earth,
    May bear the gree,[4] an' a' that.
For a' that, an' a' that,
    It's coming yet for a' that,
That man to man, the warld o'er,
    Shall brothers be for a' that.   40

O, WERT THOU IN THE CAULD BLAST

O, wert thou in the cauld blast,
    On yonder lea, on yonder lea,
My plaidie to the angry airt,[5]
    I'd shelter thee, I'd shelter thee.
Or did misfortune's bitter storms
    Around thee blaw, around thee blaw,
Thy bield[6] should be my bosom,
    To share it a', to share it a'.   8

Or were I in the wildest waste,
    Sae black and bare, sae black and bare,
The desert were a paradise,
    If thou wert there, if thou wert there.
Or were I monarch o' the globe,
    Wi' thee to reign, wi' thee to reign,
The brightest jewel in my crown
    Wad be my queen, wad be my queen.   16

1 fellow
2 fool
3 may not accomplish
4 prize
5 to the windy quarter
6 shelter

THE ROMANTIC REVIVAL

WILLIAM WORDSWORTH

(1770-1850)

DEAR NATIVE REGIONS*

Dear native regions, I foretell,
From what I feel at this farewell,
That, wheresoe'er my steps may tend,
And whensoe'er my course shall end,
If in that hour a single tie
Survive of local sympathy,
My soul will cast the backward view,
The longing look alone on you.

Thus, while the Sun sinks down to rest
Far in the regions of the west,
Though to the vale no parting beam
Be given, not one memorial gleam,
A lingering light he fondly throws
On the dear hills where first he rose.

WE ARE SEVEN†

—A simple Child,
That lightly draws its breath,
And feels its life in every limb,
What should it know of death?

I met a little cottage Girl:
She was eight years old, she said;
Her hair was thick with many a curl
That clustered round her head.   8

*Wordsworth thought it worth while to print
this "extract from the conclusion of a poem"
which was written, at the age of sixteen,
just before he left his school at Hawkshead.
It both reveals his strong local attachment
and anticipates his reliance upon what became for him a chief source of poetic inspiration, namely, "emotion recollected in
tranquillity."
†This, and the two poems that follow it, were
among those contributed by Wordsworth to
the joint volume of *Lyrical Ballads* which
he and Coleridge published in 1798 (see p.
428; also *Eng. Lit.*, pp. 232-235). This poem
was written to show "the obscurity and
perplexity which in childhood attend our
notion of death, or rather our utter inability to admit that notion."

She had a rustic, woodland air,
And she was wildly clad:
Her eyes were fair, and very fair;
—Her beauty made me glad.

"Sisters and brothers, little Maid,
How many may you be?"
"How many? Seven in all," she said
And wondering looked at me.   16

"And where are they? I pray you tell."
She answered, "Seven are we;
And two of us at Conway dwell,
And two are gone to sea.

"Two of us in the church-yard lie,
My sister and my brother;
And in the church-yard cottage, I
Dwell near them with my mother."   24

"You say that two at Conway dwell,
And two are gone to sea.
Yet ye are seven!—I pray you tell,
Sweet Maid, how this may be."

Then did the little Maid reply,
"Seven boys and girls are we;
Two of us in the church-yard lie,
Beneath the church-yard tree."   32

"You run about, my little Maid,
Your limbs they are alive;
If two are in the church-yard laid,
Then ye are only five."

"Their graves are green, they may be seen,"
The little Maid replied,
"Twelve steps or more from my mother's door,
And they are side by side.   40

"My stockings there I often knit,
My kerchief there I hem;
And there upon the ground I sit,
And sing a song to them.

"And often after sunset, Sir,
When it is light and fair,
I take my little porringer,
And eat my supper there.   48

"The first that died was sister Jane;
In bed she moaning lay,
Till God released her of her pain;
And then she went away.

"So in the church-yard she was laid;
And, when the grass was dry,
Together round her grave we played,
My brother John and I.   56

"And when the ground was white with snow,
And I could run and slide,
My brother John was forced to go,
And he lies by her side."

"How many are you, then," said I,
"If they two are in heaven?"
Quick was the little Maid's reply,
"O Master! we are seven."   64

"But they are dead; those two are dead!
Their spirits are in heaven!"
'Twas throwing words away; for still
The little Maid would have her will,
And said, "Nay, we are seven!"

LINES WRITTEN IN EARLY SPRING*

I heard a thousand blended notes,
While in a grove I sate reclined,
In that sweet mood when pleasant thoughts
Bring sad thoughts to the mind.

To her fair works did Nature link
The human soul that through me ran;
And much it grieved my heart to think
What man has made of man.   8

Through primrose tufts, in that green bower,
The periwinkle trailed its wreaths;
And 'tis my faith that every flower
Enjoys the air it breathes.

The birds around me hopped and played,
Their thoughts I cannot measure:—
But the least motion which they made
It seemed a thrill of pleasure.   16

The budding twigs spread out their fan,
To catch the breezy air;
And I must think, do all I can,
That there was pleasure there.

* This is one of the earliest and most definite
expressions of Wordsworth's faith in the essential oneness of man and nature, and of
his sorrow over man's apostasy from that
faith.

If this belief from heaven be sent,
If such be Nature's holy plan,
Have I not reason to lament
What man has made of man?   2

LINES COMPOSED A FEW MILES ABOVE TINTERN ABBEY, ON REVISITING THE BANKS OF THE WYE DURING A TOUR. JULY 13, 1798.†

Five years have past; five summers, with the
     length
Of five long winters! and again I hear
These waters, rolling from their mountain
     springs
With a soft inland murmur.‡—Once again
Do I behold these steep and lofty cliffs,
That on a wild secluded scene impress
Thoughts of more deep seclusion; and connect
The landscape with the quiet of the sky.
The day is come when I again repose
Here, under this dark sycamore, and view   1
These plots of cottage-ground, these orchard
     tufts,
Which at this season, with their unripe fruits,
Are clad in one green hue, and lose themselves
'Mid groves and copses. Once again I see
These hedge-rows, hardly hedge-rows, little lines
Of sportive wood run wild: these pastoral
     farms,
Green to the very door; and wreaths of smoke
Sent up, in silence, from among the trees!
With some uncertain notice, as might seem
Of vagrant dwellers in the houseless woods,   2
Or of some Hermit's cave, where by his fire
The Hermit sits alone.
                          These beauteous forms,
Through a long absence, have not been to me
As is a landscape to a blind man's eye:
But oft, in lonely rooms, and 'mid the din
Of towns and cities, I have owed to them
In hours of weariness, sensations sweet,
Felt in the blood, and felt along the heart;
And passing even into my purer mind,

† Note by Wordsworth: "I have not ventured
to call this poem an Ode; but it was written with a hope that in the transitions, and
the impassioned music of the versification
would be found the principal requisites of
that species of composition." Professor
Dowden remarks upon the four stages of
the poet's growth to be found described in
the poem: First, animal enjoyment of
nature in boyhood; second, passion for
beauty and sublimity; third, perception of
nature's tranquillizing and elevating influence on the spirit; and fourth, deep communion with a spiritual presence; stages
which he further describes as the periods of
the blood, of the senses, of the imagination
and of the soul.
‡ For the effect of the tides on the Wye nearer
its mouth, see Tennyson's In Memoriam
XIX.

With tranquil restoration:—feelings too   30
Of unremembered pleasure: such, perhaps,
As have no slight or trivial influence
On that best portion of a good man's life,
His little, nameless, unremembered acts
Of kindness and of love. Nor less, I trust,
To them I may have owed another gift,
Of aspect more sublime; that blessed mood
In which the burthen of the mystery,
In which the heavy and the weary weight
Of all this unintelligible world,   40
Is lightened:—that serene and blessed mood,
In which the affections gently lead us on,—
Until, the breath of this corporeal frame
And even the motion of our human blood
Almost suspended, we are laid asleep
In body, and become a living soul:
While with an eye made quiet by the power
Of harmony, and the deep power of joy,
We see into the life of things.
                              If this
Be but a vain belief, yet, oh! how oft—   50
In darkness and amid the many shapes
Of joyless daylight; when the fretful stir
Unprofitable, and the fever of the world,
Have hung upon the beatings of my heart—
How oft, in spirit, have I turned to thee,
O sylvan Wye! thou wanderer thro' the woods,
How often has my spirit turned to thee!
     And now, with gleams of half-extinguished
          thought,
With many recognitions dim and faint,
And somewhat of a sad perplexity,   60
The picture of the mind revives again:
While here I stand, not only with the sense
Of present pleasure, but with pleasing thoughts
That in this moment there is life and food
For future years. And so I dare to hope,
Though changed, no doubt, from what I was
          when first
I came among these hills; when like a roe
I bounded o'er the mountains, by the sides
Of the deep rivers, and the lonely streams,
Wherever nature led: more like a man   70
Flying from something that he dreads, than
          one
Who sought the thing he loved. For nature
          then
(The coarser pleasures of my boyish days,
And their glad animal movements all gone by)
To me was all in all.—I cannot paint
What then I was. The sounding cataract
Haunted me like a passion: the tall rock,
The mountain, and the deep and gloomy wood,
Their colours and their forms, were then to me
An appetite; a feeling and a love,   80
That had no need of a remoter charm,
By thought supplied, nor any interest

Unborrowed from the eye.—That time is past,
And all its aching joys are now no more,
And all its dizzy raptures. Not for this
Faint I, nor mourn nor murmur; other gifts
Have followed; for such loss, I would believe,
Abundant recompense. For I have learned
To look on nature, not as in the hour
Of thoughtless youth; but hearing oftentimes
The still, sad music of humanity,   91
Nor harsh nor grating, though of ample power
To chasten and subdue. And I have felt
A presence that disturbs me with the joy
Of elevated thoughts; a sense sublime
Of something far more deeply interfused,
Whose dwelling is the light of setting suns,
And the round ocean and the living air,
And the blue sky, and in the mind of man;
A motion and a spirit, that impels   100
All thinking things, all objects of all thought,
And rolls through all things. Therefore am I
          still
A lover of the meadows and the woods,
And mountains; and of all that we behold
From this green earth; of all the mighty world
Of eye, and ear,—both what they half create,
And what perceive; well pleased to recognize
In nature and the language of the sense,
The anchor of my purest thoughts, the nurse,
The guide, the guardian of my heart, and soul
Of all my moral being.
                    Nor perchance,   111
If I were not thus taught, should I the more
Suffer my genial spirits to decay:
For thou art with me here upon the banks
Of this fair river; thou my dearest Friend,
My dear, dear Friend; and in thy voice I catch
The language of my former heart, and read
My former pleasures in the shooting lights
Of thy wild eyes. Oh! yet a little while
May I behold in thee what I was once,   120
My dear, dear Sister! and this prayer I make,
Knowing that Nature never did betray
The heart that loved her; 'tis her privilege,
Through all the years of this our life, to lead
From joy to joy: for she can so inform[1]
The mind that is within us, so impress
With quietness and beauty, and so feed
With lofty thoughts, that neither evil tongues,
Rash judgments, nor the sneers of selfish men,
Nor greetings where no kindness is, nor all   130
The dreary intercourse of daily life,
Shall e'er prevail against us, or disturb
Our cheerful faith, that all which we behold
Is full of blessings. Therefore let the moon
Shine on thee in thy solitary walk;
And let the misty mountain-winds be free
To blow against thee: and, in after years,

[1] give form to, animate

When these wild ecstasies shall be matured
Into a sober pleasure; when thy mind
Shall be a mansion for all lovely forms,   140
Thy memory be as a dwelling-place
For all sweet sounds and harmonies; oh! then,
If solitude, or fear, or pain, or grief,
Should be thy portion, with what healing
    thoughts
Of tender joy wilt thou remember me,
And these my exhortations! Nor, perchance—
If I should be where I no more can hear
Thy voice, nor catch from thy wild eyes these
    gleams
Of past existence—wilt thou then forget
That on the banks of this delightful stream 150
We stood together; and that I, so long
A worshipper of Nature, hither came
Unwearied in that service: rather say
With warmer love—oh! with far deeper zeal
Of holier love. Nor wilt thou then forget,
That after many wanderings, many years
Of absence, these steep woods and lofty cliffs,
And this green pastoral landscape, were to me
More dear, both for themselves and for thy
    sake!

STRANGE FITS OF PASSION HAVE I KNOWN*

Strange fits of passion have I known:
And I will dare to tell,
But in the Lover's ear alone,
What once to me befell.

When she I loved looked every day
Fresh as a rose in June,
I to her cottage bent my way
Beneath an evening-moon.   8

Upon the moon I fixed my eye,
All over the wide lea;
With quickening pace my horse drew nigh
Those paths so dear to me.

And now we reached the orchard-plot;
And, as we climbed the hill,
The sinking moon to Lucy's cot
Came near, and nearer still.   16

In one of those sweet dreams I slept,
Kind Nature's gentlest boon!

* This little group of five poems upon an unknown
and perhaps imaginary Lucy were written in
Germany in the year 1799. Without titles or
notes, or any ornament beyond two or three
of the simplest figures, they convey absolutely their contained emotion, illustrating
that poetry which, in moments of deepest
feeling, is the natural language of man. The
fifth poem appears to sum up the preceding
four; in its two brief stanzas it presents the
two opposing and inscrutable mysteries of
life and death, and leaves them to the imagination, without further comment.

And all the while my eyes I kept
On the descending moon.

My horse moved on; hoof after hoof
He raised, and never stopped:
When down behind the cottage roof,
At once, the bright moon dropped.   2

What fond and wayward thoughts will slide
Into a Lover's head!
"O mercy!" to myself I cried,
"If Lucy should be dead!"

SHE DWELT AMONG THE UNTRODDEN WAYS

She dwelt among the untrodden ways
Beside the springs of Dove,[1]
A Maid whom there were none to praise
And very few to love:

A violet by a mossy stone
Half hidden from the eye!
—Fair as a star, when only one
Is shining in the sky.   8

She lived unknown, and few could know
When Lucy ceased to be;
But she is in her grave, and, oh,
The difference to me!

I TRAVELLED AMONG UNKNOWN MEN

I travelled among unknown men,
In lands beyond the sea;
Nor, England! did I know till then
What love I bore to thee.

'Tis past, that melancholy dream!
Nor will I quit thy shore
A second time; for still I seem
To love thee more and more.   8

Among thy mountains did I feel
The joy of my desire;
And she I cherished turned her wheel
Beside an English fire.

Thy mornings showed, thy nights concealed
The bowers where Lucy played;
And thine too is the last green field
That Lucy's eyes surveyed.   16

THREE YEARS SHE GREW IN SUN AND SHOWER

Three years she grew in sun and shower,
Then Nature said, "A lovelier flower
On earth was never sown;
This Child I to myself will take;

[1] The name of several streams in England; one
has been made famous by Izaak Walton, the
angler.

She shall be mine, and I will make
A Lady of my own.   6

"Myself will to my darling be
Both law and impulse: and with me
The Girl, in rock and plain,
In earth and heaven, in glade and bower,
Shall feel an overseeing power
To kindle or restrain.   12

"She shall be sportive as the fawn
That wild with glee across the lawn,
Or up the mountain springs;
And hers shall be the breathing balm,
And hers the silence and the calm
Of mute insensate things.   18

"The floating clouds their state shall lend
To her; for her the willow bend;
Nor shall she fail to see
Even in the motions of the Storm
Grace that shall mould the Maiden's form
By silent sympathy.   24

"The stars of midnight shall be dear
To her; and she shall lean her ear
In many a secret place
Where rivulets dance their wayward round,
And beauty born of murmuring sound
Shall pass into her face.   30

"And vital feelings of delight
Shall rear her form to stately height,
Her virgin bosom swell;
Such thoughts to Lucy I will give
While she and I together live
Here in this happy dell."   36

Thus Nature spake.—The work was done—
How soon my Lucy's race was run!
She died, and left to me
This heath, this calm, and quiet scene;
The memory of what has been,
And never more will be.   42

A SLUMBER DID MY SPIRIT SEAL

A Slumber did my spirit seal;
  I had no human fears:
She seemed a thing that could not feel
  The touch of earthly years.

No motion has she now, no force;
  She neither hears nor sees;
Rolled round in earth's diurnal course,
  With rocks, and stones, and trees.

LUCY GRAY
OR, SOLITUDE

Oft I had heard of Lucy Gray:
And, when I crossed the wild,

I chanced to see at break of day
The solitary child.

No mate, no comrade Lucy knew;
She dwelt on a wide moor,
—The sweetest thing that ever grew
Beside a human door!   8

You yet may spy the fawn at play,
The hare upon the green;
But the sweet face of Lucy Gray
Will never more be seen.

"To-night will be a stormy night—
You to the town must go;
And take a lantern, Child, to light
Your mother through the snow."   16

"That, Father! will I gladly do:
'Tis scarcely afternoon—
The minster-clock has just struck two,
And yonder is the moon!"

At this the Father raised his hook,
And snapped a faggot-band;
He plied his work;—and Lucy took
The lantern in her hand.   24

Not blither is the mountain roe:
With many a wanton stroke
Her feet disperse the powdery snow,
That rises up like smoke.

The storm came on before its time:
She wandered up and down;
And many a hill did Lucy climb:
But never reached the town.   32

The wretched parents all that night
Went shouting far and wide;
But there was neither sound nor sight
To serve them for a guide.

At daybreak on the hill they stood
That overlooked the moor;
And thence they saw the bridge of wood,
A furlong from their door.   40

They wept—and, turning homeward, cried,
"In heaven we all shall meet;"
—When in the snow the mother spied
The print of Lucy's feet.

Then downwards from the steep hill's edge
They tracked the footmarks small;
And through the broken hawthorn hedge,
And by the long stone-wall;   48

And then an open field they crossed:
The marks were still the same;
They tracked them on, nor ever lost;
And to the bridge they came.

They followed from the snowy bank
Those footmarks, one by one,
Into the middle of the plank;
And further there were none!   56

—Yet some maintain that to this day
She is a living child;
That you may see sweet Lucy Gray
Upon the lonesome wild.

O'er rough and smooth she trips along,
And never looks behind;
And sings a solitary song
That whistles in the wind.   64

THE PRELUDE; OR, GROWTH OF A POET'S MIND

From Book I. Childhood

Fair seed-time had my soul, and I grew up
Fostered alike by beauty and by fear:
Much favoured in my birth-place, and no less
In that beloved Vale[1] to which erelong
We were transplanted;—there were we let loose
For sports of wider range. Ere I had told
Ten birth-days, when among the mountain
    slopes
Frost, and the breath of frosty wind, had
    snapped
The last autumnal crocus, 'twas my joy
With store of springes o'er my shoulder hung 310
To range the open heights where woodcocks run
Along the smooth green turf. Through half the
    night,
Scudding away from snare to snare, I plied
That anxious visitation;—moon and stars
Were shining o'er my head. I was alone,
And seemed to be a trouble to the peace
That dwelt among them. Sometimes it befell
In these night wanderings, that a strong desire
O'rpowered my better reason, and the bird
Which was the captive of another's toil 320
Became my prey; and when the deed was done
I heard among the solitary hills
Low breathings coming after me, and sounds
Of undistinguishable motion, steps
Almost as silent as the turf they trod.

Nor less, when spring had warmed the cul-
    tured Vale,

[1] Esthwaite, Lancashire, where, at the village of Hawkshead, Wordsworth attended school.

Moved we as plunderers where the mother-bi
Had in high places built her lodge; thou,
    mean
Our object and inglorious, yet the end
Was not ignoble. Oh! when I have hung   3
Above the raven's nest, by knots of grass
And half-inch fissures in the slippery rock
But ill sustained, and almost (so it seemed)
Suspended by the blast that blew amain,
Shouldering the naked crag, oh, at that time
While on the perilous ridge I hung alone,
With what strange utterance did the loud d
    wind
Blow through my ear! the sky seemed not a s
Of earth—and with what motion moved t
    clouds!

Dust as we are, the immortal spirit grows   3
Like harmony in music; there is a dark
Inscrutable workmanship that reconciles
Discordant elements, makes them cling togeth
In one society. How strange, that all
The terrors, pains, and early miseries,
Regrets, vexations, lassitudes interfused
Within my mind, should e'er have borne a pa
And that a needful part, in making up
The calm existence that is mine when I
Am worthy of myself! Praise to the end! 3
Thanks to the means which Nature deigned
    employ;
Whether her fearless visitings, or those
That came with soft alarm, like hurtless light
Opening the peaceful clouds; or she would u
Severer interventions, ministry
More palpable, as best might suit her aim.

One summer evening (led by her) I found
A little boat tied to a willow tree
Within a rocky cave, its usual home.   3
Straight I unloosed her chain, and stepping
Pushed from the shore. It was an act of steal
And troubled pleasure, nor without the voice
Of mountain-echoes did my boat move on;
Leaving behind her still, on either side,
Small circles glittering idly in the moon,
Until they melted all into one track
Of sparkling light. But now, like one who row
Proud of his skill, to reach a chosen point
With an unswerving line, I fixed my view
Upon the summit of a craggy ridge,   3
The horizon's utmost boundary; far above
Was nothing but the stars and the grey sky.
She was an elfin pinnace; lustily
I dipped my oars into the silent lake,
And, as I rose upon the stroke, my boat
Went heaving through the water like a swan;
When, from behind that craggy steep till the

The horizon's bound, a huge peak, black and
  huge,
As if with voluntary power instinct,   379
Upreared its head. I struck and struck again,
And growing still in stature the grim shape
Towered up between me and the stars, and still,
For so it seemed, with purpose of its own
And measured motion like a living thing,
Strode after me. With trembling oars I turned,
And through the silent water stole my way
Back to the covert of the willow tree;
There in her mooring-place I left my bark,—
And through the meadows homeward went, in
  grave
And serious mood; but after I had seen   390
That spectacle, for many days, my brain
Worked with a dim and undetermined sense
Of unknown modes of being; o'er my thoughts
There hung a darkness, call it solitude
Or blank desertion. No familiar shapes
Remained, no pleasant images of trees,
Of sea or sky, no colours of green fields;
But huge and mighty forms, that do not live
Like living men, moved slowly through the mind
By day, and were a trouble to my dreams.   400

  Wisdom and Spirit of the universe!
Thou Soul that art the eternity of thought
That givest to forms and images a breath
And everlasting motion, not in vain
By day or star-light thus from my first dawn
Of childhood didst thou intertwine for me.
The passions that build up our human soul;
Not with the mean and vulgar works of man,
But with high objects, with enduring things—
With life and nature—purifying thus   410
The elements of feeling and of thought,
And sanctifying, by such discipline,
Both pain and fear, until we recognize
A grandeur in the beatings of the heart.
Nor was this fellowship vouchsafed to me
With stinted kindness. In November days,
When vapours rolling down the valley made
A lonely scene more lonesome, among woods,
At noon and 'mid the calm of summer nights,
When, by the margin of the trembling lake,   420
Beneath the gloomy hills homeward I went
In solitude, such intercourse was mine;
Mine was it in the fields both day and night,
And by the waters, all the summer long.

  And in the frosty season, when the sun
Was set, and visible for many a mile
The cottage windows blazed through twilight
  gloom,
I heeded not their summons: happy time
It was indeed for all of us—for me
It was a time of rapture! Clear and loud   430

The village clock tolled six,—I wheeled about,
Proud and exulting like an untired horse
That cares not for his home. All shod with
  steel,
We hissed along the polished ice in games
Confederate, imitative of the chase
And woodland pleasures,—the resounding horn,
The pack loud chiming, and the hunted hare.
So through the darkness and the cold we flew,
And not a voice was idle; with the din
Smitten, the precipices rang aloud;   440
The leafless trees and every icy crag
Tinkled like iron; while far distant hills
Into the tumult sent an alien sound
Of melancholy not unnoticed, while the stars
Eastward were sparkling clear, and in the west
The orange sky of evening died away.
Not seldom from the uproar I retired
Into a silent bay, or sportively
Glanced sideway, leaving the tumultuous throng,
To cut across the reflex of a star   450
That fled, and, flying still before me, gleamed
Upon the glassy plain; and oftentimes,
When we had given our bodies to the wind,
And all the shadowy banks on either side
Came sweeping through the darkness, spinning
  still
The rapid line of motion, then at once
Have I, reclining back upon my heels,
Stopped short; yet still the solitary cliffs
Wheeled by me—even as if the earth had rolled
With visible motion her diurnal round!   460
Behind me did they stretch in solemn train,
Feebler and feebler, and I stood and watched
Till all was tranquil as a dreamless sleep.

  Ye Presences of Nature in the sky
And on the earth! Ye Visions of the hills!
And Souls of lonely places! can I think
A vulgar hope was yours when ye employed
Such ministry, when ye, through many a year
Haunting me thus among my boyish sports,
On caves and trees, upon the woods and hills,   470
Impressed, upon all forms, the characters
Of danger or desire; and thus did make
The surface of the universal earth,
With triumph and delight, with hope and fear,
Work like a sea?
          Not uselessly employed,
Might I pursue this theme through every change
Of exercise and play, to which the year
Did summon us in his delightful round.

FROM BOOK V

  There was a Boy: ye knew him well, ye cliffs
And islands of Winander![2]—many a time

2 Winandermere, now Windermere, a lake in West-
  moreland.

At evening, when the earliest stars began
To move along the edges of the hills,
Rising or setting, would he stand alone
Beneath the trees or by the glimmering lake,   369
And there, with fingers interwoven, both hands
Pressed closely palm to palm, and to his mouth
Uplifted, he, as through an instrument,
Blew mimic hootings to the silent owls,
That they might answer him; and they would
        shout
Across the watery vale, and shout again,
Responsive to his call, with quivering peals,
And long halloos and screams, and echoes loud,
Redoubled and redoubled, concourse wild
Of jocund din; and, when a lengthened pause
Of silence came and baffled his best skill,   380
Then sometimes, in that silence while he hung
Listening, a gentle shock of mild surprise
Has carried far into his heart the voice
Of mountain-torrents; or the visible scene
Would enter unawares into his mind,
With all its solemn imagery, its rocks,
Its woods, and that uncertain heaven, received
Into the bosom of the steady lake.

    This Boy was taken from his mates, and died
In childhood, ere he was full twelve years old.
Fair is the spot, most beautiful the vale   391
Where he was born; the grassy churchyard
        hangs
Upon a slope above the village-school,
And through that churchyard when my way has
        led
On summer-evenings, I believe that there
A long half hour together I have stood
Mute, looking at the grave in which he lies!

MY HEART LEAPS UP WHEN I BEHOLD

My heart leaps up when I behold
        A rainbow in the sky:
So was it when my life began;
So is it now I am a man;
So be it when I shall grow old,
        Or let me die!
The Child is father of the Man;
And I could wish my days to be
Bound each to each by natural piety.[3]

THE SOLITARY REAPER

Behold her, single in the field,
Yon solitary Highland Lass!
Reaping and singing by herself;
Stop here, or gently pass!
Alone she cuts and binds the grain,
And sings a melancholy strain;
O listen! for the Vale profound
Is overflowing with the sound.   8

[3] religious regard for nature

No Nightingale did ever chant
More welcome notes to weary bands
Of travellers in some shady haunt,
Among Arabian sands:
A voice so thrilling ne'er was heard
In spring-time from the Cuckoo-bird,
Breaking the silence of the seas
Among the farthest Hebrides.   16

Will no one tell me what she sings?—
Perhaps the plaintive numbers flow
For old, unhappy, far-off things,
And battles long ago:
Or is it some more humble lay,
Familiar matter of to-day?
Some natural sorrow, loss, or pain,
That has been, and may be again?   24

Whate'er the theme, the Maiden sang
As if her song could have no ending;
I saw her singing at her work,
And o'er the sickle bending;—
I listened, motionless and still;
And, as I mounted up the hill
The music in my heart I bore,
Long after it was heard no more.   32

TO THE CUCKOO

O blithe New-comer! I have heard,
I hear thee and rejoice.
O Cuckoo! shall I call thee Bird,
Or but a wandering Voice?

While I am lying on the grass
Thy twofold shout I hear,
From hill to hill it seems to pass,
At once far off, and near.   8

Though babbling only to the Vale,
Of sunshine and of flowers,
Thou bringest unto me a tale
Of visionary hours.

Thrice welcome, darling of the Spring!
Even yet thou art to me
No bird, but an invisible thing,
A voice, a mystery;   16

The same whom in my school-boy days
I listened to; that Cry
Which made me look a thousand ways
In bush, and tree, and sky.

To seek thee did I often rove
Through woods and on the green;
And thou wert still a hope, a love;
Still longed for, never seen.   24

And I can listen to thee yet;
Can lie upon the plain
And listen, till I do beget
That golden time again.

O blessed Bird! the earth we pace
Again appears to be
An unsubstantial, faery place;
That is fit home for Thee!   32

SHE WAS A PHANTOM OF DELIGHT*

She was a Phantom of delight
When first she gleamed upon my sight;
A lovely Apparition sent
To be a moment's ornament;
Her eyes as stars of Twilight fair;
Like Twilight's, too, her dusky hair;
But all things else about her drawn
From May-time and the cheerful Dawn;
A dancing Shape, an Image gay,
To haunt, to startle, and way-lay.   10

I saw her upon nearer view,
A Spirit, yet a Woman too!
Her household motions light and free,
And steps of virgin-liberty;
A countenance in which did meet
Sweet records, promises as sweet;
A Creature not too bright or good
For human nature's daily food;
For transient sorrows, simple wiles,
Praise, blame, love, kisses, tears, and smiles.   20

And now I see with eye serene
The very pulse of the machine;
A Being breathing thoughtful breath,
A Traveller between life and death;
The reason firm, the temperate will,
Endurance, foresight, strength, and skill;
A perfect Woman, nobly planned,
To warn, to comfort, and command;
And yet a Spirit still, and bright
With something of angelic light.   30

I WANDERED LONELY AS A CLOUD

I wandered lonely as a cloud
That floats on high o'er vales and hills,
When all at once I saw a crowd,
A host, of golden daffodils;
Beside the lake, beneath the trees,
Fluttering and dancing in the breeze.   6

Continuous as the stars that shine
And twinkle on the milky way,
They stretched in never-ending line
Along the margin of a bay:

* Written of Mrs. Wordsworth.

Ten thousand saw I at a glance,
Tossing their heads in sprightly dance.   12

The waves beside them danced; but they
Out-did the sparkling waves in glee:
A poet could not but be gay,
In such a jocund company:
I gazed—and gazed—but little thought
What wealth the show to me had brought: 18

For oft, when on my couch I lie
In vacant or in pensive mood,
They flash upon that inward eye
Which is the bliss of solitude;
And then my heart with pleasure fills,
And dances with the daffodils.   24

ODE TO DUTY

Stern Daughter of the Voice of God!
O Duty! if that name thou love
Who art a light to guide, a rod
To check the erring, and reprove;
Thou, who art victory and law
When empty terrors overawe:
From vain temptations dost set free: 7
And calm'st the weary strife of frail humanity!

There are who ask not if thine eye
Be on them; who, in love and truth,
Where no misgiving is, rely
Upon the genial sense of youth:
Glad Hearts! without reproach or blot
Who do thy work, and know it not:
Oh! if through confidence misplaced
They fail, thy saving arms, dread Power!
      around them cast.   16

Serene will be our days and bright,
And happy will our nature be,
When love is an unerring light,
And joy its own security.
And they a blissful course may hold
Even now, who, not unwisely bold,
Live in the spirit of this creed;
Yet seek thy firm support, according to their
      need.   24

I, loving freedom, and untried,
No sport of every random gust,
Yet being to myself a guide,
Too blindly have reposed my trust:
And oft, when in my heart was heard
Thy timely mandate, I deferred
The task, in smoother walks to stray;
But thee I now would serve more strictly, if I
      may.   32

Through no disturbance of my soul,
Or strong compunction in me wrought,
I supplicate for thy control;
But in the quietness of thought:
Me this unchartered freedom tires;
I feel the weight of chance-desires:
My hopes no more must change their name,
I long for a repose that ever is the same.   40

Stern Lawgiver! yet thou dost wear
The Godhead's most benignant grace;
Nor know we anything so fair
As is the smile upon thy face:
Flowers laugh before thee on their beds
And fragrance in thy footing treads;
Thou dost preserve the stars from wrong;
And the most ancient heavens, through Thee,
    are fresh and strong.   48

To humbler functions, awful Power!
I call thee: I myself commend
Unto thy guidance from this hour;
Oh, let my weakness have an end!
Give unto me, made lowly wise,
The spirit of self-sacrifice;
The confidence of reason give;
And in the light of truth thy Bondman let me
    live!   56

TO A SKY-LARK

(1805)

Up with me! up with me into the clouds!
    For thy song, Lark, is strong;
Up with me, up with me into the clouds!
    Singing, singing,
With clouds and sky about thee ringing,
    Lift me, guide me till I find
That spot which seems so to thy mind!

I have walked through wildernesses dreary
And to-day my heart is weary;
Had I now the wings of a Faery,   10
Up to thee would I fly.
There is madness about thee, and joy divine
In that song of thine;
Lift me, guide me high and high
To thy banqueting-place in the sky.

    Joyous as morning
Thou art laughing and scorning;
Thou hast a nest for thy love and thy rest.
And, though little troubled with sloth,
Drunken Lark! thou would'st be loth   20
To be such a traveller as I.
Happy, happy Liver,
With a soul as strong as a mountain river
Pouring out praise to the Almighty Giver,
    Joy and jollity be with us both!

Alas! my journey, rugged and uneven,
Through prickly moors or dusty ways must
    wind;
But hearing thee, or others of thy kind,
As full of gladness and as free of heaven,
I, with my fate contented, will plod on,   30
And hope for higher raptures, when life's day
    is done.

TO A SKY-LARK

(1825)

Ethereal minstrel! pilgrim of the sky!
Dost thou despise the earth where cares abound?
Or, while the wings aspire, are heart and eye
Both with thy nest upon the dewy ground?
Thy nest which thou canst drop into at will,
Those quivering wings composed, that music
    still!   6

Leave to the nightingale her shady wood;
A privacy of glorious light is thine;
Whence thou dost pour upon the world a flood
Of harmony, with instinct more divine;
Type of the wise who soar, but never roam;
True to the kindred points of Heaven and
    Home!   12

ODE

INTIMATIONS OF IMMORTALITY FROM RECOLLEC-
TIONS OF EARLY CHILDHOOD*

I

There was a time when meadow, grove, and
    stream,
The earth, and every common sight,
        To me did seem
        Apparelled in celestial light,
The glory and the freshness of a dream.
It is not now as it hath been of yore;—
        Turn wheresoe'er I may,
            By night or day,
The things which I have seen I now can see no
        more.

* "To that dream-like vividness and splendour
which invest objects of sight in childhood,
every one, I believe, if he would look back,
could bear testimony, and I need not dwell
upon it here; but having in the poem regarded it as presumptive evidence of a prior
state of existence, I think it right to protest
against a conclusion, which has given pain to
some good and pious persons. It is far too
shadowy a notion to be recommended to faith,
as more than an element in our instincts of
immortality . . . A pre-existent state has
entered into the popular creeds of many nations; and, among all persons acquainted
with classic literature, is known as an in-
gredient in Platonic philosophy."—Extract
from Wordsworth's note. Compare Henry
Vaughan's *The Retreat*, p. 223.

II

The Rainbow comes and goes,   10
And lovely is the Rose,
The Moon doth with delight
Look round her when the heavens are bare;
Waters on a starry night
Are beautiful and fair;
The sunshine is a glorious birth;
But yet I know, where'er I go,
That there hath past away a glory from the
    earth.

III

Now, while the birds thus sing a joyous song,
And while the young lambs bound   20
As to the tabor's sound,
To me alone there came a thought of grief;
A timely utterance gave that thought relief,
And I again am strong:
The cataracts blow their trumpets from the
    steep;
No more shall grief of mine the season wrong;
I hear the Echoes through the mountains throng,
The Winds come to me from the fields of sleep,
And all the earth is gay;
Land and sea   30
Give themselves up to jollity,
And with the heart of May
Doth every Beast keep holiday;—
Thou Child of Joy,
Shout round me, let me hear thy shouts, thou
    happy Shepherd-boy!

IV

Ye blessèd Creatures, I have heard the call
Ye to each other make; I see
The heavens laugh with you in your jubilee;
My heart is at your festival,   40
My head hath its coronal,
The fulness of your bliss, I feel—I feel it all.
Oh evil day! if I were sullen
While Earth herself is adorning,
This sweet May-morning,
And the Children are culling
On every side,
In a thousand valleys far and wide,
Fresh flowers; while the sun shines warm,
And the Babe leaps up on his Mother's arm:—
I hear, I hear, with joy I hear!   51
—But there's a Tree, of many, one,
A single Field which I have looked upon,
Both of them speak of something that is gone:
The Pansy at my feet
Doth the same tale repeat:
Whither is fled the visionary gleam?
Where is it now, the glory and the dream?

V

Our birth is but a sleep and a forgetting:
The Soul that rises with us, our life's Star,   60
Hath had elsewhere its setting,
And cometh from afar:
Not in entire forgetfulness,
And not in utter nakedness,
But trailing clouds of glory do we come
From God, who is our home:
Heaven lies about us in our infancy!
Shades of the prison-house begin to close
Upon the growing Boy,
But he beholds the light, and whence it flows,
He sees it in his joy;   71
The Youth, who daily farther from the east
Must travel, still is Nature's Priest,
And by the vision splendid
Is on his way attended;
At length the Man perceives it die away,
And fade into the light of common day.

VI

Earth fills her lap with pleasures of her own;
Yearnings she hath in her own natural kind,
And, even with something of a Mother's mind,
And no unworthy aim,   81
The homely Nurse doth all she can
To make her Foster-child, her Inmate Man,
Forget the glories he hath known,
And that imperial palace whence he came.

VII

Behold the Child among his new-born blisses,
A six years' Darling of a pigmy size!
See, where 'mid work of his own hand he lies,
Fretted by sallies of his mother's kisses,
With light upon him from his father's eyes!   90
See, at his feet, some little plan or chart,
Some fragment from his dream of human life,
Shaped by himself with newly-learned art;
A wedding or a festival,
A mourning or a funeral;
And this hath now his heart,
And unto this he frames his song:
Then will he fit his tongue
To dialogues of business, love, or strife;
But it will not be long   100
Ere this be thrown aside,
And with new joy and pride
The little Actor cons another part;
Filling from time to time his "humorous[1]
    stage"
With all the Persons, down to palsied Age,
That Life brings with her in her equipage;
As if his whole vocation
Were endless imitation

1 humorsome

VIII

Thou, whose exterior semblance doth belie
    Thy Soul's immensity;   110
Thou best Philosopher, who yet dost keep
Thy heritage, thou Eye among the blind,
That, deaf and silent, read'st the eternal deep,
Haunted for ever by the eternal mind,—
    Mighty Prophet! Seer blest!
    On whom those truths do rest,
Which we are toiling all our lives to find,
In darkness lost, the darkness of the grave;
Thou, over whom thy Immortality
Broods like the Day, a Master o'er a Slave, 120
A Presence which is not to be put by;
Thou little Child, yet glorious in the might
Of heaven-born freedom on thy being's height,
Why with such earnest pains dost thou provoke
The years to bring the inevitable yoke,
Thus blindly with thy blessedness at strife?
Full soon thy Soul shall have her earthly freight,
And custom lie upon thee with a weight,
Heavy as frost, and deep almost as life!

IX

    O joy! that in our embers   130
    Is something that doth live,
    That nature yet remembers
    What was so fugitive!
The thought of our past years in me doth breed
Perpetual benediction; not indeed
For that which is most worthy to be blest—
Delight and liberty, the simple creed
Of Childhood, whether busy or at rest,
With new-fledged hope still fluttering in his
    breast:—
    Not for these I raise   140
    The song of thanks and praise;
    But for those obstinate questionings
    Of sense and outward things,
    Fallings from us, vanishings;
    Blank misgivings of a Creature
Moving about in worlds not realized,
High instincts before which our mortal Nature
Did tremble like a guilty Thing surprised:
    But for those first affections,
    Those shadowy recollections,   150
    Which, be they what they may,
Are yet the fountain light of all our day,
Are yet a master light of all our seeing;
    Uphold us, cherish, and have power to make
Our noisy years seem moments in the being
Of the eternal Silence: truths that wake,
    To perish never;
Which neither listlessness, nor mad endeavour,
    Nor Man nor Boy,
Nor all that is at enmity with joy,   160
Can utterly abolish or destroy!

Hence in a season of calm weather
    Though inland far we be,
Our Souls have sight of that immortal sea
    Which brought us hither,
    Can in a moment travel thither,
And see the Children sport upon the shore,
And hear the mighty waters rolling evermore.

X

Then sing, ye Birds, sing, sing a joyous song
    And let the young Lambs bound   17
    As to the tabor's sound!
We in thought will join your throng,
    Ye that pipe and ye that play,
    Ye that through your hearts to-day
    Feel the gladness of the May!
What though the radiance which was once s
    bright
Be now forever taken from my sight,
    Though nothing can bring back the hour
Of splendour in the grass, of glory in the flower
    We will grieve not, rather find   18
    Strength in what remains behind;
    In the primal sympathy
    Which having been must ever be;
    In the soothing thoughts that spring
    Out of human suffering;
    In the faith that looks through death,
In years that bring the philosophic mind.

XI

And O, ye Fountains, Meadows, Hills, and
    Groves,
Forebode not any severing of our loves!
Yet in my heart of hearts I feel your might;
I only have relinquished one delight   19
To live beneath your more habitual sway.
I love the Brooks which down their channels
    fret,
Even more than when I tripped lightly as they;
The innocent brightness of a new-born Day
    Is lovely yet;
The Clouds that gather round the setting sun
Do take a sober colouring from an eye
That hath kept watch o'er man's mortality;
Another race hath been, and other palms are
    won.   200
Thanks to the human heart by which we live,
Thanks to its tenderness, its joys, and fears,
To me the meanest flower that blows can give
Thoughts that do often lie too deep for tears.

COMPOSED UPON WESTMINSTER BRIDGE, SEPTEMBER 3, 1802

Earth has not anything to show more fair:
Dull would he be of soul who could pass by
A sight so touching in its majesty:

his City now doth, like a garment, wear
he beauty of the morning; silent, bare,
hips, towers, domes, theatres and temples lie
pen unto the fields, and to the sky;
ll bright and glittering in the smokeless air.
ever did sun more beautifully steep
n his first splendour, valley, rock, or hill;
e'er saw I, never felt, a calm so deep!
he river glideth at his own sweet will:
ear God! the very houses seem asleep;
nd all that mighty heart is lying still!

IT IS A BEAUTEOUS EVENING, CALM AND FREE

t is a beauteous evening, calm and free,
he holy time is quiet as a Nun
reathless with adoration; the broad sun
s sinking down in its tranquillity;
he gentleness of heaven broods o'er the Sea:
isten! the mighty Being is awake,
nd doth with his eternal motion make
 sound like thunder—everlastingly.
ear Child![1] dear Girl! that walkest with me here,
f thou appear untouched by solemn thought,
hy nature is not therefore less divine:
hou liest in Abraham's bosom[2] all the year;
nd worship'st at the Temple's inner shrine,
od being with thee when we know it not.

ON THE EXTINCTION OF THE VENETIAN REPUBLIC*

nce did She hold the gorgeous east in fee;
nd was the safeguard of the west: the worth
f Venice did not fall below her birth,
enice, the eldest Child of Liberty.
he was a maiden City, bright and free;
o guile seduced, no force could violate;
nd when she took unto herself a Mate,
he must espouse the everlasting Sea.†
nd what if she had seen those glories fade,
hose titles vanish, and that strength decay;
et shall some tribute of regret be paid
hen her long life hath reached its final day:
en are we, and must grieve when even the Shade
f that which once was great, is passed away.

Wordsworth's sister, Dorothy.
See *Luke* xvi, 22.
Venice threw off the yoke of the Eastern Empire as early as 809 and remained a republic or an oligarchy until conquered by Napoleon in 1797. At one time she had extensive possessions and colonies in the Levant.
The ancient Doges annually, on Ascension Day, threw a ring into the Adriatic in formal token of this espousal, or of perpetual dominion.

LONDON, 1802‡

Milton! thou should'st be living at this hour:
England hath need of thee; she is a fen
Of stagnant waters: altar, sword, and pen,
Fireside, the heroic wealth of hall and bower,
Have forfeited their ancient English dower
Of inward happiness. We are selfish men;
Oh! raise us up, return to us again;
And give us manners, virtue, freedom, power.
Thy soul was like a Star, and dwelt apart:
Thou hadst a voice whose sound was like the sea:
Pure as the naked heavens, majestic, free,
So didst thou travel on life's common way,
In cheerful godliness; and yet thy heart
The lowliest duties on herself did lay.

THE WORLD IS TOO MUCH WITH US

The world is too much with us; late and soon,
Getting and spending, we lay waste our powers:
Little we see in Nature that is ours;
We have given our hearts away, a sordid boon!
The Sea that bares her bosom to the moon;
The winds that will be howling at all hours,
And are up-gathered now like sleeping flowers;
For this, for everything, we are out of tune;
It moves us not.—Great God! I'd rather be
A Pagan suckled in a creed outworn;
So might I, standing on this pleasant lea,
Have glimpses that would make me less forlorn;
Have sight of Proteus rising from the sea;
Or hear old Triton blow his wreathéd horn.

AFTER-THOUGHTS§

I thought of Thee, my partner and my guide,
As being past away.—Vain sympathies!
For, backward, Duddon, as I cast my eyes,
I see what was, and is, and will abide;
Still glides the Stream, and shall forever glide;
The Form remains, the Function never dies;
While we, the brave, the mighty, and the wise,
We Men, who in our morn of youth defied
The elements, must vanish;—be it so!
Enough, if something from our hands have power
To live, and act, and serve the future hour;
And if, as toward the silent tomb we go,
Through love, through hope, and faith's transcendent dower,
We feel that we are greater than we know.

‡ Written in despondency over the inert attitude of England toward the hopes and ideals of the revolutionists and the opponents of Napoleon.
§ The conclusion of a series of sonnets to the river Duddon.

SAMUEL TAYLOR COLERIDGE
(1772-1834)

KUBLA KHAN*

In Xanadu[1] did Kubla Khan[2]
A stately pleasure-dome decree:
Where Alph, the sacred river, ran
Through caverns measureless to man
  Down to a sunless sea.
So twice five miles of fertile ground
With walls and towers were girdled round:
And here were gardens bright with sinuous rills,
Where blossomed many an incense-bearing tree;
And here were forests ancient as the hills,   10
Enfolding sunny spots of greenery.

But oh! that deep romantic chasm which
    slanted
Down the green hill athwart a cedarn cover!
A savage place! as holy and enchanted
As e'er beneath a waning moon was haunted
By woman wailing for her demon-lover!
And from this chasm, with ceaseless turmoil
    seething,
As if this earth in fast thick pants were
    breathing,
A mighty fountain momently was forced:
Amid whose swift half-intermitted burst   20
Huge fragments vaulted like rebounding hail,
Or chaffy grain beneath the thresher's flail:
And 'mid these dancing rocks at once and ever
It flung up momently the sacred river.
Five miles meandering with a mazy motion
Through wood and dale the sacred river ran,
Then reached the caverns measureless to man,
And sank in tumult to a lifeless ocean:
And 'mid this tumult Kubla heard from far
Ancestral voices prophesying war!   30

    The shadow of the dome of pleasure
    Floated midway on the waves;
    Where was heard the mingled measure
    From the fountain and the caves.
It was a miracle of rare device,
A sunny pleasure-dome with caves of ice!

    A damsel with a dulcimer
    In a vision once I saw:
    It was an Abyssinian maid,
    And on her dulcimer she played,   40

* Coleridge says this poem was composed when he had fallen asleep just after reading from Marco Polo in *Purchas's Pilgrimage* how "In Xandu did Cublai Can build a stately palace," etc. There were more lines which he failed to record. Charles Lamb spoke of the poem as "a vision which he [Coleridge] repeats so enchantingly that it irradiates and brings heaven and elysian bowers into my parlour when he sings or says it."

[1] A region in Tartary.   [2] Kubla the Cham, or Emperor.

    Singing of Mount Abora.
    Could I revive within me
    Her symphony and song,
To such a deep delight 'twould win me,
That with music loud and long,
I would build that dome in air,
That sunny dome! those caves of ice!
And all who heard should see them there,
And all should cry, Beware! Beware!
His flashing eyes, his floating hair!   5
Weave a circle round him thrice,
And close your eyes with holy dread,
For he on honey-dew hath fed,
And drunk the milk of Paradise.

THE RIME OF THE ANCIENT MARINER†

IN SEVEN PARTS

ARGUMENT

How a Ship having passed the Line was drive by Storms to the cold Country towards the Sout Pole; and how from thence she made her cours to the Tropical Latitude of the Great Pacif Ocean; and of the strange things that befell; an in what manner the Ancyent Marinere came bac to his own Country.

PART I.

It is an ancient Mariner,
And he stoppeth one of three.
"By thy long gray beard and glittering ey
Now wherefore stopp'st thou me?

1-12. An ancient Mariner meeteth three Ga lants bidden to a wedding-feast, and detaineth on

† From the publication, in 1798, of the *Lyric Ballads*, the joint production of Coleridg and Wordsworth, may be dated very def nitely the recognition of the new spirit English literature which is commonly spoke of as the Romantic Revival. See *Eng. Lit* pp. 232-235. Coleridge, in the fourteent chapter of his *Biographia Literaria*, writes the occasion of the *Lyrical Ballads* as follow

"During the first year that Mr. Wordsworth an I were neighbours, our conversations turned fr quently on the two cardinal points of poetry, th power of exciting the sympathy of the reader by faithful adherence to the truth of nature, an the power of giving the interest of novelty by th modifying colours of the imagination. The su den charm, which accidents of light and shad which moonlight or sunset, diffused over a know and familiar landscape, appeared to represent th practicability of combining both. These are th poetry of nature. The thought suggested itse (to which of us I do not recollect) that a seri of poems might be composed of two sorts. the one, the incidents and agents were to be, th part at least, supernatural; and the excellenc aimed at was to consist in the interesting of th affections by the dramatic truth of such emotion as would naturally accompany such situation supposing them real. And real in this sense the have been to every human being who, from what ever source of delusion, has at any time believ

he Bridegroom's doors are opened wide,
nd I am next of kin;
he guests are met, the feast is set:
ay'st hear the merry din.''

e holds him with his skinny hand,
There was a ship,'' quoth he.   10
Hold off! unhand me, gray-beard loon!''
ftsoons[1] his hand dropt he.

e holds him with his glittering eye—
he Wedding-Guest stood still,
nd listens like a three years' child:
he Mariner hath his will.

he Wedding-Guest sat on a stone:
.e cannot choose but hear;
nd thus spake on that ancient man,
he bright-eyed Mariner.   20

imself under supernatural agency. For the
econd class, subjects were to be chosen from
rdinary life; the characters and incidents were
o be such as will be found in every village and
.s vicinity where there is a meditative and feel-
ng mind to seek after them, or to notice them
hen they present themselves.
"In this idea originated the plan of the *Lyrical
allads;* in which it was agreed that my en-
eavours should be directed to persons and char-
cters supernatural, or at least romantic; yet so
s to transfer from our inward nature a human
nterest and a semblance of truth sufficient to
rocure for these shadows of imagination that
illing suspension of disbelief for the moment,
hich constitutes poetic faith. Mr. Wordsworth,
n the other hand, was to propose to himself as
is object, to give the charm of novelty to things
f every day, and to excite a feeling analogous to
e supernatural, by awakening the mind's atten-
on from the lethargy of custom, and directing it
o the loveliness and the wonders of the world
efore us; an inexhaustible treasure, but for
hich, in consequence of the film of familiarity
nd selfish solicitude, we have eyes, yet see not,
rs that hear not, and hearts that neither feel
or understand. With this view I wrote *The
ncient Mariner.*"
he poem is here given in the revised text of 1829.
As first printed in the *Lyrical Ballads,* the
diction and spelling were considerably more
archaic, as the Argument, which was not
retained in the later edition, shows. Wordsworth gives the following information:
"Much the greatest part of the story was
Mr. Coleridge's invention, but certain parts
I suggested; for example, some crime was
to be committed which should bring upon
the Old Navigator, as Coleridge afterward delighted to call him, the spectral persecution,
as a consequence of that crime and his own
wanderings. I had been reading in Shel-
vocke's *Voyages* a day or two before, that,
while doubling Cape Horn, they frequently
saw albatrosses in that latitude, the largest
sort of sea-fowl, some extending their
wings twelve or thirteen feet. 'Suppose,' said
I, 'you represent him as having killed one
of these birds on entering the South Sea,
and that the tutelary spirits of these regions take upon them to avenge the crime.'
The incident was thought fit for the purpose
and adopted accordingly." Wordsworth also
furnished several lines of the poem, especially 15-16, 226-227.

at once

''The ship was cheered, the harbour cleared,
Merrily did we drop
Below the kirk, below the hill,
Below the lighthouse top.

The sun came up upon the left,
Out of the sea came he!
And he shone bright, and on the right
Went down into the sea.

Higher and higher every day,
Till over the mast at noon—''   30
The Wedding-Guest here beat his breast,
For he heard the loud bassoon.

The bride hath paced into the hall,
Red as a rose is she;
Nodding their heads before her goes
The merry minstrelsy.

The Wedding-Guest he beat his breast,
Yet he cannot choose but hear;
And thus spake on that ancient man,
The bright-eyed Mariner.   40

''And now the Storm-blast came, and he
Was tyrannous and strong:
He struck with his o'ertaking wings,
And chased us south along.

With sloping masts and dipping prow,
As who pursued with yell and blow
Still treads the shadow of his foe,
And forward bends his head,
The ship drove fast, loud roared the blast,
And southward aye we fled.   50

And now there came both mist and snow,
And it grew wondrous cold:
And ice, mast-high, came floating by,
As green as emerald.

And through the drifts the snowy clifts
Did send a dismal sheen:
Nor shapes of men nor beasts we ken—
The ice was all between.

13-21. The Wedding-Guest is spell-bound by the
eye of the old seafaring man, and constrained to
hear his tale.
21-30. The Mariner tells how the ship sailed
southward with a good wind and fair weather, till
it reached the line.
31-40. The Wedding Guest heareth the bridal
music: but the Mariner continueth his tale.
41-50. The ship driven by a storm toward the
south pole.
51-62. The land of ice, and of fearful sounds,
where no living thing was to be seen.

The ice was here, the ice was there,
The ice was all around: 60
It cracked and growled, and roared and howled,
Like voices in a swound!²

At length did cross an Albatross,
Thorough the fog it came;
As if it had been a Christian soul,
We hailed it in God's name.

It ate the food it ne'er had eat,³
And round and round it flew.
The ice did split with a thunder-fit;
The helmsman steered us through!   70

And a good south wind sprung up behind;
The Albatross did follow,
And every day, for food or play,
Came to the mariner's hollo!

In mist or cloud, on mast or shroud,
It perched for vespers nine;⁴
Whiles all the night, through fog-smoke white,
Glimmered the white moon-shine.''

"God save thee, ancient Mariner!
From the fiends, that plague thee thus!—   80
Why look'st thou so?''—''With my cross-bow
I shot the Albatross.

PART II.

"The Sun now rose upon the right:
Out of the sea came he,
Still hid in mist, and on the left
Went down into the sea.

And the good south wind still blew behind,
But no sweet bird did follow,
Nor any day for food or play
Came to the mariner's hollo!

And I had done a hellish thing,
And it would work 'em woe:

63-70. Till a great sea bird, called the Albatross, came through the snow-fog, and was received with great joy and hospitality.
71-78. And lo! the Albatross proveth a bird of good omen, and followeth the ship as it returned northward through fog and floating ice.
79-82. The ancient Mariner inhospitably killeth the pious bird of good omen.
83-96. His shipmates cry out against the ancient Mariner, for killing the bird of good luck.
97-102. But when the fog cleared off, they justify the same, and thus make themselves accomplices in the crime.
103-106. The fair breeze continues; the ship enters the Pacific Ocean, and sails northward, even till it reaches the Line.
2 swoon, dream
3 "The marineres gave it biscuit-worms" (1798 ed.)
4 nine evenings

For all averred, I had killed the bird
That made the breeze to blow.
Ah wretch! said they, the bird to slay,
That made the breeze to blow!

Nor dim nor red, like God's own head,
The glorious Sun uprist:⁵
Then all averred, I had killed the bird
That brought the fog and mist.   10
'Twas right, said they, such birds to slay,
That bring the fog and mist.

The fair breeze blew, the white foam flew,
The furrow followed free;
We were the first that ever burst
Into that silent sea.

Down dropt the breeze, the sails dropt down
'Twas sad as sad could be;
And we did speak only to break
The silence of the sea!   11

All in a hot and copper sky,
The bloody Sun, at noon,
Right up above the mast did stand,
No bigger than the Moon.

Day after day, day after day,
We stuck, nor breath nor motion;
As idle as a painted ship
Upon a painted ocean.

Water, water, everywhere.
And all the boards did shrink;   12
Water, water, everywhere,
Nor any drop to drink.

The very deep did rot: O Christ!
That ever this should be!
Yea, slimy things did crawl with legs
Upon the slimy sea.

About, about, in reel and rout
The death-fires danced at night;
The water, like a witch's oils,
Burnt green, and blue and white.   13

And some in dreams assured were
Of the Spirit that plagued us so;
Nine fathom deep he had followed us
From the land of mist and snow.

107-118. The ship hath been suddenly becalmed
119-130. And the Albatross begins to be avenged.
131-138. A Spirit had followed them; one of the invisible inhabitants of this planet, neither departed souls nor angels; concerning whom the learned Jew, Josephus, and the Platonic Constantinopolitan, Michael Psellus, may be consulted. They are very numerous, and there is no climate or element without one or more.
5 Properly a present tense; cp. p. 61, note 16.

And every tongue, through utter drought,
Was withered at the root;
We could not speak, no more than if
We had been choked with soot.

Ah! well-a-day! what evil looks
Had I from old and young!   140
Instead of the cross, the Albatross
About my neck was hung.

PART III.

'There passed a weary time. Each throat
Was parched, and glazed each eye.
A weary time! a weary time!
How glazed each weary eye!—
When looking westward, I beheld
A something in the sky.

At first it seemed a little speck,
And then it seemed a mist;   150
It moved and moved, and took at last
A certain shape, I wist.⁶

A speck, a mist, a shape, I wist!
And still it neared and neared:
As if it dodged a water-sprite,
It plunged and tacked and veered.

With throats unslaked, with black lips baked,
We could nor laugh, nor wail;
Through utter drought all dumb we stood!
I bit my arm, I sucked the blood,   160
And cried, A sail! a sail!

With throats unslaked, with black lips baked,
Agape they heard me call:
Gramercy!⁷ they for joy did grin,
And all at once their breath drew in,
As they were drinking all.

See! see!' (I cried) 'she tacks no more!
Hither to work us weal,
Without a breeze, without a tide,
She steadies with upright keel!'   170

The western wave was all aflame.
The day was well-nigh done!
Almost upon the western wave
Rested the broad bright Sun;
When that strange shape drove suddenly
Betwixt us and the Sun.

And straight the Sun was flecked with bars,
(Heaven's Mother send us grace!)
As if through a dungeon-grate he peered
With broad and burning face.   180

Alas! (thought I, and my heart beat loud)
How fast she nears and nears!
Are those her sails that glance in the Sun,
Like restless gossameres?

Are those her ribs through which the Sun
Did peer, as through a grate?
And is that Woman all her crew?
Is that a Death? and are there two?
Is Death that woman's mate?

Her lips were red, her looks were free,   190
Her locks were yellow as gold:
Her skin was as white as leprosy,
The Night-mare, Life-in-Death, was she,
Who thicks man's blood with cold.

The naked hulk alongside came,
And the twain were casting dice;
'The game is done! I've won! I've won!'
Quoth she, and whistles thrice.

The Sun's rim dips; the stars rush out.
At one stride comes the dark;   200
With far-heard whisper, o'er the sea,
Off shot the spectre-bark.

We listened and looked sideways up!
Fear at my heart, as at a cup,
My life-blood seemed to sip!
The stars were dim, and thick the night,
The steersman's face by his lamp gleamed white;
From the sails the dew did drip—
Till clomb above the eastern bar
The hornèd Moon, with one bright star   210
Within the nether tip.

139-142. The shipmates, in their sore distress, would fain throw the whole guilt on the ancient Mariner: in sign whereof they hang the dead sea-bird round his neck.
143-156. The ancient Mariner beholdeth a sign in the element afar off.
157-163. At its nearer approach, it seemeth him to be a ship; and at a dear ransom he freeth his speech from the bonds of thirst.
164-166. A flash of joy.
167-176. And horror follows. For can it be a ship that comes onward without wind or tide?
⁶ I knew (but apparently confused in form and meaning with the old participial adverb y-wis, "surely").
great thanks

177-186. It seemeth him but the skeleton of a ship. And its ribs are seen as bars on the face of the setting Sun.
187-194. The Spectre-Woman and her Death-mate, and no other on board the skeleton-ship. Like vessel, like crew!
195-198. Death and Life-in-Death have diced for the ship's crew, and she (the latter) winneth the ancient Mariner.
199-202. No twilight within the courts of the Sun.
203-223. At the rising of the Moon, one after

One after one, by the star-dogged Moon,
Too quick for groan or sigh,
Each turned his face with a ghastly pang,
And cursed me with his eye.

Four times fifty living men,
(And I heard nor sigh nor groan)
With heavy thump, a lifeless lump,
They dropped down one by one.

The souls did from their bodies fly,—   220
They fled to bliss or woe!
And every soul, it passed me by,
Like the whizz of my cross-bow!''—

PART IV.

''I fear thee, ancient Mariner!
I fear thy skinny hand
And thou art long, and lank, and brown,
As is the ribbed sea-sand.

I fear thee and thy glittering eye,
And thy skinny hand, so brown.''—
''Fear not, fear not, thou Wedding-Guest!
This body dropt not down.   231

Alone, alone, all, all alone,
Alone on a wide wide sea!
And never a saint took pity on
My soul in agony.

The many men, so beautiful!
And they all dead did lie:
And a thousand thousand slimy things
Lived on; and so did I.

I looked upon the rotting sea,   240
And drew my eyes away;
I looked upon the rotting deck,
And there the dead men lay.

I looked to heaven, and tried to pray;
But or ever a prayer had gusht,
A wicked whisper came, and made
My heart as dry as dust.

I closed my lips, and kept them close,
And the balls like pulses beat;
For the sky and the sea, and the sea and the
    sky   250

Lay like a load on my weary eye,
And the dead were at my feet.

The cold sweat melted from their limbs,
Nor rot nor reek did they:
The look with which they looked on me
Had never passed away.

An orphan's curse would drag to hell
A spirit from on high;
But oh! more horrible than that
Is a curse in a dead man's eye!   26
Seven days, seven nights, I saw that curse.
And yet I could not die.

The moving Moon went up the sky,
And nowhere did abide;
Softly she was going up,
And a star or two beside—

Her beams bemocked the sultry main,
Like April hoar-frost spread;
But where the ship's huge shadow lay,
The charmed water burnt alway   27
A still and awful red.

Beyond the shadow of the ship,
I watched the water-snakes:
They moved in tracks of shining white,
And when they reared, the elfish light
Fell off in hoary flakes.

Within the shadow of the ship
I watched their rich attire:
Blue, glossy green, and velvet black,
They coiled and swam; and every track   28
Was a flash of golden fire.

O happy living things! no tongue
Their beauty might declare:
A spring of love gushed from my heart,
And I blessed them unaware:
Sure my kind saint took pity on me,
And I blessed them unaware.

The selfsame moment I could pray;
And from my neck so free

another his shipmates drop down dead. But Life-in-Death begins her work on the ancient Mariner.
224-235. The Wedding-Guest feareth that a Spirit is talking to him: but the ancient Mariner assureth him of his bodily life, and proceedeth to relate his horrible penance.
236-252. He despiseth the creatures of the calm, and envieth that they should live, and so many lie dead.
253-262. But the curse liveth for him in the eye of the dead men.
263-271. In his loneliness and fixedness he yearneth towards the journeying Moon, and the stars that still sojourn, yet still move onward: and everywhere the blue sky belongs to them, and is their appointed rest, and their native country and their own natural homes, which they enter unannounced, as lords that are certainly expected and yet there is a silent joy at their arrival.
272-281. By the light of the Moon he beholdeth God's creatures of the great calm.
282-283. Their beauty and their happiness.
284-287. He blesseth them in his heart.
288-291. The spell begins to break.

The Albatross fell off, and sank 290
Like lead into the sea.

PART V.

'Oh sleep! it is a gentle thing,
Beloved from' pole to pole!
To Mary Queen the praise be given!
She sent the gentle sleep from Heaven,
That slid into my soul.

The silly[8] buckets on the deck,
That had so long remained,
  I dreamt that they were filled with dew;
And when I awoke, it rained. 300

My lips were wet, my throat was cold,
My garments all were dank;
Sure I had drunken in my dreams,
And still my body drank.

I moved, and could not feel my limbs:
I was so light—almost
I thought that I had died in sleep,
And was a blessed ghost.

And soon I heard a roaring wind:
It did not come anear; 310
But with its sound it shook the sails,
That were so thin and sere.

The upper air burst into life!
And a hundred fire-flags sheen,
To and fro they were hurried about!
And to and fro, and in and out,
The wan stars danced between.

And the coming wind did roar more loud,
And the sails did sigh like sedge;
And the rain poured down from one black
  cloud; 320
The Moon was at its edge.

The thick black cloud was cleft, and still
The Moon was at its side:
Like waters shot from some high crag,
The lightning fell with never a jag,
A river steep and wide.

The loud wind never reached the ship,
Yet now the ship moved on!
Beneath the lightning and the Moon
The dead men gave a groan. 330

They groaned, they stirred, they all uprose,
Nor spake, nor moved their eyes;
It had been strange, even in a dream,
To have seen those dead men rise.

The helmsman steered, the ship moved on;
Yet never a breeze up blew:
The mariners all 'gan work the ropes,
Where they were wont to do;
They raised their limbs like lifeless tools—
We were a ghastly crew. 340

The body of my brother's son
Stood by me, knee to knee:
The body and I pulled at one rope
But he said nought to me."—

"I fear thee, ancient Mariner!"—
"Be calm, thou Wedding-Guest!
'Twas not those souls that fled in pain,
Which to their corses came again,
But a troop of spirits blest:

For when it dawned—they dropped their
  arms, 350
And clustered round the mast;
Sweet sounds rose slowly through their mouths,
And from their bodies passed.

Around, around, flew each sweet sound,
Then darted to the Sun;
Slowly the sounds came back again,
Now mixed, now one by one.

Sometimes a-dropping from the sky
I heard the sky-lark sing;
Sometimes all little birds that are, 360
How they seemed to fill the sea and air
With their sweet jargoning!

And now 'twas like all instruments,
Now like a lonely flute;
And now it is an angel's song,
That makes the heavens be mute.

It ceased; yet still the sails made on
A pleasant noise till noon,
A noise like of a hidden brook
In the leafy month of June, 370
That to the sleeping woods all night
Singeth a quiet tune.

Till noon we quietly sailed on,
Yet never a breeze did breathe:
Slowly and smoothly went the ship,
Moved onward from beneath.

292-308. By grace of the holy Mother, the
ancient Mariner is refreshed with rain.
309-326. He heareth sounds and seeth strange
sights and commotions in the sky and the element.
327-376. The bodies of the ship's crew are inspired, and the ship moves on; but not by the
souls of the men, nor by demons of earth or middle air, but by a blessed troop of angelic spirits,
sent down by the invocation of the guardian saint.
Perhaps "useless"; but the original meaning
"blessed" will fit very well.

Under the keel nine fathom deep,
From the land of mist and snow,
The spirit slid; and it was he
That made the ship to go.   380
The sails at noon left off their tune,
And the ship stood still also.

The Sun, right up above the mast,
Had fixed her to the ocean:
But in a minute she 'gan stir,
With a short uneasy motion—
Backwards and forwards half her length
With a short uneasy motion.

Then like a pawing horse let go,
She made a sudden bound: 390
It flung the blood into my head,
And I fell down in a swound.

How long in that same fit I lay,
I have not to declare;
But ere my living life returned,
I heard and in my soul discerned
Two voices in the air.

'Is it he?' quoth one, 'Is this the man?
By him who died on cross,
With his cruel bow he laid full low   400
The harmless Albatross.

The spirit who bideth by himself
In the land of mist and snow,
He loved the bird that loved the man
Who shot him with his bow.'

The other was a softer voice,
As soft as honey-dew:
Quoth he, 'The man hath penance done,
And penance more will do.'

PART VI.

FIRST VOICE

'' 'But tell me, tell me! speak again,   410
Thy soft response renewing—
What makes that ship drive on so fast?
What is the ocean doing?'

377-392. The lonesome Spirit from the south-
pole carries on the ship as far as the Line, in
obedience to the angelic troop, but still requireth
vengeance.
393-409. The Polar Spirit's fellow-demons, the
invisible inhabitants of the element, take part in
his wrong; and two of them relate one to the
other, that penance long and heavy for the ancient Mariner hath been accorded to the Polar
Spirit, who returneth southward.
410-429. The Mariner hath been cast into a
trance; for the angelic power causeth the vessel
to drive northward faster than human life could
endure.

SECOND VOICE

'Still as a slave before his lord,
The ocean hath no blast;
His great bright eye most silently
Up to the Moon is cast—

If he may know which way to go;
For she guides him smooth or grim.
See, brother, see! how graciously   420
She looketh down on him.'

FIRST VOICE

'But why drives on that ship so fast,
Without or wave or wind?'

SECOND VOICE

'The air is cut away before,
And closes from behind.

Fly, brother, fly! more high, more high!
Or we shall be belated:
For slow and slow that ship will go,
When the Mariner's trance is abated.'

I woke, and we were sailing on   430
As in a gentle weather:
'Twas night, calm night, the Moon was high
The dead men stood together.

All stood together on the deck,
For a charnel-dungeon fitter:
All fixed on me their stony eyes,
That in the Moon did glitter.

The pang, the curse, with which they died,
Had never passed away:
I could not draw my eyes from theirs,   440
Nor turn them up to pray.

And now this spell was snapt: once more
I viewed the ocean green,
And looked far forth, yet little saw
Of what had else been seen—

Like one, that on a lonesome road
Doth walk in fear and dread,
And having once turned round walks on,
And turns no more his head;
Because he knows, a frightful fiend   450
Doth close behind him tread.

But soon there breathed a wind on me,
Nor sound nor motion made:

430-441. The supernatural motion is retarded
the Mariner awakes, and his penance begins anew
442-463. The curse is finally expiated.

Its path was not upon the sea,
In ripple or in shade.

It raised my hair, it fanned my cheek
Like a meadow-gale of spring—
It mingled strangely with my fears,
Yet it felt like a welcoming.

Swiftly, swiftly flew the ship,   460
Yet she sailed softly too:
Sweetly, sweetly blew the breeze—
On me alone it blew.

Oh! dream of joy! is this indeed
The light-house top I see?
Is this the hill? is this the kirk?
Is this mine own countree?

We drifted o'er the harbour-bar,
And I with sobs did pray—
'O let me be awake, my God!   470
Or let me sleep alway.'

The harbour-bay was clear as glass,
So smoothly it was strewn!
And on the bay the moonlight lay,
And the shadow of the Moon.

The rock shone bright, the kirk no less,
That stands above the rock:
The moonlight steeped in silentness
The steady weathercock.

And the bay was white with silent light   480
Till rising from the same,
Full many shapes, that shadows were,
In crimson colours came.

A little distance from the prow
Those crimson shadows were:
I turned my eyes upon the deck—
Oh, Christ! what saw I there!

Each corse lay flat, lifeless and flat,
And, by the holy rood!9
A man all light, a seraph-man,   490
On every corse there stood.

This seraph-band, each waved his hand:
It was a heavenly sight!
They stood as signals to the land,
Each one a lovely light;

This seraph-band, each waved his hand,
No voice did they impart—
No voice; but oh! the silence sank
Like music on my heart.

But soon I heard the dash of oars,   500
I heard the Pilot's cheer:
My head was turned perforce away,
And I saw a boat appear.

The Pilot and the Pilot's boy,
I heard them coming fast:
Dear Lord in Heaven! it was a joy
The dead men could not blast.

I saw a third—I heard his voice:
It is the Hermit good!
He singeth loud his godly hymns   510
That he makes in the wood.
He'll shrieve my soul, he'll wash away
The Albatross's blood.

PART VII.

"This Hermit good lives in that wood
Which slopes down to the sea.
How loudly his sweet voice he rears!
He loves to talk with marineres
That come from a far countree.

He kneels at morn, and noon, and eve—
He hath a cushion plump: 520
It is the moss that wholly hides
The rotted old oak stump.

The skiff-boat neared: I heard them talk,
'Why, this is strange, I trow!
Where are those lights so many and fair,
That signal made but now?'

'Strange, by my faith!' the Hermit said—
'And they answered not our cheer!
The planks looked warped! and see those sails,
How thin they are and sere!   530
I never saw aught like to them,
Unless perchance it were

Brown skeletons of leaves that lag
My forest-brook along;
When the ivy-tod10 is heavy with snow,
And the owlet whoops to the wolf below,
That eats the she-wolf's young.'

'Dear Lord! it hath a fiendish look'—
(The Pilot made reply)
'I am a-feared.'—'Push on, push on!'   540
Said the Hermit cheerily.

The boat came closer to the ship,
But I nor spake nor stirred;
The boat came close beneath the ship,
And straight a sound was heard.

464-479. The ancient Mariner beholdeth his native country.
480-499. The angelic spirits leave the dead bodies and appear in their own forms of light.
9 cross

513-545. The Hermit of the Wood approacheth the ship with wonder.
10 ivy-bush

Under the water it rumbled on,
Still louder and more dread:
It reached the ship, it split the bay;
The ship went down like lead.

Stunned by that loud and dreadful sound, 550
Which sky and ocean smote,
Like one that hath been seven days drowned
My body lay afloat;
But swift as dreams, myself I found
Within the Pilot's boat.

Upon the whirl, where sank the ship,
The boat spun round and round;
And all was still, save that the hill
Was telling of the sound.

I moved my lips—the Pilot shrieked 560
And fell down in a fit;
The holy Hermit raised his eyes,
And prayed where he did sit.

I took the oars: The Pilot's boy,
Who now doth crazy go,
Laughed loud and long, and all the while
His eyes went to and fro.
'Ha! ha!' quoth he, 'full plain I see,
The Devil knows how to row.'

And now, all in my own countree, 570
I stood on the firm land!
The Hermit stepped forth from the boat,
And scarcely he could stand.

'O shrieve me, shrieve me, holy man!'
The Hermit crossed his brow.
'Say quick,' quoth he, 'I bid thee say—
What manner of man art thou?'

Forthwith this frame of mine was wrenched
With a woful agony,
Which forced me to begin my tale; 580
And then it left me free.

Since then, at an uncertain hour,
That agony returns:
And till my ghastly tale is told,
This heart within me burns.

I pass, like night, from land to land;
I have strange power of speech;
That moment that his face I see,

I know the man that must hear me: 590
To him my tale I teach.

What loud uproar bursts from that door!
The wedding-guests are there:
But in the garden-bower the bride
And bride-maids singing are:
And hark the little vesper bell,
Which biddeth me to prayer!

O Wedding-Guest! this soul hath been
Alone on a wide wide sea:
So lonely 'twas, that God himself 600
Scarce seemed there to be.

O sweeter than the marriage-feast,
'Tis sweeter far to me,
To walk together to the kirk,
With a goodly company!—

To walk together to the kirk,
And all together pray.
While each to his great Father bends,
Old men, and babes, and loving friends
And youths and maidens gay!

Farewell, farewell! but this I tell 610
To thee, thou Wedding-Guest!
He prayeth well, who loveth well
Both man and bird and beast.

He prayeth best, who loveth best
All things both great and small;
For the dear God who loveth us,
He made and loveth all.''

The Mariner, whose eye is bright,
Whose beard with age is hoar,
Is gone; and now the Wedding-Guest 620
Turned from the bridegroom's door.

He went like one that hath been stunned,
And is of sense forlorn:
A sadder and a wiser man,
He rose the morrow morn.

CHRISTABEL*

PART THE FIRST

'Tis the middle of night by the castle clock,
And the owls have awakened the crowing cock
To—whit!——Tu—whoo!
And hark, again! the crowing cock,
How drowsily it crew.

546-549. The ship suddenly sinketh.
550-573. The ancient Mariner is saved in the Pilot's boat.
574-581. The ancient Mariner earnestly entreateth the Hermit to shrieve him; and the penance of life falls on him.
582-625. And ever and anon throughout his future life an agony constraineth him to travel from land to land, and to teach, by his own example, love and reverence to all things that God made and loveth.

* Written in 1797, and published in 1816, when a second part was added, though "three parts yet to come" were never written. The first part circulated in manuscript and had considerable influence, especially in the matter of form, on Scott and other poets. See Eng. Lit., pp. 243, 262.

Sir Leoline, the Baron rich,
Hath a toothless mastiff, which
From her kennel beneath the rock
Maketh answer to the clock,
Four for the quarters, and twelve for the hour;
Ever and aye, by shine and shower, 11
Sixteen short howls, not over loud;
Some say, she sees my lady's shroud.

Is the night chilly and dark?
The night is chilly, but not dark.
The thin gray cloud is spread on high,
It covers but not hides the sky.
The moon is behind, and at the full;
And yet she looks both small and dull.
The night is chill, the cloud is gray; 20
'Tis a month before the month of May,
And the Spring comes slowly up this way.

The lovely lady, Christabel,
Whom her father loves so well,
What makes her in the woods so late,
A furlong from the castle gate?
She had dreams all yesternight
Of her own betrothed knight;
And she in the midnight wood will pray
For the weal of her lover that's far away. 30

She stole along, she nothing spoke,
The sighs she heaved were soft and low,
And naught was green upon the oak
But moss and rarest mistletoe:
She kneels beneath the huge oak tree,
And in silence prayeth she.

The lady sprang up suddenly,
The lovely lady, Christabel!
It moaned as near, as near can be,
But what it is she cannot tell.— 40
One the other side it seems to be,
Of the huge, broad-breasted, old oak tree.

The night is chill; the forest bare;
Is it the wind that moaneth bleak?
There is not wind enough in the air
To move away the ringlet curl
From the lovely lady's cheek—
There is not wind enough to twirl
The one red leaf, the last of its clan,
That dances as often as dance it can, 50
Hanging so light, and hanging so high,
On the topmost twig that looks up at the sky.

Hush, beating heart of Christabel!
Jesu, Maria, shield her well!
She folded her arms beneath her cloak,
And stole to the other side of the oak.
What sees she there?

There she sees a damsel bright,
Drest in a silken robe of white,
That shadowy in the moonlight shone; 60
The neck that made the white robe wan,
Her stately neck, and arms were bare;
Her blue-veined feet unsandal'd were,
And wildly glittered here and there
The gems entangled in her hair.
I guess, 'twas frightful there to see
A lady so richly clad as she—
Beautiful exceedingly!

Mary mother, save me now!
(Said Christabel,) And who art thou? 70

The lady strange made answer meet,
And her voice was faint and sweet:—
Have pity on my sore distress,
I scarce can speak for weariness:
Stretch forth thy hand, and have no fear!
Said Christabel, How camest thou here?
And the lady, whose voice was faint and sweet,
Did thus pursue her answer meet:

My sire is of a noble line,
And my name is Geraldine: 80
Five warriors seized me yestermorn,
Me, even me, a maid forlorn:
They choked my cries with force and fright,
And tied me on a palfrey white.
The palfrey was as fleet as wind,
And they rode furiously behind.
They spurred amain, their steeds were white:
And once we crossed the shade of night.
As sure as Heaven shall rescue me,
I have no thought what men they be; 90
Nor do I know how long it is
(For I have lain entranced I wis)
Since one, the tallest of the five,
Took me from the palfrey's back,
A weary woman, scarce alive.
Some muttered words his comrades spoke:
He placed me underneath this oak;
He swore they would return with haste;
Whither they went I cannot tell—
I thought I heard, some minutes past, 100
Sounds as of a castle bell.
Stretch forth thy hand (thus ended she),
And help a wretched maid to flee.

Then Christabel stretched forth her hand,
And comforted fair Geraldine:
O well, bright dame! may you command
The service of Sir Leoline;
And gladly our stout chivalry
Will he send forth and friends withal
To guide and guard you safe and free 110
Home to your noble father's hall.

She rose: and forth with steps they passed
That strove to be, and were not, fast.
Her gracious stars the lady blest,
And thus spake on sweet Christabel:
All our household are at rest,
The hall as silent as the cell;
Sir Leoline is weak in health,
And may not well awakened be,
But we will move as if in stealth,   120
And I beseech your courtesy,
This night, to share your couch with me.

They crossed the moat, and Christabel
Took the key that fitted well;
A little door she opened straight,
All in the middle of the gate;
The gate that was ironed within and without,
Where an army in battle array had marched
   out.
The lady sank, belike through pain,
And Christabel with might and main   130
Lifted her up, a weary weight,
Over the threshold of the gate:
Then the lady rose again,
And moved, as she were not in pain.*

So free from danger, free from fear,
They crossed the court; right glad they were.
And Christabel devoutly cried
To the lady by her side,
Praise we the Virgin all divine
Who hath rescued thee from thy distress!   140
Alas, alas! said Geraldine,
I cannot speak for weariness.
So free from danger, free from fear,
They crossed the court: right glad they were.

Outside her kennel, the mastiff old
Lay fast asleep, in moonshine cold.
The mastiff old did not awake,
Yet she an angry moan did make!
And what can ail the mastiff bitch?
Never till now she uttered yell   150
Beneath the eye of Christabel.
Perhaps it is the owlet's scritch:
For what can ail the mastiff bitch?

They passed the hall, that echoes still,
Pass as lightly as you will!
The brands were flat, the brands were dying,
Amid their own white ashes lying;
But when the lady passed, there came
A tongue of light, a fit of flame;
And Christabel saw the lady's eye,   160
And nothing else saw she thereby,

* Thresholds were often blessed to keep out evil
   spirits. The malign character of the supernatural Geraldine is clearly hinted at here
   and in the lines that follow.

Save the boss of the shield of Sir Leoline tall,
Which hung in a murky old niche in the wall.
O softly tread, said Christabel,
My father seldom sleepeth well.

Sweet Christabel her feet doth bare,
And jealous of the listening air
They steal their way from stair to stair,
Now in glimmer, and now in gloom,
And now they pass the Baron's room,   17*
As still as death, with stifled breath!
And now have reached her chamber door;
And now doth Geraldine press down
The rushes of the chamber floor.

The moon shines dim in the open air,
And not a moonbeam enters here.
But they without its light can see
The chamber carved so curiously,
Carved with figures strange and sweet,
All made out of the carver's brain,   18*
For a lady's chamber meet;
The lamp with twofold silver chain
Is fastened to an angel's feet.

The silver lamp burns dead and dim;
But Christabel the lamp will trim.
She trimmed the lamp, and made it bright,
And left it swinging to and fro,
While Geraldine, in wretched plight,
Sank down upon the floor below.

O weary lady, Geraldine,   190
I pray you, drink this cordial wine!
It is a wine of virtuous powers;
My mother made it of wild flowers.

And will your mother pity me,
Who am a maiden most forlorn?
Christabel answered—Woe is me!
She died the hour that I was born.
I have heard the gray-haired friar tell
How on her death-bed she did say,
That she should hear the castle-bell   200
Strike twelve upon my wedding-day.
O mother dear! that thou wert here!
I would, said Geraldine, she were!

But soon with altered voice, said she—
"Off, wandering mother! Peak and pine!"[1]
I have power to bid thee flee."
Alas! what ails poor Geraldine?
Why stares she with unsettled eye?
Can she the bodiless dead espy?
And why with hollow voice cries she,   210
"Off, woman, off! this hour is mine—
Though thou her guardian spirit be,
Off, woman, off! 'tis given to me."

[1] Cp. *Macbeth* I, iii, 23.

Then Christabel knelt by the lady's side,
And raised to heaven her eyes so blue—
"Alas!" said she, "this ghastly ride—
Dear lady! it hath wildered you!"
The lady wiped her moist cold brow,
And faintly said, " 'tis over now!"

Again the wild-flower wine she drank: 220
Her fair large eyes 'gan glitter bright,
And from the floor whereon she sank,
The lofty lady stood upright:
She was most beautiful to see,
Like a lady of a far countree.

And thus the lofty lady spake—
"All they who live in the upper sky,
Do love you, holy Christabel!
And you love them, and for their sake
And for the good which me befel,   230
Even I in my degree will try,
Fair maiden, to requite you well.
But now unrobe yourself; for I
Must pray, ere yet in bed I lie."

Quoth Christabel, So let it be!
And as the lady bade, did she.
Her gentle limbs did she undress,
And lay down in her loveliness.

But through her brain of weal and woe
So many thoughts moved to and fro,   240
That vain it were her lids to close;
So half-way from the bed she rose,
And on her elbow did recline
To look at the lady Geraldine.

Beneath the lamp the lady bowed,
And slowly rolled her eyes around;
Then drawing in her breath aloud,
Like one that shuddered, she unbound
The cincture from beneath her breast:
Her silken robe, and inner vest,   250
Dropt to her feet, and full in view,
Behold! her bosom and half her side——
A sight to dream of, not to tell!
O shield her! shield sweet Christabel!

Yet Geraldine nor speaks nor stirs;
Ah! what a stricken look was hers!
Deep from within she seems half-way
To lift some weight with sick assay,
And eyes the maid and seeks delay;
Then suddenly, as one defied,   260
Collects herself in scorn and pride,
And lay down by the Maiden's side!—
And in her arms the maid she took,
      Ah wel-a-day!
And with low voice and doleful look
These words did say:

"In the touch of this bosom there worketh a
      spell,
Which is lord of thy utterance, Christabel!
Thou knowest to-night, and wilt know to-mor-
      row,
This mark of my shame, this seal of my sorrow;
      But vainly thou warrest,   270
            For this is alone in
            Thy power to declare,
            That in the dim forest
            Thou heard'st a low moaning,
And found'st a bright lady, surpassingly fair;
And didst bring her home with thee in love
      and in charity,
To shield her and shelter her from the damp
      air."

THE CONCLUSION TO PART THE FIRST

It was a lovely sight to see
The lady Christabel, when she   280
Was praying at the old oak tree.
      Amid the jagged shadows
      Of mossy leafless boughs,
      Kneeling in the moonlight,
      To make her gentle vows;
Her slender palms together prest,
Heaving sometimes on her breast;
Her face resigned to bliss or bale—
Her face, oh call it fair not pale,
And both blue eyes more bright than clear,   290
Each about to have a tear.

With open eyes (ah woe is me!)
Asleep, and dreaming fearfully,
Fearfully dreaming, yet, I wis,
Dreaming that alone, which is—
O sorrow and shame! Can this be she,
The lady, who knelt at the old oak tree?
And lo! the worker of these harms,
That holds the maiden in her arms,
Seems to slumber still and mild,   300
As a mother with her child.

A star hath set, a star hath risen,
O Geraldine! since arms of thine
Have been the lovely lady's prison.
O Geraldine! one hour was thine—
Thou'st had thy will! By tairn and rill,
The night-birds all that hour were still,
But now they are jubilant anew,
From cliff and tower, tu—whoo! tu—whoo!
Tu—whoo! tu—whoo! from wood and fell!

And see! the lady Christabel   311
Gathers herself from out her trance;
Her limbs relax, her countenance
Grows sad and soft; the smooth thin lids
Close o'er her eyes! and tears she sheds—

Large tears that leave the lashes bright!
And oft the while she seems to smile
As infants at a sudden light!

Yea, she doth smile, and she doth weep,
Like a youthful hermitess,   320
Beauteous in a wilderness,
Who, praying always, prays in sleep.
And, if she move unquietly,
Perchance, 'tis but the blood so free
Comes back and tingles in her feet.
No doubt, she hath a vision sweet.
What if her guardian spirit 'twere,
What if she knew her mother near?
But this she knows, in joys and woes,
That saints will aid if men will call: 330
For the blue sky bends over all!

FRANCE: AN ODE*

I

Ye Clouds! that far above me float and pause,
    Whose pathless march no mortal may control!
    Ye Ocean Waves! that, whereso'er ye roll,
Yield homage only to eternal laws!
Ye Woods! that listen to the night-bird's
        singing,
    Midway the smooth and perilous slope re-
        clined,
Save when your own imperious branches swing-
        ing,
    Have made a solemn music of the wind!
Where, like a man beloved of God,
Through glooms, which never woodman trod,   10
    How oft, pursuing fancies holy,
My moonlight way o'er flowering weeds I
        wound,
    Inspired beyond the guess of folly,
By each rude shape and wild unconquerable
        sound!
O ye loud Waves! and O ye Forests high!
    And O ye Clouds that far above me soared!
Thou rising sun! thou blue rejoicing Sky!
    Yea, every thing that is and will be free!
Bear witness for me, wheresoe'er ye be,
    With what deep worship I have still adored
    The spirit of divinest Liberty.   21

II

When France in wrath her giant-limbs up-
        reared,
    And with that oath which smote air, earth
        and sea,
    Stamped her strong foot and said she would
        be free,

* Written in 1798; called forth by the French
  invasion of Switzerland.

Bear witness for me, how I hoped and feared!
With what a joy my lofty gratulation
    Unawed I sang, amid a slavish band:
And when to whelm the disenchanted nation,
    Like fiends embattled by a wizard's wand,
        The Monarchs marched in evil day,   30
        And Britain joined the dire array;
    Though dear her shores and circling ocean,
Though many friendships, many youthful loves
    Had swoln the patriot emotion
And flung a magic light o'er all her hills and
        groves;
Yet still my voice, unaltered, sang defeat
    To all that braved the tyrant-quelling lance,
    And shame too long delayed and vain retreat!
For ne'er, O Liberty! with partial aim   39
I dimmed thy light or damped thy holy flame;
    But blessed the pæans of delivered France,
And hung my head and wept at Britain's name.

III

"And what," I said, "though Blasphemy's
        loud scream
With that sweet music of deliverance strove!
Though all the fierce and drunken passions
        wove
A dance more wild than e'er was maniac's
        dream![1]
    Ye storms, that round the dawning east as-
        sembled,
The Sun[2] was rising, though ye hid his light!"
    And when to soothe my soul, that hoped and
        trembled,
The dissonance ceased, and all seemed calm
        and bright;   50
    When France her front deep-scarred and
        gory
Concealed with clustering wreaths of glory;
    When, insupportably advancing,
    Her arm made mockery of the warrior's
        ramp;
    While timid looks of fury glancing,
Domestic treason, crushed beneath her fatal
        stamp,
Writhed like a wounded dragon in his gore;
    Then I reproached my fears that would not
        flee;
"And soon," I said, "shall Wisdom teach her
        lore
In the low huts of them that toil and groan;
And, conquering by her happiness alone,   61
    Shall France compel the nations to be free,
Till Love and Joy look round, and call the
        earth their own."

[1] Alluding to the excesses that attended the
    French Revolution.
[2] Liberty

IV

rgive me, Freedom! O forgive those dreams!
I hear thy voice, I hear thy loud lament,
From bleak Helvetia's[3] icy caverns sent—
  hear thy groans upon her blood-stained
    streams!
Heroes, that for your peaceful country per-
    ished,
ıd ye, that fleeing, spot your mountain snows
With bleeding wounds; forgive me, that I
    cherished   70
ıe thought that ever blessed your cruel foes!
To scatter rage and traitorous guilt
Where Peace her jealous home had built;
  A patriot-race to disinherit
ɛ all that made their stormy wilds so dear;
  And with inexpiable spirit
ɔ taint the bloodless freedom of the moun-
    taineer—
France, that mockest Heaven, adulterous,
    blind,
And patriot only in pernicious toils!
ɛ these thy boasts, Champion of human
    kind?   80
To mix with Kings in the low lust of sway,
ell in the hunt, and share the murderous prey;
ɔ insult the shrine of Liberty with spoils
From freemen torn; to tempt and to betray?

V

  The Sensual and the Dark rebel in vain,
Slaves by their own compulsion! In mad
    game
They burst their manacles and wear the name
Of Freedom, graven on a heavier chain!
O Liberty! with profitless endeavour
ave I pursued thee, many a weary hour; 90
But thou nor swell'st the victor's strain nor
    ever
ıdst breathe thy soul in forms of human
    power.
Alike from all, howe'er they praise thee,
(Nor prayer, nor boastful name delays thee)
  Alike from Priestcraft's harpy minions,
And factious Blasphemy's obscener slaves,
Thou speedest on thy subtle pinions,
he guide of homeless winds, and playmate of
    the waves!
nd there I felt thee!—on that sea-cliff's
    verge,
Whose pines, scarce travelled by the breeze
    above,   100
ad made one murmur with the distant surge!
es, while I stood and gazed, my temples bare,
nd shot my being through earth, sea and air,
Possessing all things with intensest love,
  O Liberty! my spirit felt thee there.

Switzerland's

HYMN BEFORE SUNRISE IN THE VALE OF CHAMOUNI*

Hast thou a charm to stay the morning-star
In his steep course? So long he seems to pause
On thy bald awful head, O sovran Blanc!
The Arve and Arveiron at thy base
Rave ceaselessly; but thou, most awful Form!
Risest from forth thy silent sea of pines,
How silently! Around thee and above
Deep is the air and dark, substantial, black,
An ebon mass: methinks thou piercest it,
As with a wedge! But when I look again, 10
It is thine own calm home, thy crystal shrine,
Thy habitation from eternity!
O dread and silent Mount! I gazed upon thee,
Till thou, still present to the bodily sense,
Didst vanish from my thought: entranced in
    prayer
I worshipped the Invisible alone.

  Yet, like some sweet beguiling melody,
So sweet, we know not we are listening to it,
Thou, the meanwhile, wast blending with my
    Thought,
Yea, with my Life and Life's own secret joy:
Till the dilating Soul, enrapt, transfused, 21
Into the mighty vision passing—there
As in her natural form, swelled vast to
    Heaven!

  Awake, my soul! not only passive praise
Thou owest! not alone these swelling tears,
Mute thanks and secret ecstasy! Awake,
Voice of sweet song! Awake, my heart, awake!
Green vales and icy cliffs, all join my Hymn.

Thou first and chief, sole sovereign of the
    Vale!
O struggling with the darkness all the night,
And visited all night by troops of stars, 31
Or when they climb the sky or when they sink:
Companion of the morning-star at dawn,
Thyself Earth's rosy star, and of the dawn
Co-herald: wake, O wake, and utter praise!
Who sank thy sunless pillars deep in Earth?
Who filled thy countenance with rosy light?
Who made thee parent of perpetual streams?

  And you, ye five wild torrents fiercely glad!
Who called you forth from night and utter
    death,   40
From dark and icy caverns called you forth,
Down those precipitous, black, jagged rocks,
For ever shattered and the same for ever?

* This rather Ossianic poem has been perhaps
  unduly admired. Coleridge never was at
  Chamouni; his immediate model was a poem
  by the German poetess Frederike Brun.

Who gave you your invulnerable life,
Your strength, your speed, your fury, and your joy,
Unceasing thunder and eternal foam?
And who commanded (and the silence came),
Here let the billows stiffen, and have rest?

   Ye Ice-falls! ye that from the mountain's brow
Adown enormous ravines slope amain—   50
Torrents, methinks, that heard a mighty voice,
And stopped at once amid their maddest plunge!
Motionless torrents! silent cataracts!
Who made you glorious as the Gates of Heaven
Beneath the keen full moon? Who bade the sun
Clothe you with rainbows? Who, with living flowers
Of loveliest blue, spread garlands at your feet?—
God! let the torrents, like a shout of nations,
Answer! and let the ice-plains echo, God!
God! sing ye meadow-streams with gladsome voice!   60
Ye pine-groves, with your soft and soul-like sounds!
And they too have a voice, yon piles of snow,
And in their perilous fall shall thunder, God!

   Ye living flowers that skirt the eternal frost!
Ye wild goats sporting round the eagle's nest!
Ye eagles, play-mates of the mountain-storm!
Ye lightnings, the dread arrows of the clouds!
Ye signs and wonders of the element!
Utter forth God, and fill the hills with praise!

   Thou too, hoar Mount! with thy sky-pointing peaks,   70
Oft from whose feet the avalanche, unheard,
Shoots downward, glittering through the pure serene
Into the depth of clouds, that veil thy breast—
Thou too again, stupendous Mountain! thou
That as I raise my head, awhile bowed low
In adoration, upward from thy base
Slow travelling with dim eyes suffused with tears,
Solemnly seemest, like a vapoury cloud,
To rise before me—Rise, O ever rise,   79
Rise like a cloud of incense from the Earth!
Thou kingly Spirit throned among the hills,
Thou dread ambassador from Earth to Heaven,
Great Hierarch! tell thou the silent sky,
And tell the stars, and tell yon rising sun
Earth, with her thousand voices, praises God.

THE KNIGHT'S TOMB

Where is the grave of Sir Arthur O'Kellyn?
Where may the grave of that good man be?—
By the side of a spring, on the breast of Helvellyn,[1]
Under the twigs of a young birch tree!
The oak that in summer was sweet to hear,
And rustled its leaves in the fall of the year,
And whistled and roared in the winter alone,
Is gone,—and the birch in its stead is grown.—
The Knight's bones are dust,
And his good sword rust;—
His soul is with the saints, I trust.

SONG

FROM ZAPOLYA, ACT II, SCENE I

A sunny shaft did I behold,
   From sky to earth it slanted:
And poised therein a bird so bold—
   Sweet bird, thou wert enchanted!

He sunk, he rose, he twinkled, he trolled
   Within that shaft of sunny mist;
His eyes of fire, his beak of gold,
   All else of amethyst!

And thus he sang: Adieu! adieu!
Love's dreams prove seldom true.
The blossoms make no delay;
The sparkling dew-drops will not stay.
   Sweet month of May,
     We must away;
      Far far away!
      Today! today!

YOUTH AND AGE*

Verse, a breeze mid blossoms straying,
Where Hope clung feeding, like a bee—
Both were mine! Life went a-maying
   With Nature, Hope, and Poesy,
    When I was young!

When I was young?—Ah, woeful When!
Ah! for the change 'twixt Now and Then!
This breathing house not built with hands,
This body that does me grievous wrong,
O'er aery cliffs and glittering sands,
How lightly *then* it flashed along:—
Like those trim skiffs, unknown of yore,
On winding lakes and rivers wide,
That ask no aid of sail or oar,
That fear no spite of wind or tide!
Nought cared this body for wind or weather
When Youth and I lived in't together.

[1] A mountain in Cumberland.
* A first rough draft of this poem was called "Area Spontanea," and the whole still reads like a musical improvisation.

owers are lovely; Love is flower-like;
riendship is a sheltering tree;
the joys, that came down shower-like,
Friendship, Love, and Liberty,   21
    Ere I was old!

e I was old? Ah woeful Ere,
hich tells me, Youth's no longer here!
Youth! for years so many and sweet,
is known, that Thou and I were one,
ll think it but a fond conceit—
cannot be that Thou art gone!
ay vesper-bell hath not yet toll'd:—
d thou wert aye a masker bold!   30
hat strange disguise hast now put on,
make believe, that thou art gone?
see these locks in silvery slips,
is drooping gait, this altered size:
t Spring-tide blossoms on thy lips,
d tears take sunshine from thine eyes!
fe is but thought: so think I will
at Youth and I are house-mates still.

w-drops are the gems of morning,
t the tears of mournful eve!   40
here no hope is, life's a warning
at only serves to make us grieve,
    When we are old:
at only serves to make us grieve,
ith oft and tedious taking-leave,
ke some poor nigh-related guest,
at may not rudely be dismist;
t hath out-stay'd his welcome while,
d tells the jest without the smile.

WORK WITHOUT HOPE†

Nature seems at work. Slugs leave their lair—
e bees are stirring—birds are on the wing—
d Winter slumbering in the open air,
ars on his smiling face a dream of Spring!
d I the while, the sole unbusy thing,
r honey make, nor pair, nor build, nor sing.

Yet well I ken the banks where amaranths blow,
ve traced the fount whence streams of nectar flow.
om, O ye amaranths! bloom for whom ye may,
r me ye bloom not! Glide, rich streams, away!
th lips unbrightened, wreathless brow, I stroll:

ritten in 1827: the mournful *Ay de mi* of a man confronted by age and sickness and looking back over a life of defeated hopes and wasted opportunities.

And would you learn the spells that drowse my soul?
Work without Hope draws nectar in a sieve,
And Hope without an object cannot live.

SIR WALTER SCOTT
(1771-1832)
LOCHINVAR*
FROM MARMION, CANTO V

Oh! young Lochinvar is come out of the west,
Through all the wide Border his steed was the best;
And save his good broadsword he weapons had none.
He rode all unarmed and he rode all alone.
So faithful in love and so dauntless in war,
There never was knight like the young Lochinvar.   6

He stayed not for brake and he stopped not for stone,
He swam the Eske river where ford there was none,
But ere he alighted at Netherby gate
The bride had consented, the gallant came late:
For a laggard in love and a dastard in war
Was to wed the fair Ellen of brave Lochinvar.

So boldly he entered the Netherby Hall,   13
Among bridesmen, and kinsmen, and brothers, and all:
Then spoke the bride's father, his hand on his sword,—
For the poor craven bridegroom said never a word,—
'Oh! come ye in peace here, or come ye in war,
Or to dance at our bridal, young Lord Lochinvar?'—   18

'I long wooed your daughter, my suit you denied;
Love swells like the Solway,[1] but ebbs like its tide—
And now am I come, with this lost love of mine,
To lead but one measure, drink one cup of wine.
There are maidens in Scotland more lovely by far,
That would gladly be bride to the young Lochinvar.'   24

[1] Solway Firth, noted for its swift tides.
* Compare *Katharine Jaffray*, p. 79, upon which Scott "in a very slight degree founded" the present ballad.

The bride kissed the goblet: the knight took
it up,
He quaffed off the wine, and he threw down
the cup.
She looked down to blush, and she looked up to
sigh,
With a smile on her lips and a tear in her eye.
He took her soft hand ere her mother could
bar,—
'Now tread we a measure!' said young
Lochinvar.   30

So stately his form, and so lovely her face,
That never a hall such a galliard² did grace;
While her mother did fret, and her father did
fume,
And the bridegroom stood dangling his bonnet³
and plume;
And the bride-maidens whispered ' 'Twere bet-
ter by far
To have matched our fair cousin with young
Lochinvar.'   36

One touch to her hand and one word in her ear,
When they reached the hall-door, and the
charger stood near;
So light to the croupe the fair lady he swung,
So light to the saddle before her he sprung!
'She is won! we are gone, over bank, bush, and
scaur;⁴
They 'll have fleet steeds that follow,' quoth
young Lochinvar.   42

There was mounting 'mong Græmes of the
Netherby clan;
Forsters, Fenwicks, and Musgraves, they rode
and they ran:
There was racing and chasing on Cannobie
Lee,
But the lost bride of Netherby ne'er did they
see.
So daring in love and so dauntless in war,
Have ye e'er heard of gallant like young
Lochinvar?   48

SOLDIER, REST!

FROM THE LADY OF THE LAKE, CANTO I

Soldier, rest! thy warfare o'er,
  Sleep the sleep that knows not breaking!
Dream of battled fields no more,
  Days of danger, nights of waking.
In our isle's enchanted hall,
  Hands unseen thy couch are strewing,   6
Fairy strains of music fall,

Every sense in slumber dewing.
Soldier, rest! thy warfare o'er,
Dream of fighting fields no more;
Sleep the sleep that knows not breaking,
Morn of toil, nor night of waking.

No rude sound shall reach thine ear,
  Armour's clang, or war-steed champing,
Trump nor pibroch summon here
  Mustering clan or squadron tramping.
Yet the lark's shrill fife may come
  At the daybreak from the fallow,
And the bittern sound his drum,
  Booming from the sedgy shallow.
Ruder sounds shall none be near,
Guards nor warders challenge here,
Here's no war-steed's neigh and champing,
Shouting clans or squadrons stamping.

Huntsman, rest! thy chase is done;
  While our slumbrous spells assail ye,
Dream not, with the rising sun,
  Bugles here shall sound reveillé.
Sleep! the deer is in his den;
  Sleep! thy hounds are by thee lying:
Sleep! nor dream in yonder glen
  How thy gallant steed lay dying.
Huntsman, rest! thy chase is done;
Think not of the rising sun,
For at dawning to assail ye
Here no bugles sound reveillé.

CORONACH⁵

FROM THE LADY OF THE LAKE, CANTO III

He is gone on the mountain,
  He is lost to the forest,
Like a summer-dried fountain,
  When our need was the sorest.
The font, reappearing,
  From the rain-drops shall borrow,
But to us comes no cheering,
  To Duncan no morrow!

The hand of the reaper
  Takes the ears that are hoary,
But the voice of the weeper
  Wails manhood in glory.
The autumn winds rushing
  Waft the leaves that are searest,
But our flower was in flushing,
  When blighting was nearest.

Fleet foot on the correi,⁶
  Sage counsel in cumber,⁷

---

2 A brisk dance.   3 cap   4 cliff

5 A Highland dirge.
6 A hollow hillside, resort of game.
7 trouble

Red hand in the foray,
  How sound is thy slumber!
Like the dew on the mountain,
  Like the foam on the river,
Like the bubble on the fountain,
  Thou art gone, and forever!   24

THE BATTLE OF BEAL' AN DUINE*

FROM THE LADY OF THE LAKE, CANTO VI

he Chieftain reared his form on high,
nd fever's fire was in his eye;
ut ghastly, pale, and livid streaks   340
hequered his swarthy brow and cheeks.
-''Hark, Minstrel! I have heard thee play,
/ith measure bold, on festal day,
n yon lone isle,—again where ne'er
hall harper play, or warrior hear!—
hat stirring air that peals on high,
'er Dermid's race[1] our victory.—
trike it!—and then, (for well thou canst,)
ree from thy minstrel-spirit glanced,
ling me the picture of the fight,   350
'hen met my clan the Saxon[2] might.
'll listen, till my fancy hears
he clang of swords, the crash of spears!
hese grates, these walls, shall vanish then,
or the fair field of fighting men,
nd my free spirit burst away,
s if it soared from battle fray.''
he trembling Bard with awe obeyed,—
.ow on the harp his hand he laid;
ut soon remembrance of the sight   360
e witnessed from the mountain's height,
'ith what old Bertram[3] told at night,
wakened the full power of song,
nd bore him in career along;—
s shallop launched on river's tide,
hat slow and fearful leaves the side,
ut, when it feels the middle stream,
rives downward swift as lightning's beam.

The Minstrel came once more to view
he eastern ridge of Benvenue,   370
or ere he parted, he would say
arewell to lovely Loch Achray—
'here shall he find, in foreign land,
o lone a lake, so sweet a strand!—
There is no breeze upon the fern,
  No ripple on the lake,

Upon her eyrie nods the erne,[4]
  The deer has sought the brake;
The small birds will not sing aloud,
  The springing trout lies still,   380
So darkly glooms yon thunder cloud,
That swathes, as with a purple shroud,
  Benledi's distant hill.
Is it the thunder's solemn sound
  That mutters deep and dread,
Or echoes from the groaning ground
  The warrior's measured tread?
Is it the lightning's quivering glance
  That on the thicket streams,
Or do they flash on spear and lance   390
  The sun's retiring beams?—
I see the dagger-crest of Mar,[5]
I see the Moray's[5] silver star,
Wave o'er the cloud of Saxon war,
That up the lake comes winding far!
  To hero boune[6] for battle-strife,
    Or bard of martial lay,
  'Twere worth ten years of peaceful life,
    One glance at their array!

''Their light-armed archers far and near   400
    Surveyed the tangled ground,
  Their centre ranks, with pike and spear,
    A twilight forest frowned,
  Their barded[7] horsemen, in the rear,
    The stern battalia[8] crowned.
No cymbal clashed, no clarion rang,
  Still were the pipe and drum;
Save heavy tread, and armour's clang,
  The sullen march was dumb.
There breathed no wind their crests to shake,
  Or wave their flags abroad;   410
Scarce the frail aspen seemed to quake,
  That shadowed o'er their road.
Their vaward[9] scouts no tidings bring,
  Can rouse no lurking foe,
Nor spy a trace of living thing,
  Save when they stirred the roe;
The host moves, like a deep-sea wave,
Where rise no rocks its pride to brave,
  High-swelling, dark, and slow.   420
The lake is passed, and now they gain
A narrow and a broken plain,
Before the Trosachs'[10] rugged jaws:
And here the horse and spearmen pause,
While, to explore the dangerous glen,
Dive through the pass the archer-men.

''At once there rose so wild a yell
Within that dark and narrow dell,

Roderick Dhu, a marauding chieftain of the
Highland Clan-Alpine, having been wounded
in combat with the disguised King of Scotland, lies dying in prison, while the Minstrel,
Allan-bane, recites to him the story of the
conflict between his clan and the forces of
the king. The Minstrel's tale begins at line
369; he speaks of himself in the third person.

The Campbells.   3 One of the king's
Lowland   men.

4 eagle
5 A Lowland leader.
6 prepared
7 armed with plate-ar-
  mor
8 battle array
9 vanward

10 The rough moun-
  tains and pass in
  the Highlands be-
  t w e e n Lochs
  Katrine and Ach-
  ray.

As all the fiends from heaven that fell
Had pealed the banner-cry of hell!⁣   430
   Forth from the pass in tumult driven,
   Like chaff before the wind of heaven,
     The archery appear:
For life! for life! their plight they ply—
And shriek, and shout, and battle-cry,
And plaids and bonnets waving high,
And broadswords flashing to the sky,
   Are maddening in the rear.
Onward they drive, in dreadful race,
    Pursuers and pursued;   440
Before that tide of flight and chase,
How shall it keep its rooted place,
   The spearmen's twilight wood?—
'Down, down,' cried Mar, 'your lances down!
   Bear back both friend and foe!'—
Like reeds before the tempest's frown,
That serried grove of lances brown
    At once lay levelled low;
And closely shouldering side to side,
The bristling ranks the onset bide.—   450
'We'll quell the savage mountaineer,
   As their Tinchel[11] cows the game!
They come as fleet as forest deer,
   We'll drive them back as tame.'—

"Bearing before them, in their course,
The relics of the archer force,
Like wave with crest of sparkling foam,
Right onward did Clan-Alpine come.
Above the tide, each broadsword bright
Was brandishing like beam of light,   460
   Each targe was dark below;
And with the ocean's mighty swing,
When heaving to the tempest's wing,
   They hurled them on the foe.
I heard the lance's shivering crash,
As when the whirlwind rends the ash;
I heard the broadsword's deadly clang,
As if an hundred anvils rang!
But Moray wheeled his rearward rank
Of horsemen on Clan-Alpine's flank,—   470
   'My banner-man, advance!
I see,' he cried, 'their column shake.
Now, gallants! for your ladies' sake,
   Upon them with the lance!'—
The horsemen dashed among the rout,
   As deer break through the broom;
Their steeds are stout, their swords are out,
   They soon make lightsome room.
Clan-Alpine's best are backward borne—
   Where, where was Roderick then!   480
One blast upon his bugle-horn
   Were worth a thousand men.
And refluent through the pass of fear
   The battle's tide was poured;

Vanished the Saxon's struggling spear,
   Vanished the mountain-sword.
As Bracklinn's chasm, so black and steep,
   Receives her roaring linn,[12]
As the dark caverns of the deep
   Suck the wild whirlpool in,   49
So did the deep and darksome pass
Devour the battle's mingled mass:
None linger now upon the plain,
Save those who ne'er shall fight again.

"Now westward rolls the battle's din,
That deep and doubling pass within.—
Minstrel, away! the work of fate
Is bearing on: its issue wait,
Where the rude Trosachs' dread defile
Opens on Katrine's lake and isle.—   50
Gray Benvenue I soon repassed,
Loch Katrine lay beneath me cast.
   The sun is set;—the clouds are met,
     The lowering scowl of heaven
    An inky hue of livid blue
     To the deep lake has given;
Strange gusts of wind from mountain glen
Swept o'er the lake, then sunk agen.
I heeded not the eddying surge,
Mine eye but saw the Trosachs' gorge,   51
Mine ear but heard the sullen sound,
Which like an earthquake shook the ground,
And spoke the stern and desperate strife
That parts not but with parting life,
Seeming, to minstrel ear, to toll
The dirge of many a passing soul.
   Nearer it comes—the dim-wood glen
   The martial flood disgorged agen,
    But not in mingled tide;
   The plaided warriors of the North   52
   High on the mountain thunder forth
    And overhang its side;
   While by the lake below appears
   The dark'ning cloud of Saxon spears.
At weary bay each shattered band,
Eying their foemen, sternly stand;
Their banners stream like tattered sail,
That flings its fragments to the gale,
And broken arms and disarray
Marked the fell havoc of the day.   53

"Viewing the mountain's ridge askance,
The Saxon stood in sullen trance,
Till Moray pointed with his lance,
   And cried—'Behold yon isle!—
See! none are left to guard its strand,
But women weak, that wring the hand:
'Tis there of yore the robber band
    Their booty wont to pile;—

---

11 A circle of hunters surrounding game.   12 waterfall

y purse, with bonnet-pieces store,[13]
him will[14] swim a bow-shot o'er, 540
d loose a shallop from the shore.
ghtly we'll tame the war-wolf then,
rds of his mate, and brood, and den.'—
rth from the ranks a spearman sprung,
earth his casque and corslet rung,
  He plunged him in the wave:—
l saw the deed—the purpose knew,
d to their clamours Benvenue
  A mingled echo gave;
e Saxons shout, their mate to cheer, 550
e helpless females scream for fear,
d yells for rage the mountaineer.
was then, as by the outcry riven,
ured down at once the lowering heaven;
whirlwind swept Loch Katrine's breast,
r billows reared their snowy crest.
ell for the swimmer swelled they high,
  mar the Highland marksman's eye;
r round him showered, 'mid rain and hail,
e vengeful arrows of the Gael.[15]— 560
  vain.—He nears the isle—and lo!
s hand is on a shallop's bow.
st then a flash of lightning came,
tinged the waves and strand with flame;—
narked Duncraggan's widowed dame,[16]
hind an oak I saw her stand,
naked dirk gleamed in her hand:—
darkened—but amid the moan
waves, I heard a dying groan;—
other flash!—the spearman floats 570
weltering corse beside the boats,
d the stern matron o'er him stood,
r hand and dagger streaming blood.

'Revenge! revenge!' the Saxons cried,
e Gaels' exulting shout replied.
spite the elemental rage,
ain they hurried to engage;
t, ere they closed in desperate fight,
ody with spurring came a knight,
rung from his horse, and from a crag, 580
aved 'twixt the hosts a milk-white flag.
rion and trumpet by his side
ng forth a trumpet-note high and wide,
ile, in the Monarch's name, afar
herald's voice forbade the war,
r Bothwell's lord,[17] and Roderick bold,
re both, he said, in captive hold.'—

t here the lay made sudden stand,
e harp escaped the Minstrel's hand!

gold coins (stamped with the king's head) in
  plenty.
who will
Highlander
Widow of the Duncan mourned for in the
  Coronach on p. 444.
Douglas, an exile, to whom Roderick Dhu had
  given shelter.

Oft had he stolen a glance, to spy 590
How Roderick brooked his minstrelsy:
At first, the Chieftain, to the chime,
With lifted hand kept feeble time;
That motion ceased,—yet feeling strong
Varied his look as changed the song;
At length, no more his deafened ear
The minstrel melody can hear;
His face grows sharp,—his hands are clenched,
As if some pang his heart-strings wrenched;
Set are his teeth, his fading eye 600
Is sternly fixed on vacancy;
Thus, motionless and moanless, drew
His parting breath, stout Roderick Dhu!—
Old Allan-bane looked on aghast,
While grim and still his spirit passed;
But when he saw that life was fled,
He poured his wailing o'er the dead.

JOCK OF HAZELDEAN

"Why weep ye by the tide, ladie?
  Why weep ye by the tide?
I'll wed ye to my youngest son,
  And ye sall be his bride:
And ye sall be his bride, ladie,
  Sae comely to be seen"—
But aye she loot the tears down fa'
  For Jock of Hazeldean. 8

"Now let this wilfu' grief be done,
  And dry that cheek so pale;
Young Frank is chief of Errington
  And lord of Langley-dale;
His step is first in peaceful ha',
  His sword in battle keen"—
But aye she loot the tears down fa'
  For Jock of Hazeldean. 16

"A chain of gold ye sall not lack,
  Nor braid to bind your hair;
Nor mettled hound, nor managed[1] hawk,
  Nor palfrey fresh and fair;
And you, the foremost o' them a',
  Shall ride our forest queen."—
But aye she loot the tears down fa'
  For Jock of Hazeldean. 24

The kirk was decked at morning-tide,
  The tapers glimmered fair;
The priest and bridegroom wait the bride,
  And dame and knight are there.
They sought her baith by bower and ha';
  The ladie was not seen!
She's o'er the Border and awa'
  Wi' Jock of Hazeldean. 32

1 trained

PROUD MAISIE

From The Heart of Midlothian

Proud Maisie is in the wood,
　Walking so early;
Sweet Robin sits on the bush,
　Singing so rarely.

"Tell me, thou bonny bird,
　When shall I marry me?"
"When six braw[2] gentlemen
　Kirkward shall carry ye."　　8

"Who makes the bridal bed,
　Birdie, say truly?"
"The gray-headed sexton
　That delves the grave duly.

"The glow-worm o'er grave and stone
　Shall light thee steady;
The owl from the steeple sing
　'Welcome, proud lady.'"　　16

COUNTY GUY

From Quentin Durward

Ah! County Guy, the hour is nigh,
　The sun has left the lea,
The orange flower perfumes the bower,
　The breeze is on the sea.
The lark his lay who thrilled all day
　Sits hushed his partner nigh:
Breeze, bird, and flower confess the hour,
　But where is County Guy?　　8

The village maid steals through the shade
　Her shepherd's suit to hear;
To beauty shy by lattice high,
　Sings high-born Cavalier.
The star of Love, all stars above,
　Now reigns o'er earth and sky;
And high and low the influence know—
　But where is County Guy?　　16

BONNY DUNDEE*

To the Lords of Convention 't was Claver'se
　who spoke,
"Ere the King's crown shall fall there are
　crowns to be broke;
So let each Cavalier who loves honour and me,

Come follow the bonnet of Bonny Dundee.
　Come fill up my cup, come fill up my can,
　Come saddle your horses and call up yo[ur]
　　men;
　Come open the West Port and let me ga[ng]
　　free,
　And it's room for the bonnets of Bon[ny]
　　Dundee!"

Dundee he is mounted, he rides up the street,
The bells are rung backward,[3] the drums th[ey]
　are beat;
But the Provost,[4] douce[5] man, said, "Just e'[en]
　let him be,
The Gude Town is weel quit of that Deil [o']
　Dundee."
　Come fill up my cup, etc.

As he rode down the sanctified bends of t[he]
　Bow,[6]
Ilk carline[7] was flyting[8] and shaking her pow[9]
But the young plants of grace they look[ed]
　couthie and slee,[10]
Thinking, luck to thy bonnet, thou Bon[ny]
　Dundee!
　Come fill up my cup, etc.

With sour-featured Whigs the Grassmarke[t]
　was crammed
As if half the West had set tryst to be hange[d]
There was spite in each look, there was fear [in]
　each e'e,
As they watched for the bonnets of Bon[ny]
　Dundee.
　Come fill up my cup, etc.

These cowls of Kilmarnock[12] had spits and b[road]
　spears,
And lang-hafted gullies[13] to kill Cavaliers;
But they shrunk to close-heads[14] and the cau[se]way was free,
At the toss of the bonnet of Bonny Dundee.
　Come fill up my cup, etc.

He spurred to the foot of the proud Cas[tle]
　rock,[15]
And with the gay Gordon he gallantly spoke;
"Let Mons Meg[16] and her marrows[17] speak t[wa]
　words or three,

2 brave, fine
* John Graham of Claverhouse, Viscount Dundee, in support of James II. withstood the Scotch Covenanters, defied the Convention, or Scotch Parliament, which had accepted King William, and marched out of Edinburgh with a few faithful followers in 1689, thus creating the "Jacobite" party. He met the government forces at Killiecrankie and defeated them, but was killed in the battle. See Macaulay's account of that battle in the present volume.

3 reversing the chimes (as an alarm)
4 Mayor
5 sedate
6 windings of Bow street
7 each old woman
8 scolding
9 head
10 gracious and sly
11 The place of execution (see *Midlothian*, chap. II).

12 hoods made at K[il]marnock (here u[sed] for the weare[rs,] Presbyterians)
13 knives
14 blind alleys
15 The site of Ed[in]burgh Castle, th[en] held by the D[uke] of Gordon.
16 nickname of a c[an]non
17 mates

For the love of the bonnet of Bonny Dundee.''
  Come fill up my cup, etc.

The Gordon demands of him which way he
    goes—
''Where'er shall direct me the shade of Mont-
    rose![18]
Your Grace in short space shall hear tidings
    of me,
Or that low lies the bonnet of Bonny Dundee. 32
  Come fill up my cup, etc.

''There are hills beyond Pentland and lands
    beyond Forth,
If there's lords in the Lowlands, there's chiefs
    in the North;
There are wild Duniewassals[19] three thousand
    times three,
Will cry *hoigh!* for the bonnet of Bonny
    Dundee.
  Come fill up my cup, etc.

''There's brass on the target of barkened[20]
    bull-hide;
There's steel in the scabbard that dangles
    beside;
The brass shall be burnished, the steel shall flash
    free,
At a toss of the bonnet of Bonny Dundee. 40
  Come fill up my cup, etc.

''Away to the hills, to the caves, to the rocks—
Ere I own an usurper, I'll couch with the fox;
And tremble, false Whigs, in the midst of your
    glee,
You have not seen the last of my bonnet and
    me!''
  Come fill up my cup, etc.

He waved his proud hand and the trumpets
    were blown,
The kettle-drums clashed and the horsemen rode
    on,
Till on Ravelston's cliffs and on Clermiston's lea
Died away the wild war-notes of Bonny Dun-
    dee.   48
  Come fill up my cup, come fill up my can,
  Come saddle the horses and call up the men,
  Come open your gates and let me gae free,
  For its up with the bonnets of Bonny
    Dundee!

HERE'S A HEALTH TO KING CHARLES
FROM WOODSTOCK

Bring the bowl which you boast,
  Fill it up to the brim;

18 A royalist executed   19 gentlemen of minor
  in 1350.   degree
                      20 tanned

'Tis to him we love most,
  And to all who love him.
Brave gallants, stand up,
  And avaunt ye, base carles!
Were there death in the cup,
  Here's a health to King Charles.

Though he wanders through dangers,
  Unaided, unknown,
Dependent on strangers,
  Estranged from his own;
Though 't is under our breath,
  Amidst forfeits and perils,
Here's to honour and faith,
  And a health to King Charles!

Let such honours abound
  As the time can afford,
The knee on the ground,
  And the hand on the sword;
But the time shall come round
  When, 'mid Lords, Dukes, and Earls,
The loud trumpet shall sound,
  Here's a health to King Charles.

LORD BYRON
(1788-1824)

FROM ENGLISH BARDS AND SCOTCH RE-
VIEWERS*

When Vice triumphant holds her sov'reign
    sway,
Obeyed by all who nought beside obey;
When Folly, frequent harbinger of crime,
Bedecks her cap with bells of every Clime;
When knaves and fools combined o'er all pre-
    vail,   30
And weigh their Justice in a Golden Scale;
E'en then the boldest start from public sneers,
Afraid of Shame, unknown to other fears,
More darkly sin, by Satire kept in awe,
And shrink from Ridicule, though not from
    Law.

Such is the force of Wit! but not belong
To me the arrows of satiric song;
The royal vices of our age demand
A keener weapon, and a mightier hand .
Still there are follies, e'en for me to chase, 40

* This satire is in part a retort which Byron was
  stung into making by the ridicule with which
  the *Edinburgh Review* in January, 1808, received his youthful volume of verses, *Hours
  of Idleness;* though he had before planned a
  satirical poem upon contemporary English
  poets. In later years he regretted his severity, and especially his treatment of Francis
  Jeffrey, the editor of the journal, whom he
  had wrongly suspected of writing the offending
  article. See *Eng. Lit.*, p. 246.

And yield at least amusement in the race:
Laugh when I laugh, I seek no other fame,
The cry is up, and scribblers are my game:
Speed, Pegasus!—ye strains of great and small,
Ode! Epic! Elegy!—have at you all!
I, too, can scrawl, and once upon a time
I poured along the town a flood of rhyme,
A schoolboy freak, unworthy praise or blame;
I printed—older children do the same.   49
'Tis pleasant, sure, to see one's name in print;
A Book's a Book, altho' there's nothing in't.
Not that a Title's sounding charm can save
Or scrawl or scribbler from an equal grave:
This Lamb[1] must own, since his patrician name
Failed to preserve the spurious farce from
    shame.
No matter, George continues still to write,
Tho' now the name is veiled from public sight.
Moved by the great example, I pursue
The self-same road, but make my own review:
Not seek great Jeffrey's, yet like him will be   60
Self-constituted Judge of Poesy.

A man must serve his time to every trade
Save Censure—Critics all are ready made.
Take hackneyed jokes from Miller,[2] got by rote,
With just enough of learning to misquote;
A mind well skilled to find, or forge a fault;
A turn for punning—call it Attic salt;[3]
To Jeffrey go, be silent and discreet,
His pay is just ten sterling pounds per sheet:
Fear not to lie, 'twill seem a *sharper* hit;   70
Shrink not from blasphemy, 'twill pass for wit;
Care not for feeling—pass your proper jest,
And stand a Critic, hated yet caressed.

And shall we own such judgment? no—as soon
Seek roses in December—ice in June;
Hope constancy in wind, or corn in chaff,
Believe a woman or an epitaph,
Or any other thing that's false, before
You trust in Critics, who themselves are sore;
Or yield one single thought to be misled   80
By Jeffrey's heart, or Lamb's Bœotian head.[4]
To these young tyrants, by themselves mis-
    placed,
Combined usurpers on the Throne of Taste;
To these, when Authors bend in humble awe,
And hail their voice as Truth, their word as
    Law;
While these are Censors, 'twould be sin to
    spare;

1 George (son of Sir Peniston) Lamb, author of
    an unsuccessful farce.
2 "Joe" Miller, an 18th century actor and the re-
    puted author of a famous compilation of jests.
3 wit
4 The Bœotians were proverbial for dulness.

While such are Critics, why should I forbear?

. . . .

  Behold! in various throngs the scribbling
    crew,
For notice eager, pass in long review:
Each spurs his jaded Pegasus apace,
And Rhyme and Blank maintain an equal race;
Sonnets on sonnets crowd, and ode on ode;
And Tales of Terror[5] jostle on the road;
Immeasurable measures move along;*
For simpering Folly loves a varied song,   150
To strange, mysterious Dulness still the friend,
Admires the strain she cannot comprehend.
Thus Lays of Minstrels—may they be the
    last!—
On half-strung harps whine mournful to the
    blast,
While mountain spirits prate to river sprites,
That dames may listen to the sound at nights;
And goblin brats, of Gilpin Horner's brood,[6]
Decoy young Border-nobles through the wood,
And skip at every step, Lord knows how high,
And frighten foolish babes, the Lord knows
    why;   160
While high-born ladies in their magic cell,
Forbidding Knights to read who cannot spell,
Despatch a courier to a wizard's grave,
And fight with honest men to shield a knave.

  Next view in state, proud prancing on his
    roan,
The golden-crested haughty Marmion,
Now forging scrolls, now foremost in the fight,
Not quite a Felon, yet but half a Knight,
The gibbet or the field prepared to grace—
A mighty mixture of the great and base.   170
And think'st thou, Scott! by vain conceit per-
    chance,
On public taste to foist thy stale romance,
Though Murray with his Miller[7] may combine
To yield thy muse just half-a-crown per line?
No! when the sons of song descend to trade,
Their bays are sear, their former laurels fade;
Let such forego the poet's sacred name,
Who rack their brains for lucre, not for fame:
Still for stern Mammon may they toil in vain!
And sadly gaze on gold they cannot gain!   180
Such be their meed, such still the just reward
Of prostituted Muse and hireling bard!
For this we spurn Apollo's venal son,[8]
And bid a long "good night to Marmion."[9]

5 By "Monk" Lewis (*Eng. Lit.*, 204).
6 Scott's *Lay of the Last Minstrel* (1805) grew
    out of a suggestion for a ballad derived from
    an absurd old Border legend of Gilpin Horner.
7 Publishers.
8 i. e., this bought Orpheus (Scott)
9 *Marmion*, line 869.
* This is a sneer at the new anapestic metres.
    See *Eng. Lit.*, p. 243.

These are the themes that claim our plaudits now;
These are the Bards to whom the Muse must bow;
While Milton, Dryden, Pope, alike forgot,
Resign their hallowed Bays to Walter Scott.

The time has been, when yet the Muse was young,   189
When Homer swept the lyre, and Maro[10] sung,
An Epic[11] scarce ten centuries could claim,
While awe-struck nations hailed the magic name:
The work of each immortal Bard appears
The single wonder of a thousand years.
Empires have mouldered from the face of earth,
Tongues have expired with those who gave them birth,
Without the glory such a strain can give,
As even in ruin bids the language live.
Not so with us, though minor Bards, content,
On one great work a life of labour spent: 200
With eagle pinion soaring to the skies,
Behold the Ballad-monger Southey rise!
To him let Camoens, Milton, Tasso yield,
Whose annual strains, like armies, take the field.[12]
First in the ranks see Joan of Arc advance,
The scourge of England and the boast of France!
Though burnt by wicked Bedford[13] for a witch,
Behold her statue placed in Glory's niche;
Her fetters burst, and just released from prison,
A virgin Phœnix from her ashes risen.   210
Next see tremendous Thalaba come on,
Arabia's monstrous, wild, and wond'rous son;
Domdaniel's[14] dread destroyer, who o'erthrew
More mad magicians than the world e'er knew.
Immortal Hero! all thy foes o'ercome,
For ever reign—the rival of Tom Thumb![15]
Since startled Metre fled before thy face,
Well wert thou doomed the last of all thy race!
Well might triumphant Genii bear thee hence,
Illustrious conqueror of common sense!   220
Now, last and greatest, Madoc spreads his sails,
Cacique[16] in Mexico, and Prince in Wales;
Tells us strange tales, as other travellers do,
More old than Mandeville's,[17] and not so true.
Oh, Southey! Southey! cease thy varied song!

A bard may chaunt too often and too long;
As thou art strong in verse, in mercy spare!
A fourth, alas! were more than we could bear.
But if, in spite of all the world can say,
Thou still wilt verseward plod thy weary way;
If still in Berkley-Ballads most uncivil,   231
Thou wilt devote old women to the devil,[18]
The babe unborn thy dread intent may rue:
"God help thee," Southey, and thy readers too.

Next comes the dull disciple of thy school,
That mild apostate from poetic rule,
The simple Wordsworth, framer of a lay
As soft as evening in his favourite May,
Who warns his friend[19] "to shake off toil and trouble,   239
And quit his books, for fear of growing double";
Who, both by precept[20] and example, shows
That prose is verse, and verse is merely prose;
Convincing all, by demonstration plain,
Poetic souls delight in prose insane;
And Christmas stories tortured into rhyme
Contain the essence of the true sublime.
Thus, when he tells the tale of Betty Foy,
The idiot mother of "an idiot Boy",
A moon-struck, silly lad, who lost his way,
And, like his bard, confounded night with day;
So close on each pathetic part he dwells,   251
And each adventure so sublimely tells,
That all who view the "idiot in his glory"
Conceive the Bard the hero of the story.

Shall gentle Coleridge pass unnoticed here,
To turgid Ode and tumid stanza dear?
Though themes of innocence amuse him best,
Yet still Obscurity's a welcome guest.
If Inspiration should her aid refuse
To him who takes a Pixy for a muse,[21]   260
Yet none in lofty numbers can surpass
The bard who soars to elegize an ass:
So well the subject suits his noble mind,
He brays, the Laureate of the long-eared kind.

MAID OF ATHENS, ERE WE PART

Ζωη μου, σας αγαπω[1]

Maid of Athens, ere we part,
Give, oh, give me back my heart!
Or, since that has left my breast,
Keep it now, and take the rest!

---

10 Virgil
11 Object of "claim."
12 Southey's *Joan of Arc*, 1796; *Thalaba the Destroyer*, 1801; *Madoc* (in two parts: *Madoc in Wales, Madoc in Aztlan*), 1805.
13 John Plantagenet, the general of the English forces in France.
14 In Arabian tales, a cavern where magicians were schooled.
15 The hero of a farce by Fielding.
16 chieftain
17 See p. 63.

18 In Southey's ballad, *The Old Woman of Berkeley*, the old woman is carried off by the Devil.
19 In *The Tables Turned*.
20 In his preface to *Lyrical Ballads*.
21 In *Songs of the Pixies*, containing "Lines to a Young Ass."

---

1 "My life, I love you."

Hear my vow before I go,
Ζωη μου, σας αγαπω. 6

By those tresses unconfined,
Wooed by each Ægean wind;
By those lids whose jetty fringe
Kiss thy soft cheeks' blooming tinge;
By those wild eyes like the roe,
Ζωη μου, σας αγαπω. 12

By that lip I long to taste;
By that zone-encircled waist;
By all the token-flowers that tell
What words can never speak so well;
By love's alternate joy and woe,
Ζωη μου, σας αγαπω. 18

Maid of Athens! I am gone:
Think of me, sweet! when alone.
Though I fly to Istambol,[2]
Athens holds my heart and soul;
Can I cease to love thee? No!
Ζωη μου, σας αγαπω. 24

SHE WALKS IN BEAUTY

She walks in beauty, like the night
Of cloudless climes and starry skies;
And all that's best of dark and bright
Meet in her aspect and her eyes:
Thus mellowed to that tender light
Which heaven to gaudy day denies. 6

One shade the more, one ray the less,
Had half impaired the nameless grace
Which waves in every raven tress,
Or softly lightens o'er her face;
Where thoughts serenely sweet express
How pure, how dear, their dwelling-place. 12

And on that cheek, and o'er that brow,
So soft, so calm, yet eloquent,
The smiles that win, the tints that glow,
But tell of days in goodness spent,
A mind at peace with all below,
A heart whose love is innocent! 18

THE DESTRUCTION OF SENNACHERIB*

The Assyrian came down like the wolf on the
fold,
And his cohorts were gleaming in purple and
gold;
And the sheen of their spears was like stars on
the sea,
When the blue wave rolls nightly on deep
Galilee. 4

Like the leaves of the forest when Summer is
green,
That host with their banners at sunset were
seen:
Like the leaves of the forest when Autumn hath
blown,
That host on the morrow lay withered and
strown. 8

For the Angel of Death spread his wings on the
blast,
And breathed in the face of the foe as he
passed;
And the eyes of the sleepers waxed deadly and
chill,
And their hearts but once heaved, and for ever
grew still! 12

And there lay the steed with his nostril all wide,
But through it there rolled not the breath of his
pride;
And the foam of his gasping lay white on the
turf,
And cold as the spray of the rock-beating
surf. 16

And there lay the rider distorted and pale,
With the dew on his brow, and the rust on his
mail:
And the tents were all silent, the banners alone,
The lances unlifted, the trumpet unblown. 20

And the widows of Ashur are loud in their wail,
And the idols are broke in the temple of Baal;
And the might of the Gentile, unsmote by the
sword,
Hath melted like snow in the glance of the
Lord! 24

SO WE'LL GO NO MORE A ROVING

So we'll go no more a roving
So late into the night,
Though the heart be still as loving,
And the moon be still as bright.

For the sword outwears its sheath,
And the soul wears out the breast,
And the heart must pause to breathe,
And love itself have rest.

Though the night was made for loving,
And the day returns too soon,
Yet we'll go no more a roving
By the light of the moon.

2 Constantinople
* II *Kings*, xix, 35.

LORD BYRON 453

STANZAS WRITTEN ON THE ROAD BETWEEN FLORENCE AND PISA

Oh, talk not to me of a name great in story;
The days of our youth are the days of our glory;
And the myrtle and ivy of sweet two-and-twenty
Are worth all your laurels, though ever so plenty.   4

What are garlands and crowns to the brow that is wrinkled?
'Tis but as a dead flower with May-dew besprinkled.
Then away with all such from the head that is hoary!
What care I for the wreaths that can *only* give glory!   8

Oh, Fame!—if I e'er took delight in thy praises,
'Twas less for the sake of thy high-sounding phrases,
Than to see the bright eyes of the dear one discover,
She thought that I was not unworthy to love her.   12

There chiefly I sought thee, *there* only I found thee;
Her glance was the best of the rays that surround thee;
When it sparkled o'er aught that was bright in my story,
I knew it was love, and I felt it was glory.   16

TO THOMAS MOORE*

My boat is on the shore,
  And my bark is on the sea;
But, before I go, Tom Moore,
  Here's a double health to thee!

Here's a sigh to those who love me,
  And a smile to those who hate;
And, whatever sky's above me,
  Here's a heart for every fate.   8

Though the ocean roar around me,
  Yet it still shall bear me on;
Though a desert should surround me,
  It hath springs that may be won.

Were't the last drop in the well,
  As I gasped upon the brink,
Ere my fainting spirit fell,
  'Tis to thee that I would drink.   16

* The first stanza of this poem was written in 1816, when Byron left England for the last time.

With that water, as this wine,
  The libation I would pour
Should be—peace with thine and mine,
  And a health to thee, Tom Moore.   20

SONNET ON CHILLON

Eternal Spirit of the chainless Mind!
Brightest in dungeons, Liberty! thou art,
For there thy habitation is the heart—
The heart which love of thee alone can bind;
And when thy sons to fetters are consigned—
To fetters, and the damp vault's dayless gloom,
Their country conquers with their martyrdom,
And Freedom's fame finds wings on every wind.
Chillon!† thy prison is a holy place,
And thy sad floor an altar—for 't was trod,
Until his very steps have left a trace
Worn, as if thy cold pavement were a sod,
By Bonnivard! May none those marks efface!
For they appeal from tyranny to God.

THE PRISONER OF CHILLON‡

My hair is gray, but not with years,
  Nor grew it white
  In a single night,
As men's have grown from sudden fears;
My limbs are bowed, though not with toil.
  But rusted with a vile repose,
For they have been a dungeon's spoil,
  And mine has been the fate of those
To whom the goodly earth and air
Are banned, and barred—forbidden fare;   10
But this was for my father's faith
I suffered chains and courted death;
That father perished at the stake
For tenets he would not forsake;
And for the same his lineal race
In darkness found a dwelling-place;
We were seven—who now are one,
  Six in youth, and one in age,
Finished as they had begun,

† This French word has no very marked accent on either syllable. Byron usually accents the first.

‡ François de Bonivard was a republican of Geneva who resisted the domination of the Duke of Savoy and was imprisoned for six years (1530-1536) in the castle of Chillon, on the Lake of Geneva (Leman). When the castle was captured by his republican friends, he was released. Byron has greatly idealized the character and has invented the circumstance of the imprisonment and death of the brothers. The poem was composed in two days. Of it Dr. F. I. Carpenter writes: "There is very little action; there is very little ornament; the narrative evolves from within, and is presented with high dramatic fidelity, and with subtle gradation and progression. The situation in itself is bare and simple; the art with which the poet develops it is masterly Who else, except Dante perhaps, as in the Ugolino episode [*Inferno* 33], could do so much with so little?"

Proud of Persecution's rage;
One in fire, and two in field
Their belief with blood have sealed,
Dying as their father died,
For the God their foes denied;
Three were in a dungeon cast,
Of whom this wreck is left the last.

There are seven pillars of Gothic mould,
In Chillon's dungeons deep and old,
There are seven columns, massy and gray,
Dim with a dull imprisoned ray,   30
A sunbeam which hath lost its way
And through the crevice and the cleft
Of the thick wall is fallen and left;
Creeping o'er the floor so damp,
Like a marsh's meteor lamp:
And in each pillar there is a ring,
    And in each ring there is a chain;
That iron is a cankering thing,
    For in these limbs its teeth remain,
With marks that will not wear away,   40
Till I have done with this new day,
Which now is painful to these eyes,
Which have not seen the sun so rise
For years—I cannot count them o'er,
I lost their long and heavy score,
When my last brother drooped and died,
And I lay living by his side.

They chained us each to a column stone,
And we were three—yet, each alone;
We could not move a single pace,   50
We could not see each other's face,
But with that pale and livid light
That made us strangers in our sight:
And thus together—yet apart,
Fettered in hand, but joined in heart,
'Twas still some solace, in the dearth
Of the pure elements of earth,
To hearken to each other's speech,
And each turn comforter to each
With some new hope, or legend old,   60
Or song heroically bold;
But even these at length grew cold.
Our voices took a dreary tone,
An echo of the dungeon stone,
    A grating sound, not full and free,
    As they of yore were wont to be;
It might be fancy, but to me
They never sounded like our own.

I was the eldest of the three,
    And to uphold and cheer the rest   70
    I ought to do—and did my best—
And each did well in his degree.
    The youngest, whom my father loved,
Because our mother's brow was given
To him, with eyes as blue as heaven—

For him my soul was sorely moved;
And truly might it be distressed
To see such bird in such a nest;
For he was beautiful as day—
    (When day was beautiful to me   80
    As to young eagles, being free)—
    A polar day, which will not see
A sunset till its summer's gone,
    Its sleepless summer of long light,
The snow-clad offspring of the sun:
    And thus he was as pure and bright,
And in his natural spirit gay,
    With tears for nought but others' ills,
And then they flowed like mountain rills,   90
Unless he could assuage the woe
Which he abhorred to view below.

The other was as pure of mind,
But formed to combat with his kind;
Strong in his frame, and of a mood
Which 'gainst the world in war had stood,
And perished in the foremost rank
    With joy:—but not in chains to pine:
His spirit withered with their clank,
    I saw it silently decline—
    And so perchance in sooth did mine: 100
But yet I forced it on to cheer
Those relics of a home so dear.
He was a hunter of the hills,
    Had followed there the deer and wolf;
    To him this dungeon was a gulf,
And fettered feet the worst of ills.

Lake Leman lies by Chillon's walls:
A thousand feet in depth below
Its massy waters meet and flow;
Thus much the fathom-line was sent   110
From Chillon's snow-white battlement,
    Which round about the wave inthrals:
A double dungeon wall and wave
Have made—and like a living grave.
Below the surface of the lake
The dark vault lies wherein we lay:
We heard it ripple night and day;
    Sounding o'er our heads it knocked;
And I have felt the winter's spray
Wash through the bars when winds were high
And wanton in the happy sky;   121
    And then the very rock hath rocked,
    And I have felt it shake, unshocked,
Because I could have smiled to see
The death that would have set me free.

I said my nearer brother pined,
I said his mighty heart declined,
He loathed and put away his food;
It was not that 'twas coarse and rude,
For we were used to hunter's fare,   130

And for the like had little care:
The milk drawn from the mountain goat
Was changed for water from the moat,
Our bread was such as captives' tears
Have moistened many a thousand years,
Since man first pent his fellow men
Like brutes within an iron den;
But what were these to us or him?
These wasted not his heart or limb;
My brother's soul was of that mould   140
Which in a palace had grown cold,
Had his free breathing been denied
The range of the steep mountain's side;
But why delay the truth?—he died.
I saw, and could not hold his head,
Nor reach his dying hand—nor dead,—
Though hard I strove, but strove in vain
To rend and gnash my bonds in twain.
He died, and they unlocked his chain,
And scooped for him a shallow grave   150
Even from the cold earth of our cave.
I begged them as a boon to lay
His corse in dust whereon the day
Might shine—it was a foolish thought,
But then within my brain it wrought,
That even in death his freeborn breast
In such a dungeon could not rest.
I might have spared my idle prayer—
They coldly laughed, and laid him there:
The flat and turfless earth above   160
The being we so much did love;
His empty chain above it leant,
Such murder's fitting monument!

But he, the favourite and the flower,
Most cherished since his natal hour,
His mother's image in fair face,
The infant love of all his race,
His martyred father's dearest thought,
My latest care, for whom I sought
To hoard my life, that his might be   170
Less wretched now, and one day free;
He, too, who yet had held untired
A spirit natural or inspired—
He, too, was struck, and day by day
Was withered on the stalk away.
Oh, God! it is a fearful thing
To see the human soul take wing
In any shape, in any mood,
I've seen it rushing forth in blood,
I've seen it on the breaking ocean   180
Strive with a swoln convulsive motion,
I've seen the sick and ghastly bed
Of Sin delirious with its dread:
But these were horrors—this was woe
Unmixed with such—but sure and slow:
He faded, and so calm and meek,
So softly worn, so sweetly weak,

So tearless, yet so tender, kind,
And grieved for those he left behind;
With all the while a cheek whose bloom   190
Was as a mockery of the tomb,
Whose tints as gently sunk away
As a departing rainbow's ray;
An eye of most transparent light,
That almost made the dungeon bright;
And not a word of murmur, not
A groan o'er his untimely lot,—
A little talk of better days,
A little hope my own to raise,
For I was sunk in silence—lost   200
In this last loss, of all the most;
And then the sighs he would suppress
Of fainting nature's feebleness,
More slowly drawn, grew less and less:
I listened, but I could not hear;
I called, for I was wild with fear:
I knew 't was hopeless, but my dread
Would not be thus admonishèd;
I called, and thought I heard a sound—
I burst my chain with one strong bound,   210
And rushed to him:—I found him not,
I only stirred in this black spot,
I only lived, I only drew
The accursèd breath of dungeon-dew;
The last, the sole, the dearest link
Between me and the eternal brink,
Which bound me to my failing race,
Was broken in this fatal place.
One on the earth, and one beneath—
My brothers—both had ceased to breathe: 220
I took that hand which lay so still,
Alas! my own was full as chill;
I had not strength to stir, or strive,
But felt that I was still alive—
A frantic feeling, when we know
That what we love shall ne'er be so.
  I know not why
  I could not die,
I had no earthly hope—but faith,
And that forbade a selfish death.   230

What next befell me then and there
  I know not well—I never knew—
First came the loss of light, and air,
  And then of darkness too:
I had no thought, no feeling—none—
Among the stones I stood a stone,
And was, scarce conscious what I wist,
As shrubless crags within the mist;
For all was blank, and bleak, and gray;
It was not night, it was not day;   240
It was not even the dungeon-light,
So hateful to my heavy sight,
But vacancy absorbing space,
And fixedness without a place;

There were no stars, no earth, no time,
No check, no change, no good, no crime,
But silence, and a stirless breath
Which neither was of life nor death;
A sea of stagnant idleness,
Blind, boundless, mute, and motionless!   250

A light broke in upon my brain,—
  It was the carol of a bird;
It ceased, and then it came again,
  The sweetest song ear ever heard,
And mine was thankful till my eyes
Ran over with the glad surprise,
And they that moment could not see
I was the mate of misery;
But then by dull degrees came back
My senses to their wonted track;   260
I saw the dungeon walls and floor
Close slowly round me as before,
I saw the glimmer of the sun
Creeping as it before had done,
But through the crevice where it came
That bird was perched, as fond and tame,
  And tamer than upon the tree;
A lovely bird, with azure wings,
And song that said a thousand things,
  And seemed to say them all for me!   270
I never saw its like before,
I ne'er shall see its likeness more:
It seemed like me to want a mate,
But was not half so desolate,
And it was come to love me when
None lived to love me so again,
And cheering from my dungeon's brink,
Had brought me back to feel and think.
I know not if it late were free,
  Or broke its cage to perch on mine,   280
But knowing well captivity,
  Sweet bird! I could not wish for thine!
Or if it were, in winged guise,
A visitant from Paradise;
For—Heaven forgive that thought! the while
Which made me both to weep and smile—
I sometimes deemed that it might be
My brother's soul come down to me;
But then at last away it flew,
And then 'twas mortal well I knew,   290
For he would never thus have flown,
And left me twice so doubly lone,
Lone as the corse within its shroud,
Lone as a solitary cloud,—
  A single cloud on a sunny day,
While all the rest of heaven is clear,
A frown upon the atmosphere,
That hath no business to appear
  When skies are blue, and earth is gay.

A kind of change came in my fate,   300
My keepers grew compassionate;

I know not what had made them so,
They were inured to sights of woe,
But so it was:—my broken chain
With links unfastened did remain,
And it was liberty to stride
Along my cell from side to side,
And up and down, and then athwart,
And tread it over every part;
And round the pillars one by one,   310
Returning where my walk begun,
Avoiding only, as I trod,
My brothers' graves without a sod;
For if I thought with heedless tread
My step profaned their lowly bed,
My breath came gaspingly and thick,
And my crushed heart fell blind and sick.

I made a footing in the wall,
  It was not therefrom to escape,
For I had buried one and all   320
  Who loved me in a human shape;
And the whole earth would henceforth be
A wider prison unto me:
No child, no sire, no kin had I,
No partner in my misery;
I thought of this, and I was glad,
For thought of them had made me mad;
But I was curious to ascend
To my barred windows, and to bend
Once more, upon the mountains high,   330
The quiet of a loving eye.

I saw them, and they were the same,
They were not changed like me in frame;
I saw their thousand years of snow
On high—their wide long lake below,
And the blue Rhone in fullest flow;
I heard the torrents leap and gush
O'er channelled rock and broken bush;
I saw the white-walled distant town,
And whiter sails go skimming down;   340
And then there was a little isle,
Which in my very face did smile,
  The only one in view;
A small green isle, it seemed no more,
Scarce broader than my dungeon floor,
But in it there were three tall trees,
And o'er it blew the mountain breeze,
And by it there were waters flowing,
And on it there were young flowers growing,
  Of gentle breath and hue.   350
The fish swam by the castle wall,
And they seemed joyous each and all;
The eagle rode the rising blast,
Methought he never flew so fast
As then to me he seemed to fly;
And then new tears came in my eye,
And I felt troubled—and would fain

I had not left my recent chain;
And when I did descend again,
The darkness of my dim abode   360
Fell on me as a heavy load;
It was as is a new-dug grave,
Closing o'er one we sought to save,—
And yet my glance, too much opprest,
Had almost need of such a rest.

It might be months, or years, or days,
 I kept no count, I took no note,
I had no hope my eyes to raise,
 And clear them of their dreary mote;
At last men came to set me free;   370
 I asked not why, and recked not where;
It was at length the same to me,
Fettered or fetterless to be,
 I learned to love despair.
And thus when they appeared at last,
And all my bonds aside were cast,
These heavy walls to me had grown
A hermitage—and all my own!
And half I felt as they were come
To tear me from a second home: 380
With spiders I had friendship made,
And watched them in their sullen trade,
Had seen the mice by moonlight play,
And why should I feel less than they?
We were all inmates of one place,
And I, the monarch of each race,
Had power to kill—yet, strange to tell!
In quiet we had learned to dwell;
My very chains and I grew friends,
So much a long communion tends   390
To make us what we are:—even I
Regained my freedom with a sigh.

From CHILDE HAROLD

Waterloo. From Canto III*

21

There was a sound of revelry by night,
And Belgium's capital had gathered then
Her Beauty and her Chivalry, and bright
The lamps shone o'er fair women and brave
 men;
A thousand hearts beat happily; and when
Music arose with its voluptuous swell,
Soft eyes looked love to eyes which spake again,
And all went merry as a marriage-bell;
 But hush! hark! a deep sound strikes like a
  rising knell!

* Three days before the battle of Waterloo, on
 the eve of the battle of Quatre-Bras, the
 Duchess of Richmond gave a ball in Brussels, which was attended by Wellington and
 other British officers.

22

Did ye not hear it?—No; 'twas but the wind,
Or the car rattling o'er the stony street;
On with the dance! let joy be unconfined;
No sleep till morn, when Youth and Pleasure
 meet
To chase the glowing Hours with flying feet—
But hark!—that heavy sound breaks in once
 more,
As if the clouds its echo would repeat;
And nearer, clearer, deadlier than before!
 Arm! Arm! it is—it is—the cannon's open-
  ing roar!

23

Within a windowed niche of that high hall
Sate Brunswick's fated chieftain;[1] he did hear
That sound the first amidst the festival,
And caught its tone with Death's prophetic ear;
And when they smiled because he deemed it
 near,
His heart more truly knew that peal too well
Which stretched his father on a bloody bier,
And roused the vengeance blood alone could
 quell;
 He rushed into the field, and, foremost fight-
  ing, fell.

24

Ah! then and there was hurrying to and fro,
And gathering tears, and tremblings of distress,
And cheeks all pale, which but an hour ago
Blushed at the praise of their own loveliness;
And there were sudden partings, such as press
The life from out young hearts, and choking
 sighs
Which ne'er might be repeated; who could
 guess
If ever more should meet those mutual eyes,
 Since upon night so sweet such awful morn
  could rise!

25

And there was mounting in hot haste: the steed,
The mustering squadron, and the clattering car,
Went pouring forward with impetuous speed,
And swiftly forming in the ranks of war;
And the deep thunder peal on peal afar;
And near, the beat of the alarming drum
Roused up the soldier ere the morning star;
While thronged the citizens with terror dumb,
 Or whispering, with white lips—"The foe,
  they come! they come!"

[1] The Duke of Brunswick, nephew of George III.
His father was killed at Auerstädt in 1806.

26

And wild and high the ''Cameron's gathering''
  rose!
The war-note of Lochiel,[2] which Albyn's[3] hills
Have heard, and heard, too, have her Saxon[4]
  foes:—
How in the noon of night that pibroch thrills,
Savage and shrill! But with the breath which
  fills
Their mountain-pipe, so fill the mountaineers
With the fierce native daring which instils
The stirring memory of a thousand years,
  And Evan's, Donald's fame rings in each
  clansman's ears!

27

And Ardennes[5] waves above them her green
  leaves,
Dewy with nature's tear-drops as they pass,
Grieving, if aught inanimate e'er grieves,
Over the unreturning brave,—alas!
Ere evening to be trodden like the grass
Which now beneath them, but above shall grow
In its next verdure, when this fiery mass
Of living valour, rolling on the foe
  And burning with high hope shall moulder
  cold and low.

28

Last noon beheld them full of lusty life,
Last eve in Beauty's circle proudly gay,
The midnight brought the signal-sound of strife,
The morn the marshalling in arms,—the day
Battle's magnificently stern array!
The thunder-clouds close o'er it, which when
  rent
The earth is covered thick with other clay,
Which her own clay shall cover, heaped and
  pent,
  Rider and horse,—friend, foe,—in one red
  burial blent!

NIGHT ON LAKE LEMAN. FROM CANTO III

85

Clear, placid Leman![6] thy contrasted lake,
With the wild world I dwelt in, is a thing
Which warns me, with its stillness, to forsake
Earth's troubled waters for a purer spring.
This quiet sail is as a noiseless wing
To waft me from distraction; once I loved
Torn ocean's roar, but thy soft murmuring
Sounds sweet as if a Sister's voice reproved,

That I with stern delights should e'er have
  been so moved.

86

It is the hush of night, and all between
Thy margin and the mountains, dusk, yet clear,
Mellowed and mingling, yet distinctly seen,
Save darkened Jura, whose capt heights appear
Precipitously steep; and drawing near,
There breathes a living fragrance from the
  shore,
Of flowers yet fresh with childhood; on the ear
Drops the light drip of the suspended oar,
  Or chirps the grasshopper one good-night
  carol more;

87

He is an evening reveller, who makes
His life an infancy, and sings his fill;
At intervals, some bird from out the brakes
Starts into voice a moment, then is still.
There seems a floating whisper on the hill,
But that is fancy, for the starlight dews
All silently their tears of love instil,
Weeping themselves away, till they infuse
  Deep into nature's breast the spirit of her
  hues.

88

Ye stars! which are the poetry of heaven!
If in your bright leaves we would read the fate
Of men and empires,—'tis to be forgiven,
That in our aspirations to be great,
Our destinies o'erleap their mortal state,
And claim a kindred with you; for ye are
A beauty and a mystery, and create
In us such love and reverence from afar,
  That fortune, fame, power, life, have named
  themselves a star.

89

All heaven and earth are still—though not in
  sleep,
But breathless, as we grow when feeling most;
And silent, as we stand in thoughts too deep:—
All heaven and earth are still: From the high
  host
Of stars, to the lulled lake and mountain coast,
All is concentered in a life intense,
Where not a beam, nor air, nor leaf is lost,
But hath a part of being, and a sense
  Of that which is of all Creator and defence.

90

Then stirs the feeling infinite, so felt
In solitude, where we are *least* alone;
A truth, which through our being then doth
  melt,
And purifies from self: it is a tone,

---

2 Donald Cameron of Lochiel, chief of the Cameron clan.
3 Scotland's
4 Lowland and English (Sir Evan Cameron fought
  against Cromwell).
5 A forest, properly Soignies.
6 The Lake of Geneva (Latin *Lemannus*).

The soul and source of music, which makes
known
Eternal harmony, and sheds a charm
Like to the fabled Cytherea's zone,[7]
Binding all things with beauty:—'t would dis-
arm
　The spectre Death, had he substantial power
　　to harm.

91

Not vainly did the early Persian make
His altar the high places, and the peak
Of earth-o'ergazing mountains, and thus take
A fit and unwalled temple, there to seek
The Spirit, in whose honour shrines are weak,
Upreared of human hands. Come, and compare
Columns and idol-dwellings, Goth or Greek,
With Nature's realms of worship, earth and air,
　Nor fix on fond abodes to circumscribe thy
　　prayer!

92

The sky is changed!—and such a change! Oh
night,
And storm, and darkness, ye are wondrous
strong,
Yet lovely in your strength, as is the light
Of a dark eye in woman! Far along,
From peak to peak, the rattling crags among
Leaps the live thunder! Not from one lone
cloud,
But every mountain now hath found a tongue,
And Jura answers, through her misty shroud,
　Back to the joyous Alps, who call to her
　　aloud!

93

And this is in the night:—Most glorious night!
Thou wert not sent for slumber! let me be
A sharer in thy fierce and far delight,—
A portion of the tempest and of thee!
How the lit lake shines, a phosphoric sea,
And the big rain comes dancing to the earth!
And now again 'tis black,—and now, the glee
Of the loud hills shakes with its mountain-
mirth,
　As if they did rejoice o'er a young earth-
　　quake's birth.

94

Now, where the swift Rhone cleaves his way
between
Heights which appear as lovers who have
parted
In hate, whose mining depths so intervene,
That they can meet no more, though broken-
hearted;
Though in their souls, which thus each other
thwarted,
Love was the very root of the fond rage

7 The cestus of Venus, which inspired Love.

Which blighted their life's bloom, and then departed:
Itself expired, but leaving them an age,
　Of years all winters,—war within themselves
　　to wage:

95

Now, where the quick Rhone thus hath cleft his
way,
The mightiest of the storms hath ta'en his
stand:
For here, not one, but many, make their play,
And fling their thunder-bolts from hand to
hand,
Flashing and cast around; of all the band,
The brightest through these parted hills hath
forked
His lightnings,—as if he did understand,
That in such gaps as desolation worked,
　There the hot shaft should blast whatever
　　therein lurked.

96

Sky, mountains, river, winds, lake, lightnings!
ye!
With night, and clouds, and thunder, and a soul
To make these felt and feeling, well may be
Things that have made me watchful; the far
roll
Of your departing voices, is the knoll
Of what in me is sleepless,—if I rest.
But where of ye, O tempests! is the goal?
Are ye like those within the human breast?
　Or do ye find, at length, like eagles, some
　　high nest?

97

Could I embody and unbosom now
That which is most within me,—could I wreak
My thoughts upon expression, and thus throw
Soul, heart, mind, passions, feelings, strong or
weak,
All that I would have sought, and all I seek,
Bear, know, feel, and yet breathe—into *one*
word,
And that one word were Lightning, I would
speak;
But as it is I live and die unheard,
　With a most voiceless thought, sheathing it
　　as a sword.

98

The morn is up again, the dewy morn,
With breath all incense, and with cheek all
bloom,
Laughing the clouds away with playful scorn,
And living as if earth contained no tomb,—
And glowing into day: we may resume
The march of our existence: and thus I,

Still on thy shores, fair Leman! may find room
And food for meditation, nor pass by
   Much, that may give us pause, if ponder'd
    fittingly.

VENICE. FROM CANTO IV

1

I stood in Venice, on the Bridge of Sighs;[1]
A palace and a prison on each hand:
I saw from out the wave her structures rise
As from the stroke of the enchanter's wand:
A thousand years their cloudy wings expand
Around me,[2] and a dying Glory smiles
O'er the far times, when many a subject land
Looked to the winged Lion's[3] marble piles,
   Where Venice sate in state, throned on her
    hundred isles!

2

She looks a sea Cybele, fresh from ocean,
Rising with her tiara of proud towers[4]
At airy distance, with majestic motion,
A ruler of the waters and their powers;
And such she was;—her daughters had their
   dowers
From spoils of nations, and the exhaustless
   East
Poured in her lap all gems in sparkling showers.
In purple was she robed, and of her feast
   Monarchs partook, and deemed their dignity
    increased.

3

In Venice Tasso's echoes are no more,[5]
And silent rows the songless gondolier;
Her palaces are crumbling to the shore,
And music meets not always now the ear:
Those days are gone—but Beauty still is here.
States fall, arts fade—but Nature doth not die,
Nor yet forget how Venice once was dear,
The pleasant place of all festivity,
   The revel of the earth, the masque of Italy!

4

But unto us she hath a spell beyond
Her name in story, and her long array
Of mighty shadows, whose dim forms despond
Above the dogeless city's vanished sway;

Ours is a trophy which will not decay
With the Rialto;[6] Shylock and the Moor,[7]
And Pierre,[8] cannot be swept or worn away—
The keystones of the arch! though all were
   o'er,
   For us repeopled were the solitary shore.

5

The beings of the mind are not of clay;
Essentially immortal, they create
And multiply in us a brighter ray
And more beloved existence: that which Fate
Prohibits to dull life, in this our state
Of mortal bondage, by these spirits supplied,
First exiles, then replaces what we hate;
Watering the heart whose early flowers have
   died,
   And with a fresher growth replenishing the
    void.

13

Before St. Mark still glow his Steeds of brass,
Their gilded collars glittering in the sun;
But is not Doria's menace come to pass?[9]
Are they not *bridled?*—Venice, lost and won,
Her thirteen hundred years of freedom done,
Sinks, like a sea-weed, into whence she rose!
Better be whelmed beneath the waves, and shun,
Even in destruction's depth, her foreign foes,
   From whom submission wrings an infamous
    repose.

14

In youth she was all glory, a new Tyre,
Her very by-word sprung from victory,
The "Planter of the Lion," which through fire
And blood she bore o'er subject earth and sea;
Though making many slaves, herself still free,
And Europe's bulwark 'gainst the Ottomite;—
Witness Troy's rival, Candia![10] Vouch it, ye
Immortal waves that saw Lepanto's fight![11]
   For ye are names no time nor tyranny can
    blight.

15

Statues of glass—all shivered—the long file
Of her dead Doges are declined to dust;
But where they dwelt, the vast and sumptuous
   pile
Bespeaks the pageant of their splendid trust;

1 The gallery spanning the canal between the
  ducal palace and the prison.
2 See note on Wordsworth's sonnet, p. 427.
3 The Lion of St. Mark, surmounting one of the
  two pillars in the square in front of the
  palace. The Lion was also the standard of
  the republic; see st. 14.
4 In ancient art, the goddess Cybele wore a turreted crown.
5 Stanzas of Tasso's *Jerusalem Delivered* were
  once sung by the gondoliers.

6 Here evidently meaning the Bridge of the Rialto
  across the Grand Canal.
7 Othello
8 A character in Otway's *Venice Preserved.*
9 This Genoese admiral once threatened to put a
  bridle on the bronze steeds that adorn St.
  Mark's.
10 Crete, once possessed by Venice, but lost again
  to the Turks.
11 The battle of Lepanto, 1571, a victory over the
  Turks in which Venice took a leading part.

Their sceptre broken, and their sword in rust,
Have yielded to the stranger: empty halls,
Thin streets, and foreign aspects, such as must
Too oft remind her who and what enthralls,
  Have flung a desolate cloud o'er Venice'
    lovely walls.

16

When Athens' armies fell at Syracuse,
And fettered thousands bore the yoke of war,
Redemption rose up in the Attic Muse,[12]
Her voice their only ransom from afar;
See! as they chant the tragic hymn, the car
Of the o'ermastered victor stops, the reins
Fall from his hands, his idle scimitar
Starts from its belt—he rends his captive's
    chains,
  And bids him thank the bard for freedom
    and his strains.

17

Thus, Venice, if no stronger claim were thine,
Were all thy proud historic deeds forgot,
Thy choral memory of the Bard divine,
Thy love of Tasso, should have cut the knot
Which ties thee to thy tyrants; and thy lot
Is shameful to the nations,—most of all,
Albion! to thee: the Ocean queen should not
Abandon Ocean's children; in the fall
  Of Venice, think of thine, despite thy watery
    wall.

18

I loved her from my boyhood; she to me
Was as a fairy city of the heart,
Rising like water-columns from the sea,
Of joy the sojourn, and of wealth the mart;
And Otway, Radcliffe,[13] Schiller,[14] Shake-
    speare's art,
Had stamped her image in me, and even so,
Although I found her thus, we did not part,
Perchance even dearer in her day of woe,
  Than when she was a boast, a marvel and a
    show.

ROME. FROM CANTO IV

78

Oh Rome! my country! city of the soul
The orphans of the heart must turn to thee,
Lone mother of dead empires! and control
In their shut breasts their petty misery.
What are our woes and sufferance? Come and
    see

The cypress, hear the owl, and plod your way
O'er steps of broken thrones and temples, Ye!
Whose agonies are evils of a day—
  A world is at our feet as fragile as our clay.

79

The Niobe of nations![15] there she stands,
Childless and crownless, in her voiceless woe;
An empty urn within her withered hands,
Whose holy dust was scattered long ago;
The Scipios' tomb contains no ashes now;
The very sepulchres lie tenantless
Of their heroic dwellers: dost thou flow,
Old Tiber! through a marble wilderness?
  Rise, with thy yellow waves, and mantle her
    distress.

80

The Goth, the Christian, Time, War, Flood, and
    Fire,
Have dealt upon the seven-hilled city's pride;
She saw her glories star by star expire,
And up the steep barbarian monarchs ride,
Where the car climbed the Capitol; far and
    wide
Temple and tower went down, nor left a site:
Chaos of ruins! who shall trace the void,
O'er the dim fragments cast a lunar light,
  And say, "here was, or is," where all is
    doubly night?

81

The double night of ages, and of her,
Night's daughter, Ignorance, hath wrapt and
    wrap
All round us; we but feel our way to err:
The Ocean hath his chart, the stars their map,
And Knowledge spreads them on her ample lap;
But Rome is as the desert, where we steer
Stumbling o'er recollections; now we clap
Our hands, and cry "Eureka!" "it is clear"—
  When but some false mirage of ruin rises
    near.

82

Alas! the lofty city! and, alas,
The trebly hundred triumphs; and the day
When Brutus made the dagger's edge surpass
The Conqueror's sword in bearing fame away!
Alas, for Tully's[16] voice, and Virgil's lay,
And Livy's pictured page;—but these shall be
Her resurrection; all beside—decay.
Alas, for Earth, for never shall we see
  That brightness in her eye she bore when
    Rome was free!

.   .   .   .   .   .

12 It is said that the Athenian prisoners who
    could recite Euripides were set free. Cp. page
    233, note 5.
13 In *The Mysteries of Udolpho.*
14 In *The Ghost-Seer.*

15 The twelve children of Niobe were slain by
    Apollo. They are the subject of a famous
    ancient group of statuary.
16 Cicero's

96

Can tyrants but by tyrants conquered be,
And Freedom find no champion, and no child,
Such as Columbia saw arise when she
Sprung forth a Pallas, armed and undefiled?
Or must such minds be nourished in the wild,
Deep in the unpruned forest, 'midst the roar
Of cataracts, where nursing Nature smiled
On infant Washington? Has earth no more
　Such seeds within her breast, or Europe no
　　such shore?

97

But France got drunk with blood to vomit
　　crime;
And fatal have her Saturnalia been
To Freedom's cause, in every age and clime;
Because the deadly days which we have seen,
And vile Ambition, that built up between
Man and his hopes an adamantine wall,
And the base pageant last upon the scene,*
Are grown the pretext for the eternal thrall
　Which nips life's tree, and dooms man's
　　worst—his second fall.

98

Yet, Freedom! yet thy banner, torn but flying,
Streams like the thunder-storm *against* the
　　wind;
Thy trumpet voice, though broken now and
　　dying,
The loudest still the tempest leaves behind;
Thy tree hath lost its blossoms, and the rind,
Chopped by the axe, looks rough and little
　　worth,
But the sap lasts,—and still the seed we find
Sown deep, even in the bosom of the North;
　So shall a better spring less bitter fruit
　　bring forth.

THE COLISEUM. FROM CANTO IV

139

And here the buzz of eager nations ran,
In murmured pity, or loud-roared applause,
As man was slaughtered by his fellow-man,
And wherefore slaughtered? wherefore, but be-
　　cause
Such were the bloody Circus' genial laws,
And the imperial pleasure.—Wherefore not?
What matters where we fall to fill the maws
Of worms—on battle-plains or listed spot?
　Both are but theatres where the chief actors
　　rot.

* The Congress of Vienna, the "Holy Alliance"
　(into which Wellington would not enter),
　and the Second Treaty of Paris.—E. H. Cole-
　ridge.

140

I see before me the Gladiator lie:[17]
He leans upon his hand—his manly brow
Consents to death, but conquers agony,
And his drooped head sinks gradually low—
And through his side the last drops, ebbing
　　slow
From the red gash, fall heavy, one by one,
Like the first of a thunder-shower; and now
The arena swims around him—he is gone,
　Ere ceased the inhuman shout which hailed
　　the wretch who won.

141

He heard it, but he heeded not—his eyes
Were with his heart, and that was far away:
He recked not of the life he lost nor prize,
But where his rude hut by the Danube lay,
There were his young barbarians all at play,
There was their Dacian mother—he, their sire,
Butchered to make a Roman holiday—
All this rushed with his blood—Shall he expire
　And unavenged? Arise! ye Goths, and glut
　　your ire!

142

But here, where Murder breathed her bloody
　　steam:
And here, where buzzing nations choked the
　　ways,
And roared or murmured like a mountain
　　stream
Dashing or winding as its torrent strays:
Here, where the Roman million's blame or
　　praise
Was death or life, the playthings of a crowd,
My voice sounds much—and fall the stars'
　　faint rays
On the arena void—seats crushed, walls bowed—
　And galleries, where my steps seem echoes
　　strangely loud.

143

A ruin—yet what ruin! from its mass
Walls, palaces, half-cities, have been reared;
Yet oft the enormous skeleton ye pass,
And marvel where the spoil could have ap-
　　peared.
Hath it indeed been plundered, or but cleared?
Alas! developed, opens the decay,
When the colossal fabric's form is neared:
It will not bear the brightness of the day,
　Which streams too much on all years, man
　　have reft away.

17 Suggested by the statue of The Dying Gaul,
　once supposed to represent a dying gladiator

144

But when the rising moon begins to climb
Its topmost arch, and gently pauses there;
When the stars twinkle through the loops of
time,
And the low night-breeze waves along the air
The garland-forest, which the gray walls wear,
Like laurels on the bald first Cæsar's head;[18]
When the light shines serene but doth not glare,
Then in this magic circle raise the dead:
   Heroes have trod this spot—'tis on their dust
     ye tread.

145

"While stands the Coliseum, Rome shall stand;
"When falls the Coliseum Rome shall fall;
"And when Rome falls—the World." From
   our own land
Thus spake the pilgrims o'er this mighty wall
In Saxon times, which we are wont to call
Ancient; and these three mortal things are still
On their foundations, and unaltered all;
Rome and her Ruin past Redemption's skill,
   The World, the same wide den—of thieves,
     or what ye will.

THE OCEAN. FROM CANTO IV

178

There is a pleasure in the pathless woods,
There is a rapture on the lonely shore,
There is society, where none intrudes,
By the deep Sea, and music in its roar:
I love not Man the less, but Nature more,
From these our interviews, in which I steal
From all I may be, or have been before,
To mingle with the Universe, and feel
   What I can ne'er express, yet cannot all con-
     ceal.

179

Roll on, thou deep and dark blue Ocean—roll!
Ten thousand fleets sweep over thee in vain;
Man marks the earth with ruin—his control
Stops with the shore; upon the watery plain
The wrecks are all thy deed, nor doth remain
A shadow of man's ravage, save his own,
When, for a moment, like a drop of rain,
He sinks into thy depths with bubbling groan,
   Without a grave, unknelled, uncoffined, and
     unknown.

180

His steps are not upon thy paths—thy fields
Are not a spoil for him,—thou dost arise
And shake him from thee; the vile strength
   he wields

18 Cæsar was glad to cover his baldness with the
   wreath of laurel which the senate decreed
   he should wear.

For earth's destruction thou dost all despise,
Spurning him from thy bosom to the skies,
And send'st him, shivering in thy playful spray
And howling, to his Gods, where haply lies
His petty hope in some near port or bay,
   And dashest him again to earth:—there let
     him lay.*

181

The armaments which thunderstrike the walls
Of rock-built cities, bidding nations quake,
And monarchs tremble in their capitals,
The oak leviathans, whose huge ribs make
Their clay creator the vain title take
Of lord of thee, and arbiter of war—
These are thy toys, and, as the snowy flake,
They melt into thy yeast of waves, which mar
   Alike the Armada's pride or spoils of Tra-
     falgar.

182

Thy shores are empires, changed in all save
   thee—
Assyria, Greece, Rome, Carthage, what are they?
Thy waters washed them power while they
   were free,
And many a tyrant since; their shores obey
The stranger, slave, or savage; their decay
Has dried up realms to deserts: not so thou;—
Unchangeable, save to thy wild waves' play,
Time writes no wrinkle on thine azure brow:
   Such as creation's dawn beheld, thou rollest
     now.

183

Thou glorious mirror, where the Almighty's
   form
Glasses itself in tempests; in all time,—
Calm or convulsed, in breeze, or gale, or storm,
Icing the pole, or in the torrid clime
Dark-heaving—boundless, endless, and sublime,
The image of eternity, the throne
Of the Invisible; even from out thy slime
The monsters of the deep are made; each zone
   Obeys thee; thou goest forth, dread, fathom-
     less, alone.

184

And I have loved thee, Ocean! and my joy
Of youthful sports was on thy breast to be
Borne, like thy bubbles, onward; from a boy
I wantoned with thy breakers—they to me
Were a delight; and if the freshening sea
Made them a terror—'twas a pleasing fear,
For I was as it were a child of thee,
And trusted to thy billows far and near,
   And laid my hand upon thy mane—as I do
     here.

* This grammatical error, occurring in so lofty a
passage, is perhaps the most famous in our
literature. It is quite characteristic of
Byron's negligence or indifference.

FROM DON JUAN

THE SHIPWRECK. FROM CANTO II*

38

But now there came a flash of hope once more;
　Day broke, and the wind lulled: the masts
　　were gone,
The leak increased; shoals round her, but no
　shore,
　The vessel swam, yet still she held her own.
They tried the pumps again, and though before
　Their desperate efforts seemed all useless
　　grown,
A glimpse of sunshine set some hands to bale—
The stronger pumped, the weaker thrummed[1] a
　sail.

39

Under the vessel's keel the sail was past,
　And for the moment it had some effect;
But with a leak, and not a stick of mast,
　Nor rag of canvas, what could they expect?
But still 't is best to struggle to the last,
　'T is never too late to be wholly wrecked:
And though 't is true that man can only die
　once,
'T is not so pleasant in the Gulf of Lyons.

40

There winds and waves had hurled them, and
　from thence,
　Without their will, they carried them away;
For they were forced with steering to dispense,
　And never had as yet a quiet day
On which they might repose, or even commence
　A jurymast, or rudder, or could say
The ship would swim an hour, which, by good
　luck,
Still swam,—though not exactly like a duck.

41

The wind, in fact, perhaps was rather less,
　But the ship laboured so, they scarce could
　　hope
To weather out much longer; the distress
　Was also great with which they had to cope
For want of water, and their solid mess
　Was scant enough: in vain the telescope
Was used—nor sail nor shore appeared in sight,
Nought but the heavy sea, and coming night.

42

Again the weather threatened,—again blew
　A gale, and in the fore and after hold
Water appeared; yet, though the people knew

[1] wove in bits of rope-yarn (usually done to prevent chafing)
* Don Juan, with his servants and his tutor Pedrillo, meets with shipwreck in the Mediterranean.

All this, the most were patient, and some
　bold,
Until the chains and leathers were worn
　through
　Of all our pumps:—a wreck complete she
　　rolled,
At mercy of the waves, whose mercies are
Like human beings' during civil war.

43

Then came the carpenter, at last, with tears
　In his rough eyes, and told the captain he
Could do no more: he was a man in years,
　And long had voyaged through many a
　　stormy sea,
And if he wept at length, they were not fears
　That made his eyelids as a woman's be,
But he, poor fellow, had a wife and children,—
Two things for dying people quite bewildering.

44

The ship was evidently settling now
　Fast by the head; and, all distinction gone,
Some went to prayers again, and made a vow
　Of candles to their saints—but there were
　　none
To pay them with; and some looked o'er the
　bow;
　Some hoisted out the boats; and there was
　　one
That begged Pedrillo for an absolution,
Who told him to be damned—in his confusion.

45

Some lashed them in their hammocks; some
　put on
　Their best clothes, as if going to a fair;
Some cursed the day on which they saw the Sun,
　And gnashed their teeth, and, howling, tore
　　their hair;
And others went on as they had begun,
　Getting the boats out, being well aware
That a tight boat will live in a rough sea,
Unless with breakers close beneath her lee.

46

The worst of all was, that in their condition,
　Having been several days in great distress,
'T was difficult to get out such provision
　As now might render their long suffering
　　less:
Men, even when dying, dislike inanition;
　Their stock was damaged by the weather's
　　stress:
Two casks of biscuit and a keg of butter
Were all that could be thrown into the cutter.

47

ut in the long-boat they contrived to stow
  Some pounds of bread, though injured by
    the wet;
Vater, a twenty-gallon cask or so;
  Six flasks of wine; and they contrived to get
  portion of their beef up from below,
  And with a piece of pork, moreover, met,
ut scarce enough to serve them for a
    luncheon—
hen there was rum, eight gallons in a
    puncheon.

48

he other boats, the yawl and pinnace, had
  Been stove in the beginning of the gale;
nd the long-boat's condition was but bad,
  As there were but two blankets for a sail,
nd one oar for a mast, which a young lad
  Threw in by good luck over the ship's rail;
nd two boats could not hold, far less be stored,
o save one half the people then on board.

49

T was twilight, and the sunless day went down
  Over the waste of waters; like a veil,
Vhich, if withdrawn, would but disclose the
    frown
  Of one whose hate is masked but to assail.
hus to their hopeless eyes the night was shown,
  And grimly darkled o'er the faces pale,
nd the dim desolate deep: twelve days had
    Fear
een their familiar, and now Death was here.

50

ome trial had been making at a raft,
  With little hope in such a rolling sea,
  sort of thing at which one would have
    laughed
  If any laughter at such times could be,
nless with people who too much have quaffed,
  And have a kind of wild and horrid glee,
alf epileptical, and half hysterical:—
heir preservation would have been a miracle.

51

t half-past eight o'clock, booms, hencoops,
    spars,
  And all things, for a chance, had been cast
    loose
hat still could keep afloat the struggling tars,
  For yet they strove, although of no great use:
here was no light in heaven but a few stars,
  The boats put off o'ercrowded with their
    crews;
e gave a heel, and then a lurch to port,
nd, going down head-foremost—sunk, in short.

52

Then rose from sea to sky the wild farewell—
  Then shrieked the timid, and stood still the
    brave—
Then some leaped overboard with dreadful yell,
  As eager to anticipate their grave;
And the sea yawned around her like a hell,
  And down she sucked with her the whirling
    wave,
Like one who grapples with his enemy,
And strives to strangle him before he die.

53

And first one universal shriek there rushed,
  Louder than the loud ocean, like a crash
Of echoing thunder; and then all was hushed,
  Save the wild wind and the remorseless dash
Of billows; but at intervals there gushed,
  Accompanied with a convulsive splash,
A solitary shriek, the bubbling cry
Of some strong swimmer in his agony.

THE ISLES OF GREECE. FROM CANTO III*

78

And now they were diverted by their suite,
  Dwarfs, dancing girls, black eunuchs, and a
    poet,
Which made their new establishment complete;
  The last was of great fame, and liked to
    show it;
His verses rarely wanted their due feet—
  And for his theme—he seldom sung below it,
He being paid to satirize or flatter,
As the psalm says, "inditing a good matter."

79

He praised the present, and abused the past,
  Reversing the good custom of old days,
An Eastern anti-jacobin[1] at last
  He turned, preferring pudding to *no*
    praise[2]—
For some few years his lot had been o'ercast
  By his seeming independent in his lays,
But now he sung the Sultan and the Pacha
With truth like Southey, and with verse like
    Crashaw.[3]

80

He was a man who had seen many changes,
  And always changed as true as any needle;
His polar star being one which rather ranges,

[1] Anti-revolutionary, anti-democratic.
[2] See Pope *The Dunciad*, 52.
[3] Southey, as poet laureate, flattered royalty. The
  name of Crashaw serves chiefly for a rhyme.
* Juan and Haidée, the daughter of Lambro, a pi-
  rate, and lord of one of the Grecian isles,
  hold a feast in Lambro's halls during his
  absence.

And not the fixed—he knew the way to
    wheedle;
So vile he 'scaped the doom which oft avenges;
    And being fluent (save indeed when fee'd
    ill),
He lied with such a fervour of intention—
There was no doubt he earned his laureate
    pension.

  .   .   .   .   .   .

85

Thus, usually, when he was asked to sing,
    He gave the different nations something na-
    tional;
'Twas all the same to him—"God save the
    King,"
Or, "Ca ira,"[4] according to the fashion all:
His Muse made increment of anything,
    From the high lyric down to the low rational;
If Pindar[5] sang horse-races, what should hinder
Himself from being as pliable as Pindar.

86

In France, for instance, he would write a
    chanson;
    In England a six canto quarto tale;
In Spain he'd make a ballad or romance on
    The last war—much the same in Portugal;
In Germany, the Pegasus he'd prance on
    Would be old Goethe's (see what says De
    Stael[6]);
In Italy he'd ape the "Trecentisti;"[7]
In Greece, he'd sing some sort of hymn like
    this t' ye:

The isles of Greece, the isles of Greece!
    Where burning Sappho loved and sung,
Where grew the arts of war and peace,—
    Where Delos[8] rose, and Phœbus sprung!
Eternal summer gilds them yet,
But all, except their sun, is set.   6

The Scian and the Teian muse,[9]
    The hero's harp, the lover's lute,
Have found the fame your shores refuse:
    Their place of birth alone is mute

To sounds which echo further west
Than your sires' "Islands of the Blest."[10] 1

The mountains look on Marathon—
    And Marathon looks on the sea;
And musing there an hour alone,
    I dreamed that Greece might still be free;
For standing on the Persians' grave,
I could not deem myself a slave. 1

A king sate on the rocky brow
    Which looks o'er sea-born Salamis;
And ships, by thousands, lay below,
    And men in nations;—all were his!
He counted them at break of day—
And when the sun set, where were they? 2

And where are they? and where art thou,
    My country? On thy voiceless shore
The heroic lay is tuneless now—
    The heroic bosom beats no more!
And must thy lyre, so long divine,
Degenerate into hands like mine? 3

'Tis something, in the dearth of fame,
    Though linked among a fettered race,
To feel at least a patriot's shame,
    Even as I sing, suffuse my face;
For what is left the poet here?
For Greeks a blush—for Greece a tear. 3

Must *we* but weep o'er days more blest?
    Must *we* but blush?—Our fathers bled.
Earth! render back from out thy breast
    A remnant of our Spartan dead!
Of the three hundred grant but three,
To make a new Thermopylæ! 4

What, silent still? and silent all?
    Ah! no;—the voices of the dead
Sound like a distant torrent's fall,
    And answer, "Let one living head,
But one arise,—we come, we come!"
'Tis but the living who are dumb. 4

In vain—in vain: strike other chords;
    Fill high the cup with Samian wine!
Leave battles to the Turkish hordes,
    And shed the blood of Scio's vine!
Hark! rising to the ignoble call—
How answers each bold Bacchanal!

You have the Pyrrhic dance[11] as yet;
    Where is the Pyrrhic phalanx[12] gone?
Of two such lessons, why forget
    The nobler and the manlier one?

---

4 A song of the French revolutionists. "It will succeed."

5 An ancient Greek poet who composed songs in honor of the victors in the national games, for which he was doubtless well remunerated.

6 Madame de Staël had lately written a book on Germany.

7 Writers in the Italian style of the 14th century.

8 The birth-place of Phœbus Apollo.

9 Homer was sometimes said to have been born on the isle of Chios (Italian name, Scio). Anacreon was born at Teios in Asia Minor.

10 The fabled Western Isles, lying somewhere the Atlantic.

11 A war-dance.

12 The Greek phalanx as employed by the gre general, Pyrrhus.

LORD BYRON

467

You have the letters Cadmus[13] gave—
Think ye he meant them for a slave?   60

Fill high the bowl with Samian wine!
  We will not think of themes like these!
It made Anacreon's song divine;
  He served—but served Polycrates[14]—
A tyrant; but our masters then
Were still, at least, our countrymen.   66

The tyrant of the Chersonese[15]
  Was freedom's best and bravest friend;
That tyrant was Miltiades!
  Oh! that the present hour would lend
Another despot of the kind!
Such chains as his were sure to bind.   72

Fill high the bowl with Samian wine!
  On Suli's rock, and Parga's shore,[16]
Exists the remnant of a line
  Such as the Doric mothers bore;
And there, perhaps, some seed is sown,
The Heracleidan[17] blood might own.   78

Trust not for freedom to the Franks—
  They have a king who buys and sells;
In native swords and native ranks,
  The only hope of courage dwells:
But Turkish force, and Latin fraud,
Would break your shield, however broad.   84

Fill high the bowl with Samian wine!
  Our virgins dance beneath the shade—
I see their glorious black eyes shine;
  But gazing on each glowing maid,
My own the burning tear-drop laves,
To think such breasts must suckle slaves.   90

Place me on Sunium's[18] marbled steep,
  Where nothing, save the waves and I,
May hear our mutual murmurs sweep;
  There, swan-like, let me sing and die:
A land of slaves shall ne'er be mine—
Dash down yon cup of Samian wine!   96

87

Thus sung, or would, or could, or should have
    sung,
The modern Greek, in tolerable verse;
If not like Orpheus quite, when Greece was
    young,
Yet in these times he might have done much
    worse:

Cadmus was said to have introduced the Greek
    alphabet from Phœnicia.
Tyrant (ruler) of Samos, who gave refuge to
    Anacreon.
A Thracian peninsula.
In western Greece.
i. e., ancient Greek
The southernmost promontory of Attica.

His strain displayed some feeling—right or
    wrong;
  And feeling, in a poet, is the source
Of others' feeling; but they are such liars,
  And take all colours—like the hands of dyers.[19]

88

But words are things, and a small drop of ink,
  Falling like dew, upon a thought, produces
That which makes thousands, perhaps millions,
    think;
  'Tis strange, the shortest letter which man
    uses
Instead of speech, may form a lasting link
  Of ages; to what straits old Time reduces
Frail man when paper—even a rag like this,
Survives himself, his tomb, and all that's his!

.   .   .   .   .   .

101

T' our tale.—The feast was over, the slaves
    gone,
  The dwarfs and dancing girls had all retired:
The Arab lore and poet's song were done,
  And every sound of revelry expired;
The lady and her lover, left alone,
  The rosy flood of twilight's sky admired;
Ave Maria! o'er the earth and sea,
That heavenliest hour of Heaven is worthiest
    thee!

102

Ave Maria! blessed be the hour!
  The time, the clime, the spot, where I so oft
Have felt that moment in its fullest power
  Sink o'er the earth so beautiful and soft,
While swung the deep bell in the distant tower,
  Or the faint dying day-hymn stole aloft,
And not a breath crept through the rosy air,
And yet the forest leaves seemed stirred with
    prayer.

103

Ave Maria! 'tis the hour of prayer!
  Ave Maria! 'tis the hour of love!
Ave Maria! may our spirits dare
  Look up to thine and to thy Son's above!
Ave Maria! oh that face so fair!
  Those downcast eyes beneath the Almighty
    dove—
What though 't is but a pictured image?—
    strike—
That painting is no idol,—'t is too like.

104

Some kinder casuists are pleased to say,
  In nameless print—that I have no devotion;
But set those persons down with me to pray,

19 Shakespeare: Sonnet 111.

And you shall see who has the properest
notion
Of getting into heaven the shortest way;
My altars are the mountains and the ocean,
Earth, air, stars,—all that springs from the
great Whole,
Who hath produced, and will receive the soul.

105

Sweet hour of twilight!—in the solitude
Of the pine forest, and the silent shore
Which bounds Ravenna's immemorial wood,
Rooted where once the Adrian[20] wave flowed
o'er,
To where the last Cæsarean fortress stood,
Evergreen forest! which Boccaccio's lore
And Dryden's lay made haunted ground to
me,[21]
How have I loved the twilight hour and thee!

106

The shrill cicalas, people of the pine,
Making their summer lives one ceaseless song,
Were the sole echoes, save my steed's and
mine,
And vesper bell's that rose the boughs along;
The spectre huntsman of Onesti's line,
His hell-dogs, and their chase, and the fair
throng
Which learned from this example not to fly
From a true lover,—shadowed my mind's eye.

107

Oh, Hesperus! thou bringest all good things—
Home to the weary, to the hungry cheer,
To the young bird the parent's brooding wings,
The welcome stall to the o'erlaboured steer;
Whate'er of peace about our hearthstone clings,
Whate'er our household gods protect of dear,
Are gathered round us by thy look of rest;
Thou bring'st the child, too, to the mother's
breast.

108

Soft hour! which wakes the wish and melts
the heart
Of those who sail the seas, on the first day
When they from their sweet friends are torn
apart;
Or fills with love the pilgrim on his way
As the far bell of vesper makes him start,
Seeming to weep the dying day's decay;
Is this a fancy which our reason scorns?
Ah! surely, nothing dies but something
mourns!

20 The Adriatic.
21 Dryden's *Theodore and Tonoria* is a translation
from Boccaccio of the tale of a spectre huntsman who haunted this region. Byron lived
for some time at Ravenna and frequently rode
in the adjoining forest.

PERCY BYSSHE SHELLEY
(1792-1822)

ALASTOR, OR THE SPIRIT OF SOLITUDE*

Nondum amabam, et amare amabam, quærebam
quid amarem, amans amare.†—*Confes. St. August.*

PREFACE

The poem entitled *Alastor* may be considered as
allegorical of one of the most interesting situations
of the human mind. It represents a youth of uncorrupted feelings and adventurous genius led forth
by an imagination inflamed and purified through
familiarity with all that is excellent and majestic,
to the contemplation of the universe. He drinks
deep of the fountains of knowledge, and is still
insatiate. The magnificence and beauty of the
external world sinks profoundly into the frame of
his conceptions, and affords to their modifications
a variety not to be exhausted. So long as it is
possible for his desires to point towards objects
thus infinite and unmeasured, he is joyous, and
tranquil, and self-possessed. But the period arrives
when these objects cease to suffice. His mind is
at length suddenly awakened and thirsts for intercourse with an intelligence similar to itself. He
images to himself the Being whom he loves. Conversant with speculations of the sublimest and
most perfect natures, the vision in which he embodies his own imaginations unites all of wonderful, or wise, or beautiful, which the poet, the
philosopher, or the lover, could depicture. The
intellectual faculties, the imagination, the functions of sense, have their respective requisitions on
the sympathy of corresponding powers in other
human beings. The Poet is represented as uniting
these requisitions, and attaching them to a single
image. He seeks in vain for a prototype of his
conception. Blasted by his disappointment, he
descends to an untimely grave.

The picture is not barren of instruction to
actual men. The Poet's self-centred seclusion was
avenged by the furies of an irresistible passion
pursuing him to speedy ruin. But that Power
which strikes the luminaries of the world with
sudden darkness and extinction, by awakening
them to too exquisite a perception of its influ-

* The word *Alastor* means "the spirit of solitude,"
which is treated here as a spirit of evil, or
a spirit leading to disaster; it must not be
mistaken for the name of the hero of the
poem. In the introduction (lines 1-49) Shelley speaks in his own person; but the Poet
whose history he then proceeds to relate bears
very markedly his own traits, and the whole
must be considered as largely a spiritual au-
tobiography. It is difficult to resist calling
attention to some of the features of this
impressive poem; to its quiet mastery of
theme and sustained poetic power; to its
blank-verse harmonies subtler than rhymes;
to the graphic descriptions, as in lines 239-
369, whence Bryant, Poe, and Tennyson have
manifestly all drawn inspiration; to occa-
sional lines of an impelling swiftness (612,
613), or occasional phrases of startling
strength (676, 681); to the fervent exaltation of self-sacrifice in the prayer that our
life might answer for all, and the pangs of
death be henceforth banished from the world
(609-624); or to the unapproachable beauty
of the description of slow-coming death itself
—a euthanasia in which life passes away like
a strain of music or like an "exhalation."
There can be no higher definition of poetry
than is implicit in these things.

† "Not yet did I love, yet I yearned to love;
sought what I might love, yearning to love."
In this vain pursuit of ideal loveliness, says
Mrs. Shelley, is the deeper meaning of
Alastor to be found.

nces, dooms to a slow and poisonous decay those meaner spirits that dare to abjure its dominion. Their destiny is more abject and inglorious as their delinquency is more contemptible and pernicious. They who, deluded by no generous error, instigated by no sacred thirst of doubtful knowledge, duped by no illustrious superstition, loving nothing on this earth, and cherishing no hopes beyond, yet keep aloof from sympathies with their kind, rejoicing neither in human joy nor mourning with human grief; these, and such as they, have their apportioned curse. They languish, because none feel with them their common nature. They are morally dead. They are neither friends, nor lovers, nor fathers, nor citizens of the world, nor benefactors of their country. Among those who attempt to exist without human sympathy, the pure and tender-hearted perish through the intensity and passion of their search after its communities, when the vacancy of their spirit suddenly makes itself felt. All else, selfish, blind, and torpid, are those unforeseeing multitudes who constitute, together with their own, the lasting misery and loneliness of the world. Those who love not their fellow-beings live unfruitful lives, and prepare for their old age a miserable grave.

> "The good die first,
> And those whose hearts are dry as summer dust,
> Burn to the socket!"
>
> *December 14, 1815.*

Earth, ocean, air, belovèd brotherhood!
If our great Mother has imbued my soul
With aught of natural piety[1] to feel
Your love, and recompense the boon with mine;
If dewy morn, and odorous noon, and even,
With sunset and its gorgeous ministers,
And solemn midnight's tingling silentness;
If autumn's hollow sighs in the sere wood,
And winter robing with pure snow and crowns
Of starry ice the gray grass and bare boughs;
If spring's voluptuous pantings when she
    breathes   11
Her first sweet kisses,—have been dear to me;
If no bright bird, insect, or gentle beast
I consciously have injured, but still loved
And cherished these my kindred; then forgive
This boast, belovèd brethren, and withdraw
No portion of your wonted favour now!

Mother of this unfathomable world!
Favour my solemn song, for I have loved
Thee ever, and thee only; I have watched   20
Thy shadow, and the darkness of thy steps,
And my heart ever gazes on the depth
Of thy deep mysteries. I have made my bed
In charnels and on coffins,[2] where black death
Keeps record of the trophies won from thee,
Hoping to still these obstinate questionings[3]
Of thee and thine, by forcing some lone ghost,
Thy messenger, to render up the tale
Of what we are. In lone and silent hours,
When night makes a weird sound of its own
    stillness,   30

Like an inspired and desperate alchemist
Staking his very life on some dark hope,
Have I mixed awful talk and asking looks
With my most innocent love, until strange
    tears
Uniting with those breathless kisses, made
Such magic as compels the charmèd night
To render up thy charge: and, though ne'er
    yet
Thou hast unveiled thy inmost sanctuary,
Enough from incommunicable dream,
And twilight phantasms, and deep noonday
    thought,   40
Has shone within me, that serenely now
And moveless, as a long-forgotten lyre
Suspended in the solitary dome
Of some mysterious and deserted fane,
I wait thy breath, Great Parent, that my
    strain
May modulate with murmurs of the air,
And motions of the forests and the sea,
And voice of living beings, and woven hymns
Of night and day, and the deep heart of man.

There was a Poet whose untimely tomb   50
No human hands with pious reverence reared,
But the charmed eddies of autumnal winds
Built o'er his mouldering bones a pyramid
Of mouldering leaves in the waste wilderness:—
A lovely youth,—no mourning maiden decked
With weeping flowers, or votive cypress wreath,
The lone couch of his everlasting sleep:—
Gentle, and brave, and generous,—no lorn bard
Breathed o'er his dark fate one melodious sigh:
He lived, he died, he sung, in solitude.   60
Strangers have wept to hear his passionate
    notes,
And virgins, as unknown he passed, have pined
And wasted for fond love of his wild eyes.
The fire of those soft orbs has ceased to burn,
And Silence, too enamoured of that voice,
Locks its mute music in her rugged cell.

By solemn vision, and bright silver dream,
His infancy was nurtured. Every sight
And sound from the vast earth and ambient air
Sent to his heart its choicest impulses,   70
The fountains of divine philosophy
Fled not his thirsting lips, and all of great,
Or good, or lovely, which the sacred past
In truth or fable consecrates, he felt
And knew. When early youth had passed, he
    left
His cold fireside and alienated home
To seek strange truths in undiscovered lands.
Many a wide waste and tangled wilderness
Has lured his fearless steps; and he has bought

---

[1] Wordsworth's phrase; see his *My Heart Leaps Up*, p. 422.
[2] According to Hogg, Shelley had actually done this.
[3] Wordsworth's *Ode on Immortality*, line 142.

With his sweet voice and eyes, from savage
    men,   80
His rest and food. Nature's most secret steps
He like her shadow has pursued, where'er
The red volcano overcanopies
Its fields of snow and pinnacles of ice
With burning smoke, or where bitumen lakes
On black bare pointed islets ever beat
With sluggish surge, or where the secret caves
Rugged and dark, winding among the springs
Of fire and poison, inaccessible
To avarice or pride, their starry domes   90
Of diamond and of gold expand above
Numberless and immeasurable halls,
Frequent with crystal column, and clear shrines
Of pearl, and thrones radiant with chrysolite.
Nor had that scene of ampler majesty
Than gems or gold, the varying roof of heaven
And the green earth, lost in his heart its claims
To love and wonder; he would linger long
In lonesome vales, making the wild his home,
Until the doves and squirrels would partake   100
From his innocuous hand his bloodless food,
Lured by the gentle meaning of his looks,
And the wild antelope, that starts whene'er
The dry leaf rustles in the brake, suspend
Her timid steps to gaze upon a form
More graceful than her own.

                     His wandering step,
Obedient to high thoughts, has visited
The awful ruins of the days of old:
Athens, and Tyre, and Balbec, and the waste
Where stood Jerusalem, the fallen towers   110
Of Babylon, the eternal pyramids,
Memphis and Thebes, and whatsoe'er of strange
Sculptured on alabaster obelisk,
Or jasper tomb, or mutilated sphinx,
Dark Æthiopia in her desert hills
Conceals. Among the ruined temples there,
Stupendous columns, and wild images
Of more than man, where marble demons watch
The Zodiac's brazen mystery,[1] and dead men
Hang their mute thoughts on the mute walls
    around,   120
He lingered, poring on memorials
Of the world's youth, through the long burning
   · day
Gazed on those speechless shapes, nor, when the
    moon
Filled the mysterious halls with floating shades
Suspended he that task, but ever gazed
And gazed, till meaning on his vacant mind
Flashed like strong inspiration, and he saw
The thrilling secrets of the birth of time.

Meanwhile an Arab maiden brought his food,
Her daily portion, from her father's tent,   130
And spread her matting for his couch, and stole
From duties and repose to tend his steps:—
Enamoured, yet not daring for deep awe
To speak her love:—and watched his nightly
    sleep,
Sleepless herself, to gaze upon his lips
Parted in slumber, whence the regular breath
Of innocent dreams arose: then, when red morn
Made paler the pale moon, to her cold home
Wildered, and wan, and panting, she returned.

    The Poet wandering on, through Arabie   140
And Persia, and the wild Carmanian waste,[2]
And o'er the aërial mountains which pour down
Indus and Oxus from their icy caves,
In joy and exultation held his way;
Till in the vale of Cashmire,[3] far within
Its loneliest dell, where odorous plants entwine
Beneath the hollow rocks a natural bower,
Beside a sparkling rivulet he stretched
His languid limbs. A vision on his sleep   149
There came, a dream of hopes that never yet
Had flushed his cheek. He dreamed a veiled
    maid
Sate near him, talking in low solemn tones.
Her voice was like the voice of his own soul
Heard in the calm of thought; its music long,
Like woven sounds of streams and breezes, held
His inmost sense suspended in its web
Of many-coloured woof and shifting hues.
Knowledge and truth and virtue were her theme,
And lofty hopes of divine liberty,
Thoughts the most dear to him, and poesy,   160
Herself a poet. Soon the solemn mood
Of her pure mind kindled through all her frame
A permeating fire: wild numbers then
She raised, with voice stifled in tremulous sobs
Subdued by its own pathos: her fair hands
Were bare alone, sweeping from some strange
    harp
Strange symphony, and in their branching veins
The eloquent blood told an ineffable tale.
The beating of her heart was heard to fill
The pauses of her music, and her breath   170
Tumultuously accorded with those fits
Of intermitted song. Sudden she rose,
As if her heart impatiently endured
Its bursting burthen: at the sound he turned,
And saw by the warm light of their own life
Her glowing limbs beneath the sinuous veil
Of woven wind, her outspread arms now bare,
Her dark locks floating in the breath of night,
Her beamy bending eyes, her parted lips   179

[1] Figures on the temple of Denderah in Upper
    Egypt.
[2] The desert of Kirman, Persia.
[3] In central Asia; poetically regarded as an earthly
    paradise.

Outstretched, and pale, and quivering eagerly.
His strong heart sunk and sickened with excess
Of love. He reared his shuddering limbs and
   quelled
His gasping breath, and spread his arms to meet
Her panting bosom:—she drew back a while,
Then, yielding to the irresistible joy,
With frantic gesture and short breathless cry
Folded his frame in her dissolving arms.
Now blackness veiled his dizzy eyes, and night
Involved and swallowed up the vision; sleep,
Like a dark flood suspended in its course,   190
Rolled back its impulse on his vacant brain.

Roused by the shock he started from his
   trance—
The cold white light of morning, the blue moon
Low in the west, the clear and garish hills,
The distinct valley and the vacant woods,
Spread round him where he stood. Whither have
   fled
The hues of heaven that canopied his bower
Of yesternight? The sounds that soothed his
   sleep,
The mystery and the majesty of Earth,
The joy, the exultation? His wan eyes   200
Gazed on the empty scene as vacantly
As ocean's moon looks on the moon in heaven.
The spirit of sweet human love has sent
A vision to the sleep of him who spurned
Her choicest gifts. He eagerly pursues
Beyond the realms of dream that fleeting shade;
He overleaps the bounds. Alas! alas!
Were limbs, and breath, and being intertwined
Thus treacherously? Lost, lost, for ever lost,
In the wide pathless desert of dim sleep,   210
That beautiful shape! Does the dark gate of
   death
Conduct to thy mysterious paradise,
O Sleep? Does the bright arch of rainbow
   clouds,
And pendent mountains seen in the calm lake,
Lead only to a black and watery depth,
While death's blue vault, with loathliest vapours
   hung,
Where every shade which the foul grave exhales
Hides its dead eye from the detested day,
Conducts, O Sleep, to thy delightful realms?
This doubt with sudden tide flowed on his
   heart;   220
The insatiate hope which it awakened stung
His brain even like despair.

          While daylight held
The sky, the Poet kept mute conference
With his still soul. At night the passion came,
Like the fierce fiend of a distempered dream,
And shook him from his rest, and led him forth

Into the darkness.—As an eagle, grasped
In folds of the green serpent, feels her breast
Burn with the poison, and precipitates
Through night and day, tempest, and calm, and
   cloud,   230
Frantic with dizzying anguish, her blind flight
O'er the wide aëry wilderness: thus driven
By the bright shadow of that lovely dream,
Beneath the cold glare of the desolate night,
Through tangled swamps and deep precipitous
   dells,
Startling with careless step the moonlight snake,
He fled. Red morning dawned upon his flight,
Shedding the mockery of its vital hues
Upon his cheek of death. He wandered on
Till vast Aornos[1] seen from Petra's steep,   240
Hung o'er the low horizon like a cloud;
Through Balk, and where the desolated tombs
Of Parthian kings scatter to every wind
Their wasting dust, wildly he wandered on,
Day after day, a weary waste of hours,
Bearing within his life the brooding care
That ever fed on its decaying flame.
And now his limbs were lean; his scattered hair
Sered by the autumn of strange suffering
Sung dirges in the wind: his listless hand   250
Hung like dead bone within its withered skin;
Life, and the lustre that consumed it, shone
As in a furnace burning secretly
From his dark eyes alone. The cottagers,
Who ministered with human charity
His human wants, beheld with wondering awe
Their fleeting visitant. The mountaineer,
Encountering on some dizzy precipice
That spectral form, deemed that the Spirit of
   wind   259
With lightning eyes, and eager breath, and feet
Disturbing not the drifted snow, had paused
In its career: the infant would conceal
His troubled visage in his mother's robe
In terror at the glare of those wild eyes,
To remember their strange light in many a
   dream
Of after-times; but youthful maidens, taught
By nature, would interpret half the woe
That wasted him, would call him with false
   names
Brother, and friend, would press his pallid hand
At parting, and watch, dim through tears, the
   path   270
Of his departure from their father's door.

      At length upon the lone Chorasmian shore[2]
He paused, a wide and melancholy waste
Of putrid marshes. A strong impulse urged

1 Aornos was a city in Bactria (Balk).
2 The Aral Sea; apparently meant for the Caspian (Woodberry).

His steps to the sea-shore. A swan was there,
Beside a sluggish stream among the reeds.
It rose as he approached, and with strong wings
Scaling the upward sky, bent its bright course
High over the immeasurable main.
His eyes pursued its flight.—''Thou hast a
    home,   280
Beautiful bird; thou voyagest to thine home,
Where thy sweet mate will twine her downy
    neck
With thine, and welcome thy return with eyes
Bright in the lustre of their own fond joy.
And what am I that I should linger here,
With voice far sweeter than thy dying notes,
Spirit more vast than thine, frame more attuned
To beauty, wasting these surpassing powers
In the deaf air, to the blind earth, and heaven
That echoes not my thoughts?''   A gloomy
    smile   290
Of desperate hope wrinkled his quivering lips.
For sleep, he knew, kept most relentlessly
Its precious charge, and silent death exposed,
Faithless perhaps as sleep, a shadowy lure,
With doubtful smile mocking its own strange
    charms.

Startled by his own thoughts he looked around.
There was no fair fiend near him, not a sight
Or sound of awe but in his own deep mind.
A little shallop floating near the shore
Caught the impatient wandering of his gaze.
It had been long abandoned, for its sides   301
Gaped wide with many a rift, and its frail joints
Swayed with the undulations of the tide.
A restless impulse urged him to embark
And meet lone Death on the drear ocean's
    waste;
For well he knew that mighty Shadow loves
The slimy caverns of the populous deep.

The day was fair and sunny, sea and sky
Drank its inspiring radiance, and the wind
Swept strongly from the shore, blackening the
    waves.   310
Following his eager soul, the wanderer
Leaped in the boat, he spread his cloak aloft
On the bare mast, and took his lonely seat,
And felt the boat speed o'er the tranquil sea
Like a torn cloud before the hurricane.

As one that in a silver vision floats
Obedient to the sweep of odorous winds
Upon resplendent clouds, so rapidly
Along the dark and ruffled waters fled
The straining boat.—A whirlwind swept it on,
With fierce gusts and precipitate force,   321
Through the white ridges of the chafèd sea.

The waves arose. Higher and higher still
Their fierce necks writhed beneath the tempest's
    scourge
Like serpents struggling in a vulture's grasp.
Calm and rejoicing in the fearful war
Of wave ruining on wave, and blast on blast
Descending, and black flood on whirlpool driven
With dark obliterating course, he sate:
As if their genii were the ministers   330
Appointed to conduct him to the light
Of those belovèd eyes, the Poet sate
Holding the steady helm. Evening came on,
The beams of sunset hung their rainbow hues
High 'mid the shifting domes of sheeted spray
That canopied his path o'er the waste deep;
Twilight, ascending slowly from the east,
Entwined in duskier wreaths her braided locks
O'er the fair front and radiant eyes of day;
Night followed, clad with stars. On every side
More horribly the multitudinous streams   341
Of ocean's mountainous waste to mutual war
Rushed in dark tumult thundering, as to mock
The calm and spangled sky. The little boat
Still fled before the storm; still fled, like foam
Down the steep cataract of a wintry river;
Now pausing on the edge of the riven wave;
Now leaving far behind the bursting mass
That fell, convulsing ocean. Safely fled—
As if that frail and wasted human form,   350
Had been an elemental god.

                    At midnight
The moon arose: and lo! the ethereal cliffs
Of Caucasus, whose icy summits shone
Among the stars like sunlight, and around
Whose caverned base the whirlpools and the
    waves
Bursting and eddying irresistibly
Rage and resound for ever.—Who shall save?—
The boat fled on,—the boiling torrent drove,—
The crags closed round with black and jagged
    arms,
The shattered mountains overhung the sea,   360
And faster still, beyond all human speed,
Suspended on the sweep of the smooth wave,
The little boat was driven. A cavern there
Yawned, and amid its slant and winding depths
Ingulfed the rushing sea. The boat fled on
With unrelaxing speed.—''Vision and Love!''
The Poet cried aloud, ''I have beheld
The path of thy departure. Sleep and death
Shall not divide us long!''

                 The boat pursued
The windings of the cavern. Daylight shone
At length upon that gloomy river's flow;   371
Now, where the fiercest war among the waves
Is calm, on the unfathomable stream

The boat moved slowly. Where the mountain,
    riven,
Exposed those black depths to the azure sky,
Ere yet the flood's enormous volume fell
Even to the base of Caucasus, with sound
That shook the everlasting rocks, the mass
Filled with one whirlpool all that ample chasm;
Stair above stair the eddying water rose,   380
Circling immeasurably fast, and laved
With alternating dash the gnarlèd roots
Of mighty trees, that stretched their giant arms
In darkness over it. I' the midst was left,
Reflecting, yet distorting every cloud,
A pool of treacherous and tremendous calm.
Seized by the sway of the ascending stream,
With dizzy swiftness, round, and round, and
    round,
Ridge after ridge the straining boat arose,
Till on the verge of the extremest curve,   390
Where, through an opening of the rocky bank,
The waters overflow, and a smooth spot
Of glassy quiet mid those battling tides
Is left, the boat paused shuddering.—Shall it
    sink
Down the abyss? Shall the reverting stress
Of that resistless gulf embosom it?
Now shall it fall?—A wandering stream of wind,
Breathed from the west, has caught the ex-
    panded sail,
And, lo! with gentle motion, between banks
Of mossy slope, and on a placid stream,   400
Beneath a woven grove it sails, and hark!
The ghastly torrent mingles its far roar
With the breeze murmuring in the musical
    woods.
Where the embowering trees recede, and leave
A little space of green expanse, the cove
Is closed by meeting banks, whose yellow flowers
For ever gaze on their own drooping eyes,
Reflected in the crystal calm. The wave
Of the boat's motion marred their pensive task,
Which nought but vagrant bird, or wanton
    wind,   410
Or falling spear-grass, or their own decay
Had e'er disturbed before. The Poet longed
To deck with their bright hues his withered hair,
But on his heart its solitude returned,
And he forebore. Not the strong impulse hid
In those flushed cheeks, bent eyes, and shadowy
    frame
Had yet performed its ministry: it hung
Upon his life, as lightning in a cloud
Gleams, hovering ere it vanish, ere the floods
Of night close over it.

        The noonday sun   420
Now shone upon the forest, one vast mass
Of mingling shade, whose brown magnificence

A narrow vale embosoms. There, huge caves,
Scooped in the dark base of their aëry rocks,
Mocking its moans, respond and roar for ever.
The meeting boughs and implicated leaves
Wove twilight o'er the Poet's path, as led
By love, or dream, or god, or mightier Death,
He sought in Nature's dearest haunt some bank,
Her cradle, and his sepulchre. More dark   430
And dark the shades accumulate. The oak,
Expanding its immense and knotty arms,
Embraces the light beech. The pyramids
Of the tall cedar overarching frame
Most solemn domes within, and far below,
Like clouds suspended in an emerald sky,
The ash and the acacia floating hang
Tremulous and pale. Like restless serpents,
    clothed
In rainbow and in fire, the parasites,
Starred with ten thousand blossoms, flow around
The gray trunks, and, as gamesome infants'
    eyes,   441
With gentle meanings, and most innocent wiles,
Fold their beams round the hearts of those that
    love,
These twine their tendrils with the wedded
    boughs
Uniting their close union; the woven leaves
Make network of the dark blue light of day,
And the night's noontide clearness, mutable
As shapes in the weird clouds. Soft mossy
    lawns
Beneath these canopies extend their swells,
Fragrant with perfumed herbs, and eyed with
    blooms   450
Minute yet beautiful. One darkest glen
Sends from its woods of musk-rose, twined with
    jasmine,
A soul-dissolving odour, to invite
To some more lovely mystery. Through the dell,
Silence and Twilight here, twin-sisters, keep
Their noonday watch, and sail among the shades,
Like vaporous shapes half seen; beyond, a well,
Dark, gleaming, and of most translucent wave,
Images all the woven boughs above,
And each depending leaf, and every speck   460
Of azure sky, darting between their chasms;
Nor aught else in the liquid mirror laves
Its portraiture, but some inconstant star
Between one foliaged lattice twinkling fair,
Or painted bird, sleeping beneath the moon,
Or gorgeous insect floating motionless,
Unconscious of the day, ere yet his wings
Have spread their glories to the gaze of noon.

      Hither the Poet came. His eyes beheld   469
Their own wan light through the reflected lines
Of his thin hair, distinct in the dark depth
Of that still fountain: as the human heart,

Gazing in dreams over the gloomy grave,
Sees its own treacherous likeness there. He
  heard
The motion of the leaves, the grass that sprung
Startled and glanced and trembled even to feel
An unaccustomed presence, and the sound
Of the sweet brook that from the secret springs
Of that dark fountain rose. A Spirit seemed
To stand beside him—clothed in no bright robes
Of shadowy silver or enshrining light,   481
Borrowed from aught the visible world affords
Of grace, or majesty, or mystery;—
But undulating woods, and silent well,
And leaping rivulet, and evening gloom
Now deepening the dark shades, for speech
  assuming,
Held commune with him, as if he and it
Were all that was; only—when his regard
Was raised by intense pensiveness—two eyes,   489
Two starry eyes, hung in the gloom of thought,
And seemed with their serene and azure smiles
To beckon him.

Obedient to the light
That shone within his soul, he went, pursuing
The windings of the dell.—The rivulet
Wanton and wild, through many a green ravine
Beneath the forest flowed. Sometimes it fell
Among the moss with hollow harmony
Dark and profound. Now on the polished stones
It danced, like childhood laughing as it went:
Then through the plain in tranquil wanderings
  crept,   500
Reflecting every herb and drooping bud
That overhung its quietness.—"O stream!
Whose source is inaccessibly profound,
Whither do thy mysterious waters tend?
Thou imagest my life. Thy darksome stillness,
Thy dazzling waves, thy loud and hollow gulfs,
Thy searchless fountain, and invisible course
Have each their type in me: and the wide sky,
And measureless ocean may declare as soon
What oozy cavern or what wandering cloud   510
Contains thy waters, as the universe
Tell where these living thoughts reside, when
  stretched
Upon thy flowers my bloodless limbs shall waste
I' the passing wind!''

Beside the grassy shore
Of the small stream he went; he did impress
On the green moss his tremulous step, that
  caught
Strong shuddering from his burning limbs. As
  one
Roused by some joyous madness from the couch
Of fever, he did move; yet not like him
Forgetful of the grave, where, when the flame

Of his frail exultation shall be spent,   521
He must descend. With rapid steps he went
Beneath the shade of trees, beside the flow
Of the wild babbling rivulet; and now
The forest's solemn canopies were changed
For the uniform and lightsome evening sky.
Gray rocks did peep from the spare moss, and
  stemmed
The struggling brook: tall spires of windlestrae[1]
Threw their thin shadows down the rugged slope,
And nought but gnarled roots of ancient pines
Branchless and blasted, clenched with grasping
  roots   531
The unwilling soil. A gradual change was here,
Yet ghastly. For, as fast years flow away,
The smooth brow gathers, and the hair grows
  thin
And white, and where irradiate dewy eyes
Had shone, gleam stony orbs:—so from his steps
Bright flowers departed, and the beautiful shade
Of the green groves, with all their odorous winds
And musical motions. Calm, he still pursued
The stream, that with a larger volume now   540
Rolled through the labyrinthine dell, and there
Fretted a path through its descending curves
With its wintry speed. On every side now rose
Rocks, which, in unimaginable forms,
Lifted their black and barren pinnacles
In the light of evening, and, its precipice
Obscuring the ravine, disclosed above,
Mid toppling stones, black gulfs and yawning
  caves,
Whose windings gave ten thousand various
  tongues
To the loud stream. Lo! where the pass
  expands   550
Its stony jaws, the abrupt mountain breaks,
And seems, with its accumulated crags,
To overhang the world: for wide expand
Beneath the wan stars and descending moon
Islanded seas, blue mountains, mighty streams,
Dim tracts and vast, robed in the lustrous
  gloom
Of leaden coloured even, and fiery hills
Mingling their flames with twilight, on the verge
Of the remote horizon. The near scene,
In naked and severe simplicity,   560
Made contrast with the universe. A pine,
Rock-rooted, stretched athwart the vacancy
Its swinging boughs, to each inconstant blast
Yielding one only response, at each pause
In most familiar cadence, with the howl,
The thunder and the hiss of homeless streams
Mingling its solemn song, whilst the broad river
Foaming and hurrying o'er its rugged path,
Fell into that immeasurable void
Scattering its waters to the passing winds.   570

[1] withered grass-stalks

Yet the gray precipice and solemn pine
And torrent were not all;—one silent nook
Was there. Even on the edge of that vast
    mountain,
Upheld by knotty roots and fallen rocks,
It overlooked in its serenity
The dark earth, and the bending vault of stars.
It was a tranquil spot, that seemed to smile
Even in the lap of horror. Ivy clasped
The fissured stones with its entwining arms,
And did embower with leaves for ever green, 580
And berries dark, the smooth and even space
Of its inviolated floor, and here
The children of the autumnal whirlwind bore,
In wanton sport, those bright leaves, whose
    decay,
Red, yellow, or ethereally pale,
Rivals the pride of summer. 'Tis the haunt
Of every gentle wind, whose breath can teach
The wilds to love tranquillity. One step,
One human step alone, has ever broken
The stillness of its solitude:—one voice 590
Alone inspired its echoes;—even that voice
Which hither came, floating among the winds,
And led the loveliest among human forms
To make their wild haunts the depository
Of all the grace and beauty that endued
Its motions, render up its majesty,
Scatter its music on the unfeeling storm,
And to the damp leaves and blue cavern mould,
Nurses of rainbow flowers and branching moss,
Commit the colours of that varying cheek, 600
That snowy breast, those dark and drooping eyes.

    The dim and hornèd moon hung low, and
    poured
A sea of lustre on the horizon's verge
That overflowed its mountains. Yellow mist
Filled the unbounded atmosphere, and drank
Wan moonlight even to fulness: not a star
Shone, not a sound was heard; the very winds,
Danger's grim playmates, on that precipice
Slept, clasped in his embrace.—O, storm of
    Death!
Whose sightless speed divides this sullen night:
And thou, colossal Skeleton, that, still 611
Guiding its irresistible career
In thy devastating omnipotence,
Art king of this frail world! from the red field
Of slaughter, from the reeking hospital,
The patriot's sacred couch, the snowy bed
Of innocence, the scaffold and the throne,
A mighty voice invokes thee. Ruin calls
His brother Death. A rare and regal prey
He hath prepared, prowling around the world;
Glutted with which thou mayst repose, and
    men 621
Go to their graves like flowers or creeping
    worms,

Nor ever more offer at thy dark shrine
The unheeded tribute of a broken heart.

    When on the threshold of the green recess
The wanderer's footsteps fell, he knew that
    death
Was on him. Yet a little, ere it fled,
Did he resign his high and holy soul
To images of the majestic past,
That paused within his passive being now, 630
Like winds that bear sweet music, when they
    breathe
Through some dim latticed chamber. He did
    place
His pale lean hand upon the rugged trunk
Of the old pine. Upon an ivied stone
Reclined his languid head, his limbs did rest,
Diffused and motionless, on the smooth brink
Of that obscurest chasm;—and thus he lay,
Surrendering to their final impulses
The hovering powers of life. Hope and despair,
The torturers, slept; no mortal pain or fear 640
Marred his repose, the influxes of sense,
And his own being unalloyed by pain,
Yet feebler and more feeble, calmly fed
The stream of thought, till he lay breathing
    there
At peace, and faintly smiling:—his last sight
Was the great moon, which o'er the western line
Of the wide world her mighty horn suspended,
With whose dun beams inwoven darkness seemed
To mingle. Now upon the jaggèd hills
It rests, and still as the divided frame 650
Of the vast meteor sunk, the Poet's blood,
That ever beat in mystic sympathy
With nature's ebb and flow, grew feebler still:
And when two lessening points of light alone
Gleamed through the darkness, the alternate
    gasp
Of his faint respiration scarce did stir
The stagnate night:—till the minutest ray
Was quenched, the pulse yet lingered in his
    heart.
It paused—it fluttered. But when heaven re-
    mained
Utterly black, the murky shades involved 660
An image, silent, cold, and motionless,
As their own voiceless earth and vacant air.
Even as a vapour fed with golden beams
That ministered on sunlight, ere the west
Eclipses it, was now that wondrous frame—
No sense, no motion, no divinity—
A fragile lute, on whose harmonious strings
The breath of heaven did wander—a bright
    stream
Once fed with many-voicèd waves—a dream
Of youth, which night and time have quenched
    forever, 670

Still, dark, and dry, and unremembered now.

O, for Medea's wondrous alchemy,[1]
Which wheresoe'er it fell made the earth gleam
With bright flowers, and the wintry boughs
    exhale
From vernal blooms fresh fragrance! O, that
    God,
Profuse of poisons, would concede the chalice
Which but one living man[2] has drained, who
    now
Vessel of deathless wrath, a slave that feels
No proud exemption in the blighting curse
H bears, over the world wanders for ever,   680
Lone as incarnate death! O, that the dream[3]
Of dark magician in his visioned cave,
Raking the cinders of a crucible
For life and power, even when his feeble hand
Shakes in its last decay, were the true law
Of this so lovely world! But thou art fled
Like some frail exhalation; which the dawn
Robes in its golden beams,—ah! thou hast fled!
The brave, the gentle, and the beautiful,   689
The child of grace and genius. Heartless things
Are done and said i' the world, and many worms
And beasts and men live on, and mighty Earth
From sea and mountain, city and wilderness,
In vesper low or joyous orison,
Lifts still its solemn voice:—but thou art fled;
Thou canst no longer know or love the shapes
Of this phantasmal scene, who have to thee
Been purest ministers, who are, alas!
Now thou art not. Upon those pallid lips
So sweet even in their silence, on those eyes   700
That image sleep in death, upon that form
Yet safe from the worm's outrage, let no tear
Be shed—not even in thought. Nor, when those
    hues
Are gone, and those divinest lineaments,
Worn by the senseless wind, shall live alone
In the frail pauses of this simple strain,
Let not high verse, mourning the memory
Of that which is no more, or painting's woe
Or sculpture, speak in feeble imagery
Their own cold powers. Art and eloquence,   710
And all the shows o' the world are frail and
    vain
To weep a loss that turns their lights to shade.
It is a woe too "deep for tears,"[4] when all
Is reft at once, when some surpassing Spirit,
Whose light adorned the world around it, leaves
Those who remain behind, not sobs or groans,

1 magic decoction (For example of Medea's witch-
    craft, see the story of Jason.)
2 Ahasuerus, the legendary Wandering Jew, said
    to have been condemned by Christ, for his
    insolence, to wander till Christ's second com-
    ing.
3 i. e., immortal youth, the *elixir vitae*
4 Wordsworth's *Ode on Immortality*, last line.

The passionate tumult of a clinging hope;
But pale despair and cold tranquillity,
Nature's vast frame, the web of human things
Birth and the grave, that are not as they
    were.   72[0]

OZYMANDIAS

I met a traveller from an antique land
Who said: 'Two vast and trunkless legs o[f]
    stone
Stand in the desert. Near them, on the sand,
Half sunk, a shattered visage lies, whose frown
And wrinkled lip, and sneer of cold command,
Tell that its sculptor well those passions read
Which yet survive, stamped on these lifeless
    things,
The hand that mocked them and the heart tha[t]
    fed.[5]
And on the pedestal these words appear—
"My name is Ozymandias, king of kings:
Look on my works, ye Mighty, and despair!"
Nothing beside remains. Round the decay
Of that colossal wreck, boundless and bare
The lone and level sands stretch far away.'

ODE TO THE WEST WIND*

I

O wild West Wind, thou breath of Autumn'[s]
    being,
Thou, from whose unseen presence the leave[s]
    dead
Are driven, like ghosts from an enchante[r]
    fleeing,

Yellow, and black, and pale, and hectic red,
Pestilence-stricken multitudes: O thou,
Who chariotest to their dark wintry bed

The wingèd seeds, where they lie cold and low,
Each like a corpse within its grave, until
Thine azure sister of the spring shall blow

5 That is, they survived both him who image[d]
    them and him who nursed them.
* Note by Shelley: "This poem was conceive[d]
    and chiefly written in a wood that skirts th[e]
    Arno, near Florence. . . The phenomeno[n]
    alluded to at the conclusion of the thi[rd]
    stanza is well known to naturalists. T[he]
    vegetation at the bottom of the sea, of river[s]
    and of lakes, sympathizes with that of t[he]
    land in the change of seasons, and is cons[e]
    quently influenced by the winds which a[n]
    nounce it."
    The poem has something of the impet[u]
    osity of the wind—a breathless swiftne[ss]
    which seems almost to scorn rhyme, a[nd]
    which is characteristic of many of She[l]
    ley's longer poems. Characteristically, too,
    breathes his intense "passion for reformi[ng]
    the world," the combination of which wi[th]
    lyric delicacy, as here, is exceedingly rare.

Her clarion o'er the dreaming earth, and fill 10
(Driving sweet buds like flocks to feed in air)
With living hues and odours plain and hill;

Wild Spirit, which art moving everywhere;
Destroyer and preserver; hear, Oh hear!

II

Thou on whose stream, 'mid the steep sky's
    commotion,
Loose clouds like earth's decaying leaves are
    shed,
Shook from the tangled boughs of Heaven and
    Ocean,

Angels of rain and lightning: there are spread
On the blue surface of thine airy surge,
Like the bright hair uplifted from the head 20

Of some fierce Mænad,[1] even from the dim verge
Of the horizon to the zenith's height,
The locks of the approaching storm. Thou dirge

Of the dying year, to which this closing[2] night
Will be the dome of a vast sepulchre,
Vaulted with all thy congregated might

Of vapours, from whose solid atmosphere
Black rain, and fire, and hail will burst:
    Oh hear!

III

Thou who didst waken from his summer dreams
The blue Mediterranean, where he lay,   30
Lulled by the coil of his crystàlline streams,

Beside a pumice isle in Baiæ's bay,[3]
And saw in sleep old palaces and towers
Quivering within the wave's intenser day,

All overgrown with azure moss and flowers
So sweet, the sense faints picturing them! Thou
For whose path the Atlantic's level powers

Cleave themselves into chasms, while far below
The sea-blooms and the oozy woods which wear
The sapless foliage of the ocean, know   40

Thy voice, and suddenly grow gray with fear,
And tremble and despoil themselves: Oh hear!

IV

If I were a dead leaf thou mightest bear;
If I were a swift cloud to fly with thee;
A wave to pant beneath thy power, and share

The impulse of thy strength, only less free
Than thou, O uncontrollable! If even
I were as in my boyhood, and could be

The comrade of thy wanderings over heaven,
As then, when to outstrip thy skyey speed 50
Scarce seemed a vision; I would ne'er have
    striven

As thus with thee in prayer in my sore need.
Oh lift me as a wave, a leaf, a cloud!
I fall upon the thorns of life! I bleed!

A heavy weight of hours has chained and bowed
One too like thee: tameless, and swift, and
    proud.

V

Make me thy lyre, even as the forest is:
What if my leaves are falling like its own!
The tumult of thy mighty harmonies

Will take from both a deep, autumnal tone, 60
Sweet though in sadness. Be thou, spirit fierce,
My spirit! Be thou me, impetuous one!

Drive my dead thoughts over the universe
Like withered leaves to quicken a new birth!
And, by the incantation of this verse,

Scatter, as from an unextinguished hearth
Ashes and sparks, my words among mankind!
Be through my lips to unawakened earth

The trumpet of a prophecy! O Wind,
If Winter comes, can Spring be far behind? 70

THE INDIAN SERENADE

I arise from dreams of thee
In the first sweet sleep of night,
When the winds are breathing low,
And the stars are shining bright;
I arise from dreams of thee,
And a spirit in my feet
Hath led me—who knows how?
To thy chamber window, sweet!   8

The wandering airs, they faint
On the dark, the silent stream;
The champak[1] odours fail
Like sweet thoughts in a dream;
The nightingale's complaint,
It dies upon her heart,
As I must die on thine,
Oh, belovèd as thou art!   16

Oh, lift me from the grass!
I die! I faint! I fail!
Let thy love in kisses rain

---

[1] A frenzied priestess
    of Bacchus.
[2] closing in

[3] Near Naples; the site
    of many ruins of
    ancient luxury.

[1] An Indian tree of the Magnolia family.

On my lips and eyelids pale.
My cheek is cold and white, alas!
My heart beats loud and fast,
Oh! press it close to thine again,
Where it will break at last.   24

FROM PROMETHEUS UNBOUND
Song*

Life of Life, thy lips enkindle
  With their love the breath between them;
And thy smiles before they dwindle
  Make the cold air fire; then screen them
In those looks, where whoso gazes
Faints, entangled in their mazes.   6

Child of Light! thy limbs are burning
  Through the vest which seems to hide them;
As the radiant lines of morning
  Through the clouds, ere they divide them;
And this atmosphere divinest
Shrouds thee wheresoe'er thou shinest.   12

Fair are others; none beholds thee,
  But thy voice sounds low and tender
Like the fairest, for it folds thee
  From the sight, that liquid splendour,
And all feel, yet see thee never,
As I feel now, lost forever.   18

Lamp of Earth! where'er thou movest
  Its dim shapes are clad with brightness,
And the souls of whom thou lovest
  Walk upon the winds with lightness,
Till they fail, as I am failing,
Dizzy, lost, yet unbewailing!   24

Asia's Response

My soul is an enchanted boat,
  Which, like a sleeping swan, doth float
Upon the silver waves of thy sweet singing;
  And thine doth like an angel sit
  Beside a helm conducting it,
Whilst all the winds with melody are ringing.
  It seems to float ever, forever,
  Upon that many-winding river,
  Between mountains, woods, abysses,
  A paradise of wildernesses!   10
Till, like one in slumber bound,
Borne to the ocean, I float down, around,
Into a sea profound of ever-spreading sound.

  Meanwhile thy spirit lifts its pinions
  In music's most serene dominions;
Catching the winds that fan that happy heaven.

And we sail on, away, afar,
  Without a course, without a star,
But by the instinct of sweet music driven;
  Till through Elysian garden islets   20
  By thee, most beautiful of pilots,
  Where never mortal pinnace glided,
  The boat of my desire is guided;
Realms where the air we breathe is love,
Which in the winds on the waves doth move,
Harmonizing this earth with what we feel above.

  We have passed Age's icy caves,
  And Manhood's dark and tossing waves,
And Youth's smooth ocean, smiling to betray;
  Beyond the glassy gulfs we flee   30
  Of shadow-peopled Infancy,
Through Death and Birth, to a diviner day;*
  A paradise of vaulted bowers
  Lit by downward-gazing flowers,
  And watery paths that wind between
  Wildernesses calm and green,
Peopled by shapes too bright to see,
And rest, having beheld; somewhat like thee;
Which walk upon the sea, and chant melodiously!

THE CLOUD

I bring fresh showers for the thirsting flowers,
  From the seas and the streams;
I bear light shade for the leaves when laid
  In their noonday dreams.
From my wings are shaken the dews that waken
  The sweet buds every one,
When rocked to rest on their mother's breast,
  As she dances about the sun.
I wield the flail of the lashing hail,
  And whiten the green plains under,   10
And then again I dissolve it in rain,
  And laugh as I pass in thunder.

I sift the snow on the mountains below,
  And their great pines groan aghast;
And all the night 'tis my pillow white,
  While I sleep in the arms of the blast.
Sublime on the towers of my skyey bowers,
  Lightning my pilot sits;
In a cavern under is fettered the thunder,
  It struggles and howls at fits;   20
Over earth and ocean, with gentle motion,
  This pilot is guiding me,
Lured by the love of the genii that move
  In the depths of the purple sea;
Over the rills, and the crags, and the hills,
  Over the lakes and the plains,
Wherever he dream, under mountain or stream,

---

* This is the song of an unseen spirit to *Asia*,
who is the dramatic embodiment of the spirit
of love working through all nature.

* In imagination reversing the course of nature
she passes back through the portals of earthly
being to the spirit's condition of primordial
immortality.

The Spirit he loves remains;
And I all the while bask in heaven's blue smile,
  Whilst he is dissolving in rains.   30

The sanguine sunrise, with his meteor eyes,
  And his burning plumes outspread,
Leaps on the back of my sailing rack,
  When the morning star shines dead,
As on the jag of a mountain crag,
  Which an earthquake rocks and swings,
An eagle alit one moment may sit
  In the light of its golden wings.
And when sunset may breathe, from the lit sea
    beneath,
  Its ardours of rest and of love,   40
And the crimson pall of eve may fall
  From the depth of heaven above,
With wings folded I rest, on mine airy nest,
  As still as a brooding dove.

That orbèd maiden with white fire laden,
  Whom mortals call the moon,
Glides glimmering o'er my fleece-like floor,
  By the midnight breezes strewn;
And wherever the beat of her unseen feet,
  Which only the angels hear,   50
May have broken the woof of my tent's thin
    roof,
  The stars peep behind her and peer;
And I laugh to see them whirl and flee,
  Like a swarm of golden bees,
When I widen the rent in my wind-built tent,
  Till the calm rivers, lakes, and seas,
Like strips of the sky fallen through me on high,
  Are each paved with the moon and these.

I bind the sun's throne with a burning zone,
  And the moon's with a girdle of pearl;   60
The volcanoes are dim, and the stars reel and
    swim,
  When the whirlwinds my banner unfurl.
From cape to cape, with a bridge-like shape,
  Over a torrent sea,
Sunbeam-proof, I hang like a roof,—
  The mountains its columns be.
The triumphal arch through which I march
  With hurricane, fire, and snow,
When the powers of the air are chained to my
    chair,
  Is the million-coloured bow;   70
The sphere-fire above its soft colours wove,
  While the moist earth was laughing below.

I am the daughter of earth and water,
  And the nursling of the sky;
I pass through the pores of the ocean and
    shores;
  I change, but I cannot die.
For after the rain when with never a stain

The pavilion of heaven is bare,
And the winds and sunbeams with their convex
    gleams
  Build up the blue dome of air,   80
I silently laugh at my own cenotaph,[1]
  And out of the caverns of rain,
Like a child from the womb, like a ghost from
    the tomb,
  I arise and unbuild it again.

TO A SKYLARK

Hail to thee, blithe spirit!
  Bird thou never wert,
That from heaven, or near it,
  Pourest thy full heart
In profuse strains of unpremeditated art.

Higher still and higher
  From the earth thou springest
Like a cloud of fire;
  The blue deep thou wingest,
And singing still dost soar, and soaring ever
    singest.   10

In the golden lightning
  Of the sunken sun,
O'er which clouds are brightning,
  Thou dost float and run;
Like an unbodied joy whose race is just begun.

The pale purple even
  Melts around thy flight;
Like a star of heaven
  In the broad daylight
Thou art unseen, but yet I hear thy shrill
    delight,   20

Keen as are the arrows
  Of that silver sphere,
Whose intense lamp narrows
  In the white dawn clear,
Until we hardly see, we feel that it is there.

All the earth and air
  With thy voice is loud,
As, when night is bare,
  From one lonely cloud
The moon rains out her beams, and heaven is
    overflowed.   30

What thou art we know not;
  What is most like thee?
From rainbow clouds there flow not
  Drops so bright to see,
As from thy presence showers a rain of melody.

Like a poet hidden
  In the light of thought,

---

[1] An empty tomb.

Singing hymns unbidden,
   Till the world is wrought
To sympathy with hopes and fears it heeded
     not: 40

Like a high-born maiden
   In a palace-tower,
Soothing her love-laden
   Soul in secret hour
With music sweet as love, which overflows her
     bower:

Like a glow-worm golden
   In a dell of dew,
Scattering unbeholden
   Its aërial hue
Among the flowers and grass, which screen it
     from the view: 50

Like a rose embowered
   In its own green leaves,
By warm winds deflowered,
   Till the scent it gives
Makes faint with too much sweet those heavy-
     wingèd thieves:

Sound of vernal showers
   On the twinkling grass,
Rain-awakened flowers,
   All that ever was
Joyous, and clear, and fresh, thy music doth
     surpass.   60

Teach us, sprite or bird,
   What sweet thoughts are thine:
I have never heard
   Praise of love or wine
That panted forth a flood of rapture so divine.

Chorus Hymeneal,
   Or triumphal chant,
Matched with thine would be all
   But an empty vaunt,
A thing wherein we feel there is some hidden
     want.   70

What objects are the fountains
   Of thy happy strain?
What fields, or waves, or mountains?
   What shapes of sky or plain?
What love of thine own kind? what ignorance
     of pain?

With thy clear keen joyance
   Languor cannot be:
Shadow of annoyance
   Never came near thee:
Thou lovest, but ne'er knew love's sad
     satiety.   80

Waking or asleep,
   Thou of death must deem
Things more true and deep
   Than we mortals dream,
Or how could thy notes flow in such a crystal
     stream?

We look before and after,
   And pine for what is not:
Our sincerest laughter
   With some pain is fraught;
Our sweetest songs are those that tell of
     saddest thought.   90

Yet if we could scorn
   Hate, and pride, and fear;
If we were things born
   Not to shed a tear,
I know not how thy joy we ever should come
     near.

Better than all measures
   Of delightful sound,
Better than all treasures
   That in books are found,
Thy skill to poet were, thou scorner of the
     ground!   100

Teach me half the gladness
   That thy brain must know,
Such harmonious madness
   From my lips would flow,
The world should listen then, as I am listening
     now.

From ADONAIS*
The Grave of Keats
49

Go thou to Rome,—at once the Paradise,
The grave, the city, and the wilderness;

* "John Keats died at Rome of a consumption, in his twenty-fourth [twenty-sixth] year, on the [22d] day of [February], 1821; and was buried in the romantic and lonely cemetery of the Protestants in that city, under the pyramid which is the tomb of Cestius and the massy walls and towers, now mouldering and desolate, which formed the circuit of ancient Rome. The cemetery is an open space among the ruins, covered in winter with violets and daisies. It might make one in love with death to think that one should be buried in so sweet a place."—From Shelley's Preface. "Adonais" is of course a poetical name for Keats. The elegy was the outcome of Shelley's noble indignation over a death which he somewhat mistakenly supposed was immediately due to the savage criticism of Keats's reviewers—"Wretched men," as he characterized them, who "know not what they do," murderers who had "spoken daggers but used none." See *Eng. Lit.*, p. 258. The especially beautiful concluding stanzas, which are given here, are almost purely personal; Shelley is communing with himself, and thinking of his own troubled life.

And where its wrecks like shattered mountains
    rise,
And flowering weeds, and fragrant copses dress
The bones of Desolation's nakedness,
Pass, till the Spirit of the spot shall lead
Thy footsteps to a slope of green access
Where, like an infant's smile, over the dead
    A light of laughing flowers along the grass is
        spread.

50

And gray walls moulder round, on which dull
    Time
Feeds, like slow fire upon a hoary brand;
And one keen pyramid with wedge sublime,
Pavilioning the dust of him who planned
This refuge for his memory, doth stand
Like flame transformed to marble; and beneath,
A field is spread, on which a newer band
Have pitched in Heaven's smile their camp of
    death
    Welcoming him we lose with scarce extin-
        guished breath.

51

Here pause: these graves are all too young as
    yet
To have outgrown the sorrow which consigned
Its charge to each; and if the seal is set,
Here, on one fountain of a mourning mind,
Break it not thou! too surely shalt thou find
Thine own well full, if thou returnest home,
Of tears and gall.   From the world's bitter
    wind
Seek shelter in the shadow of the tomb.
    What Adonais is, why fear we to become?

52

The One remains, the many change and pass;
Heaven's light forever shines, Earth's shadows
    fly;
Life, like a dome of many-coloured glass,
Stains the white radiance of Eternity,
Until Death tramples it to fragments.—Die,
If thou wouldst be with that which thou dost
    seek!
Follow where all is fled!—Rome's azure sky,
Flowers, ruins, statues, music, words, are weak,
    The glory they transfuse with fitting truth to
        speak.

53

Why linger, why turn back, why shrink, my
    Heart?
Thy hopes are gone before: from all things here
They have departed: thou shouldst now depart!
A light is past from the revolving year,

And man, and woman; and what still is dear
Attracts to crush, repels to make thee wither.
The soft sky smiles,—the low wind whispers
    near;
'Tis Adonais calls! oh, hasten thither,
    No more let Life divide what Death can join
        together.

54

That Light whose smile kindles the Universe,
That Beauty in which all things work and move,
That Benediction which the eclipsing Curse
Of birth can quench not, that sustaining Love
Which through the web of being blindly wove
By man and beast and earth and air and sea,
Burns bright or dim, as each are mirrors of
The fire for which all thirst; now beams on me,
    Consuming the last clouds of cold mortality.

55

The breath whose might I have invoked in song
Descends on me; my spirit's bark is driven,
Far from the shore, far from the trembling
    throng
Whose sails were never to the tempest given;
The massy earth and spherèd skies are riven!
I am borne darkly, fearfully, afar;
Whilst burning through the inmost veil of
    Heaven,
The soul of Adonais, like a star,
    Beacons from the abode where the Eternal are.

From HELLAS*

CHORUS

The world's great age begins anew,
    The golden years return,
The earth doth like a snake renew
    Her winter weeds[1] outworn:
Heaven smiles, and faiths and empires[2] gleam,
Like wrecks of a dissolving dream.   6

A brighter Hellas rears its mountains
    From waves serener far;
A new Peneus rolls his fountains

---

1 robes
2 creeds and monarchies (to which, as such, Shel-
    ley was devotedly hostile)
* Shelley's drama of the modern Greeks' strug-
    gle for independence concludes with this
    Chorus, prophesying the return of that Golden
    Age when Saturn was fabled to have reigned
    over a universe of peace and love. Of the
    fulfillment of this prophecy Shelley had at
    times an ardent hope, which reaches perhaps
    its highest expression in this Chorus (with
    which compare Byron's *Isles of Greece*), and
    at other times a profound despair, which can
    easily be read in some of the lyrics that are
    given on subsequent pages.

Against the morning star.
Where fairer Tempes bloom, there sleep
Young Cyclads on a sunnier deep.   12

A loftier Argo cleaves the main,
    Fraught with a later prize;
Another Orpheus sings again,
    And loves, and weeps, and dies.
A new Ulysses leaves once more
Calypso for his native shore.   18

Oh, write no more the tale of Troy,†
If earth Death's scroll must be!
Nor mix with Laian rage the joy
    Which dawns upon the free:
Although a subtler Sphinx renew
Riddles of death Thebes never knew.   4

Another Athens shall arise,
    And to remoter time
Bequeath, like sunset to the skies,
    The splendour of its prime;
And leave, if nought so bright may live,
All earth can take or Heaven can give.   30

Saturn and Love their long repose
    Shall burst, more bright and good
Than all who fell,[3] than One who rose,[4]
    Than many unsubdued:[5]
Not gold, not blood, their altar dowers,
But votive tears and symbol flowers.   36

Oh, cease! must hate and death return?
    Cease! must men kill and die?
Cease! drain not to its dregs the urn
    Of bitter prophecy.
The world is weary of the past,
Oh, might it die or rest at last!   42

TO ―――――――

Music, when soft voices die,
    Vibrates in the memory;
Odours, when sweet violets sicken,
    Live within the sense they quicken.

Rose leaves, when the rose is dead,
    Are heaped for the belovèd's bed;
And so thy thoughts, when thou art gone,
    Love itself shall slumber on.

TO ―――――――

One word is too often profaned
    For me to profane it,
One feeling too falsely disdained

3 Pagan gods.   5 Objects   of   heathen
4 Christ.   idolatry.
† The more or less historic Trojan War, and the
    woes of the Theban house of Laius and his
    son Œdipus, belong of course to a time suc-
    ceeding the Golden Age of fable.

    For thee to disdain it;
One hope is too like despair
    For prudence to smother,
And pity from thee more dear
    Than that from another.

I can give not what men call love,
    But wilt thou accept not
The worship the heart lifts above
    And the Heavens reject not,—
The desire of the moth for the star,
    Of the night for the morrow,
The devotion to something afar
    From the sphere of our sorrow?

A LAMENT

O world! O life! O time!
On whose last steps I climb,
    Trembling at that where I had stood before;
When will return the glory of your prime?
    No more—oh, never more!

Out of the day and night
A joy has taken flight;
    Fresh spring, and summer, and winter hoar,
Move my faint heart with grief, but with delight
    No more—oh, never more!

WHEN THE LAMP IS SHATTERED

When the lamp is shattered,
The light in the dust lies dead—
    When the cloud is scattered,
The rainbow's glory is shed.
    When the lute is broken,
Sweet tones are remembered not;
    When the lips have spoken,
Loved accents are soon forgot.   8

    As music and splendour
Survive not the lamp and the lute,
    The heart's echoes render
No song when the spirit is mute:—
    No song but sad dirges,
Like the wind through a ruined cell,
    Or the mournful surges
That ring the dead seaman's knell.   16

    When hearts have once mingled,
Love first leaves the well-built nest;
    The weak one is singled
To endure what it once possessed.
    O Love! who bewailest
The frailty of all things here,
    Why choose you the frailest
For your cradle, your home, and your bier?   24

Its passions will rock thee
As the storms rock the ravens on high:
  Bright reason will mock thee,
Like the sun from a wintry sky.
  From thy nest every rafter
Will rot, and thine eagle home
  Leave thee naked to laughter,
When leaves fall and cold winds come.   32

A DIRGE

Rough wind, that moanest loud
  Grief too sad for song;
Wild wind, when sullen cloud
  Knells all the night long;
Sad storm, whose tears are vain,
Bare woods, whose branches strain,
Deep caves and dreary main,
  Wail, for the world's wrong!

JOHN KEATS

(1795-1821)

FROM ENDYMION*

PROEM. FROM BOOK I

A thing of beauty is a joy forever:
Its loveliness increases; it will never
Pass into nothingness; but still will keep
A bower quiet for us, and a sleep
Full of sweet dreams, and health, and quiet
    breathing.
Therefore, on every morrow,[1] are we wreathing
A flowery band to bind us to the earth,
Spite of despondence, of the inhuman dearth
Of noble natures, of the gloomy days,
Of all the unhealthy and o'er-darkened ways   10
Made for our searching: yes, in spite of all,
Some shape of beauty moves away the pall
From our dark spirits. Such the sun, the moon,
Trees old and young, sprouting a shady boon
For simple sheep; and such are daffodils
With the green world they live in; and clear
    rills
That for themselves a cooling covert make
'Gainst the hot season; the mid-forest brake,
Rich with a sprinkling of fair musk-rose blooms:
And such too is the grandeur of the dooms[2]   20
We have imagined for the mighty dead;
All lovely tales that we have heard or read:
An endless fountain of immortal drink,
Pouring unto us from the heaven's brink.

Nor do we merely feel these essences
For one short hour; no, even as the trees

That whisper round a temple become soon
Dear as the temple's self, so does the moon,
The passion poesy, glories infinite,
Haunt us till they become a cheering light   30
Unto our souls, and bound to us so fast,
That, whether there be shine, or gloom o'ercast,
They alway must be with us, or we die.

  Therefore, 'tis with full happiness that I
Will trace the story of Endymion.
The very music of the name has gone
Into my being, and each pleasant scene
Is growing fresh before me as the green
Of our own valleys: so I will begin
Now while I cannot hear the city's din;   40
Now while the early budders are just new,
And run in mazes of the youngest hue
About old forests; while the willow trails
Its delicate amber; and the dairy pails
Bring home increase of milk. And, as the year
Grows lush in juicy stalks, I'll smoothly steer
My little boat, for many quiet hours,
With streams that deepen freshly into bowers.
Many and many a verse I hope to write,
Before the daisies, vermeil rimmed and white,   50
Hide in deep herbage; and ere yet the bees
Hum about globes of clover and sweet peas,
I must be near the middle of my story.
O may no wintry season, bare and hoary,
See it half finished: but let Autumn bold,
With universal tinge of sober gold,
Be all about me when I make an end.
And now at once, adventuresome, I send
My herald thought into a wilderness:
There let its trumpet blow, and quickly dress   60
My uncertain path with green, that I may speed
Easily onward, thorough[3] flowers and weed.

THE EVE OF ST. AGNES

1

St. Agnes' Eve[4]—Ah, bitter chill it was!
The owl, for all his feathers, was a-cold;
The hare limped trembling through the frozen
    grass,
And silent was the flock in woolly fold:
Numb were the Beadsman's fingers, while he
    told
His rosary, and while his frosted breath,
Like pious incense from a censer old,
Seemed taking flight for heaven, without a
    death,
  Past the sweet Virgin's picture, while his
    prayer he saith.

1 morning   2 destinies
* See *Eng. Lit.*, p. 258.   3 through   4 The night preceding Jan. 21.

2

His prayer he saith, this patient, holy man;
Then takes his lamp, and riseth from his knees,
And back returneth, meagre, barefoot, wan,
Along the chapel aisle by slow degrees:
The sculptured dead, on each side, seem to
    freeze,
Emprisoned in black, purgatorial rails:
Knights, ladies, praying in dumb orat'ries,
He passeth by; and his weak spirit fails
  To think how they may ache in icy hoods and
    mails.

3

Northward he turneth through a little door,
And scarce three steps, ere Music's golden
    tongue
Flattered to tears this aged man and poor;
But no—already had his deathbell rung;
The joys of all his life were said and sung:
His was harsh penance on St. Agnes' Eve:
Another way he went, and soon among
Rough ashes sat he for his soul's reprieve,
  And all night kept awake, for sinners' sake
    to grieve.

4

That ancient Beadsman heard the prelude soft;
And so it chanced, for many a door was wide,
From hurry to and fro. Soon, up aloft,
The silver, snarling trumpets 'gan to chide:
The level chambers, ready with their pride,
Were glowing to receive a thousand guests:
The carvèd angels, ever eager-eyed,
Stared, where upon their heads the cornice rests,
  With hair blown back, and wings put cross-
    wise on their breasts.

5

At length burst in the argent revelry,
With plume, tiara, and all rich array,
Numerous as shadows, haunting fairily
The brain, new stuffed, in youth, with triumphs
    gay
Of old romance. These let us wish away,
And turn, sole-thoughted, to one Lady there,
Whose heart had brooded, all that wintry day,
On love, and winged St. Agnes' saintly care,
  As she had heard old dames full many times
    declare.

6

They told her how, upon St. Agnes' Eve,
Young virgins might have visions of delight,
And soft adorings from their loves receive
Upon the honeyed middle of the night,
If ceremonies due they did aright;
As, supperless to bed they must retire,
And couch supine their beauties, lily white;
Nor look behind, nor sideways, but require
  Of Heaven with upward eyes for all that they
    desire.

7

Full of this whim was thoughtful Madeline;
The music, yearning like a God in pain,
She scarcely heard: her maiden eyes divine,
Fixed on the floor, saw many a sweeping train[1]
Pass by—she heeded not at all: in vain
Came many a tiptoe, amorous cavalier,
And back retired; not cooled by high disdain,
But she saw not: her heart was otherwhere:
  She sighed for Agnes' dreams, the sweetest
    of the year.

8

She danced along with vague, regardless eyes,
Anxious her lips, her breathing quick and short:
The hallowed hour was near at hand: she sighs
Amid the timbrels, and the thronged resort
Of whisperers in anger, or in sport;
'Mid looks of love, defiance, hate, and scorn,
Hoodwinked[2] with faery fancy; all amort,[3]
Save to St. Agnes and her lambs unshorn,[*]
  And all the bliss to be before to-morrow morn.

9

So, purposing each moment to retire,
She lingered still. Meantime, across the moors,
Had come young Porphyro, with heart on fire
For Madeline. Beside the portal doors,
Buttressed from moonlight, stands he, and im-
  • plores
All saints to give him sight of Madeline,
But for one moment in the tedious hours,
That he might gaze and worship all unseen;
  Perchance speak, kneel, touch, kiss—in sooth
    such things have been.

10

He ventures in: let no buzzed whisper tell:
All eyes be muffled, or a hundred swords
Will storm his heart, Love's feverous citadel:
For him, those chambers held barbarian hordes,
Hyena foemen, and hot-blooded lords,
Whose very dogs would execrations howl
Against his lineage: not one breast affords
Him any mercy, in that mansion foul,
  Save one old beldame, weak in body and in
    soul.

1 i. e., of robes (Keats)   3 dead
2 blinded (to all else)
* St. Agnes was a Roman virgin who suffered
   martyrdom. At Mass, on the day sacred to
   her, while the Agnus Dei (Lamb of God) was
   chanted, two lambs were dedicated to her,
   and afterwards shorn and the wool woven
   (stanza 13).

11

Ah, happy chance! the aged creature came,
Shuffling along with ivory-headed wand,
To where he stood, hid from the torch's flame,
Behind a broad hall-pillar, far beyond
The sound of merriment and chorus bland:
He startled her; but soon she knew his face,
And grasped his fingers in her palsied hand,
Saying, "Mercy, Porphyro! hie thee from this
    place;
    They are all here to-night, the whole blood-
      thirsty race!

12

Get hence! get hence! there's dwarfish Hilde-
    brand;
He had a fever late, and in the fit
He cursèd thee and thine, both house and land:
Then there's that old Lord Maurice, not a whit
More tame for his gray hairs—Alas me! flit!
Flit like a ghost away."—"Ah, Gossip[4] dear,
We're safe enough; here in this arm-chair sit,
And tell me how"—"Good Saints! not here,
    not here;
    Follow me, child, or else these stones will
      be thy bier."

13

He followed through a lowly archèd way,
Brushing the cobwebs with his lofty plume;
And as she muttered "Well-a—well-a-day!"
He found him in a little moonlight room,
Pale, latticed, chill, and silent as a tomb.
"Now tell me where is Madeline," said he,
"O tell me, Angela, by the holy loom
Which none but secret sisterhood may see,
    When they St. Agnes' wool are weaving
      piously."

14

"St. Agnes! Ah! it is St. Agnes' Eve—
Yet men will murder upon holy days:
Thou must hold water in a witch's sieve,
And be liege-lord of all the Elves and Fays,
To venture so: it fills me with amaze
To see thee, Porphyro!—St. Agnes' Eve!
God's help! my lady fair the conjurer plays
This very night; good angels her deceive!
    But let me laugh awhile, I've mickle time to
      grieve."

15

Feebly she laugheth in the languid moon,
While Porphyro upon her face doth look,
Like puzzled urchin on an aged crone
Who keepeth closed a wond'rous riddle-book,
As spectacled she sits in chimney nook.

But soon his eyes grew brilliant, when she told
His lady's purpose; and he scarce could brook[5]
Tears, at the thought of those enchantments
    cold,
    And Madeline asleep in lap of legends old.

16

Sudden a thought came like a full-blown rose,
Flushing his brow, and in his painèd heart
Made purple riot: then doth he propose
A stratagem, that makes the beldame start:
"A cruel man and impious thou art:
Sweet lady, let her pray, and sleep, and dream
Alone with her good angels, far apart
From wicked men like thee. Go, go!—I deem
    Thou canst not surely be the same that thou
      didst seem."

17

"I will not harm her, by all saints I swear,"
Quoth Porphyro: "O may I ne'er find grace
When my weak voice shall whisper its last
    prayer,
If one of her soft ringlets I displace,
Or look with ruffian passion in her face:
Good Angela, believe me by these tears;
Or I will, even in a moment's space,
Awake, with horrid shout, my foemen's ears,
    And beard them, though they be more fanged
      than wolves and bears."

18

"Ah! why wilt thou affright a feeble soul?
A poor, weak, palsy-stricken churchyard thing,
Whose passing-bell may ere the midnight toll;
Whose prayers for thee, each morn and evening,
Were never missed." Thus plaining, doth she
    bring
A gentler speech from burning Porphyro;
So woful, and of such deep sorrowing,
That Angela gives promise she will do
    Whatever he shall wish, betide her weal or
      woe.

19

Which was, to lead him, in close secrecy,
Even to Madeline's chamber, and there hide
Him in a closet, of such privacy
That he might see her beauty unespied,
And win perhaps that night a peerless bride,
While legioned fairies paced the coverlet,
And pale enchantment held her sleepy-eyed.
Never on such a night have lovers met,
    Since Merlin paid his Demon all the mon-
      strous debt.*

---

5 Misused for "check".
* Merlin, the famous wizard, became himself a
    victim of magic. See Tennyson's *Merlin and
    Vivien*.

4 godmother

20

"It shall be as thou wishest," said the Dame;
"All cates¹ and dainties shall be storèd there
Quickly on this feast-night: by the tambour
    frame²
Her own lute thou wilt see: no time to spare,
For I am slow and feeble, and scarce dare
On such a catering trust my dizzy head.
Wait here, my child, with patience; kneel in
    prayer
The while: Ah! thou must needs the lady
    wed,
  Or may I never leave my grave among the
    dead.''

21

So saying, she hobbled off with busy fear.
The lover's endless minutes slowly pass'd;
The dame returned, and whispered in his ear
To follow her; with aged eyes aghast
From fright of dim espial. Safe at last,
Through many a dusky gallery, they gain
The maiden's chamber, silken, hushed, and
    chaste;
  Where Porphyro took covert, pleased amain.
    His poor guide hurried back with agues in
    her brain.

22

Her faltering hand upon the balustrade,
Old Angela was feeling for the stair,
When Madeline, St. Agnes' charmèd maid,
Rose, like a missioned spirit, unaware:
With silver taper's light, and pious care,
She turned, and down the aged gossip led
To a safe level matting. Now prepare,
Young Porphyro, for gazing on that bed;
  She comes, she comes again, like ringdove
    frayed and fled.

23

Out went the taper as she hurried in;
Its little smoke, in pallid moonshine, died:
She closed the door, she panted, all akin
To spirits of the air, and visions wide:
No uttered syllable, or woe betide!
But to her heart, her heart was voluble,
Paining with eloquence her balmy side;
As though a tongueless nightingale should
    swell
  Her throat in vain, and die, heart-stifled, in
    her dell.

24

A casement high and triple arched there was,
All garlanded with carven imag'ries
Of fruits, and flowers, and bunches of knot-
    grass,
And diamonded with panes of quaint device,
Innumerable of stains and splendid dyes,
As are the tiger-moth's deep-damasked wings;
And in the midst, 'mong thousand heraldries,
And twilight saints, and dim emblazonings,
  A shielded scutcheon blushed with blood of
    queens and kings.

25

Full on this casement shone the wintry moon,
And threw warm gules³ on Madeline's fair
    breast,
As down she knelt for heaven's grace and
    boon;
Rose-bloom fell on her hands, together prest,
And on her silver cross soft amethyst,
And on her hair a glory, like a saint:
She seemed a splendid angel, newly drest,
Save wings, for heaven: Porphyro grew faint:
  She knelt, so pure a thing, so free from mor-
    tal taint.

26

Anon his heart revives: her vespers done,
Of all its wreathèd pearls her hair she frees;
Unclasps her warmèd jewels one by one;
Loosens her fragrant bodice; by degrees
Her rich attire creeps rustling to her knees;
Half-hidden, like a mermaid in seaweed,
Pensive awhile she dreams awake, and sees,
In fancy, fair St. Agnes in her bed,
  But dares not look behind, or all the charm
    is fled.

27

Soon, trembling in her soft and chilly nest,
In sort of wakeful swoon, perplexed she lay,
Until the poppied warmth of sleep oppressed
Her soothèd limbs, and soul fatigued away;
Flown, like a thought, until the morrow-day;
Blissfully havened both from joy and pain;
Clasped like a missal⁴ where swart Paynims
    pray;
Blinded alike from sunshine and from rain,
  As though a rose should shut, and be a bud
    again.

28

Stol'n to this paradise, and so entranced,
Porphyro gazed upon her empty dress,
And listened to her breathing, if it chanced
To wake into a slumberous tenderness;
Which when he heard, that minute did he bless,
And breathed himself: then from the closet
    crept,
Noiseless as fear in a wide wilderness,
And over the hushed carpet, silent, stepped,

¹ delicacies   ² A drum-like embroid-ery frame.
³ red color (a heraldic term)
⁴ mass-book (which pagans would have no occa-sion to unclasp)

And 'tween the curtains peeped, where, lo!
  how fast she slept.

29

Then by the bed-side, where the faded moon
Made a dim, silver twilight, soft he set
A table, and, half-anguished, threw thereon
A cloth of woven crimson, gold, and jet:—
O for some drowsy Morphean amulet!
The boisterous, midnight, festive clarion,
The kettle-drum, and far-heard clarinet,
Affray his ears, though but in dying tone:—
  The hall door shuts again, and all the noise
    is gone.

30

And still she slept an azure-lidded sleep,
In blanchèd linen, smooth, and lavendered,
While he from forth the closet brought a heap
Of candied apple, quince, and plum, and gourd;
With jellies soother5 than the creamy curd,
And lucent syrops, tinct with cinnamon;
Manna and dates, in argosy transferred
From Fez; and spicèd dainties, every one,
  From silken Samarcand to cedared Lebanon.

31

These delicates he heaped with glowing hand
On golden dishes and in baskets bright
Of wreathèd silver: sumptuous they stand
In the retired quiet of the night,
Filling the chilly room with perfume light.—
'And now, my love, my seraph fair, awake!
Thou art my heaven, and I thine eremite;
Open thine eyes, for meek St. Agnes' sake,
  Or I shall drowse beside thee, so my soul
    doth ache.''

32

Thus whispering, his warm, unnervèd arm
Sank in her pillow. Shaded was her dream
By the dusk curtains:—'twas a midnight
  charm
Impossible to melt as icèd stream:
The lustrous salvers in the moonlight gleam:
Broad golden fringe upon the carpet lies:
It seemed he never, never could redeem
From such a stedfast spell his lady's eyes;
  So mused awhile, entoiled in woofèd phan-
    tasies.

33

Awakening up, he took her hollow lute,—
Tumultuous,—and, in chords that tenderest be,
He played an ancient ditty, long since mute,
In Provence called, ''La belle dame sans
  mercy:''6

Close to her ear touching the melody;—
Wherewith disturbed, she uttered a soft moan:
He ceased—she panted quick—and suddenly
Her blue affrayèd eyes wide open shone:
  Upon his knees he sank, pale as smooth-
    sculptured stone.

34

Her eyes were open, but she still beheld,
Now wide awake, the vision of her sleep:
There was a painful change, that nigh ex-
  pelled
The blisses of her dream so pure and deep,
At which fair Madeline began to weep,
And moan forth witless words with many a
  sigh;
While still her gaze on Porphyro would keep;
Who knelt, with joinèd hands and piteous eye,
  Fearing to move or speak, she looked so
    dreamingly.

35

''Ah, Porphyro!'' said she, ''but even now
Thy voice was at sweet tremble in mine ear,
Made tuneable with every sweetest vow;
And those sad eyes were spiritual and clear;
How changed thou art! how pallid, chill, and
  drear!
Give me that voice again, my Porphyro,
Those looks immortal, those complainings dear!
Oh leave me not in this eternal woe,
  For if thou diest, my Love, I know not where
    to go.''

36

Beyond a mortal man impassioned far
At these voluptuous accents, he arose,
Ethereal, flushed, and like a throbbing star
Seen mid the sapphire heaven's deep repose;
Into her dream he melted, as the rose
Blendeth its odour with the violet,—
Solution sweet: meantime the frost-wind blows
Like Love's alarum pattering the sharp sleet
  Against the window-panes; St. Agnes' moon
    hath set.

37

'Tis dark: quick pattereth the flaw-blown
  sleet:
''This is no dream, my bride, my Madeline!''
'Tis dark: the icèd gusts still rave and beat:
''No dream, alas! alas! and woe is mine!
Porphyro will leave me here to fade and pine.—
Cruel! what traitor could thee hither bring?
I curse not, for my heart is lost in thine,
Though thou forsakest a deceivèd thing;—
  A dove forlorn and lost with sick unprunèd
    wing.''

5 Apparently used here   6 ''The beautiful lady
  for ''smoother.''   without pity.''

38

"My Madeline! sweet dreamer! lovely bride!
Say, may I be for aye thy vassal blest?
Thy beauty's shield, heart-shaped and vermeil
    dyed?
Ah, silver shrine, here will I take my rest
After so many hours of toil and quest,
A famished pilgrim,—saved by miracle.
Though I have found, I will not rob thy nest
Saving of thy sweet self; if thou think'st well
    To trust, fair Madeline, to no rude infidel.

39

"Hark! 'tis an elfin-storm from faery land,
Of haggard seeming, but a boon indeed:
Arise—arise! the morning is at hand;—
The bloated wassaillers will never heed:—
Let us away, my love, with happy speed;
There are no ears to hear, or eyes to see,—
Drowned all in Rhenish and the sleepy mead:
Awake! arise! my love, and fearless be,
    For o'er the southern moors I have a home
        for thee."

40

She hurried at his words, beset with fears,
For there were sleeping dragons all around,
At glaring watch, perhaps, with ready spears—
Down the wide stairs a darkling way they
    found.—
In all the house was heard no human sound.
A chain-drooped lamp was flickering by each
    door;
The arras, rich with horseman, hawk, and
    hound,
Fluttered in the besieging wind's uproar;
    And the long carpets rose along the gusty
        floor.

41

They glide, like phantoms, into the wide hall;
Like phantoms, to the iron porch, they glide;
Where lay the Porter, in uneasy sprawl,
With a huge empty flagon by his side:
The wakeful bloodhound rose, and shook his
    hide,
But his sagacious eye an inmate owns:
By one and one, the bolts full easy slide:—
The chains lie silent on the footworn stones;—
    The key turns, and the door upon its hinges
        groans.

42

And they are gone: ay, ages long ago
These lovers fled away into the storm.
That night the Baron dreamt of many a woe,
And all his warrior-guests, with shade and form
Of witch, and demon, and large coffin-worm,
Were long be-nightmared. Angela the old

Died palsy-twitched, with meagre face deform
The Beadsman, after thousand aves told,
    For aye unsought for slept among his ash
        cold.

ODE TO A NIGHTINGALE

My heart aches, and a drowsy numbness pain
    My sense, as though of hemlock I had dru
Or emptied some dull opiate to the drains
    One minute past, and Lethe-wards had sun
'Tis not through envy of thy happy lot,
    But being too happy in thine happiness,—
        That thou, light-wingèd Dryad of the tre
            In some melodious plot
Of beechen green, and shadows numberless,
    Singest of summer in full-throated ease.

O, for a draught of vintage! that hath be
    Cooled a long age in the deep-delvèd earth,
Tasting of Flora and the country green,
    Dance, and Provençal song,[1] and sun-bur
        mirth!
O for a beaker full of the warm South,
    Full of the true, the blushful Hippocrene,[2]
        With beaded bubbles winking at the brim
            And purple-stainèd mouth;
    That I might drink, and leave the world u
        seen,
        And with thee fade away into the fores
            dim:

Fade far away, dissolve, and quite forget
    What thou among the leaves hast neve
        known,
The weariness, the fever, and the fret
    Here, where men sit and hear each othe
        groan;
Where palsy shakes a few, sad, last gray hairs
    Where youth grows pale, and spectre-thin
        and dies;
        Where but to think is to be full of sorrow
            And leaden-eyed despairs;
    Where Beauty cannot keep her lustrous eyes
        Or new Love pine at them beyon
            to-morrow.

Away! away! for I will fly to thee,
    Not charioted by Bacchus and his pards,[*]
But on the viewless wings of Poesy,
    Though the dull brain perplexes and retards

[1] Of southern France, the home of the troubadours.   [2] A fountain of the Muses on Mt. Heli con.
[*] The sources of Keats's classical knowledge ar interesting. The suggestion for this particu lar metaphor came, doubtless, from Titian' painting of Ariadne (with Bacchus and his leopards), which was brought to England in 1806 and of which Keats must at least have seen a print, for he describes it in his *Sleep and Poetry*, line 335. The painting was pu in the National Gallery in 1826.

Already with thee! tender is the night,
  And haply the Queen-Moon is on her throne,
    Clustered around by all her starry Fays;
      But here there is no light,
Save what from heaven is with the breezes
    blown
    Through verdurous glooms and winding
      mossy ways.   40

I cannot see what flowers are at my feet,
  Nor what soft incense hangs upon the boughs,
But, in embalmèd[3] darkness, guess each sweet
  Wherewith the seasonable month endows
The grass, the thicket, and the fruit-tree wild;
  White hawthorn, and the pastoral eglantine;
    Fast fading violets covered up in leaves;
      And mid-May's eldest child,
The coming musk-rose, full of dewy wine,
    The murmurous haunt of flies on summer
    eves.   50

Darkling I listen; and, for[4] many a time
  I have been half in love with easeful Death,
Called him soft names in many a musèd rhyme,
  To take into the air my quiet breath;
Now more than ever seems it rich to die,
  To cease upon the midnight with no pain,
    While thou art pouring forth thy soul
    abroad
        In such an ecstasy!
Still wouldst thou sing, and I have ears in
    vain—
    To thy high requiem become a sod.   60

Thou wast not born for death, immortal Bird!
  No hungry generations tread thee down;
The voice I hear this passing night was heard
  In ancient days by emperor and clown:
Perhaps the self-same song that found a path
  Through the sad heart of Ruth, when, sick
    for home,
    She stood in tears amid the alien corn;[5]
      The same that oft-times hath
Charmed magic casements, opening on the
    foam
Of perilous seas, in faery lands forlorn. 70

Forlorn! the very word is like a bell
  To toll me back from thee to my sole self!
Adieu! the fancy cannot cheat so well
  As she is famed to do, deceiving elf.
Adieu! adieu! thy plaintive anthem fades
  Past the near meadows, over the still stream,
    Up the hill-side; and now 'tis buried deep
      In the next valley-glades:
Was it a vision, or a waking dream?
    Fled is that music:—Do I wake or sleep?

3 balmy   5 *Ruth*, ii.
4 inasmuch as, while

ODE ON A GRECIAN URN*

Thou still unravished bride of quietness,
  Thou foster-child of silence and slow time,
Sylvan historian,[1] who canst thus express
  A flowery tale more sweetly than our rhyme:
What leaf-fringed legend haunts about thy
    shape
    Of deities or mortals, or of both,
      In Tempe or the dales of Arcady?
What men or gods are these? What maidens
    loth?
    What mad pursuit? What struggle to escape?
      What pipes and timbrels? What wild
      ecstasy?   10

Heard melodies are sweet, but those unheard
  Are sweeter; therefore, ye soft pipes, play
    on;
Not to the sensual ear, but, more endeared,
  Pipe to the spirit ditties of no tone:
Fair youth, beneath the trees, thou canst not
    leave
    Thy song, nor ever can those trees be bare;
      Bold Lover, never, never canst thou kiss,
Though winning near the goal—yet, do not
    grieve;
    She cannot fade, though thou hast not thy
    bliss,
      For ever wilt thou love, and she be
      fair!

Ah, happy, happy boughs! that cannot shed
  Your leaves, nor ever bid the Spring adieu;
And, happy melodist, unwearièd,
  For ever piping songs for ever new;
More happy love! more happy, happy love!
  For ever warm and still to be enjoyed,
    For ever panting, and for ever young;
All breathing human passion far above,
    That leaves a heart high-sorrowful and
    cloyed,
      A burning forehead, and a parching
      tongue.   30

Who are these coming to the sacrifice?
  To what green altar, O mysterious priest,
Lead'st thou that heifer lowing at the skies,
  And all her silken flanks with garlands
    dressed?
What little town by river or sea shore,
  Or mountain-built with peaceful citadel,
    Is emptied of this folk, this pious morn?

1 historian of sylvan scenes
* "There is some reason for thinking that the particular urn which inspired this beautiful poem
  is a somewhat weather-beaten work in marble
  still preserved in the garden of Holland House,
  and figured in Piranesi's *Vasi e Candelabri.*"
    —H. B. Forman.

And, little town, thy streets for evermore
  Will silent be; and not a soul to tell
    Why thou art desolate, can e'er return. 40

O Attic shape! Fair attitude! with brede[2]
  Of marble men and maidens overwrought,
With forest branches and the trodden weed;
  Thou, silent form, dost tease us out of
    thought[3]
As doth eternity: Cold Pastoral!
  When old age shall this generation waste,
    Thou shalt remain, in midst of other woe
Than ours, a friend to man, to whom thou
    say'st,
  "Beauty is truth, truth beauty,"—that is
    all
    Ye know on earth, and all ye need to
    know. 50

ODE ON MELANCHOLY

No, no, go not to Lethe, neither twist
  Wolf's-bane, tight-rooted, for its poisonous
    wine;
Nor suffer thy pale forehead to be kissed
  By nightshade, ruby grape of Proserpine;
Make not your rosary of yew-berries,
  Nor let the beetle, nor the death-moth be
    Your mournful Psyche,[1] nor the downy owl
A partner in your sorrow's mysteries;
  For shade to shade will come too drowsily,
    And drown the wakeful anguish of the
    soul. 10

But when the melancholy fit shall fall
  Sudden from heaven like a weeping cloud,
That fosters the droop-headed flowers all,
  And hides the green hill in an April shroud;
Then glut thy sorrow on a morning rose,
  Or on the rainbow of the salt sand-wave,
    Or on the wealth of globèd peonies;
Or if thy mistress some rich anger shows,
  Emprison her soft hand, and let her rave,
    And feed deep, deep upon her peerless
    eyes. 20

She dwells with Beauty—Beauty that must die;
  And Joy, whose hand is ever at his lips
Bidding adieu; and aching Pleasure nigh,
  Turning to poison while the bee-mouth sips:
Ay, in the very temple of Delight
  Veiled Melancholy has her sovran shrine,
    Though seen of none save him whose stren-
    uous tongue

Can burst Joy's grape against his palate fine;
  His soul shall taste the sadness of her might
    And be among her cloudy trophies
    hung. 30

TO AUTUMN

Season of mists and mellow fruitfulness,
  Close bosom-friend of the maturing sun;
Conspiring with him how to load and bless
  With fruit the vines that round the thatch-
    eaves run;
To bend with apples the mossed cottage-trees
  And fill all fruit with ripeness to the core;
    To swell the gourd, and plump the hazel
    shells
With a sweet kernel; to set budding more,
  And still more, later flowers for the bees,
  Until they think warm days will never
    cease, 10
    For Summer has o'er-brimmed their clam-
    my cells.

Who hath not seen thee oft amid thy store?
  Sometimes whoever seeks abroad may find
Thee sitting careless on a granary floor,
  Thy hair soft-lifted by the winnowing wind;
Or on a half-reaped furrow sound asleep,
  Drowsed with the fume of poppies, while
    thy hook
    Spares the next swath and all its twinèd
    flowers:
And sometimes like a gleaner thou dost keep
  Steady thy laden head across a brook; 20
  Or by a cider-press, with patient look,
    Thou watchest the last oozings hours by
    hours.

Where are the songs of Spring? Ay, where are
    they?
  Think not of them, thou hast thy music too,—
While barrèd clouds bloom the soft-dying day,
  And touch the stubble-plains with rosy hue;
Then in a wailful choir the small gnats mourn
  Among the river sallows, borne aloft
    Or sinking as the light wind lives or dies;
And full-grown lambs loud bleat from hilly
    bourn; 30
  Hedge-crickets sing; and now with treble
    soft
    The red-breast whistles from a garden-croft;
    And gathering swallows twitter in the skies.

LINES ON THE MERMAID TAVERN*

Souls of Poets dead and gone,
What Elysium have ye known,

---

2 embroidery (cp. Col-   3 draw us from our
  lins's *Ode to Even-*   anxieties
  ing, line 7, p. 346)

---

1 Psyche, the soul, was conventionally symbolized
  by the butterfly.

* The Mermaid Tavern was a favorite resort of
  Shakespeare, Jonson, and their friends.

Happy field or mossy cavern,
Choicer than the Mermaid Tavern?
Have ye tippled drink more fine
Than mine host's Canary wine?
Or are fruits of Paradise
Sweeter than those dainty pies
Of venison? O generous food!
Drest as though bold Robin Hood   10
Would, with his maid Marian,
Sup and bowse from horn and can.

I have heard that on a day
Mine host's sign-board flew away,
Nobody knew whither, till
An astrologer's old quill
To a sheepskin gave the story,
Said he saw you in your glory,
Underneath a new old sign
Sipping beverage divine,   20
And pledging with contented smack
The Mermaid in the Zodiac.

Souls of Poets dead and gone,
What Elysium have ye known,
Happy field or mossy cavern,
Choicer than the Mermaid Tavern?

IN A DREAR-NIGHTED DECEMBER

In a drear-nighted December,
  Too happy, happy tree,
Thy branches ne'er remember
  Their green felicity:
The north cannot undo them,
With a sleety whistle through them;
Nor frozen thawings glue them
  From budding at the prime.   8

In a drear-nighted December,
  Too happy, happy brook,
Thy bubblings ne'er remember
  Apollo's summer look;
But with a sweet forgetting,
They stay their crystal fretting,
Never, never petting
  About the frozen time.   16

Ah! would 'twere so with many
  A gentle girl and boy!
But were there ever any
  Writhed not at passèd joy?
To know the change and feel it,
When there is none to heal it,
Nor numbèd sense to steel it,
  Was never said in rhyme.   24

LA BELLE DAME SANS MERCI*

O what can ail thee, knight-at-arms,
  Alone and palely loitering?
The sedge has withered from the lake,
  And no birds sing.

O what can ail thee, knight-at-arms,
  So haggard and so woe-begone?
The squirrel's granary is full,
  And the harvest's done.   8

I see a lily on thy brow,
  With anguish moist and fever dew;
And on thy cheeks a fading rose
  Fast withereth too.—

I met a lady in the meads,
  Full beautiful—a faery's child;
Her hair was long, her foot was light,
  And her eyes were wild.   16

I made a garland for her head,
  And bracelets too, and fragrant zone;
She looked at me as she did love,
  And made sweet moan.

I set her on my pacing steed,
  And nothing else saw, all day long.
For sidelong would she bend, and sing
  A faery's song.   24

She found me roots of relish sweet,
  And honey wild, and manna dew;
And sure in language strange she said,
  "I love thee true."

She took me to her elfin grot,
  And there she wept, and sighed full sore;
And there I shut her wild, wild eyes
  With kisses four.   32

And there she lullèd me asleep,
  And there I dreamed, ah woe betide!
The latest dream I ever dreamt
  On the cold hill's side.

I saw pale kings, and princes too,
  Pale warriors, death-pale were they all;
They cried, "La Belle Dame sans Merci
  Hath thee in thrall!"   40

* "The Fair Lady without Pity." Cp. *The Eve of St. Agnes*, st. 33. Keats obtained the title from an old French poem, a translation of which was once attributed to Chaucer. There are two versions of Keats's poem, but the second is hardly an improvement over the first, which is the more familiar, and which is given here. The reply of the knight begins at the fourth stanza. The story has some resemblance to that of Tannhäuser and the Venusberg.

I saw their starved lips in the gloam
  With horrid warning gapèd wide—
And I awoke, and found me here,
  On the cold hill's side.

And this is why I sojourn here,
  Alone and palely loitering,
Though the sedge is withered from the lake
  And no birds sing.   48

ON FIRST LOOKING INTO CHAPMAN'S HOMER*

Much have I travelled in the realms of gold,
And many goodly states and kingdoms seen;
Round many western islands have I been
Which bards in fealty to Apollo hold.
Oft of one wide expanse had I been told
That deep-browed Homer ruled as his demesne;
Yet did I never breathe its pure serene
Till I heard Chapman speak out loud and bold:
Then felt I like some watcher of the skies
When a new planet swims into his ken;
Or like stout Cortez when with eagle eyes
He stared at the Pacific—and all his men
Looked at each other with a wild surmise—
Silent, upon a peak in Darien.

ON THE GRASSHOPPER AND CRICKET†

The poetry of earth is never dead:
When all the birds are faint with the hot sun,
And hide in cooling trees, a voice will run
From hedge to hedge about the new-mown
    mead;
That is the Grasshopper's—he takes the lead
In summer luxury,—he has never done
With his delights; for when tired out with fun
He rests at ease beneath some pleasant weed.
The poetry of earth is ceasing never:
On a lone winter evening, when the frost
Has wrought a silence, from the stove there
    shrills
The Cricket's song, in warmth increasing ever,
And seems to one in drowsiness half lost,
The Grasshopper's among some grassy hills.

* This sonnet of discovery was written after
  Keats had spent a night with a friend reading
  in Chapman's translation (*Eng. Lit.*, p. 97).
  Keats could not read Greek, but had to content himself mainly with "western islands"
  of poetry and romance. It should be noted
  that it was not Cortez, but Balboa, who discovered the Pacific.
† Written in a friendly competition with Leigh
  Hunt. See Hunt's sonnet, p. 496.

ON SEEING THE ELGIN MARBLES‡

My spirit is too weak—mortality
Weighs heavily on me like unwilling sleep,
And each imagined pinnacle and steep
Of godlike hardship tells me I must die
Like a sick Eagle looking at the sky.
Yet 'tis a gentle luxury to weep
That I have not the cloudy winds to keep,
Fresh for the opening of the morning's eye.
Such dim-conceivèd glories of the brain
Bring round the heart an undescribable feud;
So do these wonders a most dizzy pain,
That mingles Grecian grandeur with the rude
Wasting of old Time—with a billowy main—
A sun—a shadow of a magnitude.

ON THE SEA

It keeps eternal whisperings around
Desolate shores, and with its mighty swell
Gluts twice ten thousand caverns, till the spell
Of Hecate[1] leaves them their old shadowy
    sound.
Often 'tis in such gentle temper found,
That scarcely will the very smallest shell
Be moved for days from where it sometime
    fell,
When last the winds of heaven were unbound.
Oh ye! who have your eye-balls vexed and
    tired,
Feast them upon the wideness of the Sea;
Oh ye! whose ears are dinned with uproar
    rude,
Or fed too much with cloying melody—
Sit ye near some old cavern's mouth, and brood
Until ye start, as if the sea-nymphs quired!

WHEN I HAVE FEARS THAT I MAY CEASE TO BE

When I have fears that I may cease to be
Before my pen has gleaned my teeming brain,
Before high-pilèd books, in charactery,
Hold like rich garners the full ripened grain;
When I behold, upon the night's starred face,
Huge cloudy symbols of a high romance,
And think that I may never live to trace
Their shadows, with the magic hand of chance;
And when I feel, fair creature of an hour!
That I shall never look upon thee more,
Never have relish in the faery power
Of unreflecting love!—then on the shore
Of the wide world I stand alone, and think
Till Love and Fame to nothingness do sink.

1 The moon.
‡ These marbles are mainly sculptures from the
  Parthenon which were transferred from
  Athens to London by Lord Elgin in 1803.

ort=3ffort=38
rt=3rt=3t=33

BRIGHT STAR! WOULD I WERE STEDFAST AS THOU ART*

Bright star! would I were stedfast as thou
    art—
Not in lone splendour hung aloft the night,
And watching, with eternal lids apart,
Like Nature's patient, sleepless Eremite,
The moving waters at their priestlike task
Of pure ablution round earth's human shores,
Or gazing on the new soft-fallen mask
Of snow upon the mountains and the moors—
No—yet still stedfast, still unchangeable,
Pillowed upon my fair love's ripening breast,
To feel for ever its soft fall and swell,
Awake for ever in a sweet unrest,
Still, still to hear her tender-taken breath,
And so live ever—or else swoon to death.

LATE GEORGIAN BALLADS AND LYRICS†

ROBERT SOUTHEY (1774-1843)

THE BATTLE OF BLENHEIM‡

It was a summer evening;
    Old Kaspar's work was done,
And he before his cottage door
    Was sitting in the sun;
And by him sported on the green
His little grandchild Wilhelmine.   6

She saw her brother Peterkin
    Roll something large and round,
Which he beside the rivulet
    In playing there had found.
He came to ask what he had found,
That was so large, and smooth, and round.   12

Old Kaspar took it from the boy,
    Who stood expectant by;

And then the old man shook his head,
    And with a natural sigh,
" 'Tis some poor fellow's skull," said he,
"Who fell in the great victory.   18

"I find them in the garden,
    For there's many here about;
And often, when I go to plough,
    The ploughshare turns them out;
For many thousand men," said he,
"Were slain in that great victory."   24

"Now tell us what 'twas all about,"
    Young Peterkin, he cries;
And little Wilhelmine looks up
    With wonder-waiting eyes;
"Now tell us all about the war,
And what they fought each other for."   30

"It was the English," Kaspar cried,
    "Who put the French to rout;
But what they fought each other for,
    I could not well make out;
But everybody said," quoth he,
"That 'twas a famous victory.   36

"My father lived at Blenheim then,
    Yon little stream hard by;
They burnt his dwelling to the ground,
    And he was forced to fly;
So with his wife and child he fled,
Nor had he where to rest his head.   42

"With fire and sword the country round
    Was wasted far and wide,
And many a childing mother then,
    And new-born baby, died;
But things like that, you know, must be
At every famous victory.   ⸸

"They say it was a shocking sight
    After the field was won;
For many thousand bodies here
    Lay rotting in the sun;
But things like that, you know, must be
After a famous victory.   54

"Great praise the Duke of Marlboro' won,
    And our good Prince Eugene."
"Why, 'twas a very wicked thing!"
    Said little Wilhelmine.
"Nay, nay, my little girl," quoth he;
"It was a famous victory.   60

"And everybody praised the Duke
    Who this great fight did win."
"But what good came of it at last?"

* This sonnet was composed on the Dorsetshire coast just as Keats was sailing for Italy the autumn before his death. It was written in a copy of Shakespeare's poems on a blank page facing *A Lover's Complaint*.
† Under this general title are given here some minor poems of the early decades of the nineteenth century, though one or two are really post-Georgian. Hunt's *Abou ben Adhem*, for instance, is as late as 1844; but Hunt was himself a contemporary of Shelley and Keats. The poems have been selected partly for their real value as shown by their continued popularity, and partly to illustrate the character and range of the minor verse of the period.
‡ At Blenheim, in Bavaria, in 1704, the British and their German allies, under the Duke of Marlborough and the Austrian Prince Eugene, defeated the French and Bavarians with great loss.

Quoth little Peterkin.
"Why, that I cannot tell," said he;
"But 'twas a famous victory."   66

THOMAS CAMPBELL (1777-1844)

Ye Mariners of England

A Naval Ode*

Ye mariners of England!
That guard our native seas;
Whose flag has braved, a thousand years,
The battle and the breeze!
Your glorious standard launch again
To match another foe!
And sweep through the deep
While the stormy winds do blow;
While the battle rages loud and long,
And the stormy winds do blow.   10

The spirits of your fathers
Shall start from every wave!—
For the deck it was their field of fame,
And Ocean was their grave:
Where Blake and mighty Nelson fell,
Your manly hearts shall glow,
As ye sweep through the deep,
While the stormy winds do blow;
While the battle rages loud and long,
And the stormy winds do blow.   20

Britannia needs no bulwarks,
No towers along the steep;
Her march is o'er the mountain waves,
Her home is on the deep,
With thunders from her native oak,
She quells the floods below,—
As they roar on the shore,
When the stormy winds do blow;
When the battle rages loud and long,
And the stormy winds do blow.   30

The meteor flag of England
Shall yet terrific burn,
Till danger's troubled night depart,
And the star of peace return.
Then, then, ye ocean warriors!
Our song and feast shall flow
To the fame of your name,
When the storm has ceased to blow;
When the fiery fight is heard no more,
And the storm has ceased to blow.   40

* This poem was written, it is said, in 1800, on
the prospect of a war with Russia (see line
5) ; but it must have undergone some later
revision, for Nelson (line 15) fell at Trafalgar
in 1805. Admiral Robert Blake died at sea in
1657.

On Linden, when the sun was low,
All bloodless lay the untrodden snow,
And dark as winter was the flow
Of Iser, rolling rapidly:

But Linden saw another sight,
When the drum beat at dead of night,
Commanding fires of death to light
The darkness of her scenery.   8

By torch and trumpet fast arrayed,
Each horseman drew his battle blade,
And furious every charger neighed,
To join the dreadful revelry.

Then shook the hills with thunder riven,
Then rushed the steed to battle driven,
And louder than the bolts of heaven,
Far flashed the red artillery.   16

But redder yet that light shall glow
On Linden's hills of stained snow,
And bloodier yet the torrent flow
Of Iser, rolling rapidly.

'Tis morn, but scarce yon level sun
Can pierce the war-clouds, rolling dun,
Where furious Frank, and fiery Hun,
Shout in their sulphurous canopy.   24

The combat deepens. On, ye brave,
Who rush to glory, or the grave!
Wave, Munich! all thy banners wave,
And charge with all thy chivalry!

Few, few, shall part where many meet!
The snow shall be their winding-sheet,
And every turf beneath their feet
Shall be a soldier's sepulchre.   32

CHARLES WOLFE (1791-1823)

The Burial of Sir John Moore‡

Not a drum was heard, not a funeral note,
  As his corse to the rampart we hurried;
Not a soldier discharged his farewell shot
  O'er the grave where our hero we buried.

† At the Bavarian village of Hohenlinden, not far
  from Munich, the Austrian army (referred to
  in this poem as the "Hun") was defeated by
  the French (the "Frank") in December, 1800.
  Campbell did not witness the battle, as a
  pleasing tradition relates, but he was on the
  continent at the time and witnessed at least
  one skirmish. Scott greatly admired this ballad, though the author himself spoke somewhat contemptuously of its "drum and trumpet lines."
‡ Sir John Moore, a British general, was killed at
  Corunna in January, 1809, just as the British
  troops, retreating from the French, were about
  to embark, though he lived long enough to
  hear that the French were beaten back. He
  was buried at night in the citadel.

We buried him darkly, at dead of night,
  The sods with our bayonets turning;
By the struggling moonbeam's misty light,
  And the lantern dimly burning.   8

No useless coffin enclosed his breast,
  Not in sheet or in shroud we wound him,
But he lay like a warrior taking his rest,
  With his martial cloak around him.

Few and short were the prayers we said,
  And we spoke not a word of sorrow;
But we steadfastly gazed on the face that was
  dead,
  And we bitterly thought of the morrow.   16

We thought, as we hollowed his narrow bed
  And smoothed down his lonely pillow,
That the foe and the stranger would tread
  o'er his head,
  And we far away on the billow!

Lightly they'll talk of the spirit that's gone,
  And o'er his cold ashes upbraid him;
But little he'll reck, if they let him sleep on
  In the grave where a Briton has laid him.   24

But half of our weary task was done
  When the clock struck the note for retiring;
And we heard the distant and random gun
  Of the enemy sullenly firing.

Slowly and sadly we laid him down,
  From the field of his fame fresh and gory;
We carved not a line, and we raised not a stone,
  But we left him alone with his glory.   32

THOMAS MOORE (1779-1852)

The Harp that Once Through Tara's Halls§

The harp that once through Tara's halls
  The soul of music shed,
Now hangs as mute on Tara's walls
  As if that soul were fled.
So sleeps the pride of former days,
  So glory's thrill is o'er,
And hearts that once beat high for praise
  Now feel that pulse no more!   8

No more to chiefs and ladies bright
  The harp of Tara swells;
The chord alone that breaks at night
  Its tale of ruin tells.
Thus Freedom now so seldom wakes,
  The only throb she gives
Is when some heart indignant breaks,
  To show that still she lives.   16

§ Tara Hill, some twenty miles from Dublin, is
said to have been the seat of the ancient
kings of Ireland.

The Minstrel Boy

The Minstrel-boy to the war is gone,
  In the ranks of death you'll find him;
His father's sword he has girded on,
  And his wild harp slung behind him.—
"Land of song!" said the warrior-bard,
  "Though all the world betrays thee,
One sword at least thy rights shall guard,
  One faithful harp shall praise thee!"   8

The Minstrel fell!—but the foeman's chain
  Could not bring his proud soul under;
The harp he loved ne'er spoke again,
  For he tore its cords asunder;
And said, "No chains shall sully thee,
  Thou soul of love and bravery!
Thy songs were made for the brave and free,
  They shall never sound in slavery!"

Oft, in the Stilly Night
(Scotch Air)

Oft, in the stilly night,
  Ere Slumber's chain has bound me,
Fond Memory brings the light
  Of other days around me;
    The smiles, the tears,
    Of boyhood's years,
  The words of love then spoken;
    The eyes that shone,
    Now dimmed and gone,
  The cheerful hearts now broken!   10
Thus, in the stilly night,
  Ere Slumber's chain has bound me,
Sad Memory brings the light
  Of other days around me.

When I remember all
  The friends, so linked together,
I've seen around me fall,
  Like leaves in wintry weather;
    I feel like one
    Who treads alone   20
  Some banquet-hall deserted,
    Whose lights are fled,
    Whose garlands dead,
  And all but he departed!
Thus, in the stilly night,
  Ere Slumber's chain has bound me,
Sad Memory brings the light
  Of other days around me.

CHARLES LAMB (1775-1834
The Old Familiar Faces

I have had playmates, I have had companions,
In my days of childhood, in my joyful school-
  days—
All, all are gone, the old familiar faces.

I have been laughing, I have been carousing,
Drinking late, sitting late, with my bosom
    cronies—
All, all are gone, the old familiar faces.   6

I loved a love once, fairest among women;
Closed are her doors on me, I must not see
    her—
All, all are gone, the old familiar faces.

I have a friend, a kinder friend has no man;
Like an ingrate, I left my friend abruptly;
Left him, to muse on the old familiar
    faces.   12

Ghost-like I paced round the haunts of my
    childhood,
Earth seemed a desert I was bound to traverse,
Seeking to find the old familiar faces.

Friend of my bosom, thou more than a brother,
Why wert not thou born in my father's
    dwelling?
So might we talk of the old familiar faces— 18

How some they have died, and some they have
    left me,
And some are taken from me; all are departed;
All, all are gone, the old familiar faces.

WALTER SAVAGE LANDOR (1775-1864)

ROSE AYLMER*

Ah what avails the sceptred race,
    Ah what the form divine!
What every virtue, every grace!
    Rose Aylmer, all were thine.

Rose Aylmer, whom these wakeful eyes
    May weep, but never see,
A night of memories and of sighs
    I consecrate to thee.

LEIGH HUNT (1784-1859)

TO THE GRASSHOPPER AND THE CRICKET†

Green little vaulter in the sunny grass,
Catching your heart up at the feel of June,
Sole voice that's heard amidst the lazy noon,
When even the bees lag at the summoning brass;

* Rose, a daughter of Baron Aylmer, and a youthful companion of Landor, died in India in
1800.
† Written in competition with Keats, whose sonnet
may be seen on p. 492.

And you, warm little housekeeper, who class
With those who think the candles come too
    soon,
Loving the fire, and with your tricksome tune
Nick the glad silent moments as they pass;
O sweet and tiny cousins, that belong,
One to the fields, the other to the hearth,
Both have your sunshine; both, though small,
    are strong
At your clear hearts: and both seem given to
    earth
To ring in thoughtful ears this natural song—
Indoors and out, summer and winter, Mirth.

RONDEAU

Jenny kissed me when we met,
    Jumping from the chair she sat in;
Time, you thief, who love to get
    Sweets into your list, put that in:
Say I'm weary, say I'm sad,
    Say that health and wealth have missed me,
Say I'm growing old, but add,
    Jenny kissed me.

ABOU BEN ADHEM

Abou Ben Adhem (may his tribe increase!)
Awoke one night from a deep dream of peace,
And saw, within the moonlight in his room,
Making it rich, and like a lily in bloom,
An angel writing in a book of gold:
Exceeding peace had made Ben Adhem bold,
And to the presence in the room he said,
"What writest thou?"—The vision raised its
    head,
And, with a look made of all sweet accord,   9
Answered, "The names of those who love the
    Lord."
"And is mine one?" said Abou. "Nay, not
    so,"
Replied the angel. Abou spoke more low,
But cheerly still; and said, "I pray thee, then,
Write me as one that loves his fellow-men."‡

The angel wrote, and vanished. The next
    night
It came again, with a great wakening light,
And showed the names whom love of God had
    blessed,—
And lo! Ben Adhem's name led all the rest.

‡ This line is carved on Hunt's monument in
Kensal Green Cemetery.

WINTHROP MACKWORTH PRAED
(1802-1839)

LETTERS FROM TEIGNMOUTH. I.—OUR BALL§

You'll come to our ball;—since we parted
  I've thought of you more than I'll say;
Indeed, I was half broken-hearted
  For a week, when they took you away.
Fond fancy brought back to my slumbers
  Our walks on the Ness and the Den,
And echoed the musical numbers
  Which you used to sing to me then.
I know the romance, since it's over,
  'Twere idle, or worse, to recall;—
I know you're a terrible rover;
  But, Clarence, you'll come to our Ball!   12

It's only a year since, at College,
  You put on your cap and your gown;
But, Clarence, you're grown out of knowledge,
  And changed from the spur to the crown;
The voice that was best when it faltered,
  Is fuller and firmer in tone:
And the smile that should never have altered,—
  Dear Clarence,—it is not your own;
Your cravat was badly selected,
  Your coat don't become you at all;
And why is your hair so neglected?
  You must have it curled for our Ball.   24

I've often been out upon Haldon
  To look for a covey with Pup;
I've often been over to Shaldon,
  To see how your boat is laid up.
In spite of the terrors of Aunty,
  I've ridden the filly you broke;
And I've studied your sweet little Dante
  In the shade of your favourite oak:
When I sat in July to Sir Lawrence,
  I sat in your love of a shawl;
And I'll wear what you brought me from Florence,
  Perhaps, if you'll come to our Ball.   36

§ This is a specimen of the half gay, half grave *vers de société* of which Praed was a master. Teignmouth is a watering-place in Devonshire. The various places named belong to the locality. The Ness is a promontory. The Den is a promenade formed by a sand-bank between the town and the sea. Haldon is a range of hills; Shaldon, a village just across the river Teign; Dawlish, another seaside resort three miles away. As for the other allusions, Sir Thomas Lawrence was a famous portrait painter of that date (1829); National Schools (line 38) had lately been established at various places by a national society for the education of the poor; "Captain Rock" was a fictitious name signed to public notices by one of the Irish insurgents of 1822; "Hock" is a kind of wine —Hochheimer; a "Blue" is a "blue-stocking" —a woman affecting literature and politics.

You'll find us all changed since you vanished;
  We've set up a National School;
And waltzing is utterly banished;
  And Ellen has married a fool;
The Major is going to travel;
  Miss Hyacinth threatens a rout;
The walk is laid down with fresh gravel;
  Papa is laid up with the gout;
And Jane has gone on with her easels,
  And Anne has gone off with Sir Paul;
And Fanny is sick with the measles,
  And I'll tell you the rest at the Ball.   48

You'll meet all your beauties;—the Lily,
  And the Fairy of Willowbrook Farm,
And Lucy, who made me so silly
  At Dawlish, by taking your arm;
Miss Manners, who always abused you,
  For talking so much about Hock;
And her sister, who often amused you,
  By raving of rebels and Rock;
And something which surely would answer,
  An heiress quite fresh from Bengal:—
So, though you were seldom a dancer,
  You'll dance, just for once, at our Ball.   60

But out on the world!—from the flowers
  It shuts out the sunshine of truth;
It blights the green leaves in the bowers,
  It makes an old age of our youth:
And the flow of our feeling, once in it,
  Like a streamlet beginning to freeze,
Though it cannot turn ice in a minute,
  Grows harder by sudden degrees.
Time treads o'er the graves of affection;
  Sweet honey is turned into gall;
Perhaps you have no recollection
  That ever you danced at our Ball.   72

You once could be pleased with our ballads—
  To-day you have critical ears;
You once could be charmed with our salads—
  Alas! you've been dining with Peers;
You trifled and flirted with many;
  You've forgotten the when and the how;
There was one you liked better than any—
  Perhaps you've forgotten her now.
But of those you remember most newly,
  Of those who delight or inthrall,
None love you a quarter so truly
  As some you will find at our Ball.   84

They tell me you've many who flatter,
  Because of your wit and your song;
They tell me (and what does it matter?)
  You like to be praised by the throng;
They tell me you're shadowed with laurel,
  They tell me you're loved by a Blue;
They tell me you're sadly immoral—

Dear Clarence, that cannot be true!
But to me you are still what I found you
  Before you grew clever and tall;
And you'll think of the spell that once bound
    you;
  And you'll come, WON'T you come? to our
    Ball?   96

THOMAS LOVELL BEDDOES (1803-1849)

DREAM-PEDLARY*

If there were dreams to sell,
  What would you buy?
Some cost a passing-bell;
  Some a light sigh,
That shakes from Life's fresh crown
Only a rose-leaf down.
If there were dreams to sell,
Merry and sad to tell,
And the crier rang the bell,
  What would you buy?

A cottage lone and still,
  With bowers nigh,
Shadowy, my woes to still   .
  Until I die.
Such pearl from Life's fresh crown
Fain would I shake me down:
Were dreams to have at will,
This would best heal my ill,
  This would I buy.

But there were dreams to sell   20
  Ill didst thou buy;
Life is a dream, they tell,
  Waking, to die.
Dreaming a dream to prize,
Is wishing ghosts to rise;
And, if I had the spell
To call the buried well,
  Which one would I?

If there are ghosts to raise,
  What shall I call,   30
Out of hell's murky haze,
  Heaven's blue pall?
Raise my loved long-lost boy
To lead me to his joy—
There are no ghosts to raise;
Out of death lead no ways;
  Vain is the call.

Know'st thou not ghosts to sue,
  No love thou hast.
Else lie, as I will do,   40

* This poem is somewhat obscure, but to para-
  phrase it into perfect lucidity would be to
  destroy an element of its charm.

And breathe thy last.
So out of Life's fresh crown
Fall like a rose-leaf down.
Thus are the ghosts to woo;
Thus are all dreams made true,
  Ever to last!

THOMAS HOOD (1798-1845)

THE DEATH-BED

We watched her breathing through the night,
  Her breathing soft and low,
As in her breast the wave of life
  Kept heaving to and fro.

So silently we seemed to speak,
  So slowly moved about,
As we had lent her half our powers
  To eke her living out.

Our very hopes belied our fears,
  Our fears our hopes belied—
We thought her dying when she slept,
  And sleeping when she died.

For when the morn came dim and sad,
  And chill with early showers,
Her quiet eyelids closed—she had
  Another morn than ours.   16

THE SONG OF THE SHIRT

With fingers weary and worn,
  With eyelids heavy and red,
A woman sat, in unwomanly rags,
  Plying her needle and thread—
Stitch! stitch! stitch!
  In poverty, hunger, and dirt,
And still with a voice of dolorous pitch
  She sang the "Song of the Shirt".

"Work! work! work!
  While the cock is crowing aloof!
And work—work—work,
  Till the stars shine through the roof!
It's Oh! to be a slave
  Along with the barbarous Turk,
Where woman has never a soul to save,
  If this is Christian work!   16

"Work—work—work,
  Till the brain begins to swim;
Work—work—work,
  Till the eyes are heavy and dim!
Seam, and gusset, and band,
  Band, and gusset, and seam,
Till over the buttons I fall asleep,
  And sew them on in a dream!   24

"Oh, Men, with Sisters dear!
Oh, Men, with Mothers and Wives!
It is not linen you're wearing out,
But human creatures' lives!
Stitch—stitch—stitch,
In poverty, hunger, and dirt,
Sewing at once, with a double thread,
A Shroud as well as a Shirt. 32

"But why do I talk of Death?
That Phantom of grisly bone,
I hardly fear its terrible shape,
It seems so like my own—
It seems so like my own,
Because of the fasts I keep;
Oh, God! that bread should be so dear
And flesh and blood so cheap! 40

"Work—work—work!
My labour never flags;
And what are its wages? A bed of straw,
A crust of bread—and rags.
That shattered roof—this naked floor—
A table—a broken chair—
And a wall so blank, my shadow I thank
For sometimes falling there! 48

"Work—work—work!
From weary chime to chime,
Work—work—work,
As prisoners work for crime!
Band, and gusset, and seam,
Seam, and gusset, and band,
Till the heart is sick, and the brain benumbed,
As well as the weary hand. 56

"Work—work—work,
In the dull December light,
And work—work—work,
When the weather is warm and bright—
While underneath the eaves
The brooding swallows cling
As if to show me their sunny backs
And twit me with the spring. 64

'Oh! but to breathe the breath
Of the cowslip and primrose sweet—
With the sky above my head,
And the grass beneath my feet;
For only one short hour
To feel as I used to feel,
Before I knew the woes of want
And the walk that costs a meal. 72

'Oh! but for one short hour!
A respite however brief!
No blessèd leisure for Love or Hope,
But only time for Grief!

A little weeping would ease my heart,
But in their briny bed
My tears must stop, for every drop
Hinders needle and thread!'' 80

With fingers weary and worn,
With eyelids heavy and red,
A woman sat, in unwomanly rags,
Plying her needle and thread—
Stitch! stitch! stitch!
In poverty, hunger, and dirt,
And still with a voice of dolorous pitch,—
Would that its tone could reach the Rich!—
She sang this "Song of the Shirt!'' 89

ROBERT STEPHEN HAWKER (1803-1875)

THE SONG OF THE WESTERN MEN*

A good sword and a trusty hand!
A merry heart and true!
King James's men shall understand
What Cornish lads can do.

And have they fixed the where and when?
And shall Trelawny die?
Here's twenty thousand Cornish men
Will know the reason why! 8

Out spake their captain brave and bold,
A merry wight was he:
"If London Tower were Michael's hold,
We'll set Trelawny free!

"We'll cross the Tamar, land to land,
The Severn is no stay,
With 'one and all,' and hand in hand,
And who shall bid us nay? 16

"And when we come to London Wall,
A pleasant sight to view,
Come forth! come forth, ye cowards all,
Here's men as good as you!

"Trelawny he's in keep and hold,
Trelawny he may die;
But here's twenty thousand Cornish bold,
Will know the reason why!'' 24

* In 1688, Sir Jonathan Trelawny, a native of Cornwall, was, with six other bishops, thrown into the Tower of London for resisting James the Second's Declaration of Indulgence. He was soon released. It was long supposed that this ballad, which was first printed anonymously, dated from that time. The refrain is ancient, but the ballad was written by Hawker in 1825. The Tamar and Severn (lines 13 and 14) are rivers of southwestern England. Michael (line 11) is the archangel to whom was given the task of overthrowing Satan and consigning him to hell.

THE SILENT TOWER OF BOTTREAU†

Tintadgel bells ring o'er the tide,
The boy leans on his vessel side;
He hears that sound, and dreams of home
Soothe the wild orphan of the foam.
  "Come to thy God in time!"
  Thus saith their pealing chime:
  Youth, manhood, old age past,
  "Come to thy God at last."   8

But why are Bottreau's echoes still?
Her tower stands proudly on the hill;
Yet the strange chough that home hath found,
The lamb lies sleeping on the ground.
  "Come to thy God in time!"
  Should be her answering chime:
  "Come to thy God at last!"
  Should echo on the blast.   16

The ship rode down with courses free,
The daughter of a distant sea:
Her sheet was loose, her anchor stored,
The merry Bottreau bells on board.
  "Come to thy God in time!"
  Rung out Tintadgel chime;
  Youth, manhood, old age past,
  "Come to thy God at last!"   24

The pilot heard his native bells
Hang on the breeze in fitful swells;
"Thank God," with reverent brow he cried,
"We make the shore with evening's tide."
  "Come to thy God in time!"
  It was his marriage chime:
  Youth, manhood, old age past,
  His bell must ring at last.   32

"Thank God, thou whining knave, on land,
But thank, at sea, the steersman's hand,"
The captain's voice above the gale:
"Thank the good ship and ready sail."
  "Come to thy God in time!"
  Sad grew the boding chime:
  "Come to thy God at last!"
  Boomed heavy on the blast.   40

Uprose that sea! as if it heard
The mighty Master's signal-word:
What thrills the captain's whitening lip?

---

† "The rugged heights that line the sea-shore in the neighborhood of Tintadgel Castle and Church [on the coast of Cornwall] are crested with towers. Among these, that of Bottreau, or, as it is now written, Boscastle, is without bells. The silence of this wild and lonely churchyard on festive or solemn occasions is not a little striking. On enquiry I was told that the bells were once shipped for this church, but that when the vessel was within sight of the tower the blasphemy of her captain was punished in the manner related in the Poem. The bells, they told me, still lie in the bay, and announce by strange sounds the approach of a storm."—R. S. Hawker.

The death-groans of his sinking ship.
  "Come to thy God in time!"
  Swung deep the funeral chime:
  Grace, mercy, kindness past,
  "Come to thy God at last!"   48

Long did the rescued pilot tell—
When gray hairs o'er his forehead fell,
While those around would hear and weep—
That fearful judgment of the deep.
  "Come to thy God in time!"
  He read his native chime:
  Youth, manhood, old age past,
  His bell rung out at last.   56

Still when the storm of Bottreau's waves
Is wakening in his weedy caves,
Those bells, that sullen surges hide,
Peal their deep notes beneath the tide:
  "Come to thy God in time!"
  Thus saith the ocean chime:
  Storm, billow, whirlwind past,
  "Come to thy God at last!"   64

SIR WALTER SCOTT (1771-1832)

FROM OLD MORTALITY*

CHAPTER I. PRELIMINARY

"Most readers," says the Manuscript of Mr. Pattieson, "must have witnessed with delight the joyous burst which attends the dismissing of a village-school on a fine summer evening. The buoyant spirit of childhood, repressed with so much difficulty during the tedious hours of discipline, may then be seen to explode, as it were, in shout, and song, and frolic, as the little urchins join in groups on their playground, and arrange their matches of sport for the evening. But there is one individual who partakes of the relief afforded by the moment of dismission, whose feelings are not so obvious to the eye of the spectator, or so apt to receive his sympathy. I mean the teacher himself, who, stunned with the hum, and suffocated with the closeness of his school-room, has spent the whole day (himself against a host) in controlling petulance, exciting indifference to action, striving to enlighten stupidity, and labouring to soften obstinacy; and whose very powers of

---

* Old Mortality is a story of the rising of the Scotch Covenanters about 1677-9 against the English church and throne. Scott had once met, in the churchyard of Dunnottar, on Robert Paterson, familiarly known as "Old Mortality," and he chooses to make him responsible for the substance of the tale. It is one of the "Tales of My Landlord": and the Landlord of Wallace Inn, Mr. Cleishbotom the schoolmaster, and the manuscript of his assistant, the frail Mr. Pattieson, are a part of the fictitious background.

ntellect have been confounded by hearing the same dull lesson repeated a hundred times by rote, and only varied by the various blunders of the reciters. Even the flowers of classic genius, with which his solitary fancy is most gratified, have been rendered degraded, in his imagination, by their connexion with tears, with errors, and with punishment; so that the *Eclogues* of Virgil and *Odes* of Horace are each inseparably allied in association with the sullen figure and monotonous recitation of some blubbering school-boy. If to these mental distresses are added a delicate frame of body, and a mind ambitious of some higher distinction than that of being the tyrant of childhood, the reader may have some slight conception of the relief which a solitary walk, in the cool of a fine summer evening, affords to the head which has ached, and the nerves which have been shattered, for so many hours, in plying the irksome task of public instruction.

"To me these evening strolls have been the happiest hours of an unhappy life; and if any gentle reader shall hereafter find pleasure in perusing these lucubrations, I am not unwilling he should know, that the plan of them has been usually traced in those moments, when relief from toil and clamour, combined with the quiet scenery around me, has disposed my mind to the task of composition.

"My chief haunt, in these hours of golden leisure, is the banks of the small stream, which, winding through a 'lone vale of green bracken,' passes in front of the village school-house of Gandercleugh. For the first quarter of a mile, perhaps, I may be disturbed from my meditations, in order to return the scrape, or doffed bonnet, of such stragglers among my pupils as fish for trouts or minnows in the little brook, or seek rushes and wild-flowers by its margin. But, beyond the space I have mentioned, the juvenile anglers do not, after sunset, voluntarily extend their excursions. The cause is, that farther up the narrow valley, and in a recess which seems scooped out of the side of the steep heathy bank, there is a deserted burial-ground, which the little cowards are fearful of approaching in the twilight. To me, however, the place has an inexpressible charm. It has been long the favourite termination of my walks, and, if my kind patron forgets not his promise, will (and probably at no very distant day) be my final resting-place after my mortal pilgrimage.

"It is a spot which possesses all the solemnity of feeling attached to a burial-ground, without exciting those of a more unpleasing description. Having been very little used for many years, the few hillocks which rise above the level plain are covered with the same short velvet turf. The monuments, of which there are not above seven or eight, are half sunk in the ground, and overgrown with moss. No newly-erected tomb disturbs the sober serenity of our reflections by reminding us of recent calamity, and no rank-springing grass forces upon our imagination the recollection, that it owes its dark luxuriance to the foul and festering remnants of mortality which ferment beneath. The daisy which sprinkles the sod, and the harebell which hangs over it, derive their pure nourishment from the dew of heaven, and their growth impresses us with no degrading or disgusting recollections. Death has indeed been here, and its traces are before us; but they are softened and deprived of their horror by our distance from the period when they have been first impressed. Those who sleep beneath are only connected with us by the reflection, that they have once been what we now are, and that, as their relics are now identified with their mother earth, ours shall, at some future period, undergo the same transformation.

"Yet, although the moss has been collected on the most modern of these humble tombs during four generations of mankind, the memory of some of those who sleep beneath them is still held in reverent remembrance. It is true, that, upon the largest, and, to an antiquary, the most interesting monument of the group, which bears the effigies of a doughty knight in his hood of mail, with his shield hanging on his breast, the armorial bearings are defaced by time, and a few worn-out letters may be read, at the pleasure of the decipherer, *Dns. Johan - - - de Hamel, - - -* or *Johan - - - de Lamel - - -*. And it is also true, that of another tomb, richly sculptured with an ornamental cross, mitre, and pastoral staff, tradition can only aver, that a certain nameless bishop lies interred there. But upon other two stones which lie beside, may still be read in rude prose, and ruder rhyme, the history of those who sleep beneath them. They belong, we are assured by the epitaph, to the class of persecuted Presbyterians who afforded a melancholy subject for history in the times of Charles II. and his successor. In returning from the battle of Pentland Hills, a party of the insurgents had been attacked in this glen by a small detachment of the King's troops, and three or four either killed in the skirmish, or shot after being made prisoners, as rebels taken with arms in their hands. The peasantry continued to attach to the tombs of those victims of prelacy an honour which they do not render to more splendid mausoleums; and, when they point them out to their sons, and narrate the fate of the sufferers, usually conclude, by exhorting them to be ready, should times call for it, to resist to the death in the cause of civil and religious liberty, like their brave forefathers.

"Although I am far from venerating the peculiar tenets asserted by those who call themselves the followers of those men, and whose intolerance and narrow-minded bigotry are at least as conspicuous as their devotional zeal, yet it is without depreciating the memory of those sufferers, many of whom united the independent sentiments of a Hampden[1] with the suffering zeal of a Hooper or Latimer.[2] On the other hand, it would be unjust to forget, that many even of those who had been most active in crushing what they conceived the rebellious and seditious spirit of those unhappy wanderers, displayed themselves, when called upon to suffer for their political and religious opinions, the same daring and devoted zeal, tinctured, in their case, with chivalrous loyalty, as in the former with republican enthusiasm. It has often been remarked of the Scottish character, that the stubbornness with which it is moulded shows most to advantage in adversity, when it seems akin to the native sycamore of their hills, which scorns to be biased in its mode of growth, even by the influence of the prevailing wind, but, shooting its branches with equal boldness in every direction, shows no weather-side to the storm, and may be broken, but can never be bended. It must be understood that I speak of my countrymen as they fall under my own observation. When in foreign countries, I have been informed that they are more docile. But it is time to return from this digression.

"One summer evening, as in a stroll, such as I have described, I approached this deserted mansion of the dead, I was somewhat surprised to hear sounds distinct from those which usually soothe its solitude, the gentle chiding, namely, of the brook, and the sighing of the wind in the boughs of three gigantic ash-trees, which mark the cemetery. The clink of a hammer was, on this occasion, distinctly heard; and I entertained some alarm that a march-dike, long meditated by the two proprietors whose estates were divided by my favourite brook, was about to be drawn up the glen, in order to substitute its rectilinear deformity for the graceful winding of the natural boundary. As I approached, I was agreeably undeceived. An old man was

seated upon the monument of the slaughtered presbyterians, and busily employed in deepening, with his chisel, the letters of the inscription, which, announcing, in scriptural language, the promised blessings of futurity to be the lot of the slain, anathematised the murderers with corresponding violence. A blue bonnet of unusual dimensions covered the grey hairs of the pious workman. His dress was a large old-fashioned coat of the coarse cloth called *hoddin-grey*, usually worn by the elder peasants, with waistcoat and breeches of the same; and the whole suit, though still in decent repair, had obviously seen a train of long service. Strong clouted shoes, studded with hobnails, and *gramoches* or *leggins*, made of thick black cloth, completed his equipment. Beside him, fed among the graves a pony, the companion of his journey, whose extreme whiteness, as well as its projecting bones and hollow eyes, indicated its antiquity. It was harnessed in the most simple manner, with a pair of branks,[3] a hair tether, or halter, and a *sunk*, or cushion of straw, instead of bridle and saddle. A canvas pouch hung around the neck of the animal, for the purpose, probably, of containing the rider's tools, and any thing else he might have occasion to carry with him. Although I had never seen the old man before, yet from the singularity of his employment, and the style of his equipage, I had no difficulty in recognising a religious itinerant whom I had often heard talked of, and who was known in various parts of Scotland by the title of Old Mortality.

"Where this man was born, or what was his real name, I have never been able to learn; nor are the motives which made him desert his home, and adopt the erratic mode of life which he pursued, known to me except very generally. According to the belief of most people, he was a native of either the county of Dumfries or Galloway, and lineally descended from some of those champions of the Covenant, whose deeds and sufferings were his favourite theme. He is said to have held, at one period of his life, a small moorland farm; but, whether from pecuniary losses, or domestic misfortune, he had long renounced that and every other gainful calling. In the language of Scripture, he left his house, his home, and his kindred, and wandered about until the day of his death, a period of nearly thirty years.

"During this long pilgrimage, the pious enthusiast regulated his circuit so as annually to visit the graves of the unfortunate Covenanters, who suffered by the sword, or by the executioner, during the reigns of the two last mon-

1 John Hampden, who refused to pay taxes levied by Charles I.

2 John Hooper and Bishop Latimer were both burned for heresy in 1555.

3 curbs, or bridle

archs of the Stewart line. These are most numerous in the western districts of Ayr, Galloway, and Dumfries; but they are also to be found in other parts of Scotland, wherever the fugitives had fought, or fallen, or suffered by military or civil execution. Their tombs are often apart from all human habitation, in the remote moors and wilds to which the wanderers had fled for concealment. But wherever they existed, Old Mortality was sure to visit them when his annual round brought them within his reach. In the most lonely recesses of the mountains, the moor-fowl shooter has been often surprised to find him busied in cleaning the moss from the grey stones, renewing with his chisel the half-defaced inscriptions, and repairing the emblems of death with which these simple monuments are usually adorned. Motives of the most sincere, though fanciful devotion, induced the old man to dedicate so many years of existence to perform this tribute to the memory of the deceased warriors of the church. He considered himself as fulfilling a sacred duty, while renewing to the eyes of posterity the decaying emblems of the zeal and sufferings of their forefathers, and thereby trimming, as it were, the beacon-light, which was to warn future generations to defend their religion even unto blood.

"In all his wanderings, the old pilgrim never seemed to need, or was known to accept, pecuniary assistance. It is true, his wants were very few; for wherever he went, he found ready quarters in the house of some Cameronian[4] of his own sect, or of some other religious person. The hospitality which was reverentially paid to him he always acknowledged, by repairing the gravestones (if there existed any) belonging to the family or ancestors of his host. As the wanderer was usually to be seen bent on this pious task within the precincts of some country churchyard, or reclined on the solitary tombstone among the heath, disturbing the plover and the black-cock with the clink of his chisel and mallet, with his old white pony grazing by his side, he acquired from his converse among the dead, the popular appellation of Old Mortality.

"The character of such a man could have in it little connexion even with innocent gaiety. Yet, among those of his own religious persuasion, he is reported to have been cheerful. The descendants of persecutors, or those whom he supposed guilty of entertaining similar tenets, and the scoffers at religion by whom he was sometimes assailed, he usually termed the generation of vipers.[5] Conversing with others, he

was grave and sententious, not without a cast of severity. But he is said never to have been observed to give way to violent passion, excepting upon one occasion, when a mischievous truant-boy defaced with a stone the nose of a cherub's face, which the old man was engaged in retouching. I am in general a sparer of the rod, notwithstanding the maxim of Solomon, for which school-boys have little reason to thank his memory; but on this occasion I deemed it proper to show that I did not hate the child.—But I must return to the circumstances attending my first interview with this interesting enthusiast.

"In accosting Old Mortality, I did not fail to pay respect to his years and his principles, beginning my address by a respectful apology for interrupting his labours. The old man intermitted the operation of the chisel, took off his spectacles and wiped them, then, replacing them on his nose, acknowledged my courtesy by a suitable return. Encouraged by his affability, I intruded upon him some questions concerning the sufferers on whose monument he was now employed. To talk of the exploits of the Covenanters was the delight, as to repair their monuments was the business, of his life. He was profuse in the communication of all the minute information which he had collected concerning them, their wars, and their wanderings. One would almost have supposed he must have been their contemporary, and have actually beheld the passages which he related, so much had he identified his feelings and opinions with theirs, and so much had his narratives the circumstantiality of an eye-witness.

"'We,' he said, in a tone of exultation,—'we are the only true whigs. Carnal men have assumed that triumphant appellation, following him whose kingdom is of this world. Which of them would sit six hours on a wet hill-side to hear a godly sermon? I trow an hour o't wad staw[6] them. They are ne'er a hair better than them that shamena to take upon themsells the persecuting name of bludethirsty tories. Self-seekers all of them, strivers after wealth, power, and worldly ambition, and forgetters alike of what has been dree'd[7] and done by the mighty men who stood in the gap in the great day of wrath. Nae wonder they dread the accomplishment of what was spoken by the mouth of the worthy Mr. Peden[8] (that precious servant of the Lord, none of whose words fell to the ground), that the French monzies[9] sall rise as fast in the

4 An austere sect of Presbyterians.   5 *Matthew* iii, 7. |

6 disgust   7 suffered
8 Alexander Peden, an eloquent minister who was
    supposed to have prophetic gifts.
9 monsieurs (referring to a possible invasion from
    France)

glens of Ayr, and the kenns[10] of Galloway, as ever the Highlandmen did in 1677. And now they are gripping to the bow and to the spear, when they suld be mourning for a sinfu' land and a broken covenant.'

"Soothing the old man by letting his peculiar opinions pass without contradiction, and anxious to prolong conversation with so singular a character, I prevailed upon him to accept that hospitality, which Mr. Cleishbotham is always willing to extend to those who need it. In our way to the schoolmaster's house, we called at the Wallace Inn, where I was pretty certain I should find my patron about that hour of the evening. After a courteous interchange of civilities, Old Mortality was, with difficulty, prevailed upon to join his host in a single glass of liquor, and that on condition that he should be permitted to name the pledge, which he prefaced with a grace of about five minutes, and then, with bonnet doffed and eyes uplifted, drank to the memory of those heroes of the Kirk[11] who had first uplifted her banner upon the mountains. As no persuasion could prevail on him to extend his conviviality to a second cup, my patron accompanied him home, and accommodated him in the Prophet's Chamber, as it is his pleasure to call the closet which holds a spare bed, and which is frequently a place of retreat for the poor traveller.

"The next day I took leave of Old Mortality, who seemed affected by the unusual attention with which I had cultivated his acquaintance and listened to his conversation. After he had mounted, not without difficulty, the old white pony, he took me by the hand and said, 'The blessing of our Master be with you, young man! My hours are like the ears of the latter harvest, and your days are yet in the spring; and yet you may be gathered into the garner of mortality before me, for the sickle of death cuts down the green as oft as the ripe, and there is a colour in your cheek, that, like the bud of the rose, serveth oft to hide the worm of corruption. Wherefore labour as one who knoweth not when his master calleth. And if it be my lot to return to this village after ye are gane hame to your ain place, these auld withered hands will frame a stane of memorial, that your name may not perish from among the people.'

"I thanked Old Mortality for his kind intentions in my behalf, and heaved a sigh, not, I think, of regret so much as of resignation, to think of the chance that I might soon require his good offices. But though, in all human probability, he did not err in supposing that

10 From Gaelic *ceann*, head, headland, mountain.
11 The Scotch, or Presbyterian Church.

my span of life may be abridged in youth, he had over-estimated the period of his own pilgrimage on earth. It is now some years since he has been missed in all his usual haunts, while moss, lichen, and deer-hair, are fast covering those stones, to cleanse which had been the business of his life. About the beginning of this century he closed his mortal toils, being found on the highway near Lockerby, in Dumfriesshire, exhausted and just expiring. The old white pony, the companion of all his wanderings, was standing by the side of his dying master. There was found about his person a sum of money sufficient for his decent interment, which serves to show that his death was in no ways hastened by violence or by want. The common people still regard his memory with great respect; and many are of opinion, that the stones which he repaired will not again require the assistance of the chisel. They even assert that on the tombs where the manner of the martyrs' murder is recorded, their names have remained indelibly legible since the death of Old Mortality, while those of the persecutors, sculptured on the same monuments, have been entirely defaced. It is hardly necessary to say that this is a fond imagination, and that, since the time of the pious pilgrim, the monuments which were the objects of his care are hastening, like all earthly memorials, into ruin or decay.'"

CHARLES LAMB (1775-1834)

FROM ELIA*

DREAM-CHILDREN: A REVERIE

Children love to listen to stories about their elders, when *they* were children; to stretch their imagination to the conception of a traditionary great-uncle, or grandame, whom they never saw. It was in this spirit that my little ones crept about me the other evening to hear about their great-grandmother Field, who lived in a great house in Norfolk (a hundred times bigger than

* "Elia," the signature under which Lamb published his essays in the London Magazine, was the name of an Italian clerk at the South-Sea House where Lamb had been employed nearly thirty years before. The essay entitled *Dream-Children* was written some time after the death of his brother John, late in the year 1821, when he and his sister Mary ("Bridget Elia") were left alone. "Alice W——n" or "Alice Winterton" may have stood, in part at least, for one Ann Simmons (later Mrs. Bartrum) for whom Lamb seems to have felt some attachment. The "great house in Norfolk" was a manor-house in Hertfordshire where his grandmother, Mary Field, had for many years been housekeeper.

hat in which they and papa lived) which had
been the scene (so at least it was generally
believed in that part of the country) of the
tragic incidents which they had lately become
familiar with from the ballad of the Children
in the Wood. Certain it is that the whole story
of the children and their cruel uncle was to be
seen fairly carved out in wood upon the
chimney-piece of the great hall, the whole story
down to the Robin Redbreasts; till a foolish
rich person pulled it down to set up a marble
one of modern invention in its stead, with no
story upon it. Here Alice put out one of her
dear mother's looks, too tender to be called up-
braiding. Then I went on to say how religious
and how good their great-grandmother Field
was, how beloved and respected by everybody,
though she was not indeed the mistress of this
great house, but had only the charge of it
and yet in some respects she might be said to
be the mistress of it too) committed to her by
the owner, who preferred living in a newer and
more fashionable mansion which he had pur-
hased somewhere in the adjoining county; but
till she lived in it in a manner as if it had been
er own, and kept up the dignity of the great
ouse in a sort while she lived, which afterwards came to decay, and was nearly pulled
own, and all its old ornaments stripped and
arried away to the owner's other house, where
hey were set up, and looked as awkward as if
ome one were to carry away the old tombs
hey had seen lately at the Abbey,† and stick
hem up in Lady C.'s tawdry gilt drawing-
oom. Here John smiled, as much as to say,
that would be foolish indeed.'' And then I
old how, when she came to die, her funeral
was attended by a concourse of all the poor,
and some of the gentry too, of the neighbour-
ood for many miles round, to show their re-
ect for her memory, because she had been
uch a good and religious woman; so good in-
eed that she knew all the Psaltery by heart,
y, and a great part of the Testament besides.
ere little Alice spread her hands. Then I told
hat a tall, upright, graceful person their
reat-grandmother Field once was; and how in
er youth she was esteemed the best dancer—
ere Alice's little right foot played an invol-
tary movement, till, upon my looking grave,
desisted—the best dancer, I was saying, in
e county, till a cruel disease, called a cancer,
me, and bowed her down with pain; but it
uld never bend her good spirits, or make
em stoop, but they were still upright, be-

† Lamb was fond of visiting Westminster Abbey,
and he wrote an essay in protest against the
charge for admittance which had lately been
imposed.

cause she was so good and religious. Then I
told how she was used to sleep by herself in a
lone chamber of the great lone house; and how
she believed that an apparition of two infants
was to be seen at midnight gliding up and down
the great staircase near where she slept, but
she said, ''those innocents would do her no
harm;'' and how frightened I used to be,
though in those days I had my maid to sleep
with me, because I was never half so good or
religious as she—and yet I never saw the infants. Here John expanded all his eyebrows
and tried to look courageous. Then I told how
good she was to all her grandchildren, having
us to the great house in the holidays, where I
in particular used to spend many hours by myself, in gazing upon the old busts of the Twelve
Cæsars, that had been Emperors of Rome, till
the old marble heads would seem to live again,
or I to be turned into marble with them; how
I never could be tired with roaming about that
huge mansion, with its vast empty rooms, with
their worn-out hangings, fluttering tapestry,
and carved oaken panels, with the gilding almost rubbed out—sometimes in the spacious
old-fashioned gardens, which I had almost to
myself, unless when now and then a solitary
gardening man would cross me—and how the
nectarines and peaches hung upon the walls,
without my ever offering to pluck them, because they were forbidden fruit, unless now
and then,—and because I had more pleasure in
strolling about among the old melancholy-look-
ing yew-trees, or the firs, and picking up the
red berries, and the fir-apples, which were good
for nothing but to look at—or in lying about
upon the fresh grass with all the fine garden
smells around me—or basking in the orangery,
till I could almost fancy myself ripening too
along with the oranges and the limes in that
grateful warmth—or in watching the dace that
darted to and fro in the fish-pond, at the bottom
of the garden, with here and there a great sulky
pike hanging midway down the water in silent
state, as if it mocked at their impertinent frisk-
ings,—I had more pleasure in these busy-idle
diversions than in all the sweet flavours of
peaches, nectarines, oranges, and such-like common baits of children. Here John slyly deposited back upon the plate a bunch of grapes,
which, not unobserved by Alice, he had meditated dividing with her, and both seemed willing
to relinquish them for the present as irrelevant.
Then, in somewhat a more heightened tone, I
told how, though their great-grandmother Field
loved all her grandchildren, yet in an especial
manner she might be said to love their uncle,
John L——, because he was so handsome and

spirited a youth, and a king to the rest of us; and, instead of moping about in solitary corners, like some of us, he would mount the most mettlesome horse he could get, when but an imp no bigger than themselves, and make it carry him half over the county in a morning, and join the hunters when there were any out —and yet he loved the old great house and gardens too, but had too much spirit to be always pent up within their boundaries—and how their uncle grew up to man's estate as brave as he was handsome, to the admiration of everybody, but of their great-grandmother Field most especially; and how he used to carry me upon his back when I was a lame-footed boy— for he was a good bit older than me—many a mile when I could not walk for pain;—and how in after life he became lame-footed too, and I did not always (I fear) make allowances enough for him when he was impatient, and in pain, nor remember sufficiently how considerate he had been to me when I was lame-footed; and how when he died, though he had not been dead an hour, it seemed as if he had died a great while ago, such a distance there is betwixt life and death; and how I bore his death as I thought pretty well at first, but afterwards it haunted and haunted me; and though I did not cry or take it to heart as some do, and as I think he would have done if I had died, yet I missed him all day long, and knew not till then how much I had loved him. I missed his kindness, and I missed his crossness, and wished him to be alive again, to be quarrelling with him (for we quarrelled sometimes) rather than not have him again, and was as uneasy without him as he their poor uncle must have been when the doctor took off his limb. Here the children fell a crying, and asked if their little mourning which they had on was not for uncle John, and they looked up, and prayed me not to go on about their uncle, but to tell them some stories about their pretty dead mother. Then I told how for seven long years, in hope sometimes, sometimes in despair, yet persisting ever, I courted the fair Alice W——n; and, as much as children could understand, I explained to them what coyness, and difficulty, and denial, meant in maidens—when suddenly, turning to Alice, the soul of the first Alice looked out at her eyes with such a reality of re-presentment, that I became in doubt which of them stood there before me, or whose that bright hair was; and while I stood gazing, both the children gradually grew fainter to my view, receding, and still receding, till nothing at last but two mournful features were seen in the uttermost distance, which, without speech,

strangely impressed upon me the effects of speech: "We are not of Alice, nor of thee, nor are we children at all. The children of Alice call Bartrum father. We are nothing; less than nothing, and dreams. We are only what might have been, and must wait upon the tedious shores of Lethe millions of ages before we have existence and a name"——and immediately awaking, I found myself quietly seated in my bachelor arm-chair, where I had fallen asleep, with the faithful Bridget unchanged by my side—but John L. (or James Elia) was gone forever.

A DISSERTATION UPON ROAST PIG

Mankind, says a Chinese manuscript,[*] which my friend M. was obliging enough to read and explain to me, for the first seventy thousand ages ate their meat raw, clawing or biting it from the living animal, just as they do in Abyssinia to this day. This period is not obscurely hinted at by their great Confucius in the second chapter of his Mundane Mutations, where he designates a kind of golden age by the term Chofang, literally the Cooks' Holiday. The manuscript goes on to say, that the art of roasting, or rather broiling (which I take to be the elder-brother), was accidentally discovered in the manner following. The swineherd, Ho-ti, having gone out into the woods one morning, as his manner was, to collect mast for his hogs, left his cottage in the care of his eldest son Bo-bo, a great lubberly boy, who being fond of playing with fire, as younkers of his age commonly are, let some sparks escape into a bundle of straw, which kindling quickly, spread the conflagration over every part of their poor mansion, till it was reduced to ashes. Together with the cottage (a sorry antediluvian makeshift of a building, you may think it), what was of much more importance, a fine litter of new-farrowed pigs, no less than nine in number, perished. China pigs have been esteemed a luxury all over the East, from the remotest periods that we read of. Bo-bo was in the utmost consternation, as you may think, not so much for the sake of the tenement, which his father and he could easily build up again with a few dry branches, and the labour of an hour or two, at any time, as for the loss of the pigs. While he was thinking what he should say to his father, and wringing his hands over the smoking remnants of one of those untimely

[*] The manuscript, and the Chinese names (except that of Confucius the great philosopher), are fictitious, but the tradition itself, which Lamb obtained from the traveller Thomas Manning is an ancient one.

ufferers, an odour assailed his nostrils, unlike
ny scent which he had before experienced.
What could it proceed from?—not from the
urnt cottage—he had smelt that smell before
—indeed this was by no means the first acci-
ent of the kind which had occurred through
he negligence of this unlucky young fire-brand.
Much less did it resemble that of any known
erb, weed, or flower. A premonitory moisten-
ng at the same time overflowed his nether lip.
He knew not what to think. He next stooped
own to feel the pig, if there were any signs
f life in it. He burnt his fingers, and to cool
hem he applied them in his booby fashion to
is mouth. Some of the crumbs of the scorched
kin had come away with his fingers, and for
he first time in his life (in the world's life
ndeed, for before him no man had known it)
e tasted—*crackling!*[1] Again he felt and fum-
led at the pig. It did not burn him so much
ow; still he licked his fingers from a sort of
abit. The truth at length broke into his slow
nderstanding, that it was the pig that smelt so,
nd the pig that tasted so delicious; and, sur-
endering himself up to the new-born pleasure,
e fell to tearing up whole handfuls of the
corched skin with the flesh next it, and was
ramming it down his throat in his beastly
ashion, when his sire entered amid the smoking
afters, armed with retributory cudgel, and
nding how affairs stood, began to rain blows
pon the young rogue's shoulders, as thick as
ail-stones, which Bo-bo heeded not any more
han if they had been flies. The tickling
leasure, which he experienced in his lower
egions, had rendered him quite callous to any
nconveniences he might feel in those remote
uarters. His father might lay on, but he
ould not beat him from his pig, till he had
airly made an end of it, when, becoming a
ttle more sensible of his situation, something
ke the following dialogue ensued.

"You graceless whelp, what have you got
here devouring? Is it not enough that you
ave burnt me down three houses with your
og's tricks, and be hanged to you! but you
ust be eating fire, and I know not what—what
ave you got there, I say?"

"O father, the pig, the pig! do come and
aste how nice the burnt pig eats."

The ears of Ho-ti tingled with horror. He
ursed his son, and he cursed himself, that ever
e should beget a son that should eat burnt pig.

Bo-bo, whose scent was wonderfully sharp-
ned since morning, soon raked out another pig,
nd fairly rending it asunder, thrust the lesser

half by main force into the fists of Ho-ti, still
shouting out, "Eat, eat, eat the burnt pig,
father; only taste—O Lord!"—with such-like
barbarous ejaculations, cramming all the while
as if he would choke.

Ho-ti trembled every joint while he grasped
the abominable thing, wavering whether he
should not put his son to death for an unnatural young monster, when the crackling
scorching his fingers, as it had done his son's,
and applying the same remedy to them, he in
his turn tasted some of its flavour, which, make
what sour mouths he would for a pretense,
proved not altogether displeasing to him. In
conclusion (for the manuscript here is a little
tedious), both father and son fairly sat down
to the mess, and never left off till they had
despatched all that remained of the litter.

Bo-bo was strictly enjoined not to let the
secret escape, for the neighbours would certainly have stoned them for a couple of abominable wretches, who could think of improving
upon the good meat which God had sent them.
Nevertheless, strange stories got about. It was
observed that Ho-ti's cottage was burnt down
now more frequently than ever. Nothing but
fires from this time forward. Some would
break out in broad day, others in the night-
time. As often as the sow farrowed, so sure
was the house of Ho-ti to be in a blaze; and
Ho-ti himself, which was the more remarkable,
instead of chastising his son, seemed to grow
more indulgent to him than ever. At length
they were watched, the terrible mystery discovered, and father and son summoned to take
their trial at Pekin, then an inconsiderable
assize town. Evidence was given, the obnoxious
food itself produced in court, and verdict about
to be pronounced, when the foreman of the jury
begged that some of the burnt pig, of which
the culprits stood accused, might be handed int>
the box. He handled it, and they all handled
it; and burning their fingers, as Bo-bo and his
father had done before them, and nature
prompting to each of them the same remedy,
against the face of all the facts, and the clearest charge which judge had ever given,—to the
surprise of the whole court, townsfolk, strangers,
reporters, and all present—without leaving the
box, or any manner of consultation whatever,
they brought in a simultaneous verdict of Not
Guilty.

The judge, who was a shrewd fellow, winked
at the manifest iniquity of the decision; and
when the court was dismissed, went privily, and
bought up all the pigs that could be had for
love or money. In a few days his Lordship's
town-house was observed to be on fire. The

The crisp skin of roast pork.

thing took wing, and now there was nothing to be seen but fires in every direction. Fuel and pigs grew enormously dear all over the district. The insurance-offices one and all shut up shop. People built slighter and slighter every day, until it was feared that the very science of architecture would in no long time be lost to the world. Thus this custom of firing houses continued, till in process of time, says my manuscript, a sage arose, like our Locke,[2] who made a discovery, that the flesh of swine, or indeed of any other animal, might be cooked (*burnt*, as they called it) without the necessity of consuming a whole house to dress it. Then first began the rude form of a gridiron. Roasting by the string, or spit, came in a century or two later, I forget in whose dynasty. By such slow degrees, concludes the manuscript, do the most useful, and seemingly the most obvious arts, make their way among mankind.—

Without placing too implicit faith in the account above given, it must be agreed, that if a worthy pretext for so dangerous an experiment as setting houses on fire (especially in these days) could be assigned in favour of any culinary object, that pretext and excuse might be found in ROAST PIG.

Of all the delicacies in the whole *mundus edibilis*,[3] I will maintain it to be the most delicate—*princeps obsoniorum*.[4]

I speak not of your grown porkers—things between pig and pork—those hobbydehoys[5]—but a young and tender suckling—under a moon old—guiltless as yet of the sty—with no original speck of the *amor immunditiæ*,[6] the hereditary failing of the first parent, yet manifest—his voice as yet not broken, but something between a childish treble and a grumble—the mild forerunner, or *præludium*, of a grunt.

He must be roasted. I am not ignorant that our ancestors ate them seethed, or boiled—but what a sacrifice of the exterior tegument!

There is no flavour comparable, I will contend, to that of the crisp, tawny, well-watched, not over-roasted, *crackling*, as it is well called—the very teeth are invited to their share of the pleasure at this banquet in overcoming the coy, brittle resistance—with the adhesive oleaginous—O call it not fat! but an indefinable sweetness growing up to it—the tender blossoming of fat—fat cropped in the bud—taken in the shoot—in the first innocence—the cream and quintessence of the child-pig's yet pure food—the lean, no lean, but a kind of animal manna—or, rather,

fat and lean (if it must be so) so blended and running into each other, that both together make but one ambrosian result, or common substance.

Behold him, while he is "doing"—it seemeth rather a refreshing warmth, than a scorching heat, that he is so passive to. How equably he twirleth round the string!—Now he is just done. To see the extreme sensibility of that tender age! he hath wept out his pretty eyes—radiant jellies—shooting stars[7]—

See him in the dish, his second cradle, how meek he lieth!—wouldst thou have had this innocent grow up to the grossness and indocility which too often accompany maturer swinehood? Ten to one he would have proved a glutton, a sloven, an obstinate disagreeable animal—wallowing in all manner of filthy conversation. From these sins he is happily snatched away—

> Ere sin could blight or sorrow fade,
> Death came with timely care[8]—

his memory is odoriferous—no clown curseth while his stomach half rejecteth, the rank bacon—no coalheaver bolteth him in reeking sausages—he hath a fair sepulchre in the grateful stomach of the judicious epicure—and for such a tomb might be content to die.

He is the best of sapors.[9] Pine-apple is great. She is indeed almost too transcendent—a delight, if not sinful, yet so like to sinning that really a tender-conscienced person would do well to pause—too ravishing for mortal taste, she woundeth and excoriateth the lips that approach her—like lovers' kisses, she biteth—she is a pleasure bordering on pain from the fierceness and insanity of her relish—but she stoppeth at the palate—she meddleth not with the appetite—and the coarsest hunger might barter her consistently for a mutton chop.

Pig—let me speak his praise—is no less provocative of the appetite, than he is satisfactory to the criticalness of the censorious palate. The strong man may batten on him, and the weakling refuseth not his mild juices.

Unlike to mankind's mixed characters, a bundle of virtues and vices, inexplicably intertwisted and not to be unravelled without hazard, he is—good throughout. No part of him is better or worse than another. He helpeth, as far as his little means extend, all around. He is the least envious of banquets. He is all neighbours' fare.

I am one of those who freely and ungrudg-

2 John Locke, a British philosopher.
3 world of edibles
4 chief of tidbits
5 youths at the awkward age
6 love of dirt
7 Ancient superstition regarded certain jelly-like fungi as fallen shooting-stars. Compare moreover, Cornwall's "Out, vile jelly" (*King Lear*, III, vii, 83).
8 Coleridge: *Epitaph on an Infant*.
9 savors

ngly impart a share of the good things of this life which fall to their lot (few as mine are in this kind) to a friend. I protest I take as great an interest in my friend's pleasures, his relishes, and proper satisfactions, as in mine own. "Presents," I often say, "endear Absents." Hares, pheasants, partridges, snipes, barn-door chickens (those "tame villatic[10] fowl"), capons, plovers, brawn,[11] barrels of oysters, I dispense as freely as I receive them. I love to taste them, as it were, upon the tongue of my friend. But a stop must be put somewhere. One would not, like Lear, "give everything."[12] I make my stand upon[13] pig. Methinks it is an ingratitude to the Giver of all good flavours, to extra-domiciliate, or send out of the house slightingly (under pretext of friendship, or I know not what), a blessing so particularly adapted, predestined, I may say, to my individual palate—it argues an insensibility.

I remember a touch of conscience in this kind at school. My good old aunt, who never parted from me at the end of a holiday without stuffing a sweet-meat, or some nice thing, into my pocket, had dismissed me one evening with a smoking plum-cake, fresh from the oven. In my way to school (it was over London Bridge) a gray-headed old beggar saluted me (I have no doubt at this time of day that he was a counterfeit). I had no pence to console him with, and in the vanity of self-denial, and the very coxcombry of charity, schoolboy-like, I made him a present of—the whole cake! I walked on a little, buoyed up, as one is on such occasions, with a sweet soothing of self-satisfaction; but before I had got to the end of the bridge, my better feelings returned, and I burst into tears, thinking how ungrateful I had been to my good aunt, to go and give her good gift away to a stranger that I had never seen before, and who might be a bad man for aught I knew; and then I thought of the pleasure my aunt would be taking in thinking that I—I myself and not another—would eat her nice cake—and what would I say to her the next time I saw her—how naughty I was to part with her pretty present!— and the odour of that spicy cake came back upon my recollection, and the pleasure and the curiosity I had taken in seeing her make it, and her joy when she had sent it to the oven, and how disappointed she would feel that I had never had a bit of it in my mouth at last—and I blamed my impertinent spirit of alms-giving, and out-of-place hypoc-

risy of goodness; and above all, I wished never to see the face again of that insidious, good-for-nothing, old gray impostor.

Our ancestors were nice[14] in their method of sacrificing these tender victims. We read of pigs whipt to death with something of a shock, as we hear of any other obsolete custom. The age of discipline is gone by, or it would be curious to inquire (in a philosophical light merely) what effect this process might have towards intenerating and dulcifying a substance, naturally so mild and dulcet as the flesh of young pigs. It looks like refining a violet. Yet we should be cautious, while we condemn the inhumanity, how we censure the wisdom of the practice. It might impart a gusto—

I remember an hypothesis, argued upon by the young students, when I was at St. Omer's,[15] and maintained with much learning and pleasantry on both sides, "Whether, supposing that the flavour of a pig who obtained his death by whipping (*per flagellationem extremam*) superadded a pleasure upon the palate of a man more intense than any possible suffering we can conceive in the animal, is man justified in using that method of putting the animal to death?" I forget the decision.

His sauce should be considered. Decidedly a few bread crumbs, done up with his liver and brains, and a dash of mild sage. But banish, dear Mrs. Cook, I beseech you, the whole onion tribe. Barbecue your whole hogs to your palate, steep them in shalots, stuff them out with plantations of the rank and guilty garlic; you cannot poison them, or make them stronger than they are—but consider, he is a weakling—a flower.

FROM THE LAST ESSAYS OF ELIA
OLD CHINA

I have an almost feminine partiality for old china. When I go to see any great house, I inquire for the china-closet, and next for the picture-gallery. I cannot defend the order of preference, but by saying that we have all some taste or other, of too ancient a date to admit of our remembering distinctly that it was an acquired one. I can call to mind the first play, and the first exhibition, that I was taken to; but I am not conscious of a time when china jars and saucers were introduced into my imagination.

I had no repugnance then—why should I now have?—to those little, lawless, azure-tinctured

---

farm-yard (Milton: *Samson Agonistes*, line 1695)
11 pickled boar's flesh
12 *King Lear*, II, iv, 253.
13 halt at

14 particular
15 A Jesuit College (Lamb was never a student there).

grotesques, that, under the notion of men and women, float about, uncircumscribed by any element, in that world before perspective—a china tea-cup.

I like to see my old friends—whom distance cannot diminish—figuring up in the air (so they appear to our optics), yet on *terra firma* still—for so we must in courtesy interpret that speck of deeper blue, which the decorous artist, to prevent absurdity, has made to spring up beneath their sandals.

I love the men with women's faces, and the women, if possible, with still more womanish expressions.

Here is a young and courtly Mandarin, handing tea to a lady from a salver—two miles off. See how distance seems to set off respect! And here the same lady, or another—for likeness is identity on tea-cups—is stepping into a little fairy boat, moored on the hither side of this calm garden river, with a dainty mincing foot, which in a right[1] angle of incidence (as angles go in our world) must infallibly land her in the midst of a flowery mead—a furlong off on the other side of the same strange stream!

Farther on—if far or near can be predicated of their world—see horses, trees, pagodas, dancing the hays.[2]

Here—a cow and rabbit couchant and co-extensive—so objects show, seen through the lucid atmosphere of fine Cathay.[3]

I was pointing out to my cousin last evening, over our Hyson[4] (which we are old-fashioned enough to drink unmixed still of an afternoon), some of these *speciosa miracula*[5] upon a set of extraordinary old blue china (a recent purchase) which we were now for the first time using; and could not help remarking, how favourable circumstances had been to us of late years, that we could afford to please the eye sometimes with trifles of this sort—when a passing sentiment seemed to overshade the brows of my companion. I am quick at detecting these summer clouds in Bridget.[6]

"I wish the good old times would come again," she said, "when we were not quite so rich. I do not mean that I want to be poor; but there was a mid'^'e state"—so she was pleased to ramble on—' in which I am sure we were a great deal happier. A purchase is but a purchase, now tl at you have money enough and to spare. Formerly it used to be a triumph. When we coveted a cheap luxury (and O! how much ado I had to get you to consent in those times!) we were used to have a debate two or three days before, and to weigh the *fo* and *against*, and think what we might spare i out of, and what saving we could hit upon, tha' should be an equivalent. A thing was wort buying then when we felt the money that w paid for it.

"Do you remember the brown suit, which yo made to hang upon you, till all your friend cried shame upon you, it grew so threadbare—and all because of that folio Beaumont an Fletcher* which you dragged home late at nigh from Barker's in Covent Garden?[7] Do yo remember how we eyed it for weeks before w could make up our minds to the purchase, an had not come to a determination till it was nea ten o'clock of the Saturday night, when you se off from Islington,[8] fearing you should be to late—and when the old bookseller with som grumbling opened his shop, and by the twinklin taper (for he was setting bedwards) lighted ou the relic from his dusty treasures—and whe you lugged it home, wishing it were twice a cumberso^ >—and when you presented it to m —and wnen we were exploring the perfectnes of it (c ...lating, you called it)—and while I wa repairing some of the loose leaves with past which your impatience would not suffer to l left till day-break—was there no pleasure i being a poor man? or can those neat blac clothes which you wear now, and are so caref to keep brushed, since we have become rich an finical, give you half the honest vanity wit which you flaunted it about in that overwo suit—your old corbeau[9]—for four or five wee longer than you should have done, to paci your conscience for the mighty sum of fifteen or sixteen shillings was it?—a great affair v thought it then—which you had lavished on t old folio. Now that you can afford to buy any bo that pleases you, but I do not see that you ev bring me home any nice old purchases now.

"When you came home with twenty apologi for laying out a less number of shillings up that print after Lionardo,[10] which we christen the 'Lady Blanche;' when you looked at t purchase, and thought of the money—a thought of the money, and looked again at t picture—was there no pleasure in being a po man? Now, you have nothing to do but to wa into Colnaghi's, and buy a wilderness[11] Lionardos. Yet do you?

1 properly calculated
2 An old English dance.
3 Chinese Tartary (used loosely for China)
4 green tea
5 radiant wonders
6 See introductory note on "Elia."
7 A square in the heart of London, best known for its fruit and flower markets.
8 In northern London.
9 black coat
10 Leonardo da Vin the Italian paint
11 *Merchant of Veni* III, i, 128.
* This particular volume, with notes in it Coleridge, is now in the British Museum.

"Then, do you remember our pleasant walks to Enfield, and Potter's Bar, and Waltham,[12] when we had a holiday—holidays and all other fun are gone, now we are rich—and the little handbasket in which I used to deposit our day's fare of savory cold lamb and salad—and how you would pry about at noontide for some decent house, where we might go in, and produce our store—only paying for the ale that you must call for—and speculate upon the looks of the landlady, and whether she was likely to allow us a table-cloth—and wish for such another honest hostess, as Izaak Walton has described many a one on the pleasant banks of the Lea, when he went a-fishing—and sometimes they would prove obliging enough, and sometimes they would look grudgingly upon us—but we had cheerful looks still for one another, and would eat our plain food savorily, scarcely grudging Piscator[13] his Trout Hall? Now, when we go out a day's pleasuring, which is seldom moreover, we *ride* part of the way—and go into a fine inn, and order the best of dinners, never debating the expense—which, after all, never has half the relish of those chance country snaps, when we were at the mercy of uncertain usage, and a precarious welcome.

"You are too proud to see a play anywhere now but in the pit. Do you remember where it was we used to sit, when we saw the Battle of Hexam and the Surrender of Calais,[14] and Bannister[15] and Mrs. Bland in the Children in the Wood[16]—when we squeezed out our shilling-piece to sit three or four times in a season in the one-shilling gallery—where you felt all the time that you ought not to have brought me—and more strongly I felt obligation to you for having brought me—and the pleasure was the better for a little shame—and when the curtain drew up, what cared we for our place in the house, or what mattered it where we were sitting, when our thoughts were with Rosalind in Arden, or with Viola at the court of Illyria?[17] You used to say, that the gallery was the best place of all for enjoying a play socially—that the relish of such exhibitions must be in proportion to the infrequency of going—that the company we met there, not being in general readers of plays, were obliged to attend the more, and did attend, to what was going on, on the stage—because a word lost would have been a chasm, which it was impossible for them to fill up.

With such reflections we consoled our pride then —and I appeal to you, whether, as a woman, I met generally with less attention and accommodation than I have done since in more expensive situations in the house? The getting in indeed, and the crowding up those inconvenient staircases, was bad enough,—but there was still a law of civility to women recognized to quite as great an extent as we ever found in the other passages—and how a little difficulty overcome heightened the snug seat, and the play, afterwards! Now we can only pay our money, and walk in. You cannot see, you say, in the galleries now. I am sure we saw, and heard too, well enough then—but sight, and all, I think is gone with our poverty.

"There was pleasure in eating strawberries, before they became quite common—in the first dish of peas, while they were yet dear—to have them for a nice supper, a treat. What treat can we have now? If we were to treat ourselves now—that is, to have dainties a little above our means, it would be selfish and wicked. It is the very little more that we allow ourselves beyond what the actual poor can get at, that makes what I call a treat—when two people, living together as we have done, now and then indulge themselves in a cheap luxury which both like; while each apologizes, and is willing to take both halves of the blame to his single share. I see no harm in people making much of themselves, in that sense of the word. It may give them a hint how to make much of others. But now—what I mean by the word—we never do make much of ourselves. None but the poor can do it. I do not mean the veriest poor of all, but persons as we were, just above poverty.

"I know what you were going to say, that it is mighty pleasant at the end of the year to make all meet—and much ado we used to have every Thirty-first Night of December to account for our exceedings—many a long face did you make over your puzzled accounts, and in contriving to make it out how we had spent so much—or that we had not spent so much—or that it was impossible we should spend so much next year—and still we found our slender capital decreasing—but then, betwixt ways, and projects, and compromises of one sort or another, and talk of curtailing this charge, and doing without that for the future—and the hope that youth brings, and laughing spirits (in which you were never poor till now), we pocketed up our loss, and in conclusion, with 'lusty brimmers' (as you used to quote it out of *hearty cheerful Mr. Cotton,*[18] as you called

London suburbs.
See Walton's *The Complete Angler,* p. 264.
Plays by George Colman the younger.
15 John Bannister, a pupil of Garrick.
16 A comedy by Thomas Morton.
17 In *As You Like It* and *Twelfth Night.*
18 Charles Cotton: *The New Year.*

him), we used to welcome in the 'coming guest.' Now we have no reckoning at all at the end of the old year—no flattering promises about the new year doing better for us.''

Bridget is so sparing of her speech on most occasions, that when she gets into a rhetorical vein, I am careful how I interrupt it. I could not help, however, smiling at the phantom of wealth which her dear imagination had conjured up out of a clear income of poor —— hundred pounds a year. ''It is true we were happier when we were poorer, but we were also younger, my cousin. I am afraid we must put up with the excess, for if we were to shake the superflux into the sea, we should not much mend ourselves. That we had much to struggle with, as we grew up together, we have reason to be most thankful. It strengthened, and knit our compact closer. We could never have been what we have been to each other, if we had always had the sufficiency which you now complain of. The resisting power—those natural dilations of the youthful spirit, which circumstances cannot straiten—with us are long since passed away. Competence to age is supplementary youth; a sorry supplement indeed, but I fear the best that is to be had. We must ride, where we formerly walked; live better, and lie softer—and shall be wise to do so—than we had means to do in those good old days you speak of. Yet could those days return—could you and I once more walk our thirty miles a-day—could Bannister and Mrs. Bland again be young, and you and I be young to see them—could the good old one-shilling gallery days return—they are dreams, my cousin, now—but could you and I at this moment, instead of this quiet argument, by our well-carpeted fireside, sitting on this luxurious sofa—be once more struggling up those inconvenient staircases, pushed about, and squeezed, and elbowed by the poorest rabble of poor gallery scramblers—could I once more hear those anxious shrieks of yours—and the delicious *Thank God, we are safe,* which always followed when the topmost stair, conquered, let in the first light of the whole cheerful theatre down beneath us—I know not the fathom line that ever touched a descent so deep as I would be willing to bury more wealth in than Crœsus[19] had, or the great Jew R——[20] is supposed to have, to purchase it.

''And now do just look at that merry little Chinese waiter holding an umbrella, big enough for a bed-tester,[21] over the head of that pretty insipid half-Madona-ish chit of a lady in that very blue summer-house.''

19 King of Lydia. 21 bed canopy
20 Rothschild

WALTER SAVAGE LANDOR
(1775-1864)

From IMAGINARY CONVERSATIONS

METELLUS AND MARIUS*

Metellus. Well met, Caius Marius! My orders are to find instantly a centurion who shall mount the walls; one capable of observation, acute in remark, prompt, calm, active, intrepid. The Numantians are sacrificing to the gods in secrecy; they have sounded the horn only once, —and hoarsely and low and mournfully.

Marius. Was that ladder I see yonder among the caper-bushes and purple lilies, under where the fig-tree grows out of the rampart, left for me?

Metellus. Even so, wert thou willing. Wouldst thou mount it?

Marius. Rejoicingly. If none are below or near, may I explore the state of things by entering the city?

Metellus. Use thy discretion in that. What seest thou? Wouldst thou leap down? Lift the ladder.

Marius. Are there spikes in it where it sticks in the turf? I should slip else.

Metellus. How! bravest of our centurions art even thou afraid? Seest thou any one by?

Marius. Ay; some hundreds close beneath me.

Metellus. Retire, then. Hasten back; I will protect thy descent.

Marius. May I speak, O Metellus, without an offence to discipline?

Metellus. Say.

Marius. Listen! Dost thou not hear?

Metellus. Shame on thee! alight, alight! my shield shall cover thee.

Marius. There is a murmur like the hum of bees in the bean-field of Cereaté;[1] for the sun is hot, and the ground is thirsty. When will i

1 The rustic home of Marius's childhood, near Arpinum.
* The siege and capture, in 132 B. C., of the Numantians, struggling with 8,000 men against the whole power of Rome, was one of the stages in the disgraceful third Punic war which was conducted by Scipio Africanus the Younger. Caius Cæcilius Metellus, the tribune, was a comparatively unimportant personage. Marius, the centurion, of obscure birth, rose later to be seven times consul. Plutarch tells us that Scipio had marked the youth's good qualities, and when asked who should succeed himself in case of accident, had touched the shoulder of Marius, saying, "Perhaps this man;" which saying "raised the hopes of Marius like a divine oracle." On this slight historical foundation Landor constructs his dramatic scene. The Numantians, in all probability, had no regular walls; and Appian says that some of them preferred surrender to death and were led in a Roman Triumph.

have drunk up for me the blood that has run, and is yet oozing on it, from those fresh bodies!

Metellus. How! We have not fought for many days; what bodies, then, are fresh ones?

Marius. Close beneath the wall are those of infants and of girls; in the middle of the road are youths, emaciated; some either unwounded or wounded months ago; some on their spears, others on their swords: no few have received in mutual death the last interchange of friendship; their daggers unite them, hilt to hilt, bosom to bosom.

Metellus. Mark rather the living,—what are they about?

Marius. About the sacrifice, which portends them, I conjecture, but little good,—it burns sullenly and slowly. The victim will lie upon the pyre till morning, and still be unconsumed, unless they bring more fuel.

I will leap down and walk on cautiously, and return with tidings, if death should spare me.

Never was any race of mortals so unmilitary as these Numantians; no watch, no stations, no palisades across the streets.

Metellus. Did they want, then, all the wood for the altar?

Marius. It appears so—I will return anon.

Metellus. The gods speed thee, my brave, honest Marius!

Marius (returned). The ladder should have been better spiked for that slippery ground. I am down again safe, however. Here a man may walk securely, and without picking his steps.

Metellus. Tell me, Caius, what thou sawest.

Marius. The streets of Numantia.

Metellus. Doubtless; but what else?

Marius. The temples and markets and places of exercise and fountains.

Metellus. Art thou crazed, centurion? what more? Speak plainly, at once, and briefly.

Marius. I beheld, then, all Numantia.

Metellus. Has terror maddened thee? hast thou descried nothing of the inhabitants but those carcasses under the ramparts?

Marius. Those, O Metellus, lie scattered, although not indeed far asunder. The greater part of the soldiers and citizens—of the fathers, husbands, widows, wives, espoused— were assembled together.

Metellus. About the altar?

Marius. Upon it.

Metellus. So busy and earnest in devotion! but how all upon it?

Marius. It blazed under them, and over them, and round about them.

Metellus. Immortal gods! Art thou sane, Caius Marius? Thy visage is scorched: thy speech may wander after such an enterprise; thy shield burns my hand!

Marius. I thought it had cooled again. Why, truly, it seems hot: I now feel it.

Metellus. Wipe off those embers.

Marius. 'Twere better: there will be none opposite to shake them upon, for some time.

The funereal horn, that sounded with such feebleness, sounded not so from the faint heart of him who blew it. Him I saw; him only of the living. Should I say it? there was another: there was one child whom its parent could not kill, could not part from. She had hidden it in her robe, I suspect; and, when the fire had reached it, either it shrieked or she did. For suddenly a cry pierced through the crackling pinewood, and something of round in figure fell from brand to brand, until it reached the pavement, at the feet of him who had blown the horn. I rushed toward him, for I wanted to hear the whole story, and felt the pressure of time. Condemn not my weakness, O Cæcilius! I wished an enemy to live an hour longer; for my orders were to explore and bring intelligence. When I gazed on him, in height almost gigantic, I wondered not that the blast of his trumpet was so weak: rather did I wonder that Famine, whose hand had indented every limb and feature, had left him any voice articulate. I rushed toward him, however, ere my eyes had measured either his form or strength. He held the child against me, and staggered under it.

"Behold," he exclaimed, "the glorious ornament of a Roman triumph!"

I stood horror-stricken; when suddenly drops, as of rain, pattered down from the pyre. I looked; and many were the precious stones, many were the amulets and rings and bracelets, and other barbaric ornaments, unknown to me in form or purpose, that tinkled on the hardened and black branches, from mothers and wives and betrothed maids; and some, too, I can imagine, from robuster arms—things of joyance, won in battle. The crowd of incumbent bodies was so dense and heavy, that neither the fire nor the smoke could penetrate upward from among them; and they sank, whole and at once, into the smouldering cavern eaten out below. He at whose neck hung the trumpet felt this, and started.

"There is yet room," he cried, "and there is strength enough yet, both in the element and in me."

He extended his withered arms, he thrust forward the gaunt links of his throat, and upon gnarled knees, that smote each other audibly, tottered into the civic[2] fire. It—like some hungry and strangest beast on the innermost wild of Africa, pierced, broken, prostrate, motionless, gazed at by its hunter in the impatience of glory, in the delight of awe—panted once more, and seized him.

I have seen within this hour, O Metellus, what Rome in the cycle of her triumphs will never see, what the Sun in his eternal course can never show her, what the Earth has borne but now, and must never rear again for her, what Victory herself has envied her,—a Numantian.

Metellus. We shall feast to-morrow. Hope, Caius Marius, to become a tribune: trust in fortune.

Marius. Auguries are surer: surest of all is perseverance.

Metellus. I hope the wine has not grown vapid in my tent: I have kept it waiting, and must now report to Scipio the intelligence of our discovery. Come after me, Caius.

Marius (alone). The tribune is the discoverer! the centurion is the scout! Caius Marius must enter more Numantias. Lighthearted Cæcilius, thou mayest perhaps hereafter, and not with humbled but with exulting pride, take orders from this hand. If Scipio's words are fate, and to me they sound so, the portals of the Capitol may shake before my chariot, as my horses plunge back at the applauses of the people, and Jove in his high domicile[3] may welcome the citizen of Arpinum.

Leofric and Godiva*

Godiva. There is a dearth in the land, my sweet Leofric! Remember how many weeks of drought we have had, even in the deep pastures of Leicestershire; and how many Sundays we have heard the same prayers for rain, and supplications that it would please the Lord in his mercy to turn aside his anger from the poor, pining cattle. You, my dear husband, have imprisoned more than one malefactor for leaving his dead ox in the public way; and other hinds[4] have fled before you out of the traces, in which they, and their sons and their daughters, and

haply their old fathers and mothers, were dragging the abandoned wain homeward. Although we were accompanied by many brave spearmen and skilful archers, it was perilous to pass the creatures which the farm-yard dogs, driven from the hearth by the poverty of their masters, were tearing and devouring; while others, bitten and lamed, filled the air either with long and deep howls or sharp and quick barkings, as they struggled with hunger and feebleness, or were exasperated by heat and pain. Nor could the thyme from the heath, nor the bruised branches of the fir-tree, extinguish or abate the foul odour.

Leofric. And now, Godiva, my darling, thou art afraid we should be eaten up before we enter the gates of Coventry; or perchance that in the gardens there are no roses to greet thee, no sweet herbs for thy mat and pillow.

Godiva. Leofric, I have no such fears. This is the month of roses: I find them everywhere since my blessed marriage. They, and all other sweet herbs, I know not why, seem to greet me wherever I look at them, as though they knew and expected me. Surely they cannot feel that I am fond of them.

Leofric. O light, laughing simpleton! But what wouldst thou? I came not hither to pray; and yet if praying would satisfy thee, or remove the drought, I would ride up straightway to Saint Michael's and pray until morning.

Godiva. I would do the same, O Leofric! but God hath turned away his ear from holier lips than mine. Would my own dear husband hear me, if I implored him for what is easier to accomplish,—what he can do like God?

Leofric. How! what is it?

Godiva. I would not, in the first hurry of your wrath, appeal to you, my loving Lord, in behalf of these unhappy men who have offended you.

Leofric. Unhappy! is that all?

Godiva. Unhappy they must surely be, to have offended you so grievously. What a soft air breathes over us! how quiet and serene and still an evening! how calm are the heavens and the earth!—Shall none enjoy them; not even we, my Leofric? The sun is ready to set: let it never set, O Leofric, on your anger. These are not my words: they are better than mine.[5] Should they lose their virtue from my unworthiness in uttering them?

Leofric. Godiva, wouldst thou plead to me for rebels?

Godiva. They have, then, drawn the sword against you? Indeed, I knew it not.

Leofric. They have omitted to send me my dues, established by my ancestors, well knowing of our nuptials, and of the charges and festivities they require, and that in a season of such scarcity my own lands are insufficient.

Godiva. If they were starving, as they said they were——

Leofric. Must I starve too? Is it not enough to lose my vassals?

Godiva. Enough! O God! too much! too much! May you never lose them! Give them life, peace, comfort, contentment. There are those among them who kissed me in my infancy, and who blessed me at the baptismal font. Leofric, Leofric! the first old man I meet I shall think is one of those; and I shall think on the blessing he gave me, and (ah me!) on the blessing I bring back to him. My heart will bleed, will burst; and he will weep at it! he will weep, poor soul, for the wife of a cruel lord who denounces vengeance on him, who carries death into his family!

Leofric. We must hold solemn festivals.

Godiva. We must, indeed.

Leofric. Well, then?

Godiva. Is the clamorousness that succeeds the death of God's dumb creatures, are crowded halls, are slaughtered cattle, festivals?—are maddening songs, and giddy dances, and hireling praises from parti-coloured coats? Can the voice of a minstrel tell us better things of ourselves than our own internal one might tell us; or can his breath make our breath softer in sleep? O my beloved! let everything be a joyance to us: it will, if we will. Sad is the day, and worse must follow, when we hear the blackbird in the garden, and do not throb with joy. But, Leofric, the high festival is strown by the servant of God upon the heart of man. It is gladness, it is thanksgiving; it is the orphan, the starveling, pressed to the bosom, and bidden as its first commandment to remember its benefactor. We will hold this festival; the guests are ready; we may keep it up for weeks, and months, and years together, and always be the happier and the richer for it. The beverage of this feast, O Leofric, is sweeter than bee or flower or vine can give us:[6] it flows from heaven; and in heaven will it abundantly be poured out again to him who pours it out here unsparingly.

Leofric. Thou art wild.

Godiva. I have, indeed, lost myself. Some Power, some good kind Power, melts me (body and soul and voice) into tenderness and love. O

6 Honey, nectar, and wine are the constituents of mead.

my husband, we must obey it. Look upon me! look upon me! lift your sweet eyes from the ground! I will not cease to supplicate; I dare not.

Leofric. We may think upon it.

Godiva. Never say that! What! think upon goodness when you can be good? Let not the infants cry for sustenance! The mother of our blessed Lord will hear them; us never, never afterward.

Leofric. Here comes the Bishop: we are but one mile from the walls. Why dismountest thou? no bishop can expect it. Godiva! my honour and rank among men are humbled by this. Earl Godwin will hear of it. Up! up! the Bishop hath seen it: he urgeth his horse onward. Dost thou not hear him now upon the solid turf behind thee?

Godiva. Never, no, never will I rise, O Leofric, until you remit this most impious tax —this tax on hard labour, on hard life.

Leofric. Turn round: look how the fat nag canters, as to the tune of a sinner's psalm, slow and hard-breathing. What reason or right can the people have to complain, while their bishop's steed is so sleek and well caparisoned? Inclination to change, desire to abolish old usages.—Up! up! for shame! They shall smart for it, idlers! Sir Bishop, I must blush for my young bride.

Godiva. My husband, my husband! will you pardon the city?

Leofric. Sir Bishop! I could not think you would have seen her in this plight. Will I pardon? Yea, Godiva, by the holy rood, will I pardon the city, when thou ridest naked at noontide through the streets!

Godiva. O my dear, cruel Leofric, where is the heart you gave me? It was not so: can mine have hardened it?

Bishop. Earl, thou abashest thy spouse; she turneth pale, and weepeth. Lady Godiva, peace be with thee.

Godiva. Thanks, holy man! peace will be with me when peace is with your city. Did you hear my Lord's cruel word?

Bishop. I did, lady.

Godiva. Will you remember it, and pray against it?

Bishop. Wilt *thou* forget it, daughter?

Godiva. I am not offended.

Bishop. Angel of peace and purity!

Godiva. But treasure it up in your heart: deem it an incense, good only when it is consumed and spent, ascending with prayer and sacrifice. And, now, what was it?

Bishop. Christ save us! that he will pardon

the city when thou ridest naked through the streets at noon.

Godiva. Did he not swear an oath?

Bishop. He sware by the holy rood.

Godiva. My Redeemer, thou hast heard it! save the city!

Leofric. We are now upon the beginning of the pavement: these are the suburbs. Let us think of feasting: we may pray afterward; to-morrow we shall rest.

Godiva. No judgments, then, to-morrow, Leofric?

Leofric. None: we will carouse.

Godiva. The saints of heaven have given me strength and confidence; my prayers are heard; the heart of my beloved is now softened.

Leofric (aside). Ay, ay—they shall smart, though.

Godiva. Say, dearest Leofric, is there indeed no other hope, no other mediation?

Leofric. I have sworn. Beside, thou hast made me redden and turn my face away from thee, and all the knaves have seen it: this adds to the city's crime.

Godiva. I have blushed too, Leofric, and was not rash nor obdurate.

Leofric. But thou, my sweetest, art given to blushing: there is no conquering it in thee. I wish thou hadst not alighted so hastily and roughly: it hath shaken down a sheaf of thy hair. Take heed thou sit not upon it, lest it anguish thee. Well done! it mingleth now sweetly with the cloth of gold upon the saddle, running here and there, as if it had life and faculties and business, and were working thereupon some newer and cunninger device. O my beauteous Eve! there is a Paradise about thee! the world is refreshed as thou movest and breathest on it. I cannot see or think of evil where thou art. I could throw my arms even here about thee. No signs for me! no shaking of sunbeams! no reproof or frown or wonderment—I *will* say it—now, then, for worse—I could close with my kisses thy half-open lips, ay, and those lovely and loving eyes, before the people.

Godiva. To-morrow you shall kiss me, and they shall bless you for it. I shall be very pale, for to-night I must fast and pray.

Leofric. I do not hear thee; the voices of the folk are so loud under this archway.

Godiva (to herself). God help them! good kind souls! I hope they will not crowd about me so to-morrow. O Leofric! could my name be forgotten, and yours alone remembered! But perhaps my innocence may save me from reproach; and how many as innocent are in fear and famine! No eye will open on me but fresh from tears. What a young mother for so

large a family! Shall my youth harm me? Under God's hand it gives me courage. Ah! when will the morning come? Ah! when will the noon be over?

THOMAS DE QUINCEY
(1785-1859)

FROM CONFESSIONS OF AN ENGLISH OPIUM-EATER*
THE PAINS OF OPIUM

I now pass to what is the main subject of these latter confessions; to the history and journal of what took place in my dreams; for these were the immediate and proximate cause of my acutest suffering.

The first notice I had of any important change going on in this part of my physical economy, was from the re-awakening of a state of eye generally incident to childhood, or exalted states of irritability. I know not whether my reader is aware that many children, perhaps most, have a power of painting, as it were, upon the darkness, all sorts of phantoms; in some, that power is simply a mechanic affection of the eye; others have a voluntary, or semi-voluntary power to dismiss or to summon them; or, as a child once said to me when I questioned him on this matter, "I can tell them to go, and they go; but sometimes they come, when I don't tell them to come." Whereupon I told him that he had almost as unlimited a command over apparitions as a Roman centurion over his soldiers. In the middle of 1817, I think it was, that this faculty became positively distressing to me: at night, when I lay awake in bed, vast processions passed along in mournful pomp;

---

* De Quincey says: *"The Opium Confessions* were written with some slight secondary purpose of exposing the specific power of opium upon the faculty of dreaming, but much more with the purpose of displaying the faculty itself." And again: "The machinery for dreaming planted in the human brain was not planted for nothing. That faculty, in alliance with the mystery of darkness, is the one great tube through which man communicates with the shadowy. And the dreaming organ, in connection with the heart, the eye, and the ear, compose the magnificent apparatus which forces the infinite into the chambers of the human brain, and throws dark reflections from eternities below all life upon the mirrors of that mysterious *camera obscura*—the sleeping mind." Such, in substance, is De Quincey's account of what may very well be regarded as an almost unique contribution to the literature of the world. To English literature he has made, moreover, the important contribution of a style of "impassioned prose" which has no counterpart. See *Eng. Lit.* p. 275. Late in life, he revised his *Confessions*, but the early text of 1821-1822 is from a rhetorical point of view generally the superior and is here retained.

friezes of never-ending stories, that to my feel-ings were as sad and solemn as if they were stories drawn from times before Œdipus or Priam—before Tyre—before Memphis.[1] And, at the same time, a corresponding change took place in my dreams; a theatre seemed suddenly opened and lighted up within my brain, which presented nightly spectacles of more than earthly splendour. And the four following facts may be mentioned, as noticeable at this time:

1. That as the creative state of the eye in-creased, a sympathy seemed to arise between the waking and the dreaming states of the brain in one point—that whatsoever I happened to call up and to trace by a voluntary act upon the darkness was very apt to transfer itself to my dreams; so that I feared to exercise this faculty; for, as Midas turned all things to gold, that yet baffled his hopes and defrauded his human desires, so whatsoever things capable of being visually represented I did but think of in the darkness, immediately shaped themselves into phantoms of the eye; and, by a process apparently no less inevitable, when thus once traced in faint and visionary colours, like writings in sympathetic ink, they were drawn out by the fierce chemistry of my dreams, into insufferable splendour that fretted my heart.

2. For this, and all other changes in my dreams, were accompanied by deep-seated anxi-ety and gloomy melancholy, such as are wholly incommunicable by words. I seemed every night to descend, not metaphorically, but liter-ally to descend, into chasms and sunless abysses, depths below depths, from which it seemed hopeless that I could ever re-ascend. Nor did I, by waking, feel that I *had* re-ascended. This I do not dwell upon; because the state of gloom which attended these gorgeous spectacles, amounting at last to utter darkness, as of some suicidal despondency, cannot be approached by words.

3. The sense of space, and, in the end, the sense of time, were both powerfully affected. Buildings, landscapes, etc., were exhibited in proportions so vast as the bodily eye is not fit-ted to receive. Space swelled, and was ampli-fied to an extent of unutterable infinity. This, however, did not disturb me so much as the vast expansion of time; I sometimes seemed to have lived for seventy or a hundred years in one night; nay, sometimes had feelings representa-tive of a millennium passed in that time, or, however,[2] of a duration far beyond the limits of any human experience.

4. The minutest incidents of childhood, or

forgotten scenes of later years, were often re-vived; I could not be said to recollect them; for if I had been told of them when waking, I should not have been able to acknowledge them as parts of my past experience. But placed as they were before me, in dreams like intuitions, and clothed in all their evanescent circumstances and accompanying feelings, I *recognised* them instantaneously. I was once told by a near relative of mine, that having in her childhood fallen into a river, and being on the very verge of death but for the critical assistance which reached her, she saw in a moment her whole life, in its minutest incidents, arrayed before her simultaneously as in a mirror; and she had a faculty developed as suddenly for comprehend-ing the whole and every part. This, from some opium experiences of mine, I can believe; I have, indeed, seen the same thing asserted twice in modern books, and accompanied by a remark which I am convinced is true—viz., that the dread book of account, which the Scriptures speak of,[3] is, in fact, the mind itself of each individual. Of this, at least, I feel assured, that there is no such thing as *forgetting* pos-sible to the mind; a thousand accidents may and will interpose a veil between our present consciousness and the secret inscriptions on the mind; accidents of the same sort will also rend away this veil; but alike, whether veiled or unveiled, the inscription remains for ever; just as the stars seem to withdraw before the com-mon light of day, whereas, in fact, we all know that it is the light which is drawn over them as a veil, and that they are waiting to be revealed when the obscuring daylight shall have withdrawn.

Having noticed these four facts as memorably distinguishing my dreams from those of health, I shall now cite a case illustrative of the first fact; and shall then cite any others that I re-member, either in their chronological order, or any other that may give them more effect as pictures to the reader.

I had been in youth, and even since, for occa-sional amusement, a great reader of Livy, whom, I confess, that I prefer, both for style and mat-ter, to any other of the Roman historians; and I had often felt as most solemn and appalling sounds, and most emphatically representative of the majesty of the Roman people, the two words so often occurring in Livy—*Consul Romanus;* especially when the consul is introduced in his military character. I mean to say that the words king—sultan—regent, etc., or any other titles of those who embody in their own persons the collective majesty of a great people, had

---

1 Greece, Phoenicia, Egypt, form a climax of an-tiquity.   2 at any rate.   3 *Revelation,* xx, 12.

less power over my reverential feelings. I had also, though no great reader of history, made myself minutely and critically familiar with one period of English history—viz., the period of the Parliamentary War—having been attracted by the moral grandeur of some who figured in that day, and by the many interesting memoirs which survive those unquiet times. Both these parts of my lighter reading, having furnished me often with matter of reflection, now furnished me with matter for my dreams. Often I used to see, after painting upon the blank darkness a sort of rehearsal whilst waking, a crowd of ladies, and perhaps a festival, and dances. And I heard it said, or I said to myself, "These are English ladies from the unhappy times of Charles I. These are the wives and the daughters of those who met in peace, and sat at the same tables, and were allied by marriage or by blood; and yet, after a certain day in August, 1642,[4] never smiled upon each other again, nor met but in the field of battle; and at Marston Moor, at Newbury, or at Naseby, cut asunder all ties of love by the cruel sabre, and washed away in blood the memory of ancient friendship." The ladies danced, and looked as lovely as the court of George IV. Yet I knew, even in my dreams, that they had been in the grave for nearly two centuries. This pageant would suddenly dissolve; and, at a clapping of hands, would be heard the heart-quaking sound of *Consul Romanus;* and immediately came "sweeping by," in gorgeous paludaments,[5] Paulus or Marius,[6] girt round by a company of centurions, with the crimson tunic hoisted on a spear,[7] and followed by the *alalagmos*[8] of the Roman legions.

· · · · · · · ·

And now came a tremendous change, which, unfolding itself slowly like a scroll, through many months, promised an abiding torment; and, in fact, it never left me until the winding up of my case. Hitherto the human face had mixed often in my dreams, but not despotically, nor with any special power of tormenting. But now that which I have called the tyranny of the human face began to unfold itself. Perhaps some part of my London life might be answerable for this. Be that as it may, now it was that upon the rocking waters of the ocean the human face began to appear: the sea appeared

paved with innumerable faces, upturned to th[e] heavens; faces imploring, wrathful, despairing surged upwards by thousands, by myriads, b[y] generations, by centuries:—my agitation wa[s] infinite,—my mind tossed—and surged with th[e] ocean.

May, 1818.

The Malay[9] has been a fearful enemy fo[r] months. I have been every night, through hi[s] means, transported into Asiatic scenes. I know not whether others share in my feelings on thi[s] point; but I have often thought that if I wer[e] compelled to forego England, and to live i[n] China, and among Chinese manners and mode[s] of life and scenery, I should go mad. Th[e] causes of my horror lie deep; and some of them must be common to others. Southern Asia, i[n] general, is the seat of awful images and associations. As the cradle of the human race, i[t] would alone have a dim and reverential feeling connected with it. But there are other reasons No man can pretend that the wild, barbarous and capricious superstitions of Africa, or of savage tribes elsewhere, affect him in the way that he is affected by the ancient, monumental, cruel, and elaborate religions of Indostan, etc. The mere antiquity of Asiatic things, of their institutions, histories, modes of faith, etc., is so impressive, that to me the vast age of the race and name overpowers the sense of youth in the individual. A young Chinese seems to me an antediluvian man renewed. Even Englishmen, though not bred in any knowledge o[f] such institutions, cannot but shudder at the mystic sublimity of *castes* that have flowed apart, and refused to mix, through such immemorial tracts of time; nor can any man fail to be awed by the names of the Ganges, or the Euphrates. It contributes much to these feelings, that Southern Asia is, and has been for thousands of years, the part of the earth most swarming with human life; the great *officina gentium.*[10] Man is a weed in those regions. The vast empires also, in which the enormous population of Asia has always been cast, give a further sublimity to the feelings associated with all oriental names or images. In China, over and above what it has in common with the rest of Southern Asia, I am terrified by the modes of life, by the manners, and the barrier of utter abhorrence, and want of sympathy, placed between us by feelings deeper than I can analyse. I could sooner live with lunatics, or brute animals. All this, and much more than

4 Charles's standard was raised, giving the signal for civil war, August 22, 1642.
5 military cloaks
6 For this latter Consul, see note to Landor's *Metellus and Marius*, p. 512.
7 A signal of battle.
8 "A word expressing collectively the gathering of the Roman war-cries— *Alála, Alála.*"—De Quincey.

9 A Malay, as related in an earlier part of the Confessions, once knocked at De Quincey's door.
10 laboratory of nations

can say, or have time to say, the reader must
[en]ter into before he can comprehend the un-
[im]aginable horror which these dreams of orien-
[ta]l imagery, and mythological tortures, im-
[p]ressed upon me. Under the connecting feeling
[of] tropical heat and vertical sun-lights, I
[b]rought together all creatures, birds, beasts,
[re]ptiles, all trees and plants, usages and appear-
[a]nces, that are found in all tropical regions,
[a]nd assembled them together in China or Indo-
[st]an. From kindred feelings, I soon brought
[E]gypt and all her gods under the same law.
[I] was stared at, hooted at, grinned at, chat-
[t]ered at, by monkeys, by paroquets, by cocka-
[to]os. I ran into pagodas: and was fixed, for
[c]enturies, at the summit, or in secret rooms;
[I] was the idol; I was the priest; I was wor-
[s]hipped; I was sacrificed. I fled from the
[w]rath of Brama through all the forests of
[A]sia: Vishnu hated me: Seeva laid wait for
[m]e.11 I came suddenly upon Isis and Osiris:
[I] had done a deed, they said, which the ibis
[a]nd the crocodile trembled at. I was buried,
[f]or a thousand years, in stone coffins, with
[m]ummies and sphinxes, in narrow chambers
[a]t the heart of eternal pyramids. I was kissed,
[w]ith cancerous kisses, by crocodiles; and laid,
[c]onfounded with all unutterable slimy things,
[a]mongst reeds and Nilotic mud.

I thus give the reader some slight abstraction
[o]f my oriental dreams, which always filled me
[w]ith such amazement at the monstrous scenery,
[t]hat horror seemed absorbed, for a while, in
[s]heer astonishment. Sooner or later, came a
[r]eflux of feeling that swallowed up the aston-
[i]shment, and left me, not so much in terror, as
[i]n hatred and abomination of what I saw. Over
[e]very form, and threat, and punishment, and
[d]im sightless incarceration, brooded a sense of
[e]ternity and infinity that drove me into an
[o]ppression as of madness. Into these dreams
[o]nly, it was, with one or two slight exceptions,
[t]hat any circumstances of physical horror en-
[t]ered. All before had been moral and spiritual
[e]rrors. But here the main agents were ugly
[b]irds, or snakes, or crocodiles; especially the
[l]ast. The cursed crocodile became to me the
[o]bject of more horror than almost all the rest.
[I] was compelled to live with him; and (as was
[a]lways the case almost in my dreams) for cen-
[t]uries. I escaped sometimes, and found myself
[i]n Chinese houses, with cane tables, etc. All
[t]he feet of the tables, sofas, etc., soon became

instinct with life: the abominable head of the
crocodile, and his leering eyes, looked out at
me, multiplied into a thousand repetitions: and
I stood loathing and fascinated. And so often
did this hideous reptile haunt my dreams, that
many times the very same dream was broken
up in the very same way: I heard gentle voices
speaking to me (I hear everything when I am
sleeping); and instantly I awoke: it was broad
noon; and my children were standing, hand in
hand, at my bed-side; come to show me their
coloured shoes, or new frocks, or to let me see
them dressed for going out. I protest that so
awful was the transition from the damned crocodile, and the other unutterable monsters and
abortions of my dreams, to the sight of innocent *human* natures and of infancy, that, in
the mighty and sudden revulsion of mind, I
wept, and could not forbear it, as I kissed their
faces.

FROM SUSPIRIA DE PROFUNDIS*

LEVANA AND OUR LADIES OF SORROW

Oftentimes at Oxford I saw Levana in my
dreams. I knew her by her Roman symbols.
Who is Levana? Reader, that do not pretend
to have leisure for very much scholarship, you
will not be angry with me for telling you.
Levana was the Roman goddess that performed
for the new-born infant the earliest office of
ennobling kindness,—typical, by its mode, of
that grandeur which belongs to man everywhere,
and of that benignity in powers invisible which
even in Pagan worlds sometimes descends to
sustain it. At the very moment of birth, just
as the infant tasted for the first time the atmosphere of our troubled planet, it was laid on the
ground. *That* might bear different interpreta-
tions. But immediately, lest so grand a creature should grovel there for more than one
instant, either the paternal hand, as proxy for
the goddess Levana, or some near kinsman, as

---

11 Brahma the creator, Vishnu the preserver, and
Siva the destroyer, constitute the great triad
of Hindu mythology. Osiris the creator, and
Isis, his sister and wife, were Egyptian
deities, and the ibis and crocodile were regarded as sacred animals.

* *Suspiria de Profundis* (Sighs from the Depths)
is the title under which De Quincey began in
1845 to publish a series of articles which were
to have closed with a crowning succession of
"some twenty or twenty-five dreams and noonday visions." Most of the articles were either
never written or were destroyed. Of *Levana*,
one of the earliest, Professor Masson has said
that "it is a permanent addition to the mythology of the human race," typifying as it
does "the varieties and degrees of misery that
there are in the world." As for De Quincey's
own education through initiation into these
several degrees of sorrow, it is to be remembered that in childhood he lost by death his
father and two sisters, in youth he ran away
from an uncongenial school and wandered like
an outcast in Wales and London, and in manhood his body, intellect, and will became
enslaved to opium.

proxy for the father, raised it upright, bade it look erect as the king of all this world, and presented its forehead to the stars, saying, perhaps, in his heart, ''Behold what is greater than yourselves!'' This symbolic act represented the function of Levana. And that mysterious lady, who never revealed her face (except to me in dreams), but always acted by delegation, had her name from the Latin verb (as still it is the Italian verb) *levare,* to raise aloft.

This is the explanation of Levana, and hence it has arisen that some people have understood by Levana the tutelary power that controls the education of the nursery. She, that would not suffer at his birth even a prefigurative or mimic degradation for her awful ward, far less could be supposed to suffer the real degradation attaching to the non-development of his powers. She therefore watches over human education. Now the word *edŭco,* with the penultimate short, was derived (by a process often exemplified in the crystallisation of languages) from the word *edūco,* with the penultimate long. Whatsoever *educes,* or develops, *educates.* By the education of Levana, therefore, is meant,—not the poor machinery that moves by spelling-books and grammars, but that mighty system of central forces hidden in the deep bosom of human life, which by passion, by strife, by temptation, by the energies of resistance, works for ever upon children,—resting not day or night, any more than the mighty wheel of day and night themselves, whose moments, like restless spokes, are glimmering for ever as they revolve.

If, then, *these* are the ministries by which Levana works, how profoundly must she reverence the agencies of grief! But you, reader, think that children generally are not liable to grief such as mine. There are two senses in the word *generally,*—the sense of Euclid, where it means *universally* (or in the whole extent of the *genus*), and a foolish sense of this word, where it means *usually.* Now, I am far from saying that children universally are capable of grief like mine. But there are more than you ever heard of who die of grief in this island of ours. I will tell you a common case. The rules of Eton require that a boy on the *foundation*[1] should be there twelve years: he is superannuated at eighteen, consequently he must come at six. Children torn away from mothers and sisters at that age not unfrequently die. I speak of what I know. The complaint is not entered by the registrar as grief; but *that* it is. Grief of that sort, and at that age, has killed more than ever have been counted amongst its martyrs.

Therefore it is that Levana often communes with the powers that shake man's heart: therefore it is that she dotes upon grief. ''These ladies,'' said I softly to myself, on seeing the ministers with whom Levana was conversing ''these are the Sorrows; and they are three in number, as the *Graces* are three, who dress man's life with beauty; the *Parcæ*[2] are three who weave the dark arras of man's life in their mysterious loom, always with colours sad in part, sometimes angry with tragic crimson and black; the *Furies* are three, who visit with retributions called from the other side of the grave offences that walk upon this; and once even the *Muses* were but three, who fit the harp, the trumpet, or the lute, to the great burden of man's impassioned creations. These are the Sorrows, all three of whom I know.'' The last words I say *now;* but in Oxford I said, ''One of whom I know, and the others too surely *shall* know.'' For already, in my fervent youth I saw (dimly relieved upon the dark background of my dreams) the imperfect lineaments of the awful sisters. These sisters—by what name shall we call them? If I say simply, ''The Sorrows,'' there will be a chance of mistaking the term; it might be understood of individual sorrow,—separate cases of sorrow,—whereas I want a term expressing the mighty abstractions that incarnate themselves in all individual sufferings of man's heart; and I wish to have these abstractions presented as impersonations, that is, as clothed with human attributes of life, and with functions pointing to flesh. Let us call them, therefore, *Our Ladies of Sorrow.*

I know them thoroughly, and have walked in all their kingdoms. Three sisters they are, of one mysterious household; and their paths are wide apart; but of their dominion there is no end. Them I saw often conversing with Levana, and sometimes about myself. Do they talk then? O, no! Mighty phantoms like these disdain the infirmities of language. They may utter voices through the organs of man when they dwell in human hearts, but amongst themselves is no voice nor sound; eternal silence reigns in *their* kingdoms. *They* spoke not, as they talked with Levana; *they* whispered not; *they* sang not; though oftentimes methought they *might* have sung: for I upon earth had heard their mysteries oftentimes deciphered by harp and timbrel, by dulcimer and organ. Like God, whose servants they are, they utter their pleasure, not by sounds that perish, or by words that go astray, but by signs in

1 holding a scholarship provided by the foundation, or endowment

2 Fates

heaven, by changes on earth, by pulses in secret rivers, heraldries painted on darkness, and hieroglyphics written on the tablets of the brain. *They* wheeled in mazes; *I* spelled the steps. *They* telegraphed[3] from afar; *I* read the signals. *They* conspired together; and on the mirrors of darkness *my* eye traced the plots. *Theirs* were the symbols; *mine* are the words.

What is it the sisters are? What is it that they do? Let me describe their form, and their presence: if form it were that still fluctuated in its outline, or presence it were that for ever advanced to the front, or for ever receded amongst shades.

The eldest of the three is named *Mater Lachrymarum*, Our Lady of Tears. She it is that night and day raves and moans, calling for vanished faces. She stood in Rama, where a voice was heard of lamentation,—Rachel weeping for her children, and refusing to be comforted.[4] She it was that stood in Bethlehem on the night when Herod's sword swept its nurseries of Innocents, and the little feet were stiffened for ever, which, heard at times as they tottered along floors overhead, woke pulses of love in household hearts that were not unmarked in heaven.

Her eyes are sweet and subtle, wild and sleepy, by turns; oftentimes rising to the clouds, oftentimes challenging the heavens. She wears a diadem round her head. And I knew by childish memories that she could go abroad upon the winds, when she heard the sobbing of litanies or the thundering of organs, and when she beheld the mustering of summer clouds. This sister, the eldest, it is that carries keys more than papal[5] at her girdle, which open every cottage and every palace. She, to my knowledge, sat all last summer by the bedside of the blind beggar, him that so often and so gladly I talked with, whose pious daughter, eight years old, with the sunny countenance, resisted the temptations of play and village mirth to travel all day long on dusty roads with her afflicted father. For this did God send her a great reward. In the spring-time of the year, and whilst yet her own spring was budding, He recalled her to himself. But her blind father mourns for ever over *her*; still he dreams at midnight that the little guiding hand is locked within his own; and still he wakens to a darkness that is *now* within a second and a deeper darkness. This *Mater Lachrymarum* also has been sitting all this

winter of 1844-5 within the bed-chamber of the Czar,[6] bringing before his eyes a daughter (not less pious) that vanished to God not less suddenly, and left behind her a darkness not less profound. By the power of the keys it is that Our Lady of Tears glides a ghostly intruder into the chambers of sleepless men, sleepless women, sleepless children, from Ganges to Nile, from Nile to Mississippi. And her, because she is the first-born of her house, and has the widest empire, let us honour with the title of "Madonna!"

The second sister is called *Mater Suspiriorum* —Our Lady of Sighs. She never scales the clouds, nor walks abroad upon the winds. She wears no diadem. And her eyes, if they were ever seen, would be neither sweet nor subtle; no man could read their story; they would be found filled with perishing dreams, and with wrecks of forgotten delirium. But she raises not her eyes; her head, on which sits a dilapidated turban, droops for ever, for ever fastens on the dust. She weeps not. She groans not. But she sighs inaudibly at intervals. Her sister, Madonna, is oftentimes stormy and frantic, raging in the highest against heaven, and demanding back her darlings. But Our Lady of Sighs never clamours, never defies, dreams not of rebellious aspirations. She is humble to abjectness. Hers is the meekness that belongs to the hopeless. Murmur she may, but it is in her sleep. Whisper she may, but it is to herself in the twilight. Mutter she does at times, but it is in solitary places that are desolate as she is desolate, in ruined cities, and when the sun has gone down to his rest. This sister is the visitor of the Pariah,[7] of the Jew, of the bondsman to the oar in the Mediterranean galleys; and of the English criminal in Norfolk Island,[8] blotted out from the books of remembrance in sweet far-off England; of the baffled penitent reverting his eyes for ever upon a solitary grave, which to him seems the altar overthrown of some past and bloody sacrifice, on which altar no oblations can now be availing, whether towards pardon that he might implore, or towards reparation that he might attempt. Every slave that at noonday looks up to the tropical sun with timid reproach, as he points with one hand to the earth, our general mother, but for *him* a stepmother,—as he points with the other hand to the Bible, our general teacher, but against *him* sealed and sequestered;—every woman sitting in darkness, without love to shel-

3 The word was formerly used of various methods of signalling, as by beacon-fires.
4 *Jeremiah*, xxxi, 15; *Matthew*, ii, 16-18.
5 St. Peter's keys, emblem of papal power. Cp. Milton's *Lycidas*, l. 110.
6 Nicholas I., whose daughter Alexandra had lately died.
7 social outcast (Hindu term)
8 A penal colony in the south Pacific. 1825-1845.

ter her head, or hope to illumine her solitude, because the heaven-born instincts kindling in her nature germs of holy affections which God implanted in her womanly bosom, having been stifled by social necessities, now burn sullenly to waste, like sepulchral lamps amongst the ancients; every nun defrauded of her unreturning May-time by wicked kinsman, whom God will judge; every captive in every dungeon; all that are betrayed and all that are rejected; outcasts by traditionary law, and children of *hereditary* disgrace,—all these walk with Our Lady of Sighs. She also carries a key; but she needs it little. For her kingdom is chiefly amongst the tents of Shem,[9] and the houseless vagrant of every clime. Yet in the very highest ranks of man she finds chapels of her own; and even in glorious England there are some that, to the world, carry their heads as proudly as the reindeer, who yet secretly have received her mark upon their foreheads.

But the third sister, who is also the youngest ——! Hush, whisper whilst we talk of *her!* Her kingdom is not large, or else no flesh should live; but within that kingdom all power is hers. Her head, turreted like that of Cybele,[10] rises almost beyond the reach of sight. She droops not; and her eyes rising so high *might* be hidden by distance; but, being what they are, they cannot be hidden; through the treble veil of crape which she wears, the fierce light of a blazing misery, that rests not for matins or for vespers, for noon of day or noon of night, for ebbing or for flowing tide, may be read from the very ground. She is the defier of God. She also is the mother of lunacies, and the suggestress of suicides. Deep lie the roots of her power; but narrow is the nation that she rules. For she can approach only those in whom a profound nature has been upheaved by central convulsions; in whom the heart trembles, and the brain rocks under conspiracies of tempest from without and tempest from within. Madonna moves with uncertain steps, fast or slow, but still with tragic grace. Our Lady of Sighs creeps timidly and stealthily. But this youngest sister moves with incalculable motions, bounding, and with tiger's leaps. She carries no key; for, though coming rarely amongst men, she storms all doors at which she is permitted to enter at all. And *her* name is *Mater Tenebrarum*—Our Lady of Darkness.

These were the *Semnai Theai,* or Sublime Goddesses, these were the *Eumenides,*[11] or Gracious Ladies (so called by antiquity in shuddering propitiation), of my Oxford dreams. Madonna spoke. She spoke by her mysterious hand. Touching my head, she beckoned to Our Lady of Sighs; and *what* she spoke, translated out of the signs which (except in dreams) no man reads, was this:—

"Lo! here is he, whom in childhood I dedicated to my altars. This is he that once I made my darling. Him I led astray, him I beguiled, and from heaven I stole away his young heart to mine. Through me did he become idolatrous; and through me it was, by languishing desires, that he worshipped the worm, and prayed to the wormy grave. Holy was the grave to him; lovely was its darkness; saintly its corruption. Him, this young idolater, I have seasoned for thee, dear gentle Sister of Sighs! Do thou take him now to *thy* heart, and season him for our dreadful sister. And thou,"—turning to the *Mater Tenebrarum,* she said,—"wicked sister, that temptest and hatest, do thou take him from her. See that thy sceptre lie heavy on his head. Suffer not woman and her tenderness to sit near him in his darkness. Banish the frailties of hope, wither the relenting of love, scorch the fountains of tears, curse him as only thou canst curse. So shall he be accomplished[12] in the furnace, so shall he see the things that ought *not* to be seen, sights that are abominable, and secrets that are unutterable. So shall he read elder truths, sad truths, grand truths, fearful truths. So shall he rise again *before* he dies, and so shall our commission be accomplished which from God we had,—to plague his heart until we had unfolded the capacities of his spirit."

SAVANNAH-LA-MAR[*]

God smote Savannah-la-mar, and in one night, by earthquake, removed her, with all her towers standing and population sleeping, from the steadfast foundations of the shore to the coral floors of ocean. And God said,—"Pompeii did I bury and conceal from men through seventeen centuries: this city I will bury, but not conceal. She shall be a monument to men of my mysterious anger, set in azure light through generations to come; for I will enshrine her in a crystal dome of my tropic seas." This city, therefore, like a mighty galleon with all her apparel mounted, streamers flying, and tackling perfect, seems floating along the noiseless depths

9 Son of Noah, reputed ancestor of the Semitic races—the Hebrews, Arabs, etc. For the phrase, see *Genesis,* ix, 27.
10 See note on *Childe Harold,* IV, 2.
11 A euphemistic name for the Furies.

12 perfected.
* "Plain (of) the Sea"—a fanciful name adopted by De Quincey for this vision of a sunken city. The "Dark Interpreter" mentioned here gives name to another of the Suspiria papers.

of ocean; and oftentimes in glassy calms, through the translucid atmosphere of water that now stretches like an air-woven awning above the silent encampment, mariners from every clime look down into her courts and terraces, count her gates, and number the spires of her churches. She is one ample cemetery, and *has* been for many a year; but, in the mighty calms that brood for weeks over tropic latitudes, she fascinates the eye with a *Fata-Morgana*† revelation, as of human life still subsisting in submarine asylums sacred from the storms that torment our upper air.

Thither, lured by the loveliness of cerulean depths, by the peace of human dwellings privileged from molestation, by the gleam of marble altars sleeping in everlasting sanctity, oftentimes in dreams did I and the Dark Interpreter cleave the watery veil that divided us from her streets. We looked into the belfries, where the pendulous bells were waiting in vain for the summons which should awaken their marriage peals; together we touched the mighty organ-keys, that sang no *jubilates*[1] for the ear of heaven, that sang no requiems for the ear of human sorrow; together we searched the silent nurseries, where the children were all asleep, and *had* been asleep through five generations. "They are waiting for the heavenly dawn," whispered the Interpreter to himself: "and, when *that* comes, the bells and organs will utter a *jubilate* repeated by the echoes of Paradise." Then, turning to me, he said,—"This is sad, this is piteous; but less would not have sufficed for the purpose of God. Look here. Put into a Roman clepsydra[2] one hundred drops of water; let these run out as the sands in an hour-glass, every drop measuring the hundredth part of a second, so that each shall represent but the three-hundred-and-sixty-thousandth part of an hour. Now, count the drops as they race along; and, when the fiftieth of the hundred is passing, behold! forty-nine are not, because already they have perished, and fifty are not, because they are yet to come. You see, therefore, how narrow, how incalculably narrow, is the true and actual present. Of that time which we call the present, hardly a hundredth part but belongs either to a past which has fled, or to a future which is still on the wing. It has perished, or it is not born. It was, or it is not. Yet even this approximation to the truth is *infinitely* false. For again subdivide that solitary drop, which only was found to represent the present,

into a lower series of similar fractions, and the actual present which you arrest measures now but the thirty-sixth-millionth of an hour; and so by infinite declensions the true and very present, in which only we live and enjoy, will vanish into a mote of a mote, distinguishable nly by a heavenly vision. Therefore the present, which only man possesses, offers less capacity for his footing than the slenderest film that ever spider twisted from her womb. Therefore, also, even this incalculable shadow from the narrowest pencil of moonlight is more transitory than geometry can measure, or thought of angel can overtake. The time which *is* contracts into a mathematic point; and even that point perishes a thousand times before we can utter its birth. All is finite in the present; and even that finite is infinite in its velocity of flight towards death. But in God there is nothing finite; but in God there is nothing transitory; but in God there *can* be nothing that tends to death. Therefore, it follows, that for God there can be no present. The future is the present of God, and to the future it is that he sacrifices the human present. Therefore it is that he works by earthquake. Therefore it is that he works by grief. O, deep is the ploughing of earthquake! O, deep"—(and his voice swelled like a *sanctus*[3] rising from the choir of a cathedral)—"O, deep is the ploughing of grief. But oftentimes less would not suffice for the agriculture of God. Upon a night of earthquake he builds a thousand years of pleasant habitations for man. Upon the sorrow of an infant he raises oftentimes from human intellects glorious vintages that could not else have been. Less than these fierce ploughshares would not have stirred the stubborn soil. The one is needed for Earth, our planet,—for Earth itself as the dwelling-place of man; but the other is needed yet oftener for God's mightiest instrument,—yes" (and he looked solemnly at myself), "is needed for the mysterious children of the Earth!"

From JOAN OF ARC*

What is to be thought of *her?* What is to be thought of the poor shepherd girl from the hills and forests of Lorraine, that—like the Hebrew

---

1 hymns of rejoicing (specifically the 100th Psalm)
2 water-clock
† Here "mirage-like": from the *fata morgana* of the Sicilian coast—a phenomenon attributed to Morgan le Fay, or Morgana the Fairy.

3 The anthem "Holy, Holy, Holy."
* De Quincey's venture into this particular field of history, which is so obscure and so acrimoniously debated, was inspired by Michelet's *Histoire de France*, then (1847) appearing, and his avowed object was to do justice to the maligned Maid, defending her even against her own countrymen. The body of his article, which is narrative and argumentative, is here omitted, only the introduction and conclusion being given. See *Eng. Lit.*, p. 274.

shepherd boy from the hills and forests of Judea—rose suddenly out of the quiet, out of the safety, out of the religious inspiration, rooted in deep pastoral solitudes, to a station in the van of armies, and to the more perilous station at the right hand of kings? The Hebrew boy inaugurated his patriotic mission by an *act*, by a victorious *act*, such as no man could deny.[1] But so did the girl of Lorraine, if we read her story as it was read by those who saw her nearest. Adverse armies bore witness to the boy as no pretender; but so they did to the gentle girl. Judged by the voices of all who saw them *from a station of good will*, both were found true and loyal to any promises involved in their first acts. Enemies it was that made the difference between their subsequent fortunes. The boy rose to a splendour and a noonday prosperity, both personal and public, that rang through the records of his people, and became a byword among his posterity for a thousand years, until the sceptre was departing from Judah.[2] The poor forsaken girl, on the contrary, drank not herself from that cup of rest which she had secured for France. She never sang together with the songs that rose in her native Domrémy as echoes to the departing steps of invaders. She mingled not in the festal dances at Vaucouleurs[3] which celebrated in rapture the redemption of France. No! for her voice was then silent; no! for her feet were dust. Pure, innocent, noble-hearted girl! whom, from earliest youth, ever I believed in as full of truth and self-sacrifice, this was among the strongest pledges for *thy* truth, that never once —no, not for a moment of weakness—didst thou revel in the vision of coronets and honour from man. Coronets for thee! Oh, no! Honours, if they come when all is over, are for those that share thy blood. Daughter of Domrémy, when the gratitude of thy king shall awaken, thou wilt be sleeping the sleep of the dead. Call her, king of France, but she will not hear thee. Cite her by the apparitors[4] to come and receive a robe of honour, but she will be found *en contumace*.[5] When the thunders of universal France, as even yet may happen,† shall proclaim the grandeur of the poor shepherd girl that gave up all for her country, thy ear, young shepherd girl, will have been deaf for five centuries. To suffer and to do, that was thy portion in this life, that was thy destiny; and not for a moment was it hidden from thyself. Life, thou saidst, is short;

and the sleep which is in the grave is long; let me use that life, so transitory, for the glory of those heavenly dreams destined to comfort the sleep which is so long! This pure creature— pure from every suspicion of even a visionary self-interest, even as she was pure in senses more obvious—never once did this holy child, as regarded herself, relax from her belief in the darkness that was travelling to meet her. She might not prefigure the very manner of her death; she saw not in vision, perhaps, the aërial altitude of the fiery scaffold, the spectators without end, on every road, pouring into Rouen[6] as to a coronation, the surging smoke, the volleying flames, the hostile faces all around, the pitying eye that lurked but here and there, until nature and imperishable truth broke loose from artificial restraints—these might not be apparent through the mists of the hurrying future. But the voice that called her to death, *that* she heard forever.

Great was the throne of France, even in those days, and great was he that sat upon it; but well Joanna knew that not the throne, nor he that sat upon it, was for *her;* but, on the contrary, that she was for *them;* not she by them, but they by her, should rise from the dust. Gorgeous were the lilies of France,[7] and for centuries had the privilege to spread their beauty over land and sea, until, in another century, the wrath of God and man combined to wither them; but well Joanna knew, early at Domrémy she had read that bitter truth, that the lilies of France would decorate no garland for *her.* Flower nor bud, bell nor blossom, would ever bloom for *her!*

Bishop of Beauvais![8] thy victim died in fire upon a scaffold—thou upon a down bed. But, for the departing minutes of life, both are oftentimes alike. At the farewell crisis, when the gates of death are opening, and flesh is resting from its struggles, oftentimes the tortured and the torturer have the same truce from carnal torment; both sink together into sleep; together both sometimes kindle into dreams. When the mortal mists were gathering fast upon you two, bishop and shepherd girl—when the pavilions of life were closing up their shadowy curtains about you—let us try, through the gigantic glooms, to decipher the flying features of your separate visions.

The shepherd girl that had delivered France —she, from her dungeon, she, from her baiting

---

[1] The killing of Goliath; I. Samuel, xvii.
[2] *Genesis*, xlix. 10.
[3] A village near Domrémy.
[4] court summoners
[5] A legal term signifying failure to appear in court.
† Joan has lately been canonized by the church.
[6] The place of Joan's martyrdom.
[7] The royal device of the fleur-de-lis.
[8] The presiding judge at Joan's trial. He had played traitor to the French and abetted the English in this execution.

at the stake, she, from her duel with fire, as she entered her last dream—saw Domrémy, saw the fountain of Domrémy, saw the pomp of forests in which her childhood had wandered. That Easter festival which man had denied to her languishing heart—that resurrection of spring-time, which the darkness of dungeons had inter-cepted from her, hungering after the glorious liberty of forests—were by God given back into her hands as jewels that had been stolen from her by robbers. With those, perhaps (for the minutes of dreams can stretch into ages), was given back to her by God the bliss of childhood. By special privilege for her might be created, in this farewell dream, a second childhood, inno-cent as the first; but not, like that, sad with the gloom of a fearful mission in the rear. This mission had now been fulfilled. The storm was weathered; the skirts even of that mighty storm were drawing off. The blood that she was to reckon for had been exacted; the tears that she was to shed in secret had been paid to the last. The hatred to herself in all eyes had been faced steadily, had been suffered, had been survived. And in her last fight upon the scaf-fold she had triumphed gloriously; victoriously she had tasted the stings of death. For all, except this comfort from her farewell dream, she had died—died amid the tears of ten thou-sand enemies—died amid the drums and trum-pets of armies—died amid peals redoubling upon peals, volleys upon volleys, from the saluting clarions of martyrs.

Bishop of Beauvais! because the guilt-bur-dened man is in dreams haunted and waylaid by the most frightful of his crimes, and because upon that fluctuating mirror—rising (like the mocking mirrors of mirage in Arabian deserts) from the fens of death—most of all are re-flected the sweet countenances which the man has laid in ruins; therefore I know, bishop, that you also, entering your final dream, saw Domrémy. That fountain, of which the wit-nesses spoke so much, showed itself to your eyes in pure morning dews; but neither dews, nor the holy dawn, could cleanse away the bright spots of innocent blood upon its surface. By the fountain, bishop, you saw a woman seated, that hid her face. But, as you draw near, the woman raises her wasted features. Would Dom-rémy know them again for the features of her child? Ah, but you know them, bishop, well!

Oh, mercy! what a groan was that which the servants, waiting outside the bishop's dream at his bedside, heard from his labouring heart, as at this moment he turned away from the foun-tain and the woman, seeking rest in the forests afar off. Yet not so to escape the woman, whom once again he must behold before he dies. In the forests to which he prays for pity, will he find a respite? What a tumult, what a gathering of feet is there! In glades where only wild deer should run, armies and nations are assembling; towering in the fluctuating crowd are phantoms that belong to departed hours. There is the great English Prince, Regent of France. There is my Lord of Win-chester, the princely cardinal, that died and made no sign.[9] There is the Bishop of Beauvais, clinging to the shelter of thickets. What build-ing is that which hands so rapidly are raising? Is it a martyr's scaffold? Will they burn the child of Domrémy a second time? No; it is a tribunal that rises to the clouds; and two na-tions stand around it, waiting for a trial. Shall my Lord of Beauvais sit again upon the judgment-seat, and again number the hours for the innocent? Ah, no! he is the prisoner at the bar. Already all is waiting: the mighty audience is gathered, the Court is hurrying to their seats, the witnesses are arrayed, the trum-pets are sounding, the judge is taking his place. Oh, but this is sudden! My Lord, have you no counsel? "Counsel I have none; in heaven above, or on earth beneath, counsellor there is none now that would take a brief from me: all are silent." Is it, indeed, come to this? Alas! the time is short, the tumult is wondrous, the crowd stretches away into infinity; but yet I will search in it for somebody to take your brief; I know of somebody that will be your counsel. Who is this that cometh from Dom-rémy? Who is she in bloody coronation robes from Rheims?[10] Who is she that cometh with blackened flesh from walking the furnaces of Rouen? This is she, the shepherd girl, counsellor that had none for herself, whom I choose, bishop, for yours. She it is, I engage, that shall take my lord's brief. She it is, bishop, that would plead for you; yes, bishop, she—when heaven and earth are silent.

9 See Shakespeare's II Henry VI., III, iii.
10 Joan was present at the coronation of Charles VII. at Rheims—a coronation made possible by her own martial exploits.

THE VICTORIAN AGE

THOMAS CARLYLE (1795-1881)

FROM SARTOR RESARTUS

THE EVERLASTING YEA. FROM BOOK II, CHAPTER IX*

"Temptations in the Wilderness!"[1] exclaims Teufelsdröckh: "Have we not all to be tried with such? Not so easily can the old Adam, lodged in us by birth, be dispossessed. Our Life is compassed round with Necessity; yet is the meaning of Life itself no other than Freedom, than Voluntary Force; thus have we a warfare; in the beginning, especially, a hard-fought battle. For the God-given mandate, *Work thou in Welldoing*, lies mysteriously written, in Promethean[2] Prophetic Characters, in our hearts; and leaves us no rest, night or day, till it be deciphered and obeyed; till it burn forth, in our conduct, a visible, acted Gospel of Freedom. And as the clay-given mandate, *Eat thou and be filled*, at the same time persuasively proclaims itself through every nerve,—must there not be a confusion, a contest, before the better influence can become the upper?

"To me nothing seems more natural than that the Son of Man, when such God-given mandate first prophetically stirs within him, and the Clay must now be vanquished or vanquish,—

---

[1] See *Luke*, iv, 1, 2.
[2] The name of Prometheus, the fabled defender of man against Jupiter's tyranny, means "forethought."
* *Sartor Resartus*, or "The Tailor Re-Tailored," is nominally a work on clothes; in reality, it is a philosophy, or rather gospel, of life. Carlyle poses as the editor merely, professing to have received the work in manuscript from a certain German Professor "Teufelsdröckh" of the University of "Weissnichtwo" (see *Eng. Lit.*, pp. 345-346). In the Second Book he assumes to give the physical and spiritual biography of the author as culled from imaginary "Paper-bags"—bundles of loose documents—derived from the same source. The Professor, afflicted with personal sorrows, and beset by religious and speculative doubts, has set forth on a world-pilgrimage. In his mental struggle he passes from the "Everlasting No," a period of doubt and denial, through the "Centre of Indifference" to the "Everlasting Yea."

---

should be carried of the spirit into grim Solitudes, and there fronting the Tempter do grimmest battle with him; defiantly setting him at naught, till he yield and fly. Name it as we choose: with or without visible Devil, whether in the natural Desert of rocks and sands, or in the populous moral Desert of selfishness and baseness,—to such Temptation are we all called. Unhappy if we are not! Unhappy if we are but Half-men, in whom that divine handwriting has never blazed forth, all-subduing, in true sun-splendour; but quivers dubiously amid meaner lights: or smoulders, in dull pain, in darkness, under earthly vapours!—Our Wilderness is the wide World in an Atheistic Century; our Forty Days are long years of suffering and fasting: nevertheless, to these also comes an end. Yes, to me also was given, if not Victory, yet the consciousness of Battle, and the resolve to persevere therein while life or faculty is left. To me also, entangled in the enchanted forests, demon-peopled, doleful of sight and of sound, it was given, after weariest wanderings, to work out my way into the higher sunlit slopes—of that Mountain which has no summit, or whose summit is in Heaven only!"

He says elsewhere, under a less ambitious figure; as figures are, once for all, natural to him: "Has not thy Life been that of most sufficient men (*tüchtigen Männer*) thou hast known in this generation? An outflush of foolish young Enthusiasm, like the first fallow-crop, wherein are as many weeds as valuable herbs: this all parched away, under the Droughts of practical and spiritual Unbelief, as Disappointment, in thought and act, often-repeated gave rise to Doubt, and Doubt gradually settled into Denial! If I have had a second-crop, and now see the perennial greensward, and sit under umbrageous cedars, which defy all Drought (and Doubt); herein too, be the Heavens praised, I am not without examples, and even exemplars."

So that, for Teufelsdröckh also, there has been a "glorious revolution:" these mad shadow-hunting and shadow-hunted Pilgrimings of his were but some purifying "Temptation in the Wilderness," before his apostolic work (such as it was) could begin; which Temptation is now happily over, and the Devil once more worsted! Was "that high moment in the *Rue de l'Enfer*,"[3] then, properly, the turning point of the battle; when the Fiend said, *Worship me, or be torn in shreds*, and was answered valiantly with an *Apage Satana?*[4]— Singular Teufelsdröckh, would thou hadst told thy singular story in plain words! But it is fruitless to look there, in those Paper-bags, for such. Nothing but innuendoes, figurative crotchets: a typical Shadow, fitfully wavering, prophetico-satiric; no clear logical Picture. "How paint to the sensual eye," asks he once, "what passes in the Holy-of-Holies of Man's Soul; in what words, known to these profane times, speak even afar off of the unspeakable?" We ask in turn: Why perplex these times, profane as they are, with needless obscurity, by omission and by commission? Not mystical only is our Professor, but whimsical; and involves himself, now more than ever, in eye-bewildering *chiaroscuro*.[5] Successive glimpses, here faithfully imparted, our more gifted readers must endeavour to combine for their own behoof.

He says: "The hot Harmattan-wind[6] had raged itself out: its howl went silent within me; and the long-deafened soul could now hear. I paused in my wild wanderings; and sat me down to wait, and consider; for it was as if the hour of change drew nigh. I seemed to surrender, to renounce utterly, and say: Fly, then, false shadows of Hope; I will chase you no more, I will believe you no more. And ye too, haggard spectres of Fear, I care not for you; ye too are all shadows and a lie. Let me rest here: for I am way-weary and life-weary; I will rest here, were it but to die: to die or to live is alike to me; alike insignificant."—And again: "Here, then, as I lay in that CENTRE of INDIFFERENCE; cast, doubtless by benignant upper Influence, into a healing sleep, the heavy dreams rolled gradually away, and I awoke to a new Heaven and a new Earth. The first preliminary moral Act, Annihilation of Self (*Selbst-tödtung*), had been happily accomplished; and my mind's eyes were now unsealed, and its hands ungyved."

Might we not also conjecture that the following passage refers to his Locality, during this same "healing sleep;" that his Pilgrim-staff lies cast aside here on "the high table-land;" and indeed that the repose is already taking wholesome effect on him? If it were not that the tone, in some parts, has more of riancy, even of levity, than we could have expected! However, in Teufelsdröckh, there is always the strangest Dualism: light dancing, with guitar-music, will be going on in the fore-court, while by fits from within comes the faint whimpering of woe and wail. We transcribe the piece entire:

"Beautiful it was to sit there, as in my skyey Tent, musing and meditating; on the high table-land, in front of the Mountains; over me, as roof, the azure Dome, and around me, for walls, four azure flowing curtains,—namely, of the Four azure Winds, on whose bottom-fringes also I have seen gilding. And then to fancy the fair Castles, that stood sheltered in these Mountain hollows; with their green flower lawns, and white dames and damosels, lovely enough: or better still, the straw-roofed Cottages, wherein stood many a Mother baking bread, with her children round her:—all hidden and protectingly folded-up in the valley-folds; yet there and alive, as sure as if I beheld them. Or to see, as well as fancy, the nine Towns and Villages, that lay round my mountain-seat, which, in still weather, were wont to speak to me (by their steeple-bells) with metal tongue; and, in almost all weather, proclaimed their vitality by repeated Smoke-clouds; whereon, as on a culinary horologe, I might read the hour of the day. For it was the smoke of cookery, as kind housewives at morning, midday, eventide, were boiling their husbands' kettles; and ever a blue pillar rose up into the air, successively or simultaneously, from each of the nine, saying, as plainly as smoke could say: Such and such a meal is getting ready here. Not uninteresting! For you have the whole Borough, with all its love-makings and scandal-mongeries, contentions and contentments, as in miniature, and could cover it all with your hat.—If, in my wide Wayfarings, I had learned to look into the business of the World in its details, here perhaps was the place for combining it into general propositions, and deducing inferences therefrom.

"Often also could I see the black Tempest marching in anger through the Distance: round some Schreckhorn,[8] as yet grim-blue, would the eddying vapour gather, and there

3 Described in a previous chapter as a "dirty little" street in the French Capital where fresh courage had suddenly come to him. This passage Carlyle admitted to be autobiographical, and the street was Leith Walk, Edinburgh.
4 "Get thee hence, Satan." *Matthew*, iv, 10.
5 light and shade
6 A withering wind of West Africa; here figurative for Doubt.
7 laughing gayety
8 "Peak of Terror."

tumultuously eddy, and flow down like a mad witch's hair; till, after a space, it vanished, and, in the clear sunbeam, your Schreckhorn stood smiling grim-white, for the vapour had held snow. How thou fermentest and elaboratest in thy great fermenting-vat and laboratory of an Atmosphere, of a World, O Nature! Or what is Nature? Ha! why do I not name thee GOD? Art thou not the "Living Garment of God?" O Heavens, is it, in very deed, HE then that ever speaks through thee; that lives and loves in thee, that lives and loves in me?

"Fore-shadows, call them rather fore-splendours, of that Truth, and Beginning of Truths, fell mysteriously over my soul. Sweeter than Dayspring to the Shipwrecked in Nova Zembla;* ah, like the mother's voice to her little child that strays bewildered, weeping, in unknown tumults; like soft streamings of celestial music to my too-exasperated heart, came that Evangel. The Universe is not dead and demoniacal, a charnel-house with spectres: but godlike, and my Father's!

"With other eyes, too, could I now look upon my fellow man; with an infinite Love, an infinite Pity. Poor, wandering, wayward man! Art thou not tried, and beaten with stripes, even as I am? Ever, whether thou bear the royal mantle or the beggar's gabardine, art thou not so weary, so heavy-laden; and thy Bed of Rest is but a Grave. O my Brother, my Brother, why cannot I shelter thee in my bosom, and wipe away all tears from thy eyes! —Truly, the din of many-voiced Life, which in this solitude, with the mind's organ, I could hear, was no longer a maddening discord, but a melting one: like inarticulate cries, and sobbings of a dumb creature, which in the ear of Heaven are prayers. The poor Earth, with her poor joys, was now my needy Mother, not my cruel Stepdame; Man, with his so mad Wants and so mean Endeavours, had become the dearer to me; and even for his sufferings and his sins, I now first named him brother. Thus was I standing in the porch of that '*Sanctuary of Sorrow;*' by strange, steep ways, had I too been guided thither; and ere long its sacred gates would open, and the '*Divine Depth of Sorrow*' lie disclosed to me.''

The Professor says, he here first got eye on the Knot that had been strangling him, and straightway could unfasten it, and was free.

* Carlyle got the suggestion for his comparison from the journal of William Barentz, a Dutch navigator who was shipwrecked in the winter of 1596 on these Arctic islands, where the sun returns only after weeks of darkness. Compare the third note on Addison's paper on "Frozen Words," p. 298.

"A vain interminable controversy," writes he, "touching what is at present called Origin of Evil, or some such thing, arises in every soul, since the beginning of the world; and in every soul, that would pass from idle Suffering into actual Endeavouring, must first be put an end to. The most, in our time, have to go content with a simple, incomplete enough Suppression of this controversy; to a few, some Solution of it is indispensable. In every new era, too, such Solution comes out in different terms; and ever the Solution of the last era has become obsolete, and is found unserviceable. For it is man's nature to change his Dialect from century to century; he cannot help it though he would. The authentic *Church-Catechism* of our present century has not yet fallen into my hands: meanwhile, for my own private behoof, I attempt to elucidate the matter so. Man's Unhappiness, as I construe, comes of his Greatness; it is because there is an Infinite in him, which with all his cunning he cannot quite bury under the Finite. Will the whole Finance Ministers and Upholsterers and Confectioners of modern Europe undertake, in joint-stock company, to make one Shoeblack HAPPY? They cannot accomplish it, above an hour or two; for the Shoeblack also has a Soul quite other than his Stomach: and would require, if you consider it, for his permanent satisfaction and saturation, simply this allotment, no more, and no less: *God's infinite Universe altogether to himself*, therein to enjoy infinitely, and fill every wish as fast as it rose. Oceans of Hochheimer,[1] a Throat like that of Ophiuchus:[2] speak not of them; to the infinite Shoeblack they are as nothing. No sooner is your ocean filled, than he grumbles that it might have been of better vintage. Try him with half of a Universe, of an Omnipotence, he sets to quarrelling with the proprietor of the other half, and declares himself the most maltreated of men.—Always there is a black spot in our sunshine: it is even, as I said, the *Shadow of Ourselves*.

"But the whim we have of Happiness is somewhat thus. By certain valuations, and averages, of our own striking, we come upon some sort of average terrestrial lot; this we fancy belongs to us by nature, and of indefeasible right. It is simple payment of our wages, of our deserts; requires neither thanks nor complaint: only such *overplus* as there may be do we account Happiness; any *deficit* again is Misery. Now consider that we have the valuation of our own deserts ourselves, and

1 Hock.
2 See *Par. Lost*, II, 708.

what a fund of Self-conceit there is in each of us,—do you wonder that the balance should so often dip the wrong way, and many a Block-head cry: See there, what a payment; was ever worthy gentleman so used!—I tell thee, Blockhead, it all comes of thy Vanity; of what thou *fanciest* those same deserts of thine to be. Fancy that thou deservest to be hanged (as is most likely), thou wilt feel it happiness to be only shot: fancy that thou deservest to be hanged in a hair-halter, it will be a luxury to die in hemp.

"So true it is, what I then said, that *the fraction of Life can be increased in value not so much by increasing your Numerator as by lessening your Denominator.* Nay, unless my Algebra deceive me, *Unity* itself divided by *zero* will give *Infinity.* Make thy claim of wages a zero, then; thou hast the world under thy feet. Well did the Wisest of our time[3] write: 'It is only with Renunciation (*Entsagen*) that Life, properly speaking, can be said to begin.'

"I asked myself: What is this that, ever since earliest years, thou hast been fretting and fuming, and lamenting and self-tormenting, on account of? Say it in a word: is it not because thou art not HAPPY? Because the THOU (sweet gentleman) is not sufficiently honoured, nourished, soft-bedded, and lovingly cared-for? Foolish soul! What Act of Legislature was here that *thou* shouldst be Happy? A little while ago thou hadst no right to *be* at all. What if thou wert born and predestined not to be Happy, but to be Unhappy! Art thou nothing other than a Vulture, then, that fliest through the Universe seeking after somewhat to *eat;* and shrieking dolefully because carrion enough is not given thee? Close thy *Byron;*[4] open thy *Goethe.*"

"*Es leuchtet mir ein,* I see a glimpse of it!" cries he elsewhere "there is in man a HIGHER than Love of Happiness: he can do without Happiness, and instead thereof find Blessedness! Was it not to preach-forth this same HIGHER that sages and martyrs, the Poet and the Priest, in all times, have spoken and suffered; bearing testimony, through life and through death, of the Godlike that is in Man, and how in the Godlike only has he Strength and Freedom? Which God-inspired Doctrine art thou also honoured to be taught; O Heavens! and broken with manifold merciful Afflictions, even till thou become contrite, and learn it! O thank thy Destiny for these;

Goethe.
Byron's verse is full of his personal grievances. See *Eng. Lit.,* p. 251.

thankfully bear what yet remain: thou hadst need of them; the Self in thee needed to be annihilated. By benignant fever-paroxysms is Life rooting out the deep-seated chronic Disease, and triumphs over Death. On the roaring billows of Time, thou art not engulfed, but borne aloft into the azure of Eternity. Love not Pleasure; love God. This is the EVERLASTING YEA, wherein all contradiction is solved; wherein whoso walks and works, it is well with him."

NATURAL SUPERNATURALISM. FROM BOOK III, CHAPTER VIII

"But deepest of all illusory Appearances, for hiding Wonder, as for many other ends, are your two grand fundamental world-enveloping Appearances, SPACE and TIME. These, as spun and woven for us from before Birth itself, to clothe our celestial ME for dwelling here, and yet to blind it,—lie all-embracing, as the universal canvas, or warp and woof, whereby all minor Illusions, in this Phantasm Existence, weave and paint themselves. In vain, while here on Earth, shall you endeavour to strip them off; you can, at best, but rend them asunder for moments, and look through.

"Fortunatus[5] had a wishing Hat, which when he put on, and wished himself Anywhere, behold he was There. By this means had Fortunatus triumphed over Space, he had annihilated Space; for him there was no Where, but all was Here. Were a Hatter to establish himself, in the Wahngasse of Weissnichtwo,[6] and make felts of this sort for all mankind, what a world we should have of it! Still stranger, should, on the opposite side of the street, another Hatter establish himself; and, as his fellow-craftsman made Space-annihilating Hats, make Time-annihilating! Of both would I purchase, were it with my last groschen[7]; but chiefly of this latter. To clap on your felt, and, simply by wishing that you were Any*where*, straightway to be *There!* Next to clap on your other felt, and simply by wishing that you were Any*when*, straightway to be *Then!* This were indeed the grander: shooting at will from the Fire-Creation of the World to its Fire-Consummation; here historically present in the First Century, conversing face to face with Paul and Seneca;* there prophet-

[5] The hero of a popular modern legend.
[6] "Dream-lane of Know-not-where." See introductory note.
[7] A very small silver coin of Germany, now obsolete.
* Certain spurious letters have come down to us which were said to have passed between Paul and Seneca.

ically in the Thirty-first, conversing also face to face with other Pauls and Senecas, who as yet stand hidden in the depth of that late Time!

"Or thinkest thou, it were impossible, unimaginable? Is the Past annihilated, then, or only past; is the Future non-extant, or only future? Those mystic faculties of thine, Memory and Hope, already answer: already through those mystic avenues, thou the Earth-blinded summonest both Past and Future, and communest with them, though as yet darkly, and with mute beckonings. The curtains of Yesterday drop down, the curtains of To-morrow roll up; but Yesterday and To-morrow both *are*. Pierce through the Time-Element, glance into the Eternal. Believe what thou findest written in the sanctuaries of Man's Soul, even as all Thinkers, in all ages, have devoutly read it there: that Time and Space are not God, but creations of God; that with God as it is a universal HERE, so is it an everlasting Now.

"And seest thou therein any glimpse of IMMORTALITY?—O Heaven! Is the white Tomb of our Loved One, who died from our arms, and had to be left behind us there, which rises in the distance, like a pale, mournfully receding Milestone, to tell how many toilsome uncheered miles we have journeyed on alone,— but a pale spectral Illusion! Is the lost Friend still mysteriously Here, even as we are Here mysteriously with God!—Know of a truth that only the Time-shadows have perished, or are perishable; that the real Being of whatever was, and whatever is, and whatever will be, *is* even now and forever. This, should it unhappily seem new, thou mayst ponder at thy leisure; for the next twenty years, or the next twenty centuries: believe it thou must; understand it thou canst not.

"That the Thought-forms, Space and Time, wherein, once for all, we are sent into this Earth to live, should condition and determine our whole Practical reasonings, conceptions, and imagings or imaginings,—seems altogether fit, just, and unavoidable. But that they should, furthermore, usurp such sway over pure spiritual Meditation, and blind us to the wonder everywhere lying close on us, seems nowise so. Admit Space and Time to their due rank as Forms of Thought; nay, even, if thou wilt, to their quite undue rank of Realities: and consider, then, with thyself how their thin disguises hide from us the brightest God-effulgences! Thus, were it not miraculous, could I stretch forth my hand and clutch the Sun? Yet thou seest me daily stretch forth my hand, and therewith clutch many a thing, and swing it hither and thither. Art thou a grown baby then, to fancy that the Miracle lies in miles of distance, or in pounds avoirdupois of weight; and not to see that the true inexplicable God-revealing Miracle lies in this, that I can stretch forth my hand at all; that I have free Force to clutch aught therewith? Innumerable other of this sort are the deceptions, and wonder-hiding stupefactions, which Space practices on us.

"Still worse is it with regard to Time. Your grand anti-magician, and universal wonder-hider, is this same lying Time. Had we but the Time-annihilating Hat, to put on for once only, we should see ourselves in a World of Miracles, wherein all fabled or authentic Thaumaturgy, and feats of Magic, were outdone. But unhappily we have not such a Hat; and man, poor fool that he is, can seldom and scantily help himself without one.

"Were it not wonderful, for instance, had Orpheus, or Amphion, built the walls of Thebes by the mere sound of his Lyre?[8] Yet tell me Who built these walls of Weissnichtwo; summoning out all the sandstone rocks, to dance along from the *Stein-bruch*[9] (now a huge Troglodyte Chasm, with frightful green-mantled pools); and shape themselves into Doric and Ionic pillars, squared ashlar houses, and noble streets? Was it not the still higher Orpheus, or Orpheuses, who, in past centuries, by the divine Music of Wisdom, succeeded in civilising man? Our highest Orpheus walked in Judea eighteen hundred years ago: his sphere-melody, flowing in wild native tones, took captive the ravished souls of men; and, being of a true sphere-melody, still flows and sounds, though now with thousandfold accomplishments, and rich symphonies, through all our hearts; and modulates, and divinely leads them. Is that a wonder, which happens in two hours; and does it cease to be wonderful if happening in two million? Not only was Thebes built by the music of an Orpheus; but without the music of some inspired Orpheus was no city ever built, no work that man glories in ever done.

"Sweep away the Illusion of Time; glance, if thou have eyes, from the near moving-cause to its far-distant Mover: The stroke that came transmitted through a whole galaxy of elastic balls, was it less a stroke than if the last ball only had been struck, and sent flying? O, could I (with the Time-annihilating Hat) transport thee direct from the Beginnings to the Endings, how were thy eyesight unsealed, and thy heart set flaming in the Light-sea of

8 An ancient tradition. Cp. p. 228, note 30.
9 stone-quarry
10 See p. 321, note 8.

lestial wonder! Then sawest thou that this
ir Universe, were it in the meanest province
ereof, is in very deed the star-domed City of
od; that through every star, through every
ass-blade, and most through every Living
oul, the glory of a present God still beams.
it Nature, which is the Time-vesture of God,
d reveals Him to the wise, hides Him from
e foolish.

"Again, could anything be more miraculous
an an actual authentic Ghost? The English
hnson longed, all his life to see one; but
uld not, though he went to Cock Lane,[1] and
ence to the church-vaults, and tapped on cof-
s. Foolish Doctor! Did he never, with the
ind's eye as well as with the body's, look
und him into that full tide of human Life he
loved; did he never so much as look into
imself? The good Doctor was a Ghost, as
tual and authentic as heart could wish; well-
gh a million of Ghosts were travelling the
eets by his side. Once more I say, sweep
ay the illusion of Time; compress the three-
ore years into three minutes: what else was
, what else are we? Are we not Spirits, that
e shaped into a body, into an Appearance;
d that fade away again into air, and Invis-
lity? This is no metaphor, it is a simple
entific *fact;* we start out of Nothingness,
ke figure, and are Apparitions; round us, as
und the veriest spectre, is Eternity; and to
ernity minutes are as years and æons. Come
ere not tones of Love and Faith, as from
estial harp-strings, like the Song of beatified
uls? And again, do not we squeak and
ober[2] (in our discordant, screech-owlish de-
tings and recriminatings); and glide bodeful
d feeble, and fearful; or uproar (*poltern*),
d revel in our mad Dance of the Dead,—till
e scent of the morning-air[3] summons us to
r still Home; and dreamy Night becomes
ake and Day? Where now is Alexander of
acedon: does the steel Host, that yelled in
rce battle-shouts, at Issus and Arbela, remain
hind him; or have they all vanished utterly,
en as perturbed Goblins must? Napoleon too,
d his Moscow Retreats and Austerlitz Cam-
igns! Was it all other than the veriest
ectre-hunt; which has now, with its howling
mult that made night hideous, flitted away?—
osts! There are nigh a thousand million
lking the Earth openly at noontide; some
lf-hundred have vanished from it, some half-

hundred have arisen in it, ere thy watch ticks once.

"O Heaven, it is mysterious, it is awful to consider that we not only carry each a future Ghost within him; but are, in very deed, Ghosts! These Limbs, whence had we them; this stormy Force; this life-blood with its burning passion? They are dust and shadow; a Shadow-system gathered round our ME; wherein through some moments or years, the Divine Essence is to be revealed in the Flesh. That warrior on his strong war-horse, fire flashes through his eyes; force dwells in his arm and heart; but warrior and war-horse are a vision; a revealed Force, nothing more. Stately they tread the Earth, as if it were a firm substance: fool! the Earth is but a film; it cracks in twain, and warrior and war-horse sink beyond plummet's sounding. Plummet's? Fantasy herself will not follow them. A little while ago they were not; a little while and they are not, their very ashes are not.

"So has it been from the beginning, so will it be to the end. Generation after generation takes to itself the Form of a Body; and forth-issuing from Cimmerian Night,[4] on Heaven's mission APPEARS. What Force and Fire is in each he expends: one grinding in the mill of Industry; one hunter-like climbing the giddy Alpine heights of Science; one madly dashed in pieces on the rocks of Strife, in war with his fellow:—and then the Heaven-sent is re-called; his earthly Vesture falls away, and soon even to Sense becomes a Vanished Shadow. Thus, like some wild-flaming, wild-thundering train of Heaven's Artillery, does this mysterious MANKIND thunder and flame, in long-drawn, quick-succeeding grandeur, through the unknown Deep. Thus, like a God-created, fire-breathing Spirit-host, we emerge from the Inane; haste stormfully across the astonished Earth; then plunge again into the Inane. Earth's mountains are levelled, and her seas filled up, in our passage: can the Earth, which is but dead and a vision, resist Spirits which have reality and are alive? On the hardest adamant some footprint of us is stamped-in; the last Rear of the host will read traces of the earliest Van. But whence?—O Heaven, whither? Sense knows not; Faith knows not; only that it is through Mystery to Mystery, from God and to God.

"We *are such stuff*
As Dreams are made on, and our little Life
Is rounded with a sleep!"[5]

he "Cock Lane Ghost" was a notorious impos-
ture perpetrated in London in 1762.
amlet, I, i, 116.
amlet, I, v, 58.

4 Cimmeria was a fabled country of perpetual darkness.
5 *The Tempest,* IV, i, 156.

From THE FRENCH REVOLUTION

Uprising of the Populace. Storming of the Bastille. From Volume I, Book V, Chapters IV-VI*

So hangs it, dubious, fateful, in the sultry days of July. It is the passionate printed *advice* of M. Marat,† to abstain, of all things, from violence. Nevertheless the hungry poor are already burning Town Barriers,[1] where Tribute on eatables is levied; getting clamorous for food.

The twelfth July morning is Sunday: the streets are all placarded with an enormous-sized *De par le Roi*,[2] "inviting peaceable citizens to remain within doors,"‡ to feel no alarm, to gather in no crowd. Why so? What mean these "placards of enormous size?" Above all, what means this clatter of military; dragoons, hussars, rattling in from all points of the compass towards the Place Louis Quinze:[3] with a staid gravity of face, though saluted with mere nicknames, hootings and even missiles? Besenval[4] is with them. Swiss Guards of his are already in the Champs Elysées,[5] with four pieces of artillery.

Have the destroyers descended on us,§ then? From the Bridge of Sèvres to utmost Vincennes, from Saint-Denis to the Champ-de-Mars, we are begirt! Alarm, of the vague unknown, is in

[1] City gates.
[2] An order *de part le roi*, "by the authority of the king."
[3] "Square of Louis XV."; a noted square west of the Tuileries, or royal residence; now the Place de la Concorde.
[4] Then Commandant of Paris.
[5] An avenue and public park extending westward from the Place de la Concorde.

* The immediate cause of the French Revolution was a deficiency of revenue and the oppressive taxation of the people—the Commonalty, or Third Estate—to the exemption of the two other Estates, the Nobility and the Clergy. Necker, a Genevese statesman, who was Director General of Finance, convened the States-General, or legislative assemblies, at Versailles in May, 1789. As they failed to come to an agreement, the Third Estate resolved itself into a National Assembly with the object of forming a Constitution. Such in brief was the situation when this narrative opens,—the King and his court at Versailles, just outside of Paris, hopelessly at odds with the National Assembly, and the starving populace in Paris and throughout France beginning to clamor for bread.

† Jean Paul Marat, at one time the Prince d'Artois's horse-leech (horse doctor): one of the earliest inciters to revolution, and a leader of the Jacobin party after it was formed.

‡ Words thus quoted by Carlyle are taken from various memoirs and contemporary documents.

§ Carlyle speaks from the point of view of the Parisian populace, or revolutionists, whom he later calls by the collective name of "Patriotism."

every heart. The Palais Royal* has become place of awestruck interjections, silent shaking of the head: one can fancy with what dolorous sound the noontide cannon (which the Sun fires at crossing of his meridian) went off there, bodeful, like an inarticulate voice of doom. A these troops verily come out "against Brigands?" Where are the Brigands? What mystery is in the wind?—Hark! a human voice reporting articulately the Job's-news:[6] *Necker, People's Minister, Saviour of France, is dismissed.* Impossible, incredible! Treasonous the public peace! Such a voice ought to be choked in the water-works;—had not the newsbringer quickly fled. Nevertheless, friend make of it what ye will, the news is true. Necker is gone. Necker hies northward incessantly, in obedient secrecy, since yesternight. We have a new Ministry: Broglie the War god;[7] Aristocrat Breteuil; Foulon who said the people might eat grass!

Rumour, therefore, shall arise; in the Palais Royal, and in broad France. Paleness sits on every face: confused tremor and fremescence waxing into thunder-peals, of Fury stirred on by Fear.

But see Camille Desmoulins, from the Café de Foy, rushing out, sibylline[9] in face; his hair streaming, in each hand a pistol! He springs to a table: the Police satellites are eyeing him alive they shall not take him, not they alive him alive. This time he speaks without stammering:—Friends! shall we die like hunted hares? Like sheep hounded into their pinfold, bleating for mercy, where is no mercy, but only a whetted knife? The hour is come; the supreme hour of Frenchman and Man; when Oppressors are to try conclusions with Oppressed; and the word is, swift Death, or Deliverance forever. Let such hour be welcome! Us, meseems, one cry only befits: To Arms! Let universal Paris, universal France, as with the throat of the whirlwind, sound only To arms!—"To arms!" yell responsive the innumerable voices; like one great voice, as of a Demon yelling from the air: for all faces wax fire-eyed, all hearts burn up into madness. In such, or fitter words, does Camille evoke the Elemental Powers, in this great moment.

[6] disheartening news
[7] i. e., Minister of War
[8] From Latin *fremo*, to growl.
[9] like the ancient Sibyl, or inspired prophetess

* A palace, with galleries and gardens, built by Cardinal Richelieu in the heart of Paris. At this time it was occupied by the Duc d'Orléans (Philippe Égalité), one of the nobles who had joined the Commons, and its cafés were the resort of the more violent democrats

friends, continues Camille, some rallying sign! Cockades; green ones;—the colour of Hope!—As with the flight of locusts, these green tree-eaves; green ribands from the neighbouring hops; all green things are snatched, and made cockades of. Camille descends from his table; "stifled with embraces, wetted with tears;" as a bit of green ribbon handed him; sticks it in his hat. And now to Curtius' Image-hop there; to the Boulevards; to the four winds, and rest not till France be on fire!

France, so long shaken and wind-parched, is probably at the right inflammable point.—As for poor Curtius, who, one grieves to think, might be but imperfectly paid,—he cannot make two words about his Images. The Wax-bust of Necker, the Wax-bust of D'Orleans, helpers of France: these, covered with crape, is in funeral procession, or after the manner of suppliants appealing to Heaven, to Earth, and Tartarus itself, a mixed multitude bears off. For a sign! As indeed man, with his singular imaginative faculties, can do little or nothing without signs; thus Turks look to their Prophet's Banner; also Osier *Mannikins*[10] have been burnt, and Necker's Portrait has erewhile figured, aloft on its perch.

In this manner march they, a mixed, continually increasing multitude; armed with axes, staves and miscellanea; grim, many-sounding, through the streets. Be all Theatres shut; let all dancing on planked floor, or on the natural greensward, cease! Instead of a Christian Sabbath, and feast of *guinguette*[11] tabernacles, it shall be a Sorcerer's Sabbath;[12] and Paris, gone rabid, dance,—with the Fiend for piper!

. . . .

Raging multitudes surround the Hôtel-de-ville,[13] crying: Arms! Orders! The Six-and-seventy Town-Councillors, with their long gowns, have ducked under (into the raging chaos);—shall never emerge more. Besenval is painfully wriggling himself out, to the Champ-de-Mars;[14] he must sit there "in the cruellest uncertainty!" courier after courier may dash off for Versailles; but will bring back no answer, can hardly bring himself back. For the roads are all blocked with batteries and pickets, with floods of carriages arrested for examination: such was Broglie's one sole order; the Œil-de-œuf,[15] hearing in the distance such mad din, which sounded almost like invasion, will before all things keep its own head whole. A new Ministry, with, as it were, but one foot in the stirrup, cannot take leaps. Mad Paris is abandoned altogether to itself.

What a Paris, when the darkness fell! A European metropolitan City hurled suddenly forth from its old combinations and arrangements; to crash tumultuously together, seeking new. Use and wont will now no longer direct any man; each man with what of originality he has, must begin thinking; or following those that think. Seven hundred thousand individuals, on the sudden, find all their old paths, old ways of acting, and deciding, vanish from under their feet. And so there go they, with clangour and terror, they know not as yet whether running, swimming, or flying,—headlong into the New Era. With clangour and terror: from above, Broglie, the war-god, impends, preternatural, with his redhot cannon-balls; and from below a preternatural Brigand-world menaces with dirk and firebrand: madness rules the hour.

Happily, in place of the submerged Twenty-six, the Electoral Club is gathering; has declared itself a "Provisional Municipality." On the morrow, it will get Provost Flesselles, with an Echevin or two,[16] to give help in many things. For the present it decrees one most essential thing: that forthwith a "Parisian Militia" shall be enrolled. Depart, ye heads of Districts, to labour in this great work; while we here, in Permanent Committee, sit alert. Let fencible[17] men, each party in its own range of streets, keep watch and ward, all night. Let Paris court a little fever-sleep; confused by such fever-dreams, of "violent motions at the Palais Royal;"—or from time to time start awake, and look out, palpitating, in its nightcap, at the clash of discordant mutually-unintelligible Patrols; on the gleam of distant Barriers, going up all-too ruddy towards the vault of Night.

On Monday, the huge City has awoke, not to its week-day industry: to what a different one! The working man has become a fighting man; has one want only: that of arms. The industry of all crafts has paused;—except it be the smith's, fiercely hammering pikes; and, in a faint degree, the kitchener's, cooking offhand victuals, for *bouche va toujours*.[18] Women too are sewing cockades;—not now of *green*, which

Images of Guy Fawkes, for example.
tea-garden
assembly of witches or wizards
The Town Hall, which became the rallying place of the democratic party.
A military field, south of the Seine.
The hall of the king's counsellors, at Versailles.

16 The Provost of Merchants, with his municipal magistrates.
17 capable of defending
18 "Eating must go on."

being D'Artois[19] colour, the Hôtel-de-Ville has had to interfere in it; but of *red* and *blue*, our old Paris colours: these, once based on a ground of constitutional *white*, are the famed TRICOLOR,—Which (if Prophecy err not) "will go round the world."

All shops, unless it be the Bakers' and Vintners', are shut: Paris is in the streets;—rushing, foaming like some Venice wine-glass into which you had dropped poison. The tocsin, by order, is pealing madly from all steeples. Arms, ye Elector Municipals; thou Flesselles with thy Echevins, give us arms! Flesselles gives what he can: fallacious, perhaps insidious promises of arms from Charleville; order to seek arms here, order to seek them there. The new Municipals give what they can; some three hundred and sixty indifferent firelocks, the equipment of the City-watch: "a man in wooden shoes, and without coat, directly clutches one of them, and mounts guard." Also as hinted, an order to all Smiths to make pikes with their whole soul.

Heads of Districts are in fervent consultation; subordinate Patriotism roams distracted, ravenous for arms. Hitherto at the Hôtel-de-Ville was only such modicum of indifferent firelocks as we have seen. At the so-called Arsenal, there lies nothing but rust, rubbish and saltpetre,—overlooked too by the guns of the Bastille. His Majesty's Repository, what they call *Garde-Meuble*, is forced and ransacked: tapestries enough, and gauderies; but of serviceable fighting-gear small stock! Two silver-mounted cannons there are; an ancient gift from his Majesty of Siam to Louis Fourteenth; gilt sword of the Good Henri[20]; antique Chivalry arms and armour. These, and such as these, a necessitous Patriotism snatches greedily, for want of better. The Siamese cannons go trundling, on an errand they were not meant for. Among the indifferent firelocks are seen tourney-lances; the princely helm and hauberk glittering amid ill-hatted heads,—as in a time when all times and their possessions are suddenly sent jumbling!

. . . .

In such circumstances, the Aristocrat, the unpatriotic rich man is packing up for departure. But he shall not get departed. A wooden-shod force has seized all Barriers, burnt or not: all that enters, all that seeks to issue, is stopped there, and dragged to the Hôtel-de-Ville: coaches, tumbrils,[21] plate, furniture, "many

meal-sacks," in time even "flocks and herds" encumber the Place de Grève.[2]

And so it roars, and rages, and brays: drum beating, steeples pealing; criers rushing with hand-bells: "Oyez,[3] oyez, All men to their Districts to be enrolled!" The Districts have met in gardens, open squares; are getting marshalled into volunteer troops. No redhot ball has yet fallen from Besenval's Camp; on the contrary, Deserters with their arms are continually dropping in: nay now, joy of joys at two in the afternoon, the Gardes Françaises, being ordered to Saint-Denis, and flatly declining, have come over in a body! It is a fact worth many. Three thousand six hundred of the best fighting men, with complete accoutrement; with cannoneers even, and cannon! Their officers are left standing alone; could not so much as succeed in "spiking the guns." The very Swiss, it may now be hoped, Château Vieux[5] and the others, will have doubts about fighting.

Our Parisian Militia,—which some think it were better to name National Guard,—is prospering as heart could wish. It promised to be forty-eight thousand; but will in few hours double and quadruple that number: invincible, if we had only arms!

But see, the promised Charleville Boxes marked *Artillerie!* Here then are arms enough? —Conceive the blank face of Patriotism, when it found them filled with rags, foul linen, candle-ends, and bits of wood! Provost of the Merchants, how is this? Neither at the Chartreux Convent, whither we were sent with signed order, is there or ever was there any weapon of war. Nay here, in this Seine Boat, safe under tarpaulings (had not the nose of Patriotism been of the finest), are "five thousand-weight of gunpowder;" not coming *in*, but surreptitiously going out! What meanest thou, Flesselles? 'Tis a ticklish game, that of "amusing" us. Cat plays with captive mouse: but mouse with enraged cat, with enraged National Tiger?

Meanwhile, the faster, O ye black-aproned Smiths, smite; with strong arm and willing heart. This man and that, all stroke from head to heel, shall thunder alternating, and ply the great forge-hammer, till stithy reel and ring again; while ever and anon, overhead, booms the alarm-cannon,—for the City has now got gunpowder. Pikes are fabricated; fifty thou-

19 Monseigneur d'Artois was an unpopular adherent of the king.
20 Henry of Navarre.
21 two-wheeled carts

2 Now the Place de l'Hôtel-de-Ville.
3 "Hear ye!"
4 The French Guards, the chief regiment of the French army.
5 A regiment of Swiss troops.

sand of them, in six-and-thirty hours; judge whether the Black-aproned have been idle. Dig trenches, unpave the streets, ye others, assiduous, man and maid; cram the earth in barrel-barricades, at each of them a volunteer sentry; pile the whin-stones in window-sills and upper rooms. Have scalding pitch, at least boiling water ready, ye weak old women, to pour it and dash it on Royal-Allemand,[6] with your skinny arms: your shrill curses along with it will not be wanting!—Patrols of the new-born National Guard, bearing torches, scour the streets, all that night; which otherwise are vacant, yet illuminated in every window by order. Strange-looking; like some naphtha-lighted City of the Dead, with here and there a flight of perturbed Ghosts.

O poor mortals, how ye make this Earth bitter for each other; this fearful and wonderful Life fearful and horrible; and Satan has his place in all hearts! Such agonies and ragings and wailings ye have, and have had, in all times:—to be buried all, in so deep silence; and the salt sea is not swoln with your tears.

Great meanwhile is the moment, when tidings of Freedom reach us; when the long-enthralled soul, from amid its chains and squalid stagnancy, arises, were it still only in blindness and bewilderment, and swears by Him that made it, that it will be *free!* Free? Understand that well, it is the deep commandment, dimmer or clearer, of our whole being, to be *free*. Freedom is the one purport, wisely aimed at, or unwisely, of all man's struggles, toilings and sufferings, in this Earth. Yes, supreme is such a moment (if thou have known it): first vision as of a flame-girt Sinai,[1] in this our waste Pilgrimage,—which thenceforth wants not its pillar of cloud by day, and pillar of fire by night![2] Something it is even,—nay, something considerable, when the chains have grown *corrosive*, poisonous,—to be free 'from oppression by our fellow-man.' Forward, ye maddened sons of France; be it towards this destiny or towards that! Around you is but starvation, falsehood, corruption and the clam of death. Where ye are is no abiding.

Imagination may, imperfectly, figure how Commandant Besenval, in the Champ-de-Mars, has worn out these sorrowful hours. Insurrection raging all round; his men melting away! From Versailles, to the most pressing messages, comes no answer; or once only some vague word

of answer which is worse than none. A Council of Officers can decide merely that there is no decision: Colonels inform him, 'weeping,' that they do not think their men will fight. Cruel uncertainty is here: war-god Broglie sits yonder, inaccessible in his Olympus; does not descend terror-clad, does not produce his whiff of grape-shot;[*] sends no orders.

Truly, in the Château[3] of Versailles all seems mystery: in the Town of Versailles, were we there, all is rumour, alarm and indignation. An august National Assembly sits, to appearance, menaced with death; endeavouring to defy death. It has resolved 'that Necker carries with him the regrets of the Nation.' It has sent solemn Deputation over to the Château, with entreaty to have these troops withdrawn. In vain: his Majesty, with a singular composure, invites us to be busy rather with our own duty, making the Constitution! . . .

So at Versailles. But at Paris, agitated Besenval, before retiring for the night, has stept over to old M. de Sombreuil, of the *Hôtel des Invalides*[4] hard by. M. de Sombreuil has, what is a great secret, some eight-and-twenty-thousand stand of muskets deposited in his cellars there; but no trust in the temper of his Invalides. This day, for example, he sent twenty of the fellows down to unscrew those muskets; lest Sedition might snatch at them: but scarcely, in six hours, had the twenty unscrewed twenty gun-locks, or dogsheads (*chiens*) of locks,—each Invalide his dogshead! If ordered to fire, they would, he imagines, turn their cannon against himself.

Unfortunate old military gentlemen, it is your hour, not of glory! Old Marquis de Launay too, of the Bastille, has pulled up his drawbridges long since, 'and retired into his interior;' with sentries walking on his battlements, under the midnight sky, aloft over the glare of illuminated Paris;—whom a National Patrol passing that way, takes the liberty of firing at: 'seven shots towards twelve at night,' which do not take effect. This was the 13th day of July 1789; a worse day, many said, than the last 13th was, when only hail fell out of Heaven, not madness rose out of Tophet;[5] ruining worse than crops!

* * * * * *

[6] A regiment of German troops.

[1] The mountain on which the law was given to Moses. *Exodus*, xix.

[2] *Exodus*, xiii, 21.

[3] The residence of the king.

[4] An establishment for disabled soldiers, not far from the Champs de Mars.

[5] Hell.

[*] Broglie had boasted that he would settle the Third Estate with a "whiff of grape-shot" (*salve de canons*). Six years later the whiff was delivered by Napoleon, and the Revolution ended See the next to the last chapter Carlyle's *History*.

But . . . a new, Fourteenth morning dawns. Under all roofs of this distracted City is the nodus[6] of a drama, not untragical, crowding towards solution. The bustlings and preparings, the tremors and menaces; the tears that fell from old eyes! This day, my sons, ye shall quit[7] you like men. By the memory of your fathers' wrongs, by the hope of your children's rights! Tyranny impends in red wrath: help for you is none, if not in your own right hands. This day ye must do or die.

From earliest light, a sleepless Permanent Committee has heard the old cry, now waxing almost frantic, mutinous: Arms! Arms! Provost Flesselles, or what traitors there are among you, may think of those Charleville Boxes. A hundred-and-fifty-thousand of us; and but the third man furnished with so much as a pike! Arms are the one thing needful: with arms we are an unconquerable man-defying National Guard; without arms, a rabble to be whiffed with grapeshot.

Happily the word has arisen, for no secret can be kept,—that there lie muskets at the *Hôtel des Invalides*. Thither will we: King's Procureur[8] M. Ethys de Corny, and whatsoever of authority a Permanent Committee can lend, shall go with us. Besenval's Camp is there; perhaps he will not fire on us; if he kill us, we shall but die.

Alas, poor Besenval, with his troops melting away in that manner, has not the smallest humour to fire! At five o'clock this morning, as he lay dreaming, oblivious in the *École Militaire*,[9] a 'figure' stood suddenly at his bedside; 'with face rather handsome; eyes inflamed, speech rapid and curt, air audacious;' such a figure drew Priam's curtains![10] The message and monition of the figure was, that resistance would be hopeless; that if blood flowed, woe to him who shed it. Thus spoke the figure: and vanished. 'Withal there was a kind of eloquence that struck one.' Besenval admits that he should have arrested him, but did not. Who this figure with inflamed eyes, with speech rapid and curt, might be? Besenval knows, but mentions not. Camille Desmoulins? Pythagorean Marquis Valadi,[11] inflamed with 'violent motions all night at the Palais Royal'? Fame names him, 'Young M. Meillar'; then shuts her lips about him forever.

In any case, behold, about nine in the morning, our National Volunteers rolling in long wide flood, south-westward to the *Hôtel des Invalides;* in search of the one thing needful. King's Procureur M. Ethys de Corny and officials are there; the Curé of Saint-Étienne du Mont marches unpacific, at the head of his militant Parish; the Clerks of the Basoche[12] in red coats we see marching, now Volunteers of the Basoche; the Volunteers of the Palais Royal:—National Volunteers, numerable by tens of thousands; of one heart and mind. The King's muskets are the Nation's; think, old M. de Sombreuil, how, in this extremity, thou wilt refuse them! Old M. de Sombreuil would fain hold parley, send couriers; but it skills[13] not: the walls are scaled, no Invalide firing a shot; the gates must be flung open. Patriotism rushes in, tumultuous, from grunsel[14] up to ridge-tile, through all rooms and passages; rummaging distractedly for arms. What cellar, or what cranny can escape it? The arms are found; all safe there; lying packed in straw,— apparently with a view to being burnt! More ravenous than famishing lions over dead prey, the multitude, with clangour and vociferation, pounces on them; struggling, dashing, clutching:—to the jamming-up, to the pressure, fracture and probable extinction of the weaker Patriot. And so, with such protracted crash of deafening, most discordant Orchestra-music, the Scene is changed; and eight-and-twenty thousand sufficient firelocks are on the shoulders of as many National Guards, lifted thereby out of darkness into fiery light.

Let Besenval look at the glitter of these muskets, as they flash by: Gardes Françaises, it is said, have cannon levelled on him; ready to open, if need were, from the other side of the River. Motionless sits he; 'astonished,' one may flatter oneself, 'at the proud bearing (*fière contenance*) of the Parisians.'—And now to the Bastille, ye intrepid Parisians! There grapeshot still threatens: thither all men's thoughts and steps are now tending.

Old De Launay, as we hinted, withdrew 'into his interior' soon after midnight of Sunday. He remains there ever since, hampered, as all military gentlemen now are, in the saddest conflict of uncertainties. The Hôtel-de-Ville 'invites' him to admit National Soldiers, which is a soft name for surrendering. On the other hand, His Majesty's orders were precise. His garrison is but eighty-two old Invalides, reinforced by thirty-two young Swiss; his walls indeed are nine feet thick, he has cannon and

6 "knot," tangle, plot
7 acquit
8 Attorney
9 Military School; by the Champs de Mars.
10 Cp. Goldsmith's *The Haunch of Venison*, l. 110 and note.
11 Another of the nobles who had joined the people.
12 A collective term for "the Law."
13 avails
14 groundsill

owder; but, alas, only one day's provision of victuals. The city, too, is French, the poor garrison mostly French. Rigorous old De Launay, think what thou wilt do!

All morning, since nine, there has been a cry every where: To the Bastille! Repeated deputations of citizens' have been here, passionate for arms; whom De Launay has got dismissed by soft speeches through portholes. Towards noon, Elector Thuriot de la Rosière gains admittance; finds De Launay indisposed for surrender; nay, disposed for blowing up the place rather. Thuriot mounts with him to the battlements: heaps of paving-stones, old iron and missiles lie piled; cannon all duly levelled; in every embrasure a cannon,—only drawn back a little! But outwards, behold, O Thuriot, how the multitude flows on, welling through every street; tocsin furiously pealing, all drums beating the *générale*[1]: the Suburb Saint-Antoine rolling hitherward wholly, as one man!* Such vision (spectral yet real) thou, O Thuriot, as from thy Mount of Vision, beholdest in this moment: prophetic of what other Phantasmagories, and loud-gibbering Spectral Realities, which thou yet beholdest not, but shalt! "*Que voulez-vous?*"[2] said De Launay, turning pale at the sight, with an air of reproach, almost of menace. "Monsieur," said Thuriot, rising into the moral sublime, "what mean *you*? consider if I could not precipitate *both* of us from this height,"—say only a hundred feet, exclusive of the walled ditch! Whereupon De Launay fell silent. Thuriot shows himself from some pinnacle, to comfort the multitude becoming suspicious, fremescent: then descends; departs with protest; with warning addressed also to the Invalides,—on whom however, it produces but a mixed indistinct impression. The old heads are none of the clearest; besides, it is said, De Launay has been profuse of beverages (*prodigua des buissons*). They think they will not fire,—if not fired on, if they can help it; but must, on the whole, be ruled considerably by circumstances.

Wo to thee, De Launay, in such an hour, if thou canst not, taking some one firm decision, *rule* circumstances! Soft speeches will not serve; hard grapeshot is questionable; but hovering between the two is *un*questionable. Ever wilder swells the tide of men; their infinite hum waxing ever louder, into imprecations, perhaps into crackle of stray musketry,

—which latter, on walls nine feet thick, cannot do execution. The Outer Drawbridge has been lowered for Thuriot; new *deputation of citizens* (it is the third, and noisiest of all) penetrates that way into the Outer Court: soft speeches producing no clearance of these, De Launay gives fire; pulls up his Drawbridge. A slight sputter;—which has *kindled* the too combustible chaos; made it a roaring fire-chaos! Bursts forth Insurrection, at sight of its own blood (for there were deaths by that sputter of fire), into endless rolling explosion of musketry, distraction, execration;—and over head, from the Fortress, let one great gun, with its grapeshot, go booming, to show what we *could* do. The Bastille is besieged!

On, then, all Frenchmen, that have hearts in your bodies! Roar with all your throats, of cartilage and metal, ye Sons of Liberty; stir spasmodically whatsoever of utmost faculty is in you, soul, body, or spirit; for it is the hour! Smite, thou Louis Tournay, cartwright of the Marais,[3] old-soldier of the Regiment Dauphiné; smite at that Outer Drawbridge chain, though the fiery hail whistles round thee! Never, over nave or felloe, did thy axe strike such a stroke. Down with it, man; down with it to Orcus:[4] let the whole accursed Edifice sink thither, and Tyranny be swallowed up forever! Mounted, some say, on the roof of the guard-room, some 'on bayonets stuck into joints of the wall,' Louis Tournay smites, brave Aubin Bonnemère (also an old soldier) seconding him; the chain yields, breaks; the huge drawbridge slams down, thundering (*avec fracas*). Glorious: and yet, alas, it is still but the outworks. The Eight grim Towers, with their Invalide musketry, their paving stones and cannon-mouths, still soar aloft intact;—Ditch yawning impassable, stone-faced; the inner Drawbridge with its *back* towards us: the Bastille is still to take!

To describe this Siege of the Bastille (thought to be one of the most important in History) perhaps transcends the talent of mortals. Could one but, after infinite reading, get to understand so much as the plan of the building! But there is open Esplanade, at the end of the Rue Saint-Antoine; there are such Forecourts, *Cour Avancée, Cour de l'Orme*, arched Gateway (where Louis Tournay now fights); then new drawbridges, dormant-bridges, rampart-bastions, and the grim Eight Towers; a labyrinthic Mass, high-frowning there, of all ages from twenty years to four hundred and twenty;—beleaguered, in this its last hour, as

---

1 The signal for assembling, or of alarm.
2 "What do you want? What do you mean?"
* The Faubourg St. Antoine, or east side of Paris, much like the east side of London, is mainly a residence of the lower classes.

3 A manufacturing quarter of Paris.
4 Hades.

we said, by mere Chaos come again! Ordnance of all calibres; throats of all capacities; men of all plans, every man his own engineer: seldom since the war of Pygmies and Cranes[5] was there seen so anomalous a thing. Half-pay Elie is home for a suit of regimentals;[*] no one would heed him in coloured clothes: half-pay Hulin is haranguing Gardes Françaises in the Place de Grève. Frantic Patriots pick up the grapeshots; bear them, still hot (or seemingly so), to the Hôtel-de-Ville;—Paris, you perceive, is to be burnt! Flesselles is 'pale to the very lips,' for the roar of the multitude grows deep. Paris wholly has got to the acme of its frenzy; whirled, all ways, by panic madness. At every street-barricade, there whirls simmering a minor whirlpool,—strengthening the barricade, since God knows what is coming; and all minor whirlpools play distractedly into that grand Fire-Mahlstrom[6] which is lashing round the Bastille.

And so it lashes and it roars. Cholat the wine-merchant has become an impromptu cannoneer. See Georget, of the Marine Service, fresh from Brest,[7] ply the King of Siam's cannon. Singular (if we were not used to the like): Georget lay, last night, taking his ease at his inn;[8] the King of Siam's cannon also lay, knowing nothing of *him*, for a hundred years. Yet now, at the right instant, they have got together, and discourse eloquent music. For, hearing what was toward, Georget sprang from the Brest Diligence,[9] and ran. Gardes Françaises also will be here, with real artillery: were not the walls so thick!—Upwards from the Esplanade, horizontally from all neighbouring roofs and windows, flashes one irregular deluge of musketry, without effect. The Invalides lie flat, firing comparatively at their ease from behind stone; hardly through portholes show the tip of a nose. We fall, shot; and make no impression!

Let conflagration rage; of whatsoever is combustible! Guard-rooms are burnt, Invalides mess-rooms. A distracted 'Peruke-maker with two fiery torches' is for burning 'the saltpetres of the Arsenal;'—had not a woman run screaming; had not a Patriot, with some tincture of Natural Philosophy,[10] instantly struck the wind

out of him (butt of musket on pit of stomach), overturned barrels, and stayed the devouring element. A young beautiful lady, seized escaping in these Outer Courts, and thought falsely to be De Launay's daughter, shall be burnt in De Launay's sight; she lies swooned on paillasse;[11] but again a Patriot, it is brave Aubin Bonnemère the old soldier, dashes in and rescues her. Straw is burnt; three cartloads of it, hauled thither, go up in white smoke, almost to the choking of Patriotism itself; so that Elie had, with singed brows, to drag back one cart; and Réole the 'gigantic haberdasher' another. Smoke as of Tophet; confusion as of Babel; noise as of the Crack of Doom!

Blood flows; the aliment of new madness. The wounded are carried into houses of the Rue Cerisaie; the dying leave their last mandate not to yield till the accursed Stronghold fall. And yet, alas, how fall? The walls are so thick! Deputations, three in number, arrive from the Hôtel-de-Ville; Abbé Fauchat (who was of one) can say, with what almost superhuman courage of benevolence. These wave their Town-flag in the arched Gateway; and stand, rolling their drum; but to no purpose. In such Crack of Doom, De Launay cannot hear them, dare not believe them: they return, with justified rage, the whew of lead still singing in their ears. What to do? The Firemen are here, squirting with their fire pumps on the Invalides cannon, to wet the touchholes; they unfortunately cannot squirt so high; but produce only clouds of spray. Individuals of classical knowledge propose *catapults*. Santerre, the sonorous Brewer of the Suburb Saint Antoine, advises rather that the place be fired by a 'mixture of phosphorus and oil-of-turpentine spouted up through forcing pumps:' O Spinola-Santerre,[†] hast thou the mixture ready? Every man his own engineer! And still the fire-deluge abates not: even women are firing, and Turks; at least one woman (with her sweetheart), and one Turk. Gardes Françaises have come: real cannon, real cannoneers. Usher[12] Maillard is busy; half-pay Elie, half-pay Hulin rage in the midst of thousands.

How the great Bastille Clock ticks (inaudible) in its Inner Court there, at its ease, hour after hour; as if nothing special, for it or the world, were passing! It tolled One when the firing began; and is now pointing towards Five, and still the firing slakes not.—Far down, in their vaults, the seven Prisoners hear muffled

5 An ancient fable; see *Iliad*, III, 5.
6 maëlstrom, whirlpool
7 The principal naval port of France.
8 "Shall I not take mine ease in mine inn?" *1 Henry IV.*, III, iii, 93.
9 stage-coach
10 some knowledge of physics
* Carlyle is here merely reporting a glimpse of Elie as he gets it from some record. He has earlier described these two captains, Elie and Hulin, as "both with an air of half-pay."

11 straw mattress
12 *huissier*, constable
† General Spinola in 1625 took the fortress of Breda in Holland.

lin as of earthquakes; their Turnkeys answer vaguely.

Wo to thee, De Launay, with thy poor hundred Invalides! Broglie is distant, and his ears heavy: Besenval hears, but can send no help. One poor troop of Hussars has crept, reconnoitering, cautiously along the Quais, as far as the Pont Neuf.[13] "We are come to join you," said the Captain; for the crowd seems shoreless. A large-headed dwarfish individual of smoke-bleared aspect, shambles forward, opening his blue lips, for there is sense in him; and croaks: "Alight then, and give up your arms!" The Hussar-Captain is too happy to be escorted to the Barriers, and dismissed on parole. Who the squat individual was? Men answer, It is M. Marat, author of the excellent pacific *Avis au Peuple!*[14] Great truly, O thou remarkable Dogleech, is this thy day of emergence and new-birth: and yet this same day some four years——!—But let the curtains of the Future hang.[15]

What shall De Launay do? One thing only De Launay could have done: what he said he would do. Fancy him sitting, from the first, with lighted taper, within arm's length of the Powder-Magazine; motionless, like old Roman Senator, or Bronze Lamp-holder; coldly apprising Thuriot, and all men, by a slight motion of his eye, what his resolution was:—Harmless, he sat there, while unharmed; but the King's Fortress, meanwhile, could, might, would, or should, in nowise be surrendered, save to the King's Messenger: one old man's life is worthless, so it be lost with honour; but think, ye brawling *canaille*,[16] how will it be when a whole Bastille springs skyward!—In such catuesque, taper-holding attitude, one fancies De Launay might have left Thuriot, the red clerks of the Basoche, Curé of Saint-Stephen and all the tag-rag-and-bobtail of the world, to work their will.

And yet, withal, he could not do it. Hast thou considered how each man's heart is so tremulously responsive to the hearts of all men; hast thou noted how omnipotent is the very sound of many men? How their shriek of indignation palsies the strong soul; their howl of contumely withers with unfelt pangs? The bitter Gluck[17] confessed that the ground-tone of the noblest passage, in one of his noblest operas, was the voice of the Populace he had heard at Vienna, crying to their Kaiser:

Bread! Bread! Great is the combined voice of men; the utterance of their *instincts*, which are truer than their *thoughts*: it is the greatest a man encounters, among the sounds and shadows which make up this World of Time. He who can resist that, has his footing somewhere *beyond* Time. De Launay could not do it. Distracted, he hovers between two; hopes in the middle of despair; surrenders not his Fortress; declares that he will blow it up, seizes torches to blow it up, and does not blow it. Unhappy old De Launay, it is the death-agony of thy Bastille and thee! Jail, Jailoring, and Jailor, all three, such as they may have been, must finish.

For four hours now has the World-Bedlam roared: call it the World-Chimæra, blowing fire! The poor Invalides have sunk under their battlements, or rise only with reversed muskets: they have made a white flag of napkins; go beating the *chamade*,[18] or seeming to beat, for one can hear nothing. The very Swiss at the Portcullis look weary of firing; disheartened in the fire-deluge: a porthole at the drawbridge is opened, as by one that would speak. See Huissier Maillard, the shifty man! On his plank, swinging over the abyss of that stone Ditch; plank resting on parapet, balanced by weight of Patriots,—he hovers perilous: such a Dove towards such an Ark! Deftly, thou shifty Usher; one man already fell; and lies smashed, far down there, against the masonry; Usher Maillard falls not; deftly, unerring he walks, with outspread palm. The Swiss holds a paper through his porthole; the shifty Usher snatches it, and returns. Terms of surrender: Pardon, immunity to all! Are they accepted?—"*Foi d' officier*, On the word of an officer," answers half-pay Hulin,—or half-pay Elie, for men do not agree on it, "they are!" Sinks the drawbridge,—Usher Maillard bolting it when down; rushes-in the living deluge: the Bastille is fallen! *Victoire! La Bastille est prise!*[19]

THOMAS BABINGTON, LORD MACAULAY (1800-1859)

THE HISTORY OF ENGLAND

LONDON IN 1685. FROM CHAPTER III

Whoever examines the maps of London which were published towards the close of the reign of Charles the Second will see that only the nucleus of the present capital then existed.

---

[13] "New Bridge."
[14] "Advice to the People."
[15] He was assassinated by Charlotte Corday, July 13, 1793.
[16] rabble
[17] Of Germany. A *Ritter* is a knight.

[18] parley
[19] "Victory! The Bastille is taken!"—After the first anniversary of its capture, this ancient fortress and prison was razed to the ground.

The town did not, as now, fade by imperceptible degrees into the country. No long avenues of villas, embowered in lilacs and laburnums, extended from the great centre of wealth and civilization almost to the boundaries of Middlesex and far into the heart of Kent and Surrey. In the east, no part of the immense line of warehouses and artificial lakes which now stretches from the Tower to Blackwall had even been projected. On the west, scarcely one of those stately piles of building which are inhabited by the noble and wealthy was in existence; and Chelsea, which is now peopled by more than forty thousand human beings, was a quiet country village with about a thousand inhabitants. On the north, cattle fed, and sportsmen wandered with dogs and guns, over the site of the borough of Marylebone,[1] and over far the greater part of the space now covered by the boroughs of Finsbury and of the Tower Hamlets. Islington was almost a solitude; and poets loved to contrast its silence and repose with the din and turmoil of the monster London.[2] On the south the capital is now connected with its suburb by several bridges, not inferior in magnificence and solidity to the noblest works of the Cæsars. In 1685, a single line of irregular arches, overhung by piles of mean and crazy houses, and garnished, after a fashion, worthy of the naked barbarians of Dahomy,[3] with scores of mouldering heads, impeded the navigation of the river.

.   .   .   .   .   .

He who then rambled to what is now the gayest and most crowded part of Regent Street[4] found himself in a solitude, and was sometimes so fortunate as to have a shot at a woodcock. On the north the Oxford road ran between hedges. Three or four hundred yards to the south were the garden walls of a few great houses which were considered as quite out of town. On the west was a meadow renowned for a spring from which, long afterwards, Conduit Street was named. On the east was a field not to be passed without a shudder by any Londoner of that age. There, as in a place far from the haunts of men, had been dug, twenty years before, when the great plague was raging, a pit into which the dead-carts had nightly shot corpses by scores. It was popularly believed that the earth was deeply tainted with infection, and could not be disturbed without imminent risk to human life. No foundations were laid there till two generations had passed without any return of the pestilence, and till the ghastly spot had long been surrounded by buildings.

We should greatly err if we were to suppose that any of the streets and squares then bore the same aspect as at present. The great majority of the houses, indeed, have, since that time, been wholly, or in great part, rebuilt. If the most fashionable parts of the capital could be placed before us, such as they then were, we should be disgusted by their squalid appearance, and poisoned by their noisome atmosphere. In Covent Garden[5] a filthy and noisy market was held close to the dwellings of the great. Fruit women screamed, carters fought, cabbage stalks and rotten apples accumulated in heaps at the thresholds of the Countess of Berkshire and of the Bishop of Durham.

The centre of Lincoln's Inn Fields[6] was an open space where the rabble congregated every evening, within a few yards of Cardigan House and Winchester House, to hear mountebanks harangue, to see bears dance, and to set dogs at oxen. Rubbish was shot in every part of the area. Horses were exercised there. The beggars were as noisy and importunate as in the worst governed cities of the Continent. A Lincoln's Inn mumper[7] was a proverb. The whole fraternity knew the arms and liveries of every charitably disposed grandee in the neighbourhood, and, as soon as his lordship's coach and six appeared, came hopping and crawling in crowds to persecute him. These disorders lasted, in spite of many accidents, and of some legal proceedings, till, in the reign of George the Second, Sir Joseph Jekyll, Master of the Rolls, was knocked down and nearly killed in the middle of the square. Then at length palisades were set up, and a pleasant garden laid out.

Saint James's Square[8] was a receptacle for all the offal and cinders, for all the dead cats and dead dogs of Westminster.[9] At one time a cudgel player[10] kept the ring there. At another time an impudent squatter settled himself there, and built a shed for rubbish under the windows of the gilded saloons in which the first magnates of the realm, Norfolk, Ormond

---

1 Popularly pronounced Marlibun. or Maribun.
2 Cp. Cowley: *Discourse of Solitude.*
3 In West Africa. (This is a description of the famous old London Bridge.)
4 A fashionable shopping district in West London.
5 A piazza north of the Strand; a fruit and flower market.
6 The largest of London's squares, surrounded by lawyers' offices and ancient mansions.
7 beggar and impostor
8 The site of the most aristocratic mansions and clubs.
9 The portion of London which was once the city of Westminster; the site of the Government houses.
10 One skilled in contests with cudgels or staves.

Kent, and Pembroke, gave banquets and balls. It was not till these nuisances had lasted through a whole generation, and till much had been written about them, that the inhabitants applied to Parliament for permission to put up rails, and to plant trees.

When such was the state of the region inhabited by the most luxurious portion of society, we may easily believe that the great body of the population suffered what would now be considered as insupportable grievances. The pavement was detestable; all foreigners cried shame upon it. The drainage was so bad that in rainy weather the gutters soon became torrents. Several facetious poets have commemorated the fury with which these black rivulets roared down Snow Hill and Ludgate Hill, bearing to Fleet Ditch a vast tribute of animal and vegetable filth from the stalls of butchers and greengrocers. This flood was profusely thrown to right and left by coaches and carts. To keep as far from the carriage road as possible was therefore the wish of every pedestrian. The mild and timid gave the wall. The bold and athletic took it. If two roisterers met, they cocked their hats in each other's faces, and pushed each other about till the weaker was shoved towards the kennel.[11] If he was a mere bully he sneaked off, muttering that he should find a time. If he was pugnacious, the encounter probably ended in a duel behind Montague House.[12]

The houses were not numbered. There would indeed have been little advantage in numbering them; for of the coachmen, chairmen,[13] porters, and errand boys of London, a very small proportion could read. It was necessary to use marks which the most ignorant could understand. The shops were therefore distinguished by painted or sculptured signs, which gave a gay and grotesque aspect to the streets. The walk from Charing Cross to Whitechapel lay through an endless succession of Saracens' Heads, Royal Oaks, Blue Bears, and Golden Lambs, which disappeared when they were no longer required for the direction of the common people.

When the evening closed in, the difficulty and danger of walking about London became serious indeed. The garret windows were opened, and pails were emptied, with little regard to those who were passing below. Falls, bruises, and broken bones were of constant occurrence. For, till the last year of the reign of Charles the Second, most of the streets were left in

profound darkness. Thieves and robbers plied their trade with impunity: yet they were hardly so terrible to peaceable citizens as another class of ruffians. It was a favourite amusement of dissolute young gentlemen to swagger by night about the town, breaking windows, upsetting sedans, beating quiet men, and offering rude caresses to pretty women. Several dynasties of these tyrants had, since the Restoration, domineered over the streets. The Muns and Tityre Tus had given place to the Hectors, and the Hectors had been recently succeeded by the Scourers. At a later period rose the Nicker, the Hawcubite, and the yet more dreaded name of Mohawk. The machinery for keeping the peace was utterly contemptible. There was an act of Common Council which provided that more than a thousand watchmen should be constantly on the alert in the city, from sunset to sunrise, and that every inhabitant should take his turn of duty. But this Act was negligently executed. Few of those who were summoned left their homes; and those few generally found it more agreeable to tipple in alehouses than to pace the streets.

THE LONDON COFFEE HOUSES. FROM CHAPTER III

The coffee house must not be dismissed with a cursory mention. It might indeed at that time have been not improperly called a most important political institution. No Parliament had sat for years. The municipal council of the City had ceased to speak the sense of the citizens. Public meetings, harangues, resolutions, and the rest of the modern machinery of agitation had not yet come into fashion. Nothing resembling the modern newspaper existed. In such circumstances the coffee houses were the chief organs through which the public opinion of the metropolis vented itself.

The first of these establishments had been set up, in the time of the Commonwealth, by a Turkey merchant, who had acquired among the Mahometans a taste for their favourite beverage. The convenience of being able to make appointments in any part of the town, and of being able to pass evenings socially at a very small charge, was so great that the fashion spread fast. Every man of the upper or middle class went daily to his coffee house to learn the news and to discuss it. Every coffee house had one or more orators to whose eloquence the crowd listened with admiration, and who soon became, what the journalists of our own time have been called, a fourth Estate of the realm. The court had long seen with uneasiness the

1 gutter
2 In Whitehall, the region of the Government offices.
3 sedan-chair bearers

growth of this new power in the state. An attempt had been made, during Danby's[1] administration, to close the coffee houses. But men of all parties missed their usual places of resort so much that there was an universal outcry. The government did not venture, in opposition to a feeling so strong and general, to enforce a regulation of which the legality might well be questioned. Since that time ten years had elapsed, and during those years the number and influence of the coffee houses had been constantly increasing. Foreigners remarked that the coffee house was that which especially distinguished London from all other cities; that the coffee house was the Londoner's home, and that those who wished to find a gentleman commonly asked, not whether he lived in Fleet Street or Chancery Lane, but whether he frequented the Grecian or the Rainbow. Nobody was excluded from these places who laid down his penny at the bar. Yet every rank and profession, and every shade of religious and political opinion, had its own headquarters. There were houses near Saint James's Park where fops congregated, their heads and shoulders covered with black or flaxen wigs, not less ample than those which are now worn by the Chancellor and by the Speaker of the House of Commons. The wig came from Paris; and so did the rest of the fine gentleman's ornaments, his embroidered coat, his fringed gloves, and the tassel which upheld his pantaloons. The conversation was in that dialect which, long after it had ceased to be spoken in fashionable circles, continued, in the mouth of Lord Foppington,[2] to excite the mirth of theatres. The atmosphere was like that of a perfumer's shop. Tobacco in any other form than that of richly scented snuff was held in abomination. If any clown, ignorant of the usages of the house, called for a pipe, the sneers of the whole assembly and the short answers of the waiters soon convinced him that he had better go somewhere else. Nor, indeed, would he have had far to go. For, in general, the coffee rooms reeked with tobacco like a guard-room; and strangers sometimes expressed their surprise that so many people should leave their own firesides to sit in the midst of eternal fog and stench. Nowhere was the smoking more constant than at Will's. That celebrated house, situated between Covent Garden and Bow Street, was sacred to polite letters. There the talk was about poetical justice and the unities of place and time. There

was a faction for Perrault and the moderns[3] a faction for Boileau and the ancients. One group debated whether *Paradise Lost* ought not to have been in rhyme. To another an envious poetaster demonstrated that *Venice Preserved* ought to have been hooted from the stage. Under no roof was a greater variety of figures to be seen. There were Earls in stars and garters, clergymen in cassocks and bands, pert Templars,[5] sheepish lads from the Universities, translators and index makers in ragged coats of frieze. The great press was to get near the chair where John Dryden sat. In winter that chair was always in the warmest nook by the fire; in summer it stood in the balcony. To bow to the Laureate, and to hear his opinion of Racine's last tragedy or of Bossu's treatise on epic poetry, was thought a privilege. A pinch from his snuff-box was an honour sufficient to turn the head of a young enthusiast. There were coffee houses where the first medical men might be consulted. Doctor John Radcliffe, who, in the year 1685, rose to the largest practice in London, came daily, at the hour when the Exchange was full, from his house in Bow Street, then a fashionable part of the capital, to Garraway's, and was to be found, surrounded by surgeons and apothecaries, at a particular table. There were Puritan coffee houses where no oath was heard, and where lank-haired men discussed election and reprobation through their noses; Jew coffee houses where dark eyed money changers from Venice and from Amsterdam greeted each other; and Popish coffee houses where, as good Protestants believed, Jesuits planned, over their cups, another great fire, and cast silver bullets to shoot the King.

These gregarious habits had no small share in forming the character of the Londoner of that age. He was, indeed, a different being from the rustic Englishman. There was then the intercourse which now exists between the two classes. Only very great men were in the habit of dividing the year between town and country. Few esquires came to the capital thrice in their lives. Nor was it yet the practice of all citizens in easy circumstances to breathe the fresh air of the fields and woods during some weeks of every summer. A cockney, in a rural village, was stared at as much as if he had intruded into a Kraal of Hottentots

1 Thomas Osborn, Lord Treasurer under Charles II.
2 A character in Vanbrugh's *The Relapse*. As an example of the dialect Macaulay gives the word Lord, pronounced Lard.
3 Between Perrault and Boileau, two members of the French Academy, arose about 1687 famous quarrel over the respective merits modern and ancient literature.
4 By Thomas Otway, a contemporary dramatist.
5 Students or lawyers residing in the Temple.

ots. On the other hand, when the Lord of a Lincolnshire or Shropshire manor appeared in Fleet Street, he was as easily distinguished from the resident population as a Turk or a Lascar. His dress, his gait, his accent, the manner in which he stared at the shops, stumbled into the gutters, ran against the porters, and stood under the water spouts, marked him out as an excellent subject for the operations of swindlers and banterers. Bullies jostled him into the kennel. Hackney coachmen splashed him from head to foot. Thieves explored with perfect security the huge pockets of his horseman's coat, while he stood entranced by the splendour of the Lord Mayor's show. Moneydroppers,[6] sore from the cart's tail,[7] introduced themselves to him, and appeared to him the most honest, friendly gentlemen that he had ever seen. Painted women, the refuse of Lewkner Lane and Whetstone Park, passed themselves on him for countesses and maids of honour. If he asked his way to Saint James's,[8] his informants sent him to Mile End.[9] If he went into a shop, he was instantly discerned to be a fit purchaser of everything that nobody else would buy, of secondhand embroidery, copper rings, and watches that would not go. If he rambled into any fashionable coffee house, he became a mark for the insolent derision of fops and the grave waggery of Templars. Enraged and mortified, he soon returned to his mansion, and there, in the homage of his tenants, and the conversation of his boon companions, found consolation for the vexations and humiliations which he had undergone. There he was once more a great man, and saw nothing above himself except when at the assizes he took his seat on the bench near the judge, or when at the muster of the militia he saluted the Lord Lieutenant.

THE BATTLE OF KILLIECRANKIE. FROM CHAPTER XIII*

While these things were passing in the Parliament House, the civil war in the Highlands, having been during a few weeks suspended,

broke forth again more violently than before. Since the splendour of the House of Argyle[1] had been eclipsed, no Gaelic chief could vie in power with the Marquess of Athol. The district from which he took his title, and of which he might almost be called the sovereign, was in extent larger than an ordinary county, and was more fertile, more diligently cultivated, and more thickly peopled than the greater part of the Highlands. The men who followed his banner were supposed to be not less numerous than all the Macdonalds and Macleans united, and were, in strength and courage, inferior to no tribe in the mountains. But the clan had been made insignificant by the insignificance of the chief. The Marquess was the falsest, the most fickle, the most pusillanimous, of mankind. Already, in the short space of six months, he had been several times a Jacobite, and several times a Williamite. Both Jacobites and Williamites regarded him with contempt and distrust, which respect for his immense power prevented them from fully expressing. After repeatedly vowing fidelity to both parties, and repeatedly betraying both, he began to think that he should best provide for his safety by abdicating the functions both of a peer and of a chieftain, by absenting himself both from the Parliament House at Edinburgh and from his castle in the mountains, and by quitting the country to which he was bound by every tie of duty and honour at the very crisis of her fate. While all Scotland was waiting with impatience and anxiety to see in which army his numerous retainers would be arrayed, he stole away to England, settled himself at Bath, and pretended to drink the waters. His principality, left without a head, was divided against itself. The general leaning of the Athol men was towards King James. For they had been employed by him, only four years before, as the ministers of his vengeance against the House of Argyle. They had garrisoned Inverary: they had ravaged Lorn: they had demolished houses, cut down fruit trees, burned fishing boats, broken millstones, hanged Campbells, and were therefore not likely to be pleased by the prospect of MacCallum More's[2] restoration. One word from the Marquess

6 Confidence men who drop money and pretend to find it for purposes of fraud.

7 Offenders were tied to the end of a cart and whipped through the streets.

8 In West London.

9 In East London.

The events here described took place in July, 1689, during the English Revolution. James the Second had lately been deposed, but the success of the party of William was still in doubt. In Scotland, William was supported by the parliament at Edinburgh and had a body of troops commanded by General Mackay. On the other hand, John Graham of Claver-

1 The Campbells. The last Earl of Argyle had been executed for participating in Monmouth's rising against James.

2 A name given to the Dukes and Earls of Argyle.

3 broadswords

house, Viscount Dundee, had gathered about him his own Lowland adherents and a considerable force of Highland clansmen who supported James. Compare Scott's poem, *Bonny Dundee*, p. 448.

would have sent two thousand claymores[3] to the Jacobite side. But that word he would not speak; and the consequence was, that the conduct of his followers was as irresolute and inconsistent as his own.

While they were waiting for some indication of his wishes, they were called to arms at once by two leaders, either of whom might, with some show of reason, claim to be considered as the representative of the absent chief. Lord Murray, the Marquess's eldest son, who was married to a daughter of the Duke of Hamilton, declared for King William. Stewart of Ballenach, the Marquess's confidential agent, declared for King James. The people knew not which summons to obey. He whose authority would have been held in profound reverence, had plighted faith to both sides, and had then run away for fear of being under the necessity of joining either; nor was it very easy to say whether the place which he had left vacant belonged to his steward or to his heir apparent.

The most important military post in Athol was Blair Castle. The house which now bears that name is not distinguished by any striking peculiarity from other country seats of the aristocracy. The old building was a lofty tower of rude architecture which commanded a vale watered by the Garry. The walls would have offered very little resistance to a battering train, but were quite strong enough to keep the herdsmen of the Grampians[4] in awe. About five miles south of this stronghold, the valley of the Garry contracts itself into the celebrated glen of Killiecrankie. At present a highway as smooth as any road in Middlesex[5] ascends gently from the low country to the summit of the defile. White villas peep from the birch forest; and, on a fine summer day, there is scarcely a turn of the pass at which may not be seen some angler casting his fly on the foam of the river, some artist sketching a pinnacle of rock, or some party of pleasure banqueting on the turf in the fretwork of shade and sunshine. But, in the days of William the Third, Killiecrankie was mentioned with horror by the peaceful and industrious inhabitants of the Perthshire lowlands. It was deemed the most perilous of all those dark ravines through which the marauders of the hills were wont to sally forth. The sound, so musical to modern ears, of the river brawling round the mossy rocks and among the smooth pebbles, the masses of grey crag and verdure worthy of the pencil

of Wilson,[6] the fantastic peaks bathed, at sunrise and sunset, with light rich as that which glows on the canvass of Claude,[7] suggested to our ancestors thoughts of murderous ambuscades and of bodies stripped, gashed, and abandoned to the birds of prey. The only path was narrow and rugged: a horse could with difficulty be led up: two men could hardly walk abreast; and, in some places, the way ran so close by the precipice that the traveller had great need of a steady eye and foot. Many years later, the first Duke of Athol constructed a road up which it was just possible to drag his coach. But even that road was so steep and strait that a handful of resolute men might have defended it against an army; nor did any Saxon[8] consider a visit to Killiecrankie as a pleasure, till experience had taught the English Government that the weapons by which the Celtic clans could be most effectually subdued were the pickaxe and the spade.

The country which lay just above this pass was now the theatre of a war such as the Highlands had not often witnessed. Men wearing the same tartan, and attached to the same lord, were arrayed against each other. The name of the absent chief was used, with some show of reason, on both sides. Ballenach, at the head of a body of vassals who considered him as the representative of the Marquess, occupied Blair Castle. Murray, with twelve hundred followers, appeared before the walls and demanded to be admitted into the mansion of his family, the mansion which would one day be his own. The garrison refused to open the gates. Messages were sent off by the besiegers to Edinburgh and by the besieged to Lochaber.[9] In both places the tidings produced great agitation. Mackay and Dundee agreed in thinking that the crisis required prompt and strenuous exertions. On the fate of Blair Castle probably depended the fate of all Athol. On the fate of Athol might depend the fate of Scotland. Mackay hastened northward, and ordered his troops to assemble in the low country of Perthshire. Some of them were quartered at such a distance that they did not arrive in time. He soon, however, had with him the three Scotch regiments which had served in Holland, and which bore the names of their Colonels, Mackay himself, Balfour, and Ramsay. There was also a gallant regiment of infantry from England, then called Hastings's

---

[4] A mountain system in Scotland.
[5] An English county which then included a great part of the metropolis of London.
[6] Richard Wilson, English landscape painter.
[7] Claude Lorrain, French landscape painter.
[8] An Englishman or Lowlander, as opposed to the Highlanders, who are Celts.
[9] Mackay was at Edinburgh, Dundee in the district of Lochaber.

but now known as the thirteenth of the line. With these old troops were joined two regiments newly levied in the Lowlands. One of them was commanded by Lord Kenmore; the other, which had been raised on the Border, and which is still styled the King's Own Borderers, by Lord Leven. Two troops of horse, Lord Annandale's and Lord Belhaven's, probably made up the army to the number of above three thousand men. Belhaven rode at the head of his troop: but Annandale, the most factious of all Montgomery's followers, preferred the Club and the Parliament House to the field.*

Dundee, meanwhile, had summoned all the clans which acknowledged his commission to assemble for an expedition into Athol. His exertions were strenuously seconded by Lochiel.[10] The fiery crosses[11] were sent again in all haste through Appin and Ardnamurchan, up Glenmore, and along Loch Leven. But the call was so unexpected, and the time allowed was so short, that the muster was not a very full one. The whole number of broadswords seems to have been under three thousand. With this force, such as it was, Dundee set forth. On his march he was joined by succours which had just arrived from Ulster. They consisted of little more than three hundred Irish foot, ill armed, ill clothed, and ill disciplined. Their commander was an officer named Cannon, who had seen service in the Netherlands, and who might perhaps have acquitted himself well in a subordinate post and in a regular army, but who was altogether unequal to the part now assigned him. He had already loitered among the Hebrides so long that some ships which had been sent with him, and which were laden with stores, had been taken by English cruisers. He and his soldiers had with difficulty escaped the same fate. Incompetent as he was, he bore a commission which gave him military rank in Scotland next to Dundee.

The disappointment was severe. In truth James would have done better to withhold all assistance from the Highlanders than to mock them by sending them, instead of the well appointed army which they had asked and expected, a rabble contemptible in numbers and appearance. It was now evident that whatever was done for his cause in Scotland must be done by Scottish hands.

While Mackay from one side, and Dundee from the other, were advancing towards Blair Castle, important events had taken place there. Murray's adherents soon began to waver in their fidelity to him. They had an old antipathy to Whigs; for they considered the name of Whig as synonymous with the name of Campbell. They saw arrayed against them a large number of their kinsmen, commanded by a gentleman who was supposed to possess the confidence of the Marquess. The besieging army therefore melted rapidly away. Many returned home on the plea that, as their neighbourhood was about to be the seat of war, they must place their families and cattle in security. Others more ingenuously declared that they would not fight in such a quarrel. One large body went to a brook, filled their bonnets with water, drank a health to King James, and then dispersed. Their zeal for King James, however did not induce them to join the standard of his general. They lurked among the rocks and thickets which overhang the Garry, in the hope that there would soon be a battle, and that, whatever might be the event, there would be fugitives and corpses to plunder.

Murray was in a strait. His force had dwindled to three or four hundred men: even in those men he could put little trust; and the Macdonalds and Camerons were advancing fast. He therefore raised the siege of Blair Castle, and retired with a few followers into the defile of Killiecrankie. There he was soon joined by a detachment of two hundred fusileers whom Mackay had sent forward to secure the pass. The main body of the Lowland army speedily followed.

Early in the morning of Saturday the twenty-seventh of July, Dundee arrived at Blair Castle. There he learned that Mackay's troops were already in the ravine of Killiecrankie. It was necessary to come to a prompt decision. A council of war was held. The Saxon officers were generally against hazarding a battle. The Celtic chiefs were of a different opinion. Glengarry[12] and Lochiel were now both of a mind. "Fight, my Lord," said Lochiel with his usual energy; "fight immediately: fight, if you have only one to three. Our men are in heart. Their only fear is that the enemy should escape. Give them their way; and be assured that they will either perish or gain a complete victory. But if you restrain them, if you force them to remain on the defensive, I answer for nothing. If we do not fight, we had better break up and retire to our mountains."

Dundee's countenance brightened. "You hear, gentlemen," he said to his Lowland

10 Sir Ewan Cameron of Lochiel.   11 The signal for a gathering.

* Sir James Montgomery, a malcontent scheming for office, had formed a club at Edinburgh to concert plans of secret opposition to the king.

12 Macdonald of Glengarry, another Highland chieftain.

officers, "you hear the opinion of one who understands Highland war better than any of us." No voice was raised on the other side. It was determined to fight; and the confederated clans in high spirits set forward to encounter the enemy.

The enemy meanwhile had made his way up the pass. The ascent had been long and toilsome: for even the foot had to climb by twos and threes; and the baggage horses, twelve hundred in number, could mount only one at a time. No wheeled carriage had ever been tugged up that arduous path. The head of the column had emerged and was on the table land while the rearguard was still in the plain below. At length the passage was effected; and the troops found themselves in a valley of no great extent. Their right was flanked by a rising ground, their left by the Garry. Wearied with the morning's work, they threw themselves on the grass to take some rest and refreshment.

Early in the afternoon, they were roused by an alarm that the Highlanders were approaching. Regiment after regiment started up and got into order. In a little while the summit of an ascent which was about a musket shot before them was covered with bonnets and plaids. Dundee[13] rode forward for the purpose of surveying the force with which he was to contend, and then drew up his own men with as much skill as their peculiar character permitted him to exert. It was desirable to keep the clans distinct. Each tribe, large or small, formed a column separated from the next column by a wide interval. One of these battalions might contain seven hundred men, while another consisted of only a hundred and twenty. Lochiel had represented that it was impossible to mix men of different tribes without destroying all that constituted the peculiar strength of a Highland army.

On the right, close to the Garry, were the Macleans. Nearest to them were Cannon and his Irish foot. Next stood the Macdonalds of Clanronald, commanded by the guardian of their young prince. On their left were other bands of Macdonalds. At the head of one large battalion towered the stately form of Glengarry, who bore in his hand the royal standard of King James the Seventh.[14] Still further to the left were the cavalry, a small squadron consisting of some Jacobite gentlemen who had fled from the Lowlands to the mountains and of about forty of Dundee's old

troopers. The horses had been ill fed and ill tended among the Grampians, and looked miserably lean and feeble. Beyond them was Lochiel with his Camerons. On the extreme left, the men of Sky were marshalled by Macdonald of Sleat.

In the Highlands, as in all countries where war has not become a science, men thought it the most important duty of a commander to set an example of personal courage and of bodily exertion. Lochiel was especially renowned for his physical prowess. His clansmen looked big with pride when they related how he had himself broken hostile ranks and hewn down tall warriors. He probably owed quite as much of his influence to these achievements as to the high qualities which, if fortune had placed him in the English Parliament or at the French court, would have made him one of the foremost men of his age. He had the sense however to perceive how erroneous was the notion which his country men had formed. He knew that to give and to take blows was not the business of a general. He knew with how much difficulty Dundee had been able to keep together, during a few days, an army composed of several clans; and he knew that what Dundee had effected with difficulty Cannon would not be able to effect at all. The life on which so much depended must not be sacrificed to a barbarous prejudice. Lochiel therefore adjured Dundee not to run into any unnecessary danger. "Your Lordship's business," he said, "is to overlook everything, and to issue your commands. Our business is to execute those commands bravely and promptly." Dundee answered with calm magnanimity that there was much weight in what his friend Sir Ewan had urged, but that no general could effect anything great without possessing the confidence of his men. "I must establish my character for courage. Your people expect to see their leaders in the thickest of the battle; and to-day they shall see me there. I promise you, on my honour, that in future fights I will take more care of myself."

Meanwhile a fire of musketry was kept up on both sides, but more skillfully and more steadily by the regular soldiers than by the mountaineers. The space between the armies was one cloud of smoke. Not a few Highlanders dropped; and the clans grew impatient. The sun however was low in the west before Dundee gave the order to prepare for action. His men raised a great shout. The enemy, probably exhausted by the toil of the day, returned a feeble and wavering cheer. "We shall do it now," said Lochiel: "that is not

13 Here the narrative returns abruptly to the Jacobite army.

14 James Second of England was James Seventh of Scotland.

the cry of men who are going to win.'' He had walked through all his ranks, had addressed a few words to every Cameron, and had taken from every Cameron a promise to conquer or die.

It was past seven o'clock. Dundee gave the word. The Highlanders dropped their plaids. The few who were so luxurious as to wear rude socks of untanned hide spurned them away. It was long remembered in Lochaber that Lochiel took off what probably was the only pair of shoes in his clan, and charged barefoot at the head of his men. The whole line advanced firing. The enemy returned the fire and did much execution. When only a small space was left between the armies, the Highlanders suddenly flung away their firelocks, drew their broadswords, and rushed forward with a fearful yell. The Lowlanders prepared to receive the shock: but this was then a long and awkward process; and the soldiers were still fumbling with the muzzles of their guns and the handles of their bayonets when the whole flood of Macleans, Macdonalds, and Camerons came down. In two minutes the battle was lost and won. The ranks of Balfour's regiment broke. He was cloven down while struggling in the press. Ramsey's men turned their backs and dropped their arms. Mackay's own foot were swept away by the furious onset of the Camerons. His brother and nephew exerted themselves in vain to rally the men. The former was laid dead on the ground by a stroke from a claymore. The latter, with eight wounds on his body, made his way through the tumult and carnage to his uncle's side. Even in that extremity Mackay retained all his self-possession. He had still one hope. A charge of horse might recover the day! for of horse the bravest Highlanders were supposed to stand in awe. But he called on the horse in vain. Belhaven indeed behaved like a gallant gentleman: but his troopers, appalled by the rout of the infantry, galloped off in disorder; Annandale's men followed: all was over; and the mingled torrent of redcoats and tartans went raving down the valley to the gorge of Killiecrankie.

Mackay, accompanied by one trusty servant, spurred bravely through the thickest of the claymores and targets, and reached a point from which he had a view of the field. His whole army had disappeared, with the exception of some Borderers whom Leven had kept to-

gether, and of the English regiment, which had poured a murderous fire into the Celtic ranks, and which still kept unbroken order. All the men that could be collected were only a few hundreds. The general made haste to lead them across the Garry, and, having put that river between them and the enemy, paused for a moment to meditate on his situation.

He could hardly understand how the conquerors could be so unwise as to allow him even that moment for deliberation. They might with ease have killed or taken all who were with him before the night closed in. But the energy of the Celtic warriors had spent itself in one furious rush and one short struggle. The pass was choked by the twelve hundred beasts of burden which carried the provisions and baggage of the vanquished army. Such a booty was irresistibly tempting to men who were impelled to war quite as much by the desire of rapine as by the desire of glory. It is probable that few even of the chiefs were disposed to leave so rich a prize for the sake of King James. Dundee himself might at that moment have been unable to persuade his followers to quit the heaps of spoil, and to complete the great work of the day; and Dundee was no more.

At the beginning of the action he had taken his place in front of his little band of cavalry. He bade them follow him. and rode forward. But it seemed to be decreed that, on that day, the Lowland Scotch should in both armies appear to disadvantage. The horse hesitated. Dundee turned round, stood up in his stirrups, and, waving his hat, invited them to come on. As he lifted his arm, his cuirass rose, and exposed the lower part of his left side. A musket ball struck him: his horse sprang forward and plunged into a cloud of smoke and dust, which hid from both armies the fall of the victorious general. A person named Johnstone was near him and caught him as he sank down from the saddle. ''How goes the day?'' said Dundee. ''Well for King James;'' answered Johnstone: ''but I am sorry for Your Lordship.'' ''If it is well for him,'' answered the dying man, ''it matters the less for me.'' He never spoke again: but when, half an hour later, Lord Dunfermline and some other friends came to the spot, they thought that they could still discern some faint remains of life. The body wrapped in two plaids, was carried to the Castle of Blair.

THE VICTORIAN AGE

548

JOHN HENRY, CARDINAL NEWMAN (1801-1890)

SITE OF A UNIVERSITY†

If we would know what a University is, considered in its elementary idea, we must betake ourselves to the first and most celebrated home of European literature and source of European civilization, to the bright and beautiful Athens, —Athens, whose schools drew to her bosom, and then sent back again to the business of life the youth of the Western World for a long thousand years. Seated on the verge of the continent, the city seemed hardly suited for the duties of a central metropolis of knowledge; yet, what it lost in convenience of approach, it gained in its neighbourhood to the traditions of the mysterious East, and in the loveliness of the region in which it lay. Hither, then, as to a sort of ideal land, where all archetypes of the great and the fair were found in substantial being, and all departments of truth explored, and all diversities of intellectual power exhibited, where taste and philosophy were majestically enthroned as in a royal court, where there was no sovereignty but that of mind, and no nobility but that of genius, where professors were rulers, and princes did homage, hither flocked continually from the very corners of the *orbis terrarum*,[1] the many-tongued generation, just rising, or just risen into manhood, in order to gain wisdom.

Pisistratus‡ had in an early age discovered and nursed the infant genius of his people, and Cimon, after the Persian war,[2] had given it a home. That war had established the naval supremacy of Athens; she had become an imperial state; and the Ionians,[3] bound to her by the double chain of kindred and of subjection, were importing into her both their merchandise and their civilization. The arts and philosophy of the Asiatic coast were easily carried across the sea, and there was Cimon, as I have said, with his ample fortune, ready to receive

them with due honours. Not content with patronizing their professors, he built the first of those noble porticos,§ of which we hear so much in Athens, and he formed the groves, which in process of time became the celebrated Academy. Planting is one of the most graceful, as in Athens it was one of the most beneficent, of employments. Cimon took in hand the wild wood, pruned and dressed it, and laid it out with handsome walks and welcome fountains. Nor, while hospitable to the authors of the city's civilization, was he ungrateful to the instruments of her prosperity. His trees extended their cool, umbrageous branches over the merchants, who assembled in the Agora,[4] for many generations.

Those merchants certainly had deserved that act of bounty; for all the while their ships had been carrying forth the intellectual fame of Athens to the western world. Then commenced what may be called her University existence. Pericles, who succeeded Cimon both in the government and in the patronage of art, is said by Plutarch to have entertained the idea of making Athens the capital of federated Greece: in this he failed, but his encouragement of such men as Phidias[5] and Anaxagoras[6] led the way to her acquiring a far more lasting sovereignty over a far wider empire. Little understanding the sources of her own greatness, Athens would go to war; peace is the interest of a seat of commerce and the arts; but to war she went; yet to her, whether peace or war, it mattered not. The political power of Athens waned and disappeared; kingdoms rose and fell; centuries rolled away,—they did but bring fresh triumphs to the city of the poet and the sage. There at length the swarthy Moor and Spaniard were seen to meet the blue-eyed Gaul; and the Cappadocian, late subject of Mithridates, gazed without alarm at the haughty conquering Roman.* Revolution after revolution passed over the face of Europe, as well as of Greece, but still she was there,—Athens, the city of mind,—as radiant, as splendid, as delicate, as young, as ever she had been.

Many a more fruitful coast or isle is washed

1 the world
2 B. C. 500-449. Cimon, having signally defeated the Persians in 466 B. C., made liberal use of his spoils in adorning Athens.
3 Greeks of Asia Minor.
† From *The Rise and Progress of Universities*, originally published in 1854. Newman's large purpose, in this and his related works, of setting forth an ideal of University life and training, cannot be conveyed in an extract; but the present selection may afford some hint of it, besides exemplifying the author's imagination and rhetoric in their more gracious aspects.
‡ A ruler of Athens in the sixth century B. C., who established the groves and gymnasium known as the Lyceum, and who is said to have commissioned a body of scholars to collect and write down the poems of Homer.

4 The Market, or Exchange.
5 Sculptor of the frieze of the Parthenon, etc.
6 A philosopher.
§ Porches, or independent covered walks, often built in magnificent style, and used as outdoor resorts for conversation, study, or pleasure. In the Academy, mentioned just below, Plato taught for nearly fifty years.
* After the death of Mithridates, a powerful enemy of the Romans, Cappadocia passed into Roman control. The significance of the passage is that Athens was at the center of the great conflicts of races—of the South against the North, and the East against the West.

by the blue Ægean, many a spot is there more beautiful or sublime to see, many a territory more ample; but there was one charm in Attica, which, in the same perfection, was nowhere else. The deep pastures of Arcadia, the plain of Argos, the Thessalian vale, these had not the gift; Bœotia, which lay to its immediate north, was notorious for its very want of it. The heavy atmosphere of that Bœotia might be good for vegetation, but it was associated in popular belief with the dulness of the Bœotian intellect:[†] on the contrary, the special purity, elasticity, clearness, and salubrity of the air of Attica, fit concomitant and emblem of its genius, did that for it which earth did not;—it brought out every bright hue and tender shade of the landscape over which it was spread, and would have illuminated the face of even a more bare and rugged country.

A confined triangle, perhaps fifty miles its greatest length, and thirty its greatest breadth; two elevated rocky barriers, meeting at an angle; three prominent mountains, commanding the plain,—Parnes, Pentelicus, and Hymettus; an unsatisfactory soil; some streams, not always full;—such is about the report which the agent of a London company would have made of Attica. He would report that the climate was mild; the hills were limestone; there was plenty of good marble; more pasture land than at first survey might have been expected, sufficient certainly for sheep and goats; fisheries productive; silver mines once, but long since worked out; figs fair; oil first-rate; olives in profusion. But what he would not think of noting down, was, that the olive tree was so choice in nature and so noble in shape that it excited a religious veneration; and that it took so kindly to the light soil, as to expand into woods upon the open plain, and to climb up and fringe the hills. He would not think of writing word to his employers, how that clear air, of which I have spoken, brought out, yet blended and subdued, the colours on the marble, till they had a softness and harmony, for all their richness, which in a picture looks exaggerated, yet is after all within the truth. He would not tell, how that same delicate and brilliant atmosphere freshened up the pale olive, till the olive forgot its monotony, and its cheek glowed like the arbutus[1] or beech of the Umbrian hills.[2] He would say nothing of the thyme and the thousand fragrant herbs which carpeted Hymettus; he would hear noth-

ing of the hum of its bees; nor take much account of the rare flavour of its honey, since Gozo and Minorca[3] were sufficient for the English demand. He would look over the Ægean from the height he had ascended; he would follow with his eye the chain of islands, which, starting from the Sunian headland, seemed to offer the fabled divinities of Attica, when they would visit their Ionian cousins, a sort of viaduct thereto across the sea; but that fancy would not occur to him, nor any admiration of the dark violet billows with their white edges down below; nor of those graceful, fan-like jets of silver upon the rocks, which slowly rise aloft like water spirits from the deep, then shiver, and break, and spread, and shroud themselves, and disappear in a soft mist of foam; nor of the gentle, incessant heaving and panting of the whole liquid plain; nor of the long waves, keeping steady time, like a line of soldiery as they resound upon the hollow shore,—he would not deign to notice that restless living element at all except to bless his stars that he was not upon it.[4] Nor the distinct details, nor the refined colouring, nor the graceful outline and roseate golden hue of the jutting crags, nor the bold shadows cast from Otus or Laurium by the declining sun;—our agent of a mercantile firm would not value these matters even at a low figure. Rather we must turn for the sympathy we seek to yon pilgrim student, come from a semi-barbarous land to that small corner of the earth, as to a shrine, where he might take his fill of gazing on those emblems and coruscations of invisible unoriginate[5] perfection. It was the stranger from a remote province, from Britain or from Mauritania, who in a scene so different from that of his chilly, woody swamps, or of his fiery, choking sands, learned at once what a real University must be, by coming to understand the sort of country which was its suitable home.

Nor was this all that a University required, and found in Athens. No one, even there, could live on poetry. If the students at that famous place had nothing better than bright hues and soothing sounds, they would not have been able or disposed to turn their residence there to much account. Of course they must have the means of living, nay, in a certain sense, of enjoyment, if Athens was to be an Alma Mater[6] at the time, or to remain afterwards a pleasant thought in their memory. And so they had: be it recollected Athens was a port, and a mart of trade, perhaps the first

---

1 strawberry-tree, madroña.   2 In Italy.

[†] "As the nimble Attics would say, a glorious climate for eels, but a bad air for brains."—B. L. Gildersleeve. Yet Pindar was a Bœotian.

3 Islands in the Mediterranean.   5 not originated, self-existing, divine
4 The Ægean is famous for squalls.   6 fostering mother

in Greece; and this was very much to the point, when a number of strangers were ever flocking to it, whose combat was to be with intellectual, not physical difficulties, and who claimed to have their bodily wants supplied, that they might be at leisure to set about furnishing their minds. Now, barren as was the soil of Attica, and bare the face of the country, yet it had only too many resources for an elegant, nay, luxurious abode there. So abundant were the imports of the place, that it was a common saying, that the productions, which were found singly elsewhere, were brought all together in Athens. Corn and wine, the staple of subsistence in such a climate, came from the isles of the Ægean; fine wool and carpeting from Asia Minor; slaves, as now, from the Euxine, and timber too; and iron and brass from the coasts of the Mediterranean. The Athenian did not condescend to manufactures himself, but encouraged them in others; and a population of foreigners caught at the lucrative occupation both for home consumption and for exportation. Their cloth, and other textures for dress and furniture, and their hardware—for instance, armour—were in great request. Labour was cheap; stone and marble in plenty; and the taste and skill, which at first were devoted to public buildings, as temples and porticos, were in course of time applied to the mansions of public men. If nature did much for Athens, it is undeniable that art did much more.

Here some one will interrupt me with the remark: "By the by, where are we, and whither are we going?—what has all this to do with a University? at least what has it to do with education? It is instructive doubtless; but still how much has it to do with your subject?" Now I beg to assure the reader that I am most conscientiously employed upon my subject; and I should have thought every one would have seen this: however, since the objection is made, I may be allowed to pause awhile, and show distinctly the drift of what I have been saying, before I go farther. *What has this to do with my subject!* why, the question of the *site* is the very first that comes into consideration, when a *Studium Generale*[7] is contemplated; for that site should be a liberal and a noble one; who will deny it? All authorities agree in this, and very little reflection will be sufficient to make it clear. I recollect a conversation I once had on this very subject with a very eminent man.* I was a youth of eighteen, and was leaving my Uni-

versity for the Long Vacation, when I found myself in company in a public conveyance with a middle-aged person, whose face was strange to me. However, it was the great academical luminary of the day, whom afterwards I knew very well. Luckily for me, I did not suspect it; and luckily too, it was a fancy of his, as his friends knew, to make himself on easy terms especially with stage-coach companions. So, what with my flippancy and his condescension, I managed to hear many things which were novel to me at the time; and one point which he was strong upon, and was evidently fond of urging, was the material pomp and circumstance which should environ a great seat of learning. He considered it was worth the consideration of the government, whether Oxford should not stand in a domain of its own. An ample range, say four miles in diameter, should be turned into wood and meadow, and the University should be approached on all sides by a magnificent park, with fine trees in groups and groves and avenues, and with glimpses and views of the fair city, as the traveller drew near it. There is nothing surely absurd in the idea, though it would cost a round sum to realize it. What has a better claim to the purest and fairest possessions of nature, than the seat of wisdom? So thought my coach companion; and he did but express the tradition of ages and the instinct of mankind.

For instance, take the great University of Paris. That famous school engrossed as its territory the whole south bank of the Seine, and occupied one half, and that the pleasanter half, of the city. King Louis had the island pretty well as his own,—it was scarcely more than a fortification; and the north of the river was given over to the nobles and citizens to do what they could with its marshes; but the eligible south, rising from the stream which swept around its base, to the fair summit of St. Genevieve, with its broad meadows, its vineyards and its gardens, and with the sacred elevation of Montmartre[8] confronting it, all this was the inheritance of the University. There was that pleasant Pratum,[9] stretching along the river's bank, in which the students for centuries took their recreation, which Alcuin[10] seems to mention in his farewell verses

[7] School of Universal Learning.

[8] "Mount of Martyrs," north of the Seine; so named from the tradition that St. Denis, Bishop of Paris, suffered martyrdom there.
[9] Latin for "meadow"; French, *pré.*
[10] An English scholar who was Charlemagne's superintendent of education.
* Probably Dr. Edward Copleston (1776-1849) Provost of Oriel College, where Newman later became a Fellow. It was he who raised Oriel to a position of leadership at Oxford.

Paris, and which has given a name to the ~eat Abbey of St. Germain-des-Prés.[11] For ~ng years it was devoted to the purposes of ~nocent and healthy enjoyment; but evil times ~me on the University; disorder arose with-its precincts, and the fair meadow be-~me the scene of party brawls; heresy stalked ~rough Europe, and Germany and England no ~nger sending their contingent of students, a ~avy debt was the consequence to the academ-~al body. To let their land was the only source left to them: buildings rose upon it, ~d spread along the green sod, and the country length became town. Great was the grief ~d indignation of the doctors and masters, ~hen this catastrophe occurred. "A wretched ~ght," said the Proctor of the German ~tion,[12] "a wretched sight, to witness the sale ' that ancient manor, whither the Muses were ~ont to wander for retirement and pleasure. ~hither shall the youthful student now betake ~mself, what relief will he find for his eyes, ~earied with intense reading, now that the ~easant stream is taken from him?" Two ~nturies and more have passed since this com-~aint was uttered; and time has shown that ~e outward calamity, which it recorded, was ~t the emblem of the great moral revolution, ~hich was to follow; till the institution itself ~s followed its green meadows, into the region ' things which once were and now are not.[13]

CHARLES DICKENS (1812-1870)

A CHRISTMAS TREE*

I have been looking on, this evening, at a ~erry company of children assembled round at pretty German toy, a Christmas Tree. ~he tree was planted in the middle of a ~eat round table, and towered high above their ~ads. It was brilliantly lighted by a multitude little tapers; and everywhere sparkled and ~ittered with bright objects. There were rosy-~eeked dolls, hiding behind the green leaves; ~d there were real watches (with movable

Founded about 542 and dedicated to St. Ger-main, Bishop of Paris.
The Dean of the resident German students.
During the French revolution, the Faculties of the University were abolished and its organ-ization destroyed. In Newman's time it was only a member of the National University of France, but in 1896 it became once more the University of Paris.

Contributed by Dickens to *Household Words,* Dec. 21, 1850.

hands, at least, and an endless capacity of being wound up) dangling from innumerable twigs; there were French-polished tables, chairs, bedsteads, wardrobes, eight-day clocks, and various other articles of domestic furniture (wonderfully made, in tin, at Wolverhampton[1]), perched among the boughs, as if in preparation for some fairy housekeeping; there were jolly, broad-faced little men, much more agree-able in appearance than many real men—and no wonder, for their heads took off, and showed them to be full of sugar-plums; there were fiddles and drums; there were tambourines, books, work-boxes, paint-boxes, sweetmeat-boxes, peep-show boxes, and all kinds of boxes; there were trinkets for the elder girls, far brighter than any grown-up gold and jewels; there were baskets and pincushions in all de-vices; there were guns, swords, and banners; there were witches standing in enchanted rings of pasteboard, to tell fortunes; there were teetotums, humming-tops, needle-cases, pen-wipers, smelling-bottles, conversation-cards, bouquet-holders; real fruit, made artificially dazzling with goldleaf; imitation apples, pears, and walnuts, crammed with surprises; in short, as a pretty child before me delightedly whis-pered to another pretty child, her bosom friend, "There was everything, and more." This mot-ley collection of odd objects, clustering on the tree like magic fruit, and flashing back the bright looks directed towards it from every side—some of the diamond-eyes admiring it were hardly on a level with the table, and a few were languishing in timid wonder on the bosoms of pretty mothers, aunts, and nurses—made a lively realization of the fancies of childhood; and set me thinking how all the trees that grow and all the things that come into existence on the earth, have their wild adornments at that well-remembered time.

Being now at home again, and alone, the only person in the house awake, my thoughts are drawn back, by a fascination which I do not care to resist, to my own childhood. I begin to consider, what do we all remember best upon the branches of the Christmas Tree of our own young Christmas days, by which we climbed to real life.

Straight, in the middle of the room, cramped in the freedom of its growth by no encircling walls or soon-reached ceiling, a shadowy tree arises; and, looking up into the dreamy bright-ness of its top—for I observe in this tree the singular property that it appears to grow

[1] In Staffordshire; a center for the manufacture of hardware.

downward towards the earth—I look into my
youngest Christmas recollections!

All toys at first I find. Up yonder, among the
green holly and red berries, is the Tumbler
with his hands in his pockets, who wouldn't lie
down, but whenever he was put upon the floor,
persisted in rolling his fat body about, until
he rolled himself still, and brought those lobster
eyes of his to bear upon me—when I affected
to laugh very much, but in my heart of hearts
was extremely doubtful of him. Close beside
him is that infernal snuff-box, out of which
there sprang a demoniacal Counsellor in a black
gown, with an obnoxious head of hair, and a
red cloth mouth, wide open, who was not to be
endured on any terms, but could not be put
away either; for he used suddenly, in a highly
magnified state, to fly out of Mammoth Snuff-
boxes in dreams, when least expected. Nor is
the frog with cobbler's wax on his tail,
far off; for there was no knowing where he
wouldn't jump; and when he flew over the
candle, and came upon one's hand with that
spotted back—red on a green ground—he was
horrible. The cardboard lady in a blue-silk
skirt, who was stood up against the candlestick
to dance, and whom I see on the same branch,
was milder, and was beautiful; but I can't
say as much for the larger cardboard man, who
used to be hung against the wall and pulled
by a string; there was a sinister expression
in that nose of his; and when he got his legs
round his neck (which he very often did), he
was ghastly, and not a creature to be alone
with.

When did that dreadful Mask first look at
me? Who put it on, and why was I so frightened that the sight of it is an era in my life?
It is not a hideous visage in itself; it is even
meant to be droll; why then were its stolid
features so intolerable? Surely not because it
hid the wearer's face? An apron would have
done as much; and though I should have preferred even the apron away, it would not have
been absolutely insupportable, like the mask.
Was it the immovability of the mask? The
doll's face was immovable, but I was not afraid
of *her*. Perhaps that fixed and set change
coming over a real face, infused into my quickened heart some remote suggestion and dread of
the universal change that is to come on every
face, and make it still? Nothing reconciled me to
it. No drummers, from whom proceeded a melancholy chirping on the turning of a handle; no
regiment of soldiers, with a mute band, taken
out of a box, and fitted, one by one, upon a

stiff and lazy little set of lazy-tongs;[1] no o
woman, made of wires and a brown-paper cor
position, cutting up a pie for two small chi
dren; could give me a permanent comfort, f
a long time. Nor was it any satisfaction
be shown the Mask, and see that it was ma
of paper, or to have it locked up and be a
sured that no one wore it. The mere recolle
tion of that fixed face, the mere knowledge
its existence anywhere, was sufficient to awa
me in the night all perspiration and horr
with, "O I know it's coming! O the mask!

I never wondered what the dear old donk
with the panniers—there he is!—was made o
then! His hide was real to the touch, I rec
lect. And the great black horse with the rou
red spots all over him—the horse that I cou
even get upon—I never wondered what h
brought him to that strange condition,
thought that such a horse was not common
seen at Newmarket.[2] The four horses of
colour, next to him, that went into the wagg
of cheeses, and could be taken out and stabl
under the piano, appear to have bits of fu
tippet for their tails, and other bits for th
manes, and to stand on pegs instead of leg
but it was not so when they were brought ho
for a Christmas present. They were all rig
then; neither was their harness unceremo
ously nailed into their chests, as appears to
the case now. The tinkling works of the mus
cart, I *did* find out to be made of quill too
picks and wire; and I always thought th
little tumbler in his shirt sleeves, perpetua
swarming up one side of a wooden frame, a
coming down, head foremost, on the oth
rather a weak-minded person—though goo
natured; but the Jacob's Ladder,[3] next hi
made of little squares of red wood, that we
flapping and clattering over one another, ea
developing a different picture, and the wh
enlivened by small bells, was a mighty mar
and a great delight.

Ah! The Doll's house!—of which I was n
proprietor, but where I visited. I don't adm
the Houses of Parliament half so much as th
stone-fronted mansion with real glass windo
and door-steps, and a real balcony—gree
than I ever see now, except at watering-place
and even they afford but a poor imitation. A
though it *did* open all at once, the entire hou
front (which was a blow, I admit, as cancelli

1 Scissors-like, extensi-
ble tongs, common-
ly used for picking
up objects at a dis-
tance.

2 Newmarket Heat
where annual ho
races are held.

3 Name taken from G
esis, xxviii, 12.

the fiction of a staircase), it was but to shut it up again, and I could believe. Even open, there were three distinct rooms in it: a sitting-room and bedroom, elegantly furnished, and best of all, a kitchen, with uncommonly soft fire-irons, a plentiful assortment of diminutive utensils—oh, the warming-pan!—and a tin man-cook in profile, who was always going to fry two fish. What Barmecide justice[4] have I done to the noble feasts wherein the set of wooden platters figured, each with its own peculiar delicacy, as a ham or turkey, glued tight on to it, and garnished with something green, which I recollect as moss! Could all the Temperance Societies of these later days, united, give me such a tea-drinking as I have had through the means of yonder little set of blue crockery, which really would hold liquid (it ran out of the small wooden cask, I recollect, and tasted of matches), and which made tea, nectar. And if the two legs of the ineffectual little sugar-tongs did tumble over one another, and want purpose, like Punch's[5] hands, what does it matter? And if I did once shriek out, as a poisoned child, and strike the fashionable company with consternation, by reason of having drunk a little teaspoon, inadvertently dissolved in too hot tea, I was never the worse for it, except by a powder!

Upon the next branches of the tree, lower down, hard by the green roller and miniature gardening-tools, how thick the books begin to hang. Thin books, in themselves, at first, but many of them, and with deliciously smooth covers of bright red or green. What fat black letters to begin with! ''A was an archer, and shot at a frog.'' Of course he was. He was an apple-pie also, and there he is! He was a good many things in his time, was A, and so were most of his friends, except X, who had so little versatility, that I never knew him to get beyond Xerxes or Xantippe—like Y, who was always confined to a Yacht or a Yew Tree; and Z condemned for ever to be a Zebra or a Zany. But now, the very tree itself changes, and becomes a bean-stalk—the marvellous bean-stalk up which Jack climbed to the Giant's house! And now, those dreadfully interesting, double-headed giants, with their clubs over their shoulders, begin to stride along the boughs in a perfect throng, dragging knights and ladies home for dinner by the hair of their heads. And Jack—how noble, with his sword of sharp-

ness, and his shoes of swiftness! Again those old meditations come upon me as I gaze up at him; and I debate within myself whether there was more than one Jack (which I am loth to believe possible), or only one genuine original admirable Jack, who achieved all the recorded exploits.

Good for Christmas time is the ruddy colour of the cloak, in which—the tree making a forest of itself for her to trip through, with her basket—Little Red Riding-Hood comes to me one Christmas Eve to give me information of the cruelty and treachery of that dissembling Wolf who ate her grandmother, without making any impression on his appetite, and then ate her, after making that ferocious joke about his teeth. She was my first love. I felt that if I could have married Little Red Riding-Hood, I should have known perfect bliss. But, it was not to be; and there was nothing for it but to look out the Wolf in the Noah's Ark there, and put him late in the procession on the table, as a monster who was to be degraded. O the wonderful Noah's Ark! It was not found seaworthy when put in a washing-tub, and the animals were crammed in at the roof, and needed to have their legs well shaken down before they could be got in, even there—and then, ten to one but they began to tumble out at the door, which was but imperfectly fastened with a wire latch—but what was *that* against it! Consider the noble fly, a size or two smaller than the elephant: the lady-bird, the butterfly—all triumphs of art! Consider the goose, whose feet were so small, and whose balance was so indifferent, that he usually tumbled forward, and knocked down all the animal creation. Consider Noah and his family, like idiotic tobacco-stoppers;[1] and how the leopard stuck to warm little fingers; and how the tails of the larger animals used gradually to resolve themselves into frayed bits of string!

Hush! Again a forest, and somebody up in a tree—not Robin Hood, not Valentine, not the Yellow Dwarf (I have passed him and all Mother Bunch's wonders,[2] without mention), but an Eastern King with a glittering scimitar and turban. By Allah! two Eastern Kings, for I see another, looking over his shoulder! Down upon the grass, at the tree's foot, lies the full length of a coal-black Giant, stretched asleep, with his head in a lady's lap; and near them is a glass box, fastened with four locks of shining steel, in which he keeps the lady

4 In the story of the "Barber's Sixth Brother" in the *Arabian Nights*, a rich Barmecide (the name of a princely family) sets before a starving man a service of empty dishes.
5 The masculine puppet of a Punch and Judy show.

1 Plugs used to compress tobacco in a pipe.
2 In *Mother Bunch's Fairy Tales*.

prisoner when he is awake. I see the four keys at his girdle now. The lady makes signs to the two kings in the tree, who softly descend. It is the setting-in of the bright Arabian Nights.

Oh, now all common things become uncommon and enchanted to me. All lamps are wonderful; all rings are talismans. Common flower-pots are full of treasure, with a little earth scattered on the top; trees are for Ali Baba to hide in; beef-steaks are to throw down into the Valley of Diamonds, that the precious stones may stick to them, and be carried by the eagles to their nests, whence the traders, with loud cries, will scare them. Tarts are made, according to the recipe of the Vizier's son of Bussorah, who turned pastry-cook after he was set down in his drawers at the gate of Damascus; cobblers are all Mustaphas, and in the habit of sewing up people cut into four pieces, to whom they are taken blindfold.

Any iron ring let into stone is the entrance to a cave which only waits for the magician, and the little fire, and the necromancy, that will make the earth shake. All the dates imported come from the same tree as that unlucky date, with whose shell the merchant knocked out the eye of the genie's invisible son. All olives are of the stock of that fresh fruit, concerning which the Commander of the Faithful overheard the boy conduct the fictitious trial of the fraudulent olive merchant; all apples are akin to the apple purchased (with two others) from the Sultan's gardener for three sequins, and which the tall black slave stole from the child. All dogs are associated with the dog, really a transformed man, who jumped upon the baker's counter, and put his paw on the piece of bad money. All rice recalls the rice which the awful lady, who was a ghoul, could only peck by grains, because of her nightly feasts in the burial-place. My very rocking-horse,—there he is, with his nostrils turned completely inside-out, indicative of Blood!—should have a peg in his neck, by virtue thereof to fly away with me, as the wooden horse did with the Prince of Persia, in the sight of all his father's Court.

Yes, on every object that I recognize among those upper branches of my Christmas Tree, I see this fairy light! When I wake in bed, at daybreak, on the cold dark winter mornings, the white snow dimly beheld, outside, through the frost on the window-pane, I hear Dinarzade. "Sister, sister, if you are yet awake, I pray you finish the history of the Young King of the Black Islands.'' Scheherazade replies, ''If my lord the Sultan will suffer me to live another day, sister, I will not only finish that, but tell you a more wonderful story yet.'' Then, the gracious Sultan goes out, giving no orders for the execution, and we all three breathe again.[1]

At this height of my tree I begin to see, cowering among the leaves—it may be born of turkey, or of pudding, or mince-pie, or of these many fancies, jumbled with Robinson Crusoe on his desert island, Philip Quarll among the monkeys,[2] Sandford and Merton[3] with Mr. Barlow, Mother Bunch, and the Mask—or it may be the result of indigestion, assisted by imagination and over-doctoring—a prodigious nightmare. It is so exceedingly indistinct, that I don't know why it's frightful—but I know it is. I can only make out that it is an immense array of shapeless things, which appear to be planted on a vast exaggeration of the lazy-tongs that used to bear the toy soldiers, and to be slowly coming close to my eyes, and receding to an immeasurable distance. When it comes closest, it is worst. In connection with it I descry remembrances of winter nights incredibly long; of being sent early to bed, as a punishment for some small offence, and waking in two hours, with a sensation of having been asleep two nights; of the leaden hopelessness of morning ever dawning; and the oppression of a weight of remorse.

And now, I see a wonderful row of little lights rise smoothly out of the ground, before a vast green curtain. Now, a bell rings—a magic bell, which still sounds in my ears unlike all other bells—and music plays, amidst a buzz of voices, and a fragrant smell of orange-peel and oil. Anon, the magic bell commands the music to cease, and the great green curtain rolls itself up majestically, and The Play begins! The devoted dog of Montargis avenges the death of his master, foully murdered in the Forest of Bondy;[4] and a humorous Peasant

1 The stories of the *Arabian Nights* were professedly related on successive nights by Scheherazade to her sister, in order to interest the Sultan, whom she had wedded, and so prevent him from carrying out his practice of beheading his bride the day after the wedding.

2 A castaway, like Robinson Crusoe, who was solaced on his desert island by a monkey.

3 The heroes of a popular juvenile book by Thomas Day. Mr. Barlow was the boys' instructor.

4 Aubrey de Montdidier was murdered in 1371 in the forest of Bondy (or of Montargis) and avenged by his dog, which attracted such suspicion to the slayer that the king finally required the slayer to fight with the dog. The story has been dramatized.

with a red nose and a very little ha+ whom I take from this hour forth to my bosom as a friend (I think he was a Waiter or an Hostler at a village Inn, but many years have passed since he and I have met), remarks that the sassigassity of that dog is indeed surprising; and evermore this jocular conceit will live in my remembrance fresh and unfading, overtopping all possible jokes, until the end of time. Or now, I learn with bitter tears how poor Jane Shore, dressed all in white, and with her brown hair hanging down, went starving through the streets;[5] or how George Barnwell killed the worthiest uncle that ever man had, and was afterwards so sorry for it that he ought to have been let off.[6] Comes swift to comfort me, the Pantomime—stupendous Phenomenon!—when clowns are shot from loaded mortars into the great chandelier, bright constellation that it is; when Harlequins,[7] covered all over with scales of pure gold, twist and sparkle, like amazing fish; when Pantaloon (whom I deem it no irreverence to compare in my own mind to my grandfather) puts red-hot pokers in his pocket, and cries "Here's somebody coming!" or taxes the Clown with petty larceny, by saying, "Now, I sawed you do it!" when Everything is capable, with the greatest ease, of being changed into Anything; and "Nothing is, but thinking makes it so." Now, too, I perceive my first experience of the dreary sensation—often to return in after-life—of being unable, next day, to get back to the dull, settled world; of wanting to live for ever in the bright atmosphere I have quitted; of doting on the little Fairy, with the wand like a celestial Barber's Pole, and pining for a Fairy immortality along with her. Ah, she comes back in many shapes, as my eye wanders down the branches of my Christmas Tree, and goes as often, and has never yet stayed by me!

Out of this delight springs the toy-theatre,— there it is, with its familiar proscenium,[8] and ladies in feathers, in the boxes!—and all its attendant occupation with paste and glue, and gum, and water colours, in the getting-up of The Miller and His Men,[9] and Elizabeth, or the

Exile of Siberia.[10] In spite of a few besetting accidents and failures (particularly an unreasonable disposition in the respectable Kelmar, and some others, to become faint in the legs, and double up, at exciting points of the drama), a teeming world of fancies so suggestive and all-embracing, that, far below it on my Christmas Tree, I see dark, dirty, real Theatres in the day-time, adorned with these associations as with the freshest garlands of the rarest flowers, and charming me yet.

But hark! The Waits[11] are playing, and they break my childish sleep! What images do I associate with the Christmas music as I see them set forth on the Christmas Tree? Known before all the others, keeping far apart from all the others, they gather round my little bed. An angel, speaking to a group of shepherds in a field; some travellers, with eyes uplifted, following a star; a baby in a manger; a child in a spacious temple, talking with grave men; a solemn figure, with a mild and beautiful face, raising a dead girl by the hand; again, near a city gate, calling back the son of a widow, on his bier, to life; a crowd of people looking through the opened roof of a chamber where he sits, and letting down a sick person on a bed, with ropes; the same, in a tempest, walking on the water to a ship; again, on a seashore, teaching a great multitude; again, with a child upon his knee, and other children round; again, restoring sight to the blind, speech to the dumb, hearing to the deaf, health to the sick, strength to the lame, knowledge to the ignorant; again, dying upon a Cross, watched by armed soldiers, a thick darkness coming on, the earth beginning to shake, and only one voice heard, "Forgive them, for they know not what they do."

Still, on the lower and maturer branches of the Tree, Christmas associations cluster thick. School-books shut up; Ovid and Virgil silenced; the Rule of Three,[12] with its cool impertinent inquiries, long disposed of; Terence and Plautus acted no more, in an arena of huddled desks and forms, all chipped, and notched, and inked; cricket-bats, stumps,[13] and balls, left higher up, with the smell of trodden grass and the softened noise of shouts in the evening air; the tree is still fresh, still gay. If I no more come home at Christmas time, there will be

5 In a tragedy (founded on fact) by Nicholas Rowe. See also the ballad of "Jane Shore" in Percy's *Reliques.*
6 *George Barnwell, or The London Merchant,* by George Lillo; founded on another ballad.
7 The clowns, in pantomimes, who play tricks upon an absurd old man, called "Pantaloon."
8 stage
9 Originally a popular melodrama by Isaac Pocock, first played at Covent Garden in 1813. A gang of bandits, disguised as millers, try to carry off the daughter of Kelmar, an old cottager.

10 Taken from a French novel published by Madame Cottin in 1806. Elizabeth walks from Siberia to Russia to get the Czar's pardon for her exiled family.
11 Street musicians who sing from house to house on Christmas Eve.
12 The rule of "proportion."
13 The three posts constituting a wicket in the game of cricket.

boys and girls (thank Heaven!) while the World lasts; and they do! Yonder they dance and play upon the branches of my Tree, God bless them, merrily, and my heart dances and plays too!

And I *do* come home at Christmas. We all do, or we all should. We all come home, or ought to come home, for a short holiday—the longer, the better—from the great boarding-school, where we are for ever working at our arithmetical slates, to take, and give a rest. As to going a visiting, where can we not go, if we will; where have we not been, when we would; starting our fancy from our Christmas Tree!

Away into the winter prospect. There are many such upon the tree! On, by low-lying, misty grounds, through fens and fogs, up long hills, winding dark as caverns between thick plantations, almost shutting out the sparkling stars; so, out on broad heights, until we stop at last, with sudden silence, at an avenue. The gate-bell has a deep, half-awful sound in the frosty air; the gate swings open on its hinges; and, as we drive up to a great house, the glancing lights grow larger in the windows, and the opposing rows of trees seem to fall solemnly back on either side, to give us place. At intervals, all day, a frightened hare has shot across this whitened turf; or the distant clatter of a herd of deer trampling the hard frost, has, for the minute, crushed the silence too. Their watchful eyes beneath the fern may be shining now, if we could see them, like the icy dewdrops on the leaves; but they are still, and all is still. And so, the lights growing larger, and the trees falling back before us, and closing up again behind us, as if to forbid retreat, we come to the house.

There is probably a smell of roasted chestnuts and other good comfortable things all the time, for we are telling Winter Stories—Ghost Stories, or more shame for us—round the Christmas fire; and we have never stirred, except to draw a little nearer to it. But, no matter for that. We came to the house, and it is an old house, full of great chimneys where wood is burnt on ancient dogs upon the hearth, and grim portraits (some of them with grim legends, too) lower distrustfully from the oaken panels of the walls. We are a middle-aged nobleman, and we make a generous supper with our host and hostess and their guests —it being Christmas time, and the old house full of company—and then we go to bed. Our room is a very old room. It is hung with tapestry. We don't like the portrait of a cavalier in green, over the fireplace. There are great black beams in the ceiling, and there is a great black bedstead, supported at the foot by two great black figures, who seem to have come off a couple of tombs in the old baronial church in the park, for our particular accommodation. But, we are not a superstitious nobleman, and we don't mind. Well! we dismiss our servant, lock the door, and sit before the fire in our dressing-gown, musing about a great many things. At length we go to bed. Well! we can't sleep. We toss and tumble, and can't sleep. The embers on the hearth burn fitfully and make the room look ghostly. We can't help peeping out over the counterpane, at the two black figures and the cavalier — that wicked-looking cavalier — in green. In the flickering light they seem to advance and retire: which, though we are not by any means a superstitious nobleman is not agreeable. Well! we get nervous—more and more nervous. We say "This is very foolish, but we can't stand this; we'll pretend to ill, and knock up somebody." Well! we are just going to do it, when the locked door opens, and there comes in a young woman, deadly pale, and with long fair hair, who glides to the fire, and sits down in the chair we have left there, wringing her hands. Then, we notice that her clothes are wet. Our tongue cleaves to the roof of our mouth, and we can't speak; but, we observe her accurately. Her clothes are wet; her long hair is dabbled with moist mud; she is dressed in the fashion of two hundred years ago; and she has at her girdle a bunch of rusty keys. Well! there she sits, and we can't even faint, we are in such a state about it. Presently she gets up, and tries all the locks in the room with the rusty keys, which won't fit one of them; then, she fixes her eyes on the portrait of the cavalier in green, and says, in a low, terrible voice, "The stags know it!" After that, she wrings her hands again, passes the bedside, and goes out at the door. We hurry on our dressing-gown, seize our pistols (we always travel with pistols), and are following, when we find the door locked. We turn the key, look out into the dark gallery; no one there. We wander away, and try to find our servant. Can't be done. We pace the gallery till daybreak; then return to our deserted room, fall asleep, and are awakened by our servant (nothing ever haunts *him*) and the shining sun. Well! we make a wretched breakfast, and all the company say we look queer. After breakfast, we go over the house with our host, and then we take him to the portrait of the cavalier in green, and then it all comes out. He was false to a young housekeeper once attached to that family, and famous for her beauty, who drowned herself in a pond, and whose body was discovered, after a long time, because the stags refused to drink of the water. Since which, it has been whispered that she traverses the house at midnight (but goes especially to that room where the cavalier in green was wont to sleep), trying the old locks with the rusty keys. Well! we tell our host of what we have seen, and a shade comes over his features, and he begs it may be hushed up; and so it is. But, it's all true; and we said so, before we died (we are dead now) to many responsible people.

There is no end to the old houses, with resounding galleries, and dismal state-bedchambers, and haunted wings shut up for many years, through which we may ramble, with an agreeable creeping up our back, and encounter any number of ghosts, but (it is worthy of remark perhaps) reducible to a very few general types and classes; for, ghosts have little originality, and "walk" in a beaten track. Thus, it comes to pass, that a certain room in a certain old hall, where a certain bad lord, baronet, knight, or gentleman, shot himself, has certain planks in the floor from which the blood *will not* be taken out. You may scrape and scrape, as the present owner has done, or plane and plane, as his father did, or scrub and scrub, as his grandfather did, or burn and burn with strong acids, as his great-grandfather did, but, there the blood will still be—no redder and no paler—no more and no less—always just the same. Thus, in such another house there is a haunted door, that never will keep open; or another door that never will keep shut; or a haunted sound of a spinning-wheel, or a hammer, or a footstep, or a cry, or a sigh, or a horse's tramp, or the rattling of a chain. Or else, there is a turret-clock, which, at the midnight hour, strikes thirteen when the head of the family is going to die; or a shadowy, immovable black carriage which at such a time is always seen by somebody, waiting near the great gates in the stable-yard. Or thus, it came to pass how Lady Mary went to pay a visit at a large wild house in the Scottish Highlands, and, being fatigued with her long journey, retired to bed early, and innocently said, next morning, at the breakfast-table, "How odd, to have so late a party last night, in this remote place, and not to tell me of it, before I went to bed!" Then, every one asked Lady Mary what she meant? Then, Lady Mary replied, "Why, all night long, the carriages were driving round and round the terrace, underneath my window!" Then, the owner of the house turned pale, and so did his Lady, and Charles Macdoodle of Macdoodle signed to Lady Mary to say no more, and every one was silent. After breakfast, Charles Macdoodle told Lady Mary that it was a tradition in the family that those rumbling carriages on the terrace betokened death. And so it proved, for, two months afterwards, the Lady of the mansion died. And Lady Mary, who was a Maid of Honour at Court, often told this story to the old Queen Charlotte; by this token that the old King always said, "Eh, eh? What, what? Ghosts, ghosts? No such thing, no such thing!" And never left off saying so, until he went to bed.

Or, a friend of somebody's whom most of us know, when he was a young man at college, had a particular friend, with whom he made the compact that, if it were possible for the Spirit to return to this earth after its separation from the body, he of the twain who first died, should reappear to the other. In course of time, this compact was forgotten by our friend; the two young men having progressed in life, and taken diverging paths that were wide asunder. But, one night, many years afterwards, our friend being in the North of England, and staying for the night in an inn, on the Yorkshire Moors, happened to look out of bed; and there, in the moonlight, leaning on a bureau near the window, stedfastly regarding him, saw his old college friend! The appearance being solemnly addressed, replied, in a kind of whisper, but very audibly, "Do not come near me. I am dead. I am here to redeem my promise. I come from another world, but may not disclose its secrets!" Then, the whole form becoming paler, melted, as it were, into the moonlight, and faded away.

Or, there was the daughter of the first occupier of the picturesque Elizabethan house, so famous in our neighbourhood. You have heard about her? No! Why, *She* went out one summer evening at twilight, when she was a beautiful girl, just seventeen years of age, to gather flowers in the garden; and presently came running, terrified, into the hall to her father, saying, "Oh, dear father, I have met myself!" He took her in his arms, and told her it was fancy, but she said, "Oh no! I met myself in the broad walk, and I was pale and gathering withered flowers, and I turned my head, and held them up!" And, that night, she died; and a picture of her story was begun, though never finished, and they say it is somewhere in the house to this day, with its face to the wall.

Or, the uncle of my brother's wife was riding home on horseback, one mellow evening at sunset, when, in a green lane close to his own house, he saw a man standing before him, in the very centre of the narrow way. "Why does that man in the cloak stand there!" he thought. "Does he want me to ride over him?" But the figure never moved. He felt a strange sensation at seeing it so still, but slackened his trot and rode forward. When he was so close to it, as almost to touch it with his stirrup, his horse shied, and the figure glided up the bank, in a curious, unearthly manner—backward, and without seeming to use its feet—and was gone. The uncle of my brother's wife, exclaiming, "Good Heaven! It's my cousin Harry, from Bombay!" put spurs to his horse, which was suddenly in a profuse sweat, and, wondering at such strange behaviour, dashed round to the front of his house. There, he saw the same figure, just passing in at the long French window of the drawing-room, opening on the ground. He threw his bridle to a servant, and hastened in after it. His sister was sitting there, alone. "Alice, where's my cousin Harry?" "Your cousin Harry, John?" "Yes. From Bombay. I met him in the lane just now, and saw him enter here, this instant." Not a creature had been seen by any one; and in that hour and minute, as it afterwards appeared, this cousin died in India.

Or, it was a certain sensible old maiden lady, who died at ninety-nine, and retained her faculties to the last, who really did see the Orphan Boy; a story which has often been incorrectly told, but, of which the real truth is this—because it is, in fact, a story belonging to our family—and she was a connection of our family. When she was about forty years of age, and still an uncommonly fine woman (her lover died young, which was the reason why she never married, though she had many offers), she went to stay at a place in Kent, which her brother, an Indian-Merchant, had newly bought. There was a story that this place had once been held in trust, by the guardian of a young boy; who was himself the next heir, and who killed the young boy by harsh and cruel treatment. She knew nothing of that. It has been said that there was a Cage in her bedroom in which the guardian used to put the boy. There was no such thing. There was only a closet. She went to bed, made no alarm whatever in the night, and in the morning said composedly to her

maid when she came in, "Who is the pretty forlorn-looking child who has been peeping out of that closet all night?" The maid replied by giving a loud scream, and instantly decamping. She was surprised; but she was a woman of remarkable strength of mind, and she dressed herself and went downstairs, and closeted herself with her brother. "Now, Walter," she said, "I have been disturbed all night by a pretty, forlorn-looking boy, who has been constantly peeping out of that closet in my room, which I can't open. This is some trick." "I am afraid not, Charlotte," said he, "for it is the legend of the house. It is the Orphan Boy. What did he do?" "He opened the door softly," said she, "and peeped out. Sometimes, he came a step or two into the room. Then, I called to him, to encourage him, and he shrunk, and shuddered, and crept in again, and shut the door." "The closet has no communication, Charlotte," said her brother, "with any other part of the house, and it's nailed up." This was undeniably true, and it took two carpenters a whole forenoon to get it open, for examination. Then, she was satisfied that she had seen the Orphan Boy. But, the wild and terrible part of the story is, that he was also seen by three of her brother's sons, in succession, who all died young. On the occasion of each child being taken ill, he came home in a heat, twelve hours before, and said, Oh, Mamma, he had been playing under a particular oak-tree, in a certain meadow, with a strange boy—a pretty, forlorn-looking boy, who was very timid, and made signs! From fatal experience, the parents came to know that this was the Orphan Boy, and that the course of that child whom he chose for his little playmate was surely run.

Legion is the name of the German castles where we sit up alone to wait for the Spectre—where we are shown into a room, made comparatively cheerful for our reception—where we glance round at the shadows, thrown on the blank walls by the crackling fire—where we feel very lonely when the village innkeeper and his pretty daughter have retired, after laying down a fresh store of wood upon the hearth, and setting forth on the small table such supper-cheer as a cold roast capon, bread, grapes, and a flask of old Rhine wine—where the reverberating doors close on their retreat, one after another, like so many peals of sullen thunder—and where, about the small hours of the night, we come into the knowledge of divers supernatural mysteries. Legion is the name of the haunted German students, in whose society we draw yet nearer to the fire, while the schoolboy in the corner opens his eyes wide and round, and flies off the footstool he has chosen for his seat, when the door accidentally blows open. Vast is the crop of such fruit, shining on our Christmas Tree; in blossom, almost at the very top; ripening all down the boughs!

Among the later toys and fancies hanging there—as idle often and less pure—be the image once associated with the sweet old Waits, the softened music in the night, ever unalterable! Encircled by the social thoughts of Christmas time, still let the benignant figure of my childhood stand unchanged! In every cheerful image and suggestion that the season brings, may the bright star that rested above the poor roof be the star of all the Christian World! A moment's pause, O vanishing tree, of which the lower boughs are dark to me as yet, and let me look once more! I know there are blank spaces on thy branches, where eyes that I have loved have shone and smiled; from which they are departed. But, far above, I see the raiser of the dead girl, and the Widow's Son; and God is good! If Age be hiding for me in the unseen portion of thy downward growth, O may I, with a grey head, turn a child's heart to that figure yet, and a child's trustfulness and confidence!

Now, the tree is decorated with bright merriment, and song, and dance, and cheerfulness. And they are welcome. Innocent and welcome be they ever held, beneath the branches of the Christmas Tree, which cast no gloomy shadow! But, as it sinks into the ground, I hear a whisper going through the leaves. "This, in commemoration of the law of love and kindness, mercy, and compassion. This, in remembrance of Me!"

WILLIAM MAKEPEACE THACKERAY (1811-1863)

FROM THE ENGLISH HUMOURISTS OF THE EIGHTEENTH CENTURY*

GOLDSMITH

"Jeté sur cette boule,
  Laid, chétif et souffrant;
Etouffé dans la foule,
  Faute d'être assez grand:

Une plainte touchante
  De ma bouche sortit.
Le bon Dieu me dit: Chante,
  Chante, pauvre petit!

Chanter, ou je m'abuse,
  Est ma tâche ici-bas.
Tous ceux qu'ainsi j'amuse,
  Ne m'aimeront-ils pas?"†

In those charming lines of Béranger, one may fancy described the career, the sufferings, the genius, the gentle nature of Goldsmith, and the esteem in which we hold him. Who, of the millions whom he has amused, doesn't love him? To be the most beloved of English writers, what a title that is for a man! A wild youth, wayward, but full of tenderness and affection, quits the country village, where his boyhood has been passed in happy musing, in idle shelter, in fond longing to see the great world out of doors, and achieve name and fortune: and after years of dire struggle, and neglect and poverty, his heart turning back as fondly to his native place as it had longed eagerly for change when sheltered there, he writes a book and a poem, full of the recollections and feelings of home: he paints the friends and scenes of his youth, and peoples Auburn and Wakefield‡ with remembrances of Lissoy. Wander he must, but he carries away a home-relic with him, and dies with it on his breast. His nature is truant; in repose it longs for change: as on the journey it looks back for friends and quiet. He passes to-day in building an air-castle for to-morrow, or in writing yesterday's elegy; and he would fly away this hour, but that a cage and necessity keep him. What is the charm of his verse, of his style, and humour? His sweet regrets, his delicate compassion, his soft smile, his tremulous sympathy, the weakness which he owns? Your love for him is half pity. You come foot and tired from the day's battle, and this sweet minstrel sings to you. Who could harm the kind vagrant harper? Whom did he ever hurt? He carries no weapon, save the harp on which he plays to you; and with which he delights great and humble, young and old,

† Béranger (1780-1851) was a kind of French Burns, a writer of songs beloved by the people. The lines may be translated somewhat freely thus:

  Flung into life,
    Dwarfed, ugly, in pain;
  Nigh crushed in the strife
    Where I struggle in vain;

  What wonder, should spring
    To my lips my dole?
  God said to me, "Sing!
    Sing, poor little soul!"

  So my task here below
    Is a-singing to rove;
  If pleasure I sow,
    Shall I not reap love?

‡ The scenes respectively of the poem and the romance on which Goldsmith's literary reputation chiefly rests. Compare *The Deserted Village* and the notes thereon, p. 373.

* These papers, six in number, were prepared by Thackeray as lectures and were delivered in England in 1851, and in America in the winter of 1852-53. The first lecture dealt with Swift, the last with Sterne and Goldsmith.

the captains in the tents, or the soldiers round the fire, or the women and children in the villages, at whose porches he stops and sings his simple songs of love and beauty. With that sweet story of the "Vicar of Wakefield" he has found entry into every castle and every hamlet in Europe. Not one of us, however busy or hard, but once or twice in our lives has passed an evening with him, and undergone the charm of his delightful music.

Goldsmith's father was no doubt the good Doctor Primrose,[1] whom we all of us know. Swift was yet alive, when the little Oliver was born at Pallas, or Pallasmore, in the county of Longford, in Ireland. In 1730, two years after the child's birth, Charles Goldsmith removed his family to Lissoy, in the county Westmeath, that sweet "Auburn" which every person who hears me has seen in fancy. Here the kind parson brought up his eight children; and loving all the world, as his son says, fancied all the world loved him. He had a crowd of poor dependants besides those hungry children. He kept an open table; round which sat flatterers and poor friends, who laughed at the honest rector's many jokes, and ate the produce of his seventy acres of farm. Those who have seen an Irish house in the present day can fancy that one of Lissoy. The old beggar still has his allotted corner by the kitchen turf;[2] the maimed old soldier still gets his potatoes and buttermilk; the poor cottier[3] still asks his honour's charity, and prays God bless his reverence for the sixpence; the ragged pensioner still takes his place by right and sufferance. There's still a crowd in the kitchen, and a crowd round the parlour table, profusion, confusion, kindness, poverty. If an Irishman comes to London to make his fortune, he has a half-dozen of Irish dependants who take a percentage of his earnings. The good Charles Goldsmith left but little provision for his hungry race when death summoned him; and one of his daughters being engaged to a Squire of rather superior dignity, Charles Goldsmith impoverished the rest of his family to provide the girl with a dowry.

The smallpox which scourged all Europe at that time, and ravaged the roses off the cheeks of half the world, fell foul of poor little Oliver's face, when the child was eight years old, and left him scarred and disfigured for his life. An old woman in his father's village taught him his letters, and pronounced him a dunce: Paddy Byrne, the hedge-schoolmaster,[4] took him in hand: and from Paddy Byrne he was transmitted to a clergyman at Elphin. When a child was sent to school in those days, the classic phrase was that he was placed under Mr. So-and-so's *ferule*. Poor little ancestors! It is hard to think how ruthlessly you were birched; and how much of needless whipping and tears our small forefathers had to undergo! A relative—kind uncle Contarine—took the main charge of little Noll; who went through his schooldays righteously doing as little work as he could: robbing orchards, playing at ball, and making his pocket-money fly about whenever fortune sent it to him. Everybody knows the story of that famous "Mistake of a Night," when the young schoolboy, provided with a guinea and a nag, rode up to the "best house" in Ardagh, called for the landlord's company over a bottle of wine at supper, and for a hot cake for breakfast in the morning; and found, when he asked for the bill, that the best house was Squire Featherstone's, and not the inn for which he mistook it.[5] Who does not know every story about Goldsmith? That is a delightful and fantastic picture of the child dancing and capering about in the kitchen at home, when the old fiddler gibed at him for his ugliness, and called him Æsop;[6] and little Noll made his repartee of "Heralds proclaim aloud this saying—See Æsop dancing and his monkey playing." One can fancy a queer pitiful look of humour and appeal upon that little scarred face—the funny little dancing figure, the funny little brogue. In his life, and his writings, which are the honest expression of it, he is constantly bewailing that homely face and person; anon he surveys them in the glass ruefully; and presently assumes the most comical dignity. He likes to deck out his little person in splendour and fine colours. He presented himself to be examined for ordination in a pair of scarlet breeches, and said honestly that he did not like to go into the Church, because he was fond of coloured clothes. When he tried to practise as a doctor, he got by hook or by crook a black velvet suit, and looked as big and grand as he could, and kept his hat over a patch on the old coat: in better days he bloomed out in plum-colour, in blue silk, and in new velvet. For some of those splendours the

---

1 The "Vicar" (of Wakefield).
2 peat
3 A peasant renting and cultivating a small holding.
4 Open air schools, held by hedge-sides, were once common in Ireland.
5 The joke was actually played on Goldsmith, and he worked it into the plot of his play, *She Stoops to Conquer.*
6 This traditional Greek writer of fables is represented to have been deformed.

eirs and assignees of Mr. Filby, the tailor, ave never been paid to this day: perhaps the ind tailor and his creditor have met and set-led their little account in Hades.

They showed until lately a window at Trinity 'ollege, Dublin, on which the name of O. Gold-mith was engraved with a diamond. Whose iamond was it? Not the young sizar's,[7] who 1ade but a poor figure in that place of learn-1g. He was idle, penniless, and fond of pleas-re: he learned his way early to the pawn-roker's shop. He wrote ballads, they say, or the street singers, who paid him a crown or a poem: and his pleasure was to steal out t night and hear his verses sung. He was hastised by his tutor for giving a dance in his ooms, and took the box on the ear so much to eart, that he packed up his all, pawned his ooks and little property, and disappeared from ollege and family. He said he intended to go America, but when his money was spent, the oung prodigal came home ruefully, and the ood folks there killed their calf—it was but lean one—and welcomed him back.

After college he hung about his mother's ouse, and lived for some years the life of a uckeen[8]—passed a month with this relation nd that, a year with one patron, a great deal f time at the public-house. Tired of this life, was resolved that he should go to London, nd study at the Temple;[9] but he got no arther on the road to London and the wool-ack[10] than Dublin, where he gambled away the fty pounds given to him for his outfit, and hence he returned to the indefatigable for-iveness of home. Then he determined to be doctor, and uncle Contarine helped him to a ouple of years at Edinburgh. Then from Edin-urgh he felt that he ought to hear the famous rofessors of Leyden and Paris, and wrote 10st amusing pompous letters to his uncle about 1e great Farheim, Du Petit, and Duhamel du Ionceau, whose lectures he proposed to follow. f uncle Contarine believed those letters—if liver's mother believed that story which the outh related of his going to Cork, with the urpose of embarking for America, of his hav-1g paid his passage-money, and having sent his it' on board; of the anonymous captain sailing way with Oliver's valuable luggage in a name-ss ship, never to return; if uncle Contarine nd the mother at Ballymahon, believed his

stories, they must have been a very simple pair; as it was a very simple rogue indeed who cheated them. When the lad, after failing in his clerical examination, after failing in his plan for studying the law, took leave of these projects and of his parents, and set out for Edinburgh, he saw mother, and uncle, and lazy Ballymahon, and green native turf, and spark-ling river for the last time. He was never to look on old Ireland more, and only in fancy revisit her.

"But me not destined such delights to share
My prime of life in wandering spent and care,
Impelled, with steps unceasing to pursue
Some fleeting good that mocks me with the view;
That like the circle bounding earth and skies
Allures from far, yet, as I follow, flies:
My fortune leads to traverse realms alone,
And find no spot of all the world my own." [11]

I spoke in a former lecture of that high cour-age which enabled Fielding,[12] in spite of dis-ease, remorse, and poverty, always to retain a cheerful spirit and to keep his manly benevo-lence and love of truth intact, as if these treas-ures had been confided to him for the public benefit, and he was accountable to posterity for their honourable employ; and a constancy equally happy and admirable I think was shown by Goldsmith, whose sweet and friendly nature bloomed kindly always in the midst of a life's storm, and rain, and bitter weather. The poor fellow was never so friendless but he could be-friend some one; never so pinched and wretched but he could give of his crust, and speak his word of compassion. If he had but his flute left, he could give that, and make the children happy in the dreary London court. He could give the coals in that queer coal-scuttle we read of to his poor neighbour: he could give away his blankets in college to the poor widow, and warm himself as he best might in the feathers: he could pawn his coat to save his landlord from gaol: when he was a school-usher he spent his earnings in treats for the boys, and the good-natured schoolmaster's wife said justly that she ought to keep Mr. Goldsmith's money as well as the young gentlemen's. When he met his pupils in later life, nothing would satisfy the Doctor but he must treat them still. "Have you seen the print of me after Sir Joshua Rey-nolds?"[13] he asked of one of his old pupils. "Not seen it? not bought it? Sure, Jack, if your picture had been published, I'd not have

---

7 A student given free rations, usually in return for menial services.
8 An idle younger son of the poorer aris-tocracy.
9 Quarters occupied by students of law.
10 The cushion, and hence the office, of the Lord High Chancellor.
11 Goldsmith's The Trav-eller, lines 23-30.
12 Henry Fielding, the novelist.
13 Reynolds painted his portrait, and it was engraved in mezzotint by Mar-chi in 1770.

been without it half-an-hour.'' His purse and his heart were everybody's, and his friends' as much as his own. When he was at the height of his reputation, and the Earl of Northumberland, going as Lord Lieutenant to Ireland, asked if he could be of any service to Doctor Goldsmith, Goldsmith recommended his brother, and not himself, to the great man. ''My patrons,'' he gallantly said, ''are the booksellers, and I want no others.'' Hard patrons they were, and hard work he did; but he did not complain much: if in his early writings some bitter words escaped him, some allusions to neglect and poverty, he withdrew these expressions when his works were republished, and betters days seemed to open for him; and he did not care to complain that printer or publisher had overlooked his merit, or left him poor. The Court face was turned from honest Oliver, the Court patronised Beattie;[14] the fashion did not shine on him—fashion adored Sterne.[15] Fashion pronounced Kelly[16] to be the great writer of comedy of his day. A little —not ill-humour, but plaintiveness—a little betrayal of wounded pride which he showed render him not the less amiable. The author of the ''Vicar of Wakefield'' had a right to protest when Newbery[17] kept back the manuscript for two years; had a right to be a little peevish with Sterne; a little angry when Colman's[18] actors declined their parts in his delightful comedy, when the manager refused to have a scene painted for it, and pronounced its damnation before hearing. He had not the great public with him; but he had the noble Johnson, and the admirable Reynolds, and the great Gibbon, and the great Burke, and the great Fox—friends and admirers illustrious indeed, as famous as those who, fifty years before, sat round Pope's table.

Nobody knows, and I dare say Goldsmith's buoyant temper kept no account of, all the pains which he endured during the early period of his literary career. Should any man of letters in our day have to bear up against such, Heaven grant he may come out of the period of misfortune with such a pure kind heart as that which Goldsmith obstinately bore in his breast. The insults to which he had to submit are shocking to read of—slander, contumely, vulgar satire, brutal malignity perverting hi commonest motives and actions; he had hi share of these, and one's anger is roused a reading of them, as it is at seeing a woma insulted or a child assaulted, at the notion tha a creature so very gentle and weak, and ful of love, should have had to suffer so. And h had worse than insult to undergo—to own t fault and deprecate the anger of ruffians There is a letter of his extant to one Griffiths a bookseller, in which poor Goldsmith is force to confess that certain books sent by Griffith are in the hands of a friend from whom Gold smith had been forced to borrow money. ''H was wild, sir,'' Johnson said, speaking of Gold smith to Boswell, with his great, wise benev lence and noble mercifulness of heart—''Dr Goldsmith was wild, sir; but he is so no more.' Ah! if we pity the good and weak man wh suffers undeservedly, let us deal very gentl with him from whom misery extorts not onl tears, but shame; let us think humbly an charitably of the human nature that suffers s sadly and falls so low. Whose turn may it b to-morrow? What weak heart, confident befor trial, may not succumb under temptation in vincible? Cover the good man who has bee vanquished—cover his face and pass on.

For the last half-dozen years of his life Goldsmith was far removed from the pressur of any ignoble necessity: and in the receipt indeed, of a pretty large income from the book sellers his patrons. Had he lived but a fev years more, his public fame would have bee as great as his private reputation, and he migh have enjoyed alive a part of that esteem whic his country has ever since paid to the vivid an versatile genius who has touched on almos every subject of literature, and touched nothin that he did not adorn. Except in rare in stances, a man is known in our profession, an esteemed as a skillful workman, years befor the lucky hit which trebles his usual gains, an stamps him a popular author. In the strengt of his age, and the dawn of his reputatior having for backers and friends the most illus trious literary men of his time, fame and pros perity might have been in store for Goldsmit had fate so willed it, and, at forty-six, ha not sudden disease carried him off. I say pros perity rather than competence, for it is prob able that no sum could have put order into hi affairs, or sufficed for his irreclaimable habit of dissipation. It must be remembered tha he owed £2000 when he died. ''Was eve poet,'' Johnson asked, ''so trusted before?'

14 James Beattie, a Scottish poet.
15 Laurence Sterne, author of *Tristram Shandy*.
16 Hugh Kelly, author of *False Delicacy*, which
     was produced at Drury Lane just before
     Goldsmith's *The Good-Natured Man*.
17 A publisher.
18 George Colman the elder, a dramatist and manager, who brought out Goldsmith's *She Stoops to Conquer* only after much urging by Dr. Johnson and his friends.

s has been the case with many another good ellow of his nation, his life was tracked and is substance wasted by crowds of hungry beggars and lazy dependants. If they came at a cky time (and be sure they knew his affairs etter than he did himself, and watched his ay-day), he gave them of his money: if they egged on empty-purse days, he gave them his romissory bills: or he treated them to a avern where he had credit; or he obliged them ith an order upon honest Mr. Filby for coats, or which he paid as long as he could earn, and ntil the shears of Filby were to cut for him o more. Staggering under a load of debt and bour, tracked by bailiffs and reproachful creditors, running from a hundred poor dependants, hose appealing looks were perhaps the hardest all pains for him to bear, devising fevered ans for the morrow, new histories, new comees, all sorts of new literary schemes, flying om all these into seclusion, and out of seclu-on into pleasure—at last, at five-and-forty, ath seized him and closed his career. I have en many a time in the chambers in the Teme which were his, and passed up the staircase, nich Johnson and Burke and Reynolds trod see their friend, their poet, their kind Goldnith—the stair on which the poor women sat eeping bitterly when they heard that the eatest and most generous of all men was dead thin the black oak door. Ah! it was a difrent lot from that for which the poor fellow ghed, when he wrote with heart yearning for me those most charming of all fond verses, which he fancies he revisits Auburn:—

Here, as I take my solitary rounds,
midst thy tangling walks and ruined grounds,
nd, many a year elapsed, return to view
here once the cottage stood, the hawthorn grew,
emembrance wakes, with all her busy train,
wells at my breast, and turns the past to
  pain. . . ." *

In these verses, I need not say with what elody, with what touching truth, with what quisite beauty of comparison—as indeed in ndreds more pages of the writings of this nest soul—the whole character of the man told—his humble confession of faults and eakness; his pleasant little vanity, and desire at his village should admire him; his simple heme of good in which everybody was to be ppy—no beggar was to be refused his dinner nobody in fact was to work much, and he to the harmless chief of the Utopia,† and the

monarch of the Irish Yvetot.‡ He would have told again, and without fear of their failing, those famous jokes which had hung fire in London;[1] he would have talked of his great friends of the Club—of my Lord Clare and my Lord Bishop, my Lord Nugent—sure he knew them intimately, and was hand and glove with some of the best men in town—and he would have spoken of Johnson and of Burke, and of Sir Joshua who had painted him—and he would have told wonderful sly stories of Ranelagh and the Pantheon,[2] and the masquerades at Madame Cornelys;[3] and he would have toasted, with a sigh, the Jessamy Bride[4]—the lovely Mary Horneck.

The figure of that charming young lady forms one of the prettiest recollections of Goldsmith's life. She and her beautiful sister, who married Bunbury, the graceful and humorous amateur artist of those days, when Gillray[5] had but just begun to try his powers, were among the kindest and dearest of Goldsmith's many friends, cheered and pitied him, travelled abroad with him, made him welcome at their home, and gave him many a pleasant holiday. He bought his finest clothes to figure at their country house at Barton—he wrote them droll verses. They loved him, laughed at him, played him tricks and made him happy. He asked for a loan from Garrick,[6] and Garrick kindly supplied him, to enable him to go to Barton: but there were to be no more holidays and only one brief struggle more for poor Goldsmith. A lock of his hair was taken from the coffin and given to the Jessamy Bride. She lived quite into our time. Hazlitt[7] saw her an old lady, but beautiful still, in Northcote's[8] painting-room, who told the eager critic how proud she always was that Goldsmith had admired her. The younger Colman[9] has left a touching reminiscence of him (vol. i, 63, 64):—

1 Compare page 365.
2 London pleasure resorts of that time.
3 Conductress of a public place for social gatherings.
4 Goldsmith's pet name for this young girl friend of his.
5 James Gillray, a caricaturist.
6 David Garrick, the actor.
7 William Hazlitt, the essayist.
8 James Northcote, of the Royal Academy.
9 George Colman, a dramatist, son of the Colman mentioned above.

‡ A little town in Normandy whose lords were once called kings. Béranger wrote a ballad on the subject, which Thackeray translated:

There was a king of Yvetot,
  Of whom renown hath little said.
Who let all thoughts of glory go,
  And dawdled half his days abed;
And every night, as night came round,
By Jenny with a nightcap crowned,
  Slept very sound:
Sing ho, ho, ho! and he, he, he!
That's the kind of king for me. Etc.

Thackeray's quotation here from *The Deserted Village* extends through thirty lines more, for which see page 374, ll. 83-112.
See page 110 and note.

"I was only five years old," he says, "when Goldsmith took me on his knee one evening whilst he was drinking coffee with my father, and began to play with me, which amiable act I returned, with the ingratitude of a peevish brat, by giving him a very smart slap on the face: it must have been a tingler, for it left the marks of my spiteful paw on his cheek. This infantile outrage was followed by summary justice, and I was locked up by my indignant father in an adjoining room to undergo solitary imprisonment in the dark. Here I began to howl and scream most abominably, which was no bad step towards my liberation, since those who were not inclined to pity me might be likely to set me free for the purpose of abating a nuisance.

"At length a generous friend appeared to extricate me from jeopardy, and that generous friend was no other than the man I had so wantonly molested by assault and battery— it was the tender-hearted Doctor himself, with a lighted candle in his hand and a smile upon his countenance, which was still partially red from the effects of my petulance. I sulked and sobbed as he fondled and soothed, till I began to brighten. Goldsmith seized the propitious moment of returning good-humour, when he put down the candle and began to conjure. He placed three hats, which happened to be in the room, and a shilling under each. The shillings, he told me, were England, France, and Spain. 'Hey presto cockalorum!' cried the Doctor, and lo, on uncovering the shillings, which had been dispersed each beneath a separate hat, they were all found congregated under one. I was no politician at five years old, and therefore might not have wondered at the sudden revolution which brought England, France, and Spain all under one crown; but as also I was no conjurer, it amazed me beyond measure. . . . From that time, whenever the Doctor came to visit my father, 'I plucked his gown to share the good man's smile;' a game at romps constantly ensued, and we were always cordial friends and merry playfellows. Our unequal companionship varied somewhat as to sports as I grew older; but it did not last long: my senior playmate died in his forty-fifth year, when I had attained my eleventh. . . . In all the numerous accounts of his virtues and foibles, his genius and absurdities, his knowledge of nature and ignorance of the world, his 'compassion for another's woe' was always predominant; and my trivial story of his humouring a froward child weighs but as a feather in the recorded scale of his benevolence."

Think of him reckless, thriftless, vain, if yo like—but merciful, gentle, generous, full o love and pity. He passes out of our life, an goes to render his account beyond it. Thin of the poor pensioners weeping at his grave think of the noble spirits that admired an deplored him; think of the righteous pen tha wrote his epitaph—and of the wonderful an unanimous response of affection with which th world has paid back the love he gave it. Hi humour delighting us still: his song fresh an beautiful as when first he charmed with it: hi words in all our mouths: his very weaknesse beloved and familiar—his benevolent spiri seems still to smile upon us; to do gentle kin nesses: to succour with sweet charity: t soothe, caress, and forgive: to plead with th fortunate for the unhappy and the poor.

His name is the last in the list of those me of humour who have formed the themes of th discourses which you have heard so kindly.

FROM ROUNDABOUT PAPERS*

DE JUVENTUTE[1]

Our last paper of this veracious and roune about series related to a period which can onl be historical to a great number of readers o this Magazine. Four I saw at the statio to-day with orange-covered books in thei hands, who can but have known George IV by books, and statues, and pictures. Elderl gentlemen were in their prime, old men in thei middle age, when he reigned over us. Hi image remains on coins; on a picture or tw hanging here and there in a Club or ol fashioned dining-room; on horseback, as a Trafalgar Square, for example, where I def any monarch to look more uncomfortable. H turns up in sundry memoirs and histories whic may have been published in Mr. Massey's "History"; in the "Buckingham and Gre ville Correspondence"; and gentlemen wh have accused a certain writer of disloyalty a referred to those volumes to see whether th picture drawn of George is overcharge

1 "Upon Youth."
2 Died 1830.
3 William Massey, author of a history of Georg III's reign. Grenville's *Memoirs of the Cour of George IV* had just been published (1859 Thackeray's lectures on *The Four Georges* ha been delivered about five years before.

* In emulation of *Household Words*, of whic Dickens had made such a great success i the fifties, *The Cornhill Magazine* was founde in 1860 and Thackeray was engaged to edi it. The "Roundabout Papers" were his regu lar contribution for three years. The Maga zine bore an orange cover.

haron[4] has paddled him off; he has mingled
ith the crowded republic of the dead. His
figy smiles from a canvas or two. Breechless
e bestrides his steed in Trafalgar Square. I
lieve he still wears his robes at Madame Tus-
ud's[5] (Madame herself having quitted Baker
creet and life, and found him she modelled
other side the Stygian stream). On the head
: a five-shilling piece we still occasionally
me upon him, with St. George, the dragon-
ayer, on the other side of the coin.† Ah me!
d this George slay many dragons? Was he a
rave, heroic champion, and rescuer of virgins?
ell! Well! have you and I overcome all the
ragons that assail *us?* come alive and vic-
rious out of all the caverns which we have
tered in life, and succoured, at risk of life
id limb, all poor distressed persons in whose
aked limbs the dragon Poverty is about to
isten his fangs, whom the dragon Crime is
isoning with his horrible breath, and about
crunch up and devour? O my royal liege!
my gracious prince and warrior! *You* a
ampion to fight that monster? Your feeble
ear ever pierce that slimy paunch or plated
ick? See how the flames come gurgling out
: his red-hot brazen throat! What a roar!
earer and nearer he trails, with eyes flaming
ke the lamps of a railroad engine. How he
queals, rushing out through the darkness of
s tunnel! Now he is near. Now he is *here.*
nd now—what?—lance, shield, knight, feath-
s, horse and all? O horror, horror! Next
ay, round the monster's cave, there lie a few
nes more. You, who wish to keep yours in
ur skins, be thankful that you are not called
on to go out and fight dragons. Be grateful
at they don't sally out and swallow you.
eep a wise distance from their caves, lest you
ay too dearly for approaching them. Remem-
er that years passed, and whole districts were
avaged, before the warrior came who was able
· cope with the devouring monster. When
at knight *does* make his appearance, with all
y heart let us go out and welcome him with
ir best songs, huzzas, and laurel wreaths, and
agerly recognize his valour and victory. But
e comes only seldom. Countless knights were
ain before St. George won the battle. In the
attle of life are we all going to try for the
onours of championship? If we can do our

duty, if we can keep our place pretty honourably through the combat, let us say *Laus Deo!*[6]
at the end of it, as the firing ceases, and the
night falls over the field.

The old were middle-aged, the elderly were in
their prime, then, thirty years since, when yon
royal George was till fighting the dragon. As
for you, my pretty lass, with your saucy hat
and golden tresses tumbled in your net, and
you, my spruce young gentleman in your mandarin's cap (the young folks at the country-
place where I am staying are so attired), your
parents were unknown to each other, and wore
short frocks and short jackets, at the date of
this five-shilling piece. Only to-day I met a
dog-cart crammed with children—children with
moustaches and mandarin caps—children with
saucy hats and hair-nets—children in short
frocks and knickerbockers (surely the prettiest
boy's dress that has appeared these hundred
years)—children from twenty years of age to
six; and father, with mother by his side, driving in front—and on father's countenance I
saw that very laugh which I remember perfectly in the time when this crown-piece was
coined—in *his* time, in King George's time,
when we were school-boys seated on the same
form. The smile was just as broad, as bright,
as jolly, as I remember it in the past—unforgotten, though not seen or thought of, for how
many decades of years, and quite and instantly
familiar, though so long out of sight.

Any contemporary of that coin who takes
it up and reads the inscription round the lau-
relled head, "Georgius IV Britanniarum Rex.
Fid. Def.[7] 1823," if he will but look steadily
at the round, and utter the proper incantation,‡
I dare say may conjure back his life there.
Look well, my elderly friend, and tell me what
you see? First, I see a Sultan, with hair,
beautiful hair, and a crown of laurels round
his head, and his name is Georgius Rex. Fid.
Def., and so on. Now the Sultan has disappeared; and what is it that I see? A boy,—
a boy in a jacket. He is at a desk; he has
great books before him, Latin and Greek books
and dictionaries. Yes, but behind the great
books, which he pretends to read, is a little one,
with pictures, which he is really reading. It

---

[6] "Praise God."
[7] "King of Britain, Defender of the Faith."
‡ This word suggests to Thackeray's fancy the
oriental terms in which he proceeds to describe the vision. The king is a "Sultan."
The conjurer who reviews his own past life
sees himself as a school-boy under the instruction of a gowned "dervish"; later, as a college
youth in cap and gown he is himself a "dervish," disciplined by an old proctor perhaps
("moollah," judge, priest); and so on.

Ferryman of the river Styx.
The proprietress of a famous show-place containing wax effigies of various celebrities.
St. George is the great Christian hero of the
middle ages, and legendary slayer of the
dragon (the devil), whereby he delivered the
virgin Sabra (the Church); adopted as the
patron saint of England.

is—yes, I can read now—it is the "Heart of Mid Lothian," by the author of "Waverley" —or, no, it is "Life in London, or the Adventures of Corinthian Tom, Jeremiah Hawthorn, and their friend Bob Logic," by Pierce Egan; and it has pictures—oh! such funny pictures! As he reads, there comes behind the boy, a man, a dervish, in a black gown, like a woman, and a black square cap, and he has a book in each hand, and he seizes the boy who is reading the picture-book, and lays his head upon one of his books, and smacks it with the other. The boy makes faces, and so that picture disappears.

Now the boy has grown bigger. *He* has got on a black gown and cap, something like the dervish. He is at a table, with ever so many bottles on it, and fruit, and tobacco; and other young dervishes come in. They seem as if they were singing. To them enters an old moollah; he takes down their names, and orders them all to go to bed. What is this? A carriage, with four beautiful horses all galloping—a man in red is blowing a trumpet. Many young men are on the carriage—one of them is driving the horses. Surely they won't drive into that—? —ah! they have all disappeared. And now I see one of the young men alone. He is walking in a street—a dark street—presently a light comes to a window. There is the shadow of a lady who passes. He stands there till the light goes out. Now he is in a room scribbling on a piece of paper, and kissing a miniature every now and then. There seem to be lines each pretty much of a length. I can read *heart, smart, dart; Mary, fairy; Cupid, stupid; true, you;* and never mind what more. Bah! it is bosh. Now see, he has got a gown on again, and a wig of white hair on his head, and he is sitting with other dervishes in a great room full of them, and on a throne in the middle is an old Sultan in scarlet, sitting before a desk, and he wears a wig too—and the young man gets up and speaks to him. And now what is here? He is in a room with ever so many children, and the miniature hanging up. Can it be a likeness of that woman who is sitting before that copper urn with a silver vase in her hand, from which she is pouring hot liquor into cups? Was *she* ever a fairy? She is as fat as a hippopotamus now. He is sitting on a divan by the fire. He has a paper on his knees. Read the name. It is the *Superfine Review.* It inclines to think that Mr. Dickens is not a true gentleman, that Mr. Thackeray is not a true gentleman, and that when the one is pert and the other arch, we, the gentlemen of the *Superfine Review,* think, and

think rightly, that we have some cause to b indignant. The great cause why moder humour and modern sentimentalism repel u is that they are unwarrantably familiar. Now Mr. Sterne, the *Superfine Review* thinks, "wa a true sentimentalist, because he was *abou all things* a true gentleman.'' The flatterin inference is obvious; let us be thankful for a elegant moralist watching over us, and learn if not too old, to imitate his high-bred polite ness and catch his unobtrusive grace. If w are unwarrantably familiar, we know who i not. If we repel by pertness, we know wh never does. If our language offends, we kno whose is always modest. O pity! The visio has disappeared off the silver, the images o youth and the past are vanishing away! W who have lived before railways were made be long to another world. In how many hour could the Prince of Wales drive from Brighto to London, with a light carriage built ex pressly, and relays of horses longing to gallo the next stage? Do you remember Sir Some body, the coachman of the Age, who took ou half-crown so affably? It was only yesterday but what a gulf between now and then! The was the old world. Stage-coaches, more or les swift, riding-horses, pack-horses, highwaymen knights in armour, Norman invaders, Roma legions, Druids, Ancient Britons painted blue and so forth—all these belong to the old period I will concede a halt in the midst of it, an allow that gunpowder and printing tended t modernize the world. But your railroad start the new era, and we of a certain age belon to the new time and the old one. We are of th time of chivalry as well as the Black Prince or Sir Walter Manny.[2] We are of the age o steam. We have stepped out of the old worl on to "Brunel's" vast deck,[3] and across th waters *ingens patet tellus.*[4] Towards what new continent are we wending? to what new laws new manners, new politics, vast new expanse of liberties unknown as yet, or only surmised I used to know a man who had invented flying-machine. "Sir," he would say, "giv me but five hundred pounds, and I will mak it. It is so simple of construction that I trem ble daily lest some other person should ligh upon and patent my discovery." Perhaps faith was wanting; perhaps the five hundred pounds He is dead, and somebody else must make th flying-machine. But that will only be a ste

[1] The son of Edward III; hero of Poitiers, 1356.
[2] A soldier of Edward III.
[3] The steamship "Grea Eastern," designe by I. K. Brunel 1858.
[4] "A great world looms."

forward on the journey already begun since we quitted the old world. There it lies on the other side of yonder embankments. You young folks have never seen it; and Waterloo[5] is to you no more than Agincourt,[6] and George IV. than Sardanapalus.[7] We elderly people have lived in that pre-railroad world, which has passed into limbo and vanished from under us. I tell you it was firm under our feet once, and not long ago. They have raised those railroad embankments up, and shut off the old world that was behind them. Climb up that bank on which the irons are laid, and look to the other side—it is gone. There is no other side. Try and catch yesterday. Where is it? Here is a *Times* newspaper, dated Monday 26th, and this is Tuesday 27th. Suppose you deny there was such a day as yesterday.

We who lived before railways, and survive out of the ancient world, are like Father Noah and his family out of the Ark. The children will gather round and say to us patriarchs, "Tell us, grandpapa, about the old world." And we shall mumble our old stories; and we shall drop off one by one; and there will be fewer and fewer of us, and these very old and feeble. There will be but ten pre-railroadites left; then three—then two—then one—then O! If the hippopotamus had the least sensibility (of which I cannot trace any signs either in his hide or his face), I think he would go down to the bottom of his tank, and never come up again. Does he not see that he belongs to bygone ages, and that his great hulking barrel of a body is out of place in these times? What has he in common with the brisk young life surrounding him? In the watches of the night, when the keepers are asleep, when the birds are on one leg, when even the little armadillo is quiet, and the monkeys have ceased their chatter,—he, I mean the hippopotamus, and the elephant, and the long-necked giraffe, perhaps may lay their heads together and have a colloquy about the great silent antediluvian world which they remember, where mighty monsters floundered through the ooze, crocodiles basked on the banks, and dragons darted out of the eaves and waters before men were made to slay them. We who lived before railroads are antediluvians—we must pass away. We are growing scarcer every day; and old—old—very old relics of the times when George was still fighting the Dragon.

.   .   .   .

ALFRED, LORD TENNYSON
(1809-1892)

THE LADY OF SHALOTT*

PART I

On either side the river lie
Long fields of barley and of rye,
That clothe the wold and meet the sky;
And thro' the field the road runs by
    To many-tower'd Camelot;[1]
And up and down the people go,
Gazing where the lilies blow
Round an island there below,
    The island of Shalott.

Willows whiten, aspens quiver,   10
Little breezes dusk and shiver
Thro' the wave that runs for ever
By the island in the river
    Flowing down to Camelot.
Four gray walls, and four gray towers,
Overlook a space of flowers,
And the silent isle imbowers
    The Lady of Shalott.

By the margin, willow-veil'd,
Slide the heavy barges trail'd   20
By slow horses; and unhail'd
The shallop flitteth silken-sail'd
    Skimming down to Camelot;
But who hath seen her wave her hand?
Or at the casement seen her stand?
Or is she known in all the land,
    The Lady of Shalott?

Only reapers, reaping early
In among the bearded barley,
Hear a song that echoes cheerly   30
From the river winding clearly,
    Down to tower'd Camelot;
And by the moon the reaper weary,
Piling sheaves in uplands airy,
Listening, whispers " 'T is the fairy
    Lady of Shalott."

PART II

There she weaves by night and day
A magic web with colours gay.
She has heard a whisper say,
A curse is on her if she stay   40
    To look down to Camelot.

1 The place of Arthur's court.
* This is, with some variations, essentially the story of Elaine, "the lily maid of Astolat," which is told at greater length and with more fidelity in the *Idylls of the King*. It is Tennyson's earliest venture into the Arthurian field.

She knows not what the curse may be,
And so she weaveth steadily,
And little other care hath she,
    The Lady of Shalott.

And moving thro' a mirror clear
That hangs before her all the year,
Shadows of the world appear.
There she sees the highway near
    Winding down to Camelot;   50
There the river eddy whirls,
And there the surly village-churls,
And the red cloaks of market girls,
    Pass onward from Shalott.

Sometimes a troop of damsels glad,
An abbot on an ambling pad,
Sometimes a curly shepherd-lad,
Or long-hair'd page in crimson clad,
    Goes by to tower'd Camelot;
And sometimes thro' the mirror blue   60
The knights come riding two and two:
She hath no loyal knight and true,
    The Lady of Shalott.

But in her web she still delights
To weave the mirror's magic sights,
For often thro' the silent nights
A funeral, with plumes and lights
    And music, went to Camelot;
Or when the moon was overhead,
Came two young lovers lately wed: 70
"I am half sick of shadows," said
    The Lady of Shalott.†

PART III

A bow-shot from her bower-eaves,
He rode between the barley-sheaves,
The sun came dazzling thro' the leaves,
And flamed upon the brazen greaves
    Of bold Sir Lancelot.
A red-cross knight for ever kneel'd
To a lady in his shield,
That sparkled on the yellow field,   80
    Beside remote Shalott.

The gemmy bridle glitter'd free,
Like to some branch of stars we see
Hung in the golden Galaxy.[2]
The bridle bells rang merrily
    As he rode down to Camelot;
And from his blazon'd baldric slung
A mighty silver bugle hung.

[2] The Milky Way.
† In these lines, says Tennyson's son, is to be
   found the key to the poem. The allegory
   then, if one be desired, is not hard to trace.

And as he rode his armour rung,
    Beside remote Shalott.   9

All in the blue unclouded weather
Thick-jewell'd shone the saddle-leather,
The helmet and the helmet-feather
Burn'd like one burning flame together,
    As he rode down to Camelot;
As often thro' the purple night,
Below the starry clusters bright,
Some bearded meteor, trailing light,
    Moves over still Shalott.

His broad clear brow in sunlight glow'd;   10
On burnish'd hooves his war-horse trode;
From underneath his helmet flow'd
His coal-black curls as on he rode,
    As he rode down to Camelot.
From the bank and from the river
He flash'd into the crystal mirror,
"Tirra lirra," by the river
    Sang Sir Lancelot.

She left the web, she left the loom,
She made three paces thro' the room,   11
She saw the water-lily bloom,
She saw the helmet and the plume,
    She look'd down to Camelot.
Out flew the web and floated wide;
The mirror crack'd from side to side;
"The curse is come upon me," cried
    The Lady of Shalott.

PART IV

In the stormy east-wind straining,
The pale yellow woods were waning.
The broad stream in his banks complaining,   12
Heavily the low sky raining
    Over tower'd Camelot;
Down she came and found a boat
Beneath a willow left afloat,
And round about the prow she wrote
    The Lady of Shalott.

And down the river's dim expanse
Like some bold seër in a trance,
Seeing all his own mischance—
With a glassy countenance   13
    Did she look to Camelot.
And at the closing of the day
She loosed the chain, and down she lay·
The broad stream bore her far away,
    The Lady of Shalott.

Lying, robed in snowy white
That loosely flew to left and right—
The leaves upon her falling light—

Thro' the noises of the night
She floated down to Camelot; 140
And as the boat-head wound along
The willowy hills and fields among,
They heard her singing her last song,
    The Lady of Shalott.

Heard a carol, mournful, holy,
Chanted loudly, chanted lowly,
Till her blood was frozen slowly,
And her eyes were darken'd wholly,
    Turn'd to tower'd Camelot.
For ere she reach'd upon the tide 150
The first house by the water-side,
Singing in her song she died,
    The Lady of Shalott.

Under tower and balcony,
By garden-wall and gallery,
A gleaming shape she floated by,
Dead-pale between the houses high,
    Silent into Camelot.
Out upon the wharfs they came,
Knight and burgher, lord and dame, 160
And round the prow they read her name,
    The Lady of Shalott.

Who is this? and what is here?
And in the lighted palace near
Died the sound of royal cheer,
And they cross'd themselves for fear,
    All the knights at Camelot:
But Lancelot mused a little space;
He said, "She has a lovely face;
God in his mercy lend her grace, 170
    The Lady of Shalott."

ŒNONE*

There lies a vale in Ida, lovelier
Than all the valleys of Ionian hills.
The swimming vapour slopes athwart the glen,
Puts forth an arm, and creeps from pine to
    pine,
And loiters, slowly drawn. On either hand
The lawns and meadow-ledges midway down
Hang rich in flowers, and far below them roars
The long brook falling thro' the cloven ravine
In cataract after cataract to the sea.
Behind the valley topmost Gargarus 10
Stands up and takes the morning; but in front
The gorges, opening wide apart, reveal
Troas and Ilion's column'd citadel,
The crown of Troas.

* Œnone, a nymph of Mt. Ida in the Troad, early
    the beloved of the shepherd Paris, mourns his
    desertion of her, and relates the story of her,
    famous "Judgment of Paris" which led to the
    Trojan war.

        Hither came at noon
Mournful Œnone, wandering forlorn
Of Paris, once her playmate on the hills.
Her cheek had lost the rose, and round her neck
Floated her hair or seem'd to float in rest.
She, leaning on a fragment twined with vine,
Sang to the stillness, till the mountain-shade 20
Sloped downward to her seat from the upper
    cliff.

"O mother Ida, many fountain'd Ida,
Dear mother Ida, harken ere I die.
For now the noonday quiet holds the hill;
The grasshopper is silent in the grass;
The lizard, with his shadow on the stone,
Rests like a shadow, and the winds are dead.
The purple flower droops, the golden bee
Is lily-cradled: I alone awake.
My eyes are full of tears, my heart of love, 30
My heart is breaking and my eyes are dim,
And I am all aweary of my life.

"O mother Ida, many-fountain'd Ida,
Dear mother Ida, harken ere I die.
Hear me, O earth, hear me, O hills, O caves
That house the cold crown'd snake! O moun-
    tain brooks,
I am the daughter of a River-God,
Hear me, for I will speak, and build up all
My sorrow with my song, as yonder walls
Rose slowly to a music slowly breathed,† 40
A cloud that gather'd shape; for it may be
That, while I speak of it, a little while
My heart may wander from its deeper woe.

"O mother Ida, many-fountain'd Ida,
Dear mother Ida, harken ere I die.
I waited underneath the dawning hills;
Aloft the mountain-lawn was dewy-dark,
And dewy-dark aloft the mountain-pine.
Beautiful Paris, evil-hearted Paris,
Leading a jet-black goat white-horn'd. white-
    hooved, 50
Came up from reedy Simois all alone.

"O mother Ida, harken ere I die.
Far off the torrent call'd me from the cleft;
Far up the solitary morning smote
The streaks of virgin snow. With down-dropt
    eyes
I sat alone; white-breasted like a star
Fronting the dawn he moved; a leopard skin
Droop'd from his shoulder, but his sunny hair
Cluster'd about his temples like a God's;
And his cheek brighten'd as the foam-bow
    brightens 60

† According to a legend in Ovid, the walls of Troy
    rose to the music of Apollo's lyre.

When the wind blows the foam, and all my
        heart
Went forth to embrace him coming ere he came.

"Dear mother Ida, harken ere I die.
He smiled, and opening out his milk-white palm
Disclosed a fruit of pure Hesperian gold,
That smelt ambrosially, and while I look'd
And listen'd, the full-flowing river of speech
Came down upon my heart:
                        'My own Œnone,
Beautiful-brow'd Œnone, my own soul,
Behold this fruit, whose gleaming rind in-
        graven   70
"For the most fair," would seem to award it
        thine,
As lovelier than whatever Oread[1] haunt
The knolls of Ida, loveliest in all grace
Of movement, and the charm of married
        brows.'

"Dear mother Ida, harken ere I die.
He prest the blossom of his lips to mine,
And added, 'This was cast upon the board,
When all the full-faced presence of the Gods
Ranged in the halls of Peleus;[2] whereupon
Rose feud, with question unto whom 'twere
        due;   80
But light-foot Iris[3] brought it yester-eve,
Delivering, that to me, by common voice
Elected umpire, Herè comes to-day,
Pallas and Aphrodite,[4] claiming each
This meed of fairest. Thou, within the cave
Behind yon whispering tuft of oldest pine,
Mayst well behold them unbeheld, unheard
Hear all, and see thy Paris judge of Gods.'

"Dear mother Ida, harken ere I die.
It was the deep midnoon; one silvery cloud 90
Had lost his way between the piny sides
Of this long glen. Then to the bower they
        came,
Naked they came to that smooth-swarded bower,
And at their feet the crocus brake like fire,
Violet, amaracus, and asphodel,
Lotos and lilies; and a wind arose,
And overhead the wandering ivy and vine,
This way and that, in many a wild festoon
Ran riot, garlanding the gnarlèd boughs
With bunch and berry and flower thro' and
        thro'.   100

"O mother Ida, harken ere I die.
On the tree-tops a crested peacock[5] lit,

And o'er him flow'd a golden cloud, and lean'd
Upon him, slowly dropping fragrant dew.
Then first I heard the voice of her to whom
Coming thro' heaven, like a light that grows
Larger and clearer, with one mind the Gods
Rise up for reverence. She to Paris made
Proffer of royal power, ample rule
Unquestion'd, overflowing revenue   110
Wherewith to embellish state, 'from many a
        vale
And river-sunder'd champaign clothed with
        corn,
Or labour'd mine undrainable of ore.
Honour,' she said, 'and homage, tax and toll,
From many an inland town and haven large,
Mast-throng'd beneath her shadowing citadel
In glassy bays among her tallest towers.'

"O mother Ida, harken ere I die.
Still she spake on and still she spake of power,
'Which in all action is the end of all;   120
Power fitted to the season; wisdom-bred
And throned of wisdom—from all neighbour
        crowns
Alliance and allegiance, till thy hand
Fail from the sceptre-staff. Such boon from
        me,
From me, heaven's queen, Paris, to thee king-
        born,
A shepherd all thy life but yet king-born,*
Should come most welcome, seeing men, in
        power
Only, are likest Gods, who have attain'd
Rest in a happy place and quiet seats
Above the thunder, with undying bliss   130
In knowledge of their own supremacy.'

"Dear mother Ida, harken ere I die.
She ceased, and Paris held the costly fruit
Out at arm's-length, so much the thought of
        power
Flatter'd his spirit; but Pallas where she stood
Somewhat apart, her clear and barèd limbs
O'erthwarted with the brazen-headed spear
Upon her pearly shoulder leaning cold,
The while, above, her full and earnest eye
Over her snow-cold breast and angry cheek 140
Kept watch, waiting decision, made reply:
'Self-reverence, self-knowledge, self-control,
These three alone lead life to sovereign power
Yet not for power (power of herself
Would come uncall'd for) but to live by law,
Acting the law we live by without fear;
And, because right is right, to follow right
Were wisdom in the scorn of consequence.'

---

[1] Mountain nymph.
[2] The husband of the
    sea-nymph Thetis,
    and the father of
    Achilles.
[3] The messenger of the
    gods.
[4] Juno, Minerva, a n d
    Venus.
[5] Sacred to Juno.

* Paris was the son of Priam of Troy; he had
  been left exposed on the mountain-side because of the prophecy that he would bring
  ruin to Troy.

"Dear mother Ida, harken ere I die.
Again she said: 'I woo thee not with gifts.
Sequel of guerdon could not alter me 151
To fairer. Judge thou me by what I am,
So shalt thou find me fairest.
                              Yet, indeed,
If gazing on divinity disrobed
Thy mortal eyes are frail to judge of fair,
Unbias'd by self-profit, O, rest thee sure
That I shall love thee well and cleave to thee,
So that my vigour, wedded to thy blood,
Shall strike within thy pulses, like a God's,
To push thee forward thro' a life of shocks, 160
Dangers, and deeds, until endurance grow
Sinew'd with action, and the full-grown will,
Circled thro' all experiences, pure law,
Commeasure perfect freedom.'†
                      "Here she ceas'd,
And Paris ponder'd and I cried, 'O Paris,
Give it to Pallas!' but he heard me not,
Or hearing would not hear me, woe is me!

"O mother Ida, many-fountain'd Ida,
Dear mother Ida, harken ere I die.
Idalian Aphrodite beautiful, 170
Fresh as the foam, new-bathed in Paphian
          wells,‡
With rosy slender fingers backward drew§
From her warm brows and bosom her deep hair
Ambrosial, golden round her lucid throat
And shoulder; from the violets her light foot
Shone rosy-white, and o'er her rounded form
Between the shadows of the vine-bunches
Floated the glowing sunlights, as she moved.

"Dear mother Ida, harken ere I die.
She with a subtle smile in her mild eyes, 180
The herald of her triumph, drawing nigh
Half-whisper'd in his ear, 'I promise thee
The fairest and most loving wife in Greece.'
She spoke and laugh'd; I shut my sight for
          fear;
But when I look'd, Paris had raised his arm,
And I beheld great Herè's angry eyes,
As she withdrew into the golden cloud,
And I was left alone within the bower;
And from that time to this I am alone,
And I shall be alone until I die. 190

"Yet, mother Ida, harken ere I die.
Fairest—why fairest wife? am I not fair?

My love hath told me so a thousand times.
Methinks I must be fair, for yesterday,
When I past by, a wild and wanton pard,
Eyed like the evening star, with playful tail
Crouch'd fawning in the weed. Most loving is
          she?
Ah me, my mountain shepherd, that my arms
Were wound about thee, and my hot lips prest
Close, close to thine in that quick-falling dew
Of fruitful kisses, thick as autumn rains 200
Flash in the pools of whirling Simois!

"O mother, hear me yet before I die.
They came, they cut away my tallest pines,
My tall dark pines, that plumed the craggy
          ledge
High over the blue gorge, and all between
The snowy peak and snow-white cataract
Foster'd the callow eaglet—from beneath
Whose thick mysterious boughs in the dark
          morn
The panther's roar came muffled, while I sat
Low in the valley. Never, never more 210
Shall lone Œnone see the morning mist
Sweep thro' them; never see them overlaid
With narrow moonlit slips of silver cloud,
Between the loud stream and the trembling
          stars.

"O mother, hear me yet before I die.
I wish that somewhere in the ruin'd folds,
Among the fragments tumbled from the glens,
Or the dry thickets, I could meet with her
The Abominable,⁶ that uninvited came 220
Into the fair Peleïan banquet-hall,
And cast the golden fruit upon the board,
And bred this change; that I might speak my
          mind,
And tell her to her face how much I hate
Her presence, hated both of Gods and men.

"O mother, hear me yet before I die.
Hath he not sworn his love a thousand times,
In this green valley, under this green hill,
Even on this hand, and sitting on this stone?
Seal'd it with kisses? water'd it with tears? 230
O happy tears, and how unlike to these!
O happy heaven, how canst thou see my face?
O happy earth, how canst thou bear my weight?
O death, death, death, thou ever-floating cloud,
There are enough unhappy on this earth,
Pass by the happy souls, that love to live;
I pray thee, pass before my light of life,
And shadow all my soul, that I may die.
Thou weighest heavy on the heart within,
Weigh heavy on my eyelids; let me die. 240

† The will, tried and perfected by experience until
  it is redeemed from all temptation to lawless-
  ness, attains—and only then—to perfect freedom.
‡ Idalia and Paphos, in Cyprus, were places where
  Venus was especially worshiped.
§ Note the marked delaying effect of four trochaic
  words in an iambic line.
⁶ Eris, or "Strife": whence the apple was called
  the "Apple of Discord."

"O mother, hear me yet before I die.
I will not die alone,[7] for fiery thoughts
Do shape themselves within me, more and more,
Whereof I catch the issue, as I hear
Dead sounds at night come from the inmost
    hills,
Like footsteps upon wool. I dimly see
My far-off doubtful purpose, as a mother
Conjectures of the features of her child
Ere it is born. Her child!—a shudder comes
Across me: never child be born of me,   250
Unblest, to vex me with his father's eyes!

"O, mother, hear me yet before I die.
Hear me, O earth. I will not die alone,
Lest their shrill happy laughter come to me
Walking the cold and starless road of death
Uncomforted, leaving my ancient love
With the Greek woman. I will rise and go
Down into Troy, and ere the stars come forth
Talk with the wild Cassandra,[8] for she says
A fire dances before her, and a sound   260
Rings ever in her ears of armèd men.
What this may be I know not, but I know
That wheresoe'er I am by night and day,
All earth and air seem only burning fire."

THE LOTOS-EATERS*

"Courage!" he said, and pointed toward the
    land,
"This mounting wave will roll us shoreward
    soon."
In the afternoon they came unto a land
In which it seemèd always afternoon.
All round the coast the languid air did swoon,
Breathing like one that hath a weary dream.
Full-faced above the valley stood the moon;
And, like a downward smoke, the slender stream
  Along the cliff to fall and pause and fall did
    seem.   9

A land of streams! some, like a downward
    smoke,
Slow-dropping veils of thinnest lawn, did go;
And some thro' wavering lights and shadows
    broke,
Rolling a slumbrous sheet of foam below.

They saw the gleaming river seaward flow
From the inner land; far off, three mountain
    tops,
Three silent pinnacles of aged snow,
Stood sunset-flush'd; and, dew'd with showery
    drops,
  Up-clomb the shadowy pine above the woven
    copse.   18

The charmèd sunset linger'd low adown
In the red West; thro' mountain clefts the dale
Was seen far inland, and the yellow down
Border'd with palm, and many a winding vale
And meadow, set with slender galingale;[1]
A land where all things always seem'd the
    same!
And round about the keel with faces pale,
Dark faces pale against that rosy flame,   26
  The mild-eyed melancholy Lotos-eaters came.

Branches they bore of that enchanted stem,
Laden with flower and fruit, whereof they gave
To each, but whoso did receive of them
And taste, to him the gushing of the wave
Far far away did seem to mourn and rave
On alien shores; and if his fellow spake,
His voice was thin, as voices from the grave;
And deep-asleep he seem'd, yet all awake,
  And music in his ears his beating heart did
    make.   36

They sat them down upon the yellow sand,
Between the sun and moon upon the shore;
And sweet it was to dream of Fatherland,
Of child, and wife, and slave; but evermore
Most weary seem'd the sea, weary the oar,
Weary the wandering fields of barren foam.
Then some one said, "We will return no
    more;"
And all at once they sang, "Our island home
  Is far beyond the wave; we will no longer
    roam."   45

SAINT AGNES' EVE

Deep on the convent-roof the snows
  Are sparkling to the moon;
My breath to heaven like vapour goes;
  May my soul follow soon!
The shadows of the convent-towers
  Slant down the snowy sward,
Still creeping with the creeping hours
  That lead me to my lord.
Make Thou my spirit pure and clear
  As are the frosty skies,
Or this first snowdrop of the year
  That in my bosom lies.   12

7 *The Death of Œnone,* a late poem of Tennyson's,
describes her death on the funeral pyre of
Paris.
8 Sister of Paris, and a prophetess.
* This poem is founded on the story told by Ulysses (*Odyssey* IX, 83-97) of himself and his
men arriving at the land of the lotos and partaking of the "flowery food" which caused forgetfulness of home. These five Spenserian
stanzas, which are followed in the original by
a long "Choric Song," contain some distinct
echoes of Thomson's *Castle of Indolence,*
which see (p. 344).

1 A tall sedge.

s these white robes are soil'd and dark,
　To yonder shining ground;
s this pale taper's earthly spark,
　To yonder argent round;
o shows my soul before the Lamb,
　My spirit before Thee;
o in mine earthly house I am,
　To that I hope to be.
reak up the heavens, O Lord! and far,
　Thro' all yon starlight keen,
raw me, thy bride, a glittering star,
　In raiment white and clean.　　　　24

e lifts me to the golden doors;
　The flashes come and go;
ll heaven bursts her starry floors,
　And strows her lights below,
nd deepens on and up! the gates
　Roll back, and far within
or me the Heavenly Bridegroom waits,
　To make me pure of sin.
he Sabbaths of Eternity,
　One Sabbath deep and wide—
light upon the shining sea—
　The Bridegroom with his bride!　　36

SIR GALAHAD*

y good blade carves the casques of men,
　My tough lance thrusteth sure,
y strength is as the strength of ten,
　Because my heart is pure.
ne shattering trumpet shrilleth high,
　The hard brands shiver on the steel,
ne splinter'd spear-shafts crack and fly,
　The horse and rider reel;
ney reel, they roll in clanging lists,
　And when the tide of combat stands,　10
erfume and flowers fall in showers,
　That lightly rain from ladies' hands.

ow sweet are looks that ladies bend
　On whom their favours fall!
or them I battle till the end,
　To save from shame and thrall;
ut all my heart is drawn above,
　My knees are bow'd in crypt[1] and shrine;
never felt the kiss of love,
　Nor maiden's hand in mine.　　　　20
ore bounteous aspects on me beam,
　Me mightier transports move and thrill;
　keep I fair thro' faith and prayer
A virgin heart in work and will.

hen down the stormy crescent goes,
　A light before me swims,

vault, cell
See Malory's account on pages 100, 105-108.

Between dark stems the forest glows,
　I hear a noise of hymns.
Then by some secret shrine I ride;
　I hear a voice, but none are there;　30
The stalls are void, the doors are wide,
　The tapers burning fair.
Fair gleams the snowy altar-cloth,
　The silver vessels sparkle clean,
The shrill bell rings, the censer swings,
　And solemn chants resound between.

Sometimes on lonely mountain-meres
　I find a magic bark.
I leap on board; no helmsman steers;
　I float till all is dark.　　　　　40
A gentle sound, an awful light!
　Three angels bear the Holy Grail;
With folded feet, in stoles of white,
　On sleeping wings they sail.
Ah, blessed vision! blood of God!
　My spirit beats her mortal bars,
As down dark tides the glory slides,
　And starlike mingles with the stars.

When on my goodly charger borne
　Thro' dreaming towns I go,　　　　50
The cock crows ere the Christmas morn,[2]
　The streets are dumb with snow.
The tempest crackles on the leads,
　And, ringing, springs from brand and mail;
But o'er the dark a glory spreads,
　And gilds the driving hail.
I leave the plain, I climb the height;
　No branchy thicket shelter yields;
But blessed forms in whistling storms
　Fly o'er waste fens and windy fields.　60

A maiden knight—to me is given
　Such hope, I know not fear;
I yearn to breathe the airs of heaven
　That often meet me here.
I muse on joy that will not cease,
　Pure spaces clothed in living beams,
Pure lilies of eternal peace,
　Whose odours haunt my dreams;
And, stricken by an angel's hand,
　This mortal armour that I wear,　　70
This weight and size, this heart and eyes,
　Are touch'd, are turn'd to finest air.

The clouds are broken in the sky,
　And thro' the mountain-walls
A rolling organ-harmony
　Swells up and shakes and falls.
Then move the trees, the copses nod,
　Wings flutter, voices hover clear:

2 Cp. *Hamlet*, I, i, 158.

"O just and faithful knight of God!
  Ride on! the prize is near."   80
So pass I hostel, hall, and grange;
  By bridge and ford, by park and pale,
All-arm'd I ride, whate'er betide,
  Until I find the Holy Grail.

THE BEGGAR MAID*

Her arms across her breast she laid;
  She was more fair than words can say;
Barefooted came the beggar maid
  Before the king Cophetua.
In robe and crown the king stept down,
  To meet and greet her on her way;
"It is no wonder," said the lords,
  "She is more beautiful than day."

As shines the moon in clouded skies,
  She in her poor attire was seen;
One praised her ankles, one her eyes,
  One her dark hair and lovesome mien.
So sweet a face, such angel grace,
  In all that land had never been.
Cophetua sware a royal oath:
  "This beggar maid shall be my queen!"

YOU ASK ME, WHY, THO' ILL AT EASE

You ask me, why, tho' ill at ease,
  Within this region I subsist,
  Whose spirits falter in the mist,
And languish for the purple seas.

It is the land that freemen till,
  That sober-suited Freedom chose,
  The land, where girt with friends or foes
A man may speak the thing he will;   8

A land of settled government,
  A land of just and old renown,
  Where Freedom slowly broadens down†
From precedent to precedent;

Where faction seldom gathers head,
  But, by degrees to fullness wrought,
  The strength of some diffusive thought
Hath time and space to work and spread.   16

Should banded unions persecute
  Opinion, and induce a time
  When single thought is civil crime,
And individual freedom mute,

* Founded on an old ballad, which may be read
  in Percy's *Reliques*.
† The original reading, "broadens slowly down,"
  which was changed for the sake of euphony,
  gave a more correct emphasis.

Tho' power should make from land to land
  The name of Britain trebly great—
  Tho' every channel of the State
Should fill and choke with golden sand—   2

Yet waft me from the harbour-mouth,
  Wild wind! I seek a warmer sky,
  And I will see before I die
The palms and temples of the South.

OF OLD SAT FREEDOM ON THE HEIGHTS

Of old sat Freedom on the heights,
  The thunders breaking at her feet;
Above her shook the starry lights;
  She heard the torrents meet.

There in her place she did rejoice,
  Self-gather'd in her prophet-mind,
But fragments of her mighty voice
  Came rolling on the wind.

Then stepped she down thro' town and field
  To mingle with the human race,
And part by part to men reveal'd
  The fulness of her face—

Grave mother of majestic works,
  From her isle-altar gazing down,
Who, Godlike, grasps the triple forks,[1]
  And, king-like, wears the crown.   1

Her open eyes desire the truth.
  The wisdom of a thousand years
Is in them. May perpetual youth
  Keep dry their light from tears;

That her fair form may stand and shine,
  Make bright our days and light our dream
Turning to scorn with lips divine
  The falsehood of extremes!

MORTE D'ARTHUR*

So all day long the noise of battle roll'd
Among the mountains by the winter sea,
Until King Arthur's table, man by man,
Had fallen in Lyonesse[2] about their lord,
King Arthur; then, because his wound w
  deep,
The bold Sir Bedivere uplifted him,

1 Jove's thunderbolt.
2 Supposed to have been in Cornwall.
* See Malory's account on pages 108-110. Th
  fragment was the germ of the *Idylls of t
  King*. It was written in 1835, and was inc
  porated in the "Passing of Arthur" when th
  was published in 1869.

Sir Bedivere, the last of all his knights,
And bore him to a chapel nigh the field,
A broken chancel with a broken cross,
That stood on a dark strait of barren land. 10
On one side lay the ocean, and on one
Lay a great water, and the moon was full.
  Then spake King Arthur to Sir Bedivere:
"'The sequel of to-day unsolders all
The goodliest fellowship of famous knights
Whereof this world holds record. Such a sleep
They sleep—the men I loved. I think that we
Shall never more, at any future time,
Delight our souls with talk of knightly deeds,
Walking about the gardens and the halls 20
Of Camelot,3 as in the days that were.
I perish by this people which I made,—
Tho' Merlin4 sware that I should come again
To rule once more—but let what will be be,
I am so deeply smitten thro' the helm
That without help I cannot last till morn.
Thou therefore take my brand Excalibur,
Which was my pride; for thou rememberest
    how
In those old days, one summer noon, an arm
Rose up from out the bosom of the lake, 30
Clothed in white samite, mystic, wonderful,
Holding the sword—and how I row'd across
And took it, and have worn it, like a king;5
And, wheresoever I am sung or told
In aftertime, this also shall be known.
But now delay not; take Excalibur,
And fling him far into the middle mere;6
Watch what thou seest, and lightly7 bring me
    word.''
  To him replied the bold Sir Bedivere:
"'It is not meet, Sir King, to leave thee thus,
Aidless, alone, and smitten thro' the helm. 41
A little thing may harm a wounded man.
Yet I thy hest will all perform at full,
Watch what I see, and lightly bring thee
    word.''
  So saying, from the ruin'd shrine he stept
And in the moon athwart the place of tombs,
Where lay the mighty bones of ancient men,
Old knights, and over them the sea-wind sang
Shrill, chill, with flakes of foam. He, stepping
    down
By zigzag paths and juts of pointed rock, 50
Came on the shining levels of the lake.
  There drew he forth the brand Excalibur,
And o'er him, drawing it, the winter moon,
Brightening the skirts of a long cloud, ran
    forth
And sparkled keen with frost against the hilt;
For all the haft twinkled with diamond sparks,

Myriads of topaz-lights, and jacinth work
Of subtlest jewellery. He gazed so long
That both his eyes were dazzled, as he stood,
This way and that dividing the swift mind, 60
In act to throw; but at the last it seem'd
Better to leave Excalibur conceal'd
There in the many-knotted water-flags,
That whistled stiff and dry about the marge.
So strode he back slow to the wounded king.
  Then spake King Arthur to Sir Bedivere:
"'Hast thou perform'd my mission which I
    gave?
What is it thou hast seen, or what hast
    heard?''
  And answer made the bold Sir Bedivere:
"'I heard the ripple washing in the reeds, 70
And the wild water lapping on the crag.''
  To whom replied King Arthur, faint and
    pale:
"'Thou hast betray'd thy nature and thy name,
Not rendering true answer, as beseem'd
Thy fealty, nor like a noble knight;
For surer sign had follow'd, either hand,
Or voice, or else a motion of the mere.
This is a shameful thing for men to lie.
Yet now, I charge thee, quickly go again
As thou art liefs and dear, and do the thing 80
I bade thee, watch, and lightly bring me
    word.''
  Then went Sir Bedivere the second time
Across the ridge, and paced beside the mere,
Counting the dewy pebbles, fix'd in thought:
But when he saw the wonder of the hilt,
How curiously and strangely chased, he smote
His palms together, and he cried aloud:
  "'And if indeed I cast the brand away,
Surely a precious thing, one worthy note,
Should thus be lost forever from the earth, 90
Which might have pleased the eyes of many
    men.
What good should follow this, if this were
    done?
What harm, undone? deep harm to disobey,
Seeing obedience is the bond of rule.
Were it well to obey then, if a king demand
An act unprofitable, against himself?
The king is sick, and knows not what he does.
What record, or what relic of my lord
Should be to aftertime, but empty breath 99
And rumours of a doubt? but were this kept,
Stored in some treasure-house of mighty kings,
Some one might show it at a joust of arms,
Saying, 'King Arthur's sword, Excalibur,
Wrought by the lonely maiden of the lake;
Nine years she wrought it, sitting in the deeps
Upon the hidden bases of the hills.'

3 The capital of Arthur.   6 into the mid-lake
4 See pages 96, 99, etc.   7 quickly
5 See page 98.

8 beloved

So might some old man speak in the aftertime
To all the people, winning reverence;
But now much honour and much fame were
    lost.''
    So spake he, clouded with his own conceit,[9]
And hid Excalibur the second time,   111
And so strode back slow to the wounded king.
    Then spoke King Arthur, breathing heavily:
''What is it thou hast seen, or what hast
    heard?''
    And answer made the bold Sir Bedivere:
''I heard the water lapping on the crag,
And the long ripple washing in the reeds.''
    To whom replied King Arthur, much in
    wrath:
''Ah, miserable and unkind, untrue,
Unknightly, traitor-hearted! Woe is me!   120
Authority forgets a dying king,
Laid widow'd of the power in his eye
That bow'd the will. I see thee what thou art,
For thou, the latest-left of all my knights,
In whom should meet the offices of all,
Thou wouldst betray me for the precious hilt;
Either from lust of gold, or like a girl
Valuing the giddy pleasure of the eyes.
Yet, for[10] a man may fail in duty twice,
And the third time may prosper, get thee
    hence;   130
But, if thou spare to fling Excalibur,
I will arise and slay thee with my hands.''
    Then quickly rose Sir Bedivere, and ran,
And, leaping down the ridges lightly, plunged
Among the bulrush-beds, and clutch'd the
    sword,
And strongly wheel'd and threw it. The great
    brand
Made lightnings in the splendour of the moon,
And flashing round and round, and whirl'd in
    an arch,
Shot like a streamer of the northern morn,
Seen where the moving isles of winter shock   140
By night, with noises of the northern sea.
So flash'd and fell the brand Excalibur;
But ere he dipt the surface, rose an arm
Cloth'd in white samite, mystic, wonderful,
And caught him by the hilt, and brandish'd
    him
Three times, and drew him under in the mere.
And lightly went the other to the king.
    Then spoke King Arthur, drawing thicker
    breath:
''Now I see by thine eyes that this is done.
Speak out; what is it thou hast heard, or
    seen?''   150
    And answer made the bold Sir Bedivere:
''Sir King, I closed mine eyelids, lest the gems

Should blind my purpose, for I never saw,
Nor shall see, here or elsewhere, till I die,
Not tho' I live three lives of mortal men,
So great a miracle as yonder hilt.
Then with both hands I flung him, wheeling
    him;
But when I look'd again, behold an arm,
Clothed in white samite, mystic, wonderful,
That caught him by the hilt, and brandish'd
    him   160
Three times, and drew him under in the mere.''
    And answer made King Arthur, breathing
    hard:
''My end draws nigh; 't is time that I were
    gone.
Make broad thy shoulders to receive my weight
And bear me to the margin; yet I fear
My wound hath taken cold, and I shall die.'
    So saying, from the pavement he half rose
Slowly, with pain, reclining on his arm,
And looking wistfully with wide blue eyes
As in a picture. Him Sir Bedivere   170
Remorsefully regarded thro' his tears,
And would have spoken, but he found not
    words,
Then took with care, and kneeling on one knee
O'er both his shoulders drew the languid
    hands,
And rising bore him thro' the place of tombs.
But, as he walk'd, King Arthur panted hard
Like one that feels a nightmare on his bed
When all the house is mute. So sigh'd the
    king,
Muttering and murmuring at his ear, ''Quick,
    quick!
I fear it is too late, and I shall die.''   180
But the other swiftly strode from ridge to
    ridge,
Clothed with his breath, and looking, as he
    walk'd,
Larger than human on the frozen hills.
He heard the deep behind him, and a cry
Before. His own thought drove him like a
    goad.
Dry clash'd his harness in the icy caves
And barren chasms, and all to left and right
The bare black cliff clang'd round him, as he
    based
His feet on juts of slippery crag that rang
Sharp-smitten with the dint of armèd heels—
And on a sudden, lo! the level lake,   191
And the long glories of the winter moon.
    Then saw they how there hove a dusky barge,
Dark as a funeral scarf from stem to stern,
Beneath them; and descending they were ware
That all the decks were dense with stately
    forms

9 fancy   10 because

Black-stoled, black-hooded, like a dream—by
    these
Three queens with crowns of gold—and from
    them rose
A cry that shiver'd to the tingling stars,
And, as it were one voice, an agony   200
Of lamentation, like a wind that shrills
All night in a waste land, where no one comes,
Or hath come, since the making of the world.
    Then murmur'd Arthur, "Place me in the
    barge."
And to the barge they came. There those
    three queens
Put forth their hands, and took the king, and
    wept,
But she that rose the tallest of them all
And fairest, laid his head upon her lap,
And loosed his shatter'd casque, and chafed
    his hands,   209
And call'd him by his name, complaining loud,
And dropping bitter tears against his brow
Striped with dark blood; for all his face was
    white
And colourless, and like the wither'd moon
Smote by the fresh beam of the springing east;
And all his greaves and cuisses dash'd with
    drops
Of onset; and the light and lustrous curls—
That made his forehead like a rising sun
High from the dais-throne—were parch'd with
    dust;
Or, clotted into points and hanging loose,
Mix'd with the knightly growth that fringed
    his lips.   220
So like a shatter'd column lay the king;
Not like that Arthur who, with lance in rest,
From spur to plume a star of tournament,
Shot thro' the lists at Camelot, and charged
Before the eyes of ladies and of kings.
    Then loudly cried the bold Sir Bedivere:
"Ah! my Lord Arthur, whither shall I go?
Where shall I hide my forehead and my eyes?
For now I see the good old times are dead,   229
When every morning brought a noble chance,
And every chance brought out a noble knight.
Such times have not been since the light that
    led
The holy Elders with the gift of myrrh.
But now the whole Round Table is dissolved
Which was an image of the mighty world;
And I, the last, go forth companionless,
And the days darken round me, and the years,
Among new men, strange faces, other minds."
    And slowly answer'd Arthur from the barge:
"The old order changeth, yielding place to
    new,   240
And God fulfils himself in many ways,

Lest one good custom should corrupt the world.
Comfort thyself: what comfort is in me?
I have lived my life, and that which I have
    done
May He within himself make pure! but thou,
If thou shouldst never see my face again,
Pray for my soul. More things are wrought
    by prayer
Than this world dreams of. Wherefore, let thy
    voice
Rise like a fountain for me night and day.
For what are men better than sheep or goats   250
That nourish a blind life within the brain,
If, knowing God, they lift not hands of prayer
Both for themselves and those who call them
    friend?
For so the whole round earth is every way
Bound by gold chains about the feet of God.[1]
But now farewell. I am going a long way
With these thou seest—if indeed I go—
For all my mind is clouded with a doubt—
To the island-valley of Avilion;*
Where falls not hail, or rain, or any snow,   260
Nor ever wind blows loudly, but it lies
Deep-meadow'd, happy, fair with orchard lawns
And bowery hollows crown'd with summer sea,
Where I will heal me of my grievous wound."
    So said he, and the barge with oar and sail
Moved from the brink, like some full-breasted
    swan
That, fluting a wild carol ere her death,
Ruffles her pure cold plume, and takes the flood
With swarthy webs. Long stood Sir Bedivere
Revolving many memories, till the hull   270
Look'd one black dot against the verge of
    dawn,
And on the mere the wailing died away.

ULYSSES†

It little profits that an idle king,
By this still hearth, among these barren crags,
Match'd with an aged wife, I mete and dole
Unequal laws unto a savage race,
That hoard, and sleep, and feed, and know
    not me.

[1] Cp. *Paradise Lost*, II, 1051 (p. 255).
* The earthly paradise of mediæval romance, corresponding to the Grecian Isles of the Blest.
† The germ of this poem is found, not in the *Odyssey*, but in the story which Dante makes Ulysses tell of his adventures (*Inferno*, XXVI, 91 ff.). It was written shortly after the death of Tennyson's friend, Arthur Hallam (see *In Memoriam*), and voiced, said Tennyson, his "feelings about the need of going forward and braving the struggle of life more simply than anything in *In Memoriam*." (*Memoir*, I. 196). It is an admirable complement to *The Lotos-Eaters*. Of lines 62-64 Carlyle said: "These lines do not make me weep, but there is in me what would fill whole Lachrymatories as I read."

I cannot rest from travel; I will drink
Life to the lees. All times I have enjoy'd
Greatly, have suffer'd greatly, both with those
That loved me, and alone; on shore, and when
Thro' scudding drifts the rainy Hyades[2]   10
Vext the dim sea. I am become a name;
For always roaming with a hungry heart
Much have I seen and known,—cities of men
And manners, climates, councils, governments,
Myself not least, but honour'd of them all,—
And drunk delight of battle with my peers,
Far on the ringing plains of windy Troy.
I am a part of all that I have met;
Yet all experience is an arch wherethro'
Gleams that untravell'd world whose margin
     fades   20
For ever and for ever when I move.
How dull it is to pause, to make an end,
To rust unburnish'd, not to shine in use!
As tho' to breathe were life! Life piled on
     life
Were all too little, and of one to me
Little remains; but every hour is saved
From that eternal silence, something more,
A bringer of new things: and vile it were
For some three suns to store and hoard myself,
And this gray spirit yearning in desire   30
To follow knowledge like a sinking star,
Beyond the utmost bound of human thought.

This is my son, mine own Telemachus,
To whom I leave the sceptre and the isle,—
Well-loved of me, discerning to fulfil
This labour, by slow prudence to make mild
A rugged people, and thro' soft degrees
Subdue them to the useful and the good.
Most blameless is he, centred in the sphere
Of common duties, decent not to fail   40
In offices of tenderness, and pay
Meet adoration to my household gods,
When I am gone. He works his work, I mine.

There lies the port; the vessel puffs her sail;
There gloom the dark, broad seas. My mariners,
Souls that have toil'd, and wrought, and
     thought with me,—
That ever with a frolic welcome took
The thunder and the sunshine, and opposed
Free hearts, free foreheads,—you and I are old;
Old age hath yet his honour and his toil.   50
Death closes all; but something ere the end,
Some work of noble note, may yet be done,
Not unbecoming men that strove with Gods.
The lights begin to twinkle from the rocks;
The long day wanes; the slow moon climbs;
     the deep

Moans round with many voices.* Come, my
     friends,
'T is not too late to seek a newer world.
Push off, and sitting well in order smite
The sounding furrows; for my purpose holds
To sail beyond the sunset, and the baths   60
Of all the western stars, until I die.
It may be that the gulfs will wash us down;
It may be we shall touch the Happy Isles,†
And see the great Achilles, whom we knew.
Tho' much is taken, much abides; and tho'
We are not now that strength which in old days
Moved earth and heaven, that which we are,
     we are,—
One equal temper of heroic hearts,
Made weak by time and fate, but strong in
     will
To strive, to seek, to find, and not to yield.   70

LOCKSLEY HALL‡

Comrades, leave me here a little, while as yet
     't is early morn:
Leave me here, and when you want me, sound
     upon the bugle-horn.

'T is the place, and all around it, as of old, the
     curlews call,
Dreary gleams about the moorland flying over
     Locksley Hall;

Locksley Hall, that in the distance overlooks
     the sandy tracts,
And the hollow ocean-ridges roaring into
     cataracts.

Many a night from yonder ivied casement, ere
     I went to rest,
Did I look on great Orion sloping slowly to the
     west.

Many a night I saw the Pleiads, rising thro'
     the mellow shade,
Glitter like a swarm of fireflies tangled in a
     silver braid.   10

Here about the beach I wander'd, nourishing
     a youth sublime

---

2 Stars in the constellation Taurus, supposed to be
   harbingers of rain. *Æneid*, I, 744.

* Successive heavy monosyllables, long vowels, and
   full pauses, combine to make this a passage
   of remarkable weight and slowness.
† Compare note on preceding poem, l. 259.
‡ This was intended to be a purely dramatic poem,
   giving expression to the conflicting and somewhat morbid feelings characteristic perhaps
   of introspective youth at any time, but with
   particular reference both to contemporary social conditions in England (it was published
   in 1842) and to the fresh spur given to imagination by the discoveries in science and
   mechanics. Some forty years later, Tennyson
   wrote a sequel, *Locksley Hall Sixty Years
   After.*

With the fairy tales of science, and the long
    result of time;

When the centuries behind me like a fruitful
    land reposed;
When I clung to all the present for the promise
    that it closed[1];

When I dipt into the future far as human eye
    could see,
Saw the vision of the world and all the wonder
    that would be.—

In the spring a fuller crimson comes upon the
    robin's breast;
In the spring the wanton lapwing gets himself
    another crest;

In the spring a livelier iris changes on the
    burnish'd dove;
In the spring a young man's fancy lightly
    turns to thoughts of love.   20

Then her cheek was pale and thinner than
    should be for one so young,
And her eyes on all my motions with a mute
    observance hung.

And I said, "My cousin Amy, speak, and
    speak the truth to me,
Trust me, cousin, all the current of my being
    sets to thee."

On her pallid cheek and forehead came a colour
    and a light,
As I have seen the rosy red flushing in the
    northern night.

And she turn'd—her bosom shaken with a
    sudden storm of sighs—
All the spirit deeply dawning in the dark of
    hazel eyes—

Saying, "I have hid my feelings, fearing they
    should do me wrong;"
Saying, "Dost thou love me, cousin?" weeping,
    "I have loved thee long."   30

Love took up the glass of Time, and turn'd it
    in his glowing hands;
Every moment, lightly shaken, ran itself in
    golden sands.

Love took up the harp of Life, and smote on
    all the chords with might;
Smote the chord of Self, that, trembling, past
    in music out of sight.

1 enclosed

Many a morning on the moorland did we hear
    the copses ring,
And her whisper throng'd my pulses with the
    fulness of the spring.

Many an evening by the waters did we watch
    the stately ships,
And our spirits rushed together at the touching
    of the lips.

O my cousin, shallow-hearted!   O my Amy,
    mine no more!
O the dreary, dreary moorland!   O the barren,
    barren shore!   40

Falser than all fancy fathoms, falser than all
    songs have sung,
Puppet to a father's threat, and servile to a
    shrewish tongue!

Is it well to wish thee happy? having known
    me—to decline
On a range of lower feelings and a narrower
    heart than mine!

Yet it shall be; thou shalt lower to his level
    day by day,
What is fine within thee growing coarse to
    sympathize with clay.

As the husband is, the wife is; thou art mated
    with a clown,
And the grossness of his nature will have
    weight to drag thee down.

He will hold thee, when his passion shall have
    spent its novel force,
Something better than his dog, a little dearer
    than his horse.   50

What is this? his eyes are heavy; think not
    they are glazed with wine.
Go to him, it is thy duty; kiss him, take his
    hand in thine.

It may be my lord is weary, that his brain is
    overwrought;
Soothe him with thy finer fancies, touch him
    with thy lighter thought.

He will answer to the purpose, easy things to
    understand—
Better thou wert dead before me, tho' I slew
    thee with my hand!

Better thou and I were lying, hidden from the
    heart's disgrace,

Roll'd in one another's arms, and silent in a
last embrace.

Cursed be the social wants that sin against the
strength of youth!
Cursed be the social lies that warp us from
the living truth!   60

Cursed be the sickly forms that err from honest
Nature's rule!
Cursed be the gold that gilds the straiten'd
forehead of the fool!

Well—'t is well that I should bluster!—Hadst
thou less unworthy proved—
Would to God—for I had loved thee more than
ever wife was loved.

Am I mad, that I should cherish that which
bears but bitter fruit?
I will pluck it from my bosom, tho' my heart
be at the root.

Never, tho' my mortal summers to such length
of years should come
As the many-winter'd crow that leads the
clanging rookery home.

Where is comfort? in division of the records
of the mind?
Can I part her from herself, and love her, as I
knew her, kind?   70

I remember one that perish'd;[1] sweetly did she
speak and move;
Such a one do I remember, whom to look at was
to love.

Can I think of her as dead, and love her for
the love she bore?
No—she never loved me truly; love is love for
evermore.

Comfort? comfort scorn'd of devils! this is
truth the poet sings,
That a sorrow's crown of sorrow is remembering happier things.[2]

Drug thy memories, lest thou learn it, lest thy
heart be put to proof,
In the dead unhappy night, and when the rain
is on the roof.

Like a dog, he hunts in dreams, and thou ar
staring at the wall,
Where the dying night-lamp flickers, and the
shadows rise and fall.   8

Then a hand shall pass before thee, pointing
to his drunken sleep,
To thy widow'd marriage-pillows, to the tears
that thou wilt weep.

Thou shalt hear the "Never, never," whisper'd by the phantom years,
And a song from out the distance in the ringing of thine ears;

And an eye shall vex thee, looking ancient
kindness on thy pain.
Turn thee, turn thee on thy pillow; get thee to
thy rest again.

Nay, but Nature brings thee solace; for a
tender voice will cry.
'T is a purer life than thine, a lip to drain thy
trouble dry.

Baby lips will laugh me down; my latest rival
brings thee rest.
Baby fingers, waxen touches, press me from the
mother's breast.   90

O, the child too clothes the father with a dearness not his due.
Half is thine and half is his; it will be worthy
of the two.

O, I see thee old and formal, fitted to thy petty
part,
With a little hoard of maxims preaching down
a daughter's heart.

"They were dangerous guides the feelings—
she herself was not exempt—
Truly, she herself had suffer'd"[3]—Perish in
thy self-contempt!

Overlive it—lower yet—be happy! wherefore
should I care?
I myself must mix with action, lest I wither
by despair.

What is that which I should turn to, lighting
upon days like these?
Every door is barr'd with gold, and opens but
to golden keys.   100

[1] I. e., she has lost the personality which I remember.
[2] Dante: *Inferno*, V, 121. The thought may be
traced to many writers—to Pindar, among
the earliest.
[3] Amy is imagined to be talking to her daughter,
at some future time, of her own early life.

Every gate is throng'd with suitors, all the markets overflow.
I have but an angry fancy; what is that which I should do?

I had been content to perish, falling on the foeman's ground,
When the ranks are roll'd in vapour, and the winds are laid with sound.

But the jingling of the guinea helps the hurt that Honour feels,
And the nations do but murmur, snarling at each other's heels.

Can I but relive in sadness? I will turn that earlier page.
Hide me from my deep emotion, O thou wondrous Mother-Age![4]

Make me feel the wild pulsation that I felt before the strife,
When I heard my days before me, and the tumult of my life; 110

Yearning for the large excitement that the coming years would yield,
Eager-hearted as a boy when first he leaves his father's field,

And at night along the dusky highway near and nearer drawn,
Sees in heaven the light of London flaring like a dreary dawn;

And his spirit leaps within him to be gone before him then,
Underneath the light he looks at, in among the throngs of men;

Men, my brothers, men the workers, ever reaping something new;
That which they have done but earnest of the things that they shall do.

For I dipt into the future, far as human eye could see,
Saw the Vision of the world, and all the wonder that would be; 120

Saw the heavens fill with commerce, argosies of magic sails,
Pilots of the purple twilight, dropping down with costly bales;*

Heard the heavens fill with shouting, and there rain'd a ghastly dew
From the nations' airy navies grappling in the central blue;

Far along the world-wide whisper of the south-wind rushing warm,
With the standards of the peoples plunging thro' the thunder-storm;

Till the war-drum throbb'd no longer, and the battle-flags were furl'd
In the Parliament of man, the Federation of the world.

There the common sense of most shall hold a fretful realm in awe,
And the kindly earth shall slumber, lapped[5] in universal law. 130

So I triumphed ere my passion sweeping thro' me left me dry,
Left me with the palsied heart, and left me with the jaundiced eye;

Eye, to which all order festers, all things here are out of joint.
Science moves, but slowly, slowly, creeping on from point to point;

Slowly comes a hungry people, as a lion, creeping nigher,
Glares at one that nods and winks behind a slowly-dying fire.†

Yet I doubt not thro' the ages one increasing purpose runs,
And the thoughts of men are widen'd with the process of the suns.

What is that to him that reaps not harvest of his youthful joys,
Tho' the deep heart of existence beat for ever like a boy's? 140

Knowledge comes, but wisdom lingers, and I linger on the shore,
And the individual withers, and the world is more and more.[6]

4 Cp. line 185.
* Tennyson had a rare faculty for putting the hopes and achievements of science into poetic language. It is interesting, however, to observe at what a cautious distance he placed the realization of this seemingly extravagant prophecy.

5 wrapped
6 Looms forever larger by contrast. Cp. *In Memoriam*, LV.
† He of the "jaundiced eye" scoffs at science and is suspicious of democratic and socialistic tendencies. The weak point in Tennyson's picture is the connection of this large pessimism with the purely personal disappointment of his hero. It may not be altogether unfaithful, but it is undramatic.

Knowledge comes, but wisdom lingers, and he
    bears a laden breast,
Full of sad experience, moving toward the
    stillness of his rest.

Hark, my merry comrades call me, sounding
    on the bugle-horn,
They to whom my foolish passion were a target
    for their scorn.

Shall it not be scorn to me to harp on such a
    moulder'd string?
I am shamed thro' all my nature to have loved
    so slight a thing.

Weakness to be wroth with weakness! woman's
    pleasure, woman's pain—
Nature made them blinder motions[7] bounded
    in a shallower brain.   150

Woman is the lesser man, and all thy passions,
    match'd with mine,
Are as moonlight unto sunlight, and as water
    unto wine—

Here at least, where nature sickens, nothing.[8]
    Ah, for some retreat
Deep in yonder shining Orient, where my life
    began to beat,

Where in wild Mahratta-battle[9] fell my father
    evil-starred;—
I was left a trampled orphan, and a selfish
    uncle's ward.

Or to burst all links of habit—there to wander
    far away,
On from island unto island at the gateways of
    the day.

Larger constellations burning, mellow moons
    and happy skies,
Breadths of tropic shade and palms in cluster,
    knots of Paradise.[10]   160

Never comes the trader, never floats an
    European flag,
Slides the bird o'er lustrous woodland, swings
    the trailer from the crag;

Droops the heavy-blossom'd bower, hangs the
    heavy-fruited tree—

Summer isles of Eden lying in dark-purple
    spheres of sea.

There methinks would be enjoyment more than
    in this march of mind,
In the steamship, in the railway, in the
    thoughts that shake mankind.

There the passions cramp'd no longer shall
    have scope and breathing space;
I will take some savage woman, she shall rear
    my dusky race.

Iron-jointed, supple-sinew'd, they shall dive,
    and they shall run,
Catch the wild goat by the hair, and hurl their
    lances in the sun;   170

Whistle back the parrot's call, and leap the
    rainbows of the brooks,
Not with blinded eyesight poring over mis-
    erable books—

Fool, again the dream, the fancy! but I *know*
    my words are wild,
But I count the gray barbarian lower than the
    Christian child.

I, to herd with narrow foreheads, vacant of
    our glorious gains,
Like a beast with lower pleasures, like a beast
    with lower pains!

Mated with a squalid savage—what to me were
    sun or clime!
I the heir of all the ages, in the foremost files
    of time—

I that rather held it better men should perish
    one by one,
Than that earth should stand at gaze like
    Joshua's moon in Ajalon![11]

Not in vain the distance beacons. Forward,
    forward let us range,
Let the great world spin for ever down the
    ringing grooves of change.[12]

Thro' the shadow of the globe we sweep into
    the younger day;
Better fifty years of Europe than a cycle of
    Cathay.

Mother-Age,—for mine I knew not,—help me
    as when life begun;

---

7 beings
8 Implying that the inferiority of woman may be the result of the conventions of a false civilization. Compare *The Princess.*

9 The British have had many conflicts with the warlike Mahrattas of India.
10 See *Par. Lost,* iv, 242.
11 *Joshua,* x 13.
12 Tennyson drew this figure from the railway, then new, under the false impression that the car-wheels ran in grooves.

Rift. the hills, and roll the waters, flash the
    lightnings, weigh the sun.

O, I see the crescent promise of my spirit hath
    not set.
Ancient founts of inspiration well thro' all
    my fancy yet.

Howsoever these things be, a long farewell to
    Locksley Hall!
Now for me the woods may wither, now for me
    the roof-tree fall. 190

Comes a vapour from the margin, blackening
    over heath and holt,
Cramming all the blast before it, in its breast
    a thunderbolt.

Let it fall on Locksley Hall, with rain or hail,
    or fire or snow;
For the mighty wind arises, roaring seaward,
    and I go.

A FAREWELL

Flow down, cold rivulet, to the sea,
    Thy tribute wave deliver;
No more by thee my steps shall be,
    For ever and for ever.

Flow, softly flow, by lawn and lea,
    A rivulet, then a river;
Nowhere by thee my steps shall be,
    For ever and for ever.

But here will sigh thine alder-tree,
    And here thine aspen shiver;
And here by thee will hum the bee,
    For ever and for ever.

A thousand suns will stream on thee,
    A thousand moons will quiver;
But not by thee my steps shall be,
    For ever and for ever.

BREAK, BREAK, BREAK*

Break, break, break,
    On thy cold gray stones, O Sea!
And I would that my tongue could utter
    The thoughts that arise in me.

O, well for the fisherman's boy,
    That he shouts with his sister at play!

* These lines were written in memory of Arthur
Hallam, and might well have been included
among the poems of *In Memoriam* had they
not been cast in a different metre.

O, well for the sailor lad,
    That he sings in his boat on the bay!

And the stately ships go on
    To their haven under the hill;
But O for the touch of a vanish'd hand,
    And the sound of a voice that is still!

Break, break, break,
    At the foot of thy crags, O Sea!
But the tender grace of a day that is dead
    Will never come back to me.

SONGS FROM THE PRINCESS
SWEET AND LOW

Sweet and low, sweet and low,
    Wind of the western sea,
Low, low, breathe and blow,
    Wind of the western sea!
Over the rolling waters go,
Come from the dying moon, and blow,
    Blow him again to me:
While my little one, while my pretty one,
    sleeps.

Sleep and rest, sleep and rest,
    Father will come to thee soon;
Rest, rest, on mother's breast,
    Father will come to thee soon;
Father will come to his babe in the nest,
Silver sails all out of the west
    Under the silver moon;
Sleep, my little one, sleep, my pretty one,
    sleep.

THE SPLENDOUR FALLS†

The splendour falls on castle walls
    And snowy summits old in story;
The long light shakes across the lakes,
    And the wild cataract leaps in glory.
Blow, bugle, blow, set the wild echoes flying,
Blow, bugle; answer, echoes, dying, dying,
    dying.

O, hark, O, hear! how thin and clear,
    And thinner, clearer, farther going!
O, sweet and far from cliff and scar
    The horns of Elfland faintly blowing!
Blow, let us hear the purple glens replying,
Blow, bugle; answer, echoes, dying, dying,
    dying.

O love, they die in yon rich sky,
    They faint on hill or field or river;

† This song was inspired by the echoes at the
Lakes of Killarney.

Our echoes roll from soul to soul,
  And grow for ever and for ever.
Blow, bugle, blow, set the wild echoes flying,
And answer, echoes, answer, dying, dying,
      dying.

TEARS, IDLE TEARS

Tears, idle tears, I know not what they mean,
Tears from the depth of some divine despair
Rise in the heart, and gather to the eyes,
In looking on the happy autumn-fields,
And thinking of the days that are no more.

Fresh as the first beam glittering on a sail,
That brings our friends up from the under-
      world,
Sad as the last which reddens over one
That sinks with all we love below the verge;
So sad, so fresh, the days that are no more.

Ah, sad and strange as in dark summer
      dawns
The earliest pipe of half-awaken'd birds
To dying ears, when unto dying eyes
The casement slowly grows a glimmering
      square;
So sad, so strange, the days that are no more.

Dear as remember'd kisses after death,
And sweet as those by hopeless fancy feign'd
On lips that are for others; deep as love,
Deep as first love, and wild with all regret;
O Death in Life, the days that are no more!

FROM IN MEMORIAM*

I

I held it truth, with him[1] who sings
  To one clear harp in divers tones,
  That men may rise on stepping-stones
Of their dead selves to higher things.

But who shall so forecast the years
  And find in loss a gain to match?
  Or reach a hand thro' time to catch
The far-off interest of tears?

Let Love clasp Grief lest both be drown'd,
  Let darkness keep her raven gloss.[2]

1 Goethe, says Tennyson.
* Tennyson's friend, Arthur Henry Hallam, died at
  Vienna in 1833. The short poems written in
  his memory at various times and in various
  moods, Tennyson arranged and published in
  the year 1850. See Eng. Lit., p. 294. The
  earlier poems are chiefly personal in nature;
  the later treat some of the larger problems of
  human life and destiny growing out of both
  personal bereavement and the unrest produced
  by the changes that were then taking place in
  the realm of religious and scientific thought.

Ah, sweeter to be drunk with loss,
To dance with Death, to beat the ground,

Than that the victor Hours should scorn
  The long[3] result of love, and boast,
  'Behold the man that loved and lost,
But all he was is overworn.'

XXVII

I envy not in any moods
  The captive void of noble rage,
  The linnet born within the cage,
That never knew the summer woods;

I envy not the beast that takes
  His license in the field of time,
  Unfetter'd by the sense of crime,
To whom a conscience never wakes;

Nor, what may count itself as blest,
  The heart that never plighted troth
  But stagnates in the weeds of sloth;
Nor any want-begotten rest.[4]

I hold it true, whate'er befall;
  I feel it, when I sorrow most;
  'T is better to have loved and lost
Than never to have loved at all.

LIV

O, yet we trust that somehow good
  Will be the final goal of ill,
  To pangs of nature, sins of will,
Defects of doubt, and taints of blood;

That nothing walks with aimless feet;
  That not one life shall be destroy'd,
  Or cast as rubbish to the void,
When God hath made the pile complete;

That not a worm is cloven in vain;
  That not a moth with vain desire
  Is shrivell'd in a fruitless fire,
Or but subserves another's gain.

Behold, we know not anything;
  I can but trust that good shall fall
  At last—far off—at last, to all,
And every winter change to spring.

So runs my dream; but what am I?
  An infant crying in the night;

2 Cp. Milton's Comus, 251.
3 Used poetically for "ultimate." Cp. Locksley
  Hall, l. 12.
4 Content due to mere want of higher faculties.

An infant crying for the light,
And with no language but a cry.

LV

The wish, that of the living whole
  No life may fail beyond the grave,
  Derives it not from what we have
The likest God within the soul?

Are God and Nature then at strife,
  That Nature lends such evil dreams?
  So careful of the type she seems,
So careless of the single life,

That I, considering everywhere
  Her secret meaning in her deeds,
  And finding that of fifty seeds
She often brings but one to bear,

I falter where I firmly trod,
  And falling with my weight of cares
  Upon the great world's altar-stairs
That slope thro' darkness up to God,

I stretch lame hands of faith, and grope,
  And gather dust and chaff, and call
  To what I feel is Lord of all,
And faintly trust the larger hope.

LVI

"So careful of the type?" but no,
  From scarped cliff and quarried stone[1]
  She cries, "A thousand types are gone;
I care for nothing, all shall go.

"Thou makest thine appeal to me:
  I bring to life, I bring to death;
  The spirit does but mean the breath:
I know no more." And he, shall he,

Man, her last work, who seem'd so fair,
  Such splendid purpose in his eyes,
  Who roll'd the psalm to wintry skies,
Who built him fanes of fruitless prayer,

Who trusted God was love indeed
  And love Creation's final law—
  Tho' Nature, red in tooth and claw
With ravine, shriek'd against his creed—

Who loved, who suffer'd countless ills,
  Who battled for the True, the Just,
  Be blown about the desert dust,
Or seal'd within the iron hills?

No more? A monster then, a dream,
  A discord. Dragons of the prime,

That tare each other in their slime,
Were mellow music match'd with him.

O life as futile, then, as frail!
  O for thy voice to soothe and bless!
  What hope of answer, or redress?
Behind the veil, behind the veil.

LVII

Peace; come away: the song of woe
  Is after all an earthly song.
  Peace; come away: we do him wrong
To sing so wildly: let us go.

Come; let us go: your cheeks are pale;
  But half my life I leave behind.[2]
  Methinks my friend is richly shrined;[3]
But I shall pass, my work will fail.

Yet in these ears, till hearing dies,
  One set slow bell will seem to toll
  The passing of the sweetest soul
That ever look'd with human eyes.

I hear it now, and o'er and o'er,
  Eternal greetings to the dead;
  And "Ave, Ave, Ave," said,
"Adieu, adieu," for evermore.

LVIII

In those sad words I took farewell.
  Like echoes in sepulchral halls,
  As drop by drop the water falls
In vaults and catacombs, they fell;

And, falling, idly broke the peace
  Of hearts that beat from day to day,
  Half-conscious[4] of their dying clay,
And those cold crypts where they shall cease.

The high Muse answer'd: "Wherefore grieve
  Thy brethren with a fruitless tear?
  Abide a little longer here,
And thou shalt take a nobler leave."

CIV

The time draws near the birth of Christ;*
  The moon is hid, the night is still;
  A single church below the hill
Is pealing, folded in the mist.

A single peal of bells below,
  That wakens at this hour of rest

2 In the grave.   4 Only half-conscious.
3 In these poems.
* This is the third Christmas described in the
  poem. Tennyson had removed to a new home.
1 Which shows fossil remains of extinct forms.

A single murmur in the breast,
That these are not the bells I know.

Like strangers' voices here they sound,
　In lands where not a memory strays,
　Nor landmark breathes of other days,
But all is new unhallow'd ground. . .

CVI

Ring out, wild bells, to the wild sky,
　The flying cloud, the frosty light:
　The year is dying in the night;
Ring out, wild bells, and let him die.

Ring out the old, ring in the new,
　Ring, happy bells, across the snow:
　The year is going, let him go;
Ring out the false, ring in the true.

Ring out the grief that saps the mind,
　For those that here we see no more;
　Ring out the feud of rich and poor;
Ring in redress to all mankind.

Ring out a slowly dying cause,
　And ancient forms of party strife;
　Ring in the nobler modes of life,
With sweeter manners, purer laws.

Ring out the want, the care, the sin,
　The faithless coldness of the times;
　Ring out, ring out my mournful rhymes,
But ring the fuller minstrel in.

Ring out false pride in place and blood,
　The civic slander and the spite;
　Ring in the love of truth and right,
Ring in the common love of good.

Ring out old shapes of foul disease;
　Ring out the narrowing lust of gold;
　Ring out the thousand wars of old,
Ring in the thousand years of peace.

Ring in the valiant man and free,
　The larger heart, the kindlier hand;
　Ring out the darkness of the land,
Ring in the Christ that is to be.

·　·　·　·　·　·　·

CXV

Now fades the last long streak of snow,
　Now burgeons every maze of quick[1]
　About the flowering squares,[2] and thick
By ashen roots the violets blow.

Now rings the woodland loud and long,
　The distance takes a lovelier hue,
　And drown'd in yonder living blue
The lark becomes a sightless song.

Now dance the lights on lawn and lea,
　The flocks are whiter down the vale,
　And milkier every milky sail
On winding stream or distant sea;

Where now the seamew pipes, or dives
　In yonder greening gleam, and fly
　The happy birds, that change their sky
To build and brood, that live their lives

From land to land; and in my breast
　Spring wakens too, and my regret
　Becomes an April violet,
And buds and blossoms like the rest.

CXVI

Is it, then, regret for buried time
　That keenlier in sweet April wakes,
　And meets the year, and gives and takes
The colours of the crescent prime?[3]

Not all: the songs, the stirring air,
　The life re-orient out of dust,
　Cry thro' the sense to hearten trust
In that which made the world so fair.

Not all regret: the face will shine
　Upon me, while I muse alone,
　And that dear voice, I once have known,
Still speak to me of me and mine.

Yet loss of sorrow lives in me
　For days of happy commune dead.
　Less yearning for the friendship fled
Than some strong bond which is to be.

CXVII

O days and hours, your work is this,
　To hold me from my proper place,
　A little while from his embrace,
For fuller gain of after bliss;

That out of distance might ensue
　Desire of nearness doubly sweet,
　And unto meeting, when we meet,
Delight a hundredfold accrue,

For every grain of sand that runs,[4]
　And every span of shade that steals,

1 hedge (especially hawthorn)
2 fields
3 increasing spring
4 This stanza describes the various means of measuring time.

And every kiss of toothéd wheels,
And all the courses of the suns.

CXVIII

Contemplate all this work of Time,
  The giant labouring in his youth;
  Nor dream of human love and truth,
As dying Nature's earth and lime;

But trust that those we call the dead
  Are breathers of an ampler day
  For ever nobler ends.   They say,
The solid earth whereon we tread

In tracts of fluent heat began,
  And grew to seeming-random forms,
  The seeming prey of cyclic[5] storms,
Till at the last arose the man;

Who throve and branch'd from clime to clime,
  The herald of a higher race,
  And of himself in higher place,
If so he type[6] this work of time

Within himself, from more to more;
  Or, crown'd with attributes of woe
  Like glories, move his course, and show
That life is not as idle ore,

But iron dug from central gloom,
  And heated hot with burning fears,
  And dipped in baths of hissing tears,
And batter'd with the shocks of doom

To shape and use.   Arise and fly
  The reeling Faun, the sensual feast;
  Move upward, working out the beast,
And let the ape and tiger die.

. . . . .

CXXV

What ever I have said or sung,
  Some bitter notes my harp would give,
  Yea, tho' there often seem'd to live
A contradiction on the tongue.

Yet Hope had never lost her youth,
  She did but look through dimmer eyes;
  Or Love but play'd with gracious lies,
Because he felt so fix'd in truth;

And if the song were full of care,
  He breathed the spirit of the song;
  And if the words were sweet and strong
He set his royal signet there;

5 periodic. (in a large sense)
6 represent, properly

Abiding with me till I sail
  To seek thee on the mystic deeps,
  And this electric force, that keeps
A thousand pulses dancing, fail.

CXXVI

Love is and was my lord and king,
  And in his presence I attend
  To hear the tidings of my friend,
Which every hour his couriers bring.

Love is and was my king and lord,
  And will be, tho' as yet I keep
  Within the court on earth, and sleep
Encompass'd by his faithful guard,

And hear at times a sentinel
  Who moves about from place to place,
  And whispers to the worlds of space,
In the deep night, that all is well.

CXXVII

And all is well, tho' faith and form
  Be sunder'd in the night of fear;
  Well roars the storm to those that hear
A deeper voice across the storm,

Proclaiming social truth shall spread,
  And justice, even tho' thrice again
  The red fool-fury of the Seine
Should pile her barricades with dead.*

But ill for him that wears a crown,
  And him, the lazar, in his rags!
  They tremble, the sustaining crags;
The spires of ice are toppled down,

And molten up, and roar in flood;
  The fortress crashes from on high,
  The brute earth lightens to the sky,
And the great Æon sinks in blood,

And compass'd by the fires of hell;
  While thou, dear spirit, happy star,
  O'erlook'st the tumult from afar,
And smilest, knowing all is well.

. . . . .

IN THE VALLEY OF CAUTERETZ†

All along the valley, stream that flashest white,
Deepening thy voice with the deepening of the
          night,
All along the valley, where thy waters flow,

* There was a violent revolution in France in
    1830, resulting in the overthrow of Charles X.
† In 1861, Tennyson revisited this valley in the
    French Pyrenees which he had visited with
    Hallam in 1830.

I walk'd with one I loved two and thirty years
  ago.
All along the valley, while I walk'd to-day,
The two and thirty years were a mist that
    rolls away;
For all along the valley, down thy rocky bed,
Thy living voice to me was as the voice of
    the dead,
And all along the valley, by rock and cave and
    tree,
The voice of the dead was a living voice to me.

IN THE GARDEN AT SWAINSTON†

Nightingales warbled without,
  Within was weeping for thee;
Shadows of three dead men
  Walk'd in the garden with me,
  Shadows of three dead men, and thou wast
    one of the three.

Nightingales sang in his woods,
  The Master was far away;
Nightingales warbled and sang
  Of a passion that lasts but a day;
  Still in the house in his coffin the Prince of
    courtesy lay.

Two dead men have I known
  In courtesy like to thee;
Two dead men have I loved
  With a love that ever will be;
  Three dead men have I loved, and thou art
    last of the three.

SONG FROM MAUD§

Come into the garden, Maud,
  For the black bat, night, has flown,
Come into the garden, Maud,
  I am here at the gate alone;
And the woodbine spices are wafted abroad,
  And the musk of the rose is blown.   6

For a breeze of morning moves,
  And the planet of love is on high,
Beginning to faint in the light that she loves
  On a bed of daffodil sky,
To faint in the light of the sun she loves,
  To faint in his light, and to die.   12

† The home of Sir John Simeon in the Isle of
  Wight, where Tennyson also lived in the lat-
  ter part of his life. Sir John died in 1870.
  The other two friends referred to were Arthur
  Hallam (see preceding poems) and Henry
  Lushington (d. 1855), to whom Tennyson had
  dedicated The Princess. All three, by a cu-
  rious coincidence, died abroad.
§ There is a distinct echo in this song of The
  Song of Solomon; cp. chapters v and vi.

All night have the roses heard
  The flute, violin, bassoon;
All night has the casement jessamine stirr'd
  To the dancers dancing in tune;
Till a silence fell with the waking bird,
  And a hush with the setting moon.   1

I said to the lily, "There is but one,
  With whom she has heart to be gay.
When will the dancers leave her alone?
  She is weary of dance and play."
Now half to the setting moon are gone,
  And half to the rising day;
Low on the sand and loud on the stone
  The last wheel echoes away.   26

I said to the rose, "The brief night goes
  In babble and revel and wine.
O young lord-lover, what sighs are those,
  For one that will never be thine?
But mine, but mine," so I sware to the rose,
  "For ever and ever, mine."   32

And the soul of the rose went into my blood,
  As the music clash'd in the Hall;
And long by the garden lake I stood,
  For I heard your rivulet fall
From the lake to the meadow and on to the
    wood,
  Our wood, that is dearer than all;   38

From the meadow your walks have left so
    sweet
  That whenever a March-wind sighs
He sets the jewel-print of your feet
  In violets blue as your eyes,
To the woody hollows in which we meet
  And the valleys of Paradise.   44

The slender acacia would not shake
  One long milk-bloom on the tree;
The white lake-blossom fell into the lake
  As the pimpernel dozed on the lea;
But the rose was awake all night for your sake,
  Knowing your promise to me;
The lilies and roses were all awake,
  They sigh'd for the dawn and thee.   52

Queen rose of the rosebud garden of girls,
  Come hither, the dances are done,
In gloss of satin and glimmer of pearls,
  Queen lily and rose in one;
Shine out, little head, sunning over with curls,
  To the flowers, and be their sun.   58

There has fallen a splendid tear
  From the passion-flower at the gate,

She is coming, my dove, my dear;
  She is coming, my life, my fate.
The red rose cries, "She is near, she is near;"
  And the white rose weeps, "She is late;"
The larkspur listens, "I hear, I hear;"
  And the lily whispers, "I wait."   66

She is coming, my own, my sweet;
  Were it ever so airy a tread,
My heart would hear her and beat,
  Were it earth in an earthy bed;
My dust would hear her and beat,
  Had I lain for a century dead,
Would start and tremble under her feet,
  And blossom in purple and red.   74

THE CHARGE OF THE LIGHT BRIGADE*

  Half a league, half a league,
  Half a league onward,
  All in the valley of Death
    Rode the six hundred.
  "Forward the Light Brigade!
  Charge for the guns!" he said.
  Into the valley of Death
    Rode the six hundred.

  "Forward, the Light Brigade!"
  Was there a man dismay'd?   10
  Not tho' the soldier knew
    Some one had blunder'd.
  Theirs not to make reply,
  Theirs not to reason why,
  Theirs but to do and die.
  Into the valley of Death
    Rode the six hundred.

  Cannon to right of them,
  Cannon to left of them,
  Cannon in front of them   20
    Volley'd and thunder'd;
  Storm'd at with shot and shell,
  Boldly they rode and well,
  Into the jaws of Death,
  Into the mouth of hell
    Rode the six hundred.

  Flash'd all their sabres bare,
  Flash'd as they turn'd in air
  Sabring the gunners there,
  Charging an army, while   30
    All the world wonder'd.
  Plunged in the battery-smoke
  Right thro' the line they broke;

*This fatal charge, due to a misunderstanding of orders, was made at Balaklava, in the Crimea, in 1854. Less than one-third of the brigade returned alive.

  Cossack and Russian
  Reel'd from the sabre-stroke
    Shatter'd and sunder'd.
  Then they rode back, but not,
    Not the six hundred.

  Cannon to right of them,
  Cannon to left of them,   40
  Cannon behind them
    Volley'd and thunder'd;
  Storm'd at with shot and shell,
  While horse and hero fell,
  They that had fought so well
  Came thro' the jaws of Death,
  Back from the mouth of hell,
  All that was left of them,
    Left of six hundred.

  When can their glory fade?   50
  O the wild charge they made!
    All the world wonder'd.
  Honour the charge they made!
  Honour the Light Brigade,
    Noble six hundred!

THE CAPTAIN

A LEGEND OF THE NAVY

He that only rules by terror
  Doeth grievous wrong.
Deep as hell I count his error.
  Let him hear my song.
Brave the captain was; the seamen
  Made a gallant crew,
Gallant sons of English freemen,
  Sailors bold and true.
But they hated his oppression;
  Stern he was and rash,   10
So for every light transgression
  Doom'd them to the lash.
Day by day more harsh and cruel
  Seem'd the Captain's mood.
Secret wrath like smother'd fuel
  Burnt in each man's blood.
Yet he hoped to purchase glory,
  Hoped to make the name
Of his vessel great in story,
  Wheresoe'er he came.   20
So they past by capes and islands,
  Many a harbour-mouth,
Sailing under palmy highlands
  Far within the South.
On a day when they were going
  O'er the lone expanse,
In the north, her canvas flowing,
  Rose a ship of France.

Then the Captain's colour heightened,
  Joyful came his speech;   20
But a cloudy gladness lighten'd
  In the eyes of each.
"Chase," he said; the ship flew forward,
  And the wind did blow;
Stately, lightly, went she norward,
  Till she near'd the foe.
Then they look'd at him they hated,
  Had what they desired:
Mute with folded arms they waited—
  Not a gun was fired.   40
But they heard the foeman's thunder
  Roaring out their doom;
All the air was torn in sunder,
  Crashing went the boom;
Spars were splinter'd, decks were shatter'd,
  Bullets fell like rain;
Over mast and deck were scatter'd
  Blood and brains of men.
Spars were splinter'd; decks were broken;
  Every mother's son—   50
Down they dropt—no word was spoken—
  Each beside his gun.
On the decks as they were lying,
  Were their faces grim.
In their blood, as they lay dying,
  Did they smile on him.
Those in whom he had reliance
  For his noble name
With one smile of still defiance
  Sold him unto shame.   60
Shame and wrath his heart confounded,
  Pale he turn'd and red,
Till himself was deadly wounded
  Falling on the dead.
Dismal error! fearful slaughter!
  Years have wandered by;
Side by side beneath the water
  Crew and Captain lie;
There the sunlit ocean tosses
  O'er them mouldering,   70
And the lonely seabird crosses
  With one waft of the wing.

THE REVENGE*

A BALLAD OF THE FLEET

I

At Flores in the Azores Sir Richard Grenville
  lay,
And a pinnace, like a flutter'd bird, came
  flying from far away;
"Spanish ships of war at sea! we have sighted
  fifty-three!"

* See Sir Walter Raleigh's account, p. 208.

Then sware Lord Thomas Howard: "'For
  God I am no coward;
But I cannot meet them here, for my ships are
  out of gear,
And the half my men are sick. I must fly, but
  follow quick.
We are six ships of the line;† can we fight
  with fifty-three?"

II

Then spake Sir Richard Grenville: "I know
  you are no coward;
You fly them for a moment to fight with them
  again.
But I've ninety men and more that are lying
  sick ashore.   10
I should count myself the coward if I left
  them, my Lord Howard,
To these Inquisition dogs and the devildoms
  of Spain."

III

So Lord Howard past away with five ships of
  war that day,
Till he melted like a cloud in the silent summer
  heaven;
But Sir Richard bore in hand all his sick men
  from the land
Very carefully and slow,
Men of Bideford in Devon,
And we laid them on the ballast down below
For we brought them all aboard,
And they blest him in their pain, that they
  were not left to Spain,   20
To the thumb-screw and the stake, for the
  glory of the Lord.

IV

He had only a hundred seamen to work the
  ship and to fight
And he sailed away from Flores till the Span-
  iard came in sight,
With his huge sea-castles heaving upon the
  weather bow.
"Shall we fight or shall we fly?
Good Sir Richard, tell us now,
For to fight is but to die!
There'll be little of us left by the time this
  sun be set."
And Sir Richard said again: "We be all
  good English men.
Let us bang these dogs of Seville, the children
  of the devil,   30

† I. e., ships of the fighting line, the old term for
battle-ships.

For I never turn'd my back upon Don or devil
yet.''

V

Sir Richard spoke and he laughed, and we
roar'd a hurrah, and so
The little Revenge ran on sheer into the heart
of the foe,
With her hundred fighters on deck, and her
ninety sick below;
For half of their fleet to the right and half to
the left were seen,
And the little Revenge ran on thro' the long
sea-lane between.

VI

Thousands of their soldiers look'd down from
their decks and laugh'd,
Thousands of their seamen made mock at the
mad little craft
Running on and on, till delay'd
By their mountain-like San Philip that, of
fifteen hundred tons,   40
And up-shadowing high above us with her
yawning tiers of guns,
Took the breath from our sails, and we stay'd.

VII

And while now the great San Philip hung
above us like a cloud
Whence the thunderbolt will fall
Long and loud,
Four galleons drew away
From the Spanish fleet that day,
And two upon the larboard and two upon the
starboard lay,
And the battle-thunder broke from them all.

VIII

But anon the great San Philip, she bethought
herself and went,   50
Having that within her womb that had left her
ill content;
And the rest they came aboard us, and they
fought us hand to hand,
For a dozen times they came with their pikes
and musqueteers,
And a dozen times we shook 'em off as a dog
that shakes his ears
When he leaps from the water to the land.

IX

And the sun went down, and the stars came
out far over the summer sea,
But never a moment ceased the fight of the
one and the fifty-three.

Ship after ship, the whole night long, their
high-built galleons came,
Ship after ship, the whole night long, with her
battle-thunder and flame:
Ship after ship, the whole night long, drew
back with her dead and her shame.   60
For some were sunk and many were shatter'd,
and so could fight no more—
God of battles, was ever a battle like this in
the world before?

X

For he said, ''Fight on! fight on!''
Tho' his vessel was all but a wreck;
And it chanced that, when half of the short
summer night was gone,
With a grisly wound to be drest he had left
the deck,
But a bullet struck him that was dressing it
suddenly dead,
And himself he was wounded again in the side
and the head,
And he said, ''Fight on! fight on!''

XI

And the night went down, and the sun smiled
out far over the summer sea,   70
And the Spanish fleet with broken sides lay
round us all in a ring;
But they dared not touch us again, for they
fear'd that we still could sting,
So they watch'd what the end would be.
And we had not fought them in vain,
But in perilous plight were we,
Seeing forty of our poor hundred were slain,
And half of the rest of us maim'd for life
In the crash of the cannonades and the des-
perate strife:
And the sick men down in the hold were most
of them stark and cold,
And the pikes were all broken or bent, and the
powder was all of it spent;   80
And the masts and the rigging were lying over
the side;
But Sir Richard cried in his English pride:
''We have fought such a fight for a day and
a night
As may never be fought again!
We have won great glory, my men!
And a day less or more
At sea or ashore,
We die—does it matter when?
Sink me the ship, Master Gunner—sink her,
split her in twain!
Fall into the hands of God, not into the hands
of Spain!''   90

XII

And the gunner said, "Ay, ay," but the sea-
men made reply:
"We have children, we have wives,
And the Lord hath spared our lives.
We will make the Spaniard promise, if we
yield, to let us go;
We shall live to fight again and to strike an-
other blow.''
And the lion there lay dying, and they yielded
to the foe.

XIII

And the stately Spanish men to their flagship
bore him then,
Where they laid him by the mast, old Sir
Richard caught at last,
And they praised him to his face with their
courtly foreign grace;
But he rose upon their decks, and he cried: 100
"I have fought for Queen and Faith like a
valiant man and true;
I have only done my duty as a man is bound
to do.
With a joyful spirit I Sir Richard Grenville
die!''
And he fell upon their decks, and he died.

XIV

And they stared at the dead that had been so
valiant and true,
And had holden the power and glory of Spain
so cheap
That he dared her with one little ship and his
English few;
Was he devil or man? He was devil for aught
they knew,
But they sank his body with honour down into
the deep.
And they mann'd the Revenge with a swarthier
alien crew,   110
And away she sail'd with her loss and long'd
for her own;
When a wind from the lands they had ruin'd
awoke from sleep,
And the water began to heave and the weather
to moan,
And or ever that evening ended a great gale
blew,
And a wave like the wave that is raised by an
earthquake grew,
Till it smote on their hulls and their sails and
their masts and their flags,
And the whole sea plunged and fell on the shot-
shatter'd navy of Spain,
And the little Revenge herself went down by
the island crags
To be lost evermore in the main.

NORTHERN FARMER*

OLD STYLE

I

Wheer 'asta beän saw long and meä liggin
'ere aloän?
Noorse? thoort nowt o' a noorse; whoy, Doc
tor 's abeän an' agoän;
Says that I moänt 'a naw moor aäle, but I
beänt a fool;
Git ma my aäle, fur I beänt a-gawin' to breäk
my rule.

II

Doctors, they knaws nowt, fur a says what '
nawways true;
Naw soort o' koind o' use to saäy the thing
that a do.
I 've 'ed my point o' aäle ivry noight sin'
beän 'ere.
An' I 've 'ed my quart ivry market-noight fo
foorty year.

III

Parson 's a beän loikewoise, an' a sittin' er
o' my bed.
"The Amoighty 's a taäkin o' you[1] to 'issén
my friend,'' a said,
An' a towd ma my sins, an' 's toithe were due
an' I gied it in hond;
I done moy duty boy 'um, as I 'a done bo
the lond.   1

IV.

Larn'd a ma' beä. I reckons I 'annot s
mooch to larn.
But a cast oop, thot a did, 'bout Bessy Mar
ris 's barne.
Thaw a knaws I hallus voäted wi' Squoire an
choorch an' staäte,
An' i' the woost o' toimes I wur niver agi
the raäte.   1

V

An' I hallus coom'd to 's choorch afoor mo
Sally wur deäd,
An' 'eärd 'um a bummin' awaäy loike a buz
zard-clock[2] ower my 'eäd,

1 ou as in *hour*   2 cockchafer
* Note that in this dialect poem an *a* pronounce
very lightly represents *thou*, as in "'asta
(hast thou), or *he*, as in "a says"; or it is
mere prefix to a participle, as in "a beän.
"a sittin' "; or, pronounced broadly, it ma
stand for *have*, as in "as I 'a done." Furthe
toitne = tithe; barne = bairn; raäte = church
rate, or tax; 'siver = howsoever; stubbed =
grubbed; boggle = bogle (ghost); raäved an
rembled = tore out and removed; 'soize = as
sizes; yows = ewes; 'aäpoth = half-penny
worth; sewer-loy = surely; atta = art thou
hallus i' the owd taäle = always urging th
same thing. The numbered notes are Tenny
son's.

An' I niver knaw'd whot a meän'd but I
   thowt a 'ad summut to saäy,
An' I thowt a said whot a owt to 'a said, an'
   I coom'd awaäy.   20

VI

Bessy Marris's barne! tha knaws she laäid it
   to meä.
Mowt a beän, mayhap, for she wur a bad un,
   sheä.
'Siver, I kep 'um, I kep 'um, my lass, tha mun
   understond;
I done moy duty boy 'um, as I 'a done boy the
   lond.   24

VII

But Parson a cooms an' a goäs, an' a says it
   eäsy an' freä:
'The Amoighty 's a taäkin o' you to 'issén,
   my friend,'' says 'eä.
I weänt saäy men be loiars, thaw summun said
   it in 'aäste;
But 'e reäds wonn sarmin a weeäk, an' I 'a
   stubb'd Thurnaby waäste.   28

VIII

D' ya moind the waäste, my lass? naw, naw,
   tha was not born then;
Theer wur a boggle in it, I often 'eärd 'um
   mysén;
Moäst loike a butter-bump,[3] fur I 'eärd 'um
   about an' about,
But I stubb'd 'um oop wi' the lot, an' raäved
   an' rembled 'um out.   32

IX

Keäper's it wur; fo' they fun 'um theer a-laäid
   of 'is faäce
Down i' the woild 'enemies[4] afoor I coom'd to
   the plaäce.
Noäks or Thimbleby—toäner[5] 'ed shot 'um as
   deäd as a naäil.
Noäks wur 'ang'd for it oop at 'soize—but git
   ma my aäle.   36

X

Dubbut looök at the waäste; theer warn't not
   feeäd for a cow;
Nowt at all but bracken an' fuzz, an' looök at
   it now—
Warn't worth nowt a haäcre, an' now theer 's
   lots o' feeäd,
Fourscoor yows[1] upon it, an' some on it down
   i' seeäd.[6]   40

XI

Nobbut a bit on it 's left, an' I meän'd to 'a
   stubb'd it at fall,

Done it ta-year I meän'd, an' runn'd plow
   thruff it an' all,
If Godamoighty an' parson 'ud nobbut let ma
   aloän,—
Meä, wi' haäte hoonderd haäcre o' Squoire's,
   an lond o' my oän.   44

XII

Do Godamoighty knaw what a's doing a-taäkin'
   o' meä?
I beänt wonn as saws 'ere a beän an yonder a
   peä;
An' Squoire 'ull be sa mad an' all—a' dear,
   a' dear!
And I 'a managed for Squoire coom Michaelmas thutty year.   48

XIII

A mowt 'a taäen owd Joänes, as 'ant not a
   'aäpoth o' sense,
Or a mowt a' taäen young Robins—a niver
   mended a fence;
But Godamoighty a moost taäke meä an' taäke
   ma now,
Wi' aäf the cows to cauve an' Thurnaby
   hoälms to plow!   52

XIV

Looök 'ow quoloty smoiles when they seeäs
   ma a passin' boy,
Says to thessén, naw doubt, ''What a man a
   beä sewer-loy!''
Fur they knaws what I beän to Squoire sin
   fust a coom'd to the 'All;
I done moy duty by Squoire an' I done moy
   duty boy hall.   56

XV

Squoire 's i' Lunnon, an' summun I reckons
   'ull 'a to wroite,
For whoä 's to howd the lond ater meä thot
   muddles ma quoit;
Sartin-sewer I beä thot a weänt niver give it
   to Joänes,
Naw, nor a moänt to Robins—a niver rembles
   the stoäns.   60

XVI

But summun 'ull come ater meä mayhap wi' 'is
   kittle o' steäm
Huzzin' an' maäzin' the blessed feälds wi' the
   divil's oän teäm.
Sin' I mun doy I mun doy, thaw loife they
   says is sweet,
But sin' I mun doy I mun doy, for I couldn
   abeär to see it.   64

3 bittern   5 one or other
4 anemones   6 clover

XVII

What atta stannin' theer fur, an' doesn bring
    ma the aäle?
Doctor 's a 'toättler, lass, an a 's hallus i' the
    owd taäle;
I weänt breäk rules fur Doctor, a knaws naw
    moor nor a floy;
Git ma my aäle, I tell tha, an' if I mun doy I
    mun doy.   68

RIZPAH*

17—

I

Wailing, wailing, wailing, .the wind over land
    and sea—
And Willy 's voice in the wind, "O mother,
    come out to me!"
Why should he call me to-night, when he knows
    that I cannot go?
For the downs are as bright as day, and the
    full moon stares at the snow.

II

We should be seen, my dear; they would spy us
    out of the town.
The loud black nights for us, and the storm
    rushing over the down,
When I cannot see my own hand, but am led by
    the creak of the chain,[1]
And grovel and grope for my son till I find
    myself drenched with the rain.

III

Anything fallen again? nay—what was there
    left to fall?
I have taken them home, I have number'd the
    bones, I have hidden them all.   10
What am I saying? and what are *you*? do you
    come as a spy?
Falls? what falls! who knows? As the tree
    falls so must it lie.

IV

Who let her in? how long has she been? you—
    what have you heard?
Why did you sit so quiet? you never have
    spoken a word.
O—to pray with me—yes—a lady—none of
    their spies—
But the night has crept into my heart, and
    begun to darken my eyes.

* Founded on a story related in a penny magazine,
and on the fact that criminals were often
denied Christian burial. The title is taken
from the narrative in 2 *Samuel*, xxi, 1-14.
[1] See line 35.

V

Ah—you, that have lived so soft, what shoulc
    you know of the night,
The blast and the burning shame and the bit
    ter frost and the fright?
I have done it, while you were asleep—yor
    were only made for the day.
I have gather'd my baby together—and now
    you may go your way.   2

VI

Nay—for it 's kind of you, madam, to sit by ar
    old dying wife.
But say nothing hard of my boy, I have only
    an hour of life.
I kiss'd my boy in the prison, before he wen
    out to die.
"They dared me to do it," he said, and he
    never has told me a lie.
I whipt him for robbing an orchard once whei
    he was but a child—
"The farmer dared me to do it," he said; he
    was always so wild—
And idle—and could n't be idle—my Willy—
    he never could rest.
The King should have made him a soldier, he
    would have been one of his best.

VII

But he lived with a lot of wild mates, and they
    never would let him be good;
They swore that he dare not rob the mail, anc
    he swore that he would;   3
And he took no life, but he took one purse, anc
    when all was done
He flung it among his fellows—"I'll none o
    it," said my son.

VIII

I came into court to the judge and the lawyers
    I told them my tale,
God's own truth—but they kill'd him, they
    kill'd him for robbing the mail.
They hang'd him in chains for a show—we hac
    always borne a good name—
To be hang'd for a thief—and then put awa
    —is n't that enough shame?
Dust to dust—low down—let us hide! but the
    set him so high
That all the ships of the world could stare a
    him, passing by.
God 'll pardon the hell-black raven and horribl
    fowls of the air,
But not the black heart of the lawyer wh
    kill'd him and hang'd him there.   4

IX

And the jailer forced me away. I had bid him
    my last good-bye;
They had fasten'd the door of his cell. "O
    mother!" I heard him cry.
I could n't get back tho' I tried, he had some-
    thing further to say,
And now I never shall know it. The jailer
    forced me away.

X

Then since I could n't but hear that cry of my
    boy that was dead,
They seized me and shut me up: they fasten'd
    me down on my bed.
"Mother, O mother!"—he call'd in the dark
    to me year after year—
They beat me for that, they beat me—you know
    that I could n't but hear;
And then at the last they found I had grown
    so stupid and still
They let me abroad again—but the creatures
    had worked their will.   50

XI

Flesh of my flesh was gone, but bone of my
    bone was left—
I stole them all from the lawyers—and you, will
    you call it a theft?—
My baby, the bones that had suck'd me, the
    bones that had laugh'd and had cried—
Theirs? O, no! they are mine—not theirs—
    they had moved in my side.

XII

Do you think I was scared by the bones? I
    kiss'd 'em, I buried 'em all—
I can't dig deep, I am old—in the night by the
    churchyard wall.
My Willy 'll rise up whole when the trumpet of
    judgment 'll sound,
But I charge you never to say that I laid him
    in holy ground.

XIII

They would scratch him up—they would hang
    him again on the curséd tree.
Sin? O, yes, we are sinners, I know—let all
    that be,   60
And read me a Bible verse of the Lord's good-
    will toward men—
"Full of compassion and mercy, the Lord"—
    let me hear it again;
"Full of compassion and mercy—long-suffer-
    ing." Yes, O, yes!

For the lawyer is born but to murder—the
    Saviour lives but to bless.
He 'll never put on the black cap except for
    the worst of the worst,
And the first may be last—I have heard it in
    church—and the last may be first.
Suffering—O, long-suffering—yes, as the Lord
    must know,
Year after year in the mist and the wind and
    the shower and the snow.

XIV

Heard, have you? what? they have told you he
    never repented his sin.
How do they know it? are *they* his mother? are
    you of his kin?   70
Heard! have you ever heard, when the storm
    on the downs began,
The wind that 'll wail like a child and the sea
    that 'll moan like a man?

XV

Election, Election, and Reprobation—it 's all
    very well.
But I go to-night to my boy, and I shall not
    find him in hell.
For I cared so much for my boy that the Lord
    has look'd into my care,
And He means me I 'm sure to be happy with
    Willy, I know not where.

XVI

And if *he* be lost—but to save *my* soul, that is
    all your desire—
Do you think that I care for *my* soul if my boy
    be gone to the fire?
I have been with God in the dark—go, go, you
    may leave me alone—
You never have borne a child—you are just as
    hard as a stone.   80

XVII

Madam, I beg your pardon! I think that you
    mean to be kind,
But I cannot hear what you say for my Willy's
    voice in the wind—
The snow and the sky so bright—he used but
    to call in the dark,
And he calls to me now from the church and
    not from the gibbet—for hark!
Nay—you can hear it yourself—it is coming—
    shaking the walls—
Willy—the moon 's in a cloud——Good-night.
    I am going. He calls.

MILTON

(ALCAICS)*

O mighty-mouth'd inventor of harmonies,
O skill'd to sing of Time or Eternity,
  God-gifted organ-voice of England,
    Milton, a name to resound for ages:
Whose Titan angels, Gabriel, Abdiel,
Starr'd from Jehovah's gorgeous armories,
  Tower, as the deep-domed empyrean
    Rings to the roar of an angel onset!
Me rather all that bowery loneliness,
The brooks of Eden mazily murmuring,
  And bloom profuse and cedar arches
    Charm, as a wanderer out in ocean,
Where some refulgent sunset of India
Streams o'er a rich ambrosial ocean isle,
  And crimson-hued the stately palm-woods
    Whisper in odorous heights of even.

TO DANTE

(WRITTEN AT THE REQUEST OF THE FLOREN-TINES)†

King, that hast reign'd six hundred years, and
    grown
In power, and ever growest, since thine own
Fair Florence honouring thy nativity,
Thy Florence now the crown of Italy,
Hath sought the tribute of a verse from me,
I, wearing but the garland of a day,
Cast at thy feet one flower that fades away.

TO VIRGIL

(WRITTEN AT THE REQUEST OF THE MANTUANS FOR THE NINETEENTH CENTENARY OF VIRGIL'S DEATH.)

Roman Virgil, thou that singest
  Ilion's lofty temples robed in fire,
Ilion falling, Rome arising,
  wars, and filial faith, and Dido's pyre;

Landscape-lover, lord of language
  more than he that sang the "Works and
    Days,"[1]
All the chosen coin of fancy
  flashing out from many a golden phrase;

Thou that singest wheat and woodland,
  tilth and vineyard, hive and horse and herd;

All the charm of all the Muses
  often flowering in a lonely word;

Poet of the happy Tityrus[2]
  piping underneath his beechen bowers;
Poet of the poet-satyr
  whom the laughing shepherd bound with flow-
    ers;[3]

Chanter of the Pollio,[4] glorying
  in the blissful years again to be,
Summers of the snakeless meadow,
  unlaborious earth and oarless sea;   10

Thou that seest Universal
  Nature moved by Universal Mind;
Thou majestic in thy sadness
  at the doubtful doom of human kind;

Light among the vanish'd ages;
  star that gildest yet this phantom shore;
Golden branch amid the shadows,
  kings and realms that pass to rise no more;

Now thy Forum roars no longer,
  fallen every purple Cæsar's dome—
Tho' thine ocean-roll of rhythm
  sound forever of Imperial Rome—

Now the Rome of slaves hath perish'd,
  and the Rome of freemen holds her place,
I, from out the Northern Island
  sunder'd once from all the human race,

I salute thee, Mantovano,
  I that loved thee since my day began,
Wielder of the stateliest measure
  ever moulded by the lips of man.   20

"FRATER AVE ATQUE VALE"*

Row us out from Desenzano, to your Sirmione
  row!
So they row'd, and there we landed—"O
  venusta Sirmio!"

[1] Hesiod.
* This poem is one of Tennyson's experiments in the quantitative metre of the classics. The two styles of Milton here described may be found in many passages of *Paradise Lost*: see especially, for the "angel onset," Boox VI, 96 ff., and for the "bowery loneliness," IV, 214 ff.
† For a festival on the six hundredth anniversary of the birth of Dante, 1865.

[2] A shepherd piper in Virgil's first Eclogue.
[3] Eclogue sixth.
[4] Title of the fourth Eclogue, which is prophetic of a golden age.
* In these words, "Hail, brother, and farewell," the Roman poet Catullus lamented the death of his brother (*Carmina* 101, 10). Catullus had a villa on the peninsula of Sermione—"venusta (beautiful) Sirmio"—in Lake Garda, northern Italy. The last two lines of this little poem, which reproduce so well the soft music of Catullus's verse, are modelled upon lines in his thirty-first song. Catullus used the word "Lydian" in the belief that the Etruscans, who anciently had settlements near the Lake of Garda, were of Lydian origin.

There to me thro' all the groves of olive in the
summer glow,
There beneath the Roman ruin where the purple
flowers grow,
Came that "Ave atque Vale" of the Poet's
hopeless woe,
Tenderest of Roman poets nineteen hundred
years ago,
"Frater Ave atque Vale"—as we wander'd to
and fro
Gazing at the Lydian laughter of the Garda
Lake below
Sweet Catullus's all-but-island, olive-silvery
Sirmio!

FLOWER IN THE CRANNIED WALL

Flower in the crannied wall,
I pluck you out of the crannies,
I hold you here, root and all, in my hand,
Little flower—but *if* I could understand
What you are, root and all, and all in all,
I should know what God and man is.

WAGES

Glory of warrior, glory of orator, glory of song,
Paid with a voice flying by to be lost on an
endless sea—
Glory of Virtue, to fight, to struggle, to right
the wrong—
Nay, but she aim'd not at glory, no lover of
glory she:
Give her the glory of going on, and still to be.

The wages of sin is death: if the wages of Virtue be dust,
Would she have heart to endure for the life
of the worm and the fly?
She desires no isles of the blest, no quiet seats
of the just,
To rest in a golden grove, or to bask in a
summer sky:
Give her the wages of going on, and not to die.

BY AN EVOLUTIONIST

The Lord let the house of a brute to the soul
of a man,
And the man said, 'Am I your debtor?'
And the Lord—'Not yet: but make it as clean
as you can,
And then I will let you a better.'

I

If my body come from brutes, my soul uncertain or a fable,
Why not bask amid the senses while the sun
of morning shines,

I, the finer brute rejoicing in my hounds, and in
my stable,
Youth and health, and birth and wealth, and
choice of women and of wines?

II

What hast thou done for me, grim Old Age,
save breaking my bones on the rack?
Would I had past in the morning that looks
so bright from afar!

OLD AGE

Done for thee? starved the wild beast that was
linkt with thee eighty years back.
Less weight now for the ladder-of-heaven
that hangs on a star.

I

If my body come from brutes, tho' somewhat
finer than their own,
I am heir, and this my kingdom. Shall the
royal voice be mute?
No, but if the rebel subject seek to drag me
from the throne,
Hold the sceptre, Human Soul, and rule thy
province of the brute.

II

I have climb'd to the snows of Age, and I gaze
at a field in the Past,
Where I sank with the body at times in the
sloughs of a low desire,
But I hear no yelp of the beast, and the Man
is quiet at last
As he stands on the heights of his life with a
glimpse of a height that is higher.

VASTNESS

Many a hearth upon our dark globe sighs after
many a vanish'd face,
Many a planet by many a sun may roll with the
dust of a vanish'd race.

Raving politics, never at rest—as this poor
earth's pale history runs,—
What is it all but a trouble of ants in the gleam
of a million million of suns?

Lies upon this side, lies upon that side, truth-
less violence mourned by the wise,
Thousands of voices drowning his own in a
popular torrent of lies upon lies;

Stately purposes, valour in battle, glorious annals of army and fleet,
Death for the right cause, death for the wrong
cause, trumpets of victory, groans of defeat;

Innocence seethed in her mother's milk, and
    Charity setting the martyr aflame;
Thraldom who walks with the banner of Free-
    dom, and recks not to ruin a realm in her
    name.   10

Faith at her zenith, or all but lost in the gloom
    of doubts that darken the schools;
Craft with a bunch of all-heal in her hand, fol-
    low'd up by her vassal legion of fools;

Trade flying over a thousand seas with her spice
    and her vintage, her silk and her corn;
Desolate offing, sailorless harbours, famishing
    populace, wharves forlorn;

Star of the morning, Hope in the sunrise;
    gloom of the evening, Life at a close;
Pleasure who flaunts on her wide downway with
    her flying robe and her poison'd rose;

Pain that has crawl'd from the corpse of Pleas-
    ure, a worm which writhes all day, and
    at night
Stirs up again in the heart of the sleeper, and
    stings him back to the curse of the light;

Wealth with his wines and his wedded harlots;
    honest Poverty, bare to the bone;
Opulent Avarice, lean as Poverty; Flattery
    gilding the rift in a throne;   20

Fame blowing out from her golden trumpet a
    jubilant challenge to Time and to Fate;
Slander, her shadow, sowing the nettle on all
    the laurell'd graves of the great;

Love for the maiden, crown'd with marriage, no
    regrets for aught that has been,
Household happiness, gracious children, debtless
    competence, golden mean;

National hatreds of whole generations, and
    pigmy spites of the village spire;
Vows that will last to the last death-ruckle, and
    vows that are snapt in a moment of fire;

He that has lived for the lust of the minute,
    and died in the doing it, flesh without
    mind;
He that has nail'd all flesh to the Cross, till
    Self died out in the love of his kind;

Spring and Summer and Autumn and Winter,
    and all these old revolutions of earth;
All new-old revolutions of Empire—change of
    the tide—what is all of it worth?   30

What the philosophies, all the sciences, poesy,
    varying voices of prayer,
All that is noblest, all that is basest, all that is
    filthy with all that is fair?

What is it all, if we all of us end but in being
    our own corpse-coffins at last?
Swallow'd in Vastness, lost in Silence, drown'd
    in the deeps of a meaningless Past?

What but a murmur of gnats in the gloom, or a
    moment's anger of bees in their hive?—
.   .   .   .
Peace, let it be! for I loved him, and love him
    for ever: the dead are not dead but
    alive.

CROSSING THE BAR*

Sunset and evening star,
    And one clear call for me!
And may there be no moaning of the bar,
    When I put out to sea,

But such a tide as moving seems asleep,
    Too full for sound and foam,
When that which drew from out the boundless
    deep
    Turns again home.

Twilight and evening bell,
    And after that the dark!
And may there be no sadness of farewell,
    When I embark;

For tho' from out our bourne of Time and
    Place
    The flood may bear me far,
I hope to see my Pilot face to face
    When I have crost the bar.

ROBERT BROWNING (1812-1889)

FROM PIPPA PASSES

NEW YEAR'S HYMN

All service ranks the same with God:
If now, as formerly he trod
Paradise, his presence fills
Our earth, each only as God wills
Can work—God's puppets, best and worst,
Are we; there is no last nor first.

Say not "a small event!" Why "small"?
Costs it more pain that this, ye call

* Written in Tennyson's eighty-first year.

A ''great event,'' should come to pass,
Than that? Untwine me from the mass
Of deeds which make up life, one deed
Power shall fall short in or exceed!

SONG

The year's at the spring
And day's at the morn;
Morning's at seven;
The hillside's dew-pearled;
The lark's on the wing;
The snail's on the thorn;
God's in his heaven—
All's right with the world!

CAVALIER TUNES*

I. MARCHING ALONG

Kentish Sir Byng stood for his King,
Bidding the crop-headed Parliament swing:
And, pressing[1] a troop unable to stoop
And see the rogues flourish and honest folk
.droop,
Marched them along, fifty-score strong,
Great-hearted gentlemen, singing this song.

God for King Charles! Pym and such carles
To the Devil that prompts 'em their treasonous
parles[2]!
Cavaliers, up! Lips from the cup,
Hands from the pasty, nor bite take, nor sup,
Till you're—
CHORUS.—Marching along, fifty-score strong,
Great-hearted gentlemen, singing this
song!

Hampden to hell, and his obsequies' knell
Serve[3] Hazelrig, Fiennes, and young Harry, as
well!
England, good cheer! Rupert is near!
Kentish and loyalists, keep we not here,
CHO.—Marching along, fifty-score strong,
Great-hearted gentlemen, singing this
song?

Then, God for King Charles! Pym and his
snarls

1 impressing, enlisting
2 parleys, debates
3 may it serve
* These songs are meant to portray the spirit of
the adherents of Charles I., and their hatred
of the Puritans, or Roundheads. The Byngs
of Kent are famous in the annals of British
warfare. Pym, a leader of the Long Parliament, Hazelrig (or Hesilrige), Fiennes (Lord
Say), and Sir Henry Vane the Younger, were
all important figures in the rebellion against
Charles. Prince Rupert was a nephew of
Charles, and a celebrated cavalry leader.

To the Devil that pricks on such pestilent
carles!
Hold by the right, you double your might;
So, onward to Nottingham,† fresh for the fight,
CHO.—March we along, fifty-score strong,
Great-hearted gentlemen, singing this
song!

II. GIVE A ROUSE

King Charles, and who'll do him right now?
King Charles, and who's ripe for fight now?
Give a rouse; here's, in hell's despite now,
King Charles!

Who gave me the goods that went since?
Who raised me the house that sank once?
Who helped me to gold I spent since?
Who found me in wine you drank once?

CHO.—King Charles, and who'll do him right
now?
King Charles, and who's ripe for fight
now?
Give a rouse: here's, in hell's despite
now,
King Charles!

To whom used my boy George quaff else,
By the old fool's side that begot him?
For whom did he cheer and laugh else,
While Noll's[4] damned troopers shot him?
CHO.—King Charles, and who'll do him right
now?
King Charles, and who's ripe for fight
now?
Give a rouse: here's, in hell's despite
now,
King Charles!

III. BOOT AND SADDLE

Boot, saddle, to horse and away!
Rescue my castle before the hot day
Brightens to blue from its silvery gray.
CHO.—Boot, saddle, to horse and away!

Ride past the suburbs, asleep as you'd say;
Many's the friend there, will listen and pray
''God's luck to gallants that strike up the lay—
CHO.—Boot, saddle, to horse, and away!''

Forty miles off, like a roebuck at bay,
Flouts Castle Brancepeth the Roundheads' array:
Who laughs, ''Good fellows ere this, by my
fay,

4 Oliver's (i. e., Cromwell's)
† The standard of Charles was raised there in
1642, marking the beginning of the Civil War.

CHO.—Boot, saddle, to horse, and away!''

Who? My wife Gertrude; that, honest and
    gay,
Laughs when you talk of surrendering, ''Nay!
I've better counsellors; what counsel they?
    CHO.—Boot, saddle, to horse, and away!''

INCIDENT OF THE FRENCH CAMP

You know, we French stormed Ratisbon:[5]
    A mile or so away,
On a little mound, Napoleon
    Stood on our storming-day;
With neck out-thrust, you fancy how,
    Legs wide, arms locked behind,
As if to balance the prone brow
    Oppressive with its mind.   8

Just as perhaps he mused ''My plans
    That soar, to earth may fall,
Let once my army-leader Lannes
    Waver at yonder wall,''—
Out 'twixt the battery-smokes there flew
    A rider, bound on bound
Full-galloping; nor bridle drew
    Until he reached the mound.   16

Then off there flung in smiling joy,
    And held himself erect
By just his horse's mane, a boy:
    You hardly could suspect—
(So tight he kept his lips compressed,
    Scarce any blood came through)
You looked twice ere you saw his breast
    Was all but shot in two.   24

''Well,'' cried he, ''Emperor, by God's grace
    We've got you Ratisbon!
The Marshal 's in the market-place,
    And you 'll be there anon
To see your flag-bird flap his vans
    Where I, to heart's desire,
Perched him!'' The chief's eye flashed; his
    plans
    Soared up again like fire.   32

The chief's eye flashed; but presently
    Softened itself, as sheathes
A film the mother-eagle's eye
    When her bruised eaglet breathes;
''You're wounded!'' ''Nay,'' the soldier's
    pride
    Touched to the quick, he said:
''I 'm killed, Sire!'' And, his chief beside,
    Smiling the boy fell dead.   40

5 In Bavaria; stormed by Napoleon in 1809.

MY LAST DUCHESS*

FERRARA

That's my last Duchess painted on the wall,
Looking as if she were alive. I call
That piece a wonder, now: Frà Pandolf's
    hands
Worked busily a day, and there she stands.
Will 't please you sit and look at her? I said
''Frà Pandolf'' by design, for never read
Strangers like you that pictured countenance,
The depth and passion of its earnest glance,
But to myself they turned (since none puts by
The curtain I have drawn for you, but I)   10
And seemed as they would ask me, if they
    durst,
How such a glance came there; so, not the first
Are you to turn and ask thus. Sir, 't was not
Her husband's presence only, called that spot
Of joy into the Duchess' cheek: perhaps
Frà Pandolf chanced to say, ''Her mantle laps
Over my lady's wrist too much,'' or ''Paint
Must never hope to reproduce the faint
Half-flush that dies along her throat:'' such
    stuff
Was courtesy, she thought, and cause enough 20
For calling up that spot of joy. She had
A heart—how shall I say?—too soon made glad.
Too easily impressed: she liked whate'er
She looked on, and her looks went everywhere.
Sir, 't was all one! My favour at her breast,
The dropping of the daylight in the West,
The bough of cherries some officious fool
Broke in the orchard for her, the white mule
She rode with round the terrace—all and each
Would draw from her alike the approving
    speech,   30
Or blush, at least. She thanked men,—good!
    but thanked
Somehow—I know not how—as if she ranked
My gift of a nine-hundred-years-old name
With anybody's gift. Who 'd stoop to blame
This sort of trifling? Even had you skill
In speech—(which I have not)—to make your
    will
Quite clear to such an one, and say, ''Just this
Or that in you disgusts me; here you miss,
Or there exceed the mark''—and if she let
Herself be lessoned so, nor plainly set   40

* A Duke of Ferrara stands before a portrait of
his deceased Duchess, talking coolly with the
envoy of a Count whose daughter he seeks
to marry. The poem is a study in the heartless jealousy of supreme selfishness. The
nature of the commands (line 45) which such
a man might give, living at the time of the
Italian Renaissance, may be left to the imagination, as Browning leaves it. The artists
mentioned (lines 3, 56) are imaginary. On
the monologue form, see Eng. Lit., p. 301.

er wits to yours, forsooth, and made excuse,
—E'en then would be some stooping; and I
    choose
Never to stoop. Oh sir, she smiled, no doubt,
Whene'er I passed her; but who passed without
Much the same smile? This grew; I gave com-
    mands;
Then all smiles stopped together. There she
    stands
As if alive. Will 't please you rise? We 'll
    meet
The company below, then. I repeat,
The Count your master 's known munificence
Is ample warrant that no just pretence   50
Of mine for dowry will be disallowed;
Though his fair daughter 's self, as I avowed
At starting, is my object. Nay, we 'll go
Together down, sir. Notice Neptune, though,
Taming a sea-horse, thought a rarity,
Which Claus of Innsbruck cast in bronze for
    me!

IN A GONDOLA*

He sings

I send my heart up to thee, all my heart
  In this my singing.
For the stars help me, and the sea bears part;
  The very night is clinging
Closer to Venice' streets to leave one space
Above me, whence thy face
May light my joyous heart to thee its dwelling
    place.

She speaks

Say after me, and try to say
My very words, as if each word
Came from you of your own accord,   10
In your own voice, in your own way:
"This woman 's heart and soul and brain
Are mine as much as this gold chain
She bids me wear; which" (say again)
"I choose to make by cherishing
A precious thing, or choose to fling
Over the boat-side, ring by ring."
And yet once more say . . . no word more!
Since words are only words. Give o'er!

Unless you call me, all the same,   20
Familiarly by my pet name,
Which if the Three should hear you call,

Written for a picture, "The Serenade," by Daniel
Maclise. The characters are imaginary. So
also are the pictures mentioned in lines 183-
202, though the painters are well known.
Haste-thee-Luke was a nickname for the
Neapolitan, Luca Giordano. Castelfranco is
Giorgione. Tizian we know best as Titian,
and his "Ser" (Sir) would be the portrait of
an Italian gentleman.

And me reply to, would proclaim
At once our secret to them all.
Ask of me, too, command me, blame,—
Do, break down the partition-wall
'Twixt us, the daylight world beholds
Curtained in dusk and splendid folds!
What 's left but—all of me to take?
I am the Three 's: prevent them, slake   30
Your thirst! 'T is said, the Arab sage,
In practising with gems, can loose
Their subtle spirit in his cruce
And leave but ashes: so, sweet mage,
Leave them my ashes when thy use
Sucks out my soul, thy heritage!

He sings

Past we glide, and past, and past!
  What 's that poor Agnese doing
Where they make the shutters fast?
  Gray Zanobi 's just a-wooing   40
To his couch the purchased bride:
  Past we glide!

Past we glide, and past, and past!
  Why 's the Pucci Palace flaring
Like a beacon to the blast?
  Guests by hundreds, not one caring
If the dear host 's neck were wried:
  Past we glide!

She sings

The moth 's kiss, first!
Kiss me as if you made believe   50
You were not sure, this eve,
How my face, your flower, had pursed
Its petals up; so, here and there
You brush it, till I grow aware
Who wants me, and wide ope I burst.

The bee 's kiss, now!
Kiss me as if you entered gay
My heart at some noonday,
A bud that dares not disallow
The claim, so all is rendered up,   60
And passively its shattered cup
Over your head to sleep I bow.

He sings

What are we two?
I am a Jew,
And carry thee, farther than friends can pursue,
To a feast of our tribe;
Where they need thee to bribe
The devil that blasts them unless he imbibe
Thy . . . Scatter the vision forever! And
    now,
As of old, I am I, thou art thou!   70

Say again, what we are?
The sprite of a star,
I lure thee above where the destinies bar
My plumes their full play
Till a ruddier ray
Than my pale one announce there is withering
      away
Some . . . Scatter the vision forever! And
      now,
As of old, I am I, thou art thou!

He muses

Oh, which were best, to roam or rest?
The land's lap or the water's breast?   80
To sleep on yellow millet-sheaves,
Or swim in lucid shallows just
E'uding water-lily leaves,
An inch from Death's black fingers, thrust
To lock you, whom release he must;
Which life were best on Summer eves?

He speaks, musing

Lie back; could thought of mine improve you?
From this shoulder let there spring
A wing; from this, another wing;
Wings, not legs and feet, shall move you!   90
Snow-white must they spring, to blend
With your flesh, but I intend
They shall deepen to the end,
Broader, into burning gold,
Till both wings crescent-wise enfold
Your perfect self, from 'neath your feet
To o'er your head, where, lo, they meet
As if a million sword-blades hurled
Defiance from you to the world!

Rescue me thou, the only real!   100
And scare away this mad ideal
That came, nor motions to depart!
Thanks! Now, stay ever as thou art!

Still he muses

What if the Three should catch at last
Thy serenader? While there 's cast
Paul's cloak about my head, and fast
Gian pinions me, Himself has past
His stylet through my back; I reel;
And . . . is it thou I feel?

They trail me, these three godless knaves,   110
Past every church that saints and saves,
Nor stop till, where the cold sea raves
By Lido's[1] wet accurséd graves,
They scoop mine, roll me to its brink,
And . . . on thy breast I sink!

[1] A long sandy bar lying off Venice. There is a
Jewish cemetery there.

She replies, musing

Dip your arm o'er the boat-side, elbow-deep,
As I do: thus: were death so unlike sleep,
Caught this way? Death 's to fear from flam
      or steel,
Or poison doubtless; but from water—feel!
Go find the bottom! Would you stay me
      There!   12
Now pluck a great blade of that ribbon-gras
To plait in where the foolish jewel was,
I flung away: since you have praised my hai
'T is proper to be choice in what I wear.

He speaks

Row home? must we row home? Too surely
Know I where its front 's demurely
Over the Giudecca[2] piled;
Window just with window mating,
Door on door exactly waiting,
All 's the set face of a child: 1
But behind it, where 's a trace
Of the staidness and reserve,
And formal lines without a curve,
In the same child's playing-face?
No two windows look one way
O'er the small sea-water thread
Below them. Ah, the autumn day
I, passing, saw you overhead!
First, out a cloud of curtain blew,
Then a sweet cry, and last came you—   1
To catch your lory[3] that must needs
Escape just then, of all times then,
To peck a tall plant's fleecy seeds,
And make me happiest of men.
I scarce could breathe to see you reach
So far back o'er the balcony
To catch him ere he climbed too high
Above you in the Smyrna peach,
That quick the round smooth cord of gold,
This coiled hair on your head, unrolled,   1
Fell down you like a gorgeous snake
The Roman girls were wont, of old,
When Rome there was, for coolness' sake
To let lie curling o'er their bosoms.
Dear lory, may his beak retain
Ever its delicate rose stain
As if the wounded lotus-blossoms
Had marked their thief to know again!

Stay longer yet, for others' sake
Than mine! What should your chamber do?
—With all its rarities that ache   1
In silence while day lasts, but wake
At night-time and their life renew,
Suspended just to pleasure you
Who brought against their will together

[2] A Venetian canal.   [3] A kind of parrot

These objects, and, while day lasts, weave
Around them such a magic tether
That dumb they look: your harp, believe,
With all the sensitive tight strings .
Which dare not speak, now to itself   170
Breathes slumberously, as if some elf
Went in and out the chords,[4] his wings
Make murmur wheresoe'er they graze,
As an angel may, between the maze
Of midnight palace-pillars, on
And on, to sow God's plagues, have gone
Through guilty glorious Babylon.
And while such murmurs flow, the nymph
Bends o'er the harp-top from her shell
As the dry limpet for the lymph   180
Come with a tune he knows so well.
And how your statues' hearts must swell!
And how your pictures must descend
To see each other, friend with friend!
Oh, could you take them by surprise,
You'd find Schidone's eager Duke
Doing the quaintest courtesies
To that prim saint by Haste-thee-Luke!
And, deeper into her rock den,
Old Castelfranco's Magdalen   190
You'd find retreated from the ken
Of that robed counsel-keeping Ser—
As if the Tizian thinks of her,
And is not, rather, gravely bent
On seeing for himself what toys
Are these,[4] his progeny invent,
What litter now the board employs
Whereon he signed a document
That got him murdered! Each enjoys
Its night so well, you cannot break   200
The sport up, so, indeed must make
More stay with me, for others' sake.

She speaks

To-morrow, if a harp-string, say,
Is used to tie the jasmine back
That overfloods my room with sweets,
Contrive your Zorzi somehow meets
My Zanze! If the ribbon's black,
The Three are watching: keep away!

Your gondola—let Zorzi wreathe
A mesh of water-weeds about   210
Its prow, as if he unaware
Had struck some quay or bridge-foot stair!
That I may throw a paper out
As you and he go underneath.

There's Zanze's vigilant taper; safe are we.
Only one minute more to-night with me?

Supply "which" before "his".

Resume your past self of a month ago!
Be you the bashful gallant, I will be
The lady with the colder breast than snow.
Now bow you, as becomes, nor touch my hand
More than I touch yours when I step to land,
And say, "All thanks, Siora!"—   222
              Heart to heart
And lips to lips! Yet once more, ere we part,
Clasp me and make me thine, as mine thou art!
      [He is surprised, and stabbed.]
It was ordained to be so, sweet!—and best
Comes now, beneath thine eyes, upon thy breast.
Still kiss me! Care not for the cowards! Care
Only to put aside thy beauteous hair
My blood will hurt! The Three, I do not scorn
To death, because they never lived: but I   230
Have lived indeed, and so—(yet one more kiss)
    —can die!

THE PIED PIPER OF HAMELIN*

A CHILD'S STORY

I

Hamelin Town 's in Brunswick,
By famous Hanover city;
  The river Weser, deep and wide,
  Washes its wall on the southern side;
  A pleasanter spot you never spied;
But, when begins my ditty,
  Almost five hundred years ago,
  To see the townsfolk suffer so
    From vermin, was a pity.

II   10

Rats!
They fought the dogs and killed the cats,
  And bit the babies in the cradles,
And ate the cheeses out of the vats,
  And licked the soup from the cooks' own
    ladles,
Split open the kegs of salted sprats,
Made nests inside men's Sunday hats,
And even spoiled the women's chats
  By drowning their speaking
  With shrieking and squeaking
In fifty different sharps and flats.   20

III

At last the people in a body
  To the Town Hall came flocking:

* This poem was written by Browning to amuse the little son of the actor, William Macready, and furnish him a subject for drawings. The legend is an old one. John Fiske is disposed to identify it with various myths: "Goethe's Erlking is none other than the Piper of Hamelin. And the piper, in turn, is the classic Hermes or Orpheus. . . . His wonderful pipe is the horn of Oberon, the lyre of Apollo (who, like the piper, was a rat-killer), the harp stolen by Jack when he climbed the bean-stalk to the ogre's castle."

"'T is clear," cried they, "our Mayor's a
    noddy;
And as for our Corporation—shocking
To think we buy gowns lined with ermine
For dolts that can't or won't determine
What 's best to rid us of our vermin!
You hope, because you 're old and obese,
To find in the furry civic robe ease?
Rouse up, sirs! Give your brains a racking   30
To find the remedy we 're lacking,
Or, sure as fate, we 'll send you packing!"
At this the Mayor and Corporation
Quaked with a mighty consternation.

IV

An hour they sat in council;
    At length the Mayor broke silence:
"For a guilder¹ I 'd my ermine gown sell,
    I wish I were a mile hence!
It 's easy to bid one rack one's brain—
I 'm sure my poor head aches again,   40
I 've scratched it so, and all in vain.
Oh for a trap, a trap, a trap!"
Just as he said this, what should hap
At the chamber-door but a gentle tap?
"Bless us," cried the Mayor, "what 's that?"
(With the Corporation as he sat,
Looking little though wondrous fat;
Nor brighter was his eye, nor moister
Than a too-long-opened oyster,
Save when at noon his paunch grew mutinous
For a plate of turtle green and glutinous)   51
"Only a scraping of shoes on the mat?
Anything like the sound of a rat
Makes my heart go pit-a-pat!"

V

"Come in!"—the Mayor cried, looking bigger:
And in did come the strangest figure!
His queer long coat from heel to head
Was half of yellow and half of red,
And he himself was tall and thin,
With sharp blue eyes, each like a pin,   60
And light loose hair, yet swarthy skin,
No tuft on cheek nor beard on chin,
But lips where smiles went out and in:
There was no guessing his kith and kin:
And nobody could enough admire
The tall man and his quaint attire.
Quoth one: "It 's as my great-grandsire,
Starting up at the Trump of Doom 's tone,
Had walked this way from his painted tomb-
    stone!"

VI

He advanced to the council-table: 70
And, "Please your honours," said he, "I 'm
    able,

¹ A Dutch coin, worth forty cents.

By means of a secret charm, to draw
All creatures living beneath the sun,
That creep or swim or fly or run,
After me so as you never saw!
And I chiefly use my charm
On creatures that do people harm,
The mole and toad and newt and viper;
And people call me the Pied Piper."
(And here they noticed round his neck   80
A scarf of red and yellow stripe,
To match with his coat of the self-same check,
And at the scarf 's end hung a pipe;
And his fingers, they noticed, were ever stray-
    ing
As if impatient to be playing
Upon this pipe, as low it dangled
Over his vesture so old-fangled.)
"Yet," said he, "poor piper as I am,
In Tartary I freed the Cham,
Last June, from his huge swarms of gnats;   90
I eased in Asia the Nizam
Of a monstrous brood of vampire-bats:
And as for what your brain bewilders,
If I can rid your town of rats
Will you give me a thousand guilders?"
"One? fifty thousand!"—was the exclamation
Of the astonished Mayor and Corporation.

VII

Into the street the Piper stept,
    Smiling first a little smile,
As if he knew what magic slept   100
    In his quiet pipe the while;
Then, like a musical adept,
To blow the pipe his lips he wrinkled,
And green and blue his sharp eyes twinkled,
Like a candle-flame where salt is sprinkled;
And ere three shrill notes the pipe uttered,
You heard as if an army muttered;
And the muttering grew to a grumbling;
And the grumbling grew to a mighty rum-
    bling;
And out of the houses the rats came tumbling.
Great rats, small rats, lean rats, brawny rats,   110
Brown rats, black rats, gray rats, tawny rats,
Grave old plodders, gay young friskers,
    Fathers, mothers, uncles, cousins,
Cocking tails and pricking whiskers,
    Families by tens and dozens,
Brothers, sisters, husbands, wives—
Followed the Piper for their lives.
From street to street he piped advancing,
And step for step they followed dancing,   120
Until they came to the river Weser,
Wherein all plunged and perished!
—Save one who, stout as Julius Cæsar,
Swam across and lived to carry

As he, the manuscript he cherished[1])
o Rat-land home his commentary:
Which was, "At the first shrill notes of the
    pipe,
heard a sound as of scraping tripe,
nd putting apples, wondrous ripe,
to a cider-press's gripe: 130
nd a moving away of pickle-tub-boards,
nd a leaving ajar of conserve-cupboards,
nd a drawing the corks of train-oil-flasks,
nd a breaking the hoops of butter-casks:
nd it seemed as if a voice
Sweeter far than by harp or by psaltery
    breathed) called out, 'Oh rats, rejoice!
he world is grown to one vast dry-saltery!
munch on, crunch on, take your nuncheon,[2]
reakfast, supper, dinner, luncheon!'   140
nd just as a bulky sugar puncheon,
ll ready staved, like a great sun shone
orious scarce an inch before me,
ust as methought it said, 'Come, bore me!'
I found the Weser rolling o'er me."

VIII

ou should have heard the Hamelin people
nging the bells till they rocked the steeple.
Go," cried the Mayor, "and get long poles,
ke out the nests and block up the holes!
nsult with carpenters and builders,   150
d leave in our town not even a trace
the rats!"—when, suddenly, up the face
the Piper perked in the market-place,
ith a, "First, if you please, my thousand
    guilders!"

IX

thousand guilders! The Mayor looked blue;
did the Corporation too.
r council dinners made rare havoc
ith Claret, Moselle, Vin-de-Grave, Hock;
d half the money would replenish
eir cellar's biggest butt with Rhenish.   160
pay this sum to a wandering fellow
ith a gypsy coat of red and yellow!
Beside," quoth the Mayor with a knowing
    wink
Our business was done at the river's brink;
e saw with our eyes the vermin sink,
d what's dead can't come to life, I think.
, friend, we 're not the folks to shrink
om the duty of giving you something for
    drink,
d a matter of money to put in your poke;
t as for the guilders, what we spoke   170
them, as you very well know, was in joke.

This happened in Egypt, according to Plutarch,
who tells the story.
bout the same as "luncheon".

Beside, our losses have made us thrifty.
A thousand guilders! Come, take fifty!"

X

The Piper's face fell, and he cried,
"No trifling! I can't wait, beside!
I 've promised to visit by dinner time
Bagdad, and accept the prime
Of the Head-Cook's pottage, all he 's rich in,
For having left, in the Caliph's kitchen,
Of a nest of scorpions no survivor: 180
With him I proved no bargain-driver,
With you, don't think I 'll 'bate a stiver!
And folks who put me in a passion
May find me pipe after another fashion."

XI

"How?" cried the Mayor, "d'ye think I brook
Being worse treated than a Cook?
Insulted by a lazy ribald
With idle pipe and vesture piebald?
You threaten us, fellow? Do your worst,
Blow your pipe there till you burst!"   190

XII

Once more he stept into the street,
    And to his lips again
Laid his long pipe of smooth straight cane;
    And ere he blew three notes (such sweet
Soft notes as yet musician's cunning
    Never gave the enraptured air)
There was a rustling that seemed like a bust-
    ling
Of merry crowds justling at pitching and hust-
    ling;
Small feet were pattering, wooden shoes clatter-
    ing,
Little hands clapping and little tongues chat-
    tering,   200
And, like fowls in a farm-yard when barley is
    scattering,
Out came the children running.
All the little boys and girls,
With rosy cheeks and flaxen curls,
And sparkling eyes and teeth like pearls,
Tripping and skipping, ran merrily after
The wonderful music with shouting and laugh-
    ter.

XIII

The Mayor was dumb, and the Council stood
As if they were changed into blocks of wood,
Unable to move a step, or cry   210
To the children merrily skipping by,
—Could only follow with the eye
That joyous crowd at the Piper's back.
But how the Mayor was on the rack,
And the wretched Council's bosoms beat,

As the Piper turned from the High Street
To where the Weser rolled its waters
Right in the way of their sons and daughters!
However, he turned from South to West,
And to Koppelberg Hill his steps addressed, 220
And after him the children pressed;
Great was the joy in every breast.
"He never can cross that mighty top!
He's forced to let the piping drop,
And we shall see our children stop!"
When, lo, as they reached the mountain-side,
A wondrous portal opened wide,
As if a cavern was suddenly hollowed;
And the Piper advanced and the children fol-
    lowed,
And when all were in to the very last,   230
The door in the mountain-side shut fast.
Did I say all? No! One was lame,
And could not dance the whole of the way;
And in after years if you would blame
His sadness, he was used to say,—
"It's dull in our town since my playmates
    left!
I can't forget that I'm bereft
Of all the pleasant sights they see,
Which the Piper also promised me.
For he led us, he said, to a joyous land,   240
Joining the town and just at hand,
Where waters gushed and fruit-trees grew
And flowers put forth a fairer hue,
And everything was strange and new;
The sparrows were brighter than peacocks here,
And their dogs outran our fallow deer,
And honey-bees had lost their stings,
And horses were born with eagles' wings;
And just as I became assured
My lame foot would be speedily cured,   250
The music stopped and I stood still,
And found myself outside the hill,
Left alone against my will,
To go now limping as before,
And never hear of that country more!"

XIV

Alas, alas for Hamelin!
    There came into many a burgher's pate
    A text which says that heaven's gate
    Opes to the rich at as easy rate
As the needle's eye takes a camel in!   260
The Mayor sent East, West, North and South,
To offer the Piper, by word of mouth,
    Wherever it was men's lot to find him,
Silver and gold to his heart's content,
    If he'd only return the way he went,
    And bring the children behind him.
But when they saw 't was a lost endeavour,
And Piper and dancers were gone forever,

They made a decree that lawyers never
    Should think their records dated duly   2
If, after the day of the month and year,
These words did not as well appear,
"And so long after what happened here
    On the Twenty-second of July,
Thirteen hundred and seventy-six:"
And the better in memory to fix
The place of the children's last retreat,
They called it, the Pied Piper's Street—
Where any one playing on pipe or tabour
Was sure for the future to lose his labour.   2
Nor suffered they hostelry or tavern
    To shock with mirth a street so solemn;
But opposite the place of the cavern
    They wrote the story on a column.
And on the great church-window painted
The same, to make the world acquainted
How their children were stolen away,
And there it stands to this very day.
And I must not omit to say
That in Transylvania there's a tribe   2
Of alien people who ascribe
The outlandish ways and dress
On which their neighbours lay such stress,
To their fathers and mothers having risen
Out of some subterraneous prison
Into which they were trepanned[3]
Long time ago in a mighty band
Out of Hamelin town in Brunswick land,
But how or why, they don't understand.

XV

So, Willy, let me and you be wipers   3
Of scores out with all men—especially pipers
And, whether they pipe us free fróm rats or
    fróm mice,
If we've promised them aught, let us keep our
    promise!

HOW THEY BROUGHT THE GOOD NEW
FROM GHENT TO AIX[*]

I sprang to the stirrup, and Joris, and he;
I galloped, Dirck galloped, we galloped
    three;
"Good speed!" cried the watch, as the gate-
    bolts undrew;
"Speed!" echoed the wall to us galloping
    through;
Behind shut the postern, the lights sank to rest,
And into the midnight we galloped abreast.

3 ensnared
* This poem has no historical foundation. It sug-
    gests comparison with Longfellow's Paul Re-
    vere's Ride, which was written later. Ghent
    (g hard) is in Belgium, and Aix-la-Chapelle
    in Prussia, about ninety miles distant.

ot a word to each other; we kept the great
   pace
eck by neck, stride by stride, never changing
   our place;
 turned in my saddle and made its girths
   tight,
hen shortened each stirrup, and set the pique‡
   right,   10
ebuckled the cheek-strap, chained slacker the
   bit,
or galloped less steadily Roland a whit.

' was moonset at starting; but while we drew
   near
okeren, the cocks crew and twilight dawned
   clear;
t Boom, a great yellow star came out to see;
t Düffeld, 't was morning as plain as could
   be;
nd from Mecheln church-steeple we heard the
   half-chime,
o Joris broke silence with, "Yet there is
   time!"

t Aershot, up leaped of a sudden the sun,
nd against him the cattle stood black every
   one,   20
o stare through the mist at us galloping past,
nd I saw my stout galloper Roland at last,
ith resolute shoulders, each butting away
he haze, as some bluff river headland its
   spray:

nd his low head and crest, just one sharp ear
   bent back
or my voice, and the other pricked out on his
   track;
nd one eye's black intelligence,—ever that
   glance
) 'er its white edge at me, his own master,
   askance!
nd the thick heavy spume-flakes which aye
   and anon   29
lis fierce lips shook upwards in galloping on.

3y Hasselt, Dirck groaned; and cried Joris,
   "Stay, spur!
our Roos galloped bravely, the fault's not in
   her.
Ve'll remember at Aix"—for one heard the
   quick wheeze
)f her chest, saw the stretched neck and staggering knees,
nd sunk tail, and horrible heave of the flank,
s down on her haunches she shuddered and
   sank.

peak, pommel

So, we were left galloping, Joris and I,
Past Looz and past Tongres, no cloud in the sky;
The broad sun above laughed a pitiless laugh,
'Neath our feet broke the brittle bright stubble
   like chaff;   40
Till over by Dalhem a dome-spire sprang white,
And "Gallop," gasped Joris, "for Aix is in
   sight!"

"How they'll greet us!"—and all in a moment
   his roan
Rolled neck and croup over, lay dead as a
   stone;
And there was my Roland to bear the whole
   weight
Of the news which alone could save Aix from
   her fate,
With his nostrils like pits full of blood to the
   brim,
And with circles of red for his eye-sockets'
   rim.

Then I cast loose my buffcoat, each holster
   let fall,
Shook off both my jack-boots, let go belt and
   all,   50
Stood up in the stirrup, leaned, patted his ear,
Called my Roland his pet-name, my horse without peer;
Clapped my hands, laughed and sang, any
   noise, bad or good,
Till at length into Aix Roland galloped and
   stood.

And all I remember is—friends flocking round
As I sat with his head 'twixt my knees on the
   ground;
And no voice but was praising this Roland of
   mine,
As I poured down his throat our last measure
   of wine,
Which (the burgesses voted by common consent)
Was no more than his due who brought good
   news from Ghent.   60

THE LOST LEADER*

Just for a handful of silver he left us,
   Just for a riband to stick in his coat—
Found the one gift of which fortune bereft us,
   Lost all the others she lets us devote;

* This poem was suggested by Wordsworth's
change from very radical views to conservatism and Toryism. Browning later apologized
for its great injustice to Wordsworth: it was
the effusion of "hasty youth," and was, moreover, not intended as an exact characterization. Compare Browning's poem, *Why I am a
Liberal*, below. Whittier's poem, *Ichabod*, on
the defection of Daniel Webster, is written
in a similar strain.

They, with the gold to give, doled him out
    silver,
  So much was theirs who so little allowed:
How all our copper had gone[1] for his service!
  Rags—were they purple,[2] his heart had been
    proud!
We that had loved him so, followed him, hon-
    oured him,
  Lived in his mild and magnificent eye,   10
Learned his great language, caught his clear
    accents,
  Made him our pattern to live and to die!
Shakespeare was of us, Milton was for us,
  Burns, Shelley, were with us,—they watch
    from their graves!
He alone breaks from the van and the freemen,
  —He alone sinks to the rear and the slaves!
We shall march prospering,—not through his
    presence;
  Songs may inspirit us,—not from his lyre;
Deeds will be done,—while he boasts his quies-
    cence,
  Still bidding crouch whom the rest bade
    aspire: 20
Blot out his name, then, record one lost soul
    more,
  One task more declined, one more footpath
    untrod,
One more devils'-triumph and sorrow for
    angels,
  One wrong more to man, one more insult to
    God!
Life's night begins: let him never come back
    to us!
  There would be doubt, hesitation and pain,
Forced praise on our part—the glimmer of twi-
    light,
  Never glad confident morning again!
Best fight on well,[3] for we taught him—strike
    gallantly,
  Menace our heart ere we master his own;   30
Then let him receive the new knowledge and
    wait us,
  Pardoned in heaven, the first by the throne!

HOME-THOUGHTS, FROM ABROAD

Oh, to be in England
Now that April's there,
And whoever wakes in England
Sees, some morning, unaware,
That the lowest boughs and the brushwood
    sheaf
Round the elm-tree bole are in tiny leaf,

While the chaffinch sings on the orchard bough
In England—now!

And after April, when May follows,
And the whitethroat builds, and all the swal-
    lows!
Hark, where my blossomed pear-tree in the
    hedge
Leans to the field and scatters on the clover
Blossoms and dewdrops—at the bent spray's
    edge—
That's the wise thrush; he sings each song
    twice over,
Lest you should think he never could recapture
The first fine careless rapture!
And though the fields look rough with hoary
    dew,
All will be gay when noontide wakes anew
The buttercups, the little children's dower
—Far brighter than this gaudy melon-flower!

HOME-THOUGHTS, FROM THE SEA

Nobly, nobly Cape Saint Vincent to the North-
    west died away;[4]
Sunset ran, one glorious blood-red, reeking into
    Cadiz Bay;
Bluish 'mid the burning water, full in face
    Trafalgar lay;
In the dimmest Northeast distance dawned
    Gibraltar grand and gray;
"Here and here did England help me: how
    can I help England?"—say,
Whoso turns as I, this evening, turn to God
    to praise and pray,
While Jove's planet rises yonder, silent over
    Africa.

THE BOY AND THE ANGEL*

Morning, evening, noon and night,
"Praise God!" sang Theocrite.

Then to his poor trade he turned,
Whereby the daily meal was earned.

Hard he laboured, long and well;
O'er his work the boy's curls fell.

But ever, at each period,
He stopped and sang, "Praise God!"

[1] would have gone (gladly)
[2] had they been royal robes (spoken in sarcasm)
[3] i. e., against us

[4] The scene is that of Nelson's great victory.
* This legend is a pure invention, in the mediæval
    spirit. The moral is the same as that of the
    "New Year's Hymn" from *Pippa Passes* above.
    Or, in the words of Emerson,
        "There is no great and no small
        To the Soul that maketh all."

Then back again his curls he threw,
And cheerful turned to work anew.   10

Said Blaise, the listening monk, "Well done;
I doubt not thou art heard, my son:

"As well as if thy voice to-day
Were praising God, the Pope's great way.

"This Easter Day, the Pope at Rome
Praises God from Peter's dome."

Said Theocrite, "Would God that I
Might praise him that great way, and die!"

Night passed, day shone,
And Theocrite was gone.   20

With God a day endures alway,
A thousand years are but a day.

God said in heaven, "Nor day nor night
Now brings the voice of my delight."

Then Gabriel, like a rainbow's birth,
Spread his wings and sank to earth;

Entered, in flesh, the empty cell,
Lived there, and played the craftsman well;

And morning, evening, noon and night,
Praised God in place of Theocrite.   30

And from a boy, to youth he grew:
The man put off the stripling's hue:

The man matured and fell away
Into the season of decay:

And ever o'er the trade he bent,
And ever lived on earth content.

(He did God's will; to him, all one
If on the earth or in the sun.)

God said "A praise is in mine ear;
There is no doubt in it, no fear: 40

"So sing old worlds, and so
New worlds that from my footstool go.

"Clearer loves sound other ways:
I miss my little human praise."

Then forth sprang Gabriel's wings, off fell
The flesh disguise, remained the cell.

'Twas Easter Day: he flew to Rome,
And paused above St. Peter's dome.

In the tiring-room close by
The great outer gallery,   50

With his holy vestments dight,[5]
Stood the new Pope, Theocrite:

And all his past career
Came back upon him clear,

Since when, a boy, he plied his trade,
Till on his life the sickness weighed;

And in his cell, when death drew near,
An angel in a dream brought cheer:

And rising from the sickness drear,
He grew a priest, and now stood here.   60

To the East with praise he turned,
And on his sight the angel burned.

"I bore thee from thy craftsman's cell,
And set thee here; I did not well.

"Vainly I left my angel-sphere,
Vain was thy dream of many a year.

"Thy voice's praise seemed weak; it dropped—
Creation's chorus stopped!

"Go back and praise again
The early way, while I remain.   70

"With that weak voice of our disdain,
Take up creation's pausing strain.

"Back to the cell and poor employ:
Resume the craftsman and the boy!"

Theocrite grew old at home;
A new Pope dwelt in Peter's dome.

One vanished as the other died:
They sought God side by side.

SAUL*

I

Said Abner,[1] "At last thou art come!   Ere I
  tell, ere thou speak,
Kiss my cheek, wish me well!"   Then I wished
  it, and did kiss his cheek.

[5] arrayed

---

[1] The captain of Saul's host. David is the speaker throughout.

* In *I Samuel*, xvi. 14-23, David, the shepherd boy, is summoned to play on his harp and drive away the evil spirit which troubles Saul. Browning has availed himself of the theme to set forth, in majestic anapests, the range and power of music in its various kinds; thence passing to a view of the boundlessness of spiritual influence, and rising in the end to a vision of the ultimate oneness of human sympathy and love with divine. A. J. George writes: "The severity, sweetness, and beauty of the closing scene where David returns to his simple task of tending his flocks, when all nature is alive with the new impulse and pronounces the benediction on his efforts, is not surpassed by anything in our literature."

And he: "Since the King, O my friend, for
thy countenance sent,
Neither drunken nor eaten have we; nor until
from his tent
Thou return with the joyful assurance the
King liveth yet,
Shall our lip with the honey be bright, with
the water be wet,
For out of the black mid-tent's silence, a space
of three days,
Not a sound hath escaped to thy servants, of
prayer nor of praise,
To betoken that Saul and the Spirit have ended
their strife,
And that, faint in his triumph, the monarch
sinks back upon life.   10

II

"Yet now my heart leaps, O beloved! God's
child with his dew
On thy gracious gold hair, and those lilies still
living and blue
Just broken to twine round thy harp-strings,
as if no wild heat
Were now raging to torture the desert!"

III
                    Then I, as was meet,
Knelt down to the God of my fathers, and
rose on my feet,
And ran o'er the sand burnt to powder. The
tent was unlooped;
I pulled up the spear that obstructed, and
under I stooped;
Hands and knees on the slippery grass-patch,
all withered and gone,
That extends to the second enclosure, I groped
my way on
Till I felt where the foldskirts fly open. Then
once more I prayed,   20
And opened the foldskirts and entered, and
was not afraid
But spoke, "Here is David, thy servant!"
And no voice replied.
At the first I saw naught but the blackness:
but soon I descried
A something more black than the blackness—
the vast, the upright
Main prop which sustains the pavilion: and
slow into sight
Grew a figure against it, gigantic and blackest
of all.
Then a sunbeam, that burst through the tent-
roof, showed Saul.

IV

He stood as erect as that tent-prop, both arms
stretched out wide

On the great cross-support in the centre, that
goes to each side;
He relaxed not a muscle, but hung there as,
caught in his pangs   30
And waiting his change, the king-serpent all
heavily hangs,
Far away from his kind, in the pine, till
deliverance come
With the spring-time,[2]—so agonized Saul, drear
and stark, blind and dumb.

V

Then I tuned my harp,—took off the lilies we
twine round its chords
Lest they snap 'neath the stress of the noontide—those sunbeams like swords!
And I first played the tune all our sheep know,
as, one after one,
So docile they come to the pen-door till folding
be done.
They are white and untorn by the bushes, for
lo, they have fed
Where the long grasses stifle the water within
the stream's bed;
And now one after one seeks its lodging, as
star follows star   40
Into eve and the blue far above us,—so blue
and so far!

VI

—Then the tune for which quails on the corn-
land will each leave his mate
To fly after the player; then, what makes the
crickets elate
Till for boldness they fight one another; and
then, what has weight
To set the quick jerboa[3] a-musing outside his
sand house—
There are none such as he for a wonder, half
bird and half mouse!
God made all the creatures and gave them our
love and our fear,
To give sign, we and they are his children, one
family here.

VII

Then I played the help-tune of our reapers,
their wine-song, when hand
Grasps at hand, eye lights eye in good friend-
ship, and great hearts expand   50
And grow one in the sense of this world's life.
    —And then, the last song
When the dead man is praised on his journey
    —"Bear, bear him along,
With his few faults shut up like dead flowerets!
Are balm seeds not here

[2] Through the sloughing of his old skin.
[3] A rodent with long hind legs, with which it can
spring like a bird.

To console us? The land has none left such
    as he on the bier.
Oh, would we might keep thee, my brother!''—
    And then, the glad chaunt
Of the marriage,—first go the young maidens,
    next, she whom we vaunt
As the beauty, the pride of our dwelling.—
    And then, the grand march
Wherein man runs to man to assist him and
    buttress an arch
Naught can break; who shall harm them, our
    friends? Then, the chorus intoned
As the Levites go up to the altar in glory
    enthroned.   60
But I stopped here: for here in the darkness
    Saul groaned.

VIII

And I paused, held my breath in such silence,
    and listened apart:
And the tent shook, for mighty Saul shud-
    dered: and sparkles 'gan dart
From the jewels that woke in his turban, at
    once, with a start.
All its lordly male-sapphires,[4] and rubies cour-
    ageous at heart.
So the head: but the body still moved not,
    still hung there erect.
And I bent once again to my playing, pursued
    it unchecked,
As I sang:—

IX

    ''Oh, our manhood's prime vigour! No
    spirit feels waste,
Not a muscle is stopped in its playing nor
    sinew unbraced.
Oh, the wild joys of living! the leaping from
    rock up to rock,   70
The strong rending of boughs from the fir-
    tree, the cool silver shock
Of the plunge in a pool's living water, the hunt
    of the bear,
And the sultriness showing the lion is couched
    in his lair.
And the meal, the rich dates yellowed over
    with gold dust divine,
And the locust-flesh[5] steeped in the pitcher,
    the full draught of wine,
And the sleep in the dried river-channel where
    bulrushes tell
That the water was wont to go warbling so
    softly and well.
How good is man's life, the mere living! how
    fit to employ

All the heart and the soul and the senses for-
    ever in joy!
Hast thou loved the white locks of thy father,
    whose sword thou didst guard   80
When he trusted thee forth with the armies,
    for glorious reward?
Didst thou see the thin hands of thy mother,
    held up as men sung
The low song of the nearly-departed, and hear
    her faint tongue
Joining in while it could to the witness, ''Let
    one more attest,
I have lived, seen God's hand through a life-
    time, and all was for best?''
Then they sung through their tears in strong
    triumph, not much, but the rest.
And thy brothers, the help and the contest, the
    working whence grew
Such result as, from seething grape-bundles,
    the spirit strained true:
And the friends of thy boyhood—that boyhood
    of wonder and hope,
Present promise and wealth of the future be-
    yond the eye's scope,—   90
Till lo, thou art grown to a monarch: a people
    is thine;
And all gifts, which the world offers singly,
    on one head combine!
On one head, all the beauty and strength, love
    and rage (like the throe
That, a-work in the rock, helps its labour and
    lets the gold go)
High ambition and deeds which surpass it,
    fame crowning them,—all
Brought to blaze on the head of one creature
    —King Saul!''

X

And lo, with that leap of my spirit,—heart,
    hand, harp and voice,
Each lifting Saul's name out of sorrow, each
    bidding rejoice
Saul's fame in the light it was made for—as
    when, dare I say,
The Lord's army, in rapture of service, strains
    through its array,[6]   100
And upsoareth the cherubim-chariot—''Saul!''
    cried I, and stopped,
And waited the thing that should follow. Then
    Saul, who hung propped
By the tent's cross-support in the centre, was
    struck by his name.
Have ye seen when Spring's arrowy summons
    goes right to the aim,
And some mountain, the last to withstand her,
    that held (he alone,

---

4 Sapphires of superior hardness and brilliancy.
5 The meat of John the Baptist in the wilderness.
    See page 41, and the note on Wyclif's mis-
    translation.

6 See *Ezekiel,* x.

While the vale laughed in freedom and flowers) on a broad bust of stone
A year's snow bound about for a breast-plate,
—leaves grasp of the sheet?
Fold on fold all at once it crowds thunderously
down to his feet,
And there fronts you, stark, black, but alive
yet, your mountain of old,
With his rents, the successive bequeathings of
ages untold—   110
Yea, each harm got in fighting your battles,
each furrow and scar
Of his head thrust 'twixt you and the tempest
—all hail, there they are!
—Now again to be softened with verdure,
again hold the nest
Of the dove, tempt the goat and its young to
the green on his crest
For their food in the ardours of summer. One
long shudder thrilled
All the tent till the very air tingled, then
sank and was stilled
At the King's self left standing before me,
released and aware.
What was gone, what remained? All to trav-
verse 'twixt hope and despair.
Death was past, life not come: so he waited.
Awhile his right hand
Held the brow, helped the eyes left too vacant
forthwith to remand   120
To their place what new objects should enter:
't was Saul as before.
I looked up and dared gaze at those eyes, nor
was hurt any more
Than by slow pallid sunsets in autumn, ye
watch from the shore,
At their sad level gaze o'er the ocean—a sun's
slow decline
Over hills which, resolved¹ in stern silence,
o'erlap and entwine
Base with base to knit strength more intensely:
so, arm folded arm
O'er the chest whose slow heavings subsided.

XI

       What spell or what charm,
(For awhile there was trouble within me),
what next should I urge
To sustain him where song had restored him?—
Song filled to the verge
His cup with the wine of this life, pressing all
that it yields   130
Of mere fruitage, the strength and the beauty:
beyond, on what fields,
Glean a vintage more potent and perfect to
brighten the eye

¹ separated in outline

And bring blood to the lip, and commend them
the cup they put by?
He saith, "It is good;" still he drinks not:
he lets me praise life,
Gives assent, yet would die for his own part.

XII

       Then fancies grew rife
Which had come long ago on the pasture,
when round me the sheep
Fed in silence—above, the one eagle wheeled
slow as in sleep;
And I lay in my hollow and mused on the
world that might lie
'Neath his ken, though I saw but the strip
'twixt the hill and the sky:
And I laughed—"Since my days are ordained
to be passed with my flocks,   140
Let me people at least, with my fancies, the
plains and the rocks,
Dream the life I am never to mix with, and
image the show
Of mankind as they live in those fashions I
hardly shall know!
Schemes of life, its best rules and right uses,
the courage that gains,
And the prudence that keeps what men strive
for." And now these old trains
Of vague thought came again; I grew surer;
so, once more the string
Of my harp made response to my spirit, as
thus—

XIII

       "Yea, my King,"
I began—"thou dost well in rejecting mere
comforts that spring
From the mere mortal life held in common by
man and by brute:
In our flesh grows the branch of this life, in
our soul it bears fruit.   150
Thou hast marked the slow rise of the tree,—
how its stem trembled first
Till it passed the kid's lip, the stag's antler;
then safely outburst
The fan-branches all round; and thou mindest
when these too, in turn,
Broke a-bloom and the palm-tree seemed perfect: yet more was to learn,
E'en the good that comes in with the palm-
fruit. Our dates shall we slight,
When their juice brings a cure for all sorrow?
or care for the plight
Of the palm's self whose slow growth produced
them? Not so! stem and branch
Shall decay, nor be known in their place, while
the palm-wine shall stanch

very wound of man's spirit in winter. I pour
  thee such wine,
eave the flesh to the fate it was fit for! the
  spirit be thine! 160
y the spirit, when age shall o'ercome thee,
  thou still shalt enjoy
ore indeed, than at first when inconscious,
  the life of a boy.
rush that life, and behold its wine running!
  Each deed thou hast done
ies, revives, goes to work in the world! until
  e'en as the sun
ooking down on the earth, though clouds spoil
  him, though tempests efface,
an find nothing his own deed produced not,
  must everywhere trace
he results of his past summer-prime,—so, each
  ray of thy will,
very flash of thy passion and prowess, long
  over, shall thrill
hy whole people, the countless, with ardour,
  till they too give forth
like cheer to their sons, who in turn, fill the
  South and the North 170
'ith the radiance thy deed was the germ of.
  Carouse in the past!
ut the license of age has its limit; thou diest
  at last:
s the lion when age dims his eyeball, the rose
  at her height,
• with man—so .his power and his beauty
  forever take flight.
o! Again a long draught of my soul-wine!
  Look forth o'er the years!
hou hast done now with eyes for the actual;
  begin with the seer's!
Saul dead? In the depth of the vale make
  his tomb—bid arise
gray mountain of marble heaped four-square,
  till, built to the skies,
et it mark where the great First King¹ slumbers: whose fame would ye know?
p above see the rock's naked face, where the
  record shall go 180
a great characters cut by the scribe.—Such
  was Saul, so he did;
'ith the sages directing the work, by the populace chid,—
or not half, they'll affirm, is comprised there!
  Which fault to amend,
a the grove with his kind grows the cedar,
  whereon they shall spend
See, in tablets 't is level before them) their
  praise, and record
'ith the gold of the graver, Saul's story,—the
  statesman's great word

Of Israel.

Side by side with the poet's sweet comment.
  The river's a-wave
With smooth paper-reeds grazing each other
  when prophet-winds² rave:
So the pen gives unborn generations their due
  and their part
In thy being! Then, first of the mighty, thank
  God that thou art!'' 190

XIV

And behold while I sang . . . but O Thou
  who didst grant me that day,
And before it not seldom hast granted thy
  help to essay, .
Carry on and complete an adventure,—my
  shield and my sword
In that act where my soul was thy servant, thy
  word was my word,—
Still be with me, who then at the summit of
  human endeavour
And scaling the highest man's thought could,
  gazed hopeless as ever
On the new stretch of heaven above me—till,
  mighty to save,
Just one lift of thy hand cleared that distance
  —God's throne from man's grave!
Let me tell out my tale to its ending—my
  voice to my heart
Which can scarce dare believe in what marvels
  last night I took part, 200
As this morning I gather the fragments, alone
  with my sheep,
And still fear lest the terrible glory evanish
  like sleep!
For I wake in the gray dewy covert, while
  Hebron³ upheaves
The dawn, struggling with night, on his shoul-
  der, and Kidron retrieves
Slow the damage of yesterday's sunshine.*

XV

I say then,—my song
While I sang thus, assuring the monarch, and
  ever more strong
Made a proffer of good to console him—he
  slowly resumed
His old motions and habitudes kingly. The
  right hand replumed
His black locks to their wonted composure, adjusted the swathes
Of his turban, and see—the huge sweat that
  his countenance bathes, 210

² The winds of prophecy; divine inspiration, demanding to be recorded on papyrus.
³ The city which became for a time David's royal
  residence.
* The Kidron is a nearly dry water-course at the
  foot of Mt. Olivet. In dry countries, small
  streams are always perceptibly fuller at
  morning than at night.

He wipes off with the robe; and he girds now
    his loins as of yore,
And feels slow for the armlets of price, with
    the clasp set before.
He is Saul, ye remember in glory,—ere error
    had bent
The broad brow from the daily communion;
    and still, though much spent
Be the life and the bearing that front you, the
    same God did choose
To receive what a man may waste, desecrate,
    never quite lose.
So sank he along by the tent-prop till, stayed
    by the pile
Of his armour and war-cloak and garments,
    he leaned there awhile,
And sat out my singing,—one arm round the
    tent-prop, to raise
His bent head, and the other hung slack—till
    I touched on the praise   220
I foresaw from all men in all time, to the man
    patient there;
And thus ended, the harp falling forward.
    Then first I was 'ware
That he sat, as I say, with my head just above
    his vast knees
Which were thrust out on each side around me,
    like oak roots which please
To encircle a lamb when it slumbers. I looked
    up to know
If the best I could do had brought solace; he
    spoke not, but slow
Lifted up the hand slack at his side, till he
    laid it with care
Soft and grave, but in mild settled will, on my
    brow: through my hair
The large fingers were pushed, and he bent
    back my head, with kind power—
All my face back, intent to peruse it, as men
    do a flower.   230
Thus held he me there with his great eyes that
    scrutinized mine—
And oh, all my heart how it loved him! but
    where was the sign?
I yearned—"Could I help thee, my father,
    inventing a bliss,
I would add, to that life of the past, both the
    future and this;
I would give thee new life altogether, as good,
    ages hence,
As this moment,—had love but the warrant,
    love's heart to dispense!"

XVI

Then the truth came upon me. No harp more
    —no song more! outbroke—

XVII

"I have gone the whole round of creation:
    saw and I spoke:
I, a work of God's hand for that purpo[se]
    received in my brain
And pronounced on the rest of his handwork
    returned him again   2
His creation's approval or censure: I spo[ke]
    as I saw:
I report, as a man may of God's work—all[']
    love, yet all's law.
Now I lay down the judgeship he lent n[e]
    Each faculty tasked
To perceive him, has gained an abyss, where[']
    dewdrop was asked.
Have I knowledge? confounded it shrivels
    Wisdom laid bare.
Have I forethought? how purblind, how bla[nk]
    to the Infinite Care!
Do I task any faculty highest, to ima[ge]
    success?
I but open my eyes,—and perfection, no mo[re]
    and no less,
In the kind I imagined, full-fronts me, a[nd]
    God is seen God
In the star, in the stone, in the flesh, in t[he]
    soul and the clod.   2
And thus looking within and around me,
    ever renew
(With that stoop of the soul which in bendi[ng]
    upraises it too)
The submission of man's nothing-perfect
    God's all-complete,
As by each new obeisance in spirit, I climb
    his feet.
Yet with all this abounding experience, th[is]
    deity known,
I shall dare to discover some province, so[me]
    gift of my own.
There's a faculty pleasant to exercise, ha[rd]
    to hoodwink,
I am fain to keep still in abeyance, (I lau[gh]
    as I think)
Lest, insisting to claim and parade in it, w[ear]
    ye, I worst
E'en the Giver in one gift.—Behold, I cou[ld]
    love if I durst!   2
But I sink the pretension as fearing a m[an]
    may o'ertake
God's own speed in the one way of love:
    abstain for love's sake.
—What, my soul? see thus far and no farthe[r]
    when doors great and small,
Nine-and-ninety flew ope at our touch, shou[ld]
    the hundredth appal?
In the least things have faith, yet distrust
    the greatest of all?

I find love so full in my nature, God's ultimate gift,
at I doubt his own love can compete with
it? Here, the parts shift?
re, the creature surpass the Creator,—the
end, what Began?
uld I fain in my impotent yearning do all
for this man,
d dare doubt He alone shall not help him,
who yet alone can?   270
uld it ever have entered my mind, the bare
will, much less power,
bestow on this Saul what I sang of, the
marvellous dower
the life he was gifted and filled with? to
make such a soul,
ch a body, and then such an earth for in-
sphering the whole?
d doth it not enter my mind (as my warm
tears attest)
ese good things being given, to go on, and
give one more, the best?
, to save and redeem and restore him, maintain at the height
is perfection,—succeed with life's day-spring,
death's minute of night?
erpose at the difficult minute, snatch Saul
the mistake,
il the failure, the ruin he seems now,—and
bid him awake   280
om the dream, the probation, the prelude, to
find himself set
ar and safe in new light and new life,—a
new harmony yet
be run, and continued, and ended—who
knows?—or endure!
e man taught enough by life's dream, of the
rest to make sure;
the pain-throb, triumphantly winning intensified bliss,
d the next world's reward and repose, by
the struggles in this.

XVIII

believe it!   'T is thou, God, that givest,
't is I who receive:
the first is the last, in thy will is my power
to believe.
's one gift: thou canst grant it moreover,
as prompt to my prayer
I breathe out this breath, as I open these
arms to the air.   290
om thy will stream the worlds, life and
nature, thy dread Sabaoth:1
vill?—the mere atoms despise me! Why am
I not loth

'he armies of the Lord.

To look that, even that in the face too? Why
is it I dare
Think but lightly of such impuissance? What
stops my despair?
This;—'t is not what man Does which exalts
him, but what man Would do!
See the King—I would help him but cannot,
the wishes fall through.
Could I wrestle to raise him from sorrow, grow
poor to enrich,
To fill up his life, starve my own out, I would
—knowing which,
I know that my service is perfect. Oh, speak
through me now!
Would I suffer for him that I love? So
wouldst thou—so wilt thou!   300
So shall crown thee the topmost, ineffablest,
uttermost crown—
And thy love fill infinitude wholly, nor leave
up nor down
One spot for the creature to stand in! It is by
no breath,
Turn of eye, wave of hand, that salvation joins
issue with death!
As thy Love is discovered almighty, almighty
be proved
Thy power, that exists with and for it, of
being Beloved!
He who did most, shall bear most; the strongest
shall stand the most weak.
'T is the weakness in strength, that I cry for!
my flesh, that I seek
In the Godhead! I seek and I find it. O Saul,
it shall be
A Face like my face that receives thee; a Man
like to me,   310
Thou shalt love and be loved by, forever: a
Hand like this hand
Shall throw open the gates of new life to thee!
See the Christ stand!''

XIX

I know not too well how I found my way
home in the night.
There were witnesses, cohorts about me, to left
and to right,
Angels, powers, the unuttered, unseen, the alive,
the aware:
I repressed, I got through them as hardly, as
strugglingly there,
As a runner beset by the populace famished
for news—
Life or death. The whole earth was awakened,
hell loosed with her crews;
And the stars of night beat with emotion, and
tingled and shot

Out in fire the strong pain of pent knowledge:
    but I fainted not,   320
For the Hand still impelled me at once and
    supported, suppressed
All the tumult, and quenched it with quiet, and
    holy behest,
Till the rapture was shut in itself, and the
    earth sank to rest.
Anon at the dawn, all that trouble had with-
    ered from earth—
Not so much, but I saw it die out in the day's
    tender birth;
In the gathered intensity brought to the gray
    of the hills,
In the shuddering forests' held breath; in the
    sudden wind-thrills;
In the startled wild beasts that bore off, each
    with eye sidling still
Though averted with wonder and dread; in
    the birds stiff and chill
That rose heavily, as I approached them, made
    stupid with awe;   330
E'en the serpent that slid away silent,—he felt
    the new law.
The same stared in the white humid faces up-
    turned by the flowers;
The same worked in the heart of the cedar and
    moved the vine-bowers;
And the little brooks witnessing murmured, per-
    sistent and low,
With their obstinate, all but hushed voices—
    "E'en so, it is so!"

EVELYN HOPE

BEAUTIFUL Evelyn Hope is dead!
    Sit and watch by her side an hour.
That is her book-shelf, this her bed;
    She plucked that piece of geranium-flower,
Beginning to die too, in the glass;
    Little has yet been changed, I think:
The shutters are shut, no light may pass   7
    Save two long rays through the hinge's chink.

Sixteen years old when she died!
    Perhaps she had scarcely heard my name;
It was not her time to love; beside,
    Her life had many a hope and aim,
Duties enough and little cares,
    And now was quiet, now astir,
Till God's hand beckoned unawares,—
    And the sweet white brow is all of her.   16

Is it too late then, Evelyn Hope?
    What, your soul was pure and true,
The good stars met in your horoscope,
    Made you of spirit, fire and dew—

And, just because I was thrice as old
    And our paths in the world diverged so wi█
Each was naught to each, must I be told?
    We were fellow mortals, naught beside?

No, indeed! for God above
    Is great to grant, as mighty to make,
And creates the love to reward the love:
    I claim you still, for my own love's sake!
Delayed it may be for more lives yet,
    Through worlds I shall traverse, not a fe█
Much is to learn, much to forget
    Ere the time be come for taking you.

But the time will come,—at last it will,
    When, Evelyn Hope, what meant (I sh█
    say)
In the lower earth, in the years long still,
    That body and soul so pure and gay?
Why your hair was amber, I shall divine,
    And your mouth of your own geranium
    red—
And what you would do with me, in fine,
    In the new life come in the old one's ste█

I have lived (I shall say) so much since then,
    Given up myself so many times,
Gained me the gains of various men,
    Ransacked the ages, spoiled the climes;
Yet one thing, one, in my soul's full scope,
    Either I missed or itself missed me:
And I want and find you, Evelyn Hope!
    What is the issue? let us see!

I loved you, Evelyn, all the while!
    My heart seemed full as it could hold;
There was place and to spare for the fra█
    young smile,
    And the red young mouth, and the hai█
    young gold.
So, hush,—I will give you this leaf to keep:
    See, I shut it inside the sweet cold hand!
There, that is our secret: go to sleep!
    You will wake, and remember, and und█
    stand.

FRA LIPPO LIPPI*

I AM poor brother Lippo, by your leave!
You need not clap your torches to my face.
Zooks, what's to blame? you think you see█
    monk!

* This, like *My Last Duchess*, is another of Brow█
ing's dramatic monologues. It portrays
mirably that period of the Italian Rena█
sance when men were growing more kee█
awake to the charm of physical life, and
ciety began to break through the restraints
which it had long submitted. In painti█

What, 't is past midnight, and you go the
    rounds,
And here you catch me at an alley's end
Where sportive ladies leave their doors ajar?
The Carmine's my cloister: hunt it up.
Do,—harry out, if you must show your zeal,
Whatever rat, there, haps on his wrong hole,
And nip each softling of a wee white mouse, 10
Weke, weke, that 's crept to keep him company!
Aha, you know your betters! Then, you'll take
Your hand away that 's fiddling on my throat,
And please to know me likewise. Who am I?
Why, one, sir, who is lodging with a friend
Three streets off—he's a certain . . . how d'
    ye call?
Master—a . . . Cosimo of the Medici,
I' the house that caps the corner. Boh! you
    were best!
Remember and tell me, the day you're hanged,
How you affected such a gullet's-gripe! 20
But you, sir, it concerns you that your knaves
Pick up a manner[1] nor discredit you:
Zooks, are we pilchards,[2] that they sweep the
    streets
And count fair prize what comes into their
    net?
He's Judas to a tittle, that man is!
Just such a face! Why, sir, you make amends.
Lord, I'm not angry! Bid your hang-dogs go
Drink out this quarter-florin to the health
Of the munificent House that harbours me
(And many more beside, lads! more beside!) 30
And all 's come square again. I'd like his
    face—
His, elbowing on his comrade in the door
With the pike and lantern,—for the slave that
    holds
John Baptist's head a-dangle by the hair
With one hand ("Look you, now," as who
    should say)

[1] mend a little
[2] Mediterranean sardines.

the new spirit was manifested in the change
from religious and symbolical subjects—haloed
saints and choiring angels—to portraits and
scenes from human life and the world of nature, or to religious pictures thoroughly humanized. The poem was suggested by a picture of the "Coronation of the Virgin" (described in lines 347 ff.) which is in the
Academy of Fine Arts at Florence; the incidents of the life of Fra Filippo Lippi (1406?-
1469) were obtained from Vasari's *Lives of
the Painters.* He was first a monk, but he
broke away from the Carmine, or Carmelite
monastery, and came under the patronage of
Cosimo de' Medici the Elder, the great banker,
patron of art and literature, and practical
ruler of the Florentine Republic. It is said
that his patron once shut him up in his
palace in order to restrain his roving propensities and keep him at work on some frescoes
he was painting. The poem opens with his
capture on this escapade by the watchmen.

And his weapon in the other, yet unwiped!
It 's not your chance to have a bit of chalk,
A wood-coal or the like? or you should see!
Yes, I'm the painter, since you style me so.
What, brother Lippo's doings, up and down, 40
You know them and they take you? like enough!
I saw the proper twinkle in your eye—
'Tell you, I liked your looks at very first.
Let 's sit and set things straight now, hip to
    haunch.
Here's spring come, and the nights one makes
    up bands
To roam the town and sing out carnival,
And I've been three weeks shut within my mew,
A-painting for the great man, saints and saints
And saints again. I could not paint all night—
Ouf! I leaned out of window for fresh air. 50
There came a hurry of feet and little feet,
A sweep of lute strings, laughs, and whiffs of
    song,—
Flower o' the broom,
Take away love, and our earth is a tomb!
Flower o' the quince,
I let Lisa go, and what good in life since?
Flower o' the thyme—and so on. Round they
    went.[3]
Scarce had they turned the corner when a titter
Like the skipping of rabbits by moonlight,—
    three slim shapes,
And a face that looked up . . . zooks, sir, flesh
    and blood, 60
That 's all I'm made of! Into shreds it went,
Curtain and counterpane and coverlet,
All the bed-furniture—a dozen knots,
There was a ladder! Down I let myself,
Hands and feet, scrambling somehow, and so
    dropped,
And after them. I came up with the fun
Hard by Saint Laurence,[4] hail fellow, well
    met,—
Flower o' the rose,
If I've been merry, what matter who knows?
And so as I was stealing back again 70
To get to bed and have a bit of sleep
Ere I rise up to-morrow and go work
On Jerome[5] knocking at his poor old breast
With his great round stone to subdue the flesh,
You snap me of the sudden. Ah, I see!
Though your eye twinkles still, you shake your
    head—
Mine's shaved—a monk, you say—the sting's in
    that!
If Master Cosimo announced himself,
Mum's the word naturally; but a monk!
Come, what am I a beast for? tell us, now! 80

[3] I. e., took up the song in turn.
[4] The Church of San Lorenzo.
[5] St. Jerome, one of the early church fathers.

I was a baby when my mother died
And father died and left me in the street.
I starved there, God knows how, a year or two
On fig-skins, melon-parings, rinds and shucks,
Refuse and rubbish. One fine frosty day,
My stomach being empty as your hat,
The wind doubled me up and down I went.
Old Aunt Lapaccia trussed me with one hand,
(Its fellow was a stinger as I knew)
And so along the wall, over the bridge,   90
By the straight cut to the convent. Six words there,
While I stood munching my first bread that month:
"So, boy, you're minded," quoth the good fat father,
Wiping his own mouth, 't was refection-time,—
"To quit this very miserable world?
Will you renounce" . . . "the mouthful of bread?" thought I;
By no means! Brief, they made a monk of me;
I did renounce the world, its pride and greed,
Palace, farm, villa, shop, and banking-house,
Trash, such as these poor devils of Medici   100
Have given their hearts to—all at eight years old.
Well, sir, I found in time, you may be sure,
'T was not for nothing—the good bellyful,
The warm serge and the rope that goes all round,
And day-long blessed idleness beside!
"Let's see what the urchin's fit for"—that came next.
Not overmuch their way, I must confess.
Such a to-do! They tried me with their books;
Lord, they'd have taught me Latin in pure waste!
Flower o' the clove,   110
All the Latin I construe is "amo," I love!
But, mind you, when a boy starves in the streets
Eight years together, as my fortune was,
Watching folk's faces to know who will fling
The bit of half-stripped grape-bunch he desires,
And who will curse or kick him for his pains,—
Which gentleman processional⁶ and fine,
Holding a candle to the Sacrament,
Will wink and let him lift a plate and catch
The droppings of the wax to sell again,   120
Or holla for the Eight⁷ and have him whipped,—
How say I?—nay, which dog bites, which lets drop
His bone from the heap of offal in the street,—
Why, soul and sense of him grow sharp alike,
He learns the look of things, and none the less
For admonition from the hunger-pinch.

I had a store of such remarks, be sure,
Which, after I found leisure, turned to use.
I drew men's faces on my copy-books,   129
Scrawled them within the antiphonary's⁸ marge,
Joined legs and arms to the long music-notes,
Found eyes and nose and chin for A's and B's,
And made a string of pictures of the world
Betwixt the ins and outs of verb and noun,
On the wall, the bench, the door. The monks looked black.
"Nay," quoth the Prior, "turn him out, d'ye say?
In no wise. Lose a crow and catch a lark.
What if at last we get our man of parts,
We Carmelites, like those Camaldolese⁹
And Preaching Friars,¹⁰ to do our church up fine   140
And put the front on it that ought to be!"
And hereupon he bade me daub away.
Thank you! my head being crammed, the walls a blank,
Never was such prompt disemburdening.
First, every sort of monk, the black and white,¹¹
I drew them, fat and lean: then, folk at church,
From good old gossips waiting to confess
Their cribs¹² of barrel-droppings, candle-ends,—
To the breathless fellow at the altar-foot,
Fresh from his murder, safe and sitting there
With the little children round him in a row 151
Of admiration, half for his beard and half
For that white anger of his victim's son
Shaking a fist at him with one fierce arm,
Signing himself with the other because of Christ
(Whose sad face on the cross sees only this
After the passion of a thousand years)
Till some poor girl, her apron o'er her head,
(Which the intense eyes looked through) came at eve
On tiptoe, said a word, dropped in a loaf, 160
Her pair of earrings and a bunch of flowers
(The brute took growling), prayed, and so was gone.
I painted all, then cried " 'T is ask and have;
Choose, for more's ready!"—laid the ladder flat,
And showed my covered bit of cloister-wall.
The monks closed in a circle and praised loud
Till checked, taught what to see and not to see,
Being simple bodies,—"That's the very man!
Look at the boy who stoops to pat the dog!
That woman's like the Prior's niece who comes

⁶ taking part in a religious procession (as at one of the sacraments)
⁷ The city magistrates.
⁸ A book of antiphons, or responsive songs.
⁹ A monastic order founded by St. Romuald at Camaldoli, near Florence.
¹⁰ Dominicans.
¹¹ The Dominicans wore black robes, the Carmelites white.
¹² pilferings

To care about his asthma: it's the life!''   171
But there my triumph's straw-fire flared and
    funked;
Their betters took their turn to see and say:
The Prior and the learned pulled a face
And stopped all that in no time. ''How?
    what's here?
Quite from the mark of painting, bless us all!
Faces, arms, legs, and bodies like the true
As much as pea and pea! it's devil's-game!
Your business is not to catch men with show,
With homage to the perishable clay,   180
But lift them over it, ignore it all,
Make them forget there's such a thing as flesh.
Your business is to paint the souls of men—
Man's soul, and it's a fire, smoke . . . no, it's
    not . . .
It's vapour done up like a new-born babe—
(In that shape when you die it leaves your
    mouth[13])
It's . . . well, what matters talking, it's the
    soul!
Give us no more of body than shows soul!
Here's Giotto,[14] with his Saint a-praising God,
That sets us praising,—why not stop with him?
Why put all thoughts of praise out of our
    head   191
With wonder at lines, colours, and what not?
Paint the soul, never mind the legs and arms!
Rub all out, try at it a second time.
Oh, that white smallish female with the
    breasts,
She's just my niece . . . Herodias,[15] I would
    say,—
Who went and danced and got men's heads
    cut off!
Have it all out!'' Now, is this sense, I ask?
A fine way to paint soul, by painting body
So ill, the eye can't stop there, must go fur-
    ther   200
And can't fare worse! Thus, yellow does for
    white
When what you put for yellow's simply black,
And any sort of meaning looks intense
When all beside itself means and looks naught.
Why can't a painter lift each foot in turn,
Left foot and right foot, go a double step,
Make his flesh liker and his soul more like,
Both in their order? Take the prettiest face,
The Prior's niece . . . patron-saint—is it so
    pretty

You can't discover if it means hope, fear,   210
Sorrow or joy? won't beauty go with these?
Suppose I've made her eyes all right and blue,
Can't I take breath and try to add life's flash,
And then add soul and heighten them three-
    fold?
Or say there's beauty with no soul at all—
(I never saw it—put the case the same—)
If you get simple beauty and naught else,
You get about the best thing God invents:
That's somewhat: and you'll find the soul you
    have missed,
Within yourself, when you return him thanks.
''Rub all out!'' Well, well, there's my life, in
    short,   221
And so the thing has gone on ever since.
I'm grown a man no doubt, I've broken
    bounds:
You should not take a fellow eight years old
And make him swear to never kiss the girls.
I'm my own master, paint now as I please—
Having a friend, you see, in the Corner-house!
Lord, it's fast holding by the rings in front—
Those great rings serve more purposes than just
To plant a flag in, or tie up a horse!   230
And yet the old schooling sticks, the old grave
    eyes
Are peeping o'er my shoulder as I work,
The heads shake still—''It's art's decline, my
    son!
You're not of the true painters, great and old;
Brother Angelico's[16] the man, you'll find;
Brother Lorenzo[17] stands his single peer:
Fag on at flesh, you'll never make the third!''
Flower o' the pine,
You keep your mistr . . . manners, and I'll
    stick to mine!
I'm not the third, then: bless us, they must
    know!   240
Don't you think they're the likeliest to know,
They with their Latin? So, I swallow my rage,
Clench my teeth, suck my lips in tight, and
    paint
To please them—sometimes do and sometimes
    don't;
For, doing most, there's pretty sure to come
A turn, some warm eve finds me at my saints—
A laugh, a cry, the business of the world—
(Flower o' the peach,
Death for us all, and his own life for each!)
And my whole soul revolves, the cup runs
    over,   250
The world and life's too big to pass for a
    dream,
And I do these wild things in sheer despite,

13 Frequently represented so in early paintings,
    e. g., in the "Triumph of Death," ascribed to
    Orcagna, in the Campo Santo of Pisa.
14 Sometimes called "the father of modern Italian
    art": he flourished at the beginning of the
    14th century.
15 It was not Herodias, but her daughter, Salome,
    who danced before Herod and obtained the
    head of John the Baptist. See *Matthew*, 14.

16 Fra Angelico (1387-1415), who painted in the
    earlier manner; famous for his paintings of
    angels. Cp. what Ruskin says, p. 684.
17 Lorenzo Monaco, another contemporary painter.

And play the fooleries you catch me at,
In pure rage! The old mill-horse, out at grass
After hard years, throws up his stiff heels so,
Although the miller does not preach to him
The only good of grass is to make chaff.
What would men have? Do they like grass
or no—
May they or may n't they? all I want's the
thing
Settled forever one way. As it is,   260
You tell too many lies and hurt yourself;
You don't like what you only like too much,
You do like what, if given you at your word,
You find abundantly detestable.
For me, I think I speak as I was taught;
I always see the garden and God there
A-making man's wife: and, my lesson learned,
The value and significance of flesh,
I can't unlearn ten minutes afterwards.

You understand me: I'm a beast, I know. 270
But see, now—why, I see as certainly
As that the morning-star 's about to shine,
What will hap some day. We've a youngster
here
Comes to our convent, studies what I do,
Slouches and stares and lets no atom drop:
His name is Guidi[18]—he 'll not mind the
monks—
They call him Hulking Tom, he lets them talk—
He picks my practice up—he 'll paint apace.
I hope so—though I never live so long,
I know what 's sure to follow. You be
judge!   280
You speak no Latin more than I, belike;
However, you 're my man, you 've seen the
world
—The beauty and the wonder and the power,
The shapes of things, their colours, lights and
shades,
Changes, surprises,—and God made it all!
—For what? Do you feel thankful, ay or no,
For this fair town's face, yonder river's line,
The mountain round it and the sky above,
Much more the figures of man, woman, child,
These are the frame to? What 's it all about? 290
To be passed over, despised? or dwelt upon,
Wondered at? oh, this last of course!—you say.
But why not do as well as say,—paint these
Just as they are, careless what comes of it?
God's works—paint any one, and count it crime
To let a truth slip. Don't object, "His works
Are here already; nature is complete:
Suppose you reproduce her—(which you can't)"

There's no advantage! you must beat her
then.''
For, don't you mark? we 're made so that we
love   300
First when we see them painted, things we have
passed
Perhaps a hundred times nor cared to see;
And so they are better, painted—better to us
Which is the same thing. Art was given for
that;
God uses us to help each other so,
Lending our minds out. Have you noticed,
now,
Your cullion's hanging face? A bit of chalk,
And trust me but you should, though! How
much more,
If I drew higher things with the same truth!
That were to take the Prior's pulpit-place, 310
Interpret God to all of you! Oh, oh,
It makes me mad to see what men shall do
And we in our graves! This world 's no blot
for us,
Nor blank; it means intensely, and means
good:
To find its meaning is my meat and drink.
"Ay, but you don't so instigate to prayer!"
Strikes in the Prior: "when your meaning 's
plain
It does not say to folk—remember matins,
Or, mind you fast next Friday!" Why, for this,
What need of art at all? A skull and bones, 320
Two bits of stick nailed crosswise, or, what's
best,
A bell to chime the hour with, does as well.
I painted a Saint Laurence[19] six months since
At Prato,[20] splashed the fresco in fine style:
"How looks my painting, now the scaffold 's
down?"
I ask a brother: "Hugely," he returns—
"Already not one phiz of your three slaves
Who turn the Deacon off his toasted side,
But 's scratched and prodded to our heart's
content,
The pious people have so eased their own   330
With coming to say prayers there in a rage:
We get on fast to see the bricks beneath.
Expect another job this time next year,
For pity and religion grow i' the crowd—
Your painting serves its purpose!" Hang the
fools!

—That is—you 'll not mistake an idle word
Spoke in a huff by a poor monk, God wot,
Tasting the air this spicy night which turns

18 Tommaso Guidi, better known as Masaccio (i. e.
   Tommasaccio, "Careless Tom"), the great
   pioneer of the Renaissance period, and the
   master of Filippo Lippi, not the pupil.

19 A Christian martyr of the 3d century who was
   roasted alive on a gridiron, or iron chair.
20 A town near Florence.

The unaccustomed head like Chianti[21] wine!
Oh, the church knows! don't misreport me,
    now!
It 's natural a poor monk out of bounds
Should have his apt word to excuse himself:
And harken how I plot to make amends.
I have bethought me: I shall paint a piece
. . . There 's for you![22] Give me six months,
    then go, see
Something in Sant' Ambrogio's![23] Bless the
    nuns!
They want a cast o' my office.[24] I shall paint
God in the midst, Madonna and her babe,
Ringed by a bowery, flowery angel-brood,
Lilies and vestments and white faces, sweet 350
As puff on puff of grated orris-root
When ladies crowd to Church at mid-summer.
And then i' the front, of course a saint or
    two—
Saint John,[25] because he saves the Florentines,
Saint Ambrose, who puts down in black and
    white
The convent's friends and gives them a long
    day,
And Job, I must have him there past mistake,
The man of Uz (and Us without the z,
Painters who need his patience). Well, all
    these
Secured at their devotion, up shall come   360
Out of a corner when you least expect,
As one by a dark stair into a great light,
Music and talking, who but Lippo! I!—
Mazed, motionless, and moonstruck—I'm the
    man!
Back I shrink—what is this I see and hear?
I, caught up with my monk's-things by mistake,
My old serge gown and rope that goes all round,
I, in this presence, this pure company!
Where 's a hole, where 's a corner for escape?
Then steps a sweet angelic slip of a thing   370
Forward, puts out a soft palm—"Not so
    fast!"
—Addresses the celestial presence, "nay—
He made you and devised you, after all,
Though he 's none of you! Could Saint John
    there draw—
His camel-hair[26] make up a painting-brush?
We come to brother Lippo for all that,
Iste perfecit opus!"[27] So, all smile—
I shuffle sideways with my blushing face
Under the cover of a hundred wings

21 A famous vineyard region near Florence.
22 Giving them money.
23 St. Ambrose's, a Florentine convent.
24 A stroke of my skill.
25 The patron saint of Florence.
26 See page 41 (*Matthew*, iii, 4).
27 *Is perfecit opus* ("This is he who made it") is
    the inscription on a scroll in the painting de-
    scribed, indicating the portrait of Lippi.

Thrown like a spread of kirtles when you 're
    gay   380
And play hot cockles, all the doors being shut,
Till, wholly unexpected, in there pops
The hothead husband! Thus I scuttle off
To some safe bench behind, not letting go
The palm of her, the little lily thing
That spoke the good word for me in the nick,
Like the Prior's niece . . . Saint Lucy, I
    would say,
And so all 's saved for me, and for the church
A pretty picture gained. Go, six months hence!
Your hand, sir, and good-by: no lights, no
    lights!   390
The street 's hushed, and I know my own way
    back,
Don't fear me! There 's the gray beginning.
    Zooks!

UP AT A VILLA—DOWN IN THE CITY

(AS DISTINGUISHED BY AN ITALIAN PERSON OF QUALITY)

Had I but plenty of money, money enough and
    to spare,
The house for me, no doubt, were a house in
    the city-square;
Ah, such a life, such a life, as one leads at the
    window there!

Something to see, by Bacchus, something to
    hear, at least!
There, the whole day long, one 's life is a per-
    fect feast;
While up at a villa one lives, I maintain it, no
    more than a beast.

Well now, look at our villa! stuck like the
    horn of a bull
Just on a mountain-edge as bare as the crea-
    ture's skull,
Save a mere shag of a bush with hardly a leaf
    to pull!
—I scratch my own, sometimes, to see if the
    hair 's turned wool.   10

But the city, oh the city—the square with the
    houses! Why,
They are stone-faced, white as a curd, there 's
    something to take the eye!
Houses in four straight lines, not a single front
    awry;
You watch who crosses and gossips, who saun-
    ters, who hurries by;
Green blinds, as a matter of course, to draw
    when the sun gets high;
And the shops with fanciful signs which are
    painted properly.

What of a villa? Though winter be over in
    March by rights,
'T is May perhaps ere the snow shall have
    withered well off the heights:
You 've the brown ploughed land before, where
    the oxen steam and wheeze,
And the hills over-smoked behind by the faint
    gray olive-trees.					20

Is it better in May, I ask you? You 've sum-
    mer all at once;
In a day he leaps complete with a few strong
    April suns.
'Mid the sharp short emerald wheat, scarce
    risen three fingers well,
The wild tulip, at end of its tube, blows out
    its great red bell
Like a thin clear bubble of blood, for the
    children to pick and sell.

Is it ever hot in the square? There 's a
    fountain to spout and splash!
In the shade it sings and springs: in the shine
    such foambows flash
On the horses with curling fish-tails, that
    prance and paddle and pash
Round the lady atop in her conch—fifty gazers
    do not abash,
Though all that she wears is some weeds round
    her waist in a sort of sash.					30

All the year long at the villa, nothing to see
    though you linger,
Except yon cypress that points like death's
    lean lifted forefinger.
Some think fireflies pretty, when they mix i' the
    corn and mingle,
Or thrid the stinking hemp till the stalks of it
    seem a-tingle.
Late August or early September, the stunning
    cicala is shrill,
And the bees keep their tiresome whine round
    the resinous firs on the hill.
Enough of the seasons,—I spare you the months
    of the fever and chill.

Ere you open your eyes in the city, the blessed
    church-bells begin:
No sooner the bells leave off than the diligence
    rattles in:
You get the pick of the news, and it costs you
    never a pin.					40
By and by there 's the travelling doctor gives
    pills, lets blood, draws teeth:
Or the Pulcinello[1]-trumpet breaks up the mar-
    ket beneath.
At the post-office such a scene-picture—the new
    play, piping hot!

[1] English "Punch" (Punch and Judy show).

And a notice how, only this morning, three
    liberal thieves were shot.[2]
Above it, behold the Archbishop 's most fatherly
    of rebukes,
And beneath, with his crown and his lion, some
    little new law of the Duke 's!
Or a sonnet with flowery marge, to the Rev-
    erend Don So-and-so,
Who is Dante, Boccaccio, Petrarca, Saint
    Jerome, and Cicero.
"And moreover," (the sonnet goes rhyming,)
    "the skirts of Saint Paul has reached,
Having preached us those six Lent-lectures
    more unctuous than ever he preached." 50
Noon strikes,—here sweeps the procession! our
    Lady borne smiling and smart
With a pink gauze gown all spangles, and
    seven swords stuck in her heart!
Bang-whang-whang goes the drum, *tootle-te-*
    tootle the fife;
No keeping one 's haunches still: it 's the great-
    est pleasure in life.

But bless you, it 's dear—it 's dear! fowls,
    wine, at double the rate.
They have clapped a new tax upon salt, and
    what oil pays passing the gate
It 's a horror to think of. And so, the villa
    for me, not the city!

Beggars can scarcely be choosers: but still—
    ah, the pity, the pity!
Look, two and two go the priests, then the
    monks with cowls and sandals.
And the penitents dressed in white shirts,
    a-holding the yellow candles;					60
One, he carries a flag up straight, and another
    a cross with handles,
And the Duke 's guard brings up the rear, for
    the better prevention of scandals:
Bang-whang-whang goes the drum, *tootle-te-*
    tootle the fife.
Oh, a day in the city-square, there is no such
    pleasure in life!

MEMORABILIA*

Ah, did you once see Shelley plain,
    And did he stop and speak to you,
And did you speak to him again?
    How strange it seems and new!

[2] There is subtle irony in making this soulless
civilian betray his childish contempt for the
liberal or republican party.

* Once, in a bookstore, Browning overheard some
one mention the fact that he had once seen
Shelley. Browning was a youthful admirer
of Shelley; having received from certain volumes of him and Keats—a chance-found
"eagle-feather," as it were,—some of his
earliest inspiration. On Keats, see the next
poem.

But you were living before that,
　　And also you are living after;
And the memory I started at—
　　My starting moves your laughter!

I crossed a moor, with a name of its own
　　And a certain use in the world no doubt,
Yet a hand's breadth of it shines alone
　　'Mid the blank miles round about:

For there I picked up on the heather
　　And there I put inside my breast
A moulted feather, an eagle-feather!
　　Well, I forget the rest.

POPULARITY

Stand still, true poet that you are! †
　　I know you; let me try and draw you.
Some night you'll fail us; when afar
　　You rise, remember one man saw you,
Knew you, and named a star!

My star, God's glow-worm! Why extend
　　That loving hand of his which leads you,
Yet locks you safe from end to end
　　Of this dark world, unless he needs you,
Just saves your light to spend?　　　　　10

His clenched hand shall unclose at last,
　　I know, and let out all the beauty:
My poet holds the future fast,
　　Accepts the coming ages' duty,
Their present for this past.

That day the earth's feast-master's brow
　　Shall clear, to God the chalice raising;
"Others give best at first, but thou
　　Forever set'st our table praising,
Keep'st the good wine till now!"　　　　20

Meantime, I'll draw you as you stand,
　　With few or none to watch and wonder:
I'll say—a fisher, on the sand
　　By Tyre the old, with ocean-plunder,
A netful, brought to land.

Who has not heard how Tyrian shells
　　Enclosed the blue, that dye of dyes

Whereof one drop worked miracles,
　　And coloured like Astarte's[1] eyes
Raw silk the merchant sells?　　　　　30

And each bystander of them all
　　Could criticise, and quote tradition
How depths of blue sublimed some pall[2]
　　—To get which, pricked a king's ambition;
Worth sceptre, crown and ball.[3]

Yet there's the dye, in that rough mesh,
　　The sea has only just o'er-whispered!
Live whelks, each lip's beard dripping fresh,
　　As if they still the water's lisp heard
Through foam the rock-weeds thresh.　　40

Enough to furnish Solomon
　　Such hangings for his cedar-house,
That, when gold-robed he took the throne
　　In that abyss of blue, the Spouse[4]
Might swear his presence shone.

Most like the centre-spike of gold
　　Which burns deep in the bluebell's womb
What time, with ardours manifold,
　　The bee goes singing to her groom,
Drunken and overbold.　　　　　　　50

Mere conchs! not fit for warp or woof!
　　Till cunning come to pound and squeeze
And clarify,—refine to proof
　　The liquor filtered by degrees,
While the world stands aloof.

And there's the extract, flasked and fine,
　　And priced and salable at last!
And Hobbs, Nobbs, Stokes and Nokes combine
　　To paint the future from the past,
Put blue into their line.[5]　　　　　60

Hobbs hints blue,—straight he turtle eats:
　　Nobbs prints blue,—claret crowns his cup:
Nokes outdares Stokes in azure feats,—
　　Both gorge. Who fished the murex up?
What porridge had John Keats?

THE PATRIOT*

AN OLD STORY.

It was roses, roses, all the way,
　　With myrtle mixed in my path like mad:
The house-roofs seemed to heave and sway,
　　The church-spires flamed, such flags they had,
A year ago on this very day.

† This poet is not necessarily Keats, but Keats
is a type of the great man who, missing
popularity in his own life, dies obscurely—
like the ancient obscure discoverer of the
murex, the fish whose precious purple dyes
made the fortune of many a mere trader or
artisan who came after him. (Without in-
timating for a moment that Tennyson was a
mere artisan, it may be freely acknowledged
that much of his popularity, in which at this
time, 1855, he quite exceeded Browning, was
due to qualities which he derived from Keats.)

[1] The Syrian Aphrodite.
[2] coronation robe
[3] The golden orb borne with the sceptre as em-
　　blem of sovereignty.
[4] *The Song of Solomon*, v, i.
[5] I. e., aspire to the aristocracy.
* The poem is purely dramatic, not historical.

The air broke into a mist with bells,
  The old walls rocked with the crowd and
    cries.
Had I said, "Good folk, mere noise repels—
  But give me your sun from yonder skies!"
They had answered, "And afterward, what
  else?"   10

Alack, it was I who leaped at the sun
  To give it my loving friends to keep!
Naught man could do, have I left undone:
  And you see my harvest, what I reap
This very day, now a year is run.

There's nobody on the house-tops now—
  Just a palsied few at the windows set;
For the best of the sight is, all allow,
  At the Shambles' Gate—or, better yet,
By the very scaffold's foot, I trow.   20

I go in the rain, and, more than needs,
  A rope cuts both my wrists behind;
And I think, by the feel, my forehead bleeds,
  For they fling, whoever has a mind,
Stones at me for my year's misdeeds.

Thus I entered, and thus I go!
  In triumphs, people have dropped down dead.
"Paid by the world, what dost thou owe
  Me?"—God might question; now instead,
'T is God shall repay: I am safer so.   30

"CHILDE ROLAND TO THE DARK
TOWER CAME"*

My first thought was, he lied in every word,
  That hoary cripple, with malicious eye
  Askance to watch the working of his lie
On mine, and mouth scarce able to afford
Suppression of the glee, that pursed and scored
  Its edge, at one more victim gained thereby.

What else should he be set for, with his staff?
  What, save to waylay with his lies, ensnare
  All travellers who might find him posted
    there,
And ask the road? I guessed what skull-like
  laugh   10
Would break, what crutch 'gin write my
  epitaph
  For pastime in the dusty thoroughfare,

* The title is a line of Edgar's song, *King Lear*,
III, iv, 187. "Childe" is an old title for a
youth of noble birth. There has been much
discussion over the question whether the
knight's pilgrimage, which is here so vividly
and yet so mystically portrayed, is allegorical
or not. Doubtless there is no elaborate allegory in it, though there may well be a
moral—something like constancy to an ideal,
Browning admitted.

If at his counsel I should turn aside
  Into that ominous tract which, all agree,
  Hides the Dark Tower. Yet acquiescingly
I did turn as he pointed: neither pride
Nor hope rekindling at the end descried,
  So much as gladness that some end might be.

For, what with my whole world-wide wandering,
  What with my search drawn out through
    years, my hope   20
  Dwindled into a ghost not fit to cope
With that obstreperous joy success would
  bring,—
I hardly tried now to rebuke the spring
  My heart made, finding failure in its scope.

As when a sick man very near to death
  Seems dead indeed, and feels begin and end
The tears, and takes the farewell of each friend,
And hears one bid the other go, draw breath
Freelier outside, ("since all is o'er," he saith,
  "And the blow fallen no grieving can
    amend;")   30

While some discuss if near the other graves
  Be room enough for this, and when a day
  Suits best for carrying the corpse away,
With care about the banners, scarves and
  staves:
And still the man hears all, and only craves
  He may not shame such tender love and stay.

Thus, I had so long suffered in this quest,
  Heard failure prophesied so oft, been writ
  So many times among "The Band"—to wit,
The knights who to the Dark Tower's search
  addressed   40
Their steps—that just to fail as they, seemed
  best,
  And all the doubt was now—should I be fit?

So, quiet as despair, I turned from him,
  That hateful cripple, out of his highway
  Into the path he pointed. All the day
Had been a dreary one at best, and dim
Was settling to its close, yet shot one grim
  Red leer to see the plain catch its estray.

For mark! no sooner was I fairly found
  Pledged to the plain, after a pace or two, 50
  Than, pausing to throw backward a last view
O'er the safe road, 't was gone; gray plain
  all round:
Nothing but plain to the horizon's bound.
  I might go on; naught else remained to do.

So, on I went. I think I never saw
  Such starved ignoble nature; nothing throve:
  For flowers—as well expect a cedar grove!

t cockle, spurge, according to their law
ght propagate their kind, with none to awe,
You'd think: a burr had been a treasure
trove.   60

! penury, inertness and grimace,
In some strange sort, were the land's portion.
   "See
Or shut your eyes," said Nature peevishly,
t nothing skills:1 I cannot help my case:
is the Last Judgment's fire must cure this
    place,
Calcine its clods and set my prisoners free."

there pushed any ragged thistle-stalk
Above its mates, the head was chopped; the
    bents2
Were jealous else. What made those holes
    and rents
the dock's harsh swarth leaves, bruised as
    to balk   70
hope of greenness? 't is a brute must walk
Pashing their life out, with a brute's intents.

for the grass, it grew as scant as hair ·
In leprosy; thin dry blades pricked the mud
Which underneath looked kneaded up with
    blood.
e stiff blind horse, his every bone a-stare,
ood stupefied, however he came there:
Thrust out past service from the devil's stud!

ive? he might be dead for aught I know,
With that red gaunt and colloped3 neck
    a-strain,   80
And shut eyes underneath the rusty mane;
dom went such grotesqueness with such woe;
never saw a brute I hated so!
He must be wicked to deserve such pain.

shut my eyes and turned them on my heart.
As a man calls for wine before he fights,
I asked one draught of earlier, happier sights,
e fitly I could hope to play my part.
ink first, fight afterwards—the soldier's art:
One taste of the old time sets all to rights.

t it! I fancied Cuthbert's reddening face 91
Beneath its garniture of curly gold,
Dear fellow, till I almost felt him fold
a arm in mine to fix me to the place,
at way he used. Alas, one night's disgrace!
Out went my heart's new fire and left it cold.

les then, the soul of honour—there he stands
Frank as ten years ago when knighted first.

vails nothing   2 grass stalks
dged

What honest man should dare (he said) he
    durst.
Good—but the scene shifts—faugh! what hang-
    man hands   100
Pin to his breast a parchment? His own bands
Read it. Poor traitor, spit upon and curst!

Better this present than a past like that;
Back therefore to my darkening path again!
No sound, no sight as far as eye could strain.
Will the night send a howlet or a bat?
I asked: when something on the dismal flat
Came to arrest my thoughts and change their
    train.

A sudden little river crossed my path
As unexpected as a serpent comes.   110
No sluggish tide congenial to the glooms;
This, as it frothed by, might have been a bath
For the fiend's glowing hoof—to see the wrath
Of its black eddy bespate* with flakes and
    spumes.

So petty, yet so spiteful! All along,
Low scrubby alders kneeled down over it;
Drenched willows flung them headlong in a fit
Of mute despair, a suicidal throng:
The river which had done them all the wrong,
Whate'er that was, rolled by, deterred no
    whit.   120

Which, while I forded,—good saints, how I
    feared
To set my foot upon a dead man's cheek,
Each step, or feel the spear I thrust to seek
For hollows, tangled in his hair or beard!
—It may have been a water-rat I speared,
But, ugh, it sounded like a baby's shriek.

Glad was I when I reached the other bank.
Now for a better country. Vain presage!
Who were the strugglers, what war did they
    wage,
Whose savage trample thus could pad the dank
Soil to a plash? Toads in a poisoned tank, 131
Or wild-cats in a red-hot iron cage—

The fight must so have seemed in that fell
    cirque.
What penned them there, with all the plain to
    choose?
No footprint leading to that horrid mews,
None out of it. Mad brewage set to work
Their brains, no doubt, like galley-slaves the
    Turk

* That is, bespit, bespattered: from the archaic *bespete*. The rather unusual diction employed throughout the poem helps to heighten its grotesque character.

Pits for his pastime, Christians against Jews.

And more than that—a furlong on—why, there!
  What bad use was that engine for, that wheel,   140
  Or brake, not wheel—that harrow fit to reel
Men's bodies out like silk? with all the air
Of Tophet's¹ tool, on earth left unaware.
  Or brought to sharpen its rusty teeth of steel.

Then came a bit of stubbed ground, once a wood,
  Next a marsh, it would seem, and now mere earth
  Desperate and done with: (so a fool finds mirth,
Makes a thing and then mars it, till his mood
Changes and off he goes!) within a rood—
  Bog, clay and rubble, sand and stark black dearth.   150

Now blotches rankling, coloured gay and grim,
  Now patches where some leanness of the soil's
  Broke into moss or substances like boils;
Then came some palsied oak, a cleft in him
Like a distorted mouth that splits its rim
  Gaping at death, and dies while it recoils.

And just as far as ever from the end!
  Naught in the distance but the evening, naught
  To point my footstep further! At the thought,
A great black bird, Apollyon's² bosom-friend,
Sailed past, nor beat his wide wing dragon-penned³   161
  That brushed my cap—perchance the guide I sought.

For, looking up, aware I somehow grew,
  'Spite of the dusk, the plain had given place
  All round to mountains—with such name to grace
Mere ugly heights and heaps now stolen in view.
How thus they had surprised me,—solve it, you!
  How to get from them was no clearer case.

Yet half I seemed to recognize some trick
  Of mischief happened to me, God knows when—   170
In a bad dream perhaps. Here ended, then,
Progress this way. When, in the very nick
Of giving up, one time more, came a click
  As when a trap shuts—you're inside the den!

¹ hell's   ² Satan's
³ with pinions like a dragon's

Burningly it came on me all at once,
  This was the place! those two hills on right,
  Crouched like two bulls locked horn in h[orn] in fight;
While to the left, a tall scalped mountain . . .
  Dunce,
Dotard, a-dozing at the very nonce,⁴
  After a life spent training for the sight!

What in the midst lay but the Tower itself
  The round squat turret, blind as the fo[ol's] heart,
  Built of brown stone, without a counterp[art]
In the whole world. The tempest's mocking [elf]
Points to the shipman thus the unseen she[lf]
  He strikes on, only when the timbers star[t]

Not see? because of night perhaps?—why,
  Came back again for that! before it left
  The dying sunset kindled through a cleft
The hills, like giants at a hunting, lay,
Chin upon hand, to see the game at bay,—
  "Now stab and end the creature—to heft!"

Not hear? when noise was everywhere! it tol[led]
  Increasing like a bell. Names in my ears,
  Of all the lost adventurers my peers,—
How such a one was strong, and such was b[old,]
And such was fortunate, yet each of old
  Lost, lost! one moment knelled the woe years.

There they stood, ranged along the hillsi[de,] met
  To view the last of me, a living frame
  For one more picture! in a sheet of flame
I saw them and I knew them all. And yet
Dauntless the slug-horn⁵ to my lips I set,
  And blew: "*Childe Roland to the D[ark] Tower came.*"

RABBI BEN EZRA*

Grow old along with me!
The best is yet to be,
The last of life, for which the first was ma[de:]
Our times are in his hand

⁴ critical moment
⁵ Not properly the name of a horn, if the w[ord]
  is a corruption of "slogan." It was t[hus]
  misused by Chatterton frequently, and Bro[wn-]
  ing may have obtained it from that source[.]
* There was a certain Rabbi, Ben Ezra (or Ab[en]
  ezra, or Ibn Ezra), who was a great scho[lar]
  and theologian of the twelfth century. [He]
  was born at Toledo and traveled wide[ly]
  dwelling at Rome, London, Palestine, and el[se-]
  where. Browning here makes him the mou[th-]
  piece of a noble philosophy.

o saith, "A whole I planned,
uth shows but half: trust God: see all, nor
  be afraid!"

t that, amassing flowers,
uth sighed, "Which rose make ours,
nich lily leave and then as best recall?"
t that, admiring stars,   10
yearned, "Nor Jove, nor Mars;
ne be some figured flame which blends,
  transcends them all!"

t for such hopes and fears†
nnulling youth's brief years,
 I remonstrate: folly wide the mark!
ther I prize the doubt‡
w kinds exist without,
nished and finite clods, untroubled by a spark.

or vaunt of life indeed,
ere man but formed to feed   20
 joy, to solely seek and find and feast:
ch feasting ended, then
 sure an end to men:
ks care[1] the crop-full bird? Frets doubt the
  maw-crammed beast?

joice we are allied
 that which doth provide
nd not partake, effect and not receive!
 spark disturbs our clod;
earer we hold of God
ho gives, than of his tribes that take, I must
  believe.   30

en, welcome each rebuff
hat turns earth's smoothness rough,
ach sting that bids nor sit nor stand but go!
e our joys three-parts pain!
rive, and hold cheap the strain;
earn, nor account the pang; dare, never
  grudge the throe!

or thence,—a paradox
hich comforts while it mocks,—
hall life succeed in that it seems to fail:
hat I aspired to be,   40
nd was not, comforts me:
 brute I might have been, but would not sink
  i' the scale.

hat is he but a brute
hose flesh has soul to suit,

Subject of "irks."
I. e., such as those just mentioned, which seem
  to make youth ineffectual.
Supply "that." This is exactly the thought
  which Tennyson had already expressed in *In
  Memoriam*, XXVII.

Whose spirit works lest arms and legs want
  play?
To man, propose this test—
Thy body at its best,
How far can that project thy soul on its lone
  way?

Yet gifts should prove their use:
I own the Past profuse   50
Of power each side, perfection every turn:
Eyes, ears took in their dole,
Brain treasured up the whole;
Should not the heart beat once "How good to
  live and learn"?

Not once beat "Praise be thine!
I see the whole design,
I, who saw power, see now Love perfect too;
Perfect I call thy plan:
Thanks that I was a man!
Maker, remake, complete,—I trust what thou
  shalt do!"   60

For pleasant is this flesh;
Our soul, in its rose-mesh
Pulled ever to the earth, still yearns for rest:
Would we some prize might hold
To match those manifold
Possessions of the brute,—gain most, as we did
  best!

Let us not always say,
"Spite of this flesh to-day
I strove, made head, gained ground upon the
  whole!"
As the bird wings and sings,   70
Let us cry, "All good things
Are ours, nor soul helps flesh more, now, than
  flesh helps soul!"

Therefore I summon age
To grant youth's heritage,
Life's struggle having so far reached its term:
Thence shall I pass, approved
A man, for aye removed
From the developed brute; a God though in the
  germ.

And I shall thereupon
Take rest, ere I be gone   80
Once more on my adventure brave and new:
Fearless and unperplexed,
When I wage battle next,
What weapons to select, what armour to indue.[1]

Youth ended, I shall try
My gain or loss thereby;

1 put on

Leave the fire ashes, what survives is gold:
And I shall weigh the same,
Give life its praise or blame:
Young, all lay in dispute; I shall know, being
    old.   90

For note, when evening shuts,
A certain moment cuts
The deed off, calls the glory from the gray:
A whisper from the west
Shoots—''Add this to the rest,
Take it and try its worth: here dies another
    day.''

So, still within this life,
Though lifted o'er its strife,
Let me discern, compare, pronounce at last,
''This rage was right i' the main,   100
That acquiescence vain:
The Future I may face now I have proved the
    Past.''

For more is not reserved
To man, with soul just nerved
To act to-morrow what he learns to-day:
Here, work enough to watch
The Master work, and catch
Hints of the proper craft, tricks of the tool's
    true play.

As it was better, youth
Should strive, through acts uncouth,   110
Toward making, than repose on aught found
    made:
So, better, age, exempt
From strife, should know, than tempt
Further. Thou waitedst age: wait death nor
    be afraid!

Enough now, if the Right
And Good and Infinite
Be named here, as thou callest thy hand thine
    own,
With knowledge absolute,
Subject to no dispute
From fools that crowded youth, nor let thee
    feel alone.   120

Be there, for once and all,
Severed great minds from small,
Announced to each his station in the Past!
Was I,[2] the world arraigned,
Were they,[2] my soul disdained,
Right? Let age speak the truth and give us
    peace at last!

[2] Supply "whom."

Now, who shall arbitrate?
Ten men love what I hate,
Shun what I follow, slight what I receive;
Ten, who in ears and eyes   1
Match me; we all surmise,
They this thing, and I that: whom shall m
    soul believe?

Not on the vulgar mass
Called ''work'' must sentence pass,
Things done, that took the eye and had t
    price;
O'er which, from level stand,
The low world laid its hand,
Found straightway to its mind, could value
    a trice:

But all, the world's coarse thumb
And finger failed to plumb,   1
So passed in making up the main account;
All instincts immature,
All purposes unsure,
That weighed not as his work, yet swelled t
    man's amount:

Thoughts hardly to be packed
Into a narrow act,
Fancies that broke through language a
    escaped;
All I could never be,
All, men ignored in me,
This, I was worth to God, whose wheel t
    pitcher shaped.   1

Ay, note that Potter's wheel,
That metaphor! and feel
Why time spins fast, why passive lies o
    clay,—
Thou, to whom fools propound,
When the wine makes its round,
''Since life fleets, all is change; the Past gor
    seize to-day!''*

Fool! All that is, at all,
Lasts ever, past recall;
Earth changes, but thy soul and God sta
    sure:
What entered into thee,   1
That was, is, and shall be:
Time's wheel runs back or stops: Potter a
    clay endure.

He fixed thee 'mid this dance
Of plastic[3] circumstance,

[3] shaping
* Both the figure and the philosophy here obviou
    ly suggest Omar Khayyam, though both a
    very much older.

This Present, thou, forsooth, would fain arrest:
Machinery just meant
To give thy soul its bent,
Try thee and turn thee forth, sufficiently
    impressed.[4]

What though the earlier grooves,
Which ran the laughing loves   170
Around thy base, no longer pause and press?
What though, about thy rim,
Skull-things in order grim
Grow out, in graver mood, obey the sterner
    stress?

Look not thou down but up!
To uses of a cup,
The festal board, lamp's flash and trumpet's
    peal,
The new wine's foaming flow,
The Master's lips aglow!
Thou, heaven's consummate cup, what needst
    thou with earth's wheel?   180

But I need, now as then,
Thee, God, who mouldest men;
And since, not even while the whirl was worst,
Did I—to the wheel of life
With shapes and colours rife,
Bound dizzily—mistake my end, to slake thy
    thirst:

So, take and use thy work:
Amend what flaws may lurk,
What strain o' the stuff, what warpings past
    the aim!
My times be in thy hand!   190
Perfect the cup as planned!
Let age approve of youth, and death complete
    the same!

PROSPICE*

Fear death?—to feel the fog in my throat,
    The mist in my face,
When the snows begin, and the blasts denote
    I am nearing the place,
The power of the night, the press of the storm,
    The post of the foe;
Where he stands, the Arch Fear in a visible
    form,
    Yet the strong man must go:
For the journey is done and the summit
    attained,
    And the barriers fall,   10

4 moulded and figured
* This poem was written in 1861, shortly after
    Mrs. Browning's death. The title means
    "Look forward."

Though a battle's to fight ere the guerdon be
    gained,
    The reward of it all.
I was ever a fighter, so—one fight more,
    The best and the last!
I would hate that death bandaged my eyes, and
    forbore,
    And bade me creep past.
No! let me taste the whole of it, fare like my
    peers
    The heroes of old,
Bear the brunt, in a minute pay glad life's
    arrears
    Of pain, darkness and cold.   20
For sudden the worst turns the best to the
    brave,
    The black minute's at end,
And the elements' rage, the fiend-voices that
    rave,
    Shall dwindle, shall blend,
Shall change, shall become first a peace out of
    pain,
    Then a light, then thy breast,
O thou soul of my soul! I shall clasp thee
    again,
    And with God be the rest!

HERVÉ RIEL†

I

On the sea and at the Hogue, sixteen hundred
    ninety-two,
    Did the English fight the French,—woe to
    France!
And, the thirty-first of May, helter-skelter
    through the blue,
Like a crowd of frightened porpoises[1] a shoal
    of sharks pursue,
    Came crowding ship on ship to Saint Malo
    on the Rance,
With the English fleet in view.

II

'T was the squadron that escaped, with the vic-
    tor in full chase;
    First and foremost of the drove, in his great
    ship, Damfreville;
Close on him fled, great and small,
Twenty-two good ships in all;   10
And they signalled to the place
"Help the winners of a race!

1 Supply "which."
† The victory of La Hogue was won off the north
    coast of Normandy by the British and Dutch
    Allies against Louis XIV. Hervé Riel, a Bre-
    ton sailor from the village of Croisic, saved
    many of the fleeing French vessels by pilot-
    ing them through the shallows at the mouth
    of the river Rance to the roadstead at St.
    Malo.

Get us guidance, give us harbour, take us
    quick—or, quicker still,
Here 's the English can and will!"

III

Then the pilots of the place put out brisk and
    leapt on board;
"Why what hope or chance have ships like
    these to pass?" laughed they:
"Rocks to starboard, rocks to port, all the
    passage scarred and scored,
Shall the 'Formidable' here with her twelve
    and eighty guns
    Think to make the river-mouth by the single
    narrow way,
Trust to enter where 't is ticklish for a craft
    of twenty tons,   20
And with flow at full beside?
Now, 't is slackest ebb of tide.
    Reach the mooring? Rather say,
While rock stands or water runs,
    Not a ship will leave the bay!"

IV

Then was called a council straight.
Brief and bitter the debate:
"Here's the English at our heels; would you
    have them take in tow
All that 's left us of the fleet, linked together
    stern and bow,
For a prize to Plymouth Sound?   30
Better run the ships aground!"
    (Ended Damfreville his speech).
"Not a minute more to wait!
    Let the Captains all and each
Shove ashore, then blow up, burn the vessels
    on the beach!
France must undergo her fate.

V

"Give the word!" But no such word
Was ever spoke or heard
For up stood, for out stepped, for in struck
    amid all these
—A Captain? A Lieutenant? A Mate—first,
    second, third?   40
No such man of mark, and meet
With his betters to compete!
But a simple Breton sailor pressed by Tourville
    for the fleet,
A poor coasting pilot he, Hervé Riel the Croi-
    sickese.

VI

And "What mockery or malice have we here?"
    cries Hervé Riel:
"Are you mad, you Malouins? Are you cow-
    ards, fools, or rogues?
Talk to me of rocks and shoals, me who took
    the soundings, tell

On my fingers every bank, every shallow, ever
    swell,
    'Twixt the offing here and Grève where th
    river disembogues?
Are you bought by English gold? Is it lov
    the lying's for?   5
Morn and eve, night and day,
Have I piloted your bay,
Entered free and anchored fast at the foot o
    Solidor.
    Burn the fleet and ruin France? That wer
    worse than fifty Hogues!
Sirs, they know I speak the truth! Sirs, believ
    me there 's a way!
Only let me lead the line,
    Have the biggest ship to steer,
    Get this 'Formidable' clear,
Make the others follow mine.
And I lead them, most and least, by a passag
    I know well,
    Right to Solidor past Grève,
And there lay them safe and sound:
And if one ship misbehave,
—Keel so much as grate the ground,
Why I've nothing but my life,—here 's m
    head!" cries Hervé Riel.

VII

Not a minute more to wait.
"Steer us in, then, small and great!
    Take the helm, lead the line, save th
    squadron!" cried its chief.
Captains, give the sailor place!
He is Admiral, in brief.
Still the north-wind, by God's grace!
See the noble fellow's face
As the big ship, with a bound,
Clears the entry like a hound,
Keeps the passage as its inch of way were th
    wide sea's profound!
    See, safe through shoal and rock,
    How they follow in a flock,
Not a ship that misbehaves, not a keel tha
    grates the ground,
    Not a spar that comes to grief!
The peril, see, is past,
All are harboured to the last,
And just as Hervé Riel hollas "Anchor!"—
    sure as fate,
Up the English come—too late!

VIII

So, the storm subsides to calm:
    They see the green trees wave
    On the heights o'erlooking Grève.
Hearts that bled are stanched with balm.
"Just our rapture to enhance,
    Let the English rake the bay,

ᵃash their teeth and glare askance   90
  As they cannonade away!
ᵀeath rampired Solidor pleasant riding on the
    Rance!''
ᵒw hope succeeds despair on each Captain's
    countenance!
ᵘt burst all with one accord,
  "This is Paradise for Hell!
ᵉt France, let France's King
  ᵗhank the man that did ᵗhe thing!''
ᵂhat a shout, and all one word,
  "Hervé Riel!''
ˢ he stepped in front once more,   100
  Not a symptom of surprise
  In the frank blue Breton eyes,
ᵘst the same man as before.

                IX

ᵗhen said Damfreville, "My friend,
  ᴵ must speak out at the end,
  Though I find the speaking hard.
ᵖraise is deeper than the lips:
  ᵒu have saved the King his ships,
  You must name your own reward.
ᶠaith, our sun was near eclipse!   110
ᵈemand whate'er you will,
ᶠrance remains your debtor still.
ˢk to heart's content and have! or my name's
    not Damfreville.''

                X

ᵗhen a beam of fun outbroke
ᵒn the bearded mouth that spoke,
ˢ the honest heart laughed through
ᵗhose frank eyes of Breton blue:
  Since I needs must say my say,
  Since on board the duty 's done,
  And from Malo Roads to Croisic Point, what
    is it but a run?—   120
ᶤnce 't is ask and have, I may—
  Since the others go ashore—
ᵒme! A good whole holiday!
  Leave to go and see my wife, whom I call
    the Belle Aurore!''
  That he asked and that he got,—nothing
    more.

                XI

ᵃme and deed alike are lost:
ᵒt a pillar nor a post
  In his Croisic keeps alive the feat as it be-
    fell;
ᵒt a head in white and black
ᵒn a single fishing-smack,   130
ᵃ memory of the man but for whom had gone
    to wrack
  All that France saved from the **fight whence**
    England bore the bell.[1]

ʰad the victory

Go to Paris: rank on rank
  Search the heroes flung pell-mell
On the Louvre,[1] face and flankᵢ
  You shall look long enough ere you come to
    Hervé Riel.
So, for better and for worse,
Hervé Riel, accept my verse!
In my verse, Hervé Riel, do thou once more
Save the squadron, honour France, love thy
    wife, the Belle Aurore!   140

WANTING IS—WHAT?

  Wanting is—what?
  Summer redundant,
  Blueness abundant,
  —Where is the blot?
Beamy the world, yet a blank all the same,
  —Framework which waits for a picture to
    frame:
What of the leafage, what of the flower?
Roses embowering with naught they embower!
Come then, complete incompletion, O comer,
Pant through the blueness, perfect the summer!
  Breathe but one breath
  Rose-beauty above,
  And all that was death
  Grows life, grows love,
  Grows love!

WHY I AM A LIBERAL

"Why?'' Because all I haply can and do,
All that I am now, all I hope to be,—
Whence comes it save from fortune setting free
Body and soul the purpose to pursue,
God traced for both? If fetters not a few,
Of prejudice, convention, fall from me,
These shall I bid men—each in his degree
Also God-guided—bear, and gayly, too?

But little do or can the best of us:
That little is achieved through Liberty.
Who, then, dares hold, emancipated thus,
His fellow shall continue bound? Not I,
Who live, love, labour freely, nor discuss
A brother's right to freedom. That is "Why.''

EPILOGUE*

At the midnight in the silence of the sleep-time,
  When you set your fancies free,
Will they pass to where—by death, fools think,
  imprisoned—

[1] An ancient royal palace, now mainly an art-
  gallery, adorned with the statues of eminent
  Frenchmen.
* This is the Epilogue to *Asolando*, which was
  published at London on the day when Browning died at Venice.

Low he lies who once so loved you, whom you
    loved so,
      —Pity me?

Oh to love so, be so loved, yet so mistaken!
    What had I on earth to do
With the slothful, with the mawkish, the un-
    manly?
Like the aimless, helpless, hopeless, did I drivel
      —Being—who?

One who never turned his back but marched
    breast forward,
    Never doubted clouds would break,
Never dreamed, though right were worsted,
    wrong would triumph,
Held we fall to rise, are baffled to fight better,
    Sleep to wake.

No, at noonday in the bustle of man's work-
    time
    Greet the unseen with a cheer!
Bid him forward, breast and back as either
    should be,
"Strive and thrive!" cry "Speed,—fight on,
    fare ever
      There as here!"

ELIZABETH BARRETT BROWN-ING (1809-1861)

SONNETS FROM THE PORTUGUESE*

I

I thought once how Theocritus had sung[1]
Of the sweet years, the dear and wished-for
    years,
Who each one in a gracious hand appears
To bear a gift for mortals, old or young:
And, as I mused it in his antique tongue,
I saw, in gradual vision through my tears,
The sweet, sad years, the melancholy years,
Those of my own life, who by turns had flung
A shadow across me. Straightway I was 'ware,

[1] *Idyls,* xv, 104.

* These Sonnets, forty-four in number, were
written by Miss Barrett during the time of
Mr. Browning's courtship, but were not shown
to him until after their marriage in 1846.
The title under which they were published
(1850) was adopted as a disguise. To understand them aright, it must be remembered
that Miss Barrett was in middle life and
had long been an invalid. See *Eng. Lit.,* p.
307. F. G. Kenyon, in his edition of Mrs.
Browning's *Letters,* writes: "With the single exception of Rossetti, no modern English
poet has written of love with such genius,
such beauty, and such sincerity, as the two
who gave the most beautiful example of it in
their own lives."

So weeping, how a mystic Shape did move
Behind me, and drew me backward by the hair
And a voice said in mastery, while I strove,—
"Guess now who holds thee?"—"Death," I
    said. But, there,
The silver answer rang,—"Not Death, but
    Love."

III

Unlike are we, unlike, O princely Heart!
Unlike our uses and our destinies.
Our ministering two angels look surprise
On one another, as they strike athwart
Their wings in passing. Thou, bethink thee, art
A guest for queens to social pageantries,
With gages from a hundred brighter eyes
Than tears even can make mine, to play thy
    part
Of chief musician. What hast *thou* to do
With looking from the lattice-lights at me,
A poor, tired, wandering singer, singing through
The dark, and leaning up a cypress tree?
The chrism[2] is on thine head,—on mine, the
    dew,—
And Death must dig the level where these agree.

IV

Thou hast thy calling to some palace-floor,
Most gracious singer of high poems! where
The dancers will break footing, from the care
Of watching up thy pregnant lips for more.
And dost thou lift this house's latch too poor
For hand of thine? and canst thou think and
    bear
To let thy music drop here unaware
In folds of golden fulness at my door?
Look up and see the casement broken in,
The bats and owlets builders in the roof!
My cricket chirps against thy mandolin.
Hush, call no echo up in further proof
Of desolation! there's a voice within
That weeps—as thou must sing—alone, aloof.

XIV

If thou must love me, let it be for nought
Except for love's sake only. Do not say
"I love her for her smile—her look—her way
Of speaking gently,—for a trick of thought
That falls in well with mine, and certes brought
A sense of pleasant ease on such a day"—
For these things in themselves, Belovèd, may
Be changed, or change for thee,—and love, so
    wrought,
May be unwrought so. Neither love me for
Thine own dear pity's wiping my cheeks dry,
A creature might forget to weep, who bore
Thy comfort long, and lose thy love thereby!

[2] The sacred ointment; here figurative for poetic
consecration.

But love me for love's sake, that evermore
Thou may'st love on, through love's eternity.

XXII

When our two souls stand up erect and strong,
Face to face, silent, drawing nigh and nigher,
Until the lengthening wings break into fire
At either curvèd point,—what bitter wrong
Can the earth do to us, that we should not long
Be here contented? Think. In mounting
    higher,
The angels would press on us and aspire
To drop some golden orb of perfect song
Into our deep, dear silence. Let us stay
Rather on earth, Belovèd,—where the unfit
Contrarious moods of men recoil away
And isolate pure spirits, and permit
A place to stand and love in for a day,
With darkness and the death-hour rounding it.

XLIII

How do I love thee? Let me count the ways.
I love thee to the depth and breadth and height
My soul can reach, when feeling out of sight
For the ends of Being and ideal Grace.
I love thee to the level of everyday's
Most quiet need, by sun and candle-light.
I love thee freely, as men strive for Right;
I love thee purely, as they turn from Praise.
I love thee with the passion put to use
In my old griefs, and with my childhood's
    faith.
I love thee with a love I seemed to lose
With my lost saints,—I love thee with the
    breath,
Smiles, tears, of all my life!—and, if God
    choose,
I shall but love thee better after death.

EDWARD FITZGERALD
(1809-1883)

RUBÁIYÁT OF OMAR KHAYYÁM*

I

Wake! For the Sun, who scatter'd into flight
The Stars before him from the Field of Night,
    Drives Night along with them from Heav'n,
      and strikes
The Sultán's Turret with a Shaft of Light.†

1 "False Dawn," preceding the real dawn about
  an hour; "a well known phenomenon in the
  East." (This note, and many that follow,
  are condensed from Fitzgerald's notes.)
2 The Vernal equinox.
3 See *Exodus*, iv, 6. A strong figure for the
  miracle of spring blossoms.
4 "According to the Persians, the healing power
  of Jesus resided in his breath."

II

Before the phantom of False morning died,[1]
Methought a Voice within the Tavern cried,
    "When all the Temple is prepared within,
Why nods the drowsy Worshipper outside?"

III

And, as the Cock crew, those who stood before
The Tavern shouted—"Open then the Door!
    You know how little while we have to stay,
And, once departed, may return no more."

IV

Now the New Year[2] reviving old Desires,
The thoughtful Soul to Solitude retires,
    Where the WHITE HAND OF MOSES on the
      Bough
Puts out,[3] and Jesus from the Ground suspires.[4]

V

Iram indeed is gone with all his Rose,
And Jamshyd's Sev'n-ring'd Cup where no one
    knows;
    But still a Ruby kindles in the Vine,
And many a Garden by the Water blows.‡

* Omar Khayyám (i. e., Omar the Tent-maker)
  was a Persian astronomer and poet of the
  12th century, who dwelt at Naishápúr.
  Rubáiyát is a Persian word, the plural of
  rubái, which signifies "a quatrain." These
  rubáiyát are therefore short, epigrammatic
  poems, virtually independent of each other.
  From among the numerous quatrains left by
  Omar, Edward Fitzgerald selected and freely translated a number, and printed them in
  1859 (see *Eng. Lit.*, p. 309). The number in
  that edition was seventy-five. The third edition (1873) contained one hundred and one;
  the fourth edition, which is reproduced here,
  had a few further verbal changes. There are
  two widely divergent views of the philosophy
  contained in them, the one regarding it as
  wholly materialistic, raising questions of the
  "Two Worlds" only to dismiss them and take
  refuge in the pleasures of sense—an Epi-
  curean philosophy of "Eat, drink, and be
  merry." The other regards it as an example
  of Oriental mysticism, employing Wine and
  the like as poetic symbols of deity. Fitzgerald held firmly to the former view, content, however, "to believe that, while the
  wine Omar celebrates is simply the juice of
  the grape, he bragged more than he drank of
  it, in very defiance perhaps of that spiritual
  wine which left its votaries sunk in hypocrisy
  or disgust."
† The opening stanza of the first edition is considerably more daring in its imagery, drawing
  one of its figures from the practice, in the
  desert, of flinging a stone into the cup as a
  signal "To Horse!"—

  Awake! for Morning in the Bowl of Night
  Has flung the Stone that puts the Stars to Flight:
    And Lo! the Hunter of the East has caught
  The Sultán's Turret in a Noose of Light.

‡ Iram was an ancient garden, planted by King
  Shaddád. Jamshyd was a legendary king of
  Persia's golden age; his seven-ringed cup was
  "typical of the seven heavens, etc., and was
  a divining cup." Other kings and heroes
  are mentioned in quatrains X and XVIII.
  Hátim was "a well known type of oriental
  generosity." For Zál and Rustum, see Arnold's poem of *Sohrab and Rustum*.

VI

And David's lips are lockt; but in divine
High-piping Pehleví,[5] with "Wine! Wine!
  Wine!
  Red Wine!"—the Nightingale cries to the
    Rose
That sallow cheek of hers to' incarnadine.

VII

Come, fill the Cup, and in the fire of Spring
Your Winter-garment of Repentance fling:
  The Bird of Time has but a little way
To flutter—and the Bird is on the Wing.

VIII

Whether at Naishápúr or Babylon,
Whether the Cup with sweet or bitter run,
  The Wine of Life keeps oozing drop by drop,
The Leaves of Life keep falling one by one.

IX

Each Morn a thousand Roses brings, you say;
Yes, but where leaves the Rose of Yesterday?
  And this first Summer month that brings the
    Rose
Shall take Jamshyd and Kaikobád away.

X

Well, let it take them! What have we to do
With Kaikobád the Great, or Kaikhosrú?
  Let Zál and Rustum bluster as they will,
Or Hátim call to Supper—heed not you.

XI

With me along the strip of Herbage strown
That just divides the desert from the sown,
  Where name of Slave and Sultán is forgot—
And Peace to Mahmúd[6] on his golden Throne!

XII

A Book of Verses underneath the Bough,
A Jug of Wine, a Loaf of Bread—and Thou
  Beside me singing in the Wilderness—
Oh, Wilderness were Paradise enow!

XIII

Some for the Glories of This World; and some
Sigh for the Prophet's Paradise to come;
  Ah, take the Cash, and let the Credit go,
Nor heed the rumble of a distant Drum![7]

XIV

Look to the blowing Rose about us—"Lo,
Laughing," she says, "into the world I blow,
  At once the silken tassel of my Purse
Tear, and its Treasure on the Garden throw."

XV

And those who husbanded the Golden Grain,
And those who flung it to the winds like Rain
  Alike to no such aureate Earth are turn'd
As, buried once, Men want dug up again.

XVI

The Worldly Hope men set their Hearts upon
Turns Ashes—or it prospers; and anon,
  Like Snow upon the Desert's dusty Face,
Lighting a little hour or two—was gone.

XVII

Think, in this batter'd Caravanserai[8]
Whose Portals are alternate Night and Day,
  How Sultán after Sultán with his Pomp
Abode his destin'd Hour, and went his way.

XVIII

They say the Lion and the Lizard keep
The Courts where Jamshyd gloried and drank
    deep:[9]
  And Bahrám, that great Hunter—the Wild
    Ass
Stamps o'er his Head, but cannot break his
    Sleep.

XIX

I sometimes think that never blows so red
The Rose as where some buried Cæsar[10] bled;
  That every Hyacinth the Garden wears
Dropt in her Lap from some once lovely Head.

XX

And this reviving Herb whose tender Green
Fledges the River-Lip on which we lean—
  Ah, lean upon it lightly! for who knows
From what once lovely Lip it springs unseen!

XXI

Ah, my Belovéd, fill the Cup that clears
TO-DAY of past Regrets and future Fears:
  To-morrow!—Why, To-morrow I may be
Myself with Yesterday's Sev'n thousand
    Years.[11]

XXII

For some we loved, the loveliest and the best
That from his Vintage rolling Time hath prest,
  Have drunk their Cup a Round or two before,
And one by one crept silently to rest.

XXIII

And we that now make merry in the Room
They left, and Summer dresses in new bloom,
  Ourselves must we beneath the Couch of
    Earth
Descend—ourselves to make a couch—for
    whom?

5 An ancient literary language of Persia.
6 See quatrain LX.
7 "Beaten outside a palace."

8 inn   9 Persepolis.
10 emperor
11 "A thousand years to each Planet."

XXIV

h, make the most of what we yet may spend,
efore we too into the Dust descend;
  Dust into Dust, and under Dust to lie,
ans[12] Wine, sans Song, sans Singer, and—sans
    End!

XXV

like for those who for TO-DAY prepare,
nd those that after some TO-MORROW stare,
  A Muezzín[13] from the Tower of Darkness
    cries,
"Fools! your Reward is neither Here nor
    There.''

XXVI

Vhy, all the Saints and Sages who discuss'd
Of the Two Worlds so wisely—they are thrust
  Like foolish Prophets forth; their Words to
    Scorn
Are scatter'd, and their Mouths are stopt with
    Dust.

XXVII

Myself when young did eagerly frequent
Doctor and Saint, and heard great argument
  About it and about: but evermore
Came out by the same door where in I went.

XXVIII

With them the seed of Wisdom did I sow,
And with mine own hand wrought to make it
    grow;
  And this was all the Harvest that I reap'd—
'I came like Water, and like Wind I go.''

XXIX

Into this Universe, and *Why* not knowing
Nor *Whence*, like Water willy-nilly flowing;
  And out of it, as Wind along the Waste,
I know not *Whither*, willy-nilly, blowing.

XXX

What, without asking, hither hurried *Whence?*
And, without asking, *Whither* hurried hence!
  Oh, many a Cup of this forbidden Wine
Must drown the memory of that insolence!

XXXI

Up from Earth's Centre through the Seventh
    Gate
I rose, and on the Throne of Saturn[14] sate,
  And many a Knot unravell'd by the Road;
But not the Master-knot of Human Fate.

XXXII

There was the Door to which I found no
    Key;

There was the Veil through which I might not
    see:
  Some little talk awhile of ME and THEE[15]
There was—and then no more of THEE and ME.

XXXIII

Earth could not answer; nor the Seas that
    mourn
In flowing Purple, of their Lord forlorn;
  Nor rolling Heaven, with all his Signs re-
    veal'd
And hidden by the sleeve of Night and Morn.

XXXIV

Then of the THEE IN ME who works behind
The Veil, I lifted up my hands to find
  A Lamp amid the Darkness; and I heard,
As from Without—"THE ME WITHIN THEE
    BLIND!''

XXXV

Then to the Lip of this poor earthen Urn
I lean'd, the Secret of my Life to learn:
  And Lip to Lip it murmur'd—"While you
    live,
Drink!—for, once dead, you never shall re-
    turn.''

XXXVI

I think the Vessel, that with fugitive
Articulation answer'd, once did live,
  And drink; and Ah! the passive Lip I kiss'd,
How many Kisses might it take—and give!

XXXVII

For I remember stopping by the way
To watch a Potter thumping his wet Clay:
  And with its all-obliterated Tongue
It murmur'd—"Gently, Brother, gently,
    pray!''

XXXVIII

And has not such a Story from of Old
Down Man's successive generations roll'd
  Of such a clod of saturated Earth
Cast by the Maker into Human mould?

XXXIX

And not a drop that from our Cups we throw
For Earth to drink of, but may steal below
  To quench the fire of Anguish in some Eye
There hidden—far beneath, and long ago.

XL

As then the Tulip for her morning sup
Of Heav'nly Vintage from the soil looks up,
  Do you devoutly do the like, till Heav'n
To Earth invert you—like an empty Cup.

---

12 without
13 A summoner to prayer.
14 "Lord of the Seventh Heaven."

15 "Some dividual Existence or Personality dis-
    tinct from the Whole."

XLI

Perplext no more with Human or Divine,
To-morrow's tangle to the winds resign,
    And lose your fingers in the tresses of
The Cypress-slender Minister of Wine.

XLII

And if the Wine you drink, the Lip you press,
End in what All begins and ends in—Yes;
    Think then you are TO-DAY what YESTERDAY
You were—TO-MORROW you shall not be less.

XLIII

So when the Angel of the darker Drink
At last shall find you by the river-brink,
    And, offering his Cup, invite your Soul
Forth to your Lips to quaff—you shall not
    shrink.

XLIV

Why, if the Soul can fling the Dust aside,
And naked on the Air of Heaven ride,
    Were 't not a Shame—were 't not a Shame
        for him
In this clay carcase crippled to abide?

XLV

'Tis but a Tent where takes his one day's rest
A Sultán to the realm of Death addrest;
    The Sultán rises, and the dark Ferrásh[1]
Strikes, and prepares it for another Guest.

XLVI

And fear not lest Existence closing your
Account, and mine, should know the like no
        more;
    The Eternal Sákí[2] from that Bowl has pour'd
Millions of Bubbles like us, and will pour.

XLVII

When You and I behind the Veil are past,
Oh, but the long, long while the World shall
        last,
    Which of our Coming and Departure heeds
As the Sea's self should heed a pebble-cast.

XLVIII

A Moment's Halt—a momentary taste
Of BEING from the Well amid the Wast?—
    And Lo!—the phantom Caravan has reach'd
The NOTHING it set out from—Oh, make haste!

XLIX

Would you that spangle of Existence spend
About THE SECRET—quick about it, Friend!
    A Hair perhaps divides the False and True—
And upon what, prithee, does life depend?

L

A Hair perhaps divides the False and True;
Yes; and a single Alif[3] were the clue—
    Could you but find it—to the Treasure-house
And peradventure to THE MASTER too;

LI

Whose secret Presence, through Creation's
        veins
Running Quicksilver-like eludes your pains;
    Taking all shapes from Máh to Máhi;[4] and
They change and perish all—but He remains;

LII

A moment guess'd—then back behind the Fold
Immerst of Darkness round the Drama roll'd
    Which, for the Pastime of Eternity,
He doth Himself contrive, enact, behold.

LIII

But if in vain, down on the stubborn floor
Of Earth, and up to Heav'n's unopening Door
    You gaze TO-DAY, while You are You—how
        then
TO-MORROW, You when shall be You no more?

LIV

Waste not your Hour, nor in the vain pursuit
Of This and That endeavour and dispute;
    Better be jocund with the fruitful Grape
Than sadden after none, or bitter, Fruit.

LV

You know, my Friends, with what a brave
        Carouse
I made a Second Marriage in my house;
    Divorced old barren Reason from my Bed,
And took the Daughter of the Vine to Spouse.

LVI

For "Is" and "Is-NOT" though with Rule and
        Line,
And "UP-AND-DOWN" by Logic I define,
    Of all that one should care to fathom, I
Was never deep in anything but—Wine.

LVII

Ah, but my Computations, People say,
Reduced the Year to better reckoning?[5]—Nay
    'Twas only striking from the Calendar
Unborn To-morrow, and dead Yesterday.

LVIII

And lately, by the Tavern Door agape,
Came shining through the Dusk an Angel Shape

---

[3] The letter *a*, often represented by a slight mark
    like an apostrophe, the presence or absence of
    which could change the meaning of a word.
[4] from fish to moon
[5] Omar assisted in reforming the calendar.

[1] attendant   [2] wine-bearer

Bearing a Vessel on his Shoulder; and
He bid me taste of it; and 't was—the Grape!

LIX

The Grape that can with Logic absolute
The Two-and-Seventy jarring Sects[6] confute:
  The sovereign Alchemist that in a trice
Life's leaden metal into Gold transmute:

LX

The mighty Mahmúd, Allah-breathing Lord,[7]
That all the misbelieving and black Horde
  Of Fears and Sorrows that infest the Soul
Scatters before him with his whirlwind Sword.

LXI

Why, be this Juice the growth of God, who dare
Blaspheme the twisted tendril as a Snare?
  A Blessing, we should use it, should we not?
And if a Curse—why, then, Who set it there?

LXII

I must abjure the Balm of Life, I must,
Scared by some After-reckoning ta'en on trust,
  Or lured with Hope of some Diviner Drink,
To fill the Cup—when crumbled into Dust!

LXIII

Oh, threats of Hell and Hopes of Paradise!
One thing at least is certain—*This* Life flies;
  One thing is certain and the rest is Lies;
The Flower that once has blown for ever dies.

LXIV

Strange, is it not? that of the myriads who
Before us pass'd the door of Darkness through,
  Not one returns to tell us of the Road,
Which to discover we must travel too.

LXV

The Revelations of Devout and Learn'd
Who rose before us, and as Prophets burn'd,
  Are all but Stories, which, awoke from Sleep
They told their comrades, and to Sleep return'd.

LXVI

I sent my Soul through the Invisible,
Some letter of that After-life to spell:
  And by and by my Soul return'd to me,
And answer'd "I Myself am Heav'n and Hell:"

LXVII

Heav'n but the Vision of fulfill'd Desire,
And Hell the Shadow from a Soul on fire,

Cast on the Darkness into which Ourselves,
So late emerged from, shall so soon expire.

LXVIII

We are no other than a moving row
Of Magic Shadow-shapes that come and go
  Round with the Sun-illumined Lantern[8] held
In Midnight by the Master of the Show;

LXIX

But helpless Pieces of the Game He plays
Upon this Chequer-board of Nights and Days;
  Hither and thither moves, and checks, and slays,
And one by one back in the Closet lays.

LXX

The Ball no question makes of Ayes and Noes,
But Here or There as strikes the Player goes;
  And He that toss'd you down into the Field,
He knows about it all—HE knows—HE knows!

LXXI

The Moving Finger writes; and, having writ,
Moves on: nor all your Piety nor Wit
  Shall lure it back to cancel half a Line,
Nor all your Tears wash out a Word of it.

LXXII

And that inverted Bowl they call the Sky,
Whereunder crawling coop'd we live and die,
  Lift not your hands to *It* for help—for It
As impotently moves as you or I.

LXXIII

With Earth's first Clay They did the Last Man knead,
And there of the Last Harvest sow'd the Seed:
  And the first Morning of Creation wrote
What the Last Dawn of Reckoning shall read.

LXXIV

YESTERDAY *This* Day's Madness did prepare;
TO-MORROW'S Silence, Triumph, or Despair:
  Drink! for you know not whence you came, nor why:
Drink! for you know not why you go, nor where.

LXXV

I tell you this—When, started from the Goal,
Over the flaming shoulders of the Foal
  Of Heav'n Parwín and Mushtarí[9] they flung,
In my predestined Plot of Dust and Soul

LXXVI

The Vine had struck a fibre: which about
If clings my Being—let the Dervish[10] flout;

6 "The seventy-two religions supposed to divide
    the world."
7 "Alluding to Sultan Mahmúd's conquest of India
    and its dark people." By "Allah-breathing"
    is meant that the Sultan was a Mohamme-
    dan, or worshiper of Allah.

8 i. e., the earth
9 The Pleiads and Jupiter.
10 A Mohammedan devotee.

Of my Base metal may be filed a Key,
That shall unlock the Door he howls without.

LXXVII

And this I know: whether the one True Light
Kindle to Love, or Wrath-consume me quite,
   One Flash of It within the Tavern caught
Better than in the Temple lost outright.

LXXVIII

What! out of senseless Nothing to provoke
A conscious Something to resent the yoke
   Of unpermitted Pleasure, under pain
Of Everlasting Penalties, if broke!

LXXIX

What! from his helpless Creature be repaid
Pure Gold for what he lent him dross-allay'd—
   Sue for a Debt we never did contract,
And cannot answer—Oh, the sorry trade!

LXXX

Oh Thou, who didst with pitfall and with gin
Beset the Road I was to wander in,
   Thou wilt not with Predestined Evil round
Enmesh, and then impute my Fall to Sin!

LXXXI

Oh Thou, who Man of baser Earth didst make,
And ev'n with Paradise devise the Snake:
   For all the Sin wherewith the Face of Man
Is blacken'd—Man's forgiveness give—and
   take!

.   .   .   .   .   .

LXXXII

As under cover of departing Day
Slunk hunger-stricken Ramazán[11] away,
   Once more within the Potter's house alone
I stood, surrounded by the Shapes of Clay.

LXXXIII

Shapes of all Sorts and Sizes, great and small,
That stood along the floor and by the wall;
   And some loquacious Vessels were; and some
Listen'd perhaps, but never talk'd at all.

LXXXIV

Said one among them—"Surely not in vain
My substance of the common Earth was ta'en
   And to this Figure moulded, to be broke,
Or trampled back to shapeless Earth again."

LXXXV

Then said a Second—"Ne'er a peevish Boy
Would break the Bowl from which he drank in
   joy;

And He that with his hand the Vessel mad[e]
Will surely not in after Wrath destroy."

LXXXVI

After a momentary silence spake
Some Vessel of a more ungainly Make:
   "They sneer at me for leaning all awry:
What! did the Hand then of the Potte[r]
   shake?"

LXXXVII

Whereat some one of the loquacious Lot—
I think a Súfi[12] pipkin—waxing hot—
   "All this of Pot and Potter—Tell me the[n]
Who is the Potter, pray, and who the Pot?"

LXXXVIII

"Why," said another, "Some there are wh[o]
   tell
Of one who threatens he will toss to Hell
   The luckless Pots he marr'd in making—
   Pish!
He's a Good Fellow, and 't will all be well."

LXXXIX

"Well," murmur'd one, "Let whoso make o[r]
   buy,
My Clay with long Oblivion is gone dry:
   But fill me with the old familiar Juice,
Methinks I might recover by and by."

XC

So while the Vessels one by one were speakin[g,]
The little Moon[13] look'd in that all were seek[-]
   ing:
   And then they jogg'd each other, "Brother[!]
   Brother!
Now for the Porter's shoulder-knot[14] a-creak[-]
   ing!"

.   .   .   .   .   .

XCI

Ah, with the Grape my fading Life provide,
And wash the Body whence the Life has die[d,]
   And lay me, shrouded in the living Leaf,
By some not unfrequented Garden-side.

XCII

That ev'n my buried Ashes such a snare
Of Vintage shall fling up into the Air
   As not a True-believer passing by
But shall be overtaken unaware.

---

12 The allusion here is to a sect of oriental mysti[cs]
   who held a pantheistic doctrine.
13 Marking the new month and the end of t[he]
   fast.
14 A shoulder-strap in which the jars of wi[ne]
   were slung.

1 The month of fasting, during which no food is
  taken between sunrise and sunset.

XCIII

Indeed the Idols I have loved so long
Have done my credit in this World much wrong:
  Have drown'd my Glory in a shallow Cup,
And sold my Reputation for a Song.

XCIV

Indeed, indeed, Repentance oft before
I swore—but was I sober when I swore?
  And then and then came Spring, and Rose-in-hand
My thread-bare Penitence apieces tore.

XCV

And much as Wine has play'd the Infidel,
And robb'd me of my Robe of Honour—Well,
  I wonder often what the Vintners buy
One half so precious as the stuff they sell.

XCVI

Yet Ah, that Spring should vanish with the Rose!
That Youth's sweet-scented manuscript should close!
  The Nightingale that in the branches sang,
Ah whence, and whither flown again, who knows!

XCVII

Would but the Desert of the Fountain yield
One glimpse—if dimly, yet indeed, reveal'd,
  To which the fainting Traveller might spring,
As springs the trampled herbage of the field.

XCVIII

Would but some wingéd Angel ere too late
Arrest the yet unfolded Roll of Fate,
  And make the stern Recorder otherwise
Enregister, or quite obliterate!

XCIX

Ah Love! could you and I with Him conspire
To grasp this sorry Scheme of Things Entire,
  Would not we shatter it to bits—and then
Re-mould it nearer to the Heart's desire!

.   .   .   .

C

Yon rising Moon that looks for us again—
How oft hereafter will she wax and wane;
  How oft hereafter rising look for us
Through this same Garden—and for *one* in vain!

CI

And when like her, oh Sákí, you shall pass
Among the Guests Star-scatter'd on the Grass,
  And in your joyous errand reach the spot

Where I made One—turn down an empty Glass!

TAMAM[15]

ARTHUR HUGH CLOUGH
(1819-1861)

IN A LECTURE-ROOM

Away, haunt thou not me,
Thou vain Philosophy!
Little hast thou bestead,
Save to perplex the head,
And leave the spirit dead.
Unto thy broken cisterns wherefore go,
While from the secret treasure-depths below,
Fed by the skyey shower,
And clouds that sink and rest on hill-tops high,
Wisdom at once, and Power,
Are welling, bubbling forth, unseen, incessantly?
Why labour at the dull mechanic oar,
When the fresh breeze is blowing,
And the strong current flowing,
Right onward to the Eternal Shore?

QUA CURSUM VENTUS*

As ships, becalmed at eve, that lay
  With canvas drooping, side by side,
Two towers of sail at dawn of day
  Are scarce long leagues apart descried;

When fell the night, upsprung the breeze,
  And all the darkling hours they plied,
Nor dreamt but each the self-same seas
  By each was cleaving, side by side: 8

E'en so, but why the tale reveal
  Of those, whom year by year unchanged,
Brief absence joined anew to feel,
  Astounded, soul from soul estranged?

At dead of night their sails were filled,
  And onward each rejoicing steered—
Ah, neither blame, for neither willed,
  Or wist, what first with dawn appeared!   16

To veer, how vain! On, onward strain,
  Brave barks! In light, in darkness too,
Through winds and tides one compass guides—
  To that, and your own selves, be true.

---

15 "The end."
* "As the wind (directs) the course." The poem is metaphorical of the divergence of men's creeds. See *Eng. Lit.*, p. 315.

But O blithe breeze! and O great seas,
   Though ne'er, that earliest parting past,
On your wide plain they join again,
   Together lead them home at last.   24

One port, methought, alike they sought,
   One purpose hold where'er they fare,—
O bounding breeze, O rushing seas!
   At last, at last, unite them there!

SAY NOT THE STRUGGLE NOUGHT AVAILETH

Say not the struggle nought availeth,
   The labour and the wounds are vain,
The enemy faints not, nor faileth,
   And as things have been they remain.

If hopes were dupes, fears may be liars;
   It may be, in yon smoke concealed,
Your comrades chase e'en now the fliers,
   And, but for you, possess the field.   8

For while the tired waves, vainly breaking,
   Seem here no painful inch to gain,
Far back, through creeks and inlets making,
   Comes silent, flooding in, the main.†

And not by eastern windows only,
   When daylight comes, comes in the light,
In front, the sun climbs slow, how slowly,
   But westward, look, the land is bright.   16

ITE DOMUM SATURÆ, VENIT HESPERUS‡

The skies have sunk, and hid the upper snow
(Home, Rose, and home, Provence and La
      Palie¹),
The rainy clouds are filing fast below,
And wet will be the path, and wet shall we.
Home, Rose, and home, Provence and La Palie.

Ah dear, and where is he, a year agone,
Who stepped beside and cheered us on and on?
My sweetheart wanders far away from me,
In foreign land or on a foreign sea,   9
Home, Rose, and home, Provence and La Palie.

The lightning zigzags shoot across the sky
(Home, Rose, and home, Provence and La
      Palie),
And through the vale the rains go sweeping by;
Ah me, and when in shelter shall we be?
Home, Rose, and home, Provence and La Palie.

1 "The Pale One"—a name of obvious significance,
   like "Blanche" or "Brindle."
† "Perhaps Clough's greatest title to poetic fame
   is this exquisite and exquisitely expressed
   image of the rising tide."—George Saintsbury.
‡ "Go home, now that you have fed, evening
   comes."—Virgil, Eclog. x, 77.

Cold, dreary cold, the stormy winds feel they
O'er foreign lands and foreign seas that stra⋯
(Home, Rose, and home, Provence and La
      Palie).
And doth he e'er, I wonder, bring to mind
The pleasant huts and herds he left behind?   20
And doth he sometimes in his slumbering see
The feeding kine, and doth he think of me,
My sweetheart wandering wheresoe'er it be?
Home, Rose, and home, Provence and La Palie.

The thunder bellows far from snow to snow
(Home, Rose, and home, Provence and La
      Palie),
And loud and louder roars the flood below.
Heigho! but soon in shelter shall we be:
Home, Rose, and home, Provence and La Palie.

Or shall he find before his term be sped   30
Some comelier maid that he shall wish to wed?
(Home, Rose, and home, Provence and La
      Palie.)
For weary is work, and weary day by day
To have your comfort miles on miles away.
Home, Rose, and home, Provence and La Palie.

Or may it be that I shall find my mate,
And he returning see himself too late?
For work we must, and what we see, we see,
And God he knows, and what must be, must be,
When sweethearts wander far away from me.   40
Home, Rose, and home, Provence and La Palie.

The sky behind is brightening up anew
(Home, Rose, and home, Provence and La
      Palie),
The rain is ending, and our journey too:
Heigho! aha! for here at home are we:—
In, Rose, and in, Provence and La Palie.

ALL IS WELL

Whate'er you dream, with doubt possessed,
Keep, keep it snug within your breast,
And lay you down and take your rest;
Forget in sleep the doubt and pain,
And when you wake, to work again.
The wind it blows, the vessel goes,
And where and whither, no one knows.

'Twill all be well: no need of care;
Though how it will, and when, and where,
We cannot see, and can't declare.   1
In spite of dreams, in spite of thought,
'Tis not in vain, and not for nought,
The wind it blows, the ship it goes,
Though where and whither, no one knows.

MATTHEW ARNOLD
(1822-1888)

THE FORSAKEN MERMAN*

Come, dear children, let us away;
Down and away below!
Now my brothers call from the bay,
Now the great winds shoreward blow,
Now the salt tides seaward flow;
Now the wild white horses[1] play,
Champ and chafe and toss in the spray.
Children dear, let us away!
This way, this way!

Call her once before you go—   10
Call once yet!
In a voice that she will know:
"Margaret! Margaret!"
Children's voices should be dear
(Call once more) to a mother's ear;
Children's voices, wild with pain—
Surely she will come again!
Call her once and come away;
This way, this way!
"Mother dear, we cannot stay!   20
The wild white horses foam and fret."
Margaret! Margaret!

Come, dear children, come away down;
Call no more!
One last look at the white-walled town,
And the little gray church on the windy shore,
Then come down!
She will not come though you call all day;
Come away, come away!

Children dear, was it yesterday   30
We heard the sweet bells over the bay?
In the caverns where we lay,
Through the surf and through the swell,
The far-off sound of a silver bell?
Sand-strewn caverns, cool and deep,
Where the winds are all asleep;
Where the spent lights quiver and gleam,
Where the salt weed sways in the stream,
Where the sea-beasts, ranged all round,
Feed in the ooze of their pasture ground;   40
Where the sea-snakes coil and twine,
Dry their mail and bask in the brine;
Where great whales come sailing by,
Sail and sail, with unshut eye,

Round the world for ever and aye?
When did music come this way?
Children dear, was it yesterday?

Children dear, was it yesterday
(Call yet once) that she went away?
Once she sate with you and me,   50
On a red gold throne in the heart of the sea,
And the youngest sate on her knee.
She combed its bright hair, and she tended it
     well,
When down swung the sound of a far-off bell.
She sighed, she looked up through the clear
     green sea;
She said: "I must go, for my kinsfolk pray
In the little gray church on the shore to-day.
'Twill be Easter-time in the world—ah me!
And I lose my poor soul, Merman! here with
     thee."
I said: "Go up, dear heart, through the
     waves;   60
Say thy prayer, and come back to the kind
     sea-caves!"
She smiled, she went up through the surf in
     the bay.
Children dear, was it yesterday?

Children dear, were we long alone?
"The sea grows stormy, the little ones moan;
Long prayers," I said, "in the world they
     say;
Come!" I said; and we rose through the surf
     in the bay.
We went up the beach, by the sandy down
Where the sea-stocks bloom, to the white-walled
     town;
Through the narrow-paved streets, where all
     was still,   70
To the little gray church on the windy hill.
From the church came a murmur of folk at
     their prayers,
But we stood without in the cold blowing
     airs.
We climbed on the graves, on the stones worn
     with rains,
And we gazed up the aisle through the small
     leaded panes.
She sate by the pillar; we saw her clear:
"Margaret, hist! come quick, we are here!
Dear heart," I said, "we are long alone;
The sea grows stormy, the little ones moan."
But, ah, she gave me never a look,   80
For her eyes were sealed to the holy book!
Loud prays the priest; shut stands the door.
Come away, children, call no more!
Come away, come down, call no more!

Down, down, down!
Down to the depths of the sea!

[1] The breakers.
* This poem is based on a legend which is found
   in the literature of various nations. See
   Eng. Lit., p. 311.

She sits at her wheel in the humming town,
Singing most joyfully.
Hark what she sings: "O joy, O joy,
For the humming street, and the child with its
    toy!   90
For the priest, and the bell, and the holy well;
For the wheel where I spun,
And the blessed light of the sun!"
And so she sings her fill,
Singing most joyfully,
Till the spindle drops from her hand,
And the whizzing wheel stands still.
She steals to the window, and looks at the
    sand,
And over the sand at the sea;
And her eyes are set in a stare;   100
And anon there breaks a sigh,
And anon there drops a tear,
From a sorrow-clouded eye,
And a heart sorrow-laden,
A long, long sigh;
For the cold strange eyes of a little Mermaiden
And the gleam of her golden hair.

   Come away, away children ;
Come children, come down!
The hoarse wind blows coldly;   110
Lights shine in the town.
She will start from her slumber
When gusts shake the door;
She will hear the winds howling,
Will hear the waves roar.
We shall see, while above us
The waves roar and whirl,
A ceiling of amber,
A pavement of pearl.
Singing: "Here came a mortal,   120
But faithless was she!
And alone dwell forever
The kings of the sea."

But, children, at midnight,
When soft the winds blow,
When clear falls the moonlight,
When spring tides are low;
When sweet airs come seaward
From heaths starred with broom,
And high rocks throw mildly   130
On the blanched sands a gloom;
Up the still, glistening beaches,
Up the creeks we will hie,
Over banks of bright seaweed
The ebb-tide leaves dry.
We will gaze, from the sand-hills,
At the white, sleeping town;
At the church on the hillside—
And then come back down.

Singing: "There dwells a loved one,   140
But cruel is she!
She left lonely forever
The kings of the sea."

TO A FRIEND*

Who prop, thou ask'st, in these bad days, my
    mind?—
He much, the old man, who, clearest-souled of
    men,
Saw The Wide Prospect, and the Asian Fen,
And Tmolus hill, and Smyrna bay, though blind.
Much he, whose friendship I not long since won,
That halting slave, who in Nicopolis
Taught Arrian, when Vespasian's brutal son
Cleared Rome of what most shamed him. But
    be his
My special thanks, whose even-balanced soul,
From first youth tested up to extreme old age,
Business could not make dull, nor passion wild;
Who saw life steadily, and saw it whole;
The mellow glory of the Attic stage,
Singer of sweet Colonus, and its child.

SHAKESPEARE

Others abide our question. Thou art free.
We ask and ask—Thou smilest and art still,
Out-topping knowledge. For the loftiest hill,
Who to the stars uncrowns his majesty,
Planting his steadfast footsteps in the sea,
Making the heaven of heavens his dwelling-
    place,
Spares but the cloudy border of his base
To the foiled searching of mortality;
And thou, who didst the stars and sunbeams
    know,
Self-schooled, self-scanned, self-honoured, self-
    secure,
Didst tread on earth unguessed at.—Better so!
All pains the immortal spirit must endure,
All weakness which impairs, all griefs which
    bow,
Find their sole speech in that victorious brow.

* This sonnet gives expression to. Arnold's steady
reliance, for mental and moral support, upon
the great poets and philosophers—his constant recourse to "the best that is known and
thought in the world." The three "props"
mentioned here are Homer, the blind bard
whom the city of Smyrna in Asia Minor
claimed as her son; Epictetus, the lame
philosopher who had been a slave, and who,
when Domitian banished the philosophers
from Rome, went to Nicopolis in Greece and
taught his Stoic principles to Arrian; and
Sophocles, the Athenian dramatist, author of
Œdipus at Colonus and other tragedies. Arnold explains the third line by pointing out
that the name Europe means "the wide prospect," and Asia probably means "marshy."
The twelfth line has passed into familiar
quotation.

AUSTERITY OF POETRY

That son of Italy who tried to blow,[1]
Ere Dante came, the trump of sacred song,
In his light youth amid a festal throng
Sat with his bride to see a public show.
Fair was the bride, and on her front did glow
Youth like a star; and what to youth belong—
Gay raiment, sparkling gauds, elation strong.
A prop gave way! crash fell a platform! lo,
'Mid struggling sufferers, hurt to death, she
    lay!
Shuddering, they drew her garments off—and
    found
A robe of sackcloth next the smooth, white skin.
Such, poets, is your bride, the Muse! young,
    gay,
Radiant, adorned outside; a hidden ground
Of thought and of austerity within.

MEMORIAL VERSES

April, 1850

Goethe in Weimar sleeps, and Greece,
Long since, saw Byron's struggle cease.
But one such death remained to come;
The last poetic voice is dumb—
We stand to-day by Wordsworth's tomb.

When Byron's eyes were shut in death,
We bowed our head and held our breath.
He taught us little; but our soul
Had *felt* him like the thunder's roll.
With shivering heart the strife we saw   10
Of passion with eternal law;
And yet with reverential awe
We watched the fount of fiery life
Which served for that Titanic strife.

When Goethe's death was told, we said:
Sunk, then, is Europe's sagest head.
Physician of the iron age,
Goethe has done his pilgrimage.
He took the suffering human race,
He read each wound, each weakness clear;   20
And struck his finger on the place,
And said: *Thou ailest here, and here!*
He looked on Europe's dying hour
Of fitful dream and feverish power;
His eye plunged down the weltering strife,
The turmoil of expiring life—
He said: *The end is everywhere,*
Art still has truth, take refuge there!

1 Jacopone da Todi, who was, says Gaspary, a
"true type of the mediaeval Christian ascetic."
According to the legend, he was turned by the
incident which Arnold relates from a life of
gayety to one of rigorous self-imposed penances.

And he was happy, if to know
Causes of things, and far below   30
His feet to see the lurid flow
Of terror, and insane distress,
And headlong fate, be happiness.

And Wordsworth!—Ah, pale ghosts, rejoice!
For never has such soothing voice
Been to your shadowy world conveyed,
Since erst, at morn, some wandering shade
Heard the clear song of Orpheus come
Through Hades, and the mournful gloom.
Wordsworth has gone from us—and ye,   40
Ah, may ye feel his voice as we!
He too upon a wintry clime
Had fallen—on this iron time
Of doubts, disputes, distractions, fears.
He found us when the age had bound
Our souls in its benumbing round;
He spoke, and loosed our heart in tears.
He laid us as we lay at birth
On the cool flowery lap of earth,
Smiles broke from us and we had ease;   50
The hills were round us, and the breeze
Went o'er the sun-lit fields again;
Our foreheads felt the wind and rain.
Our youth returned; for there was shed
On spirits that had long been dead,
Spirits dried up and closely furled,
The freshness of the early world.

Ah! since dark days still bring to light
Man's prudence and man's fiery might,
Time may restore us in his course   60
Goethe's sage mind and Byron's force;
But where will Europe's latter hour
Again find Wordsworth's healing power?
Others will teach us how to dare,
And against fear our breast to steel;
Others will strengthen us to bear—
But who, ah! who, will make us feel?
The cloud of mortal destiny,
Others will front it fearlessly—
But who, like him, will put it by?   70

Keep fresh the grass upon his grave,
O Rotha,[1] with thy living wave!
Sing him thy best! for few or none
Hears thy voice right, now he is gone.

SELF-DEPENDENCE

Weary of myself, and sick of asking
What I am, and what I ought to be,
At this vessel's prow I stand, which bears me
Forwards, forwards, o'er the starlit sea.

1 The stream which flows past the churchyard of
Grasmere where Wordsworth is buried.

And a look of passionate desire
O'er the sea and to the stars I send:
"Ye who from my childhood up have calmed
me,
Calm me, ah, compose me to the end!   8

"Ah, once more," I cried, "ye stars, ye
waters,
On my heart your mighty charm renew;
Still, still let me, as I gaze upon you,
Feel my soul becoming vast like you!"

From the intense, clear, star-sown vault of
heaven,
Over the lit sea's unquiet way,
In the rustling night-air came the answer:
"Wouldst thou *be* as these are? *Live* as
they.   16

"Unaffrighted by the silence round them,
Undistracted by the sights they see,
These demand not that the things without them
Yield them love, amusement, sympathy.

"And with joy the stars perform their shining,
And the sea its long moon-silvered roll;
For self-poised they live, nor pine with noting
All the fever of some differing soul.   24

"Bounded by themselves, and unregardful
In what state God's other works may be,
In their own tasks all their powers pouring,
These attain the mighty life you see."

O air-born voice! long since, severely clear,
A cry like thine in mine own heart I hear:
"Resolve to be thyself; and know that he,
Who finds himself, loses his misery!"   32

LINES WRITTEN IN KENSINGTON GARDENS[2]

In this lone, open glade I lie,
Screened by deep boughs on either hand;
And at its end, to stay the eye,
Those black-crowned, red-boled pine-trees stand!

Birds here make song, each bird has his,
Across the girdling city's hum.
How green under the boughs it is!
How thick the tremulous sheep-cries come!   8

Sometimes a child will cross the glade
To take his nurse his broken toy;
Sometimes a thrush flit overhead
Deep in her unknown day's employ.

Here at my feet what wonders pass,
What endless, active life is here!

2 An extensive London park.

What blowing daisies, fragrant grass!
An air-stirred forest, fresh and clear.   16

Scarce fresher is the mountain-sod
Where the tired angler lies, stretched out,
And, eased of basket and of rod,
Counts his day's spoil, the spotted trout.

In the huge world, which roars hard by,
Be others happy if they can!
But in my helpless cradle I
Was breathed on by the rural Pan.[3]   24

I, on men's impious uproar hurled,
Think often, as I hear them rave,
That peace has left the upper world
And now keeps only in the grave.

Yet here is peace for ever new!
When I who watch them am away,
Still all things in this glade go through
The changes of their quiet day.   32

Then to their happy rest they pass!
The flowers upclose, the birds are fed,
The night comes down upon the grass,
The child sleeps warmly in his bed.

Calm soul of all things! make it mine
To feel, amid the city's jar,
That there abides a peace of thine,
Man did not make, and cannot mar.   40

The will to neither strive nor cry,
The power to feel with others give!
Calm, calm me more! nor let me die
Before I have begun to live.

REQUIESCAT[4]

Strew on her roses, roses,
    And never a spray of yew!
In quiet she reposes;
    Ah, would that I did too!

Her mirth the world required;
    She bathed it in smiles of glee.
But her heart was tired, tired,
    And now they let her be.

Her life was turning, turning,
    In mazes of heat and sound.
But for peace her soul was yearning,
    And now peace laps her round.

Her cabined, ample spirit,
    It fluttered and failed for breath.
To-night it doth inherit
    The vasty hall of death.

3 Arnold was born at Laleham in the Thames valley, and grew up amid country scenes.
4 "May she rest."

SOHRAB AND RUSTUM*

And the first gray of morning filled the east,
And the fog rose out of the Oxus stream.[5]
But all the Tartar camp along the stream
Was hushed, and still the men were plunged in
    sleep;
Sohrab alone, he slept not; all night long
He had lain wakeful, tossing on his bed;
But when the gray dawn stole into his tent,
He rose, and clad himself, and girt his sword,
And took his horseman's cloak, and left his
    tent,
And went abroad into the cold wet fog,   10
Through the dim camp to Peran-Wisa's[6] tent.
    Through the black Tartar tents he passed,
    which stood
Clustering like beehives on the low flat strand
Of Oxus, where the summer-floods o'erflow
When the sun melts the snows in high Pamere;
Through the black tents he passed, o'er that
    low strand,
And to a hillock came, a little back
From the stream's brink—the spot where first
    a boat,
Crossing the stream in summer, scrapes the
    land.
The men of former times had crowned the top 20
With a clay fort; but that was fallen, and now
The Tartars built there Peran-Wisa's tent,
A dome of laths, and o'er it felts were spread.
And Sohrab came there, and went in, and stood
Upon the thick piled[7] carpets in the tent,
And found the old man sleeping on his bed
Of rugs and felts, and near him lay his arms.
And Peran-Wisa heard him, though the step
Was dulled; for he slept light, an old man's
    sleep;
And he rose quickly on one arm, and said:— 30
"Who art thou? for it is not yet clear dawn.
Speak! is there news, or any night alarm?"
    But Sohrab came to the bedside, and said:—
"Thou know'st me, Peran-Wisa! it is I.
The sun is not yet risen, and the foe
Sleep; but I sleep not; all night long I lie

Tossing and wakeful, and I come to thee.
For so did King Afrasiab bid me seek
Thy counsel, and to heed thee as thy son,
In Samarcand, before the army marched;   40
And I will tell thee what my heart desires.
Thou know'st if, since from Ader-baijan[8] first
I came among the Tartars and bore arms,
I have still served Afrasiab well, and shown,
At my boy's years, the courage of a man.
This too thou know'st, that while I still bear on
The conquering Tartar ensigns through the
    world,
And beat the Persians back on every field,
I seek one man, one man, and one alone—   49
Rustum, my father; who I hoped should greet,
Should one day greet, upon some well-fought
    field,
His not unworthy, not inglorious son.
So I long hoped, but him I never find.
Come then, hear now, and grant me what I ask.
Let the two armies rest to-day; but I
Will challenge forth the bravest Persian lords
To meet me, man to man; if I prevail,
Rustum will surely hear it; if I fall—
Old man, the dead need no one, claim no kin.
Dim is the rumour of a common fight,   60
Where host meets host, and many names are
    sunk;
But of a single combat fame speaks clear.''
    He spoke; and Peran-Wisa took the hand
Of the young man in his, and sighed, and
    said:—
    "O Sohrab, an unquiet heart is thine!
Canst thou not rest among the Tartar chiefs,
And share the battle's common chance with us
Who love thee, but must press for ever first,
In single fight incurring single risk,
To find a father thou hast never seen?   70
That were far best, my son, to stay with us
Unmurmuring; in our tents, while it is war,
And when 't is truce, then in Afrasiab's towns.
But, if this one desire indeed rules all,
To seek out Rustum—seek him not through
    fight!
Seek him in peace, and carry to his arms,
O Sohrab, carry an unwounded son!
But far hence seek him, for he is not here.
For now it is not as when I was young,
When Rustum was in front of every fray;   80
But now he keeps apart, and sits at home,
In Seistan,[9] with Zal, his father old.
Whether that his own mighty strength at last
Feels the abhorred approaches of old age,
Or in some quarrel with the Persian King.
There go!—Thou wilt not? Yet my heart fore-
    bodes

---

5 Now the Amu-Daria, flowing from the plateau
    of Pamir, in central Asia, to the Aral Sea.
6 A Turanian chieftain.
7 From "pile"—fur, or hair-like nap.
* Founded on a story in the Persian epic, *Shah
    Nameh*, or "Book of Kings." Rustum is the
    great legendary warrior-hero of Iran, or Per-
    sia. In the Turanian, or Tartar land, which
    is ruled over by Afrasiab, an enemy of the Per-
    sians, Rustum's son Sohrab has grown up
    without ever having seen his father; nor does
    the father know of the existence of his son,
    having been told that the child born to him
    was a girl. The rest of the tragic tale may
    be left to tell itself in the simple and digni-
    fied language which Arnold, in professed imi-
    tation of the Homeric poems, has chosen.
    See *Eng. Lit.*, p. 312.

8 A northerly province of Persia.
9 Three syllables, *Se-is-tan;* in eastern Persia.

Danger or death awaits thee on this field.
Fain would I know thee safe and well, though
    lost
To us! fain therefore send thee hence, in peace
To seek thy father, not seek single fights   90
In vain;— but who can keep the lion's cub
From ravening, and who govern Rustum's son?
Go, I will grant thee what thy heart desires.''
    So said he, and dropped Sohrab's hand, and
    left
His bed, and the warm rugs whereon he lay;
And o'er his chilly limbs his woollen coat
He passed, and tied his sandals on his feet,
And threw a white cloak round him, and he took
In his right hand a ruler's staff, no sword;
And on his head he set his sheep-skin cap, 100
Black, glossy, curled, the fleece of Kara-Kul;[10]
And raised the curtain of his tent, and called
His herald to his side, and went abroad.
    The sun by this had risen, and cleared the
    fog
From the broad Oxus and the glittering sands.
And from their tents the Tartar horsemen filed
Into the open plain; so Haman bade—
Haman, who next to Peran-Wisa ruled
The host, and still was in his lusty prime.
From their black tents, long files of horse, they
    streamed;   110
As when some gray November morn the files,
In marching order spread, of long-necked cranes
Stream over Casbin and the southern slopes
Of Elburz, from the Aralian estuaries,
Or some frore[11] Caspian reed-bed, southward
    bound
For the warm Persian sea-board—so they
    streamed.
The Tartars of the Oxus, the King's guard,
First, with black sheep-skin caps and with long
    spears;
Large men, large steeds; who from Bokhara
    come
And Khiva, and ferment the milk of mares.[12]
Next, the more temperate Toorkmuns of the
    south,   121
The Tukas, and the lances of Salore,
And those from Attruck and the Caspian sands;
Light men and on light steeds, who only drink
The acrid milk of camels, and their wells.
And then a swarm of wandering horse, who
    came
From far, and a more doubtful service owned;
The Tartars of Ferghana, from the banks
Of the Jaxartes, men with scanty beards
And close-set skull-caps; and those wilder
    hordes   130

Who roam o'er Kipchak and the northern waste,
Kalmucks and unkempt Kuzzaks, tribes who
    stray
Nearest the Pole, and wandering Kirghizzes,
Who come on shaggy ponies from Pamere;
These all filed out from camp into the plain.
And on the other side the Persians formed;—
First a light cloud of horse, Tartars they
    seemed,
The Ilyats of Khorassan; and behind,
The royal troops of Persia, horse and foot,
Marshalled battalions bright in burnished steel.
But Peran-Wisa with his herald came,   141
Threading the Tartar squadrons to the front,
And with his staff kept back the foremost
    ranks.
And when Ferood, who led the Persians, saw
That Peran-Wisa kept the Tartars back,
He took his spear, and to the front he came,
And checked his ranks, and fixed them where
    they stood.
And the old Tartar came upon the sand
Betwixt the silent hosts, and spake, and said:—
  ''Ferood, and ye, Persians and Tartars,
    hear!   150
Let there be truce between the hosts to-day.
But choose a champion from the Persian lords
To fight our champion Sohrab, man to man.''
    As, in the country, on a morn in June,
When the dew glistens on the pearlèd ears,
A shiver runs through the deep corn for joy—
So, when they heard what Peran-Wisa said,
A thrill through all the Tartar squadron ran
Of pride and hope for Sohrab, whom they loved.
    But as a troop of pedlars, from Cabool,   160
Cross underneath the Indian Caucasus,
That vast sky-neighbouring mountain of milk
    snow;
Crossing so high, that, as they mount, they pass
Long flocks of travelling birds dead on the
    snow,
Choked by the air, and scarce can they them-
    selves
Slake their parched throats with sugared mul-
    berries—
In single file they move, and stop their breath,
For fear they should dislodge the o'erhanging
    snows—
So the pale Persians held their breath with fear.
    And to Ferood his brother chiefs came up   170
To counsel; Gudurz and Zoarrah came,
And Feraburz, who ruled the Persian host
Second, and was the uncle of the King;
These came and counselled, and then Gudurz
    said:—
  ''Ferood, shame bids us take their challenge
    up,
Yet champion have we none to match this youth.

10 A town in Bokhara.
11 See *Par. Lost*, ii, 595.
12 Making the drink called kumiss.

He has the wild stag's foot, the lion's heart.
But Rustum came last night; aloof he sits
And sullen, and has pitched his tents apart.
Him will I seek, and carry to his ear   180
The Tartar challenge, and this young man's
    name.
Haply he will forget his wrath, and fight.13
Stand forth the while, and take their challenge
    up.''

  So spake he; and Ferood stood forth and
    cried:—
''Old man, be it agreed as thou hast said!
Let Sohrab arm, and we will find a man.''

  He spake: and Peran-Wisa turned, and
    strode
Back through the opening squadrons to his tent.
But through the anxious Persians Gudurz ran,
And crossed the camp which lay behind, and
    reached,   190
Out on the sands beyond it, Rustum's tents.
Of scarlet cloth they were, and glittering gay,
Just pitched; the high pavilion in the midst
Was Rustum's, and his men lay camped around.
And Gudurz entered Rustum's tent, and found
Rustum; his morning meal was done, but still
The table stood before him, charged with
    food—
A side of roasted sheep, and cakes of bread,
And dark green melons; and there Rustum sate
Listless, and held a falcon on his wrist,   200
And played with it; but Gudurz came and stood
Before him; and he looked, and saw him stand,
And with a cry sprang up and dropped the bird,
And greeted Gudurz with both hands, and
    said:—
''Welcome! these eyes could see no better
    sight.
What news? but sit down first, and eat and
    drink.''

  But Gudurz stood in the tent door, and
    said:—
''Not now! a time will come to eat and drink,
But not to-day; to-day has other needs.
The armies are drawn out, and stand at gaze;
For from the Tartars is a challenge brought 211
To pick a champion from the Persian lords
To fight their champion—and thou know'st his
    name—
Sohrab men call him, but his birth is hid.
O Rustum, like thy might is this young man's!
He has the wild stag's foot, the lion's heart;
And he is young, and Iran's chiefs are old,
Or else too weak; and all eyes turn to thee.
Come down and help us, Rustum, or we lose!''
  He spoke; but Rustum answered with a
    smile:—   220

''Go to! if Iran's chiefs are old, then I
Am older; if the young are weak, the King
Errs strangely; for the King, for Kai Khosroo,
Himself is young, and honours younger men,
And lets the aged moulder to their graves.
Rustum he loves no more, but loves the young—
The young may rise at Sohrab's vaunts, not I.
For what care I, though all speak Sohrab's
    fame?
For would that I myself had such a son,
And not that one slight helpless girl I have—
A son so famed, so brave, to send to war,   231
And I to tarry with the snow-haired Zal,*
My father, whom the robber Afghans vex,
And clip his borders short, and drive his herds,
And he has none to guard his weak old age.
There would I go, and hang my armour up,
And with my great name fence that weak old
    man,
And spend the goodly treasures I have got,
And rest my age, and hear of Sohrab's fame,
And leave to death the hosts of thankless
    kings,   240
And with these slaughterous hands draw sword
    no more.''
  He spoke and smiled; and Gudurz made re-
    ply:—
''What then, O Rustum, will men say to this,
When Sohrab dares our bravest forth, and seeks
Thee most of all, and thou, whom most he seeks,
Hidest thy face? Take heed lest men should
    say:
Like some old miser, Rustum hoards his fame,
And shuns to peril it with younger men.''
  And greatly moved, then Rustum made re-
    ply:—
''O Gudurz, wherefore dost thou say such
    words?   250
Thou knowest better words than this to say.
What is one more, one less, obscure or famed,
Valiant or craven, young or old, to me?
Are not they mortal, am not I myself?
But who for men of nought would do great
    deeds?
Come, thou shalt see how Rustum hoards his
    fame!
But I will fight unknown, and in plain arms;
Let not men say of Rustum, he was matched
In single fight with any mortal man.''
  He spoke, and frowned; and Gudurz turned,
    and ran   260
Back quickly through the camp in fear and
    joy—
Fear at his wrath, but joy that Rustum came.

13 This is a distinct echo of the *Iliad*.

* Zal was born with white hair, and on that account had been cast out to die, but was fostered by a marvelous bird, the simburg, or roc.
Cp. l. 679.

But Rustum strode to his tent-door, and called
His followers in, and bade them bring his arms,
And clad himself in steel; the arms he chose
Were plain, and on his shield was no device,
Only his helm was rich, inlaid with gold,
And, from the fluted spine atop, a plume
Of horsehair waved, a scarlet horsehair plume.
So armed, he issued forth; and Ruksh, his
    horse,   270
Followed him like a faithful hound at heel—
Ruksh, whose renown was noised through all the
    earth,
The horse, whom Rustum on a foray once
Did in Bokhara by the river find
A colt beneath its dam, and drove him home,
And reared him; a bright bay, with lofty crest,
Dight with a saddle-cloth of broidered green
Crusted with gold, and on the ground were
    worked
All beasts of chase, all beasts which hunters
    know.   280
So followed, Rustum left his tents, and crossed
The camp, and to the Persian host appeared.
And all the Persians knew him, and with shouts
Hailed; but the Tartars knew not who he was.
And dear as the wet diver to the eyes
Of his pale wife who waits and weeps on shore,
By sandy Bahrein, in the Persian Gulf,
Plunging all day in the blue waves, at night,
Having made up his tale of precious pearls,
Rejoins her in their hut upon the sands—
So dear to the pale Persians Rustum came.   290
    And Rustum to the Persian front advanced,
And Sohrab armed in Haman's tent, and came.
And as afield the reapers cut a swath
Down through the middle of a rich man's corn,
And on each side are squares of standing corn,
And in the midst a stubble, short and bare—
So on each side were squares of men, with
    spears
Bristling, and in the midst, the open sand.
And Rustum came upon the sand, and cast
His eyes toward the Tartar tents, and saw   300
Sohrab come forth, and eyed him as he came.
    As some rich woman, on a winter's morn,
Eyes through her silken curtains the poor
    drudge
Who with numb blackened fingers makes her
    fire—
At cock-crow, on a starlit winter's morn,
When the frost flowers the whitened window-
    panes—
And wonders how she lives, and what the
    thoughts
Of that poor drudge may be; so Rustum eyed
The unknown adventurous youth, who from afar
Came seeking Rustum, and defying forth   310
All the most valiant chiefs; long he perused

His spirited air, and wondered who he was.
For very young he seemed, tenderly reared;
Like some young cypress, tall, and dark, and
    straight,*
Which in a queen's secluded garden throws
Its slight dark shadow on the moonlit turf,
By midnight, to a bubbling fountain's sound—
So slender Sohrab seemed, so softly reared.
And a deep pity entered Rustum's soul
As he beheld him coming; and he stood,   320
And beckoned to him with his hand, and said:—
  "O thou young man, the air of Heaven is
    soft,
And warm, and pleasant; but the grave is cold!
Heaven's air is better than the cold dead grave.
Behold me! I am vast, and clad in iron,
And tried; and I have stood on many a field
Of blood, and I have fought with many a foe—
Never was that field lost, or that foe saved.
O Sohrab, wherefore wilt thou rush on death?
Be governed! quit the Tartar host, and come 330
To Iran, and be as my son to me,
And fight beneath my banner till I die!
There are no youths in Iran brave as thou."
    So he spake, mildly; Sohrab heard his voice,
The mighty voice of Rustum, and he saw
His giant figure planted on the sand,
Sole, like some single tower, which a chief
Hath builded on the waste in former years
Against the robbers; and he saw that head,
Streaked with its first gray hairs;—hope filled
    his soul,   340
And he ran forward and embraced his knees,
And clasped his hand within his own, and
    said:—
  "O, by thy father's head! by thine own soul!
Art thou not Rustum? speak! art thou not he?"
    But Rustum eyed askance the kneeling youth,
And turned away, and spake to his own soul:—
  "Ah me, I muse what this young fox may
    mean!
False, wily, boastful, are these Tartar boys.
For if I now confess this thing he asks,
And hide it not, but say: Rustum is here!   350
He will not yield indeed, nor quit our foes,
But he will find some pretext not to fight,
And praise my fame, and proffer courteous gifts,
A belt or sword perhaps, and go his way.
And on a feast-tide, in Afrasiab's hall,
In Samarcand, he will arise and cry:
'I challenged once, when the two armies
    camped
Beside the Oxus, all the Persian lords
To cope with me in single fight; but they
Shrank, only Rustum dared; then he and I   360
Changed gifts, and went on equal terms away.'

* For this oriental figure, compare the *Rubáiyát*,
  st. xli.

So will he speak, perhaps, while men applaud;
Then were the chiefs of Iran shamed through
    me.''
    And then he turned, and sternly spake
    aloud:—
''Rise! wherefore dost thou vainly question
    thus
Of Rustum? I am here, whom thou hast called
By challenge forth; make good thy vaunt, or
    yield!
Is it with Rustum only thou wouldst fight?
Rash boy, men look on Rustum's face and flee!
For well I know, that did great Rustum stand
Before thy face this day, and were re-
    vealed, 371
There would be then no talk of fighting more.
But being what I am, I tell thee this—
Do thou record it in thine inmost soul:
Either thou shalt renounce thy vaunt and yield,
Or else thy bones shall strew this sand, till
    winds
Bleach them, or Oxus with his summer-floods,
Oxus in summer wash them all away.''
    He spoke; and Sohrab answered, on his
    feet:—
''Art thou so fierce? Thou wilt not fright me
    so! 380
I am no girl, to be made pale by words.
Yet this thou hast said well, did Rustum stand
Here on this field, there were no fighting then.
But Rustum is far hence, and we stand here.
Begin! thou art more vast, more dread than I,
And thou art proved, I know, and I am young—
But yet success sways with the breath of
    Heaven.
And though thou thinkest that thou knowest
    sure
Thy victory, yet thou canst not surely know,
For we are all, like swimmers in the sea, 390
Poised on the top of a huge wave of fate,
Which hangs uncertain to which side to fall.
And whether it will heave us up to land,
Or whether it will roll us out to sea,
Back out to sea, to the deep waves of death,
We know not, and no search will make us know;
Only the event will teach us in its hour.''
    He spoke, and Rustum answered not, but
    hurled
His spear; down from the shoulder, down it
    came,
As on some partridge in the corn a hawk, 400
That long has towered in the airy clouds,
Drops like a plummet; Sohrab saw it come,
And sprang aside, quick as a flash; the spear
Hissed, and went quivering down into the sand,
Which it sent flying wide;—then Sohrab threw
In turn, and full struck Rustum's shield; sharp
    rang,

The iron plates rang sharp, but turned the
    spear.
And Rustum seized his club, which none but he
Could wield; an unlopped trunk it was, and
    huge,
Still rough—like those which men in treeless
    plains 410
To build them boats fish from the flooded rivers,
Hyphasis or Hydaspes, when, high up
By their dark springs, the wind in winter-time
Hath made in Himalayan forests wrack,
And strewn the channels with torn boughs—so
    huge
The club which Rustum lifted now, and struck
One stroke; but again Sohrab sprang aside,
Lithe as the glancing snake, and the club came
Thundering to earth, and leapt from Rustum's
    hand.
And Rustum followed his own blow, and fell
To his knees, and with his fingers clutched the
    sand; 421
And now might Sohrab have unsheathed his
    sword,
And pierced the mighty Rustum while he lay
Dizzy, and on his knees, and choked with sand;
But he looked on, and smiled, nor bared his
    sword,
But courteously drew back, and spoke, and
    said:—
''Thou strik'st too hard! that club of thine
    will float
Upon the summer-floods, and not my bones.
But rise, and be not wroth! not wroth am I;
No, when I see thee, wrath forsakes my soul.
Thou say'st, thou art not Rustum; be it so! 431
Who art thou then, that canst so touch my soul?
Boy as I am, I have seen battles too—
Have waded* foremost in their bloody waves,
And heard their hollow roar of dying men;
But never was my heart thus touched before.
Are they from Heaven, these softenings of the
    heart?
O thou old warrior, let us yield to Heaven!
Come, plant we here in earth our angry spears,
And make a truce, and sit upon this sand, 440
And pledge each other in red wine, like friends,
And thou shalt talk to me of Rustum's deeds.
There are enough foes in the Persian host,
Whom I may meet, and strike, and feel no
    pang;
Champions enough Afrasiab has, whom thou
Mayst fight; fight *them*, when they confront
    thy spear!
But oh, let there be peace 'twixt thee and
    me!''

* The word originally meant only "walked"; with
the change in meaning grew up the hyperbole
of "seas of blood," "bloody waves," etc.

He ceased, but while he spake, Rustum had
    risen,
And stood erect, trembling with rage; his club
He left to lie, but had regained his spear,   450
Whose fiery point now in his mailed right-
    hand
Blazed bright and baleful, like that autumn-
    star,
The baleful sign of fevers; dust had soiled
His stately crest, and dimmed his glittering
    arms.
His breast heaved, his lips foamed, and twice
    his voice
Was choked with rage; at last these words
    broke way:—
    "Girl! nimble with thy feet, not with thy
    hands!
Curled minion, dancer, coiner of sweet words!
Fight, let me hear thy hateful voice no more!
Thou art not in Afrasiab's gardens now   460
With Tartar girls, with whom thou art wont to
    dance;
But on the Oxus-sands, and in the dance
Of battle, and with me, who make no play
Of war; I fight it out, and hand to hand.
Speak not to me of truce, and pledge, and wine!
Remember all thy valour; try thy feints
And cunning! all the pity I had is gone;
Because thou hast shamed me before both the
    hosts
With thy light skipping tricks, and thy girl's
    wiles.''   469
    He spoke, and Sohrab kindled at his taunts,
And he too drew his sword; at once they
    rushed
Together, as two eagles on one prey
Come rushing down together from the clouds,
One from the east, one from the west; their
    shields
Dashed with a clang together, and a din
Rose, such as that the sinewy wood-cutters
Make often in the forest's heart at morn,
Of hewing axes, crashing trees—such blows
Rustum and Sohrab on each other hailed.
And you would say that sun and stars took
    part   480
In that unnatural conflict; for a cloud
Grew suddenly in Heaven, and darked the sun
Over the fighters' heads; and a wind rose
Under their feet, and moaning swept the plain,
And in a sandy whirlwind wrapped the pair.
In gloom they twain were wrapped, and they
    alone;
For both the on-looking hosts on either hand
Stood in broad daylight, and the sky was pure,
And the sun sparkled on the Oxus stream.
But in the gloom they fought, with bloodshot
    eyes   490

And labouring breath; first Rustum struck the
    shield
Which Sohrab held stiff out; the steel-spiked
    spear
Rent the tough plates, but failed to reach the
    skin,
And Rustum plucked it back with angry groan.
Then Sohrab with his sword smote Rustum's
    helm,
Nor clove its steel quite through; but all the
    crest
He shore away, and that proud horsehair plume,
Never till now defiled, sank to the dust;
And Rustum bowed his head; but then the
    gloom
Grew blacker, thunder rumbled in the air,   500
And lightnings rent the cloud; and Ruksh, the
    horse,
Who stood at hand, uttered a dreadful cry;—
No horse's cry was that, most like the roar
Of some pained desert-lion, who all day
Hath trailed the hunter's javelin in his side,
And comes at night to die upon the sand.
The two hosts heard that cry, and quaked for
    fear,
And Oxus curdled as it crossed his stream.
But Sohrab heard, and quailed not, but rushed
    on,
And struck again; and again Rustum bowed 510
His head; but this time all the blade, like glass,
Sprang in a thousand shivers on the helm,
And in the hand the hilt remained alone.
Then Rustum raised his head; his dreadful
    eyes
Glared, and he shook on high his menacing
    spear,
And shouted: *Rustum!*—Sohrab heard that
    shout,
And shrank amazed; back he recoiled one step,
And scanned with blinking eyes the advancing
    form;
And then he stood bewildered; and he dropped
His covering shield, and the spear pierced his
    side.   520
He reeled, and staggering back, sank to the
    ground,
And then the gloom dispersed, and the wind
    fell,
And the bright sun broke forth, and melted all
The cloud; and the two armies saw the pair—
Saw Rustum standing, safe upon his feet,
And Sohrab, wounded, on the bloody sand.
    Then, with a bitter smile, Rustum began:—
"Sohrab, thou thoughtest in thy mind to kill
A Persian lord this day, and strip his corpse,
And bear thy trophies to Afrasiab's tent. 530
Or else that the great Rustum would come down
Himself to fight, and that thy wiles would move

His heart to take a gift, and let thee go.
And then that all the Tartar host would praise
Thy courage or thy craft, and spread thy fame,
To glad thy father in his weak old age.
Fool, thou art slain, and by an unknown man!
Dearer to the red jackals shalt thou be
Than to thy friends, and to thy father old.''
   And, with a fearless mien, Sohrab re-
      plied:—   540
''Unknown thou art; yet thy fierce vaunt is
      vain.
Thou dost not slay me, proud and boastful
      man!
No! Rustum slays me, and this filial heart.
For were I matched with ten such men as thee,
And I were that which till to-day I was,
They should be lying here, I standing there.
But that belovèd name unnerved my arm—
That name, and something, I confess, in thee,
Which troubles all my heart, and made my
      shield
Fall; and thy spear transfixed an unarmed
      foe.   550
And now thou boastest, and insult'st my fate.
But hear thou this, fierce man, tremble to hear
The mighty Rustum shall avenge my death!
My father, whom I seek through all the world,
He shall avenge my death, and punish thee!''
   As when some hunter in the spring hath
      found
A breeding eagle sitting on her nest,
Upon the craggy isle of a hill-lake,
And pierced her with an arrow as she rose,
And followed her to find her where she fell 560
Far off;—anon her mate comes winging back
From hunting, and a great way off descries
His huddling young left sole; at that, he checks
His pinion, and with short uneasy sweeps
Circles above his eyry, with loud screams
Chiding his mate back to her nest; but she
Lies dying, with the arrow in her side,
In some far stony gorge out of his ken,
A heap of fluttering feathers—never more
Shall the lake glass her, flying over it;   570
Never the black and dripping precipices
Echo her stormy scream as she sails by—
As that poor bird flies home, nor knows his loss,
So Rustum knew not his own loss, but stood
Over his dying son, and knew him not.
   But, with a cold incredulous voice, he said:—
''What prate is this of fathers and revenge?
The mighty Rustum never had a son.''
   And, with a failing voice, Sohrab replied:—
''Ah yes, he had! and that lost son am I. 580
Surely the news will one day reach his ear,
Reach Rustum, where he sits, and tarries long,
Somewhere, I know not where, but far from
      here,

And pierce him like a stab, and make him leap
To arms, and cry for vengeance upon thee.
Fierce man, bethink thee, for an only son!
What will that grief, what will that vengeance
      be?
Oh, could I live, till I that grief had seen!
Yet him I pity not so much, but her,
My mother, who in Ader-baijan dwells   590
With that old king, her father, who grows gray
With age, and rules over the valiant Koords.
Her most I pity, who no more will see
Sohrab returning from the Tartar camp,
With spoils and honour, when the war is done.
But a dark rumour will be bruited up,
From tribe to tribe, until it reach her ear;
And then will that defenceless woman learn
That Sohrab will rejoice her sight no more,
But that in battle with a nameless foe,   600
By the far-distant Oxus, he is slain.''
   He spoke; and as he ceased, he wept aloud,
Thinking of her he left, and his own death.
He spoke; but Rustum listened, plunged in
      thought.
Nor did he yet believe it was his son
Who spoke, although he called back names he
      knew;
For he had had sure tidings that the babe,
Which was in Ader-baijan born to him,
Had been a puny girl, no boy at all—
So that sad mother sent him word, for fear 610
Rustum should seek the boy, to train in arms.
And so he deemed that either Sohrab took,
By a false boast, the style of Rustum's son;
Or that men gave it him, to swell his fame.
So deemed he; yet he listened, plunged in
      thought.
And his soul set to grief, as the vast tide
Of the bright rocking Ocean sets to shore
At the full moon; tears gathered in his eyes;
For he remembered his own early youth,
And all its bounding rapture; as, at dawn, 620
The shepherd from his mountain-lodge descries
A far, bright city, smitten by the sun,
Through many rolling clouds—so Rustum saw
His youth; saw Sohrab's mother, in her bloom;
And that old king, her father, who loved well
His wandering guest, and gave him his fair
      child
With joy; and all the pleasant life they led,
They three, in that long-distant summer-time—
The castle, and the dewy woods, and hunt
And hound, and morn on those delightful hills
In Ader-baijan. And he saw that Youth,   631
Of age and looks to be his own dear son,
Piteous and lovely, lying on the sand,
Like some rich hyacinth which by the scythe
Of an unskilful gardener has been cut,
Mowing the garden grass-plots near its bed.

And lies, a fragrant tower of purple bloom,
On the mown, dying grass—so Sohrab lay,
Lovely in death, upon the common sand.
And Rustum gazed on him with grief, and
  said:— 640
  "O Sohrab, thou indeed art such a son
Whom Rustum, wert thou his, might well have
  loved.
Yet here thou errest, Sohrab, or else men
Have told thee false—thou art not Rustum's
  son.
For Rustum had no son; one child he had—
But one—a girl; who with her mother now
Plies some light female task, nor dreams of
  us—
Of us she dreams not, nor of wounds, nor war.'
  But Sohrab answered him in wrath; for now
The anguish of the deep-fixed spear grew
  fierce, 650
And he desired to draw forth the steel.
And let the blood flow free, and so to die—
But first he would convince his stubborn foe;
And, rising sternly on one arm, he said:—
  "Man, who art thou who dost deny my
  words?
Truth sits upon the lips of dying men,
And falsehood, while I lived, was far from
  mine.
I tell thee, pricked upon this arm I bear
That seal which Rustum to my mother gave,
That she might prick it on the babe she bore."
  He spoke; and all the blood left Rustum's
  cheeks, 661
And his knees tottered, and he smote his hand
Against his breast, his heavy mailèd hand,
That the hard iron corslet clanked aloud:
And to his heart he pressed the other hand,
And in a hollow voice he spake, and said:—
  "Sohrab, that were a proof which could not
  lie!
If thou show this, then art thou Rustum's
  son."
  Then, with weak hasty fingers, Sohrab loosed
His belt, and near the shoulder bared his arm,
And showed a sign in faint vermilion points 671
Pricked; as a cunning workman, in Pekin,
Pricks with vermilion some clear porcelain
  vase,
An emperor's gift—at early morn he paints,
And all day long, and, when night comes, the
  lamp
Lights up his studious forehead and thin
  hands—
So delicately pricked the sign appeared
On Sohrab's arm, the sign of Rustum's seal.
It was that griffin, which of old reared Zal,
Rustum's great father, whom they left to die,
A helpless babe, among the mountain-rocks; 681

Him that kind creature found, and reared, and
  loved—
Then Rustum took it for his glorious sign.
And Sohrab bared that image on his arm,
And himself scanned it long with mournful
  eyes,
And then he touched it with his hand and
  said:—
  "How say'st thou? Is that sign the proper
  sign
Of Rustum's son, or of some other man's?"
  He spoke; but Rustum gazed, and gazed, and
  stood
Speechless; and then he uttered one sharp
  cry: 690
O boy—thy father!—and his voice choked there.
And then a dark cloud passed before his eyes,
And his head swam, and he sank down to earth.
But Sohrab crawled to where he lay, and cast
His arms about his neck, and kissed his lips,
And with fond faltering fingers stroked his
  cheeks,
Trying to call him back to life; and life
Came back to Rustum, and he oped his eyes,
And they stood wide with horror; and he seized
In both his hands the dust which lay around,
And threw it on his head, and smirched his
  hair,— 701
His hair, and face, and beard, and glittering
  arms;
And strong convulsive groanings shook his
  breast,
And his sobs choked him; and he clutched his
  sword,
To draw it, and for ever let life out.
But Sohrab saw his thought, and held his
  hands,
And with a soothing voice he spake, and
  said:—
  "Father, forbear! for I but meet to-day
The doom which at my birth was written down
In Heaven, and thou art Heaven's unconscious
  hand. 710
Surely my heart cried out that it was thou,
When first I saw thee; and thy heart spoke too,
I know it! but fate trod those promptings
  down
Under its iron heel; fate, fate engaged
The strife, and hurled me on my father's spear.
But let us speak no more of this! I find
My father; let me feel that I have found!
Come, sit beside me on this sand, and take
My head betwixt thy hands, and kiss my cheeks,
And wash them with thy tears, and say: My
  son! 720
Quick! quick! for numbered are my sands of
  life,
And swift; for like the lightning to this field

I came, and like the wind I go away—
Sudden, and swift, and like a passing wind.
But it was writ in Heaven that this should be.''
  So said he, and his voice released the heart
Of Rustum, and his tears broke forth; he cast
His arms round his son's neck, and wept aloud,
And kissed him. And awe fell on both the
    hosts,
When they saw Rustum's grief; and Ruksh, the
    horse,   730
With his head bowing to the ground and mane
Sweeping the dust, came near, and in mute woe
First to the one, then to the other moved
His head, as if inquiring what their grief
Might mean; and from his dark, compassionate
    eyes,
The big warm tears rolled down, and caked the
    sand.*
But Rustum chid him with stern voice, and
    said:—
  ''Ruksh, now thou grievest; but, O Ruksh,
    thy feet
Should first have rotted on their nimble joints,
Or ere they brought thy master to this field!''
  But Sohrab looked upon the horse and
    said:—   741
''Is this, then, Ruksh? How often, in past
    days,
My mother told me of thee, thou brave steed,
My terrible father's terrible horse! and said,
That I should one day find thy lord and thee.
Come, let me lay my hand upon thy mane!
O Ruksh, thou art more fortunate than I;
For thou hast gone where I shall never go,
And snuffed the breezes of my father's home,
And thou hast trod the sands of Seistan,   750
And seen the River of Helmund, and the Lake
Of Zirrah; and the aged Zal himself
Has often stroked thy neck, and given thee
    food,
Corn in a golden platter soaked with wine,
And said: O Ruksh! bear Rustum well!—but I
Have never known my grandsire's furrowed
    face,
Nor seen his lofty house in Seistan,
Nor slaked my thirst at the clear Helmund
    stream;
But lodged among my father's foes, and seen
Afrasiab's cities only, Samarcand,   760
Bokhara, and lone Khiva in the waste,
And the black Toorkmun tents; and only drunk
The desert rivers, Moorghab and Tejend,
Kohik, and where the Kalmuks feed their sheep,
The northern Sir; and this great Oxus stream,
The yellow Oxus, by whose brink I die.''

* Compare the action of the horse of Achilles,
  Iliad, xix, end.

  Then, with a heavy groan, Rustum be-
    wailed:—
''Oh, that its waves were flowing over me!
Oh, that I saw its grains of yellow silt
Roll tumbling in the current o'er my head!''
  But, with a grave mild voice, Sohrab re-
    plied:—   771
''Desire not that, my father! thou must live.
For some are born to do great deeds, and live,
As some are born to be obscured, and die.
Do thou the deeds I die too young to do,
And reap a second glory in thine age;
Thou art my father, and thy gain is mine.
But come! thou seest this great host of men
Which follow me; I pray thee, slay not these!
Let me entreat for them; what have they
    done?   780
They followed me, my hope, my fame, my star.
Let them all cross the Oxus back in peace.
But me thou must bear hence, not send with
    them,
But carry me with thee to Seistan,
And place me on a bed, and mourn for me,
Thou, and the snow-haired Zal, and all thy
    friends.
And thou must lay me in that lovely earth,
And heap a stately mound above my bones,
And plant a far-seen pillar over all.
That so the passing horseman on the waste 790
May see my tomb a great way off, and cry:
Sohrab, the mighty Rustum's son, lies there,
Whom his great father did in ignorance kill!
And I be not forgotten in my grave.''
  And, with a mournful voice, Rustum re-
    plied:—
''Fear not! as thou hast said, Sohrab, my son,
So shall it be; for I will burn my tents,
And quit the host, and bear thee hence with me,
And carry thee away to Seistan,
And place thee on a bed, and mourn for thee,
With the snow-headed Zal, and all my friends,
And I will lay thee in that lovely earth,   802
And heap a stately mound above thy bones,
And plant a far-seen pillar over all,
And men shall not forget thee in thy grave.
And I will spare thy host; yea, let them go!
Let them all cross the Oxus back in peace!
What should I do with slaying any more?
For would that all that I have ever slain
Might be once more alive; my bitterest foes, 810
And they who were called champions in their
    time,
And through whose death I won that fame I
    have—
And I were nothing but a common man,
A poor, mean soldier, and without renown,
So thou mightest live too, my son, my son!
Or rather would that I, even I myself,

Might now be lying on this bloody sand,
Near death, and by an ignorant stroke of thine,
Not thou of mine; and I might die, not thou;
And I, not thou, be borne to Seistan;　　820
And Zal might weep above my grave, not thine;
And say: *O son, I weep thee not too sore,*
For willingly, I know, thou met'st thine end!
But now in blood and battles was my youth,
And full of blood and battles is my age,
And I shall never end this life of blood.''

　　Then, at the point of death, Sohrab re-
　　plied:—
''A life of blood indeed, thou dreadful man!
But thou shalt yet have peace; only not now,
Not yet! but thou shalt have it on that day,
When thou shalt sail in a high-masted ship,　831
Thou and the other peers of Kai Khosroo,
Returning home over the salt blue sea,
From laying thy dear master in his grave.''

　　And Rustum gazed in Sohrab's face, and
　　said:—
''Soon be that day, my son, and deep that sea!
Till then, if fate so wills, let me endure.''

　　He spoke; and Sohrab smiled on him, and
　　took
The spear, and drew it from his side, and eased
His wound's imperious anguish; but the blood
Came welling from the open gash, and life　841
Flowed with the stream;—all down his cold
　　white side
The crimson torrent ran, dim now and soiled,
Like the soiled tissue of white violets
Left, freshly gathered, on their native bank,
By children whom their nurses call with haste
Indoors from the sun's eye; his head drooped
　　low,
His limbs grew slack; motionless, white, he
　　lay—
White, with eyes closed; only when heavy gasps,
Deep heavy gasps quivering through all his
　　frame,　　　　　　　　　　　　　　850
Convulsed him back to life, he opened them,
And fixed them feebly on his father's face;
Till now all strength was ebbed, and from his
　　limbs
Unwillingly the spirit fled away,
Regretting the warm mansion which it left,
And youth, and bloom, and this delightful
　　world.

　　So, on the bloody sand, Sohrab lay dead;
And the great Rustum drew his horseman's
　　cloak
Down o'er his face, and sate by his dead son.
As those black granite pillars, once high-
　　reared　　　　　　　　　　　　　　860
By Jemshid[1] in Persepolis, to bear

His house, now 'mid their broken flights of
　　steps
Lie prone, enormous, down the mountain side—
So in the sand lay Rustum by his son.

　　And night came down over the solemn waste,
And the two gazing hosts, and that sole pair,
And darkened all; and a cold fog, with night,
Crept from the Oxus. Soon a hum arose
As of a great assembly loosed, and fires
Began to twinkle through the fog; for now　870
Both armies moved to camp, and took their
　　meal;
The Persians took it on the open sands
Southward, the Tartars by the river marge;
And Rustum and his son were left alone.

　　But the majestic river floated on,
Out of the mist and hum of that low land,
Into the frosty starlight, and there moved,
Rejoicing, through the hushed Chorasmian
　　waste,
Under the solitary moon;—he flowed
Right for the polar star, past Orgunjè,[2]　880
Brimming, and bright, and large; then sands
　　begin
To hem his watery march, and dam his streams,
And split his currents; that for many a league
The shorn and parcelled Oxus strains along
Through beds of sand and matted rushy isles—
Oxus, forgetting the bright speed he had
In his high mountain-cradle in Pamere,
A foiled circuitous wanderer—till at last
The longed-for dash of waves is heard, and wide
His luminous home of waters opens, bright　890
And tranquil, from whose floor the new-bathed
　　stars
Emerge, and shine upon the Aral Sea.

PHILOMELA*

Hark! ah, the nightingale—
The tawny-throated!
Hark, from that moonlit cedar what a burst!
What triumph! hark!—what pain!

O wanderer from a Grecian shore,
Still, after many years, in distant lands,
Still nourishing in thy bewildered brain
That wild, unquenched, deep-sunken, old-world
　　pain—
Say, will it never heal?
And can this fragrant lawn　　　　　　　10
With its cool trees, and night,
And the sweet, tranquil Thames,
And moonshine, and the dew,

[2] A village near Khiva.

* See the familiar story of Philomela and Procne in Greek mythology. The poem is evidently addressed to a friend, "Eugenia."

[1] Or Jamshid; a mythical king of Persia. Persepolis is noted for its ruins of ancient grandeur.

To thy racked heart and brain
Afford no balm?

Dost thou to-night behold,
Here, through the moonlight on this English
    grass,
The unfriendly palace in the Thracian wild?
Dost thou again peruse
With hot cheeks and seared eyes   20
The too clear web, and thy dumb sister's
    shame?
Dost thou once more assay
Thy flight, and feel come over thee,
Poor fugitive, the feathery change
Once more, and once more seem to make re-
    sound
With love and hate, triumph and agony,
Lone Daulis, and the high Cephissian vale?

Listen, Eugenia—
How thick the bursts come crowding through
    the leaves!
Again—thou hearest?   30
Eternal passion!
Eternal pain!

KAISER DEAD

APRIL 6, 1887.

What, Kaiser dead? The heavy news
Post-haste to Cobham[1] calls the Muse,
From where in Farringford[2] she brews
    The ode sublime,
Or with Pen-bryn's bold bard[3] pursues
    A rival rhyme.

Kai's bracelet tail, Kai's busy feet,
Were known to all the village-street.
"What, poor Kai dead?" say all I meet;
    "A loss indeed!"
O for the croon pathetic, sweet,
    Of Robin's reed![4]   12

Six years ago I brought him down,
A baby dog, from London town;
Round his small throat of black and brown
    A ribbon blue,
And vouched by glorious renown
    A dachshound true.

His mother, most majestic dame,
Of blood-unmixed, from Potsdam[5] came;
And Kaiser's race we deemed the same—
    No lineage higher.

And so he bore the imperial name.
    But ah, his sire!   24

Soon, soon the days conviction bring.
The collie hair, the collie swing,
The tail's indomitable ring,
    The eye's unrest—
The case was clear; a mongrel thing
    Kai stood confest.

But all those virtues, which commend
The humbler sort who serve and tend,
Were thine in store, thou faithful friend.
    What sense, what cheer!
To us, declining towards our end,
    A mate how dear!   36

For Max, thy brother-dog, began
To flag, and feel his narrowing span.
And cold, besides, his blue blood ran,
    Since, 'gainst the classes,
He heard, of late, the Grand Old Man
    Incite the Masses.[6]

Yes, Max and we grew slow and sad;
But Kai, a tireless shepherd-lad,
Teeming with plans, alert, and glad
    In work or play,
Like sunshine went and came, and bade
    Live out the day!   48

Still, still I see the figure smart—
Trophy in mouth, agog to start,
Then, home returned, once more depart;
    Or prest together
Against thy mistress, loving heart,
    In winter weather.

I see the tail, like bracelet twirled,
In moments of disgrace uncurled,
Then at a pardoning word re-furled,
    A conquering sign;
Crying, "Come on, and range the world,
    And never pine."   60

Thine eye was bright, thy coat it shone;
Thou hadst thine errands, off and on;
In joy thy last morn flew; anon,
    A fit! All's over;
And thou art gone where Geist[7] hath gone,
    And Toss, and Rover.

Poor Max, with downcast, reverent head,
Regards his brother's form outspread;

1 In Surrey, where Arnold was then living.
2 Tennyson's home on the Isle of Wight.
3 Sir Lewis Morris lived at Pen-bryn, in Wales.
4 Adapted from Burns's *Poor Mailie's Elegy,* which
    Arnold is imitating.
5 A residence of the German emperor.

6 A mild thrust at Gladstone and his Home Rule
    Bill.
7 Mourned in a previous elegy, *Geist's Grave.*

Full well Max knows the friend is dead
    Whose cordial talk,
And jokes, in doggish language said,
    Beguiled his walk.   72

And Glory, stretched at Burwood gate,
Thy passing by doth vainly wait;
And jealous Jock, thy only hate,
    The chiel from Skye,
Lets from his shaggy Highland pate
    Thy memory die.

Well, fetch his graven collar fine,
And rub the steel, and make it shine,
And leave it round thy neck to twine,
    Kai, in thy grave.
There of thy master keep that sign,
    And this plain stave.   84

DOVER BEACH*

The sea is calm to-night,
The tide is full, the moon lies fair
Upon the straits;—on the French coast the
    light
Gleams and is gone; the cliffs of England
    stand,
Glimmering and vast, out in the tranquil bay.
Come to the window, sweet is the night-air!
Only, from the long line of spray
Where the sea meets the moon-blanched land,
Listen! you hear the grating roar
Of pebbles which the waves draw back, and
    fling,   10
At their return, up the high strand,
Begin, and cease, and then again begin,
With tremulous cadence slow, and bring
The eternal note of sadness in.

Sophocles long ago
Heard it on the Ægæan, and it brought
Into his mind the turbid ebb and flow
Of human misery; we
Find also in the sound a thought,
Hearing it by this distant northern sea.   20

The Sea of Faith
Was once, too, at the full, and round earth's
    shore
Lay like the folds of a bright girdle furled.
But now I only hear
Its melancholy, long, withdrawing roar,
Retreating, to the breath
Of the night-wind, down the vast edges drear
And naked shingles of the world.

---

* Another expression of Arnold's Stoic creed. See
note on his sonnet *To a Friend*, p. 642.

Ah, love, let us be true
To one another; for the world, which seems   30
To lie before us like a land of dreams,
So various, so beautiful, so new,
Hath really neither joy, nor love, nor light,
Nor certitude, nor peace, nor help for pain;
And we are here as on a darkling plain
Swept with confused alarms of struggle and
    flight,
Where ignorant armies clash by night.

THE LAST WORD

Creep into thy narrow bed,
Creep, and let no more be said!
Vain thy onset! all stands fast.
Thou thyself must break at last.

Let the long contention cease!
Geese are swans, and swans are geese.
Let them have it how they will!
Thou art tired; best be still.

They out-talked thee, hissed thee, tore thee?
Better men fared thus before thee;
Fired their ringing shot and passed,
Hotly charged—and sank at last.

Charge once more, then, and be dumb!
Let the victors, when they come,
When the forts of folly fall,
Find thy body by the wall!

CULTURE AND HUMAN PERFECTION*

The disparagers of culture make its motive
curiosity; sometimes, indeed, they make its
motive mere exclusiveness and vanity. The culture which is supposed to plume itself on a
smattering of Greek and Latin is a culture
which is begotten by nothing so intellectual as
curiosity; it is valued either out of sheer vanity
and ignorance, or else as an engine of social
and class distinction, separating its holder, like
a badge or title, from other people who have
not got it. No serious man would call this *culture*, or attach any value to it, as culture, at all.
To find the real ground for the very different
estimate which serious people will set upon culture, we must find some motive for culture in
the terms of which may lie a real ambiguity;
and such a motive the word *curiosity* gives us.

I have before now pointed out that we English do not, like the foreigners, use this word

---

* From the first chapter of *Culture and Anarchy*
(1867), entitled "Sweetness and Light."

in a good sense as well as in a bad sense. With us the word is always used in a somewhat disapproving sense. A liberal and intelligent eagerness about the things of the mind may be meant by a foreigner when he speaks of curiosity, but with us the word always conveys a certain notion of frivolous and unedifying activity. In the *Quarterly Review*, some little time ago, was an estimate of the celebrated French critic, M. Sainte-Beuve, and a very inadequate estimate it in my judgment was. And its inadequacy consisted chiefly in this: that in our English way it left out of sight the double sense really involved in the word *curiosity*, thinking enough was said to stamp M. Sainte-Beuve with blame if it was said that he was impelled in his operations as a critic by curiosity, and omitting either to perceive that M. Sainte-Beuve himself, and many other people with him, would consider that this was praiseworthy and not blameworthy, or to point out why it ought really to be accounted worthy of blame and not of praise. For, as there is a curiosity about intellectual matters which is futile and merely a disease, so there is certainly a curiosity,—a desire after the things of the mind simply for their own sakes and for the pleasure of seeing them as they are,—which is, in an intelligent being, natural and laudable. Nay, and the very desire to see things as they are† implies a balance and regulation of mind which is not often attained without fruitful effort, and which is the very opposite of the blind and diseased impulse of mind which is what we mean to blame when we blame curiosity. Montesquieu[1] says: "The first motive which ought to impel us to study is the desire to augment the excellence of our nature, and to render an intelligent being yet more intelligent." This is the true ground to assign for the genuine scientific passion, however manifested, and for culture, viewed simply as a fruit of this passion; and it is a worthy ground, even though we let the term *curiosity* stand to describe it.

But there is of culture another view, in which not solely the scientific passion, the sheer desire to see things as they are, natural and proper in an intelligent being, appears as the ground of it. There is a view in which all the love of our neighbour, the impulses towards action, help,

and beneficence, the desire for removing human error, clearing human confusion, and diminishing human misery, the noble aspiration to leave the world better and happier than we found it, —motives eminently such as are called social,— come in as part of the grounds of culture, and the main and pre-eminent part. Culture is, then, properly described, not as having its origin in curiosity, but as having its origin in the love of perfection; it is *a study of perfection*. It moves by the force, not merely or primarily of the scientific passion for pure knowledge, but also of the moral and social passion for doing good. As, in the first view of it, we took for its worthy motto Montesquieu's words, "To render an intelligent being yet more intelligent!" so, in the second view of it, there is no better motto which it can have than these words of Bishop Wilson[2]: "To make reason and the will of God prevail!"

Only, whereas the passion for doing good is apt to be over-hasty in determining what reason and the will of God say, because its turn is for acting rather than thinking, and it wants to be beginning to act; and whereas it is apt to take its own conceptions, which proceed from its own state of development and share in all the imperfections and immaturities of this, for a basis of action; what distinguishes culture is, that it is possessed by the scientific passion, as well as by the passion of doing good; that it demands worthy notions of reason and the will of God, and does not readily suffer its own crude conceptions to substitute themselves for them. And knowing that no action or institution can be salutary and stable which is not based on reason and the will of God, it is not so bent on acting and instituting, even with the great aim of diminishing human error and misery ever before its thoughts, but that it can remember that acting and instituting are of little use, unless we know how and what we ought to act and to institute.

This culture is more interesting and more far-reaching than that other, which is founded solely on the scientific passion for knowing. But it needs times of faith and ardour, times when the intellectual horizon is opening and widening all round us, to flourish in. And is not the close and bounded intellectual horizon within which we have long lived and moved now lifting up, and are not new lights finding free passage to shine in upon us? For a long time there was no passage for them to make their way in upon us, and then it was of no

---

1 A French writer of the 18th century, author of the celebrated philosophical work on *The Spirit of the Laws*.

† This phrase, derived from Wordsworth, has been given wide currency by Arnold. See Wordsworth's Supplementary Essay to his Preface to the *Lyrical Ballads*.

2 Thomas Wilson, Bishop of the Isle of Man (d. 1765).

use to think of adapting the world's action to them. Where was the hope of making reason and the will of God prevail among people who had a routine which they had christened reason and the will of God, in which they were inextricably bound, and beyond which they had no power of looking? But now the iron force of adhesion to the old routine,—social, political religious,—has wonderfully yielded; the iron force of exclusion of all which is new has wonderfully yielded. The danger now is, not that people should obstinately refuse to allow anything but their old routine to pass for reason and the will of God, but either that they should allow some novelty or other to pass for these too easily, or else that they should underrate the importance of them altogether, and think it enough to follow action for its own sake, without troubling themselves to make reason and the will of God prevail therein. Now, then, is the moment for culture to be of service, culture which believes in making reason and the will of God prevail; believes in perfection; is the study and pursuit of perfection; and is no longer debarred, by a rigid invincible exclusion of whatever is new, from getting acceptance for its ideas, simply because they are new.

The moment this view of culture is seized, the moment it is regarded not solely as the endeavour to see things as they are, to draw towards a knowledge of the universal order which seems to be intended and aimed at in the world, and which it is a man's happiness to go along with or his misery to go counter to,—to learn, in short, the will of God,—the moment, I say, culture is considered not merely as the endeavour to *see* and *learn* this, but as the endeavour, also, to make it *prevail*, the moral, social, and beneficent character of culture becomes manifest. The mere endeavour to see and learn the truth for our own personal satisfaction is indeed a commencement for making it prevail, a preparing the way for this, which always serves this, and is wrongly, therefore, stamped with blame absolutely in itself and not only in its caricature and degeneration. But perhaps it has got stamped with blame and disparaged with the dubious title of curiosity because, in comparison with this wider endeavour of such great and plain utility, it looks selfish, petty, and unprofitable.

And religion, the greatest and most important of the efforts by which the human race has manifested its impulse to perfect itself,—religion, that voice of the deepest human experience,—does not only enjoin and sanction the aim which is the great aim of culture, the

aim of setting ourselves to ascertain what perfection is, and to make it prevail; but also, in determining generally in what human perfection consists, religion comes to a conclusion identical with that which culture,—culture seeking the determination of this question through *all* the voices of human experience which have been heard upon it, of art, science, poetry, philosophy, history, as well as of religion, in order to give a greater fullness and certainty to its solution,—likewise reaches. Religion says: *The kingdom of God is within you*; and culture, in like manner, places human perfection in an *internal* condition, in the growth and predominance of our humanity proper, as distinguished from our animality. It places it in the ever-increasing efficacy and in the general harmonious expansion of those gifts of thought and feeling which make the peculiar dignity, wealth, and happiness of human nature. As I have said on a former occasion: "It is in making endless additions to itself, in the endless expansion of its powers, in endless growth in wisdom and beauty, that the spirit of the human race finds its ideal. To reach this ideal, culture is an indispensable aid, and that is the true value of culture." Not a having and a resting, but a growing and a becoming, is the character of perfection as culture conceives it; and here, too, it coincides with religion. . . . .

But the point of view of culture, keeping the mark of human perfection simply and broadly in view, and not assigning to this perfection, as religion or utilitarianism assigns to it, a special and limited character, this point of view, I say, of culture is best given by these words of Epictetus[1]: "It is a sign of ἀφυΐα," says he,—that is, of a nature not finely tempered,—"to give yourselves up to things which relate to the body; to make, for instance, a great fuss about exercise, a great fuss about eating, a great fuss about drinking, a great fuss about walking, a great fuss about riding. All these things ought to be done merely by the way; the formation of the spirit and character must be our real concern." This is admirable; and, indeed, the Greek word εὐφυΐα, a finely tempered nature, gives exactly the notion of perfection as culture brings us to conceive it: a harmonious perfection, a perfection in which the characters of beauty and intelligence are both present, which unites "the two noblest of things,"—as Swift, who of one of the two, at any rate, had himself all too little, most happily calls them in his *Battle of*

[1] See note on Arnold's sonnet *To a Friend*.

the Books,—''the two noblest of things, *sweetness and light.*''* The εὐφυής[2] is the man who tends toward sweetness and light; the ἀφυής[3] on the other hand, is our Philistine.[4] The immense spiritual significance of the Greeks is due to their having been inspired with this central and happy idea of the essential character of human perfection; and Mr. Bright's[5] misconception of culture, as a smattering of Greek and Latin, comes itself, after all, from this wonderful significance of the Greeks having affected the very machinery of our education, and is in itself a kind of homage to it.

In thus making sweetness and light to be characters of perfection, culture is of like spirit with poetry, follows one law with poetry. Far more than on our freedom, our population, and our industrialism, many amongst us rely upon our religious organizations to save us. I have called religion a yet more important manifestation of human nature than poetry, because it has worked on a broader scale for perfection, and with greater masses of men. But the idea of beauty and of a human nature perfect on all its sides, which is the dominant idea of poetry, is a true and invaluable idea, though it has not yet had the success that the idea of conquering the obvious faults of our animality, and of a human nature perfect on the moral side,—which is the dominant idea of religion,—has been enabled to have; and it is destined, adding to itself the religious idea of a devout energy, to transform and govern the other.

The best art and poetry of the Greeks, in which religion and poetry are one, in which the idea of beauty and of a human nature perfect on all sides adds to itself a religious and devout energy, and works in the strength of that, is on this account of such surpassing interest and instructiveness for us, though it was,—as having regard to the human race in general, and, indeed, having regard to the Greeks themselves, we must own,—a premature attempt, an attempt which for success needed the moral and religious fibre in humanity to be more braced and developed than it had yet been. But Greece did not err in having the idea of beauty, harmony, and complete human perfection, so present and paramount. It is impossible to have this idea too present and paramount; only, the moral fibre must be braced too. And we, because we have braced the moral fibre, are not on that account in the right way, if at the same time the idea of beauty, harmony, and complete human perfection is wanting or misapprehended amongst us.

NATURAL MAGIC IN CELTIC LITERATURE†

The Celt's quick feeling for what is noble and distinguished gave his poetry style; his indomitable personality gave it pride and passion; his sensibility and nervous exaltation gave it a better gift still, the gift of rendering with wonderful felicity the magical charm of nature. The forest solitude, the bubbling spring, the wild flowers, are everywhere in romance. They have a mysterious life and grace there; they are Nature's own children, and utter her secret in a way which makes them something quite different from the woods, waters, and plants of Greek and Latin poetry. Now of this delicate magic, Celtic romance is so pre-eminent a mistress, that it seems impossible to believe the power did not come into romance from the Celts. Magic is just the word for it,—the magic of nature; not merely the beauty of nature,—that the Greeks and Latins had; not merely an honest smack of the soil, a faithful realism,—that the Germans had; but the intimate life of Nature, her weird power and her fairy charm. As the Saxon names of places, with the pleasant wholesome smack of the soil in them,—Weathersfield, Thaxted, Shalford,—are to the Celtic names of places, with their penetrating, lofty beauty,—Velindra, Tyntagel, Caernarvon,—so is the homely realism of German and Norse nature to the fairy-like loveliness of Celtic nature. Gwydion wants a wife for his pupil: ''Well,'' says Math, ''we will seek, I and thou, by charms and illusions, to form a wife for him out of flowers. So they took the blossoms of the oak, and the blossoms of the broom, and the blossoms of the meadow-sweet, and produced from them a maiden, the fairest and most graceful that man ever saw. And they baptized her, and gave her the name of Flower-Aspect.''‡ Celtic romance is full of exquisite

2 "Well endowed by nature."
3 "Ill endowed by nature."
4 Arnold's name for the middle class of English society, whose defect he declares to be narrowness.
5 John Bright, a Liberal statesman, who had scoffed at Arnold's advocacy of culture.
* Swift derived the words from the labor of the bees, that fill their hives "with honey and wax, thus furnishing mankind with the two noblest of things, sweetness and light." The terms stand for spiritual beauty and intellectual breadth.

† From *On the Study of Celtic Literature* (1866). The Celtic race is represented mainly by the Welsh, the Irish, and the Highland Scotch.
‡ This and the following quotations are taken from the Welsh *Mabinogion*, translated by Lady Charlotte Guest.

touches like that, showing the delicacy of the Celt's feeling in these matters, and how deeply Nature lets him come into her secrets. The quick dropping of blood is called "faster than the fall of the dewdrop from the blade of reed-grass upon the earth, when the dew of June is at the heaviest." And thus is Olwen described: "More yellow was her hair than the flower of the broom, and her skin was whiter than the foam of the wave, and fairer were her hands and her fingers than the blossoms of the wood-anemony amidst the spray of the meadow fountains." For loveliness it would be hard to beat that; and for magical clearness and nearness take the following:—

"And in the evening Peredur entered a valley, and at the head of the valley he came to a hermit's cell, and the hermit welcomed him gladly, and there he spent the night. And in the morning he arose, and when he went forth, behold! a shower of snow had fallen the night before, and a hawk had killed a wild-fowl in front of the cell. And the noise of the horse scared the hawk away, and a raven alighted upon the bird. And Peredur stood and compared the blackness of the raven and the whiteness of the snow, and the redness of the blood, to the hair of the lady whom best he loved, which was blacker than the raven, and to her skin, which was whiter than the snow, and to her two cheeks, which were redder than the blood upon the snow appeared to be."

And this, which is perhaps less striking, is not less beautiful:

"And early in the day Geraint and Enid left the wood, and they came to an open country, with meadows on one hand and mowers mowing the meadows. And there was a river before them, and the horses bent down and drank the water. And they went up out of the river by a steep bank, and there they met a slender stripling with a satchel about his neck; and he had a small blue pitcher in his hand, and a bowl on the mouth of the pitcher."

And here the landscape, up to this point so Greek in its clear beauty, is suddenly magicalized by the romance touch:

"And they saw a tall tree by the side of the river, one-half of which was in flames from the root to the top, and the other half was green and in full leaf."

Magic is the word to insist upon,—a magically vivid and near interpretation of nature; since it is this which constitutes the special charm and power of the effect I am calling attention to, and it is for this that the Celt's sensibility gives him a peculiar aptitude.

WORDSWORTH*

"But turn we," as Wordsworth says, "from these bold, bad men," the haunters of Social Science Congresses. And let us be on our guard, too, against the exhibitors and extollers of a "scientific system of thought" in Wordsworth's poetry. The poetry will never be seen aright while they thus exhibit it. The cause of its greatness is simple, and may be told quite simply. Wordsworth's poetry is great because of the extraordinary power with which Wordsworth feels the joy offered to us in nature, the joy offered to us in the simple primary affections and duties; and because of the extraordinary power with which, in case after case, he shows us this joy, and renders it so as to make us share it.

The source of joy from which he thus draws is the truest and most unfailing source of joy accessible to man. It is also accessible universally. Wordsworth brings us word, therefore, according to his own strong and characteristic line, he brings us word

"Of joy in widest commonalty spread."[1]

Here is an immense advantage for a poet. Wordsworth tells of what all seek, and tells of it at its truest and best source, and yet a source where all may go and draw from it.

Nevertheless, we are not to suppose that everything is precious which Wordsworth, standing even at this perennial and beautiful source, may give us. Wordsworthians are apt to talk as if it must be. They will speak with the same reverence of *The Sailor's Mother*, for example, as of *Lucy Gray*. They do their master harm by such lack of discrimination. *Lucy Gray* is a beautiful success; *The Sailor's Mother* is a failure.† To give aright what he wishes to give, to interpret and render successfully, is not always within Wordsworth's own command. It is within no poet's command; here is the part of the Muse, the inspiration, the God, the "not ourselves."[2] In Wordsworth's case, the accident, for so it may almost be called, of inspiration, is of peculiar importance. No poet, perhaps, is so evidently filled with a new

[1] *The Recluse*, line 771.
[2] Arnold elsewhere speaks of deity as the "tendency not ourselves that makes for righteousness."

* From the Preface to *The Poems of Wordsworth*, chosen and edited by Arnold (1879). In the passage just preceding, Arnold deprecates the attempt to make Wordsworth sponsor for any complete philosophical or social system, such, for instance, as a Social Science congress might dryly and dismally quote and discuss.
† Swinburne thought otherwise. See his *Miscellanies*.

and sacred energy when the inspiration is upon him; no poet, when it fails him, is so left "weak as is a breaking wave." I remember hearing him say tha' "Goethe's poetry was not inevitable[3] enough." The remark is striking and true; no line in Goethe, as Goethe said himself, but its maker knew well how it came there. Wordsworth is right, Goethe's poetry is not inevitable; not inevitable enough. But Wordsworth's poetry, when he is at his best, is inevitable, as inevitable as Nature herself. It might seem that Nature not only gave him the matter for his poem, but wrote his poem for him. He has no style. He was too conversant with Milton not to catch at times his master's manner, and he has fine Miltonic lines; but he has no assured poetic style of his own, like Milton. When he seeks to have a style, he falls into ponderosity and pomposity. In the *Excursion* we have his style, as an artistic product of his own creation; and although Jeffrey[4] completely failed to recognize Wordsworth's real greatness, he was yet not wrong in saying of the *Excursion*, as a work of poetic style: "This will never do." And yet magical as is that power, which Wordsworth has not, of assured and possessed poetic style, he has something which is an equivalent for it.

Every one who has any sense for these things feels the subtle turn, the heightening, which is given to a poet's verse by his genius for style. We can feel it in the

"After life's fitful fever, he sleeps well"[5]

of Shakespeare; in the

" . . . though fallen on evil days,
On evil days though fallen, and evil tongues"[6]—

of Milton. It is the incomparable charm of Milton's power of poetic style which gives such worth to *Paradise Regained*, and makes a great poem of a work in which Milton's imagination does not soar high. Wordsworth has in constant possession, and at command, no style of this kind; but he had too poetic a nature, and had read the great poets too well, not to catch, as I have already remarked, something of it occasionally. We find it not only in his Miltonic lines; we find it in such a phrase as this, where the manner is his own, not Milton's:

" . . . the fierce confederate storm
Of sorrow barricadoed evermore
Within the walls of cities;"[7]

although even here, perhaps, the power of style, which is undeniable, is more properly that of eloquent prose than the subtle heightening and

i. e., spontaneous
Francis Jeffrey, first editor of the *Edinburgh Review*.
Macbeth, III, ii, 23.
Par. Lost, vii, 25.
The Recluse, ll. 831-83?

change wrought by genuine poetic style. It is style, again, and the elevation given by style, which chiefly makes the effectiveness of *Laodamia*. Still, the right sort of verse to choose from Wordsworth, if we are to seize his true and most characteristic form of expression, is a line like this from *Michael:*

"And never lifted up a single stone."

There is nothing subtle in it, no heightening, no study of poetic style, strictly so called, at all; yet it is expression of the highest and most truly expressive kind.

Wordsworth owed much to Burns, and a style of perfect plainness, relying for effect solely on the weight and force of that which with entire fidelity it utters, Burns could show him:

"The poor inhabitant below
Was quick to learn and wise to know
And keenly felt the friendly glow
        And softer flame;
But thoughtless follies laid him low
        And stained his name."[8]

Every one will be conscious of a likeness here to Wordsworth; and if Wordsworth did great things with this nobly plain manner, we must remember, what indeed he himself would always have been forward to acknowledge, that Burns used it before him.

Still, Wordsworth's use of it has something unique and unmatchable. Nature, herself, seems, I say, to take the pen out of his hand, and to write for him with her own bare, sheer, penetrating power. This arises from two causes; from the profound sincereness with which Wordsworth feels his subject, and also from the profoundly sincere and natural character of his subject itself. He can and will treat such a subject with nothing but the most plain, first-hand, almost austere naturalness. His expression may often be called bald, as, for instance, in the poem of *Resolution and Independence;* but it is bald as the bare mountain tops are bald, with a baldness which is full of grandeur.

Wherever we meet with the successful balance, in Wordsworth, of profound truth of subject with profound truth of execution, he is unique. His best poems are those which most perfectly exhibit this balance. I have a warm admiration for *Laodamia* and for the great *Ode;* but if I am to tell the very truth, I find *Laodamia* not wholly free from something artificial, and the great *Ode* not wholly free from something declamatory. If I had to pick out poems of a kind most perfectly to show Wordsworth's unique power, I should rather choose poems such as *Michael, The Fountain, The High-*

8 *A Bard's Epitaph*, st. 4.

land Reaper. And poems with the peculiar and unique beauty which distinguishes these, Wordsworth produced in considerable number; besides very many other poems of which the worth, although not so rare as the worth of these, is still exceedingly high.

On the whole, then, as I said at the beginning, not only is Wordsworth eminent by reason of the goodness of his best work, but he is eminent also by reason of the great body of good work which he has left to us. With the ancients I will not compare him. In many respects the ancients are far above us, and yet there is something that we demand which they can never give. Leaving the ancients, let us come to the poets and poetry of Christendom. Dante, Shakespeare, Molière, Milton, Goethe, are altogether larger and more splendid luminaries in the poetical heaven than Wordsworth. But I know not where else, among the moderns, we are to find his superiors. . . . . He is one of the very chief glories of English Poetry; and by nothing is England so glorious as by her poetry. Let us lay aside every weight which hinders our getting him recognized as this, and let our one study be to bring to pass, as widely as possible and as truly as possible, his own word concerning his poems: "They will coöperate with the benign tendencies in human nature and society, and will, in their degree, be efficacious in making men wiser, better and happier."

JAMES ANTHONY FROUDE
(1818-1894)
THE SAILING OF THE SPANISH ARMADA*

The weather moderating, the fleet was again collected in the Bay of Ferrol[1] by the 6th-16th[2] of July. All repairs were completed by the 11th-21st, and the next day, 12th-22nd, the

[1] Off northwestern Spain.   [2] The first date is Old Style; see note on p. 323.

* The story of the spectacular but ill-fated expedition of the Spanish Armada has often been told, but by no one perhaps more graphically than by Froude. His first account is that in the 36th chapter of his *History of England* (1856-1870), from which has been taken this description of the sailing of the Armada. Later in life, after much additional research, Froude wrote and published *The Spanish Story of the Armada* (1892). About the same time he was appointed to a lectureship at Oxford, where he delivered some lectures on the subject which were published after his death (*English Seamen in the XVIth Century*, 1895). From these the second selection above has been taken.

In the summer of 1588, Philip II. of Spain, who

Armada took leave of Spain for the last time.

The scene as the fleet passed out of the harbour must have been singularly beautiful. It was a treacherous interval of real summer. The early sun was lighting the long chain of the Galician mountains, marking with shadows the cleft defiles, and shining softly on the white walls and vineyards of Coruña. The wind was light, and falling towards a calm; the great galleons drifted slowly with the tide on the purple water, the long streamers trailing from the trucks, the red crosses, the emblem of the crusade, showing bright upon the hanging sails. The fruit boats were bringing off the last fresh supplies, and the pinnaces hastening to the ships with the last loiterers on shore. Out of thirty thousand men who that morning stood upon the decks of the proud Armada, twenty thousand and more were never again to see the hills of Spain. Of the remnant who in two short months crept back ragged and torn, all but a few hundred returned only to die.

The Spaniards, though a great people, were usually over conscious of their greatness, and boasted too loudly of their fame and prowess; but among the soldiers and sailors of the doomed expedition against England, the national vainglory was singularly silent. They were the flower of the country, culled and chosen over the entire Peninsula, and they were going with a modest nobility upon a service which they knew to be dangerous, but which they believed to be peculiarly sacred. Every one, seaman, officer, and soldier, had confessed and communicated before he went on board. Gambling, swearing, profane language of all kinds had been peremptorily forbidden. Private quarrels and differences had been made up or suspended. . . In every vessel, and in the whole fleet, the strictest order was prescribed and observed. Medina Sidonia led the way in the *San Martin*, showing lights at night, and firing guns when the weather was hazy. Mount's

was trying to restore the Catholic faith through the Protestant countries of Europe, fitted out his "Invincible Armada" with the purpose of invading England. His great Admiral, Santa Cruz, had just died, and the expedition was given into the command of the Duke of Medina Sidonia, a wealthy nobleman of little experience and less ability, who ought to have been allowed to remain at home among his orange groves. His instructions were to effect a junction with the Duke of Parma, a general in the Spanish service in the Low Countries, and to assist the latter in transporting his army to the English shores. The obvious tactics for the English to pursue was to cripple and if possible defeat the fleet as it sailed through the English Channel. The fleet started from Lisbon on the 29th of May, but was delayed on the route six weeks by bad weather.

Bay[3] was to be the next place of rendezvous if they were again separated.

On the first evening the wind dropped to a calm. The morning after, the 13th-23rd, a fair fresh breeze came up from the south and southwest; the ships ran flowingly before it; and in two days and nights they had crossed the bay,[4] and were off Ushant.[5] The fastest of the pinnaces was dispatched from thence to Parma, with a letter bidding him expect the Duke's immediate coming.

But they had now entered the latitude of the storms which through the whole season had raged round the English shore. The same night a southwest gale overtook them. They lay-to, not daring to run further. The four galleys unable to keep the sea were driven in upon the French coast, and wrecked. The *Santa Aña, a* galleon of eight hundred tons, went down, carrying with her ninety seamen, three hundred soldiers, and fifty thousand ducats in gold. The weather was believed to be under the peculiar care of God, and this first misfortune was of evil omen for the future. The storm lasted two days, and then the sky cleared, and again gathering into order they proceeded on their way. On the 19th-29th they were in the mouth of the Channel. At daybreak on the morning of the 20th-30th the Lizard was under their lee, and an English fishing-boat was hanging near them, counting their numbers. They gave chase, but the boat shot away down wind and disappeared. They captured another an hour or two later, from which they learnt the English fleet was in Plymouth, and Medina Sidonia called a council of war to consider whether they should go in, and fall upon it while at anchor. Philip's orders, however, were peremptory that they should turn neither right nor left, and make straight for Margate roads† and Parma. The Duke was unenterprising, and consciously unequal to his work; and already bending under his responsibilities, he hesitated to add to them.

Had he decided otherwise it would have made no difference, for the opportunity was not allowed him. Long before the Spaniards saw the Lizard they had themselves been seen, and on the evening of the 19th-29th, the beacons along the coast had told England that the hour of its trial was come.

DEFEAT OF THE ARMADA

In the gallery at Madrid there is a picture, painted by Titian, representing the Genius of Spain coming to the delivery of the afflicted Bride of Christ. Titian was dead, but the temper of the age survived, and in the study of that great picture you will see the spirit in which the Spanish nation had set out for the conquest of England. The scene is the seashore. The Church a naked Andromeda,‡ with dishevelled hair, fastened to the trunk of an ancient disbranched tree. The cross lies at her feet, the cup overturned, the serpents of heresy biting at her from behind with uplifted crests. Coming on before a leading breeze is the sea monster, the Moslem fleet, eager for their prey, while in front is Perseus, the Genius of Spain, banner in hand, with the legions of the faithful laying not raiment before him, but shield and helmet, the apparel of war for the Lady of Nations to clothe herself with strength and smite her foes.

In the Armada the crusading enthusiasm had reached its point and focus. England was the stake to which the Virgin, the daughter of Sion, was bound in captivity. Perseus had come at last in the person of the Duke of Medina Sidonia, and with him all that was best and brightest in the countrymen of Cervantes,[1] to break her bonds and replace her on her throne. They had sailed into the channel in pious hope, with the blessed banner waving over their heads.

To be the executor of the decrees of Providence is a lofty ambition, but men in a state of high emotion overlook the precautions which are not to be dispensed with even on the sublimest of errands. Don Quixote, when he set out to redress the wrongs of humanity, forgot that a change of linen might be necessary, and that he must take money with him to pay his hotel bills. Philip II., in sending the Armada to England, and confident in supernatural protection, imagined an unresisted triumphal procession. He forgot that contractors might be rascals, that water four months in the casks in a hot climate turned putrid, and that putrid water would poison his ships' companies, though

3 On the English coast of Cornwall, between Land's End on the west and Lizard Head on the east.
4 Of Biscay.
5 An island off the extreme northwestern coast of France.
† Just north of Dover, opposite Calais. Vessels sailing up the English Channel and through Dover Strait would round the North Foreland and Margate to pass into the Thames. The passage of the fleet up the Channel was virtually a running fight, beginning at Plymouth and lasting for a week.

1 Creator of Don Quixote, the half-mad knight-errant.
‡Andromeda, according to the Greek legend, was exposed to be devoured by a sea-monster, but was rescued by Perseus.

his crews were companies of angels. He forgot that the servants of the evil one might fight for their mistress after all, and that he must send adequate supplies of powder, and, worst forgetfulness of all, that a great naval expedition required a leader who understood his business. Perseus, in the shape of the Duke of Medina Sidonia, after a week of disastrous battles, found himself at the end of it in an exposed roadstead,[2] where he ought never to have been, nine-tenths of his provisions thrown overboard as unfit for food, his ammunition exhausted by the unforeseen demands upon it, the seamen and soldiers harassed and dispirited, officers the whole week without sleep, and the enemy, who had hunted him from Plymouth to Calais, anchored within half a league of him.

Still, after all his misadventures, he had brought the fleet, if not to the North Foreland,[3] yet within a few miles of it, and to outward appearance not materially injured. Two of the galleons had been taken; a third, the *Santa Aña*, had strayed; and his galleys had left him, being found too weak for the channel sea, but the great armament had reached its destination substantially uninjured so far as English eyes could see. Hundreds of men had been killed and hundreds more wounded, and the spirit of the rest had been shaken. But the loss of life could only be conjectured on board the English fleet. The English admiral* could only see that the Duke was now in touch with Parma. Parma, they knew, had an army at Dunkirk[4] with him, which was to cross to England. He had been collecting men, barges, and transports all the winter and spring, and the backward state of Parma's preparations could not be anticipated, still less relied upon. The Calais anchorage was unsafe; but at that season of the year, especially after a wet summer, the weather usually settled; and to attack the Spaniards in a French port might be dangerous for many reasons. It was uncertain after the day of the Barricades[5] whether the Duke of Guise or Henry of Valois was master of France, and a violation of the neutrality laws might easily at that moment bring Guise and France into the field on the Spaniards' side. It was, no doubt, with some such expectation that the

Duke and his advisers had chosen Calais as the point at which to bring up. It was now Saturday, the 7th of August. The governor of the town came off in the evening to the *San Martin*. He expressed surprise to see the Spanish fleet in so exposed a position, but he was profuse in his offers of service. Anything which the Duke required should be provided, especially every facility for communicating with Dunkirk and Parma. The Duke thanked him, said that he supposed Parma to be already embarked with his troops, ready for the passage, and that his own stay in the roads would be but brief. On Monday morning at latest he expected that the attempt to cross would be made. The governor took his leave, and the Duke, relieved from his anxieties, was left to a peaceful night. He was disturbed on the Sunday morning by an express from Parma informing him that, so far from being embarked, the army could not be ready for a fortnight. The barges were not in condition for sea. The troops were in camp. The arms and stores were on the quays at Dunkirk. As for the fly-boats[6] and ammunition which the Duke had asked for, he had none to spare. He had himself looked to be supplied from the Armada. He promised to use his best expedition, but the Duke, meanwhile, must see to the safety of the fleet.

Unwelcome news to a harassed landsman thrust into the position of an admiral and eager to be rid of his responsibilities. If by evil fortune the northwester should come down upon him, with the shoals and sandbanks close under his lee, he would be in a bad way. Nor was the view behind him calculated for comfort. There lay the enemy almost within gunshot, who, though scarcely more than half his numbers, had hunted him like a pack of bloodhounds, and, worse than all, in double strength; for the Thames squadron—three Queen's ships and thirty London adventurers—under Lord H Seymour and Sir John Hawkins, had crossed in the night. There they were between him and Cape Grisnez,[7] and the reinforcements meant plainly enough that mischief was in the wind.

After a week so trying the Spanish crew would have been glad of a Sunday's rest if they could have had it; but the rough handling which they had gone through had thrown everything into disorder. The sick and wounded had to be cared for, torn rigging looked to, splintered timbers mended, decks scoured, and gun and arms cleaned up and put to rights. And so it was that no rest could be allowed; so

2 Calais Roads.
3 See last note of preceding selection.
4 A port twenty miles east of Calais.
5 May 12, when the Duke of Guise entered Paris in an attempt to depose Henry III.

* Lord Charles Howard. Sir Francis Drake, vice admiral, commanded a second division of the British fleet; Sir Henry Seymour a third. Commanders of squadrons were Sir John Hawkins and Sir Martin Frobisher.

6 "Gunboats worked with oars."
7 Eighteen miles S. W. of Calais.

much had to be done, and so busy was every one, that the usual rations were not served out and the Sunday was kept as a fast. In the afternoon the stewards went ashore for fresh meat and vegetables. They came back with their boats loaded, and the prospect seemed a little less gloomy. Suddenly, as the Duke and a group of officers were watching the English fleet from the *San Martin's* poop deck, a small smart pinnace, carrying a gun in her bow, shot out from Howard's lines, bore down on the *San Martin*, sailed round her, sending in a shot or two as she passed, and went off unhurt. The Spanish officers could not help admiring such airy impertinence. Hugo de Monçada[8] sent a ball after the pinnace, which went through her mainsail, but did no damage, and the pinnace again disappeared behind the English ships.

So a Spanish officer describes the scene. The English story says nothing of the pinnace, but she doubtless came and went as the Spaniard says, and for sufficient purpose. The English, too, were in straits, though the Duke did not dream of it. You will remember that the last supplies which the Queen had allowed to the fleet had been issued in the middle of June. They were to serve for a month, and the contractors were forbidden to prepare more. The Queen had clung to her hope that her differences with Philip were to be settled by the Commission at Ostend;[9] and she feared that if Drake and Howard were too well furnished they would venture some fresh rash stroke on the coast of Spain, which might mar the negotiations. Their month's provisions had been stretched to serve for six weeks, and when the Armada appeared but two full days' rations remained. On these they had fought their way up Channel. Something had been brought out by private exertion on the Dorsetshire coast, and Seymour had, perhaps, brought a little more. But they were still in extremity. The contractors had warned the Government that they could provide nothing without notice, and notice had not been given. The adventurers were in better state, having been equipped by private owners. But the Queen's ships in a day or two more must either go home or their crews would be starving. They had been on reduced rations for near two months. Worse than that, they were still poisoned by the sour beer. The Queen had changed her mind so

often, now ordering the fleet to prepare for sea, then recalling her instructions and paying off the men, that those whom Howard had with him had been enlisted in haste, had come on board as they were, and their clothes were hanging in rags on them. The fighting and the sight of the flying Spaniards were meat and drink, and clothing, too, and had made them careless of all else. There was no fear of mutiny; but there was a limit to the toughest endurance. If the Armada was left undisturbed, a long struggle might be still before them. The enemy would recover from its flurry, and Parma would come out from Dunkirk. To attack them directly in French waters might lead to perilous complications, while delay meant famine. The Spanish fleet had to be started from the roads in some way. Done it must be, and done immediately.

Then, on that same Sunday afternoon a memorable council of war was held in the *Ark's*[10] main cabin. Howard, Drake, Seymour, Hawkins, Martin Frobisher and two or three others met to consult, knowing that on them at that moment the liberties of England were depending. Their resolution was taken promptly. There was no time for talk. After nightfall a strong flood tide would be setting up along shore to the Spanish anchorage. They would try what could be done with fire ships, and the excursion of the pinnace, which was taken for bravado, was probably for a survey of the Armada's exact position. Meantime eight useless vessels were coated with pitch—hulls, spars and rigging. Pitch was poured on the decks and over the sides, and parties were told off to steer them to their destination and then fire and leave them.

The hours stole on, and twilight passed into dark. The night was without a moon. The Duke paced his deck late with uneasy sense of danger. He observed lights moving up and down the English lines, and imagining that the *endemoniada gente*—the infernal devils—might be up to mischief, ordered a sharp lookout. A faint westerly air was curling the water, and towards midnight the watchers on board the galleons made out dimly several ships which seemed to be drifting down upon them. Their experience since the action off Plymouth had been so strange and unlooked for that anything unintelligible which the English did was alarming.

The phantom forms drew nearer, and were almost among them when they broke into a blaze from water-line to truck, and the two fleets were seen by the lurid light of the conflagration; the anchorage, the walls and windows of Calais, and the sea shining red as far as eye could reach, as if the ocean itself was burning. Among the dangers which they might have to encounter, English fireworks had been especially dreaded by the Spaniards. Fire ships —a fit device of heretics—had worked havoc among the Spanish troops, when the bridge was blown up at Antwerp.[11] They imagined that similar infernal machines were approaching the Armada. A capable commander would have sent a few launches to grapple the burning hulks, which of course were now deserted, and tow them out of harm's way. Spanish sailors were not cowards, and would not have flinched from duty because it might be dangerous; but the Duke and Diego Florez[12] lost their heads again. A signal gun from the *San Martin* ordered the whole fleet to slip their cables and stand out to sea.

Orders given in panic are doubly unwise, for they spread the terror in which they originate. The danger from the fire ships was chiefly from the effect on the imagination, for they appear to have drifted by and done no real injury. And it speaks well for the seamanship and courage of the Spaniards that they were able, crowded together as they were, at midnight, and in sudden alarm, to set their canvas and clear out without running into one another. They buoyed their cables, expecting to return for them at daylight, and with only a single accident, to be mentioned directly, they executed successfully a really difficult manœuvre.

The Duke was delighted with himself. The fire ships burned harmlessly out. He had baffled the inventions of the *endemoniada gente*. He brought up a league outside the harbour, and supposed that the whole Armada had done the same. Unluckily for himself, he found it at daylight divided into two bodies. The *San Martin* with forty of the best appointed of the galleons were riding together at their anchors. The rest, two-thirds of the whole, having no second anchors ready, and inexperienced in Channel tides and currents, had been lying to. The west wind was blowing up. Without seeing where they were going they had drifted to leeward and were two leagues off, towards Gravelines, dangerously near the shore. The Duke was too ignorant to realize the full peril of his situation. He signalled to them to return and join him. As the wind and tide stood it was impossible. He proposed to follow them. The pilots told him that if he did the

whole fleet might be lost on the banks. Towards the land the look of things was not more encouraging.

One accident only had happened the night before. The *Capitana* galleass, with Don Hugo de Monçada and eight hundred men on board, had fouled her helm in a cable in getting under way and had become unmanageable. The galley slaves disobeyed orders, or else Don Hugo was as incompetent as his commander-in-chief. The galleass had gone on the sands, and as the tide ebbed had fallen over on her side. Howard, seeing her condition, had followed her in the *Ark* with four or five other of the Queen's ships, and was furiously attacking her with his boats, careless of neutrality laws. Howard's theory was, as he said, to pluck the feathers one by one from the Spaniard's wing, and here was a feather worth picking up. The galleass was the most splendid vessel of her kind afloat, Don Hugo one of the greatest of Spanish grandees.

Howard was making a double mistake. He took the galleass at last after three hours' fighting. Don Hugo was killed by a musket ball. The vessel was plundered and Howard's men took possession, meaning to carry her away when the tide rose. The French authorities ordered him off, threatening to fire upon him; and after wasting the forenoon, he was obliged at last to leave her where she lay. Worse than this, he had lost three precious hours, and had lost along with them, in the opinion of the Prince of Parma, the honours of the great day.

Drake and Hawkins knew better than to waste time plucking single feathers. The fire ships had been more effective than they could have dared to hope. The enemy was broken up. The Duke was shorn of half his strength, and the Lord had delivered him into their hand. He had got under way, still signalling wildly, and uncertain in which direction to turn. His uncertainties were ended for him by seeing Drake bear down upon him with the whole English fleet, save those which were loitering about the galleass. The English had now the advantage of numbers. The superiority of their guns he knew already, and their greater speed allowed him no hope to escape a battle. Forty ships alone were left to him to defend the banner of the crusade and the honour of Castile; but those forty were the largest and most powerfully armed and manned that he had, and on board them were Oquendo, De Leyva, Recalde, Bretandona, the best officers in the Spanish navy next to the lost Don Pedro.[1]

It was now or never for England. The scene of the action which was to decide the future of Europe was between Calais and Dunkirk, a few miles off shore, and within sight of Parma's camp. There was no more manœuvring for the weather-gage, no more fighting at long range. Drake dashed straight upon his prey as the falcon stoops upon its quarry. A chance had fallen to him which might never return; not for the vain distinction of carrying prizes into English ports, not for the ray of honour which would fall on him if he could carry off the sacred banner itself and hang it in the Abbey at Westminster, but a chance so to handle the Armada that it should never be seen again in English waters, and deal such a blow on Philip that the Spanish Empire should reel with it. The English ships had the same superiority over the galleons which steamers have now over sailing vessels. They had twice the speed; they could lie two points nearer to the wind. Sweeping around them at cable's length, crowding them in one upon the other, yet never once giving them a chance to grapple, they hurled in their cataracts of round shot. Short as was the powder supply, there was no sparing it that morning. The hours went on, and still the battle raged, if battle it could be called where the blows were all dealt on one side and the suffering was all on the other. Never on sea or land did the Spaniards show themselves worthier of their great name than on that day. But from the first they could do nothing. It was said afterwards in Spain that the Duke showed the white feather, that he charged his pilot to keep him out of harm's way, that he shut himself up in his cabin, buried in woolpacks, and so on. The Duke had faults enough, but poltroonery was not one of them. He, who till he entered the English Channel had never been in action on sea or land, found himself, as he said, in the midst of the most furious engagement recorded in the history of the world. As to being out of harm's way, the standard at his masthead drew the hottest of the fire upon him. The *San Martin's* timbers were of oak and a foot thick, but the shot, he said, went through them enough to shatter a rock. Her deck was a slaughterhouse; half his company were killed or wounded, and no more would have been heard or seen of the *San Martin* or her commander had not Oquendo and De Leyva pushed in to the rescue and enabled him to creep away under their cover. He himself saw nothing more of the action after this. The smoke, he said, was so thick that he could make out nothing, even from his masthead.

But all round it was but a repetition of the same scene. The Spanish shot flew high, as before, above the low English hulls, and they were themselves helpless butts to the English guns. And it is noticeable and supremely creditable to them that not a single galleon struck her colours. One of them, after a long duel with an Englishman, was on the point of sinking. An English officer, admiring the courage which the Spaniards had shown, ran out upon his bowsprit, told them that they had done all which became men, and urged them to surrender and save their lives. For answer they cursed the English as cowards and chickens because they refused to close. The officer was shot. His fall brought a last broadside on them, which finished the work. They went down, and the water closed over them. Rather death to the soldiers of the Cross than surrender to a heretic.

The deadly hail rained on. In some ships blood was seen streaming out of the scupper holes. Yet there was no yielding; all ranks showed equal heroism. The priests went up and down in the midst of the carnage, holding the crucifix before the eyes of the dying. At midday Howard came up to claim a second share in a victory which was no longer doubtful. Towards the afternoon the Spanish fire slackened. Their powder was gone, and they could make no return to the cannonade which was still overwhelming them. They admitted freely afterwards that if the attack had been continued but two hours more they must all have struck or gone ashore. But the English magazines were empty also; the last cartridge was shot away, and the battle ended from mere inability to keep it up. It had been fought on both sides with peculiar determination. In the English there was the accumulated resentment of thirty years of menace to their country and their creed, with the enemy in tangible shape at last to be caught and grappled with; in the Spanish, the sense that if their cause had not brought them the help they looked for from above, the honour and faith of Castile should not suffer in their hands.

It was over. The English drew off, regretting that their thrifty mistress had limited their means of fighting for her, and so obliged them to leave their work half done. When the cannon ceased the wind rose, the smoke rolled away, and in the level light of the sunset they could see the results of the action.

A galleon in Recalde's squadron was sinking with all hands. The *San Philip* and the *San Matteo* were drifting dismasted towards the

Dutch coast, where they were afterwards wrecked. Those which were left with canvas still showing were crawling slowly after their comrades who had not been engaged, the spars and rigging so cut up that they could scarce bear their sails. The loss of life could only be conjectured, but it had been obviously terrible. The nor'-wester was blowing up and was pressing the wounded ships upon the shoals, from which, if it held, it seemed impossible in their crippled state they would be able to work off.

In this condition Drake left them for the night, not to rest, but from any quarter to collect, if he could, more food and powder. The snake had been scotched, but not killed.[1] More than half the great fleet were far away, untouched by shot, perhaps able to fight a second battle if they recovered heart. To follow, to drive them on the banks if the wind held, or into the North Sea, anywhere so that he left them no chance of joining hands with Parma again, and to use the time before they had rallied from his blows, that was the present necessity. His own poor fellows were famished and in rags; but neither he nor they had leisure to think of themselves. There was but one thought in the whole of them, to be again in chase of the flying foe. Howard was resolute as Drake. All that was possible was swiftly done. Seymour and the Thames squadron were to stay in the straits and watch Parma. From every obtainable source food and powder were collected for the rest—far short in both ways of what ought to have been, but, as Drake said, 'we were resolved to put on a brag and go on as if we needed nothing.' Before dawn the admiral and he were again off on the chase.

The brag was unneeded. What man could do had been done, and the rest was left to the elements. Never again could Spanish seamen be brought to face the English guns with Medina Sidonia to lead them. They had a fool at their head. The Invisible Powers in whom they had been taught to trust had deserted them. Their confidence was gone and their spirit broken. Drearily the morning broke on the Duke and his consorts the day after the battle. The Armada had collected in the night. The nor'-wester had freshened to a gale, and they were labouring heavily along, making fatal leeway towards the shoals.

It was St. Lawrence's Day, Philip's patron saint, whose shoulder-bone he had lately added to the treasures of the Escurial;[2] but St. Lawrence was as heedless as St. Dominic.[3] The *San Martin* had but six fathoms under her. Those nearer to the land signalled five, and right before them they could see the brown foam of the breakers curling over the sands, while on their weather-beam, a mile distant and clinging to them like the shadow of death, were the English ships which had pursued them from Plymouth like the dogs of the Furies. The Spanish sailors and soldiers had been without food since the evening when they anchored at Calais. All Sunday they had been at work, no rest allowed them to eat. On the Sunday night they had been stirred out of their sleep by the fire ships. Monday they had been fighting, and Monday night committing their dead to the sea. Now they seemed advancing directly upon inevitable destruction. As the wind stood there was still room for them to wear and thus escape the banks, but they would then have to face the enemy, who seemed only refraining from attacking them because while they continued on their present course the winds and waves would finish the work without help from man. Recalde, De Leyva, Oquendo, and other officers were sent for to the *San Martin* to consult. Oquendo came last. 'Ah, Señor Oquendo,' said the Duke as the heroic Biscayan stepped on board, 'que haremos?' (what shall we do?) 'Let your Excellency bid load the guns again,' was Oquendo's gallant answer. It could not be. De Leyva himself said that the men would not fight the English again. Florez advised surrender. The Duke wavered. It was said that a boat was actually lowered to go off to Howard and make terms, and that Oquendo swore that if the boat left the *San Martin* on such an errand he would fling Florez into the sea. Oquendo's advice would have, perhaps, been the safest if the Duke could have taken it. There were still seventy ships in the Armada little hurt. The English were 'bragging,' as Drake said, and in no condition themselves for another serious engagement. But the temper of the entire fleet made a courageous course impossible. There was but one Oquendo. Discipline was gone. The soldiers in their desperation had taken the command out of the hands of the seamen. Officers and men alike abandoned hope, and, with no human prospect of salvation left to them, they flung themselves on their knees upon the decks and prayed the Almighty to have pity on them. But two weeks were gone since they had knelt on those same decks on the first sight of the

---

[1] *Macbeth*, III, ii, 13.
[2] The palace of Philip II.

[3] Referring to a disastrous engagement five days before, on St. Dominic's Day, Aug. 4.

English shore to thank Him for having brought them so far on an enterprise so glorious. Two weeks; and what weeks! Wrecked, torn by cannon shot, ten thousand of them dead or dying—for this was the estimated loss by battle—the survivors could now but pray to be delivered from a miserable death by the elements. In cyclones the wind often changes suddenly back from northwest to west, from west to south. At that moment, as if in answer to their petition, one of these sudden shifts of wind saved them from the immediate peril. The gale backed round to S.S.W., and ceased to press them on the shoals. They could ease their sheets, draw off into open water, and steer a course up the middle of the North Sea.

So only that they went north, Drake was content to leave them unmolested. Once away into the high latitudes they might go where they would. Neither Howard nor he, in the low state of their own magazines, desired any unnecessary fighting. If the Armada turned back they must close with it. If it held its present course they must follow it till they could be assured it would communicate no more for that summer with the Prince of Parma. Drake thought they would perhaps make for the Baltic or some port in Norway. They would meet no hospitable reception from either Swedes or Danes, but they would probably try. One only imminent danger remained to be provided against. If they turned into the Forth, it was still possible for the Spaniards to redeem their defeat, and even yet shake Elizabeth's throne. Among the many plans which had been formed for the invasion of England, a landing in Scotland had long been the favourite. Guise had always preferred Scotland when it was intended that Guise should be the leader. Santa Cruz had been in close correspondence with Guise on this very subject, and many officers in the Armada must have been acquainted with Santa Cruz's views. The Scotch Catholic nobles were still savage at Mary Stuart's execution, and had the Armada anchored in Leith Roads[4] with twenty thousand men, half a million ducats, and a Santa Cruz at its head, it might have kindled a blaze at that moment from John o'Groat's Land[5] to the Border.

But no such purpose occurred to the Duke of Medina Sidonia. He probably knew nothing at all of Scotland or its parties. Among the many deficiencies which he had pleaded to Philip as unfitting him for the command, he had said that Santa Cruz had acquaintances among the English and Scotch peers. He had himself none. The small information which he had of anything did not go beyond his orange gardens and his tunny fishing. His chief merit was that he was conscious of his incapacity; and, detesting a service into which he had been fooled by a hysterical nun,[*] his only anxiety was to carry home the still considerable fleet which had been trusted to him without further loss. Beyond Scotland and the Scotch isles there was the open ocean, and in the open ocean there were no sandbanks and no English guns. Thus, with all sail set, he went on before the wind. Drake and Howard attended him till they had seen him past the Forth, and knew then that there was no more to fear. It was time to see to the wants of their own poor fellows, who had endured so patiently and fought so magnificently. On the 13th day of August they saw the last of the Armada, turned back, and made their way to the Thames.[†]

THOMAS HENRY HUXLEY
(1825-1895)

ON A PIECE OF CHALK.[‡]

If a well were to be sunk at our feet in the midst of the city of Norwich, the diggers would very soon find themselves at work in that white substance, almost too soft to be called rock, with which we are all familiar as "chalk." Not only here, but over the whole county of Norfolk, the well-sinker might carry his shaft down many hundred feet without coming to the end of the chalk; and, on the sea-coast, where the waves have pared away the face of the land which breasts them, the scarped faces of the high cliffs are often wholly formed of the same material. Northward, the chalk may be followed as far as Yorkshire; on the south

---

[*] A nun at Lisbon had told the wavering Duke that "Our Lady had sent her to promise him success."

[†] The remainder of the narrative is the story of the disasters that attended the Spanish in their voyage around Scotland and Ireland. Many died from exposure, scanty food, and poisonous water; many were wrecked; even of those who reached Spain alive, few ever rallied from the experience.

[‡] A lecture delivered to the working men of Norwich, England, and printed in *Macmillan's Magazine,* 1868; now in *Lay Sermons, Addresses and Reviews.* Some changes have here been made in paragraphing and punctuation. For clearness of exposition Huxley has few or no superiors, but the system of paragraphing employed in his works as they are ordinarily printed not infrequently has an obscuring effect.

---

[4] On the Firth of Forth, near Edinburgh.   [5] The northwestern extremity of Scotland.

coast it appears abruptly in the picturesque western bays of Dorset, and breaks into the Needles[1] of the Isle of Wight; while on the shores of Kent it supplies that long line of white cliffs to which England owes her name of Albion.[2]

Were the thin soil which covers it all washed away, a curved band of white chalk, here broader and there narrower, might be followed diagonally across England from Lulworth in Dorset to Flamborough Head in Yorkshire—a distance of over two hundred and eighty miles as the crow flies. From this band to the North Sea, on the east, and the Channel, on the south, the chalk is largely hidden by other deposits; but, except in the Weald[†] of Kent and Sussex, it enters into the very foundation of all the south-eastern counties.

Attaining, as it does in some places, a thickness of more than a thousand feet, the English chalk must be admitted to be a mass of considerable magnitude. Nevertheless, it covers but an insignificant portion of the whole area occupied by the chalk formation of the globe, which has precisely the same general characters as ours, and is found in detached patches, some less and others more extensive than the English. Chalk occurs in northwest Ireland; it stretches over a large part of France,—the chalk which underlies Paris being, in fact, a continuation of that of the London basin; runs through Denmark and Central Europe, and extends southward to North Africa; while eastward, it appears in the Crimea and in Syria, and may be traced as far as the shores of the Sea of Aral, in Central Asia. If all the points at which true chalk occurs were circumscribed, they would lie within an irregular oval about three thousand miles in long diameter, the area of which would be as great as that of Europe, and would many times exceed that of the largest existing inland sea—the Mediterranean.

Thus the chalk is no unimportant element in the masonry of the earth's crust, and it impresses a peculiar stamp, varying with the conditions to which it is exposed, on the scenery of the districts in which it occurs. The undulating downs and rounded coombs[3], covered with sweet-grassed turf, of our inland chalk country, have a peacefully domestic and mutton-suggesting prettiness, but can hardly be called either grand or beautiful. But on our southern coasts,

the wall-sided cliffs, many hundred feet high, with vast needles and pinnacles standing out in the sea, sharp and solitary enough to serve as perches for the wary cormorant, confer a wonderful beauty and grandeur upon the chalk headlands. And in the East, chalk has its share in the formation of some of the most venerable of mountain ranges, such as the Lebanon.

What is this wide-spread component of the surface of the earth? and whence did it come?

You may think this no very hopeful inquiry. You may not unnaturally suppose that the attempt to solve such problems as these can lead to no result, save that of entangling the inquirer in vague speculations, incapable of refutation and of verification. If such were really the case, I should have selected some other subject than a "piece of chalk" for my discourse. But in truth, after much deliberation, I have been unable to think of any topic which would so well enable me to lead you to see how solid is the foundation upon which some of the most startling conclusions of physical science rest. A great chapter in the history of the world is written in the chalk. Few passages in the history of man can be supported by such an overwhelming mass of direct and indirect evidence as that which testifies to the truth of the fragment of the history of the globe which I hope to enable you to read, with your own eyes, tonight.

Let me add that few chapters of human history have a more profound significance for ourselves. I weigh my words well when I assert that the man who should know the true history of the bit of chalk which every carpenter carries about in his breeches-pocket, though ignorant of all other history, is likely, if he will think his knowledge out to its ultimate results, to have a truer, and therefore a better, conception of this wonderful universe, and of man's relation to it, than the most learned student who is deep read in the records of humanity and ignorant of those of Nature. The language of the chalk is not hard to learn, not nearly so hard as Latin, if you only want to get at the broad features of the story it has to tell; and I propose that we now set to work to spell that story out together. . . .

[In the intervening portion of his address Huxley sets forth the following facts:

First. Chemically, chalk consists of carbonic acid and quicklime. Under the microscope it is seen to be made up of granules in which are imbedded numerous calcareous skeletons known as *Globigerinæ*.

Second. The bed of the North Atlantic, be-

---

[1] Three white rocks rising abruptly from the sea to the height of 100 feet.
[2] Latin *albus*, "white."
[3] Or combs; bowl-shaped valleys.
[†] This name for the region is old: Anglo-Saxon *weald* (German *Wald*) means "forest." Compare Caxton's account of his birth, p. 95.

tween Ireland and Newfoundland, is found to be a vast plain of deep-sea mud which is substantially chalk, deposited there by multitudes of organisms *(Globigerinæ)*, which in life have the power of separating from the ocean the small proportion of carbonate of lime which is dissolved in sea-water, and of building that substance into skeletons for themselves.

Third. The living *Globigerinæ* are exclusively marine animals, and this, along with other evidence, compels the conclusion that the chalk beds of the dry land are the dried mud of an ancient deep sea.

Fourth. The thickness of the chalk bed and the character of its fossil remains prove that the period of deposit—the cretaceous epoch—was of great duration.]

Thus not only is it certain that the chalk is the mud of an ancient sea-bottom; but it is no less certain that the chalk sea existed during an extremely long period, though we may not be prepared to give a precise estimate of the length of that period in years. The relative duration is clear, though the absolute duration may not be definable. The attempt to affix any precise date to the period at which the chalk sea began, or ended, its existence, is baffled by difficulties of the same kind. But the relative age of the cretaceous epoch may be determined with as great ease and certainty as the long duration of that epoch.

You will have heard of the interesting discoveries recently made in various parts of Western Europe of flint implements, obviously worked into shape by human hands, under circumstances which show conclusively that man is a very ancient denizen of these regions. It has been proved that the old populations of Europe, whose existence has been revealed to us in this way, consisted of savages, such as the Esquimaux are now; that, in the country which is now France, they hunted the reindeer, and were familiar with the ways of the mammoth and the bison. The physical geography of France was in those days different from what it is now—the river Somme, for instance, having cut its bed a hundred feet deeper between that time and this; and it is probable that the climate was more like that of Canada or Siberia than that of Western Europe.

The existence of these people is forgotten even in the traditions of the oldest historical nations. The name and fame of them had utterly vanished until a few years back; and the amount of physical change which has been effected since their day renders it more than probable that, venerable as are some of the historical nations, the workers of the chipped flints of Hoxne[1] or of Amiens[2] are to them, as they are to us, in point of antiquity.

But if we assign to these hoar relics of long-vanished generations of men the greatest age that can possibly be claimed for them, they are not older than the drift, or boulder clay, which, in comparison with the chalk, is but a very juvenile deposit. You need go no further than your own sea-board for evidence of this fact. At one of the most charming spots on the coast of Norfolk, Cromer, you will see the boulder clay forming a vast mass, which lies upon the chalk, and must consequently have come into existence after it. Huge boulders of chalk are, in fact, included in the clay, and have evidently been brought to the position they now occupy by the same agency as that which has planted blocks of syenite from Norway side by side with them.

The chalk, then, is certainly older than the boulder clay. If you ask how much, I will again take you no further than the same spot upon your own coasts for evidence. I have spoken of the boulder clay and drift as resting upon the chalk. That is not strictly true. Interposed between the chalk and the drift is a comparatively insignificant layer, containing vegetable matter. But that layer tells a wonderful history. It is full of stumps of trees standing as they grew. Fir-trees are there with their cones, and hazel-bushes with their nuts; there stand the stools[3] of oak and yew trees, beeches and alders. Hence this stratum is appropriately called the "forest-bed."

It is obvious that the chalk must have been upheaved and converted into dry land before the timber trees could grow upon it. As the boles of some of these trees are from two to three feet in diameter, it is no less clear that the dry land thus formed remained in the same condition for long ages. And not only do the remains of stately oaks and well-grown firs testify to the duration of this condition of things, but additional evidence to the same effect is afforded by the abundant remains of elephants, rhinoceroses, hippopotamuses and other great wild beasts, which it has yielded to the zealous search of such men as the Rev. Mr. Gunn.[4] When you look at such a collection as he has formed, and bethink you that these elephantine bones did veritably carry their owners about, and these great grinders crunch, in the dark

[1] In Suffolk. England. where an important discovery of flint implements was made in 1797.
[2] In northern France.
[3] stumps
[4] Robert Campbell Gunn (1808-1881), a British naturalist.

woods of which the forest-bed is now the only trace, it is impossible not to feel that they are as good evidence of the lapse of time as the annual rings of the tree-stumps.

Thus there is a writing upon the walls of cliffs at Cromer, and whoso runs may read it. It tells us, with an authority which cannot be impeached, that the ancient sea-bed of the chalk sea was raised up, and remained dry land until it was covered with forest, stocked with the great game whose spoils have rejoiced your geologists. How long it remained in that condition cannot be said; but "the whirligig of time brought its revenges"[5] in those days as in these. That dry land, with the bones and teeth of generations of long-lived elephants hidden away among the gnarled roots and dry leaves of its ancient trees, sank gradually to the bottom of the icy sea, which covered it with huge masses of drift and boulder clay. Sea-beasts, such as the walrus, now restricted to the extreme north, paddled about where birds had twittered among the topmost twigs of the fir-trees. How long this state of things endured we know not, but at length it came to an end. The upheaved glacial mud hardened into the soil of modern Norfolk. Forests grew once more, the wolf and the beaver replaced the reindeer and the elephant; and at length what we call the history of England dawned.

Thus you have, within the limits of your own county, proof that the chalk can justly claim a very much greater antiquity than even the oldest physical traces of mankind. But we may go further and demonstrate, by evidence of the same authority as that which testifies to the existence of the father of men, that the chalk is vastly older than Adam himself.

The Book of Genesis informs us that Adam, immediately upon his creation, and before the appearance of Eve, was placed in the Garden of Eden. The problem of the geographical position of Eden has greatly vexed the spirits of the learned in such matters, but there is one point respecting which, so far as I know, no commentator has ever raised a doubt. This is, that of the four rivers which are said to run out of it, Euphrates and Hiddekel are identical with the rivers now known by the names of Euphrates and Tigris. But the whole country in which these mighty rivers take their origin, and through which they run, is composed of rocks which are either of the same age as the chalk, or of later date. So that the chalk must not only have been formed, but, after its formation, the time required for the deposit of these later rocks, and for their upheaval into dry land, must have elapsed before the smallest brook which feeds the swift stream of "the great river, the river of Babylon,"[6] began to flow.

Thus, evidence which cannot be rebutted, and which need not be strengthened, though if time permitted I might indefinitely increase its quantity, compels you to believe that the earth, from the time of the chalk to the present day, has been the theater of a series of changes as vast in their amount as they were slow in their progress. The area on which we stand has been first sea and then land, for at least four alternations; and has remained in each of these conditions for a period of great length. Nor have these wonderful metamorphoses of sea into land, and of land into sea, been confined to one corner of England. During the chalk period, or "cretaceous epoch," not one of the present great physical features of the globe was in existence. Our great mountain ranges, Pyrenees, Alps, Himalayas, Andes, have all been upheaved since the chalk was deposited, and the cretaceous sea flowed over the sites of Sinai and Ararat. All this is certain, because rocks of cretaceous, or still later date, have shared in the elevatory movements which gave rise to these mountain chains; and may be found perched up, in some cases, many thousand feet high upon their flanks. And evidence of equal cogency demonstrates that, though in Norfolk the forest-bed rests directly upon the chalk, yet it does so, not because the period at which the forest grew immediately followed that at which the chalk was formed, but because an immense lapse of time, represented elsewhere by thousands of feet of rock, is not indicated at Cromer.

I must ask you to believe that there is no less conclusive proof that a still more prolonged succession of similar changes occurred before the chalk was deposited. Nor have we any reason to think that the first term in the series of these changes is known. The oldest sea-beds preserved to us are sands, and mud, and pebbles, the wear and tear of rocks which were formed in still older oceans.

But, great as is the magnitude of these physical changes of the world, they have been accompanied by a no less striking series of modifications in its living inhabitants. All the great classes of animals, beasts of the field, fowls of the air, creeping things, and things which dwell in the waters, flourished upon the globe long ages before the chalk was deposited. Very few, however, if any, of these ancient forms of animal life were identical with those which now live. Certainly not one of the higher animals was of the same species as any of those now in existence. The beasts of the field, in the days before the chalk, were not our beasts of the field, nor the fowls of the air such as those which the eye of man has seen flying, unless his antiquity dates infinitely further back than we at present surmise. If we could be carried back into those times, we should be as one suddenly set down in Australia before it was colonized. We should see mammals, birds, reptiles, fishes, insects, snails, and the like, clearly recognizable as such, and yet not one of them would be just the same as those with which we are familiar, and many would be extremely different.

From that time to the present, the population of the world has undergone slow and gradual, but incessant changes. There has been no grand catastrophe—no destroyer has swept away the forms of life of one period and replaced them by a totally new creation; but one species has vanished and another has taken its place; creatures of one type of structure have diminished, those of another have increased, as time has passed on. And thus, while the differences between the living creatures of the time before the chalk and those of the present day appear startling if placed side by side, we are led from one to the other by the most gradual progress if we follow the course of Nature through the whole series of those relics of her operations which she has left behind.

And it is by the population of the chalk sea that the ancient and the modern inhabitants of the world are most completely connected. The groups which are dying out flourish side by side with the groups which are now the dominant forms of life. Thus the chalk contains remains of those strange flying and swimming reptiles, the pterodactyl, the ichthyosaurus, and the plesiosaurus, which are found in no later deposits, but abounded in preceding ages. The chambered shells called ammonites and belemnites, which are so characteristic of the period preceding the cretaceous, in like manner die with it. But amongst these fading remainders of a previous state of things are some very modern forms of life, looking like Yankee pedlars among a tribe of Red Indians. Crocodiles of modern type appear; bony fishes, many of them very similar to existing species, almost supplant the forms of fish which predominate in more ancient seas; and many kinds of living shellfish first become known to us in the chalk. The

vegetation acquires a modern aspect. A few living animals are not even distinguishable as species from those which existed at that remote epoch. The *Globigerina* of the present day, for example, is not different specifically from that of the chalk; and the same may be said of many other *Foraminifera*. I think it probable that critical and unprejudiced examination will show that more than one species of much higher animals have had a similar longevity; but the only example which I can at present give confidently is the snake's-head lamp-shell (*Terebratulina caput serpentis*), which lives in our English seas and abounded (as *Terebratulina striata* of authors) in the chalk.

The longest line of human ancestry must hide its diminished head[7] before the pedigree of this insignificant shell-fish. We Englishmen are proud to have an ancestor who was present at the Battle of Hastings.[8] The ancestors of *Terebratulina caput serpentis* may have been present at a battle of *Ichthyosauria* in that part of the sea which, when the chalk was forming, flowed over the site of Hastings. While all around has changed, this *Terebratulina* has peacefully propagated its species from generation to generation, and stands, to this day, as a living testimony to the continuity of the present with the past history of the globe.

Up to this moment I have stated, so far as I know, nothing but well-authenticated facts, and the immediate conclusions which they force upon the mind. But the mind is so constituted that it does not willingly rest in facts and immediate causes, but seeks always after a knowledge of the remoter links in the chain of causation. Taking the many changes of any given spot of the earth's surface, from sea to land and from land to sea, as an established fact, we cannot refrain from asking ourselves how these changes have occurred. And when we have explained them—as they must be explained—by the alternate slow movements of elevation and depression which have affected the crust of the earth, we go still further back and ask, Why these movements?

I am not certain that anyone can give you a satisfactory answer to that question. Assuredly I cannot. All that can be said, for certain, is that such movements are part of the ordinary course of nature, inasmuch as they are going on at the present time. Direct proof may be given that some parts of the land of the northern hemisphere are at this moment in-

7 *Paradise Lost*. IV, 35.
8 The Norman Conquest, 1066.

sensibly rising and others insensibly sinking; and there is indirect, but perfectly satisfactory, proof that an enormous area now covered by the Pacific has been deepened thousands of feet since the present inhabitants of that sea came into existence. Thus there is not a shadow of a reason for believing that the physical changes of the globe in past times have been effected by other than natural causes. Is there any more reason for believing that the concomitant modifications in the forms of the living inhabitants of the globe have been brought about in other ways?

Before attempting to answer this question, let us try to form a distinct mental picture of what has happened in some special case. The crocodiles are animals which, as a group, have a very vast antiquity. They abounded ages before the chalk was deposited; they throng the rivers in warm climates at the present day. There is a difference in the form of the joints of the backbone, and in some minor particulars, between the crocodiles of the present epoch and those which lived before the chalk; but in the cretaceous epoch, as I have already mentioned, the crocodiles had assumed the modern type of structure. Notwithstanding this, the crocodiles of the chalk are not identically the same as those which lived in the times called ''older tertiary,'' which succeeded the cretaceous epoch, and the crocodiles of the older tertiaries are not identical with those of the newer tertiaries, nor are these identical with existing forms. (I leave open the question whether particular species may have lived on from epoch to epoch.) Thus each epoch has had its peculiar crocodiles; though all, since the chalk, have belonged to the modern type, and differ simply in their proportions, and in such structural particulars as are discernible only to trained eyes.

How is the existence of this long succession of different species of crocodiles to be accounted for? Only two suppositions seem to be open to us—Either each species of crocodile has been specially created, or it has arisen out of some pre-existing form by the operation of natural causes. Choose your hypothesis; I have chosen mine. I can find no warranty for believing in the distinct creation of a score of successive species of crocodiles in the course of countless ages of time. Science gives no countenance to such a wild fancy; nor can even the perverse ingenuity of a commentator pretend to discover this sense in the simple words in which the writer of Genesis records the proceedings of the fifth and sixth days of the Creation. On the other hand, I see no good reason for doubting the necessary alternative, that all these varied species have been evolved from pre-existing crocodilian forms, by the operation of causes as completely a part of the common order of nature as those which have effected the changes of the inorganic world. Few will venture to affirm that the reasoning which applies to crocodiles loses its force among other animals, or among plants. If one series of species has come into existence by the operation of natural causes, it seems folly to deny that all may have arisen in the same way.

A small beginning has led us to a great ending. If I were to put the bit of chalk with which we started into the hot but obscure flame of burning hydrogen, it would presently shine like the sun. It seems to me that this physical metamorphosis is no false image of what has been the result of our subjecting it to a jet of fervent, though nowise brilliant, thought tonight. It has become luminous, and its clear rays, penetrating the abyss of the remote past, have brought within our ken some stages of the evolution of the earth. And in the shifting ''without haste, but without rest''[9] of the land and sea, in the endless variation of the forms assumed by living beings, we have observed nothing but the natural product of the forces originally possessed by the substance of the universe.

JOHN RUSKIN (1819-1900)

From THE SEVEN LAMPS OF ARCHITECTURE*

The Lamp of Memory.

Among the hours of his life to which the writer looks back with peculiar gratitude as having been marked by more than ordinary fulness of joy or clearness of teaching, is one passed, now some years ago, near time of sunset, among the broken masses of pine forest which skirt the course of the Ain, above the village of Champagnole, in the Jura.[1] It is a spot which has all the solemnity, with none of the savage-

[9] *"Ohne Hast, aber ohne Rast."*—Goethe.

---

[1] A chain of mountains in eastern France.

* Published in 1849, some time after the first two volumes of *Modern Painters*. The seven "Lamps" are Sacrifice, Truth, Power, Beauty, Life, Memory, and Obedience. The word "lamp" is used in allusion to the story of Aladdin's magic lamp; and the book was written, said Ruskin, "to show that certain right states of temper and moral feeling were the magic powers by which all good architecture, without exception, had been produced." The selection here given illustrates Ruskin's early exuberant style and also contains his fundamental doctrine of the necessity of relating art to life and morality.

ness, of the Alps; where there is a sense of a great power beginning to be manifested in the earth, and of a deep and majestic concord in the rise of the long low lines of piny hills; the first utterance of those mighty mountain symphonies, soon to be more loudly lifted and wildly broken along the battlements of the Alps. But their strength is as yet restrained; and the far-reaching ridges of pastoral mountain succeed each other, like the long and sighing swell which moves over quiet waters from some far-off stormy sea. And there is a deep tenderness pervading that vast monotony. The destructive forces and the stern expression of the central ranges are alike withdrawn. No frost-ploughed, dust-encumbered paths of ancient glacier fret the soft Jura pastures; no splintered heaps of ruin break the fair ranks of her forests; no pale, defiled, or furious rivers rend their rude and changeful ways among her rocks. Patiently, eddy by eddy, the clear green streams wind along their well-known beds; and under the dark quietness of the undisturbed pines, there spring up, year by year, such company of joyful flowers as I know not the like of among all the blessings of the earth. It was spring time, too; and all were coming forth in clusters crowded for very love; there was room enough for all, but they crushed their leaves into all manner of strange shapes only to be nearer each other. There was the wood anemone, star after star, closing every now and then into nebulæ; and there was the oxalis, troop by troop, like virginal processions of the Mois de Marie,[2] the dark vertical clefts in the limestone choked up with them as with heavy snow, and touched with ivy on the edges—ivy as light and lovely as the vine; and, ever and anon, a blue gush of violets, and cowslip bells in sunny places; and in the more open ground the vetch and comfrey, and mezereon, and the small sapphire buds of the Polygala Alpina,[3] and the wild strawberry, just a blossom or two all showered amidst the golden softness of deep, warm, amber-coloured moss. I came out presently on the edge of the ravine; the solemn murmur of its waters rose suddenly from beneath, mixed with the singing of the thrushes among the pine boughs; and on the opposite side of the valley, walled all along as it was by gray cliffs of limestone, there was a hawk sailing slowly off their brow, touching them nearly with his wings, and with the shadows of the pines flickering upon his plumage from above; but with the fall of a hundred fathoms under his breast, and the

curling pools of the green river gliding and glittering dizzily beneath him, their foam globes moving with him as he flew. It would be difficult to conceive a scene less dependent upon any other interest than that of its own secluded and serious beauty; but the writer well remembers the sudden blankness and chill which were cast upon it when he endeavoured, in order more strictly to arrive at the sources of its impressiveness, to imagine it, for a moment, a scene in some aboriginal forest of the New Continent. The flowers in an instant lost their light, the river its music; the hills became oppressively desolate; a heaviness in the boughs of the darkened forest showed how much of their former power had been dependent upon a life which was not theirs, how much of the glory of the imperishable, or continually renewed, creation is reflected from things more precious in their memories than it, in its renewing. Those ever springing flowers and ever flowing streams had been dyed by the deep colours of human endurance, valour, and virtue; and the crests of the sable hills that rose against the evening sky received a deeper worship, because their far shadows fell eastward over the iron wall of Joux,[4] and the four-square keep of Granson.[5]

It is as the centralization and protectress of this sacred influence, that Architecture is to be regarded by us with the most serious thought. We may live without her, and worship without her, but we cannot remember without her. How cold is all history, how lifeless all imagery, compared to that which the living nation writes, and the uncorrupted marble bears!—how many pages of doubtful record might we not often spare, for a few stones left one upon another! The ambition of the old Babel builders was well directed for this world:[6] there are but two strong conquerors of the forgetfulness of men, Poetry and Architecture; and the latter in some sort includes the former, and is mightier in its reality; it is well to have, not only what men have thought and felt, but what their hands have handled, and their strength wrought, and their eyes beheld, all the days of their life. The age of Homer is surrounded with darkness, his very personality with doubt. Not so that of Pericles:[7] and the day is coming when we shall

2 "Mary's Month." The reference is to May processions in honor of the Virgin.
3 A milkwort.

4 In the Fort de Joux, Mirabeau, the French orator, was once imprisoned; and Toussaint L'Ouverture, the Haitian revolutionist, died there.
5 A village and castle on the Lake of Neuchâtel, Switzerland. A Swiss garrison was treacherously put to death there by Charles the Bold in 1476 and gloriously avenged by the Swiss army.
6 See *Genesis*, xi. 4.
7 It was during the ascendency of Pericles that the Parthenon was built.

confess that we have learned more of Greece out of the crumbled fragments of her sculpture than even from her sweet singers or soldier historians. And if indeed there be any profit in our knowledge of the past, or any joy in the thought of being remembered hereafter, which can give strength to present exertion, or patience to present endurance, there are two duties respecting national architecture whose importance it is impossible to overrate; the first, to render the architecture of the day historical; and the second, to preserve, as the most precious of inheritances, that of past ages.

It is in the first of these two directions that Memory may truly be said to be the Sixth Lamp of Architecture; for it is in becoming memorial or monumental that a true perfection is attained by civil and domestic buildings; and this partly as they are, with such a view, built in a more stable manner, and partly as their decorations are consequently animated by a metaphorical or historical meaning.

As regards domestic buildings, there must always be a certain limitation to views of this kind in the power, as well as in the hearts, of men; still I cannot but think it an evil sign of a people when their houses are built to last for one generation only. There is a sanctity in a good man's house which cannot be renewed in every tenement that rises on its ruins; and I believe that good men would generally feel this; and that having spent their lives happily and honourably, they would be grieved, at the close of them, to think that the place of their earthly abode, which had seen, and seemed almost to sympathize in, all their honour, their gladness or their suffering,—that this, with all the record it bare of them, and of all material things that they had loved and ruled over, and set the stamp of themselves upon—was to be swept away, as soon as there was room made for them in the grave; that no respect was to be shown to it, no affection felt for it, no good to be drawn from it by their children; that though there was a monument in the church, there was no warm monument in the heart and house to them; that all that they ever treasured was despised, and the places that had sheltered and comforted them were dragged down to the dust. I say that a good man would fear this; and that, far more, a good son, a noble descendant, would fear doing it to his father's house. I say that if men lived like men indeed, their houses would be temples—temples which we should hardly dare to injure, and in which it would make us holy to be permitted to live; and there must be a strange dissolution of natural affection, a strange unthankfulness for all that homes have

given and parents taught, a strange consciousness that we have been unfaithful to our fathers' honour, or that our own lives are not such as would make our dwellings sacred to our children, when each man would fain build to himself, and build for the little revolution of his own life only. And I look upon those pitiful concretions of lime and clay which spring up, in mildewed forwardness, out of the kneaded fields about our capital—upon those thin, tottering, foundationless shells of splintered wood and imitated stone—upon those gloomy rows of formalized minuteness, alike without difference and without fellowship, as solitary as similar—not merely with the careless disgust of an offended eye, not merely with sorrow for a desecrated landscape, but with a painful foreboding that the roots of our national greatness must be deeply cankered when they are thus loosely struck in their native ground; that those comfortless and unhonoured dwellings are the signs of a great and spreading spirit of popular discontent; that they mark the time when every man's aim is to be in some more elevated sphere than his natural one, and every man's past life is his habitual scorn; when men build in the hope of leaving the places they have built, and live in the hope of forgetting the years that they have lived; when the comfort, the peace, the religion of home have ceased to be felt, and the crowded tenements of a struggling and restless population differ only from the tents of the Arab or the Gipsy by their less healthy openness to the air of heaven, and less happy choice of their spot of earth; by their sacrifice of liberty without the gain of rest, and of stability without the luxury of change.

This is no slight, no consequenceless evil; it is ominous, infectious, and fecund of other fault and misfortune. When men do not love their hearths, nor reverence their thresholds, it is a sign that they have dishonoured both, and that they have never acknowledged the true universality of that Christian worship which was indeed to supersede the idolatry, but not the piety, of the pagan. Our God is a household God, as well as a heavenly one; He has an altar in every man's dwelling; let men look to it when they rend it lightly and pour out its ashes. It is not a question of mere ocular delight, it is no question of intellectual pride, or of cultivated and critical fancy, how, and with what aspect of durability and of completeness, the domestic buildings of a nation shall be raised. It is one of those moral duties, not with more impunity to be neglected because the perception of them depends on a finely toned and balanced conscientiousness, to build our dwellings with care, and patience, and fondness, and diligent completion, and with a view to their duration at least for such a period as, in the ordinary course of national revolutions, might be supposed likely to extend to the entire alteration of the direction of local interests. This at the least; but it would be better if, in every possible instance, men built their own houses on a scale commensurate rather with their condition at the commencement, than their attainments at the termination, of their worldly career; and built them to stand as long as human work at its strongest can be hoped to stand; recording to their children what they have been, and from what, if so it had been permitted them, they had risen. And when houses are thus built, we may have that true domestic architecture, the beginning of all other, which does not disdain to treat with respect and thoughtfulness the small habitation as well as the large, and which invests with the dignity of contented manhood the narrowness of worldly circumstance.

FROM THE STONES OF VENICE.

THE THRONE. VOLUME II, CHAPTER I*

In the olden days of travelling, now to return no more, in which distance could not be vanquished without toil, but in which that toil was rewarded, partly by the power of deliberate survey of the countries through which the journey lay, and partly by the happiness of the evening hours, when from the top of the last hill he had surmounted, the traveller beheld the quiet village where he was to rest, scattered among the meadows beside its valley stream; or, from the long hoped for turn in the dusty perspective of the causeway, saw, for the first time, the towers of some famed city, faint in the rays of sunset—hours of peaceful and thoughtful pleasure, for which the rush of the arrival in the railway station is perhaps not always, or to all men, an equivalent,—in those days, I say, when there was something more to be anticipated and remembered in the first aspect of each successive halting-place, than a new arrangement of glass roofing and iron girder, there were few moments of which the recollection was more fondly cherished by the traveller, than that

*In this "faithful view of the site of the Venetian Throne," we have both an illustration of Ruskin's descriptive and narrative powers, and an expression of the deep religious convictions which informed his earlier writings. In the selection that follows will be found his defence and praise of Gothic art, together with his central social theory.

which, as I endeavoured to describe in the close of the last chapter, brought him within sight of Venice, as his gondola shot into the open lagoon from the canal of Mestre. Not but that the aspect of the city itself was generally the source of some slight disappointment, for, seen in this direction, its buildings are far less characteristic than those of the other great towns of Italy; but this inferiority was partly disguised by distance, and more than atoned for by the strange rising of its walls and towers out of the midst, as it seemed, of the deep sea, for it was impossible that the mind or the eye could at once comprehend the shallowness of the vast sheet of water which stretched away in leagues of rippling lustre to the north and south, or trace the narrow line of islets bounding it to the east. The salt breeze, the white roaning sea-birds, the masses of black weed separating and disappearing gradually, in knots of heaving shoal, under the advance of the steady tide, all proclaimed it to be indeed the ocean on whose bosom the great city rested so calmly; not such blue, soft, lake-like ocean as bathes the Neapolitan promontories, or sleeps beneath the marble rocks of Genoa, but a sea with the bleak power of our own northern waves, yet subdued into a strange spacious rest, and changed from its angry pallor into a field of burnished gold, as the sun declined behind the belfry tower of the lonely island church, fitly named "St. George of the Seaweed." As the boat drew nearer to the city, the coast which the traveller had just left sank behind him into one long, low, sad-coloured line, tufted irregularly with brushwood and willows; but at what seemed its northern extremity, the hills of Arqua rose in a dark cluster of purple pyramids, balanced on the bright mirage of the lagoon; two or three smooth surges of inferior hill extended themselves about their roots, and beyond these, beginning with the craggy peaks above Vicenza, the chain of the Alps girded the whole horizon to the north—a wall of jagged blue, here and there showing through its clefts a wilderness of misty precipices, fading far back into the recesses of Cadore, and itself rising and breaking away eastward, where the sun struck opposite upon its snow into mighty fragments of peaked light, standing up behind the barred clouds of evening, one after another, countless, the crown of the Adrian Sea, until the eye turned back from pursuing them, to rest upon the nearer burning of the campaniles[1] of Murano, and on the great city,

[1] bell-towers (Murano is an island just north of Venice.)

where it magnified itself along the waves, as the quick silent pacing of the gondola drew nearer and nearer. And at last, when its walls were reached, and the outmost of its untrodden streets was entered, not through towered gate or guarded rampart, but as a deep inlet between two rocks of coral in the Indian sea; when first upon the traveller's sight opened the long ranges of columned palaces,—each with its black boat moored at the portal,—each with its image cast down beneath its feet upon that green pavement which every breeze broke into new fantasies of rich tessellation; when first, at the extremity of the bright vista, the shadowy Rialto threw its colossal curve slowly forth from behind the palace of the Camerlenghi;[2] that strange curve, so delicate, so adamantine, strong as a mountain cavern, graceful as a bow just bent; when first, before its moonlike circumference was all risen, the gondolier's cry, "Ah! Stalì,"[3] struck sharp upon the ear, and the prow turned aside under the mighty cornices that half met over the narrow canal, where the plash of the water followed close and loud, ringing along the marble by the boat's side; and when at last that boat darted forth upon the breadth of silver sea, across which the front of the Ducal Palace, flushed with its sanguine veins, looks to the snowy dome of Our Lady of Salvation,[4] it was no marvel that the mind should be so deeply entranced by the visionary charm of a scene so beautiful and so strange, as to forget the darker truths of its history and its being. Well might it seem that such a city had owed her existence rather to the rod of the enchanter than the fear of the fugitive; that the waters which encircled her had been chosen for the mirror of her state, rather than the shelter of her nakedness; and that all which in nature was wild or merciless,—Time and Decay, as well as the waves and tempests,—had been won to adorn her instead of to destroy, and might still spare, for ages to come, that beauty which seemed to have fixed for its throne the sands of the hour-glass as well as of the sea.

And although the last few eventful years, fraught with change to the face of the whole earth, have been more fatal in their influence on Venice than the five hundred that preceded them; though the noble landscape of approach to her can now be seen no more, or seen only by a glance, as the engine slackens its rushing on the iron line; and though many of her palaces are forever defaced, and many in desecrated ruins, there is still so much of magic in her aspect that the hurried traveller, who must leave her before the wonder of that first aspect has been worn away, may still be led to forget the humility of her origin, and to shut his eyes to the depth of her desolation. They, at least, are little to be envied, in whose hearts the great charities of the imagination lie dead, and for whom the fancy has no power to repress the importunity of painful impressions, or to raise what is ignoble, and disguise what is discordant, in a scene so rich in its remembrances, so surpassing in its beauty. But for this work of the imagination there must be no permission during the task which is before us. The impotent feelings of romance, so singularly characteristic of this century, may indeed gild, but never save, the remains of those mightier ages to which they are attached like climbing flowers; and they must be torn away from the magnificent fragments, if we would see them as they stood in their own strength. Those feelings, always as fruitless as they are fond, are in Venice not only incapable of protecting, but even of discerning, the objects to which they ought to have been attached. The Venice of modern fiction and drama is a thing of yesterday, a mere efflorescence of decay, a stage dream which the first ray of daylight must dissipate into dust. No prisoner, whose name is worth remembering, or whose sorrow deserved sympathy, ever crossed that "Bridge of Sighs," which is the centre of the Byronic ideal of Venice;[5] no great merchant of Venice ever saw that Rialto under which the traveller now passes with breathless interest; the statue which Byron makes Faliero address as one of his great ancestors was erected to a soldier of fortune a hundred and fifty years after Faliero's death;[6] and the most conspicuous parts of the city have been so entirely altered in the course of the last three centuries, that if Henry Dandolo or Francis Foscari[7] could be summoned from their tombs, and stood each on the deck of his galley at the entrance of the Grand Canal, that renowned entrance, the painter's favourite subject, the novelist's favourite scene, where the water first narrows by the steps of the Church of La Salute,—the mighty Doges would not know in what part of the world they stood, would literally not recognize one stone of the

2 The Bridge of the Rialto, across the Grand Canal, consists of a single marble arch of 74 feet span and 32 feet in height.

3 Indicating that the gondolier meant to turn to the right.

4 The Church of Santa Maria della Salute, on the right side of the mouth of the Grand Canal.

5 See *Childe Harold*, IV. i.

6 See *Marino Faliero*, III. i. 36.

7 Early Doges of Venice; the one was blinded by the Byzantine emperor, the other compelled to abdicate.

great city, for whose sake, and by whose ingratitude, their grey hairs had been brought down with bitterness to the grave. The remains of *their* Venice lie hidden behind the cumbrous masses which were the delight of the nation in its dotage; hidden in many a grass-grown court, and silent pathway, and lightless canal, where the slow waves have sapped their foundations for five hundred years, and must soon prevail over them for ever. It must be our task[s] to glean and gather them forth, and restore out of them some faint image of the lost city; more gorgeous a thousandfold than that which now exists, yet not created in the day-dream of the prince, nor by the ostentation of the noble, but built by iron hands and patient hearts, contending against the adversity of nature and the fury of man, so that its wonderfulness cannot be grasped by the indolence of imagination, but only after frank inquiry into the true nature of that wild and solitary scene, whose restless tides and trembling sands did indeed shelter the birth of the city, but long denied her dominion.

When the eye falls casually on a map of Europe, there is no feature by which it is more likely to be arrested than the strange sweeping loop formed by the junction of the Alps and Apennines, and enclosing the great basin of Lombardy. This return of the mountain chain upon itself causes a vast difference in the character of the distribution of its débris on its opposite sides. The rock fragments and sediment which the torrents on the other side of the Alps bear into the plains are distributed over a vast extent of country, and, though here and there lodged in beds of enormous thickness, soon permit the firm substrata to appear from underneath them; but all the torrents which descend from the southern side of the High Alps, and from the northern slope of the Apennines, meet concentrically in the recess or mountain bay which the two ridges enclose; every fragment which thunder breaks out of their battlements, and every grain of dust which the summer rain washes from their pastures, is at last laid at rest in the blue sweep of the Lombardic plain; and that plain must have risen within its rocky barriers as a cup fills with wine, but for two contrary influences which continually depress, or disperse from its surface, the accumulation of the ruins of ages.

I will not tax the reader's faith in modern science by insisting on the singular depression of the surface of Lombardy, which appears for many centuries to have taken place steadily and continually; the main fact with which we have to do is the gradual transport, by the Po and its great collateral rivers, of vast masses of the finer sediment to the sea. The character of the Lombardic plain is most strikingly expressed by the ancient walls of its cities, composed for the most part of large rounded Alpine pebbles alternating with narrow courses of brick; and was curiously illustrated in 1848, by the ramparts of these same pebbles thrown up four or five feet high round every field, to check the Austrian cavalry in the battle under the walls of Verona. The finer dust among which these pebbles are dispersed is taken up by the rivers, fed into continual strength by the Alpine snow, so that, however pure their waters may be when they issue from the lakes at the foot of the great chain, they become of the colour and opacity of clay before they reach the Adriatic; the sediment which they bear is at once thrown down as they enter the sea, forming a vast belt of low land along the eastern coast of Italy. The powerful stream of the Po of course builds forward the fastest; on each side of it, north and south, there is a tract of marsh, fed by more feeble streams, and less liable to rapid change than the delta of the central river. In one of these tracts is built RAVENNA, and in the other VENICE.

What circumstances directed the peculiar arrangement of this great belt of sediment in the earliest times, it is not here the place to inquire. It is enough for us to know that from the mouths of the Adige to those of the Piave there stretches, at a variable distance of from three to five miles from the actual shore, a bank of sand, divided into long islands by narrow channels of sea. The space between this bank and the true shore consists of the sedimentary deposits from these and other rivers, a great plain of calcareous mud,[9] covered, in the neighbourhood of Venice, by the sea at high water, to the depth in most places of a foot or a foot and a half, and nearly everywhere exposed at low tide, but divided by an intricate network of narrow and winding channels, from which the sea never retires. In some places, according to the run of the currents, the land has risen into marshy islets, consolidated, some by art, and some by time, into ground firm enough to be built upon, or fruitful enough to be cultivated: in others, on the contrary, it has not reached the sea level; so that, at the average low water, shallow lakelets glitter among its irregularly exposed fields of seaweed. In the midst of the largest of these, increased in importance

[s] I. e., Ruskin's task, in this intended work on Venetian architecture and sculpture.

[9] Compare what Huxley says on the chalk formation of Europe, p. 670.

by the confluence of several large river channels towards one of the openings in the sea bank, the city of Venice itself is built, on a crowded cluster of islands; the various plots of higher ground which appear to the north and south of this central cluster, have at different periods been also thickly inhabited, and now bear, according to their size, the remains of cities, villages, or isolated convents and churches, scattered among spaces of open ground, partly waste and encumbered by ruins, partly under cultivation for the supply of the metropolis.

The average rise and fall of the tide is about three feet (varying considerably with the seasons); but this fall, on so flat a shore, is enough to cause continual movement in the waters, and in the main canals to produce a reflux which frequently runs like a mill stream. At high water no land is visible for many miles to the north or south of Venice, except in the form of small islands crowned with towers or gleaming with villages: there is a channel, some three miles wide, between the city and the mainland, and some mile and a half wide between it and the sandy breakwater called the Lido, which divides the lagoon from the Adriatic, but which is so low as hardly to disturb the impression of the city's having been built in the midst of the ocean, although the secret of its true position is partly, yet not painfully, betrayed by the clusters of piles set to mark the deep-water channels, which undulate far away in spotty chains like the studded backs of huge sea-snakes, and by the quick glittering of the crisped and crowded waves that flicker and dance before the strong winds upon the uplifted level of the shallow sea. But the scene is widely different at low tide. A fall of eighteen or twenty inches is enough to show ground over the greater part of the lagoon; and at the complete ebb the city is seen standing in the midst of a dark plain of seaweed, of gloomy green, except only where the larger branches of the Brenta and its associated streams converge towards the port of the Lido. Through this salt and sombre plain the gondola and the fishing-boat advance by tortuous channels, seldom more than four or five feet deep, and often so choked with slime that the heavier keels furrow the bottom till their crossing tracks are seen through the clear sea water like the ruts upon a wintry road, and the oar leaves blue gashes upon the ground at every stroke, or is entangled among the thick weed that fringes the banks with the weight of its sullen waves, leaning to and fro upon the uncertain sway of the exhausted tide. The scene is often profoundly oppressive, even at this day,

when every plot of higher ground bears some fragment of fair building: but, in order to know what it was once, let the traveller follow in his boat at evening the windings of some unfrequented channel far into the midst of the melancholy plain; let him remove, in his imagination, the brightness of the great city that still extends itself in the distance, and the walls and towers from the islands that are near; and so wait, until the bright investiture and sweet warmth of the sunset are withdrawn from the waters, and the black desert of their shore lies in its nakedness beneath the night, pathless, comfortless, infirm, lost in dark languor and fearful silence, except where the salt runlets plash into the tideless pools, or the sea-birds flit from their margins with a questioning cry; and he will be enabled to enter in some sort into the horror of heart with which this solitude was anciently chosen by man for his habitation. They little thought, who first drove the stakes into the sand, and strewed the ocean reeds for their rest, that their children were to be the princes of that ocean, and their palaces its pride; and yet, in the great natural laws that rule that sorrowful wilderness, let it be remembered what strange preparation had been made for the things which no human imagination could have foretold, and how the whole existence and fortune of the Venetian nation were anticipated or compelled, by the setting of those bars and doors to the rivers and the sea. Had deeper currents divided their islands, hostile navies would again and again have reduced the rising city into servitude; had stronger surges beaten their shores, all the richness and refinement of the Venetian architecture must have been exchanged for the walls and bulwarks of an ordinary sea-port. Had there been no tide, as in other parts of the Mediterranean, the narrow canals of the city would have become noisome, and the marsh in which it was built pestiferous. Had the tide been only a foot or eighteen inches higher in its rise, the water-access to the doors of the palaces would have been impossible: even as it is, there is sometimes a little difficulty, at the ebb, in landing without setting foot upon the lower and slippery steps; and the highest tides sometimes enter the courtyards, and overflow the entrance halls. Eighteen inches more of difference between the level of the flood and ebb would have rendered the doorsteps of every palace, at low water, a treacherous mass of weeds and limpets, and the entire system of water-carriage for the higher classes, in their easy and daily intercourse, must have been done away with. The streets of the city would have been widened, its network of canals filled up, and all the peculiar character of the place and the people destroyed.

The reader may perhaps have felt some pain in the contrast between this faithful view of the site of the Venetian Throne, and the romantic conception of it which we ordinarily form; but this pain, if he have felt it, ought to be more than counterbalanced by the value of the instance thus afforded to us at once of the inscrutableness and the wisdom of the ways of God. If, two thousand years ago, we had been permitted to watch the slow settling of the slime of those turbid rivers into the polluted sea, and the gaining upon its deep and fresh waters of the lifeless, impassable, unvoyageable plain, how little could we have understood the purpose with which those islands were shaped out of the void, and the torpid waters enclosed with their desolate walls of sand! How little could we have known, any more than of what now seems to us most distressful, dark, and objectless, the glorious aim which was then in the mind of Him in whose hand are all the corners of the earth! how little imagined that in the laws which were stretching forth the gloomy margins of those fruitless banks, and feeding the bitter grass among their shallows, there was indeed a preparation, and *the only preparation possible*, for the founding of a city which was to be set like a golden clasp on the girdle of the earth, to write her history on the white scrolls of the sea-surges, and to word it in their thunder, and to gather and give forth, in world-wide pulsation, the glory of the West and of the East, from the burning heart of her Fortitude and Splendour.

The Mediaeval and the Modern Workman. From Volume II, Chapter VI

Now, in the make and nature of every man, however rude or simple, whom we employ in manual labour, there are some powers for better things: some tardy imagination, torpid capacity of emotion, tottering steps of thought, there are, even at the worst; and in most cases it is all our own fault that they *are* tardy or torpid. But they cannot be strengthened, unless we are content to take them in their feebleness, and unless we prize and honour them in their imperfection above the best and most perfect manual skill. And this is what we have to do with all our labourers; to look for the *thoughtful* part of them, and get that out of them, whatever we lose for it, whatever faults and errors we are obliged to take with it. For the best that is in them cannot manifest itself, but in company with much error. Understand this clearly: You can teach a man to draw a straight line, and to cut one; to strike a curved line, and to carve it; and to copy and carve any number of given lines or forms, with admirable speed and perfect precision; and you find his work perfect of its kind: but if you ask him to think about any of those forms, to consider if he cannot find any better in his own head, he stops; his execution becomes hesitating; he thinks, and ten to one he thinks wrong; ten to one he makes a mistake in the first touch he gives to his work as a thinking being. But you have made a man of him for all that. He was only a machine before, an animated tool.

And observe, you are put to stern choice in this matter. You must either make a tool of the creature, or a man of him. You cannot make both. Men were not intended to work with the accuracy of tools, to be precise and perfect in all their actions. If you will have that precision out of them, and make their fingers measure degrees like cog-wheels, and their arms strike curves like compasses, you must unhumanize them. All the energy of their spirits must be given to make cogs and compasses of themselves. All their attention and strength must go to the accomplishment of the mean act. The eye of the soul must be bent upon the finger-point, and the soul's force must fill all the invisible nerves that guide it, ten hours a day, that it may not err from its steely precision, and so soul and sight be worn away, and the whole human being be lost at last—a heap of sawdust, so far as its intellectual work in this world is concerned; saved only by its Heart, which cannot go into the form of cogs and compasses, but expands, after the ten hours are over, into fireside humanity. On the other hand, if you will make a man of the working creature, you cannot make a tool. Let him but begin to imagine, to think, to try to do anything worth doing; and the engine-turned precision is lost at once. Out come all his roughness, all his dulness, all his incapability; shame upon shame, failure upon failure, pause after pause: but out comes the whole majesty of him also; and we know the height of it only when we see the clouds settling upon him. And, whether the clouds be bright or dark, there will be transfiguration behind and within them.

And now, reader, look round this English room of yours, about which you have been so proud so often, because the work of it was so good and strong, and the ornaments of it so finished. Examine again all those accurate mouldings, and perfect polishings, and unerring adjustments of the seasoned wood and tempered steel. Many a time you have exulted over them, and thought how great England was, because her slightest work was done so thoroughly. Alas! if read rightly, these perfectnesses are signs of a slavery in our England a thousand times more bitter and more degrading than that of the scourged African, or helot[1] Greek. Men may be beaten, chained, tormented, yoked like cattle, slaughtered like summer flies, and yet remain in one sense, and the best sense, free. But to smother their souls within them, to blight and hew into rotting pollards the suckling branches of their human intelligence, to make the flesh and skin which, after the worm's work on it, is to see God,[2] into leathern thongs to yoke machinery with,—this it is to be slave-masters indeed; and there might be more freedom in England, though her feudal lords' lightest words were worth men's lives, and though the blood of the vexed husbandman dropped in the furrows of her fields, than there is while the animation of her multitudes is sent like fuel to feed the factory smoke, and the strength of them is given daily to be wasted into the fineness of a web, or racked into the exactness of a line.

And, on the other hand, go forth again to gaze upon the old cathedral front, where you have smiled so often at the fantastic ignorance of the old sculptors: examine once more those ugly goblins, and formless monsters, and stern statues, anatomiless and rigid; but do not mock at them, for they are signs of the life and liberty of every workman who struck the stone; a freedom of thought, and rank in scale of being, such as no laws, no charters, no charities can secure; but which it must be the first aim of all Europe at this day to regain for her children.

Let me not be thought to speak wildly or extravagantly. It is verily this degradation of the operative into a machine, which, more than any other evil of the times, is leading the mass of the nations everywhere into vain, incoherent, destructive struggling for a freedom of which they cannot explain the nature to themselves. Their universal outcry against wealth, and against nobility, is not forced from them either by the pressure of famine, or the sting of mortified pride. These do much, and have done much in all ages; but the foundations of society were never yet shaken as they are at this day. It is not that men are ill fed, but that they have no pleasure in the work by which they make their bread, and therefore look to wealth as the only means of pleasure. It is not that men are pained by the scorn of the upper classes, but they cannot endure their own; for they feel that the kind of labour to which they are condemned is verily a degrading one, and makes them less than men. Never had the upper classes so much sympathy with the lower, or charity for them, as they have at this day, and yet never were they so much hated by them: for, of old, the separation between the noble and the poor was merely a wall built by law; now it is a veritable difference in level of standing, a precipice between upper and lower grounds in the field of humanity, and there is pestilential air at the bottom of it. I know not if a day is ever to come when the nature of right freedom will be understood, and when men will see that to obey another man, to labour for him, yield reverence to him or to his place, is not slavery. It is often the best kind of liberty,—liberty from care. The man who says to one, Go, and he goeth, and to another, Come, and he cometh,[3] has, in most cases, more sense of restraint and difficulty than the man who obeys him. The movements of the one are hindered by the burden on his shoulder; of the other, by the bridle on his lips: there is no way by which the burden may be lightened; but we need not suffer from the bridle if we do not champ at it. To yield reverence to another, to hold ourselves and our lives at his disposal, is not slavery; often it is the noblest state in which a man can live in this world. There is, indeed, a reverence which is servile, that is to say irrational or selfish: but there is also noble reverence, that is to say, reasonable and loving; and a man is never so noble as when he is reverent in this kind; nay, even if the feeling pass the bounds of mere reason, so that it be loving, a man is raised by it. Which had, in reality, most of the serf nature in him,—the Irish peasant who was lying in wait yesterday for his landlord, with his musket muzzle thrust through the ragged hedge; or that old mountain servant, who 200 years ago, at Inverkeithing, gave up his own life and the lives of his seven sons for his chief?—as each fell, calling forth his brother to the death, "Another for Hector!"[4] And therefore, in all ages and all countries, reverence has been paid and sacrifice made by men to each other, not only without complaint, but rejoicingly; and famine, and peril, and sword, and all evil, and all shame, have been borne willingly in the causes of masters and

---

1 A slave in ancient Sparta, owned by the state, and attached to the soil.
2 See *Job*, xix, 26.

3 See *Matthew*, viii, 9.
4 See the Preface to Scott's *The Fair Maid of Perth*.

kings; for all these gifts of the heart ennobled the men who gave, not less than the men who received, them, and nature prompted, and God rewarded the sacrifice. But to feel their souls withering within them, unthanked, to find their whole being sunk into an unrecognized abyss, to be counted off into a heap of mechanism, numbered with its wheels, and weighed with its hammer strokes;—this nature bade not,—this God blesses not,—this humanity for no long time is able to endure.

We have much studied and much perfected, of late, the great civilized invention of the division of labour; only we give it a false name. It is not, truly speaking, the labour that is divided; but the men:—Divided into mere segments of men—broken into small fragments and crumbs of life; so that all the little piece of intelligence that is left in a man is not enough to make a pin, or a nail, but exhausts itself in making the point of a pin or the head of a nail. Now it is a good and desirable thing, truly, to make many pins in a day; but if we could only see with what crystal sand their points were polished,—sand of human soul, much to be magnified before it can be discerned for what it is,—we should think there might be some loss in it also. And the great cry that rises from all our manufacturing cities, louder than their furnace blast, is all in very deed for this,—that we manufacture everything there except men; we blanch cotton, and strengthen steel, and refine sugar, and shape pottery; but to brighten, to strengthen, to refine, or to form a single living spirit, never enters into our estimate of advantages. And all the evil to which that cry is urging our myriads can be met only in one way: not by teaching nor preaching, for to teach them is but to show them their misery, and to preach to them, if we do nothing more than preach, is to mock at it. It can be met only by a right understanding, on the part of all classes, of what kinds of labour are good for men, raising them, and making them happy; by a determined sacrifice of such convenience, or beauty, or cheapness as is to be got only by the degradation of the workman; and by equally determined demand for the products and results of healthy and ennobling labour.

FROM MODERN PAINTERS

OF THE TRUE IDEAL:—FIRST, PURIST. PART IV, CHAPTER VI

Having thus glanced at the principal modes in which the imagination works for evil, we must rapidly note also the principal directions in which its operation is admissible, even in changing or strangely combining what is brought within its sphere.

For hitherto we have spoken as if every change wilfully wrought by the imagination was an error; apparently implying that its only proper work was to summon up the memories of past events, and the anticipations of future ones, under aspects which would bear the sternest tests of historical investigation, or abstract reasoning. And in general this is, indeed, its noblest work. Nevertheless, it has also permissible functions peculiarly its own, and certain rights of feigning, and adorning, and fancifully arranging, inalienable from its nature. Everything that is natural is, within certain limits, right; and we must take care not, in over-severity, to deprive ourselves of any refreshing or animating power ordained to be in us for our help.

(A). It was noted in speaking above of the Angelican[1] or passionate ideal, that there was a certain virtue in it dependent on the expression of its loving enthusiasm.

(B). In speaking of the pursuit of beauty as one of the characteristics of the highest art, it was also said that there were certain ways of showing this beauty by gathering together, without altering, the finest forms, and marking them by gentle emphasis.

(C). And in speaking of the true uses of imagination it was said that we might be allowed to create for ourselves, in innocent play, fairies and naiads, and other such fictitious creatures.

Now this loving enthusiasm, which seeks for a beauty fit to be the object of eternal love; this inventive skill, which kindly displays what exists around us in the world; and this playful energy of thought which delights in various conditions of the impossible, are three forms of idealism more or less connected with the three tendencies of the artistical mind which I had occasion to explain in the chapter on the Nature of Gothic, in the *Stones of Venice*. It was there pointed out, that, the things around us containing mixed good and evil, certain men chose the good and left the evil (thence properly called Purists); others received both good and evil together (thence properly called Naturalists); and others had a tendency to choose the evil and leave the good, whom, for convenience' sake, I termed Sensualists. I do not mean to say that painters of fairies and naiads must belong to this last and lowest class, or habitually choose the evil and leave the good; but there is, nevertheless, a strange connection between the reinless play of the imagination, and a sense of the presence of evil, which is usually more or less developed in those creations of the imagination to which we properly attach the word *Grotesque*.

For this reason, we shall find it convenient to arrange what we have to note respecting true idealism under the three heads—

A. Purist Idealism.
B. Naturalist Idealism.
C. Grotesque Idealism.

A. Purist Idealism.—It results from the unwillingness of men whose dispositions are more than ordinarily tender and holy, to contemplate the various forms of definite evil which necessarily occur in the daily aspects of the world around them. They shrink from them as from pollution, and endeavour to create for themselves an imaginary state, in which pain and imperfection either do not exist, or exist in some edgeless and enfeebled condition.

As, however, pain and imperfection are, by eternal laws, bound up with existence, so far as it is visible to us, the endeavour to cast them away invariably indicates a comparative childishness of mind, and produces a childish form of art. In general, the effort is most successful when it is most naïve, and when the ignorance of the draughtsman is in some frank proportion to his innocence. For instance, one of the modes of treatment, the most conducive to this ideal expression, is simply drawing everything without shadows, as if the sun were everywhere at once. This, in the present state of our knowledge, we could not do with grace, because we could not do it without fear or shame. But an artist of the thirteenth century did it with no disturbance of conscience,—knowing no better, or rather, in some sense, we might say, knowing no worse. It is, however, evident, at the first thought, that all representations of nature without evil must either be ideals of a future world, or be false ideals, if they are understood to be representations of facts. They can only be classed among the branches of the true ideal, in so far as they are understood to be nothing more than expressions of the painter's personal affections or hopes.

Let us take one or two instances in order clearly to explain our meaning.

The life of Angelico was almost entirely spent in the endeavour to imagine the beings belonging to another world. By purity of life, habitual elevation of thought, and natural sweetness of disposition, he was enabled to express the sacred affections upon the human countenance as no one ever did before or since. In order to effect clearer distinction between heavenly beings and those of this world, he represents the former as clothed in draperies of the purest colour, crowned with glories of burnished gold, and entirely shadowless. With exquisite choice of gesture, and disposition of folds of drapery, this mode of treatment gives perhaps the best idea of spiritual beings which the human mind is capable of forming. It is, therefore, a true ideal; but the mode in which it is arrived at (being so far mechanical and contradictory of the appearances of nature) necessarily precludes those who practise it from being complete masters of their art. It is always childish, but beautiful in its childishness.

The works of our own Stothard[2] are examples of the operation of another mind, singular in gentleness and purity, upon mere worldly subject. It seems as if Stothard could not conceive wickedness, coarseness, or baseness; every one of his figures looks as if it had been copied from some creature who had never harboured an unkind thought, or permitted itself in an ignoble action. With this intense love of mental purity is joined, in Stothard, a love of mere physical smoothness and softness, so that he lived in a universe of soft grass and stainless fountains, tender trees, and stones at which no foot could stumble.

All this is very beautiful, and may sometimes urge us to an endeavour to make the world itself more like the conception of the painter. At least, in the midst of its malice, misery, and baseness, it is often a relief to glance at the graceful shadows, and take, for momentary companionship, creatures full only of love, gladness, and honour. But the perfect truth will at last vindicate itself against the partial truth; the help which we can gain from the unsubstantial vision will be only like that which we may sometimes receive, in weariness, from the scent of a flower or the passing of a breeze. For all firm aid, and steady use, we must look to harder realities; and, as far as the painter himself is regarded, we can only receive such work as the sign of an amiable imbecility. It is indeed ideal; but ideal as a fair dream is in the dawn of morning, before the faculties are astir. The apparent completeness of grace can never be attained without much definite falsification as well as omission; stones, over which we cannot stumble, must be ill-drawn

[2] Thomas Stothard (1755-1834), best known perhaps for his painting of the "Canterbury Pilgrims."

stones; trees, which are all gentleness and soft-ness, cannot be trees of wood; nor companies without evil in them, companies of flesh and blood. The habit of falsification (with what-ever aim) begins always in dulness and ends always in incapacity: nothing can be more pitiable than any endeavour by Stothard to express facts beyond his own sphere of soft pathos or graceful mirth, and nothing more unwise than the aim at a similar ideality by any painter who has power to render a sin-cerer truth.

I remember another interesting example of ideality on this same root, but belonging to another branch of it, in the works of a young German painter, which I saw some time ago in a London drawing-room. He had been travel-ling in Italy, and had brought home a port-folio of sketches remarkable alike for their fidelity and purity. Every one was a laborious and accurate study of some particular spot. Every cottage, every cliff, every tree, at the site chosen, had been drawn; and drawn with palpable sincerity of portraiture, and yet in such a spirit that it was impossible to conceive that any sin or misery had ever entered into one of the scenes he had represented; and the volcanic horrors of Radicofani,[3] the pestilent gloom of the Pontines,[4] and the boundless despondency of the Campagna[5] became, under his hand, only various appearances of Paradise.

It was very interesting to observe the minute emendations or omissions by which this was effected. To set the tiles the slightest degree more in order upon a cottage roof; to insist upon the vine leaves at the window, and let the shadow which fell from them naturally conceal the rent in the wall; to draw all the flowers in the foreground, and miss the weeds; to draw all the folds of the white clouds, and miss those of the black ones; to mark the graceful branches of the trees, and, in one way or another, beguile the eye from those which were ungainly; to give every peasant-girl whose face was visible the expression of an angel, and every one whose back was turned the bearing of a princess; finally, to give a general look of light, clear organization, and serene vitality to every feature in the landscape;—such were his artifices, and such his delights. It was impossible not to sympathize deeply

with the spirit of such a painter; and it was just cause for gratitude to be permitted to travel, as it were, through Italy with such a friend. But his work had, nevertheless, its stern limitations and marks of everlasting in-feriority. Always soothing and pathetic, it could never be sublime, never perfectly nor entrancingly beautiful; for the narrow spirit of correction could not cast itself fully into any scene; the calm cheerfulness which shrank from the shadow of the cypress, and the dis-tortion of the olive, could not enter into the brightness of the sky that they pierced, nor the softness of the bloom that they bore: for every sorrow that his heart turned from, he lost a consolation; for every fear which he dared not confront, he lost a portion of his hardiness; the unsceptred sweep of the storm-clouds, the fair freedom of glancing shower and flickering sunbeam, sank into sweet recti-tudes and decent formalisms; and, before eyes that refused to be dazzled or darkened, the hours of sunset wreathed their rays unheeded, and the mists of the Apennines spread their blue veils in vain.

To this inherent shortcoming and narrow-ness of reach the farther defect was added, that this work gave no useful representation of the state of facts in the country which it pre-tended to contemplate. It was not only want-ing in all the higher elements of beauty, but wholly unavailable for instruction of any kind beyond that which exists in pleasurableness of pure emotion. And considering what cost of labour was devoted to the series of drawings, it could not but be matter for grave blame, as well as for partial contempt, that a man of amiable feeling and considerable intellectual power should thus expend his life in the declaration of his own petty pieties and pleas-ant reveries, leaving the burden of human sor-row unwitnessed, and the power of God's judg-ments unconfessed; and, while poor Italy lay wounded and moaning at his feet, pass by, in priestly calm, lest the whiteness of his decent vesture should be spotted with unhallowed blood.

Of several other forms of Purism I shall have to speak hereafter, more especially of that exhibited in the landscapes of the early re-ligious painters; but these examples are enough, for the present, to show the general principle that the purest ideal, though in some measure true, in so far as it springs from the true long-ings of an earnest mind, is yet necessarily in many things deficient or blamable, and *always* an indication of some degree of weakness in

3 A town in the province of Siena, Italy, situated on a hill at the foot of a basaltic rock.
4 A marshy region in central Italy.
5 The Roman Campagna. In his preface to the second edition of the first volume of *Modern Painters*, Ruskin has a remarkable description of this "wild and wasted plain."

the mind pursuing it. But, on the other hand, it is to be noted that entire scorn of this purist ideal is the sign of a far greater weakness. Multitudes of petty artists, incapable of any noble sensation whatever, but acquainted, in a dim way, with the technicalities of the schools, mock at the art whose depths they cannot fathom, and whose motives they cannot comprehend, but of which they can easily detect the imperfections, and deride the simplicities. Thus poor fumigatory Fuseli,[6] with an art composed of the tinsel of the stage and the panics of the nursery, speaks contemptuously of the name of Angelico as "dearer to sanctity than to art." And a large portion of the resistance to the noble Pre-Raphaelite movement of our own days[7] has been offered by men who suppose the entire function of the artist in this world to consist in laying on colour with a large brush, and surrounding dashes of flake white with bituminous brown; men whose entire capacities of brain, soul, and sympathy, applied industriously to the end of their lives, would not enable them, at last, to paint so much as one of the leaves of the nettles, at the bottom of Hunt's picture of the Light of the World.[8]

It is finally to be remembered, therefore, that Purism is always noble when it is *instinctive.* It is not the greatest thing that can be done, but it is probably the greatest thing that the man who does it can do, provided it comes from his heart. True, it is a sign of weakness, but it is not in our choice whether we will be weak or strong; and there is a certain strength which can only be made perfect in weakness. If he is working in humility, fear of evil, desire of beauty, and sincere purity of purpose and thought, he will produce good and helpful things; but he must be much on his guard against supposing himself to be greater than his fellows, because he has shut himself into this calm and cloistered sphere. His only safety lies in knowing himself to be, on the

contrary, *less* than his fellows, and in always striving, so far as he can find it in his heart, to extend his delicate narrowness toward the great naturalist ideal. The whole group of modern German purists have lost themselves because they founded their work not on humility, nor on religion, but on small self-conceit. Incapable of understanding the great Venetians, or any other masters of true imaginative power, and having fed what mind they had with weak poetry and false philosophy, they thought themselves the best and greatest of artistic mankind, and expected to found a new school of painting in pious plagiarism and delicate pride. It is difficult at first to decide which is the more worthless, the spiritual affectation of the petty German, or the composition and chiaroscuro of the petty Englishman; on the whole, however, the latter have lightest weight, for the pseudo-religious painter must, at all events, pass much of his time in meditation upon solemn subjects, and in examining venerable models; and may sometimes even cast a little useful reflected light, or touch the heart with a pleasant echo.

DANTE GABRIEL ROSSETTI
(1828-1882)

THE BLESSED DAMOZEL*

The blessed damozel leaned out
  From the gold bar of Heaven;
Her eyes were deeper than the depth
  Of waters stilled at even;
She had three lilies in her hand,
  And the stars in her hair were seven. 6

Her robe, ungirt from clasp to hem,
  No wrought flowers did adorn,
But a white rose of Mary's gift,
  For service meetly worn;
Her hair that lay along her back
  Was yellow like ripe corn. 12

Herseemed she scarce had been a day
  One of God's choristers;
The wonder was not yet quite gone
  From that still look of hers;
Albeit, to them she left, her day
  Had counted as ten years. 18

---

6 A Swiss-English painter and art-critic (1741-1825). He had a powerful but ill-regulated fancy, being both a fantastic designer and a reckless colorist. Perhaps Ruskin means something like this by calling him "fumigatory," but his meaning is not very clear.

7 The movement led by Rossetti, Millais, and Hunt. See *Eng. Lit.,* pp. 369, 370. Holman Hunt's well-known "Light of the World" (now at Keble College, Oxford) is a painting representing Christ, with a lantern in his hand, standing at a door and knocking.

8 "Not that the Pre-Raphaelite is a purist movement, it is stern naturalist; but its unfortunate opposers, who neither know what nature is, nor what purism is, have mistaken the simple nature for morbid purism, and therefore cried out against it."—Ruskin's note.

* Slight in substance as this poem is, it has two unusual sources of charm—a very definite pictorial character which stamps it as the work of a poet who was also a painter, and a mystical quality springing from an imagination that dared to portray earthly love in heavenly surroundings. Those who are interested in sources may consult Virgil, *Eclogue* v. 56; and Petrarch, Sonnets *In Morte,* 74.

(To one, it is ten years of years.
   . . . Yet now, and in this place,
Surely she leaned o'er me—her hair
   Fell all about my face. . . .
Nothing: the autumn fall of leaves.
   The whole year sets apace.)   24

It was the rampart of God's house
   That she was standing on;
By God built over the sheer depth
   The which is Space begun;
So high, that looking downward thence
   She scarce could see the sun.   30

It lies in Heaven, across the flood
   Of ether, as a bridge.
Beneath, the tides of day and night
   With flame and darkness ridge
The void, as low as where this earth
   Spins like a fretful midge.   36

Around her, lovers, newly met
   'Mid deathless love's acclaims,
Spoke evermore among themselves
   Their heart-remembered names;
And the souls mounting up to God
   Went by her like thin flames.   42

And still she bowed herself and stooped
   Out of the circling charm;
Until her bosom must have made
   The bar she leaned on warm,
And the lilies lay as if asleep
   Along her bended arm.   48

From the fixed place of Heaven she saw
   Time like a pulse shake fierce
Through all the worlds. Her gaze still strove
   Within the gulf to pierce
Its path; and now she spoke as when
   The stars sang in their spheres.   54

The sun was gone now; the curled moon
   Was like a little feather
Fluttering far down the gulf; and now
   She spoke through the still weather.
Her voice was like the voice the stars
   Had when they sang together.   60

(Ah sweet! Even now, in that bird's song,
   Strove not her accents there,
Fain to be hearkened? When those bells
   Possessed the mid-day air,
Strove not her steps to reach my side
   Down all the echoing stair?)   66

"I wish that he were come to me,
   For he will come," she said.

"Have I not prayed in Heaven?—on earth,
   Lord, Lord, has he not prayed?
Are not two prayers a perfect strength?
   And shall I feel afraid?   72

"When round his head the aureole clings,
   And he is clothed in white,
I'll take his hand and go with him
   To the deep wells of light;
As unto a stream we will step down,
   And bathe there in God's sight.   78

"We two will stand beside that shrine,
   Occult, withheld, untrod,
Whose lamps are stirred continually
   With prayer sent up to God;
And see our old prayers, granted, melt
   Each like a little cloud.   84

"We two will lie i' the shadow of
   That living mystic tree
Within whose secret growth the Dove[1]
   Is sometimes felt to be,
While every leaf that His plumes touch
   Saith His Name audibly.   90

"And I myself will teach to him,
   I myself, lying so,
The songs I sing here; which his voice
   Shall pause in, hushed and slow,
And find some knowledge at each pause,
   Or some new thing to know."   96

(Alas! We two, we two, thou say'st!
   Yea, one wast thou with me
That once of old. But shall God lift
   To endless unity
The soul whose likeness with thy soul
   Was but its love for thee?)   102

"We two," she said, "will seek the groves
   Where the lady Mary is,
With her five handmaidens, whose names
   Are five sweet symphonies,
Cecily, Gertrude, Magdalen,
   Margaret and Rosalys.   108

"Circlewise sit they, with bound locks
   And foreheads garlanded;
Into the fine cloth white like flame
   Weaving the golden thread,
To fashion the birth-robes for them
   Who are just born, being dead.   114

"He shall fear, haply, and be dumb:
   Then will I lay my cheek

---

[1] The Dove typifies the third member of the Trinity, the Holy Spirit.

To his, and tell about our love,
  Not once abashed or weak:
And the dear Mother will approve
  My pride, and let me speak.   120

"Herself shall bring us, hand in hand.
  To Him round whom all souls
Kneel, the clear-ranged unnumbered heads
  Bowed with their aureoles:
And angels meeting us shall sing
  To their citherns and citoles.   126

"There will I ask of Christ the Lord
  Thus much for him and me:—
Only to live as once on earth
  With Love, only to be,
As then awhile, for ever now
  Together, I and he."   132

She gazed and listened and then said,
  Less sad of speech than mild,—
"All this is when he comes." She ceased.
  The light thrilled towards her, filled
With angels in strong level flight.
  Her eyes prayed, and she smiled.   138

(I saw her smile.) But soon their path
  Was vague in distant spheres:
And then she cast her arms along
  The golden barriers,
And laid her face between her hands,
  And wept. (I heard her tears.)   144

SISTER HELEN*

"Why did you melt your waxen man,
           Sister Helen?
To-day is the third since you began."
"The time was long, yet the time ran,
           Little brother."
        (O Mother, Mary Mother,
Three days to-day, between Hell and Heaven!)

"But if you have done your work aright,
           Sister Helen,
You'll let me play, for you said I might." 10
"Be very still in your play to-night,
           Little brother."
        (O Mother, Mary Mother,

* This ballad is founded on an old superstition.
Holinshed, for example, tells a story of an attempt upon the life of King Duffe—how certain soldiers breaking into a house, "found
one of the witches roasting upon a wooden
broach an image of wax at the fire, resembling
in each feature the king's person, ...
by the which means it should have come to
pass that when the wax was once clean consumed, the death of the king should immediately follow."

Third night, to-night, between Hell and
  Heaven!)

"You said it must melt ere vesper-bell,
           Sister Helen;
If now it be molten, all is well."
"Even so,—nay, peace! you cannot tell,
           Little brother."
        (O Mother, Mary Mother, 2
O what is this, between Hell and Heaven?)

"Oh the waxen knave was plump to-day,
           Sister Helen;
How like dead folk he has dropped away!"
"Nay now, of the dead what can you say,
           Little brother?"
        (O Mother, Mary Mother,
What of the dead, between Hell and Heaven?

"See, see, the sunken pile of wood,
           Sister Helen, 3
Shines through the thinned wax red as blood!"
"Nay now, when looked you yet on blood,
           Little brother?"
        (O Mother, Mary Mother,
How pale she is, between Hell and Heaven!

"Now close your eyes, for they're sick and
  sore,
           Sister Helen,
And I'll play without the gallery door."
"Aye, let me rest,—I'll lie on the floor,
           Little brother." 4
        (O Mother, Mary Mother,
What rest to-night, between Hell and Heaven?

"Here high up in the balcony,
           Sister Helen,
The moon flies face to face with me."
"Aye, look and say whatever you see,
           Little brother."
        (O Mother, Mary Mother,
What sight to-night, between Hell and
  Heaven?)

"Outside it's merry in the wind's wake, 5
           Sister Helen;
In the shaken trees the chill stars shake."
"Hush, heard you a horse-tread as you spake?
           Little brother?"
        (O Mother, Mary Mother,
What sound to-night, between Hell and
  Heaven?)

"I hear a horse-tread, and I see,
           Sister Helen,
Three horsemen that ride terribly."

"Little brother, whence come the three, 60
    Little brother?"
        (*O Mother, Mary Mother,*
Whence should they come, between Hell and
    Heaven?)

"They come by the hill-verge from Boyne Bar,
    Sister Helen,
And one draws nigh, but two are afar."
"Look, look, do you know them who they are,
    Little brother?"
        (*O Mother, Mary Mother,*
Who should they be, between Hell and
    Heaven?) 70

"Oh, it's Keith of Eastholm rides so fast,
    Sister Helen,
For I know the white mane on the blast."
"The hour has come, has come at last,
    Little brother!"
        (*O Mother, Mary Mother,*
Her hour at last, between Hell and Heaven!)

"He has made a sign and called Halloo!
    Sister Helen,
And he says that he would speak with you." 80
"Oh tell him I fear the frozen dew,
    Little brother."
        (*O Mother, Mary Mother,*
Why laughs she thus, between Hell and
    Heaven?)

"The wind is loud, but I hear him cry,
    Sister Helen,
That Keith of Ewern's like to die."
"And he and thou, and thou and I,
    Little brother."
        (*O Mother, Mary Mother,* 90
And they and we, between Hell and Heaven!)

"Three days ago, on his marriage-morn,
    Sister Helen,
He sickened, and lies since then forlorn."
"For bridegroom's side is the bride a thorn,
    Little brother?"
        (*O Mother, Mary Mother,*
Cold bridal cheer, between Hell and Heaven!)

"Three days and nights he has lain abed,
    Sister Helen, 100
And he prays in torment to be dead."
"The thing may chance, if he have prayed,
    Little brother!"
        (*O Mother, Mary Mother,*
If he have prayed, between Hell and Heaven!)

"But he has not ceased to cry to-day,
    Sister Helen,
That you should take your curse away."
"*My* prayer was heard,—he need but pray,
    Little brother!" 110
        (*O Mother, Mary Mother,*
Shall God not hear, between Hell and
    Heaven?)

"But he says, till you take back your ban,
    Sister Helen,
His soul would pass, yet never can."
"Nay then, shall I slay a living man,
    Little brother?"
        (*O Mother, Mary Mother,*
A living soul, between Hell and Heaven!)

"But he calls for ever on your name, 120
    Sister Helen,
And says that he melts before a flame."
"My heart for his pleasure fared the same,
    Little brother."
        (*O Mother, Mary Mother,*
Fire at the heart, between Hell and Heaven!)

"Here's Keith of Westholm riding fast,
    Sister Helen,
For I know the white plume on the blast."
"The hour, the sweet hour I forecast, 130
    Little brother!"
        (*O Mother, Mary Mother,*
Is the hour sweet, between Hell and Heaven?)

"He stops to speak, and he stills his horse,
    Sister Helen;
But his words are drowned in the wind's
    course."
"Nay hear, nay hear, you must hear perforce,
    Little brother!"
        (*O Mother, Mary Mother,*
What word now heard, between Hell and
    Heaven?) 140

"Oh he says that Keith of Ewern's cry,
    Sister Helen,
Is ever to see you ere he die."
"In all that his soul sees, there am I,
    Little brother!"
        (*O Mother, Mary Mother,*
The soul's one sight, between Hell and
    Heaven!)

"He sends a ring and a broken coin,
    Sister Helen,
And bids you mind the banks of Boyne." 150

"What else he broke will he ever join,
          Little brother?''
          (*O Mother, Mary Mother,*
No, never joined, between Hell and Heaven!)

"He yields you these and craves full fain,
          Sister Helen,
You pardon him in his mortal pain.''
"What else he took will he give again,
          Little brother?''
          (*O Mother, Mary Mother,*   160
Not twice to give, between Hell and Heaven!)

"He calls your name in an agony,
          Sister Helen,
That even dead Love must weep to see.''
"Hate, born of Love, is blind as he,
          Little brother!''
          (*O Mother, Mary Mother,*
Love turned to hate, between Hell and
*   Heaven!*)

"Oh it's Keith of Keith now that rides fast,
          Sister Helen,   170
For I know the white hair on the blast.''
"The short, short hour will soon be past,
          Little brother!''
          (*O Mother, Mary Mother,*
Will   soon   be   past, between Hell and
*   Heaven!*)

"He looks at me and he tries to speak,
          Sister Helen,
But oh! his voice is sad and weak!''
"What here should the mighty Baron seek,
          Little brother?''   180
          (*O Mother, Mary Mother,*
Is this the end, between Hell and Heaven?)

"Oh his son still cries, if you forgive,
          Sister Helen,
The body dies, but the soul shall live.''
"Fire shall forgive me as I forgive,
          Little brother!''
          (*O Mother, Mary Mother,*
As she forgives, between Hell and Heaven!)

"Oh he prays you, as his heart would rive,   190
          Sister Helen,
To save his dear son's soul alive.''
"Fire cannot slay it, it shall thrive,
          Little brother!''
          (*O Mother, Mary Mother,*
Alas, alas, between Hell and Heaven!)

"He cries to you, kneeling in the road,
          Sister Helen,
To go with him for the love of God!''
"The way is long to his son's abode,   200
          Little brother.''
          (*O Mother, Mary Mother,*
The way is long, between Hell and Heaven!)

"A lady's here, by a dark steed brought,
          Sister Helen,
So darkly clad, I saw her not.''
"See her now or never see aught,
          Little brother!''
          (*O Mother, Mary Mother,*
What   more   to   see, between Hell and
*   Heaven?*)   210

"Her hood falls back, and the moon shines
     fair,
          Sister Helen,
On the Lady of Ewern's golden hair.''
"Blest hour of my power and her despair,
          Little brother!''
          (*O Mother, Mary Mother,*
Hour blest and banned, between Hell and
*   Heaven!*)

"Pale, pale her cheeks, that in pride did glow,
          Sister Helen,
'Neath the bridal-wreath three days ago.''   220
"One morn for pride and three days for woe,
          Little brother!''
          (*O Mother, Mary Mother,*
Three days, three nights, between Hell and
*   Heaven!*)

"Her clasped hands stretch from her bending
     head,
          Sister Helen;
With the loud wind's wail her sobs are wed.''
"What wedding-strains hath her bridal-bed,
          Little brother?''   229
          (*O Mother, Mary Mother,*
What   strain but death's, between Hell and
*   Heaven?*)

"She may not speak, she sinks in a swoon,
          Sister Helen,
She lifts her lips and gasps on the moon.''
"Oh! might I but hear her soul's blithe tune,
          Little brother!''
          (*O Mother, Mary Mother,*
Her   woe's   dumb   cry, between Hell and
*   Heaven!*)

"They've caught her to Westholm's saddle-
     bow,
          Sister Helen,   240
And her moonlit hair gleams white in its flow.''
"Let it turn whiter than winter snow,
          Little brother!''
          (*O Mother, Mary Mother,*
Woe-withered gold, between Hell and Heaven!)

"O Sister Helen, you heard the bell,
         Sister Helen!
More loud than the vesper-chime it fell."
"No vesper-chime, but a dying knell,
         Little brother!"   250
         (O Mother, Mary Mother,
His dying knell, between Hell and Heaven!)

"Alas! but I fear the heavy sound,
         Sister Helen;
Is it in the sky or in the ground?"
"Say, have they turned their horses round,
         Little brother?"
         (O Mother, Mary Mother,
What would she more, between Hell and
    Heaven?)

"They have raised the old man from his knee,
         Sister Helen,   261
And they ride in silence hastily."
"More fast the naked soul doth flee,
         Little brother!"
         (O Mother, Mary Mother,
The naked soul, between Hell and Heaven!)

"Flank to flank are the three steeds gone,
         Sister Helen,
But the lady's dark steed goes alone."
"And lonely her bridegroom's soul hath flown,
         Little brother."   271
         (O Mother, Mary Mother,
The lonely ghost, between Hell and Heaven!)

"Oh the wind is sad in the iron chill,
         Sister Helen,
And weary sad they look by the hill."
"But he and I are sadder still,
         Little brother!"
         (O Mother, Mary Mother,
Most sad of all, between Hell and Heaven!)   280

"See, see, the wax has dropped from its place,
         Sister Helen,
And the flames are winning up apace!"
"Yet here they burn but for a space,
         Little brother!"
         (O Mother, Mary Mother,
Here for a space, between Hell and Heaven!)

"Ah! what white thing at the door has crossed,
         Sister Helen?
Ah! what is this that sighs in the frost?"   290
"A soul that's lost as mine is lost,
         Little brother!"
         (O Mother, Mary Mother,
Lost, lost, all lost, between Hell and Heaven!)

LA BELLA DONNA*

She wept, sweet lady,
And said in weeping:
"What spell is keeping
The stars so steady?
Why does the power
Of the sun's noon-hour
To sleep so move me?
And the moon in heaven,
Stained where she passes
As a worn-out glass is,—
Why walks she above me?

"Stars, moon, and sun too,
I'm tired of either
And all together!
Whom speak they unto
That I should listen?
For very surely,
Though my arms and shoulders
Dazzle beholders,
And my eyes glisten,
All's nothing purely!
What are words said for
At all about them,
If he they are made for
Can do without them?"

She laughed, sweet lady,
And said in laughing:
"His hand clings half in
My own already!
Oh! do you love me?
Oh! speak of passion
In no new fashion,
But the old sayings
You once said of me.

"You said: 'As summer,
Through boughs grown brittle,
Comes back a little
Ere frosts benumb her,—
So bring'st thou to me
All leaves and flowers,
Though autumn's gloomy
To-day in the bowers.'

"Oh! does he love me,
When my voice teaches
The very speeches
He then spoke of me?
Alas! what flavour

* This is a translation, by Rossetti, of an Italian
  song (probably also written by him) in his
  poem, The Last Confession. Though apparently little more than a tour de force of
  rhyme, it has a quality, and portrays a mood,
  not common in our literature.

Still with me lingers—''
(But she laughed as my kisses
Glowed in her fingers
With love's old blisses)
''Oh! what one favour
Remains to woo him,
Whose whole poor savour
Belongs not to him?''

THE WOODSPURGE

The wind flapped loose, the wind was still,
Shaken out dead from tree and hill:
I had walked on at the wind's will,—
I sat now, for the wind was still.

Between my knees my forehead was,—
My lips, drawn in, said not Alas!
My hair was over in the grass,
My naked ears heard the day pass.

My eyes, wide open, had the run
Of some ten weeds to fix upon;
Among those few, out of the sun,
The woodspurge flowered, three cups in one.

From perfect grief there need not be
Wisdom or even memory:
One thing then learnt remains to me,
The woodspurge has a cup of three.

THE SONG OF THE BOWER

Say, is it day, is it dusk in thy bower,
   Thou whom I long for, who longest for me?
Oh! be it light, be it night, 'tis Love's hour,
   Love's that is fettered as Love's that is free.
Free Love has leaped to that innermost chamber,
   Oh! the last time, and the hundred before:
Fettered Love, motionless, can but remember,
   Yet something that sighs from him passes
      the door.   8

Nay, but my heart when it flies to thy bower,
   What does it find there that knows it again?
There it must droop like a shower-beaten flower,
   Red at the rent core and dark with the rain.
Ah! yet what shelter is still shed above it,—
   What waters still image its leaves torn apart?
Thy soul is the shade that clings round it to
      love it,
   And tears are its mirror deep down in thy
      heart.   16

What were my prize, could I enter the bower,
   This day, to-morrow, at eve or at morn?

Large lovely arms and a neck like a tower,
   Bosom then heaving that now lies forlorn.
Kindled with love-breath, (the sun's kiss is
      colder!)
   Thy sweetness all near me, so distant to-day;
My hand round thy neck and thy hand on my
      shoulder,
   My mouth to thy mouth as the world melts
      away.   24

What is it that keeps me afar from thy
      bower,—
   My spirit, my body, so fain to be there?
Waters engulfing or fires that devour?—
   Earth heaped against me or death in the air?
Nay, but in day-dreams, for terror, for pity,
   The trees wave their heads with an omen to
      tell;
Nay, but in night-dreams, throughout the dark
      city,
   The hours, clashed together, lose count in the
      bell.   32

Shall I not one day remember thy bower,
   One day when all days are one day to me?—
Thinking, 'I stirred not, and yet had the
      power,'
   Yearning, 'Ah God, if again it might be!'
Peace, peace! such a small lamp illumes, on
      this highway,
   So dimly so few steps in front of my feet,—
Yet shows me that her way is parted from my
      way. . . .
   Out of sight, beyond light, at what goal may
      we meet?   40

THE CLOUD CONFINES

The day is dark and the night
   To him that would search their heart;
No lips of cloud that will part
   Nor morning song in the light:
      Only, gazing alone,
      To him wild shadows are shown,
      Deep under deep unknown
And height above unknown height.
      Still we say as we go,—
      ''Strange to think by the way,
      Whatever there is to know,
         That shall we know one day.''

The Past is over and fled;
   Named new, we name it the old;
Thereof some tale hath been told,
   But no word comes from the dead;
      Whether at all they be,
      Or whether as bond or free,
      Or whether they too were we,

Or by what spell they have sped.
   Still we say as we go,—
     "Strange to think by the way,
     Whatever there is to know,
     That shall we know one day."

What of the heart of hate
   That beats in thy breast, O Time?—
   Red strife from the furthest prime,
And anguish of fierce debate;
   War that shatters her slain,
   And peace that grinds them as grain,
And eyes fixed ever in vain
On the pitiless eyes of Fate.
   Still we say as we go,—
     "Strange to think by the way,
     Whatever there is to know,
     That shall we know one day."

What of the heart of love
   That bleeds in thy breast, O Man?
   Thy kisses snatched 'neath the ban
Of fangs that mock them above;
   Thy bells prolonged unto knells,
   Thy hope that a breath dispels,
   Thy bitter forlorn farewells
And the empty echoes thereof?
   Still we say as we go,—
     "Strange to think by the way,
     Whatever there is to know,
     That shall we know one day."

The sky leans dumb on the sea,
   Aweary with all its wings;
   And oh! the song the sea sings
Is dark everlastingly.
   Our past is clean forgot,
   Our present is and is not,
   Our future's a sealed seedplot,
And what betwixt them are we?—
   We who say as we go,—
     "Strange to think by the way,
     Whatever there is to know,
     That shall we know one day."

From THE HOUSE OF LIFE*
The Sonnet

A Sonnet is a moment's monument,—
Memorial from the Soul's eternity
To one dead deathless hour. Look that it be,
Whether for lustral rite or dire portent,

---

* The "house of life" was the first of the twelve
divisions of the heavens made by old astrol-
ogers in casting the horoscope of a man's destiny. This series of a hundred and one sonnets is a faithful record, drawn from Rossetti's own inward experience, "of the mysterious conjunctions and oppositions wrought by
Love, Change, and Fate in the House of
Life."—*Eng. Lit.*, p. 373.

Of its own arduous fulness reverent:
Carve it in ivory or in ebony,
As Day or Night may rule; and let Time see
Its flowering crest impearled and orient.
A Sonnet is a coin: its face reveals
The Soul,—its converse, to what Power 'tis
    due:—
Whether for tribute to the august appeals
Of Life, or dower in Love's high retinue,
It serve; or 'mid the dark wharf's cavernous
    breath,
In Charon's palm it pay the toll to Death.

IV. LOVESIGHT

When do I see thee most, beloved one?
When in the light the spirits of mine eyes
Before thy face, their altar, solemnize
The worship of that Love through thee made
    known?
Or when in the dusk hours, (we two alone,)
Close-kissed and eloquent of still replies
Thy twilight-hidden glimmering visage lies,
And my soul only sees thy soul its own?
O love, my love! if I no more should see
Thyself, nor on the earth the shadow of thee,
Nor image of thine eyes in any spring,—
How then should sound upon Life's darkening
    slope
The ground-whirl of the perished leaves of
    Hope,
The wind of Death's imperishable wing?

XIX. SILENT NOON

Your hands lie open in the long fresh grass,
The finger-points look through like rosy blooms;
Your eyes smile peace. The pasture gleams and
    glooms
'Neath billowing skies that scatter and amass.
All round our nest, far as the eye can pass,
Are golden kingcup-fields with silver edge
Where the cow-parsley skirts the hawthorn-
    hedge.
'Tis visible silence, still as the hour-glass.
Deep in the sun-searched growths the dragon-fly
Hangs like a blue thread loosened from the
    sky:—
So this wing'd hour is dropt to us from above
Oh! clasp we to our hearts, for deathless dower
This close-companioned inarticulate hour
When twofold silence was the song of love.

XLIX—LII. WILLOWWOOD

I

I sat with Love upon a woodside well,
Leaning across the water, I and he;
Nor ever did he speak nor looked at me,

But touched his lute wherein was audible
The certain secret thing he had to tell:
Only our mirrored eyes met silently
In the low wave; and that sound came to be
The passionate voice I knew; and my tears fell.
And at their fall, his eyes beneath grew hers;
And with his foot and with his wing-feathers
He swept the spring that watered my heart's
 drouth.
Then the dark ripples spread to waving hair,
And as I stooped, her own lips rising there
Bubbled with brimming kisses at my mouth.

II

And now Love sang: but his was such a song,
So meshed with half-remembrance hard to free,
As souls disused in death's sterility
May sing when the new birthday tarries long.
And I was made aware of a dumb throng
That stood aloof, one form by every tree,
All mournful forms, for each was I or she,
The shades of those our days that had no
 tongue.
They looked on us, and knew us and were
 known;
While fast together, alive from the abyss,
Clung the soul-wrung implacable close kiss;
And pity of self through all made broken moan
Which said, "For once, for once, for once
 alone!"
And still Love sang, and what he sang was
 this:—

III

"O ye, all ye that walk in Willowwood,
That walk with hollow faces burning white;
What fathom-depth of soul-struck widowhood,
What long, what longer hours, one life-long
 night,
Ere ye again, who so in vain have wooed
Your last hope lost, who so in vain invite
Your lips to that their unforgotten food,
Ere ye, ere ye again shall see the light!
Alas! the bitter banks in Willowwood,
With tear-spurge wan, with blood-wort burning
 red:
Alas! if ever such a pillow could
Steep deep the soul in sleep till she were
 dead,—
Better all life forget her than this thing,
That Willowwood should hold her wandering!"

IV

So sang he: and as meeting rose and rose
Together cling through the wind's wellaway[1]
Nor change at once, yet near the end of day

[1] An archaic expression of grief.

The leaves drop loosened where the heart-stain
 glows,—
So when the song died did the kiss unclose;
And her face fell back drowned, and was as
 gray
As its gray eyes; and if it ever may
Meet mine again I know not if Love knows.
Only I know that I leaned low and drank
A long draught from the water where she sank,
Her breath and all her tears and all her soul:
And as I leaned, I know I felt Love's face
Pressed on my neck with moan of pity and
 grace,
Till both our heads were in his aureole.

LXV. KNOWN IN VAIN

As two whose love, first foolish, widening scope,
Knows suddenly, to music high and soft,
The Holy of holies; who because they scoff'd
Are now amazed with shame, nor dare to cope
With the whole truth aloud, lest heaven should
 ope;
Yet, at their meetings, laugh not as they
 laugh'd
In speech; nor speak, at length; but sitting oft
Together, within hopeless sight of hope
For hours are silent:—So it happeneth
When Work and Will awake too late, to gaze
After their life sailed by, and hold their breath.
Ah! who shall dare to search through what sad
 maze
Thenceforth their incommunicable ways
Follow the desultory feet of Death?

LXVI. THE HEART OF THE NIGHT

From child to youth; from youth to arduous
 man;
From lethargy to fever of the heart;
From faithful life to dream-dowered days
 apart;
From trust to doubt; from doubt to brink of
 ban;—
Thus much of change in one swift cycle ran
Till now. Alas, the soul!—how soon must she
Accept her primal immortality,—
The flesh resume its dust whence it began?
O Lord of work and peace! O Lord of life!
O Lord, the awful Lord of will! though late,
Even yet renew this soul with duteous breath:
That when the peace is garnered in from strife,
The work retrieved, the will regenerate,
This soul may see thy face, O Lord of death!

LXVII. THE LANDMARK

Was *that* the landmark? What—the foolish
 well

Whose wave, low down, I did not stoop to
    drink,
But sat and flung the pebbles from its brink
In sport to send its imaged skies pell-mell,
(And mine own image, had I noted well!)—
Was that my point of turning?—I had thought
The stations of my course should rise unsought,
As altar-stone or ensigned citadel,
But lo! the path is missed, I must go back,
And thirst to drink when next I reach the
    spring
Which once I stained, which since may have
    grown black.
Yet though no light be left nor bird now sing
As here I turn, I'll thank God, hastening,
That the same goal is still on the same track.

LXX. THE HILL SUMMIT

This feast-day of the sun, his altar there
In the broad west has blazed for vesper-song;
And I have loitered in the vale too long
And gaze now a belated worshipper.
Yet may I not forget that I was 'ware,
So journeying, of his face at intervals
Transfigured where the fringed horizon falls,—
A fiery bush with coruscating hair.
And now that I have climbed and won this
    height,
I must tread downward through the sloping
    shade
And travel the bewildered tracks till night.
Yet for this hour I still may here be stayed
And see the gold air and the silver fade
And the last bird fly into the last light.

LXXIX. THE MONOCHORD*

Is it this sky's vast vault or ocean's sound
That is Life's self and draws my life from me,
And by instinct ineffable decree
Holds my breath quailing on the bitter bound?
Nay, is it Life or Death, thus thunder-crowned,
That 'mid the tide of all emergency
Now notes my separate wave, and to what sea
Its difficult eddies labour in the ground?
Oh! what is this that knows the road I came,
The flame turned cloud, the cloud returned to
    flame,
The lifted shifted steeps and all the way?—
That draws round me at last this wind-warm
    space,
And in regenerate rapture turns my face
Upon the devious coverts of dismay?

* A musical instrument of one string, hence, unity,
harmony: here apparently used to symbolize
the ultimate merging of separate lives into
one Life.

CHRISTINA ROSSETTI (1830-1894)

GOBLIN MARKET*

Morning and evening
Maids heard the goblins cry:
'Come buy our orchard fruits,
Come buy, come buy:
Apples and quinces,
Lemons and oranges,
Plump unpecked cherries,
Melons and raspberries,
Bloom-down-cheeked peaches,
Swart-headed mulberries,   10
Wild free-born cranberries,
Crab-apples, dewberries,
Pine-apples, blackberries,
Apricots, strawberries;—
All ripe together
In summer weather,—
Morns that pass by,
Fair eves that fly;
Come buy, come buy:
Our grapes fresh from the vine,   20
Pomegranates full and fine,
Dates and sharp bullaces,
Rare pears and greengages,
Damsons and bilberries,
Taste them and try:
Currants and gooseberries,
Bright-fire-like barberries,
Figs to fill your mouth,
Citrons from the South,
Sweet to tongue and sound to eye;   30
Come buy, come buy.'

Evening by evening
Among the brookside rushes,
Laura bowed her head to hear,
Lizzie veiled her blushes:
Crouching close together
In the cooling weather,
With clasping arms and cautioning lips,
With tingling cheeks and finger tips.
'Lie close,' Laura said,   40
Pricking up her golden head:

* Of this poem, William M. Rossetti, Christina's
brother, writes: "I have more than once
heard Christina say that she did not mean
anything profound by this fairy tale—it is
not a moral apologue consistently carried out
in detail. Still the incidents are . . .
suggestive, and different minds may be likely
to read different messages into them." He
remarks further that the central point of the
story, read merely as a story, is often missed.
Lizzie's service to her sister lies in procuring
for her a *second* taste of the goblin fruits,
such as those who have once tasted them ever
afterward long for, and pine away with longing, but which the goblins themselves will
not voluntarily accord.

'We must not look at goblin men,
We must not buy their fruits:
Who knows upon what soil they fed
Their hungry thirsty roots?'
'Come buy,' call the goblins
Hobbling down the glen.
'Oh,' cried Lizzie, 'Laura, Laura,
You should not peep at goblin men.'
Lizzie covered up her eyes,   50
Covered close lest they should look;
Laura reared her glossy head,
And whispered like the restless brook:
'Look, Lizzie, look, Lizzie,
Down the glen tramp little men.
One hauls a basket,
One bears a plate,
One lugs a golden dish
Of many pounds' weight.
How fair the vine must grow   60
Whose grapes are so luscious;
How warm the wind must blow
Through those fruit bushes.'
'No,' said Lizzie: 'No, no, no;
Their offers should not charm us,
Their evil gifts would harm us.'
She thrust a dimpled finger
In each ear, shut eyes and ran:
Curious Laura chose to linger
Wondering at each merchant man.   70
One had a cat's face,
One whisked a tail,
One tramped at a rat's pace,
One crawled like a snail,
One like a wombat[1] prowled obtuse and furry,
One like a ratel[2] tumbled hurry skurry.
She heard a voice like voice of doves
Cooing all together:
They sounded kind and full of loves
In the pleasant weather.   80

Laura stretched her gleaming neck
Like a rush-imbedded swan,
Like a lily from the beck,[3]
Like a moonlit poplar branch,
Like a vessel at the launch
When its last restraint is gone.

Backwards up the mossy glen
Turned and trooped the goblin men,
With their shrill repeated cry,
'Come buy, come buy.'   90
When they reached where Laura was
They stood stock still upon the moss,

[1] An Australian marsupial, something like a small bear.
[2] A honey-badger; a nocturnal animal which feeds on rats, birds, and honey
[3] brook

Leering at each other,
Brother with queer brother;
Signalling each other,
Brother with sly brother.
One set his basket down,
One reared his plate,
One began to weave a crown
Of tendrils, leaves, and rough nuts brown   100
(Men sell not such in any town);
One heaved the golden weight
Of dish and fruit to offer her:
'Come buy, come buy,' was still their cry.
Laura stared but did not stir,
Longed but had no money.
The whisk-tailed merchant bade her taste
In tones as smooth as honey,
The cat-faced purr'd,
The rat-paced spoke a word   110
Of welcome, and the snail-paced even was heard;
One parrot-voiced and jolly
Cried 'Pretty Goblin' still for 'Pretty Polly';
One whistled like a bird.

But sweet-tooth Laura spoke in haste:
'Good Folk, I have no coin;
To take were to purloin:
I have no copper in my purse,
I have no silver either,
And all my gold is on the furze   . 120
That shakes in windy weather
Above the rusty heather.'
'You have much gold upon your head,'
They answered all together:
'Buy from us with a golden curl.'
She clipped a precious golden lock,
She dropped a tear more rare than pearl,
Then sucked their fruit globes fair or red.
Sweeter than honey from the rock,
Stronger than man-rejoicing wine,   130
Clearer than water flowed that juice;
She never tasted such before,
How should it cloy with length of use?
She sucked and sucked and sucked the more
Fruits which that unknown orchard bore
She sucked until her lips were sore;
Then flung the emptied rinds away
But gathered up one kernel stone,
And knew not was it night or day
As she turned home alone.   140

Lizzie met her at the gate
Full of wise upbraidings:
'Dear, you should not stay so late,
Twilight is not good for maidens;
Should not loiter in the glen
In the haunts of goblin men.
Do you not remember Jeanie,

How she met them in the moonlight,
Took their gifts both choice and many,
Ate their fruits and wore their flowers 150
Plucked from bowers
Where summer ripens at all hours?
But ever in the moonlight
She pined and pined away;
Sought them by night and day,
Found them no more, but dwindled and grew
    grey;
Then fell with the first snow,
While to this day no grass will grow
Where she lies low:
I planted daisies there a year ago 160
That never blow.
You should not loiter so.'
'Nay, hush,' said Laura:
'Nay, hush, my sister:
I ate and ate my fill,
Yet my mouth waters still:
To-morrow night I will
Buy more;' and kissed her.
'Have done with sorrow;
I'll bring you plums to-morrow 170
Fresh on their mother twigs,
Cherries worth getting;
You cannot think what figs
My teeth have met in,
What melons icy-cold
Piled on a dish of gold
Too huge for me to hold,
What peaches with a velvet nap,
Pellucid grapes without one seed:
Odorous indeed must be the mead 180
Whereon they grow, and pure the wave they
    drink
With lilies at the brink,
And sugar-sweet their sap.'

Golden head by golden head,
Like two pigeons in one nest
Folded in each other's wings,
They lay down in their curtained bed:
Like two blossoms on one stem,
Like two flakes of new-fall'n snow,
Like two wands of ivory 190
Tipped with gold for awful kings.
Moon and stars gazed in at them,
Wind sang to them lullaby,
Lumbering owls forebore to fly,
Not a bat flapped to and fro
Round their nest:
Cheek to cheek and breast to breast
Locked together in one nest.

Early in the morning
When the first cock crowed his warning, 200

Neat like bees, as sweet and busy,
Laura rose with Lizzie:
Fetched in honey, milked the cows,
Aired and set to rights the house,
Kneaded cakes of whitest wheat,
Cakes for dainty mouths to eat,
Next churned butter, whipped up cream,
Fed their poultry, sat and sewed;
Talked as modest maidens should:
Lizzie with an open heart, 210
Laura in an absent dream,
One content, one sick in part;
One warbling for the mere bright day's delight,
One longing for the night.

At length slow evening came:
They went with pitchers to the reedy brook;
Lizzie most placid in her look,
Laura most like a leaping flame.
They drew the gurgling water from its deep.
Lizzie plucked purple and rich golden flags, 220
Then turning homeward said: 'The sunset
    flushes
Those furthest loftiest crags;
Come, Laura, not another maiden lags.
No wilful squirrel wags,
The beasts and birds are fast asleep.'

But Laura loitered still among the rushes,
And said the bank was steep,
And said the hour was early still,
The dew not fallen, the wind not chill;
Listening ever, but not catching 230
The customary cry,
'Come buy, come buy,'
With its iterated jingle
Of sugar-baited words:
Not for all her watching
Once discerning even one goblin
Racing, whisking, tumbling, hobbling—
Let alone the herds
That used to tramp along the glen,
In groups or single, 240
Of brisk fruit-merchant men.

Till Lizzie urged, 'O Laura, come;
I hear the fruit-call, but I dare not look:
You should not loiter longer at this brook:
Come with me home.
The stars rise, the moon bends her arc,
Each glow-worm winks her spark,
Let us go home before the night grows dark;
For clouds may gather
Though this is summer weather, 250
Put out the lights and drench us through;
Then if we lost our way what should we do?'

Laura turned cold as stone
To find her sister heard that cry alone,
That goblin cry,
'Come buy our fruits, come buy.'
Must she then buy no more such dainty fruit?
Must she no more such succous pasture⁴ find,
Gone deaf and blind?
Her tree of life drooped from the root: 260
She said not one word in her heart's sore ache:
But peering thro' the dimness, nought discerning,
Trudged home, her pitcher dripping all the
          way;
So crept to bed, and lay
Silent till Lizzie slept;
Then sat up in a passionate yearning,
And gnashed her teeth for baulked desire, and
          wept
As if her heart would break.

Day after day, night after night,
Laura kept watch in vain   270
In sullen silence of exceeding pain.
She never caught again the goblin cry,
'Come buy, come buy;'—
She never spied the goblin men
Hawking their fruits along the glen:
But when the noon waxed bright
Her hair grew thin and grey;
She dwindled, as the fair full moon doth turn
To swift decay and burn
Her fire away.   280

One day remembering her kernel-stone
She set it by a wall that faced the south;
Dewed it with tears, hoped for a root,
Watched for a waxing shoot,
But there came none.
It never saw the sun,
It never felt the trickling moisture run:
While with sunk eyes and faded mouth
She dreamed of melons, as a traveller sees
False waves in desert drouth   290
With shade of leaf-crowned trees,
And burns the thirstier in the sandful breeze.

She no more swept the house,
Tended the fowls or cows,
Fetched honey, kneaded cakes of wheat,
Brought water from the brook:
But sat down listless in the chimney-nook
And would not eat.

Tender Lizzie could not bear
To watch her sister's cankerous care,   300
Yet not to share.

She night and morning
Caught the goblin's cry:
'Come buy our orchard fruits,
Come buy, come buy:'—
Beside the brook, along the glen,
She heard the tramp of goblin men,
The voice and stir
Poor Laura could not hear;
Longed to buy fruit to comfort her,   310
But feared to pay too dear.
She thought of Jeanie in her grave,
Who should have been a bride;
But who for joys brides hope to have
Fell sick and died
In her gay prime,
In earliest winter time,
With the first glazing rime,
With the first snow-fall of crisp winter time.

Till Laura dwindling   320
Seemed knocking at Death's door.
Then Lizzie weighed no more
Better and worse;
But put a silver penny in her purse,
Kissed Laura, crossed the heath with clumps of
          furze
At twilight, halted by the brook:
And for the first time in her life
Began to listen and look.

Laughed every goblin
When they spied her peeping: 330
Came towards her hobbling,
Flying, running, leaping,
Puffing and blowing,
Chuckling, clapping, crowing,
Clucking and gobbling,
Mopping and mowing,⁵
Full of airs and graces.
Pulling wry faces,
Demure grimaces,
Cat-like and rat-like,   340
Ratel- and wombat-like,
Snail-paced in a hurry,
Parrot-voiced and whistler,
Helter skelter, hurry skurry,
Chattering like magpies,
Fluttering like pigeons,
Gliding like fishes,—
Hugged her and kissed her:
Squeezed and caressed her:
Stretched up their dishes,   350
Panniers, and plates:
'Look at our apples
Russet and dun,
Bob at our cherries,

---

⁴ juicy feasting

⁵ See *The Tempest*, IV, i, 47, and note (page 184).

Bite at our peaches,
Citrons and dates,
Grapes for the asking,
Pears red with basking
Out in the sun,
Plums on their twigs; 360
Pluck them and suck them,—
Pomegranates, figs.'

Good folk,' said Lizzie,
Mindful of Jeanie:
'Give me much and many:'
Held out her apron,
Tossed them her penny.
'Nay, take a seat with us,
Honour and eat with us,'
They answered grinning: 370
'Our feast is but beginning.
Night yet is early,
Warm and dew-pearly,
Wakeful and starry:
Such fruits as these
No man can carry;
Half their bloom would fly,
Half their dew would dry,
Half their flavour would pass by.
Sit down and feast with us, 380
Be welcome guest with us,
Cheer you and rest with us.'—
'Thank you,' said Lizzie: 'But one waits
At home alone for me:
So without further parleying,
If you will not sell me any
Of your fruits though much and many,
Give me back my silver penny
    I tossed you for a fee.'—
They began to scratch their pates, 390
No longer wagging, purring,
But visibly demurring,
Grunting and snarling.
One called her proud,
Cross-grained, uncivil;
Their tones waxed loud,
Their looks were evil.
Lashing their tails
They trod and hustled her,
Elbowed and jostled her, 400
Clawed with their nails,
Barking, mewing, hissing, mocking,
Tore her gown and soiled her stocking,
Twitched her hair out by the roots,
Stamped upon her tender feet,
Held her hands and squeezed their fruits
Against her mouth to make her eat.

White and golden Lizzie stood,
Like a lily in a flood,—

Like a rock of blue-veined stone 410
Lashed by tides obstreperously,—
Like a beacon left alone
In a hoary roaring sea,
Sending up a golden fire,—
Like a fruit-crowned orange-tree
White with blossoms honey-sweet
Sore beset by wasp and bee,—
Like a royal virgin town
Topped with gilded dome and spire
Close beleaguered by a fleet 420
Mad to tug her standard down.

One may lead a horse to water,
Twenty cannot make him drink.
Though the goblins cuffed and caught her,
Coaxed and fought her,
Bullied and besought her,
Scratched her, pinched her black as ink,
Kicked and knocked her,
Mauled and mocked her,
Lizzie uttered not a word; 430
Would not open lip from lip
Lest they should cram a mouthful in:
But laughed in heart to feel the drip
Of juice that syruped all her face,
And lodged in dimples of her chin,
And streaked her neck which quaked like curd.
At last the evil people,
Worn out by her resistance,
Flung back her penny, kicked their fruit
Along whichever road they took, 440
Not leaving root or stone or shoot;
Some writhed into the ground,
Some dived into the brook
With ring and ripple,
Some scudded on the gale without a sound,
Some vanished in the distance.

In a smart, ache, tingle,
Lizzie went her way;
Knew not was it night or day;
Sprang up the bank, tore thro' the furze, 450
Threaded copse and dingle,
And heard her penny jingle
Bouncing in her purse,—
Its bounce was music to her ear.
She ran and ran
As if she feared some goblin man
Dogged her with gibe or curse
Or something worse:
But not one goblin skurried after,
Nor was she pricked by fear; 460
The kind heart made her windy-paced
That urged her home quite out of breath with
    haste
And inward laughter.

She cried, 'Laura,' up the garden,
'Did you miss me?
Come and kiss me.
Never mind my bruises,
Hug me, kiss me, suck my juices
Squeezed from goblin fruits for you,
Goblin pulp and goblin dew.   470
Eat me, drink me, love me;
Laura, make much of me;
For your sake I have braved the glen
And had to do with goblin merchant men.'

Laura started from her chair,
Flung her arms up in the air,
Clutched her hair:
'Lizzie, Lizzie, have you tasted
For my sake the fruit forbidden?
Must your light like mine be hidden,   480
Your young life like mine be wasted,
Undone in mine undoing,
And ruined in my ruin,
Thirsty, cankered, goblin-ridden?'—
She clung about her sister,
Kissed and kissed and kissed her:
Tears once again
Refreshed her shrunken eyes,
Dropping like rain
After long sultry drouth;   490
Shaking with aguish fear, and pain,
She kissed and kissed her with a hungry mouth.

Her lips began to scorch,
That juice was wormwood to her tongue,
She loathed the feast:
Writhing as one possessed she leaped and sung,
Rent all her robe, and wrung
Her hands in lamentable haste,
And beat her breast.
Her locks streamed like the torch   500
Borne by a racer at full speed,
Or like the mane of horses in their flight,
Or like an eagle when she stems the light
Straight toward the sun,
Or like a caged thing freed,
Or like a flying flag when armies run.

Swift fire spread through her veins, knocked
     at her heart,
Met the fire smouldering there
And overbore its lesser flame;
She gorged on bitterness without a name: 510
Ah fool, to choose such part
Of soul-consuming care!
Sense failed in the mortal strife:
Like the watch-tower of a town
Which an earthquake shatters down,

Like a lightning-stricken mast,
Like a wind-uprooted tree
Spun about,
Like a foam-topped waterspout
Cast down headlong in the sea,   520
She fell at last;
Pleasure past and anguish past,
Is it death or is it life?

Life out of death.
That night long, Lizzie watched by her,
Counted her pulse's flagging stir,
Felt for her breath,
Held water to her lips, and cooled her face
With tears and fanning leaves.
But when the first birds chirped about their
     eaves,   530
And early reapers plodded to the place
Of golden sheaves,
And dew-wet grass
Bowed in the morning winds so brisk to pass,
And new buds with new day
Opened of cup-like lilies on the stream,
Laura awoke as from a dream,
Laughed in the innocent old way,
Hugged Lizzie but not twice or thrice;
Her gleaming locks showed not one thread of
     grey,   .   540
Her breath was sweet as May,
And light danced in her eyes.

Days, weeks, months, years
Afterwards, when both were wives
With children of their own;
Their mother-hearts beset with fears,
Their lives bound up in tender lives;
Laura would call the little ones
And tell them of her early prime,
Those pleasant days long gone   550
Of not-returning time:
Would talk about the haunted glen,
The wicked quaint fruit-merchant men,
Their fruits like honey to the throat
But poison in the blood
(Men sell not such in any town):
Would tell them how her sister stood
In deadly peril to do her good,
And win the fiery antidote:
Then joining hands to little hands   560
Would bid them cling together,—
'For there is no friend like a sister
In calm or stormy weather;
To cheer one on the tedious way,
To fetch one if one goes astray,
To lift one if one totters down,
To strengthen whilst one stands.'

THE THREE ENEMIES

THE FLESH

'Sweet, thou art pale.'
                    'More pale to see,
Christ hung upon the cruel tree
And bore His Father's wrath for me.'

'Sweet, thou art sad.'
                    'Beneath a rod
More heavy, Christ for my sake trod
The winepress of the wrath of God.'   6

'Sweet, thou art weary.'
                    'Not so Christ;
Whose mighty love of me sufficed
For Strength, Salvation, Eucharist.'

'Sweet, thou art footsore.'
                    'If I bleed,
His feet have bled; yea in my need
His Heart once bled for mine indeed.'   12

THE WORLD

'Sweet, thou art young.'
                    'So He was young
Who for my sake in silence hung
Upon the Cross with Passion wrung.'

'Look, thou art fair.'
                    'He was more fair
Than men, Who deigned for me to wear
A visage marred beyond compare.'   18

'And thou hast riches.'
                    'Daily bread:
All else is His: Who, living, dead,
For me lacked where to lay His Head.'

'And life is sweet.'
                    'It was not so
To Him, Whose Cup did overflow
With mine unutterable woe.'   24

THE DEVIL

'Thou drinkest deep.'
                    'When Christ would sup
He drained the dregs from out my cup:
So how should I be lifted up?'

'Thou shalt win Glory.'
                    'In the skies,
Lord Jesus, cover up mine eyes
Lest they should look on vanities.'   30

'Thou shalt have Knowledge.'
                    'Helpless dust!

In Thee, O Lord, I put my trust:
Answer Thou for me, Wise and Just.'

'And Might.'—
                    'Get thee behind me. Lord,
Who hast redeemed and not abhorred
My soul, oh keep it by Thy Word.'   36

AN APPLE GATHERING

I plucked pink blossoms from mine apple-tree
    And wore them all that evening in my hair:
Then in due season when I went to see
    I found no apples there.

With dangling basket all along the grass
    As I had come I went the selfsame track:
My neighbours mocked me while they saw me pass
    So empty-handed back.   8

Lilian and Lilias smiled in trudging by,
    Their heaped-up basket teased me like a jeer;
Sweet-voiced they sang beneath the sunset sky,
    Their mother's home was near.

Plump Gertrude passed me with her basket full,
    A stronger hand than hers helped it along;
A voice talked with her through the shadows cool
    More sweet to me than song.   16

Ah Willie, Willie, was my love less worth
    Than apples with their green leaves piled above?
I counted rosiest apples on the earth
    Of far less worth than love.

So once it was with me you stooped to talk
    Laughing and listening in this very lane;
To think that by this way we used to walk
    We shall not walk again!   24

I let my neighbours pass me, ones and twos
    And groups; the latest said the night grew chill,
And hastened: but I loitered; while the dews
    Fell fast I loitered still.

MONNA INNOMINATA*

1

Come back to me, who wait and watch for you:—
Or come not yet, for it is over then,
And long it is before you come again,
So far between my pleasures are, and few.

* "Lady Unnamed"; a series of fourteen sonnets
   in which the personal utterance, as in Mrs.
   Browning's *Sonnets from the Portuguese,*
   wears a titular disguise.

While, when you come not, what I do I do
Thinking 'Now when he comes,' my sweetest
    'when':
For one man is my world of all the men
This wide world holds; O love, my world is you.
Howbeit, to meet you grows almost a pang
Because the pang of parting comes so soon;
My hope hangs waning, waxing, like a moon
Between the heavenly days on which we meet:
Ah me, but where are now the songs I sang
When life was sweet because you called them
    sweet?

2

I wish I could remember that first day,
First hour, first moment of your meeting me,
If bright or dim the season,—it might be
Summer or Winter for aught I can say;
So unrecorded did it slip away,
So blind was I to see and to foresee,
So dull to mark the budding of my tree
That would not blossom yet for many a May.
If only I could recollect it, such
A day of days! I let it come and go
As traceless as a thaw of bygone snow;
It seemed to mean so little, meant so much;
If only now I could recall that touch,
First touch of hand in hand—Did one but
    know!

11

Many in aftertimes will say of you
'He loved her'—while of me what will they
    say?
Not that I loved you more than just in play,
For fashion's sake as idle women do.
Even let them prate; who know not what we
    knew
Of love and parting in exceeding pain,
Of parting hopeless here to meet again,
Hopeless on earth, and heaven is out of view.
But by my heart of love laid bare to you,
My love that you can make not void nor vain,
Love that foregoes you but to claim anew
Beyond this passage of the gate of death,
I charge you at the Judgment make it plain
My love of you was life and not a breath.

UP-HILL

Does the road wind up-hill all the way?
    Yes, to the very end.
Will the day's journey take the whole long
    day?
    From morn to night, my friend.

But is there for the night a resting-place?
    A roof for when the slow dark hours begin.

May not the darkness hide it from my face?
    You cannot miss that inn.

Shall I meet other wayfarers at night?
    Those who have gone before.
Then must I knock, or call when just in sight?
    They will not keep you standing at that door.

Shall I find comfort, travel-sore and weak?
    Of labour you shall find the sum.
Will there be beds for me and all who seek?
    Yea, beds for all who come.

WILLIAM MORRIS (1834-1896)

THE GILLIFLOWER OF GOLD.

A golden gilliflower to-day
I wore upon my helm alway,
And won the prize of this tourney.
    Hah! hah! la belle jaune giroflée.[1]

However well Sir Giles might sit,
His sun was weak to wither it;
Lord Miles's blood was dew on it:
    Hah! hah! la belle jaune giroflée.

Although my spear in splinters flew,
From John's steel-coat, my eye was true;
I wheeled about, and cried for you,
    Hah! hah! la belle jaune giroflée.

Yea, do not doubt my heart was good,
Though my sword flew like rotten wood,
To shout, although I scarcely stood,
    Hah! hah! la belle jaune giroflée.

My hand was steady, too, to take
My axe from round my neck, and break
John's steel-coat up for my love's sake.
    Hah! hah! la belle jaune giroflée.

When I stood in my tent again,
Arming afresh, I felt a pain
Take hold of me, I was so fain—
    Hah! hah! la belle jaune giroflée—

To hear: *"Honneur aux fils des preux!*[2]*"*
Right in my ears again, and shew
The gilliflower blossomed new.
    Hah! hah! la belle jaune giroflée.

The Sieur Guillaume against me came,
His tabard bore three points of flame
From a red heart; with little blame[3]—
    Hah! hah! la belle jaune giroflée—

1 "Hah! hah! the beautiful yellow gilliflower!"
2 "Honor to the sons of the brave!"
3 hurt

Our tough spears crackled up like straw;
He was the first to turn and draw
His sword, that had nor speck nor flaw;
   Hah! hah! la belle jaune giroflée.

But I felt weaker than a maid,
And my brain, dizzied and afraid,
Within my helm a fierce tune played,
   Hah! hah! la belle jaune giroflée,   40

Until I thought of your dear head,
Bowed to the gilliflower bed,
The yellow flowers stained with red;
   Hah! hah! la belle jaune giroflée.

Crash! how the swords met; *"giroflée!"*
The fierce tune in my helm would play,
"La belle! la belle jaune giroflée!"
   Hah! hah! la belle jaune giroflée.   48

Once more the great swords met again:
"La belle! la belle!" but who fell then?
Le Sieur Guillaume, who struck down ten;
   Hah! hah! la belle jaune giroflée.

And as with mazed and unarmed face,
Toward my own crown and the Queen's place,
They led me at a gentle pace,—
   Hah! hah! la belle jaune giroflée,—   56

I almost saw your quiet head
Bowed o'er the gilliflower bed,
The yellow flowers stained with red,
   Hah! hah! la belle jaune giroflée.

THE SAILING OF THE SWORD.

Across the empty garden-beds,
   When the Sword went out to sea,
I scarcely saw my sisters' heads
   Bowed each beside a tree.
I could not see the castle leads,
   When the Sword went out to sea.   6

Alicia wore a scarlet gown,
   When the Sword went out to sea,
But Ursula's was russet brown:
   For the mist we could not see
The scarlet roofs of the good town,
   When the Sword went out to sea.   12

Green holly in Alicia's hand,
   When the Sword went out to sea;
With sere oak-leaves did Ursula stand;
   Oh! yet alas for me!
I did but bear a peeled white wand,
   When the Sword went out to sea.   18

O, russet brown and scarlet bright,
   When the Sword went out to sea,
My sisters wore; I wore but white;
   Red, brown, and white, are three;
Three damozels; each had a knight,
   When the Sword went out to sea.   24

Sir Robert shouted loud, and said,
   When the Sword went out to sea,
"Alicia, while I see thy head,
   What shall I bring for thee?"
"O, my sweet Lord, a ruby red:"
   The Sword went out to sea.   30

Sir Miles said, while the sails hung down,
   When the Sword went out to sea,
"O, Ursula! while I see the town,
   What shall I bring for thee?"
"Dear knight, bring back a falcon brown:"
   The Sword went out to sea.   36

But my Roland, no word he said,
   When the Sword went out to sea,
But only turned away his head;
   A quick shriek came from me:
"Come back, dear lord, to your white maid!"
   The Sword went out to sea.   42

The hot sun bit the garden-beds
   When the Sword came back from sea;
Beneath an apple-tree our heads
   Stretched out toward the sea;
Gray gleamed the thirsty castle-leads,
   When the Sword came back from sea.   48

Lord Robert brought a ruby red,
   When the Sword came back from sea;
He kissed Alicia on the head:
   "I am come back to thee;
'Tis time, sweet love, that we were wed,
   Now the Sword is back from sea!"   54

Sir Miles he bore a falcon brown,
   When the Sword came back from sea;
His arms went round tall Ursula's gown:
   "What joy, O love, but thee?
Let us be wed in the good town,
   Now the Sword is back from sea!"   60

My heart grew sick, no more afraid,
   When the Sword came back from sea;
Upon the deck a tall white maid
   Sat on Lord Roland's knee;
His chin was pressed upon her head,
   When the Sword came back from sea!   66

THE BLUE CLOSET.*

The Damozels.

Lady Alice, lady Louise,
Between the wash of the tumbling seas
We are ready to sing, if so ye please:
So lay your long hands on the keys;
  Sing, "*Laudate pueri.*"[1]

And ever the great bell overhead
Boomed in the wind a knell for the dead,
Though no one tolled it, a knell for the dead.

Lady Louise.

Sister, let the measure swell
Not too loud; for you sing not well 10
If you drown the faint boom of the bell;
  He is weary, so am I.

And ever the chevron[2] overhead
Flapped on the banner of the dead;
(Was he asleep, or was he dead?)

Lady Alice

Alice the Queen, and Louise the Queen,
Two damozels wearing purple and green,
Four lone ladies dwelling here
From day to day and year to year;
And there is none to let us go, 20
To break the locks of the doors below,
Or shovel away the heaped-up snow;
And when we die no man will know
That we are dead; but they give us leave,
Once every year on Christmas-eve,
To sing in the Closet Blue one song;
And we should be so long, so long,
If we dared, in singing; for dream on dream,
They float on in a happy stream;
Float from the gold strings, float from the
  keys, 30
Float from the opened lips of Louise;
But, alas! the sea-salt oozes through
The chinks of the tiles of the Closet Blue;

And ever the great bell overhead
Booms in the wind a knell for the dead,
The wind plays on it a knell for the dead.

They Sing All Together

How long ago was it, how long ago,
He came to this tower with hands full of snow?

"Kneel down, O love Louise, kneel down!" he
  said,
And sprinkled the dusty snow over my head. 40

He watched the snow melting, it ran through my
  hair,
Ran over my shoulders, white shoulders and
  bare.

"I cannot weep for thee, poor love Louise,
For my tears are all hidden deep under the
  seas;
In a gold and blue casket she keeps all my
  tears,
But my eyes are no longer blue, as in old
  years;

"Yea, they grow gray with time, grow small
  and dry,
I am so feeble now, would I might die."

And in truth the great bell overhead
Left off his pealing for the dead, 50
Perchance, because the wind was dead.

Will he come back again, or is he dead?
O! is he sleeping, my scarf round his head?

Or did they strangle him as he lay there,
With the long scarlet scarf I used to wear?

Only I pray thee, Lord, let him come here!
Both his soul and his body to me are most
  dear.

Dear Lord, that loves me, I wait to receive
Either body or spirit this wild Christmas-eve.

Through the floor shot up a lily red, 60
With a patch of earth from the land of the
  dead,
For he was strong in the land of the dead.

What matter that his cheeks were pale,
 His kind kissed lips all gray?
"O, love Louise, have you waited long?"
 "O, my lord Arthur, yea."

What if his hair that brushed her cheek
 Was stiff with frozen rime?
His eyes were grown quite blue again,
 As in the happy time. 70

"O, love Louise, this is the key
 Of the happy golden land!
O, sisters, cross the bridge with me,
 My eyes are full of sand.
What matter that I cannot see,
 If ye take me by the hand?"

And ever the great bell overhead,
And the tumbling seas mourned for the dead;
For their song ceased, and they were dead!

FROM THE EARTHLY PARADISE

AN APOLOGY

Of Heaven or Hell I have no power to sing,
I cannot ease the burden of your fears,
Or make quick-coming death a little thing,
Or bring again the pleasure of past years,
Nor for my words shall ye forget your tears,
Or hope again for aught that I can say,
The idle singer of an empty day.　　　7

But rather, when aweary of your mirth,
From full hearts still unsatisfied ye sigh,
And, feeling kindly unto all the earth,
Grudge every minute as it passes by,
Made the more mindful that the sweet days
　die—
—Remember me a little then I pray,
The idle singer of an empty day.　　　14

The heavy trouble, the bewildering care
That weighs us down who live and earn our
　bread,
These idle verses have no power to bear;
So let me sing of names rememberéd,
Because they, living not, can ne'er be dead,
Or long time take their memory quite away
From us poor singers of an empty day.　　21

Dreamer of dreams, born out of my due time,
Why should I strive to set the crooked straight?
Let it suffice me that my murmuring rhyme
Beats with light wing against the ivory gate,[1]
Telling a tale not too importunate
To those who in the sleepy region stay,
Lulled by the singer of an empty day.　　28

Folk say, a wizard to a northern king
At Christmas-tide such wondrous things did
　show,
That through one window men beheld the
　spring,
And through another saw the summer glow,
And through a third the fruited vines a-row,
While still, unheard, but in its wonted way,
Piped the drear wind of that December day.　35

So with this Earthly Paradise it is,
If ye will read aright, and pardon me,
Who strive to build a shadowy isle of bliss
Midmost the beating of the steely sea,
Where tossed about all hearts of men must be;

[1] According to Greek legend, false dreams come
　through the gate of ivory, true dreams
　through the gate of horn.

Whose ravening monsters mighty men shall
　slay,
Not the poor singer of an empty day.　　42

FROM LOVE IS ENOUGH

SONG FOR MUSIC

Love is enough: though the world be a-waning,
And the woods have no voice but the voice of
　complaining,
　Though the sky be too dark for dim eyes to
　　discover
The gold-cups and daisies fair blooming there-
　under,
Though the hills be held shadows, and the sea
　a dark wonder,
　And this day draw a veil over all deeds passed
　　over,
Yet their hands shall not tremble, their feet
　shall not falter,
The void shall not weary, the fear shall not
　alter
　These lips and these eyes of the loved and
　　the lover.

FROM SIGURD THE VOLSUNG*

OF THE PASSING AWAY OF BRYNHILD

Once more on the morrow-morning fair
　shineth the glorious sun,
And the Niblung children labour on a deed that
　shall be done;
For out in the people's meadows they raise a
　bale[2] on high,
The oak and the ash together, and thereon shall
　the Mighty lie;

* The *Volsunga Saga* is an older, Norse version of
the legend which appears in German literature
as the *Nibelungenlied,* and which has been
made familiar in modern times by Wagner's
opera *Der Ring des Nibelungen.* It is the
great Teutonic race epic. Sigurd (Siegfried,
in the German version) is the grandson of Volsung, who was a descendant of Odin. Brynhild was originally a Valkyrie, one of Odin's
"Choosers of the Slain," maidens who rode
on white cloud-horses and visited battle-fields
to select heroes for Odin's great hall, Valhalla.
Sigurd wakened Brynhild from an enchanted
sleep to the doom of mortal life and love, and
they plighted troth. But their love was
thwarted at the court of the Niblung princes,
Gunnar, Hogni, and Guttorm, and their sister
Gudrun, the children of Giuki. Through the
witchcraft of Grimhild, Gudrun's mother,
Sigurd is made to lose all memory of Brynhild and to marry Gudrun. Moreover, he is
made to assist in bringing about the marriage
of Brynhild to Gunnar. Later, as a result
of rivalry, Guttorm surprises and slays
Sigurd, but is himself slain by Sigurd's sword,
the "Wrath." Then follows the portion of the
tale here given—the pathetic story of the
means taken by Brynhild to rejoin Sigurd.
Morris's metrical rendering of the entire
legend extends to about ten thousand lines.

[2] funeral pile

Nor gold nor steel shall be lacking, nor savour
of sweet spice,
Nor cloths in the Southlands woven, nor webs
of untold price:
The work grows, toil is as nothing; long blasts
of the mighty horn
From the topmost tower out-wailing o'er the
woeful world are borne.

But Brynhild lay in her chamber, and her
women went and came,
And they feared and trembled before her, and
none spake Sigurd's name;   10
But whiles[3] they deemed her weeping, and
whiles they deemed indeed
That she spake, if they might but hearken, but
no words their ears might heed;
Till at last she spake out clearly: "I know not
what ye would;
For ye come and go in my chamber, and ye
seem of wavering mood
To thrust me on, or to stay me; to help my
heart in woe,
Or to bid my days of sorrow midst nameless
folly go."

None answered the word of Brynhild, none
knew of her intent;
But she spake: "Bid hither Gunnar, lest the
sun sink o'er the bent,[4]
And leave the words unspoken I yet have will
to speak."

Then her maidens go from before her, and
that lord of war they seek,   20
And he stands by the bed of Brynhild and
strives to entreat and beseech,
But her eyes gaze awfully on him, and his lips
may learn no speech.
And she saith: "I slept in the morning, or I
dreamed in the waking-hour,
And my dream was of thee, O Gunnar, and the
bed in thy kingly bower,
And the house that I blessed in my sorrow, and
cursed in my sorrow and shame,
The gates of an ancient people, the towers of
a mighty name;
King, cold was the hall I have dwelt in, and
no brand burned on the hearth;
Dead-cold was thy bed, O Gunnar, and thy land
was parched with dearth:
But I saw a great King riding, and a master
of the harp,
And he rode amidst of the foemen, and the
swords were bitter-sharp,   30
But his hand in the hand-gyves smote not, and
his feet in the fetters were fast,

While many a word of mocking at his speech-
less face was cast."[5]
Then I heard a voice in the world: 'O woe
for the broken troth,
And the heavy Need of the Niblungs,[6] and the
Sorrow of Odin the Goth!'[7]
Then I saw the halls of the strangers, and the
hills, and the dark-blue sea,
Nor knew of their names and their nations, for
earth was afar from me,
But brother rose up against brother, and blood
swam over the board,
And women smote and spared not, and the fire
was master and lord.
Then, then was the moonless mid-mirk, and I
woke to the day and the deed—
The deed that earth shall name not, the day of
its bitterest need.   40
Many words have I said in my life-days, and
little more shall I say;
Ye have heard the dream of a woman, deal with
it as ye may;
For meseems the world-ways sunder, and the
dusk and the dark is mine,
Till I come to the hall of Freyia,[8] where the
deeds of the Mighty shall shine."

So hearkened Gunnar the Niblung, that her
words he understood,
And he knew she was set on the death-stroke,
and he deemed it nothing good;
But he said: "I have hearkened, and heeded
thy death and mine in thy words:
I have done the deed and abide it, and my face
shall laugh on the swords;
But thee, woman, I bid thee abide here till thy
grief of soul abate;
Meseems nought lowly nor shameful shall be the
Niblung fate;   50
And here shalt thou rule and be mighty, and
be Queen of the measureless Gold,[9]
And abase the Kings and upraise them; and
anew shall thy fame be told,
And as fair shall thy glory blossom as the fresh
fields under the spring."

Then he casteth his arms about her, and hot
is the heart of the King
For the glory of Queen Brynhild and the hope
of her days of gain,

5 A prophecy of Gunnar's fate at the hands of
Atli, the Eastern King, who afterward married Gudrun.
6 That is, their time of need, when punishment
began to overtake them.
7 The sorrows of the race of Odin.
8 The goddess of love.
9 The hoard of the Niblungs, won from the
Dwarfs, or smiths who dwelt in the caverns
of the earth. The curse attached to this treasure brought sorrow on all who shared in it.

3 at times   4 heath, field

And he clean forgetteth Sigurd and the foster-
brother slain;
But she shrank aback from before him, and
cried: "Woe worth the while[10]
For the thoughts ye drive back on me, and the
memory of your guile!
The Kings of Earth were gathered, the wise of
men were met;
On the death of a woman's pleasure their glorious hearts were set,[11]   60
And I was alone amidst them—ah, hold thy
peace hereof!
Lest the thought of the bitterest hours this little
hour should move."

He rose abashed from before her, and yet he
lingered there;
Then she said: "O King of the Niblungs,
what noise do I hearken and hear?
Why ring the axes and hammers, while feet of
men go past,
And shields from the walls are shaken, and
swords on the pavement cast,
And the door of the treasure is opened, and the
horn cries loud and long,
And the feet of the Niblung children to the
people's meadows throng?"

His face was troubled before her, and again
she spake and said:
"Meseemeth this is the hour when men array
the dead;   70
Wilt thou tell me tidings, Gunnar, that the
children of thy folk
Pile up the bale for Guttorm, and the hand
that smote the stroke?"

He said: "It is not so, Brynhild; for that
Giuki's son[12] was burned
When the moon of the middle heaven last night
toward dawning turned."

They looked on each other and spake not;
but Gunnar gat him gone,
And came to his brother Hogni, the wise-heart
Giuki's son,
And spake: "Thou art wise, O Hogni; go in
to Brynhild the Queen,
And stay her swift departing; or the last of her
days hath she seen."

"It is nought, thy word," said Hogni; "wilt
thou bring dead men aback,

Or the souls of Kings departed midst the battle
and the wrack?   80
Yet this shall be easier to thee than the turning Brynhild's heart;
She came to dwell among us, but in us she had
no part;
Let her go her ways from the Niblungs, with
her hand in Sigurd's hand.
Will the grass grow up henceforward where her
feet have trodden the land?"

"O evil day!" said Gunnar, "when my
Queen must perish and die!"
"Such oft betide," saith Hogni, "as the lives
of men flit by;
But the evil day is a day, and on each day
groweth a deed,
And a thing that never dieth; and the fateful
tale shall speed.
Lo, now, let us harden our hearts and set our
brows as the brass,
Lest men say it, 'They loathed the evil and they
brought the evil to pass'."   90

So they spake, and their hearts were heavy,
and they longed for the morrow morn,
And the morrow of tomorrow, and the new day
yet to be born.

But Brynhild cried to her maidens: "Now
open ark and chest,
And draw forth queenly raiment of the loveliest
and the best;
Red rings that the Dwarf-lords fashioned, fair
cloths that Queens have sewed,
To array the bride for the Mighty, and the traveller for the road."

They wept as they wrought her bidding and
did on her goodliest gear;
But she laughed 'mid the dainty linen, and the
gold-rings fashioned fair;
She arose from the bed of the Niblungs, and
her face no more was wan;
As a star in the dawn-tide heavens, 'mid the
dusky house she shone;   109
And they that stood about her, their hearts
were raised aloft
Amid their fear and wonder. Then she spake
them kind and soft:

"Now give me the sword, O maidens, wherewith I sheared the wind
When the Kings of Earth were gathered to
know the Chooser's mind."[13]

10 woe betide the time
11 When Sigurd, in the guise of Gunnar, walked
   through the flame and won Brynhild for
   Gunnar
12 Guttorm.

13 See introductory note. p. 705.

All sheathed the maidens brought it, and
  feared the hidden blade,
But the naked blue-white edges across her knees
  she laid,
And spake: "The heaped-up riches, the gear
  my fathers left,
All dear-bought woven wonders, all rings from
  battle reft,
All goods of men desired, now strew them on
  the floor,
And so share among you, maidens, the gifts of
  Brynhild's store."   110

They brought them 'mid their weeping, but
  none put forth a hand
To take that wealth desired, the spoils of many
  a land:
There they stand and weep before her, and
  some are moved to speech,
And they cast their arms about her and strive
  with her and beseech
That she look on her loved-ones' sorrow and the
  glory of the day.
It was nought; she scarce might see them, and
  she put their hands away,
And she said: "Peace, ye that love me! and
  take the gifts and the gold
In remembrance of my fathers and the faithful deeds of old."

Then she spake: "Where now is Gunnar,
  that I may speak with him?
For new things are mine eyes beholding and
  the Niblung house grows dim,   120
And new sounds gather about me, that may
  hinder me to speak
When the breath is near to flitting, and the
  voice is waxen weak."

Then upright by the bed of the Niblungs
  for a moment doth she stand,
And the blade flasheth bright in the chamber,
  but no more they hinder her hand
Than if a god were smiting to rend the world
  in two;
Then dulled are the glittering edges, and the
  bitter point cleaves through
The breast of the all-wise Brynhild, and her
  feet from the pavement fail,
And the sigh of her heart is hearkened 'mid
  the hush of the maidens' wail.
Chill, deep is the fear upon them, but they
  bring her aback to the bed,
And her hand is yet on the hilts, and sidelong
  droopeth her head.   130

Then there cometh a cry from withoutward,
  and Gunnar's hurrying feet

Are swift on the kingly threshold, and Bryn-
  hild's blood they meet.
Low down o'er the bed he hangeth and heark-
  eneth for her word,
And her heavy lids are opened to look on the
  Niblung lord,
And she saith: "I pray thee a prayer, the last
  word in the world I speak,
That ye bear me forth to Sigurd, and the hand
  my hand would seek;
The bale for the dead is builded, it is wrought
  full wide on the plain,
It is raised for Earth's best Helper, and there-
  on is room for twain:
Ye have hung the shields about it, and the
  Southland hangings spread;
There lay me adown by Sigurd and my head
  beside his head;   140
But ere ye leave us sleeping draw his Wrath
  from out the sheath,
And lay that Light of the Branstock* and the
  blade that frighted death
Betwixt my side and Sigurd's, as it lay that
  while agone,
When once in one bed together we twain were
  laid alone:
How then when the flames flare upward may I
  be left behind?
How then may the road he wendeth be hard
  for my feet to find?
How then in the gates of Valhall may the door
  of the gleaming ring
Clash to on the heel of Sigurd, as I follow on
  my King?"

Then she raised herself on her elbow, but
  again her eyelids sank,
And the wound by the sword-edge whispered,
  as her heart from the iron shrank,   150
And she moaned: "O lives of man-folk, for
  unrest all overlong
By the Father were ye fashioned; and what
  hope amendeth wrong?
Now at last, O my beloved, all is gone; none
  else is near,
Through the ages of all ages, never sundered,
  shall we wear."

Scarce more than a sigh was the word, as
  back on the bed she fell,
Nor was there need in the chamber of the passing of Brynhild to tell;

* Another name for Sigurd's sword. The Branstock was a great oak tree about which was
built the ancestral home of the Volsungs. The
sword, set by Odin, was drawn from the
Branstock by Sigurd's father. It was later
broken into pieces, but reforged as Bram, or
the Wrath of Sigurd.

And no more their lamentation might the maidens hold aback,
But the sound of their bitter mourning was as if red-handed wrack
Ran wild in the Burg of the Niblungs, and the fire were master of all.

Then the voice of Gunnar, the war-king, cried out o'er the weeping hall: 160
"Wail on, O women forsaken, for the mightiest woman born!
Now the hearth is cold and joyless, and the waste bed lieth forlorn.
Wail on, but amid your weeping lay hand to the glorious dead,
That not alone for an hour may lie Queen Brynhild's head:
For here have been heavy tidings, and the Mightiest under shield
Is laid on the bale high-builded in the Niblungs' hallowed field.
Fare forth! for he abideth, and we do All-father wrong
If the shining Valhall's pavement await their feet o'erlong.''

Then they took the body of Brynhild in the raiment that she wore,
And out through the gate of the Niblungs the holy corpse they bore,   170
And thence forth to the mead of the people, and the high-built shielded bale:
Then afresh in the open meadows breaks forth the women's wail
When they see the bed of Sigurd and the glittering of his gear;
And fresh is the wail of the people as Brynhild draweth anear,
And the tidings go before her that for twain the bale is built,
That for twain is the oak-wood shielded and the pleasant odours spilt.

There is peace on the bale of Sigurd, and the gods look down from on high,
And they see the lids of the Volsung close shut against the sky,
As he lies with his shield beside him in the hauberk all of gold,
That has not its like in the heavens, nor has earth of its fellow told;   180
And forth from the Helm of Aweing[14] are the sunbeams flashing wide,

And the sheathéd Wrath of Sigurd lies still by his mighty side.
Then cometh an elder of days, a man of the ancient times,
Who is long past sorrow and joy, and the steep of the bale he climbs;
And he kneeleth down by Sigurd, and bareth the Wrath to the sun
That the beams are gathered about it, and from hilt to blood-point run,
And wide o'er the plain of the Niblungs doth the Light of the Branstock glare,
Till the wondering mountain-shepherds on that star of noontide stare,
And fear for many an evil; but the ancient man stands still
With the war-flame on his shoulder, nor thinks of good or of ill,   190
Till the feet of Brynhild's bearers on the topmost bale are laid,
And her bed is dight[15] by Sigurd's; then he sinks the pale white blade
And lays it 'twixt the sleepers, and leaves them there alone—
He, the last that shall ever behold them,—and his days are well-nigh done.

Then is silence over the plain; in the noon shine the torches pale,
As the best of the Niblung Earl-folk[16] bear fire to the builded bale:
Then a wind in the west ariseth, and the white flames leap on high,
And with one voice crieth the people a great and mighty cry,
And men cast up hands to the Heavens, and pray without a word,
As they that have seen God's visage, and the voice of the Father have heard.   200

They are gone—the lovely, the mighty, the hope of the ancient Earth:
It shall labour and bear the burden as before that day of their birth;
It shall groan in its blind abiding for the day that Sigurd hath sped,
And the hour that Brynhild hath hastened, and the dawn that waketh the dead;
It shall yearn, and be oft-times holpen, and forget their deeds no more,
Till the new sun beams on Baldur, and the happy sealess shore.*

---

14 Or the Helm of Dread, won by the slaying of the dragon Fafnir.

15 prepared
16 The nobles, or warriors, as opposed to the churls.
* Alluding to the new heaven, that is to arise after the Twilight of the Gods, when Baldur the Good shall be released from Hel and reign in the seats of the old gods.

THE VOICE OF TOIL*

I heard men saying, Leave hope and praying,
All days shall be as all have been;
To-day and to-morrow bring fear and sorrow,
The never-ending toil between.

When Earth was younger mid toil and hunger,
In hope we strove, and our hands were strong;
Then great men led us, with words they fed us,
And bade us right the earthly wrong.   8

Go read in story their deeds and glory,
Their names amidst the nameless dead;
Turn then from lying to us slow-dying
In that good world to which they led;

Where fast and faster our iron master,
The thing we made, for ever drives,
Bids us grind treasure and fashion pleasure
For other hopes and other lives.   16

Where home is a hovel and dull we grovel,
Forgetting that the world is fair;
Where no babe we cherish, lest its very soul
    perish;
Where mirth is crime, and love a snare.

Who now shall lead us, what god shall heed us
As we lie in the hell our hands have won?
For us are no rulers but fools and befoolers,
The great are fallen, the wise men gone.   24

I heard men saying, Leave tears and praying,
The sharp knife heedeth not the sheep;
Are we not stronger than the rich and the
    wronger,
When day breaks over dreams and sleep?

Come, shoulder to shoulder ere the world grows
    older!
Help lies in nought but thee and me;
Hope is before us, the long years that bore us
Bore leaders more than men may be.   32

Let dead hearts tarry and trade and marry,
And trembling nurse their dreams of mirth,
While we the living our lives are giving
To bring the bright new world to birth.

Come, shoulder to shoulder ere earth grows
    older!
The Cause spreads over land and sea;
Now the world shaketh, and fear awaketh,
And joy at last for thee and me.   40

* This poem, now printed in Morris's *Poems by
  the Way*, was first published, in 1885, in a
  pamphlet called *Chants for Socialists*. "The
  Cause" mentioned in the last stanza is of
  course Socialism, in which Morris was much
  interested in his later life.

ALGERNON CHARLES SWINBURNE (1837-1909)

FROM ATALANTA IN CALYDON

CHORUS

When the hounds of spring are on winter's
    traces,
    The mother of months† in meadow or plain
Fills the shadows and windy places
    With lisp of leaves and ripple of rain;
And the brown bright nightingale amorous
Is half assuaged for Itylus,[1]
For the Thracian ships and the foreign faces,
    The tongueless vigil, and all the pain.   8

Come with bows bent and with emptying of
    quivers,
    Maiden most perfect, lady of light,
With a noise of winds and many rivers,
    With a clamour of waters, and with might;
Bind on thy sandals, O thou most fleet,
Over the splendour and speed of thy feet;
For the faint east quickens, the wan west
    shivers,
    Round the feet of the day and the feet of
        the night.   16

Where shall we find her, how shall we sing
    to her,
    Fold our hands round her knees, and cling?
O that man's heart were as fire and could
    spring to her,
    Fire, or the strength of the streams that
        spring!
For the stars and the winds are unto her
As raiment, as songs of the harp-player;
For the risen stars and the fallen cling to her,
    And the southwest-wind and the west-wind
        sing.   24

For winter's rains and ruins are over,
    And all the season of snows and sins;
The days dividing lover and lover,
    The light that loses, the night that wins;
And time remembered is grief forgotten,
And frosts are slain and flowers begotten,
And in green underwood and cover
    Blossom by blossom the spring begins.   32

The full streams feed on flower of rushes,
    Ripe grasses trammel a travelling foot,

† Artemis, or Diana, the goddess of the moon—
  also the goddess of the hunt—see next stanza.
  Compare Shelley's *Prometheus Unbound*, iv
  207.
[1] Alluding to the old Thracian legend of Philomela and Procne.

he faint fresh flame of the young year
flushes
From leaf to flower and flower to fruit;
nd fruit and leaf are as gold and fire,
nd the oat is heard above the lyre,‡
nd the hoofèd heel of a satyr crushes
The chestnut-husk at the chestnut-root. 40

nd Pan by noon and Bacchus by night,
Fleeter of foot than the fleet-foot kid,
'ollows with dancing and fills with delight
The Mænad and the Bassarid;[2]
nd soft as lips that laugh and hide,
he laughing leaves of the trees divide,
nd screen from seeing and leave in sight
The god pursuing, the maiden hid. 48

he ivy falls with the Bacchanal's hair
Over her eyebrows hiding her eyes;
he wild vine slipping down leaves bare
Her bright breast shortening into sighs;
he wild vine slips with the weight of its
leaves,
But the berried ivy catches and cleaves
To the limbs that glitter, the feet that scare
The wolf that follows, the fawn that flies. 56

A LEAVE-TAKING

Let us go hence, my songs; she will not hear.
Let us go hence together without fear;
Keep silence now, for singing-time is over,
And over all old things and all things dear.
She loves not you nor me as all we love her.
Yea, though we sang as angels in her ear,
She would not hear. 7

Let us rise up and part; she will not know.
Let us go seaward as the great winds go,
Full of blown sand and foam; what help is
here?
There is no help, for all these things are so,
And all the world is bitter as a tear;
And how these things are, though ye strove to
show,
She would not know. 14

Let us go home and hence; she will not weep.
We gave love many dreams and days to keep,
Flowers without scent, and fruits that would
not grow,
Saying, "If thou wilt, thrust in thy sickle and
reap."

2 Names for bacchanals, or frenzied votaries of
Bacchus.
‡ That is, pastoral, out-of-door music takes the
place of indoor, festal song; Pan supplants
Apollo. An oat is a shepherd's pipe made of
an oat stem.

All is reaped now; no grass is left to mow;
And we that sowed, though all we fell on
sleep,
She would not weep. 21

Let us go hence and rest; she will not love.
She shall not hear us if we sing hereof,
Nor see love's ways, how sore they are and
steep.
Come hence, let be, lie still; it is enough.
Love is a barren sea, bitter and deep;
And though she saw all heaven in flower above,
She would not love. 28

Let us give up, go down; she will not care.
Though all the stars made gold of all the air,
And the sea moving saw before it move
One moon-flower making all the foam-flowers
fair,
Though all those waves went over us, and drove
Deep down the stifling lips and drowning hair,
She would not care. 35

Let us go hence, go hence; she will not see.
Sing all once more together; surely she,
She, too, remembering days and words that
were,
Will turn a little toward us, sighing; but we,
We are hence, we are gone, as though we had
not been there.
Nay, and though all men seeing had pity on me,
She would not see. 42

HYMN TO PROSERPINE*

(AFTER THE PROCLAMATION IN ROME OF THE
CHRISTIAN FAITH)

Vicisti, Galilæe

I have lived long enough, having seen one thing,
that love hath an end;
Goddess and maiden and queen, be near me
now and befriend.
Thou art more than the day or the morrow, the
seasons that laugh or that weep;
For these give joy and sorrow; but thou, Proserpina, sleep.
Sweet is the treading of wine, and sweet the
feet of the dove;

But a goodlier gift is thine than foam of the
grapes or love.

Yea, is not even Apollo, with hair and harp-
string of gold,

A bitter God to follow, a beautiful God to
behold?

I am sick of singing; the bays burn deep and
chafe; I am fain

To rest a little from praise and grievous pleasure and pain.   10

For the Gods we know not of, who give us our
daily breath,

We know they are cruel as love or life, and
lovely as death.

O Gods dethroned and deceased, cast forth,
wiped out in a day!

From your wrath is the world released, redeemed from your chains, men say.

New Gods are crowned in the city, their flowers have broken your rods;

They are merciful, clothed with pity, the young
compassionate Gods.

But for me their new device is barren, the days
are bare;

Things long past over suffice, and men forgotten that were.

Time and the Gods are at strife: ye dwell in
the midst thereof,

Draining a little life from the barren breasts
of love.   20

I say to you, cease, take rest; yea, I say to you
all, be at peace,

Till the bitter milk of her breast and the barren bosom shall cease.

Wilt thou yet take all, Galilean? but these thou
shalt not take,

The laurel, the palms, and the pæan, the breasts
of the nymphs in the brake;

Breasts more soft than a dove's, that tremble
with tenderer breath;

And all the wings of the Loves, and all the joy
before death;

All the feet of the hours that sound as a single
lyre,

Dropped and deep in the flowers, with strings
that flicker like fire.

More than these wilt thou give, things fairer
than all these things?

Nay, for a little we live, and life hath mutable
wings.   30

A little while and we die; shall life not thrive
as it may?

For no man under the sky lives twice, outliving
his day.

And grief is a grievous thing, and a man hath
enough of his tears:

Why should he labour and bring fresh grief to
blacken his years?

Thou hast conquered, O pale Galilean; the world
has grown gray from thy breath;

We have drunken of things Lethean, and fed
on the fulness of death.

Laurel is green for a season, and love is sweet
for a day;

But love grows bitter with treason, and laurel
outlives not May.

Sleep, shall we sleep after all? for the world
is not sweet in the end;

For the old faiths loosen and fall, the new
years ruin and rend.   40

Fate is a sea without shore, and the soul is a
rock that abides;

But her ears are vexed with the roar and her
face with the foam of the tides.

O lips that the live blood faints in, the leavings
of racks and rods!

O ghastly glories of saints, dead limbs of gib-
beted Gods!

Though all men abase them before you in
spirit, and all knees bend,

I kneel not, neither adore you, but standing,
look to the end.

All delicate days and pleasant, all spirits and
sorrows are cast

Far out with the foam of the present that
sweeps to the surf of the past;

Where beyond the extreme sea-wall, and between the remote sea-gates,

Waste water washes, and tall ships founder,
and deep death waits: 50

Where, mighty with deepening sides, clad about
with the seas as with wings,

And impelled of invisible tides, and fulfilled
of unspeakable things,

White-eyed and poisonous-finned, shark-toothed
and serpentine-curled,

Rolls, under the whitening wind of the future,
the wave of the world.

The depths stand naked in sunder behind it,
the storms flee away;

In the hollow before it the thunder is taken
and snared as a prey;

In its sides is the north-wind bound; and its
salt is of all men's tears;

With light of ruin, and sound of changes, and
pulse of years;

With travail of day after day, and with trouble
of hour upon hour;

And bitter as blood is the spray; and the
crests are as fangs that devour: 60

And its vapour and storm of its steam as the
sighing of spirits to be;

And its noise as the noise in a dream; and its
   depth as the roots of the sea:
And the height of its heads as the height of the
   utmost stars of the air;
And the ends of the earth at the might thereof
   tremble, and time is made bare.
Will ye bridle the deep sea with reins, will ye
   chasten the high sea with rods?
Will ye take her to chain her with chains, who
   is older than all ye Gods?
All ye as a wind shall go by, as a fire shall ye
   pass and be past;
Ye are Gods, and behold ye shall die, and the
   waves be upon you at last.
In the darkness of time, in the deeps of the
   years, in the changes of things,
Ye shall sleep as a slain man sleeps, and the
   world shall forget you for kings.   70
Though the feet of thine high priests tread
   where thy lords and our forefathers trod,
Though these that were Gods are dead, and
   thou being dead art a God,
Though before thee the throned Cytherean be
   fallen, and hidden her head,
Yet thy kingdom shall pass, Galilean, thy dead
   shall go down to thee dead.
Of the maiden thy mother, men sing as a goddess with grace clad around;
Thou art throned where another was king;
   where another was queen she is crowned.
Yea, once we had sight of another; but now
   she is queen, say these.
Not as thine, not as thine was our mother, a
   blossom of flowering seas,[1]
Clothed round with the world's desire as with
   raiment, and fair as the foam,
And fleeter than kindled fire, and a goddess
   and mother of Rome.   80
For thine came pale and a maiden, and sister
   to sorrow; but ours,
Her deep hair heavily laden with odour and
   colour of flowers,
White rose of the rose-white water, a silver
   splendour, a flame,
Bent down unto us that besought her, and earth
   grew sweet with her name.
For thine came weeping, a slave among slaves,
   and rejected; but she
Came flushed from the full-flushed wave, and
   imperial, her foot on the sea,
And the wondering waters knew her, the winds
   and the viewless ways,
And the roses grew rosier, and bluer the sea-
   blue stream of the bays.
Ye are fallen, our lords, by what token? we wist
   that ye should not fall.

[1] Venus, born of the foam.

Ye were all so fair that are broken; and one
   more fair than ye all.   90
But I turn to her still, having seen she shall
   surely abide in the end;
Goddess and maiden and queen, be near me
   now and befriend.
O daughter of earth, of my mother, her crown
   and blossom of birth,
I am also, I also, thy brother; I go as I came
   unto earth.
In the night where thine eyes are as moons are
   in heaven, the night where thou art,
Where the silence is more than all tunes, where
   sleep overflows from the heart,
Where the poppies are sweet as the rose in our
   world, and the red rose is white,
And the wind falls faint as it blows with the
   fume of the flowers of the night,
And the murmur of spirits that sleep in the
   shadow of Gods from afar
Grows dim in thine ears and deep as the deep
   dim soul of a star,   100
In the sweet low light of thy face, under heav-
   ens untrod by the sun,
Let my soul with their souls find place, and
   forget what is done and undone.
Thou art more than the Gods who number the
   days of our temporal breath;
For these give labour and slumber; but thou,
   Proserpina, death.
Therefore now at thy feet I abide for a season
   in silence. I know
I shall die as my fathers died, and sleep as they
   sleep; even so.
For the glass of the years is brittle wherein we
   gaze for a span;
A little soul for a little bears up this corpse
   which is man.[2]
So long I endure, no longer; and laugh not
   again, neither weep.
For there is no God found stronger than death;
   and death is a sleep.   110

PRELUDE OF SONGS BEFORE SUNRISE*

Between the green bud and the red
Youth sat and sang by Time, and shed
   From eyes and tresses flowers and tears,
   From heart and spirit hopes and fears,

[2] Adapted from Epictetus.
* Swinburne's *Songs Before Sunrise*, published in
   1871, and dedicated to Joseph Mazzini, the
   Italian patriot, are a noteworthy contribution
   to the poetry of political and religious freedom. They were mainly inspired by the long
   struggle for a free and united Italy. The partial union of Italy, effected in 1861, was completed by the occupation of Rome in 1870,
   but the government was monarchical, and
   not republican, as the more ardent revolutionists had hoped.

Upon the hollow stream whose bed
  Is channelled by the foamless years;
And with the white the gold-haired head
  Mixed running locks, and in Time's ears
Youth's dreams hung singing, and Time's truth
Was half not harsh in the ears of Youth.   10

Between the bud and the blown flower
Youth talked with joy and grief an hour,
  With footless joy and wingless grief
  And twin-born faith and disbelief
Who share the seasons to devour;
  And long ere these made up their sheaf
Felt the winds round him shake and shower
  The rose-red and the blood-red leaf,
Delight whose germ grew never grain,
And passion dyed in its own pain.   20

Then he stood up, and trod to dust
Fear and desire, mistrust and trust,
  And dreams of bitter sleep and sweet,
  And bound for sandals on his feet
Knowledge and patience of what must
  And what things may be, in the heat
And cold of years that rot and rust
  And alter; and his spirit's meat
Was freedom, and his staff was wrought
Of strength, and his cloak woven of thought. 30

For what has he whose will sees clear
To do with doubt and faith and fear,
  Swift hopes and slow despondencies?
  His heart is equal with the sea's
And with the sea-wind's, and his ear
  Is level to the speech of these,
And his soul communes and takes cheer
  With the actual earth's equalities,
Air, light, and night, hills, winds, and streams,
And seeks not strength from strengthless
      dreams.   40

His soul is even with the sun
Whose spirit and whose eyes are one,
  Who seeks not stars by day nor light
  And heavy heat of day by night.
Him can no God cast down, whom none
  Can lift in hope beyond the height
Of faith and nature and things done
  By the calm rule of might and right
That bids men be and bear and do,
And die beneath blind skies or blue.   50

To him the lights of even and morn
Speak no vain things of love or scorn,
  Fancies and passions miscreate
  By man in things dispassionate.
Nor holds he fellowship forlorn
  With souls that pray and hope and hate,

And doubt they had better not been born,
  And fain would lure or scare off fate
And charm their doomsman from their doom
And make fear dig its own false tomb.   60

He builds not half of doubts and half
Of dreams his own soul's cenotaph,
  Whence hopes and fears with helpless eyes,
  Wrapt loose in cast-off cerecloths, rise
And dance and wring their hands and laugh,
  And weep thin tears and sigh light sighs,
And without living lips would quaff
  The living spring in man that lies,
And drain his soul of faith and strength
It might have lived on a life's length.   70

He hath given himself and hath not sold
To God for heaven or man for gold,
  Or grief for comfort that it gives,
  Or joy for grief's restoratives.
He hath given himself to time, whose fold
  Shuts in the mortal flock that lives
On its plain pasture's heat and cold
  And the equal year's alternatives.
Earth, heaven, and time, death, life, and he,
Endure while they shall be to be.   80

"Yet between death and life are hours
To flush with love and hide in flowers;
  What profit save in these?" men cry:
  "Ah, see, between soft earth and sky,
What only good things here are ours!"
  They say, "What better wouldst thou try,
What sweeter sing of? or what powers
  Serve, that will give thee ere thou die
More joy to sing and be less sad,
More heart to play and grow more glad?"   90

Play then and sing; we too have played,
We likewise, in that subtle shade.
  We too have twisted through our hair
  Such tendrils as the wild Loves wear,
And heard what mirth the Mænads[1] made,
  Till the wind blew our garlands bare
And left their roses disarrayed,
  And smote the summer with strange air,
And disengirdled and discrowned   99
The limbs and locks that vine-wreaths bound.

We too have tracked by star-proof trees
The tempest of the Thyiades[1]
  Scare the loud night on hills that hid
  The blood-feasts of the Bassarid,[1]
Heard their song's iron cadences
  Fright the wolf hungering from the kid,
Outroar the lion-throated seas,
  Outchide the north-wind if it chid,
And hush the torrent-tongued ravines
With thunders of their tambourines.   110

1 Ancient names of votaries of Bacchus.

But the fierce flute whose notes acclaim
Dim goddesses of fiery fame,
  Cymbal and clamorous kettledrum,
  Timbrels and tabrets, all are dumb
That turned the high chill air to flame;
  The singing tongues of fire are numb
That called on Cotys[2] by her name
  Edonian, till they felt her come
And maddened, and her mystic face
Lightened along the streams of Thrace.   120

For Pleasure slumberless and pale,
And Passion with rejected veil,
  Pass, and the tempest-footed throng
  Of hours that follow them with song
Till their feet flag and voices fail,
  And lips that were so loud so long
Learn silence, or a wearier wail;
  So keen is change, and time so strong,
To weave the robes of life and rend
And weave again till life have end.   130

But weak is change, but strengthless time,
To take the light from heaven, or climb
  The hills of heaven with wasting feet.
  Songs they can stop that earth found meet,
But the stars keep their ageless rhyme;
  Flowers they can slay that spring thought sweet,
But the stars keep their spring sublime,
  Passions and pleasures can defeat,
Actions and agonies control,
And life and death, but not the soul.   140

Because man's soul is man's God still,
What wind soever waft his will
  Across the waves of day and night
  To port or shipwreck, left or right,
By shores and shoals of good and ill;
  And still its flame at mainmast height
Through the rent air that foam-flakes fill
  Sustains the indomitable light
Whence only man hath strength to steer
Or helm to handle without fear.   150

Save his own soul's light overhead,
None leads him, and none ever led,
  Across birth's hidden harbour-bar,
  Past youth where shoreward shallows are,
Through age that drives on toward the red
  Vast void of sunset hailed from far,
To the equal waters of the dead;
  Save his own soul he hath no star,
And sinks, except his own soul guide,
Helmless in middle turn of tide.   160

No blast of air or fire of sun
Puts out the light whereby we run

With girdled loins our lamplit race,[3]
And each from each takes heart of grace
And spirit till his turn be done,
  And light of face from each man's face
In whom the light of trust is one;
  Since only souls that keep their place
By their own light, and watch things roll,
And stand, have light for any soul.   170

A little time we gain from time
To set our seasons in some chime,
  For harsh or sweet or loud or low,
  With seasons played out long ago
And souls that in their time and prime
  Took part with summer or with snow,
Lived abject lives out or sublime,
  And had their chance of seed to sow
For service or disservice done
To those days dead and this their son.   180

A little time that we may fill
Or with such good works or such ill
  As loose the bonds or make them strong
  Wherein all manhood suffers wrong.
By rose-hung river and light-foot rill
  There are who rest not; who think long
Till they discern as from a hill
  At the sun's hour of morning song,
Known of souls only, and those souls free,
The sacred spaces of the sea.   190

LINES ON THE MONUMENT OF GIUSEPPE MAZZINI[*]

Italia, mother of the souls of men,
    Mother divine,
Of all that served thee best with sword or pen,
    All sons of thine,

Thou knowest that here the likeness of the best
    Before thee stands:
The head most high, the heart found faithfullest,
    The purest hands.

Above the fume and foam of time that flits,
    The soul, we know,   10
Now sits on high where Alighieri sits
    With Angelo.

Not his own heavenly tongue hath heavenly speech
    Enough to say

---

3 In allusion to the ancient torch race.
* Joseph Mazzini, the Italian patriot, died in 1872. A monument was erected to him at Genoa (Genoa "La Superba"), where there is also a monument to Columbus. Alighieri (line 11) is Dante, Angelo is Michelangelo.

2 An Edonian, or Thracian, divinity, worshiped with licentious revelry.

What this man was, whose praise no thought
    may reach,
      No words can weigh.

Since man's first mother brought to mortal
    birth
      Her first-born son,
Such grace befell not ever man on earth
      As crowns this One.   20

Of God nor man was ever this thing said:
      That he could give
Life back to her who gave him, whence his dead
      Mother might live.

But this man found his mother dead and slain,
      With fast-sealed eyes,
And bade the dead rise up and live again,
      And she did rise:

And all the world was bright with her through
    him:
      But dark with strife,   30
Like heaven's own sun that storming clouds
    bedim,
      Was all his life.

Life and the clouds are vanished; hate and fear
      Have had their span
Of time to hurt and are not: He is here,
      The sunlike man.

City superb, that hadst Columbus first
      For sovereign son,
Be prouder that thy breast hath later nurst
      This mightier One.   40

Glory be his for ever, while his land
      Lives and is free,
As with controlling breath and sovereign hand
      He bade her be.

Earth shows to heaven the names by thousands
    told
      That crown her fame,
But highest of all that heaven and earth be-
    hold,
      Mazzini's name.

THE PILGRIMS*

Who is your lady of love, O ye that pass
Singing? and is it for sorrow of that which was
That ye sing sadly, or dream of what shall be?
    For gladly at once and sadly it seems ye
    sing.

* The poem is in the form of a dialogue, as indi-
  cated by the dashes,—a speech and a reply
  in each stanza. For form, compare with it
  Tennyson's *The Two Voices*; for thought,
  Wordsworth's *Ode to Duty*, Tennyson's
  Wages, and Browning's *Rabbi Ben Ezra*.

—Our lady of love by you is unbeholden;
For hands she hath none, nor eyes, nor lips, nor
    golden
Treasure of hair, nor face nor form; but we
    That love, we know her more fair than any-
      thing.   8

—Is she a queen, having great gifts to give?
—Yea, these: that whoso hath seen her shall not
    live
Except he serve her sorrowing, with strange
    pain,
    Travail and bloodshedding and bitterer tears;
And when she bids die he shall surely die.
And he shall leave all things under the sky,
And go forth naked under sun and rain,
    And work and wait and watch out all his
      years.   16

—Hath she on earth no place of habitation?
—Age to age calling, nation answering nation,
Cries out, Where is she? and there is none to
    say;
    For if she be not in the spirit of men,
For if in the inward soul she hath no place,
In vain they cry unto her, seeking her face,
In vain their mouths make much of her; for
    they
    Cry with vain tongues, till the heart lives
      again.   24

—O ye that follow, and have ye no repentance?
For on your brows is written a mortal sentence,
An hieroglyph of sorrow, a fiery sign,
    That in your lives ye shall not pause or rest,
Nor have the sure sweet common love, nor keep
Friends and safe days, nor joy of life nor
    sleep.
—These have we not, who have one thing, the
    divine
    Face and clear eyes of faith and fruitful
      breast.   32

—And ye shall die before your thrones be won.
—Yea, and the changed world and the liberal
    sun
Shall move and shine without us, and we lie
    Dead; but if she too move on earth, and live,
But if the old world with all the old irons rent
Laugh and give thanks, shall we not be content?
Nay, we shall rather live, we shall not die,
    Life being so little, and death so good to
      give.   40

—And these men shall forget you.—Yea, but we
Shall be a part of the earth and the ancient sea,
And heaven-high air august, and awful fire,
    And all things good; and no man's heart
    shall beat

But somewhat in it of our blood once shed
Shall quiver and quicken, as now in us the dead
Blood of men slain and the old same life's de-
    sire
    Plants in their fiery footprints our fresh
        feet.   48

—But ye that might be clothed with all things
    pleasant,
Ye are foolish that put off the fair soft present,
That clothe yourselves with the cold future
    air;
    When mother and father, and tender sister
        and brother
And the old live love that was shall be as ye,
Dust, and no fruit of loving life shall be.
—She shall be yet who is more than all these
    were,
    Than sister or wife or father unto us or
        mother.   56

—Is this worth life, is this, to win for wages?
Lo, the dead mouths of the awful grey-grown
    ages,
The venerable, in the past that is their prison,
    In the outer darkness, in the unopening
        grave,
Laugh, knowing how many as ye now say have
    said,
How many, and all are fallen, are fallen and
    dead:
Shall ye dead rise, and these dead have not
    risen?
    —Not we but she, who is tender, and swift to
        save.   64

—Are ye not weary and faint not by the way,
Seeing night by night devoured of day by day,
Seeing hour by hour consumed in sleepless fire?
    Sleepless; and ye too, when shall ye too
        sleep?
—We are weary in heart and head, in hands and
    feet,
And surely more than all things sleep were
    sweet,—
Than all things save the inexorable desire
    Which whoso knoweth shall neither faint nor
        weep.   72

—Is this so sweet that one were fain to follow?
Is this so sure where all men's hopes are hol-
    low,
Even this your dream, that by much tribulation
    Ye shall make whole flawed hearts, and
        bowed necks straight?
—Nay, though our life were blind, our death
    were fruitless,

Not therefore were the whole world's high hope
    rootless;
But man to man, nation would turn to nation,
    And the old life live, and the old great word
        be great.   80

—Pass on, then, and pass by us, and let us be,
For what light think ye after life to see?
And if the world fare better will ye know?
    And if man triumph who shall seek you and
        say?
—Enough of light is this for one life's span,
That all men born are mortal, but not man;
And we men bring death lives by night to sow,
    That men may reap and eat and live by
        day.   88

A FORSAKEN GARDEN

In a coign of the cliff between lowland and
    highland,
    At the sea-down's edge between windward
        and lee,
Walled round with rocks as an inland island,
    The ghost of a garden fronts the sea.
A girdle of brushwood and thorn encloses
    The steep square slope of the blossomless bed
Where the weeds that grew green from the
    graves of its roses
        Now lie dead.   8

The fields fall southward, abrupt and broken,
    To the low last edge of the long lone land.
If a step should sound or a word be spoken,
    Would a ghost not rise at the strange guest's
        hand?
So long have the grey bare walks lain guestless,
    Through branches and briars if a man make
        way,
He shall find no life but the sea-wind's, rest-
    less
        Night and day.   16

The dense hard passage is blind and stifled
    That crawls by a track none turn to climb
To the straight waste place that the years have
    rifled
    Of all but the thorns that are touched not of
        time.
The thorns he spares when the rose is taken;
    The rocks are left when he wastes the plain;
The wind that wanders, the weeds wind-shaken,
        These remain.   24

Not a flower to be pressed of the foot that falls
    not;
    As the heart of a dead man the seed-plots are
        dry;

From the thicket of thorns whence the nightin-
gale calls not,
　Could she call, there were never a rose to
　　reply.
Over the meadows that blossom and wither,
　Rings but the note of a sea-bird's song.
Only the sun and the rain come hither
　　　　All year long.　　　　　　　　32

The sun burns sere, and the rain dishevels
　One gaunt bleak blossom of scentless breath.
Only the wind here hovers and revels
　In a round where life seems barren as death.
Here there was laughing of old, there was
　weeping,
　Haply, of lovers none ever will know,
Whose eyes went seaward a hundred sleeping
　　　　Years ago.　　　　　　　　40

Heart handfast in heart as they stood, "Look
　thither,"
　Did he whisper? "Look forth from the flow-
　　ers to the sea;
For the foam-flowers endure when the rose-
　blossoms wither,
　And men that love lightly may die—But
　　we?"
And the same wind sang, and the same waves
　whitened,
　And or ever the garden's last petals were
　　shed,
In the lips that had whispered, the eyes that
　had lightened,
　　　　Love was dead.　　　　　　　48

Or they loved their life through, and then went
　whither?
　And were one to the end—but what end who
　　knows?
Love deep as the sea as a rose must wither,
　As the rose-red seaweed that mocks the rose.
Shall the dead take thought for the dead to
　love them?
　What love was ever as deep as a grave?
They are loveless now as the grass above them
　　　　Or the wave.　　　　　　　56

All are at one now, roses and lovers,
　Not known of the cliffs and the fields and the
　　sea.
Not a breath of the time that has been hovers
　In the air now soft with a summer to be.
Not a breath shall there sweeten the seasons
　hereafter
　Of the flowers or the lovers that laugh now
　　or weep,
When, as they that are free now of weeping
　and laughter,
　　　　We shall sleep.　　　　　　　64

Here death may deal not again forever;
　Here change may come not till all change
　　end.
From the graves they have made they shall rise
　up never,
　Who have left naught living to ravage and
　　rend.
Earth, stones, and thorns of the wild ground
　growing,
　While the sun and the rain live, these shall
　　be;
Till a last wind's breath upon all these blow-
　ing
　　　　Roll the sea.　　　　　　　72

Till the slow sea rise and the sheer cliff crum-
　ble,
　Till terrace and meadow the deep gulfs drink,
Till the strength of the waves of the high tides
　humble
　The fields that lessen, the rocks that shrink,
Here now in his triumph where all things falter,
　Stretched out on the spoils that his own hand
　　spread,
As a god self-slain on his own strange altar,
　　　　Death lies dead.　　　　　　　80

A BALLAD OF DREAMLAND

I hid my heart in a nest of roses,
　Out of the sun's way, hidden apart;
In a softer bed than the soft white snow's is,
　Under the roses I hid my heart.
　Why would it sleep not? why should it start,
When never a leaf of the rose-tree stirred?
　What made sleep flutter his wings and part?
Only the song of a secret bird.　　　　　8

Lie still, I said, for the wind's wing closes,
　And mild leaves muffle the keen sun's dart;
Lie still, for the wind on the warm sea dozes,
　And the wind is unquieter yet than thou art.
　Does a thought in thee still as a thorn's
　　wound smart?
Does the fang still fret thee of hope deferred?
　What bids the lids of thy sleep dispart?
Only the song of a secret bird.　　　　　16

The green land's name that a charm encloses,
　It never was writ in the traveller's chart,
And sweet on its trees as the fruit that grows is,
　It never was sold in the merchant's mart.
　The swallows of dreams through its dim fields
　　dart,
And sleep's are the tunes in its tree-tops heard;
　No hound's note wakens the wildwood hart,
Only the song of a secret bird.　　　　　24

ENVOI*

In the world of dreams I have chosen my part,
  To sleep for a season and hear no word
Of true love's truth or of light love's art,
  Only the song of a secret bird.

UPON A CHILD

Of such is the kingdom of heaven.
  No glory that ever was shed
From the crowning star of the seven
  That crown the north world's head,

No word that ever was spoken
  Of human or godlike tongue,
Gave ever such godlike token
  Since human harps were strung.

No sign that ever was given
  To faithful or faithless eyes
Showed ever beyond clouds riven
  So clear a Paradise.

Earth's creeds may be seventy times seven
  And blood have defiled each creed:
If of such be the kingdom of heaven,
  It must be heaven indeed.

A CHILD'S LAUGHTER

  All the bells of heaven may ring,
  All the birds of heaven may sing,
  All the wells on earth may spring,
  All the winds on earth may bring
    All sweet sounds together;
  Sweeter far than all things heard,
  Hand of harper, tone of bird,
  Sound of woods at sundawn stirr'd,
  Welling water's winsome word,
    Wind in warm wan weather,

  One thing yet there is, that none
  Hearing ere its chime be done
  Knows not well the sweetest one
  Heard of man beneath the sun,
    Hoped in heaven hereafter;
  Soft and strong and loud and light,
  Very sound of very light
  Heard from morning's rosiest height,
  When the soul of all delight
    Fills a child's clear laughter.

  Golden bells of welcome roll'd
  Never forth such notes, nor told

Hours so blithe in tones so bold,
As the radiant mouth of gold
  Here that rings forth heaven.
If the golden-crested wren
Were a nightingale—why, then
Something seen and heard of men
Might be half as sweet as when
  Laughs a child of seven.

A BABY'S DEATH*

I

A little soul scarce fledged for earth
Takes wing with heaven again for goal
Even while we hailed as fresh from birth
  A little soul.

Our thoughts ring sad as bells that toll,
Not knowing beyond this blind world's girth
What things are writ in heaven's full scroll.

Our fruitfulness is there but dearth,
And all things held in time's control
Seem there, perchance, ill dreams, not worth
  A little soul.

II

The little feet that never trod
Earth, never strayed in field or street,
What hand leads upward back to God
  The little feet?

A rose in June's most honied heat,
When life makes keen the kindling sod,
Was not so soft and warm and sweet.

Their pilgrimage's period
A few swift moons have seen complete
Since mother's hands first clasped and shod
  The little feet.

III

The little hands that never sought
Earth's prizes, worthless all as sands,
What gift has death, God's servant, brought
  The little hands?

We ask: but love's self silent stands,
Love, that lends eyes and wings to thought
To search where death's dim heaven expands.

Ere this, perchance, though love knew nought,
Flowers fill them, grown in lovelier lands,
Where hands of guiding angels caught
  The little hands.

* L'envoi, or "the despatch," was the name formerly given to the closing lines of a *ballade*, containing an address to some prince, or poet's patron; see *The Compleynt of Chaucer to his Purse*, p. 62. In modern imitations, this address can be only a formula and is frequently omitted, the *envoi* being merely a summary, or an appended stanza completing the metrical scheme.

* From *A Century of Roundels*. Of the poem here given in part there are seven sections, each in the form of a roundel with regularly recurring refrain. The last three sections, however, vary in length of line, and being of a personal nature detract from the universal appeal of the first four.

IV

The little eyes that never knew
Light other than of dawning skies,
What new life now lights up anew
    The little eyes?

Who knows but on their sleep may rise
Such light as never heaven let through
To lighten earth from Paradise?

No storm, we know, may change the blue
Soft heaven that haply death descries;
No tears, like these in ours, bedew
    The little eyes.

FROM TRISTRAM OF LYONESSE†

PRELUDE. TRISTRAM AND ISEULT

Love, that is first and last of all things made,
The light that has the living world for shade,
The spirit that for temporal veil has on
The souls of all men woven in unison,
One fiery raiment with all lives inwrought
And lights of sunny and starry deed and
    thought,
And alway through new act and passion new
Shines the divine same body and beauty
    through,
The body spiritual of fire and light
That is to worldly noon as noon to night; 10
Love, that is flesh upon the spirit of man
And spirit within the flesh whence breath be-
    gan;
Love, that keeps all the choir of lives in chime;
Love, that is blood within the veins of time;
That wrought the whole world without stroke of
    hand,
Shaping the breadth of sea, the length of land,
And with the pulse and motion of his breath
Through the great heart of the earth strikes life
    and death,
The sweet twain chords that make the sweet
    tune live
Through day and night of things alternative, 20
Through silence and through sound of stress
    and strife,

† In the long lyrical epic thus named, Swinburne
tells again the story of Tristram and Iseult,
which shares with that of Siegfried and
Brunhild the distinction of being one of the
greatest love stories of the world. "The
world of Swinburne," says Professor Woodberry, "is well symbolized by that Zodiac of
the burning signs of love that he named in
the prelude to *Tristram of Lyonesse*,—the
signs of Helen, Hero, Alcyone, Iseult, Rosamond, Dido, Juliet, Cleopatra, Francesca,
Thisbe, Angelica, Guenevere; under the
heavens of these starry names the poet moves
in his place apart and sees his visions of
woe and wrath and weaves his dream of the
loves and the fates of men."

And ebb and flow of dying death and life;
Love, that sounds loud or light in all men's
    ears,
Whence all men's eyes take fire from sparks of
    tears,
That binds on all men's feet or chains or wings;
Love, that is root and fruit of terrene things;
Love, that the whole world's waters shall not
    drown,
The whole world's fiery forces not burn down;
Love, that what time his own hands guard his
    head
The whole world's wrath and strength shall not
    strike dead; 30
Love, that if once his own hands make his grave
The whole world's pity and sorrow shall not
    save;
Love, that for very life shall not be sold,
Nor bought nor bound with iron nor with gold;
So strong that heaven, could love bid heaven
    farewell,
Would turn to fruitless and unflowering hell;
So sweet that hell, to hell could love be given,
Would turn to splendid and sonorous heaven;
Love that is fire within thee and light above,
And lives by grace of nothing but of love; 40
Through many and lovely thoughts and much
    desire
Led these twain to the life of tears and fire;
Through many and lovely days and much de-
    light
Led these twain to the lifeless life of night.
    Yea, but what then? albeit all this were thus,
And soul smote soul and left it ruinous,
And love led love as eyeless men lead men,
Through chance by chance to deathward—Ah,
    what then?
Hath love not likewise led them further yet,
Out through the years where memories rise and
    set, 50
Some large as suns, some moon-like warm and
    pale,
Some starry-sighted, some through clouds that
    sail
Seen as red flame through spectral float of
    fume,
Each with the blush of its own special bloom
On the fair face of its own coloured light,
Distinguishable in all the host of night,
Divisible from all the radiant rest
And separable in splendour? Hath the best
Light of love's all, of all that burn and move,
A better heaven than heaven is? Hath not
    love 60
Made for all these their sweet particular air
To shine in, their own beams and names to bear,
Their ways to wander and their wards to keep,

Till story and song and glory and all things
  sleep?
Hath he not plucked from death of lovers dead
Their musical soft memories, and kept red
The rose of their remembrance in men's eyes,
The sunsets of their stories in his skies,
The blush of their dead blood in lips that speak
Of their dead lives, and in the listener's cheek
That trembles with the kindling pity lit   71
In gracious hearts for some sweet fever-fit,
A fiery pity enkindled of pure thought
By tales that make their honey out of nought,
The faithless faith that lives without belief
Its light life through, the griefless ghost of
  grief?
Yea, as warm night refashions the sere blood
In storm-struck petal or in sun-struck bud,
With tender hours and tempering dew to cure
The hunger and thirst of day's distemperature
And ravin of the dry discolouring hours,   81
Hath he not bid relume their flameless flowers
With summer fire and heat of lamping song
And bid the short-lived things, long dead, live
  long,
And thought remake their wan funereal fames,
And the sweet shining signs of women's names,
That mark the months out and the weeks anew
He moves in changeless change of seasons
  through
To fill the days up of his dateless year,
Flame from Queen Helen to Queen Guenevere?
For first of all the sphery signs whereby   91
Love severs light from darkness, and most high,
In the white front of January there glows
The rose-red sign of Helen like a rose:[1]
And gold-eyed as the shore-flower shelterless
Whereon the sharp-breathed sea blows bitter-
  ness,
A storm-star that the seafarers of love
Strain their wind-wearied eyes for glimpses of,
Shoots keen through February's grey frost and
  damp
The lamp-like star of Hero for a lamp;   100
The star that Marlowe[2] sang into our skies
With mouth of gold, and morning in his eyes;
And in clear March across the rough blue sea
The signal sapphire of Alcyone[3]
Makes bright the blown brows of the wind-foot
  year;
And shining like a sunbeam-smitten tear
Full ere it fall, the fair next sign in sight
Burns opal-wise with April-coloured light
When air is quick with song and rain and flame,
My birth-month star that in love's heaven hath
  name   110

Iseult,[4] a light of blossom and beam and
  shower,
My singing sign that makes the song-tree
  flower;
Next like a pale and burning pearl beyond
The rose-white sphere of flower-named Rosa-
  mond[5]
Signs the sweet head of Maytime; and for June
Flares like an angered and storm-reddening
  moon
Her signal sphere, whose Carthaginian pyre
Shadowed her traitor's flying sail with fire;[6]
Next, glittering as the wine-bright jacinth-
  stone,
A star south-risen that first to music shone,   120
The keen girl-star of golden Juliet[7] bears
Light northward to the month whose forehead
  wears
Her name for flower upon it, and his trees
Mix their deep English song with Veronese;
And like an awful sovereign chrysolite
Burning, the supreme fire that blinds the night,
The hot gold head of Venus kissed by Mars,
A sun-flower among small sphered flowers of
  stars,
The light of Cleopatra[8] fills and burns
The hollow of heaven whence ardent August
  yearns;   130
And fixed and shining as the sister-shed
Sweet tears for Phaethon disorbed and dead,[9]
The pale bright autumn's amber-coloured
  sphere,
That through September sees the saddening
  year
As love sees change through sorrow, hath to
  name
Francesca's; and the star that watches flame
The embers of the harvest overgone
Is Thisbe's, slain of love in Babylon,[10]
Set in the golden girdle of sweet signs
A blood-bright ruby; last save one light shines
An eastern wonder of sphery chrysopras,   141
The star that made men mad, Angelica's;[11]
And latest named and lordliest, with a sound

1 Homer : *The Iliad.*
2 In his *Hero and Leander.*
3 Ovid's *Metamorphoses,* xi.

4 Her story has been told by Malory, Tennyson
  (*Idylls of the King,* "The Last Tournament"),
  Arnold, Wagner, etc.
5 The "Fair Rosamond" of Henry II. See Scott's
  The Talisman and *Woodstock.*
6 Virgil : *Aeneid,* iv.
7 Shakespeare : *Romeo and Juliet.*
8 Shakespeare : *Antony and Cleopatra.*
9 Alluding to the story that after Phaethon's fatal
  fall with the chariot of the sun, his sisters,
  the Heliades, mourned for him until they
  were changed into poplars and their tears
  into amber. The story of Paolo and Francesca is immortalized in Dante's *Inferno.*
10 Chaucer : *Legend of Good Women* (see p. 60).
11 Boiardo : *Orlando Innamorato ;* Ariosto : *Orlando
  Furioso.* Angelica's coquetry drove Orlando
  mad.

Of swords and harps in heaven that ring it
  round,
Last love-light and last love-song of the year's,
Gleams like a glorious emerald Guenevere's.[12]
These are the signs wherethrough the year sees
  move,
Full of the sun, the sun-god which is love,
A fiery body blood-red from the heart
Outward, with fire-white wings made wide apart,
That close not and unclose not, but upright   151
Steered without wind by their own light and
  might,
Sweep through the flameless fire of air that
  rings
From heaven to heaven with thunder of wheels
  and wings
And antiphones of motion-moulded rhyme
Through spaces out of space and timeless time.
So shine above dead chance and conquered
  change
The spherèd signs, and leave without their
  range
Doubt and desire, and hope with fear for wife,
Pale pains, and pleasures long worn out of life.
Yea, even the shadows of them spiritless,   161
Through the dim door of sleep that seem to
  press,
Forms without form, a piteous people and
  blind,
Men and no men, whose lamentable kind
The shadow of death and shadow of life compel
Through semblances of heaven and false-faced
  hell,
Through dreams of light and dreams of dark-
  ness tost
On waves innavigable, are these so lost?
Shapes that wax pale and shift in swift strange
  wise,
Void faces with unspeculative eyes,   170
Dim things that gaze and glare, dead mouths
  that move,
Featureless heads discrowned of hate and love,
Mockeries and masks of motion and mute
  breath,
Leavings of life, the superflux of death—
If these things and no more than these things be
Left when man ends or changes, who can see?
Or who can say with what more subtle sense
Their subtler natures taste in air less dense
A life less thick and palpable than ours,
Warmed with faint fires and sweetened with
  dead flowers   180
And measured by low music? how time fares
In that wan time-forgotten world of theirs,
Their pale poor world too deep for sun or star
To live in, where the eyes of Helen are,

And hers[13] who made as God's own eyes t
  shine
The eyes that met them of the Florentine,
Wherein the godhead thence transfigured lit
All time for all men with the shadow of it;
Ah, and these too felt on them as God's grac
The pity and glory of this man's breathin
  face;   19
For these too, these my lovers, these my twain
Saw Dante,[14] saw God visible by pain,
With lips that thundered and with feet tha
  trod
Before men's eyes incognisable God;
Saw love and wrath and light and night and fir
Live with one life and at one mouth respire,
And in one golden sound their whole soul hear
Sounding, one sweet immitigable word.
  They have the night, who had like us th
    day;[*]
We, whom day binds, shall have the night a
  they.   20
We, from the fetters of the light unbound,
Healed of our wound of living, shall slee
  sound.
All gifts but one the jealous God may keep
From our soul's longing, one he cannot—sleep
This, though he grudge all other grace t
  prayer,
This grace his closed hand cannot choose bu
  spare.
This, though his ear be sealed to all that live
Be it lightly given or lothly, God must give.
We, as the men whose name on earth is none
We too shall surely pass out of the sun;   21
Out of the sound and eyeless light of things,
Wide as the stretch of life's time-wandering
  wings,
Wide as the naked world and shadowless,
And long-lived as the world's own weariness.
Us too, when all the fires of time are cold,
The heights shall hide us and the depths shal
  hold.
Us too, when all the tears of time are dry,
The night shall lighten from her tearless eye.
Blind is the day and eyeless all its light,
But the large unbewildered eye of night   22
Hath sense and speculation; and the sheer
Limitless length of lifeless life and clear,
The timeless space wherein the brief world
  move

12 Cf. Mallory, Tennyson, etc.

13 Dante's Beatrice.
14 *Inferno*, v, 7.
* In this passage, with its rapt contemplation and
  solemn music, Swinburne has surely attaine
  to that "high seriousness" which Matthew
  Arnold regarded as the mark of the greates
  poetry. A portion of it reads not unlike a
  expansion of *Paradise Lost*, Book II, line
  149, 150.

Clothed with light life and fruitful with light
love,
With hopes that threaten, and with fears that
cease,
Past fear and hope, hath in it only peace.
  Yet of these lives inlaid with hopes and
fears,
Spun fine as fire and jewelled thick with tears,
These lives made out of loves that long since
were,
Lives wrought as ours of earth and burning
air,   230
Fugitive flame, and water of secret springs,
And clothed with joys and sorrows as with
wings,
Some yet are good, if aught be good, to save
Some while from washing wreck and wrecking
wave.
Was such not theirs, the twain I take, and give
Out of my life to make their dead life live
Some days of mine, and blow my living breath
Between dead lips forgotten even of death?
So many and many ere me have given my twain
Love and live song and honey-hearted pain, 240
Whose root is sweetness and whose fruit is
sweet,
So many and with such joy have tracked their
feet,
What should I do to follow? yet I too,
I have the heart to follow, many or few
Be the feet gone before me; for the way,
Rose-red with remnant roses of the day
Westward, and eastward white with stars that
break,
Between the green and foam is fair to take
For any sail the sea-wind steers for me
From morning into morning, sea to sea.   250

WALTER PATER (1839-1894)

THE CHILD IN THE HOUSE*

As Florian Deleal walked, one hot afternoon,
he overtook by the wayside a poor aged man,
and, as he seemed weary with the road, helped
him on with the burden which he carried, a
certain distance. And as the man told his
story, it chanced that he named the place, a
little place in the neighbourhood of a great city,
where Florian had passed his earliest years,
but which he had never since seen, and, the

* When originally published in 1878 this essay
was denominated an "Imaginary Portrait,"
though it is doubtless in some measure autobiographical. As an account of the development of an extremely sensitive and impres-
sionable youth, it holds a unique place in our
literature. On Pater's philosophy and style,
see *Eng. Lit.*, p. 382.

story told,[1] went forward on his journey comforted. And that night, like a reward for his
pity, a dream of that place came to Florian, a
dream which did for him the office of the finer
sort of memory, bringing its object to mind
with a great clearness, yet, as sometimes happens in dreams, raised a little above itself, and
above ordinary retrospect. The true aspect of
the place, especially of the house there in which
he had lived as a child, the fashion of its doors,
its hearths, its windows, the very scent upon
the air of it, was with him in sleep for a season; only, with tints more musically[2] blent on
wall and floor, and some finer light and shadow
running in and out along its curves and angles,
and with all its little carvings daintier. He
awoke with a sigh at the thought of almost
thirty years which lay between him and that
place, yet with a flutter of pleasure still within
him at the fair light, as if it were a smile, upon
it. And it happened that this accident of his
dream was just the thing needed for the beginning of a certain design he then had in view,
the noting, namely, of some things in the story
of his spirit—in that process of brain-building
by which we are, each one of us, what we are.
With the image of the place so clear and
favourable upon him, he fell to thinking of
himself therein, and how his thoughts had
grown up to him. In that half-spiritualised
house he could watch the better, over again,
the gradual expansion of the soul which had
come to be there—of which indeed, through
the law which makes the material objects about
them so large an element in children's lives, it
had actually become a part; inward and outward being woven through and through each
other into one inextricable texture—half, tint
and trace and accident of homely colour and
form, from the wood and the bricks; half,
mere[3] soul-stuff, floated thither from who knows
how far. In the house and garden of his dream
he saw a child moving, and could divide the
main streams at least of the winds that had
played on him, and study so the first stage in
that mental journey.

The *old house*, as when Florian talked of it
afterwards he always called it, (as all children
do, who can recollect a change of home, soon
enough but not too soon to mark a period in
their lives) really was an old house; and an
element of French descent in its inmates—

1 Pater's fondness for participles partakes rather
   more of Latin than of English style. Note,
   too, the difficulty of resuming, in the close of
   this sentence, the grammatical subject of the
   beginning.
2 harmoniously
3 pure, unmixed

descent from Watteau, the old court-painter,* one of whose gallant pieces still hung in one of the rooms—might explain, together with some other things, a noticeable trimness and comely whiteness about everything there—the curtains, the couches, the paint on the walls with which the light and shadow played so delicately; might explain also the tolerance of the great poplar in the garden, a tree most often despised by English people, but which French people love, having observed a certain fresh way its leaves have of dealing with the wind, making it sound, in never so slight a stirring of the air, like running water.

The old-fashioned, low wainscoting went round the rooms, and up the staircase with carved balusters and shadowy angles, landing half-way up at a broad window, with a swallow's nest below the sill, and the blossom of an old pear-tree showing across it in late April, against the blue, below which the perfumed juice of the find of fallen fruit in autumn was so fresh. At the next turning came the closet which held on its deep shelves the best china. Little angel faces and reedy flutings stood out round the fireplace of the children's room. And on the top of the house, above the large attic, where the white mice ran in the twilight—an infinite, unexplored wonderland of childish treasures, glass beads, empty scent-bottles still sweet, thrum of coloured silks, among its lumber—a flat space of roof, railed round, gave a view of the neighbouring steeples; for the house, as I said, stood near a great city, which sent up heavenwards, over the twisting weather-vanes, not seldom, its beds of rolling cloud and smoke, touched with storm or sunshine. But the child of whom I am writing did not hate the fog, because of the crimson lights which fell from it sometimes upon the chimneys, and the whites which gleamed through its openings, on summer mornings, on turret or pavement. For it is false to suppose that a child's sense of beauty is dependent on any choiceness or special fineness, in the objects which present themselves to it, though this indeed comes to be the rule with most of us in later life; earlier, in some degree, we see inwardly; and the child finds for itself, and with unstinted delight, a difference for the sense, in those whites and reds through the smoke on very homely buildings, and in the gold of the dandelions at the road-side, just beyond the houses, where not a handful of earth is virgin and untouched, in the lack of better ministries to its desire of beauty.†

This house then stood not far beyond the gloom and rumours of the town, among high garden-walls, bright all summer-time with Golden-rod, and brown-and-golden Wall-flower —*Flos Parietis,* as the children's Latin-reading father taught them to call it, while he was with them. Tracing back the threads of his complex spiritual habit, as he was used in after years to do, Florian found that he owed to the place many tones of sentiment afterwards customary with him, certain inward lights under which things most naturally presented themselves to him. The coming and going of travellers to the town along the way, the shadow of the streets, the sudden breath of the neighbouring gardens, the singular brightness of bright weather there, its singular darknesses which linked themselves in his mind to certain engraved illustrations in the old big Bible at home, the coolness of the dark, cavernous shops round the great church, with its giddy winding stair up to the pigeons and the bells—a citadel of peace in the heart of the trouble—all this acted on his childish fancy, so that ever afterwards the like aspects and incidents never failed to throw him into a well-recognised imaginative mood, seeming actually to have become a part of the texture of his mind. Also, Florian could trace home to this point a pervading preference in himself for a kind of comeliness and dignity, an *urbanity* literally, in modes of life, which he connected with the pale people of towns, and which made him susceptible to a kind of exquisite satisfaction in the trimness and well-considered grace of certain things and persons he afterwards met with, here and there, in his way through the world.

So the child of whom I am writing lived on there quietly; things without thus ministering to him, as he sat daily at the window with the birdcage hanging below it, and his mother taught him to read, wondering at the ease with which he learned, and at the quickness of his memory. The perfume of the little flowers of the lime-tree fell through the air upon them like rain; while time seemed to move ever more slowly to the murmur of the bees in it, till it almost stood still on June afternoons. How insignificant, at the moment, seem the influences of the sensible things which are tossed and fall and lie about us, so, or so, in the

---

* There may have been some family connection between Pater and Jean Baptiste Pater, a French painter of Watteau's time.

† This last clause is to be attached to the subject, "child." Pater's sentences often wind thus, by a devious route, to an unexpected end.

environment of early childhood. How indelibly, as we afterwards discover, they affect us; with what capricious attractions and associations they figure themselves on the white paper,‡ the smooth wax, of our ingenuous souls, as "with lead in the rock for ever,"[1] giving form and feature, and as it were assigned house-room in our memory, to early experiences of feeling and thought, which abide with us ever afterwards, thus, and not otherwise. The realities and passions, the rumours of the greater world without, steal in upon us, each by its own special little passage-way, through the wall of custom about us; and never afterwards quite detach themselves from this or that accident, or trick, in the mode of their first entrance to us. Our susceptibilities, the discovery of our powers, manifold experiences—our various experiences of the coming and going of bodily pain, for instance—belong to this or the other well-remembered place in the material habitation—that little white room with the window across which the heavy blossoms could beat so peevishly in the wind, with just that particular catch or throb, such a sense of teasing in it, on gusty mornings; and the early habitation thus gradually becomes a sort of material shrine or sanctuary of sentiment; a system of visible symbolism interweaves itself through all our thoughts and passions; and irresistibly, little shapes, voices, accidents—the angle at which the sun in the morning fell on the pillow— become parts of the great chain wherewith we are bound.

Thus far, for Florian, what all this had determined was a peculiarly strong sense of home —so forcible a motive with all of us—prompting to us our customary love of the earth, and the larger part of our fear of death, that revulsion we have from it, as from something strange, untried, unfriendly; though life-long imprisonment, they tell you, and final banishment from home is a thing bitterer still; the looking forward to but a short space, a mere childish *goûter*[2] and dessert of it, before the end, being so great a resource of effort to pilgrims and wayfarers, and the soldier in distant quarters, and lending, in lack of that, some power of solace to the thought of sleep in the home churchyard, at least—dead cheek by dead cheek, and with the rain soaking in upon one from above.

1 *Job*, xix. 24.
2 a slight repast, a taste
‡ Referring to Locke's familiar figure for the state of mind at birth (Locke did not believe in innate ideas). The next figure is derived from the ancient practice of writing on tablets of wax.

So powerful is this instinct, and yet accidents like those I have been speaking of so mechanically determine it; its essence being indeed the early familiar, as constituting our ideal, or typical conception, of rest and security. Out of so many possible conditions, just this for you and that for me, brings ever the unmistakable realisation of the delightful *chez soi;*[3] this for the Englishman, for me and you, with the closely-drawn white curtain and the shaded lamp; that, quite other, for the wandering Arab, who folds his tent every morning, and makes his sleeping-place among haunted ruins, or in old tombs.

With Florian then the sense of home became singularly intense, his good fortune being that the special character of his home was in itself so essentially home-like. As after many wanderings I have come to fancy that some parts of Surrey and Kent are, for Englishmen, the true landscape, true home-counties, by right, partly, of a certain earthy warmth in the yellow of the sand below their gorse-bushes, and of a certain gray-blue mist after rain, in the hollows of the hills there, welcome to fatigued eyes, and never seen farther south; so I think that the sort of house I have described, with precisely those proportions of red-brick and green, and with a just perceptible monotony in the subdued order of it, for its distinguishing note, is for Englishmen at least typically home-like. And so for Florian that general human instinct was reinforced by this special home-likeness in the place his wandering soul had happened to light on, as, in the second degree, its body and earthly tabernacle; the sense of harmony between his soul and its physical environment became, for a time at least, like perfectly played music, and the life led there singularly tranquil and filled with a curious sense of self-possession. The love of security, of an habitually undisputed standing-ground or sleeping-place, came to count for much in the generation and correcting of his thoughts, and afterwards as a salutary principle of restraint in all his wanderings of spirit. The wistful yearning towards home, in absence from it, as the shadows of evening deepened, and he followed in thought what was doing there from hour to hour, interpreted to him much of a yearning and regret he experienced afterwards, towards he knew not what, out of strange ways of feeling and thought in which, from time to time, his spirit found itself alone; and in the tears shed in such absences there seemed always to

3 at home

be some soul-subduing foretaste of what his last tears might be.

And the sense of security could hardly have been deeper, the quiet of the child's soul being one with the quiet of its home, a place "inclosed" and "sealed." But upon this assured place, upon the child's assured soul which resembled it, there came floating in from the larger world without, as at windows left ajar unknowingly, or over the high garden walls, two streams of impressions, the sentiments of beauty and pain—recognitions of the visible, tangible, audible loveliness of things, as a very real and somewhat tyrannous element in them —and of the sorrow of the world, of grown people and children and animals, as a thing not to be put by in them. From this point he could trace two predominant processes of mental change in him—the growth of an almost diseased sensibility to the spectacle of suffering, and, parallel with this, the rapid growth of a certain capacity of fascination by bright colour and choice form—the sweet curvings, for instance, of the lips of those who seemed to him comely persons, modulated in such delicate unison to the things they said or sang,—marking early the activity in him of a more than customary sensuousness, "the lust of the eye," as the Preacher says,* which might lead him, one day, how far! Could he have foreseen the weariness of the way! In music sometimes the two sorts of impressions came together, and he would weep, to the surprise of older people. Tears of joy too the child knew, also to older people's surprise; real tears, once, of relief from long-strung, childish expectation, when he found returned at evening, with new roses in her cheeks, the little sister who had been to a place where there was a wood, and brought back for him a treasure of fallen acorns, and black crow's feathers, and his peace at finding her again near him mingled all night with some intimate sense of the distant forest, the rumour of its breezes, with the glossy blackbirds aslant and the branches lifted in them, and of the perfect nicety of the little cups that fell. So those two elementary apprehensions of the tenderness and of the colour in things grew apace in him, and were seen by him afterwards to send their roots back into the beginnings of life. Let me note first some of the occasions of his recognition of the element of pain in things—incidents, now and again, which seemed suddenly to awake in him the whole force of that sentiment which Goethe has called the

Weltschmerz,[1] and in which the concentrated sorrow of the world seemed suddenly to lie heavy upon him. A book lay in an old bookcase, of which he cared to remember one picture—a woman sitting, with hands bound behind her, the dress, the cap, the hair, folded with a simplicity which touched him strangely, as if not by her own hands, but with some ambiguous care at the hands of others—Queen Marie Antoinette, on her way to execution—we all remember David's[2] drawing, meant merely to make her ridiculous. The face that had been so high had learned to be mute and resistless; but out of its very resistlessness, seemed now to call on men to have pity, and forbear; and he took note of that, as he closed the book, as a thing to look at again, if he should at any time find himself tempted to be cruel. Again, he would never quite forget the appeal in the small sister's face, in the garden under the lilacs, terrified at a spider lighted on her sleeve. He could trace back to the look then noted a certain mercy he conceived always for people in fear, even of little things, which seemed to make him, though but for a moment, capable of almost any sacrifice of himself. Impressible, susceptible persons, indeed, who had had their sorrows, lived about him; and this sensibility was due in part to the tacit influence of their presence, enforcing upon him habitually the fact that there are those who pass their days, as a matter of course, in a sort of "going quietly." Most poignantly of all he could recall, in unfading minutest circumstance, the cry on the stair, sounding bitterly through the house, and struck into his soul for ever, of an aged woman, his father's sister, come now to announce his death in distant India; how it seemed to make the aged woman like a child again; and, he knew not why, but this fancy was full of pity to him. There were the little sorrows of the dumb animals too—of the white angora, with a dark tail like an ermine's, and a face like a flower, who fell into a lingering sickness, and became quite delicately human in its valetudinarianism, and came to have a hundred different expressions of voice—how grew worse and worse, till it began to feel light too much for it, and at last, after a wild morning of pain, the little soul flickered away from the body, quite worn to death already, and now but feebly retaining it.

So he wanted another pet; and as there were starlings about the place, which could be taught

*The Preacher is Ecclesiastes, but the phrase "lust of the eyes" is in *I John*, ii, 16.

1 world-sorrow
2 Jacques Louis David, court-painter to Louis XVI. and to Napoleon.

to speak, one of them was caught, and he meant to treat it kindly; but in the night its young ones could be heard crying after it, and the responsive cry of the mother-bird towards them; and at last, with the first light, though not till after some debate with himself, he went down and opened the cage, and saw a sharp bound of the prisoner up to her nestlings; and therewith came the sense of remorse,—that he too was become an accomplice in moving, to the limit of his small power, the springs and handles of that great machine in things, constructed so ingeniously to play pain-fugues on the delicate nerve-work of living creatures.

I have remarked how, in the process of our brain-building, as the house of thought in which we live gets itself together, like some airy bird's-nest of floating thistle-down and chance straws, compact at last, little accidents have their consequence; and thus it happened that, as he walked one evening, a garden gate, usually closed, stood open; and lo! within, a great red hawthorn in full flower, embossing heavily the bleached and twisted trunk and branches, so aged that there were but few green leaves thereon—a plumage of tender, crimson fire out of the heart of the dry wood. The perfume of the tree had now and again reached him, in the currents of the wind, over the wall, and he had wondered what might be behind it, and was now allowed to fill his arms with the flowers—flowers enough for all the old blue-china pots along the chimney-piece, making *fête* in the children's room. Was it some periodic moment in the expansion of soul within him, or mere trick of heat in the heavily-laden summer air? But the beauty of the thing struck home to him feverishly; and in dreams all night he loitered along a magic roadway of crimson flowers, which seemed to open ruddily in thick, fresh masses about his feet, and fill softly all the little hollows in the banks on either side. Always afterwards, summer by summer, as the flowers came on, the blossom of the red hawthorn still seemed to him absolutely the reddest of all things; and the goodly crimson, still alive in the works of old Venetian masters or old Flemish tapestries, called out always from afar the recollection of the flame in those perishing little petals, as it pulsed gradually out of them, kept long in the drawers of an old cabinet. Also then, for the first time, he seemed to experience a passionateness in his relation to fair outward objects, an inexplicable excitement in their presence, which disturbed him, and from which he half longed to be free. A touch of regret or desire mingled all night

with the remembered presence of the red flowers, and their perfume in the darkness about him; and the longing for some undivined, entire possession of them was the beginning of a revelation to him, growing ever clearer, with the coming of the gracious summer guise of fields and trees and persons in each succeeding year, of a certain, at times seemingly exclusive, predominance in his interests, of beautiful physical things, a kind of tyranny of the senses over him.

In later years he came upon philosophies which occupied him much in the estimate of the proportion of the sensuous and the ideal elements in human knowledge, the relative parts they bear in it; and, in his intellectual scheme, was led to assign very little to the abstract thought, and much to its sensible vehicle or occasion. Such metaphysical speculation did but reinforce what was instinctive in his way of receiving the world, and for him, everywhere, that sensible vehicle or occasion became, perhaps only too surely, the necessary concomitant of any perception of things, real enough to be of any weight or reckoning, in his house of thought. There were times when he could think of the necessity he was under of associating all thoughts to touch and sight, as a sympathetic link between himself and actual, feeling, living objects; a protest in favour of real men and women against mere gray, unreal abstractions; and he remembered gratefully how the Christian religion, hardly less than the religion of the ancient Greeks, translating so much of its spiritual verity into things that may be seen, condescends in part to sanction this infirmity, if so it be, of our human existence, wherein the world of sense is so much with us,[1] and welcomed this thought as a kind of keeper and sentinel over his soul therein. But certainly, he came more and more to be unable to care for, or think of soul but as in an actual body, or of any world but that wherein are water and trees, and where men and women look, so or so, and press actual hands. It was the trick even his pity learned, fastening those who suffered in anywise to his affections by a kind of sensible attachments. He would think of Julian, fallen into incurable sickness, as spoiled in the sweet blossom of his skin like pale amber, and his honey-like hair; of Cecil, early dead, as cut off from the lilies, from golden summer days, from women's voices; and then what comforted him a little was the thought of the turning of the child's flesh to violets in the turf above him. And thinking of

[1] See Wordsworth's sonnet, p. 427.

the very poor, it was not the things which most men care most for that he yearned to give them; but fairer roses, perhaps, and power to taste quite as they will, at their ease and not task-burdened, a certain desirable, clear light in the new morning, through which sometimes he had noticed them, quite unconscious of it, on their way to their early toil.

So he yielded himself to these things, to be played upon by them like a musical instrument, and began to note with deepening watchfulness, but always with some puzzled, unutterable longing in his enjoyment, the phases of the seasons and of the growing or waning day, down even to the shadowy changes wrought on bare wall or ceiling—the light cast up from the snow, bringing out their darkest angles; the brown light in the cloud, which meant rain; that almost too austere clearness, in the protracted light of the lengthening day, before warm weather began, as if it lingered but to make a severer workday, with the school-books opened earlier and later; that beam of June sunshine, at last, as he lay awake before the time, a way of gold-dust across the darkness; all the humming, the freshness, the perfume of the garden seemed to lie upon it—and coming in one afternoon in September, along the red gravel walk, to look for a basket of yellow crab-apples left in the cool, old parlour, he remembered it the more, and how the colours struck upon him, because a wasp on one bitten apple stung him, and he felt the passion of sudden, severe pain. For this too brought its curious reflexions; and, in relief from it, he would wonder over it— how it had then been with him—puzzled at the depth of the charm or spell over him, which lay, for a little while at least, in the mere absence of pain; once, especially, when an older boy taught him to make flowers of sealing-wax, and he had burnt his hand badly at the lighted taper, and been unable to sleep. He remembered that also afterwards, as a sort of typical thing—a white vision of heat about him, clinging closely, through the languid scent of the ointments put upon the place to make it well.

Also, as he felt this pressure upon him of the sensible world, then, as often afterwards, there would come another sort of curious questioning how the last impressions of eye and ear might happen to him, how they would find him —the scent of the last flower, the soft yellowness of the last morning, the last recognition of some object of affection, hand or voice; it could not be but that the latest look of the eyes, before their final closing, would be strangely vivid; one would go with the hot tears, the cry,

the touch of the wistful bystander, impressed how deeply on one! or would it be, perhaps, a mere frail retiring of all things, great or little, away from one, into a level distance?

For with this desire of physical beauty mingled itself early the fear of death—the fear of death intensified by the desire of beauty. Hitherto he had never gazed upon dead faces, as sometimes, afterwards, at the *Morgue* in Paris, or in that fair cemetery at Munich, where all the dead must go and lie in state before burial, behind glass windows, among the flowers and incense and holy candles—the aged clergy with their sacred ornaments, the young men in their dancing-shoes and spotless white linen—after which visits, those waxen, resistless faces would always live with him for many days, making the broadest sunshine sickly. The child had heard indeed of the death of his father, and how, in the Indian station, a fever had taken him, so that though not in action he had yet died as a soldier; and hearing of the "resurrection of the just,"[1] he could think of him as still abroad in the world, somehow, for his protection—a grand, though perhaps rather terrible figure, in beautiful soldier's things, like the figure in the picture of Joshua's Vision in the Bible[2]—and of that, round which the mourners moved so softly, and afterwards with such solemn singing, as but a worn-out garment left at a deserted lodging. So it was, until on a summer day he walked with his mother through a fair churchyard. In a bright dress he rambled among the graves, in the gay weather, and so came, in one corner, upon an open grave for a child—a dark space on the brilliant grass—the black mould lying heaped up round it, weighing down the little jewelled branches of the dwarf rosebushes in flower. And therewith came, full-grown, never wholly to leave him, with the certainty that even children do sometimes die, the physical horror of death, with its wholly selfish recoil from the association of lower forms of life, and the suffocating weight above. No benign, grave figure in beautiful soldier's things any longer abroad in the world for his protection! only a few poor, piteous bones; and above them, possibly, a certain sort of figure he hoped not to see. For sitting one day in the garden below an open window, he heard people talking, and could not but listen, how, in a sleepless hour, a sick woman had seen one of the dead sitting beside her, come to call her hence; and from the broken talk evolved with much clearness the notion that not all those dead people had really

1 *Luke*, xiv. 14.   2 *Joshua*, v. 13.

departed to the churchyard, nor were quite so motionless as they looked, but led a secret, half-fugitive life in their old homes, quite free by night, though sometimes visible in the day, dodging from room to room, with no great goodwill towards those who shared the place with them. All night the figure sat beside him in the reveries of his broken sleep, and was not quite gone in the morning—an odd, irreconcilable new member of the household, making the sweet familiar chambers unfriendly and suspect by its uncertain presence. He could have hated the dead he had pitied so, for being thus. Afterwards he came to think of those poor, home-returning ghosts, which all men have fancied to themselves—the *revenants*—pathetically, as crying, or beating with vain hands at the doors, as the wind came, their cries distinguishable in it as a wilder inner note. But, always making death more unfamiliar still, that old experience would ever, from time to time, return to him; even in the living he sometimes caught its likeness; at any time or place, in a moment, the faint atmosphere of the chamber of death would be breathed around him, and the image with the bound chin, the quaint smile, the straight, stiff feet, shed itself across the air upon the bright carpet, amid the gayest company, or happiest communing with himself.

To most children the sombre questionings to which impressions like these attach themselves, if they come at all, are actually suggested by religious books, which therefore they often regard with much secret distaste, and dismiss, as far as possible, from their habitual thoughts as a too depressing element in life. To Florian such impressions, these misgivings as to the ultimate tendency of the years, of the relationship between life and death, had been suggested spontaneously in the natural course of his mental growth by a strong innate sense for the soberer tones in things, further strengthened by actual circumstances; and religious sentiment, that system of biblical ideas in which he had been brought up, presented itself to him as a thing that might soften and dignify, and light up as with a "lively hope,"[3] a melancholy already deeply settled in him. So he yielded himself easily to religious impressions, and with a kind of mystical appetite for sacred things; the more as they came to him through a saintly person who loved him tenderly, and believed that this early preoccupation with them already marked the child out for a saint. He began to love, for their own sakes, church lights, holy days, all that

belonged to the comely order of the sanctuary, the secrets of its white linen, and holy vessels, and fonts of pure water; and its hieratic purity and simplicity became the type of something he desired always to have about him in actual life. He pored over the pictures in religious books, and knew by heart the exact mode in which the wrestling angel grasped Jacob, how Jacob looked in his mysterious sleep, how the bells and pomegranates were attached to the hem of Aaron's vestment, sounding sweetly as he glided over the turf of the holy place.[4] His way of conceiving religion came then to be in effect what it ever afterwards remained—a sacred history indeed, but still more a sacred ideal, a transcendent version or representation, under intenser and more expressive light and shade, of human life and its familiar or exceptional incidents, birth, death, marriage, youth, age, tears, joy, rest, sleep, waking—a mirror, towards which men might turn away their eyes from vanity and dullness, and see themselves therein as angels, with their daily meat and drink, even, become a kind of sacred transaction—a complementary strain or burden, applied to our every-day existence, whereby the stray snatches of music in it re-set themselves, and fall into the scheme of some higher and more consistent harmony. A place adumbrated itself in his thoughts, wherein those sacred personalities, which are at once the reflex and the pattern of our nobler phases of life, housed themselves; and this region in his intellectual scheme all subsequent experience did but tend still further to realise and define. Some ideal, hieratic persons he would always need to occupy it and keep a warmth there. And he could hardly understand those who felt no such need at all, finding themselves quite happy without such heavenly companionship, and sacred double of their life, beside them.

Thus a constant substitution of the typical for the actual took place in his thoughts. Angels might be met by the way, under English elm or beech-tree; mere messengers seemed like angels, bound on celestial errands; a deep mysticity brooded over real meetings and partings; marriages were made in heaven; and deaths also, with hands of angels thereupon, to bear soul and body quietly asunder, each to its appointed rest. All the acts and accidents of daily life borrowed a sacred colour and significance; the very colours of things became themselves weighty with meanings like the sacred stuffs of Moses' tabernacle,[5] full of

3 *I Peter*, i, 3.

4 *Genesis*, xxxii, 24; xxviii, 11; *Exodus*, xxviii, 33-35.
5 *Exodus*, xxvi.

penitence or peace. Sentiment, congruous in the first instance only with those divine transactions, the deep, effusive unction of the House of Bethany,[6] was assumed as the due attitude for the reception of our every-day existence; and for a time he walked through the world in a sustained, not unpleasurable awe, generated by the habitual recognition, beside every circumstance and event of life, of its celestial correspondent.

Sensibility—the desire of physical beauty—a strange biblical awe, which made any reference to the unseen act on him like solemn music—these qualities the child took away with him, when, at about the age of twelve years, he left the old house, and was taken to live in another place. He had never left home before, and, anticipating much from this change, had long dreamed over it, jealously counting the days till the time fixed for departure should come; had been a little careless about others even, in his strong desire for it—when Lewis fell sick, for instance, and they must wait still two days longer. At last the morning came, very fine; and all things—the very pavement with its dust, at the roadside—seemed to have a white, pearl-like lustre in them. They were to travel by a favourite road on which he had often walked a certain distance, and on one of those two prisoner days, when Lewis was sick, had walked farther than ever before, in his great desire to reach the new place. They had started and gone a little way when a pet bird was found to have been left behind, and must even now—so it presented itself to him —have already all the appealing fierceness and wild self-pity at heart of one left by others to perish of hunger in a closed house; and he returned to fetch it, himself in hardly less stormy distress. But as he passed in search of it from room to room, lying so pale, with a look of meekness in their denudation, and at last through that little, stripped white room, the aspect of the place touched him like the face of one dead; and a clinging back towards it came over him, so intense that he knew it would last long, and spoiling all his pleasure in the realisation of a thing so eagerly anticipated. And so, with the bird found, but himself in an agony of home-sickness, thus capriciously sprung up within him, he was driven quickly away, far into the rural distance, so fondly speculated on, of that favourite country-road.

6 The house of Simon the leper, where the woman poured the box of ointment on Jesus' head— a "deep, effusive unction." See *Matthew,* xxvi, 7.

ROBERT LOUIS STEVENSON
(1850-1894)
EL DORADO*

It seems as if a great deal were attainable in a world where there are so many marriages and decisive battles, and where we all, at certain hours of the day, and with great gusto and despatch, stow a portion of victuals finally and irretrievably into the bag which contains us. And it would seem also, on a hasty view, that the attainment of as much as possible was the one goal of man's contentious life. And yet, as regards the spirit, this is but a semblance. We live in an ascending scale when we live happily, one thing leading to another in an endless series. There is always a new horizon for onward-looking men,[1] and although we dwell on a small planet, immersed in petty business and not enduring beyond a brief period of years, we are so constituted that our hopes are inaccessible, like stars, and the term of hoping is prolonged until the term of life. To be truly happy is a question of how we begin and not of how we end, of what we want and not of what we have. An aspiration is a joy forever,[2] a possession as solid as a landed estate, a fortune which we can never exhaust and which gives us year by year a revenue of pleasurable activity. To have many of these is to be spiritually rich. Life is only a very dull and ill-directed theatre unless we have some interests in the piece; and to those who have neither art nor science, the world is a mere arrangement of colours, or a rough footway where they may very well break their shins. It is in virtue of his own desires and curiosities that any man continues to exist with even patience, that he is charmed by the look of things and people, and that he wakens every morning with a renewed appetite for work and pleasure. Desire and curiosity are the two eyes through which he sees the world in the most enchanted colours: it is they that make women beautiful or fossils interesting: and the man may squander his estate and come to beggary, but if he keeps these two amulets he is still rich in the possibilities of pleasure. Suppose he

1 Cp. Tennyson's famous figure, *Ulysses,* 19-21.
2 Echoed from Keats's *Endymion,* 1.

* Spanish : The Gilded, or Golden. The name was originally given to a fabulous king of a wealthy city supposed to exist somewhere in South America, the object of much search in the 16th century. It was later applied to the city, and has now become a name for the object of any visionary quest. The essay is from *Virginibus Puerisque,* 1881, and is reprinted, along with the selections that follow, by permission of Messrs. Charles Scribner's Sons, who hold the copyright.

could take one meal so compact and comprehensive that he should never hunger any more; suppose him, at a glance, to take in all the features of the world and allay the desire for knowledge; suppose him to do the like in any province of experience—would not that man be in a poor way for amusement ever after?

One who goes touring on foot with a single volume in his knapsack reads with circumspection, pausing often to reflect, and often laying the book down to contemplate the landscape or the prints in the inn parlour; for he fears to come to an end of his entertainment, and be left companionless on the last stages of his journey. A young fellow recently finished the works of Thomas Carlyle, winding up, if we remember aright, with the ten note-books upon Frederick the Great. "What!" cried the young fellow, in consternation, "is there no more Carlyle? Am I left to the daily papers?" A more celebrated instance is that of Alexander, who wept bitterly because he had no more worlds to subdue. And when Gibbon had finished the *Decline and Fall*,[3] he had only a few moments of joy; and it was with a "sober melancholy" that he parted from his labours.

Happily we all shoot at the moon with ineffectual arrows; our hopes are set on inaccessible El Dorado; we come to an end of nothing here below. Interests are only plucked up to sow themselves again, like mustard. You would think, when the child was born, there would be an end to trouble; and yet it is only the beginning of fresh anxieties; and when you have seen it through its teething and its education, and at last its marriage, alas! it is only to have new fears, new quivering sensibilities, with every day; and the health of your children's children grows as touching a concern as that of your own. Again, when you have married your wife, you would think you were got upon a hilltop, and might begin to go downward by an easy slope. But you have only ended courting to begin marriage. Falling in love and winning love are often difficult tasks to overbearing and rebellious spirits; but to keep in love is also a business of some importance, to which both man and wife must bring kindness and goodwill. The true love story commences at the altar, when there lies before the married pair a most beautiful contest of wisdom and generosity, and a life-long struggle towards an unattainable ideal. Unattainable? Ay, surely unattainable, from the very fact that they are two instead of one.

"Of making books there is no end," complained the Preacher;[4] and did not perceive how highly he was praising letters as an occupation. There is no end, indeed, to making books or experiments, or to travel, or to gathering wealth. Problem gives rise to problem. We may study for ever, and we are never as learned as we would. We have never made a statue worthy of our dreams. And when we have discovered a continent, or crossed a chain of mountains, it is only to find another ocean or another plain upon the further side. In the infinite universe there is room for our swiftest diligence and to spare. It is not like the works of Carlyle, which can be read to an end. Even in a corner of it, in a private park, or in the neighbourhood of a single hamlet, the weather and the seasons keep so deftly changing that although we walk there for a lifetime there will be always something new to startle and delight us.

There is only one wish realisable on the earth; only one thing that can be perfectly attained: Death. And from a variety of circumstances we have no one to tell us whether it be worth attaining.

A strange picture we make on our way to our chimæras, ceaselessly marching, grudging ourselves the time for rest; indefatigable, adventurous pioneers. It is true that we shall never reach the goal; it is even more than probable that there is no such place; and if we lived for centuries and were endowed with the powers of a god, we should find ourselves not much nearer what we wanted at the end. O toiling hands of mortals! O unwearied feet, travelling ye know not whither! Soon, soon, it seems to you, you must come forth on some conspicuous hilltop, and but a little way further, against the setting sun, descry the spires of El Dorado. Little do ye know your own blessedness; for to travel hopefully is a better thing than to arrive, and the true success is to labour.

THE MAROON*

Of the beauties of Anaho books might be written. I remember waking about three, to find the air temperate and scented. The long swell brimmed into the bay, and seemed to fill

[3] A twenty-four years' labor. See *Eng. Lit.*, p. 213.

[4] *Ecclesiastes*, xii, 12.
* A maroon is one who has been "marooned," or abandoned on an island. This chapter is taken from *In the South Seas*, 1891. Stevenson made a cruise among the South Sea Islands in the yacht *Casco*, which he chartered at San Francisco in 1888. Anaho is a native village of Nuka-hiva, the chief island of the Marquesas. Kanaka, properly a Sandwich-Islander, is a general name for a South Sea Islander or his speech.

it full and then subside. Gently, deeply, and silently the *Casco* rolled; only at times a block[1] piped like a bird. Oceanward, the heaven was bright with stars and the sea with their reflections. If I looked to that side, I might have sung with the Hawaiian poet:

Ua maomao ka lani, ua kahaea luna,
Ua pipi ka maka o ka hoku.
(The heavens were fair, they stretched above,
Many were the eyes of the stars.)

And then I turned shoreward, and high squalls were overhead; the mountains loomed up black; and I could have fancied I had slipped ten thousand miles away and was anchored in a Highland loch; that when the day came, it would show pine, and heather, and green fern, and roofs of turf sending up the smoke of peats; and the alien speech that should next greet my ears must be Gaelic, not Kanaka.

And day, when it came, brought other sights and thoughts. I have watched the morning break in many quarters of the world; it has been certainly one of the chief joys of my existence, and the dawn that I saw with most emotion shone upon the bay of Anaho. The mountains abruptly overhang the port with every variety of surface and of inclination, lawn, and cliff, and forest. Not one of these but wore its proper tint of saffron, of sulphur, of the clove, and of the rose. The lustre was like that of satin; on the lighter hues there seemed to float an efflorescence; a solemn bloom appeared on the more dark. The light itself was the ordinary light of morning, colourless and clean; and on this ground of jewels, pencilled out the least detail of drawing. Meanwhile, around the hamlet, under the palms, where the blue shadow lingered, the red coals of cocoa-husk and the light trails of smoke betrayed the awakening business of the day; along the beach men and women, lads and lasses, were returning from the bath in bright raiment, red and blue and green, such as we delighted to see in the coloured little pictures of our childhood; and presently the sun had cleared the eastern hill, and the glow of the day was over all.

The glow continued and increased, the business, from the main part, ceased before it had begun. Twice in the day there was a certain stir of shepherding along the seaward hills. At times a canoe went out to fish. At times a woman or two languidly filled a basket in the cotton patch. At times a pipe would sound out of the shadow of a house, ringing the changes on its three notes, with an effect like *Que le jour me dure*[2] repeated endlessly. Or at times, across a corner of the bay, two natives might communicate in the Marquesan manner with conventional whistlings. All else was sleep and silence. The surf broke and shone around the shores; a species of black crane fished in the broken water; the black pigs were continually galloping by on some affair; but the people might never have awaked, or they might all be dead.

My favourite haunt was opposite the hamlet, where was a landing in a cove under a lianaed[3] cliff. The beach was lined with palms and a tree called the purao, something between the fig and mulberry in growth, and bearing a flower like a great yellow poppy with a maroon heart. In places rocks encroached upon the sand; the beach would be all submerged; and the surf would bubble warmly as high as to my knees, and play with cocoa-nut husks as our more homely ocean plays with wreck and wrack and bottles. As the reflux drew down, marvels of colour and design streamed between my feet; which I would grasp at, miss, or seize: now to find them what they promised, shells to grace a cabinet or be set in gold upon a lady's finger; now to catch only *maya*[4] of coloured sand, pounded fragments and pebbles, that, as soon as they were dry, became as dull and homely as the flints upon a garden path. I have toiled at this childish pleasure for hours in the strong sun, conscious of my incurable ignorance; but too keenly pleased to be ashamed. Meanwhile, the blackbird (or his tropical understudy) would be fluting in the thickets overhead.

A little further, in the turn of the bay, a streamlet trickled in the bottom of a den,[5] thence spilling down a stair of rock into the sea. The draught of air drew down under the foliage in the very bottom of the den, which was a perfect arbour for coolness. In front it stood open on the blue bay and the *Casco* lying there under her awning and her cheerful colours. Overhead was a thatch of puraos, and over these again palms brandished their bright fans, as I have seen a conjurer make himself a halo out of naked swords. For in this spot, over a neck of low land at the foot of the mountains, the trade-wind streams into Anaho Bay in a flood of almost constant volume and velocity, and of a heavenly coolness.

It chanced one day that I was ashore in the cove with Mrs. Stevenson and the ship's cook.

1 pulley
2 "How heavy hangs the day on me!"
3 Covered with lianas, or tropical vines.
4 illusion (Hindu philosophy)
5 glen, dingle

Except for the *Casco* lying outside, and a crane or two, and the ever-busy wind and sea, the face of the world was of a prehistoric emptiness; life appeared to stand stockstill, and the sense of isolation was profound and refreshing. On a sudden, the trade-wind, coming in a gust over the isthmus, struck and scattered the fans of the palms above the den; and, behold! in two of the tops there sat a native, motionless as an idol, and watching us, you would have said, without a wink. The next moment the tree closed, and the glimpse was gone. This discovery of human presences latent overhead in a place where we had supposed ourselves alone, the immobility of our tree-top spies, and the thought that perhaps at all hours we were similarly supervised, struck us with a chill. Talk languished on the beach. As for the cook (whose conscience was not clear), he never afterwards set foot on shore, and twice, when the *Casco* appeared to be driving on the rocks, it was amusing to observe that man's alacrity; death, he was persuaded, awaiting him upon the beach. It was more than a year later, in the Gilberts, that the explanation dawned upon myself. The natives were drawing palm-tree wine, a thing forbidden by law; and when the wind thus suddenly revealed them, they were doubtless more troubled than ourselves.

At the top of the den there dwelt an old, melancholy, grizzled man of the name of Tari (Charlie) Coffin. He was a native of Oahu, in the Sandwich Islands; and had gone to sea in his youth in the American whalers; a circumstance to which he owed his name, his English, his down-east twang, and the misfortune of his innocent life. For one captain, sailing out of New Bedford, carried him to Nuka-hiva and marooned him there among the cannibals. The motive for this act was inconceivably small; poor Tari's wages, which were thus economised, would scarce have shook the credit of the New Bedford owners. And the act itself was simply murder. Tari's life must have hung in the beginning by a hair. In the grief and terror of that time, it is not unlikely he went mad, an infirmity to which he was still liable; or perhaps a child may have taken a fancy to him and ordained him to be spared. He escaped at least alive, married in the island, and when I knew him was a widower with a married son and a granddaughter. But the thought of Oahu haunted him; its praise was for ever on his lips; he beheld it, looking back, as a place of ceaseless feasting, song and dance; and in his dreams I dare say he revisits it with joy. I wonder what he would think if he could be

carried there indeed, and see the modern town of Honolulu brisk with traffic, and the palace with its guards, and the great hotel, and Mr. Berger's band with their uniforms and outlandish instruments; or what he would think to see the brown faces grown so few and the white so many; and his father's land sold for planting sugar, and his father's house quite perished, or perhaps the last of them struck leprous and immured between the surf and the cliffs on Molokai.[1] So simply, even in South Sea Islands, and so sadly, the changes come.

Tari was poor, and poorly lodged. His house was a wooden frame, run up by Europeans; it was indeed his official residence, for Tari was the shepherd of the promontory sheep. I can give a perfect inventory of its contents: three kegs, a tin biscuit-box, an iron sauce-pan, several cocoa-shell cups, a lantern, and three bottles, probably containing oil; while the clothes of the family and a few mats were thrown across the open rafters. Upon my first meeting with this exile he had conceived for me one of the baseless island friendships, had given me nuts to drink, and carried me up the den "to see my house"—the only entertainment that he had to offer. He liked the "Amelican," he said, and the "Inglisman," but the "Flessman" was his abhorrence; and he was careful to explain that if he had thought us "Fless," we should have had none of his nuts, and never a sight of his house. His distaste for the French I can partly understand, but not at all his toleration of the Anglo-Saxon. The next day he brought me a pig, and some days later one of our party going ashore found him in act to bring a second. We were still strange to the islands; we were pained by the poor man's generosity, which he could ill afford; and by a natural enough but quite unpardonable blunder, we refused the pig. Had Tari been a Marquesan we should have seen him no more; being what he was, the most mild, long-suffering, melancholy man, he took a revenge a hundred times more painful. Scarce had the canoe with the nine villagers put off from their farewell[2] before the *Casco* was boarded from the other side. It was Tari; coming thus late because he had no canoe of his own, and had found it hard to borrow one; coming thus solitary (as indeed we always saw him), because he was a stranger in the land, and the dreariest of company. The rest of my family basely fled from the encounter. I must

[1] An island on which the lepers are isolated, a little to the southeast of Oahu.
[2] The farewell visit of the natives, mentioned in a preceding chapter.

receive our injured friend alone; and the interview must have lasted hard upon an hour, for he was loath to tear himself away. "You go 'way. I see you no more—no, sir!" he lamented; and then looking about him with rueful admiration, "This goodee ship!—no, sir!—goodee ship!" he would exclaim: the "no, sir," thrown out sharply through the nose upon a rising inflection, an echo from New Bedford and the fallacious whaler. From these expressions of grief and praise, he would return continually to the case of the rejected pig. "I like give give plesent all the same you," he complained; "only got pig: you no take him!" he was a poor man; he had no choice of gifts; he had only a pig, he repeated; and I had refused it. I have rarely been more wretched than to see him sitting there, so old, so grey, so poor, so hardly fortuned, of so rueful a countenance, and to appreciate, with growing keenness, the affront which I had so innocently dealt him; but it was one of those cases in which speech is vain.

Tari's son was smiling and inert; his daughter-in-law, a girl of sixteen, pretty, gentle, and grave, more intelligent than most Anaho women, and with a fair share of French; his grandchild, a mite of a creature at the breast. I went up the den one day when Tari was from home, and found the son making a cotton sack, and madame suckling mademoiselle. When I had sat down with them on the floor, the girl began to question me about England; which I tried to describe, piling the pan and the cocoa shells one upon another to represent the houses, and explaining, as best I was able, and by word and gesture, the over-population, the hunger, and the perpetual toil. "*Pas de cocotiers? pas de popoi?*"[3] she asked. I told her it was too cold, and went through an elaborate performance, shutting out draughts, and crouching over an imaginary fire, to make sure she understood. But she understood right well; remarked it must be bad for the health, and sat a while gravely reflecting on that picture of unwonted sorrows. I am sure it roused her pity, for it struck in her another thought always uppermost in the Marquesan bosom; and she began with a smiling sadness, and looking on me out of melancholy eyes, to lament the decease of her own people. "*Ici pas de Kanaques,*"[4] said she; and taking the baby from her breast, she held it out to me with both her hands. "*Tenez*[5]—a little baby like this;

then dead. All the Kanaques die. Then no more." The smile, and this instancing by the girl-mother of her own tiny flesh and blood, affected me strangely; they spoke of so tranquil a despair. Meanwhile the husband smilingly made his sack; and the unconscious babe struggled to reach a pot of raspberry jam, friendship's offering, which I had just brought up the den; and in a perspective of centuries I saw their case as ours, death coming in like a tide, and the day already numbered when there should be no more Beretani,[6] and no more of any race whatever, and (what oddly touched me) no more literary works and no more readers.

THE VAGABOND

Give to me the life I love,
    Let the lave[7] go by me,
Give the jolly heaven above
    And the byway nigh me.
Bed in the bush with stars to see,
    Bread I dip in the river—
There's the life for a man like me,
    There's the life for ever.

Let the blow fall soon or late,
    Let what will be o'er me;
Give the face of earth around
    And the road before me.
Wealth I seek not, hope nor love,
    Nor a friend to know me;
All I seek the heaven above
    And the road below me.

Or let autumn fall on me
    Where afield I linger,
Silencing the bird on tree,
    Biting the blue finger:
White as meal the frosty field—
    Warm the fireside haven—
Not to autumn will I yield,
    Not to winter even!

Let the blow fall soon or late,
    Let what will be o'er me;
Give the face of earth around,
    And the road before me.
Wealth I ask not, hope nor love,
    Nor a friend to know me.
All I ask the heaven above,
    And the road below me.

---

3 "No cocoa-palms? no bread-fruit trees?"
4 "Here no more Kanakas!"
5 "See here!"
6 I. e., Britanni, Britons. The language of the Kanakas being so largely vocalic, they find it difficult to pronounce two consonants in succession without interposing a vowel.
7 The leave, the rest; a familiar word in Burns.

THE MORNING DRUM-CALL ON MY EAGER EAR

The morning drum-call on my eager ear
Thrills unforgotten yet; the morning dew
　Lies yet undried along my field of noon.
But now I pause at whiles in what I do,
And count the bell, and tremble lest I hear
　(My work untrimmed) the sunset gun too
　　soon.

EVENSONG

The embers of the day are red
Beyond the murky hill.
The kitchen smokes: the bed
In the darkling house is spread:
The great sky darkens overhead,
And the great woods are shrill.
So far have I been led,
Lord, by Thy will:

So far I have followed, Lord, and wondered
　still.

The breeze from the embalmèd land
Blows sudden toward the shore,
And claps my cottage door.
I hear the signal, Lord—I understand.
The night at Thy command
Comes. I will eat and sleep and will not question more.

REQUIEM

Under the wide and starry sky,
Dig the grave and let me lie.
Glad did I live and gladly die,
　And I laid me down with a will.

This be the verse you grave for me:
Here he lies where he longed to be;
Home is the sailor, home from sea,
　And the hunter home from the hill.

INDEX TO NOTES, AND GLOSSARY

The page number is given first; a superior numeral or character indicates the note. When it is necessary to distinguish columns, the letters *a* and *b* are used. Occasionally the references are to numbered lines on a page.

Not all notes are indexed. Notes upon authors and titles may be found through the indexes to authors and titles. In general this index has been restricted to such notes as are likely to be wanted for purposes of cross-reference and comparison (see Introduction); but a few others, that seemed of especial intrinsic importance, have been added.

The glossary is inserted here in one alphabetical order with the index, but the words begin with small letters. It has likewise been restricted to the items of most importance. Since practically every strange or archaic usage is explained as it occurs, it seemed useless to repeat them all here, especially those that occur only once, or have only a contextual significance. Thus, the vocabulary of Chaucer has been largely omitted from the glossary, and so also have the Scotticisms. But all such archaisms as are to be found widely scattered through our literature are given, with nearly always one or more references to illustrate their use.

Scylding, 1*.
Scylla, 251*. Another Scylla, 318⁵.
secular, marking or completing a century, 286b.
Sedge, 231²⁷.
seen, skilled, 111¹.
Semi-cope, 46³⁰, 354¹⁹.
Semiramis, 60⁹.
Seneca, 192⁵, 529*.
sensible, sensitive, 174²⁷.
sentence, sense, opinion, judgment, 95².
Sequin, 195¹³.
Seraphim, 139¹³.
Sessions, Courts of, 293*.
Setebos, 170⁶⁶.
Seven Deadly Sins, 135†.
Shadwell, Thomas, 280* ff.
Shaftesbury, Earl of, 277*.
Shah Nameh, 645*.
Shakespeare, Epitaph on, 191†.
shell = lyre, 349¹, 351³.
Shelley, 622*.
Sher-Thursday, 106³⁶.
Shooting-stars, 508⁷.
Sicilian Muse, 232⁴⁰.
Siege Perilous, 101¹⁵.
Siegfried, Sigurd, 705*, 720†.
Signs, London, 369², 541a.
Sigurd, The "Wrath" of, 705*, 708*.
silly (German selig, blessed), innocent, simple, 224¹⁷, 433⁸.
Sion, 234⁷.
Sinai, Mt., 225²⁴, 234⁴, 535¹.
sith, sithens, since, 103⁸.
Sizar, 561⁷.
skills, (impersonal), matters, avails, 113¹¹, 625¹.
Slug-horn, 626⁵.
Sock = Comedy, 192⁶, 228²⁸, 281¹⁹.
Soho Square, 292⁷.
Solway Firth, 443¹.
Song of Solomon, 588§, 623⁴.
Sonnet, Introduction of, 125*.
Sonnet sequences, 142*, 632*, 693*, 701*.
sooth, soth, sothe, truth, 87⁷.
sop, soupe, sup, small portion of a liquid, 162⁶, 402¹.
Sophocles, 642*.
Souls, Pictorial representation of, 619¹³.
Spairges, 404†.
speir, ask, 402¹³.
Spheres, Music of, 255*, 225²², 321⁸, 530¹⁰. See Ptolemaic Astronomy.
Sphinx, Theban, 482a line 23.
Stang, 336¹.
Stella, 362¹⁶.
stole, robe, 229¹⁰, 577 line 197.
Storied, 348², 230⁴².
Stothard, Thomas, 684².
Strappado, 299⁵.
Straw, Jack, 59²⁵.
Stratford atte Bowe, 44*.
style = name, 247¹⁸.
sublime = uplifted, 249³⁹, 350⁵.
Summoner, 49⁴⁴, 524⁴.
Sunium, 467¹⁵, 549b.
Swan-song, 318⁵.

"Sweetness and light," 659*.
Switzerland, Invasion of, 440*.
Sword of King David, 103†.
Sylvanus, 230³⁵.
syne, since, 405¹.
Synonyms in early prose style, 111§.

Tabard, 43²⁷, 702b line 30.
tale, number, 227¹⁴.
Tanaquil, 127⁷.
Tara Hill, 495§.
Tartarus, 253 line 858.
Tasso, 460⁵.
Taurus, 343¹, 578².
teen, grief, 166²⁴.
Telegraph, 521³.
tell, count, 227¹⁴.
Tempe. A vale in Thessaly, near Mt. Olympus, 482a, 489b line 7.
Templars, 542⁵.
Temple, The, 50¹², 293¹¹, 542⁵, 561¹.
Tethys, 131⁵³.
Thalia, 227⁵.
Thammuz, 239⁵².
thane, war-companion, retainer, 3 line 234.
that = that which, what, 212⁷.
that pleonastic (when that = when, because that = because, etc.), 43¹.
that serving to repeat a preceding connective, 207³.
Theatre, Customs of Elizabethan, 197*.
Thebes, Walls of, 157b line 26, 173¹⁰, 530⁸. Cp. 569†.
Theocritus, 231²⁰, 632¹.
Third Estate, 535*. See Estates.
tho, then, 136¹¹.
thorough, through, 483³.
thou in familiar address, 165¹⁴.
Thresholds, Blessing of, 438*.
Thrones, 139¹³.
Timotheus, 283b².
Titan, 240 line 510; = the sun, 221†.
Titans, 236†.
to intensive: to-burst, burst to pieces, 93b line 814.
Toad-eater, 371⁹.
Tophet = hell 535⁵, 626¹. See 239, lines 402-405.
Touchstone, 133¹.
Tournament, 97¹⁰.
Transubstantiation, 278⁸.
Travellers' insurance, 182*.
Trelawny, Sir Jonathan, 499*.
Triple Alliance, 278¹¹.
Triton, 231²².
Triumphal processions, 228²⁸, 512*, 514³.
Trosachs, 445¹⁰.
Troubadours, 488¹.
Tuileries, 532³.
Tully, 293¹⁵.
Tussaud, Madame, 565⁵.
Twelfth-day, 98¹⁷.
Twelve good rules, 375⁸.
Tyler, Wat, 59²⁵.
Typhon, 226⁴², 236†.
Tyrian purple, 287⁶.

INDEX TO TITLES AND FIRST LINES

746